Professional SQL Server 2000 Programming

Robert Vieira

Wrox Press Ltd. ®

Professional SQL Server 2000 Programming

Latest Reprint December 2002

wrox

Published by Wrox Press Ltd,
Arden House, 1102 Warwick Road, Acocks Green,
Birmingham, B27 6BH, UK
Printed in the United States
ISBN 1-861004-48-6

Trademark Acknowledgements

Wrox has endeavored to provide trademark information about all the companies and products mentioned in this book by the appropriate use of capitals. However, Wrox cannot guarantee the accuracy of this information.

Credits

Author
Robert Vieira

Additional Material
Bruce Bachelor
Robin Dewson
Charles Fairchild
Hope Hatfield
Brian Knight
Michael Maston
Brian Matsik
John Reid
Rick Tempestini
Sakhr Youness

Technical Reviewers
Itzik Ben-Gan
David Bosley
Mark Cassorla
Steve Danielson
Scott Hanselman
Greg Jackson
Tim Johnson
Paul Morris
Mark Smith

Technical Architect
Kate Hall

Category Manager
Bruce Lawson

Technical Editors
Catherine Alexander
Claire Brittle
Benjamin Egan
Gary Evans
Paul Jeffcoat
Gareth Oakley
Adrian Young

Author Agents
Tony Berry
Sarah Bowers

Project Administrator
Cilmara Lion

Production Coordinator
Tom Bartlett

Index
Michael Brinkman
Bill Johncocks

Figures
Shabnam Hussain

Cover
Shelley Frazier

Production Manager
Simon Hardware

About the Author

Experiencing his first bout with computing in 1978, Robert Vieira knew right away that this was something "really cool". In 1980 he began immersing himself into the computing world more fully – splitting time between building and repairing computer kits, and programming in BASIC as well as Z80 and 6502 assembly languages. In 1983, he began studies for a degree in Computer Information Systems, but found the professional mainframe environment too rigid for his tastes, dropping out in 1985 to pursue other interests. Later that year, he caught the "PC bug" and began the long road of programming in database languages from dBase to SQL Server. Rob completed a degree in Business Administration in 1990, and has since typically worked in roles that allow him to combine his knowledge of business and computing. Beyond his Bachelor's degree, he has been certified as a Certified Management Accountant as well as Microsoft Certified as a Solutions Developer (MCSD), Trainer (MCT), and Database Administrator (MCDBA).

Rob is currently the Principal Consultant for Database and Storage Technologies with the Technology and Innovation Group at STEP Technology in Portland, Oregon – a position that offers the high-end consulting and team support he craves.

He resides with his wife Nancy, elder daughter Ashley, and new addition Adrianna, in Vancouver, WA.

Acknowledgements

Wow! What a ride the last year has been. It's had both heartache and happiness. It's had way too much to squeeze into one year – that's for sure (just ask my wife who says she "can't wait to have a husband again").

As always, there is a ton of people to thank. I'll start with my wife, who has had what would have been a stressful year even if her husband wasn't writing a book. The thank you's definitely need to begin there.

You – the readers. You've written me mail and told me how I helped you out in some way. That was and continues to be the number one reason I wrote this book, and the one before it. The original version of this book has, to date, sold roughly three times what I expected, and more than twice what I thought was the best we could hope for. We struck a chord – I'm glad. Here's to hoping we help make your SQL Server experience a little less frustrating and a lot more successful.

Thank you to all the Wrox Press staff, with special thanks to the following:

- ❑ **Kate Hall** – who, although she was probably ready to kill me by the end of each book, somehow guided me through the edit process to build a better book the first time, and repeated the feat plus somehow helped me to just plain survive the second time.

- ❑ **Dominic Shakeshaft** – who got me writing in the first place (then again, given some nights filled with writing instead of sleep lately, maybe it's not thanks I owe him…).

- ❑ **Dominic Lowe** – who saw me on my way with the first book and talked me into round two, then bailed out on me (I owe him much for the first, but I may never forgive him for the last…). Best of luck on the new endeavors.

- ❑ **Tony Berry** – who tells me I need to be properly "wedged" (thank goodness it wasn't "wedgied") when I hook up with him so I can buy the ale…

- ❑ **Catherine Alexander** – who has managed to play Kate's more than able-bodied sidekick for me twice now, and has also done such a great job of fielding so many questions that come in through feedback@wrox.com.

- ❑ **Helen Stroud** – who helped everyone get to know the first book – I wish she was going to be around for part two…

- ❑ **Cilmara Lion** – who made sure enough eyes looked over this book to make it as accurate as possible – best wishes for the little editor on the way!

Much like last time, there are so many other people who deserve mentioning that I'm sure I'll miss one or two – if you're among those missed, please accept my humblest apologies and my assurance that your help was appreciated. That said, people who deserve some additional thanks include **Sakhr Youness** (x2 buddy), **Michael Maston, Brian Matsik, Brian Knight, Steve Danielson, Itzik Ben-Gan, Hal Berenson, Kalen Delaney, Patrick Cauldwell, Fernando Guerrero, Tibor Karaszi, Gert Drapers,** and **Richard Waymire**. Thanks also to **Scott Hanselman** – the king of the techno-geeks – who is the only one of the bunch bold enough to say "feel free to thank me profusely in the notes baby!" – consider it done Scott!

And back to the wife again (and more): This book is dedicated in the grandest possible fashion to my wife **Nancy** and daughter **Ashley**, who, once again, put up with me "disappearing" into my home office for days at a time during the several months that I worked on this book. It is also dedicated to the newest member of the clan, **Adrianna**, who doesn't yet know what a book is, but sure knows how to give me a big smile when I emerge from hours of writing. I only wish Wrox would let me print a picture of the three women in my life on the cover of this book rather than my ugly mug.

Finally, I would also like to dedicate this book to the memory of my father-in-law, Joe Turner, who left us last spring for what I'm sure is a better place. I spent many hours during the writing of this book pondering his memory as well as the memory of many others that I've lost over the years – there are a good many questions in life I'll miss the chance to ask them.

Table of Contents

Table of Contents

Table of Contents

Table of Contents

Table of Contents

Table of Contents

Table of Contents

Table of Contents

Table of Contents

Online discussion at http://p2p.wrox.com

Introduction

SQL Server 7.0 was a major leap forward from SQL Server 6.5. SQL Server 2000 continues that trend in the grandest possible way. While SQL Server 7.0 added a host of interesting new utilities and features, a tremendous amount of the effort put into 7.0 was directed towards the rewrite of the product – that is, just getting the new code to work in a fashion that was reasonably compatible with the 6.5 version product.

With SQL Server 2000, the development team was able to focus almost exclusively on new features: XML integration, distributed partitioned views, indexed views, INSTEAD OF triggers, User Defined Functions, a two stage data pump (for DTS), data mining – the list goes on and on.

For developers coming from a solid knowledge of version 7.0, you'll feel right at home immediately – yet you'll quickly find yourself yelling "Cool!" as you bump into the usefulness of new features on a regular basis. Things that weren't possible before are now often trivial. But where to find out about these new features – well, I hope you'll be glad you picked up this book!

If you're coming from version 6.5 or older, there's even more in store for you – it's literally a whole new world inside SQL Server.

And for the beginner – who still holds a rather special place in my heart – or the person who may have some relational database experience, but is new to SQL Server: this book does not leave you out either. For the approach of this book is actually rather simple – start at the beginning and work to the end. This book can't hope to be everything to everyone. It can, however, provide a ton of information on every day-to-day topic associated with developing on SQL Server, and still find time to toss in solid introductions into parts of SQL Server that deserve their own books (DTS, English Query, and OLAP for example).

What's Covered in this Book

The book is designed to become progressively more advanced as you read through it, but, from the very beginning, I'm assuming that you are already an experienced developer – just not necessarily with databases. In order to make it through this book you do need to already have understanding of programming basics such as variables, data types, and procedural programming. You do not have to have ever seen a query before in your life (though I suspect you have).

This book is something of a blend of both the beginning and the advanced in the SQL Server database development world. If you're already familiar with RDBMS systems – SQL Server in particular – then several of the beginning chapters may be sort of "Ho Hum" to you. I would still strongly suggest reading Chapters 2 and 3, but Chapter 4 and, perhaps, 5 may be worth skipping. From there, we're getting into areas where SQL Server 2000 has some variance from other RDBMS products and version 6.5 and even 7.0 of SQL Server.

The focus of the book is highly developer-oriented. This means that we will, for the sake of both brevity and sanity, sometimes gloss over, or even totally ignore, items that are more the purview of the database administrator than the developer. We will, however, remember administration issues as they either affect the developer or as they need to be thought of during the development process – we'll also take a brief look at several administration-related issues in Chapter 30.

In the 7.0 version of this book, I made a serious attempt to keep the book relatively language independent outside of SQL Server's own Active Scripting (used with DTS) and T-SQL (SQL Server's own brand of SQL) language requirements. Use of client-side languages was pretty much limited to a single chapter for that version of the book. Given feedback that I've gotten (yes, I do listen!), we've necessarily added additional scripting and client-side information in a few places (most notably in Chapters 22, 27, 31, and 32). In these cases, we will use Visual Basic since it is typically a bit easier to understand for the generic reader of this book (I find that C programmers tend to read VB better than VB programmers tend to read C). Several items are pointed out with references to similarities and differences vs. two of the more popular programming languages today – C++ and Visual Basic.

So let's take a brief look at the chapters of this book:

Chapter 1 provides some background information on the history of SQL Server along with a comparison of the features of the various SQL Server editions and data access technologies.

In *Chapter 2*, we explore the **database objects** present in SQL Server 2000. We'll look in detail at the databases installed by default, and more generally, at the other objects including stored procedures, rules, and views. We also look at SQL Server data types – including the data types added in SQL Server 2000.

Chapter 3 introduces the tools used by a developer working in SQL Server 2000. By the time you finish this chapter you'll be familiar with the **Enterprise Manager**, **Performance Monitor**, and **Query Analyzer** (among others).

Chapter 4 begins the **Transact-SQL** tutorial with an introduction to basic queries.

Chapter 5 follows on from the previous chapter and introduces the concept of **joins** (INNER, OUTER, FULL, and CROSS).

Chapter 6 deals with **tables**, both creating and altering them.

Chapter 7 introduces **constraints**. Included in this chapter are explanations and examples of primary keys and foreign keys, as well as rules and defaults. CASCADE actions – newly added with SQL Server 2000 – are also covered in this chapter.

In *Chapter 8*, we turn our attention to **database design** and consider normalization. We will discuss the three normal forms (as well as a few extra rarely used and academic forms).

Chapter 9 is another theoretical chapter and covers the **index structures** used in SQL Server as well as rules of thumb as to when to use indexes and when not to.

In *Chapter 10*, we'll turn our attention to simple **views** – virtual tables that allow you to partition off parts of your tables from readers. Indexed views are also fully discussed in this chapter.

Chapter 11 discusses SQL **scripts** and **batches**. We'll look at the USE and GO statements, SQL Server variable usage, system functions, **OSQL** (which allows you to run SQL from a windows command prompt) and wrap up the chapter with a discussion of **Dynamic SQL**.

Chapter 12 is concerned with **stored procedures** – one of the fundamental tools of a database developer's kit. In this chapter, we see how to create, alter, and drop stored procedures. **Extended** and **system stored procedures** are discussed in this chapter, as is error handling. The chapter will conclude with a brief discussion of debugging.

Chapter 13 deals with a feature that is entirely new with SQL Server 2000 – **User Defined Functions**. We'll examine in detail the differences between UDFs and stored procedures.

Chapter 14 covers **transactions** and **locks**. We'll discuss the BEGIN, COMMIT, ROLLBACK, and SAVE TRAN statements. Then we'll see how the **SQL Server log** works, before moving on to a discussion of the various forms of locks and how to deal with deadlocks.

In *Chapter 15* we'll cover **triggers**, we'll discuss how to create and alter them, and also when to use them and when to avoid them. We'll also examine the new capability to add triggers to views and also the concept of a INSTEAD OF trigger.

Chapter 16 introduces concepts behind advanced queries. We'll look at how to create **nested subqueries** and **correlated subqueries**.

In *Chapter 17*, we'll discuss **distributed transactions** and queries and the role of **linked** and **remote servers**. We'll also examine the highly touted ability to use **distributed partitioned views** that was added with this release.

In *Chapter 18*, we'll see how to navigate a recordset using **cursors**. While cursors should be avoided whenever possible, there are times where the "whenever possible" doesn't apply, and the cursor is the only solution available – if you're in that boat, this chapter's for you.

Chapter 19 will provide a hyper-speed introduction to XML.

Moving on to *Chapter 20*, we'll use our newfound XML basics to dive into the new XML integration features that are now part of SQL Server 2000.

Chapter 21 is all about moving large chunks of data in and out of your server utilizing an old friend – the **bulk copy program**, or **bcp**.

Chapter 22 will be the first of two chapters covering **Data Transformation Services** – or **DTS**. In this chapter, we'll learn the fundamentals of building and using DTS packages.

Chapter 23 is devoted to **replication**, after discussing what it is and why you might need to use it, we'll run through all the replication wizards supplied along with the new replication features in SQL Server 2000.

Chapter 24 deals with advanced database design issues such as advanced diagramming, dealing with large file-based information and sub-categories.

Chapter 25 provides an introduction to the **Analysis Services** (including the new data mining tools) that are provided with SQL Server 2000.

Chapter 26 finds us looking into **Full-Text Search**. Utilizing the MSSearch service (which is also found in Index Server and Site Server Search), Full Text provides wonderful word and phrase searches for a wide variety of needs. This chapter also looks into the new features in SQL Server 2000 that are meant to help improve performance.

In *Chapter 27* we'll look at **English Query.** This too allows you to map English words and phrases against your database to allow questions in basic English to be translated into functional queries.

Chapter 28 is concerned with **security**. We'll consider Windows security as well as that provided by SQL Server itself. We'll also explore some overall security strategies and other things to consider.

Chapter 29 covers a mix of issues. The core principle behind it, though, is **performance tuning** and you'll find that all the topics mentioned will need to be considered to get the most out of your SQL Server.

We continue our SQL-Server-fest with an overview of **administration** in *Chapter 30*. This chapter will take something of a minimalist approach to administration (there are tons of admin books out there), but will provide an overview of the things you'll need, in order to deal with your own development environment as well as do planning for the administration of your applications.

Chapter 31 brings us to the second of our promised two chapters on DTS. In this chapter, we'll explore the basics of the programmability in DTS.

Chapter 32 wraps things up with something many SQL Server people have never heard of – **Windows Management Instrumentation** (**WMI**). SQL Server 2000 reportedly marks the last release of SQL Server's previous management API (SQL-DMO), but WMI is here to take its place. In this chapter, we'll get you familiar with the basics of managing your server using WMI programming.

Version Issues

This book was first written from the ground up for SQL Server 7.0. It has been entirely updated to deal with the many changes of SQL Server 2000, but retains a sharp eye out for backward compatibility issues with 7.0, and, to a smaller degree, version 6.5.

What You Need to Use this Book

Nearly everything discussed in this book has examples with it. All the code is written out and there are plenty of screenshots where they are appropriate (and none where they are inappropriate!). However, you'll want to make sure that you have a system available (and by that I mean one that you can have administrative-level access to) to run the examples on, in order to get the most out of it. Your system should be equipped with:

- ❑ SQL Server 2000
- ❑ Windows NT 4.0 SP5 or better – Windows 2000 Server preferred (Win 9x will work, but you'll miss out on some things)

Conventions Used

I've used a number of different styles of text and layout in the book, to help differentiate between different kinds of information. Here are some of the styles I've used and an explanation of what they mean:

> **These boxes hold important, not-to-be forgotten, mission-critical details that are directly relevant to the surrounding text.**

Background information, asides, and references appear in text like this.

- ❑ **Important Words** are in a bold font
- ❑ Words that appear on the screen, such as menu options, are in a similar font to the one used on screen, for example, the Tools menu
- ❑ All object names, function names, and other code snippets are in this style: SELECT

Code that is new or important is presented like this:

```
SELECT CustomerID, ContactName, Phone
FROM Customers
```

whereas code that we've seen before or has little to do with the matter being discussed, looks like this:

```
SELECT ProductName FROM Products
```

In Case of a Crisis...

There are number of places you can turn to if you encounter a problem:

- ❏ Books Online
- ❏ http://www.wrox.com – for the downloadable source code and support
- ❏ http://www.microsoft.com/sql/ – for up-to-the-minute news and support
- ❏ http://msdn.microsoft.com/sqlserver/ – for developer news and good articles about how to work with SQL Server
- ❏ http://www.microsoft.com/technet – for Microsoft Knowledge Base articles, security information, and a bevy of other more admin-related items
- ❏ http://www.ProfessionalSQL.com – for source code and examples

Feedback

I've tried, as far as possible, to write this book as though we were sitting down next to each other going over this stuff. I've made a concerted effort to keep it from getting "too heavy" while still maintaining a fairly quick pace. I'd like to think that I've been successful at it, but I encourage you to e-mail me and let me know what you think one way or the other. Constructive criticism is always appreciated, and can only help future versions of this book. You can contact me either by e-mail (feedback@wrox.com) or via the Wrox web site.

Questions?

Seems like there are always some, eh? From the last edition of this book, I received hundreds of questions. Some were simple – others hard! Wrox and I have tried to respond to every one of them as best as possible. What I ask is that you give it your best shot to understand the problem based on the explanations in the book. If the book fails you, then you can either e-mail Wrox (feedback@wrox.com) or me personally (robv@ProfessionalSQL.com). Wrox has a dedicated team of support staff and I personally *try* (no guarantees!) to answer all the mail that comes to me. For the last book, I responded to about 98% of the questions asked of me – but life sometimes becomes demanding enough that I can't get to them all. Just realize that the response may take a few days (as I get an awful lot of mail).

1

SQL Server 2000 – Particulars and History

So you want to learn something about **databases** – **SQL Server** in particular? That's great because databases are pervasive – they are everywhere, though you may not have really thought about this up until now.

In this chapter, we'll be looking at some of the different varieties and brands of databases available both today and throughout history. We'll examine some of the advantages and disadvantages of each, and how they fit into the grand picture of life, so to speak.

Moving on from there, we'll take a look at SQL Server 2000 specifically – the different editions that are currently available and what each one does or doesn't include.

In addition, we'll take some time to examine the database development process and how it fits into your overall development cycle. In this same section, we'll talk at an entry level about some system architecture issues and how these affect our database thinking.

This book is focused on trying to successfully prepare you to develop applications using SQL Server 2000. It should also act as good preparation for some of the exams in the Microsoft certification process, so we'll round off the chapter with a brief look at this.

A Brief History of Databases

SQL Server is an **RDBMS** – or **Relational Database Management System**. RDBMS systems are at the pinnacle of their popularity at the moment. Using an RDBMS as the basis for data storage is plainly "the way it's done" for most applications nowadays – but it wasn't always this way.

In this section, we're going to take a look back in time and examine some of the other databases used in the past. We'll try not to dwell on this "Old News", but it's critical to understand where database technology has come from if you want to understand where you're going today, and why.

Types of Databases

Databases are not just limited to the computer-based systems that we typically think about when we hear the term – they are much, much more. A database is really any collection of *organized* data. Even Webster's dictionary puts a qualifier on any computer notion:

> *Database: A usually large collection of data organized especially for rapid search and retrieval (as by a computer).*

The file drawers in your office are really something of a database (that is, if they are better organized than mine at home). In fact, databases have existed throughout most of the history of the "civilized" world, going back to the days of the early philosophers and academics (Socrates, Aristotle, Hippocrates, etc.).

That being said, there's a reason why databases are so closely associated with computers. It's because, for most database situations (virtually, but not quite, all of them), computers are simply the fastest and most efficient way to store data. Indeed, the term database is thought to have originated from the computing community in 1962 or so.

Databases, then, fall into a number of common categories:

❑ **Paper-based**: These, although often not thought of as databases, probably still make up the largest proportion of databases in the world today. There are literally billions and billions of tons of paper out there that are still meticulously organized, but haven't been anywhere near a computer.

❑ **Legacy mainframe** – often **VSAM** (**Virtual Storage Access Method** – common to IBM mainframes) databases: Don't underestimate the number of legacy mainframes still out there, and their importance. Connectivity to host systems and the vast amounts of data they still contain is one of the major opportunity areas in database and systems development today. There are still many situations where I recommend a host system solution rather than a client-server or web-based model. It's worth noting though that I still believe in using a true RDBMS – albeit one that's located on a host system.

❑ **dBase** and other file-based databases: Typically, these include any of the older **Indexed Sequential Access Method** – or **ISAM** – databases. These normally use a separate file for each table, but the ISAM name comes from the physical way the data is stored and accessed more than anything else. Examples of ISAM databases that are still in widespread legacy use – and even in some new developments in certain cases – include dBase, FoxPro, Excel, Paradox, and Access. (Yes, Access is an ISAM with a relational feel and several relational features – it is not, however, a true relational database system.) These systems had most of their heyday well before RDBMS systems. (There is something of a paradox in this since RDBMS systems appeared first.) These systems are still quite often great for small, stand-alone databases where you will never have more than a small number of users accessing the data at a time.

❏   **RDBMS systems**: Data for the masses, but with much better data integrity. These systems do more than just store and retrieve data. They can be thought of as actually caring for the integrity of the data. Whereas VSAM and ISAM databases typically store data very well, the database itself has no control over what goes in and out (OK, Access has some, but not like a true RDBMS). The programs that use the database are responsible for implementing any data integrity rules. If five programs are accessing the data, you'd better make sure that they are all programmed correctly. RDBMS systems, on the other hand, take the level of responsibility for data integrity right down to the database level. You still want your programs to know about the data integrity rules to avoid getting errors from the database, but the database now takes some of the responsibility itself and the data is much safer.

❏   **Object-oriented databases**: These have been around for a while now, but are only recently beginning to make a splash. They are really a completely different way of thinking about your data and, to date, have only found fairly specialized use. Examples would be something similar to a document management system. Instead of storing the document in several tables, the document would be stored as a single object, and would have properties whose state would be maintained. **ODBMS** systems often provide for such object-oriented concepts as inheritance and encapsulation.

RDBMS systems are clearly king these days. They are designed from the ground up with the notion that they are not going to be working with just one table that has it all, but with data that relates to data in completely different tables. They facilitate the notion of combining data in many different ways. They eliminate the repetitive storage of data and increase speed in transactional environments.

The Evolution of Relational Databases

E.F. Codd of IBM first introduced the principles behind relational database structures and a Structured English QUEry Language – or SEQUEL – back in the late 1960's (the name was later shortened to just **Structured Query Language** or **SQL**). The concept was actually pretty simple – increase data integrity and decrease costs by reducing repetitive data as well as other database problems that were common at the time.

Nothing really happened in the relational world as far as a real product was concerned until the mid to late 70's, though. Around that time, companies such as Oracle and Sybase became the first to create true relational database systems. It might surprise you to learn that these systems got their start in mainframe – not client-server – computing. These systems offered a new way of looking at database architecture and, since they ran on multiple platforms, they also often offered a higher potential for sharing data across multiple systems.

In the 80's, the **American National Standards Institute** (**ANSI**) finally weighed in with a specification for SQL, and **ANSI-SQL** was born. This was actually a key moment in RDBMS computing because it meant that there would be better compatibility between vendors. That, in turn, meant that more of the expertise built up in one RDBMS was also usable in a competing system. This has greatly aided the process of trying to increase the number of developers in the SQL community. The ANSI specification called for several different levels of compliance. Most of the major RDBMS products available today are classified as being **Entry-Level ANSI compliant** (like SQL Server, for example). Entry-level ANSI compliance means that a database meets the basic defined ANSI standards for the SQL syntax.

> *ANSI compliance is a double-edged sword. I'm going to encourage you to make use of ANSI compliant code where feasible – it's particularly important if you may be migrating your code between different database servers. But you also need to realize that many of the performance and functionality features that each of the high performance database vendors offers are not ANSI compliant. Each vendor extends their product beyond the ANSI spec in order to differentiate their product and meet needs that ANSI hasn't dealt with yet. For example, SQL Server 2000 has expanded on the basic SQL with its own additions, which are called T-SQL. This leaves you with a choice – ANSI compliance or performance.*

> *Use ANSI compliance not as a religion but, rather, where it makes sense. Go for ANSI code where it means little or no difference in performance (such as with queries), but also don't be afraid to make judicious use of specialized features that may offer some functionality or performance gain that ANSI can't give you. Just document these areas where you use them so that, if you are faced with porting to a new RDBMS, you know where to look for code that may not run on the new system.*

Microsoft SQL Server (referred to in this book as simply **SQL Server**) was originally born from Sybase SQL Server (referred to in this book simply as **Sybase**). Microsoft partnered with Sybase in 1989 to develop a version of SQL Server for, of all things, OS/2. SQL Server was migrated to Windows NT back in 1993 with version 4.2. The relationship ended with the release of version 6.0. From 6.5 forward, SQL Server has been a Microsoft-only product. The highly successful version 7.0 was essentially a complete rewrite of the product and was the first version available for Windows 9x (there was now virtually no Sybase code left in SQL Server). Finally, we reach today's version – SQL Server 2000.

While there are unmistakable similarities, there are now substantial differences in implementation and feature support between version 4.21 (the oldest version you're actually likely to find installed somewhere) and version 2000. Version 6.0 added such details as cursor support. Version 6.5 added distributed transactions, replication, and ANSI compatibility. The rewrite with version 7.0 enabled the loss of problem areas such as the devices defined for data storage.

About SQL Server 2000

SQL Server 2000 comes with far more than just the usual RDBMS – it has additional components that would, for many products, be sold entirely separately or with add-on pricing. Instead, Microsoft has seen fit to toss in these extras at no additional charge.

SQL Server 2000 is now available in five **editions** (CE, Personal, Desktop Engine, Standard, Developer, and Enterprise), which are discussed in more detail later.

> *There is also an Enterprise Evaluation Edition, which can be downloaded from the Web for a 120 day trial period.*

The full suite that makes up SQL Server 2000 includes:

System/Subsystem	Description	Editions
SQL Server 2000 (the main RDBMS)	This is the "guts" of the system, and is required for anything else to work. It is a very robust relational database system. With the exception of the Desktop Engine, which only has the main RDBMS, you will find that this part of the system also includes several different services and utilities, such as the **SQL Server Agent** (Scheduler), the **Distributed Transaction Coordinator** (**DTC**), the **SQL Server Profiler** (trouble-shooting), and the **Enterprise Manager** (**EM**) – one of the best built-in management tools in the business, regardless of price-range. If you're coming from the Access world or some other desktop database, strap on your seatbelt, because you have just seen a glimpse of what's possible.	Desktop Engine Personal Standard Developer Enterprise

System/Subsystem	Description	Editions
Full-Text Search	This is an optional part of the main installation. If you want this functionality, you need to actively choose it – it's not installed by default. **Full-Text Search** provides the functionality to support more robust word lookups. If you've used an Internet search engine and been left in awe of the words and phrases that you can find, Full-Text Search is the tool for you. It ranges from being able to quickly locate small phrases in large bodies of text to being able to tell that "drink" is pretty much the same word as "drunk" or that "swam" is just the past tense of that word "swim" you were looking for. This one is not available in the Personal version (Win 9x) of SQL Server. We'll look at it extensively in Chapter 26.	Personal (except Win 9x) Standard Developer Enterprise
English Query	Featured in Chapter 27, **English Query** (**EQ**) allows you to develop applications for even the most non-technical of users. EQ allows users to ask questions or give commands in plain English and have them translated into a query that's usable by SQL Server. A great tool, but keep in mind that this is a completely separate installation from the rest of SQL Server.	Personal Standard Developer Enterprise
Analysis Services	Yet another tool that isn't part of the main installation, but gives great extras to the product. Analysis Services comprises of **OLAP** (**On Line Analytical Processing**), data warehousing, and data mining tools. It's something that many companies try to do from their main server – we'll look into why that's a mistake and how to make use of SQL Server's Analysis Services in detail in Chapter 25. The editions listed on the right all support OLAP, although only Enterprise and Developer have the full Analysis Services functionality. The Standard and Personal editions only contain the main functionality, which consists of Analysis Services itself, custom rollups, data mining, and actions (end user operation on data). Additionally, Analysis Services can only be installed on Windows NT/2000.	Personal Standard Developer Enterprise
Replication	This function allows data to be replicated to another SQL Server instance, usually found on another server as part of a recovery strategy, or to a remote server in another physical location, to reduce data transfer traffic. Replication is covered in Chapter 23.	Desktop Engine Personal Standard Developer Enterprise

Table continued on following page

System/Subsystem	Description	Editions
Data Transformation Services	**Data Transformation Services (DTS)** has expanded enormously in SQL Server 2000. A great range of different functionality in transforming data, either within a database, or transferring information in or out, is now available, including the ability to customize tasks and workflows. DTS is a greatly under-utilized product that reduces the need for companies to use a programmatic approach to transform data (for example, with Visual Basic), or even a basic Bulk Copy Program (bcp). We will cover DTS in Chapter 22.	Personal Standard Developer Enterprise

There are a few additional differences between the various editions of SQL Server 2000. These include:

- **Symmetric Multiprocessing (SMP)**: Support for SMP has increased a great deal through the different editions of SQL Server 2000 (though Win 98 and NT4 Workstation can't support this). There is support for up to four processors in the Standard edition if installed on NT Server or Enterprise, and support for up to 32 processors with the Enterprise edition if it is installed on Windows 2000 Datacenter Server.

  SMP distributes the workload of the server over multiple processors symmetrically – that is, it tries to balance the load as opposed to running on just one CPU per process.

- **Clustering Support** (Enterprise/Developer editions only): Clustering allows load-balancing across servers and automatic fail-over support (if one server dies, another one automatically picks up where the other left off). Currently, you can only cluster two servers with all operating systems, with the exception of Windows NT Enterprise edition, Windows 2000 Enterprise edition, and Windows 2000 Datacenter edition which can have up to four cluster servers.

Which Edition Should You Use?

The answer to this is like the answer to most things in life: it depends.

Each of the various editions has a particular target "market" that it's designed for. Usually, I find some exceptions to the rules on how things should best be used but, for these products, I would say that what Microsoft designed them for really is their best use. Let's take a quick look at the editions, one by one. The following section gives my summary of each edition. Obviously, Microsoft makes its own comparisons, which it might be useful for you to see. Don't forget that there is a Microsoft slant to all of these.

- http://www.Microsoft.com/sql/productinfo/sqlcompdata.htm – gives an overall comparison on data warehousing

- http://www.Microsoft.com/sql/productinfo/sqlcompecom.htm – gives an overall comparison on e-commerce

- http://www.Microsoft.com/sql/productinfo/sqlcomplob.htm – gives an overall comparison on Line-of-Business

- http://www.Microsoft.com/sql/productinfo/feaover.htm – gives a features overview with links to specific areas

Windows CE Edition

The **Windows CE Edition** will be used on Windows CE devices. It will be extremely limited in its functionality as, obviously, these devices have an extremely limited capacity. Applications using Windows CE and SQL Server are still quite limited at present and it's really only possible to have any sort of useful application built on the more expensive CE products.

Desktop Engine Edition

The **Desktop Engine Edition** of SQL Server 2000 was known as the Microsoft Data Engine (MSDE) in SQL Server 7.0. Don't get confused by thinking that this is still the same version as the SQL Server 7.0 Desktop version. It isn't. Desktop with SQL Server 7.0 is now Personal with SQL Server 2000. The Desktop Engine Edition consists only of the main RDBMS. It has none of the administration tools – not even the Enterprise Manager or Query Analyzer.

Contrary to popular belief, this is not a different version of SQL Server – all editions use the same binary executable that the Enterprise Edition uses. The difference is more in what auxiliary services are supported.

This edition is small and freely distributable, and Microsoft is pushing it as the new database engine for Access (replacing Jet). This makes it great for salespeople who need a database to take on the road with them.

Personal Edition

The **Personal Edition** is a rename of the Desktop Edition found with SQL Server 7.0 (not to be confused with the Desktop Engine Edition in SQL Server 2000). It was created to serve a couple of purposes: to provide a more robust desktop database solution than that provided with Access (even on Windows 9x); and to provide a version of SQL Server that could be used in "unplugged" situations. The latter is the big advantage – it is proving to be really popular in remote situations, like for sales reps who are on the road all the time. They can have their own version of the customer database and just "synchronize" using replication when they are able to connect back up with the network.

The Personal Edition is excellent when you want a small stand-alone database or when you have the need to be disconnected from a central data source, but want to be able to take some of that data with you. You could also use the Personal Edition to run a small server on Windows NT/2000 – this latter configuration even has support for multiple processors. Keep in mind though that, even with multiprocessing active, there is no support for parallel queries (which run different parts of the same query at the same time).

> *I'm told (I haven't tried it myself) that several of the tools that are not supposed to work with the Personal Edition actually do work just fine – particularly if you're running under NT Workstation. I strongly discourage you from implementing things this way. If you need the extra features, then use the right O/S to support them. Otherwise, you may find that everything works OK for a while, but you'll also find that you have no support from Microsoft when you want to ask why something broke.*

Confusingly, the Personal Edition cannot be bought, but if you buy the Standard or Enterprise Editions you'll get it for free. It is part of the Client Access License (CAL) and client software. Useful if you are running Windows 2000 Professional or Windows 98 and you need access to the GUI Admin tools (Standard and Enterprise editions don't run on Win2K Pro or 98, and no edition supports 95).

Standard Edition

The **Standard Edition** is the mainstream edition of SQL Server. This is the edition that's going to be installed for the majority of SQL Server users. The Standard Edition supports multiprocessing with up to four CPUs and 2GB of RAM. However, it doesn't support some of the more advanced features. For example, only a subset of the Analysis Services features is supported. You need to purchase a separate license for each Standard Edition instance you install on a machine.

Developer Edition

Readers of this book will probably see the **Developer Edition** as the default installation. Enterprise and Standard Editions should be seen as the production server solution, with developing and testing of applications performed on the Developer Edition. This has all the features of the Enterprise edition and, therefore, once a solution has been developed using the Developer Edition, there should be no problems in moving this to a production environment.

The only difference between this edition and the Enterprise Edition is the licensing of the product – the Developer Edition can only be used as a development environment.

Enterprise Edition

To run the **Enterprise Edition**, you must have NT Enterprise Edition, Windows 2000 Advanced Server, or Windows 2000 Datacenter Server installed. SQL Server Enterprise Edition adds support for multiprocessing with up to 32 CPUs, there is support for clustering (where two separate servers provide fail-over and can otherwise share a workload), and it allows for HTTP access to OLAP cubes (cubes are fully described in Chapter 25).

Whether to go with Enterprise Edition or not is usually an easy choice because the outcome is almost always decided for you, based on a requirement for one of the Enterprise Edition features, or costs and licensing (the per-processor license for the Enterprise Edition is four times the price of that for the Standard Edition). If you need clustering, then you need the Enterprise Edition. Enterprise edition special features include:

- Clustering
- Distributed partitioned views
- Indexed views
- Partitioned cubes
- Support for more than 4GB of RAM
- Log shipping (a fail-over strategy)
- Support for more than 4 CPUs

In addition, there is a long list of more obscure features that are only supported in the Enterprise edition, but it would be rare that one of those is needed if you don't also need one of the above items. Basically, if you need one of these, then you need Enterprise edition – it's that simple.

Hardware and OS Requirements

The stated **minimum hardware requirements** for SQL Server are pretty easy to reach these days:

- ❏ Pentium 166 or better (Alpha is no longer an option, and Microsoft has stated that there will be no future development for that platform).

- ❏ At least 64MB memory, although 128MB is recommended for the Enterprise Edition.

    You can get away with only 32MB for the Desktop Engine and Personal Editions on all but Windows 2000 – where 64MB is required.

- ❏ Between 95MB hard disk space (minimum installation) and 270MB (full installation).

    You will also need a further 50-130MB if you want to install Analysis Services, and another 80MB for English Query.

    The Desktop Engine Edition requires only 44MB.

- ❏ Enterprise and Standard Editions run on Windows NT Server version 4.0 with Service Pack 5 (SP5) or later, Windows NT Server 4.0 Enterprise Edition with SP5 or later, Windows 2000 Server, Windows 2000 Advanced Server, and Microsoft Windows 2000 Datacenter Server.

    Developer Edition runs on the operating systems listed above for the Enterprise and Standard Editions, as well as on Windows 2000 Professional and Windows NT Workstation 4.0 with SP5 or later.

    Personal Edition and Desktop Engine run on the operating systems listed above for the Enterprise and Standard Editions, as well as on Windows 98 (Second Edition if the computer doesn't have a network card), Windows Millennium Edition, Windows 2000 Professional, and Windows NT Workstation 4.0 with SP5 or later.

    This information can be found at http://www.microsoft.com/sql/productinfo/sysreq.htm.

- ❏ VGA Video in 800 x 600 mode (some of the graphical tools require it)
- ❏ IE 5.0 or later

In reality, you'll want to have a bit beefier machine than the recommendation. Even for a stand-alone development server, I recommend a minimum of 128MB of RAM and a Pentium II 500 or better processor. For production systems, no less than 256MB of RAM even for the smallest systems – and more likely 512MB to 2GB.

Building Database Connected Systems

At this juncture, we're ready to go into the holy-war territory of architectural issues. It seems like everybody's got an idea of what the best architecture is for everything.

Before we even get too deep into this I'll give you my first soapbox diatribe.

The perfect architecture to use is the one that is right for the particular solution you are working towards. There are very few easy answers in life, and what system architecture to use for a project is rarely one of them. Don't allow anyone to mislead you into thinking, "You should always use n-tier architecture", or that, "The mainframe is dead – anyone who installs a host-based system today is nuts!"

I have a definite belief in the power and flexibility of the n-tier approach we'll be talking about shortly – but don't believe for a minute that I think it's the only solution. The moment you let yourself be backed into thinking one approach is the right one for everything, will be the moment that you start turning out sub-standard work. Both traditional client-server and host technology still very much have their place, and I'll try to address some of the "wheres" and "whys" as we go through this section.

There have been a few models to come around through the years, but today we usually group things depending on how they handle three groups of **services**:

- ❑ **User Services**: This usually includes aspects like drawing the user interface (UI) and basic formatting and field rules. An example of facets that might be handled by User Services is proper formatting of a date – including making it known that a given field is a date field and pre-validating that any value entered into this field is actually a date. User services is all about presentation and making sure that each field has at least the type of data it's supposed to have in it.

- ❑ **Business Services**: This part knows about various business rules. An example of a business service is one that connects with your credit card company to validate a customer's credit card purchase. In a 3-tier or n-tier system, the Business Services objects may reside on their own server, be split across several servers, or, in smaller installations, share a server with Data Services.

- ❑ **Data Services**: This is all about storage and retrieval of data. Data services know about data integrity rules (say, that an inventory value can't go below zero), but don't care where the credit card approval came from. This is where SQL Server lies.

Let's take a look at some of the classic architectures used, both past and present, and see how our services fit in.

Single Tier (Host) Systems

This is the old mainframe and mini-computer model. There was virtually no logic at the desktop – instead, there was a dumb terminal. All that was sent down the wire to the terminal was the screen layout information, which included the data to display, of course.

Advantages	Disadvantages
Requires very little bandwidth on your network in order to have fast response times – great for international or WAN situations where bandwidth can be expensive.	Very expensive hardware-wise. In the old days, these often required special plumbing for cooling water – although I'm not aware of any systems which still require this being produced today.
Also exceptionally reliable. You'll find mainframes out there that haven't been "down" in years, literally.	Typically proprietary in nature – much more difficult to share information with other systems.
Deployment of new software is extremely easy. Just install on the host system, and every user has the new version – no running from machine to machine for the upgrade.	Very limited number of "off-the-shelf" software packages available. Since the number of potential customers is few, the cost of these packages tends to be extremely high.

2-Tier Architecture (Client-Server)

2-tier, or **client-server** systems, first started becoming popular in the early 90's. There were actually two sub-types to this architecture: client-centric (smart client) and server-centric (smart server).

Client-Centric

The **client-centric** version of client-server was based on the notion that PCs are cheap (the driving force behind most client-server development) and that you're going to get the most power when you distribute the computing requirements as much as possible. As such, whenever possible, only the data services part was performed on the server. The business and UI side of things was performed at the client – thus ensuring that no one system had to do all that much of the work. Every computer did its fair share (at least, that was the idea).

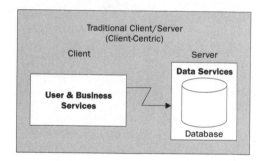

The big problem with client-centric client-server was (and still is) bandwidth. If all the business logic is on the client, then there tends to be a very large number of round trips (network sends and receives) between the client and the server. Frequently, large chunks of raw data are sent to the client – quickly clogging the network and slowing down everyone else trying to get their own huge blocks of data back and forth.

Advantages	Disadvantages
Distributes the workload to a large number of relatively cheap clients.	Is a terrible bandwidth hog – clogs networks up very quickly.
If you have one user who needs more speed, you can purchase a faster system for just them rather than a large expensive host system that everyone is going to take a piece of.	Installations are time consuming and difficult to coordinate. New software or versions of software must be installed on multiple machines. Version upgrades can be particularly problematic since old clients are not always compatible with the new server components and vice versa. All clients may have to be upgraded at one time, which can create quite a serious logistics problem.
The same money that buys the computing power on the client side also buys power for other productivity applications, such as word processing and spreadsheet applications.	Each client, depending on the vendor, may need a separate license for each seat or connection. This can increase costs.

Server-Centric

This lives on the notion that computing power is cheaper in PCs than in host systems, but tries to gain some of the advantages of centralized systems. Only user services are distributed to the client. Only information that actually needs to be displayed on the screen is sent to the client. Business and data services remain at the server. Network bandwidth is far more host system like.

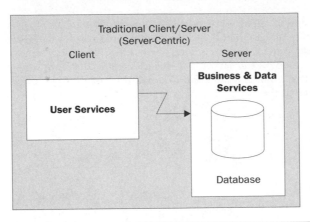

Advantages	Disadvantages
Some upgrades can be done entirely at the server level.	Other upgrades still require a "touch" on every client computer – upgrades and new installs are both very tedious and difficult logistically.
A large number of homogeneous products are available off-the-shelf – pre-made software is cheap.	Long-running and heavy-load jobs by one user affect all users.
Since only the information to be displayed is sent on the network, there is little network bandwidth used compared to the client-centric model.	Large servers grow exponentially in price. Some are every bit as expensive as host systems.
	Though the model starts to look like a host system model, there is usually considerably more downtime.

Three-Tier

This model, and the closely related one that follows (n-tier), are the much-hyped architectures of today. If you hear someone talking about how everything needs to be done one way regardless of what it is – they are almost certainly talking **three-tier** or n-tier computing.

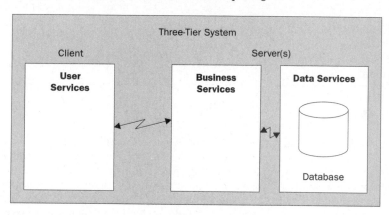

This model takes the approach of breaking up all three service levels into completely separate logical models. Clients are responsible for UI issues only – just as they were under server-centric client-server. The difference is that the business and data services are logically separated from each other. In addition, this approach moves the logical model into a distinctly separate realm from the physical model. This means that business and data services can run on the same server, but do not have to. This adds a significant level of stability and scalability since you can split the workload onto two (and, depending on how it's done, more) servers. In addition, this model has a tendency to be more extensible, since changes and additions affect smaller pieces of code (instead of one huge build of everything, you can just rebuild the affected components).

Since everything is component based, you can, if you use DCOM, take an approach where you distribute the components over many servers. If you use Microsoft Transaction Server (MTS), or COM+, which comes with Windows 2000, you can even keep copies of the same component on multiple servers for load balancing.

Advantages	Disadvantages
Some upgrades can be done entirely at the server level.	Other upgrades still require a "touch" on every client computer – upgrades and new installs are both very tedious and difficult logistically.
An increasing number of homogeneous products are available off the shelf – pre-made software is cheap.	Typically there is still considerably more downtime than with a host system.
Since only the information to be displayed is sent on the network, there is little network bandwidth used compared to the client-centric model. The load may, however, be higher between the business-logic and data-services systems if they are on different servers.	Performance can be degraded due to COM and marshalling, especially across servers or even networks. This includes any access over the Internet.

Table continued on following page

Advantages	Disadvantages
Allows for (actually encourages) component-based development, which *can* increase reusability. Two medium servers are often cheaper than one large server. The separation of business and data services makes two servers an option.	There is a much greater need for security and infrastructure. For example, MTS/COM+ for the whole process of looking after your COM modules, or MSMQ if you are using any sort of messaging.

N-Tier

N-tier is essentially like 3-tier and, theoretically, the best of all worlds. Frankly, I like this model a lot, but I still have to caution you about taking the "one size fits all" approach. This model gets serious about implementing what looks like a three-tier model logically, but instead breaks the components down to their smallest reasonable logical units of work. If the data services layer is done properly, even the database can be spread across multiple servers and moved around as needed. The only impact is on the data services components that provide access to the moved data. The business services components are oblivious to the move (less re-development here folks!), since they only need to know the name of the data services component that supplies the data and what specific method to call.

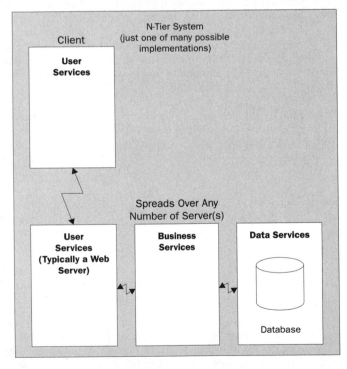

Similarly, you can change UI implementations fairly easily – you only need to redevelop the UI. You still call the same business logic components regardless of what UI (say, web vs. true client?) you are using.

Advantages	Disadvantages
Even more upgrades can be done entirely at the server level.	Often increases the number of network connections (which are frequently the slowest and most unreliable part of your system).
An increasing number of homogeneous products are available off-the-shelf – pre-made software is cheap.	Typically there is still considerably more downtime than with a host system.
Since only the information to be displayed is sent on the network (rather than an entire, not yet filtered, data set), there is little network bandwidth used compared to the client-centric model. The load may, however, be higher between the business-logic and data-services systems if they are on different servers.	The more layers of course, the more marshalling of data and requests, and so speed limitations can creep in.
Allows for (actually encourages) component-based development, which *can* increase reusability.	As with 3-tier, more infrastructure with MTS/COM+ and MSMQ.
Multiple medium servers are often cheaper than one large server. The separation of business and data services makes two servers an option.	

About .NET

.NET (pronounced "dot net") is a new development strategy being pushed by Microsoft. The latest updates of Microsoft's server products (including SQL Server 2000) are now being called the **.NET servers**. Microsoft will also be producing new versions of Visual Studio that will seek to simplify implementing .NET.

.NET is, as of this writing, still not a fully rounded-out vision, but it does have a number of proposed notions that are important for your architecture considerations. For now, what I would say is that it is important to recognize that all of the .NET servers are increasing their support for XML, and that they are doing a better job of talking to each other. For your component development, there are changes coming that will allow you to do an in-place replacement of a component without having to bring down your server to do it (remember I said, "There is typically still more downtime than a host system" when talking about n-tier?). This addresses one of the serious problems in development today – how to perform system upgrades gracefully.

More information will be coming about .NET over the next few years. The first implementations will only be the beginning of what appears to be a coming revolution in development on the Microsoft Platform. Microsoft has even indicated that it may take .NET onto Linux (could you imagine?). We'll see! In the mean time, watch .NET closely – not only for its first arrival, but also as it matures.

Data Access Models

Certainly one of the biggest issues to deal with these days is how to access your database within the various options in Microsoft's "Alphabet Soup" of **data access architectures**. Which models are available in what circumstances depends primarily on the version of SQL Server, and the choice and version of your programming language.

There are four different access models that Microsoft considers as being current for accessing SQL Server. These are:

❑ **ADO: ActiveX Data Objects**. The new RDO – or at least that's what Microsoft would like you to believe. Don't – ADO is its own animal. Each new version seems to improve performance and add features. Unlike RDO, which was based on ODBC, ADO is based on OLE DB. This provides a level of flexibility that ODBC alone can't offer, but it comes with more than just a few headaches (note that ADO can still indirectly use ODBC for connectivity by using the OLE DB provider for ODBC). RDO had a few features that will never be in ADO, but ADO has some really cool features – with persistent recordsets, filters, sorts (without going back to the server), and others – that RDO never had.

It's tough to take just a brief look at ADO, but since I have to, I'll say this much: ADO is now competitive, if not faster, in terms of speed compared with RDO, and has a very robust feature set. It is still nowhere near RDO in reliability as of writing this, but Microsoft has and continues to make a substantial investment in ADO and OLE DB. This is where they are saying the future is, and I would suggest any new non-C++ based development uses this access method (there'll be more for the C++ crowd shortly).

❑ **ODBC: Open Database Connectivity**. If you've been developing for any length of time at all (say, for more than a week), you have to have heard of ODBC. It is a Microsoft-pushed standard, but it is most definitely a standard – and a very good one at that. ODBC provides a way of gaining cross-platform access to database information. It is quite fast (often as fast as or faster than the native driver for your database) and allows you to use most of the mainstream standard SQL statements regardless of what the back-end expects for syntax. In short, ODBC is very cool. The major shortcoming for ODBC is that it is very much oriented to tabular data (columns and rows), and doesn't deal with non-standard data such as a directory structure or a multi-sheet database.

❑ **OLE DB**. The primary competitor to ODBC at this point, OLE DB is an attempt at having an open standard to communicate with both tabular and non-tabular data. OLE DB uses what is called a **provider**. A provider is a lot like an ODBC driver except that it is relatively self-describing. That is, it is able to tell the application that uses it what kind of functionality it supports. As mentioned earlier, OLE DB is the foundation under ADO. It is very fast indeed when not being used with ADO (that extra layer adds some overhead) but, since it deals with a number of items that aren't compatible with VB, you'll typically only see OLE DB being used directly by C++ programmers. It is far more of a pain to program in than ADO, but it is much faster by itself than when used in conjunction with ADO. If you're a non-C++ programmer, stick with ADO at this point. If you're a C++ programmer though, you're going to need to figure out whether the extra speed is worth the hassle.

❑ **Java Database Connectivity: (JDBC)**. OK, so I said there were five, and there are, but I have to say that JDBC is still something of an outcast at this point. It is used primarily in the web arena and by non-Microsoft users. The last time I saw much of anything done with it, it was fairly simple to use, but had very little functionality and was very slow. In short – unless for some reason you absolutely have to, don't go there.

In addition to these current object models, there are a few others that you may run across and should know about:

❑ **RDO: Remote Data Objects**. This was the speed leader for a couple of years. DAO and ODBC used to be the only options for VB programmers. DAO was easier than ODBC to develop in, but it was slow, and the object model was still too deep and complex. ODBC on the other hand, was fast, but required tons of code just to get ready to make a connection.

RDO recognized that most of the "set-up" code for ODBC was always the same, or was predictable based on a few other settings. It was created by using a very thin wrapper around ODBC that substantially simplified the code while giving most of the performance benefit of ODBC.

❑ **DB-Lib**. Prior to version 7.0, this was the native way in which SQL Server did all of its talking between the main host and client and utility applications (SQL Server now uses OLE DB natively in this role). It is still actively supported, but will only be enhanced to the extent necessary to maintain backward compatibility as SQL Server moves forward. Microsoft has said that it will pull support for this access method at some point in the future, but it also acknowledges that there are too many legacy applications out there using DB-Lib to figure on dropping support for it anytime soon.

❑ **VB-SQL**. This was only briefly available, but still found its way into several applications. This was based on an old wrapper that was written for VB to make many DB-Lib functions available for VB programmers.

If you're still using VB-SQL, move off it as soon as possible. It is slow and, if it breaks, you'll get no help with it.

❑ **DAO: Data Access Objects**. This is actually native to Microsoft Access (more specifically, the Jet database that is at the heart of Access). There are a lot of applications written in VB and Access that use this technology. Too bad! This object model can be considered clunky, slow, and just plain outdated (believe me, I'm being nice and not saying what I really think). It's still the fastest way to access things if you're using a Jet (Access) database but, if you're using this technology to access SQL Server, I would suggest putting some serious effort into migrating away from it as soon as possible. Microsoft was calling DAO a "legacy" model more than a year before the end of the Office 97 lifecycle. They want people to stop using it, and I have to agree with them.

There are several books out there on accessing SQL Server and the data access side of the database relationship – I'm going to leave you to look through those for more information, but I will recommend that you check out Bill Vaughn's *The Hitchhikers Guide to Visual Basic and SQL Server,* Microsoft Press, ISBN 1-572318-48-1. It is the relative bible of the connectivity side of Visual Basic programming. Another source you may want to check out is *Professional Visual Basic 6 Databases,* Wrox Press, ISBN 1-861002-02-5. C++ programmers should look at *Visual C++ Database Programming Tutorial,* Wrox Press, ISBN 1-861002-41-6.

Microsoft Certification

There are three SQL Server related exams that participate in different certifications offered by Microsoft. These include exams on **development, administration,** and **data warehousing**. Note that, at the time of writing, there are only exams for SQL Server 7.0. The SQL Server 2000 exams are due to go to Beta in January 2001. If you are interested in becoming certified visit http://www.microsoft.com/ technet/training/default.asp, where there is a wealth of information on how to study and get up to date.

Each of these exams has some relevance to the MCP, MCSD, MCDBA, and MCSE certifications. Indeed, the development and administration exams are core to the MCDBA certification process.

This book was not purposely written to address any Microsoft exam – it is focused on trying to successfully prepare you to develop applications using SQL Server 2000. Even so, the development exam (70-029 for SQL Server 7 and 70-229 for SQL Server 2000) was written to try and test to see if you are ready to do just that – and almost everything I can think of that's covered in the exam is addressed somewhere in this book.

I am not going to tell you that if you read this book you will pass that exam. I participated in the authoring of that exam, and I have had to take it myself – it is one seriously nasty exam. Still, the topics covered in this book happen to speak right to the heart of the exam – if you do well going through this book, the odds are you'll do just fine on the exam (sorry folks – this isn't exam cram so no guarantees on that!).

Summary

We've made a start and talked briefly about where the database world has been, database access, and a few other miscellaneous items. This is really just conducting some bookkeeping and preparation to get you ready to go.

In our next few chapters, we're going to take a deeper look into many of the basics of building and making use of a SQL Server database. I strongly encourage you to run through the many examples in this book. As I mentioned earlier, there are very few concepts in this book that do not have specific examples associated with them – take advantage of that and you'll be taking full advantage of this book.

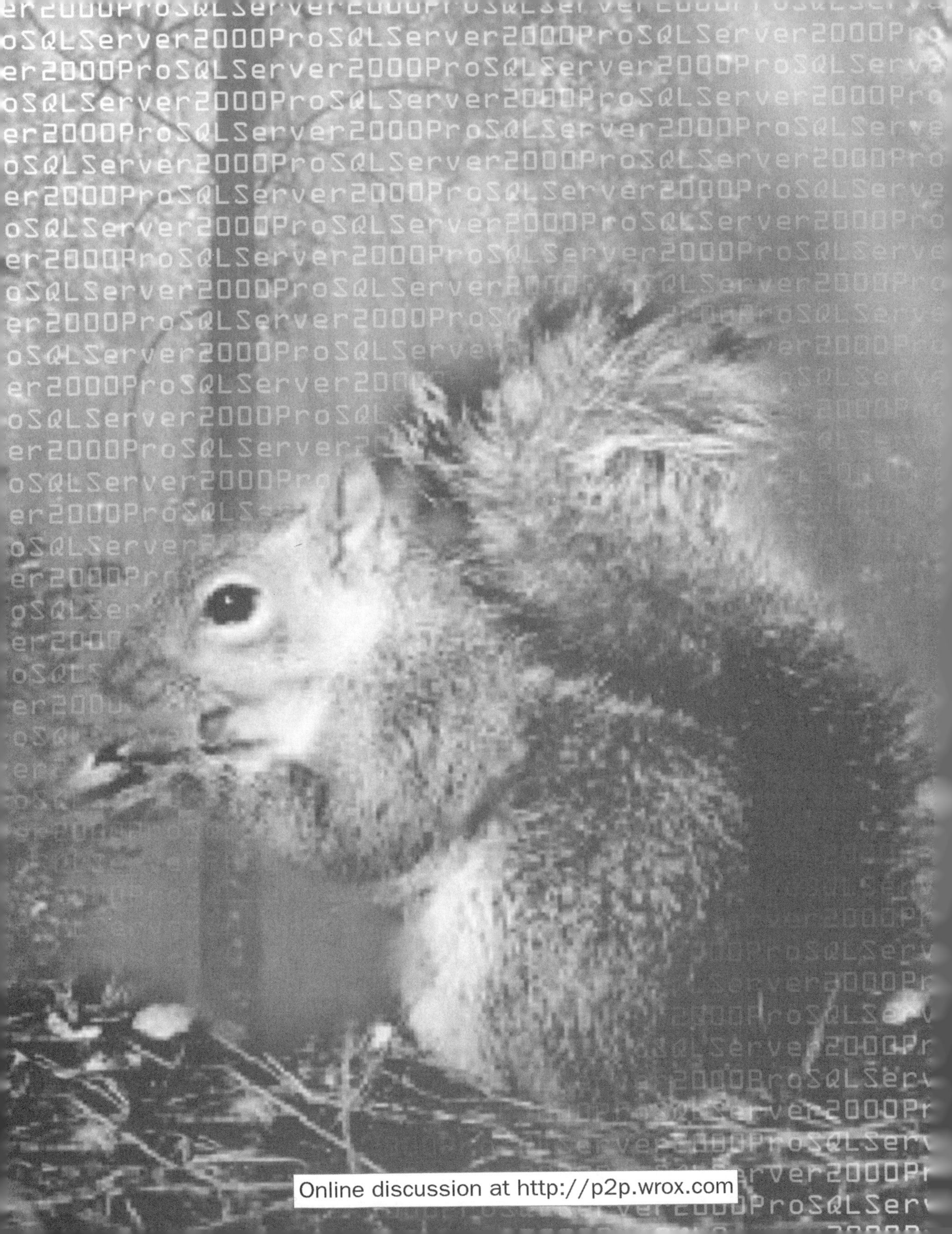
Online discussion at http://p2p.wrox.com

2

RDBMS Basics: What Makes Up a SQL Server Database?

What makes up a database? Data for sure (what use is a database that doesn't store anything?), but a **Relational Database Management System** (**RDBMS**) is actually much more than that. Today's advanced RDBMSs not only store your data, they also manage that data for you – restricting what kind of data can go into the system, and also facilitating getting data out of the system. If all you wanted was to tuck the data away somewhere safe, you could use just about any data storage system. RDBMSs allow you to go beyond the storage of the data into the realm of defining what that data should look like, or the **business rules** of the data.

Don't confuse what I'm calling the "business rules of data" as being the more generalized business rules that drive your entire system (for example, someone can't see anything until they've logged on, or automatically adjusting the current period in an accounting system on the first of the month). Those types of rules can be enforced at virtually any level of the system (these days, it's usually in the middle tier of an n-tier system). Instead, what we're talking about here are the business rules that specifically relate to the data, such as that you can't have a sales order with a negative amount. With an RDBMS, we can incorporate these rules right into the integrity of the database itself.

This chapter will provide an overview to the rest of the book. Everything discussed in this chapter will be covered again in later chapters, but this chapter is intended to provide you with a roadmap or plan to bear in mind as we progress through the book. Therefore, in this chapter, we will take a high-level look into:

- ❑ Database objects
- ❑ Data types
- ❑ Other database concepts that ensure data integrity

An Overview of Database Objects

An RDBMS such as SQL Server contains many **objects**. Object purists out there may quibble with whether Microsoft's choice of what to call an object (and what not to) actually meets the normal definition of an object, but, for SQL Server's purposes, the list of database objects can be said to contain:

- ❏   The database itself
- ❏   The transaction log
- ❏   Tables
- ❏   Filegroups
- ❏   Diagrams
- ❏   Views
- ❏   Stored procedures
- ❏   User Defined Functions
- ❏   Users
- ❏   Roles
- ❏   Rules
- ❏   Defaults
- ❏   User-defined data types
- ❏   Full-text catalogs

The Database Object

The database is effectively the highest-level object that you can refer to within a given SQL Server (technically speaking, the server itself can be considered to be an object, but not from any real "programming" perspective, so we're not going there). Most, but not all, other objects in a SQL Server are children of the database object.

> *If you are familiar with old versions of SQL Server you may now be saying, "What? What happened to logins? What happened to Remote Servers and SQL Agent Tasks?" SQL Server has several other objects (as listed above) that exist in support of the database. With the exception of linked servers, and perhaps DTS packages, these are primarily the domain of the database administrator and as such, we generally do not give them significant thought during the design and programming processes. (They are programmable via something called the SQL Distributed Management Objects (SQL-DMO) object model or through Windows Management Instrumentation (WMI), but are usually set up manually.)*

A database is typically a group of at least a set of table objects and, more often than not, other objects (such as stored procedures and views) that pertain to the particular grouping of data that is stored in the tables of that database.

What types of tables do we store in just one database and what goes in a separate database? We'll discuss that in some detail later in the book, but for now we'll take the simple approach of saying that any data that is generally thought of as belonging to just one system, or is significantly related, will be stored in a single database. An RDBMS such as SQL Server may have multiple user databases on just one server, or it may have only one. How many can reside on one SQL Server will depend on such factors as capacity (CPU power, disk I/O limitations, memory, etc.), autonomy (you want one person to have management rights to the server this system is running on, and someone else to have admin rights to a different server), or just how many databases your company or client has. Many servers only have one production database – others may have many. Also keep in mind that, with SQL Server 2000, we now have the ability to have multiple instances of SQL Server – complete with separate logins and management rights – all on the same physical server.

When you first load SQL Server, you begin with six databases installed by default:

❑ master

❑ model

❑ msdb

❑ tempdb

❑ pubs

❑ Northwind

Some of these have to be installed or your SQL Server won't run. Others are there to give you sample databases to work with. Let's look at these one by one.

The master Database

Every SQL Server, regardless of version or custom modifications, has the **master** database. This database holds a special set of tables (system tables) that keeps track of the system as a whole. For example, when you create a new database on the server, an entry is placed in the sysdatabases table in the master database. All extended and system stored procedures, regardless of what database they are intended for use with, are stored in this database. Obviously, since almost everything that describes your server is stored in here, this database is critical to your system and cannot be deleted.

The system tables – including those found in the master database – can, in a pinch, be extremely useful. They can allow you to determine whether certain objects exist before you perform operations on them. For example, if you try to create an object that already exists in any particular database, you will get an error. If you want to force the issue, you could test to see whether the table already has an entry in the sysobjects table for that database. If it does, then you would delete that object before re-creating it.

> If you're quite cavalier, you may be saying to yourself, "Cool, I can't wait to mess around in there!" *Don't go there!* Using the system tables in any form is fraught with peril. Microsoft has recommended against using the system tables for at least the last two versions of SQL Server. They make absolutely no guarantees about compatibility in the **master** database between versions – indeed, they virtually guarantee that they will change. The worst offense comes when performing updates on objects in the **master** database. Trust me when I tell you that altering these tables in any way is asking for a SQL Server that no longer functions. Fortunately, there are a number of alternatives (for example, system functions, system stored procedures, and information_schema views) for retrieving much of the meta data that is stored in the system tables.

> All that said, there are still times where nothing else will do. We will discuss a few situations where you can't avoid using the system tables, but in general, you should consider them to be evil cannibals from another tribe and best left alone.

The model Database

The model database is aptly named, in the sense that it's the model on which a copy can be based. The model database forms a template for any new database that you create. This means that you can, if you wish, alter the model database if you want to change what standard, newly created databases look like. For example, you could add a set of audit tables that you include in every database you build. You could also include a few user groups that would be cloned into every new database that was created on the system. Note that since this database serves as the template for any other database, it is a required database and must be left on the system – you cannot delete it.

There are several things to keep in mind when altering the model database. First, any database you create has to be at least as large as the model database. That means that if you alter the model database to be 100MB in size, you can't have any database smaller than 100MB. There are several other similar pitfalls. As such, for 90% of installations, I strongly recommend leaving this one alone.

The msdb Database

So far we've discussed the databases that are installed along with SQL Server which are required – if you delete master or model your system will fail. msdb is different.

msdb is where the **SQL Agent** process stores any system tasks. If you schedule backups to be run on a database nightly, then there is an entry in msdb. Schedule a stored procedure for one time execution – yes, it has an entry in msdb. msdb can, however, be deleted and not cause a complete system crash. Although, if you have any, you will lose any scheduled task entries, job history, DTS packages stored in the server (as opposed to as an external file), and your meta data repository (used for MS Repository), and will also not be able to use SQL Agent.

> If you remove **msdb** and then decide that you want to re-install it, good luck. The one time I had to re-install it, it messed my server up pretty well (can you say, "Complete Reload?"). In short, while you can remove this, I would strongly suggest you don't.

The tempdb Database

tempdb is one of the key working areas for your server. Whenever you issue a complex query that SQL Server needs to build interim tables to solve – it does so in tempdb. Whenever you create a temporary table of your own – it is created in tempdb (even though you think you're creating it in the current database). Whenever there is a need for data to be stored temporarily, it is probably stored in tempdb.

tempdb is very different from any other database in that, not only are the objects within it temporary, the database itself is temporary. It has the distinction of being the only database in your system that is completely rebuilt from scratch every time you start your SQL Server.

> Technically speaking, you can actually create objects yourself in `tempdb` – I strongly recommend against this practice. You can create temporary objects from within any database you have access to in your system – it will be stored in `tempdb`. Creating objects directly in `tempdb` gains you nothing, but adds the confusion of referring to things across databases. This is another of those, "Don't go there!" kind of things.

The pubs Database

Ahhhh pubs! It's almost like an old friend. pubs is now installed mostly to support training articles and books like this. pubs has absolutely nothing to do with the operation of SQL Server. It is merely there to provide a consistent place for your training and experimentation. We will make use of pubs occasionally in this book.

pubs can be deleted with no significant consequences. Indeed, many database administrators delete it from their production database servers. Since it takes up such a small amount of space, I usually leave it. (It comes in quite handy for doing small proof of concept experiments. These are better done on a non-production server, but the production server is often the only server, particularly in small shops.)

This brings up the point of test databases. If possible, you really want to have a complete copy of your database available to serve as nothing more than a test bed for making changes or working on new procedures before you try them in the "live" database.

The Northwind Database

If your past programming experience has involved Access or Visual Basic, then you are probably already somewhat familiar with the Northwind database. Northwind was new to SQL Server beginning in version 7.0. It is, like pubs, a training database. The advantage of Northwind is that it is significantly more complex than pubs. That means that you can explore SQL Server more fully than with pubs. This turns out to be something of a good news/bad news story. It's a much better training ground, but it also takes up more space. Still, by default, it only takes up about 4MB for both the database and the log, so in this age of cheap hard drives, I usually leave it in place. The Northwind database will serve as one of the major testing grounds for this book.

> **pubs** and **Northwind** are both installed as part of the SQL Server installation. However, you can re-install them at anytime by running the scripts `instpubs.sql` (for **pubs**) and `instnwnd.sql` (for **Northwind**).

The Transaction Log

Believe it or not, the database file itself isn't where most things happen. While the data is certainly read in from there, any changes you make don't initially go to the database itself – instead, they are written serially to the **transaction log**. At some later point in time, the database is issued a **checkpoint** – it is at that point in time that all the changes in the log are propagated to the actual database file.

The database is in a random access arrangement, but the log is serial in nature. While the random nature of the database file allows for speedy access, the serial nature of the log allows things to be tracked in the proper order. The log accumulates changes that are deemed as having been committed, and then writes several of them to the physical database file(s) at a time.

We'll take a much closer look at how things are logged in our chapter on transactions and locking, but for now, remember that the log is the first place on disk that the data goes, and it is only propagated to the actual database at a later time – you need both the database file and the transaction log in order to have a functional database.

The Most Basic Database Object – Table

Databases are made up of many things, but none are more central to the make-up of a database than tables. A table can be thought of as equating to an accountant's ledger or an Excel spreadsheet. It is made up of what is called **domain** data (columns) and **entity** data (rows). The actual data for the database is stored in the tables.

Each table definition also contains the **meta data** (descriptive information about data) that describes the nature of the data it is to contain. Each column has its own set of rules about what can be stored in that column. A violation of the rules of any one column can cause the system to reject an inserted row or an update to an existing row, or prevent the deletion of a row.

Let's take a look at the `publishers` table in the `pubs` database. (The view presented is from SQL Server's Enterprise Manager. We will look at how to make use of this tool in the next chapter.)

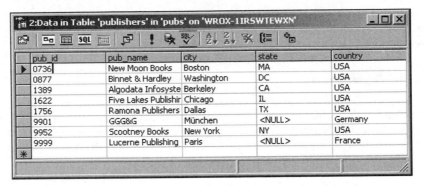

This table is made up of five columns of data. The number of columns remains constant regardless of how much data (even zero) is in the table. Currently, the table has eight records. The number of records will go up and down as we add or delete data, but the nature of the data in each record (or row) will be described and restricted by the **data type** of the column. Let's look at the definition for this table:

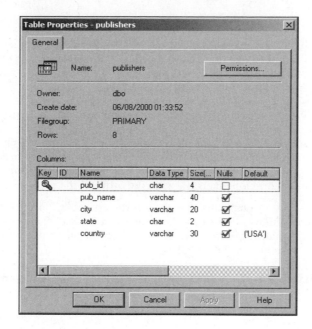

Working from left to right, we can tell:

- ❑ Whether a column is part of the **primary key** for the table
- ❑ Whether it is an **IDENTITY** column
- ❑ The column's name
- ❑ The data type for the column
- ❑ The size in bytes that column takes up
- ❑ Whether the column allows null values or not
- ❑ Whether the column has a default value (in case one isn't provided during an insert)

We will discuss the meaning of each of these and the other column choices in Chapter 6.

> **I'm going to take this as my first opportunity to launch into a diatribe on the naming of objects. Beginning with version 7.0, SQL Server added the ability to embed spaces in names, and in some cases, to use keywords as names. Resist the temptation to do this! Columns with embedded spaces in their name have nice headers when you make a SELECT statement, but there are other ways to achieve the same result. Using embedded spaces and keywords for column names is literally begging for bugs, confusion, and other disasters. I'll discuss later why Microsoft has elected to allow this, but for now, just remember to associate embedded spaces or keywords in names with evil empires, torture, and certain death. (This won't be the last time you hear from me on this one.)**

Indexes

An **index** is an object that exists only within the framework of a particular table or view. An index works much like the index does in the back of an encyclopedia – there is some sort of lookup (or "key") value that is sorted in a particular way, and, once you have that, you are provided another key with which you can look up the actual information you were after.

An index provides us ways of speeding the lookup of our information. Indexes fall into two categories:

❑ **Clustered** – you can only have one of these per table. If an index is clustered, it means that the table on which the clustered index is based is physically sorted according to that index. If you were indexing an encyclopedia, the clustered index would be the page numbers; the information in the encyclopedia is stored in the order of the page numbers.

❑ **Non-clustered** – you can have many of these for every table. This is more along the lines of what you probably think of when you hear the word "index". This kind of index points to some other value that will let you find the data. For our encyclopedia, this would be the keyword index at the back of the book.

Note that views that have indexes – or **indexed views** – can only have clustered indexes.

Triggers

A **trigger** is an object that exists only within the framework of a table. Triggers are pieces of logical code that are automatically executed when certain things happen to your table (such as inserts, updates, or deletes).

Triggers can be used for a great variety of things, but are mainly used for either copying data as it is entered or checking the update to make sure that it meets some criteria. However, with SQL Server 2000, there is a new kind of trigger (called an INSTEAD OF trigger) that allows us to substitute a totally different action in the place of whatever the user was trying to do – we will see that this becomes very important when we deal with views in Chapter 10.

Constraints

A **constraint** is yet another object that only exists within the confines of a table. Constraints are much like they sound – they confine the data in your table to meeting certain conditions. Constraints, in a way, compete with triggers as possible solutions to data integrity issues. They are not, however, the same thing – each has its own distinct advantages.

Filegroups

Filegroups are probably the closest thing that versions 7.0 and beyond have to previous versions' concepts of devices and segments. By default, all your tables and everything else about your database (except the log) are stored in a single file. That file is a member of what's called the **primary filegroup**. However, you are not stuck with this arrangement.

SQL Server allows you to define a little over 32,000 **secondary files** (if you need more than that, perhaps it isn't SQL Server that has the problem). These secondary files can be added to the primary filegroup or created as part of one or more **secondary filegroups**. While there is only one primary filegroup (and it is actually called "Primary"), you can have up to 255 secondary filegroups. A secondary filegroup is created as an option to a CREATE DATABASE or ALTER DATABASE command.

If you worked with SQL Server 6.5 devices, but didn't use multiple devices in one database, you may be saying something like, "Hey, we got rid of devices – Hallelujah! Why would we need anything similar to those?" If only it were as simple as that.

Devices were indeed a rather nasty pain in the neck for perhaps 95% or more of all installations. For the other 5% or so, they were a saving grace. Devices allowed you to break up the database onto multiple physical devices – to spread out the I/O loading and improve performance. Beginning with version 7.0, we began using files – which are generally easier to manage, but filegroups give us the ability to group together our files for administrative purposes – it means that we can easily back up an entire group rather than one file at a time. In short, they are here to make our lives easier – honest!

Diagrams

The ability to make database diagrams was added with SQL Server 7.0. We will discuss database diagramming in some detail when we discuss normalization and database design, but for now, suffice it to say that a database diagram is a visual representation of the database design, including the various tables, the column names in each table, and the relationships between tables. Prior to this version, you had very few choices in making what's referred to as an **entity-relationship** (or ER) diagram. In an ER diagram the database is divided into two parts – entities (such as "supplier" and "product") and relations (such as "supplies", "purchases").

One could say that we still have few choices in making ER diagrams. Those of us who are fortunate enough to work with a more serious database design tool consider the database design tools that are now part of SQL Server to be sparse. Indeed, the diagramming methodology the tools use does not adhere to any of the accepted standards in ER diagramming.

Still, these diagramming tools, or the "da Vinci Tools" as they are known within Microsoft, are light years ahead of what we had in version 6.5 – which is to say that we didn't have anything. I have had jobs where I would have killed for anything with as much as the da Vinci tools provide. Still, if you're doing any serious design work, I strongly suggest paying for a more serious ER diagramming tool.

Overleaf is a diagram that shows the various tables that make up the Northwind database. The diagram also describes many other properties about the database. Notice the tiny icons for keys and the infinity sign. These depict the nature of the relationship between two tables. We'll talk about relationships extensively in Chapters 7 and 8 and we'll look further into diagrams later in the book.

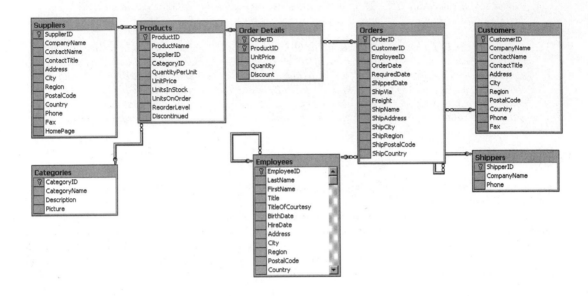

Views

A view is something of a virtual table. A view, for the most part, is used just like a table, except that it doesn't contain any data itself. Instead, a view is merely a preplanned mapping and representation of the data stored in tables. The plan is stored in the database in the form of a query. This query calls for data from some columns (but not necessarily all columns) to be retrieved from one or more tables. The data retrieved may or may not (depending on the view definition) have to meet special criteria in order to be shown as data in that view.

Until SQL Server 2000, the primary purpose of views was to control what the user of the view sees. This has two major impacts – security and ease of use. With views you can control what the users see, so if there is a section of a table that should be accessed by only a few users (for example, salary details), you can create a view that includes only those columns to which everyone is allowed access. In addition, the view can be tailored so that the user does not have to search through any unneeded information.

New with SQL Server 2000, however, is the ability to create what is called an **indexed view** (which is very similar to what Oracle refers to as a **materialized view**). This is the same as any other view, except that we can now create an index against the view. This results in a couple of performance impacts (some positive, one negative):

- ❑ Views that reference multiple tables will generally perform *much* faster with an indexed view since the join between the tables is pre-constructed

- ❑ Aggregations performed in the view are pre-calculated and stored as part of the index – again, this means that the aggregation is performed one time (when the row is inserted or updated), and then can be read directly from the index information

❑ Inserts and deletes have higher overhead since the index on the view has to be updated immediately – updates will also have higher overhead if the key column of the index is affected by the update

Also new with SQL Server 2000 is a special kind of updateable view that allows tables from different databases or even different servers to act in unison – creating one logical table. This allows us to spread out the work across multiple servers or just across different databases (which can later be moved to a different server or just kept separate for manageability).

We will look into these much deeper in Chapter 10.

Stored Procedures

Stored procedures (or **sprocs**) continue to be the bread and butter of programmatic functionality in SQL Server. Stored procedures are an ordered series of Transact-SQL (the language used to query Microsoft SQL Server) statements bundled up into a single logical unit. They allow for variables and parameters as well as selection and looping constructs. Sprocs offer several advantages over just sending individual statements to the server in the sense that they:

❑ Are referred to using short names, rather than a long string of text, therefore less network traffic is required in order to run the code within the sproc

❑ Are pre-optimized and pre-compiled, saving a small amount of time each time the sproc is run

❑ Encapsulate a process – usually for security reasons or just to hide the complexity of the database

❑ Can be called from other sprocs, thus making them reusable in a somewhat limited sense

In short, sprocs are the closest things that SQL Server has to a "program".

There has been something of a trend in recent years to "avoid sprocs at all costs!" This has been brought about by the popularity of 3- and n-tier architectures, and a move towards portability. I have to say that I disagree with this point of view.

Many developers erroneously believe that they should just pass through raw SQL to the server, that way it won't matter what the server is as long as it is ANSI (American National Standards Institute) compliant – and all major RDBMSs are. Good n-tier development says that your data layer should insulate the middle tier(s) from the actual implementation of the database. This is certainly true and doing so limits, for the most part, the risks involved with moving to a new platform to just the data layer. However, this can be done with a component approach. You should create a component that knows how to get the most out of your back-end. For SQL Server, that way is, more often than not, by using sprocs or their close cousin, User Defined Functions.

N-tier purists may scowl nastily at me for saying so, but you're nuts if you don't use every reasonable optimization available to whatever back-end you choose – regardless of what back-end that is. If you're building an n-tier system, you should build your middle tier(s) to talk to a data tier. This lets the data tier know the best way to talk to the database. You'll get a faster performing system, and the only things that will have to be modified if you change back-ends (or decide to support more than one) are just the data components.

User Defined Functions

User Defined Functions (or **UDFs**), are new to SQL Server with SQL Server 2000. They have a tremendous number of similarities to sprocs, except that they:

- ❑ Can return a value of most SQL Server data types. Excluded return types include text, ntext, image, cursor, and timestamp.

- ❑ Can't have "side effects" (basically, they can't do anything that reaches outside the scope of the function – such as changing tables, sending e-mails, or system or database parameter changes).

UDFs are similar to the functions that you would use in a standard programming language such as VB or C++. You can pass more than one variable in, and get a value out. UDFs vary from the functions found in many procedural languages, however, in that *all* variables passed into the function are passed in by value. If you're familiar with passing in variables By Ref in VB, or passing in pointers in C++ – sorry, there is no equivalent here. There is, however, some good news in that you can return a special data type called a table. We'll examine the impact of this in Chapter 13.

Although they are new, it is my strong prediction that UDFs will become something of a staple of SQL Server development to the same degree that sprocs have. UDFs allow us to perform functions in-line to a SELECT statement or other query in a far more flexible manner than we could with sprocs alone.

Users and Roles

These two go hand in hand. Prior to SQL Server 7.0, their equivalents were referred to as logins and groups, but they were not exactly the same as their current version counterparts. **Users** are pretty much the equivalent of logins. In short, this object represents an identifier for someone to login into the SQL Server. Anyone logging into SQL Server has to map (directly or indirectly depending on the security model you're using) to a user. Users, in turn, belong to one or more **roles**. Rights to perform certain actions in SQL Server can then be granted either directly to a user or to a role to which that one or more users belong.

If you are familiar with the NT security arena, you may be noticing that the format added in 7.0 has a striking resemblance to NT groups – this is not by accident. Microsoft is making a serious effort to increase the security compatibility within the BackOffice suite of products. The new roles concept in SQL Server moves solidly into the NT camp in the way that it's implemented. Perhaps the nicest side effect though is that they actually made things both simpler and more flexible in the process. The effect that Active Directory will have on all this is, as yet, unknown (SQL Server 2000 was way too far along the development trail to be significantly affected by Win2K – at least in this area).

Rules

Rules and constraints provide restriction information on what can go into a table. If an updated or inserted record violates a rule, then that insertion or update will be rejected. In addition, a rule can be used to define a restriction on a **user-defined data type**. (Unlike rules, constraints are not really objects unto themselves, but rather pieces of meta data describing a particular table.)

Defaults

There are two types of defaults. There is the default that is an object unto itself, and the default that is not really an object, but rather meta data describing a particular column in a table (in much the same way as we have constraints, which are objects, and rules, which are not objects but meta data). They both serve the same purpose. If, when inserting a record, you don't provide the value of a column and that column has a default defined, then a value will be inserted automatically as defined in the default. We will examine both types of defaults in our chapter on constraints.

User-Defined Data Types

User-defined data types are extensions to the system-defined data types. You can take a system-defined data type, such as `integer`, and bind a rule to it. For example, you could create a rule that states that a value must be greater than 5,000, bind that rule to a user-defined data type built using an `integer` and you would wind up with a data type that automatically ensures that any column where that data type is used will always have a value greater than 5,000.

User-defined data types are limited in scope to just the database in which they are created.

> This is one of those odd areas where it can actually make sense to modify the `model` database. If your development group has a data type that they use consistently across all their databases, then you could create the user-defined data type in the `model` database of all the servers you want to ensure have this data type. The data type would then be automatically added to any new database you created.

Full-Text Catalogs

First introduced in version 7.0, there have been some terrific changes made in this area for SQL Server 2000. Full-text catalogs are mappings of data that speed the search for specific blocks of text within columns that have had full-text searching enabled. While these objects are tied at the hip to the tables and columns that they map, they are separate objects, and are therefore not automatically updated when changes happen to the database.

Some of the highlights in terms of changes to full-text search in SQL Server 2000 include:

- ❑ Change tracking – giving us something along the lines of "real enough" time updates

- ❑ Improvements in the threading model (it used to peak at 8 threads, which could cause performance issues)

- ❑ The ability to perform full-text searches against several recognized types of `image` data (such as Word, Excel, and Acrobat files)

For this revision of this book, full-text search has been moved into its own chapter to give us enough room to fully explore this excellent tool. In that chapter, we will take a look at the special quirks of full-text catalogs, and what full-text search has to offer.

SQL Server Data Types

Now that you're familiar with the base objects of a SQL Server database, let's take a look at the options that SQL Server has for one of the fundamental items of any environment that handles data – data types. Note that, since this book is intended for developers, and that no developer could survive for 60 seconds without an understanding of data types, I'm going to assume that you already know how data types work, and just need to know the particulars of SQL Server data types.

With SQL Server 2000, several new data types are introduced. Some are just adding new capacity to existing data types (for example, the addition of a new, larger int data type), and a few are totally new to SQL Server for this release.

SQL Server 2000 has the following intrinsic data types:

Data Type Name	Class	Size in Bytes	Nature of the Data
Bit	Integer	1	The size is somewhat misleading. The first bit data type in a table takes up one byte; the next seven make use of the same byte. Nulls were allowed for the first time in SQL Server 7.0, although allowing nulls causes an additional byte to be used.
Bigint	Integer	8	This just deals with the fact that we use larger and larger numbers on a more frequent basis. This one allows you to use whole numbers from -2^{63} to 2^{63}-1. That's plus or minus about 92 quintrillion.
Int	Integer	4	Whole numbers from -2,147,483,648 to 2,147,483,647.
SmallInt	Integer	2	Whole numbers from -32,768 to 32,767.
TinyInt	Integer	1	Whole numbers from 0 to 255.
Decimal or Numeric	Decimal/ Numeric	Varies	Fixed precision and scale from -10^{38}-1 to 10^{38}-1. The two names are synonymous.
Money	Money	8	Monetary units from -2^{63} to 2^{63} plus precision to four decimal places. Note that this could be any monetary unit, not just dollars.
SmallMoney	Money	4	Monetary units from -214,748.3648 to +214,748.3647.
Float (also a synonym for ANSI Real)	Approximate Numerics	Varies	Accepts an argument (e.g. Float(20)) that determines size and precision. Note that the argument is in bits, not bytes. Ranges from -1.79E + 308 to 1.79E + 308.

Data Type Name	Class	Size in Bytes	Nature of the Data
DateTime	Date/Time	8	Date and time data from January 1, 1753 to December 31, 9999 with an accuracy of three-hundredths of a second. Allowed nulls for the first time in SQL Server 7.0.
Small DateTime	Date/Time	4	Date and time data from January 1, 1900 to June 6, 2079, with an accuracy of one minute.
Cursor	Special Numeric	1	Pointer to a cursor. While the pointer only takes up a byte, keep in mind that the result set that makes up the actual cursor also takes up memory – exactly how much will vary depending on the result set.
Timestamp/ rowversion	Special Numeric (binary)	8	Special value that is unique within a given database. Value is set by the database itself automatically every time the record is either inserted or updated – even though the timestamp column wasn't referred to by the UPDATE statement (you're actually not allowed to update the timestamp field directly).
Unique Identifier	Special Numeric (binary)	16	Special Globally Unique Identifier. Is guaranteed to be unique across space and time.
Char	Character	Varies	Fixed-length character data. Values shorter than the set length are padded with spaces to the set length. Data is non-Unicode. Maximum length is 8,000 characters.
VarChar	Character	Varies	Variable-length character data. Values are not padded with spaces. Data is non-Unicode. Maximum length is 8,000 characters.
Text	Character	Varies	Maximum length is 2,147,483,647 characters. Data is non-Unicode. Space is allocated in 8K pages.
NChar	Unicode	Varies	Fixed-length Unicode character data. Values shorter than the set length are padded with spaces. Maximum length is 4,000 characters.
NVarChar	Unicode	Varies	Variable-length Unicode character data. Values are not padded. Maximum length is 4,000 characters.

Table continued on following page

Data Type Name	Class	Size in Bytes	Nature of the Data
Ntext	Unicode	Varies	Variable-length Unicode character data, maximum of 1,073,741,823 characters. Data is allocated in 8K pages.
Binary	Binary	Varies	Fixed-length binary data with a maximum length of 8,000 bytes.
VarBinary	Binary	Varies	Variable-length binary data with a maximum length of 8,000 bytes.
Image	Binary	Varies	Variable-length binary data with a maximum length of $2^{31} - 1$ (2,147,483,647) bytes. Data is allocated in 8K pages. Don't confuse this with the word "image" as used in a picture. While pictures could be stored in an image field, so can any other binary data, or even text data – it's an all purpose kind of data type but has huge overhead.
Table	Other	Special	Brand new with SQL Server 2000. This is primarily for use in working with result sets –typically passing one out of a User Defined Function.
Sql_variant	Other	Special	This is loosely related to the Variant in VB and C++. Essentially, it is a container that allows you to hold most other SQL Server data types in it. That means you can use this when one column or function needs to be able to deal with multiple data types. Unlike VB, using this data type forces you to *explicitly* cast it in order to convert it to a more specific data type.

Most of these have equivalent data types in other programming languages. For example, an int in SQL Server is equivalent to a Long in Visual Basic, and for most systems and compiler combinations in C++, is equivalent to an int.

In general, SQL Server data types work much as you would expect given experience in most other modern programming languages. Adding numbers yields you a sum, but adding strings concatenates them. When you mix the usage or assignment of variables or fields of different data types, there are a number of types that convert implicitly (or automatically). Most other types can be converted explicitly (you specifically say what type you want to convert to). A few cannot be converted between at all. Opposite is a chart that shows the various possible conversions:

Data type conversion chart. Legend: **E** = Explicit Conversion, **I** = Implicit Conversion, **N** = Conversion not allowed, ***** = Requires explicit CAST or CONVERT function usage to prevent the loss of precision or scale that might occur in an implicit conversion. Blank cell = same data type (diagonal).

From \ To	binary	varbinary	char	varchar	nchar	nvarchar	datetime	smalldatetime	decimal	numeric	float	real	int(INT4)	smallint(INT2)	tinyint(INT1)	money	smallmoney	bit	timestamp	uniqueidentifier	image	ntext	text
binary		I	I	I	I	I	I	I	I	I	N	N	I	I	I	I	I	I	I	I	I	N	N
varbinary	I		I	I	I	I	I	I	I	I	N	N	I	I	I	I	I	I	I	I	I	N	N
char	E	E		I	I	I	I	I	I	I	I	I	I	I	I	E	E	I	E	I	N	I	I
varchar	E	E	I		I	I	I	I	I	I	I	I	I	I	I	E	E	I	E	I	N	I	I
nchar	E	E	I	I		I	I	I	I	I	I	I	I	I	I	E	E	I	E	N	N	I	I
nvarchar	E	E	I	I	I		I	I	I	I	I	I	I	I	I	E	E	I	E	I	N	I	I
datetime	E	E	I	I	I	I		I	I	I	E	E	E	E	E	E	E	E	I	N	N	N	N
smalldatetime	E	E	I	I	I	I	I		E	E	E	E	E	E	I	E	E	E	I	N	N	N	N
decimal	I	I	I	I	I	I	I	I	*	*	I	I	I	I	I	I	I	I	I	N	N	N	N
numeric	I	I	I	I	I	I	I	I	*	*	I	I	I	I	I	I	I	I	I	N	N	N	N
float	I	I	I	I	I	I	I	I	I	I		I	I	I	I	I	I	I	I	N	N	N	N
real	I	I	I	I	I	I	I	I	I	I	I		I	I	I	I	I	I	I	N	N	N	N
int(INT4)	I	I	I	I	I	I	I	I	I	I	I	I		I	I	I	I	I	I	N	N	N	N
smallint(INT2)	I	I	I	I	I	I	I	I	I	I	I	I	I		I	I	I	I	I	N	N	N	N
tinyint(INT1)	I	I	I	I	I	I	I	I	I	I	I	I	I	I		I	I	I	I	N	N	N	N
money	I	I	E	E	E	E	I	I	I	I	I	I	I	I	I		I	I	I	N	N	N	N
smallmoney	I	I	E	E	E	E	I	I	I	I	I	I	I	I	I	I		I	I	N	N	N	N
bit	I	I	I	I	I	I	I	I	I	I	I	I	I	I	I	I	I		I	N	N	N	N
timestamp	I	I	I	I	N	N	I	I	I	I	N	N	I	I	I	I	I	I		N	N	N	N
uniqueidentifier	I	I	I	I	I	I	N	N	N	N	N	N	N	N	N	N	N	N	N		N	N	N
image	I	I	N	N	N	N	N	N	N	N	N	N	N	N	N	N	N	N	N	N	I	N	N
ntext	N	N	E	E	I	I	N	N	N	N	N	N	N	N	N	N	N	N	N	N	N		N
text	N	N	I	I	E	E	N	N	N	N	N	N	N	N	N	N	N	N	N	N	N	N	

- ● Explicit Conversion
- ◐ Implicit Conversion
- ○ Conversion not allowed
- ***** Requires explicit CAST or CONVERT function usage to prevent the loss of precision or scale that might occur in an implicit conversion

Why would we have to convert a data type? Well, let's try a simple example. If I wanted to output the phrase, "Today's date is ##/##/####", where ##/##/#### is the current date, I could write it like this:

```
SELECT 'Today''s date is ' + GETDATE()
```

We will discuss Transact-SQL statements such as this in much greater detail later in the book, but the expected results of the above example should be fairly obvious to you.

The problem is that this statement would yield the following result:

Server: Msg 241, Level 16, State 1, Line 1
Syntax error converting datetime from character string.

Not exactly what we were after, is it? Now let's try it with the CONVERT() function:

```
SELECT "Today's date is " + CONVERT(varchar(12), GETDATE(),101)
```

This yields something like:

```
------------------------------------
Today's date is 01/01/2000
```

(1 row(s) affected)

Date and time data types (such as the output of the GETDATE() function) are not implicitly convertible to a string data type (such as "Today's date is "), yet we run into these conversions on a regular basis. Fortunately, the CAST and CONVERT() functions allow us to convert between many SQL Server data types. We will discuss the CAST and CONVERT() functions more in a later chapter.

In short, data types in SQL Server perform much the same function that they do in other programming environments. They help prevent programming bugs by ensuring that the data supplied is of the same nature that the data is supposed to be (remember 1/1/1980 means something different as a date than as a number) and ensures that the kind of operation performed is what you expect.

NULL Data

What if you have a row where you don't have any data for a particular column – that is, what if you simply don't know the value? For example, let's say that we have a record that is trying to store the company performance information for a given year. Now, imagine that one of the fields is a percentage growth over the prior year, but you don't have records for the year before the first record in your database. You might be tempted to just enter a zero in the PercentGrowth column. Would that provide the right information though? People who didn't know better might think that meant you had zero percent growth, when the fact is that you simply don't know the value for that year.

Values that are indeterminate are said to be **NULL**. It seems that every time I teach a class in programming, at least one student asks me to define the value of NULL. Well, that's a tough one, because, by definition, a NULL value means that you don't know what the value is. It could be 1, it could be 347, it could be -294 for all we know. In short, it means "undefined".

Prior to version 7.0, several data types did not accept NULL values. For example, bit fields didn't accept NULLs. This was very problematic. Typically, the way this was handled was to define an arbitrary number to serve as the "I don't know" value. The problem with this is that you are assigning a specific value to something and the specific value that you've assigned is wrong! By rule, you are sticking inaccurate data into your database! Thankfully, all data types now accept NULLs.

Be aware that the RTM version of version 7.0 contained a bug that wouldn't let you set a bit column to nullable when you were working from within Enterprise Manager (you could do it just fine if you used the T-SQL command directly). This has since been fixed, but it's something to watch out for.

SQL Server Identifiers for Objects

Now you've heard all sorts of things about objects in SQL Server. You've even heard my first soapbox diatribe on column names. But let's take a closer look at naming objects in SQL Server.

What Gets Named?

Basically, everything has a name in SQL Server. Here's a partial list:

Stored procedures	Tables	Columns
Views	Rules	Constraints
Defaults	Indexes	Filegroups
Triggers	Databases	Servers
User Defined Functions	Logins	Roles
Full-text catalogs	Files	User Defined Types

And the list goes on. Most things I can think of except rows (which aren't really objects) have a name. The trick is to make every name both useful and practical.

Rules for Naming

As I mentioned earlier in the chapter, the rules for naming in SQL Server became substantially more relaxed in version 7.0 than they were prior to that time. Like most freedoms, however, it's easy to make some bad choices and get yourself into trouble.

In SQL Server 6.5, you were usually limited to 20 characters for object names. This often generated problems in creating clear names that truly described the object that was being named. For example, let's say we had tables called `Organization` and `Characteristic`. If we created a linking table between these tables, we might want to call it something like `OrganizationCharacteristic` – that is, simply combine the names of the significant tables that we are linking. The problem would make itself apparent rather quickly when we got a message indicating that the identifier was too long (26 characters). The limit was increased to 128 characters for normal objects and 116 for temporary objects beginning with version 7.0. It should be a very rare day indeed when you run into a problem with that limit – we'll explore this in more detail later.

Here are the main rules:

❑ The name of your object must start with any letter as defined by the specification for Unicode 2.0. This will include the letters most westerners are used to – A-Z and a-z. Whether "A" is different than "a" will depend on how you have your server configured, but either makes for a valid beginning to an object name. After that first letter, you're pretty much free to run wild – almost any character will do.

❑ Any names that are the same as SQL Server keywords or contain embedded spaces must be enclosed in either double quotes (" ") or square brackets ([ ]). What words are considered to be keywords will vary depending on the compatibility level to which you have set your database.

Note that double quotes are only acceptable as a delimiter for column names if you have SET QUOTED_IDENTIFIER ON. Using square brackets ([and]) avoids the chance that your users will have the wrong setting.

These rules are generally referred to as the rules for identifiers and are in force for any objects you name in SQL Server. Additional rules may exist for specific object types.

> **Again – I can't stress enough the importance of avoiding the use of SQL Server keywords or embedded spaces in names. While both are technically legal as long as you qualify them, naming things this way will cause you no end of grief.**

Summary

Like most things in life, the little things do matter when thinking about an RDBMS. Sure, almost anyone who knows enough to even think about picking up this book at least has an idea of the *concept* of storing data in columns and rows (even if they don't know that these groupings of columns and rows should be called "tables"), but a few tables seldom make a real database. The things that make today's RDBMSs great are the extra things – the objects that allow you to place both functionality and business rules that are associated with the data right into the database with the data.

Database data has *type* – just as most other programming environments do. Most things that you do in SQL Server are going to have at least some consideration of type. Review the types that are available, and think about how these types map to the data types in whatever programming environment with which you are familiar.

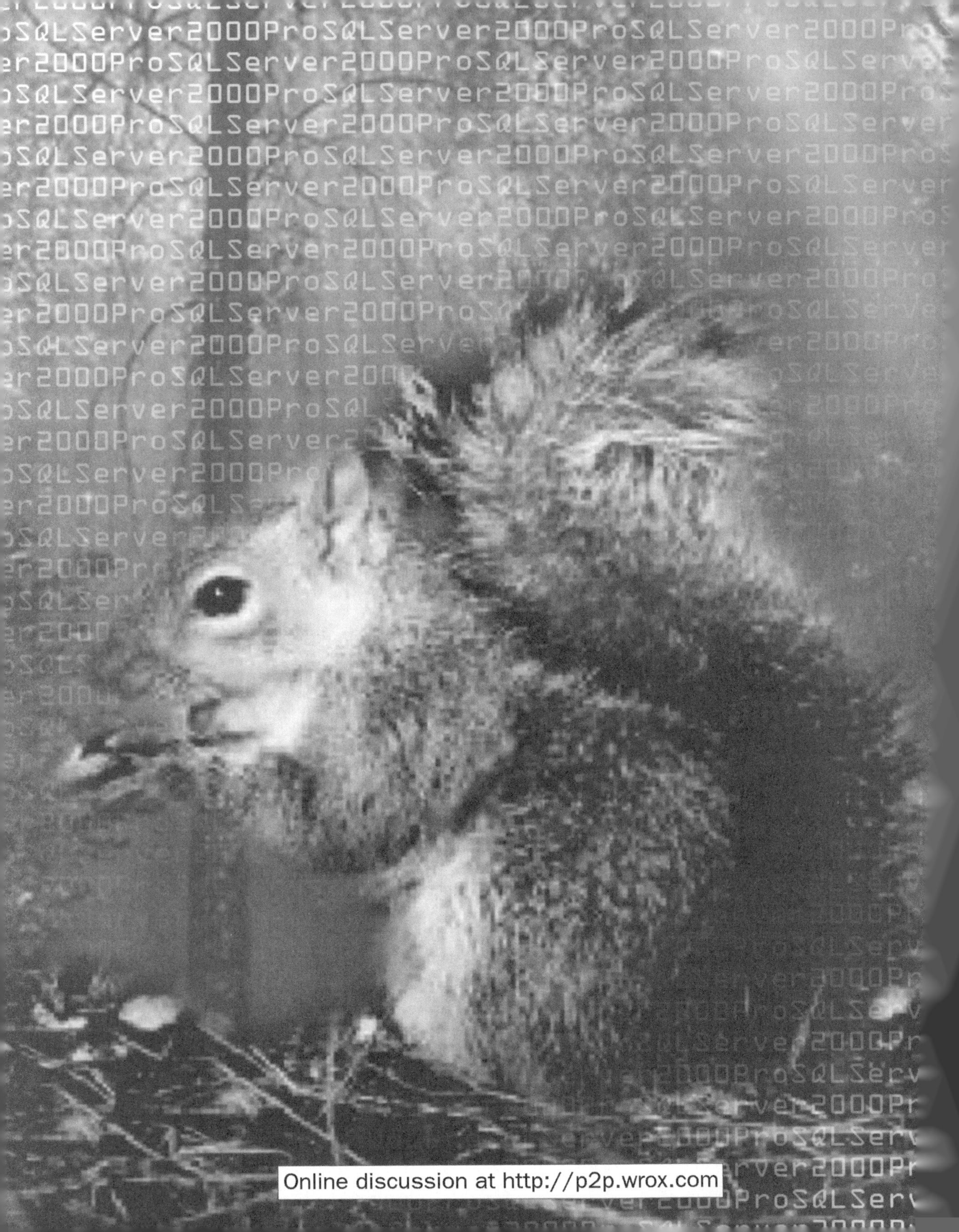
Online discussion at http://p2p.wrox.com

3

Tools of the Trade

Now that we know something about the many types of objects that exist on SQL Server, we probably should get to know something about how to find these objects, and how to monitor our system in general.

In this chapter, we will look into the tools that SQL Server has to offer. Some of them offer only a small number of highly specialized tasks – others do many different things. Most of them have been around in SQL Server for a long time, a few were new or highly revised in the last version (7.0), but a few of the old reliable tools have gone through some major changes (believe me, this is a good thing) for SQL Server 2000.

The tools we will look at in this chapter will be:

- ❑ SQL Server Books Online
- ❑ The Client and Server Network Utilities
- ❑ The Enterprise Manager
- ❑ Data Transformation Services (DTS)
- ❑ The Bulk Copy Program (bcp)
- ❑ MS DTC Administrative Console
- ❑ Profiler
- ❑ Query Analyzer
- ❑ OSQL
- ❑ Service Manager
- ❑ `sqlmaint`

Books Online

Is **Books Online** a tool? I think so. Let's face it, it doesn't matter how many times you read this or any other book on SQL Server, you're not going to remember everything you'll ever need to know about SQL Server. SQL Server is one of my mainstay products, and I still can't remember it all. Books Online is simply one of the most important tools you're going to find in SQL Server.

My general philosophy about books or any other reference material related to programming is that I can't have enough of it. I first began programming in 1980 or so, and back then it was possible to remember most things (but not everything). Today, it's simply impossible. If you have any diversification at all (something that is, in itself, rather difficult these days), there are just too many things to remember, and the things you don't use everyday get lost in dying brain cells.

Here's a simple piece of advice: Don't even try to remember it all. Remember what you've seen is possible. Remember what is an integral foundation to what you're doing. Remember what you work with everyday. Then remember to build a good reference library (starting with this book) for the rest.

Books Online in SQL Server uses the online help interface, which is becoming standard among the Microsoft technical product line (Back Office, MSDN, Visual Studio):

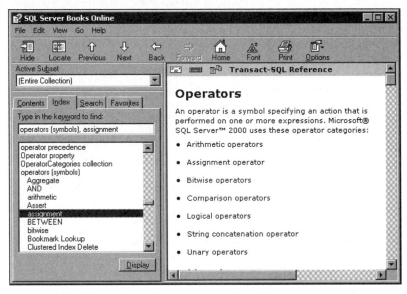

Everything works pretty much as one would expect here, so I'm not going to go into the details of how to operate a help system. Suffice it to say that SQL Server Books Online is a great quick reference that follows you to whatever machine you're working on at the time. Books Online also has the added benefit of often having information that is more up to date than the printed documentation.

> Technically speaking, it's quite possible that not every system that you move to will have the Books Online (BOL) installed. This is because you can manually de-select BOL at the time of installation. Even in tight space situations however, I strongly recommend that you always install the BOL. It really doesn't take up all that much space when you consider cost per megabyte these days, and it can save you a fortune in time by having that quick reference available wherever you are running SQL Server. (On my machine, Books Online takes up 34.5MB of space.)

The Client and Server Network Utilities

Administrators who configure computers for database access are the main users of these tools, but it is still important for us to understand the tools. A fair percentage of the time, any of the connectivity issues discovered are the result of client network configuration or how that configuration matches with that of the server.

SQL Server provides several of what are referred to as **Net-Libraries** (network libraries), or **NetLibs**. These are dynamic-link libraries (DLLs) that SQL Server uses to communicate with certain **network protocols**. NetLibs serve as something of an insulator between your client application and the network protocol (which is essentially the language that one network card uses to talk to another) that is to be used – they serve the same function at the server end too. The NetLibs supplied with SQL Server 2000 include:

❑ Named Pipes

❑ TCP/IP

❑ Multiprotocol

❑ NWLink IPX/SPX

❑ AppleTalk

❑ Banyan VINES

❑ Shared Memory

❑ VIA

> *VIA is a special net library that is made for use with some very special (and expensive) hardware. If you're running in a VIA environment, you'll know about the special requirements associated with it. For those of you that aren't running in that environment, it suffices to say that VIA offers a very fast but expensive solution to high-speed communication between servers. It would not usually be used for a normal client.*

The same NetLib must be available on both the client and server computers so that they can communicate with each other via the network protocol. Choosing a client NetLib that is not also supported on the server will result in your connection attempt failing (with a Specified SQL Server Not Found error).

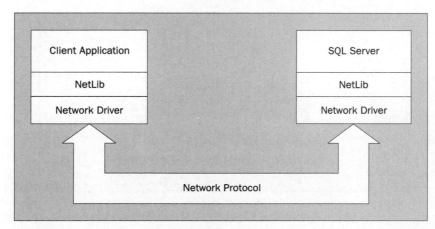

Regardless of the data access method and kind of driver used (ODBC, OLE DB, or DB-Lib), it will always be the driver that talks to the NetLib. The process works like this:

1. The client app talks to the driver (DB-Lib, ODBC, or OLE DB)

2. The driver calls the client NetLib

3. This NetLib calls the appropriate network protocol and transmits the data to a server NetLib

4. The server NetLib then passes the requests from the client to the SQL Server

Replies from SQL Server to the client follow the same sequence, only in reverse.

Prior to SQL Server 2000, the default NetLib was Named Pipes (which is the default used by NT networks). The TCP/IP client has replaced Named Pipes as the default. Beginning with version 7.0, the TCP/IP NetLib was also activated on the server by default.

> **In case you're familiar with TCP/IP, the default port that the IP NetLib will listen on is 1433. A port can be thought of as being like a channel on the radio – signals are bouncing around on all sorts of different frequencies, but they only do you any good if you're "listening" on the right channel. We'll go into the importance of ports further when we talk about security later in the book. For now, what we're interested in is what libraries our client and server each have available, and which one(s) they are actually using.**

The Protocols

Let's start off with that "What are the available choices?" question. If you run the Server Network Utility under the Microsoft SQL Server program group on the Start menu, you'll see something like this:

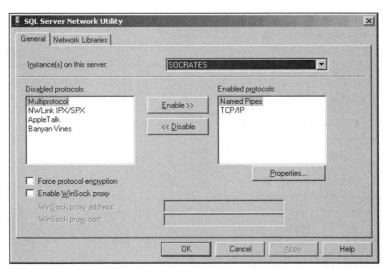

Notice the original two default protocols enabled – this is with Windows NT/2000. For Windows 95/98 we get Shared Memory instead of Named Pipes (TCP/IP remains the same). Under 7.0, we would have three choices installed by default (the extra one being Multiprotocol).

Now let's see what our server *could* be listening for by clicking on the **Network Libraries** tab:

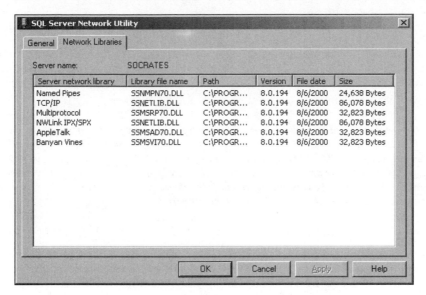

Keep in mind that, in order for your client to gain a connection to the server, the server has to be listening for the protocol with which the client is trying to communicate. Therefore, if we were in a Novell environment, we might need to add a new library. To do that, we would go back to the **General** tab, select **NWLink IPX/SPX** and click on **Enable>>**. We could then, if necessary, select the NWLink NetLib and set the properties for it.

> *At this point, you might be tempted to say, "Hey, why don't I just enable every NetLib? Then I won't have to worry about it." This situation is like anything you add onto your server – more overhead. In this case, it would both slow down your server (not terribly, but every little bit counts) and expose you to unnecessary openings in your security (why leave an extra door open if nobody is supposed to be using that door?).*

OK, now let's take a look at what we can support and why we would want to choose a particular protocol.

Named Pipes

Named Pipes is, for an NT/2000 server installation, not only a default, but is also – at least at installation time – required. Named Pipes is not supported at all for *server* installations running under Windows 9x (it is, however, supported for *client* use in Win 9x to allow connections to servers running under NT/2000). The requirement under NT lasts, however, only until SQL Server is actually installed, and then the NetLib can, if you choose, be removed (although it isn't recommended). Named Pipes can be very useful in situations where TCP/IP is either not available, or where there is no Domain Name Service (DNS) server to allow naming of servers under TCP/IP.

> Technically speaking, you can connect to a SQL Server running TCP/IP by using its IP address in the place of the name. This will work all the time as long as you have a route from the client to the server – even if there is no DNS service (if it has the IP address, then it doesn't need the name).

Named Pipes comes in two flavors: **Local Pipes** and **Network Pipes**. Local Pipes are used when you run the client using Named Pipes to a server that is located on the same machine. It is extremely fast and is the best choice for NT clients local to the server machine (under Win 9x, the Shared Memory NetLib is the best option). Network Pipes are used with Named Pipes over a Local Area Network (LAN) environment. It will resolve server locations by the server name, and can be a very easy-to-use connection option.

In case you want to test using both local and network pipes, you can run either way from your local system. If you use the true network name for your system (the system name used for most of the examples in this book is SOCRATES), then you'll use network pipes. If you use the "(local)" or ". " alias, then SQL Server knows that it is the local system and will use local pipes . Between the two, local pipes is going to be much faster, so that's the choice if you want to connect to the local server and don't have a specific reason for using the network pipes.

TCP/IP

TCP/IP has become something of the de facto standard networking protocol, and is now one of the default NetLibs installed with SQL Server. TCP/IP has the advantages of both running on any server type (NT or Windows 9x – being the default for 9x) and out-performing Named Pipes in situations where the client and server are on different computers (which is the case most of the time). Last, but not least, it is also the only option if you want to connect directly to your SQL Server via the Internet (which, of course, only uses IP).

Don't confuse the need to have your database server available to a web server with the need to have your database server directly accessible to the Internet. You can have a web server that is exposed to the Internet, but also has access to a database server that is not directly exposed to the Internet (the only way for an Internet connection to see the data server is through the web server).

Connecting your data server directly to the Internet is a security hazard in a big way. If you insist on doing it (and there can be valid reasons for doing so), then pay particular attention to security precautions – this is discussed to some degree in Chapter 28.

Multiprotocol

Multiprotocol rides on top of the other protocols that are currently installed – just automating the process of what protocol needs to be selected for which server. Multiprotocol is handy in two instances:

- ❑ You have multiple servers that do not have consistent NetLib support. (Multiprotocol will essentially figure out what NetLib to use for you in this case).

- ❑ You want to be able to access your SQL Server directly over the Internet through a firewall.

We will cover the second instance further in the security chapter later in the book, along with another very special capability that Multiprotocol offers – encryption (this is available only on the client side for Windows 9x).

Keep in mind that, when using Multiprotocol, you are still using the other base protocols. This means that Multiprotocol adds overhead in order to figure out which NetLib to use when connecting to a server. Personally, I like the idea of just taking the time to explicitly configure the NetLib to use for specific connections to each server.

> *Prior to SQL Server 2000, the only way to get encryption in your network packets from SQL Server was to use Multiprotocol – it was required if you wanted encryption turned on. Beginning with this version, you can now use Kerberos (a widely recognized encryption method) over TCP/IP – note that this requires you to be running under Windows 2000.*

NW Link IPX/SPX

IPX equates to Novell. If you're running on a Novell network, then you're going to want to check with your network administrator to see if they are using IPX. If they support both IPX and IP (as many Novell networks now do), then I would suggest that you configure for IP and don't even activate the IPX NetLib. The performance is better under IP, and you avoid a series of bugs that have plagued the IPX NetLib over the years.

AppleTalk

This one is pretty close to self-descriptive, but let's hit the highlights anyway. Use this one for older Macintosh networks that are still only utilizing **AppleTalk**. The AppleTalk NetLib is not supported on Windows 95/98.

> *There was no small amount of talk before SQL Server 7.0 came out that Microsoft was going to terminate support for the AppleTalk NetLib. They didn't, but the fact that the talk was there should give you a head's up for what may be inevitable. If you are thinking of using SQL Server in an environment that has a Macintosh presence, then you may want to verify that your Mac environment is not limited to AppleTalk for communication. Most Mac's have had IP support added, but it's a question worth asking up front.*

Banyan VINES

Hard to believe, but not that long ago, this was a very mainstream networking product. It is currently dying a rather slow death, but, fortunately, it continues to have support under SQL Server. In short, if your network is running **VINES**, then this NetLib is for you.

Shared Memory

This lovely gem was new with version 7.0, but is only available for Win 9x clients (NT can do the same thing via Named Pipes). In short, **shared memory** removes the need for inter-process marshaling (which is a way of packaging information before transferring it across process boundaries) between the client and the server if they are running on the same box. The client has direct access to the same memory-mapped file where the server is storing data. This removes a substantial amount of overhead and is *very* fast.

On to the Client

Now, we've seen all the possible protocols and we know how to choose which ones to offer. Once we know what our server is offering, we can go and configure the client. Most of the time, the defaults are going to work just fine, but let's take a look at what we've got. Select Client Network Utility from the Microsoft SQL Server program group:

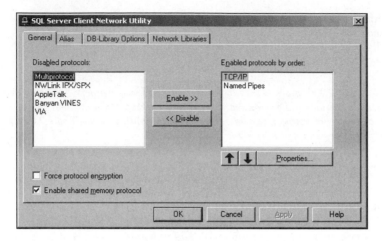

New with SQL Server 2000 is the ability for the client to start with one protocol, then, if that doesn't work, move on to another. In the dialog above, we are first using TCP/IP, and then trying Named Pipes if TCP/IP doesn't work. Unless you change the default (changing the priority by using the up and down arrows), TCP/IP is the NetLib that will be used first for connections to any server not listed in the Server alias configurations list.

> **If you have TCP/IP support on your network, leave your server configured to use it. IP has less overhead and just plain runs faster – there is no reason not to use it unless your network doesn't support it. It's worth noting, however, that for local servers (where the server is on the same physical system as the client), the Local Pipes/Shared Memory NetLibs will be quicker, as you do not need to go across the network to view your local SQL server.**

The Server alias configurations list is a listing of all the servers where you have defined a specific NetLib to be used when contacting that particular server. This means that you can contact one server using IP and another using IPX – whatever you need to get to that particular server. In this case, we've configured our client to use the NW Link NetLib for requests from the server named ARISTOTLE, and to use whatever we've set up as our default for contact with any other SQL Server:

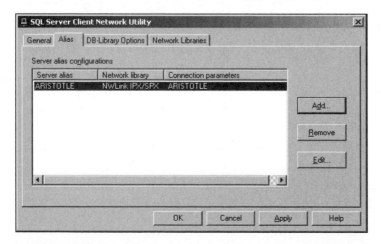

Again, remember that the Client Network Utility on the network machine must either have a default protocol that matches one supported by the server, or it must have an entry in the Server alias configurations to specifically choose a NetLib supported by that server.

> *If you are connecting to your SQL Server over the Internet (which is not a good idea from a security standpoint, but people do it), then you'll probably want to use the Server's actual IP address rather than the name of the Server. This gets around some name resolution issues you can have when dealing with SQL Server and the Internet.*

The Enterprise Manager

The **Enterprise Manager**, or **EM**, is pretty much home base when administering a SQL Server. It provides a variety of functionality to manage your server using a relatively easy-to-use graphical user interface. Beginning with version 7.0, it also added tools to assist the development side of the equation. EM supports **Entity Relationship** (**ER**) **diagramming** (which we'll look into in Chapter 8 and again in Chapter 24 – albeit with somewhat non-standard ER diagrams) as well as greatly improved tools for creating tables, views, triggers, user defined functions, and stored procedures. In addition, EM supports access to most of the other tools covered in this chapter.

For the purposes of this book, we're not going to cover everything that EM has to offer, but let's take a quick run down of the things you can do from EM:

- ❑ Create, edit, and delete databases and database objects
- ❑ Create, edit, and delete Data Transformation (DTS) packages
- ❑ Manage scheduled tasks such as backups and the execution of DTS package runs
- ❑ Display current activity, such as who is logged on, what objects are locked, and from which client they are running
- ❑ Set up web publishing jobs
- ❑ Manage security, including such items as roles, logins, and remote and linked servers.
- ❑ Initiate and manage the SQL Mail Service
- ❑ Create and manage Full-Text Search Catalogs
- ❑ Manage configuration settings for the server
- ❑ Create and manage both publishing and subscribing databases for replication

In addition to the tasks that truly belong to EM, you can also run several of the other SQL Server tools, such as the Query Analyzer and the SQL Server Profiler from EM menu choices.

We will be seeing a great deal of the EM throughout this book.

Data Transformation Services (DTS)

Your friend and mine – that's what **DTS** is. I simply sit back in amazement every time I look at this addition to SQL Server. To give you a touch of perspective here, I've done a couple of Decision Support Systems (DSS) projects over the years. (These are usually systems that don't have online data going in and out, but instead pull data together to help management make decisions.) A DSS project gathers data from a variety of sources and pumps it into one centralized database to be used for centralized reporting.

These projects can get very expensive very quickly, as they attempt to deal with the fact that not every system calls what is essentially the same data by the same name. There can be an infinite number of issues to be dealt with. These can include data integrity (what if the field has a NULL and we don't allow NULLs?) or differences in business rules (one system deals with credits by allowing a negative order quantity, another doesn't allow this and has a separate set of tables to deal with credits). The list can go on and on – so can the expense.

With the advent of DTS, a tremendous amount of the coding (usually in some client-side language) that had to be done for these situations can either be eliminated or, at least, simplified. DTS allows you to take data from any data source that has an OLE DB provider, and pump it into a SQL Server table.

> While DTS depends on OLE DB to perform data transfer, be aware that there is a special OLE DB provider for ODBC. This provider allows you to map your OLE DB access directly to an ODBC driver – that means anything that ODBC can access can also be accessed by OLE DB (and, therefore, DTS).
>
> While we're at it, it's also worth pointing out that DTS, while part of SQL Server, can work against any OLE DB source and any OLE DB destination – that means that SQL Server doesn't need to be involved in the process at all other than providing the data pump. You could, for example, push data from Oracle to Excel, or even Sybase to DB/2.

While transferring our data, we can also apply what are referred to as **transformations** to that data. Transformations essentially alter the data according to some logical rule(s). The alteration can be as simple as changing a column name, or as complex as an analysis of the integrity of the data and application of rules to change it if necessary. To think about how this is applied, consider the example I gave earlier of taking data from a field that allows nulls and moving it to a table that does not allow nulls. With DTS, you can automatically change out any null values to some other value you choose during the transfer process (for a number, that might be zero, or, for a character, it might be something like "unknown").

We will be looking into DTS in some depth in Chapters 22 and 31.

Bulk Copy Program (bcp)

If DTS is "your friend and mine", then The Bulk Copy Program, or bcp, would be that old friend that we may not see that much any more, but we really appreciate when we do see them.

bcp is a command line program that's sole purpose in life is to move formatted data in and out of SQL Server en masse. It was around long before DTS was thought of, and while DTS is replacing bcp for most import/export activity, bcp still has a certain appeal to people who like command line utilities . In addition, you'll find an awful lot of SQL Server installations out there that still depend on bcp to move data around fast.

We will look at bcp in Chapter 21.

The MS DTC Administrative Console

What is the **Distributed Transaction Coordinator** (**DTC**) you ask? A **transaction** is a group of things that you want to apply an "all or nothing" rule to – either all succeed or all fail. So, the *Reader's Digest* version is that DTC makes sure that a group of statements that you're running either happen in their entirety, or are "rolled back" such that they appear to never have happened at all. SQL Server has its own way of managing this kind of stuff, but DTC is special in that it can deal with more than one data source – even non-SQL Server data sources.

Let's say that you're running a bank. You want to transfer $100 from account "A" in your bank to account "B" in another bank. You wouldn't want the $100 dollars to be removed from the account in your bank unless it really is *for sure* going to be deposited in the other bank account – right? DTC is all about being sure that it happens this way.

The MS DTC Admin Console is actually more of a monitoring application than something that allows you to change much. Mostly, it just allows you to see what transactions are going through the DTC, and change the rules for logging transactions. I know I'm repeating myself here, but we will learn much more about transactions and DTC in Chapter 17.

SQL Server Profiler

I can't tell you how many times this one has saved my bacon by telling me what was going on with my server when nothing else would. It's not something a developer (or even a DBA for that matter) will tend to use everyday, but it's extremely powerful, and can be your salvation when you're sure nothing can save you. In SQL Server 2000, the number of different events and counters that are available have been greatly expanded – making this an even more important tool in our troubleshooting arsenal.

SQL Server Profiler is, in short, a real-time tracing tool. Whereas the Performance Monitor is all about tracking what's happening at the macro level – system configuration stuff – the Profiler is concerned with tracking specifics. This is both a blessing and a curse. The Profiler can, depending on how you configure your trace, give you the specific syntax of every statement executed on your server. Now, imagine that you are doing performance tuning on a system with 1000 users. I'm sure you can imagine the reams of paper that would be used to print out the statements executed by so many people in just a minute or two. Fortunately, the Profiler has a vast array of filters to help you narrow things down and track more specific problems – for example: long running queries, or the exact syntax of a query being run within a stored procedure (which is nice when your procedure has conditional statements that cause it to run different things under different circumstances).

We will be looking into SQL Server Profiler in some detail in Chapter 29 on *Performance Tuning*.

The Query Analyzer

This tool will be your home base when you are developing and trouble shooting. The **Query Analyzer** is your tool for interactive sessions with a given SQL Server. It is where you can execute statements using **Transact-SQL** (**T-SQL**, I pronounce it "Tee-Sequel"). T-SQL is the native language of SQL Server. It is a dialect of Structured Query Language (SQL), and is entry-level ANSI SQL 92 compliant. Entry-level compliant means that SQL Server meets a first tier of requirements that a product needs to meet to be called ANSI compliant. You'll find that most RDBMS products only support ANSI to entry-level.

Again, those of you who have some experience with older versions of SQL Server (6.5 and prior) may recall this tool under a different name – **ISQL/W**. Microsoft has renamed this tool to make the name more representative of its purpose. There were substantial enhancements to the Query Analyzer in version 7.0, and even more have been added in SQL Server 2000.

Since the Query Analyzer is where we will spend a fair amount of time in this book, let's take a more in-depth look at this tool and get familiar with how to use it.

Getting Connected

Well, we've been doing plenty of talking about things in this book, and it's high time we started doing something. To that end, start the Query Analyzer by selecting it from the **Microsoft SQL Server** program group on the **Start** menu. When it first starts up, you should see something like this:

Your login screen may look a little bit different from this, depending on whether you've logged in before, what machine you logged into, and what login name you used. Most of these are pretty self-descriptive, but let's look at a couple in more depth.

SQL Server

As you might guess, this is the SQL Server into which you're asking to be logged. In our illustration, we have chosen (local). This doesn't mean that there is a server named (local), but rather that we want to log into the default instance of SQL Server that is on this same machine, regardless of what it is named. Selecting (local) not only automatically identifies which server (and instance) you want to use, but also how you're going to get there.

> **Multi-instancing is new with SQL Server 2000. Previously, you could only have one SQL Server running per physical box. SQL Server now allows multiple "instances" of SQL Server to be running at one time. These are just separate loads into memory of the SQL Server engine running independently from each other.**

Note that the default instance of your server will almost certainly be named the same as your machine is named on the network. There are ways to change the server name after the time of installation, but they are problematic at best, and deadly to your server at worst. Additional instances of SQL Server will be named the same as the default (SOCRATES or ARISTOTLE in many of the examples in this book) followed by a dollar sign, then the instance name – for example, ARISTOTLE$POMPEII.

You may recall when we were discussing NetLibs that the Named Pipes option would vary in the method it actually used to connect depending on whether you were connecting to the same machine or going out over the network. If you select (local), then your system will use Local Pipes (one brand of Named Pipes – it bypasses the network stack), regardless of what NetLib you have selected. This is a bad news/good news story. The bad news is that you give up a little bit of control (SQL Server will always use Shared Memory to connect – you can't choose anything else). The good news is that you don't have to remember what server you're on, and you get a high-performance option for work on the same machine. If you use your local PC's actual server name, then your communications will still go through the network stack and incur the overhead associated with that just as if you were communicating with another system, regardless of the fact that it is on the same machine.

Now, what if you can't remember the specifics of how that server you want was named? If you look just to the right of the server name box, you'll see an ellipsis (...) – try clicking on it. You should see a box come up that allows you to select search criteria. You can search by name or even by version:

You can select one of these servers and click **OK**, or just double-click the one you want.

> **Watch out when using the server selection dialog. While it is usually pretty reliable, there are ways of configuring a SQL Server so that it doesn't "broadcast". When a server has been configured this way, it won't show up in the list. Also, servers that are only listening on the TCP/IP NetLib and do not have a DNS entry will not show up. You must, in this case, already know your IP address and refer to the server using it.**

Start SQL Server if Stopped

This one pretty much does as it says, but you have to have administrative control over the target server in order to do this.

Authentication Type

You can choose between **Windows authentication** (formerly NT Authentication) and **SQL Server authentication**. Version 6.5 of SQL Server and prior also had an option called "Mixed" security. Beginning with SQL Server 7.0, NT authentication was changed to always be active on the server side of the equation and SQL Server authentication became optional. This means that SQL Server authentication is now pretty much what Mixed used to be (it gave you the option of using either approach). The default for 7.0 and prior was SQL Server authentication (which is essentially mixed). For SQL Server 2000 and beyond, Windows authentication has taken over as the default.

NT Authentication

NT authentication is just as it sounds. You have NT/Windows 2000 users and groups. Those NT users are mapped into SQL Server "Logins" in their NT user profile. When they attempt to log into SQL Server, they are validated through the NT domain and mapped to "roles" according to the Login. These roles identify what the user is allowed to do.

The best part of this model is that you only have one password (if you change it in the NT domain, then it's changed for your SQL Server logins too); you pretty much don't have to fill in anything to log in (it just takes the login information from how you're currently logged into the NT network). Additionally, the administrator only has to administer users in one place. The downside is that mapping out this process can get complex and, to administer the NT user side of things, it requires that you are a domain administrator.

SQL Server Authentication

This one is really more about micro-level control and is the only option for servers running Windows 9x or ME. The security does not care at all about what the user's rights to the network are, but rather what you have explicitly set up in SQL Server. The authentication process does not take into account the current network login at all – instead, the user provides a SQL Server-specific login and password.

This can be nice since the administrator for a given SQL Server does not need to be a domain administrator in order to give rights to users on the SQL Server. The process also tends to be somewhat simpler than under NT authentication. Finally, it means that one user can have multiple logins that give different rights to different things.

> Beginning with SQL Server 7.0, giving a user multiple logins became much less desirable than before. It used to be a common practice to do this. A user would have one login for utilizing the full power of an application (including insert, update, and delete rights) and another, read-only login for doing reporting. The latter didn't really make any serious security improvement (the user could always use the login they use with an application and gain full access). It did, however, give the user an alternative "safety" login that, by only allowing read-only access, provided them a safe login for building reports and looking directly at data without fear of corrupting that data.
>
> This was a major security risk, but it was very frequently used due to how simple it was to implement. In version 7.0 and beyond, we can now automatically grant different rights to a user depending on whether they are logged in directly, or whether they are using the login in conjunction with what is called an application role .

We will discuss authentication types and application roles further in our chapter on security.

Making the Connection

Let's get logged on. If you are starting up your SQL Server for the first time, set everything just as it is in our example screen. Choose the (local) option for the SQL Server, select Use SQL Server authentication, a Login name of sa (which stands for **System Administrator** – remember this), and whatever the sa password was set to when you installed SQL Server. On case-sensitive servers, the login is also case-sensitive, so make sure you enter it in lowercase. If you're connecting to a server that has been installed by someone else, or where you have changed the default information, then you will need to provide login information that matches those changes. After you click OK, you should see the main Query Analyzer screen:

> **Don't forget to change the password for the "sa" user. This is a super-user with full access to everything. If you don't place any kind of security on it, then you're opening yourself up to just anyone coming into your system with full rights to add and drop objects or insert, update, and delete data. In version 7.0 and prior, the default password for the sa user was no password at all. You can technically still set it that way, but SQL Server 2000 will hassle you about setting it to nothing (you can force it to a blank password, but it will tell you rather nicely that you're being an idiot).**
>
> **Curious about how many people forgot to do this prior to SQL Server 2000? To date, about 25% of the active production SQL Servers I have come across still have the sa password left null. That is to say that 25% of the servers I've come across effectively had no security.**

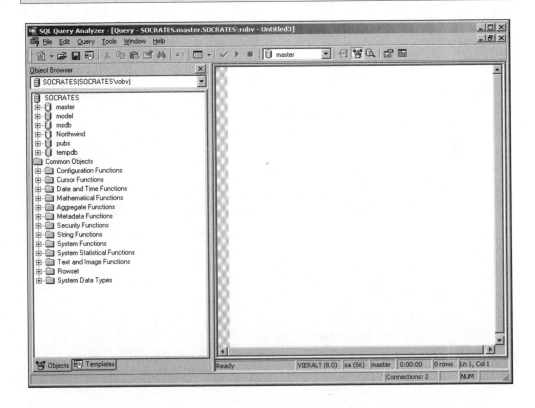

Again, many of the items here (New, Open, Save, Cut, Paste, etc.) are things that you will have seen plenty of times in other Windows applications, and should be familiar with, but there's also a fair amount that's specific to SQL Server. We'll look at these shortly, but let's get our very first query out of the way.

Type the following code into the main window of the Query Analyzer:

```
SELECT * FROM INFORMATION_SCHEMA.TABLES
```

Now click on the green arrow in the tool bar. The Query Analyzer changes a bit:

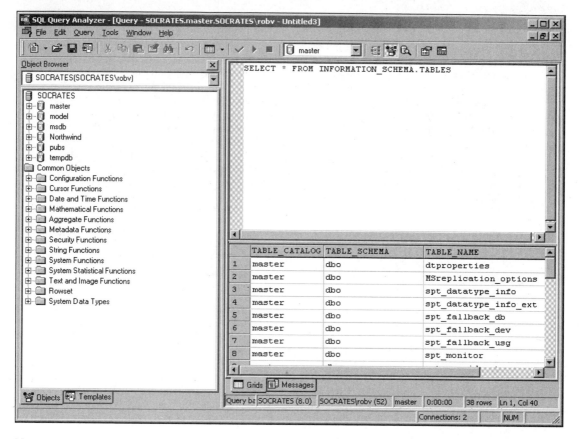

Notice that the main window has been automatically divided into two panes. The top is your original query text; the bottom is called the **results pane**. In addition, notice that the results pane has a tab at the bottom of it. Later on, after we've run queries that return multiple sets of data, you'll see that we can get each of these results on separate tabs – this can be rather handy since you often don't know how long each set of data, or **result set**, is.

> The terms result set and recordset are frequently used to refer to a set of data that is returned as a result of some command being run. You can think of these words as being interchangeable.

Now, let's change a setting or two and see how what we get varies. Click on the small down arrow on the toolbar (right after the Execute Mode icon – 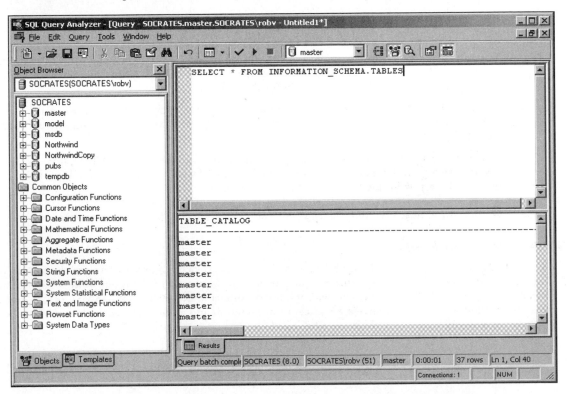 – this lets us select our execute mode for the query. The same choice can also be made from the Query menu. We have six choices for our results, but the ones we will concern ourselves with here are: Results in text, Results in Grid (which I prefer 99% of the time), and Show Execution Plan. We will look at each of these now, and return to the other options in later chapters.

Results in Text

This was the default previous to SQL Server 2000, and there was also no way to change the default. Each time you started up Query Analyzer, you had to change this setting if you want to get results in a grid. Thankfully, Microsoft has added an option to change the default behavior to whatever you want it to be (you can find it in the Results tab of the Query Analyzer's Options dialog under the heading of Default results target).

The Results in Text option takes all the output from your query and puts it into one page of text results. The page can be of virtually infinite length (limited by the available memory in your system).

Before discussing this further, let's re-run that last query using this option and see what we get. Choose the Results in Text option and re-run the previous query by clicking on the green arrow:

The data that we get back is exactly the same – it's just given to us in a somewhat different format. I use this output method in a couple of different scenarios:

❏ When I'm only getting one result set and the results have only fairly narrow columns.

❏ When I want to be able to easily save my results in a single text file.

❏ When I'm going to have multiple result sets, but the results are expected to be small, and I want to be able to see more than one result set on the same page. This one I foresee as doing a little less often with SQL Server 2000, since Microsoft has now changed the grid results to appear on one page rather than in a tabbed format as it was in 7.0.

Results in Grid

This one divides up the columns and rows into a grid arrangement. Under 7.0, it also took each result set and put it into its own tab. Unfortunately, Microsoft decided to change that behavior so result sets now appear one after the other much as they do with the results in text option.

Personally, I wish they had left well enough alone with the 7.0 format. When you get multiple long result sets back, it can be a pain to find where one ends and the next begins – the separate tabs made that very easy.

Specific things that this option gives us that the Results in Text doesn't, include:

❏ You can resize the column by hovering your mouse pointer on the right border of the column header, and then clicking and dragging the column border to its new size. Double-clicking on the right border will result in the auto-fit for the column.

❏ If you select several cells, and then cut and paste them into another grid (say, Microsoft Excel), they will be treated as individual cells (under the Results in Text option, the cut data would have been pasted all into one cell).

❏ You can select just one or two columns of multiple rows (under Results in Text, if you select several rows all of the inner rows have every column selected – you can only select in the middle of the row for the first and last row selected).

I use this option for almost everything since I find that I usually want one of the above benefits.

Show Execution Plan

Every time you run a query, SQL Server parses your query into its component parts and then sends it to the **query optimizer**. The query optimizer is the part of SQL Server that figures out what is the best way to run your query to balance fast results with minimum impact to other users. When you use the Show Execution Plan option, you receive a graphical representation and additional information on how SQL Server plans to run your query. Let's see what one looks like on our query:

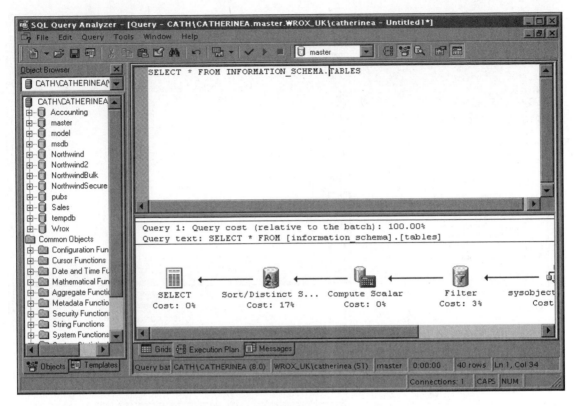

Note that you have to actually click on the Execution Plan tab for it to come up, and that your results are still displayed in whichever way you had selected.

We won't spend any more time on the Show Execution Plan option right here, other than to point out that there is another execution plan option on the toolbar – the Estimated Execution Plan. This toolbar button will give you the same output as a Show Execution Plan with two exceptions:

❑   You get the plan immediately rather than after your query executes.

❑   While what you see is the actual "plan" for the query, all the cost information is estimated, and the query is not actually run. Under Show Query Plan, the query was physically executed and the cost information you get is actual, rather than estimated.

The DB Combo Box

Finally, let's take a look at the **DB combo box**. In short, this is where you select the default database that you want your queries to run against for the current window. Initially, the Query Analyzer will start with whatever the default database is for the user that's logged in (for sa, that is the master database unless someone has changed it on your system). You can then change it to any other database that the current login has permission to access. Since we're using the sa user ID, every database on the current server should have an entry in the DB combo box.

Let's change our current database to Northwind and re-run the query:

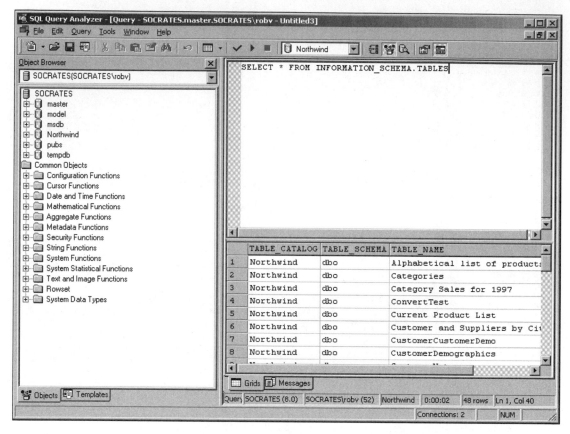

As you can see, the data has changed to represent the data from the newly queried database.

There is one more thing that I want to mention about the Query Analyzer. In SQL Server 7.0, Query Analyzer received the first set of enhanced tools for debugging. The most obvious of these was the coloring of words and phrases as you type them into the code window. Statement keywords should appear in blue; unidentifiable items, such as column and table names (these vary with every table in every database on every server), are in black; and statement arguments and connectors are in red. Pay attention to how these work and learn them – they can help you catch many bugs before you've even run the statement (and seen the resulting error). The check mark icon on the toolbar represents another simple debugging item – this quickly parses the query for you without the need to actually attempt to run the statement. If there are any syntax errors, this should catch them before you see error messages. SQL Server 2000 adds an honest-to-goodness debugger to the mix (hurray!) – we'll look at that in depth when we first start looking into variables and scripting.

The Object Browser

New with SQL Server 2000 is the Object Browser. This allows us to navigate our database, look up object names, and even perform actions like scripting and looking at the underlying data. In addition, there is a templates table available in the object browser that will pre-populate your query window with templates to perform many of the most common data scripting activities.

OSQL

You won't see **OSQL** in your SQL Server program group. Indeed, it's amazing how many people don't even know that this utility (or its older brother – **ISQL**) is around; that's because it's a console rather than a Windows program.

This is the tool to use when you want to include SQL commands and management tasks in command line batch files. Prior to version 7.0 and the advent of DTS, OSQL (then known as ISQL) was often used in conjunction with the **Bulk Copy Program** (**bcp**), to manage the import of data from external systems. This type of use is decreasing as administrators and developers everywhere learn the power and simplicity of DTS. Even so, there are occasionally items that you want to script into a larger command line process. OSQL gives you that capability.

OSQL can be very handy – particularly if you make use of files that contain the scripts you want to run under OSQL. Keep in mind, however, that there are usually tools that can do what you're after from OSQL much more effectively, and with a user interface that is more consistent with the other things you're doing with your SQL Server.

The Service Manager

This one is as simple as they come. Depending on the options you chose when installing your SQL Server, you have anywhere from two to five services available that are SQL Server related. These are:

- ❑ The **SQL Server Service**: this is the main service that forms the backbone of SQL Server. It is what stores and retrieves data.

- ❑ **SQL Server Agent**: formerly known as SQL Executive, this is the task scheduler for SQL Server. This service watches the clock and runs backups, replication publishing, and other items you have set the SQL Server to do on an automated schedule.

- ❑ **MS DTC** (the **Distributed Transaction Coordinator**): this is installed with SQL Server or Microsoft Transaction Server under NT, and installed by default (and called Component Services) under Windows 2000. We've already hit the highlights of this one, so we'll just point out here that you can use the Service Manager to start and stop MS DTC.

- ❑ **Full-Text Search**: the engine that provides the full-text search capabilities is actually an entirely separate service. To be more specific, these services are provided by **Microsoft Index Server** (which originally came with Site Server, then became part of the NT option pack, then finally became standard in Win2K), but a high level of integration has been established, so you can not only install it with SQL Server, but also manage that service from the SQL Server tools as well. Index Server was originally designed to make searching of file-based text content easy (largely on web pages, but also in things like Word documents, text files, or any other supported format). When installed as part of SQL Server, it adds some integration that greatly enhances SQL Server's power with respect to large blocks of text. Full-text search has had some serious improvements added in SQL Server 2000 – we'll explore this in Chapter 26.

- ❑ **OLAP Services:** this is the service that powers the Analysis Services part of SQL Server. Like Full Text Search, it is completely separate from SQL Server. This service will not appear unless you run the Analysis Services installation – which is completely different from the main SQL Server installation.

The SQL Server Service Manager really has only one function – to allow you to start, stop, or pause any of these services. It can be selected either from the **Microsoft SQL Server** program group or via the icon for the service that SQL Server sets up on the far right of the Windows Task Bar by default. Just right-click on it and a list of options will come up.

sqlmaint.exe

This is another holdover from days of yore. It's purpose in life is to enable command-line access to run a wide variety of maintenance tasks such as rebuilding indexes, backing up databases, running database checks, and more. `sqlmaint` is mostly considered legacy in nature at this point. Its use is largely in the domain of the database administrator, and, as such, we will consider it outside the scope of this book.

Summary

Most of the tools that you've been exposed to here are not ones you'll use every day. Indeed, for the average developer, only the Query Analyzer and Enterprise Manager will get daily use. Nevertheless, it is important to have some idea of the role that each one can play. Each has something significant to offer you. We will see each of these tools again in our journey through this book.

Note that there are some other utilities available that don't have shortcuts on your **Start** menu (connectivity tools, server diagnostics and maintenance utilities), which are mostly admin related.

The Foundation Statements of
T-SQL

4

At last! We've finally disposed of the most boring stuff. It doesn't get any worse than basic objects and tools, does it? Unfortunately, we have to lay down a foundation before we can build the house. The nice thing is that the foundation is now down. Having used the clichéd example of building a house, I'm going to turn it all upside down by talking about the things that let you enjoy living in it before we've even talked about the plumbing. You see, when working with databases, you have to get to know how data is going to be accessed before you can learn all that much about the best ways to store it.

In this chapter, we will discuss the most fundamental **Transact-SQL** (or **T-SQL**) statements. T-SQL is SQL Server's own dialect of **Structured Query Language** (or **SQL**). The T-SQL statements that we will learn in this chapter are:

- ❏ SELECT
- ❏ INSERT
- ❏ UPDATE
- ❏ DELETE

These four statements are the bread and butter of T-SQL. We'll learn plenty of other statements as we go along, but these statements make up the basis of T-SQL's **Data Manipulation Language** – or **DML**. Since you'll, generally, issue far more commands meant to manipulate (that is, read and modify) data than other types of commands (such as those to grant user rights or create a table), you'll find that these will become like old friends in no time at all.

In addition, SQL provides for many operators and keywords that help refine your queries. We'll learn some of the most common of these in this chapter.

While T-SQL is unique to SQL Server, the statements you use most of the time are not. T-SQL is entry-level ANSI SQL-92 compliant, which means that it complies up to a certain level of a very wide open standard. What this means to you as a developer is that much of the SQL you're going to learn in this book is directly transferable to other SQL-based database servers such as Sybase (which used to share the same code base as SQL Server), Oracle, DB2, and Informix. Be aware, however, that every RDBMS has different extensions and performance enhancements that it uses above and beyond the ANSI standard. I will try to point out the ANSI vs. non-ANSI ways of doing things where applicable. In some cases, you'll have a choice to make – performance vs. portability to other RDBMS systems. Most of the time, however, the ANSI way is as fast as any other option. In such a case, the choice should be clear – stay ANSI compliant.

Getting Started with a Basic SELECT Statement

If you haven't used SQL before, or don't really feel like you've really understood it yet – pay attention here! The SELECT statement and the structures used within it form the basis for the lion's share of all the commands we will perform with SQL Server. Let's look at the basic syntax rules for a SELECT statement:

```
SELECT <column list>
[FROM <source table(s)>]
[WHERE <restrictive condition>]
[GROUP BY <column name or expression using a column in the SELECT list>]
[HAVING <restrictive condition based on the GROUP BY results>]
[ORDER BY <column list>]
[[FOR XML {RAW|AUTO|EXPLICIT}[, XMLDATA][, ELEMENTS][, BINARY base 64]]
[OPTION (<query hint>, [, ...n])]
```

Wow – that's a lot to decipher, so let's look at the parts.

The SELECT Statement and FROM Clause

The "verb" – in this case a SELECT – is the part of the overall statement that tells SQL Server what we are doing. A SELECT indicates that we are merely reading information, as opposed to modifying it. What we are selecting is identified by an expression or column list immediately following the SELECT – you'll see what I mean by this in a moment.

Next, we add in more specifics, such as from where we are getting this data. The FROM statement specifies the name of the table or tables from which we are getting our data. With these, we have enough to create a basic SELECT statement. Fire up the Query Analyzer and let's take another look at the SELECT statement we ran during the last chapter:

```
SELECT * FROM INFORMATION_SCHEMA.TABLES
```

Let's look at what we've asked for here. We've asked to SELECT information – you can also think of this as requesting to display information. The * may seem odd, but it actually works pretty much as * does everywhere – it's a wildcard. When we say SELECT *, we're saying we want to select every column from the table. Next, the FROM indicates that we've finished saying what items to output, and that we're about to say what the source of the information is supposed to be – in this case, INFORMATION_SCHEMA.TABLES.

INFORMATION_SCHEMA is a special access path that is used for displaying meta data about your system's databases and their contents. INFORMATION_SCHEMA has several parts that can be specified after a period, such as INFORMATION_SCHEMA.SCHEMATA or INFORMATION_SCHEMA.VIEWS. These special access paths to the meta data of your system have been put there so you won't have to use what are called "system tables".

Let's play around with this some more. Change the current database to be the Northwind database. Recall that, to do this, you need only select the Northwind entry from the combo box at the top right of the Query Analyzer window:

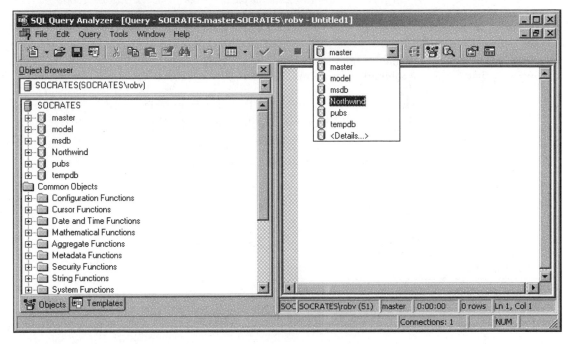

Now that we have the Northwind database selected, let's start looking at some real data from our database. Try this query:

```
SELECT * FROM Customers
```

This query will list every row of data in every column of the Customers table in the current database (in our case, Northwind). If you haven't altered any of the settings on your system or the data in the Northwind database before you ran this query, then you should see the following information line after the data:

(91 row(s) affected)

> *Note that if you're viewing the data in grid format, you'll need to click on the Messages tab to view this line.*

For a SELECT statement, the number shown here is the number of rows that your query returned.

Let's look at a few specifics of our SELECT statement. Notice that I capitalized the SELECT and FROM. This is not a requirement of SQL Server – we could run them as SeLeCt and frOM and they would work just fine. I capitalized them purely for purposes of convention and readability. You'll find that many SQL coders will use the convention of capitalizing all commands and keywords, while using mixed case for table, column, and non-constant variable names. The standards you choose or have forced upon you may vary, but live by at least one rule – be consistent.

> *OK, time for my next soapbox diatribe. Nothing is more frustrating for the person that has to read your code or remember your table names than lack of consistency. When someone looks at your code or, more importantly, uses your column and table names, it shouldn't take him or her long to guess most of the way you do things just by experience with the parts that he or she has already worked with. Being consistent is one of those incredibly simple things that have been missed to at least some degree in almost every database I've ever worked with. Break the trend – be consistent.*

The SELECT is telling the Query Analyzer what we are doing and the * is saying what we want (remember that * = every column). Then comes the FROM.

A FROM clause does just what it says – that is, it defines the place from which our data should come. Immediately following the FROM will be the names of one or more tables. In our query, all of the data came from the table called Customers.

Now let's try taking a little bit more specific information. Let's say all we want is a list of all our customers by name:

```
SELECT CompanyName FROM Customers
```

Your results should look something like:

```
CompanyName
--------------------------------------------------
Alfreds Futterkiste
Ana Trujillo Emparedados y helados
...
...
Wilman Kala
Wolski  Zajazd

(91 row(s) affected)
```

Note that I've snipped the rows out of the middle for brevity – you should have 91 rows there. Since the name of each customer is all that we want, that's all that we've selected.

> *Many SQL writers have the habit of cutting their queries short and always selecting every column by using a * in their selection criteria. This is another one of those habits to resist. While typing in a * saves you a few moments of typing out the column names that you want, it also means that more data has to be retrieved than is really necessary. In addition, SQL Server must go and figure out just how many columns "*" amounts to and what specifically they are. You would be surprised at just how much this can drag down your application's performance and that of your network. In short, a good rule to live by is to select what you need – that is, exactly what you need. No more, no less.*

Let's try another simple query. How about:

```
SELECT ProductName FROM Products
```

Again, assuming that you haven't modified the data that came with the sample database, SQL Server should respond by returning a list of 77 different products that are available in the Northwind database:

```
ProductName
---------------------------------------
Alice Mutton
Aniseed Syrup
...
...
Wimmers gute Semmelknödel
Zaanse koeken

(77 row(s) affected)
```

The columns that you have chosen right after your SELECT clause are known as the **SELECT list**. In short, the SELECT list is made up of the columns that you have requested to be output from your query.

The WHERE Clause

Well, things are starting to get boring again, aren't they? So let's add in the WHERE clause. The WHERE clause allows you to place conditions on what is returned to you. What we have seen thus far is unrestricted information in the sense that every row in the table specified has been included in our results. Unrestricted queries such as these are very useful for populating things like list boxes and combo boxes, and in other scenarios where you are trying to provide a **domain listing**.

> **For our purposes, don't confuse a domain with that of an NT domain. A domain listing is an exclusive list of choices. For example, if you want someone to provide you with information about a state in the US, you might provide them with a list that limits the domain of choices to just the fifty states. That way, you can be sure that the option selected will be a valid one. We will see this concept of domains further when we begin talking about database design.**

Now we want to try looking for more specific information. We don't want a listing of customer names – we want information on a specific customer. Try this – see if you can come up with a query that returns the company name, contact name, and phone number for a customer with the customer number "ROMEY".

Let's break it down and build a query one piece at a time. First, we're asking for information to be returned, so we know that we're looking at a SELECT statement. Our statement of what we want indicates that we would like the company name, contact name, and phone number, so we're going to have to know what the column names are for these pieces of information. We're also going to need to know out of which table or tables we can retrieve these columns.

Now, we'll take a look at the tables that are available. Since we've already used the Customers table once before, we know that it's there (later on in the chapter, we'll take a look at how we could find out what tables are available if we didn't already know). The Customers table has several columns. To give us a quick listing of our column options we can study the design view of the Customers table from Enterprise Manager. To open this screen in EM, click on the **Tables** member underneath the **Northwind** database. Then right-click on the **Customers** table (in the right-hand pane of EM) and choose **Design Table**. Again, we'll see some other methods of finding this information a little later in the chapter.

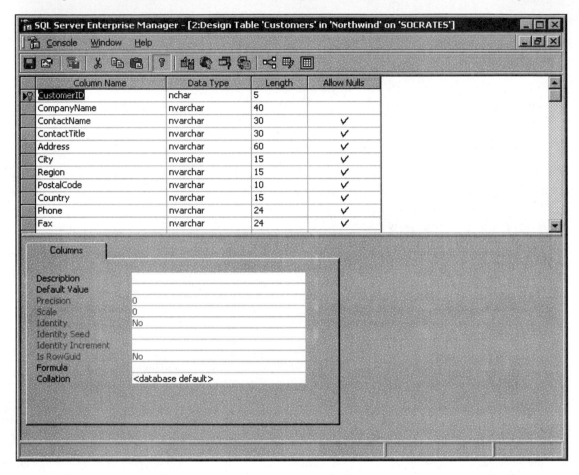

We don't have a column called customer number, but we do have one that's probably what we're looking for: CustomerID. The other two columns are, save for the missing space in between the two words, pretty easy to identify.

Therefore, our Customers table is going to be the place we get our information FROM, and the CompanyName, ContactName, and Phone columns will be the specific columns from which we'll get our information:

```
SELECT CompanyName, ContactName, Phone
FROM Customers
```

This query, however, still won't give us the results that we're after – it will still return too much information. Run it – you'll see that it still returns every record in the table rather than just the one we want.

If the table only has a few records and all we want to do is take a quick look at it, this might be fine. After all, we can look through a small list ourselves – right? But that's a pretty big "if" there. In any significant system, very few of your tables will have small record counts. You don't want to have to go scrolling through 10,000 records. What if you had 100,000 or 1,000,000? Even if you felt like scrolling through them all, the time before the results were back would be increasing dramatically. Finally, what do you do when you're designing this into your application and you need a quick result that gets straight to the point?

What we're after is a conditional statement that will limit the results of our query to just one customer – "ROMEY". That's where the WHERE clause comes in. The WHERE clause immediately follows the FROM clause and defines what conditions a record has to meet before it will be shown. For our query, we would want the CustomerID to be equal to 'ROMEY', so let's finish our query:

```
SELECT CompanyName, ContactName, Phone
FROM Customers
WHERE CustomerID = 'ROMEY'
```

Run this query against the Northwind database and you should come up with:

CompanyName	ContactName	Phone
Romero y tomillo	Alejandra Camino	(91) 745 6200

(1 row(s) affected)

This time we've gotten back precisely what we wanted – nothing more, nothing less. In addition, this query runs much faster than the first query.

Let's take a look at all the operators we can use with the WHERE clause:

Operator	Example Usage	Effect

=, >, <, >=, <=, <>, !=, !>, !<	`<Column Name> = <Other Column Name>`
	
	`<Column Name> = 'Bob'`
		Standard Comparison Operators – these work as they do in pretty much any programming language with a couple of notable points:
		
		1. What constitutes "greater than", "less than", and "equal to" can change depending on the collation order you have selected. For example, "ROMEY" = "romey" in places where case-insensitive sort order has been selected, but "ROMEY" <> "romey" in a case-sensitive situation.
		2. != and <> both mean "not equals". !< and !> mean "not less than" and "not greater than" respectively.

Table continued on following page

Operator	Example Usage	Effect

AND, OR, NOT	`<Column1> = <Column2> AND <Column3> >= <Column 4>`
	
	`<Column1> != "MyLiteral" OR <Column2> = "MyOtherLiteral"`
		Standard Boolean logic. You can use these to combine multiple conditions into one WHERE clause. NOT is evaluated first, then AND, then OR. If you need to change the evaluation order, you can use parentheses. Note that XOR is not supported.

BETWEEN	`<Column1> BETWEEN 1 AND 5`	Comparison is TRUE if the first value is between the second and third values inclusive. It is the functional equivalent of A>=B AND A<=C. Any of the specified values can be column names, variables, or literals.
LIKE	`<Column1> LIKE "ROM%"`	Uses the % and _ characters for wildcarding. % indicates a value of any length can replace the % character. _ indicates any one character can replace the _ character. Enclosing characters in [ ] symbols indicates any single character within the [ ] is OK ([a-c] means a, b, and c are OK. [ab] indicates a or b are OK). ^ operates as a NOT operator – indicating that the next character is to be excluded.

IN	`<Column1> IN (List of Numbers)`
	
	`<Column1> IN ("A", "b", "345")`
		Returns TRUE if the value to the left of the IN keyword matches any of the values in the list provided after the IN keyword. This is frequently used in subqueries, which we will look at in Chapter 16.

ALL, ANY, SOME	`<column|expression> (comparision operator) <ANY|SOME> (subquery)`	These return TRUE if any or all (depending on which you choose) values in a subquery meet the comparison operator (e.g. <, >, =, >=) condition. ALL indicates that the value must match all the values in the set. ANY and SOME are functional equivalents and will evaluate to TRUE if the expression matches any value in the set.
EXISTS	`EXISTS (subquery)`	Returns TRUE if at least one row is returned by the subquery. Again, we'll look into this one further in Chapter 16.

ORDER BY

In the queries that we've run thus far, most of them have come out in something resembling alphabetical order. Is this by accident? It will probably come as somewhat of a surprise to you, but the answer to that is yes. If you don't say you want a specific sorting on the results of a query, then you get the data in the order that SQL Server decides to give it to you. This will always be based on how SQL Server decided was the lowest cost way to gather the data. It will usually be based either on the physical order of a table, or on one of the indexes SQL Server used to find your data.

Think of an ORDER BY clause as being a "sort by". It gives you the opportunity to define the order in which you want your data to come back. You can use any combination of columns in your ORDER BY clause as long as they are columns (or derivations of columns) found in the tables within your FROM clause.

Let's look at this query:

```
SELECT CustomerID, ContactName, Phone
FROM Customers
```

This will produce the following results:

CustomerID	ContactName	Phone
ALFKI	Maria Anders	030-0074321
ANATR	Ana Trujillo	(5) 555-4729
...		
WILMK	Matti Karttunen	90-224 8858
WOLZA	Zbyszek Piestrzeniewicz	(26) 642-7012

(91 row(s) affected)

As it happened, our query result set was sorted in CustomerID order. Why? Because SQL Server decided that the best way to look at this data was by using an index that sorts the data by CustomerID. That just happened to be what created the lowest cost (in terms of CPU and I/O) query. Were we to run this exact query when the table had grown to a much larger size, SQL Server might have chosen an entirely different execution plan, and therefore might sort the data differently. We could force this sort order by changing our query to this:

```
SELECT CustomerID, ContactName, Phone
FROM Customers
ORDER BY CustomerID
```

Note that the WHERE clause isn't required. It can either be there or not depending on what you're trying to accomplish – just remember that, if you do have a WHERE clause, it goes before the ORDER BY clause.

Unfortunately, that last query doesn't really give us anything different, so we don't see what's actually happening. Let's change the query to sort the data differently – by the ContactName:

```
SELECT CustomerID, ContactName, Phone
FROM Customers
ORDER BY ContactName
```

Now our results are quite different. It's the same data, but it's been substantially rearranged:

CustomerID	ContactName	Phone
ROMEY	Alejandra Camino	(91) 745 6200
MORGK	Alexander Feuer	0342-023176
ANATR	Ana Trujillo	(5) 555-4729
TRADH	Anabela Domingues	(11) 555-2167
...		
...		
LAUGB	Yoshi Tannamuri	(604) 555-3392
OCEAN	Yvonne Moncada	(1) 135-5333
WOLZA	Zbyszek Piestrzeniewicz	(26) 642-7012

(91 row(s) affected)

SQL Server still chose the least cost method of giving us our desired results, but the particular set of tasks it actually needed to perform changed somewhat because the nature of the query changed.

We can also do our sorting using numeric fields. Let's try one on the `Products` table of `Northwind`:

```
SELECT ProductID, ProductName, UnitsInStock, UnitsOnOrder
FROM Products
WHERE UnitsOnOrder > 0
AND UnitsInStock < 10
ORDER BY UnitsOnOrder DESC
```

This one results in:

ProductID	ProductName	UnitsInStock	UnitsOnOrder
66	Louisiana Hot Spiced Okra	4	100
31	Gorgonzola Telino	0	70
45	Rogede sild	5	70
21	Sir Rodney's Scones	3	40
32	Mascarpone Fabioli	9	40
74	Longlife Tofu	4	20
68	Scottish Longbreads	6	10

(7 row(s) affected)

Notice several things in this query. First, we've made use of many of the things that we've talked about up to this point. We've combined multiple WHERE clause conditions and we also have an ORDER BY clause in place. Second, we've added something new in our ORDER BY clause – the DESC keyword. This tells SQL Server that our ORDER BY should work in descending order, rather than the default of ascending. (If you want to explicitly state that you want it to be ascending, use ASC.)

OK, let's do one more, but this time, let's sort based on multiple columns. To do this, all we have to do is add a comma followed by the next column by which we want to sort.

Suppose, for example, that we want to get a listing of every order that was placed between December 10th and 20th in 1996. To add a little bit to this though, let's further say that we want the orders sorted by date, and we want a secondary sort based on the CustomerID. Just for grins, we'll toss in yet another little twist: we want the CustomerIDs sorted in descending order.

Our query would look like this:

```
SELECT OrderDate, CustomerID
FROM Orders
WHERE OrderDate BETWEEN '12-10-1996' AND '12-20-1996'
ORDER BY OrderDate, CustomerID DESC
```

This time, we get data that is sorted two ways:

```
OrderDate                   CustomerID
-----------------------------------   ----------------
1996-12-10 00:00:00.000     FOLKO
1996-12-11 00:00:00.000     QUEDE
1996-12-12 00:00:00.000     LILAS
1996-12-12 00:00:00.000     HUNGO
1996-12-13 00:00:00.000     ERNSH
1996-12-16 00:00:00.000     BERGS
1996-12-16 00:00:00.000     AROUT
1996-12-17 00:00:00.000     SPLIR
1996-12-18 00:00:00.000     SANTG
1996-12-18 00:00:00.000     FAMIA
1996-12-19 00:00:00.000     SEVES
1996-12-20 00:00:00.000     BOTTM
```

(12 row(s) affected)

Our dates, since we didn't say anything to the contrary, were still sorted in ascending order (the default), but, if you look at the 16th as an example, you can see that our CustomerIDs were indeed sorted last to first – descending order.

> While we usually sort the results based on one of the columns that we are returning, it's worth noting that the ORDER BY clause can be based on any column in any table used in the query regardless of whether it is included in the SELECT list.

Aggregating Data Using the GROUP BY Clause

With ORDER BY, we have kind of taken things out of order compared with how the SELECT statement reads at the top of the chapter. Let's review the overall statement structure:

```
SELECT <column list>
[FROM <source table(s)>]
[WHERE <restrictive condition>]
[GROUP BY <column name or expression using a column in the SELECT list>]
[HAVING <restrictive condition based on the GROUP BY results>]
[ORDER BY <column list>]
[[FOR XML] [RAW, AUTO, EXPLICIT][, XMLDATA][, ELEMENTS][, BINARY base 64]]
[OPTION (<query hint>, [, ...n])]
```

Why, if ORDER BY comes last, did we look at it before the GROUP BY? There are two reasons:

❑   ORDER BY is used far more often than GROUP BY, so I want you to have more practice with it

❑   I want to make sure that you understand that you can mix and match all of the clauses after the FROM clause as long as you keep them in the order that SQL Server expects them (as defined in the syntax definition)

The GROUP BY clause is used to aggregate information. Let's look at a simple query without a GROUP BY. Let's say that we want to know how many parts were ordered on a given set of orders:

```
SELECT OrderID, Quantity
FROM [Order Details]
WHERE OrderID BETWEEN 11000 AND 11002
```

> **Note the use of the square brackets in this query. Remember back from Chapter 2 that, if an object name (a table in this case) has embedded spaces in it, we must delimit the name by using either square brackets or single quotes – this lets SQL Server know where the start and the end of the name is. Again, I highly recommend *against* the use of embedded spaces in your names in real practice.**

This yields a result set of:

OrderID	Quantity
11000	25
11000	30
11000	30
11001	60
11001	25
11001	25
11001	6
11002	56
11002	15
11002	24
11002	40

(11 row(s) affected)

Even though we've only asked for three orders, we're seeing each individual line of detail from the order. We can either get out our adding machine, or we can make use of the GROUP BY clause with an aggregator – in this case we'll use SUM():

```
SELECT OrderID; SUM(Quantity)
FROM [Order Details]
WHERE OrderID BETWEEN 11000 AND 11002
GROUP BY OrderID
```

This gets us what we were looking for:

```
OrderID
---------------- -----
11000       85
11001       116
11002       135
```

(3 row(s) affected)

As you would expect, the SUM function returns totals – but totals of what? If we didn't supply the GROUP BY clause, the SUM would have been of all the values in all of the rows for the named column. In this case, however, we did supply a GROUP BY, and so the total provided by the SUM function is the total in each group.

We can also group based on multiple columns. To do this, we just add a comma and the next column name.

Let's say, for example, that we're looking for the number of orders each employee has taken for customers with CustomerIDs between A and AO. We can use both the EmployeeID and CustomerID columns in our GROUP BY (I'll explain how to use the COUNT() function shortly):

```
SELECT CustomerID, EmployeeID, COUNT(*)
FROM Orders
WHERE CustomerID BETWEEN 'A' AND 'AO'
GROUP BY CustomerID, EmployeeID
```

This gets us counts, but the counts are pulled together based on how many orders a given employee took from a given customer:

```
CustomerID EmployeeID
---------------- -------------------- --
ALFKI       1           2
ANTON       1           1
ALFKI       3           1
ANATR       3           2
ANTON       3           3
ALFKI       4           2
ANATR       4           1
ANTON       4           1
ALFKI       6           1
ANATR       7           1
ANTON       7           2
```

(11 row(s) affected)

Note that, once we use a GROUP BY, every column in the SELECT list has to either be part of the GROUP BY or it must be an aggregate. What does this mean? Let's find out.

Aggregates

When you consider that they usually get used with a GROUP BY clause, it's probably not surprising that aggregates are functions that work on groups of data. For example, in one of the queries above, we got the sum of the Quantity column. The sum is calculated and returned on the selected column for each group defined in the GROUP BY clause – in this case, just OrderID. There are a wide range of aggregates available, but let's play with the most common.

> While aggregates show their power when used with a **GROUP BY** clause, they are not limited to grouped queries – if you include an aggregate without a **GROUP BY**, then the aggregate will work against the entire result set (all the rows that match the **WHERE** clause). The catch here is that, when not working with a **GROUP BY**, some aggregates can only be in the **SELECT** list with other aggregates – that is, they can't be paired with a column name in the **SELECT** list unless you have a **GROUP BY**. For example, unless there is a **GROUP BY**, AVG can be paired with SUM, but not a specific column.

AVG

This one is for computing averages. Let's try running that same query we ran before, only now we'll modify it to return the average quantity per order rather than the total for each order:

```
SELECT OrderID, AVG(Quantity)
FROM [Order Details]
WHERE OrderID BETWEEN 11000 AND 11002
GROUP BY OrderID
```

Notice that our results changed substantially:

```
OrderID
----------------   ---
11000              28
11001              29
11002              33
```

(3 row(s) affected)

You can check the math – on order number 11000 there were three line items totaling 85 altogether. 85 ÷ 3 = 28.33. I can just hear some of you out there squealing right now. You're probably saying something like, "Hey, if it's 28.33, then why did it round the value to 28?" Good question. The answer lies in the rules of **casting**. If you're from the C++ world, then you probably understand casting very well. Those of you from the Visual Basic camp may not be as well versed in it. We'll cover casting in some detail in the chapter on advanced query topics (Chapter 16), but for now just realize that since the number that we were calculating the average on was an integer, then the result is an integer.

MIN/MAX

Bet you can guess these two. Yes, these grab the minimum and maximum amounts for each grouping for a selected column. Again, let's use that same query modified for the MIN function:

```
SELECT OrderID, MIN(Quantity)
FROM [Order Details]
WHERE OrderID BETWEEN 11000 AND 11002
GROUP BY OrderID
```

Which gives us the following results:

```
OrderID
--------------- ---
11000          25
11001          6
11002          15
```

(3 row(s) affected)

Modify it one more time for the MAX function:

```
SELECT OrderID, MAX(Quantity)
FROM [Order Details]
WHERE OrderID BETWEEN 11000 AND 11002
GROUP BY OrderID
```

And you come up with this:

```
OrderID
--------------- ---
11000          30
11001          60
11002          56
```

(3 row(s) affected)

What if, however, we wanted both the MIN and the MAX? Simple! Just use both in your query:

```
SELECT OrderID, MIN(Quantity),MAX(Quantity)
FROM [Order Details]
WHERE OrderID BETWEEN 11000 AND 11002
GROUP BY OrderID
```

Now, this will yield you an additional column and a bit of a problem:

```
OrderID
--------------- --------- ----
11000          25        30
11001          6         60
11002          15        56
```

(3 row(s) affected)

Can you spot the issue here? We've gotten back everything that we've asked for, but now that we have more than one aggregate column, we have a problem identifying which column is which. Sure, in this particular example, we can be sure that the columns with the largest numbers are the columns generated by the MAX and the smallest by the MIN, but the answer to which column is which is not always so apparent. So let's make use of an **alias**. An alias allows you to change the name of a column in the result set, and is created by using the AS keyword:

```
SELECT OrderID, MIN(Quantity) AS Minimum, MAX(Quantity) AS Maximum
FROM [Order Details]
WHERE OrderID BETWEEN 11000 AND 11002
GROUP BY OrderID
```

Now our results are somewhat easier to make sense of:

OrderID	Minimum	Maximum
11000	25	30
11001	6	60
11002	15	56

(3 row(s) affected)

It's worth noting that the AS keyword is actually optional. Indeed, prior to version 6.5, it wasn't even a valid keyword. If you like, you can execute the same query as before, except remove the two AS keywords from the query – you'll see that you wind up with exactly the same results. It's also worth noting that you can alias any column (and even, as we'll see in the next chapter, table names) – not just aggregates.

Let's re-run this last query, but this time we'll not use the AS keyword in some places, and we'll alias every column:

```
SELECT OrderID AS "Order Number", MIN(Quantity) Minimum, MAX(Quantity) Maximum
FROM [Order Details]
WHERE OrderID BETWEEN 11000 AND 11002
GROUP BY OrderID
```

Despite the AS keyword being missing in some places, we've still changed the name output for every column:

Order Number	Minimum	Maximum
11000	25	30
11001	6	60
11002	15	56

(3 row(s) affected)

I must admit that I usually don't include the AS keyword in my aliasing, but I would also admit that it's a bad habit on my part. I've been working with SQL Server since before the AS keyword was available and have unfortunately got set in my ways about it (I simply forget to use it). I would, however, strongly encourage you to go ahead and make use of this "extra" word. Why? Well, first, because it reads somewhat more clearly, and second because it's the ANSI standard way of doing things.

So then, why did I even tell you about it? Well, I got you started doing it the right way – with the AS *keyword – but I want you to be aware of alternate ways of doing things so that you aren't confused when you see something that looks a little different.*

COUNT(Expression | *)

The COUNT(*) function is about counting the rows in a query. To begin with, let's go with one of the most common varieties of queries:

```
SELECT COUNT(*)
FROM Employees
WHERE EmployeeID = 5
```

The recordset you get back looks a little different from what you're used to from earlier queries:

```
-----------
1
```

(1 row(s) affected)

Let's look at the differences. First, as with all columns that are returned as a result of a function call, there is no default column name – if you want there to be a column name, then you need to supply an alias. Next, you'll notice that we haven't really returned much of anything. So what does this recordset represent? It is the number of rows that matched the WHERE condition in the query for the table(s) in the FROM clause.

> **Keep this query in mind. This is a basic query that you can use to verify that the exact number of rows that you expect to be in a table and match your WHERE condition are indeed in there.**

Just for fun, try running the query without the WHERE clause:

```
SELECT COUNT(*)
FROM Employees
```

If you haven't done any deletions or insertions into the Employees table, then you should get a recordset that looks something like this:

```
-----------
9
```

(1 row(s) affected)

What is that number? It's the total number of rows in the Employees table. This is another one to keep in mind for future use.

Now, we're just getting started! If you look back at the header for this section (the COUNT section), you'll see that there are two different ways of using COUNT. We've already discussed using COUNT with the * option. Now it's time to look at it with an expression – usually a column name.

First, try running the COUNT the old way, but against a new table:

```
SELECT COUNT(*)
FROM Customers
```

This is a slightly larger table, so you get a higher count:

```
-----------
91
```

(1 row(s) affected)

Now alter your query to select the count for a specific column:

```
SELECT COUNT(Fax)
FROM Customers
```

You'll get a result that is a bit different to the one before:

```
-----------
69
```

(1 row(s) affected)

Warning: Null value is eliminated by an aggregate or other SET operation.

This new result brings with it a question: why, since the Fax column exists for every row, is there a different count for Fax than there is for the row count in general? The answer is fairly obvious when you stop to think about it – there isn't a value, as such, for the Fax column in every row. In short, the COUNT, when used in any form other than COUNT(*), ignores NULL values. Let's verify that NULL values are the cause of the discrepancy:

```
SELECT COUNT(*)
FROM Customers
WHERE Fax IS NULL
```

This should yield you the following recordset:

```
-----------
22
```

(1 row(s) affected)

Now, let's do the math:

$69 + 22 = 91$

That's 69 records with a defined value in the Fax field and 22 rows where the value in the Fax field is NULL, making a total of 91 rows.

Actually, all aggregate functions ignore NULLs except for COUNT(*). Think about this for a minute – it can have a very significant impact on your results. Many users expect NULL values in numeric fields to be treated as zero when performing averages, but a NULL does not equal zero, and as such, shouldn't be used as one. If you perform an AVG or other aggregate function on a column with NULLs, the NULL values will not be part of the aggregation unless you manipulate them into a non-NULL value inside the function (using COALESCE() or ISNULL() for example). We'll explore this further in Chapter 16, but beware of this when coding in T-SQL and when designing your database.

Why does it matter in your database design? Well, it can have a bearing on whether you decide to allow NULL values in a field or not by thinking about the way that queries are likely to be run against the database and how you want your aggregates to work.

Before we leave the COUNT function, we had better see it in action with the GROUP BY clause.

Let's say our boss has asked us to find out the number of employees that report to each manager. The statements that we've done this far would either count up all the rows in the table (COUNT(*)) or all the rows in the table that didn't have null values (COUNT(ColumnName)). When we add a GROUP BY clause, these aggregators perform exactly as they did before, except that they return a count for each grouping rather than the full table – we can use this to get our number of reports:

```
SELECT ReportsTo, COUNT(*)
FROM Employees
GROUP BY ReportsTo
```

Notice that we only are grouping by the ReportsTo – the COUNT() function is an aggregator, and therefore does not have to be included in the GROUP BY clause.

```
ReportsTo
---------------- --
NULL            1
2               5
5               3
```

(3 row(s) affected)

Our results tell us that the manager with 2 as his/her ManagerID has five people reporting to him or her, and that three people report to the manager with ManagerID 5. We are also able to tell that one Employees record had a NULL value in the ReportsTo field – this employee apparently doesn't report to anyone (hmmm, president of the company I suspect?).

It's probably worth noting that we, technically speaking, could use a GROUP BY clause without any kind of aggregator, but this wouldn't make sense. Why not? Well, SQL Server is going to wind up doing work on all the rows in order to group them up, but, functionally speaking, you would get the same result with a DISTINCT option (which we'll look at shortly), and it would operate much faster.

Now that we've seen how to operate with groups, let's move on to one of the concepts that a lot of people have problems with. Of course, after reading the next section, you'll think it's a snap.

Placing Conditions on Groups with the HAVING Clause

Up to now, all of our conditions have been against specific rows. If a given column in a row doesn't have a specific value or isn't within a range of values, then the entire row is left out. All of this happens before the groupings are really even thought about.

What if we want to place conditions on what the groups themselves look like? In other words, what if we want every row to be added to a group, but then we want to say that only after the groups are fully accumulated are we ready to apply the condition. Well, that's where the HAVING clause comes in.

The HAVING clause is only used if there is also a GROUP BY in your query. Whereas the WHERE clause is applied to each row before they even have a chance to become part of a group, the HAVING clause is applied to the aggregated value for that group.

Let's start off with a slight modification to the GROUP BY query we used at the end of the last section – the one that tells us the number of employees assigned to each manager's EmployeeID:

```
SELECT ReportsTo AS Manager, COUNT(*) AS Reports
FROM Employees
GROUP BY ReportsTo
```

Now let's look at the results again:

```
Manager          Reports
---------------- --
NULL             1
2                5
5                3
```

(3 row(s) affected)

In the next chapter, we'll learn how to put names on the EmployeeIDs that are in the Manager column. For now though, we'll just note that there appear to be two different managers in the company. Apparently, everyone reports to these two people except for one person who doesn't have a manager assigned – that is probably our company's president (we could write a query to verify that, but we'll just trust in our assumptions for the time being).

We didn't put a WHERE clause in this query, so the GROUP BY was operating on every row in the table and every row is included in a grouping. To test out what would happen to our counts, let's add a WHERE clause:

```
SELECT ReportsTo AS Manager, COUNT(*) AS Reports
FROM Employees
WHERE EmployeeID != 5
GROUP BY ReportsTo
```

This yields us one slight change that we probably expected:

```
Manager          Reports
--------------- ---------
NULL             1
2                4
5                3
```

(3 row(s) affected)

The groupings were relatively untouched, but one row was eliminated before the GROUP BY clause was even considered. You see, the WHERE clause filtered out the one row where the EmployeeID was 5. As it happens, EmployeeID 5 reports to ManagerID 2. When EmployeeID 5 was no longer part of the query, the number of rows that were eligible to be in ManagerID 2's group was reduced by one.

I want to look at things a bit differently though. See if you can work out how to answer the following question. Which managers have more than four people reporting to them? You can look at the query without the WHERE clause and tell by the count, but how do you tell programmatically? That is, what if we need this query to return only the managers with more than four people reporting to them? If you try to work this out with a WHERE clause, you'll find that there isn't a way to return rows based on the aggregation – the WHERE clause is already completed by the system before the aggregation is executed. That's where our HAVING clause comes in:

```
SELECT ReportsTo AS Manager, COUNT(*) AS Reports
FROM Employees
GROUP BY ReportsTo
HAVING COUNT(*) > 4
```

Try it out and you'll come up with something a little bit more like what we were after:

```
Manager           Reports
----------------  ----------
2                 5
```

(1 row(s) affected)

There is only one manager that has more than four employees reporting to him or her.

As I mentioned before – we could have gone and picked this out of the original listing fairly quickly, but the list is not always so short, and when dealing with things programmatically, you often need an exact answer that requires no further analysis.

Let's try a somewhat larger recordset, and then we'll leave this topic until we look at multi-table queries in the next chapter. If we want a query that will look at the total quantity of items ordered on each order in the system, it's a reasonably easy query:

```
SELECT OrderID, SUM(Quantity) AS Total
FROM [Order Details]
GROUP BY OrderID
```

```
OrderID           Total
----------------  -------
10248             27
...
...
11075             42
11076             50
11077             72
```

(830 row(s) affected)

Unfortunately, it's somewhat difficult to do analysis on such a large list. So, let's have SQL Server do some paring down of this list to help us do our analysis. Assume that we're only interested in larger order quantities. Can you modify the query to return the same information, but limited to orders where the total quantity of product ordered was over 300? It's as easy as adding the HAVING clause:

```
SELECT OrderID, SUM(Quantity) AS Total
FROM [Order Details]
GROUP BY OrderID
HAVING SUM(Quantity) > 300
```

Now we get a substantially shorter list:

```
OrderID          Total
---------------  -------
10895            346
11030            330
```

(2 row(s) affected)

As you can see, we can very quickly pare the list down to just the few in which we are most interested. We could perform additional queries now, specifically searching for OrderIDs 10895 and 11030, or as you'll learn in later chapters, we can JOIN the information from this query with additional information to yield information that is even more precise.

Outputting XML Using the FOR XML Clause

New with SQL Server 2000 is the ability to have your results sent back in an XML format rather than the traditional result set. This is very powerful – particularly in web or cross-platform environments.

I'm going to shy away from the details of this clause for now since XML is a discussion unto itself – we'll dedicate Chapter 19 to just talking about what XML is all about later on, and then we'll spend Chapter 20 looking at how to make it work for you in SQL Server. So for now just trust me that it's better to learn the basics first.

Making Use of Hints Using the OPTION Clause

The OPTION clause is a way of overriding some of SQL Server's ideas of how to best run your query. Since SQL Server really does usually know what's best for your query, using the OPTION clause will more often hurt you rather than help you. Still, it's nice to know that it's there just in case.

This is another one of those "I'll get there later" subjects. We talk about query hints extensively when we talk about locking strategies later in the book, but, until you understand what you're affecting with your hints, I'm going to again shy away from fully explaining the OPTION clause at this point.

> Back in version 6.5 and earlier, it wasn't unheard of (though it was uncommon) for SQL Server to make the wrong choice of indexes to use or some other strategy problem. A tremendous amount of time and effort was spent in version 7.0 to improve the query optimizer (the part of SQL Server that figures out how best to run your query), and Microsoft did a positively wonderful job (still not perfect, but much better). For SQL Server 2000, Microsoft has upped the ante even further – building the best query optimizer yet.

The DISTINCT and ALL Predicates

There's just one more major concept to get through and we'll be ready to move from the SELECT statement on to action statements. It has to do with repeated data.

Let's say, for example, that we wanted a list of the IDs of the suppliers of all of the products that we have in stock currently. We can easily get that information from the Products table with the following query:

```
SELECT SupplierID
FROM Products
WHERE UnitsInStock > 0
```

What we get back is one row matching the SupplierID for every row in the Products table:

```
SupplierID
--------------
1
1
1
2
3
3
3
...
...
12
23
12
```

(72 row(s) affected)

While this meets our needs from a technical standpoint, it doesn't really meet our needs from a reality standpoint. Look at all those duplicate rows! As we've seen in other queries in this chapter, this particular table is small, but the number of rows returned and the number of duplicates can quickly become overwhelming. Like the problems we've discussed before – we have an answer. It comes in the form of the DISTINCT predicate on your SELECT statement.

Try re-running the query with a slight change:

```
SELECT DISTINCT SupplierID
FROM Products
WHERE UnitsInStock > 0
```

Now you come up with a true list of the SupplierIDs from which we currently have stock:

```
SupplierID
--------------
1
2
3
...
...
27
28
29
```

(29 row(s) affected)

As you can see, this cut down the size of our list substantially and made the contents of the list more relevant. Another side benefit of this query is that it will actually perform better than the first one. Why? Well, we'll go into that later in the book when we discuss performance issues further, but for now, suffice it to say that not having to return every single row means that SQL Server doesn't have to do quite as much work in order to meet the needs of this query.

As the old commercials on television go, "But wait! There's more!" We're not done with DISTINCT yet. Indeed, the next example is one that you might be able to use as a party trick to impress your programmer friends. You see, this is one that an amazing number of SQL programmers don't even realize you can do – DISTINCT can be used as more than just a predicate for a SELECT statement. It can also be used in the expression for an aggregate. What do I mean? Let's compare three queries.

First, grab a row count for the Order Details table:

```
SELECT COUNT(*)
FROM [Order Details]
```

If you haven't modified the Order Details table, this should yield you 2,155 rows.

Now run the same query using a specific column to count:

```
SELECT COUNT(OrderID)
FROM [Order Details]
```

Since the OrderID column is part of the key for this table, it can't contain any NULLs (more on this in Chapter 7). Therefore, the net count for this query is always going to be the same as the COUNT(*) – in this case, it's 2,155.

> *Key* is a term used to describe a column or combination of columns that can be used to identify a row within a table. There are actually several different kinds of keys (we'll see much more on these in Chapters 7-9), but when the word "key" is used by itself, it is usually referring to the table's primary key. A primary key is a column or group of columns that are effectively the unique name for that row – when you refer to a row using its primary key, you can be certain that you will only get back one row, because no two rows are allowed to have the same primary key within the same table.

Now for the fun part. Modify the query again:

```
SELECT COUNT(DISTINCT OrderID)
FROM [Order Details]
```

Now we get a substantially different result:

```
-----------
830

(1 row(s) affected)
```

All duplicate rows were eliminated before the aggregation occurred, so you have substantially fewer rows.

> Note that you can use **DISTINCT** with any aggregate function, though I question whether many of the functions have any practical use for it. For example, I can't imagine why you would want an average of just the **DISTINCT** rows.

That takes us to the ALL predicate. With one exception, it is a very rare thing indeed to see someone actually including an ALL in a statement. ALL is perhaps best understood as being the opposite of DISTINCT. Where DISTINCT is used to filter out duplicate rows, ALL says to include every row. ALL is the default for any SELECT statement except for situations where there is a UNION. We will discuss the impact of ALL in a UNION situation in the next chapter, but for now, realize that ALL is happening anytime you don't ask for a DISTINCT.

Adding Data with the INSERT Statement

By now, you should have pretty much got the hang of basic SELECT statements. We would be doing well to stop here save for a pretty major problem – we wouldn't have very much data to look at if we didn't have some way of getting it into the database in the first place. That's where the INSERT statement comes in.

The basic syntax for an INSERT statement looks like this:

```
INSERT [INTO] <table> [(column_list)] VALUES (data_values)
```

Let's look at the parts:

INSERT is the action statement. It tells SQL Server what it is that we're going to be doing with this statement and everything that comes after this keyword is merely spelling out the details of that action.

The INTO keyword is pretty much just fluff. Its sole purpose in life is to make the overall statement more readable. It is completely optional, but I highly recommend its use for the very reason that they added it to the statement – it makes things much easier to read. As we go through this section, try a few of the statements both with and without the INTO keyword. It's a little less typing if you leave it out, but it's also quite a bit stranger to read – it's up to you.

Next comes the table into which you are inserting.

Until this point, things have been pretty straightforward – now comes the part that's a little more difficult: the column list. An explicit column list (where you specifically state the columns to receive values) is optional, but not supplying one means that you have to be extremely careful. If you don't provide an explicit column list, then each value in your INSERT statement will be assumed to match up with a column in the same ordinal position of the table in order (1st value to 1st column, 2nd value to 2nd column, etc.). Additionally, a value must be supplied for every column, in order, until you reach the last column that both does not accept nulls and has no default (you'll see more about what I mean shortly). In summary, this will be a list of one or more columns that you are going to be providing data for in the next part of the statement.

Finally, you'll supply the values to be inserted. There are two ways of doing this, but for now, we'll focus on single line inserts that use data that you explicitly provide. To supply the values, we'll start with the VALUES keyword, and then follow that with a list of values, separated by commas and enclosed in parentheses. The number of items in the value list must exactly match the number of columns in the column list. The data type of each value must match or be implicitly convertible to the type of the column with which it corresponds (they are taken in order).

> *On the issue of, "Should I specifically state a value for all columns or not?" I really recommend naming every column every time – even if you just use the DEFAULT keyword or explicitly state NULL. DEFAULT will tell SQL Server to use whatever the default value is for that column (if there isn't one, you'll get an error).*
>
> *What's nice about this is the readability of code – this way it's really clear what you are doing. In addition, I find that explicitly addressing every column leads to fewer bugs.*

Whew! That's confusing, so let's practice with this some. Let's make use of the pubs database. This is a different database than we've been using, so don't forget to make the change.

OK, most of the inserts we're going to do in this chapter will be to the stores table, so let's take a look at the properties for that table. To do this, click on the Tables node of the pubs database in the EM. Then, in the right-hand pane of EM (which should now have a list of all the tables in pubs), double-click on the stores table:

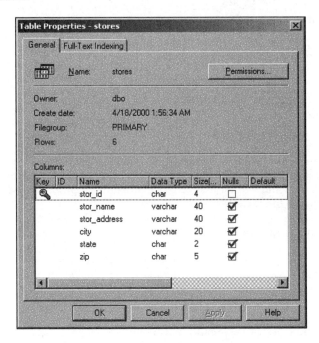

In this table, every column happens to be a char or varchar.

For our first insert, we'll eliminate the optional column list and allow SQL Server to assume we're providing something for every column:

```
INSERT INTO stores
VALUES
    ('TEST', 'Test Store', '1234 Anywhere Street', 'Here', 'NY', '00319')
```

As stated earlier, unless we provide a different column list (we'll cover how to provide a column list shortly), all the values have to be supplied in the same order as the columns are defined in the table. After executing this query, you should see a statement that tells you that one row was affected by your query. Now, just for fun, try running the exact same query a second time. You'll get the following error:

Server: Msg 2627, Level 14, State 1, Line 1
Violation of PRIMARY KEY constraint 'UPK_storeid'. Cannot insert duplicate key in object 'stores'. The statement has been terminated.

Why did it work the first time and not the second? Because this table has a primary key that does not allow duplicate values for the stor_id field. As long as we changed that one field, we could have left the rest of the columns alone and it would have taken the new row. We'll see more of primary keys in the chapters on design and constraints.

So let's see what we inserted:

```
SELECT *
FROM stores
WHERE stor_id = 'TEST'
```

This query yields us exactly what we inserted:

stor_id	stor_name	stor_address	city	state	zip
TEST	Test Store	1234 Anywhere Street	Here	NY	00319

(1 row(s) affected)

Note that I've trimmed a few spaces off the end of each column to help it fit on a page neatly, but the true data is just as we expected it to be.

Now let's try it again with modifications for inserting into specific columns:

```
INSERT INTO stores
    (stor_id, stor_name, city, state, zip)
VALUES
    ('TST2', 'Test Store', 'Here', 'NY', '00319')
```

Note that, on the line with the data values, we've changed just two things. First, we've changed the value we are inserting into the primary key column so it won't generate an error. Second, we eliminated the value that was associated with the stor_address column since we have omitted that column in our column list. There are a few different instances where we can skip a column in a column list and not provide any data for it in the INSERT statement. For now, we're just taking advantage of the fact that the stor_address column is not a required column – that is, it accepts NULLs. Since we're not providing a value for this column and since it has no default (we'll see more on defaults later on), this column will be set to NULL when we perform our insert.

Let's verify that by re-running our test SELECT statement with one slight modification:

```
SELECT *
FROM stores
WHERE stor_id = 'TST2'
```

Now we see something a little different:

stor_id	stor_name	stor_address	city	state	zip
TST2	Test Store	NULL	Here	NY	00319

(1 row(s) affected)

Notice that a NULL was inserted for the column that we skipped.

Note that the columns have to be **nullable** in order to do this. What does that mean? Pretty much what it sounds like – it means that you are allowed to have NULL values for that column. Believe me, we will be discussing the nullability of columns at great length in this book, but for now, just realize that some columns allow NULLs and some don't. We can always skip providing information for columns that allow NULLs.

If, however, the column is not nullable, then one of two conditions must exist, or we will receive an error and the INSERT will be rejected:

❑	The first condition is that the column has been defined with a **default value**. A default is a constant value that is inserted if no other value is provided. We will learn how to define defaults in Chapter 7.

❑	The second condition is, of course, that we supply a value for the column.

Just for completeness, let's perform one more INSERT statement. This time, we'll insert a new sale into the sales table. To view the properties of the sales table, we can either open its **Properties** dialog as we did with the stores table, or we can run a system stored procedure called sp_help. sp_help will report information about any database object, user-defined data type, or SQL Server data type. The syntax for using sp_help is as follows:

EXEC sp_help <name>

To view the properties of the sales table, we just have to type the following into the Query Analyzer:

```
EXEC sp_help sales
```

Which returns (among other things):

Column_name	Type	Length	Nullable
stor_id	char	4	no
ord_num	varchar	20	no
ord_date	datetime	8	no
qty	smallint	2	no
payterms	varchar	12	no
title_id	tid	6	no

The `sales` table has six columns in it, but pay particular attention to the `qty` and `ord_date` columns – they are of types that we haven't done inserts with up to this point (the `title_id` column is of type `tid`, but that is actually just a user defined type that is still a character type with a length of 6).

What you need to pay attention to in this query is how to format the types as you're inserting them. We do *not* use quotes for numeric values as we have with our character data. However, the `datetime` data type does require quotes (essentially, it goes in as a string and it then gets converted to a datetime).

```
INSERT INTO sales
    (stor_id, ord_num, ord_date, qty, payterms, title_id)
VALUES
    ('TEST', 'TESTORDER', '01/01/1999', 10, 'NET 30', 'BU1032')
```

This gets us back the now familiar (1 row(s) affected) message.

> Note that, while I've used the MM/DD/YYYY format that is popular in the US, you can use a wide variety of other formats (such as the internationally more popular YYYY-MM-DD) with equal success. The default for your server will vary depending on if you purchase a localized copy of SQL Server or if the setting has been changed on the server.

The INSERT INTO...SELECT Statement

Well, this "one row at a time" business is all fine and dandy, but what if we have a block of data that we want inserted? Over the course of the book, we'll look at lots of different scenarios where that can happen, but for now, we're going to focus on the case where what we want to insert into our table can be obtained by selecting it from another source such as:

- ❑ Another table in our database

- ❑ A totally different database on the same server

- ❑ A heterogeneous query from another SQL Server or other data source (more on that in Chapter 17)

- ❑ From the same table (usually, you're doing some sort of math or other adjustment in your `SELECT` statement in this case)

The `INSERT INTO...SELECT` statement can do all of these. The syntax for this statement comes from a combination of the two statements we've seen thus far – the `INSERT` statement and the `SELECT` statement. It looks something like this:

```
INSERT INTO <table name>
[<column list>]
<SELECT statement>
```

The result set created from the `SELECT` statement becomes the data that is added in your `INSERT` statement.

Let's check this out by doing something that, if you get into advanced coding, you'll find yourself doing all too often – selecting some data into some form of temporary table. In this case, we're going to declare a variable of type `table` and fill it with rows of data from our `Orders` table:

> **This next block of code is what is called a script. This particular script is made up of one batch. We will be examining batches at length in Chapter 11.**

```
/* This next statement is going to use code to change the "current" database
** to Northwind. This makes certain, right in the code that we are going
** to the correct database.
*/

USE Northwind

/* This next statement declares our working table.
** This particular table is actually a variable we are declaring on the fly.
** Table variables are new with SQL Server 2000.
*/

DECLARE @MyTable Table
(
    OrderID      int,
    CustomerID   char(5)
)

/* Now that we have our table variable, we're ready to populate it with data
** from our SELECT statement. Note that we could just as easily insert the
** data into a permanent table (instead of a table variable).
*/
INSERT INTO @MyTable
    SELECT OrderID, CustomerID
    FROM Northwind.dbo.Orders
    WHERE OrderID BETWEEN 10240 AND 10250

-- Finally, let's make sure that the data was inserted like we think
SELECT *
FROM @MyTable
```

This should yield you results that look like this:

```
(3 row(s) affected)

OrderID           CustomerID
----------------  ----------
10248             VINET
10249             TOMSP
10250             HANAR

(3 row(s) affected)
```

The first (3 row(s) affected) we see is the effect of the INSERT...SELECT statement at work – our SELECT statement returns three rows, so that's what got inserted into our table. We then use a straight SELECT statement to verify the insert.

Note that if you try running a **SELECT** against **@MyTable** by itself (that is, outside this script), you're going to get an error. **@MyTable** is a variable that we have declared, and it only exists as long as our batch is running. After that, it is automatically destroyed.

It's also worth noting that using a table variable like this is a new feature in SQL Server 2000. In previous versions, we would have to create what's called a "temporary table" – this is similar in nature, but doesn't work in quite the same way. Personally, I am a fan of the new **table** variable type, but stay away from it if you want compatibility with previous versions of SQL Server. Again, we will revisit temp tables and table variables in Chapters 11-13.

Changing What You've Got with the UPDATE Statement

The UPDATE statement, like most SQL statements, does pretty much what it sounds like it does – it updates existing data. The structure is a little bit different from a SELECT, though you'll notice definite similarities. Let's look at the syntax:

```
UPDATE <table name>
SET <column> = <value> [,<column> = <value>]
[FROM <source table(s)>]
[WHERE <restrictive condition>]
```

An UPDATE can be created from multiple tables, but can only affect one table. What do I mean by that? Well, we can build a condition, or retrieve values from any number of different tables, but only one table at a time can be the subject of the update action. Don't sweat this one too much – we haven't looked at joining multiple tables yet (next chapter folks!), so we won't get into complex UPDATE statements here. For now, we'll look at simple updates.

Let's start off by doing some updates to the data that we inserted in the INSERT statement section. Let's re-run that query to look at one row of inserted data (don't forget to switch back to the pubs database):

```
SELECT *
FROM stores
WHERE stor_id = 'TEST'
```

Which returns the following to us:

stor_id	stor_name	stor_address	city	state	zip
TEST	Test Store	1234 Anywhere Street	Here	NY	00319

Let's update the value in the `city` column:

```
UPDATE stores
SET city = 'There'
WHERE stor_id = 'TEST'
```

Much like when we ran the `INSERT` statement, we don't get much back from SQL Server:

(1 row(s) affected)

Yet, when we again run our `SELECT` statement, we see that the value has indeed changed:

stor_id	stor_name	stor_address	city	state	zip
TEST	Test Store	1234 Anywhere Street	There	NY	00319

Note that we could have changed more than one column just by adding a comma and the additional column expression. For example, the following statement would have updated both columns:

```
UPDATE stores
SET city = 'There', state = 'CA'
WHERE stor_id = 'TEST'
```

If we choose, we can use an expression for the `SET` clause instead of the explicit values we've used thus far. For example, take a look at a few records from the `titles` table of the `pubs` database:

```
SELECT title_id, price
FROM titles
WHERE title_id LIKE 'BU%'
```

Our `LIKE` operator used here is going to provide us with the rows that start with 'BU', but which have any value after that (since we've used a `%`). Assuming you haven't been playing around with the data in the `pubs` database, you should end up with results similar to these:

title_id	price
BU1032	19.9900
BU1111	11.9500
BU2075	2.9900
BU7832	19.9900

(4 row(s) affected)

Now that we've seen what the data looks like, let's try a somewhat different update by using an expression in our `UPDATE` statement:

```
UPDATE titles
SET price = price * 1.1
WHERE title_id LIKE 'BU%'
```

After executing that update, run the SELECT statement again:

```
SELECT title_id, price
FROM titles
WHERE title_id LIKE 'BU%'
```

You should see the price increased by 10% for every title ID that starts with BU:

title_id	price
BU1032	21.9890
BU1111	13.1450
BU2075	3.2890
BU7832	21.9890

(4 row(s) affected)

Let's take this a little further to show you how much we can manipulate our results. For example, let's say that we have a business rule that says our prices need to be evenly payable with US currency. The prices we came up with don't meet our criteria, so we need to do something to get our prices rounded to the nearest whole cent (0.01 dollars). From the point that we're at, we could round to the nearest cent by running another update that does the rounding, but let's go back to the beginning. First, let's undo our last update:

```
UPDATE titles
SET price = price / 1.1
WHERE title_id LIKE 'BU%'
```

Notice that we only had to change just the one line of code. After you execute this, the SELECT statement should yield you the results with which we started:

title_id	price
BU1032	19.9900
BU1111	11.9500
BU2075	2.9900
BU7832	19.9900

(4 row(s) affected)

Now we're ready to start from the beginning with a more advanced query. This time, we're going to perform pretty much the same update, but we'll round the updated data:

```
UPDATE titles
SET price = ROUND(price * 1.1, 2)
WHERE title_id LIKE 'BU%'
```

We've actually performed two mathematical operations before the UPDATE is actually written to each record. First, we perform the equivalent of our first query (increasing the price by 10%). Then we round it to match our business rule (must be to the cent) by indicating that our ROUND() function should round data off to two decimal places (hence the number 2 right after our 1.1,). The great thing is that we've been able to do this in just one operation rather than two.

Let's verify that result:

title_id	price
BU1032	21.9900
BU1111	13.1500
BU2075	3.2900
BU7832	21.9900

(4 row(s) affected)

As you can see, a single UPDATE statement can be fairly powerful. Even so, this is really just the beginning. We'll see even more advanced updates in later chapters.

> While SQL Server is nice enough to let us update pretty much any column (there are a few that we can't, such as timestamps), be very careful about updating primary keys. Doing so puts you at very high risk of "orphaning" other data (data that has a reference to the data you're changing).
>
> For example, the stor_id field in the stores table of the pubs database is a primary key. If we decide to change stor_id 10 to 35 in stores, then any data in the sales table that relates to that store may be orphaned and lost to us if the stor_id value in all of the records relating to stor_id 10 is not also updated to 35. As it happens, there is a constraint that references the stores table, so SQL Server would prevent such an orphaning situation in this case (we'll investigate constraints in Chapter 7), but updating primary keys is risky at best.

The DELETE Statement

The version of the DELETE statement that we'll cover in this chapter may be one of the easiest statements of them all. There's no column list – just a table name and, usually, a WHERE clause. The syntax couldn't be much easier:

```
DELETE <table_name>
[WHERE <search condition>]
```

The WHERE clause works just like all of the WHERE clauses we've seen thus far. We don't need to provide a column list because we are deleting the entire row (you can't delete half a row for example).

Since this is so easy, we'll only perform a couple of quick deletes that are focused on cleaning up the inserts that we performed earlier in the chapter. First, let's run a SELECT to make sure the first of those rows is still there:

```
SELECT *
FROM stores
WHERE stor_id = 'TEST'
```

If you haven't already deleted it, you should come up with a single row that matches what we added with our original INSERT statement. Now let's get rid of it:

```
DELETE stores
WHERE stor_id = 'TEST'
```

Note that we've run into a situation where SQL Server is refusing to delete this row due to referential integrity violations:

Server: Msg 547, Level 16, State 1, Line 1
DELETE statement conflicted with COLUMN REFERENCE constraint
'FK__sales__stor_id__1BFD2C07'. The conflict occurred in database 'pubs', table 'sales', column 'stor_id'.
The statement has been terminated.

SQL Server won't let us delete a row if it is referenced as part of a foreign key constraint. We'll see much more on foreign keys in Chapter 7, but for now, just keep in mind that, if one row references another row (either in the same or a different table – it doesn't matter) using a foreign key, then the referencing row must be deleted before the referenced row can be deleted. Our last INSERT statement inserted a record into the sales table that had a stor_id of 'TEST' – this record is referencing the record we have just attempted to delete.

Before we can delete the record from our stores table, we must delete the record it is referencing in the sales table:

```
DELETE sales
WHERE stor_id = 'TEST'
```

Now we can successfully re-run the first DELETE statement:

```
DELETE stores
WHERE stor_id = 'TEST'
```

You can do two quick checks to verify that the data was indeed deleted. The first happens automatically when the DELETE statement was executed – you should get a message telling you that one row was affected. The other quick check is to re-run the SELECT statement – you should get zero rows back.

For one more easy practice DELETE, we'll also kill off that second row by making just a slight change:

```
DELETE stores
WHERE stor_id = 'TST2'
```

That's it for simple deletes! Like the other statements in this chapter, we'll come back to the DELETE statement when we're ready for more complex search conditions.

Summary

T-SQL is SQL Server's own brand of ANSI SQL or Structured Query Language. T-SQL is entry-level ANSI 92 compliant, but it also has a number of its own extensions to the language – we'll see more of those in later chapters.

Even though, for backward compatibility, SQL Server has a number of different syntax choices that are effectively the same, wherever possible, you ought to use the ANSI form. Where there are different choices available, I will usually show you all of the choices, but again, stick with the ANSI version wherever possible. This is particularly important for situations where you think your back-end – or database server – might change at some point. Your ANSI code will, more than likely, run on the new database server – however, code that is only T-SQL definitely will not.

In this chapter, you have gained a solid taste of making use of single table statements in T-SQL, but the reality is that you often need information from more than one table. In the next chapter, we will learn how to make use of JOINs to allow us to use multiple tables.

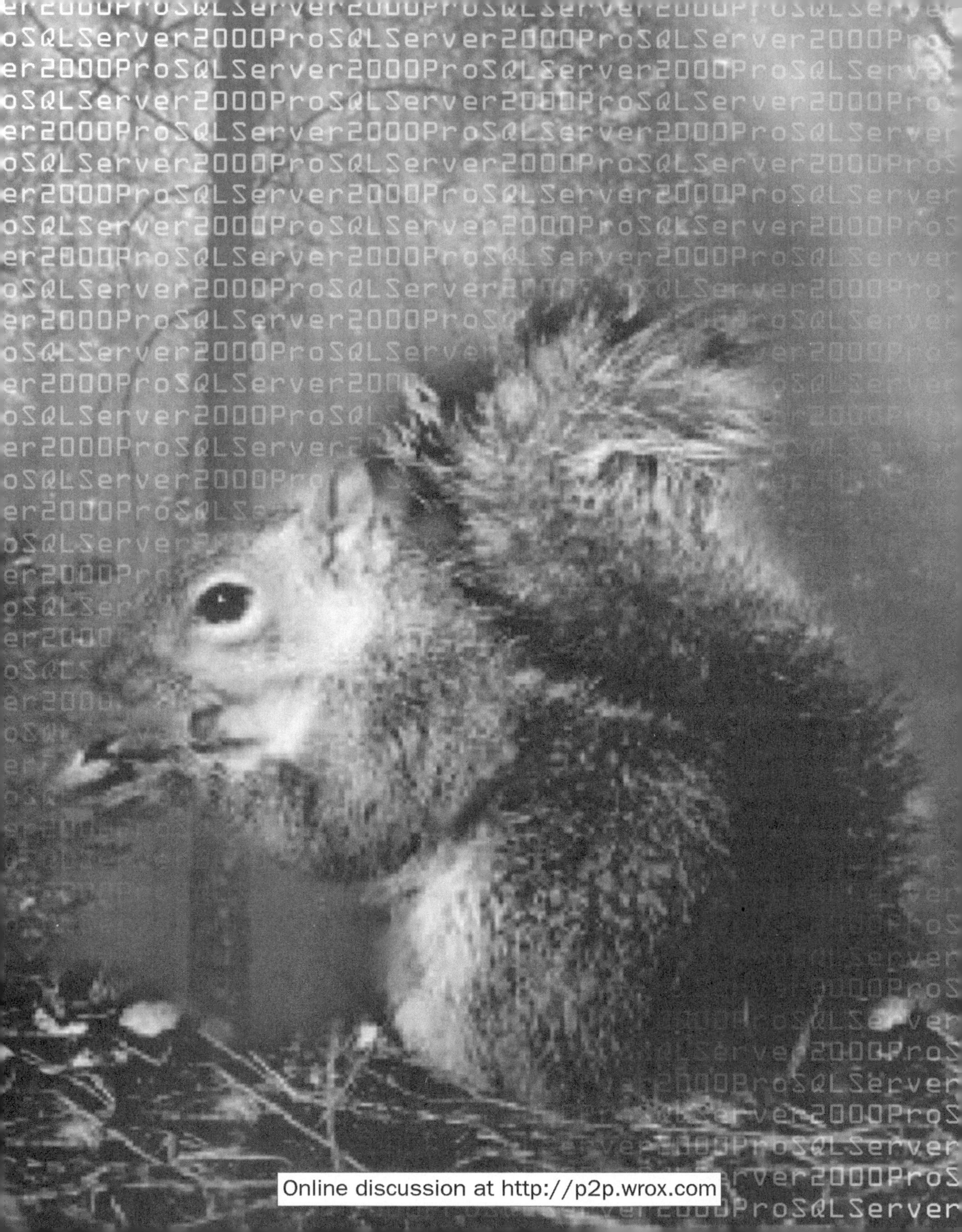
Online discussion at http://p2p.wrox.com

5

Joining Tables

As the Carpenters said in the 70s – we've only just begun. We've now got the basic statements under our belt, but they are only a small part of the bigger picture of the statements we will run. To put it simply, there is often not that much you can do with just one table – especially in a highly normalized database.

A **normalized** database is one where the data has been broken out from larger tables into many smaller tables for the purpose of eliminating repeating data, saving space, improving performance, and increasing data integrity. It's great stuff and vital to relational databases; however, it also means that you wind up getting your data from here, there, and everywhere.

> *We will be looking into the concepts of normalization extensively in Chapter 8. For now, though, just keep in mind that, the more normalized your database is, the more likely that you're going to have to join multiple tables together in order to get all the data you want.*

In this chapter, we're going to introduce you to the process of combining tables into one result set by using the various forms of the JOIN clause. These will include:

- ❑ INNER JOIN
- ❑ OUTER JOIN (both LEFT and RIGHT)
- ❑ FULL JOIN
- ❑ CROSS JOIN

We'll also learn that there is more than one syntax available to use for joins, and that one particular syntax is the right choice. In addition, we'll take a look at the UNION operator, which allows us to combine the results of two queries into one.

JOINs

When we are operating in a normalized environment, we frequently run into situations where not all of the information that we want is in one table. In other cases, all the information we want returned is in one table, but the information we want to place conditions on is in another table. In these situations, this is where the JOIN clause comes in.

A JOIN does just what it sounds like – it puts the information from two tables together into one result set. We can think of a result set as being a "virtual" table. It has both columns and rows, and the columns have data types. Indeed, in Chapter 16, we'll see how to treat a result set as if it was a table and use it for other queries.

How exactly does a JOIN put the information from two tables into a single result set? Well, that depends on how you tell it to put the data together – that's why there are four different kinds of JOINs. The thing that all JOINs have in common is that they match one record up with one or more other records to make a record that is a superset created by the combined columns of both records.

For example, let's take a record from a table we'll call Films:

FilmID	FilmName	YearMade
1	My Fair Lady	1964

Now let's follow that up with a record from a table called Actors:

FilmID	FirstName	LastName
1	Rex	Harrison

With a JOIN, we could create one record from two records found in totally separate tables:

FilmID	FilmName	YearMade	FirstName	LastName
1	My Fair Lady	1964	Rex	Harrison

This JOIN (at least apparently) joins records in a one-to-one relationship. We have one Films record joining to one Actors record.

Let's expand things just a bit and see if you can see what's happening. I've added another record to the Actors table:

FilmID	FirstName	LastName
1	Rex	Harrison
1	Audrey	Hepburn

Now let's see what happens when we join that to the very same (only one record) `Films` table:

FilmID	FilmName	YearMade	FirstName	LastName
1	My Fair Lady	1964	Rex	Harrison
1	My Fair Lady	1964	Audrey	Hepburn

As you can see, the effect has changed a bit – we are no longer seeing things as being one-to-one, but rather one-to-two, or more appropriately, what we would call one-to-many. We can use that single record in the `Films` table as many times as necessary in order to have complete (joined) information about the matching records in the `Actors` table.

Have you noticed how they are matching up? It is, of course, by matching up the `FilmID` field from the two tables to create one record out of two.

The examples we have used here with such a limited data set, would actually yield the same results no matter what kind of `JOIN` we have. Let's move on now and look at the specifics of the different `JOIN` types.

INNER JOINs

`INNER JOINs` are far and away the most common kind of `JOIN`. They match records together based on one or more common fields, as do most `JOINs`, but an `INNER JOIN` only returns the records where there are matches for whatever field(s) you have said are to be used for the `JOIN`. In our previous examples, every record has been included in the result set at least once, but this situation is rarely the case in the real world.

Let's modify our tables and see what we would get with an `INNER JOIN`. Here's our `Films` table:

FilmID	FilmName	YearMade
1	My Fair Lady	1964
2	Unforgiven	1992

And our `Actors` table:

FilmID	FirstName	LastName
1	Rex	Harrison
1	Audrey	Hepburn
2	Clint	Eastwood
5	Humphrey	Bogart

Using an INNER JOIN, our result set would look like this:

FilmID	FilmName	YearMade	FirstName	LastName
1	My Fair Lady	1964	Rex	Harrison
1	My Fair Lady	1964	Audrey	Hepburn
2	Unforgiven	1992	Clint	Eastwood

Notice that Bogey was left out of this result set. That's because he didn't have a matching record in the Films table. If there isn't a match in both tables, then the record isn't returned. Enough theory – let's try this out in code.

The preferred code for an INNER JOIN looks something like this:

```
SELECT <select list>
FROM <first_table>
<join_type> <second_table>
        [ON <join_condition>]
```

This is the ANSI syntax, and you'll have much better luck with it on non-SQL Server database systems than you will with the proprietary syntax that was the way things had to be done through version 6.0. We'll take a look at the other syntax later in the chapter.

Fire up the Query Analyzer and take a test drive of INNER JOINs using the following code against Northwind:

```
SELECT *
FROM Products
INNER JOIN Suppliers
        ON Products.SupplierID = Suppliers.SupplierID
```

The results of this query are too wide to print in this book, but if you run this, you should get something in the order of 77 rows back. There are several things worth noting about the results:

❑ The SupplierID column appears twice, but there's nothing to say which one is from which table

❑ All columns were returned from both tables

❑ The first columns listed were from the first table listed

We can figure out which SupplierID is which just by looking at what table we selected first and matching it with the first SupplierID column that shows up, but this is tedious at best, and at worst, prone to errors. That's one of many reasons why using the plain * operator in JOINs is ill advised. In the case of an INNER JOIN though, it's not really that much of a problem since we know that both SupplierID columns, even though they came from different tables, will be exact duplicates of each other. How do we know that? Think about it – since we're doing an INNER JOIN on those two columns, they have to match or the record wouldn't have been returned! Don't get in the habit of counting on this though. When we look at other JOIN types, we'll find that we can't depend on the JOIN values being equal.

As for all columns being returned from both tables, that is as expected. We used the * operator, which as we've learned before is going to return all columns to us. As I mentioned earlier, the use of the * operator in joins is a bad habit. It's quick and easy, but it's also dirty – it is error-prone and can result in poor performance.

> *One good principle to adopt early on is this: to select what you need, and need what you select. What I'm getting at here is that every additional record or column that you return takes up additional network bandwidth, and often, additional query processing on your SQL Server. The upshot is that selecting unnecessary information hurts performance not only for the current user, but also for every other user of the system and for users of the network on which the SQL Server resides.*
>
> *Select only the columns that you are going to be using and make your WHERE clause as restrictive as possible.*

If you must insist on using the * operator, you should use it only for the tables from which you need all the columns. That's right – the * operator can be used on a per-table basis. For example, if we want all of our product information, but only the name of the supplier, we could have changed our query to read:

```
SELECT Products.*, CompanyName
FROM Products
INNER JOIN Suppliers
        ON Products.SupplierID = Suppliers.SupplierID
```

If you scroll over to the right in the results of this query, you'll see that most of the supplier information is now gone. Indeed, we also only have one instance of the SupplierID column. What we got in our result set was all the columns from the Products table (since we used the * qualified for just that table – our one instance of SupplierID came from this part of the SELECT list) and the only column that had the name CompanyName (which happened to be from the Suppliers table). Now let's try it again, with only one slight change:

```
SELECT Products.*, SupplierID
FROM Products
INNER JOIN Suppliers
        ON Products.SupplierID = Suppliers.SupplierID
```

Uh, oh – this is a problem. We get an error back:

Server: Msg 209, Level 16, State 1, Line 1
Ambiguous column name 'SupplierID'.

Why did CompanyName work and SupplierID not work? For just the reason SQL Server has indicated – our column name is ambiguous. While CompanyName only exists in the Suppliers table, SupplierID appears in both tables. SQL Server has no way of knowing which one we want. All the instances where we have returned SupplierID up to this point have been resolvable, that is SQL Server could figure out which table was which. In the first query (where we used a plain * operator), we asked SQL Server to return everything – that would include *both* SupplierID columns, so no name resolution was necessary. In our second example (where we qualified the * to be only for Products), we again said nothing specifically about which SupplierID column to use – instead, we said pull everything from the Products table and SupplierID just happened to be in that list. CompanyName was resolvable because there was only one CompanyName column, so that was the one we wanted.

When we want to refer to a column where the column name exists more than once in our JOIN result, we must **fully qualify** the column name. We can do this in one of two ways:

- ❏ Provide the name of the table that the desired column is from, followed by a period and the column name (*Table.ColumnName*)
- ❏ Alias the tables, and provide that alias, followed by a period and the column name (*Alias.ColumnName*)

The task of providing the names is straightforward enough – we've already seen how that works with the qualified * operator, but let's try our SupplierID query again with a qualified column name:

```
SELECT Products.*, Suppliers.SupplierID
FROM Products
INNER JOIN Suppliers
        ON Products.SupplierID = Suppliers.SupplierID
```

Now things are working again and we have the SupplierID from the Suppliers table added back to the far right-hand side of the result set.

Aliasing the table is only slightly trickier, but can cut down on the wordiness and help the readability of your query. It works almost exactly the same as aliasing a column in the simple SELECTs that we did in the last chapter – right after the name of the table, we simply state the alias we want to use to refer to that table. Note that, just as with column aliasing, we can use the AS keyword (but for some strange reason, this hasn't caught on in practice):

```
SELECT p.*, s.SupplierID
FROM Products p
INNER JOIN Suppliers s
        ON p.SupplierID = s.SupplierID
```

Run this code and you'll see that we receive the exact same results as we did in the last query.

Be aware that using an alias is an all-or-nothing proposition. Once you decide to alias a table, you must use that alias in every part of the query. This is on a table-by-table basis, but try running some mixed code and you'll see what I mean:

```
SELECT p.*, Suppliers.SupplierID
FROM Products p
INNER JOIN Suppliers s
        ON p.SupplierID = s.SupplierID
```

This seems like it should run fine, but it will give you an error:

Server: Msg 107, Level 16, State 3, Line 1
The column prefix 'Suppliers' does not match with a table name or alias name used in the query.

Again, you can mix and match which tables you choose to use aliasing on and which you don't, but once you make a decision, you have to be consistent.

Think back to those bullet points we saw a few pages earlier; we noticed that the columns from the first table listed in the JOIN were the first columns returned. Take a break for a moment and think about why that is, and what you might be able to do to control it.

SQL Server always uses a column order that is the best guess it can make at how you want the columns returned. In our first query, we used one global * operator, so SQL Server didn't have much to go on. In that case, it goes on the small amount that it does have – the order of the columns as they exist physically in the table, and the order of tables that you specified in your query. The nice thing is that it is extremely easy to reorder the columns – we just have to be explicit about it. The simplest way to reorder the columns would be to change which table is mentioned first, but we can actually mix and match our column order by simply explicitly stating the columns that we want (even if it is every column), and the order in which we want them. Let's try a smaller query to demonstrate the point:

```
SELECT p.ProductID, s.SupplierID, p.ProductName, s.CompanyName
FROM Products p
INNER JOIN Suppliers s
        ON p.SupplierID = s.SupplierID
WHERE p.ProductID < 4
```

This yields a pretty simple result set:

ProductID	SupplierID	ProductName	CompanyName
1	1	Chai	Exotic Liquids
2	1	Chang	Exotic Liquids
3	1	Aniseed Syrup	Exotic Liquids

(3 row(s) affected)

Again, the columns have come out in exactly the order that we've specified in our SELECT list.

How an INNER JOIN is Like a WHERE Clause

In the INNER JOINs that we've done so far, we've really been looking at the concepts that will work for any JOIN type – the column ordering and aliasing is exactly the same for any JOIN. The part that makes an INNER JOIN different from other JOINs is that it is an **exclusive join** – that is, it excludes all records that don't have a value in both tables (the first named, or left table, and the second named, or right table).

Our first example of this was seen with our imaginary Films and Actors tables. Bogey was left out because he didn't have a matching movie in the Films table. Let's look at a real example or two to show how this works.

We have a Customers table, and it is full of customer names and addresses. This does not mean, however, that the customers have actually ordered anything. Indeed, I'll give you a hint up front and tell you that there are some customers that have *not* ordered anything, so let's take a question and turn it into a query – the question I've picked calls for an INNER JOIN, but we'll see how slight changes to the question will change our choice of JOINs later on.

Here's a question you might get from a sales manager: "Can you show me all the customers who have placed orders with us?"

You can waste no time in saying, "Absolutely!" and starting to dissect the parts of the query. What are the things we need? Well, the sales manager asked about both customers and orders, so we can take a guess that we will need information from both of those tables. The sales manager only asked for a list of customers, so the `CompanyName` and perhaps the `CustomerID` are the only columns we need. Note that while we need to include the `Orders` table to figure out whether a customer has ordered anything or not, we do not need to return anything from it to make use of it (that's why it's not in the `SELECT` list shown below). The sales manager has asked for a list of customers where there has been an order, so the question calls for a solution where there is both a `Customers` record and an `Orders` record – that's our `INNER JOIN` scenario, so we should now be ready to write the query:

```
SELECT DISTINCT c.CustomerID, c.CompanyName
FROM Customers c
INNER JOIN Orders o
        ON c.CustomerID = o.CustomerID
```

If you haven't altered any data in the `Northwind` database, this should give you 89 rows. Note that we used the `DISTINCT` keyword because we only need to know that the customers have made orders (once was sufficient), not how many orders. Without the `DISTINCT`, a customer who ordered multiple times would have had a separate record returned for each `Orders` record to which it joined.

Now let's see if we got all the customers back. Try running a simple `COUNT` query:

```
SELECT COUNT(*) AS "No. Of Records" FROM Customers
```

And you'll get back a different count on the number of rows:

```
No. Of Records
--------------------
91

(1 row(s) affected)
```

Where did the other two rows go? As expected, they were excluded from the result set because there were no corresponding records in the `Orders` table. It is for this reason that an `INNER JOIN` is comparable to a `WHERE` clause. Just as an `INNER JOIN` will exclude rows because they had no corresponding match in the other table, the `WHERE` clause also limits the rows returned to those that match the criteria specified.

Just for a little more proof and practice, consider the following tables from the pubs database:

authors	Titles	titleauthor
au_id	title_id	au_id
au_lname	Title	title_id
au_fname	Type	au_ord
Phone	pub_id	royaltyper
address	Price	
City	Advance	
State	Royalty	
Zip	ytd_sales	
contract	notes	
	pubdate	

What we're looking for this time is a query that returns all the authors that have written books and the titles of the books that they have written. Try coming up with this query on your own for a few minutes, then we'll dissect it a piece at a time.

The first thing to do is to figure out what data we need to return. Our question calls for two different pieces of information to be returned: the author's name and the book's title. The author's name is available (in two parts) from the authors table. The book's title is available in the titles table, so we can write the first part of our SELECT statement:

```
SELECT au_lname + ', ' + au_fname AS "Author", title
```

Like many languages, the "+" operator can be used for concatenation of strings as well as the addition of numbers. In this case, we are just connecting the last name to the first name with a comma separator in between.

What we need now is something to join the two tables on, and that's where we run into our first problem – there doesn't appear to be one. The tables don't seem to have anything in common on which we can base our JOIN.

This brings us to the third table listed. Depending on which database architect you're talking to, a table like titleauthor will be called a number of different things. The most common names that I've come across for this type of table are **linking table** or **associate table**.

A linking table is any table for which the primary purpose is not to store its own data, but rather to relate the data stored in other tables. You can consider it to be "linking" or "associating" the two or more tables. These tables are used to get around the common situation where you have what is called a "many-to-many" relationship between the tables. This is where two tables relate, but either table can have many records that potentially match many records in the other table. SQL Server can't implement such relationships directly, so the linking table breaks down the many-to-many relationship into two "one-to-many" relationships – which SQL Server can handle. We will see much more on this subject in Chapter 8.

This particular table doesn't meet the criteria for a linking table in the strictest sense of the term, but it still serves that general purpose, and I, not being a purist, consider it such a table. By using this third table, we are able to indirectly join the `authors` and `titles` tables by joining each to the linking table, `titleauthor`. `authors` can join to `titleauthor` based on `au_id`, and `titles` can join to `titleauthor` based on `title_id`. Adding this third table into our `JOIN` is no problem – we just keep on going with our `FROM` clause and `JOIN` keywords (don't forget to switch the database to `pubs`):

```
SELECT a.au_lname + ', ' + a.au_fname AS "Author", t.title
FROM authors a
JOIN titleauthor ta
   ON a.au_id = ta.au_id
JOIN titles t
   ON t.title_id = ta.title_id
```

Notice that, since we've used aliases on the tables, we had to go back and change our `SELECT` clause to use the aliases, but our `SELECT` statement with a three-table join is now complete! If we execute this (I'm using the grid mode here), we get:

Author	title
Bennet, Abraham	The Busy Executive's Database Guide
Blotchet-Halls, Reginald	Fifty Years in Buckingham Palace Kitchens
Carson, Cheryl	But Is It User Friendly?
DeFrance, Michel	The Gourmet Microwave
del Castillo, Innes	Silicon Valley Gastronomic Treats
Dull, Ann	Secrets of Silicon Valley
Green, Marjorie	The Busy Executive's Database Guide
Green, Marjorie	You Can Combat Computer Stress!
Gringlesby, Burt	Sushi, Anyone?
Hunter, Sheryl	Secrets of Silicon Valley
Karsen, Livia	Computer Phobic AND Non-Phobic Individuals: Behavior Variations
Locksley, Charlene	Net Etiquette
Locksley, Charlene	Emotional Security: A New Algorithm
MacFeather, Stearns	Cooking with Computers: Surreptitious Balance Sheets
MacFeather, Stearns	Computer Phobic AND Non-Phobic Individuals: Behavior Variations
O'Leary, Michael	Cooking with Computers: Surreptitious Balance Sheets
O'Leary, Michael	Sushi, Anyone?
Panteley, Sylvia	Onions, Leeks, and Garlic: Cooking Secrets of the Mediterranean

Author	title
Ringer, Albert	Is Anger the Enemy?
Ringer, Albert	Life Without Fear
Ringer, Anne	The Gourmet Microwave
Ringer, Anne	Is Anger the Enemy?
Straight, Dean	Straight Talk About Computers
White, Johnson	Prolonged Data Deprivation: Four Case Studies
Yokomoto, Akiko	Sushi, Anyone?

Note that your sort order may differ from what you see here – remember, SQL Server makes no promises about the order your results will arrive in unless you use an ORDER BY clause – since we didn't use ORDER BY, the old adage "Actual results may vary" comes into play.

If we were to do a simple SELECT * against the authors table, we would find that several authors were left out because, although they have been entered into the authors table, they apparently haven't written any matching books (at least not that we have in our database). Indeed, we've even left one title (The Psychology of Computer Cooking) out because we can't match it up with an author!

Once again, the key to INNER JOINs is that they are exclusive.

> Notice that we did not use the **INNER** keyword in this last query. That is because an **INNER JOIN** is the default **JOIN** type. Schools of thought vary on this, but I believe that because leaving the **INNER** keyword out has dominated the way code has been written for so long, that it is almost more confusing to put it in – that's why you won't see me use it again in this book.

OUTER JOINs

This type of JOIN is something of the exception rather than the rule. This is definitely not because they don't have their uses, but rather because:

- ❑ We, more often than not, want the kind of exclusiveness that an INNER JOIN provides
- ❑ Many SQL writers learn INNER JOINs and never go any further – they simply don't understand the OUTER variety
- ❑ There are often other ways to accomplish the same thing
- ❑ They are often simply forgotten about as an option

Whereas INNER JOINs are exclusive in nature; OUTER and, as we'll see later in this chapter, FULL JOINs are inclusive. It's a tragedy that people don't get to know how to make use of OUTER JOINs because they make seemingly difficult questions simple. They can also often speed performance when used instead of nested subqueries (which we will look into in Chapter 16).

Earlier in this chapter, we briefly introduced the concept of a JOIN having sides – a left and a right. With INNER JOINs these are a passing thought at most, but with OUTER JOINs, understanding your left from your right is absolutely critical. When you look at it, it seems very simple because it is very simple, yet many query mistakes involving OUTER JOINs stem from not thinking through your left from your right.

To learn how to construct OUTER JOINs correctly, we're going to use two syntax illustrations. The first deals with the simple scenario of a two-table OUTER JOIN. The second will deal with the more complex scenario of mixing OUTER JOINs with any other JOIN.

The Simple OUTER JOIN

The first syntax situation is the easy part – most people get this part just fine.

```
SELECT <SELECT list>
FROM <the table you want to be the "LEFT" table>
<LEFT|RIGHT> [OUTER] JOIN <table you want to be the "RIGHT" table>
                 ON <join condition>
```

> *In the examples, you'll find that I tend to use the full syntax – that is, I include the OUTER keyword (for example LEFT OUTER JOIN). Note that the OUTER keyword is optional – you need only include the LEFT or RIGHT (for example LEFT JOIN).*

What I'm trying to get across here is that the table that comes before the JOIN keyword is considered to be the LEFT table, and the table that comes after the JOIN keyword is considered to be the RIGHT table.

OUTER JOINs are, as we've said, inclusive in nature. What specifically gets included depends on which side of the join you have emphasized. A LEFT OUTER JOIN includes all the information from the table on the left, and a RIGHT OUTER JOIN includes all the information from the table on the right. Let's put this into practice with a small query so that you can see what I mean.

Let's say we want to know what all our discounts are; the amount of each discount, and which stores use them. Looking over our pubs database, we have tables called discounts and stores as follows:

Discounts	stores
discounttype	stor_id
stor_id	stor_name
Lowqty	stor_address
Highqty	city
Discount	state
	zip

We can directly join these tables based on the stor_id. If we did this using a common INNER JOIN, it would look something like:

```
SELECT discounttype, discount, s.stor_name
FROM discounts d
JOIN stores s
   ON d.stor_id = s.stor_id
```

This yields us just one record:

discounttype	discount	stor_name
Customer Discount	5.00	Bookbeat

(1 row(s) affected)

Think about this though. We wanted results based on the discounts we have – not which ones were actually in use. This query only gives us discounts that we have matching stores for – it doesn't answer the question!

What we need is something that's going to return every discount and the stores where applicable. In order to make this happen, we only need to change the JOIN type in the query:

```
SELECT discounttype, discount, s.stor_name
FROM discounts d
LEFT OUTER JOIN stores s
            ON d.stor_id = s.stor_id
```

This yields us somewhat different results:

discounttype	discount	stor_name
Initial Customer	10.50	NULL
Volume Discount	6.70	NULL
Customer Discount	5.00	Bookbeat

(3 row(s) affected)

If you were to perform a SELECT * against the Discounts table, you'd quickly find that we have included every row from that table. We are doing a LEFT JOIN, and the discounts table is on the left side of the JOIN. But what about the stores table? If we are joining, and we don't have a matching record for the stores table, then what happens? Since it is not on the inclusive side of the join (in this case, the LEFT side), SQL Server will fill in a NULL for any value that comes from the opposite side of the join if there is no match with the inclusive side of the join. In this case, all but one of our rows has a stor_name that is NULL. What we can discern from that is that two of our discounts records (the two with NULLs in the column from the stores table) do not have matching store records – that is, no stores are using that discount type.

We've answered the question then; of the three discount types, only one is being used (Customer Discount) and it is only being used by one store (Bookbeat).

Now, let's see what happens if we change the join to a RIGHT OUTER JOIN:

```
SELECT discounttype, discount, s.stor_name
FROM discounts d
RIGHT OUTER JOIN stores s
            ON d.stor_id = s.stor_id
```

Even though this seems like a very small change, it actually changes our results rather dramatically:

```
discounttype          discount          stor_name
--------------------  ----------------  -------------------------------------------------
NULL                  NULL              Eric the Read Books
NULL                  NULL              Barnum's
NULL                  NULL              News & Brews
NULL                  NULL              Doc-U-Mat: Quality Laundry and Books
NULL                  NULL              Fricative Bookshop
Customer Discount     5.00              Bookbeat
```

(6 row(s) affected)

If you were to perform a SELECT * on the stores table now, you would find that all of the records from stores have been included in the query. Where there is a matching record in discounts, the appropriate discount record is displayed. Everywhere else, the columns that are from the discounts table are filled in with NULLs. Assuming that we always name the discounts table first, and the stores table second, then we would use a LEFT JOIN if we want all the discounts, and a RIGHT JOIN if we want all the stores.

Finding Orphan or Non-Matching Records

We can actually use the inclusive nature of OUTER JOINs to find non-matching records in the exclusive table. What do I mean by that? Let's look at an example.

Let's change our discount question. We want to know the store name for all the stores that do not have any kind of discount record. Can you come up with a query to perform this based on what we know this far? Actually, the very last query we ran has us 90% of the way there. Think about it for a minute; an OUTER JOIN returns a NULL value in the discounts-based columns wherever there is no match. What we are looking for is pretty much the same result set as we received in the last query, except that we want to filter out any records that do have a discount, and we only want the store name. To do this, we simply change our SELECT list and add a WHERE clause. To make it a touch prettier to give to our manager, we also alias the stor_name field to be the more expected "Store Name":

```
SELECT s.stor_name AS "Store Name"
FROM discounts d
RIGHT OUTER JOIN stores s
            ON d.stor_id = s.stor_id
WHERE d.stor_id IS NULL
```

As expected, we have exactly the same stores that had NULL values before:

```
Store Name
---------------------------------------------------
Eric the Read Books
Barnum's
News & Brews
Doc-U-Mat: Quality Laundry and Books
Fricative Bookshop
```

(5 row(s) affected)

There is one question you might be thinking at the moment that I want to answer in anticipation, so that you're sure you understand why this will always work. The question is: "What if the discount record really has a NULL value?" Well, that's why we built a WHERE clause on the same field that was part of our join. If we are joining based on the stor_id columns in both tables, then only three conditions can exist:

- ❑   If the stores.stor_id column has a non-NULL value, then, according to the ON operator of the JOIN clause, if a discounts record exists, then discounts.stor_id must also have the same value as stores.stor_id (look at the ON d.stor_id = s.stor_id).

- ❑   If the stores.stor_id column has a non-NULL value, then, according to the ON operator of the JOIN clause, if a discounts record does not exist, then discounts.stor_id will be returned as NULL.

- ❑   If the stores.stor_id happens to have a NULL value, and discounts.stor_id also has a NULL value – there will be no join, and discounts.stor_id will return NULL because there is no matching record.

A value of NULL does not join to a value of NULL. Why? Think about what we've already said about comparing NULLs – a NULL does not equal NULL. Be extra careful of this when coding. One of the more common questions I am asked is, "Why isn't this working?" in a situation where people are using an "equal to" operation on a NULL – it simply doesn't work because they are not equal. If you want to test this, try executing some simple code:

```
IF (NULL=NULL)
    PRINT 'It Does'
ELSE
    PRINT 'It Doesn''t'
```

If you execute this, you'll get the answer to whether your SQL Server thinks a NULL equals a NULL – that it "It Doesn't".

> *This is actually a change of behavior vs. prior versions of SQL Server. Be aware that if you are running in SQL Server 6.5 compatibility mode, or if you have ANSI_NULLS set to off (through server options or a SET statement), then you will get a different answer (your server will think that a NULL equals a NULL). This is considered non-standard at this point. It is a violation of the ANSI standard, and it is no longer compatible with the default configuration for SQL Server. (Even the Books Online will tell you a NULL is not equal to a NULL.)*

Let's use this notion of being able to identify non-matching records to locate some of the missing records from one of our earlier INNER JOINs. Remember these two queries, which we ran against Northwind?

```
SELECT DISTINCT c.CustomerID, c.CompanyName
FROM Customers c
INNER JOIN Orders o
        ON c.CustomerID = o.CustomerID
```

And...

```
SELECT COUNT(*) AS "No. Of Records" FROM Customers
```

The first was one of our queries where we explored the INNER JOIN. We discovered by running the second query that the first had excluded (by design) some rows. Now let's identify the excluded rows by using an OUTER JOIN.

We know from our SELECT COUNT(*) query that our first query is missing some records from the Customers table. (It may also be missing records from the Orders table, but we're not interested in that at the moment.) The implication is that there are records in the Customers table that do not have corresponding Orders records. While our manager's first question was about all the customers that had placed orders, it would be a very common question to ask just the opposite, "What customers haven't placed an order?" That question is answered with the same result as asking the question, "What records exist in Customers that don't have corresponding records in the Orders table?" The solution has the same structure as our query to find stores without discounts:

```
USE Northwind

SELECT c.CustomerID, CompanyName
FROM Customers c
LEFT OUTER JOIN Orders o
          ON c.CustomerID = o.CustomerID
WHERE o.CustomerID IS NULL
```

Just that quick we are able to not only find out how many customers haven't placed orders, but now we know which customers they are (I suspect the sales department will contact them shortly...):

CustomerID	CompanyName
PARIS	Paris spécialités
FISSA	FISSA Fabrica Inter. Salchichas S.A.

(2 row(s) affected)

> Note that whether you use a **LEFT** or a **RIGHT JOIN** doesn't matter as long as the correct table or group of tables is on the corresponding side of the **JOIN**. For example, we could have run the above query using a **RIGHT JOIN** as long as we also switched which sides of the **JOIN** the **Customers** and **Orders** tables were on. For example this would have yielded exactly the same results:
>
> ```
> SELECT c.CustomerID, CompanyName
> FROM Orders o
> RIGHT OUTER JOIN Customers c
>           ON c.CustomerID = o.CustomerID
> WHERE o.CustomerID IS NULL
> ```

When we take a look at even more advanced queries, we'll run into a slightly more popular way of finding records that exist in one table without there being corresponding records in another table. Allow me to preface that early by saying that using JOINs is usually our best bet in terms of performance. There are exceptions to the rule that we will cover as we come across them, but in general, the use of JOINs will be the best when faced with multiple options.

Dealing with More Complex OUTER JOINs

Now we're on to our second illustration and how to make use of it. This scenario is all about dealing with an OUTER JOIN mixed with some other JOIN (no matter what the variety).

It is when combining an OUTER JOIN with other JOINs that the concept of sides becomes even more critical. What's important to understand here is that everything to the "left" – or before – the JOIN in question will be treated just as if it was a single table for the purposes of inclusion or exclusion from the query. The same is true for everything to the "right" – or after – the JOIN. The frequent mistake here is to perform a LEFT OUTER JOIN early in the query and then use an INNER JOIN late in the query. The OUTER JOIN includes everything up to that point in the query, but the INNER JOIN may still create a situation where something is excluded! My guess is that you will, like most people (including me for a while), find this exceptionally confusing at first, so let's see what we mean with some examples. Since none of the databases that come along with SQL Server has any good scenarios for demonstrating this, we're going to have to create a database and sample data of our own.

If you want to follow along with the examples, the example database called `Chapter5DB` can be created by running `Chapter5.sql` from the downloaded source code.

What we are going to do is to build up a query step-by-step and watch what happens. The query we are looking for will return a vendor name and the address of that vendor. The example database only has a few records in it; so let's start out by selecting all the choices from the central item of the query – the vendor. We're going to go ahead and start aliasing from the beginning, since we will want to do this in the end:

```
SELECT v.VendorName
FROM Vendors v
```

This yields us a scant three records:

```
VendorName
----------------------------------------
Don's Database Design Shop
Dave's Data
The SQL Sequel

(3 row(s) affected)
```

These are the names of every vendor that we have at this time. Now let's add in the address information – there are two issues here. First, we want the query to return every vendor no matter what, so we'll make use of an OUTER JOIN. Next, a vendor can have more than one address and vice versa, so the database design has made use of a linking table. This means that we don't have anything to directly join the `Vendors` and `Address` table – we must instead join both of these tables to our linking table, which is called `VendorAddress`. Let's start out with the logical first piece of this join:

```
SELECT v.VendorName
FROM Vendors v
LEFT OUTER JOIN VendorAddress va
        ON v.VendorID = va.VendorID
```

Since `VendorAddress` doesn't itself have the address information, we're not including any columns from that table in our `SELECT` list. `VendorAddress`' sole purpose in life is to be the connection point of a many-to-many relationship (one vendor can have many addresses, and, as we've set it up here, an address can be the home of more than one vendor). Running this, as we expect, gives us the same results as before:

```
VendorName
--------------------------------------
Don's Database Design Shop
Dave's Data
The SQL Sequel

(3 row(s) affected)
```

Let's take a brief time-out from this particular query to check on the table against which we just joined. Try selecting out all the data from the `VendorAddress` table:

```
SELECT *
FROM VendorAddress
```

Just two records are returned:

```
VendorID          AddressID
----------------  -------------
1                 1
2                 3

(2 row(s) affected)
```

We know, therefore, that our `OUTER JOIN` is working for us. Since there are only two records in the `VendorAddress` table, and three vendors are returned, we must be returning at least one row from the `Vendors` table that didn't have a matching record in the `VendorAddress` table. While we're here, we'll just verify that by briefly adding one more column back to our vendors query:

```
SELECT v.VendorName, va.VendorID
FROM Vendors v
LEFT OUTER JOIN VendorAddress va
          ON v.VendorID = va.VendorID
```

Sure enough, we wind up with a `NULL` in the `VendorID` column from the `VendorAddress` table:

```
VendorName                            VendorID
--------------------------------------  -------------
Don's Database Design Shop            1
Dave's Data                           2
The SQL Sequel                        NULL

(3 row(s) affected)
```

The vendor named "The SQL Sequel" would not have been returned if we were using an `INNER` or `RIGHT JOIN`. Our use of a `LEFT JOIN` has ensured that we get all vendors in our query result.

Now that we've tested things out a bit, let's return to our original query, and then add in the second JOIN to get the actual address information. Since we don't care if we get all addresses, no special JOIN is required – at least, it doesn't appear that way at first...

```
SELECT v.VendorName, a.Address
FROM Vendors v
LEFT OUTER JOIN VendorAddress va
          ON v.VendorID = va.VendorID
JOIN Address a
    ON va.AddressID = a.AddressID
```

We get back the address information as expected, but there's a problem:

```
VendorName                          Address
-----------------------------       ------------------------
Don's Database Design Shop          1234 Anywhere
Dave's Data                         567 Main St.
```

(2 row(s) affected)

Somehow, we've lost one of our vendors. That's because SQL Server is applying the rules in the order that we've stated them. We have started with an OUTER JOIN between Vendors and VendorAddress. SQL Server does just what we want for that part of the query – it returns all vendors. The issue comes when it applies the next set of instructions. We have a result set that includes all the vendors, but we now apply that result set as part of an INNER JOIN. Since an INNER JOIN is exclusive to both sides of the JOIN, only records where the result of the first JOIN has a match with the second JOIN will be included. Since only two records match up with a record in the Address table, only two records are returned in the final result set. We have two ways of addressing this:

- ❑ Add yet another OUTER JOIN
- ❑ Change the ordering of the JOINs

Let's try it both ways. We'll add another OUTER JOIN first:

```
SELECT v.VendorName, a.Address
FROM Vendors v
LEFT OUTER JOIN VendorAddress va
          ON v.VendorID = va.VendorID
LEFT OUTER JOIN Address a
          ON va.AddressID = a.AddressID
```

And now we get to our expected results:

```
VendorName                          Address
-----------------------------       --------------------
Don's Database Design Shop          1234 Anywhere
Dave's Data                         567 Main St.
The SQL Sequel                      NULL
```

(3 row(s) affected)

Now let's do something slightly more dramatic and reorder our original query:

```
SELECT v.VendorName, a.Address
FROM VendorAddress va
JOIN Address a
    ON va.AddressID = a.AddressID
RIGHT OUTER JOIN Vendors v
            ON v.VendorID = va.VendorID
```

And we still get our desired result:

```
VendorName                             Address
------------------------------------   --------------------
Don's Database Design Shop             1234 Anywhere
Dave's Data                            567 Main St.
The SQL Sequel                         NULL
```

(3 row(s) affected)

The question you should be asking now is, "Which way is best?" Quite often in SQL, there are several ways of executing the query without one having any significant advantage over the other – this is not one of those times.

I would most definitely steer you to the second of the two solutions.

> **The rule of thumb is to get all of the INNER JOINs you can out of the way first, you will then find yourself using the minimum number of OUTER JOINs, and decreasing the number of errors in your data.**

The reason has to do with navigating as quickly as possible to your data. If you keep adding OUTER JOINs not because of what's happening with the current table you're trying to add in, but because you're trying to carry through an earlier JOIN result, you are much more likely to include something you don't intend, or make some sort of mistake in your overall logic. The second solution addresses this by only using the OUTER JOIN where necessary – just once. You can't always create a situation where the JOINs can be moved around to this extent, but you often can.

I can't stress enough how often I see errors with JOIN order. It is one of those areas that just seem to give developers fits. Time after time I will get called in to look over a query that someone has spent hours verifying each section of, and it seems that at least half the time I get asked whether I know about this SQL Server "bug". The bug isn't in SQL Server in this case – it's with the developer. If you take anything away from this section, I hope it is that JOIN order is one of the first places to look for errors when the results aren't coming up as you expect.

Seeing Both Sides with FULL JOINs

Like many things in SQL, a FULL JOIN (also known as a FULL OUTER JOIN) is basically what it sounds like – it is a matching up of data on both sides of the JOIN with everything included no matter what side of the JOIN it is on.

FULL JOINs are one of those things that seem really cool at the time you learn it and then almost never get used. You'll find an honest politician more often than you'll find a FULL JOIN in use. Their main purpose in life is to look at the complete relationship between data without giving preference to one side or the other. You want to know about every record on both sides of the equation – with nothing left out.

A FULL JOIN is perhaps best expressed as what you would get if you could do a LEFT JOIN and a RIGHT JOIN in the same JOIN. You get all the records that match, based on the JOIN field(s). You also get any records that exist only in the left side, with NULLs being returned for columns from the right side. Finally, you get any records that exist only in the right side, with NULLs being returned for columns from the left side. Note that, when I say "finally", I don't mean to imply that they'll be last in the query. The result order you get will (unless you use an ORDER BY clause) depend entirely on what SQL Server thinks is the least costly way to retrieve your records.

Let's just get right to it by looking back at our last query from our section on OUTER JOINs:

```
SELECT v.VendorName, a.Address
FROM VendorAddress va
JOIN Address a
    ON va.AddressID = a.AddressID
RIGHT OUTER JOIN Vendors v
            ON v.VendorID = va.VendorID
```

What we want to do here is take it a piece at a time again, and add some fields to the SELECT list that will let us see what's happening. First, we'll take the first two tables using a FULL JOIN:

```
SELECT a.Address, va.AddressID
FROM VendorAddress va
FULL JOIN Address a
        ON va.AddressID = a.AddressID
```

As it happens, a FULL JOIN on this section doesn't yield us any more than a RIGHT JOIN would have:

```
Address                     AddressID
-------------------------   -------------
1234 Anywhere               1
567 Main St.                3
999 1st St.                 NULL
1212 Smith Ave              NULL
364 Westin                  NULL

(5 row(s) affected)
```

But wait – there's more! Now let's add in the second JOIN:

```
SELECT a.Address, va.AddressID, v.VendorID, v.VendorName
FROM VendorAddress va
FULL JOIN Address a
     ON va.AddressID = a.AddressID
FULL JOIN Vendors v
     ON va.VendorID = v.VendorID
```

Now we have everything:

Address	AddressID	VendorID	VendorName
1234 Anywhere	1	1	Don's Database Design Shop
567 Main St.	3	2	Dave's Data
999 1st St.	NULL	NULL	NULL
1212 Smith Ave	NULL	NULL	NULL
364 Westin	NULL	NULL	NULL
NULL	NULL	3	The SQL Sequel

(6 row(s) affected)

As you can see, we have the same two rows that we would have had with an INNER JOIN clause. Those are then followed by the three Address records that aren't matched with anything in either table. Last, but not least, we have the one record from the Vendors table that wasn't matched with anything.

Again, use a FULL JOIN when you want all records from both sides of the JOIN – matched where possible, but included even if there is no match.

CROSS JOINs

CROSS JOINs are very strange critters indeed. A CROSS JOIN differs from other JOINs in that there is no ON operator, and that it joins every record on one side of the JOIN with every record on the other side of the JOIN. In short, you wind up with a Cartesian product of all the records on both sides of the JOIN. The syntax is the same as any other JOIN except that it uses the keyword CROSS (instead of INNER, OUTER, or FULL), and that it has no ON operator. Here's a quick example:

```
SELECT v.VendorName, a.Address
FROM Vendors v
CROSS JOIN Address a
```

Think back now – we had three records in the Vendors table, and five records in the Address table. If we're going to match every record in the Vendors table with every record in the Address table, then we should end up with 3 x 5 = 15 records in our CROSS JOIN:

VendorName	Address
Don's Database Design Shop	1234 Anywhere
Don's Database Design Shop	567 Main St.
Don's Database Design Shop	999 1st St.
Don's Database Design Shop	1212 Smith Ave
Don's Database Design Shop	364 Westin
Dave's Data	1234 Anywhere
Dave's Data	567 Main St.
Dave's Data	999 1st St.
Dave's Data	1212 Smith Ave
Dave's Data	364 Westin
The SQL Sequel	1234 Anywhere
The SQL Sequel	567 Main St.
The SQL Sequel	999 1st St.
The SQL Sequel	1212 Smith Ave
The SQL Sequel	364 Westin

(15 row(s) affected)

Indeed, that's exactly what we get.

Every time I teach a SQL class, I get asked the same question about CROSS JOINs, "Why in the world would you use something like this?" I'm told there are scientific uses for it – this makes sense to me since I know there are a number of high-level mathematical functions that make use of Cartesian products. I presume that you could read a large number of samples into table structures, and then perform your CROSS JOIN to create a Cartesian product of your sample. There is, however, a much more frequently occurring use for CROSS JOINs – the creation of test data.

When you are building up a database, that database is quite often part of a larger scale system that will need substantial testing. A reoccurring problem in testing of large-scale systems is the creation of large amounts of test data. By using a CROSS JOIN, you can do smaller amounts of data entry to create your test data in two or more tables, and then perform a CROSS JOIN against the tables to produce a much larger set of test data. You have a great example in our last query – if you needed to match a group of addresses up with a group of vendors, then that simple query yields 15 records from 8. Of course, the numbers can become far more dramatic. For example, if we created a table with 50 first names, and then created a table with 250 last names, we could CROSS JOIN them together to create a table with 12,500 unique name combinations. By investing in keying in 300 names, we suddenly get a set of test data with 12,500 names.

Exploring Alternative Syntax for Joins

What we're going to look at in this section is what many people still consider to be the "normal" way of coding joins. Until SQL Server 6.5, the alternative syntax we'll look at here was the only join syntax in SQL Server, and what is today called the "standard" way of coding joins wasn't even an option.

Until now, we have been using the ANSI syntax for all of our SQL statements. I'm going to hold the Microsoft party line on this one and recommend that you use the ANSI method since it should, over the long run, have much better portability between systems and is also much more readable. The funny thing about this is that the old syntax is actually reasonably well supported across platforms at the current time.

The primary reason I am covering the old syntax at all is that there is absolutely no doubt that, sooner or later, you will run into it in legacy code. I don't want you staring at that code saying, "What the heck is this?"

That being said, it is my strong recommendation that you use the ANSI syntax wherever possible. It is substantially more readable and Microsoft has indicated that they may not continue to support the old syntax indefinitely. I find it very hard to believe, given the amount of legacy code out there, that Microsoft will dump the old syntax anytime soon, but you never know.

Perhaps the biggest reason is that the ANSI syntax is actually more functional. Under old syntax, it was actually possible to create ambiguous query logic – where there was more than one way to interpret the query. The new syntax eliminates this problem.

Remember when I compared a JOIN to a WHERE clause earlier in this chapter? Well, there was a reason. The old syntax expresses all of the JOINs within the WHERE clause.

The old syntax supports all of the joins that we've done using ANSI with the exception of a FULL JOIN. If you need to perform a full join, I'm afraid you'll have to stick with the ANSI version.

An Alternative INNER JOIN

Let's do a déjà vu thing and look back at the first INNER JOIN we did in this chapter:

```
SELECT *
FROM Products
INNER JOIN Suppliers
        ON Products.SupplierID = Suppliers.SupplierID
```

This got us 77 rows back (again, assuming that Northwind is still as it was when it was shipped with SQL Server). Instead of using the ANSI JOIN though, let's rewrite it using a WHERE clause-based join syntax. It's actually quite easy – just eliminate the words INNER JOIN and add a comma, and replace the ON operator with a WHERE clause:

```
SELECT *
FROM Products, Suppliers
WHERE Products.SupplierID = Suppliers.SupplierID
```

It's a piece of cake, and it yields us the same 77 rows we got with the other syntax.

An Alternative OUTER JOIN

The alternative syntax for OUTER JOINs works pretty much the same as the INNER JOIN, except that, since we don't have the LEFT or RIGHT keywords (and no OUTER or JOIN for that matter), we need some special operators especially built for the task. These look like this:

Alternative	ANSI
*=	LEFT JOIN
=*	RIGHT JOIN

Let's pull up the first OUTER JOIN we did this chapter. It made use of the pubs database and looked something like this:

```
SELECT discounttype, discount, s.stor_name
FROM discounts d
LEFT OUTER JOIN stores s
          ON d.stor_id = s.stor_id
```

Again, we just lose the words LEFT OUTER JOIN, and replace the ON operator with a WHERE clause:

```
SELECT discounttype, discount, s.stor_name
FROM discounts d, stores s
WHERE d.stor_id *= s.stor_id
```

Sure enough, we wind up with the same results as before:

discounttype	discount	stor_name
Initial Customer	10.50	NULL
Volume Discount	6.70	NULL
Customer Discount	5.00	Bookbeat

(3 row(s) affected)

A RIGHT JOIN looks pretty much the same:

```
SELECT discounttype, discount, s.stor_name
FROM discounts d, stores s
WHERE d.stor_id =* s.stor_id
```

Again, we come up with the same six rows we would have under the ANSI syntax.

An Alternative CROSS JOIN

This is far and away the easiest of the bunch. To create a cross join using the old syntax, you just do nothing. That is, you don't put anything in the WHERE clause of the form: *TableA.ColumnA = TableB.ColumnA*.

So, for an ultra quick example, let's take our first example from the CROSS JOIN section earlier in the chapter. The ANSI syntax looked like this:

```
SELECT v.VendorName, a.Address
FROM Vendors v
CROSS JOIN Address a
```

To convert it to the old syntax, we just strip out the CROSS JOIN keywords and add a comma:

```
SELECT v.VendorName, a.Address
FROM Vendors v, Address a
```

Just as with the other examples in this section, we get back the same results that we got with the ANSI syntax:

```
VendorName                              Address
---------------------------------------   --------------------
Don's Database Design Shop              1234 Anywhere
Don's Database Design Shop              67 Main St.
Don's Database Design Shop              999 1st St.
Don's Database Design Shop              1212 Smith Ave
Don's Database Design Shop              364 Westin
Dave's Data                             1234 Anywhere
Dave's Data                             567 Main St.
Dave's Data                             999 1st St.
Dave's Data                             1212 Smith Ave
Dave's Data                             364 Westin
The SQL Sequel                          1234 Anywhere
The SQL Sequel                          567 Main St.
The SQL Sequel                          999 1st St.
The SQL Sequel                          1212 Smith Ave
The SQL Sequel                          364 Westin

(15 row(s) affected)
```

The UNION

OK, enough with all the "old syntax" vs. "new syntax" stuff – now we're into something that's the same regardless of what other join syntax you prefer – the UNION operator. UNION is a special operator we can use to cause two or more queries to generate one result set.

A UNION isn't really a JOIN, like the previous options we've been looking at – instead it's more of an appending of the data from one query right onto the end of another query (functionally, it works a little differently than this, but this is the easiest way to look at the concept). Where a JOIN combined information horizontally (adding more columns), a UNION combines data vertically (adding more rows).

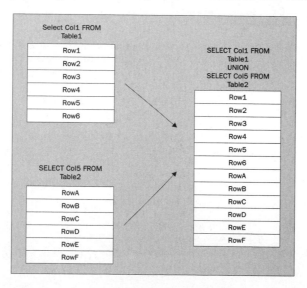

When dealing with queries that use a UNION, there are just a few key points:

- ❏ All the UNIONed queries must have the same number of columns in the SELECT list. If your first query has three columns in the SELECT list, then the second (and any subsequent queries being UNIONed) must also have three columns. If the first has five, then the second must have five too. Regardless of how many columns are in the first query, there must be the same number in the subsequent query(s).

- ❏ The headings returned for the combined result set will be taken only from the first of the queries. If your first query has a SELECT list that looks like SELECT Col1, Col2 AS Second, Col3 FROM..., then, regardless of how your columns are named or aliased in the subsequent queries, the headings on the columns returned from the UNION will be Col1, Second and Col3 respectively.

- ❏ The data types of each column in a query must be implicitly compatible with the data type in the same relative column in the other queries. Note that I'm *not* saying they have to be the same data type – they just have to be implicitly convertible (a conversion table that shows implicit vs. explicit conversions can be found in Chapter 2). If the second column in the first query is of type char(20), then it would be fine that the second column in the second query is varchar(50). However, since things are based on the first query, any rows longer than 20 would be truncated for data from the second result set.

- ❏ Unlike non-UNION queries, the default return option for UNIONs is DISTINCT rather than ALL. This can really be confusing to people. In our other queries, all rows were returned regardless of whether they were duplicated with another row or not, but the results of a UNION do not work that way. Unless you use the ALL keyword in your query, then only one of any repeating rows will be returned.

As always, let's take a look at this with an example or two.

First, let's look at a UNION that has some practical use to it (it's something I could see happening in the real world – albeit not all that often). For this example, we're going to assume that it's time for the holidays, and we want to send out a New Year's card to everyone that's involved with Northwind. We want to return a list of full addresses to send our cards to including our employees, customers, and suppliers. We can do this in just one query with something like this:

```
USE Northwind

SELECT CompanyName AS Name,
       Address,
       City,
       Region,
       PostalCode,
       Country
FROM Customers

UNION

SELECT CompanyName,
       Address,
       City,
       Region,
       PostalCode,
       Country
FROM Suppliers
```

```
UNION

SELECT FirstName + ' ' + LastName,
       Address,
       City,
       Region,
       PostalCode,
       Country
FROM Employees
```

This gets us back just one result set, but it has data from all three queries:

Name	Address	City	Region	PostalCode	Country
Alfreds Futterkiste	Obere Str. 57	Berlin	NULL	12209	Germany
Ana Trujillo Emparedados y helados	Avda. de la Constitución 2222	México D.F.	NULL	5021	Mexico
Andrew Fuller	908 W. Capital Way	Tacoma	WA	98401	USA
...					
...					
...					
Wilman Kala	Keskuskatu 45	Helsinki	NULL	21240	Finland
Wolski Zajazd	ul. Filtrowa 68	Warszawa	NULL	01-012	Poland
Zaanse Snoepfabriek	Verkoop Rijnweg 22	Zaandam	NULL	9999 ZZ	Netherlands

We've got something for everyone here. Alfreds is a customer, Andrew Fuller is an employee, and Zaanse is a supplier. We have our one result set from what would have been three. Again, notice that the headings for the returned columns all came from the SELECT list of the first of the queries.

> *As I played with this, I got some rather inconsistent results on the sorting of the query, so don't be surprised if the order of your query looks a lot different from mine. The big thing is that you should have approximately 129 rows depending on what modifications you've made to the Northwind database previously. If you want the results to be returned in a specific order, then don't forget the ORDER BY clause – for UNION statements, the ORDER BY clause needs to be part of the last query being UNIONed.*

Moving on to a second example, I want to show you how a UNION deals with duplicate rows – it's actually just the inverse of a normal query in that it assumes you want to throw out duplicates (in our previous queries, the assumption was that you wanted to keep everything unless you used the DISTINCT keyword). This demo has no real-world potential, but it's quick and easy to run and see how things work.

In this case, we are creating two tables from which we will select. We'll then insert three rows into each table, with one row being identical between the two tables. If our query is performing an ALL, then every row (six of them) will show up. If the query is performing a DISTINCT, then it will only return five rows (tossing out one duplicate):

```
CREATE TABLE UnionTest1
(
    idcol    int          IDENTITY,
    col2     char(3),
)

CREATE TABLE UnionTest2
(
    idcol    int          IDENTITY,
    col4     char(3),
)

INSERT INTO UnionTest1
VALUES
    ('AAA')

INSERT INTO UnionTest1
VALUES
    ('BBB')

INSERT INTO UnionTest1
VALUES
    ('CCC')

INSERT INTO UnionTest2
VALUES
    ('CCC')

INSERT INTO UnionTest2
VALUES
    ('DDD')

INSERT INTO UnionTest2
VALUES
    ('EEE')

SELECT col2
FROM UnionTest1

UNION

SELECT col4
FROM UnionTest2

PRINT 'Divider Line--------------------------'

SELECT col2
FROM UnionTest1

UNION ALL

SELECT col4
FROM UnionTest2

DROP TABLE UnionTest1
DROP TABLE UnionTest2
```

Now, let's look at the heart of what's returned (you'll see some "one row affects" in there – just ignore them until you get to where the results of your query are visible):

```
col2
------
DDD
EEE
AAA
BBB
CCC

(5 row(s) affected)

Divider Line-------------------------
col2
-----
AAA
BBB
CCC
CCC
DDD
EEE

(6 row(s) affected)
```

The first result set returned was a simple UNION statement with no additional parameters. You can see that one row was eliminated – even though we inserted "CCC" into both tables, only one makes an appearance since the duplicate record is eliminated by default.

The second return changed things a bit. This time we used a UNION ALL and the ALL keyword ensured that we get every row back. As such, our eliminated row from the last query suddenly reappears.

Summary

In an RDBMS, the data we want is quite frequently spread across more than one table. JOINs allow us to combine the data from multiple tables in a variety of ways:

❑ Use an INNER JOIN when you want to exclude non-matching fields.

❑ Use an OUTER JOIN when you want to retrieve matches wherever possible, but also want a fully inclusive data set on one side of the JOIN.

❑ Use a FULL JOIN when you want to retrieve matches wherever possible, but also want a fully inclusive data set of both sides of the JOIN.

❑ Use a CROSS JOIN when you want a Cartesian product based on the records in two tables. This is typically used in scientific environments and when you want to create test data.

❑ Use a UNION when you want the combination of the result of a second query appended to the first query.

There are two different forms of JOIN syntax available for INNER and OUTER JOINs. We provided the legacy syntax here to help you deal with legacy code, but the newer ANSI format presented through most of this chapter is highly preferable, as it is more readable, is not prone to the ambiguities of the older syntax, and will be supported in SQL Server for the indefinite future.

Over the course of the next few chapters, we will be learning how to build our own tables and "relate" them to each other. As we do this, the concepts of knowing what columns to join on will become even clearer.

Online discussion at http://p2p.wrox.com

6

Creating and Altering Tables

Every time I teach the T-SQL code for creating databases, tables, keys, and constraints, I am asked the same question, "Can't you just do this in the GUI tool?" The answer is an unequivocal Yes! Therefore, the next question usually follows quite shortly behind, "Then why are we spending all this time learning stuff I'll never use?" The answer is just as unequivocal – you will use the regular syntax on a quasi-regular basis. The reality is you probably won't actually write the code from scratch that often, but you'll verify and edit it on the majority of all larger database projects you work on – that means that you had better know how it works.

In this chapter, we will be studying the syntax to create our own tables. We will also take a look at how to make use of the Enterprise Manager to help us with this (after we know how to do it for ourselves).

However, before we get too deep in the actual statements that create tables and other objects, we need to digress far enough to deal with the convention for a fully qualified object name, and, to a lesser extent, object ownership.

Object Names in SQL Server

In all the queries that we've been performing so far in this book, you've seen simple naming at work. I've had you switch the active database in the Query Analyzer before running any queries and that has helped your queries to work. How? Well, SQL Server only looks at a very narrow scope when trying to identify and locate the objects you name in your queries and other statements. For example, we've only been providing the names of tables without any additional information, but there are actually four levels in the naming convention for any SQL Server table (and any other SQL Server object for that matter). A fully qualified name is as follows:

```
[ServerName.[DatabaseName.[OwnerName.]]]ObjectName
```

You must provide an object name whenever you are performing an operation on that object, but all parts of the name to the left of the object name are optional. Indeed, most of the time, they are not needed, and are therefore left off. Still, before we start creating objects, it's a good idea for us to get a solid handle on each part of the name. So let's move from the object name left.

Ownership

Ownership of objects is a sticky one. If I thought I could get away with it, I'd skip it entirely and try to keep you from even knowing it exists. Some people really like using ownership, but I'm definitely not one of them. It's my personal experience that use of ownership always creates *far* more problems than solutions. Why? Well, we'll get to that in due time. For now, let's instead worry about what it is and how it works.

Ownership is actually a great deal like what it sounds – it is a recognition, right within the fully qualified name, of who "owns" the object. Usually, this will be either the person who created the object or the database owner (more commonly referred to as the dbo – I'll get to describing the dbo shortly).

By default, only users who have the sysadmin system role or the db_owner, or db_ddladmin database roles can create objects in a database.

> *The roles mentioned here are just a few of many system and database roles that are available in SQL Server 2000. These roles have a logical set of permissions granted to them according to how that role might be used. When you assign a particular role to someone, you are giving that person the ability to have all the permissions that the role has. This is looked into much more extensively in Chapter 28.*

Individual users can also be given the right to create certain types of both database and system objects. If such individuals do indeed create an object, then, by default, they will be assigned as the owner for that object.

> We'll talk much more about this in the chapter on security, but let me say that just because a feature is there it doesn't mean it should be used! Giving CREATE authority to individual users is nothing short of nightmarish. Trying to keep track of who created what, when, and for what reason becomes near impossible. As we'll see in this and later chapters, you start a wild mix of ownership chains (where someone owns an object, which refers to an object that is owned by someone else, which refers to an object that is owned by a third person, and so on) that will break people's will, their minds, and most of all, their queries. In short, keep CREATE access limited to the sa account or members of the sysadmins or db_owner security roles.

Ownership by Default: The dbo

Whoever creates the database is considered to be the "database owner", or **dbo**. Any objects that they create within that database shall be listed with an ownership of dbo rather than their individual user name. Any objects created by anyone else will have an ownership listed with that user's login name.

For example, let's say that I am an everyday user of a database, my login name is GIJoe, and I have been granted CREATE TABLE authority to a given database. If I create a table called MyTable, the owner qualified object name would be GIJoe.MyTable. Note that, since the table has a specific owner, any user other than me (remember, I'm GIJoe here) of GIJoe.MyTable would need to provide the owner qualified name in order for SQL Server to resolve the table name.

Now, let's say that there is also a user with a login name of Fred. Fred is the database owner (as opposed to just any member of db_owner). If Fred creates a table called MyTable using an identical CREATE statement to that used by GIJoe, the owner qualified table name will be dbo.MyTable. In addition, as dbo also happens to be the default owner, any user could just refer to the table as MyTable.

It's worth pointing out that sa (or members of the sysadmin role) always aliases to the dbo. That is, no matter who actually owns the database, sa will always have full access as if it was the dbo, and any objects created by the sa login will show ownership belonging to the dbo. Not only that, but objects created by members of the db_owner database role do *not* default to dbo as the object owner.

> Only the actual **dbo** (not just any **db_owner** role member) or **sysadmins** will have their objects automatically default to the **dbo** as the owner.

Weird but true!

Personally, I used to create all objects using sa whenever possible. It removes any doubt about who the dbo is, and keeps things cleaner. With version 7, however, my attitude shifted to having specific logins for each user – even for your system administrator – and then assigning them the db_owner role for any databases for which they are responsible. If they need full-blown sa-level access, then you can assign them the sysadmins role. You can find your own way on what works best for you.

Why the change? Well, in some ways it isn't a change. I've always tried to set things up where every user – including people with system administrator roles – had their own logins. If they needed sa-level access, then they should log in separately as sa, do what they need to do, then log out. This is a hassle, but it makes it much easier to audit who's doing what in the system (if five people are all logged in as sa, then how do you tell who's who?). Still, that meant a lot of people spent a lot of time logged in as sa (if they are a sysadmin, then they frequently need that level of access). Beginning with 7.0, we gained the ability to assign sa-level access to someone other than the sa account. This means we can safely put sa to bed, and let our system administrators use their own accounts together with the sysadmin role.

The Database Name

The next item in the fully qualified naming convention is the database name. Prior to SQL Server 7.0, this was actually the top of the name hierarchy, but more on that shortly.

Sometimes you want to retrieve data from a database other than the default, or current, database. Indeed, you may actually want to JOIN data from across databases. A database-qualified name gives you that ability. For example, if you were logged in with pubs as your current database, and you wanted to refer to the Orders table in the Northwind database, then you could refer to it by Northwind.dbo.Orders. Since dbo is the default owner, you could also use Northwind..Orders. If the login GIJoe owns a table named MyTable in MyDatabase, then you could refer to that table as MyDatabase.GIJoe.MyTable. Remember that the current database is always the default, so, if you only want data from the current database, then you do not need to include the database name in your fully qualified name.

Naming by Server

Beginning with SQL Server 7.0, the server name became the top of the fully qualified name game. Also with 7.0 came the possibility of linked servers (do not confuse these with remote servers). Linked servers give you the capability to perform a JOIN across not just different databases, but different servers – even different types of servers (SQL Server, Oracle, DB2, Access – just about anything with an OLE DB provider). We'll see much more about linked servers later in the book, but for now, just realize that there is one more level in our naming hierarchy, that it lets you access different servers, and that it works pretty much like the database and ownership levels work.

Now, let's just add to our previous example. If we want to retrieve information from a server we have created a link with called MyServer, a database called MyDatabase, and a table called MyTable owned by GIJoe, then the fully qualified name would be MyServer.MyDatabase.GIJoe.MyTable.

Reviewing the Defaults

So let's look one last time at how the defaults work at each level of the naming hierarchy from right to left:

- ❑ Object Name: there isn't a default – you must supply an object name.

- ❑ Ownership: you can leave this off, in which case it will resolve first using the current user's name, and then, if the object name in question doesn't exist with the current user as owner, then it will try the dbo as the owner.

- ❑ Database Name: this can also be left off unless you are providing a Server Name – in which case you must provide the Database Name for SQL Servers (other server types vary depending on the specific kind of server).

- ❑ Server Name: you can provide the name of a linked server here, but most of the time you'll just leave this off, which will cause SQL Server to default to the server you are logged into.

If you want to skip the object owner, but still provide information regarding the database or server, then you must still provide the extra "." for the position where the owner would be. For example, if we are logged in using the Northwind database on our local server, but want to refer to the Orders table in the Northwind database on a linked server called MyOtherServer, then we could refer to that table by using MyOtherServer.Northwind..Orders. Since we didn't provide a specific owner name, it will assume that either the user ID that is used to log on to the linked server or the dbo (in that order) is the owner of the object you want (in this case, Orders).

The CREATE Statement

In the Bible, God said, "Let there be light!" And there was light! Unfortunately, creating things isn't quite as simple for us mere mortals. We need to provide a well-defined syntax in order to create the objects in our database. To do that, we make use of the CREATE statement.

Let's look at the full structure of a CREATE statement, starting with the utmost in generality. You'll find that all the CREATE statements start out the same, and then get into the specifics. The first part of the CREATE will always look like:

CREATE <object type> <object name>

This will be followed by the details that will vary by the nature of the object that you're creating.

CREATE DATABASE

For this part of things, we'll need to create a database called `Accounting` that we will also use when we start to create tables. The most basic syntax for the CREATE DATABASE statement looks like the example above.

```
CREATE DATABASE <database name>
```

> It's worth pointing out that, when you create a new object, no one can access it except for the person that created it, the system administrator and the database owner (which, if the object created was a database, is the same as the person that created it). This allows you to create things and make whatever adjustments you need to make before you explicitly allow access to your object. We will look further into how to "grant" access and security in general in Chapter 28.
>
> It's also worth noting that you can only use the **CREATE** statement to create objects on the local server (adding in a specific server name doesn't work).

This will yield a database that looks exactly like your `model` database (we discussed the `model` database in Chapter 2). The reality of what you want is almost always different, so let's look at a more full syntax listing:

```
CREATE DATABASE <database name>
[ON [PRIMARY]
    ([NAME = <'logical file name'>,]
      FILENAME = <'file name'>
      [, SIZE = <size in megabytes or kilobytes>]
      [, MAXSIZE = <size in megabytes or kilobytes>]
      [, FILEGROWTH = <No of megabytes or kilobytes|percentage>])]
[LOG ON
    ([NAME = <'logical file name'>,]
      FILENAME = <'file name'>
      [, SIZE = <size in megabytes or kilobytes>]
      [, MAXSIZE = <size in megabytes or kilobytes>]
      [, FILEGROWTH = <No of megabytes or kilobytes|percentage>])]
[ COLLATE <collation name> ]
[ FOR LOAD | FOR ATTACH ]
```

There's a lot there, so let's break down the parts.

ON

ON is used in two places: to define the location of the file where the data is stored, and to define the same information for where the log is stored. You'll notice the PRIMARY keyword there – this means that what follows is the primary (or main) filegroup in which to physically store the data. You can also store data in what are called secondary filegroups, but we'll defer discussion of those until we get to performance tuning. For now, stick with the default notion that you want everything in one file.

> SQL Server allows you to store your database in multiple files; furthermore, it allows you to collect those files into logical groupings called filegroups.

NAME

This one isn't quite what it sounds like. It is a name for the file you are defining, but only a logical name – that is, the name that SQL Server will use internally to refer to that file. You will use this name when you want to resize (expand or shrink) the database and/or file.

FILENAME

This one is what it sounds like – the physical name on the disk of the actual operating system file in which the data and log (depending on what section you're defining) will be stored. The default here (assuming you used the simple syntax we looked at first) depends on whether you are dealing with the database itself or the log. Your file will be located in the \Data subdirectory under your main Program Files\MSSQL directory (or whatever you called your main SQL Server directory if you changed it at install). If we're dealing with the physical database file, it will be named the same as your database with an .mdf extension. If we're dealing with the log, it will be named the same as the database file only with a suffix of _Log and an .ldf extension. You are allowed to specify other extensions if you explicitly name the files, but I strongly encourage you to stick with the defaults of mdf (database) and ldf (log file).

Keep in mind that, while FILENAME is an optional parameter, it is only optional as long as you go with the extremely simple syntax (the one that creates a new database based on the model database) that I introduced first. If you provide any of the additional information, then you must include an explicit file name – be sure to provide a full path.

> *Prior to version 7.0, SQL Server used a much different paradigm for the physical storage of both the data and log information. The old method made use of what was called a device, and actually operated somewhat outside the realm of the normal storage system. Thankfully, this way of doing things has gone the way of the dinosaur.*
>
> *Devices were not automatically created when you created a database – indeed, you needed to make sure that you created them in advance of your CREATE DATABASE statement. You could potentially store many databases in one device.*
>
> *Perhaps the trickiest issue regarding the old device concept was that the physical operating system file for the device was not deleted from the system when the logical SQL Server device was. You needed to manually go to the Windows Explorer and delete the operating system file. This often led to very large disk drives being inexplicably full.*

SIZE

No mystery here. It is what it says – the size of the database. By default, the size is in megabytes, but you can make it kilobytes by using a KB instead of MB after the numeric value for the size. Keep in mind that this value must be at least as large as the model database is, or you will receive an error. If you do not supply a value for SIZE, then the database will initially be the same size as the model database.

> **The value you supply for size (if any) is exactly the size that is indicated by your CREATE statement – this is unlike previous versions that used to round the size of your device to a set increment level.**

MAXSIZE

This one is still pretty much what it sounds like, with only a slight twist vs. the SIZE parameter. SQL Server has a mechanism to allow your database to automatically allocate additional disk space (to grow) when necessary. MAXSIZE is the maximum size to which the database can grow. Again, the number is, by default, in megabytes, but it can be set in kilobytes by using the KB suffix. The slight twist is that there is no firm default. If you don't supply a value for this parameter, then there is considered to be no maximum – the practical maximum becomes when your disk drive is full.

If your database reaches the value set in the MAXSIZE parameter, your users will start getting errors back saying that their inserts can't be performed. If your log reaches its maximum size, you will not be able to perform any logged activity (which is most activities) in the database. Personally, I recommend setting up what is called an **alert**. You can use alerts to tell you when certain conditions exist (such as a database or log that's almost full). We'll see how to create alerts in Chapter 30.

> I recommend that you always include a value for **MAXSIZE**, and that you make it at least several megabytes smaller than would fill up the disk. I suggest this because a completely full disk can cause situations where you can't commit any information to permanent storage. If the log was trying to expand, the results could potentially be disastrous. In addition, even the operating system can occasionally have problems if it runs completely out of disk space.
>
> One more thing – if you decide to follow my advice on this issue, be sure to keep in mind that you may have multiple databases on the same system. If you size each of them to be able to take up the full size of the disk less a few megabytes, then you will still have the possibility of a full disk (if they all expand).

FILEGROWTH

Where SIZE set the initial size of the database, and MAXSIZE determined just how large the database file could get, FILEGROWTH essentially determines just how fast it gets to that maximum. You provide a value that indicates by how many megabytes (or kilobytes) at a time you want the file to be enlarged. Alternatively, you can provide a percentage value by which you want the database file to increase. With this option, the size will go up by the stated percentage of the current database file size. Therefore, if you set a database file to start out at 1GB with a FILEGROWTH of 20%, then the first time it expands it will grow to 1.2GB, the second time to 1.44, and so on.

LOG ON

The LOG ON option allows you to establish that you want your log to go to a specific set of files and where exactly those files are to be located. If this option is not provided, then SQL Server will create the log in a single file and default it to a size equal to 25% of the data file size. In most other respects, it has the same file specification parameters as the main database file does.

COLLATE

This one is totally new with SQL Server 2000, and has to do with the issue of sort order, case sensitivity, and sensitivity to accents. Prior to this version of SQL Server, the collation order was set at the server level. All objects (even password sensitivity) were set by the collation of the server – if you had applications that needed separate collations, you needed separate servers. Well, fear no more! Not only has Microsoft seen fit to give us collation at the database level, but now you can even set your collation to be different for any specific column of a table inside your database (if you're someone who has to do localization work – you have to really love this!).

FOR LOAD

This one is only here for backward compatibility at this point. It was used under 6.5 and older servers to initially create the framework for the database to facilitate a load from a backup. If you used this option, then SQL Server would leave off some of the database create process since you were explicitly saying you wanted to load a backup over it anyway.

FOR ATTACH

You can use this option to attach an existing set of database files to the current server. The files in question must be part of a database that was, at some point, properly detached using sp_detach_db. Normally, you would use sp_attach_db for this functionality, but the CREATE DATABASE command with FOR ATTACH has the advantage of being able to access as many as 32,000+ files – sp_attach_db is limited to just 16.

Building a Database

At this point, we're ready to begin building our database. Below is the statement to create it, but keep in mind that the database itself is only one of many objects that we will create on our way to a fully functional database:

```
CREATE DATABASE Accounting
ON
   (NAME = 'Accounting',
    FILENAME = 'c:\Program Files\Microsoft SQL
Server\mssql\data\AccountingData.mdf',
    SIZE = 10,
    MAXSIZE = 50,
    FILEGROWTH = 5)
LOG ON
   (NAME = 'AccountingLog',
    FILENAME = 'c:\Program Files\Microsoft SQL
Server\mssql\data\AccountingLog.ldf',
    SIZE = 5MB,
    MAXSIZE = 25MB,
    FILEGROWTH = 5MB)

GO
```

Now is a good time to start learning about some of the informational utilities that are available with SQL Server. We saw sp_help in Chapter 4, but in this case, let's try running a command called sp_helpdb. This one is especially tailored for database structure information, and often provides better information if we're more interested in the database itself than the objects it contains. sp_helpdb takes one parameter – the database name:

```
EXEC sp_helpdb 'Accounting'
```

This actually yields you two separate result sets. The first is based on the combined (data and log) information about your database:

name	db_size	owner	dbid	created	status	compatibility_level
Accounting	15.00 MB	sa	9	May 28 2000	Status=ONLINE, Updateability=READ_WRITE, UserAccess=MULTI_USER, Recovery=FULL, Version=538, Collation=SQL_Latin1_ General_CP1_CI_AS, SQLSortOrder=52, IsTornPageDetectionEnabled, IsAutoCreateStatistics, IsAutoUpdateStatistics	80

The actual values you receive for each of these fields may vary somewhat from mine. For example, the DBID value will vary depending on how many databases you've created and in what order you've created them. The various status messages will vary depending on what server options were in place at the time you created the database as well as any options you changed for the database along the way.

Note that the **db_size** property is the *total* of the size of the database and the size of the log.

The second provides specifics about the various files that make up your database – including their current size and growth settings:

name	fileid	Filename	filegroup	size	maxsize	growth	usage
Accounting	1	C:\Program Files\Microsoft SQL Server\mssql\data\ AccountingData.mdf	PRIMARY	10240 KB	51200 KB	5120 KB	data only
AccountingLog	2	C:\Program Files\Microsoft SQL Server\mssql\data\ AccountingLog.ldf	NULL	5120 KB	25600 KB	5120 KB	log only

After you create tables and insert data, the database will begin to automatically grow on an as-needed basis – this is much different from the way things worked back in version 6.5, and was one of the many features added since then to make life easier for the database administrator.

CREATE TABLE

The first part of creating a table is pretty much the same as creating any object – remember that line I showed you? Well, here it is again:

CREATE <*object type*> <*object name*>

Since a table is what we want, we can be more specific:

```
CREATE TABLE Customers
```

With CREATE DATABASE, we could have stopped with just these first three keywords, and it would have built the database based on the guidelines established in the model database. With tables however, there is no model, so we need to provide some more specifics in the form of columns, data types, and special operators.

Let's look at more extended syntax:

```
CREATE TABLE [database_name.[owner].]table_name
(<column name> <data type>
[[DEFAULT <constant expression>]
   |[IDENTITY [(seed, increment) [NOT FOR REPLICATION]]]]
   [ROWGUIDCOL]
   [COLLATE <collation name>]
   [NULL|NOT NULL]
   [<column constraints>]
   |[column_name AS computed_column_expression]
   |[<table_constraint>]
   [,...n]
)
[ON {<filegroup>|DEFAULT}]
[TEXTIMAGE_ON {<filegroup>|DEFAULT}]
```

Now that's a handful – and it still has sections taken out of it for simplicity's sake! As usual, let's look at the parts, starting with the second line (we've already seen the top line).

Table and Column Names

What's in a name? Frankly – a lot. You may recall that one of my first soapbox diatribes was back in Chapter 2 and was about names. I promised then that it wouldn't be the last you heard from me on the subject, and this won't be either.

The rules for naming tables and columns are, in general, the same rules that apply to all database objects. The SQL Server documentation will refer to these as the **rules for identifiers**, and they are the same rules we observed at the end of Chapter 2. The rules are actually pretty simple; what we want to touch on here though, are some notions about how exactly to name your objects – not specific rules of what SQL Server will and won't accept for names, but how you want to go about naming your tables and columns so that they are useful and make sense.

There are a ton of different "standards" out there for naming database objects – particularly tables and columns. My rules are pretty simple:

❑ For each word in the name, capitalize the first letter and use small case for the remaining letters.

❑ Keep the name short, but make it long enough to be descriptive.

❑ Limit the use of abbreviations. The only acceptable use of abbreviations is when the chosen abbreviation will be recognized by anyone. Examples of abbreviations I use include "ID" to take the place of identification, "No" to take the place of number, and "Org" to take the place of organization. Keeping your names of reasonable length will require you to be more cavalier about your abbreviations sometimes, but keep in mind that, first and foremost, you want clarity in your names.

❑ When building tables based on other tables (usually called linking or associate tables), you should include the names of all of the parent tables in your new table name. For example, say you have a movie database where many stars can appear in many movies. If you have a Movies table and a Stars table, you may want to tie them together using a table called MovieStars.

❑ When you have two words in the name, do not use any separators (run the words together) – use the fact that you capitalize the first letter of each new word to figure out how to separate words.

I can't begin to tell you the battles I've had with other database people about naming issues. For example, you will find that a good many people believe that you should separate the words in your names with an underscore (_). Why don't I do it that way? Well, it's an ease of use issue. Underscores present a couple of different problems:

❑ First, many people have a difficult time typing an underscore without taking their hand away from the proper keyboard position – this leads to lots of typos.

❑ Second, in documentation it is not uncommon to run into situations where the table or column name is underlined. Underscores are, depending on the font, impossible to see when the text is underlined – this leads to confusion and more errors.

❑ Finally (and this is a nit pick), it's just more typing.

Beginning with SQL Server 7.0, it also became an option to separate the words in the name using a regular space. If you recall my first soapbox diatribe back in Chapter 2, you'll know that isn't really much of an option – it is extremely bad practice and creates an unbelievable number of errors. It was added to facilitate Access upsizing, and I continue to curse the person(s) who decided to put it in – I'm sure they were well-meaning, but they are now part of the cause of much grief in the database world.

This list is certainly not set in stone, rather it is just a Reader's Digest version of the rules I use when naming tables. I find that they save me a great deal of grief. I hope they'll do the same for you.

> **Consistency, consistency, consistency. Every time I teach, I always warn my class that it's a word I'm going to repeat over and over, and in no place is it more important than in naming. If you have to pick one rule to follow, then pick a rule that says that, whatever your standards are – make them just that: standard. If you decide to abbreviate for some reason, then abbreviate that word every time (the same way). Regardless of what you're doing in your naming, make it apply to the entire database consistently. This will save a ton of mistakes, and it will save your users time in terms of how long it takes for them to get to know the database.**

Data Types

There isn't much to this – the data types are as I described them in Chapter 2. You just need to provide a data type immediately following the column name – there is no default data type.

DEFAULT

We'll cover this in much more detail in our chapter on constraints, but for now, suffice to say that this is the value you want to be used for any rows that are inserted without a user-supplied value for this particular column. The default, if you use one, should immediately follow the data type.

IDENTITY

The concept of an **identity** value is a very important concept in database design. We will cover how to use identity columns in some detail in our chapters on design. What is an identity column? Well, when you make a column an identity column, SQL Server automatically assigns a sequenced number to this column with every row you insert. The number that SQL Server starts counting from is called the **seed** value, and the amount that the value increases or decreases by with each row is called the **increment**. The default is for a seed of 1 and an increment of 1, and most designs call for it to be left that way. As an example though, you could have a seed of 3 and an increment of 5. In this case, you would start counting from 3, and then add 5 each time for 8, 13, 18, 23, and so on.

An identity column must be numeric, and, in practice, it is almost always implemented with an integer data type. The historical exception to this was to use a fixed length numeric column if you needed to use larger numbers than an integer allows for. Beginning with SQL Server 2000, you now have the option of using the bigint data type, so the need to use non-integer related data types should be rare indeed.

The usage is pretty simple; you simply include the IDENTITY keyword right after the data type for the column. An identity option cannot be used in conjunction with a default constraint. This makes sense if you think about it – how can there be a constant default if you're counting up or down every time?

> *It's worth noting that an identity column works sequentially. That is, once you've set a seed (the starting point) and the increment, your values only go up (or down if you set the increment to a negative number). There is no automatic mechanism to go back and fill in the numbers for any rows you may have deleted. If you want to fill in blank spaces like that, you need to use SET IDENTITY_INSERT ON, which allows you to turn off (yes, turning it "on" turns it off – that is, you are turning on the ability to insert your own values, which has the effect of turning off the automatic value) the identity process for inserts from the current connection.*

The most common use for an identity column is to generate a new value to be used as an identifier for each row – that is, identity columns are commonly used to create a primary key for a table. Keep in mind, however, that an IDENTITY column and a PRIMARY KEY are completely separate notions – that is, just because you have an IDENTITY column doesn't mean that the value is unique (for example, you can reset the seed value and count back up through values you've used before). IDENTITY values are *usually* used as the PRIMARY KEY column, but they don't *have* to be used that way.

> If you've come from the Access world, you'll notice that an **IDENTITY** column is much like an **AutoNumber** column. The major difference is that you have a bit more control over it in SQL Server.

NOT FOR REPLICATION

This one is very tough to deal with at this point, so I am, at least in part, going to skip it until we come to the chapter on replication.

> Briefly, replication is the process of automatically doing what, in a very loose sense, amounts to copying some or all of the information in your database to some other database. The other database may be on the same physical machine as the original, or it may be located remotely.

The NOT FOR REPLICATION parameter determines whether a new identity value for the new database is assigned when the column is published to another database (via replication), or whether it keeps its existing value. There will be much more on this at a later time.

ROWGUIDCOL

This is also replication related and, in many ways, is the same in purpose to an identity column. We've already seen how using an identity column can provide you with an easy way to make sure that you have a value that is unique to each row and can, therefore, be used to identify that row. However, this can be a very error-prone solution when you are dealing with replicated or other distributed environments.

Think about it for a minute – while an identity column will keep counting upwards from a set value, what's to keep the values from overlapping on different databases? Now, think about when you try to replicate the values such that all the rows that were previously in separate databases now reside in one database – uh oh! You now will have duplicate values in the column that is supposed to uniquely identify each row!

Over the years, the common solution for this was to use separate seed values for each database you were replicating to and from. For example, you may have database A that starts counting at 1, database B starts at 10,000, and database C starts at 20,000. You can now publish them all into the same database safely – for a while. As soon as database A has more than 9,999 records inserted into it, you're in big trouble.

"Sure," you say, "why not just separate the values by 100,000 or 500,000?" If you have tables with a large amount of activity, you're still just delaying the inevitable – that's where a ROWGUIDCOL comes into play.

What is a ROWGUIDCOL? Well, it's quite a bit like an identity column in that it is usually used to uniquely identify each row in a table. The difference is to what lengths the system goes to make sure that the value used is truly unique. Instead of using a numerical count, SQL Server instead uses what is known as a **GUID**, or a **Globally Unique Identifier**. While an identity value is usually (unless you alter something) unique across time, it is not unique across space. Therefore, we can have two copies of our table running, and have them both assigned an identical identity value. While this is just fine to start with, it causes big problems when we try to bring the rows from both tables together as one replicated table. A GUID is unique across both space and time.

> GUIDs are actually in increasingly widespread use in computing today. For example, if you check the registry, you'll find tons of them. A GUID is a 128-bit value – for you math types, that's 38 zeros in decimal form. If I generated a GUID every second, it would, theoretically speaking, take me millions of years to generate a duplicate given a number of that size.
>
> GUIDs are generated using a combination of information – each of which is designed to be unique in either space or time. When you combine them, you come up with a value that is guaranteed, statistically speaking, to be unique across space and time.

There is a Win32 API call to generate a GUID in normal programming, but, in addition to the ROWGUIDCOL option on a column, SQL has a special function to return a GUID – it is called the NEWID() function, and can be called at any time.

COLLATE

As I indicated back in the CREATE DATABASE section, this one is new with SQL Server 2000. It works pretty much just as it did for the CREATE DATABASE command, with the primary difference being in terms of scope (here, we define at the column level rather than the database level).

NULL/NOT NULL

This one is pretty simple – it states whether the column in question accepts NULL values or not. The default, when you first install SQL Server, is to set a column to NOT NULL if you don't specify nullability. There are, however, a very large number of different settings that can affect this default, and change its behavior. For example, setting a value by using the sp_dbcmptlevel stored procedure or setting ANSI-compliance options can change this value.

> I highly recommend explicitly stating the NULL option for every column in every table you ever build. Why? As I mentioned before, there are a large number of different settings that can affect what the system uses for a default for the nullability of a column. If you rely on these defaults, then you may find later that your scripts don't seem to work right (because you, or someone else, has changed a relevant setting without realizing its full effect).

Column Constraints

We have a whole chapter coming up on constraints, so we won't spend that much time on it here. Still, it seems like a good time to review the question of what column constraints are – in short, they are restrictions and rules that you place on individual columns about the data that can be inserted into that column.

For example, if you have a column that's supposed to store the month of the year, you might define that column as being of type tinyint – but that wouldn't prevent someone from inserting the number 54 in that column. Since 54 would give us bad data (it doesn't refer to a month), we might provide a constraint that says that data in that column must be between 1 and 12. We'll see how to do this in our next chapter.

Computed Columns

New with version 7.0 was the ability to have what amounts to a "virtual" column. That is, a column that doesn't have any data of its own, but whose value is derived on the fly from other columns in the table. This is something of a boon for many applications.

For example, let's say that we're working on an invoicing system. We want to store information on the quantity of an item we have sold, and at what price. It used to be fairly commonplace to go ahead and add columns to store this information, along with another column that stored the extended value (price times quantity). However, that leads to unnecessary wasting of disk space and maintenance hassles associated with when the totals and the base values get out of synch with each other. With a computed column, we can get around that by defining the value of our computed column to be whatever multiplying price by quantity creates.

Let's look at the specific syntax:

```
<column name> AS <computed column expression>
```

The first item is a little different – we're providing a column name to go with our value. This is simply the alias that we're going to use to refer to the value that is computed, based on the expression that follows the AS keyword.

Next comes the computed column expression. The expression can be any normal expression that uses either literals or column values from the same tables. Therefore, in our example of price and quantity, we might define this column as:

```
ExtendedPrice AS Price * Quantity
```

For an example using a literal, let's say that we always charge a fixed markup on our goods that is 20% over our cost. We could simply keep track of cost in one column, and then use a computed column for the ListPrice column:

```
ListPrice AS Cost * 1.2
```

Pretty easy eh? There are a few caveats and provisos though:

❑   You cannot use a subquery, and the values cannot come from a different table.

❑   Prior to SQL Server 2000, you could not use a computed column as any part of any key (primary, foreign, or unique) or with a default constraint. For SQL Server 2000, you can now use a computed column as a primary key or unique constraint – foreign keys and defaults are still "no-no"s.

❑   Another problem for previous versions (but added as a new feature for SQL Server 2000) is the ability to create indexes on computed columns. We will discuss each of these changes to computed columns further when we explore constraints in Chapter 7 and indexing in Chapter 9.

We'll look at specific examples of how to use computed columns a little later in this chapter.

I'm actually surprised that I haven't heard much debate about the use of computed columns. Rules for normalization of data say that we should not have a column in our table for information that can be derived from other columns – that's exactly what a computed column is!

I'm glad the religious zealots of normalization haven't weighed into this one much, as I like computed columns as something of a compromise. By default, you aren't storing the data twice, and you don't have issues with the derived values not agreeing with the base values because they are calculated on the fly directly from the base values. However, you still get the end result you wanted. Note that, if you index the computed column, you are indeed actually storing the data (you have to for the index). This, however, has its own benefits when it comes to read performance.

This isn't the way to do everything related to derived data, but it sure is an excellent helper for most situations.

Table Constraints

Table constraints are quite similar to column constraints, in that they place restrictions on the data that can be inserted into the table. What makes them a little different is that they may be based on more than one column.

Again, we will be covering these in the constraints chapter, but examples of table-level constraints include PRIMARY and FOREIGN KEY constraints, as well as CHECK constraints.

> OK, so why is a **CHECK** constraint a table constraint? Isn't it a column constraint since it affects what you can place in a given column? The answer is that it's both. If it is based on solely one column, then it meets the rules for a column constraint. If, however (as **CHECK** constraints can) it is dependent on multiple columns, then you have what would be referred to as a table constraint.

ON

Remember when we were dealing with database creation, and we said we could create different filegroups? Well, the ON clause in a table definition is a way of specifically stating on which filegroup (and, therefore, physical device) you want the table located. You can place a given table on a specific physical device, or, as you will want to do in most cases, just leave the ON clause out, and it will be placed on whatever the default filegroup is (which will be the PRIMARY unless you've set it to something else). We will be looking at this usage extensively in our chapter on performance tuning.

TEXTIMAGE_ON

This one is basically the same as the ON clause we just looked at, except that it lets you move a very specific part of the table to yet a different filegroup. This clause is only valid if your table definition has text, ntext, or image column(s) in it. When you use the TEXTIMAGE_ON clause, you move only the BLOB information into the separate filegroup – the rest of the table stays either on the default filegroup or with the filegroup chosen in the ON clause.

> There can be some serious performance increases to be had by splitting your database up into multiple files, and then storing those files on separate physical disks. When you do this, it means you get the I/O from both drives. We'll look into this more in Chapter 29, but, for now, I would suggest you leave well enough alone unless you know exactly why you're going to move things.

Creating a Table

All right, we've seen plenty; we're ready for some action, so let's build a few tables.

When we started this section, we looked at our standard CREATE syntax of:

```
CREATE <object type> <object name>
```

And then we moved on to a more specific start (indeed, it's the first line of our statement that will create the table) on creating a table called Customers:

```
CREATE TABLE Customers
```

Our Customers table is going to be the first table in a database we will be putting together to track our company's accounting. We'll be looking at designing a database in a couple of chapters, but we'll go ahead and get started on our database by building a couple of tables to learn our CREATE TABLE statement. We'll look at most of the concepts of table construction in this section, but we'll save a few for later on in the book. That being said, let's get started building the first of several tables.

I'm going to add in a USE <database name> line prior to my CREATE code so that I'm sure that, when I run the script, the table is created in the proper database. We'll then follow up that first line that we've already seen with a few columns.

Any script you create for regular use with a particular database should include a USE command with the name of that database. This ensures that you really are creating, altering, and dropping the objects in the database you intend. More than once have I been the victim of my own stupidity when I blindly opened up a script and executed it only to find that the wrong database was current, and any tables with the same name had been dropped (thus losing all data) and replaced by a new layout. You can also tell when other people have done this by taking a look around the master database – you'll often find several extraneous tables in that database from people running CREATE scripts that were meant to go somewhere else.

```
USE Accounting
CREATE TABLE Customers
(
    CustomerNo      int             IDENTITY  NOT NULL,
    CustomerName    varchar(30)               NOT NULL,
    Address1        varchar(30)               NOT NULL,
    Address2        varchar(30)               NOT NULL,
    City            varchar(20)               NOT NULL,
    State           char(2)                   NOT NULL,
    Zip             varchar(10)               NOT NULL,
    Contact         varchar(25)               NOT NULL,
    Phone           char(15)                  NOT NULL,
    FedIDNo         varchar(9)                NOT NULL,
    DateInSystem    smalldatetime             NOT NULL
)
```

This is a somewhat simplified table vs. what we would probably use in real life, but there's plenty of time to change it later (and we will).

Once we've built the table, we want to verify that it was indeed created, and that it has all the columns and types that we expect. To do this, we can make use of several commands, but perhaps the best is one that will seem like an old friend before you're done with this book: sp_help. The syntax is simple:

EXEC sp_help <*object name*>

To specify the table object that we just created, try executing the following code:

```
EXEC sp_help Customers
```

The EXEC command is used in two different ways. This rendition is used to execute a stored procedure – in this case, a system stored procedure. We'll see the second version later when we are dealing with advanced query topics and stored procedures.

> **Technically speaking, you can execute a stored procedure by simply calling it (without using the EXEC keyword). The problem is that this only works if the sproc being called is the first statement of any kind in the batch. Just having sp_help Customers would have worked in the place of the code above, but if you tried to run a SELECT statement before it – it would blow up on you. With SQL Server 2000 you get a different behavior depending on whether the sproc is the first thing in the batch (in which case it works) or in the middle of the batch (in which case it varies between blowing up or getting ignored depending on the specifics of the situation). Not using EXEC leads to very unpredictable behavior and should be avoided.**

Try executing the command, and you'll find that you get back several result sets one after another. The information retrieved includes separate result sets for:

❑   Table name, owner, type of table (system vs. user), and creation date

❑   Column names, data types, nullability, size, and collation

❑   The identity column (if one exists) including the *initial* seed and increment values

❑   The RowGUIDCol (if one exists)

❑   Filegroup information

❑   Index names (if any exist), types, and included columns

❑   Constraint names (if any), types, and included columns

❑   Foreign key (if any) names and columns

❑   The names of any schema bound views (more on this in Chapter 10) that depend on the table

Now that we're certain that we have our table created, let's take a look at creating yet another table – the Employees table. This time, let's talk about what we want in the table first, and then see how you do trying to code the CREATE script for yourself.

The Employees table is another fairly simple table. It should include information on:

❑   The employee's ID – this should be automatically generated by the system

❑   First name

❑   Optionally, middle initial

❑   Last name

❑   Title

❑   Social Security Number

❑   Salary

❑   The previous salary

❑   The amount of the last raise

❑   Date of hire

❑   Date terminated (if there is one)

❑   The employee's manager

❑   Department

Start off by trying to figure out a layout for yourself.

Before we start looking at this together, let me tell you not to worry too much if your layout isn't exactly like mine. There are as many database designs as there are database designers – and that all begins with table design. We all can have different solutions to the same problem. What you want to look for is whether you have all the concepts that needed to be addressed. That being said, let's take a look at one way to build this table.

We have a special column here. The `EmployeeID` is to be generated by the system and therefore is an excellent candidate for either an identity column or a RowGUIDCol. There are several reasons you might want to go one way or the other between these two, but we'll go with an identity column for a couple of reasons:

❑ It's going to be used by an average person. (Would you want to have to remember a GUID?)

❑ It incurs lower overhead.

We're now ready to start constructing our script:

```
CREATE TABLE Employees
(
    EmployeeID        int             IDENTITY  NOT NULL,
```

For this column, the `NOT NULL` option has essentially been chosen for us by virtue of our use of an `IDENTITY` column. You cannot allow `NULL` values in an `IDENTITY` column. Note that, depending on our server settings, we will, most likely, still need to include our `NOT NULL` option (if we leave it to the default we may get an error depending on whether the default allows `NULL`s).

Next up, we want to add in our name columns. I usually allow approximately 25 characters for names. Most names are far shorter than that, but I've bumped into enough that were rather lengthy (especially since hyphenated names have become so popular) that I allow for the extra room. In addition, I make use of a variable-length data type for two reasons:

❑ To recapture the space of a column that is defined somewhat longer than the actual data usually is (retrieve blank space)

❑ To simplify searches in the `WHERE` clause – fixed-length columns are padded with spaces which requires extra planning when performing comparisons against fields of this type

> **For the code that you write directly in T-SQL, SQL Server will automatically adjust to the padded spaces issue – that is, an 'xx' placed in a char(5) will be treated as being equal (if compared) to an 'xx' placed in a varchar(5) – this is not, however, true in your client APIs such as ADO. If you connect to a char(5) in ADO, then an 'xx' will evaluate to xx with three spaces after it – if you compare it to 'xx', it will evaluate to False. An 'xx' placed in a varchar(5), however, will automatically have any trailing spaces trimmed, and comparing it to 'xx' in ADO will evaluate to True.**

The exception in this case is the middle initial. Since we really only need to allow for one character here, recapture of space is not an issue. Indeed, a variable-length data type would actually use more space in this case, since a `varchar` needs not only the space to store the data, but also a small amount of overhead space to keep track of how long the data is. In addition, ease of search is also not an issue since, if we have any value in the field at all, there isn't enough room left for padded spaces.

Since a name for an employee is a critical item, we will not allow any NULL values in the first and last name columns. Middle initial is not nearly so critical (indeed, some people in the US don't have a middle name at all, while my editor tells me that it's not uncommon for Brits to have several), so we will allow a NULL for that field only:

```
FirstName        varchar(25)           NOT NULL,
MiddleInitial    char(1)               NULL,
LastName         varchar(25)           NOT NULL,
```

Next up is the employee's title. We must know what they are doing if we're going to be cutting them a paycheck, so we will also make this a required field:

```
Title            varchar(25)           NOT NULL,
```

In that same paycheck vein, we must know their Social Security Number (or similar identification number outside the US) in order to report for taxes. In this case, we'll use a varchar and allow up to eleven characters, as these identification numbers are different lengths in different countries. If you know your application is only going to require SSNs from the US then you'll probably want to make it char(11) instead:

```
SSN              varchar(11)           NOT NULL,
```

We must know how much to pay the employees – that seems simple enough – but what comes next is a little different. When we add in the prior salary and the amount of the last raise, we get into a situation where we could use a computed column. The new salary is the sum of the previous salary and the amount of the last raise. The Salary amount is something that we might use quite regularly – indeed we might want an index on it to help with ranged queries. In version 7.0, we wouldn't have had the possibility of an index on a computed column. We do have this option with SQL Server 2000 (this is a good thing!), but for various reasons I don't want to do that here (we'll talk about the ramifications of indexes on computed columns in Chapter 9), so I'm going to use LastRaise as my computed column:

```
Salary              money                NOT NULL,
PriorSalary         money                NOT NULL,
LastRaise AS Salary - PriorSalary,
```

If we hired them, then we must know the date of hire – so that will also be required:

```
HireDate         smalldatetime         NOT NULL,
```

Note that I've chosen to use a smalldatetime data type rather than the standard datetime to save space. The datetime data type will store information down to additional fractions of seconds, plus it will save a wider range of dates. Since we're primarily interested in the date of hire, not the time, and since we are dealing with a limited range of calendar dates (say, back 50 years and ahead a century or so), the smalldatetime will meet our needs and take up half the space.

> **Date and time fields are somewhat of a double-edged sword. On one hand, it's very nice to save storage space and network bandwidth by using the smaller data type. On the other hand, you'll find that smalldatetime is incompatible with some other language data types (including Visual Basic). Even going with the normal datetime is no guarantee of safety from this last problem though – some data access models pretty much require you to pass a date in as a varchar and allow for implicit conversion to a datetime field.**

The date of termination is something we may not know (we'd like to think that some employees are still working for us), so we'll need to leave it nullable:

```
    TerminationDate  smalldatetime            NULL,
```

We absolutely want to know who the employee is reporting to (somebody must have hired them!) and what department they are working in:

```
    ManagerEmpID     int                      NOT NULL,
    Department       varchar(25)              NOT NULL
)
```

So, just for clarity, let's look at the entire script to create this table:

```
USE Accounting

CREATE TABLE Employees
(
    EmployeeID       int          IDENTITY   NOT NULL,
    FirstName        varchar(25)             NOT NULL,
    MiddleInitial    char(1)                 NULL,
    LastName         varchar(25)             NOT NULL,
    Title            varchar(25)             NOT NULL,
    SSN              varchar(11)             NOT NULL,
    Salary           money                   NOT NULL,
    PriorSalary      money                   NOT NULL,
    LastRaise AS Salary - PriorSalary,
    HireDate         smalldatetime           NOT NULL,
    TerminationDate  smalldatetime           NULL,
    ManagerEmpID     int                     NOT NULL,
    Department       varchar(25)             NOT NULL
)
```

Again, I would recommend executing sp_help on this table to verify that the table was created as you expected.

The ALTER Statement

OK, so now we have a database and a couple of nice tables – isn't life grand? If only things always stayed the same, but they don't. Sometimes (actually, far more often than we would like), we get requests to *change* a table rather than recreate it. Likewise, we have needs to change the size, file locations, or some other feature of our database. That's where our ALTER statement comes in.

Much like the CREATE statement, our ALTER statement pretty much always starts out the same:

ALTER <object type> <object name>

This is totally boring so far, but it won't stay that way. We'll see the beginnings of issues with this statement right away, and things will get really interesting (read: convoluted and confusing!) when we deal with this even further in our next chapter (when we deal with constraints).

ALTER DATABASE

Let's get right into it by taking a look at changing our database. We'll actually make a couple of changes just so we can see the effects of different things and how their syntax can vary.

Perhaps the biggest trick with the ALTER statement is to remember what you already have. With that in mind, let's take a look again at what we already have:

```
EXEC sp_helpdb Accounting
```

Notice that I didn't put the quotation marks in this time like I did when we used this stored proc earlier. That's because this system procedure, like many of them, accepts a special data type called sysname. As long as what you pass in is a name of a valid object in the system, the quotes are optional for this data type.

So, the results should be just like they were when we created the database:

Name	db_size	owner	dbid	created	status	compatibility_level
Accounting	15.00 MB	sa	9	May 28 2000	Status=ONLINE, Updateability=READ_WRITE, UserAccess=MULTI_USER, Recovery=FULL, Version=538, Collation=SQL_Latin1_General_CP1_CI_AS, SQLSortOrder=52, IsTornPageDetectionEnabled, IsAutoCreateStatistics, IsAutoUpdateStatistics	80

And...

Name	fileid	filename	filegroup	size	maxsize	growth	usage
Accounting	1	c:\Program Files\ Microsoft SQL Server\ mssql\data\ AccountingData.mdf	PRIMARY	10240 KB	51200 KB	5120 KB	data only
AccountingLog	2	c:\Program Files\ Microsoft SQL Server\ mssql\data\ AccountingLog.ldf	NULL	5120 KB	25600 KB	5120 KB	log only

Let's say we want to change things a bit. For example, let's say that we know that we are going to be doing a large import into our database. Currently, our database is only 15MB in size – that doesn't hold much these days. Since we have Autogrow turned on, we could just start our import, and SQL Server would automatically enlarge the database 5MB at a time. Keep in mind, however, that it's actually a fair amount of work to reallocate the size of the database. If we were inserting 100MB worth of data, then the server would have to deal with that reallocation at least 16 times (at 20MB, 25MB, 30MB, etc.). Since we know that we're going to be getting up to 100MB of data, why not just do it in one shot? To do this, we would use the ALTER DATABASE command.

The general syntax looks like this:

```
ALTER DATABASE <database name>
   ADD FILE
       ([NAME = <'logical file name'>,]
        FILENAME = <'file name'>
        [, SIZE = <size in megabytes or kilobytes>]
        [, MAXSIZE = <size in megabytes or kilobytes>]
        [, FILEGROWTH = <No of megabytes or kilobytes/percentage>]) [,...n]
             [ TO FILEGROUP filegroup_name]
   |ADD LOG FILE
       ([NAME = <'logical file name'>,]
        FILENAME = <'file name'>
        [, SIZE = <size in megabytes or kilobytes>]
        [, MAXSIZE = <size in megabytes or kilobytes>]
        [, FILEGROWTH = <No of megabytes or kilobytes/percentage>])
   |REMOVE FILE <logical file name> [WITH DELETE]
   |ADD FILEGROUP <filegroup name>
   |REMOVE FILEGROUP <filegroup name>
   |MODIFY FILE <filespec>
   |MODIFY NAME = <new dbname>
   |MODIFY FILEGROUP <filegroup name> {<filegroup property>|NAME =
             <new filegroup name>}
   |SET <optionspec> [,...n ][WITH <termination>]
   |COLLATE <collation name>
```

The reality is that you will very rarely use all that stuff – sometimes I think Microsoft just puts it there for the sole purpose of confusing the heck out of us (just kidding!).

So, after looking at all that gobbledygook, let's just worry about what we need to expand our database out to 100MB:

```
ALTER DATABASE Accounting
   MODIFY FILE
   (NAME = Accounting,
    SIZE = 100MB)
```

Note that, unlike when we created our database, we don't get any information about the allocation of space – instead, we get the rather non-verbose:

The command(s) completed successfully.

Gee – how informative... So, we'd better check on things for ourselves:

```
EXEC sp_helpdb Accounting
```

name	db_size	Owner	dbid	created	status	compatibility_ level
Accounting	105.00 MB	Sa	9	May 28 2000	Status=ONLINE, Updateability=READ_WRITE, UserAccess=MULTI_USER, Recovery=FULL, Version=538, Collation=SQL_Latin1_ General_CP1_CI_AS, SQLSortOrder=52, IsTornPageDetectionEnabled, IsAutoCreateStatistics, IsAutoUpdateStatistics	80

name	fileid	Filename	filegroup	size	maxsize	growth	usage
Accounting	1	C:\Program Files\ Microsoft SQL Server\ mssql\data\ AccountingData.mdf	PRIMARY	102400 KB	102400 KB	5120 KB	data only
AccountingLog	2	C:\Program Files\ Microsoft SQL Server\ mssql\data\ AccountingLog.ldf	NULL	5120 KB	25600 KB	5120 KB	log only

As you can see, we've succeeded in increasing our size up to 100MB. One thing worth noticing is that, even though we exceeded the previous maximum size of 51,200KB, we didn't get an error. This is because we *explicitly* increased the size. It was, therefore, implied that we must have wanted to increase the maximum too. If we had done things our original way of just letting SQL Server expand things as necessary, our import would have blown up in the middle because of the size restriction. One other item worth noting here is that the maxsize was only increased to our new explicit value – there now isn't any room for growth left.

Things pretty much work the same for any of the more common database-level modifications you'll make. The permutations are, however, endless. The more complex filegroup modifications and the like are outside the scope of this book, but, if you need more information on them, I would recommend one of the more administrator-oriented books out there (and there are a ton of them).

Option and Termination Specs

SQL Server 2000 has brought along a few new options that can be set with an ALTER DATABASE statement. Among these are database-specific defaults for most of the SET options that are available (such as ANSI_PADDING, ARITHABORT – handy if you're dealing with indexed or partitioned views), state options (for example, single user mode or read-only), and recovery options. The effects of the various SET options are discussed where they are relevant throughout the book. This new ALTER functionality simply gives you an additional way to change the defaults for any particular database.

Also added with SQL Server 2000 is the ability to control the implementation of some of the changes you are trying to make on your database. Many changes require that you have exclusive control over the database – something that can be hard to deal with if other users are already in the system. With SQL Server 2000 we now have the ability to gracefully force other users out of the database so that we may complete our database changes. The strength of these actions ranges from waiting a number of seconds (you decide how long) before kicking other users out, all the way up to immediate termination of any option transactions (automatically rolling them back). Relatively uncontrolled (from the clients perspective) termination of transactions is not something to be taken lightly. Such an action is usually in the realm of the database administrator. As such, we will consider further discussion out of the scope of this book.

ALTER TABLE

A far, far more common need is the situation where we need to change the makeup of our table. This can range from simple things like adding a new column to more complex issues such as changing a data type.

Let's start out by taking a look at the basic syntax for changing a table:

```
ALTER TABLE table_name
    {[ALTER COLUMN <column_name>
          {<new_data_type> [(precision [, scale])]]
          [COLLATE <collation_name>]
          [NULL|NOT NULL]
        |[{ADD|DROP} ROWGUIDCOL]}]
      |ADD
          <column name> <data_type>
          [[DEFAULT <constant_expression>]
          |[IDENTITY [(<seed>, <increment>) [NOT FOR REPLICATION]]]]]
          [ROWGUIDCOL]
          [COLLATE <collation_name>]
            [NULL|NOT NULL]
          [<column_constraints>]
          |[<column_name> AS <computed_column_expression>]
      |ADD
         [CONSTRAINT <constraint_name>]
         {[{PRIMARY KEY|UNIQUE}
             [CLUSTERED|NONCLUSTERED]
             {(<column_name>[ ,...n ])}
             [WITH FILLFACTOR = <fillfactor>]
             [ON {<filegroup> | DEFAULT}]
             ]
             |FOREIGN KEY
                [(<column_name>[ ,...n])]
                REFERENCES <referenced_table> [(<referenced_column>[ ,...n])]
                [ON DELETE {CASCADE|NO ACTION}]
                [ON UPDATE {CASCADE|NO ACTION}]
                [NOT FOR REPLICATION]
             |DEFAULT <constant_expression>
                [FOR <column_name>]
             |CHECK [NOT FOR REPLICATION]
                (<search_conditions>)
           [,...n][ ,...n]
           |[WITH CHECK|WITH NOCHECK]}
      |DROP
         {[CONSTRAINT] <constraint_name>
            |COLUMN <column_name>}[ ,...n]
         |{CHECK|NOCHECK} CONSTRAINT
            {ALL|<constraint_name>[ ,...n]}
         |{ENABLE|DISABLE} TRIGGER
            {ALL|<trigger_name>[ ,...n]}
    }
```

As with the CREATE TABLE command, there's quite a handful there to deal with.

So let's start an example of using this by looking back at our Employees table in the Accounting database:

```
EXEC sp_help Employees
```

For the sake of saving a few trees, I'm going to edit the results that I show here to just the part we care about – you'll actually see much more than this:

Column_name	Type	Computed	Length	Prec	Scale	Nullable
EmployeeID	int	no	4	10	0	no
FirstName	varchar	no	25			no
MiddleInitial	char	no	1			yes
LastName	varchar	no	25			no
Title	varchar	no	25			no
SSN	varchar	no	11			no
Salary	money	no	8	19	4	no
PriorSalary	money	no	8	19	4	no
LastRaise	money	yes	8	19	4	yes
HireDate	smalldatetime	no	4			no
TerminationDate	smalldatetime	no	4			yes
ManagerEmpID	int	no	4	10	0	no
Department	varchar	no	25			no

Let's say that we've decided we'd like to keep previous employer information on our employees (probably so we know who will be trying to recruit the good ones back!). That just involves adding another column, and really isn't all that tough. The syntax looks much like it did with our CREATE TABLE statement except that it has obvious alterations to it:

```
ALTER TABLE Employees
    ADD
        PreviousEmployer   varchar(30)    NULL
```

Not exactly rocket science – is it? Indeed, we could have added several additional columns at one time if we had wanted to. It would look something like this:

```
ALTER TABLE Employees
    ADD
        DateOfBirth     datetime    NULL,
        LastRaiseDate   datetime    NOT NULL
            DEFAULT '2000-01-01'
```

Notice the DEFAULT I slid in here. We haven't really looked at these yet (they are in our next chapter), but I wanted to use one here to point out a special case.

Back in Version 6.5, we weren't allowed to add columns with the NOT NULL option after the table was originally created. At issue was how to handle the data that was already in your table. Beginning in Version 7.0, we gained the ability to define an added column as NOT NULL – we just had to provide a default value for that column. The default is then used to populate the new column for any row that is already in our table.

Before we go away from this topic for now, let's take a look at what we've added:

```
EXEC sp_help Employees
```

Column_name	Type	Computed	Length	Prec	Scale	Nullable
EmployeeID	int	no	4	10	0	no
FirstName	varchar	no	25			no
MiddleInitial	char	no	1			yes
LastName	varchar	no	25			no
Title	varchar	no	25			no
SSN	varchar	no	11			no
Salary	money	no	8	19	4	no
PriorSalary	money	no	8	19	4	no
LastRaise	money	yes	8	19	4	yes
HireDate	smalldatetime	no	4			no
TerminationDate	smalldatetime	no	4			yes
ManagerEmpID	int	no	4	10	0	no
Department	varchar	no	25			no
PreviousEmployer	varchar	no	30			yes
DateOfBirth	datetime	no	8			yes
LastRaiseDate	datetime	no	8			no

As you can see, all of our columns have been added. The thing to note, however, is that they all went to the end of the column list. There is no way to add a column to a specific location in SQL Server. If you want to move a column to the middle, you need to create a completely new table (with a different name), copy the data over to the new table, DROP the existing table, and then rename the new one.

> *This issue of moving columns around can get very sticky indeed. Even some of the tools that are supposed to automate this often have problems with it. Why? Well, any foreign key constraints you have that reference this table must first be dropped before you are allowed to delete the current version of the table. That means that you have to drop all your foreign keys, make the changes, and then add all your foreign keys back. It doesn't end there, however, any indexes you have defined on the old table are automatically dropped when you drop the existing table – that means that you must remember to recreate your indexes as part of the build script to create your new version of the table – yuck!*

> *But wait! There's more! While we haven't really looked at views yet, I feel compelled to make a reference here to what happens to your views when you add a column. You should be aware that, even if your view is built using a SELECT * as its base statement, your new column will not appear in your view until you rebuild the view. Column names in views are resolved at the time the view is created for performance reasons. That means any views that have already been created when you add your columns have already resolved using the previous column list – you must either DROP and recreate the view or use an ALTER VIEW statement to rebuild it.*

The DROP Statement

Performing a DROP is the same as deleting whatever object(s) you reference in your DROP statement. It's very quick and easy, and the syntax is exactly the same for all of the major SQL Server objects (tables, views, sprocs, triggers, etc.). It goes like this:

```
DROP <object type> <object name> [, ...n]
```

Actually, this is about as simple as SQL statements get. We could drop both of our tables at the same time if we wanted:

```
USE Accounting

DROP TABLE Customers, Employees
```

And this deletes them both.

> Be *very* careful with this command. There is no, "Are you sure?" kind of question that goes with this – it just assumes you know what you're doing and deletes the object(s) in question.

Remember my comment at the beginning of this chapter about putting a USE statement at the top of your scripts? Well, here's an example of why it's so important – the Northwind database also has tables called Customers and Employees. You wouldn't want those gone, now, would you? As it happens, some issues of drop order would prevent you from accidentally dropping those tables with the above command, but it wouldn't prevent you from dropping the [Order Details] table, or, say, Shipments.

The syntax is very much the same for dropping the entire database. Now let's drop the Accounting database:

```
USE master

DROP DATABASE Accounting
```

You should see the following in the Results pane:

Deleting database file 'c:\Program Files\Microsoft SQL Server\mssql\data\AccountingLog.ldf'.
Deleting database file 'c:\Program Files\Microsoft SQL Server\mssql\data\AccountingData.mdf'.

You may run into a situation where you get an error that says that the database cannot be deleted because it is in use. If this happens, check a couple of things:

❑ Make sure that the database that you have as current in Query Analyzer is something other than the database you're trying to drop (that is, make sure you're not using the database as you're trying to drop it).

❑ Ensure you don't have any other connections open (using EM or sp_who) that are showing the database you're trying to drop as the current database.

I usually solve the first one just as we did in the code example – I switch to using the master database. The second you have to check manually – I usually close other sessions down entirely just to be sure.

Using the GUI Tool

We've just spent a lot of time pounding in perfect syntax for creating a database and a couple of tables – that's enough of that for a while. Let's take a look at the graphical tool in Enterprise Manager (EM) that allows us to build and relate tables. From this point on, we'll not only be dealing with code, but with the tool that can generate much of that code for us.

Creating a Database Using EM

If you run EM and expand the **Databases** node, you should see something like this:

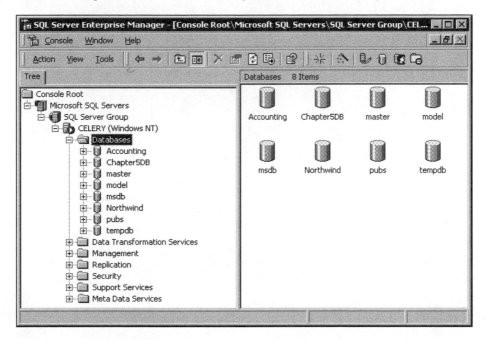

If you look closely at this screen shot, you'll see that my Accounting *database is still showing even though we just dropped it in the previous example. You may or may not wind up seeing this, depending on whether you already had EM open when you dropped the database or you opened EM after you dropped the database in QA.*

Why the difference? Well, before version 7.0, the EM used to refresh information such as the available databases regularly. Now it only updates when it knows it has a reason to (for example, you deleted something by using EM instead of QA, or perhaps you explicitly chose to refresh). The reason for the change was performance. The old 6.5 EM used to be a slug performance-wise because it was constantly making round trips to "poll" the server. The new EM performs much better, but doesn't necessarily have the most up-to-date information.

The bottom line on this is that, if you see something in EM that you don't expect to, try pressing F5 (refresh), and it should update things for you.

Now try right-clicking on the **Databases** node, and choose the **New Database...** option:

This will pull up the **Database Properties** dialog box, and allow you to fill in the information on how you want your database created. We'll use the same choices that we did when we created the `Accounting` database at the beginning of the chapter. First comes basic info and name:

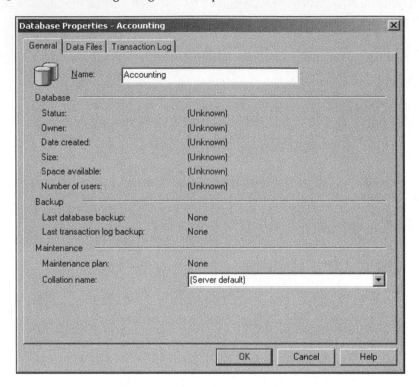

This entire tab on the dialog is new, so let's take a look at things.

First, the name – this is pretty basic. We called it `Accounting` before, and, since we deleted the first one we created, there's no reason not to call it that again.

Next comes database, backup, and maintenance information. Since this is an entirely new database, there really isn't any of this to show us (the same dialog is used to display property information after the database is created).

Perhaps the most interesting thing here though is the collation name. In 7.0 and prior versions of SQL Server, we only had one collation, and that applied to the entire server (every database, every table, every column). With SQL Server 2000, we finally have choices! For the vast majority of installs, you'll want to stick with whatever the server default was set to when the server was installed (presumably, someone had already thought this out fairly well). However, you can change it for just the current database by setting it here.

"Why", you may ask, "would I want a different collation?" Well, in the English-speaking world, a common need for specific collations would be that some applications are written expecting an "a" to be the same as an "A" – while others are expecting case sensitivity ("a" is not the same as "A"). In the old days, we would have to have separate servers set up in order to handle this. Another, non-English example would be dialect differences that are found within many countries of the world – even where they speak the same general language.

Next comes the information about the database itself on the Data Files tab – in version 7.0 and prior, this actually would have been the first tab you would have seen – other than now being second, it's basically unchanged:

Last, but not least, we switch tabs to see the information on the log:

Click OK and, after a brief pause to actually create the database, you'll see it added to the tree:

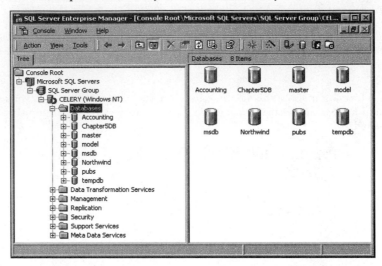

Now expand the tree to show the various items underneath the Accounting node, and select the Diagrams node. Right-click it, and choose the New Database Diagram menu choice.

New in this release of SQL Server is the Create Database Diagram Wizard. I'm actually not a fan of this one. In 7.0, you would have gotten a simple message indicating that there weren't any tables in your database. It would have further told you that you could create them within the database. With SQL Server 2000, the new wizard brings up a list of tables – the problem is that we didn't create any of them. The second screen looks like this:

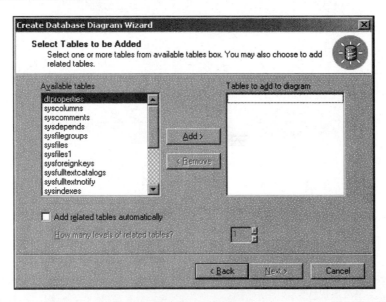

So then, what are these tables? Well, every database in SQL Server has a set of **system tables**. Virtually all of them will start with sys, and they are used for such things as keeping track of your tables, data types, relationships, dependencies, etc., etc., etc.

Before we move on, however, there is one more thing worth noticing here – the **Add related tables automatically** checkbox. This causes any tables that are related to a table you select to also be selected. The **How many levels of related tables?** box lets you define how deep into the relationship you want to go (for example, do you pull in the tables related to the tables that were related to the table you selected). Don't sweat this one too much for now – we'll look at it more after we've introduced relationships later in the book.

For now, just click **Cancel** – you should get the diagram screen:

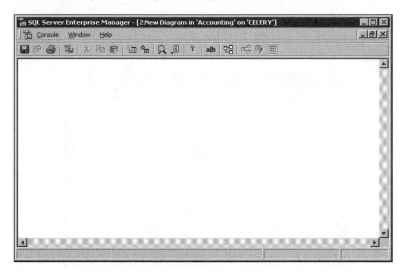

It can't be much less interesting than that. The nice part is that you can add a table by either right-clicking and choosing the appropriate option, or by clicking on the **New table** icon in the tool bar. When you choose to add a new table, SQL Server will ask you for the name you want to give your new table. You will then get a mildly helpful dialog box that lets you fill in your table one piece at a time – complete with labels for what you need to fill out:

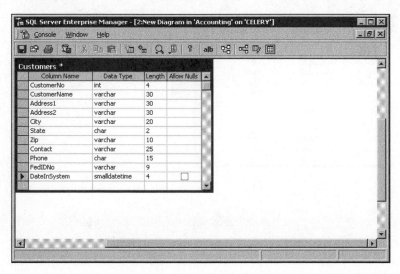

This dialog isn't quite as useful out of the box as it was under 7.0. On one hand, they've tried to make things a bit more compact. The old dialog had a bunch of columns – many of which were not used or only used for one field or two. The new version is more succinct, but it also is not very intuitive when you want to add more to your data column.

In our case, we need to define our first column as being an identity column, but we don't have any way of doing that with the default grid here. To change what items we can define for our table, we need to right-click in the editing dialog, and select Table View | Modify Custom.

We then get a list of items from which we can choose. For now, we'll just select the extra item we need – Identity. The default of a seed of one and an increment of one is great for our needs here, so we'll ignore those items for now:

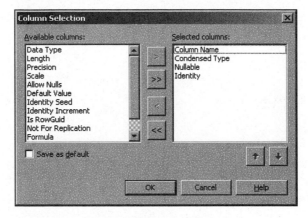

Now go back to our editing dialog and select Table View | Custom to view the identity column, and we're ready to fill in our table definition.

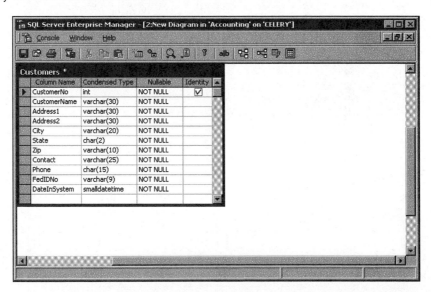

Once you have the table filled out, you can save the changes, and that will create your table for you.

This is really a point of personal preference, but I prefer to set the view down to just column names at this point. You can do this by clicking on the Show icon on the toolbar or, as I prefer, by right-clicking the table and choosing Table View | Column Names. *I find that this saves a lot of screen real-estate, and makes more room for me to work on additional tables.*

After you add in the Employees table, you'll see a different response when you go to save it – it will want confirmation that you want to add the new table. I have no idea why it asks you this time (and every subsequent time for that matter) when it didn't on the first save, but it is actually a nice confirmation of what you wanted to do before going on. After accepting that dialog's question, your diagram should have two tables in it:

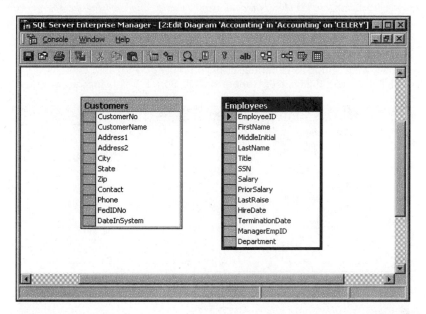

It's worth noting that you can bring up similar dialogs by going to the tables section in EM (right-click on the Tables node and select New Table) rather than the diagrams. The reason I wanted you to use the dialogs screen is that it will become your home for doing more advanced database development as we continue through this book. It's also worth noting that SS2K has added the ability to add descriptions to your tables – while seemingly simple, this is actually a rather cool new feature in terms of assisting your ability to document your database.

It's very important to understand that the diagramming tool that is included with SQL Server (you may sometimes hear this tool and the similar tools that show up in Microsoft's development suites referred to as "The da Vinci Tools") is not designed to be everything to everyone.

Presumably, since you are reading this part of this book, you are just starting out on your database journey – this tool will probably be adequate for you for a while. Eventually, you may want to take a look at some more advanced (and far more expensive) tools to help you with your database design.

Backing into the Code:
The Basics of Creating Scripts with EM

One last quick introduction before we exit this chapter— we want to see the basics of having EM write our scripts for us. For now, we are going to do this as something of a quick and dirty introduction. Later on, after we've learned about the many objects that the scripting tool references, we will take a more advanced look.

> *Beginning with SQL Server 2000, the Query Analyzer also has the ability to script objects. It is available by right-clicking on the object that you want to script and choosing the appropriate options. The scripting in EM is somewhat more robust, and that's why we'll focus on it here.*

To generate scripts, we go into EM and right-click on the database for which we want to generate scripts. (In this case, we're going to generate scripts on our Accounting database.) On the pop-up menu, choose All Tasks, and then select Generate SQL Script. EM brings up a special dialog:

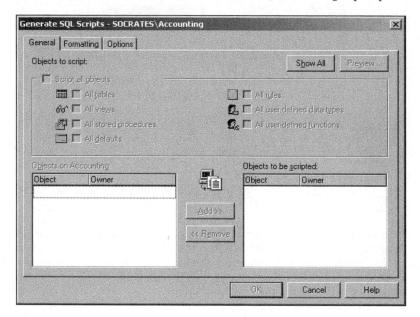

Back in 7.0, the default was to script all of the objects in our database. When you think about it, this made perfect sense – if you wanted to script the database, then you probably wanted to also script the objects that made up your database. For SQL Server 2000, some very strange user interface choices were made in this area.

First, notice that absolutely nothing is pre-selected to be scripted – not even the database itself! Indeed, if you want to script the database, you need to switch over to the Options tab (we'll get there in a moment) and check the Script database box. Wait for that one for a moment, however, and let's take care of selecting our tables.

The changes in what is pre-selected when you bring up the scripting dialog are something of a good news/bad news story. The old behavior brought up all the objects in the left hand list box – for large databases, that could make for a pretty daunting list.

The original idea was great – they would, by default, only show the object that you had selected in the left hand list box unless you clicked on the Show All button. Indeed, this is how it works if you select something smaller than the database itself. The bad news is what happens when you are trying to select the database itself. The default probably should have been to show all right from the start – that is, unfortunately, not what happened. Microsoft has acknowledged this as something of a usability problem, but, as of this writing, there was no ETA for when it might get changed. There was some thought that it might be changed in a service pack, but service packs usually do not include user interface changes – as such, I'm guessing we're stuck with this behavior until Yukon (the code name for the next release of SQL Server).

Notice that the **Objects on Accounting** list box is empty? Don't let it confuse you – you'll need to first click on the **Show All** button before you see the objects that your database holds. After that, you can select all of our objects (for now, it's just two) for scripting by clicking on them and then selecting the **Add>>** button. As another option, you could simply select the **All tables** option:

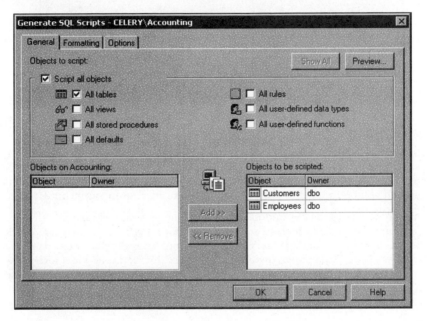

Moving on to the **Formatting** tab, we can see that SQL Server gives us a number of different formatting options about how we want our script to look:

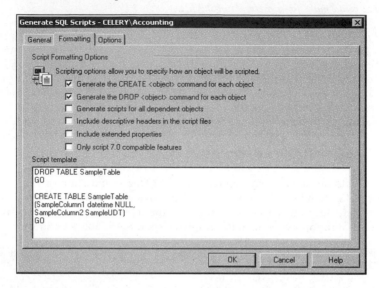

The options on this tab allow us to deal with some of the specifics of our script. Let's look at each individually.

- ❑ **Generate the CREATE <object> command for each object:** this does pretty much what it says. If you select this option, then SQL Server will generate script to recreate each of the objects you have selected (from both the **General** and **Options** tabs).

- ❑ **Generate the DROP <object> command for each object:** again, this does pretty much what it says. This one will generate an IF statement to test for the existence of the object and, if the object already exists, DROP the object. If the CREATE option was also selected, the DROP command will be scripted to go first (to make sure there aren't any conflicts).

- ❑ **Generate scripts for all dependent objects:** turning on this option will tell SQL Server to go look for any dependent objects and script those also. Perhaps the biggest significance to this option is that, without it, SQL Server makes no promises of what order it will script this in. This means that, if one object depends on another (for example, via a foreign key constraint), then the dependent object may be mistakenly scripted first – which may generate errors (how can you create a dependency if the object you're depending on isn't there yet?). If your table has foreign keys, then you'll want to pay particular attention to this option.

- ❑ **Include descriptive headers in the script files:** well, this one amounts to "insert a very simple comment". The emphasis is on *very* simple – all that will be included in the comment is the object name and the time the script was generated. Still, a simple comment can be better than no comment at all.

- ❑ **Include extended properties:** back to the "it does what it says" line. This one just scripts in things like any descriptions you've added to the object.

- ❑ **Only script 7.0 compatible features:** backwards compatibility is what this one's all about. This one is just about making sure that, whatever script gets generated, it will run successfully on a version 7.0 server.

Moving on to the Options tab, we are presented with an additional slew of objects that can be scripted:

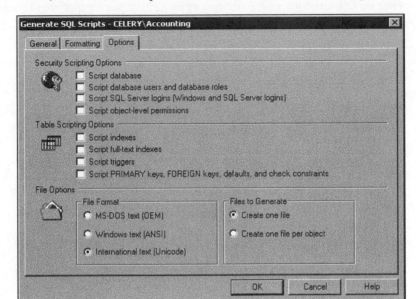

This tab is largely about scripting those "extra" things that are easy to forget about when scripting a database. These include:

- **Script database:** this does just what it says it will do – it scripts the actual database object.

- **Script database users and database roles:** scripts the addition of all the users you currently have with permissions to access the database as well as any custom database roles that you may have set up. Note that this option is separate from scripting the login to the SQL Server and assumes that necessary logins already exist on the server.

- **Script SQL Server logins (Windows and SQL Server logins):** usually, if you're scripting the users and roles, you'll want to find a way to get the logins created first. The problem with this option is that it resets the password to NULL (you wouldn't want people to see the current passwords of the users would you?). This means that, until you get your users to re-enter something, you have a ton of users with a NULL password – oops! That's why I don't like this option.

- **Script object-level permissions:** this one just makes sure that whatever access the user or role has in the current database, they will have the same access once your generated script is run.

- **Table Scripting Options:** I'm going to take these as a group. Essentially, this decides what kinds of table-dependent objects are going to also be scripted along with their parent table.

- **File Options:** I'm also going to take this set as a group – essentially, these just decide what format you want your output to be in.

Now, as a reminder, we selected our two objects on the first tab. Now we're ready to script them. We can either just click on OK (in which case it will ask us for a file to save to), or we can go back to the General tab and click on Preview:

```
CREATE TABLE [dbo].[Customers] (
 [CustomerNo] [int] IDENTITY (1, 1) NOT NULL ,
 [CustomerName] [varchar] (30) COLLATE SQL_Latin1_General_CP1_CI_AS NOT NULL ,
 [Address1] [varchar] (30) COLLATE SQL_Latin1_General_CP1_CI_AS NOT NULL ,
 [Address2] [varchar] (30) COLLATE SQL_Latin1_General_CP1_CI_AS NOT NULL ,
 [City] [varchar] (20) COLLATE SQL_Latin1_General_CP1_CI_AS NOT NULL ,
 [State] [char] (2) COLLATE SQL_Latin1_General_CP1_CI_AS NOT NULL ,
 [Zip] [varchar] (10) COLLATE SQL_Latin1_General_CP1_CI_AS NOT NULL ,
 [Contact] [varchar] (25) COLLATE SQL_Latin1_General_CP1_CI_AS NOT NULL ,
 [Phone] [char] (15) COLLATE SQL_Latin1_General_CP1_CI_AS NOT NULL ,
 [FedIDNo] [varchar] (9) COLLATE SQL_Latin1_General_CP1_CI_AS NOT NULL ,
 [DateInSystem] [smalldatetime] NOT NULL
) ON [PRIMARY]
GO

CREATE TABLE [dbo].[Employees] (
 [EmployeeID] [int] IDENTITY (1, 1) NOT NULL ,
 [FirstName] [varchar] (25) COLLATE SQL_Latin1_General_CP1_CI_AS NOT NULL ,
 [MiddleInitial] [char] (1) COLLATE SQL_Latin1_General_CP1_CI_AS NULL ,
 [LastName] [varchar] (25) COLLATE SQL_Latin1_General_CP1_CI_AS NOT NULL ,
 [Title] [varchar] (25) COLLATE SQL_Latin1_General_CP1_CI_AS NOT NULL ,
 [SSN] [varchar] (11) COLLATE SQL_Latin1_General_CP1_CI_AS NOT NULL ,
 [Salary] [money] NOT NULL ,
 [PriorSalary] [money] NOT NULL ,
 [LastRaise] AS ([Salary] - [PriorSalary]) ,
 [HireDate] [smalldatetime] NOT NULL ,
 [TerminationDate] [smalldatetime] NULL ,
 [ManagerEmpID] [int] NOT NULL ,
 [Department] [varchar] (25) COLLATE SQL_Latin1_General_CP1_CI_AS NOT NULL
) ON [PRIMARY]
GO
```

If you go back and compare these to the scripts that we wrote by hand, you'll see that they are nearly identical, with the major differences related to qualified naming and the addition of collation. SQL Server likes to use the squared brackets every time so there is no doubt about the use of keywords as names or embedded spaces.

As you can see, scripting couldn't be much easier. Once you get a complex database put together, it still isn't quite as easy as it seems in this particular demonstration, but it is a lot easier than writing it all out by hand. The reality is that it really is pretty simple once you learn what the scripting options are, and we'll learn much more about those later in the book.

Summary

In this chapter, we've covered the basics of the CREATE, ALTER, and DROP statements as they relate to creating a database and tables. There are, of course, many other renditions of these that we will cover as we continue through the book. We have also taken a look at the wide variety of options that we can use in databases and tables to have full control over our data. Finally, we have begun to see the many things that we can use the Enterprise Manager for in order to simplify our lives, and make design and scripting simpler.

At this point, you're ready to start getting into some hardcore details about how to lay out your tables, and a discussion on the concepts of normalization and more general database design. I am, however, actually going to make you wait another chapter before we get there, so that we can talk about constraints and keys somewhat before hitting the design issues.

Online discussion at http://p2p.wrox.com

7

Constraints

You've heard me talk about them, but now it's time to look at them seriously – it's time to deal with constraints. For those of you who are already somewhat familiar with SQL Server, I'll warn you – this is an area that has significantly changed with SQL Server 2000. A few things that we have been waiting a long time for have been added – but enough of that for the moment (we'll get there soon enough).

We've talked a couple of times already about what constraints are, but let's review in case you decided to skip straight to this chapter.

> **A constraint is a restriction. Placed at either column or table level, a constraint ensures that your data meets certain data integrity rules.**

This gets back to the notion that I talked about back in Chapters 1 and 2, where ensuring data integrity is not the responsibility of the programs that use your database, but rather the responsibility of the database itself. If you think about it, this is really cool. Data is inserted, updated, and deleted from the database by many sources. Even in stand-alone applications (situations where only one program accesses the database) the same table may be accessed from many different places in the program. It doesn't stop there though. Your database administrator (that might mean you if you're a dual role kind of person) may be altering data occasionally to deal with problems that arise. In more complex scenarios, you can actually run into situations where literally hundreds of different access paths exist for altering just one piece of data, let alone your entire database.

Moving the responsibility for data integrity into the database itself has been revolutionary to database management. There are still many different things that can go wrong when you are attempting to insert data into your database, but your database is now *proactive* rather than *reactive* to problems. Many problems with what programs allow into the database are now caught much earlier in the development process because, although the client program allowed the data through, the database knows to reject it. How does it do it? Primarily with constraints (data types and triggers are among the other worker bees of data integrity). Well let's take a look.

In this chapter, we'll be looking at the three different types of constraints at a high level:

- ❑ Entity constraints
- ❑ Domain constraints
- ❑ Referential integrity constraints

At a more specific level, we'll be looking at the specific methods of implementing each of these types of constraints, including:

- ❑ PRIMARY KEY constraints
- ❑ FOREIGN KEY constraints
- ❑ UNIQUE constraints (also known as alternate keys)
- ❑ CHECK constraints
- ❑ DEFAULT constraints
- ❑ Rules
- ❑ Defaults (similar to, yet different from, DEFAULT constraints)

> **New with SQL Server 2000 is support for two of the most commonly requested forms of referential integrity actions – cascade updates and cascade deletes. These have, for the longest time, been one of the most blatant feature omissions in SQL Server, but it has been taken care of in this release. We'll look at cascading actions in detail when we look at FOREIGN KEY constraints.**

We'll also take a very cursory look at triggers and stored procedures (there will be much more on these later) as a method of implementing data integrity rules.

Types of Constraints

There are a number of different ways to implement constraints, but each of them falls into one of three categories – entity, domain, or referential integrity constraints:

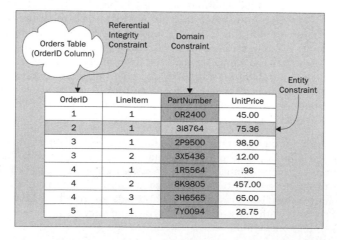

Domain Constraints

Domain constraints deal with one or more columns. What we're talking about here is ensuring that a particular column or set of columns meets particular criteria. When you insert or update a row, the constraint is applied without respect to any other row in the table – it's the column's data you're interested in.

For example, if we want to confine the `UnitPrice` column only to values that are greater than or equal to zero, that would be a domain constraint. While any row that had a `UnitPrice` that didn't meet the constraint would be rejected, we're actually enforcing integrity to make sure that entire column (no matter how many rows) meets the constraint. The domain is the column, and our constraint is a domain constraint.

We'll see this kind of constraint in dealing with `CHECK` constraints, rules, defaults, and `DEFAULT` constraints.

Entity Constraints

Entity constraints are all about individual rows. This form of constraint doesn't really care about a column as a whole, it's interested in a particular row, and would best be exemplified by a constraint that requires every row to have a unique value for a column or combination of problems.

"What," you say, "a unique column? Doesn't that mean it's a domain constraint?" No, it doesn't. We're not saying that a column has to meet any particular format, or that the value has to be greater or less than anything. What we're saying is that for *this* row, the same value can't already exist in some other row.

We'll see this kind of constraint in dealing with `PRIMARY KEY` and `UNIQUE` constraints.

Referential Integrity Constraints

Referential integrity constraints are created when a value in one column must match the value in another column – in either the same table or, far more typically, a different table.

Let's say that we are taking orders for a product, and that we accept credit cards. In order to be paid by the credit card company, we need to have some form of merchant agreement with that company. We don't want our employees to take credit cards from companies from which we're not going to be paid back. That's where referential integrity comes in – it allows us to build what we would call a **domain table**. A domain table is a table whose sole purpose in life is to provide a limited list of acceptable values. In our case, we might build a table that looks something like this:

CreditCardID	CreditCard
1	VISA
2	MasterCard
3	Discover Card
4	American Express

We can then build one or more tables that *reference* the `CreditCardID` column of our domain table. With referential integrity, any table (such as our `Orders` table) that is defined as referencing our `CreditCard` table will have to have a column that matches up to the `CreditCardID` column of our `CreditCard` table. For each row that we insert into the referencing table, it will have to have a value that is in our domain list (it will have to have a corresponding row in the `CreditCard` table).

We'll see more of this as we learn about `FOREIGN KEY` constraints later in this chapter.

Constraint Naming

Before we get down to the nitty-gritty of constraints, we'll digress for a moment and address the issue of naming constraints.

> **For each of the different types of constraints that we will be dealing with in this chapter, you can elect not to supply a name – that is, you can have SQL Server provide a name for you. Resist the temptation to do this. You'll quickly find that when SQL Server creates its own name it isn't particularly useful.**

An example of a useful generated name might be something like `PK__Employees__145C0A3F`. This is a SQL Server generated name for a primary key on the `Employees` table of the `Accounting` database, which we will create later in the chapter – the `PK` is for primary key (which is the major thing that makes it useful), the `Employees` is for the `Employees` table that it is on, and the rest is a randomly generated value to ensure uniqueness. You only get this type of naming if you create the primary key through script. If you created this table through Enterprise Manager, it would have a name of `PK_Employees`.

That one isn't too bad, but you get less help on other constraints, for example, a `CHECK` constraint used later in the chapter might generate something like `CK__Customers__22AA2996`. From this, we know that it's a `CHECK` constraint, but we know nothing of what the nature of the `CHECK` is.

Since we can have multiple `CHECK` constraints on a table, you could wind up with all these as names of constraints on the same table:

```
CK__Customers__22AA2996
CK__Customers__25869641
CK__Customers__267ABA7A
```

Needless to say, if you needed to edit one of these constraints, it would be a pain to figure out which was which.

Personally, I either use a combination of type of constraint together with a phrase to indicate what it does or the name(s) of the column(s) it affects. For example, I might use `CKPriceExceedsCost` if I have a constraint to ensure that my users can't sell a product at a loss, or perhaps something as simple as `CKCustomerPhoneNo` on a column that ensures that phone numbers are formatted properly.

As with the naming of anything that we'll use in this book, how exactly you name things is really not all that important. What is important is that you:

- ❑ Be consistent
- ❑ Make it something that everyone can understand
- ❑ Keep it as short as you can while still meeting the above rules
- ❑ Did I mention to be consistent?

Key Constraints

There are four different types of common keys that you may hear about in your database endeavors. These are primary keys, foreign keys, alternate keys, and inversion keys. For this chapter, we'll only take a look at the first three of these, as they provide constraints on the database.

> *An inversion key is basically just any index (we cover indexes in Chapter 9) that does not apply some form of constraint to the table (primary key, foreign key, unique). Inversion keys, rather than enforcing data integrity, are merely an alternative way of sorting the data.*

Keys are one of the cornerstone concepts of database design and management, so fasten your seatbelt and hold on tight – this will be one of the most important concepts you'll read about in this book, and will become absolutely critical as we move on to normalization in our next chapter.

PRIMARY KEY Constraints

Before we define what a primary key actually is, let's deviate slightly into a brief discussion of relational databases. Relational databases are constructed on the idea of being able to "relate" data. Therefore, it becomes critical in relational databases for most tables (there are exceptions, but they are very rare) to have a unique identifier for each row. A unique identifier allows you to accurately reference a record from another table in the database – so forming a relation between those two tables.

> *This is a wildly different concept from what we had with our old mainframe environment or the ISAM databases (dBase, FoxPro, Clipper, etc.) of the 80s and early 90s. In those environments, we dealt with one record at a time – we would generally open the entire table, and go one record at a time until we found what we were looking for.*

Primary keys are the unique identifiers for each row. They must contain unique values (and hence cannot be NULL). Due to their importance in relational databases, primary keys are the most fundamental of all keys and constraints.

> **Don't confuse the primary key, which uniquely identifies each row in a table, with a GUID, which is a more generic tool typically used to identify something (more than just rows) across all space and time. While a GUID can certainly be used as a primary key, they incur some overhead, and are usually not called for when we're only dealing with the contents of a table. Indeed, the only common place that a GUID becomes particularly useful in a database environment is as a primary key when dealing with replicated or other distributed data. We'll see more about this in the *Replication* chapter.**

A table can have a maximum of one primary key. As I mentioned earlier, it is rare to have a table on which you don't want a primary key.

> *When I say "rare" here – I mean very rare. A table that doesn't have a primary key severely violates the concept of relational data – it means that you can't guarantee that you can relate to a specific record. The data in your table no longer has anything that gives it distinction.*

Situations where you can have multiple rows that are logically identical are actually not that uncommon, but that doesn't mean that you don't want a primary key. In these instances, you'll want to take a look at fabricating some sort of key – this approach has most often been implemented using an identity column, though using a GUID now makes more sense in some situations.

A primary key ensures uniqueness within the columns declared as being part of that primary key, and that unique value serves as an identifier for each row in that table. How do we create a primary key? Actually, there are two ways. You can create the primary key either in your CREATE TABLE command or with an ALTER TABLE command.

Before version 7.0, there was yet another method for establishing a primary key. This method used a stored procedure called sp_primarykey. Microsoft warned for a very long time that sp_primarykey (and a similar option for foreign keys) would go away – and it did in version 7.0. I only mention it here in case you see it in legacy code.

Creating the Primary Key at Table Creation

Let's review one of our CREATE TABLE statements from the last chapter:

```
CREATE TABLE Customers
(
    CustomerNo      int   IDENTITY    NOT NULL,
    CustomerName    varchar(30)       NOT NULL,
    Address1        varchar(30)       NOT NULL,
    Address2        varchar(30)       NOT NULL,
    City            varchar(20)       NOT NULL,
    State           char(2)           NOT NULL,
    Zip             varchar(10)       NOT NULL,
    Contact         varchar(25)       NOT NULL,
    Phone           char(15)          NOT NULL,
    FedIDNo         varchar(9)        NOT NULL,
    DateInSystem    smalldatetime     NOT NULL
)
```

This CREATE statement should seem old hat by now, but it's missing a very important piece – our PRIMARY KEY constraint. We want to identify CustomerNo as our primary key. Why CustomerNo? Well, we'll look into what makes a good primary key in the next chapter, but for now, just think about it a bit – do we want two customers to have the same CustomerNo? Definitely not – it makes perfect sense for a CustomerNo to be used as an identifier for a customer. Indeed, such a system has been used for years, so there's really no sense in re-inventing the wheel here.

To alter our CREATE TABLE statement to include a PRIMARY KEY constraint, we just add in the constraint information right after the column(s) that we want to be part of our primary key. In this case, we would use:

```
CREATE TABLE Customers
(
    CustomerNo      int   IDENTITY    NOT NULL
        PRIMARY KEY,
    CustomerName    varchar(30)       NOT NULL,
    Address1        varchar(30)       NOT NULL,
    Address2        varchar(30)       NOT NULL,
```

```
    City              varchar(20)       NOT NULL,
    State             char(2)           NOT NULL,
    Zip               varchar(10)       NOT NULL,
    Contact           varchar(25)       NOT NULL,
    Phone             char(15)          NOT NULL,
    FedIDNo           varchar(9)        NOT NULL,
    DateInSystem      smalldatetime     NOT NULL
)
```

Note that, if you want to try out this code, you may need to first DROP the existing table by issuing a DROP TABLE Customers command. Notice that we altered one line (all we did was remove the comma) and added some code on a second line for that column. In a word, it was easy! Again, we just added one simple keyword (OK, so it's two words, but they operate as one) and we now have ourselves a primary key.

Creating a Primary Key on an Existing Table

Now, what if we already have a table and we want to set the primary key? That's also easy – we'll do that for our Employees table:

```
USE Accounting

ALTER TABLE Employees
    ADD CONSTRAINT PK_EmployeeID
    PRIMARY KEY (EmployeeID)
```

Our ALTER command tells SQL Server:

❑   That we are adding something to the table (we could also be dropping something from the table if we so chose)

❑   What it is that we're adding (a constraint)

❑   What we want to name the constraint (to allow us to address the constraint directly later)

❑   The type of constraint (PRIMARY KEY)

❑   The column(s) that the constraint applies to

FOREIGN KEY Constraints

Foreign keys are both a method of ensuring data integrity and a manifestation of the relationships between tables. When you add a foreign key to a table, you are creating a dependency between the table for which you define the foreign key (the **referencing** table) and the table your foreign key references (the **referenced** table). After adding a foreign key, any record you insert into the referencing table must either have a matching record in the referenced column(s) of the referenced table, or the value of the foreign key column(s) must be set to NULL. This can be a little confusing, so let's do it by example.

Let's create another table in our Accounting database called Orders. One thing you'll notice in this CREATE script is that we're going to use both a primary key and a foreign key. A primary key, as we will see as we continue through the design, is a critical part of a table. Our foreign key is added to the script in almost exactly the same way as our primary key was, except that we must say what we are referencing. The syntax goes on the column or columns that we are placing our FOREIGN KEY constraint on, and looks something like this:

```
<column name> <data type> <nullability>
FOREIGN KEY REFERENCES <table name>(<column name>)
    [ON DELETE {CASCADE|NO ACTION}]
    [ON UPDATE {CASCADE|NO ACTION}]
```

For the moment, we're going to ignore the ON clause. That leaves us, for our Orders table, with a script that looks something like this:

```
USE Accounting

CREATE TABLE Orders
(
    OrderID       int      IDENTITY     NOT NULL
        PRIMARY KEY,
    CustomerNo    int                   NOT NULL
        FOREIGN KEY REFERENCES Customers(CustomerNo),
    OrderDate     smalldatetime    NOT NULL,
    EmployeeID    int              NOT NULL
)
```

Note that the actual column being referenced must have either a PRIMARY KEY or a UNIQUE constraint defined on it (we'll discuss UNIQUE constraints later in the chapter).

It's also worth noting that primary and foreign keys can exist on the same column. You can see an example of this in the Northwind database with the Order Details table. The primary key is composed of both the OrderID and ProductID columns – both of these are also foreign keys, and reference the Orders and Products tables respectively. We'll actually create a table later in the chapter that has a column that is both a primary key and a foreign key.

Once you have successfully run the above code, run sp_help and you should see your new constraint reported under the constraints section of the sp_help information. If you want to get even more to the point, you can run sp_helpconstraint – the syntax is easy:

EXEC sp_helpconstraint <table name>

Run sp_helpconstraint on our new Orders table, and you'll get information back giving you the names, criteria, and status for all the constraints on the table. At this point, our Orders table has one FOREIGN KEY constraint and one PRIMARY KEY constraint.

> **When you run sp_helpconstraint on this table, the word (clustered) will appear right after the reporting of the PRIMARY KEY – this just means it has a clustered index. We will explore the meaning of this farther in Chapter 9.**

Unlike primary keys, we are not limited to just one foreign key on a table. We can have between 0 and 253 foreign keys in each table. The only limitation is that a given column can only reference one foreign key. However, you can have more than one column participate in a single foreign key. A given column that is the target of a reference by a foreign key can also be referenced by many tables.

Adding a Foreign Key to an Existing Table

Just like with primary keys, or any constraint for that matter, we have situations where we want to add our foreign key to a table that already exists. This process is similar to creating a primary key.

Let's add another foreign key to our Orders table to restrict the EmployeeID field (which is intended to have the ID of the employee who entered the order) to valid employees as defined in the Employees table. To do this, we need to be able to uniquely identify a target record in the referenced table. As I've already mentioned, you can do this by referencing either a primary key or a column with a UNIQUE constraint. In this case, we'll make use of the existing primary key that we placed on the Employees table earlier in the chapter:

```
ALTER TABLE Orders
    ADD CONSTRAINT FK_EmployeeCreatesOrder
    FOREIGN KEY (EmployeeID) REFERENCES Employees(EmployeeID)
```

Now execute sp_helpconstraint again against the Orders table and you'll see that our new constraint has been added.

> *Note that while we've added two foreign keys, there is still a line down at the bottom of our sp_helpconstraint results (or under the messages tab if you have Results in Grid selected) that says No foreign keys reference this table – this is telling us that, while we do have foreign keys in this table that reference other tables, there are no other tables out there that reference this table. If you want to see the difference, just run sp_helpconstraint on the Customers or Employees tables at this point and you'll see that each of these tables is now referenced by our new Orders table.*

Making a Table be Self-Referencing

What if the column you want to refer to isn't in another table, but is actually right within the table in which you are building the reference? Can a table be both the referencing and the referenced table? You bet! Indeed, while this is far from the most common of situations, it is actually used with regularity.

> *Before we actually create this self-referencing constraint that references a required (non-nullable) field that's based on an identity column, it's rather critical that we get at least one row in the table prior to the foreign key being added. Why? Well, the problem stems from the fact that the identity value is chosen and filled in after the foreign key has already been checked and enforced – that means that you don't have a value yet for that first row to reference when the check happens. The only other option here is to go ahead and create the foreign key, but then disable it when adding the first row. We'll learn about disabling constraints a little later in this chapter.*

OK – since this is a table that's referencing a column based on an identity column, we need to get a primer row into the table before we add our constraint:

```
INSERT INTO Employees
    (
    FirstName,
    LastName,
    Title,
    SSN,
    Salary,
```

```
            PriorSalary,
            HireDate,
            ManagerEmpID,
            Department
            )
VALUES
            (
            'Billy Bob',
            'Boson',
            'Head Cook & Bottle Washer',
            '123-45-6789',
            100000,
            80000,
            '1990-01-01',
            1,
            'Cooking and Bottling'
            )
```

Now that we have a primer row in, we can add in our foreign key. In an ALTER situation, this works just the same as any other foreign key definition. We can now try this out:

```
ALTER TABLE Employees
    ADD CONSTRAINT FK_EmployeeHasManager
    FOREIGN KEY (ManagerEmpID) REFERENCES Employees(EmployeeID)
```

There is one difference with a CREATE statement. The only trick to it is that you can (but you don't have to) leave out the FOREIGN KEY phrasing and just use the REFERENCES clause. We already have our Employees table set up at this point, but if we were creating it from scratch, here would be the script (pay particular attention to the foreign key on the ManagerEmpID column):

```
CREATE TABLE Employees (
    EmployeeID          int   IDENTITY    NOT NULL
        PRIMARY KEY,
    FirstName           varchar (25)      NOT NULL,
    MiddleInitial       char (1)          NULL,
    LastName            varchar (25)      NOT NULL,
    Title               varchar (25)      NOT NULL,
    SSN                 varchar (11)      NOT NULL,
    Salary              money             NOT NULL,
    PriorSalary         money             NOT NULL,
    LastRaise AS Salary - PriorSalary,
    HireDate            smalldatetime     NOT NULL,
    TerminationDate     smalldatetime     NULL,
    ManagerEmpID        int               NOT NULL
        REFERENCES Employees(EmployeeID),
    Department          varchar (25)      NOT NULL
)
```

It's worth noting that, if you try to DROP the Employees table at this point (to run the second example above), you're going to get an error. Why? Well, when we established the reference in our Orders table to the Employees table, the two tables became "schema bound" – that is, the Employees table now knows that it has what is called a dependency on it. SQL Server will not let you drop a table that is referenced by another table. You have to drop the foreign key in the Orders table before SQL Server will allow you to delete the Employees table (or the Customers table for that matter).

> In addition, doing the self-referencing foreign key in the constraint doesn't allow us to get our primer row in, so it's important that you only do it this way when the column the foreign key constraint is placed on allows NULLs – that way you can have the first row have a NULL in that column and avoid the need for a primer row.

Cascading Updates and Deletes

Those readers who are coming to SQL Server from some other database platform such as Oracle, or even Access, may be familiar with the concept of cascading updates and deletes. If you're new to larger RDBMS systems or are coming from a previous version of SQL Server, then cascading may be a new concept to you (CASCADE actions are new with SQL Server 2000).

Before we get too far into this, it's important to realize that foreign keys are bi-directional, that is, they have effects not only in restricting the child table to values that exist in the parent, but they also check for child rows whenever we do something to the parent (by doing so, they avoid orphans). The default behavior is for SQL Server to "restrict" the parent row from being deleted if any child rows exist. Sometimes, however, we would rather automatically delete any dependent records than prevent the deletion of the referenced record. The same notion applies to updates to records where we would like the dependent record to automatically reference to the newly updated record.

The process of making such automatic deletions and updates is known as **cascading**. This process, especially for deletes, can actually run through several layers of dependencies (where one record depends on another, which depends on another, and so on). Amazingly, this process was not inherently supported in SQL Server's declarative referential integrity (even Access had this!) prior to SQL Server 2000. Fortunately, cascading is here now, and we should never have to look back again (other than for legacy code, of course).

Technically speaking, there was a way in SQL Server 7.0 and prior to achieve a cascading action – you needed to use triggers for referential integrity instead of "declarative" referential integrity (foreign keys). This was lame – pure and simple. Triggers, which we will look at in Chapter 15, are reactive rather than proactive in nature, and, as such, did not perform as well. In addition, there were some instances in which triggers would not be fired (most notably, bulk copies and bulk inserts), and, therefore, you would not have your referential integrity enforced.

So, how do we implement cascading actions in SQL Server? All we need is a modification to the syntax we use when declaring our foreign key – we just add the ON clause that we skipped at the beginning of this section.

Let's check this out by adding a new table to our Accounting database. We'll make this a table to store the individual line items in an order, and we'll call it OrderDetails:

```
CREATE TABLE OrderDetails
(
    OrderID        int            NOT NULL,
    PartNo         varchar(10)    NOT NULL,
    Description    varchar(25)    NOT NULL,
    UnitPrice      money          NOT NULL,
    Qty            int            NOT NULL,
    CONSTRAINT     PKOrderDetails
```

```
        PRIMARY KEY    (OrderID, PartNo),
    CONSTRAINT     FKOrderContainsDetails
    FOREIGN KEY    (OrderID)
        REFERENCES Orders(OrderID)
        ON UPDATE  NO ACTION
        ON DELETE  CASCADE
)
```

This time we have a whole lot going on, so let's take it apart piece by piece.

> Before we get too far into looking at the foreign key aspects of this – notice something about how the primary key was done here. Instead of placing the declaration immediately after the key, I decided to declare it as a separate constraint item. This helps facilitate both the multi-column primary key (which therefore could not be declared as a column constraint) and the clarity of the overall **CREATE TABLE** statement. Likewise, I could have declared the foreign key either immediately following the column or, as I did here, as a separate constraint item. I'll touch on this a little bit latter in the chapter.

First, notice that our foreign key is also part of our primary key – this is not at all uncommon in child tables, and is actually almost always the case for associate tables (more on this next chapter). Just remember that each constraint stands alone – you add, change, or delete each of them independently.

Next, look at our foreign key declaration:

```
    FOREIGN KEY    (OrderID)
    REFERENCES     Orders(OrderID)
```

We've declared our OrderID as being dependent on a "foreign" column. In this case, it's for a column (also called OrderID) in a separate table (Orders), but, as we saw earlier in the chapter, it could just as easily have been in the same table if that's what our need was.

> There is something of a gotcha when creating foreign keys that reference the same table the foreign key is being defined on. foreign keys of this nature are not allowed to have declarative **CASCADE** actions. The reason for this restriction is to avoid cyclical updates or deletes – that is, situations where the first update causes another, which in turn tries to update the first. The result could be a never ending loop.

Now, to get to the heart of our cascading issue though, we need to look at our ON clauses:

```
    ON UPDATE    NO ACTION
    ON DELETE    CASCADE
```

We've defined two different **referential integrity actions**. As you might guess, a referential integrity action is what you want to have happen whenever the referential integrity rule you've defined is invoked. For situations where the parent record (in the Orders table) is updated, we've said that we would not like that update to be cascaded to our child table (OrderDetails). For illustration purposes, however, I've chosen a CASCADE for deletes.

Note that NO ACTION is the default, and so specifying this in our code is optional.

Let's try an insert into our `OrderDetails` table:

```
INSERT INTO OrderDetails
VALUES
    (1, '4X4525', 'This is a part', 25.00, 2)
```

Unless you've been playing around with your data some, this generates an error:

Server: Msg 547, Level 16, State 1, Line 1
INSERT statement conflicted with COLUMN FOREIGN KEY constraint 'FKOrderContainsDetails'.
The conflict occurred in database 'Accounting', table 'Orders', column 'OrderID'.
The statement has been terminated.

Why? Well, we haven't inserted anything into our `Orders` table yet, so how can we refer to a record in the `Orders` table if there isn't anything there?

> *This is going to expose you to one of the hassles of relational database work – dependency chains. A dependency chain is a situation where you have something that is, in turn, dependent on something else, which may yet be dependent on something else, and so on... There's really nothing you can do about this – it's just something that comes along with database work. You have to start at the top of the chain and work your way down to what you need inserted. Fortunately, the records you need are often already there save for one or two dependency levels.*

OK, so, in order to get our row into our `OrderDetails` table, we must also have a record already in the `Orders` table. Unfortunately, getting a row into the `Orders` table requires that we have one in the `Customers` table (remember that foreign key we built on `Orders`?). So, let's take care of it a step at a time:

```
INSERT INTO Customers  -- Our Customer.
                       -- Remember that CustomerNo is
                       -- an Identity column
VALUES
    ('Billy Bob''s Shoes',
    '123 Main St.',
    ' ',
    'Vancouver',
    'WA',
    '98685',
    'Billy Bob',
    '(360) 555-1234',
    '931234567',
    GETDATE()
    )
```

Now we have a customer, so let's select the record back out just to be sure:

Customer No	1
Customer Name	Billy Bob's Shoes
Address 1	123 Main Street
Address 2	
City	Vancouver
State	WA
Zip	98685
Contact	Billy Bob
Phone	(360) 555-1234
FedIDNo	931234567
DateInSystem	2000-07-1021:17:00

So – we have a `CustomerID` of 1 (your number may be different depending on what experimentation you've done). We'll take that number and use it in our next INSERT (into `Orders` finally). Let's insert an order for `CustomerID` 1:

```
INSERT INTO Orders
    (CustomerNo, OrderDate, EmployeeID)
VALUES
    (1, GETDATE(), 1)
```

This time, things should work fine.

> It's worth noting that the reason that we don't still get one more error here is that we already inserted that primer row in the **Employees** table; otherwise, we would have needed to get a row into that table before SQL Server would have allowed the insert into **Orders** (remember that **Employees'** foreign key?).

At this point, we're ready for our insert into the `OrderDetails` table. Just to help with a CASCADE example we're going to be doing in the moment, we're actually going to insert not one, but two rows:

```
INSERT INTO OrderDetails
VALUES
    (1, '4X4525', 'This is a part', 25.00, 2)

INSERT INTO OrderDetails
VALUES
    (1, '0R2400', 'This is another part', 50.00, 2)
```

So, let's verify things by running a SELECT:

```
SELECT OrderID, PartNo FROM OrderDetails
```

This gets us back our expected two rows:

```
OrderID    PartNo
----------------------------
1          0R2400
1          4X4525
```

(2 row(s) affected)

Now that we have our data in all the way, let's look at the effect a CASCADE has on the data. We'll delete a row from the Orders table, and then see what happens in OrderDetails:

```
USE Accounting

-- First, let's look at the rows in both tables
SELECT *
FROM Orders

SELECT *
FROM OrderDetails

-- Now, let's delete the Order record
DELETE Orders
WHERE OrderID = 1

-- Finally, look at both sets of data again
-- and see the CASCADE effect
SELECT *
FROM Orders

SELECT *
FROM OrderDetails
```

This yields us some interesting results:

OrderID	CustomerNo	OrderDate	EmployeeID
1	1	2000-07-13 22:18:00	1

(1 row(s) affected)

OrderID	PartNo	Description	UnitPrice	Qty
1	0R2400	This is another part	50.0000	2
1	4X4525	This is a part	25.0000	2

(2 row(s) affected)

(1 row(s) affected)

```
OrderID  CustomerNo  OrderDate  EmployeeID
------------------------------------------------------------------------

(0 row(s) affected)

OrderID  PartNo  Description  UnitPrice  Qty
-----------------------------------------------------------------

(0 row(s) affected)
```

Notice that, even though we only issued a DELETE against the Orders table, the DELETE also CASCADEd to our matching records in the OrderDetails table. Records in both tables were deleted. If we had defined our table with a CASCADE update and updated a relevant record, then that too would have been propagated to the child table.

> It's worth noting that there is no limit to the depth that a CASCADE action can affect. For example, if we had a ShipmentDetails table that referenced rows in OrderDetails with a CASCADE action, then those too would have been deleted just by our one DELETE in the Orders table.
>
> This is actually one of the danger areas of cascading actions – it's very, very easy to not realize all the different things that one DELETE or UPDATE statement may do in your database. For this and other reasons, I'm not a huge fan of cascading actions – they allow people to get lazy, and that's something that's not usually a good thing when doing something like deleting data! Don't get me wrong, they have their place, and we'll investigate that more in our Advanced Design chapter.

Other Things to Think about with Foreign Keys

There are some other things to think about before we're done with foreign keys. We will be coming back to this subject over and over again throughout the book, but for now, I just want to get in a couple of finer points:

- ❑ What makes values in foreign keys required versus optional
- ❑ How foreign keys are bi-directional

What Makes Values in Foreign Keys Required vs. Optional

By the nature of a foreign key itself, you have two possible choices on what to fill into a column or columns that have a foreign key defined for them:

- ❑ Fill the column in with a value that matches the corresponding column in the referenced table
- ❑ Do not fill in a value at all and leave the value NULL

You can make the foreign key completely required (limit your users to just the first option above) by simply defining the referencing column as NOT NULL. Since a NULL value won't be valid in the column and the foreign key requires any non-NULL value to have a match in the referenced table, you know that every row will have a match in your referenced table. In other words, the reference is required.

Allowing the referencing column to have NULLs will create the same requirement, except that the user will also have the option of supplying no value – even if there is not a match for NULL in the referenced table, the insert will still be allowed.

How Foreign Keys are Bi-Directional

We touched on this some when we discussed CASCADE actions, but when defining foreign keys, I can't stress enough that they effectively place restrictions on *both* tables. Up to this point, we've been talking about things in terms of the referencing table; however, once the foreign key is defined, the referenced table must also live by a rule:

> By default, you cannot delete a record or update the referenced column in a referenced table if that record is referenced from the dependent table. If you want to be able to delete or update such a record, then you need to set up a CASCADE action for the delete and/or update.

Let's illustrate this "You can't delete or update a referenced record" idea.

We just defined a couple of foreign keys for the Orders table. One of those references the EmployeeID columns of the Employees table. Let's say, for instance, that we have an employee with an EmployeeID of 10 who takes many orders for us for a year or two, and then decides to quit and move on to another job. Our tendency would probably be to delete the record in the Employees table for that employee, but that would create a rather large problem – we would get what are called **orphaned** records in the Orders table. Our Orders table would have a large number of records that still have an EmployeeID of 10. If we are allowed to delete EmployeeID 10 from the Employees table, then we will no longer be able to tell which employee entered in all those orders – the value for the EmployeeID column of the Orders table will become worthless!

Now let's take this example one step further. Say now, that the employee did not quit. Instead, for some unknown reason, we wanted to change that employee's ID number. If we made the change (via an UPDATE statement) to the Employees table, but did not make the corresponding update to the Orders table, then we would again have orphaned records – we would have records with a value of 10 in the EmployeeID column of the Orders table with no matching employee.

Now, let's take it one more step further! Imagine that someone comes along and inserts a new record with an EmployeeID of 10 – we now have a number of records in our Orders table that will be related to an employee who didn't take those orders. We would have bad data (yuck!).

Instead of allowing orphaned records, SQL Server, by default, restricts us from deleting or updating records from the referenced table (in this case, the Employees table) unless any dependent records have already been deleted from or updated in the referencing (in this case, Orders) table.

> This is actually not a bad segue into a brief further discussion of when a CASCADE action makes sense and when it doesn't. Data-integrity-wise, we probably wouldn't want to allow the deletion of an employee if there are dependent rows in the Orders table. Not being able to trace back to the employee would degrade the value of our data. On the other hand, it may be perfectly valid (for some very strange reason) to change an employee's ID. We could CASCADE that update to the Orders table with little ill effects. Another moral to the story here is not to think that you need the same CASCADE decision for both UPDATE and DELETE – think about each separately (and carefully).

As you can see, although the foreign key is defined on one table, it actually placed restrictions on both tables (if the foreign key is self-referenced, then both sets of restrictions are on the one table).

UNIQUE Constraints

These are relatively easy. UNIQUE constraints are essentially the younger sibling of primary keys in that they require a unique value throughout the named column (or combination of columns) in the table. You will often hear UNIQUE constraints referred to as **alternate keys**. The major differences are that they are not considered to be *the* unique identifier of a record in that table (even though you could effectively use it that way) and that you *can* have more than one UNIQUE constraint (remember that you can only have one primary key per table).

Once you establish a UNIQUE constraint, every value in the named columns must be unique. If you go to update or insert a row with a value that already exists in a column with a unique constraint, SQL Server will raise an error and reject the record.

> Unlike a primary key, a **UNIQUE** constraint does not automatically prevent you from having a **NULL** value. Whether **NULLs** are allowed or not depends on how you set the **NULL** option for that column in the table. Keep in mind though that, if you do allow **NULLs**, you will only be able to insert one of them (although a **NULL** doesn't equal another **NULL**, they are still considered to be duplicate from the perspective of a **UNIQUE** constraint).

Since there is nothing novel about this (we've pretty much already seen it with primary keys), let's get right to the code. Let's create yet another table in our Accounting database – this time, it will be our Shippers table:

```
CREATE TABLE Shippers
(
    ShipperID       int     IDENTITY    NOT NULL
        PRIMARY KEY,
    ShipperName     varchar(30)         NOT NULL,
    Address         varchar(30)         NOT NULL,
    City            varchar(25)         NOT NULL,
    State           char(2)             NOT NULL,
    Zip             varchar(10)         NOT NULL,
    PhoneNo         varchar(14)         NOT NULL
        UNIQUE
)
```

Now run sp_helpconstraint against the Shippers table, and verify that your Shippers table has been created with the proper constraints.

Creating UNIQUE Constraints on Existing Tables

Again, this works pretty much the same as with primary and foreign keys. We will go ahead and create a UNIQUE constraint on our Employees table:

```
ALTER TABLE Employees
    ADD CONSTRAINT AK_EmployeeSSN
    UNIQUE (SSN)
```

A quick run of sp_helpconstraint verifies that our constraint was created as planned, and on what columns the constraint is active.

In case you're wondering, the AK I used in the constraint name here is for Alternate Key – much like we used PK and FK for Primary and Foreign Keys. You will also often see a UQ or just U prefix used for UNIQUE constraint names.

CHECK Constraints

The nice thing about CHECK constraints is that they are not restricted to a particular column. They can be related to a column, but they can also be essentially table-related in that they can check one column against another as long as all the columns are within a single table, and the values are for the same row being updated or inserted. They may also check that any combination of column values meets a criterion.

The constraint is defined using the same rules that you would use in a WHERE clause. Examples of the criteria for a CHECK constraint include:

Goal	SQL
Limit Month column to appropriate numbers	BETWEEN 1 AND 12
Proper SSN formatting	LIKE '[0-9][0-9][0-9]-[0-9][0-9]-[0-9][0-9][0-9][0-9]'
Limit to a specific list of Shippers	IN ('UPS', 'Fed Ex', 'USPS')
Price must be positive	UnitPrice >= 0
Referencing another column in the same row	ShipDate >= OrderDate

This really only scratches the surface and the possibilities are virtually endless. Almost anything you could put in a WHERE clause you can also put in your constraint. What's more, CHECK constraints are very fast performance-wise as compared to the alternatives (rules and triggers).

Still building on our Accounting database, let's add a modification to our Customers table to check for a valid date in our DateInSystem field (you can't have a date in the system that's in the future):

```
ALTER TABLE Customers
   ADD CONSTRAINT CN_CustomerDateInSystem
   CHECK
   (DateInSystem <= GETDATE ())
```

Now try to insert a record that violates the CHECK constraint, you'll get an error:

```
INSERT INTO Customers
   (CustomerName, Address1, Address2, City, State, Zip, Contact,
   Phone, FedIDNo, DateInSystem)
VALUES
   ('Customer1', 'Address1', 'Add2', 'MyCity', 'NY', '55555',
   'No Contact', '553-1212', '930984954', '12-31-2049')
```

Server: Msg 547, Level 16, State 1, Line 1
INSERT statement conflicted with COLUMN CHECK constraint 'CN_CustomerDateInSystem'. The conflict occurred in database 'Accounting', table 'Customers', column 'DateInSystem'.
The statement has been terminated.

Now if we change things to use a DateInSystem that meets the criterion used in the CHECK (anything with today's date or earlier), the INSERT works fine.

DEFAULT Constraints

This will be the first of two different types of data integrity tools that will be called something to do with "default". This is, unfortunately very confusing, but I'll do my best to make it clear (and I think it will become so).

We'll see the other type of default when we look at rules and defaults later in the chapter.

A DEFAULT constraint, like all constraints, becomes an integral part of the table definition. It defines what to do when a new row is inserted that doesn't include data for the column on which you have defined the default constraint. You can either define it as a literal value (say, setting a default salary to zero or "UNKNOWN" for a string column) or as one of several system values such as GETDATE().

The main things to understand about a DEFAULT constraint are that:

❑ Defaults are only used in INSERT statements – they are ignored for UPDATE and DELETE statements

❑ If any value is supplied in the INSERT, then the default is not used

❑ If no value is supplied, the default will always be used

Defaults are only made use of in INSERT statements. I cannot express enough how much this is a confusion point for many SQL Server beginners. Think about it this way – when you are first inserting the record, SQL Server doesn't have any kind of value for your column except what you supplied (if anything) or the default. If neither of these is supplied, then SQL Server will either insert a NULL (essentially amounting to "I don't know"), or, if your column definition says NOT NULL, then SQL Server will reject the record. After that first insert, however, SQL Server already has some value for that column. If you are updating that column, then it has your new value. If the column in question isn't part of an UPDATE statement, then SQL Server just leaves what is already in the column.

If a value was provided for the column, then there is no reason to use the default – the supplied value is used.

If no value is supplied, then the default will always be used. Now this seems simple enough until you think about the circumstance where a NULL value is what you actually wanted to go into that column for a record. If you don't supply a value on a column that has a default defined, then the default will be used. What do you do if you really wanted it to be NULL? Say so – insert NULL as part of your INSERT statement.

> Under the heading of "One more thing," it's worth noting that there is an exception to the rule about an **UPDATE** command not using a default. The exception happens if you explicitly say that you want a default to be used. You do this by using the keyword **DEFAULT** as the value you want the column updated to.

Defining a DEFAULT Constraint in Your CREATE TABLE Statement

At the risk of sounding repetitious, this works pretty much like all the other column constraints we've dealt with thus far. You just add it to the end of the column definition.

To work an example, start by dropping the existing `Shippers` table that we created earlier in the chapter. This time, we'll create a simpler version of that table including a default:

```
CREATE TABLE Shippers
(
    ShipperID       int     IDENTITY    NOT NULL
        PRIMARY KEY,
    ShipperName     varchar(30)         NOT NULL,
    DateInSystem    smalldatetime       NOT NULL
        DEFAULT GETDATE ()
)
```

After you have run your CREATE script, you can again make use of `sp_helpconstraint` to show you what you have done. You can then test out how your default works by inserting a new record:

```
INSERT INTO Shippers
    (ShipperName)
VALUES
    ('United Parcel Service')
```

Then run a SELECT statement on your `Shippers` table:

```
SELECT * FROM Shippers
```

The default value has been generated for the `DateInSystem` column since we didn't supply a value ourselves:

ShipperID	ShipperName	DateInSystem
1	United Parcel Service	2000-07-13 23:26:00

(1 row(s) affected)

Adding a DEFAULT Constraint to an Existing Table

While this one is still pretty much more of the same, there is a slight twist. We make use of our ALTER statement and ADD the constraint as before, but we add a FOR operator to tell SQL Server what column is the target for the DEFAULT:

```
ALTER TABLE Customers
    ADD CONSTRAINT CN_CustomerDefaultDateInSystem
        DEFAULT GETDATE() FOR DateInSystem
```

And an extra example:

```
ALTER TABLE Customers
   ADD CONSTRAINT CN_CustomerAddress
      DEFAULT 'UNKNOWN' FOR Address1
```

As with all constraints except for a PRIMARY KEY, we are able to add more than one per table.

> You can mix and match any and all of these constraints as you choose – just be careful not to create constraints that have mutually exclusive conditions. For example, don't have one constraint that says that col1 > col2 and another one that says that col2 > col1. SQL Server will let you do this, and you wouldn't see the issues with it until run time.

Disabling Constraints

Sometimes we want to eliminate the constraint checking, either just for a time or permanently. It probably doesn't take much thought to realize that SQL Server must give us some way of deleting constraints, but SQL Server also allows us to just deactivate a FOREIGN KEY or CHECK constraint while otherwise leaving it intact.

The concept of turning off a data integrity rule might seem rather ludicrous at first. I mean, why would you want to turn off the thing that makes sure you don't have bad data? The usual reason is the situation where you already have bad data. This data usually falls into two categories:

❑ Data that's already in your database when you create the constraint

❑ Data that you want to add after the constraint is already built

> You cannot disable PRIMARY KEY or UNIQUE constraints.

Ignoring Bad Data when You Create the Constraint

All this syntax has been just fine for the circumstances where you create the constraint at the same time as you create the table. Quite often however, data rules are established after the fact. Let's say, for instance, that you missed something when you were designing your database, and you now have some records in an Invoicing table that show a negative invoice amount. You might want to add a rule that won't let any more negative invoice amounts into the database, but at the same time, you want to preserve the existing records in their original state.

To add a constraint, but have it not apply to existing data, you make use of the WITH NOCHECK option when you perform the ALTER TABLE statement that adds your constraint. As always, let's look at an example.

The Customers table we created in the Accounting database has a field called Phone. The Phone field was created with a data type of char because we expected all of the phone numbers to be of the same length. We also set it with a length of 15 in order to ensure that we have enough room for all the formatting characters. However, we have not done anything to make sure that the records inserted into the database do indeed match the formatting criteria that we expect. To test this out, we'll insert a record in a format that is not what we're expecting, but might be a very honest mistake in terms of how someone might enter a number:

```
INSERT INTO Customers
    (CustomerName,
    Address1,
    Address2,
    City,
    State,
    Zip,
    Contact,
    Phone,
    FedIDNo,
    DateInSystem)
VALUES
    ('MyCust',
    '123 Anywhere',
    '',
    'Reno',
    'NV',
    80808,
    'Joe Bob',
    '555-1212',
    '931234567',
    GETDATE ())
```

Now let's add a constraint to control the formatting of the Phone field:

```
ALTER TABLE Customers
    ADD CONSTRAINT CN_CustomerPhoneNo
    CHECK
    (Phone LIKE '([0-9][0-9][0-9]) [0-9][0-9][0-9]-[0-9][0-9][0-9][0-9]')
```

When we run this, we have a problem:

Server: Msg 547, Level 16, State 1, Line 1
ALTER TABLE statement conflicted with COLUMN CHECK constraint 'CN_CustomerPhoneNo'. The conflict occurred in database 'Accounting', table 'Customers', column 'Phone'.

SQL Server will not create the constraint unless the existing data meets the constraint criteria. To get around this long enough to install the constraint, either we need to correct the existing data or we must make use of the WITH NOCHECK option in our ALTER statement. To do this, we just add WITH NOCHECK to the statement as follows:

```
ALTER TABLE Customers
    WITH NOCHECK
    ADD CONSTRAINT CN_CustomerPhoneNo
    CHECK
    (Phone LIKE '([0-9][0-9][0-9]) [0-9][0-9][0-9]-[0-9][0-9][0-9][0-9]')
```

Now if we run our same INSERT statement again (remember it inserted without a problem last time), the constraint works and the data is rejected:

Server: Msg 547, Level 16, State 1, Line 1
INSERT statement conflicted with COLUMN CHECK constraint 'CN_CustomerPhoneNo'. The conflict occurred in database 'Accounting', table 'Customers', column 'Phone'.
The statement has been terminated.

However, if we modify our INSERT statement to adhere to our constraint and then re-execute it, the row will be inserted normally:

```
INSERT INTO Customers
    (CustomerName,
     Address1,
     Address2,
     City,
     State,
     Zip,
     Contact,
     Phone,
     FedIDNo,
     DateInSystem)
VALUES
    ('MyCust',
     '123 Anywhere',
     '',
     'Reno',
     'NV',
     80808,
     'Joe Bob',
     '(800)555-1212',
     '931234567',
     GETDATE ())
```

Try running a SELECT on the Customers table at this point. You'll see data that both does and does not adhere to our CHECK constraint criterion:

```
SELECT CustomerNo, CustomerName, Phone FROM Customers
```

CustomerNo	CustomerName	Phone
1	Billy Bob's Shoes	(360) 555-1234
2	Customer1	553-1212
3	MyCust	555-1212
5	MyCust	(800) 555-1212

(2 row(s) affected)

The old data is retained for backward reference, but any new data is restricted to meeting the new criteria.

Temporarily Disabling an Existing Constraint

All right – so you understand why we need to be able to add new constraints that do not check old data, but why would we want to temporarily disable an existing constraint? Why would we want to let data that we know is bad be added to the database? Actually, the most common reason is basically the same reason for which we make use of the WITH NOCHECK option – old data.

Old data doesn't just come in the form of data that has already been added to your database. It may also be data that you are importing from a legacy database or some other system. Whatever the reason, the same issue still holds – you have some existing data that doesn't match up with the rules, and you need to get it into the table.

Certainly one way to do this would be to drop the constraint, add the desired data, and then add the constraint back using a WITH NOCHECK. But what a pain! Fortunately, we don't need to do that. Instead, we can run an ALTER statement with an option called NOCHECK that turns off the constraint in question. Here's the code that disables the CHECK constraint that we just added in the last section:

```
ALTER TABLE Customers
    NOCHECK
    CONSTRAINT CN_CustomerPhoneNo
```

Now we can run that INSERT statement again – the one we proved wouldn't work if the constraint was active:

```
INSERT INTO Customers
    (CustomerName,
    Address1,
    Address2,
    City,
    State,
    Zip,
    Contact,
    Phone,
    FedIDNo,
    DateInSystem)
VALUES
    ('MyCust',
    '123 Anywhere',
    '',
    'Reno',
    'NV',
    80808,
    'Joe Bob',
    '555-1212',
    '931234567',
    GETDATE())
```

Once again, we are able to INSERT non-conforming data to the table.

By now, the question may have entered your mind asking how do you know whether you have the constraint turned on or not. It would be pretty tedious if you had to create a bogus record to try to insert in order to test whether your constraint is active or not. Like most (but not all) of these kinds of dilemmas, SQL Server provided a procedure to indicate the status of a constraint, and it's a procedure we've already seen, sp_helpconstraint. To execute it against our Customers table is easy:

```
EXEC sp_helpconstraint Customers
```

The results are a little too verbose to fit into the pages of this book, but the second result set this procedure generates includes a column called status_enabled. Whatever this column says the status is can be believed – in this case, it should currently be Disabled.

When we are ready for the constraint to be active again, we simply turn it back on by issuing the same command with a CHECK in the place of the NOCHECK:

```
ALTER TABLE Customers
    CHECK
    CONSTRAINT CN_CustomerPhoneNo
```

If you run the INSERT statement to verify that the constraint is again functional, you will see a familiar error message:

Server: Msg 547, Level 16, State 1, Line 1
INSERT statement conflicted with COLUMN CHECK constraint 'CN_CustomerPhoneNo'. The conflict occurred in database 'Accounting', table 'Customers', column 'Phone'.
The statement has been terminated.

Our other option, of course, is to run sp_helpconstraint again, and check out the status_enabled column. If it shows as Enabled, then our constraint must be functional again.

Rules and Defaults – Cousins of Constraints

Rules and **defaults** have been around much longer than CHECK and DEFAULT constraints have been. They are something of an old SQL Server stand-by, and are definitely not without their advantages.

That being said, I'm going to digress from explaining them long enough to recommend that you look them over for backward compatibility and legacy code familiarity only. Rules and defaults are not ANSI compliant (bringing about portability issues), and they do not perform as well as constraints do. As if that's not enough, they are described in the Books Online as "a backward compatibility feature" – not an encouraging thing if you're asking yourself whether this feature is going to continue to be supported in the future. I wouldn't go so far as to suggest that you start sifting through and replacing any old code that you may already have in place, but you should use constraints for any new code you generate.

The primary thing that sets rules and defaults apart from constraints is in their very nature; constraints are features of a table – they have no existence on their own – while rules and defaults are actual objects in and of themselves. Whereas a constraint is defined in the table definition, rules and defaults are defined independently and are then "bound" to the table after the fact.

The independent object nature of rules and defaults gives them the ability to be reused without being redefined. Indeed, rules and defaults are not limited to being bound to just tables; they can also be bound to data types – vastly improving your ability to make highly functional user-defined data types. Let's look at them individually.

Rules

A rule is incredibly similar to a CHECK constraint. The only difference beyond those I've already described is that rules are limited to working with just one column at a time. You can bind the same rule separately to multiple columns in a table, but the rule will work independently with each column, and will not be aware of the other columns at all. A constraint defined as (QtyShipped <= QtyOrdered) would not work for a rule (it refers to more than one column), whereas LIKE ([0-9][0-9][0-9]) would (it applies only to whatever column the rule is bound to).

Let's define a rule so that you can see the differences first hand:

```
CREATE RULE SalaryRule
    AS @Salary > 0
```

Notice that what we are comparing is shown as a variable – whatever the value is of the column being checked, that is the value that will be used in the place of @Salary. Thus, in this example, we're saying that any column our rule is bound to, would have to have a value greater than zero.

If you want to go back and see what your rule looks like, you can make use of sp_helptext:

```
EXEC sp_helptext SalaryRule
```

And it will show you your exact rule definition:

```
Text
-------------------------------------
CREATE RULE SalaryRule
    AS @Salary > 0
```

Now we've got a rule, but it isn't doing anything. If we tried to insert a record in our Employees table, we could still insert any value right now without any restrictions beyond data type.

In order to activate the rule, we need to make use of a special stored procedure called sp_bindrule. We want to bind our SalaryRule to the Salary column of our Employees table. The syntax looks like this:

sp_bindrule <'rule'>, <'object_name'>, [<'futureonly_flag'>]

The rule part is simple enough – that's the rule we want to bind. The object_name is also simple enough – it's the object (column or user-defined data type) to which we want to bind the rule. The only odd parameter is the futureonly_flag and it applies only when the rule is bound to a user-defined data type. The default is for this to be off. However, if you set it to True or pass in a 1, then the binding of the rule will only apply to new columns to which you bind the user-defined data type. Any columns that already have the data type in its old form will continue to use that form.

Since we're just binding this rule to a column, our syntax only requires the first two parameters:

```
sp_bindrule 'SalaryRule', 'Employees.Salary'
```

Take a close look at the object_name parameter – we have both Employees and Salary separated by a "." – why is that? Since the rule isn't associated with any particular table until you bind it, you need to state the table and column to which the rule will be bound. If you do not use the tablename.column naming structure, then SQL Server will assume that what you're naming must be a user-defined data type – if it doesn't find one, you'll get back an error message that can be a bit confusing if you hadn't intended to bind the rule to a data type:

Server: Msg 15105, Level 16, State 1, Procedure sp_bindrule, Line 185
You do not own a data type with that name.

In our case, trying to insert or update an Employees record with a negative value violates the rule and generates an error.

If we want to remove our rule from use with this column, we make use of sp_unbindrule:

```
EXEC sp_unbindrule 'Employees.Salary'
```

The futureonly_flag parameter is again an option, but doesn't apply to this particular example. If you use sp_unbindrule with the futureonly_flag turned on, and it is used against a user-defined data type (rather than a specific column), then the unbinding will only apply to future uses of that data type – existing columns using that data type will still make use of the rule.

Dropping Rules

If you want to completely eliminate a rule from your database, you use the same DROP syntax that we've already become familiar with for tables

```
DROP RULE <rule name>
```

Defaults

Defaults are even more similar to their cousin – a default constraint – than a rule is to a CHECK constraint. Indeed, they work identically, with the only real differences being in the way that they are attached to a table and the default's (the object, not the constraint) support for a user-defined data type.

> **The concept of defaults vs. DEFAULT constraints is wildly difficult for a lot of people to grasp. After all, they have almost the same name. If we refer to "default", then we are referring to either the object-based default (what we're talking about in this section), or as shorthand to the actual default value (that will be supplied if we don't provide an explicit value). If we refer to a "DEFAULT constraint", then we are talking about the non-object based solution – the solution that is an integral part of the table definition.**

The syntax for defining a default works much as it did for a rule:

```
CREATE DEFAULT <default name>
AS <default value>
```

Therefore, to define a default of zero for our Salary:

```
CREATE DEFAULT SalaryDefault
   AS 0
```

Again, a default is worthless without being bound to something. To bind it we make use of sp_bindefault, which is, other than the procedure name, identical syntax to the sp_bindrule procedure:

```
EXEC sp_bindefault 'SalaryDefault', 'Employees.Salary'
```

To unbind the default from the table, we use sp_unbindefault:

```
EXEC sp_unbindefault 'Employees.Salary'
```

Keep in mind that the futureonly_flag also applies to this stored procedure; it is just not used here.

Dropping Defaults

If you want to completely eliminate a default from your database, you use the same DROP syntax that we've already become familiar with for tables and rules:

```
DROP DEFAULT <default name>
```

Determining Which Tables and Data Types Use a Given Rule or Default

If you ever go to delete or alter your rules or defaults, you may first want to take a look at which tables and data types are making use of them. Again, SQL Server comes to the rescue with a system stored procedure. This one is called sp_depends. Its syntax looks like this:

```
EXEC sp_depends <object name>
```

sp_depends provides a listing of all the objects that depend on the object you've requested information about.

> Beginning with version 7.0, using **sp_depends** was no longer a sure bet to tell you about every object that depends on a parent object. Version 7.0 and beyond support something called "deferred name resolution". Basically, deferred name resolution means that you can create objects (primary stored procedures) that depend on another object – even before the second (target of the dependency) object is created. For example, SQL Server will now allow you to create a stored procedure that refers to a table even before the said table is created. In this instance, SQL Server isn't able to list the table as having a dependency on it. Even after you add the table, it will not have any dependency listing if you use **sp_depends**.

Triggers for Data Integrity

We've got a whole chapter coming up on triggers, but any discussion of constraints, rules, and defaults would not be complete without at least a mention of triggers.

One of the most common uses of triggers is to implement data integrity rules. Since we have that chapter coming up, I'm not going to get into it very deep here other than to say that triggers have a very large number of things they can do data-integrity-wise that a constraint or rule could never hope to do. The downside (and you knew there had to be one) is that they incur substantial additional overhead and are, therefore, much (very much) slower in almost any circumstance. They are procedural in nature (which is where they get their power), but they also happen after everything else is done, and should only be used as a relatively last resort.

Choosing What to Use

Wow. Here you are with all these choices, and now how do you figure out which is the right one to use? Some of the constraints are fairly independent (PRIMARY and FOREIGN KEYS, UNIQUE constraints) – you are using either them or nothing. The rest have some level of overlap with each other and it can be rather confusing when making a decision on what to use. You've got some hints from me as we've been going through this chapter about what some of the strengths and weaknesses are of each of the options, but it will probably make a lot more sense if we look at them all together for a bit.

Restriction	Pros	Cons
Constraints	Fast. Can reference other columns. Happens before the command occurs. ANSI Compliant.	Must be re-defined for each table. Can't reference other tables. Can't be bound to data types.
Rules, Defaults	Independent objects. Reusable. Can be bound to data types. Happens before the command occurs.	Slightly slower. Can't reference across columns. Can't reference other tables. Really only meant for backward compatibility.
Triggers	Ultimate flexibility. Can reference other columns and other tables.	Happens after the command occurs. High overhead.

The main time to use rules and defaults is if you are implementing a rather robust logical model, and are making extensive use of user-defined data types. In this instance, rules and defaults can provide a lot of functionality and ease of management without much programmatic overhead – you just need to be aware that they may go away in a future release someday. Probably not soon, but someday.

Triggers should only be used when a constraint is not an option. Like constraints, they are attached to the table, and must be re-defined with every table you create. On the bright side, they can do most things that you are likely to want to do data-integrity-wise. Indeed, they can even take the place of foreign keys if required (I don't recommend; there are still a few referential integrity actions defined by ANSI that SQL Server doesn't support except through triggers). We will cover these in some detail later in the book.

That leaves us with constraints, which should become your data integrity solution of choice. They are fast and not that difficult to create. Their downfall is that they can be limiting (not being able to reference other tables except for a FOREIGN KEY), and they can be tedious to re-define over and over again if you have a common constraint logic.

> **Regardless of what kind of integrity mechanism you're putting in place (keys, triggers, constraints, rules, defaults), the thing to remember can best be summed up in just one word – balance.**
>
> **Every new thing that you add to your database adds additional overhead, so you need to make sure that whatever you're adding honestly has value to it before you stick it in your database. Avoid things like redundant integrity implementations (for example, I can't tell you how often I've come across a database that has both foreign keys defined for referential integrity and triggers to do the same thing). Make sure you know what constraints you have before you put the next one on, and make sure you know exactly what you hope to accomplish with it.**

Summary

The different types of data integrity mechanisms described in this chapter are part of the backbone of a sound database. Perhaps the biggest power of RDBMSs is that the database can now take responsibility for data integrity rather than depending on the application. This means that even ad hoc queries are subject to the data rules, and that multiple applications are all treated equally with regard to data integrity issues.

In the chapters to come, we will look at the tie between some forms of constraints and indexes, along with taking a look at the advanced data integrity rules than can be implemented using triggers. We'll also begin looking at how the choices between these different mechanisms affect our design decisions.

Online discussion at http://p2p.wrox.com

8

Normalization and Other Basic Design Issues

If this book is your first real foray into databases, then I can imagine you as being somewhat perplexed about the how and why of some of the tables we've constructed thus far. With the exception of a chapter or two, this book is being primarily focused on an **online transaction-processing**, or **OLTP**, environment. Don't get me wrong; I'm going to be spending time throughout the book on dealing with the differences between OLTP and its more analysis-oriented cousin **OLAP (Online Analytical Processing)**. My point is that you will, in most of the examples, be seeing a table design that is optimized for the most common kind of database – OLTP. As such, you will typically have a database layout that is, for the most part, **normalized** to what is called the third normal form.

So what is "normal form"? We'll be taking a very solid look at that in this chapter, but, for the moment, let's just say that it means that your data has been broken out into a logical, non-repetitive format that can easily be reassembled into the whole. In addition to normalization (which is the process of putting your database into normal form), we'll also be examining the characteristics of OLTP and OLAP databases. And, as if we didn't have enough between those two topics, we'll also be looking at many examples of how the constraints we've already seen are implemented in the overall solution.

This is probably going to be one of the toughest chapters in the book to grasp because of a paradox in what to learn first. Some of the concepts used in this chapter refer to things we'll be covering later – such as triggers and stored procedures. On the other hand, it is difficult to relate those topics without understanding their role in database design.

I strongly recommend reading this chapter through, and then coming back to it again after you've read several of the subsequent chapters (perhaps through to Chapter 17).

Tables

This is going to seem beyond basic, but let's make a brief review of what exactly a table is. We're obviously not talking about the kind that sits in your kitchen, but, rather, the central object of any database.

A table is a collection of instances of data that have the same general **attributes**. These instances of data are organized into **rows** and **columns** of data. A table should represent a "real-world" collection of data (often referred to as an **entity**), and will have **relationships** with information in other tables. A drawing of the various entities (tables) and relationships (how they work together) is usually referred to as an **Entity-Relationship diagram** – or **ER Diagram**. Sometimes the term "ER Diagram" will even be shortened further down to **ERD**.

By connecting two or more tables through their various relationships, you are able to temporarily create other tables as needed from the combination of the data in both tables (we've already seen this to some degree in Chapters 4 and 5). A collection of related entities are then grouped together into a database.

Keeping Your Data "Normal"

Normalization is something of the cornerstone model of modern OLTP database design. Normalization first originated along with the concept of relational databases. Both came from the work of E.F. Codd (IBM) in 1969. Codd put forth the notion that a database "consists of a series of unordered tables that can be manipulated using non-procedural operations that return tables".

Several things are key about this:

❑ Order must be unimportant

❑ The tables would be able to "relate" to each other in a non-procedural way (indeed, Codd called tables, "relations")

❑ That, by relating these base tables, you would be able to create a virtual table to meet a new need

Normalization was a natural offshoot of the design of a database of "relations".

The concept of normalization has to be one of most over-referenced and yet misunderstood concepts in programming. Everyone thinks they understand it, and many do in at least its academic form. Unfortunately, it also tends to be one of those things that many database designers wear like a cross – it is somehow their symbol that they are "real" database architects. What it really is though is a symbol that they know what the normal forms are – and that's all. Normalization is really just one piece of a larger database design picture. Sometimes you need to normalize your data – then again, sometimes you need to deliberately de-normalize your data. Even within the normalization process, there are often many ways to achieve what is technically a normalized database.

My point in this latest soapbox diatribe is that normalization is a theory, and that's all it is. Once you choose to either implement a normalized strategy or not, what you have is a database – hopefully the best one you could possibly design. Don't get stuck on what the books (including this one) say you're supposed to do – do what's right for the situation that you're in. As the author of this book, all I can do is relate concepts to you – I can't implement them for you, and neither can any other author (at least not with the written word). You need to pick and choose between these concepts in order to achieve the best fit and the best solution. Now, excuse me while I put that soapbox away, and we'll get on to talking about the normal forms and what they purportedly do for us.

Let's start off by saying that there are six normal forms. For those of you who have dealt with databases and normalization some before, that number may come as a surprise. You are very likely to hear that a fully normalized database is one that is normalized to the third normal form – doesn't it then follow that there must be only three normal forms? Perhaps it will make those same people who thought there were only three normal forms feel better that in this book we're only going to be looking to any extent at the three forms you've heard about, as they are the only three that are put to any regular use in the real world. I will, however, take a brief (very brief) skim over the other three forms just for posterity.

We've already looked at how to create a primary key and some of the reasons for using one in our tables – if we want to be able to act on just one row, then we need to be able to uniquely identify that row. The concepts of normalization are highly dependent on issues surrounding the definition of the primary key and what columns are dependent on it. One phrase you might hear frequently in normalization is:

The key, the whole key, and nothing but the key.

This is a super-brief summarization of what normalization is about out to the third normal form. When you can say that all your columns are dependent only on the whole key and nothing more or less, then you are at third normal form.

Let's take a look at the various normal forms, and what each does for us.

Before the Beginning

You actually need to begin by getting a few things in place even before you try to get your data into first normal form. You have to have a thing or two in place before you can even consider the table to be a true entity in the relational database sense of the word:

❑　The table should describe one entity (no trying to short cut and combine things!)

❑　All rows must be unique, and there must be a primary key

❑　The column and row order must not matter

The place to start, then, is by identifying the right entities to have. Some of these will be fairly obvious, others will not. Many of them will be exposed and refined as you go through the normalization process. At the very least, go through and identify all the obvious entities.

> *If you're familiar with object-oriented programming, then you can liken the most logical top-level entities to objects in an object model.*

Let's think about a hyper simple model – our sales model again. To begin with, we're not going to worry about the different variations possible, or even what columns we're going to have – instead, we're just going to worry about identifying the basic entities of our system.

First, think about the most basic process. What we want to do is create an entity for each atomic unit that we want to be able to maintain data on in the process. Our process then, looks like this: a customer calls or comes in and talks to an employee who takes an order.

A first pass on this might have one entity: Orders.

As you become more experienced at normalization, your first pass at something like this is probably going to yield you quite a few more entities right from the beginning. For now though, we'll just take this one and see how the normalization process shows us the others that we need.

Assuming you've got your concepts down of what you want your entities to be, the next place to go is to figure out your beginning columns and, from there, a primary key. Remember that a primary key provides a unique identifier for each row.

We can peruse our list of columns and come up with **key candidates**. Your list of key candidates should include any column that can potentially be used to uniquely identify each row in your entity. There is, otherwise, no hard and fast rule on what column has to be the primary key (this is one of many reasons you'll see such wide variation in how people design databases that are meant to contain the same basic information). In some cases, you will not be able to find even one candidate key, and you will need to make one up (remember `Identity` and `rowguid()` columns?).

We've already created an Orders table in the last chapter, but for example purposes let's take a look at a very common implementation of an Orders table in the old flat file design:

Orders
OrderNo
CustomerNo
CustomerName
CustomerAddress
CustomerCity
CustomerState
CustomerZip
OrderDate
ItemsOrdered
Total

Since this is an Orders table, and logically, an order number is meant to be one to an order, I'm going go with OrderNo as my primary key.

OK, so now we have a basic entity. Nothing about this entity cares about the ordering of columns (tables are, by convention, usually organized as having the primary key as the first column(s), but, technically speaking, it doesn't have to be that way). Nothing in the basic makeup of this table cares about the ordering of the rows. The table, at least superficially, describes just one entity. In short, we're ready to begin our normalization process (actually, we sort of already have).

The First Normal Form

The first normal form (**1NF**) is all about eliminating repeating groups of data and guaranteeing **atomicity** (the data is self-contained and independent). At a high level, it works by creating a primary key (which we already have), then moving any repeating data groups into new tables, creating new keys for those tables, and so on. In addition, we break out any columns that combine data into separate rows for each piece of data.

In the more traditional flat file designs, repeating data was commonplace – as was multiple pieces of information in a column – this was rather problematic in a number of ways:

❑   At that time, disk storage was extremely expensive. Storing data multiple times means wasted space. Data storage has become substantially less expensive, so this isn't as big an issue as it once was.

❑   Repetitive data means more data to be moved, and larger I/O counts. This means that performance is hindered as large blocks of data must be moved through the data bus and or network. This, even with today's much faster technology, can have a substantial negative impact on performance.

❑   The data between rows of what should have been repeating data often did not agree, creating something of a data paradox and a general lack of data integrity.

❑   If you wanted to query information out of a column that has combined data, then you had to first come up with a way to parse the data in that column (this was extremely slow).

Now, there are a lot of columns in our table, and I probably could have easily tossed in a few more. Still, the nice thing about it is that I could query everything out of one place when I wanted to know about orders.

Just to explore what this means though, let's take a look at what some data in this table might look like. Note that I'm going to cut out a few columns here just to help things fit on a page, but I think you'll still be able to see the point:

Order No	Order Date	Customer No	Customer Name	Customer Address	ItemsOrdered
100	1/1/99	54545	ACME Co	1234 1st St.	1A4536, Flange, 7lbs, $75; 4-OR2400, Injector, .5lbs, $108; 4-OR2403, Injector, .5lbs, $116; 1-4I5436, Head, 63lbs, $750
101	1/1/99	12000	Sneed Corp.	555 Main Ave.	1-3X9567, Pump, 5lbs, $62.50
102	1/1/99	66651	ZZZ & Co.	4242 SW 2nd	7-8G9200; Fan, 3lbs, $84; 1-8G5437, Fan, 3lbs, $15; 1-3H6250, Control, 5lbs, $32
103	1/2/99	54545	ACME Co	1234 1st St.	40-8G9200, Fan, 3lbs, $480; 1-2P5523, Housing, 1lbs, $165; 1-3X9567, Pump, 5lbs, $42

We have a number of issues to deal with in this table if we're going to normalize it. While we have a functional primary key (yes, these existed long before relational systems), we have problems with both of the main areas of the first normal form.

❑ I have repeating groups of data (customer information). I need to break that out into a different table.

❑ The ItemsOrdered column does not contain data that is atomic in nature.

We can start by moving several columns out of the table:

OrderNo (PK)	Order Date	CustomerNo	ItemsOrdered
100	1/1/1999	54545	1A4536, Flange, 7lbs, $75; 4-OR2400, Injector, .5lbs, $108; 4-OR2403, Injector, .5lbs, $116; 1-4I5436, Head, 63lbs, $750
101	1/1/1999	12000	1-3X9567, Pump, 5lbs, $62.50
102	1/1/1999	66651	7-8G9200; Fan, 3lbs, $84; 1-8G5437, Fan, 3lbs, $15; 1-3H6250, Control, 5lbs, $32
103	1/2/1999	54545	40-8G9200, Fan, 3lbs, $480; 1-2P5523, Housing, 1lbs, $165; 1-3X9567, Pump, 5lbs, $42

And putting it into its own table:

CustomerNo (PK)	CustomerName	CustomerAddress
54545	ACME Co	1234 1st St.
12000	Sneed Corp.	555 Main Ave.
66651	ZZZ & Co.	4242 SW 2nd

There are several things to notice about both the old and new tables:

❑ We must have a primary key for our new table to ensure that each row is unique. For our Customers table, there are two candidate keys – CustomerNo and CustomerName. CustomerNo was actually created just to serve this purpose and seems the logical choice – after all, it's entirely conceivable that you could have more than one customer with the same name. (For example, there have to be hundreds of AA Auto Glass companies in the US.)

❑ Although we've moved the data out of the Orders table, we still need to maintain a reference to the data in the new Customers table. This is why you still see the CustomerNo (the primary key) column in the Orders table. Later on, when we build our references, we'll create a foreign key constraint to force all orders to have valid customer numbers.

❑ We were able to eliminate an instance of the information for ACME Co. That's part of the purpose of moving data that appears in repetitive groups – to just store it once. This both saves us space and prevents conflicting values.

❑ We only moved repeating *groups* of data. We still see the same order date several times, but it doesn't really fit into a group – it's just a relatively random piece of data that has no relevance outside of this table.

So, we've dealt with our repeating data, next, we're ready to move onto the second violation of first normal form – atomicity. If you take a look at the ItemsOrdered column, you'll see that there are actually several different pieces of data there:

❑ Anywhere from one to many individual part numbers

❑ Quantity weight information on each of those parts

Part number, weight, and price are each atomic pieces of data if kept to themselves, but combined into one lump grouping you no longer have atomicity.

Believe it or not, things were sometimes really done this way. At first glance, it seemed the easy thing to do – paper invoices often had just one big block area for writing up what the customer wanted, and computer based systems were often just as close to a clone of paper as someone could make it.

We'll go ahead and break things up – and, while we're at it, we'll add in a new piece of information in the form of a unit price. The problem is that, once we break up this information, our primary key no longer uniquely identifies our rows – our rows are still unique, but the primary key is now inadequate.

OrderNo (PK)	OrderDate	CustomerNo	PartNo	Description	Qty	UnitPrice	TotalPrice	Wt
100	1/1/1999	54545	1A4536	Flange	5	15	75	6
100	1/1/1999	54545	OR2400	Injector	4	27	108	.5
100	1/1/1999	54545	OR2403	Injector	4	29	116	.5
100	1/1/1999	54545	4I5436	Head	1	750	750	3
101	1/1/1999	12000	3X9567	Pump	1	62.50	62.50	5
102	1/1/1999	66651	8G9200	Fan	7	12	84	3
102	1/1/1999	66651	8G5437	Fan	1	15	15	3
102	1/1/1999	66651	3H6250	Control	1	32	32	5
103	1/2/1999	54545	8G9200	Fan	40	12	480	3
103	1/2/1999	54545	2P5523	Housing	1	165	165	1
103	1/2/1999	54545	3X9567	Pump	1	42	42	5

For now, we'll address this by adding a line item number to our table so we can, again, uniquely identify our rows:

OrderNo (PK)	LineItem (PK)	OrderDate	CustomerNo	PartNo	Description	Qty	UnitPrice	TotalPrice	Wt
100	1	1/1/1999	54545	1A4536	Flange	5	15	75	6
100	2	1/1/1999	54545	OR2400	Injector	4	27	108	.5
100	3	1/1/1999	54545	OR2403	Injector	4	29	116	.5
100	4	1/1/1999	54545	4I5436	Head	1	750	750	3
101	1	1/1/1999	12000	3X9567	Pump	1	62.50	62.50	5
102	1	1/1/1999	66651	8G9200	Fan	7	12	84	3
102	2	1/1/1999	66651	8G5437	Fan	1	15	15	3
102	3	1/1/1999	66651	3H6250	Control	1	32	32	5
103	1	1/2/1999	54545	8G9200	Fan	40	12	480	3
103	2	1/2/1999	54545	2P5523	Housing	1	165	165	1
103	3	1/2/1999	54545	3X9567	Pump	1	42	42	5

> Rather than create another column as we did here, we also could have taken the
> approach of making PartNo part of our primary key. The fallout from this would have
> been that we could not have had the same part number appear twice in the same
> order. We'll briefly discuss keys based on more than one column – or composite keys –
> in our next chapter.

At this point, we meet our criteria for first normal form. We have no repeating groups of data, and all
columns are atomic. We do have issues with data having to be repeated within a column (because it's
the same for all rows for that primary key), but we'll deal with that shortly.

The Second Normal Form

The next phase in normalization is to go to the second normal form (**2NF**). Second normal form further
reduces the incidence of repeated data (not necessarily groups).

Second normal form has two rules to it:

❑ The table must meet the rules for first normal form (normalization is a building block kind of
process – you can't stack the third block on if you don't have the first two there already)

❑ Each column must depend on the *whole* key

Our example has a problem – actually, it has a couple of them – in this area. Let's look at the first
normal form version of our Orders table again – is every column dependent on the whole key? Are
there any that only need part of the key?

OrderNo (PK)	LineItem (PK)	OrderDate	CustomerNo	PartNo	Description	Qty	UnitPrice	TotalPrice	Wt
100	1	1/1/1999	54545	1A4536	Flange	5	15	75	6
100	2	1/1/1999	54545	OR2400	Injector	4	27	108	.5
100	3	1/1/1999	54545	OR2403	Injector	4	29	116	.5
100	4	1/1/1999	54545	4I5436	Head	1	750	750	3
101	1	1/1/1999	12000	3X9567	Pump	1	62.50	62.50	5
102	1	1/1/1999	66651	8G9200	Fan	7	12	84	3
102	2	1/1/1999	66651	8G5437	Fan	1	15	15	3
102	3	1/1/1999	66651	3H6250	Control	1	32	32	5
103	1	1/2/1999	54545	8G9200	Fan	40	12	480	3
103	2	1/2/1999	54545	2P5523	Housing	1	165	165	1
103	3	1/2/1999	54545	3X9567	Pump	1	42	42	5

The answers are no and yes respectively. There are two columns that only depend on the OrderNo
column – not the LineItem column. The columns in question are OrderDate and CustomerNo; both are
the same for the entire order regardless of how many line items there are. Dealing with these requires
that we introduce yet another table. At this point, we run across the concept of a **header** vs. a **detail**
table for the first time.

Sometimes what is, in practice, one entity still needs to be broken out into two tables and, thus, two entities. The header is something of the parent table of the two tables in the relationship. It contains information that only needs to be stored once while the detail table stores the information that may exist in multiple instances. The header usually keeps the name of the original table, and the detail table usually has a name that starts with the header table name and adds on something to indicate that it is a detail table (for example, OrderDetails). For every one header record, you usually have at least one detail record and may have many, many more. This is one example of a kind of relationship (a one-to-many relationship) that we will look at in the next major section.

So let's take care of this by splitting our table again. We'll actually start with the detail table since it's keeping the bulk of the columns. From this point forward, we'll call this table OrderDetails:

OrderNo (PK)	LineItem (PK)	PartNo	Description	Qty	Unit Price	Total Price	Wt
100	1	1A4536	Flange	5	15	75	6
100	2	OR2400	Injector	4	27	108	.5
100	3	OR2403	Injector	4	29	116	.5
100	4	4I5436	Head	1	750	750	3
101	1	3X9567	Pump	1	62.50	62.50	5
102	1	8G9200	Fan	7	12	84	3
102	2	8G5437	Fan	1	15	15	3
102	3	3H6250	Control	1	32	32	5
103	1	8G9200	Fan	40	12	480	3
103	2	2P5523	Housing	1	165	165	1
103	3	3X9567	Pump	1	42	42	5

Then we move on to what, although you could consider it to be the new table of the two, will serve as the header table and thus keep the Orders name:

OrderNo (PK)	OrderDate	CustomerNo
100	1/1/1999	54545
101	1/1/1999	12000
102	1/1/1999	66651
103	1/2/1999	54545

So, now we have second normal form. All of our columns depend on the entire key. I'm sure you won't be surprised to hear that we still have a problem or two though – we'll deal with them next.

The Third Normal Form

This is the relative end of the line. There are technically levels of normalization beyond this, but none that get much attention outside of academic circles. We'll look at those extremely briefly next, but first we need to finish the business at hand.

I mentioned at the end of our discussion of second normal form that we still had problems – we still haven't reached third normal form (**3NF**). Third normal form deals with the issue of having all the columns in our table not just be dependent on something – but the right thing. Third normal form has just three rules to it:

❑   The table must be in 2NF (I told you this was a building block thing)

❑   No column can have any dependency on any other non-key column

❑   You cannot have derived data

We already know that we're in second normal form, so let's look at the other two rules.

First, do we have any columns that have dependencies other than the primary key? Yes! Actually, there are a couple of columns that are dependent on the PartNo as much as, if not more than, the primary key of this table. Weight and Description are both entirely dependent on the PartNo column – we again need to split into another table.

> *Your first tendency here might be to also lump UnitPrice into this category, and you would be partially right. The Products table that we will create here can and should have a UnitPrice column in it – but it will be of a slightly different nature. Indeed, perhaps it would be better named ListPrice, as it is the cost we have set in general for that product. The difference for the UnitPrice in the OrderDetails table is twofold. First, we may offer discounts that would change the price at time of sale. This means that the price in the OrderDetails record may be different than the planned price that we will keep in the Products table. Second, the price we plan to charge will change over time with factors such as inflation, but changes in future prices will not change what we have charged on our actual orders of the past. In other words, price is one of those odd circumstances where there are really two flavors of it – one dependent on the PartNo, and one dependent on the primary key for the OrderDetails table (in other words OrderID and LineItem).*

First, we need to create a new table (we'll call it Products) to hold our part information. This new table will hold the information that we had in OrderDetails that was more dependent on PartNo than on OrderID or LineItem:

PartNo (PK)	Description	Wt
1A4536	Flange	6
OR2400	Injector	.5
OR2403	Injector	.5
4I5436	Head	3
3X9567	Pump	5
8G9200	Fan	3
8G5437	Fan	3
3H6250	Control	5
8G9200	Fan	3
2P5523	Housing	1
3X9567	Pump	5

We can then chop all but the foreign key out of the OrderDetails table:

OrderNo (PK)	LineItem (PK)	PartNo	Qty	UnitPrice	TotalPrice
100	1	1A4536	5	15	75
100	2	OR2400	4	27	108
100	3	OR2403	4	29	116
100	4	4I5436	1	750	750
101	1	3X9567	1	62.50	62.50
102	1	8G9200	7	12	84
102	2	8G5437	1	15	15
102	3	3H6250	1	32	32
103	1	8G9200	40	12	480
103	2	2P5523	1	165	165
103	3	3X9567	1	42	42

That takes care of problem number 1 (cross-column dependency), but doesn't deal with derived data. We have a column called TotalPrice that contains data that can actually be derived from multiplying Qty by UnitPrice. This is a no-no in normalization.

> Derived data is one of the places that you'll see me "de-normalize" data most often. Why? Speed! A query that reads WHERE TotalPrice > $100 runs faster than one that reads WHERE Qty * UnitPrice > 50.
>
> On the other side of this, however, I started doing a bit more of a hybrid version beginning with SQL Server 7.0. SQL Server added support for "computed" columns (virtual columns that are defined as being computed from the contents of other columns). In SQL Server 2000, Microsoft has taken things even further into my way of thinking and added the ability to index the computed column. The significance of this is that we can now "materialize" the computed data. What does that mean? Well, it means that even SQL Server doesn't have to calculate the computed column on the fly – instead, it calculates it once when the row is stored in the index, and, thereafter, uses the precalculated column. It can be very fast indeed, and we'll examine it further in Chapter 9.

So, to reach third normal form, we just need to drop off the TotalPrice column and compute it when needed.

Other Normal Forms

There are a few other forms out there that are considered, at least by academics, to be part of the normalization model. These include:

- ❑ **Boyce-Codd** (considered to really just be a variation on third normal form): this one tries to address situations where you have multiple overlapping candidate keys. This can only happen if:

    a. All the candidate keys are composite keys (that is, it takes more than one column to make up the key)

    b. There is more than one candidate key

    c. The candidate keys each have at least one column that is in common with another candidate key

    This is typically a situation where any number of solutions works, and almost never gets logically thought of outside the academic community.

- ❑ **Fourth Normal Form**: this one tries to deal with issues surrounding multi-valued dependence. This is the situation where, for an individual row, no column depends on a column other than the primary key and depends on the whole primary key (meeting third normal form). However, there can be rather odd situations where one column in the primary key can depend separately on other columns in the primary key. These are rare, and don't usually cause any real problem. As such, they are largely ignored in the database world, and we will not address them here.

- ❑ **Fifth Normal Form**: deals with non-loss and loss decompositions. Essentially, there are certain situations where you can decompose a relationship such that you cannot logically recompose it into its original form. Again, these are rare, largely academic, and we won't deal with them any further here.

- ❑ **Sixth Normal Form** – or **Domain-Key Normal Form**: this is achieved only when you have eliminated any possibility of **modification anomalies** (so that modifying data in one place propagates the change everywhere needed with no risk of being out of sync with other data in the system). This is virtually impossible in the real world.

This is, of course, just a really quick look at these – and that's deliberate on my part. The main reason you need to know these in the real world is either to impress your friends (or prove to them you're a "know it all") and to not sound like an idiot when some database guru comes to town and starts talking about them.

Relationships

Well, I've always heard from women that men immediately leave the room if you even mention the word "relationship". With that in mind, I hope that I didn't just lose about half my readers.

I am, of course, kidding – but not by as much as you might think. Experts say the key to successful relationships is that you know the role of both parties and that everyone understands the boundaries and rules of the relationship that they are in. I can be talking about database relationships with that statement every bit as much as people relationships.

There are three different kinds of major relationships:

- ❑ One-to-one
- ❑ One-to-many
- ❑ Many-to-many

Each of these has some variations depending on whether one side of the relationship is nullable or not. For example, instead of a one-to-one relationship, you might have a zero or one-to-one relationship.

One-to-One

This is exactly what it says it is. A one-to-one relationship is one where the fact that you have a record in one table means that you have exactly one matching record in another table.

To illustrate a one-to-one relationship, let's look at a slight variation of a piece of our earlier example. Imagine that you have customers – just as we did in our earlier example. This time, however, we're going to imagine that we are a subsidiary of a much larger company. Our parent company wants to be able to track all of its customers, and to be able to tell the collective total of each customer's purchases – regardless of which subsidiary(s) the customer made purchases with.

Even if all the subsidiaries run out of one server at the main headquarters, there's a very good chance that the various subsidiaries would be running with their own databases. One way to track all customer information, which would facilitate combining it later, would be to create a master customer database owned by the parent company. The subsidiaries would then maintain their own customer table, but do so with a one-to-one relationship to the parent company's customer table. Any customer record created in the parent company would imply that you needed to have one in the subsidiaries also. Any creation of a customer record in a subsidiary would require that one was also created in the parent company's copy.

A second example – one that used to apply frequently to SQL Server prior to version 7.0 – is the situation where you have too much information to fit in one row. Remember that the maximum row size for SQL Server is 8060 bytes of non-BLOB data. That's a lot harder to fill than version 6.5's 1962 bytes, but you can still have situations where you need to store a very large number of columns or even fewer very wide columns. One way to get around this problem was to actually create two different tables and split our rows between the tables. We could then impose a one-to-one relationship. The combination of the matching rows in the two tables then meets our larger rowsize requirement.

> **SQL Server has no inherent method of enforcing a true one-to-one relationship. You can say that table A requires a matching record in table B, but when you then add that table B must have a matching record in table A, you create a paradox – which table gets the record first? If you need to enforce this kind of relationship in SQL Server, the best you can do is force all inserts to be done via a stored procedure. The stored procedure can have the logic to insert into both tables or neither table. Neither foreign key constraints nor triggers can handle this circular relationship.**

Zero or One-to-One

SQL Server can handle the instance of zero or one-to-one relationships. This is essentially the same as a one-to-one, with the difference that one side of the relationship has the option of either having a record or not.

Going back to our parent company vs. subsidiary example, you might prefer to create a relationship where the parent company needs to have a matching record for each subsidiary's records, but the subsidiary doesn't need the information from the parent. You could, for example, have subsidiaries that have very different customers (such as a railroad and a construction company). The parent company wants to know about *all* the customers regardless of what business they came from, but your construction company probably doesn't care about your railroad customers. In such a case, you would have *zero or one* construction customers to *one* parent company customer record.

Zero or one-to-one relationships can be enforced in SQL Server through:

❏ A combination of a unique or primary key with a foreign key constraint. A foreign key constraint can enforce that *at least* one record must exist in the "one" (or parent company in our example) table, but it can't ensure that *only* one exists (there could be more than one). Using a primary key or unique constraint would ensure that one was indeed the limit.

❏ Triggers. Note that triggers would be required in both tables.

> The reason SQL Server can handle a zero or one-to-one, but not a one-to-one relationship is due to the "which goes first" problem. In a true one-to-one relationship, you can't insert into either table because the record in the other table isn't there – it's a paradox. However, with a zero or one-to-one, you can insert into the required table first (the "one"), and the optional table (the zero or one), if desired, second. This same problem will hold true for the "one-to-one or many", and the "one to zero, one, or many" relationships also.

One-to-One or Many

This is one form of your run-of-the-mill, average, every-day foreign key kind of relationship. Usually, this is found in some form of header/detail relationship. A great example of this would be our Orders situation. OrderDetails (the one or many side of the relationship) doesn't make much sense without an Orders header to belong to (does it do you much good to have an order for a part if you don't know who the order is for?). Likewise, it doesn't make much sense to have an order if there wasn't anything actually ordered (for example, "Gee, look, ACME company ordered absolutely nothing yesterday.").

Order No (PK)	Order Date	Customer No
100	1/1/1999	54545
101	1/1/1999	12000
102	1/1/1999	66651
103	1/1/1999	54545

Order No (PK)	Line Item (PK)	Part No	Qty	Unit Price	Total Price
100	1	1A4536	5	15	75
100	2	OR2400	4	27	108
100	3	OR2403	4	29	116
100	4	4I5436	1	750	750
101	1	3X9567	1	62.50	62.50
102	1	8G9200	7	12	84
102	2	8G5437	1	15	15
102	3	3H6250	1	32	32
103	1	8G9200	40	12	480
103	2	2P5523	1	165	165
103	3	3X9567	1	42	42

This one, however, gives us the same basic problem that we had with one-to-one relationships. It's still that chicken or egg thing – which came first? Again, in SQL Server, the only way to fully implement this is by restricting all data to be inserted or deleted via stored procedures.

One-to-Zero, One, or Many

This is the other, and perhaps even more common, form of the run-of-the-mill, average, every-day foreign key relationship. The only real difference in implementation here is that the referencing field (the one in the table that has the foreign key constraint) is allowed to be null– that is, the fact that you have a record in the "one" table, doesn't necessarily mean that you have any instances of matching records in the referencing table.

An example of this can be found in the `Northwind` database in the relationship between `Suppliers` and `Orders`. The `Orders` table tracks which shipper was used to ship the order – but what if the order was picked up by the customer? If there is a shipper, then we want to limit it to our approved list of shippers, but it's still quite possible that there won't be any shipper at all:

ShipperID	CompanyName	Phone
1	Speedy Express	(503) 555-9831
2	United Package	(503) 555-3199
3	Federal Shipping	(503) 555-9931

No Match ◄

OrderID	OrderDate	CustomerID	ShipperID	ShipToAddress
10500	1997-04-09	LAMAI	1	1 rue Alsace-Lorraine
10501	1997-04-09	BLAUS	3	Forsterstr. 57
10502	1997-04-10	PERIC	1	Calle Dr. Jorge...

> This kind of relationship usually sets up what is called a *domain relationship*. A *domain* is a limited list of values that the dependent table must choose from – nothing outside the domain list is considered a valid option. The table that holds the rows that make up the domain list is commonly referred to as a *domain* or *lookup table*. Nearly all databases you create are going to have at least one, and probably many, domain tables in them. Our Shippers table is a domain table – the purpose of having it isn't just to store the information on the name and phone number of the shipper, but also to limit the list of possible shippers in the Orders table.

In SQL Server, we can enforce this kind of relationship through two methods:

❑ FOREIGN KEY constraint: you simply declare a FOREIGN KEY constraint on the table that serves as the "many" side of the relationship, and reference the table and column that is to be the "one" side of the relationship (you'll be guaranteed of only one in the referenced table since you must have a PRIMARY KEY or UNIQUE constraint on the column(s) referenced by a foreign key) .

❑ Triggers: actually, for all the early versions of SQL Server, this was the only option for true referential integrity. You actually need to add two triggers – one for each side of the relationship. Add a trigger to the table that is the "many" side of the relationship and check that any row inserted or changed in that table has a match in the table it depends on (the "one" side of the relationship). Then, you add a delete and update triggers to the other table – this trigger checks records that are being deleted (or changed) from the referenced table to make sure that it isn't going to **orphan** (make it so it doesn't have a reference).

We've previously discussed the performance ramifications of the choices between the two in our chapter on constraints. Using a FOREIGN KEY constraint is generally faster – particularly when there is a violation. That being said, triggers may still be the better option in situations where you're going to have a trigger executing anyway (or some other special constraint need).

Many-to-Many

In this type of relationship, both sides of the relationship may have several records – not just one – that match. An example of this would be the relationship of products to orders. A given order may have many different products in the order. Likewise, any given product may be ordered many times. We still may, however, want to relate the tables in question – for example, to ensure that an order is for a product that we know about (it's in our Products table).

SQL Server has no way of physically establishing a direct many-to-many relationship, so we cheat by having an intermediate table to organize the relationship. Some tables create our many-to-many relationships almost by accident as a normal part of the normalization process – others are created entirely from scratch for the sole purpose of establishing this kind of relationship. This latter "middleman" kind of table is often called either a **linking table** or an **associate table**. Let's look at both instances.

First, let's look at a many-to-many relationship that is created in the normal course of normalization. An example of this can be found in our OrderDetails table, which creates a many-to-many relationship between our Orders and Products tables:

Order No (PK)	Order Date	Customer No
100	1/1/1999	54545
101	1/1/1999	12000
102	1/1/1999	66651
103	1/2/1999	54545

Order No (PK)	Line Item (PK)	Part No	Qty	Unit Price	Total Price
100	1	1A4536	5	15	75
100	2	OR2400	4	27	108
100	3	OR2403	4	29	116
100	4	4I5436	1	750	750
101	1	3X9567	1	62.50	62.50
102	1	8G9200	7	12	84
102	2	8G5437	1	15	15
102	3	3H6250	1	32	32
103	1	8G9200	40	12	480
103	2	2P5523	1	165	165
103	3	3X9567	1	42	42

Part No (PK)	Description	Wt
1A4536	Flange	6
OR2400	Injector	.5
OR2403	Injector	.5
4I5436	Head	3
3X9567	Pump	5
8G9200	Fan	3
8G5437	Fan	3
3H6250	Control	5
2P5523	Housing	1

By using the join syntax that we learned back in Chapter 5, we can relate one product to the many orders that it's been part of, or we can go the other way and relate an order to all the products on that order.

Let's move on now to our second example – one where we create an associate table from scratch just so we can have a many-to-many relationship. We'll take the example of a user and a group of rights that a user can have on the system.

We might start with a Permissions table that looks something like this:

PermissionID	Description
1	Read
2	Insert
3	Update
4	Delete

Then we add a Users table:

UserID	Full Name	Password	Active
JohnD	John Doe	Jfz9..nm3	1
SamS	Sam Spade	klk93)md	1

Now comes the problem – how do we define what users have which permissions? Our first inclination might be to just add a column called Permissions to our Users table:

UserID	Full Name	Password	Permissions	Active
JohnD	John Doe	Jfz9..nm3	1	1
SamS	Sam Spade	klk93)md	3	1

This seems fine for only a split second, and then a question begs to be answered – what about when our users have permission to do more than one thing?

In the older, flat file days, you might have just combined all the permissions into the one cell, like:

UserID	Full Name	Password	Permissions	Active
JohnD	John Doe	Jfz9..nm3	1,2,3	1
SamS	Sam Spade	klk93)md	1,2,3,43	1

This violates our first normal form, which said that the values in any column must be atomic. In addition, this would be very slow because you would have to procedurally parse out each individual value within the cell.

What we really have between these two tables, Users and Permissions, is a many-to-many relationship – we just need a way to establish that relationship within the database. We do this by adding an associate table. Again, this is a table that, in most cases, doesn't add any new data to our database other than establishing the association between rows in two other tables:

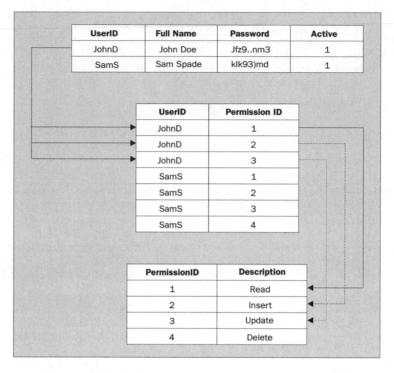

UserID	Full Name	Password	Active
JohnD	John Doe	Jfz9..nm3	1
SamS	Sam Spade	klk93)md	1

UserID	Permission ID
JohnD	1
JohnD	2
JohnD	3
SamS	1
SamS	2
SamS	3
SamS	4

PermissionID	Description
1	Read
2	Insert
3	Update
4	Delete

With the addition of our new table (we'll call it UserPermissions), we can now mix and match our permissions to our users.

Note that, for either example, the implementation of referential integrity is the same – each of the base tables (the tables that hold the underlying data and have the many-to-many relationship) has a one-to-many relationship with the associate table. This can be done via either a trigger or a FOREIGN KEY constraint.

Diagramming

Entity Relationship Diagrams (ERDs) are an important tool in good database design. Small databases can usually be easily created from a few scripts and implemented directly without drawing things out at all. The larger your database gets however, the faster it becomes very problematic to just do things "in your head". ERDs solve a ton of problems because they allow you to quickly visualize and understand both the entities and their relationships.

Before the first time I wrote this section, I debated for a long while about how I wanted to handle this. On one hand, serious ER diagramming is usually done with an application that is specifically designed to be an ER diagramming tool (we talk about a few of these in Appendix C). These tools almost always support at least one of a couple of industry standard diagramming methods. Even some of the more mass-market diagramming tools – such as Visio – support a couple of ERD methodologies. With SQL Server version 7.0 and beyond, Microsoft has given you an option for diagramming right within the EM – and therein lies the problem.

The tools included in EM are a variation on a tool set that appears in a number of other Microsoft development products, and has been code named the daVinci tools. The problem is that the daVinci tools don't comply with any ERD standard. After thinking about this for some time, and after also having one rendition of this book already out and tested, I've decided to again stick with what I know that you have – the daVinci tools. I will, however, provide a bit more information on other tools in Appendix C.

The daVinci Tools

You can open up the daVinci tools in Enterprise Manager by navigating to the Diagrams node of your database (expand your server first, then the database). Some of what we are going to see you'll find familiar – some of the dialogs are the same as we saw in Chapter 6 when we were creating tables.

The daVinci tools don't give you all that many options, so you'll find that you'll get to know them fairly quickly. Indeed, if you're familiar with the relationship editor in Access, then much of the daVinci tools will look very familiar.

Let's start by creating our diagram. You can create your new diagram by right-clicking on the Diagrams node underneath the Northwind database and choosing New Database Diagram.... This brings you to the **Create Database Diagram Wizard**. Click Next to move on to the Select Tables to be Added dialog:

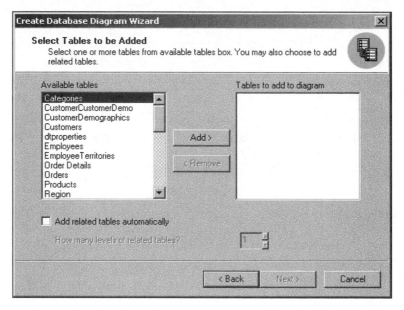

This dialog allows us to choose which tables we want to include in our diagram. If you scroll through the tables on the left, you'll see a number of tables there that you might not recognize. The table starting with dt is used by the daVinci tools. Tables starting with sys are system tables.

> *Note that there is a distinct possibility that the behavior of including the system tables may change during a service pack. The issue of including system tables all the time is, in this author's not so humble opinion, a major usability issue for people new to SQL Server. For most diagramming efforts, these tables are going to just be in the way for even an experienced developer.*

Microsoft provided the ability to add system tables to the diagrams at the request of developers – that's great. The problem is that they show up by default, but only a small fraction of diagrams are going to need inclusion of system tables. This problem has been reported to and acknowledged by Microsoft, but not in time for a change to make the release of the product. I hope to see another checkbox added (something like "include system tables") in a service pack – we'll see...

We're only interested in the user tables at this point. We could just select the tables that we were interested in and click next; however, let's try something a little extra. Click on the Add related tables automatically checkbox, and then scroll the How many levels of related tables? box up to 8. Now choose Categories and click on the Add button – you'll see *all* of our user tables move over to the right (the dt and sys tables will not move):

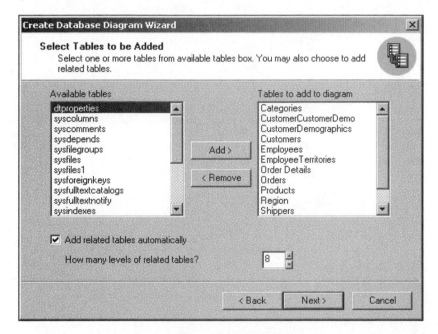

Why did the other tables move? Because all of the other tables are either directly or indirectly related to the Categories table. In our case, we needed to go to relationships eight tables deep (for example, Customers is related to Orders, which is related to Order Details). SQL Server determines these relationships by examining the foreign key definitions on all the tables.

Go ahead and click Next, and you'll get a confirmation dialog – just click on Finish, and SQL Server will build and display your diagram, which should look something like:

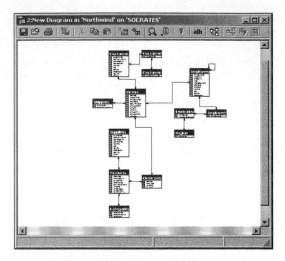

This is a little hard to see (even when you're looking at the screen and not the book!), so I'm going to rearrange things a bit plus change the zoom size. To move items around, just drag and drop them. To change the zoom size, just click on the magnifying glass on the tool bar or right-click and choose zoom.

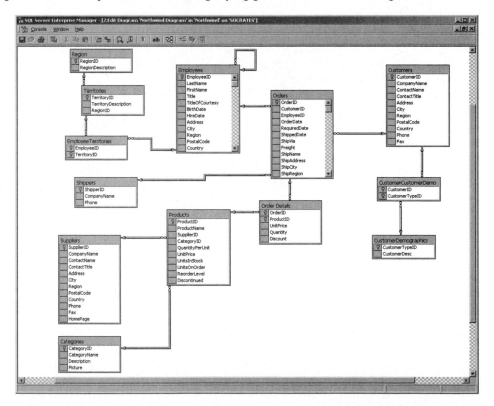

Save this diagram by clicking on the disk icon on the toolbar or right-clicking in a white-space area and choosing Save. We'll use this diagram as a launching point for explaining how the diagramming tool works and building a few tables here and there.

Tables

So, as we've seen while creating the diagram, each table has its own window you can move around. The primary key is shown with the little symbol of a key in the column to the left of the name:

This is just a default view for a table though – you can select from several others that allow you to edit the very makeup of the table. To check out your options for views of a table, just right-click on the table that you're interested in:

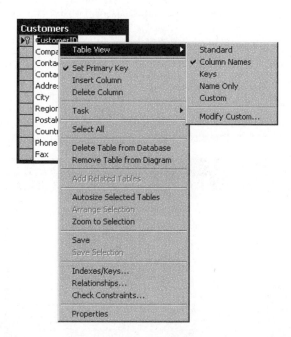

The default is names only, but you should also take an interest in the choice of Standard – this is what you would use when you want to edit the properties of the columns from right within the diagram (yes, you can do that!).

Adding and Deleting Tables

You can add a new table to the diagram in one of two ways:

❑ If you have a table that already exists in the database (but not in the diagram), but now you want to add it to your diagram, you simply click the Add table on Diagram button on the diagramming window's toolbar. You'll be presented with a list of all the tables in the database – just choose the one that you want to add, and it will appear along with any relationships it has to other tables in the diagram. If you're still using 7.0, then you'll find that, even though tables that are already in the diagram will appear in the table list, you cannot add them to the diagram a second time. This has been fixed in 2000 so that once a table is in use in the diagram it is no longer shown on the list. New to SQL Server 2000 is the ability to add the system tables to your diagram as well.

❑ If you want to add a completely new table, click on the New table button on the diagramming window's toolbar or right-click in the diagram and choose New Table... – you'll be asked for a name for the new table, and the table will be added to the diagram in Standard view. Simply edit the properties to have the column names, data types, etc. that you want, and you have a new table in the database.

> **Let me take a moment to point out a couple of gotchas in this process.**
>
> **First, don't forget to add a primary key to your table. SQL Server does not automatically do this, nor does it even prompt you (as Access does). This is a somewhat less than intuitive process. To add a primary key, you must select the columns that you want to have in the key. Then right-click and choose Set Primary Key.**
>
> **Next, be aware that your new table is not actually added to the database until you choose to save – this is also true of any edits that you make along the way.**

Let's go ahead and add a table to our database just to show how it works.

Start by clicking on the New table button in the diagramming window's toolbar. When prompted, enter a name of CustomerNotes. You should then get a new window table up using the Standard view:

CustomerNotes *				
Column Name	Data Type	Length	Allow Nulls	
CustomerID	nchar	5		
NoteDate	datetime	8		
EmployeeID	int	4		
Note	varbinary	8000		

Notice that I've added several columns to my table along with a primary key. Before you click to save this, let's try something out – open up Query Analyzer, and try to run a query against our new table:

```
SELECT * FROM CustomerNotes
```

Back comes an error message:

> Server: Msg 208, Level 16, State 1, Line 1
> Invalid object name 'CustomerNotes'.

That's because our table exists only as an edited item on the diagram – it won't be added until we actually save our changes.

> If you look at the **CustomerNotes** table in the diagram at this point, you should see a * to the right of the name – that's there to tell you that there are unsaved changes in that table.

Now, switch back to EM and right-click in the white space (not on a table or relationship) of the diagram window. Notice that there are two save options:

❑ **Save**: this saves the changes to both the diagram and to the database

❑ **Save Change Script**: this saves the changes to a script so it can be run at a later time

Go ahead and just select **Save**, and you'll be prompted for confirmation (after all, you're about to alter your database – there's no "undo" for this):

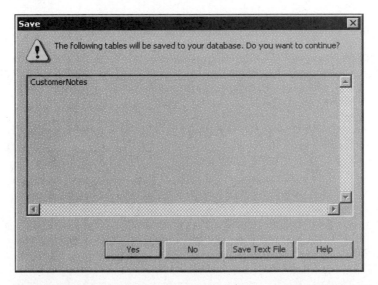

Go ahead and confirm the changes, then try running that query again against the CustomerNotes table. You should not receive an error this time since the table has now been created (you won't get any rows back, but the query should still run).

> You may notice that the "*" in the title bar of the `CustomerNotes` table has gone away at this point. The asterisk is there to tell you that you have unsaved changes on that table. Since we've just saved all the changes, the asterisk goes away.

OK, we've got our `CustomerNotes` table into the database, but now we notice a problem – the way our primary key is declared, we can only have one note per customer. More than likely, we are going to keep taking more and more notes on the customer over time. That means that we need to change our primary key, and leaves us with a couple of options depending on our requirements:

❑ **Make the date part of our primary key.** This is problematic from two standpoints:

    a. First, we're tracking what employee took the note – what if two different employees wanted to add notes at the same time? We could, of course, potentially address this by also adding `EmployeeID` to the primary key.

    b. Second, what's to say that even the same employee wouldn't want to enter two completely separate notes on the same day? (OK, so, since this is a `datetime` field, they could do it as long as they didn't get two rows inserted at the same millisecond – but just play along with me here. The point is that this is more complex than it needs to be.) Oops, now even our `EmployeeID` being in the key doesn't help us.

❑ **Add another column to help with the key structure.** We could either do this by adding a counter column for each note per customer. As yet another alternative, we could just add an identity column to ensure uniqueness – it means that our primary key doesn't really relate to anything, but that isn't always a big deal (though it does mean that we have one more index that has to be maintained) and it does allow us to have a relatively unlimited number of notes per customer.

Let's take the approach of adding a new column, which we'll call `Sequence` to the table.

By convention (it's not a requirement and not everyone does it this way), primary keys are normally the first columns in your table. If we were going to be doing this by script ourselves, we'd probably just issue an `ALTER TABLE` statement and `ADD` the column – this would stick our new column down at the end of our column list. If we wanted to reorder our columns, we'd have to copy all the data out to a holding table, drop any relationships to or from the old table, drop the old table, create a new table that has the columns and column order we want, then re-establish the relationships and copy the data back in (a long and tedious process). With the daVinci tools, however, SQL Server takes care of all that for us.

To insert a new row in the middle of everything, we just need to right-click on the row that is to immediately follow the row we want to insert and select Insert Column. The tool is nice enough to bump everything down for us to create space:

	Column Name	Data Type	Length	Allow Nulls
🔑	CustomerID	nchar	5	
	NoteDate	datetime	8	
	EmployeeID	int	4	
	Note	varbinary	8000	

We can then add in our new column, and reset the primary key by selecting both CustomerID and Sequence, right-clicking, and then selecting Set Primary Key:

CustomerNotes *			
Column Name	Condensed Type	Nullable	Identity
▶🔑 CustomerID	nchar(5)	NOT NULL	
🔑 Sequence	int	NOT NULL	✓
NoteDate	datetime	NOT NULL	
EmployeeID	int	NOT NULL	
Note	varbinary(8000)	NOT NULL	

Now save CustomerNotes and you have a table with the desired column order. Just to verify this, try using sp_help:

```
EXEC sp_help CustomerNotes
```

You'll see that we have the column order we expect:

```
....
CustomerID
Sequence
NoteDate
EmployeeID
Note
....
```

> **Making things like column order changes happens to be one area where the daVinci tools positively excel. I've used a couple of other ERD tools, and they all offered the promise of synchronizing a change in column order between the database and the diagram – the success has been pretty hit and miss. (In other words, be very careful about doing it around live data.) The tools are getting better, but this is an area where the daVinci tools show some of the genius of their namesake.**
>
> **Also, under the heading of "one more thing" – use the scripting option rather than the live connection to the database to make changes like this if you're operating against live data. That way you can fully test the script against test databases before risking your real data. Be sure to also fully back up your database before making this kind of change and make sure you have at least as much free space as the size of the table you are moving columns in – it will copy the data to a new table as part of the change, and you don't want it to blow up for lack of enough space.**

Editing Table Properties

Beyond the basic attributes that we've looked at thus far, we can also edit many other properties of our table. To check these out, right-click on our table and select Properties from the menu. We get a dialog with a ton of information that we haven't seen up to this point. This dialog has five tabs, so let's take a quick look at them:

The Tables Tab

Here you can see the name of the selected table and its owner. The Tables tab is used to change the filegroups that both your BLOB and non-BLOB information are stored on by selecting something other than PRIMARY for the Text Filegroup. You can also change and create identity and ROWGUID columns:

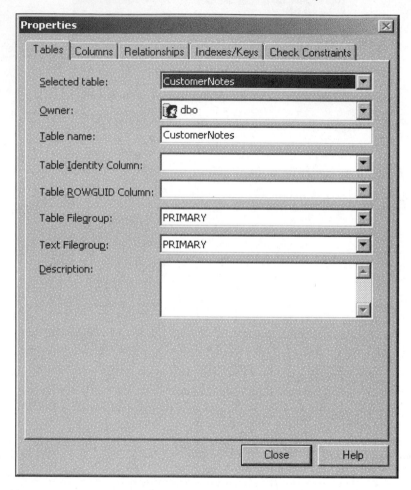

In addition, notice the Description item. This is new with SQL Server 2000, and allows you to make text notations about your table for documentation purposes. This is nice since it provides documentation about your database that will go wherever the database goes if you back up and restore or use the detach/attach system stored procedures.

The Columns Tab

The Columns tab was added as part of SQL Server 2000, and is pretty straightforward given what we've discussed thus far:

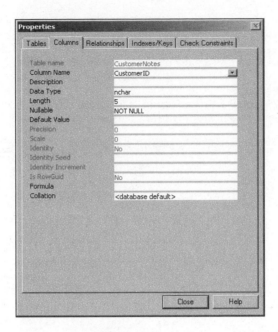

Essentially, it's just a way of editing all of our basic column information. Note the ability to create a computed column using the Formula field, and also the ability to edit the collation at the column level. This latter piece is particularly nice since, if you click on the ellipsis (...), it will give you a listing of all available collations (something you don't always have available when you're writing the code from scratch). Also, notice that we have another description box – this time for the column level rather than the table.

The Relationships Tab
Much like it sounds, the Relationships tab allows us to edit the nature of the relationships between tables:

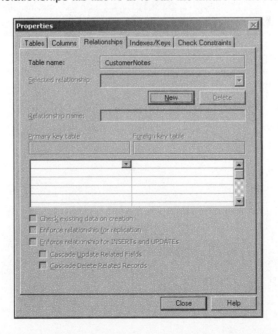

At this point, most of this tab is grayed out. We'll look into adding things to it in the next subsection, but for now, just realize that we can edit just about anything to do with relationships here. For example, we could create a relationship to another table just by clicking New and filling out the various boxes. Again, we'll look into this further in a page or two.

The Indexes/Keys Tab

A lot of the Indexes/Keys tab may be something of a mystery to you at this point – we haven't gotten to our chapter on indexing yet, so some of the terms may seem a bit strange:

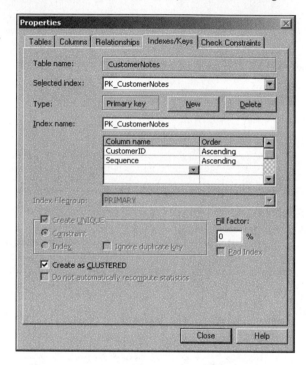

From here, we can create, edit, and delete indexes. We can also establish what filegroup we want the index to be stored on (in most instances, you'll just want to leave this alone). We'll look further into indexes in our next chapter.

The Check Constraints Tab

Notice that we're concerned with *CHECK* constraints on this tab (keys and defaults have been dealt with in the other tabs):

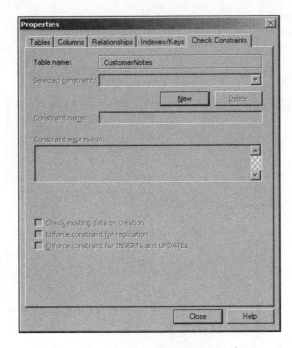

Again, this one is pretty much grayed out. Why? Well, there aren't any constraints of any kind other than a primary key defined for our CustomerNotes table, and that is dealt with on the **Indexes/Keys** tab. This one is for CHECK constraints only – if you want to see this tab in full action, then you need to click on **New** and add a constraint.

As this is our final tab, click on **Close** to return to our diagram.

Relationships

Next up on our list of features of the daVinci tools to discuss is the relationship line:

The side with the key is the side that is the "one" side of a relationship. The side that has the infinity symbol represents the "many" side. The daVinci tools have no relationship line available to specifically represent:

- ❑ Relationships where zero is possible (it still uses the same line)

- ❑ One-to-one relationships

- ❑ Many-to-many relationships

In addition, the only relationships that actually show in the diagram are ones that are declared using FOREIGN KEY constraints. Any relationship that is enforced via triggers – regardless of the type of relationship – will not cause a relationship line to appear.

Looking at our `Northwind` diagram again, try right-clicking on the relationship line between the `Customers` and `Orders` tables. You'll be given the option to either delete the relationship, show the relationship labels (names), or to view the properties. Select **Properties**, and you'll get the same **Properties** dialog box that we saw in the last section – it lets us edit a variety of things about our table as well as its indexes and relationships. This time around, we're a bit more interested in the **Relationships** tab:

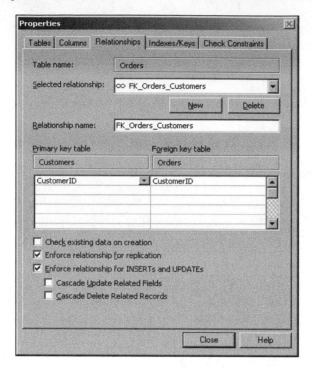

From here, we can edit the nature of our relationship, including such things as cascading actions. We can also disable it (for example, if we want to deliberately add data in that violates the relationship). Last, but not least, we can change the name of the relationship.

> **Database designers seem to vary widely in their opinion regarding names for relationships. Some don't care what they are named, but I prefer to use a verb phrase to describe my relationships – for example, in our `Customers/Orders` relationship, I would probably name it `CustomerHasOrders` or something of that ilk. It's nothing critical – most of the time you won't even use it – but I find that it can be really helpful when I'm looking at a long object list or a particularly complex ER diagram where the lines may run across the page past several unrelated entities.**

If you're working in a mixed version environment, then you'll find a few things different about this dialog in SQL Server 2000 than in 7.0. The most obvious has got to be the addition of the cascading actions, but it doesn't end there. Also new is the addition of an icon in the front of the relationship name in the combo box. Any relationship with a key symbol in front of the name indicates that the current table (the one under **Selected table** in the **Tables** tab) is the table that is referenced. Any relationship with a ∞ symbol in front of the name is indicating that the current table is the referencing table (the one with the `FOREIGN KEY` constraint defined on it).

Adding Relationships in the Diagramming Tool

Just drag and drop – it's that easy. The only trick is making sure that you start and end your drag in the places you meant to. If in doubt, select the column(s) you're interested in before starting your drag.

Let's add a relationship between our new `CustomerNotes` table (we created it in the last section) and the `Customers` table – after all, if it's a customer note we probably want to make sure that we are taking notes on a valid customer. To do this, click and hold in the gray area to the left of the `CustomerID` column in the `Customers` table, then drag your mouse until it is pointing at the `CustomerID` column in the `CustomerNotes` table. A now familiar dialog box should pop up to confirm the column mapping between the related tables:

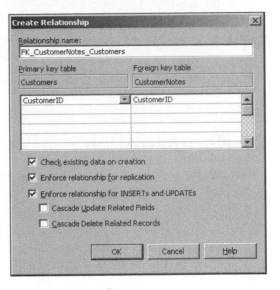

Don't worry too much about it if the names on both columns didn't come up right – just click the combo box for the table you want to change columns for and select the correct column. Let's change the name of the relationship from the default of FK_CustomerNotes_Customers to CustomerHasNotes. As soon as we click on OK, we'll see the new relationship line in our diagram – if we hover over that relationship, we'll even see a tooltip with the relationship's name and nature:

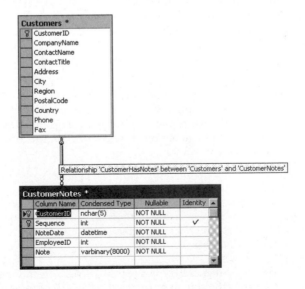

There is an instance where the way the line is displayed will change – when we "disable" the foreign key. We saw this briefly in our last chapter, and we can do it in the Relationships tab of the table's Properties dialog by unchecking the Enforce relationship for INSERTs and UPDATEs box. When we do that, our line will change to let us know that the constraint has been disabled. It will now look something like this:

If you see one of these, your first question should be, "Why is that disabled?" Maybe it was intentional, but you'll want to be sure.

De-Normalization

I'm going to keep this relatively short since we'll be dealing with this issue again in both the advanced design chapter and the Analysis Services chapter, but remember not to get carried away with the normalization of your data.

As I stated early in this chapter, normalization is one of those things that database designers sometimes wear like a cross. It's somehow turned into a religion for them, and they begin normalizing data for the sake of normalization rather than for good things it does to their database. Here are a couple of things to think about in this regard:

❑ If declaring a computed column or storing some derived data is going to allow you to run a report more effectively, then by all means put it in. Just remember to take into account the benefit vs. the risk. (For example, what if your "summary" data gets out of synch with the data it can be derived from? How will you determine that it happened, and how will you fix it if it does happen?)

❑ Sometimes, by including just one (or more) de-normalized column in a table, you can eliminate or significantly cut down the number of joins necessary to retrieve information. Watch for these scenarios – they actually come up reasonably frequently. I've dealt with situations where adding one column to one commonly used base table cut a nine-table join down to just three, and cut the query time by about 90% in the process.

❑ If you are keeping historical data – data that will largely go unchanged and is just used for reporting – then the integrity issue becomes a much smaller consideration. Once the data is written to a read-only area and verified, you can be reasonably certain that you won't have the kind of "out of sync" problems that is one of the major things that data normalization addresses. At that point, it may be much nicer (and faster) to just "flatten" (de-normalize) the data out into a few tables, and speed things up.

❑ The fewer tables that have to be joined, the happier your users who do their own reports are going to be. The user base out there continues to get more and more savvy with the tools they are using. Increasingly often, users are coming to their DBA and asking for direct access to the database to be able to do their own custom reporting. For these users, a highly-normalized database can look like a maze and become virtually useless. De-normalizing your data can make life much easier for these users.

All that said, if in doubt, normalize things. There is a reason why that is the way relational systems are typically designed. When you err on the side of normalizing, you are erring on the side of better data integrity, and on the side of better performance in a transactional environment.

Beyond Normalization

In this section, we're going to look into a basic set of "beyond normalization" rules of the road in design. Very few of these are hard and fast kind of rules – they are just things to think about. The most important thing to understand here is that, while normalization is a big thing in database design, it is not the only thing.

Keep It Simple

I run into people on a regular basis that have some really slick way to do things differently than it's ever been done before. Some of the time, I wind up seeing some ideas that are incredibly cool and incredibly useful. Other times I see ideas that are incredibly cool, but not very useful. As often as not though, I see ideas that are neither – they may be new, but that doesn't make them good.

Before I step too hard on your creative juices here, let me clarify what I'm trying to get across – don't accept the "because we've always done it that way" approach to things, but also recognize that the tried and true probably continues to be tried for a reason – it usually works.

Try to avoid instilling more complexity in your database than you really need to. A minimalist approach usually (but not always) yields something that is not only easier to edit, but also runs a lot faster.

Choosing Data Types

In keeping with the minimalist idea, choose what you need, but only what you need.

For example, if you're trying to store months (as the number, 1-12) – those can be done in a single byte by using a `tinyint`. Why then, do I regularly come across databases where a field that's only going to store a month is declared as an `int` (which is 4 bytes)? Don't use an `nchar` or `nvarchar` if you're never going to do anything that requires Unicode – these data types take up two bytes for every one as compared to their non-Unicode cousins.

> There is a tendency to think about this as being a space issue. When I bring this up in person, I sometimes hear the argument, "Ah, disk space is cheap these days!" Well, beyond the notion that a name-brand SCSI hard drive still costs more than I care to throw away on laziness, there's also a network bandwidth issue. If you're passing an extra 100 bytes down the wire for every row, and you pass a 100 record result, then that's about 10K worth of extra data you just clogged your network with. Still not convinced? Now, say that you have just 100 users performing 50 transactions per hour – that's over 50MB of wasted network bandwidth per hour.
>
> The bottom line is, most things that happen with your database will happen repetitively – that means that small mistakes snowball and can become rather large.

Err on the Side of Storing Things

There was an old movie called *The Man Who Knew Too Much* – Hitchcock I believe – that man wasn't keeping data.

Every time that you're building a database, you're going to come across the question of, "Are we going to need that information later?" Here's my two-bit advice on that – if in doubt, keep it. You see, most of the time you can't get back the data that has already come and gone.

I guarantee that at least once (and probably many, many more times than that), there will be a time where a customer (remember, customers are basically anyone who needs something from you – there is such a thing as an internal customer, not just the ones in Accounts Receivable) will come to you and say something like, "Can you give me a report on how much we paid each non-incorporated company last year?"

OK, so are you storing information on whether your vendor is a corporation or not? You had better be if you are subject to US tax law (1099 reporting). So you turn around and say that you can handle that, and the customer replies, "Great! Can you print that out along with their address as of the end of the year?"

Ooops – I'm betting that you don't have past addresses, or at the very least, aren't storing the date that the address changed. In short, you never know what a user of your system is going to ask for – try and make sure you have it. Just keep in mind that you don't want to be moving unnecessary amounts of data up and down your network wire (see my comments on choosing a data type). If you're storing the data just for posterity, then make sure you don't put it in any of your application's SELECT statements if it isn't needed (actually, this should be your policy regardless of why you're storing the data).

> If you think that there may be legal ramifications either way (both in keeping it and in getting rid of it), consult your attorney. Sometimes you're legally obligated to keep data a certain amount of time, other times it's best to get rid of information as soon as legally possible.

Drawing up a Quick Example

Let's walk quickly through a process of designing the invoicing database that we've already started with during our section on normalization. For the most part, we're going to just be applying the daVinci tools to what we've already designed, but we'll also toss in a few new issues to show how they affect our design.

Creating the Database

Unlike a lot of the third party diagramming tools out there, the daVinci tools will not create the database for you – you have to already have it created in order to get as far as having the diagram available to work with.

We're not going to be playing with any data to speak of, so just create a small database called Invoice. Feel free to use either T-SQL or EM. I'll go ahead and use EM for the sake of this example.

After right-clicking on the Databases node of my server in EM and selecting New Database..., I enter information in for a database called Invoice that is set up as 3MB in size:

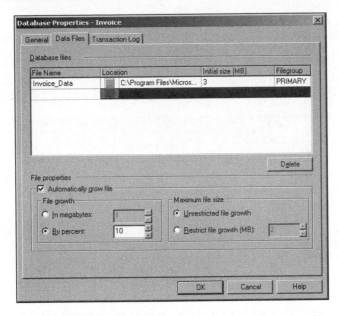

Since we've already had a chapter on creating databases (and for the sake of brevity), I'm just going to accept the defaults on all the other options.

Adding the Diagram and Our Initial Tables

As we did when creating our Northwind diagram, expand the node for our database (it should have been added underneath the Databases node). Then right-click on the Diagrams node and select New Database Diagram... The Create Database Diagram Wizard immediately starts. Click through to the second dialog:

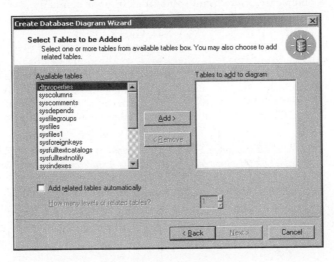

This is different than SQL Server 7.0, which would have given us a warning that there currently aren't any tables in the database. If we had some, it would try to start up a wizard to help us build a diagram after the fact.

Since there are no user tables in our database, we wind up with just a list of system tables available to add to the diagram. So, for us, we'll just want to click Cancel so we wind up with a clean sheet.

Now we're ready to start adding new tables. You can either click the New table icon on the toolbar, or right-click anywhere in the diagram and select New Table... Let's start off by adding in the Orders table.

Orders *					
Column Name	Data Type	Length	Allow Nulls	Default Value	Identity
OrderID	int	4			✓
OrderDate	datetime	8		GETDATE()	
CustomerNo	int	4			

Note that I've changed from the default view – which doesn't have **Default Value** and **Identity** as part of it – over to the "custom" view. I also had to choose to **Modify Custom** and select the **Default Value** and **Identity** columns to be added to my custom view.

Let's stop long enough to look at a couple of the decisions that we made here. While we had addressed the issue of normalization, we hadn't addressed any of the other basics yet. First up of those was the question of data types.

Since OrderID is the primary key for the table, we need to be sure that we allow enough room for our values to be unique as we insert more and more data. If this was a table we weren't going to be making very many inserts into, we might choose a smaller data type, but since it is our Orders table (and we hope to be entering lots of orders), we'll push the size up a bit. In addition, numeric order numbers seem suitable (make sure you ask your customers about issues like this) and facilitate the use of an automatic numbering mechanism in the form of an identity column. If you need more than 2 billion or so order numbers (in which case, I may want some stock in your company), you can take a look at the new BigInt data type that has been added in SQL Server 2000.

With OrderDate, the first thing to come to mind was a smalldatetime field. After all, we don't need the kind of precision that a datetime field offers, and we also don't need to go back all that far in history (maybe a few years at most). Why, then, did we go for datetime rather than smalldatetime? To show mercy on Visual Basic programmers! Visual Basic 6.0 and earlier throws fits when you start playing around with smalldatetime fields. You can get around the problems, but it's a pain. We used a datetime column for nothing more than making the client coding easy.

It's hard to say whether the .NET version of VB will have a problem with this or not. From what I've seen of VB7 thus far, I suspect we'll be fine, but I can't claim to have tested this particular issue as yet.

Our customer has told us (and we've seen in the earlier sample data), that CustomerNo is five digits, all numeric. This is one of those areas where you start saying to your customer, "Are you sure you're never going to be using alpha characters in there?" Assuming the answer is yes, we can go with an integer since it is:

❑ Faster on lookups

❑ Smaller in size – 4 bytes will cover a 5-digit number easily, but it takes 5 bytes minimum (6 if you're using variable-length fields) to handle 5 characters

Note that we're kind of cheating on this one – realistically, the customer number for this table is really being defined by the relationship we're going to be building with the Customers table. Since that's the last table we'll see in this example, we're going ahead and filling in the blanks for this field now.

After data types, we also had to decide on the size of the column – this was a no-brainer for this particular table since all the data types have fixed sizes.

Next on the hit list is whether the rows can be null or not. In this case, we're sure that we want all this information and that it should be available at the time we enter the order, so we won't allow nulls.

I've touched on this before, but you just about have to drag me kicking and screaming in order to get me to allow nulls in my databases. There are situations where you just can't avoid it – "undefined" values are legitimate. I'll still often fill text fields with actual text saying "Value Unknown" or something like that.

The reason I do this is because nullable fields promote errors in much the same way that undeclared variables do. Whenever you run across null values in the table you wind up asking yourself, "Gee, did I mean for that to be there, or did I forget to write a value into the table for that row" – that is, do I have a bug in my program?

The next issue we faced was default values. We couldn't have a default for OrderID because we're making it an identity column (the two are mutually exclusive). For OrderDate, however, a default made some level of sense. If an OrderDate isn't provided, then we're going to assume that the order date is today. Last, but not least, is the CustomerNo – which customer would we default to? Nope – can't do that here.

Next up was the issue of an identity column. OrderID is an ideal candidate for an identity column – the value has no meaning other than keeping the rows unique. Using a counter like an identity field gives us a nice, presentable, and orderly way to maintain that unique value. We don't have any reason to change the identity seed and increment, so we won't. We'll leave it starting at one and incrementing by one.

Last, but not least, is IsRowGuid. A table in SQL Server can have several columns with the uniqueidentifier (GUID) data type, but only one that is considered to be "the" GUID for a particular row. If you define a column as being IsRowGuid, then you're saying that row is the one for this table. This item would usually only be used in a replication situation. We don't have a GUID data type in there, so this is pretty much a self-answering question. Without a GUID data type, we must not be planning on using the IsRowGuid column.

Now we're ready to move on to our next table – the `OrderDetails` table:

OrderDetails *			
Column Name	Data Type	Length	Allow Nulls
OrderID	int	4	
LineItem	int	4	
PartNo	char	6	
Qty	int	4	
UnitPrice	money	8	

For this table, the `OrderID` column is going to have a foreign key to it, so our data type is decided for us – it must be of the same type and size as the field it's referencing, so it's going to be an int.

The `LineItem` is going to start over again with each row, so we probably could have gotten as little as a tinyint here. We're going to go with an int on this one just for safety's sake (I've had people exceed limits that have been set on this sort of thing before).

`PartNo` is, for this table, actually going to be defined by the fact that it needs to match up with the `PartNo` in the `Products` table. It's going to be using a `char(6)` in that table (we'll come to it shortly), so that's what we'll make it here.

`Qty` is guesswork. The question is, what's the largest order you can take as far as quantity for one line-time goes? Since we don't know what we're selling, we can't really make a guess on a maximum quantity (for example, if we were selling barrels of oil, it might be bought literally millions of barrels at a time). We're also using an int here, but we would have needed a data type that accepted decimals if we were selling things like gallons of fuel or things by weight.

`UnitPrice` is easy, as this field is going to hold a monetary value its data type must be `money`.

Moving along, we're again (no surprise here) considering all data fields to be required. No, we're not allowing nulls anywhere.

No defaults seem to make sense for this table, so we're skipping that part also.

Identity? The temptation might be to mark `OrderID` as an identity column again. Don't do that! Remember that `OrderID` is a value that we're going to match to a column in another table. That table will already have a value (as it happens, set by identity, but it didn't necessarily have to be that way), so setting our column to identity would cause a collision. We would be told that we can't do our insert because we're trying to set an identity value. All the other columns either get their data from another table or require user input of the data. IsRowGuid does not apply again.

That takes us to our `Products` and `Customers` tables:

Products *			
Column Name	Data Type	Length	Allow Nulls
PartNo	char	6	
Description	varchar	15	
Weight	tinyint	1	

Customers *				
Column Name	Data Type	Length	Allow Nulls	▲
CustomerNo	int	4		
CustomerName	varchar	50		
CustomerAddress	varchar	50		▼

Let's hit the highlights on the choices here and move on.

PartNo has been defined by the data that we saw when we were looking at normalization. It's a numeric, followed by an alpha, followed by four numerics. That's six characters, and it seems to be fixed. We would want to hold the customer to the cross about the notion that the size of the part number can't get any larger, but, assuming that's OK, we'll go with a char(6) here. That's because a char takes up slightly less overhead than a varchar, and we know that the length is going to always remain the same (this means that there's no benefit from the variable size).

Description is one of those guessing games. Sometimes a field like this is going to be driven by your user interface requirements (don't make it wider than can be displayed on the screen), other times you're just going to be truly guessing at what is "enough" space. We're using a variable-length char over a regular char for two reasons:

❑   To save a little space

❑   So we don't have to deal with trailing spaces (look at the char vs. varchar data types back in Chapter 2 if you have questions on this)

We haven't used an nchar or nvarchar because this is a simple invoicing system for a US business, and we're not concerned about localization issues.

Weight is similar to Description in that it is going to be somewhat of a guess. We've chosen a tinyint here because our products will not be over 255 pounds. Note that we are also preventing ourselves from keeping decimal places in my weight (integers only).

We described the CustomerNo field back when we were doing the Orders table.

CustomerName and CustomerAddress are pretty much the same situation as Description – the question is, how much is enough? But we need to be sure that we don't give too much...

As before, all fields are required (there will be no nulls in either table) and no defaults are called for. Identity columns also do not seem to fit the bill here as both the customer number and part number have special formats that do not lend themselves to the automatic numbering system that an identity provides.

Adding the Relationships

OK, to make the diagram less complicated, I've gone through all four of my tables and changed the view on them down to just Column Names. You can do this too, by simply right-clicking on the table and selecting the Column Names menu choice.

You should get a diagram that looks like this:

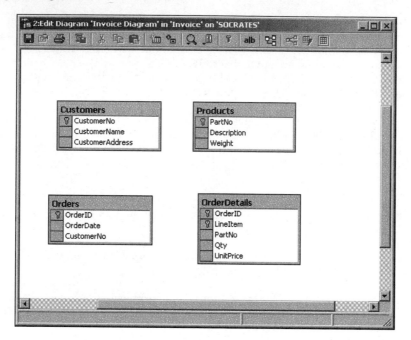

You may not have the exact same positions for your table, but the contents should be the same. We're now ready to start adding relationships, but we probably ought to stop and think about what kind of relationships we need.

All the relationships that we'll draw with the relationship lines in our SQL Server diagram tool are going to be one-to-zero, one, or many relationships. SQL Server doesn't really know how to do any other kind of relationship implicitly. As we discussed earlier in the chapter, you can add things like unique constraints and triggers to augment what SQL Server will do naturally with relations, but, assuming you don't do any of that, you're going to wind up with a one-to-zero, one, or many relationship.

> *The bright side is that this is by far the most common kind of relationship out there. In short, don't sweat it that SQL Server doesn't cover every base here. The standard foreign key constraint (which is essentially what our reference line represents) fits the bill for most things that you need to do, and the rest can usually be simulated via some other means.*

We're going to start with the central table in our system – the Orders table. First, we'll look at any relationships that it may need. In this case, we have one – it needs to reference the Customers table. This is going to be a one-to-many relationship with Customers as the parent (the one) and Orders as the child (the many) table.

To build the relationship (and a foreign key constraint to serve as the foundation for that relationship), we're going to simply click and hold in the leftmost column of the Customers table (in the gray area) right where the CustomerNo column is. We'll then drag to the same position (the gray area) next to the CustomerNo column in the Orders table and let go of the mouse button. SQL Server promptly pops up with a dialog to confirm the configuration of this relationship:

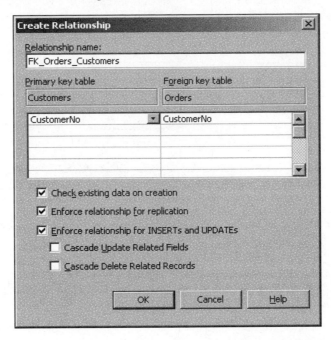

As I pointed out earlier in the chapter, don't sweat it if the names that come up don't match with what you intended – just use the combo boxes to change them back so both sides have CustomerNo in them. Note also that the names don't have to be the same – keeping them the same just helps ease confusion in situations where they really are the same.

As soon as we click OK, we have our first relationship in our new database:

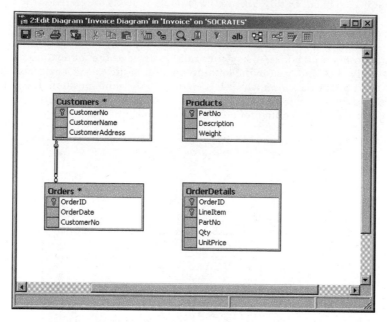

Now we'll just do the same thing for our other two relationships. We need to establish a one-to-many relationship from Orders to OrderDetails (there will be one order header for one or more order details). Also, we need a similar relationship going from Products to OrderDetails (there will be one Products record for many OrderDetails records):

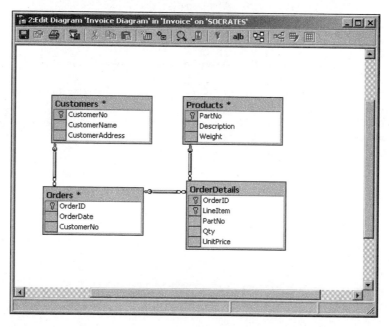

Adding Some Constraints

As we were going through the building of our tables and relationships, I mentioned a requirement that we still haven't addressed. This requirement needs a constraint to enforce it: **the part number is formatted as 9A9999 where "9" indicates a numeric digit 0-9 and "A" indicates an alpha (non-numeric) character**.

Let's add that requirement now by right-clicking on the Products table and selecting Properties. This will bring up a dialog box. When it first comes up, the dialog will be on the wrong tab. We need to switch over to the Check Constraints tab – even then most of what we want will be grayed out:

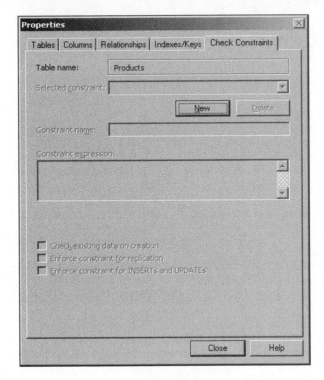

This occurs because there aren't currently any constraints to show. We can fix this by clicking on the New button.

It is at this point that we are given the opportunity to define our constraint. In order to restrict part numbers entered to the format we've established, we're going to need to make use of the LIKE operator:

```
(PartNo LIKE '[0-9][A-Z][0-9][0-9][0-9][0-9]')
```

This will essentially evaluate each character that the user is trying to enter in the PartNo column of our table. The first character will have to be zero through nine (a numeric digit), the second A through Z (an alpha), and the next four will again have to be numeric digits (the zero through nine thing again). We just enter this into the large text box labeled Constraint expression. In addition, we're going to change the default name for our constraint from CK_Products to CK_PartNo:

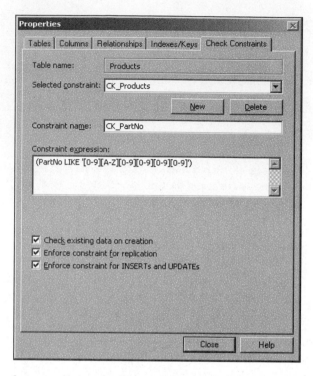

That didn't take us too long – and we now have our first database that we designed!!!

This was, of course, a relatively simple model – but we've now done the things that make up perhaps 90% or more of the actual data architecture.

Summary

Database design is a huge concept, and one that has many excellent books dedicated to it as their sole subject. It is essentially impossible to get across every database design notion in just a chapter or two.

In this chapter, we have, however, gotten you off to a solid start. We've seen that data is considered to be normalized when we take it out to the third normal form. At that level, repetitive information has been eliminated and our data in entirely dependent on our key – in short, the data is dependent on: "The key, the whole key, and nothing but the key". We've seen that normalization is, however, not always the right answer – strategic de-normalization of our data can simplify the database for users and speed reporting performance. Finally, we've looked at some non-normalization related concepts in our database design, plus how to make use of the daVinci tools to design our database.

In our next chapter, we will be taking a very close look at how SQL Server stores information and how to make the best use of indexes.

9

SQL Server Storage and Index Structures

Indexes are a critical part of your database planning and system maintenance. They provide SQL Server (and any other database system for that matter) with additional ways to look up data and take short cuts to that data's physical location. Adding the right index can cut huge percentages of time off your query executions. Unfortunately, too many poorly planned indexes can actually increase the time it takes for your query to run. Indeed, indexes tend to be one of the most misunderstood objects that SQL Server offers and, therefore, also tend to be one of the most mismanaged.

We will be studying indexes rather closely in this chapter from both a developer's and an administrator's point of view, but in order to fully understand indexes, you also need to understand how data is stored in SQL Server. For that reason, we will also take a look at SQL Server's data storage, past and present.

SQL Server Storage: Past and Present

The method of physically storing data to disk that was used for SQL Server prior to version 7.0 had been around for perhaps 20 years or more. While there's something to be said for time-tested technologies, this particular technology was not ideally suited to either the NT storage or security systems, nor would it have been a good choice for building a Windows 9x capable product. Something had to be done if Microsoft was to provide some of the features it wanted to supply for SQL Server 7.0 and beyond.

Many users of SQL Server today do not realize that the product, until version 7.0, was deeply rooted in Sybase. Microsoft and Sybase formed a cooperative to offer SQL Server on OS/2 back in the days before even NT was around. Indeed, it wasn't until version 4.2 of SQL Server that it came to Windows NT. After version 6.0 (which, incidentally, is what came after version 4.21), Sybase and Microsoft decided to go their separate ways. Microsoft kept the NT version of SQL Server; Sybase kept the UNIX version and all the other non-NT based versions (it then came out with its own NT version).

Prior to the split, Microsoft had decided it wanted to be a serious player in the enterprise database management market. Essentially, it wanted to take Oracle, Informix, and DB2 head on, but it didn't feel it had the product to do it with, so it embarked on a complete and utter re-write.

Re-writing a mission critical system like SQL Server is no small task, nor is it a quick one. Especially when you consider that you're going to have to deal with issues of backward-compatibility as well as adding new features (not many customers will buy something just because you've entirely re-written it – you have to throw them a bone in the form of new features). This being the case, Microsoft decided to throw out an interim release – SQL Server 6.5. This version offered a number of bug fixes from version 6.0 (and added a few new bugs for that matter), plus added replication (which didn't work very well), the Microsoft Distributed Transaction Coordinator (MS DTC), and several ANSI compatibility changes (most notably the new JOIN syntax).

Then came SQL Server 7.0. In building this product, Microsoft went out in search of the best and brightest RDBMS systems designers the world had to offer. The development team was (and is) an amazing collection of people who were hired away from the likes of Oracle, IBM, Informix, SAP, and more. A totally new approach was needed, and Microsoft went after the people who could give that. By the time SQL Server 7.0 was released, they had totally redesigned and rebuilt the storage engine, the relational engine, and the query engine – in short, they had re-written everything. Now, yet another release later, there is virtually no code left from the 6.5 era.

What's the point of this lengthy study in history? We've looked at the development history, and we'll look at storage in 6.5 so that you are better equipped to understand the various differences you are going to run into with the new product. SQL Server already has a very large installed base. Even with the release of SQL Server 2000, version 6.5 continues to hold a very substantial percentage of all SQL Server installations, and I suspect you will see legacy code from 4.x and 6.x developed apps for many years into the future. That said, let's take a look at how versions 6.5 and earlier, and how versions 7.0 and above handle storage.

SQL Server Storage – What All Versions Have in Common

Even with all the changes that we will investigate in SQL Server storage past and present, it's worth noting that they actually have a large number of things in common. Primarily, these similarities are in the logical way that data is stored. The data can be thought of, in both new and old versions, as existing in something of a hierarchy of structures.

The hierarchy is pretty simple. Some of the objects within the hierarchy are things that you will deal with directly, and will therefore know easily. A few others exist under the cover, and while they can be directly addressed in some cases, they usually are not. Let's take a look at them one by one.

The Database

OK – this one is easy. I can just hear people out there saying, "Duh! I knew that." Yes, you probably did, but I point it out as a unique entity here because it is the highest level of the definition of storage (for a given server) that is common to both new and old storage paradigms. How exactly the storage space for the database is defined is actually one of the biggest areas of change between the new and old versions of the product. This is the highest level that a **lock** can be established at, although you cannot explicitly create a database level lock.

A lock is something of both a hold and a place marker that is used by the system. As you do development using SQL Server – or any other database for that matter – you will find that understanding and managing locks is absolutely critical to your system.

We will be looking into locking extensively in Chapter 14, but we will see the lockability of objects within SQL Server discussed in passing as we look at storage.

The Extent

An **extent** is the basic unit of storage used to allocate space for tables and indexes. It is made up of eight contiguous data **pages**, the size of which varies by version (16K for SQL Server 6.5 and before, 64K for 7.0 and beyond). When you create the first table in your database in version 7.0, only two data pages are allocated. As new rows are inserted into the table, new pages are allocated until the table consumes eight pages. From this point on, additional space is never allocated by less than an eight-page extent at a time. In SQL Server 2000, the table does not even allocate the first two pages upon creation. These are added only on the first row insertion.

The concept of allocating space based on extents, rather than actual space used, can be somewhat difficult to understand for people used to operating system storage principles. For those of you who are indeed familiar with the concept of clustered storage, you can think of extents as being somewhat similar to a cluster. The important points about an extent include:

❑ Once an extent is full, the next record will take up not just the size of the record, but the size of a whole new extent. Many people who are new to SQL Server get tripped up in their space estimations in part due to the allocation of an extent at a time rather than a record at a time.

❑ By pre-allocating this space, SQL Server saves the time of allocating new space with each record.

❑ Extents are lockable resources. However, extents are only locked when new extents are being allocated or deallocated.

It may seem like a waste that a whole extent is taken up just because one too many rows were added to fit on the currently allocated extent(s), but the amount of space wasted this way is typically not that much. Still, it can add up – particularly in a highly fragmented environment – so it's definitely something of which you should be aware.

The good news in taking up all this space is that SQL Server skips some of the allocation time overhead. Instead of worrying about allocation issues every time it writes a row, SQL Server only deals with additional space allocation when a new extent is needed.

> *Don't confuse the space that an extent is taking up with the space that a database takes up. Whatever space is allocated to the database (or device, prior to version 7.0) is what you'll see disappear from your disk drive's available space number. An extent is merely how things are, in turn, allocated within the total space reserved by the database.*

An extent is also a lockable resource. If you have an extent lock, then you have a lock on all the data within that extent. Data may be part of the same table as that in the extent, but still be available (not have a lock on it) as long as it is not in the locked extent.

The Page

Much like an extent is a unit of allocation within the database, a page is the unit of allocation within a specific extent. There are eight pages to every extent, though the size of those pages (and the extent for that matter) depends on what version of the product you are running (pre, or post 7.0).

A page is the last level you reach before you are at the actual data row. Whereas the number of pages per extent is fixed, the number of rows per page is not – that depends entirely on the size of the row, which can vary. You can think of a page as being something of a container for both table and index row data. A row is not allowed to be split between pages.

A page is made up of several components beyond the individual rows: the **page header**, the actual row data, and the **row offsets**.

The following is an illustration of this:

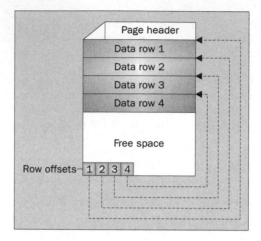

Notice how, for every row we insert, we have to place the row offset down at the end of the page to indicate where in the page that particular row's data begins.

There are a number of different **page types**:

- ❑ Data
- ❑ Index
- ❑ Binary Large Object (BLOB) – for image as well as most text and ntext data
- ❑ Global and Shared Global Allocation Map (GAM and SGAM)
- ❑ Page Free Space (PFS)
- ❑ Index Allocation Map (IAM)

Data Pages

Data pages are pretty self-explanatory – they are the actual data in your table, with the exception of any BLOB data that is not defined with the **text in row** option. In the case of a row that has a column that contains BLOB data, the regular data is stored in a data page – usually with a 16-byte pointer to where to find the BLOB page that contains the binary information that makes up the BLOB. In a situation where you are using the text in row option, the text will be stored with the data if the text is short enough to fit in the available page space (otherwise, you get the 16-byte pointer business again).

Index Pages

Index pages are also pretty straightforward: they hold both the non-leaf and leaf level pages (we'll examine what these are later in the chapter) of a non-clustered index, as well as the non-leaf level pages of a clustered index. These index types will become much clearer as we continue through this chapter.

BLOB Pages

BLOB pages are for storing Binary Large Objects. For SQL Server, these amount to any data stored in an image field as well as the vast majority of text and ntext data. BLOB pages are special as far as data storage pages go, in that they don't have any rows as such. Since a BLOB can be as large as 2GB, they have to be able to go on more than one page – for this portion of things it doesn't matter what the version is. SQL Server will allocate as many pages as it needs in order to store the entire BLOB, but there is no guarantee that these pages will be contiguous – the pages could be located anywhere within the database file(s).

As mentioned before, the connection between the non-BLOB data for a row and any BLOB related to that row comes in the form of a pointer. The nature of that pointer and how SQL Server navigates to the BLOB data was changed for version 7.0 of SQL Server. In version 6.5 and before, the BLOB pages were put together in a chain – similar to a linked list. In order to find a page that was part of the BLOB, you needed to start at the beginning and navigate through the BLOB page by page. If you were trying to perform some form of text or binary search, this kind of arrangement was deadly, given that you were forced into a serial scan of the data. Beginning with version 7.0 however, the pages were changed to be organized into a Balanced Tree (or B-Tree) structure (which we will discuss fully a little later in the chapter). B-Trees provide more of a branching structure, and therefore a more direct path for larger BLOBs. This has made quite a difference to how quickly text operations can be performed.

Even with the significant improvements made in version 7.0, BLOBs are very slow performance-wise, so we will talk about alternative storage methods when we look at advanced design issues later on.

Global Allocation Map, Shared Global Allocation Map, and Page Free Space Pages

Global Allocation Map (**GAM**), **Shared Global Allocation Map** (**SGAM**), and **Page Free Space** (**PFS**) page types are involved with figuring out which extents and pages are in use, and which are not. Essentially, these pages store records that indicate where there is space available. Understanding these page types is not really necessary in order to do high quality development or systems administration, and is beyond the scope of this book. If, however, you're just dying to know about them (or you're having problems with insomnia), then you can find more information on them in the Books Online – just look up GAM in the index.

Page Splits

When a page becomes full, it splits. This means more than just a new page being allocated – it also means that approximately half the data from the existing page is moved to the new page.

The exception to this process is when a clustered index is in use. If there is a clustered index, and the next inserted row would be physically located as the last record in the table, then a new page is created and the new row is added to the new page without relocating any of the existing data. We will see much more on page splits as we investigate indexes.

Now that we have an idea of what the versions of SQL Server have in common, let's look at the specifics.

SQL Server Storage in Version 6.5 and Below

Since this book is focused on SQL Server 2000 and, therefore, the storage engine used by version 7.0 and beyond, I am not going to go into every detail of how 6.5 did things. Still, we need to have a generalized understanding of prior versions of SQL Server if we are to be able to deal with the many legacy servers out there – not to mention a very large amount of legacy code that will try to do things that version 7.0 won't like.

In versions after 7.0, the database is the absolute highest level of space allocation that you have available. I mention that here because 6.5 doesn't work that way at all. Version 6.5 has its own brand of space allocation, and we'll see how that ends up making a large difference in the way things are stored.

The Device

In version 6.5 and earlier, there was the concept of a **device**. A device was something like another pre-allocation of space but, in this case, SQL Server was telling the operating system (remember, this goes back to the Sybase days, so we're talking a couple of different operating systems) to set aside disk space in what amounted to a named storage area. SQL Server was then responsible for what did and didn't go into that area. It could be one database, a database and its log, or multiple databases and logs – any mix of data and logs was fine as long as there was still room in the device. The trick was that you needed to say how much of that device you wanted to allocate to each database or log. When you ran out of space in your database, you needed to allocate additional space to it. If there was no room left in the device, then you needed to either expand the device, or create a new one and put a portion of your database into the new device.

What was particularly tricky was that any restore from backup had to be done using the same device names in the same sizes and order of creation as was originally performed. For many shops, there was a sad day when they had a good set of backups, but didn't know what the device names, sizes, or creation order was. This rendered the backups relatively useless if you lacked the information to rebuild the device structures to be exactly as they were.

> *This belongs in the "way back" files but, if you have a 6.5 server and run into this "we don't know what or when" device issue, there are system tables (sysdevices, sysobjects, and sysdatabases) that you can query to find the information you need – as long as you still have the original master database.*

The Database

Because 6.5 and earlier versions of SQL Server used the notion of devices, databases were somewhat simpler animals in terms of definition than they are under post 7.0 versions. At creation time, everything was defined in terms of what device the database and log were going on, and how much of that space you wanted to take up. In short, you were dealing only with the logical device, rather than the physical component that you reference in 7.0 and 2000 (where you refer to the physical file rather than a logical device). In practice though, we had to deal with two different things (a device and a database), which actually made things quite a pain. Post 7.0 databases, while being more complex in the actual database definition, actually simplify things when you compare them to the combination of device and database in 6.5 and prior versions.

In most other ways though, pre-7.0 databases work just as the post 7.0 databases do from a storage standpoint. The database is full of extents, pages, and so on. The database is a lockable resource – nothing has changed except for how we actually create the database, and that a 6.5 database works on devices rather than files.

Extents and Pages

Extents in 6.5 and earlier held eight pages just as later versions do, but the pages were only 2KB in size, and so the extent was only 16KB in size. Any table you created meant that you also created at least one extent – extents were limited to dealing with one table at a time.

BLOB data was stored in special pages, but any BLOB page would be referring to data for only one record. That record may have had many pages of BLOB data associated with it, but the reverse was not true – if your BLOB information was only 10 bytes in size, it still took up an entire 2KB page.

BLOB information in SQL Server 6.5 and earlier was stored using a chain approach. This is actually a beneficial approach from a raw I/O standpoint, but also creates what was, and is, extremely poor performance for string manipulation exercises.

Both extents and pages were lockable resources.

Rows

The primary difference in the area of rows has to do with size and lockability.

The rule of rows not spanning pages (except for BLOB data) meant that the maximum row size was a little less than 2KB (1,962 bytes; the rest of the 2,048 bytes contained page header and row-offset information).

Rows were only a quasi-lockable resource. You will read many things about how row-level locking wasn't available in SQL Server 6.5 and before. While this is true of 6.0 and earlier databases, version 6.5 did have a limited form of row-level locking. The limitation was to INSERT statements only. What's more, by default, row-level locking on inserts was turned off. Indeed, most people didn't realize it had been added. Those who knew about it usually didn't make use of it because it required some special syntax usage in your INSERT statement. In short, you could lock at the row level, but only on inserts, only if you had turned on the option, and only if you used the required syntax.

SQL Server Storage in 7.0 and Beyond

The Device

Hooray! There aren't any. Everything the device did in previous versions is either no longer necessary, or has been incorporated directly into the database and/or database file(s).

The Database

We've already seen how the database in 7.0 becomes the center point for declaring physical space needs. Beyond that, it works much as it did in 6.5. The database is still a lockable resource.

> **For those of you who are coming from the 6.5 and earlier versions of SQL Server, be aware that deleting a database on post 7.0 servers also deletes the physical files. This is a significant change from how deleting a device worked in 6.5.**

The File

Files are probably the closest thing that 7.0 and later versions have to a device. If, however, you notice the way that I'm presenting things here (which is following a hierarchy), you'll realize that we're talking about files after the database rather than before.

With devices, you could have multiple databases; it works the other way around with files – that is, you can have multiple files for one database. A file cannot hold multiple databases.

By default, your database has two files associated with it:

❑   The first is the primary physical database file – that's where your data is ultimately stored. This file should be named with an .mdf extension (this is a recommendation, not a requirement – but I think you'll find doing it in other ways will become confusing over time).

❑   The second is something of an offshoot of the database file – the log. We'll dive into the log quite a bit when we deal with transactions and locks in Chapter 14, but you should be aware that it resides in its own file (which should end with a n .ldf extension), and that your database will not operate without it. The log is the serial recording of what's happened to your database since the last time that data was "committed" to the database. The database isn't really your complete set of data. The log isn't your complete set of data either. Instead, if you start with the database and then "apply" (add in all the activities from) the log, you have your complete set of data.

There is no restriction about where these files are located relative to each other. It is possible (actually, it's even quite desirable) to place each file on a separate physical device. This not only allows the activity in one file not to interfere with that in the other file, but it also creates a situation where losing the file with the database does not cause you to lose your work – you can restore a backup and then re-apply the log (that was safe on the other drive). Likewise, if you lose the drive with the log, you'll still have a valid database up until the time of the last **checkpoint** (checkpoints are fully covered in Chapter 14).

The Extent

An extent has had several changes made to it since the 6.5 days. Prior to version 7.0, there was only a single table to one or many extents – that's been slightly changed.

SQL Server no longer considers an extent to be exclusive to one table. Instead, we now have two different kinds of extents:

❑   Shared extents

❑   Uniform extents

Shared extents are extents that can have up to eight different objects in them (up to eight different objects on the eight different pages that exist within the extent). New tables and indexes start off with shared extents. Once they have at least eight pages then they are moved to uniform extents.

Uniform extents are just that – uniform. Every page in the extent is from the same object. Here's an example of how shared and uniform extents might have data allocated:

Page	Shared Extent	Uniform Extent
1	MyTable1	MyTable1
2	1st Index on MyTable1	MyTable1
3	2nd Index on MyTable1	MyTable1
4	MyTable2	MyTable1
5	MyTable3	MyTable1
6	1st Index on MyTable3	MyTable1
7	4th Index on MyTable1	MyTable1
8	1st Index on MyTable2	MyTable1

This new way of doing things has some advantages over the previous method.

❑ First, you save space. If SQL Server was still using the "one table or index per extent" rule that was in place under 6.5, then the objects listed in our table on shared extent usage would have taken up to eight times as much space as with the new system. Think about that for a moment – if SQL Server has 64KB extents, then that means that you would save over 400KB (8 x 64K for the 8 extents, minus 8 x 8K for the 8 pages actually in use) for every shared extent.

❑ Second, you gain speed. Fewer extents means that you switch between extents less often, which in turn means that you have fewer reads. Fewer reads mean less time taken performing reads, which in turn means that you take less time on whatever task you are performing.

The larger extent and page sizes do, however, increase the risk of **fragmentation**. Fragmentation creates a situation where you have small amounts of data residing on lots of otherwise empty pages. This means that you end up incurring the overhead of switching between pages and extents for even small record counts. Fragmentation occurs in situations where you are doing a lot of deletions in your database, and is discussed further later in this chapter when we deal with the concept of a fill factor.

Pages

Pages are another area of huge change in the way that post 7.0 versions work as compared to previous versions. Some of the major changes include:

❑ Size is now 8KB instead of 2KB

❑ BLOB pages can now be used for the data of more than one row

❑ The method of linking to BLOB pages has changed

A data page can now contain BLOB data as long as that data is of the text or ntext data type (special declarations are required in your table's CREATE statement).

The 8KB size change has to be the biggest in terms of everyday effect. The rule on a given row not spanning a page is still in effect, so a bigger page means the potential for bigger rows. In addition, the larger size cuts down on the number of page changes, which in turn cuts down on logical reads. Fewer logical reads usually means less time and effort spent in I/O, and better performance.

There is a downside to larger pages however. First, it means that even when SQL Server knows on which page your data is, it has more rows to sift through in order to find the specific row (Microsoft has, however, implemented some ways around this problem). More importantly though, you have a larger number of rows within the page and, therefore, a larger number of rows are included when you lock the page. We will see more about how this can have a negative effect when we look at locks.

As for BLOB data, we now have the potential for more than one row to have data on the same BLOB page. Indeed, the data on that page is all stored in something of a general BLOB format, and does not need to even be of the same type – you can mix text, ntext, and image data with no problems.

In 7.0, Microsoft changed the storage method to make use of what is essentially a Balanced Tree structure. For those of you who are not familiar with B-Trees (which is probably most of you), we will take a detailed look at them shortly when we deal with indexes. The abbreviated version of how it works, in this case, is that a text pointer is stored with the actual data row. That text pointer does not point to the actual data but, rather, to what is called a root structure. This root structure is the first place that might actually point to the real data but, if the BLOB is too large, then the root structure may need to point at what is called an intermediate node. If the B-Tree gets larger than 32KB, then the tree must split, and additional layers of the tree will need to be navigated in order to get to the end data. As the BLOB gets larger and larger, the number of tree-branch level nodes also grows – the B-Tree gets larger.

As you might expect, there was a purpose in going with this new design. The fact is that text operations should run much faster in this structure, since SQL Server can navigate to a particular point within the structure just by traversing the B-Tree. Under 6.5, you would have had to go page by page, in order, until you got to the page you wanted.

Rows

If there is a single area where Microsoft took a huge leap forward with the version 7.0 re-write, it has to have been in the changes surrounding rows. The biggest changes were:

❑ Rows can be up to 8KB

❑ Row-level locking is now supported on all statements – in 6.5, you could only have row-level locking on INSERT statements, and then only if you knew the right set of hoops to jump through

Beginning in SQL Server 2000, we also gained the ability to perform even more varieties of locks at the row level. For example, in 7.0 we could ask for a rowlock, but we couldn't explicitly state that we wanted an exclusive lock (again, more on these in our chapter on locking). Now we can.

Larger Row Sizes

Beginning with version 7.0, rows can be up to slightly less than 8KB (8,060 bytes to be more specific) in size. This is just over 4 times as large as with 6.5, and it has a much larger impact on table and database design than many people realize.

Under 6.5, it was not at all uncommon to have tables that needed to be broken out into a one-to-one relationship just so you had enough room to store everything. This was problematic both in terms of database complexity and in the performance costs of needing to perform a join in order to get at data that should have all been in one table. While this can still certainly be a problem under post 7.0 versions, it is far less likely.

Another benefit of the larger row sizes becomes apparent when you realize that the maximum length of many field types also went up. Under 6.5 for example, the maximum length for a non-BLOB character type was 255 characters. This was very problematic – even things as common as a description field on a form quite often need more than 255 characters to be of any use whatsoever. By allowing these to now be up to 8,060 characters, we can often avoid needing to use `text` fields, which are both slower and more unwieldy than `char`, `varchar`, `nchar`, or `nvarchar`.

> **In addition to the limit of 8,060 characters, there is also a maximum of 1,024 columns (up from just 250 in version 6.5). In practice, you'll find it very unusual to run into a situation where you run out of columns before you run into the 8060 character limit. 1,024 gives you an average column width of 8 bytes. For most uses, you'll easily exceed that. The exception to this tends to be in measurement and statistical information – where you have a large number of different things that you are storing numeric samples of. Still, even those applications will find it a rare day when they bump into the 1,024 column count limit.**

Row-Level Locking

As I've mentioned several times now, we have an entire chapter coming up on the subject of locking, but I want to point this piece out here because of its sheer importance. Locking at the row level means that we are placing a hold on only that one row – not all the rows on a page or in the extent. This becomes a huge issue when we start to talk about contention issues in Chapter 14. For now though, what I want you to understand is that the concept of row-level locking applies not only to the actual data, but also to the index rows we will be working with throughout this chapter.

Understanding Indexes

Webster's dictionary defines an index as:

A list (as of bibliographical information or citations to a body of literature) arranged usually in alphabetical order of some specified datum (as author, subject, or keyword).

I'll take a simpler approach in the context of databases, and say it's a way of potentially getting to data a heck of a lot quicker. Still, the Webster's definition isn't too bad – even for our specific purposes.

Perhaps the key thing to point out in the Webster's definition is the word "usually" that's in there. The definition of "alphabetical order" changes depending on a number of rules. For example, in SQL Server, we have a number of different collation options available to us. Among these options are:

❑ **Binary**: sorts by the numeric representation of the character (for example, in ASCII, a space is represented by the number 32, the letter "D" is 68, but the letter "d" is 100). Because everything is numeric, this is the fastest option – unfortunately, it's also not at all the way in which people think, and can also really wreak havoc with comparisons in your WHERE clause.

❑ **Dictionary order**: this sorts things just as you would expect to see in a dictionary, with a twist – you can set a number of different additional options to determine sensitivity to case, accent, and character set.

It's fairly easy to understand that, if we tell SQL Server to pay attention to case, then "A" is not going to be equal to "a". Likewise, if we tell it to be case insensitive, then "A" will be equal to "a". Things get a bit more confusing when you add accent sensitivity – that is, SQL Server pays attention to diacritical marks, and therefore "a" is different from "á", which is different from "à". Where many people get even more confused is in how collation order affects not only the equality of data, but also the sort order (and, therefore, the way it is stored in indexes).

By way of example, let's look at the equality of a couple of collation options, and what they do to our sort order and equality information:

Collation Order	Comparison Values	Index Storage Order
Dictionary order, case-insensitive, accent-insensitive (the default)	A = a = à = á = â = Ä = ä = Å = å	a, A, à, â, á, Ä, ä, Å, å
Dictionary order, case-insensitive, accent-insensitive, uppercase preference	A = a = à = á = â = Ä = ä = Å = å	A, a, à, â, á, Ä, ä, Å, å
Dictionary order, case-sensitive	A ≠ a, Ä ≠ ä, Å ≠ å, a ≠ à ≠ á ≠ â ≠ ä ≠ å, A ≠ Ä ≠ Å	A, a, à, á, â, Ä, ä, Å, å

The point here is that what happens in your indexes depends on the collation information you have established for your data. Beginning with SQL Server 2000, you can change collation at the database and column level, so you have a fairly fine granularity in your level of control. For earlier versions however (even 7.0), the collation is set at the server level, and that's it. For such older installations, your system may see some rather radical changes if a server is installed as case sensitive rather than insensitive. If you're going to assume that your server is case insensitive, then you need to be sure that the documentation for your system deals with this if you plan to support earlier versions of SQL Server. Imagine, if you're an independent software vendor (ISV), and you sell your product – now imagine that your customer installs it on their existing server (which is going to seem like an entirely reasonable thing to them), but that existing server happens to be an older server that's set up as case sensitive. You're going to get a support call from one very unhappy customer.

> Once the collation order has been set for previous versions of SQL Server, it is a major pain to change it, so be certain of the collation order you want before you set it. SQL Server 2000 makes this a lot easier, but it's still a hassle to change collation orders mid development cycle.

B-Trees

The concept of a **Balanced Tree**, or **B-Tree**, is certainly not one that was created with SQL Server. Indeed, B-Trees are used in a very large number of indexing systems both in and out of the database world.

A B-Tree simply attempts to provide a consistent and relatively low cost method of finding your way to a particular piece of information. The *Balanced* in the name is pretty much self-descriptive – a B-Tree is, with the odd exception, self-balancing, meaning that every time the tree branches, approximately half the data is on one side, and half on the other side. The *Tree* in the name is also probably pretty obvious at this point (hint: tree, branch – see a trend here?) – it's there because, when you draw the structure, then turn it upside down, it has the general form of a tree.

A B-Tree starts at the **root node** (another stab at the tree analogy there, but not the last). This root node can, if there is a small amount of data, point directly to the actual location of the data. In such a case, you would end up with a structure that looked something like this:

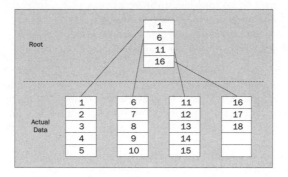

So, we start at the root and look through the records until we find the last page that starts with a value less than what we're looking for. We then obtain a pointer to that node, and look through it until we find the row that we want.

In most situations though, there is too much data to reference from the root node, so the root node points at intermediate nodes – or what are called **non-leaf level nodes**. Non-leaf level nodes are nodes that are somewhere in between the root and the node that tells you where the data is physically stored. Non-leaf level nodes can then point to other non-leaf level nodes, or to **leaf level nodes** (last tree analogy reference – I promise). Leaf level nodes are the nodes where you obtain the real reference to the actual physical data. Much like the leaf is the end of the line for navigating the tree, the node we get to at the leaf level is the end of the line for our index – from here, we can go straight to the actual data node that has our data on it.

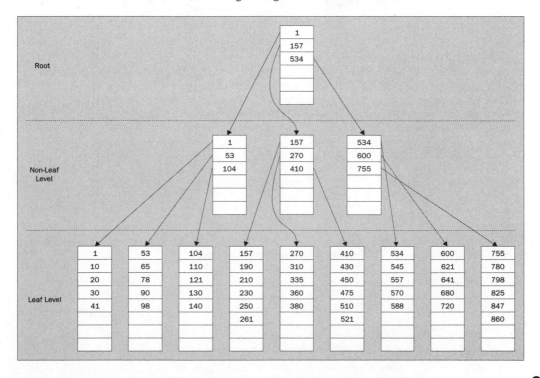

Again, we start with the root node, then move to the node that starts with the highest value that is equal to or less than what we're looking for and is also in the next level down. We then repeat the process – look for the node that has the highest starting value at or below the value for which we're looking. We keep doing this, level by level down the tree, until we get to the leaf level – from there we know the physical location of the data, and can quickly navigate to it.

Page Splits – A First Look

All of this works quite nicely on the read side of the equation – it's the insert that gets a little tricky. Recall that the *B* in B-Tree stands for *balanced*. You may also recall that I mentioned that a B-Tree is balanced because about half the data is on either side every time you run into a branch in the tree. B-Trees are sometimes referred to as **self-balancing** because the way new data is added to the tree prevents them from becoming lopsided.

When data is added to the tree, a node will eventually become full, and will need to split. Since, in SQL Server, a node equates to a page – this is called a **page split**.

When a page split occurs, data is automatically moved around to keep things balanced. The first half of the data is left on the old page, and the rest of the data is added to a new page – thus you have about a 50-50 split, and your tree remains balanced:

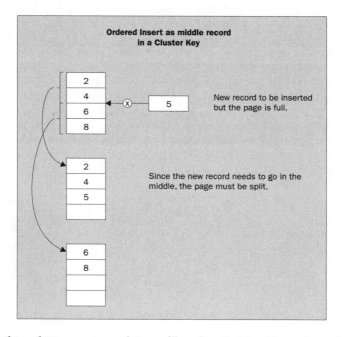

If you think about this splitting process a bit, you'll realize that it adds a substantial amount of overhead at the time of the split. Instead of inserting just one page, you are:

- ❑   Creating a new page
- ❑   Migrating rows from the existing page to the new page
- ❑   Adding your new row to one of the pages
- ❑   Adding another entry in the parent node

But the overhead doesn't stop there. Since we're in a tree arrangement, you have the possibility for something of a cascading action. When you create the new page (because of the split), you need to make another entry in the parent node. This entry in the parent node also has the potential to cause a page-split at that level, and the process starts all over again. Indeed, this possibility extends all the way up to and can even affect the root node.

If the root node splits, then you actually end up creating two additional pages. Since there can only be one root node, the page which was formerly the root node is split into two pages, and becomes a new intermediate level of the tree. An entirely new root node is then created, and will have two entries (one to the old root-node, one to the split page).

Needless to say, page splits can have a very negative impact on system performance, and are characterized by behavior where your process on the server seems to just pause for a few seconds (while the pages are being split and re-written).

We will talk about page-split prevention before we're done with this chapter.

> *While page splits at the leaf level are a common fact of life, page splits at intermediate nodes happen far less frequently. As your table grows, every layer of the index will experience page splits, but, since the intermediate nodes only have one entry for several entries on the next lower node, the number of page splits gets less and less frequent as you move further up the tree. Still, for a split to occur above the leaf level, there must have already been a split at the next lowest level – this means that page splits up the tree are cumulative (and expensive performance-wise) in nature.*

SQL Server has a number of different types of index (which we will discuss shortly), but they all make use of this B-Tree approach in some way or another. Indeed, they are all very similar in structure thanks to the flexible nature of a B-Tree. Still, we shall see that there are indeed some significant differences, and these can have an impact on the performance of our system.

> *For a SQL Server index, the nodes of the tree come in the form of pages, but you can actually apply this concept of a root node, the non-leaf level, the leaf level, and the tree structure to more than just SQL Server or even just databases.*

How Data is Accessed in SQL Server

In the broadest sense, there are only two ways in which SQL Server retrieves the data you request:

- ❑ Using a table scan
- ❑ Using an index

Which method SQL Server will use to run your particular query will depend on what indexes are available, what columns you are asking about, what kind of joins you are doing, and the size of your tables.

Use of Table Scans

A table scan is a pretty straightforward process. When a table scan is performed, SQL Server starts at the physical beginning of the table looking through every row in the table. As it finds rows that match the criteria of your query, it includes them in the result set.

You may hear lots of bad things about table scans, and in general, they will be true. However, table scans can actually be the fastest method of access in some instances. Typically, this is the case when retrieving data from rather small tables. The exact size where this becomes the case will vary widely according to the width of your table and what the specific nature of the query is.

> *After you've read up through the advanced query topics chapter, you may want to come back and think about how this works for a bit. See if you can spot why the use of EXISTS in the WHERE clause of your queries has so much to offer performance-wise where it fits the problem. When you use the EXISTS operator, SQL Server stops as soon as it finds one record that matches the criteria. If you had a million record table, and it found a matching record on the third record, then use of the EXISTS option would have saved you the reading of 999,997 records! NOT EXISTS works in much the same way.*

Use of Indexes

When SQL Server decides to use an index, the process actually works somewhat similarly to a table scan, but with a few shortcuts.

During the query optimization process, the optimizer takes a look at all the available indexes and chooses the best one (this is primarily based on the information you specify in your joins and WHERE clause, combined with statistical information SQL Server keeps on index makeup). Once that index is chosen, SQL Server navigates the tree structure to the point of data that matches your criteria and again extracts only the records it needs. The difference is that, since the data is sorted, the query engine knows when it has reached the end of the current range it is looking for. It can then end the query, or move on to the next range of data as necessary.

If you've read ahead about query topics at all (to Chapter 16 specifically), you may notice some striking resemblances to how the EXISTS option worked. The EXISTS keyword allowed a query to quit running the instant that it found a match. The performance gains using an index are similar or even better since the process of searching for data can work in a similar fashion – that is, the server is able to know when there is nothing left that's relevant, and can stop things right there. Even better, however, is that by using an index, we don't have to limit ourselves to Boolean situations (does the piece of data I was after exist – yes or no?). We can apply this same notion to both the beginning and end of a range – we are able to gather ranges of data with essentially the same benefits that using an index gives to finding data. What's more, we can do a very fast lookup (called a SEEK) of our data rather than hunting through the entire table.

> *Don't get the impression from my comparing what indexes do for us to the EXISTS operator that indexes replace the EXISTS operator altogether (or vice versa). The two are not mutually exclusive - they can be used together, and often are. I mention them here together only because they have the similarity of being able to tell when their work is done, and quit before getting to the physical end of the table.*

Index Types and Index Navigation

Although there are nominally two types of indexes in SQL Server (**clustered** and **non-clustered**), there are actually, internally speaking, three different types:

- ❑ Clustered indexes
- ❑ Non-clustered indexes – which comprise:
  - ❑ Non-clustered indexes on a heap
  - ❑ Non-clustered indexes on a clustered index

The way the physical data is stored varies between clustered and non-clustered indexes. The way SQL Server traverses the B-Tree to get to the end data varies between all three index types.

All SQL Server indexes have leaf level and non-leaf level pages. As we mentioned when we discussed B-Trees, the leaf level is the level that holds the "key" to identifying the record, and the non-leaf level pages are guides to the leaf level.

The indexes are built over either a clustered table or what is called a heap.

Clustered Tables

A **clustered table** is any table that has a clustered index on it. Clustered indexes are discussed in detail shortly, but what they mean to the table is that the data is physically stored in a designated order. Individual rows are uniquely identified through the use of the **cluster-key** – the columns which define the clustered index.

> *This should bring to mind the question of, "What if the clustered index is not unique?" That is, how can a clustered index be used to uniquely identify a row if the index is not a unique index? The answer lies under the covers – SQL Server forces any clustered indexes to be unique – even if you don't define it that way. Fortunately, it does this in a way that doesn't change how you use the index. You can still insert duplicate rows if you wish, but SQL Server will add a suffix to the key internally to ensure that the row has a unique identifier.*

Heaps

A **heap** is any table that does not have a clustered index on it. In this case, a unique identifier, or row ID (RID) is created based on a combination of the extent, pages, and row offset (places from the top of the page) for that row. A RID is only necessary if there is no cluster key available (no clustered index).

Clustered Indexes

A **clustered index** is unique for any given table – you can only have one per table. You don't have to have a clustered index, but you'll find it to be one of the most commonly chosen types as the first index, for a variety of reasons that will become apparent as we look at our index types.

What makes a clustered index special is that the leaf level of a clustered index is the actual data – that is, the data is re-sorted to be stored in the same physical order that the index sort criteria state. This means that, once you get to the leaf level of the index, you're done – you're at the data. Any new record is inserted according to its correct physical order in the clustered index. How new pages are created changes depending on where the record needs to be inserted.

In the case of a new record that needs to be inserted into the middle of the index structure, a normal page split occurs. The last half of the records from the old page are moved to the new page and the new record is inserted into the new or old page as appropriate.

In the case of a new record that is logically at the end of the index structure, a new page is created, but only the new record is added to the new page.

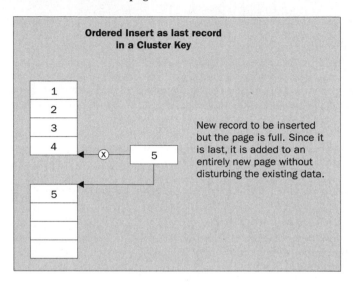

Navigating the Tree

As I've indicated previously, even the indexes in SQL Server are stored in a B-Tree. Theoretically, a B-Tree always has half of the remaining information in each possible direction as the tree branches. Let's take a look at a visualization of what a B-Tree looks like for a clustered index:

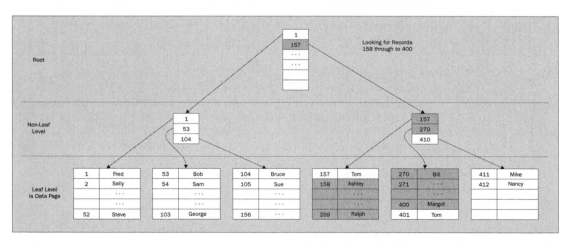

As you can see, it looks essentially identical to the more generic B-Trees we discussed earlier in the chapter. In this case, we're doing a range search (something clustered indexes are particularly good at) for numbers 158-400. All we have to do is:

Navigate to the first record, and include all remaining records on that page – we know we need the rest of that page because the information from one node up lets us know that we'll also need data from a few other pages. Since this is an ordered list, we can be sure it's continuous – that means if the next page has records which should be included, then the rest of this page must be included. We can just start spewing out data from those pages without having to do the verification side of things.

We start off by navigating to the root node. SQL Server is able to locate the root node based on an entry that is kept in the system table called sysindexes.

> **Every index in your database has an entry in sysindexes. This system table is part of your database (as opposed to being in the master database), and stores the location information for all the indexes in your database and on which columns they are based.**

By looking through the page that serves as the root node, we can figure out which the next page we need to examine is (the second page on the second level as we have it drawn here). We then continue the process. With each step we take down the tree, we are getting to smaller and smaller subsets of data.

Eventually, we will get to the leaf level of the index. In the case of our clustered index, getting to the leaf level of the index means that we are also at our desired row(s) and our desired data.

> **I can't stress enough the importance of the distinction that, with a clustered index, when you've fully navigated the index, that means that you've fully navigated to your data. How much of a performance difference this can make will really show its head as we look at non-clustered indexes – particularly when the non-clustered index is built over a clustered index.**

Non-Clustered Indexes on a Heap

Non-clustered indexes on a heap work very similarly to clustered indexes in most ways. They do, however, have a few notable differences:

The leaf level is not the data – instead, it is the level at which you are able to obtain a pointer to that data. This pointer comes in the form of the RID, which, as we described earlier in the chapter, is made up of the extent, page, and row offset for the particular row being pointed to by the index. Even though the leaf level is not the actual data (instead, it has the RID), we only have one more step than with a clustered index – because the RID has the full information on the location of the row, we can go directly to the data.

Don't, however, misunderstand this "one more step" to mean that there's only a small amount of overhead difference, and that non-clustered indexes on a heap will run close to as fast as a clustered index. With a clustered index, the data is physically in the order of the index. That means, for a range of data, when you find the row that has the beginning of your data on it, there's a good chance that the other rows are on that page with it (that is, you're already physically almost to the next record since they are stored together). With a heap, the data is not linked together in any way other than through the index. From a physical standpoint, there is absolutely no sorting of any kind. This means that, from a physical read standpoint, your system may have to retrieve records from all over the file. Indeed, it's quite possible (possibly even probable) that you will wind up fetching data from the same page several separate times – SQL Server has no way of knowing it will have to come back to that physical location because there was no link between the data. With the clustered index, it knows that's the physical sort, and can therefore grab it all in just one visit to the page.

Just to be fair to the non-clustered index on a heap here vs. the clustered index, the odds are extremely high that any page that was already read once will still be in the memory cache, and, as such, will be retrieved extremely quickly. Still, it does add some additional logical operations to retrieve the data.

Here's the same search we did with the clustered index, only with a non-clustered index on a heap this time:

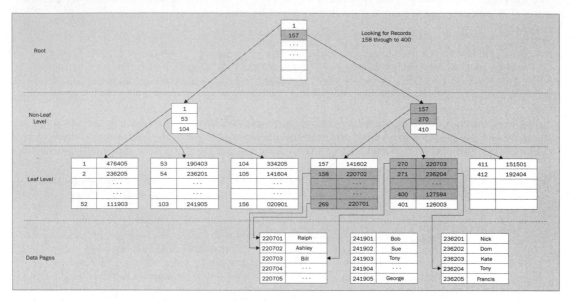

Through most of the index navigation, things work exactly as they did before. We start out at the same root node, and we traverse the tree dealing with more and more focused pages until we get to the leaf level of our index. This is where we run into the difference. With a clustered index, we could have stopped right here, but, with a non-clustered index, we have more work to do. If the non-clustered index is on a heap, then we have just one more level to go. We take the Row ID from the leaf level page, and navigate to it – it is not until that point that we are at our actual data.

Non-Clustered Indexes on a Clustered Table

With **non-clustered indexes on a clustered table**, the similarities continue – but so do the differences. Just as with non-clustered indexes on a heap, the non-leaf level of the index looks pretty much as it did for a clustered index. The difference does not come until we get to the leaf level.

At the leaf level, we have a rather sharp difference from what we've seen with the other two index structures – we have yet another index to look over. With clustered indexes, when we got to the leaf level, we found the actual data. With non-clustered indexes on a heap, we didn't find the actual data, but did find an identifier that let us go right to the data (we were just one step away). With non-clustered indexes on a clustered table, we find the **cluster-key**. That is, we find enough information to go and make use of the clustered index.

We end up with something that looks like this:

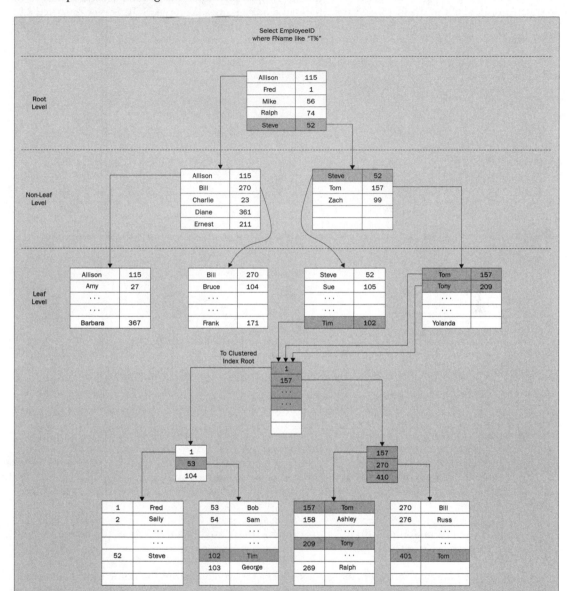

What we end up with is two entirely different kinds of lookups.

In the example from our diagram, we start off with a ranged search – we do one single lookup in our index and are able to look through the non-clustered index to find a continuous range of data that meets our criterion (LIKE 'T%'). This kind of lookup, where we can go right to a particular spot in the index, is called a **seek**.

The second kind of lookup then starts – the lookup using the clustered index. This second lookup is very fast; the problem lies in the fact that it must happen multiple times. You see, SQL Server retrieved a list from the first index lookup (a list of all the names that start with "T"), but that list doesn't logically match up with the cluster key in any continuous fashion – each record needs to be looked up individually:

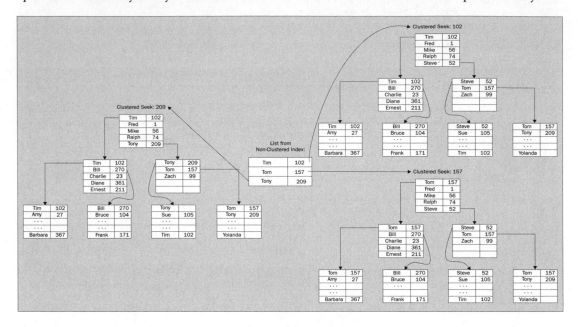

Needless to say, this multiple lookup situation introduces more overhead than if we had just been able to use the clustered index from the beginning. The first index search – the one through our non-clustered index – is going to require very few logical reads.

For example, if I have a table with 1,000 bytes per row, and I did a lookup similar to the one in our drawing (say, something that would return 5 or 6 rows); it would only take something to the order of 8-10 logical reads to get the information from the non-clustered index. However, that only gets me as far as being ready to look up the rows in the clustered index. Those lookups would cost approximately 3-4 logical reads *each*, or 15-24 additional reads. That probably doesn't seem like that big a deal at first, but look at it this way:

Logical reads went from 3 minimum to 24 maximum – that's an 800% increase in the amount of work that had to be done.

Now expand this thought out to something where the range of values from the non-clustered index wasn't just 5 or 6 rows, but 5 or 6 thousand, or 5 or 6 *hundred* thousand rows – that's going to be a huge impact.

> *Don't let the extra overhead vs. a clustered index scare you – the point isn't meant to scare you away from using indexes, but rather to recognize that a non-clustered index is not going to be as efficient as a clustered index from a read perspective (it can, in some instances, actually be a better choice at insertion time). An index of any kind is usually (there are exceptions) the fastest way to do a lookup. We'll explain what index to use and why later in the chapter.*

Creating and Dropping Indexes

You might have noticed that there is no ALTER option listed in that section title – that's because there is no ALTER statement for indexes. You can create them and drop them, but to change them you must first drop the index, and then recreate it.

Indexes can be created in two ways:

❑   Through an explicit CREATE INDEX command

❑   As an implied object when a constraint is created

Each of these has its own quirks about what it can and can't do, so let's look at each of them individually.

The CREATE INDEX Statement

The CREATE INDEX statement does exactly what it sounds like – it creates an index on the specified table or view based on the stated columns. Prior to version 7.0, tables were the only thing you could create indexes on – views don't contain any data of their own (they only point to data in tables), so there was really nothing to index. Beginning with SQL Server 2000, we now have the ability to index views – the upshot of this is that, through the index, we essentially "materialize" our view. We'll look more into the specifics of this in our next chapter.

The syntax to create an index is somewhat drawn out, and introduces several items that we haven't really talked about up to this point:

```
CREATE [UNIQUE] [CLUSTERED|NONCLUSTERED]
INDEX <index name> ON <table or view name>(<column name> [ASC|DESC] [,...n])
[WITH
[PAD_INDEX]
[[,] FILLFACTOR = <fillfactor>]
[[,] IGNORE_DUP_KEY]
[[,] DROP_EXISTING]
[[,] STATISTICS_NORECOMPUTE]
[[,] SORT_IN_TEMPDB]
]
[ON <filegroup>]
```

Loosely speaking, this statement follows the same CREATE <object type> <object name> syntax that we've seen plenty of already (and will see even more of). The primary hitch in things is that we have a few intervening parameters that we haven't seen elsewhere.

Just as we'll see with views in our next chapter, we do have to add an extra clause onto our CREATE statement to deal with the fact that an index isn't really a stand-alone kind of object. It has to go together with a table or view, and we need to state the table that our column(s) are "ON".

After the ON <table or view name>(<column name>) clause, everything is optional. You can mix and match these options. Many of them are seldom used, but some (such as FILLFACTOR) can have a significant impact on system performance and behavior, so let's look at them one by one.

ASC/DESC

These two allow you to choose between an ascending and a descending sort order for your index. The default is ASC, which is, as you might guess, ascending order. The ability to do this is brand new with SQL Server 2000, so, if you want backward compatibility with prior versions, stay away from this one entirely (just leave it out).

A question that might come to mind is why ascending vs. descending matters – you see, SQL Server can just look at an index backwards if it needs the reverse sort order. Life is not, however, always quite so simple. Looking at the index in reverse order works just fine if you're only dealing with one column, or if your sort is always the same for all columns – but what if you needed to mix sort orders within an index? That is, what if you need one column to be sorted ascending, but the other descending? Since the indexed columns are stored together, reversing the way you look at the index for one column would also reverse the order for the additional columns. If you explicitly state that one column is ascending, and the other is descending, then you invert the second column right within the physical data – there is suddenly no reason to change the way that you access your data.

As a quick example, imagine a reporting scenario where you want to order your employee list by the hire date, beginning with the most recent (a descending order), but you also want to order by their last name (an ascending order). In previous versions, SQL Server would have to do two operations – one for the first column and one for the second. By allowing us to control the physical sort order of our data, we gain flexibility in the way we combine columns.

Generally speaking, you'll want to leave this one alone (again, remember backward compatibility). Some likely exceptions are:

❏ You need to mix ascending and descending order across multiple columns.

❏ Backward compatibility is not an issue.

WITH

WITH is an easy one – it just tells SQL Server that you will indeed be supplying one or more of the options that follow.

PAD_INDEX

In the syntax list, this one comes first – but that will seem odd when you understand what PAD_INDEX does. In short, it determines just how full the non-leaf level pages of your index are going to be (as a percentage), when the index is first created. You don't state a percentage on PAD_INDEX because it will use whatever percentage is specified in the FILLFACTOR option that follows. PAD_INDEX is meaningless without a FILLFACTOR (which is why it seems odd that it comes first). This will become clearer when we look deeper into page splits, fragmentation, and fillfactors later in the chapter.

FILLFACTOR

When SQL Server first creates an index, the pages are, by default, filled as full as they can be, minus two records. You can set the FILLFACTOR to be any value between 1 and 100. This number will be how full your pages are as a percentage, once index construction is completed. Keep in mind though that, as your pages split, your data will still be distributed 50-50 between the two pages – you cannot control the fill percentage on an ongoing basis other than regularly rebuilding the indexes (something you should do – setting up a maintenance schedule for this is covered in Chapter 30).

We use a FILLFACTOR when we need to adjust the page densities. We will discuss the issue of page densities shortly, but for now, think about things this way:

❑ If it's an OLTP system, you want the FILLFACTOR to be low

❑ If it's an OLAP or other very stable (in terms of changes – very few additions and deletions) system, you want the FILLFACTOR to be as high as possible

❑ If you have something that has a medium transaction rate and a lot of report type queries against it, then you probably want something in the middle (not too low, not too high)

If you don't provide a value, then SQL Server will fill your pages to two rows short of full, with a minimum of one row per page (for example, if your row is 8000 characters wide, you can only fit one row per page – so leaving things two rows short wouldn't work).

IGNORE_DUP_KEY

The IGNORE_DUP_KEY option is a way of doing little more than circumventing the system. In short, it causes a UNIQUE constraint to have a slightly different action from that which it would otherwise have.

Normally, a unique constraint, or unique index, does not allow any duplicates of any kind – if a transaction tried to create a duplicate based on a column that is defined as unique, then that transaction would be rolled back and rejected. Once you set the IGNORE_DUP_KEY option, however, you'll get something of a mixed behavior. You will still receive an error message, but the error will only be of a warning level – the record is still not inserted.

This last line – "the record is still not inserted" – is a critical concept from an IGNORE_DUP_KEY standpoint. A rollback isn't issued for the transaction (the error is a warning error rather than a critical error), but the duplicate row will have been rejected.

Why would you do this? Well, it's a way of storing unique values, but not disturbing a transaction that tries to insert a duplicate. For whatever process is inserting the would-be duplicate, it may not matter at all that it's a duplicate row (no logical error from it). Instead, that process may have an attitude that's more along the lines of, "Well, as long as I know there's one row like that in there, I'm happy – I don't care whether it's the specific row that I tried to insert or not".

DROP_EXISTING

If you specify the DROP_EXISTING option, any existing index with the name in question will be dropped prior to construction of the new index. This option is much more efficient than simply dropping and recreating an existing index when you use it with a clustered index. If you rebuild an exact match of the existing index SQL server knows that it need not touch the non-clustered indexes, while an explicit drop and create would involve rebuilding all of the non-clustered indexes twice in order to accommodate the different row locations. If you change the structure of the index using DROP_EXISTING, the NCI's are rebuilt only once instead of twice. Furthermore, you cannot simply drop and recreate an index created by a constraint, for example, to implement a certain fillfactor. DROP_EXISTING is a workaround to this.

STATISTICS_NORECOMPUTE

Under version 7.0, SQL Server attempts to automate the process of updating the statistics on your tables and indexes. By selecting the STATISTICS_NORECOMPUTE option, you are saying that you will take responsibility for the updating of the statistics. In order to turn this option off, you need to run the UPDATE STATISTICS command, but not use the NORECOMPUTE option.

I strongly recommend against using this option. Why? Well, the statistics on your index are what the query optimizer uses to figure out just how helpful your index is going to be for a given query. The statistics on an index are changing constantly as the data in your table goes up and down in volume and as the specific values in a column change. When you combine these two facts, you should be able to see that not updating your statistics means that the query optimizer is going to be running your queries based on out of date information. Leaving the automatic statistics feature on means that the statistics will be updated regularly (just how often depends on the nature and frequency of your updates to the table). Conversely, turning automatic statistics off means that you will either be out of date, or you will need to set up a schedule to manually run the UPDATE STATISTICS command.

SORT_IN_TEMPDB

The SORT_IN_TEMPDB option is new with SQL Server 2000 and only makes sense when your tempdb is stored on a physically separate drive from the database that is to contain the new index. This is largely an administrative function, so I'm not going to linger on this topic for more than a brief overview of what it is and why it only makes sense when tempdb is on a separate physical device.

When SQL Server builds an index, it has to perform multiple reads to take care of the various index construction steps:

1. Read through all the data, constructing a leaf row corresponding to each row of actual data. Just like the actual data and final index, these go into pages for interim storage. These intermediate pages are not the final index pages, but rather a holding place to temporarily store things every time the sort buffers fill up.

2. A separate run is made through these intermediate pages to merge them into the final leaf pages of the index.

3. Non-leaf pages are built as the leaf pages are being populated.

If the SORT_IN_TEMPDB option is not used, then the intermediate pages are written out to the same physical files that the database is stored in. This means that the reads of the actual data have to compete with the writes of the build process. The two cause the disk heads to move to different places from those the other (read vs. write) needs. The result is that the disk heads are constantly moving back and forth – this takes time.

If, on the other hand, SORT_IN_TEMPDB is used, then the intermediate pages will be written to tempdb rather than the database's own file. If they are on separate physical drives, this means that there is no competition between the read and write operations of the index build. Keep in mind though that this only works if tempdb is on a separate physical drive from your database file; otherwise, the change is only in name, and the competition for I/O is still a factor.

> Note: If you're going to use SORT_IN_TEMPDB, make sure that there is enough space in tempdb for large files.

ON <filegroup>

SQL Server gives you the option of storing your indexes separately from the data by using the ON <filegroup> option. This can be nice from a couple of perspectives:

❑   The space that is required for the indexes can be spread across other drives

❑   The I/O for index operations does not burden the physical data retrieval

Implied Indexes Created with Constraints

I guess I call this one "index by accident". It's not that the index shouldn't be there – it has to be there if you want the constraint that created the index. It's just that I've seen an awful lot of situations where the only indexes on the system were those created in this fashion. Usually, this implies that the administrators and/or designers of the system are virtually oblivious to the concept of indexes.

However, you'll also find yet another bizarre twist on this one – the situation where the administrator or designer knows how to create indexes, but doesn't really know how to tell what indexes are already on the system and what they are doing. This kind of situation is typified by duplicate indexes. As long as they have different names, SQL Server will be more than happy to create them for you.

Implied indexes are created when one of two constraints is added to a table:

❑   A PRIMARY KEY

❑   A UNIQUE constraint (aka, an **alternate key**)

We've seen plenty of the CREATE syntax up to this point, so I won't belabor it – however, it should be noted that all the options except for {CLUSTERED|NONCLUSTERED} and FILLFACTOR are not allowed when creating an index as an implied index to a constraint.

Choosing Wisely: Deciding What Index Goes Where and When

By now, you're probably thinking to yourself, "Gee, I'm always going to create clustered indexes!" There are plenty of good reasons to think that way. Just keep in mind that there are also some reasons not to.

Choosing what indexes to include and what not to can be a tough process, and, in case that wasn't enough, you have to make some decisions about what type you want them to be. The latter decision is made simultaneously easier and harder in the fact that you can only have one clustered index. It means that you have to choose wisely to get the most out of it.

Selectivity

Indexes, particularly non-clustered indexes, are primarily beneficial in situations where there is a reasonably high level of **selectivity** within the index. By selectivity, I'm referring to the percentage of values in the column that are unique. The higher the percentage of unique values within a column, the higher the selectivity is said to be, and the greater the benefit of indexing.

If you think back to our sections on non-clustered indexes – particularly the section on non-clustered indexes over a clustered index – you will recall that the lookup in the non-clustered index is really only the beginning. You still need to make another loop through the clustered index in order to find the real data. Even with the non-clustered index on a heap, you still end up with multiple physically separate reads to perform.

If one lookup in your non-clustered index is going to generate multiple additional lookups in a clustered index, then you are probably better off with the table scan. The exponential effect that's possible here is actually quite amazing. Consider that the looping process created by the non-clustered index is not worth it if you don't have somewhere in the area of 90-95% uniqueness in the indexed column.

293

Clustered indexes are substantially less affected by this, since, once you're at the start of your range of data – unique or not – you're there. There are no additional index pages to read. Still, more than likely, your clustered index has other things that it could be put to greater use on.

One other exception to the rule of selectivity has to do with foreign keys. If your table has a column that is a foreign key, then, in all likelihood, you're going to benefit from having an index on that column. Why foreign keys and not other columns? Well, foreign keys are frequently the target of joins with the table they reference. Indexes, regardless of selectivity, can be very instrumental in join performance because they allow what is called a **merge join**. *A merge join obtains a row from each table and compares them to see if they match the join criteria (what you're joining on). Since there are indexes on the related columns in both tables, the seek for both rows is very fast.*

The point here is that selectivity is not everything, but it is a big issue to consider. If the column in question is not in a foreign key situation, then it is almost certainly the second only to the, "How often will this be used?" question in terms of issues you need to consider.

Watching Costs: When Less is More

Remember that, while indexes speed up performance when reading data, they are actually very costly when modifying data. Indexes are not maintained by magic. Every time that you make a modification to your data, any indexes related to that data also need to be updated.

When you insert a new row, a new entry must be made into every index on your table. Remember too that when you update a row, this is handled as a delete and insert – again, your indexes have to be updated. But wait! There's more! (Feeling like a late night infomercial here.) When you delete records – again, you must update all the indexes too – not just the data. For every index that you create, you are creating one more block of entries that have to be updated.

Notice, by the way, that I said entries plural – not just one. Remember that a B-Tree has multiple levels to it. Every time that you make a modification to the leaf level, there is a chance that a page split will occur, and that one or more non-leaf level pages must also be modified to have the reference to the proper leaf page.

Sometimes – quite often actually – not creating that extra index is the thing to do. Sometimes, the best thing to do is choose your indexes based on the transactions that are critical to your system and use the table in question. Does the code for the transaction have a WHERE clause in it? What column(s) does it use? Is there a sorting required?

Choosing that Clustered Index

Remember that you can only have one, so you need to choose it wisely.

By default, your primary key is created with a clustered index. This is often the best place to have it, but not always (indeed, it can seriously hurt you in some situations), and if you leave things this way, you won't be able to use a clustered index anywhere else. The point here is don't just accept the default. Think about it when you are defining your primary key – do you really want it to be a clustered index?

If you decide that you indeed want to change things – that is, you don't want to declare things as being clustered, just add the NONCLUSTERED keyword when you create your table. For example:

```
CREATE TABLE MyTableKeyExample
(
    Column1    intIDENTITY
      PRIMARY KEY NONCLUSTERED,
    Column2    int
)
```

Once the index is created, the only way to change it is to drop and rebuild it, so you want to get it set correctly up front.

Keep in mind that, if you change which column(s) your clustered index is on, SQL Server will need to do a complete resorting of your entire table (remember, for a clustered index, the table sort order and the index order are the same). Now, consider a table you have that is 5,000 characters wide and has a million rows in it – that is an awful lot of data that has to be reordered. Several questions should come to mind from this:

❑ How long will it take? It could be a long time, and there really isn't a good way to estimate that time.

❑ Do I have enough space? Figure that, in order to do a resort on a clustered index, you will, on average, need an *additional* 1.2 times (the working space plus the new index) the amount of space your table is already taking up. This can turn out to be a very significant amount of space if you're dealing with a large table – make sure you have the room to do it in. All this activity will, by the way, happen in the database itself – so this will also be affected by how you have your maximum size and growth options set for your database.

❑ Should I use the SORT_IN_TEMPDB option? If tempdb is on a separate physical array from your main database and it has enough room, then the answer is probably yes.

The Pros

Clustered indexes are best for queries when the column(s) in question will frequently be the subject of a ranged query. This kind of query is typified by use of the BETWEEN statement or the < or > symbols. Queries that use a GROUP BY and make use of the MAX, MIN, and COUNT aggregators are also great examples of queries that use ranges and love clustered indexes. Clustering works well here, because the search can go straight to a particular point in the physical data, keep reading until it gets to the end of the range, and then stop. It is extremely efficient.

Clusters can also be excellent when you want your data sorted (using ORDER BY) based on the cluster key.

The Cons

There are two situations where you don't want to create that clustered index. The first is fairly obvious – when there's a better place to use it. I know I'm sounding repetitive here, but don't use a clustered index on a column just because it seems like the thing to do (primary keys are the common culprit here) – be sure that you don't have another column that it's better suited to first.

Perhaps the much bigger no-no use for clustered indexes, however, is when you are going to be doing a lot of inserts in a non-sequential order. Remember that concept of page splits? Well, here's where it can come back and haunt you big time.

Imagine this scenario: you are creating an accounting system. You would like to make use of the concept of a transaction number for your primary key in your transaction files, but you would also like those transaction numbers to be somewhat indicative of what kind of transaction it is (it really helps troubleshooting for your accountants). So you come up with something of a scheme – you'll place a prefix on all the transactions indicating what sub-system they come out of. They will look something like this:

```
ARXXXXXX            Accounts Receivable Transactions
GLXXXXXX            General Ledger Transactions
APXXXXXX            Accounts Payable Transactions
```

Where XXXXXX will be a sequential numeric value

This seems like a great idea, so you implement it, leaving the default of the clustered index going on the primary key.

At first look, everything about this setup looks fine. You're going to have unique values, and the accountants will love the fact that they can infer where something came from based on the transaction number. The clustered index seems to make sense since they will often be querying for ranges of transaction IDs.

Ah, if only it were that simple. Think about your inserts for a bit. With a clustered index, we originally had a nice mechanism to avoid much of the overhead of page splits. When a new record was inserted that was to go after the last record in the table, then, even if there was a page split, only that record would go to the new page – SQL Server wouldn't try and move around any of the old data. Now we've messed things up though.

New records inserted from the General Ledger will wind up going on the end of the file just fine (GL is last alphabetically, and the numbers will be sequential). The AR and AP transactions have a major problem though – they are going to be doing non-sequential inserts. When AP000025 gets inserted and there isn't room on the page, SQL Server is going to see AR000001 in the table, and know that it's not a sequential insert. Half the records from the old page will be copied to a new page before AP000025 is inserted.

The overhead of this can be staggering. Remember that we're dealing with a clustered index, and that the clustered index is the data. The data is in index order. This means that, when you move the index to a new page, you are also moving the data. Now imagine that you're running this accounting system in a typical OLTP environment (you don't get much more OLTP-like than an accounting system) with a bunch of data-entry people keying in vendor invoices or customer orders as fast as they can. You're going to have page splits occurring constantly, and every time you do, you're going to see a brief hesitation for users of that table while the system moves data around.

Fortunately, there are a couple of ways to avoid this scenario:

❑ Choose a cluster key that is going to be sequential in its inserting. You can either create an identity column for this, or you may have another column that logically is sequential to any transaction entered regardless of system.

❑ Choose not to use a clustered index on this table. This is often the best option in a situation like in this example, since an insert into a non-clustered index on a heap is usually faster than one on a cluster key.

Even as I've told you to lean toward sequential cluster keys to avoid page splits, you also have to realize that there's a cost there. Among the downsides of sequential cluster keys are concurrency (two or more people trying to get to the same object at the same time). It's all about balancing out what you want, what you're doing, and what it's going to cost you elsewhere.

This is perhaps one of the best examples of why I have gone into so much depth as to how things work. You need to think through how things are actually going to get done before you have a good feel for what the right index to use (or not to use) is.

Column Order Matters

Just because an index has two columns in, it doesn't mean that the index is useful for any query that refers to either column.

An index is only considered for use if the first column listed in the index is used in the query. The bright side is that there doesn't have to be an exact one-for-one match to every column – just the first. Naturally, the more columns that match (in order), the better, but only the first creates a definite do-not-use situation.

Think about things this way. Imagine that you are using a phone book. Everything is indexed by last name, and then first name – does this sorting do you any real good if all you know is that the person you want to call is named Fred? On the other hand, if all you know is that his last name is Blake, the index will still serve to narrow the field for you.

One of the more common mistakes that I see in index construction is to think that one index that includes all the columns is going to be helpful for all situations. Indeed, what you're really doing is storing all the data a second time. The index will totally be ignored if the first column of the index isn't mentioned in the JOIN, ORDER BY, or WHERE clauses of the query.

Dropping Indexes

If you're constantly re-analyzing the situation and adding indexes, don't forget to drop indexes too. Remember the overhead on inserts – it doesn't make much sense to look at the indexes that you need and not also think about which indexes you do not need. Always ask yourself: "Can I get rid of any of these?"

The syntax to drop an index is pretty much the same as dropping a table. The only hitch is that you need to qualify the index name with the table or view it is attached to:

```
DROP INDEX <table or view name>.<index name>
```

And it's gone.

Use the Index Tuning Wizard

It would be my hope that you'll learn enough about indexes not to need the **Index Tuning Wizard**, but it still can be quite handy. It works by taking a workload file, which you generate using the SQL Server Profiler (discussed in Chapter 29), and looking over that information for what indexes will work best on your system.

The Index Tuning Wizard is found as part of the Wizards option within the Tools menu of Enterprise Manager. Like all wizards, I don't recommend using this tool as the sole way you decide what indexes to build, but it can be quite handy in terms of making some suggestions that you may not have thought of.

Maintaining Your Indexes

As developers, we often tend to forget about our product after it goes out the door. For many kinds of software, that's something you can get away with just fine – you ship it, then you move on to the next product or next release. However, with database-driven projects, it's virtually impossible to get away with. You need to take responsibility for the product well beyond the delivery date.

Please don't take me to be meaning that you have to go serve a stint in the tech support department – I'm actually talking about something even more important: **maintenance planning**.

There are really two issues to be dealt with in terms of the maintenance of indexes:

❏ Page splits
❏ Fragmentation

Both are related to page density and, while the symptoms are substantially different, the trouble-shooting tool is the same, as is the cure.

Fragmentation

We've already talked about page splits quite a bit, but we haven't really touched on fragmentation. I'm not talking about the fragmentation that you may have heard of with your O/S files and the defrag tool you use, because that won't help with database fragmentation.

Fragmentation happens when your database grows, pages split, and then data is eventually deleted. While the B-Tree mechanism is really not that bad at keeping things balanced from a growth point of view, it doesn't really have a whole lot to offer as you delete data. Eventually, you may get down to a situation where you have one record on this page, a few records on that page – a situation where many of your data pages are holding only a small fraction of the amount of data that they could hold.

The first problem with this is probably the first you would think about – wasted space. Remember that SQL Server allocates an extent of space at a time. If only one page has one record on it, then that extent is still allocated.

The second problem is the one that is more likely to cause you grief – records that are spread out all over the place cause additional overhead in data retrieval. Instead of just loading up one page and grabbing the ten rows it requires, SQL Server may have to load ten separate pages in order to get that same information. It isn't just reading the row that causes effort – SQL Server has to read that page in first. More pages = more work on reads.

That being said, database fragmentation does have its good side – OLTP systems positively love fragmentation. Any guesses as to why? Page splits. Pages that don't have much data in them can have data inserted with little or no fear of page splits.

So, high fragmentation equates to poor read performance, but it also equates to excellent insert performance. As you might expect, this means that OLAP systems really don't like fragmentation, but OLTP systems do.

Identifying Fragmentation vs. Likelihood of Page Splits

SQL Server gives us a command to help us identify just how full the pages and extents in our database are. We can then use that information to make some decisions about what we want to do to maintain our database. The command is actually an option for the **Database Consistency Checker** – or **DBCC**.

The syntax is pretty simple:

```
DBCC SHOWCONTIG
    [({<table name>|<table id>|<view name>|<view id>}
    [, <index name>|<index id>])]
    [WITH {ALL_INDEXES|FAST [, ALL_INDEXES ]|TABLERESULTS [, ALL_INDEXES]}]
    [ , { FAST | ALL_LEVELS } ]

DBCC SHOWCONTIG ([<table object id>], [<index id>])
```

The ability to directly state a table or view name was added with this release. Previously, we had to supply the table ID and index ID values rather than their names. If you're in an exclusively SQL Server 2000 environment, then you can skip this little helper routine and move on to what SHOWCONTIG actually does (right after the routine). If you're just plain curious, this code does work under SQL Server 2000 – you just don't need it.

For versions prior to SQL Server 2000, we have to use the OBJECT_ID(<object name>) function for the table, and we have to get the index ID out of sysindexes. I usually ran SHOWCONTIG as part of a script to package everything up, or, on some systems, I just packaged it up into a stored procedure for more frequent use. For example, to get the information from the PK_Order_Details index in the Order Details table, we would run a script like this:

```
USE Northwind
GO

-- Declare my holding variables
DECLARE @ID int,
@IdxID int,
@IndexName  varchar(128)

-- Set what I'm looking for
SELECT @IndexName = 'PK_Order_Details'
SET @ID = OBJECT_ID('Order Details')
-- Get the index id valeus
SELECT @IdxID = IndID
FROM sysindexes
WHERE id = @ID
    AND name = @IndexName

-- Get the info I'm really after
DBCC SHOWCONTIG (@id, @IdxID)
GO
```

Later on, we'll take a look at how to make our own system stored procedure out of this – that way you can install it on pre-SQL Server 2000 systems and you'll only need to pass the table and index names in as parameters and the sproc will do the rest!

The output is not really all that self-describing:

```
DBCC SHOWCONTIG scanning 'Order Details' table...
Table: 'Order Details' (325576198); index ID: 1, database ID: 6
TABLE level scan performed.
- Pages Scanned...........................................: 9
- Extents Scanned........................................:6
- Extent Switches..........................................: 5
- Avg. Pages per Extent................................: 1.5
- Scan Density [Best Count:Actual Count]........: 33.33% [2:6]
- Logical Scan Fragmentation .........................: 0.00%
- Extent Scan Fragmentation ..........................: 16.67%
- Avg. Bytes Free per Page............................: 673.2
- Avg. Page Density (full)...............................: 91.68%
DBCC execution completed. If DBCC printed error messages, contact your system administrator.
```

Some of this is probably pretty straightforward, but let's walk through what everything means:

Stat	What it means
Pages Scanned	The number of pages in the table (for a clustered index) or index.
Extents Scanned	The number of extents in the table or index. This will be a minimum of the number of pages divided by 8 and then rounded up. The more extents for the same number of pages, the higher the fragmentation.
Extent Switches	The number of times DBCC moved from one extent to another as it traversed the pages of the table or index. This is another one for fragmentation – the more switches it has to make to see the same amount of pages, the more fragmented we are.
Avg. Pages per Extent	The average number of pages per extent. A fully populated extent would have 8.
Scan Density [Best Count: Actual Count]	The best count is the ideal number of extent changes if everything is perfectly linked. Actual count is the actual number of extent changes. Scan density is the percentage found by dividing the best count by the actual count.
Logical Scan Fragmentation	The percentage of pages that are out-of-order as checked by scanning the leaf pages of an index. Only relevant to scans related to a clustered table. An out-of-order page is one for which the next page indicated in the index allocation map (IAM) is different from that pointed to by the next page pointer in the leaf page.
Extent Scan Fragmentation	This one is telling us whether an extent is not physically located next to the extent that it is logically located next to. This just means that the leaf pages of your index are not physically in order (though they still can be logically), and just what percentage of the extents this problem pertains to.
Avg. Bytes free per page	Average number of free bytes on the pages scanned. This number can get artificially high if you have large row sizes. For example, if your row size was 4,040 bytes, then every page could only hold one row, and you would always have an average number of free bytes of about 4,020 bytes. That would seem like a lot, but, given your row size, it can't be any less than that.

Stat	What it means
Avg. Page density (full)	Average page density (as a percentage). This value takes into account row size and is, therefore, a more accurate indication of how full your pages are. The higher the percentage, the better.

Now, the question is how do we use this information once we have it? The answer is, of course, that it depends.

Using the output from our SHOWCONTIG, we have a decent idea of whether our database is full, fragmented, or somewhere in between (the latter is, most likely, what we want to see). If we're running an OLAP system, then seeing our pages full would be great – fragmentation would bring on depression. For an OLTP system, we would want much the opposite (although only to a point).

So, how do we take care of the problem? To answer that we need to look into the concept of index rebuilding and fillfactors.

DBREINDEX and FILLFACTOR

As we saw earlier in the chapter, SQL Server gives us an option for controlling just how full our leaf level pages are, and, if we choose, another option to deal with non-leaf level pages. Unfortunately, these are proactive options – they are applied once, and then you need to re-apply them as necessary by rebuilding your indexes and reapplying the options.

To rebuild indexes, we can either drop them and create them again (if you do, using the DROP_EXISTING option usually is a good ideal), or make use of DBREINDEX. DBREINDEX is another DBCC command, and the syntax looks like this:

```
DBCC DBREINDEX (<'database.owner.table_name'>[, <index name>
[, <fillfactor>]]) [WITH NO_INFOMSGS]
```

Executing this command completely rebuilds the requested index. If you supply a table name with no index name, then it rebuilds all the indexes for the requested table. There is no single command to rebuild all the indexes in a database.

Rebuilding your indexes restructures all the information in those indexes, and re-establishes a base percentage that your pages are full. If the index in question is a clustered index, then the physical data is also reorganized.

By default, the pages will be reconstituted to be full minus two records. Just as with the CREATE TABLE syntax, you can set the FILLFACTOR to be any value between 0 and 100. This number will be the percent full that your pages are once the database reorganization is complete. Remember though that, as your pages split, your data will still be distributed 50-50 between the two pages – you cannot control the fill percentage on an on-going basis other than regularly rebuilding the indexes.

> There is something of an exception on the number matching the percent full that occurs if you use zero as your percentage. It will go to full minus two rows (it's a little deceiving – don't you think?).

We use a FILLFACTOR when we need to adjust the page densities. As we've already discussed, lower page densities (and therefore lower FILLFACTORs) are ideal for OLTP systems where there are a lot of insertions – this helps avoid page splits. Higher page densities are desirable with OLAP systems (fewer pages to read, but no real risk of page splitting due to few to no inserts).

If we wanted to rebuild the index that serves as the primary key for the Order Details table we were looking at earlier with a fill factor of 65, we would issue a DBCC command as follows:

```
DBCC DBREINDEX ([Order Details], PK_Order_Details, 65)
```

We can then re-run the DBCC SHOWCONTIG to see the effect:

```
DBCC SHOWCONTIG scanning 'Order Details' table...
Table: 'Order Details' (325576198); index ID: 1, database ID: 6
TABLE level scan performed.
- Pages Scanned............................................: 13
- Extents Scanned.........................................: 2
- Extent Switches...........................................: 1
- Avg. Pages per Extent..................................: 6.5
- Scan Density [Best Count:Actual Count]........: 100.00% [2:2]
- Logical Scan Fragmentation .........................: 0.00%
- Extent Scan Fragmentation ..........................: 50.00%
- Avg. Bytes Free per Page.............................: 2957.2
- Avg. Page Density (full)................................: 63.46%
DBCC execution completed. If DBCC printed error messages, contact your system administrator.
```

The big one to notice here is the change in Avg. Page Density. The number didn't quite reach 65% because SQL Server has to deal with page and row sizing, but it gets as close as it can.

Several things to note about DBREINDEX and FILLFACTOR:

❑ If a FILLFACTOR isn't provided, then the DBREINDEX will use whatever setting was used to build the index previously. If one has never been specified, then the fillfactor will make the page full less two records (which is too full for most situations).

❑ If a FILLFACTOR is provided, then that value becomes the default FILLFACTOR for that index.

❑ While DBREINDEX can be done live, I strongly recommend against it – it locks resources and can cause a host of problems. At the very least, look at doing it at non-peak hours.

Summary

Indexes are sort of a cornerstone topic in SQL Server or any other database environment, and are not something to be taken lightly. They can drive your performance successes, but they can also drive your performance failures.

Top-level things to think about with indexes:

- ❏ Clustered indexes are usually faster than non-clustered indexes (one could come very close to saying always, but there are exceptions).

- ❏ Only place non-clustered indexes on columns where you are going to get a high level of selectivity (that is, 95% or more of the rows are unique).

- ❏ All Data Manipulation Language (DML: INSERT, UPDATE, DELETE, SELECT) statements can benefit from indexes, but inserts, deletes, and updates (remember, they use a delete and insert approach) are slowed by indexes. The lookup part of a query is helped by the index, but anything that modifies data will have extra work to do (to maintain the index in addition to the actual data).

- ❏ Indexes take up space.

- ❏ Indexes are only used if the first column in the index is relevant to your query.

- ❏ Indexes can hurt as much as they help – know why you're building the index, and don't build indexes you don't need.

When you're thinking about indexes, ask yourself these questions:

Question	Response
Are there a lot of inserts or modifications to this table?	If yes, keep indexes to a minimum. This kind of table usually has modifications done through single record lookups of the primary key – usually, this is the only index you want on the table. If the inserts are non-sequential, think about not having a clustered index.
Is this a reporting table? That is, not many inserts, but reports run lots of different ways?	More indexes are fine. Target the clustered index to frequently used information that is likely to be extracted in ranges. OLAP installations will often have many times the number of indexes seen in an OLTP environment.
Is there a high level of selectivity on the data?	If yes, and it is frequently the target of a WHERE clause, then add that index.
Have I dropped the indexes I no longer need?	If not, why not?
Do I have a maintenance strategy established?	If not, why not?

In our next chapter, we'll be looking at views. Before SQL Server 2000, you could not build an index over a view. We will see, however, that a very powerful new feature – called **indexed views** – brings indexes and views together to help not only our queries against a particular view, but also selected queries performed directly against the tables that an indexed view references.

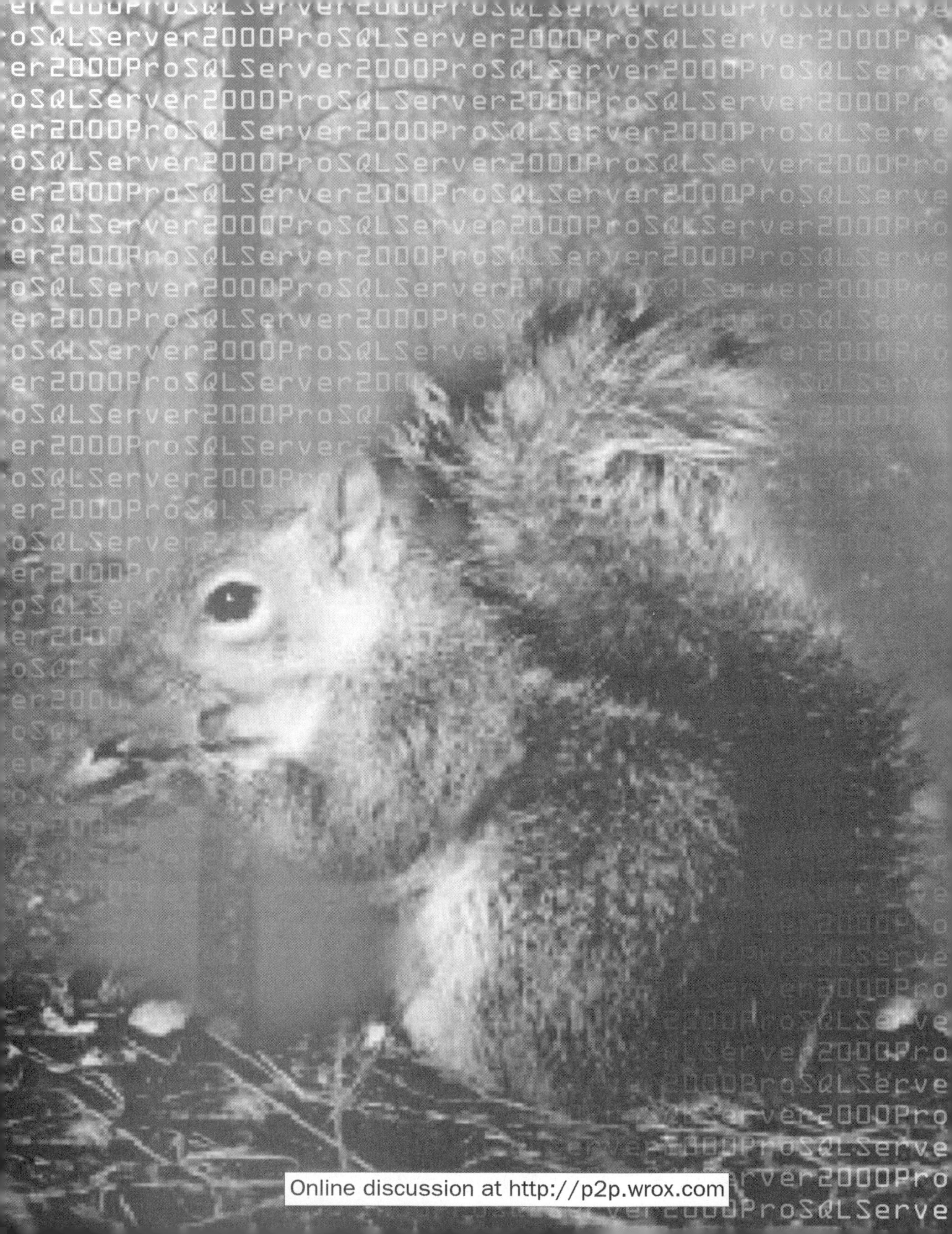
Online discussion at http://p2p.wrox.com

10

Views

Up to this point, we've been dealing with base objects – objects that have some level of substance of their own. In this chapter, we're going to go virtual (well, mostly anyway), and take a look at views.

Views have a tendency to be used either too much, or not enough – rarely just right. When we're done with this chapter, you should be able to use views to:

- ❑ Reduce apparent database complexity for end users
- ❑ Prevent sensitive columns from being selected, while still affording access to other important data
- ❑ Add additional indexing to your database to speed query performance – even when you're not using the view the index is based on

A view is, at its core, really nothing more than a stored query. What's great is that you can mix and match your data from base tables (or other views) to create what will, in most respects, function just like another base table. You can create a simple query that selects from only one table and leaves some columns out, or you can create a complex query that joins several tables and makes them appear as one.

Simple Views

The syntax for a view, in its most basic form, is a combination of a couple of things we've already seen in the book – the basic CREATE statement that we saw back in Chapter 6, plus a SELECT statement like we've used over and over again:

```
CREATE VIEW <view name>
AS
<SELECT statement>
```

The above syntax just represents the minimum, of course, but it's still all we need in a large percentage of the situations. The more extended syntax looks like this:

```
CREATE VIEW <view name> [(<column name list>)]
[WITH [ENCRYPTION] [,SCHEMABINDING] [, VIEW_METADATA]]
AS
<SELECT statement>
WITH CHECK OPTION
```

We'll be looking at each piece of this individually, but, for now, let's go ahead and dive right in with an extremely simple view. We'll call this one our customer phone list, and create it as `CustomerPhoneList_vw` in our `Accounting` database:

```
USE Accounting
GO


CREATE VIEW CustomerPhoneList_vw
AS
    SELECT CustomerName, Contact, Phone
    FROM Customers
```

Notice that when you execute the CREATE statement in the Query Analyzer, it works just like all the other CREATE statements we've done – it doesn't return any rows. It just lets us know that the view has been created:

The command(s) completed successfully.

Now switch to using the grid view (if you're not already there) to make it easy to see more than one result set. Then run a SELECT statement against your view – using it just as you would for a table – and another against the Customers table directly:

```
SELECT * FROM CustomerPhoneList_vw

SELECT * FROM Customers
```

What you get back looks almost identical – indeed, in the columns that they have in common, the two result sets *are* identical. To clarify how SQL Server is looking at your query on the view, let's break it down logically a bit.

The SELECT statement in your view is defined as:

```
SELECT CustomerName, Contact, Phone
FROM Customers
```

So when you run:

```
SELECT * FROM CustomerPhoneList_vw
```

You are essentially saying to SQL Server:

"Give me all of the rows and columns you get when you run the statement SELECT CustomerName, Contact, Phone FROM Customers."

We've created something of a pass-through situation. What's nice about that is that we have reduced the complexity for the end user. In this day and age, where we have so many tools to make life easier for the user, this may not seem like all that big of deal – but to the user, it is.

> **Be aware that, by default, there is nothing special done for a view. The view runs just as if it were run from the command line – there is no pre-optimization of any kind. This means that you are adding one more layer of overhead between the request for data and the data being delivered. That means that a view is never going to run as fast as if you had just run the underlying SELECT statement directly.**

Let's go with another view that illustrates what we can do in terms of hiding sensitive data. For this example, let's go back to our Employees table in our Accounting database. Take a look at the table layout:

Employees
EmployeeID
FirstName
MiddleInitial
LastName
Title
SSN
Salary
HireDate
TerminationDate
ManagerEmpID
Department

Federal law in the US protects some of this information – we must limit access to a "need to know" basis. Other columns though are free for anyone to see. What if we want to expose the unrestricted columns to a group of people, but don't want them to be able to see the general table structure or data? One solution would be to keep a separate table that includes only the columns that we need:

Employees
EmployeeID
FirstName
MiddleInitial
LastName
Title
HireDate
TerminationDate
ManagerEmpID
Department

While on the surface this would meet our needs, it is extremely problematic:

❑   We use disk space twice

❑   We have a synchronization problem if one table gets updated and the other doesn't

❑   We have double I/O operations (you have to read and write the data in two places instead of one) whenever we need to insert, update, or delete rows

Views provide an easy and relatively elegant solution to this problem. By using a view, the data is only stored once (in the underlying table or tables) – eliminating all of the problems described above. Instead of building our completely separate table, we can just build a view that will function in a nearly identical fashion.

Our Employees table is currently empty. To add some rows to it, load the Chapter10.sql file (supplied with the source code) into Query Analyzer and run it. Then add the following view to the Accounting database:

```
USE Accounting
GO

CREATE VIEW Employees_vw
AS
SELECT    EmployeeID,
          FirstName,
          MiddleInitial,
          LastName,
          Title,
          HireDate,
          TerminationDate,
          ManagerEmpID,
          Department
FROM Employees
```

We are now ready to let everyone have access – directly or indirectly – to the data in the Employees table. Users who have the "need to know" can now be directed to the Employees table, but we continue to deny access to other users. Instead, the users who do not have that "need to know" can have access to our Employees_vw view. If they want to make use of it, they do it just the same as they would against a table:

```
SELECT *
FROM Employees_vw
```

> This actually gets into one of the sticky areas of naming conventions. Because I've been using the _vw suffix, it's pretty easy to see that this is a view and not a table. Sometimes, you'd like to make things a little more hidden than that, so you might want to deliberately leave the _vw off. Doing so means that you have to use a different name (Employees is already the name of the base table), but you'd be surprised how many users won't know that there's a difference between a view and a table if you do it this way.

Views as Filters

This will probably be one of the shortest sections in the book. Why? Well, it doesn't get much simpler than this.

You've already seen how to create a simple view – you just use an easy SELECT statement. How do we filter the results of our queries? With a WHERE clause. Views are no different.

Let's take our Employees_vw view from the last section, and beef it up a bit by making it a list of only current employees. To do this, there are really only two changes that need to be made.

First, we have to filter out employees who no longer work for the company. Would a current employee have a termination date? Probably not, so, if we limit our results to rows with a NULL TerminationDate, then we've got what we're after.

The second change illustrates another simple point about views working just like queries – the column(s) contained in the WHERE clause do not need to be included in the SELECT list. In this case, it doesn't make any sense to include the termination date in the result set as we're talking about current employees.

With these two things in mind, let's create a new view by changing our old view around just a little bit:

```
CREATE VIEW CurrentEmployees_vw
AS
SELECT    EmployeeID,
          FirstName,
          MiddleInitial,
          LastName,
          Title,
          HireDate,
          ManagerEmpID,
          Department
FROM Employees
WHERE TerminationDate IS NULL
```

In addition to the name change and the WHERE clause we've added, note that we've also eliminated the TerminationDate column from the SELECT list.

Let's test out how this works a little bit by running a straight SELECT statement against our Employees table and limiting our SELECT list to the things that we care about:

```
SELECT    EmployeeID,
          FirstName,
          LastName,
          TerminationDate
FROM Employees
```

This gets us back a few columns from all the rows in the entire table:

EmployeeID	FirstName	LastName	TerminationDate
1	Joe	Dokey	NULL
2	Peter	Principle	NULL
3	Steve	Smith	1997-01-31 00:00:00
4	Howard	Kilroy	NULL
5	Mary	Contrary	1998-06-15 00:00:00
6	Billy	Bob	NULL

(6 row(s) affected)

Now let's check out our view:

```
SELECT   EmployeeID,
         FirstName,
         LastName
FROM CurrentEmployees_vw
```

Our result set has become a bit smaller:

EmployeeID	FirstName	LastName
1	Joe	Dokey
2	Peter	Principle
4	Howard	Kilroy
6	Billy	Bob

(4 row(s) affected)

A few people are missing versus our first select – just the way we wanted it.

More Complex Views

Even though I use the term "complex" here – don't let that scare you. The toughest thing in views is still, for the most part, simpler than most other things in SQL.

What we're doing with more complex views is really just adding joins, summarization, and perhaps some column renaming.

For those of you who will be applying this information to versions of SQL Server prior to 7.0, be aware that there is a limit to the number of joins that you can do. This might bring in the question of, "What that has to do with views?" Everything!

As I've mentioned before, views are nothing more than stored queries. For versions prior to 7.0, your queries that are part of views (and all queries for that matter) are limited to 16 joins. It doesn't stop there though – when you do a query that makes use of views, the joins that happen inside the view also count toward your 16 joins limit. That means that if you try to join 4 views that each join 5 tables, you're at 20 joins, and you're over the limit. Versions 7.0 and beyond have a limit of 256 tables – a limit you should never bump into.

You can get around this limit by performing multiple queries and creating temporary working tables that summarize some of the joins in your query. In the end, you join the working tables for a final result. Just be aware that there is a performance penalty to be paid when you take such a long route to your results.

Perhaps one of the most common uses of views is to flatten data – that is, the removal of complexity that we outlined at the beginning of the chapter. Imagine that we are providing a view for management to make it easier to check on sales information. No offense to managers who are reading this book, but managers who write their own complex queries are still a rather rare breed – even in the information age.

For an example, let's briefly go back to using the Northwind database. Our manager would like to be able to do simple queries that will tell him or her what orders have been placed for what parts and who placed them. So, we create a view that they can perform very simple queries on – remember that we are creating this one in Northwind:

```
USE Northwind
GO

CREATE VIEW CustomerOrders_vw
AS
SELECT    cu.CompanyName,
          o.OrderID,
          o.OrderDate,
          od.ProductID,
          p.ProductName,
          od.Quantity,
          od.UnitPrice,
          od.Quantity * od.UnitPrice AS ExtendedPrice
FROM      Customers AS cu
INNER JOIN   Orders AS o
      ON cu.CustomerID = o.CustomerID
INNER JOIN   [Order Details] AS od
      ON o.OrderID = od.OrderID
INNER JOIN   Products AS p
      ON od.ProductID = p.ProductID
```

Now do a SELECT:

```
SELECT *
FROM CustomerOrders_vw
```

You wind up with a bunch of rows – over 2000 – but you also wind up with information that is far simpler for the average manager to comprehend and sort out. What's more, with not that much training, the manager (or whoever the user might be) can get right to the heart of what they are looking for:

```
SELECT CompanyName, ExtendedPrice
FROM CustomerOrders_vw
WHERE OrderDate = '9/3/1996'
```

The user didn't need to know how to do a four-table join – that was hidden in the view. Instead, they only need limited skill (and limited imagination for that matter) in order to get the job done.

```
CompanyName          ExtendedPrice
--------------------------------------------------
LILA-Supermercado    201.6000
LILA-Supermercado    417.0000
LILA-Supermercado    432.0000
```

(3 row(s) affected)

However, we could make our query even more targeted. Let's say that we only want our view to return yesterday's sales. We'll make only slight changes to our query:

```
USE Northwind
GO

CREATE VIEW YesterdaysOrders_vw
AS
SELECT    cu.CompanyName,
          o.OrderID,
          o.OrderDate,
          od.ProductID,
          p.ProductName,
          od.Quantity,
          od.UnitPrice,
          od.Quantity * od.UnitPrice AS ExtendedPrice
FROM      Customers AS cu
INNER JOIN    Orders AS o
       ON cu.CustomerID = o.CustomerID
INNER JOIN    [Order Details] AS od
       ON o.OrderID = od.OrderID
INNER JOIN    Products AS p
       ON od.ProductID = p.ProductID
WHERE CONVERT(varchar(12),o.OrderDate,101) =
       CONVERT(varchar(12),DATEADD(day,-1,GETDATE()),101)
```

All the dates in the Northwind database are old enough that this view wouldn't return any data, so let's add a row to test it. Execute the following script all at one time:

```
USE Northwind

DECLARE @Ident int

INSERT INTO Orders
(CustomerID,OrderDate)
VALUES
('ALFKI', DATEADD(day,-1,GETDATE()))

SELECT @Ident = @@IDENTITY

INSERT INTO [Order Details]
(OrderID, ProductID, UnitPrice, Quantity)
VALUES
(@Ident, 1, 50, 25)

SELECT 'The OrderID of the INSERTed row is ' + CONVERT(varchar(8),@Ident)
```

I'll be explaining all of what is going on here in our chapter on scripts and batches. For now, just trust me that you'll need to run all of this in order for us to have a value in `Northwind` that will come up for our view. You should see a result from the Query Analyzer that looks something like this:

```
(1 row(s) affected)


(1 row(s) affected)


-------------------------------------------
The OrderID of the INSERTed row is 11087

(1 row(s) affected)
```

> *Be aware that some of the messages shown above will only appear on the **Messages** tab if you are using Query Analyzer's **Results In Grid** mode.*

The `OrderID` might vary, but the rest should hold pretty true.

Now let's run a query against our view and see what we get:

```
SELECT CompanyName, OrderID, OrderDate FROM YesterdaysOrders_vw
```

You can see that the **11087** does indeed show up:

CompanyName	OrderID	OrderDate
Alfreds Futterkiste	11087	2000-08-05 17:37:52.520

```
(1 row(s) affected)
```

> Don't get stuck on the notion that your `OrderID` numbers are going to be the same as mine – these are set by the system (since `OrderID` is an identity column), and are dependent on just how many rows have already been inserted into the table. As such, your numbers will vary.

The DATEADD and CONVERT Functions

The join, while larger than most of the ones we've done this far, is still pretty straightforward. We keep adding tables, joining a column in each new table to a matching column in the tables that we've already named. As always, note that the columns do not have to have the same name – they just have to have data that relates to one another.

Since this was a relatively complex join, let's take a look at what we are doing in the query that supports this view.

The WHERE clause is where things get interesting:

```
WHERE CONVERT(varchar(12),o.OrderDate,101) =
       CONVERT(varchar(12),DATEADD(day,-1,GETDATE()),101)
```

It's a single comparison, but we have several functions that are used to come up with our result.

It would be very tempting to just compare the OrderDate in the Orders table to GETDATE() (today's date) minus one day – the subtraction operation is what the DATEADD function is all about. DATEADD can add (you subtract by using negative numbers) any amount of time you want to deal with. You just tell it what date you want to operate on, what unit of time you want to add to it (days, weeks, years, minutes, etc.). On the surface, you should just be able to grab today's date with GETDATE() and then use DATEADD to subtract one day. The problem is that GETDATE() includes the current time of day, so we would only get back rows from the previous day that happened at the same time of day down to 3.3333 milliseconds – not a likely match. So we took things one more step and used the CONVERT function to equalize the dates on both sides of the equation to the same time-of-day-less format before comparison. Therefore, the view will show any sale that happened any time on the previous date.

Using a View to Change Data – Before INSTEAD OF Triggers

As we've said before, a view works *mostly* like a table does from an in-use perspective (obviously, creating them works quite a bit differently). Now we're going to come across some differences though.

It's surprising to many, but you can run INSERT, UPDATE, and DELETE statements against a view successfully. There are several things, however, that you need to keep in mind when changing data through a view:

❑ If the view contains a join, you won't, in most cases, be able to INSERT or DELETE data unless you make use of an INSTEAD OF trigger (discussed in Chapter 15). An UPDATE can, in some cases (as long as you are only updating columns that are sourced from a single table), work without INSTEAD OF triggers, but it requires some planning, or you'll bump into problems very quickly.

❑ If your view references only a single table, then you can INSERT data using a view without the use of an INSTEAD OF trigger provided all the required fields in the table are exposed in the view or have defaults. Even for single table views, if there is a column not represented in the view that does not have a default value, then you must use an INSTEAD OF trigger if you want to allow an INSERT.

❑ You can, to a limited extent, restrict what is and isn't inserted or updated in a view.

Thanks to the addition of INSTEAD OF triggers with this release, the subject of changing data using views is one with big changes this time around. Realize that you need to be very careful about updating, inserting, or deleting through views if you need to maintain compatibility with SQL Server 7.0 or earlier versions. As we will see, we can indeed INSERT, UPDATE, and DELETE data in pre-SQL Server 2000 views, but there are far more restrictions to deal with.

Now – I've already mentioned INSTEAD OF triggers several times, and I'll do it again before the chapter is done. The problem here is that we haven't discussed triggers to any significant extent yet, and, as is often the case in SQL Server items, we have something of the old chicken vs. egg thing going ("Which came first?"). I need to discuss INSTEAD OF triggers because of their relevance to views, but we're also not ready to talk about INSTEAD OF triggers unless we understand both of the objects (tables and views) that they can be created against.

The way we are going to handle things for this chapter is to address views the way they used to be – before there was such a thing as INSTEAD OF triggers. While we won't deal with the specifics of INSTEAD OF triggers in this chapter, we'll make sure we understand when they must be used. We'll then come back and address these issues more fully when we look at INSTEAD OF triggers in Chapter 15.

Dealing with Changes in Views with Joined Data

If the view has more than one table, then using a view to modify data is, in many cases, out – sort of anyway – unless you use an INSTEAD OF trigger (more on this in a moment). Since it creates some ambiguities in the key arrangements, Microsoft used to just lock you out when there are multiple tables. Beginning with SQL Server 2000, you can now use an INSTEAD OF trigger to examine the altered data and explicitly tell SQL Server what you want to do with it – thus alleviating the ambiguity issue. If you need 7.0 or earlier compatibility, then action statements against views with joins are pretty restricted.

Now, what did I mean by "sort of...", earlier? Well, technically you can't use a view to update data when you have multiple tables in the underlying query. The instance that keeps this from being completely true is if you open a view in the Enterprise Manager. It seems that SQL Server bypasses the view in EM when doing updates and, instead, goes directly to the tables. This "going directly to the table" business creates some problems (also known as bugs) when using the WITH CHECK OPTION that we'll be discussing in the next section.

Required Fields Must Appear in the View or Have Default Value

By default, if you are using a view to insert data (there must be a single table SELECT in the underlying query or at least you must limit the insert to affecting just one table and have all required columns represented), then you must be able to supply some value for all required fields (fields that don't allow NULLs) . Note that by "supply some value" I don't mean that it has to be in the SELECT list – a Default covers the bill rather nicely. Just be aware that any columns that do not have Defaults and do not accept NULL values will need to appear in the view in order to perform INSERTs through the view. The only way to get around this is – you guessed it – with an INSTEAD OF trigger.

Limit What's Inserted into Views – WITH CHECK OPTION

The WITH CHECK OPTION is one of those lesser known to almost completely unknown features in SQL Server. The rules are simple – in order to update or insert data using the view, the resulting row must qualify to appear in the view results. Restated, the inserted or updated row must meet any WHERE criterion that's used in the SELECT statement that underlies your view.

To illustrate this, let's continue working with the Northwind database, and create a view to show only Oregon shippers. We only have limited fields to work with in our Shippers table, so we're going to have to make use of the Area Code in order to figure out where the shipper is from (make sure that you use Northwind):

```
CREATE VIEW OregonShippers_vw
AS
SELECT    ShipperID,
          CompanyName,
          Phone
FROM      Shippers
WHERE Phone LIKE '(503)%'
WITH CHECK OPTION
```

Run a SELECT * against this view, and, as it happens, you return all the rows in the table (because all the rows in the table meet the criteria):

ShipperID	CompanyName	Phone
1	Speedy Express	(503) 555-9831
2	United Package	(503) 555-3199
3	Federal Shipping	(503) 555-9931
4	Speedy Shippers, Inc.	(503) 555-5566

(4 row(s) affected)

Now try to update one of the rows using the view – set the phone value to have anything other than a value starting with (503):

```
UPDATE OregonShippers_vw
SET Phone = '(333) 555 9831'
WHERE ShipperID = 1
```

SQL Server promptly tells you that you are a scoundrel, and that you should be burned at the stake for your actions – well, not really, but it does make its point...

Server: Msg 550, Level 16, State 1, Line 1
The attempted insert or update failed because the target view either specifies WITH CHECK OPTION or spans a view that specifies WITH CHECK OPTION and one or more rows resulting from the operation did not qualify under the CHECK OPTION constraint.
The statement has been terminated.

Sort of reminds one of an old Arnold Schwarzenegger flick – doesn't it? Since our update wouldn't meet the WHERE clause criteria, it is thrown out; however, if we insert the row right into the base table:

```
UPDATE Shippers
SET Phone = '(333) 555 9831'
WHERE ShipperID = 1
```

SQL Server is a lot friendlier:

(1 row(s) affected)

The restriction applies only to the view – not to the underlying table. This can actually be quite handy in a rare circumstance or two. Imagine a situation where you want to allow some users to insert or update data in a table, but only when the updated or inserted data meets certain criteria. We could easily deal with this restriction by adding a CHECK constraint to our underlying table – but this might not always be an ideal solution.

Imagine now that we've added a second requirement – we still want other users to be able to INSERT data into the table without meeting these criteria. Uh oh, the CHECK constraint will not discriminate between users. By using a view together with a WITH CHECK OPTION, we can point the restricted users to the view, and let the unrestricted users make use of the base table or a view that has no such restriction.

Just for confirmation – this works on an INSERT too. Run an INSERT that violates the WHERE clause:

```
INSERT INTO OregonShippers_vw
VALUES
('My Freight Inc.', '(555) 555-5555')
```

And you see your old friend, the "terminator" error, exactly as before:

Server: Msg 550, Level 16, State 1, Line 1
The attempted insert or update failed because the target view either specifies WITH CHECK OPTION or spans a view that specifies WITH CHECK OPTION and one or more rows resulting from the operation did not qualify under the CHECK OPTION constraint.
The statement has been terminated.

> A student in one of my SQL Server courses discovered a bug in Release Candidate 1 of 7.0 (this was December of 1998!) that, much to my amazement still existed in the RTM of SQL Server 2000. The issue is only with editing and inserting data through views while using Enterprise Manager.
>
> Despite the fact that you open the view, EM still does its inserts and updates directly to the underlying table. This means that the WITH CHECK OPTION is bypassed when using EM to edit data through a view. Perhaps an even bigger issue with this use of the underlying table instead of the actual view is that if the user does not have rights to update or insert into the underlying table, then any editing through EM will fail – even if they have the proper rights to the view.
>
> The bug has been reported and acknowledged, but I have no idea when it will be fixed – test your release before you depend on this feature in EM.

Editing Views with T-SQL

The main thing to remember when you edit views with T-SQL is that you are completely replacing the existing view. The only differences between using the ALTER VIEW statement and the CREATE VIEW statement are:

❏ ALTER VIEW expects to find an existing view, where CREATE doesn't

❏ ALTER VIEW retains any permissions that have been established for the view

❏ ALTER VIEW retains any dependency information

The second of these is the biggie. If you perform a DROP, and then use a CREATE, you have *almost* the same effect as using an ALTER VIEW statement. The problem is that you will need to entirely re-establish your permissions on who can and can't use the view.

Dropping Views

It doesn't get much easier than this:

```
DROP VIEW <view name>, [<view name>,[ …n]]
```

And it's gone.

Creating and Editing Views in EM

For people who really don't know what they are doing, this has to be a rather cool feature in EM. Building views is a snap, and you really don't have to know all that much about queries in order to get it done.

To take a look at this, fire up EM, open up the Northwind database sub-node of the Databases node and right-click on Views:

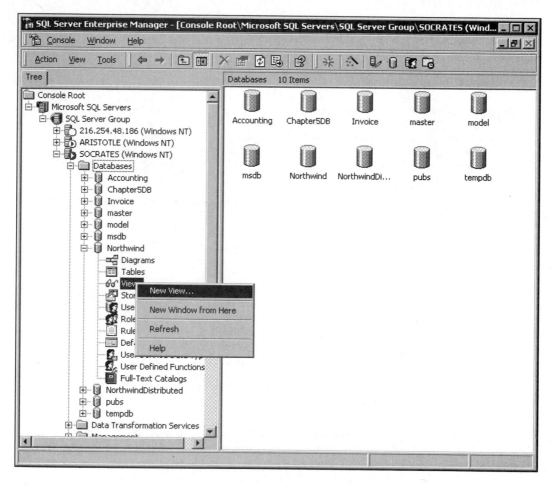

Now select New View...:

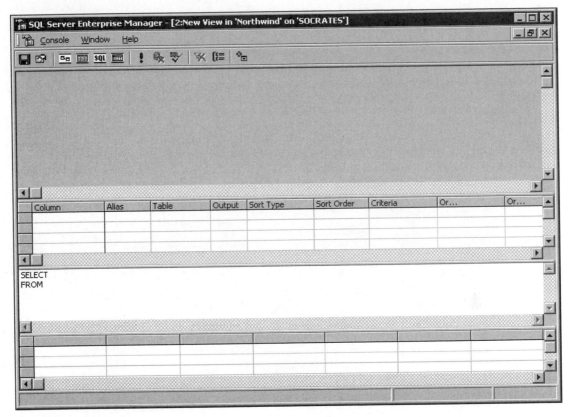

This View Builder is part of the daVinci tools that became part of SQL Server back in 7.0. There are four panes – each of which can be independently turned on or off:

❑ The Diagram pane

❑ The Grid pane

❑ The SQL pane

❑ The Results pane

For those of you who have worked with Access at all, the Diagram pane works much as it does in Access queries. You can add and remove tables, and even define relationships. Each of those added tables, checked columns, and defined relationships will automatically be reflected in the SQL pane in the form of the SQL required to match the diagram. To identify each of the icons on the toolbar, just hover your mouse pointer over them for a moment or two, and you will get a Tooltip that indicates the purpose of each button.

For demonstration purposes, add the `Customers`, `Orders`, `Order Details`, and `Products` tables.

> You can add tables either by right-clicking in the Diagram pane (the top one in the picture on the previous page) and choosing **Add Table** or by clicking on the **Add table** toolbar button (the rightmost one). Note that, for version 7.0, in order to be able to add a table, the Diagram pane must be the active pane. If in doubt, just click your mouse with the pointer somewhere inside the Diagram pane – the **Add table** toolbar button should then become enabled (if it wasn't already). This works just fine in 2000 without worrying about which pane is active.

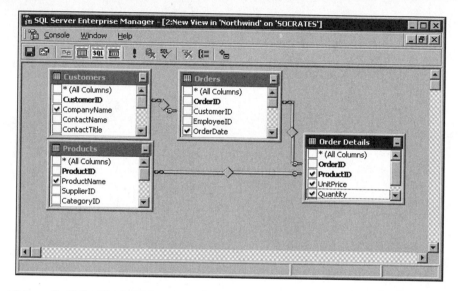

Note that I turned off the Grid, SQL, and Results panes to save space here. I then went through and checked the boxes for the columns that I wanted to include. If I had the Grid pane up, then you would have seen each column appear in the Grid pane as I selected it. With the SQL pane up, you would have also seen it appear in the SQL code.

In case you haven't recognized it yet, we're building the same view that we built as our first complex view (`CustomerOrders_vw`). The only thing that's tricky at all is the computed column (`ExtendedPrice`). To do that one, either we have to manually type the equation into the SQL pane, or we can type it into the **Column** column in the Grid pane along with its alias:

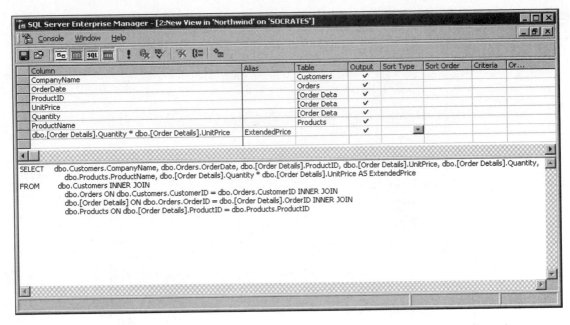

When all is said and done, the view builder gives us the following SQL code:

```
SELECT  dbo.Customers.CompanyName, dbo.Orders.OrderDate,
        dbo.[Order Details].ProductID, dbo.[Order Details].UnitPrice,
        dbo.[Order Details].Quantity, dbo.Products.ProductName,
        dbo.[Order Details].Quantity * dbo.[Order Details].UnitPrice AS
            ExtendedPrice
FROM    dbo.Customers INNER JOIN
        dbo.Orders ON dbo.Customers.CustomerID = dbo.Orders.CustomerID
            INNER JOIN
        dbo.[Order Details] ON dbo.Orders.OrderID = dbo.[Order
            Details].OrderID
            INNER JOIN
        dbo.Products ON dbo.[Order Details].ProductID = dbo.Products.ProductID
```

While it's not formatted the same, if you look it over, you'll find that it's basically the same code we wrote by hand!

> If you've been struggling with learning your T-SQL query syntax, you can use this tool to play around with the syntax of a query. Just drag and drop some tables into the Diagram pane, select the column you want from each table, and, for the most part, SQL Server will build you a query – you can then use the syntax from the view builder to learn how to build it yourself next time.

Now go ahead and save it as CustomerOrders2_vw and close the view builder.

Editing Views in EM

To edit a view, we have a couple of choices.

First, we can just double-click on it. If we double-click on our new `CustomerOrders2_vw` view, we'll get something a little different from we might expect at this point:

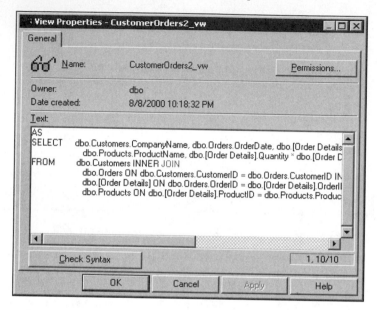

We're back to straight code. From a user interface standpoint, this stinks. Not because we're back to code, but that we have an inconsistent interface. Oh well, again – they didn't consult with me first....

You can edit the code as you see fit, then just click **OK** or **Apply** in order to make the change.

Your other option is probably going to be a bit more appealing – it's back to the editor we used the first time around. To use this, just right-click on your view and choose **Design View**. You'll be greeted with the same friendly query designer that we used with our query when it was created.

Auditing: Displaying Existing Code

What do you do when you have a view, but you're not sure what it does? The first option should be easy at this point – just go into EM like you're going to edit the view. Go to the Views sub-node and double-click. You'll see the code behind the view complete with color-coding.

Unfortunately, we don't always have the option of having EM around to hold our hand through this stuff. The bright side is that we have two ways of getting at the actual view definition:

❑ `sp_helptext`

❑ The `syscomments` system table

Using sp_helptext is highly preferable, as when new releases come out, it will automatically be updated for changes to the system tables.

Let's run sp_helptext against one of the supplied views in the Northwind database – Alphabetical List of Products:

```
EXEC sp_helptext [Alphabetical list of products]
```

SQL Server obliges us with the code for the view:

```
Text
-----------------------------------------------------------
create view "Alphabetical list of products" AS
SELECT Products.*, Categories.CategoryName
FROM Categories INNER JOIN Products ON Categories.CategoryID = Products.CategoryID
WHERE (((Products.Discontinued)=0))
```

I must admit to finding this one of the more peculiar examples that Microsoft supplies – I attribute it to this database being migrated from Access. Why? Well, the one seemingly simple thing that we *cannot* do in views is use an ORDER BY clause. The exception to the rule on the ORDER BY clause is that you can use ORDER BY as long as you also use the TOP predicate. Microsoft say this view is in alphabetical order, but there is no guarantee of that. Indeed, if you run the query, odds are it won't come out in alphabetical order!

> Note that the restriction on using the ORDER BY clause only applies to the code within the view. Once the view is created, you can still use an ORDER BY clause when you reference the view in a query.

Now let's try it the other way – using syscomments. Beyond the compatibility issues with using system tables, using syscomments (and most other system tables for that matter) comes with the extra added hassle of everything being coded in object IDs.

> Object IDs are SQL Server's internal way of keeping track of things. They are integer values rather than the names that you're used to for your objects.

Fortunately, you can get around this by joining to the sysobjects table:

```
SELECT sc.text
FROM syscomments sc
JOIN sysobjects so
    ON sc.id = so.id
WHERE so.name = 'Alphabetical list of products'
```

Again, you get the same block of code (indeed, all sp_helptext does is run what amounts to this same query):

```
Text
----------------------------------------------------------------
create view "Alphabetical list of products" AS
SELECT Products.*, Categories.CategoryName
FROM Categories INNER JOIN Products ON Categories.CategoryID = Products.CategoryID
WHERE (((Products.Discontinued)=0))

(1 row(s) affected)
```

I can't stress enough my recommendation that you avoid the system tables where possible – but I do like you to know your options.

Protecting Code: Encrypting Views

If you're building any kind of commercial software product, odds are that you're interested in protecting your source code. Views are the first place we see the opportunity to do just that.

All you have to do to encrypt your view is use the WITH ENCRYPTION option. This one has a couple of tricks to it if you're used to the WITH CHECK OPTION clause:

❑ WITH ENCRYPTION goes after the name of the view, but *before* the AS keyword

❑ WITH ENCRYPTION does not use the OPTION keyword

In addition, remember that if you use an ALTER VIEW statement, you are entirely replacing the existing view except for access rights. This means that the encryption is also replaced. If you want the altered view to be encrypted, then you must use the WITH ENCRYPTION clause in the ALTER VIEW statement.

Let's do an ALTER VIEW on our CustomerOrders_vw view that we created in Northwind. If you haven't yet created the CustomerOrders_vw view, then just change the ALTER to CREATE (don't forget to run this against Northwind):

```
ALTER VIEW CustomerOrders_vw
WITH ENCRYPTION
AS
SELECT    cu.CompanyName,
          o.OrderDate,
          od.ProductID,
          p.ProductName,
          od.Quantity,
          od.UnitPrice,
          od.Quantity * od.UnitPrice AS ExtendedPrice
FROM      Customers AS cu
INNER JOIN    Orders AS o
      ON cu.CustomerID = o.CustomerID
INNER JOIN    [Order Details] AS od
      ON o.OrderID = od.OrderID
INNER JOIN    Products AS p
      ON od.ProductID = p.ProductID
```

Now do an sp_helptext on our CustomerOrders_vw:

```
EXEC sp_helptext CustomerOrders_vw
```

SQL Server promptly tells us that it can't do what we're asking:

The object comments have been encrypted.

The heck you say, and promptly go to the `syscomments` table:

```
SELECT sc.text FROM syscomments sc
JOIN sysobjects so
    ON sc.id = so.id
WHERE so.name = 'CustomerOrders_vw'
```

But that doesn't get you very far either:

text

                                          Û

(1 row(s) affected)

Note that I've chopped off the right hand side of this for brevity's sake, but I think you get the point – the data is pretty useless.

In short – your code is safe and sound. Even if you pull it up in EM you'll find it useless.

> Make sure you store your source code somewhere before using the **WITH ENCRYPTION** option. Once it's been encrypted, there is no easy way to get it back. If you haven't stored your code away somewhere and you need to change it, then you may find yourself re-writing it from scratch.

About Schema Binding

Schema binding essentially takes the things that your view is dependent upon (tables or other views), and "binds" them to that view. The significance of this is that no one can make alterations to those objects (CREATE, ALTER) unless they drop the schema-bound view first.

Why would you want to do this? Well, there are a few reasons why this can come in handy:

- It prevents your view from becoming "orphaned" by alterations in underlying objects. Imagine, for a moment, that someone performs a DROP or makes some other change (even deleting a column could cause your view grief), but doesn't pay attention to your view. Oops. If the view is Schema Bound, then this is prevented from happening.

- To allow Indexed Views: If you want an index on your view, you *must* create it using the SCHEMABINDING option (We'll look at Indexed Views just a few paragraphs from now).

- If you are going to create a schema bound user defined function (and there are instances where your UDF *must* be schema bound) that references your view, then your view must also be schema bound.

Keep these in mind as you are building your views.

Making Your View Look Like a Table with VIEW_METADATA

This option has the effect of making your view look very much like an actual table to DB-LIB, ODBC and OLE-DB clients. Without this option, the meta-data passed back to the client API is that of the base table(s) that your view relies on.

Providing this metadata information is required to allow for any client-side cursors (cursors your client applications manages) to be updateable. Note that, if you want to support such cursors, you're also going to need to use an INSTEAD OF trigger.

Indexed (Materialized) Views

This one is brand new with SQL Server 2000 and is, unfortunately, only supported in the Enterprise Edition (OK, the Developer and Evaluation Editions also support it, but you aren't allowed to use these in production systems). Simply put, this is a spectacular new feature. Until fairly recently, the concept of an index on a view seemed pretty ludicrous – after all, how do you index data that isn't really there? Remember, a view is a *virtual* table – that is, it is only a way of looking at the data in base tables, and it doesn't have any "real" data of its own. Well, as I said, that was until recently – then someone got a much better idea.

> It probably deserves to be reiterated: Indexed Views are only supported by the Enterprise, Developer, and Evaluation Editions of SQL Server. The other editions (Standard and Personal) will allow you to create an index on a view (to avoid syntax errors when migrating to one of the other editions), but the query optimiser will not use the Indexed View in the query plan!

When a view is referred to, the logic in the query that makes up the view is essentially incorporated into the calling query. Crucially, the calling query just gets that much more complex. The extra overhead of figuring out the impact of the view (and what data it represents) on the fly can actually get very high. What's more, you're often adding additional joins into your query in the form of the tables that are joined in the view.

Lamenting this issue often made me wish for a concept I made use of on the AS/400 several years ago. The concept in question was referred to as a "join file", and it essentially allowed multiple tables to have an index built over them that was made up of data from all of participating tables. The "joined" tables could effectively act as one without the normal overhead involved in joining the tables – the index essentially made the relationship between the tables a quick and easy access thing rather than a sort process every time a query ran against the combined set of data.

I don't know who was the first to bring this concept to the RDBMS world, but it's easy to say that Larry Ellison of Oracle was certainly the most vocal about it. Around the time of the release of SQL Server 7.0, Mr. Ellison issued the infamous "Million Dollar Challenge". The challenge was relatively simple – Oracle would pay a million dollars to anyone who could show that SQL Server could perform within 100 times the speed of Oracle on a particular query run on a 1TB database that Oracle had constructed. This was, of course, one of those contrived challenges meant to highly utilize a feature that Oracle had and SQL Server didn't. The feature in question was something that Oracle refers to as a "Materialized" view. Not surprisingly, the challenge was "closed" just a few weeks before Microsoft demonstrated a system to meet the challenge.

For those readers who may be among the Oracle zealot crowd, please don't take this as a knock on Oracle. They had a cool feature that SQL Server didn't have an equivalent for. I'm not knocking that – in fact, I love it. The fact that one product has something another doesn't (and usually vice versa) is simply great. In the end, both products get better as they rush to try to both match and beat each other. Frankly, I say "Go Oracle!" because it makes Oracle that much better of a product, and, in addition, that invariably means that SQL Server is also going to be spurred on to new heights.

SQL Server now has something that is, in many ways, equivalent to Oracle's Materialized View from a user standpoint. An Indexed View is essentially a view that has had a set of unique values "materialized" into the form of a clustered index. The advantage of this is that it provides a very quick lookup in terms of pulling the information behind a view together. After the first index (which must be a clustered index against a unique set of values), SQL Server can also build additional indexes on the view using the cluster key from the first index as a reference point. That said, nothing comes for free – there are some restrictions about when you can and can't build indexes on views (I hope you're ready for this one – it's an awfully long list!):

❑ The view must use the SCHEMABINDING option

❑ If it references any User Defined Functions (more on these in Chapter 13), then these must also be schema bound

❑ The view must not reference any other views – just tables and UDFs

❑ All tables and UDFs referenced in the view must utilize a two part (not even three part and four part names are allowed) naming convention (for example dbo.Customers, BillyBob.SomeUDF) and must also have the same owner as the view

❑ The view must be in the same database as all objects referenced by the view

❑ The ARITHABORT option must be turned on (using the SET command) at the time the index is created

To create an example Indexed View, let's start by making a few alterations to the CustomerOrders_vw object that we created earlier in the chapter:

```
ALTER VIEW CustomerOrders_vw
WITH SCHEMABINDING
AS
SELECT    cu.CompanyName,
          o.OrderID,
          o.OrderDate,
          od.ProductID,
          p.ProductName,
          od.Quantity,
          od.UnitPrice
FROM      dbo.Customers AS cu
INNER JOIN    dbo.Orders AS o
          ON cu.CustomerID = o.CustomerID
INNER JOIN    dbo.[Order Details] AS od
          ON o.OrderID = od.OrderID
INNER JOIN    dbo.Products AS p
          ON od.ProductID = p.ProductID
```

The big things to notice here are:

❑ We had to make our view use the SCHEMABINDING option

❑ In order to utilize the SCHEMABINDING option, we had to go to two part naming for the objects (in this case, all tables) that we reference

We had to remove our calculated column – while you can build indexed views with non-aggregate expressions, the query optimiser will ignore them. The only way to utilize such a view is by using a direct query hint (we will learn more about optimiser hints in Chapter 17).

This is really just the beginning – we don't have an indexed view as yet. Instead, what we have is a view that *can* be indexed. When we create the index, the first index created on the view must be both clustered and unique.

```
SET ARITHABORT ON

CREATE UNIQUE CLUSTERED INDEX ivCustomerOrders
ON CustomerOrders_vw(CompanyName, OrderID, ProductID)
```

Once this command has executed, we have a clustered view. We also, however, have a small problem that will become clear in just a moment.

Let's test our view by running a simple SELECT against it:

```
SELECT * FROM CustomerOrders_vw
```

If you execute this, everything appears to be fine – but try displaying the graphical showplan (Display Estimated Execution Plan is the tool tip for this, and you'll find it towards the right-hand side of the toolbar):

Query 1: Query cost (relative to the batch): 100.00%
Query text: SELECT * FROM CustomerOrders_vw

I mentioned a paragraph or two ago that we had a small problem – the evidence is in this showplan. If you look through all the parts of this, you'll see that our index isn't being used at all!

At issue here is the size of our tables. The `Northwind` database doesn't have enough data. You see, the optimiser runs a balance between how long it will take to run the first plan that it finds versus the amount of work it takes to keep looking for a better plan. For example, does it make sense to spend two more seconds thinking about the plan when the plan you already know about could be done in less than one second?

In our example above, SQL Server looks at the underlying table, sees that there really isn't that much data out there, and decides that the plan it has is "good enough" before the optimiser gets far enough to see that the index on the view might be faster.

> *Keep this issue of "just how much data is there" versus "what will it cost to keep looking for a better plan" in mind when deciding on any index – not just indexed views. For small datasets, there's a very high possibility that SQL Server will totally ignore your index in favor of the first plan that it comes upon. In such a case, you pay the cost of maintaining the index (slower INSERT, UPDATE, and DELETE executions) without any benefit in the SELECT.*

Just so we get a chance to see a difference, however, let's create a database that will have enough data to make our index more interesting. You can download and execute a population script called `CreateAndLoadNorthwindBulk.sql`.

> *Figure that, if you load the default amount of data, you're going to use up somewhere in the area of 55MB of disk space for NorthwindBulk. Also, be aware that the population script can take a while to run, as it has to generate and load thousands and thousands of rows of data.*

Now just recreate your view and index in your new `NorthwindBulk` database.

```
USE NorthwindBulk
GO

CREATE VIEW CustomerOrders_vw
WITH SCHEMABINDING
AS
SELECT     cu.CompanyName,
           o.OrderID,
           o.OrderDate,
           od.ProductID,
           p.ProductName,
           od.Quantity,
           od.UnitPrice
FROM       dbo.Customers AS cu
INNER JOIN  dbo.Orders AS o
    ON cu.CustomerID = o.CustomerID
INNER JOIN  dbo.[Order Details] AS od
    ON o.OrderID = od.OrderID
INNER JOIN  dbo.Products AS p
    ON od.ProductID = p.ProductID
GO

SET ARITHABORT ON

CREATE UNIQUE CLUSTERED INDEX ivCustomerOrders
ON CustomerOrders_vw(CompanyName, OrderID, ProductID)
```

Now re-run the original query, only against `NorthwindBulk`:

```
USE NorthwindBulk

SELECT * FROM CustomerOrders_vw
```

And check out your new queryplan:

```
Query 1: Query cost (relative to the batch): 100.00%
Query text: SELECT * FROM CustomerOrders_vw
```

```
    SELECT              CustomerOrders_...
   Cost: 0%               Cost: 100%
```

This time, SQL Server has enough data that it does a more thorough query plan. In this case, it accepts the index view that exists on our table. The overall performance of this view is now much faster (row for row) than the previous model would have been.

> *OK Folks! One more time (just in case)! If you're using the Standard or Personal Editions of SQL Server 2000, you will still see the old query plan here! The query optimizer in those editions will not make use of the new index – if you want to see this example work, you have to be using the Enterprise, Evaluation, or Developer Edition.*

Summary

Views tend to be either the most over- or most under-used tools in most of the databases I've seen. Some people like to use them to abstract seemingly everything (often forgetting that they are adding another layer to the process when they do this). Others just seem to forget that views are even an option. Personally, like most things, I think you should use a view when it's the right tool to use – not before, not after. Things to remember with views include:

- ❑ Stay away from building views based on views – instead, adapt the appropriate query information from the first view into your new view.

- ❑ Remember that a view using the WITH CHECK OPTION provides some flexibility that can't be duplicated with a normal CHECK constraint.

- ❑ Encrypt views when you don't want others to be able to see your source code – either for commercial products or general security reasons.

- ❑ Prior to 7.0, there was a 16 table join limit – any query that includes views needs to include the tables within those views as being part of the table count.

- ❑ Using an ALTER VIEW completely replaces the existing view other than permissions. This means you must include the WITH ENCRYPTION and WITH CHECK OPTION clauses in the ALTER statement if you want encryption and restrictions to be in effect in the altered view.

- ❑ Use sp_helptext to display the supporting code for a view – avoid using the system tables.

- ❑ Minimize the user of views for production queries – they add additional overhead and hurt performance.

Common uses for views include:

- ❑ Filtering rows

- ❑ Protecting sensitive data

- ❑ Reducing database complexity

- ❑ Abstracting multiple physical databases into one logical database

In our next chapter, we'll take a look at batches and scripting. We got a brief taste when we ran the INSERT script in this chapter to insert a row into the Orders table, and then used information from the freshly inserted row in an insert into the Order Details table. Batches and scripting will lead us right into stored procedures – the closest thing that SQL Server has to its own programs.

11

Writing Scripts and Batches

Whether you've realized it or not, you've already been writing SQL **scripts**. Every CREATE statement that you write, every ALTER, every SELECT is all (if you're running a single statement) or part (multiple statements) of a script. It's hard to get excited though, over a script with one line in it – could you imagine Hamlet's "To be, or not to be…?" if it had never had the following lines – we wouldn't have any context for what he was talking about.

SQL scripts are much the same way. Things get quite a bit more interesting when we string several commands together into a longer script – a full play or at least an act to finish our Shakespeare analogy.

Scripts generally have a unified goal. That is, all the commands that are in a script are usually building up to one overall purpose. Examples include scripts to build a database (these might be used for a system installation), scripts for system maintenance (backups, Database Consistency Checker utilities (DBCCs)) – scripts for anything where several commands are usually run together.

We will be looking into scripts during this chapter, and adding in the notion of **batches** – which control how SQL Server groups your commands together. In addition, we will take a look at **OSQL** – the command line utility, and how it relates to scripts.

Script Basics

A script technically isn't a script until you store it in a file where it can be pulled up and reused. SQL scripts are stored as text files and, prior to 7.0, many of the people I knew actually wrote their scripts in Notepad rather than the ISQL/W utility. The case against that now is pretty high given that the new ISQL/W (now called the Query Analyzer, but still `isqlw.exe` on the executable) has so many things to help you edit your code. Color-coding, parse without executing, graphical query plan display – these are just a few of the things that were either added or made easier to use in 7.0. Now, with SQL Server 2000, we've also picked up a step debugger, code templates, the object browser, and more. Even if you do elect not to use the Query Analyzer, then you should take a look at the increasing number of SQL editing tools that are available.

Scripts are usually treated as a unit. That is, you are normally executing the entire script or nothing at all. They can make use of both system functions and local variables. As an example, let's look at the script that we used to INSERT order records in our chapter on views (Chapter 10):

```
USE Northwind

DECLARE @Ident int

INSERT INTO Orders
(CustomerID,OrderDate)
VALUES
('ALFKI', DATEADD(day,-1,GETDATE()))

SELECT @Ident = @@IDENTITY

INSERT INTO [Order Details]
(OrderID, ProductID, UnitPrice, Quantity)
VALUES
(@Ident, 1, 50, 25)

SELECT 'The OrderID of the INSERTed row is ' + CONVERT(varchar(8),@Ident)
```

We have six distinct commands working here, covering a range of different things that we might do in a script. We're using both system functions and local variables, the USE statement, INSERT statements, and both assignment and regular versions of the SELECT statement. They are all working in unison to accomplish one task – to insert complete orders into the database.

> *What SQL Server used to refer to as global variables (and still does in many places in the documentation) are not really variables at all (you can't store anything in them) and are more correctly referred to as "system functions" or "parameterless system functions". All such references in this book will use the term "system functions". However it should be realized that old habits die hard, and that I or anyone else may well refer in conversation to global variables or "globals" in SQL Server, when what we are really dealing with are system functions that return a value – it just happens that you retrieve the value by referring to @@<variable name>. The uses for individual globals – excuse me, system functions – are covered in Appendix A.*

The USE Statement

The USE statement sets the current database. This affects any place where we are making use of default values for the database portion of our fully qualified object name. In this particular example, we have not indicated what database the tables in our INSERT or SELECT statements are from, but, since we've included a USE statement prior to our INSERT and SELECT statements, they will use that database (in this case, Northwind). Without our USE statement, we would be at the mercy of whoever executes the script to make certain that the correct database was current when the script was executed.

> Don't take this as meaning that you should always include a USE statement in your script – it depends on what the purpose of the script is. If your intent is to have a general-purpose script, then leaving out the USE statement might actually be helpful.
>
> Usually, if you are naming database-specific tables in your script (that is, non-system tables), then you want to use the USE command. I also find it very helpful if the script is meant to modify a specific database – I can't tell you how many times I've accidentally created a large number of tables in the **master** database that were intended for a user database.

Next we have a DECLARE statement to declare a variable. We've talked about DECLARE statements briefly before, but let's expand on this some.

Declaring Variables

The DECLARE statement has a pretty simple syntax:

```
DECLARE @<variable name> <variable type>[,
        @<variable name> <variable type>[,
        @<variable name> <variable type>]]
```

You can declare just one variable at a time, or several. It's not at all uncommon to see people reuse the DECLARE statement with each variable they declare, rather than using the comma separated method. It's up to you, but no matter which method you choose, the value of your variable will always be NULL until you explicitly set it to some other value.

In our case, we've declared a local variable called @ident as an integer. Technically, we could have got away without declaring this variable – instead, we could have chosen to just use @@IDENTITY directly. @@IDENTITY is a system function. It is always available, and supplies the last identity value that was assigned in the current connection. As with most system functions, you should make a habit of explicitly moving the value in @@IDENTITY to a local variable. That way, you're sure that it won't get changed accidentally. There was no danger of that in this case, but, as always, be consistent.

> I like to move a value I'm taking from a system function into my own variable. That way I can safely use the value and know that it's only being changed when I change it. With the system function itself, you sometimes can't be certain when it's going to change because most system functions are not set by you, but by the system. That creates a situation where it would be very easy to have the system change a value at a time you weren't expecting it, and wind up with the most dreaded of all computer terms: unpredictable results.

Setting the Value in Your Variables

Well, we now know how to declare our variables, but the question that follows is, "How do we change their values?" There are currently two ways to set the value in a variable. You can use a SELECT statement or a SET statement. Functionally, they work almost the same, except that a SELECT statement has the power to have the source value come from a column within the SELECT statement.

So why have two ways of doing this? Actually, I still don't know. I thought after the last edition someone would e-mail me and give me a good answer – they didn't. Suffice to say that SET is now part of the ANSI standard, and that's why it's been put in there. However, I can't find anything wrong with the same functionality in SELECT – even ANSI seems to think that it's OK. I'm sure there's a purpose in the redundancy, but what it is I can't tell you. That said; there are some differences in the way they are typically put to use.

Setting Variables Using SET

SET is usually used for setting variables in the fashion that you would see in more procedural languages. Examples of typical uses would be:

```
SET @TotalCost = 10
SET @TotalCost = @UnitCost * 1.1
```

Notice that these are all straight assignments that use either explicit values or another variable. With a SET, you cannot assign a value to a variable from a query – you have to separate the query from the SET. For example:

```
USE Northwind

DECLARE @Test money

SET @Test = MAX(UnitPrice) FROM [Order Details]
SELECT @Test
```

Causes an error, but:

```
USE Northwind

DECLARE @Test money

SET @Test = (SELECT MAX(UnitPrice) FROM [Order Details])
SELECT @Test
```

Works just fine.

> *Although this latter syntax works, by convention, code is never implemented this way. Again, I don't know for sure why it's "just not done that way", but I suspect that it has to do with readability – you want a SELECT statement to be related to retrieving table data, and a SET to be about simple variable assignments.*

Setting Variables Using SELECT

SELECT is usually used to assign variable values when the source of the information you're storing in the variable is from a query. For example, our last illustration above would be far more typically done using a SELECT:

```
USE Northwind

DECLARE @Test money

SELECT @Test = MAX(UnitPrice) FROM [Order Details]
SELECT @Test
```

Notice that this is a little cleaner (it takes less verbiage to do the same thing).

So again, the convention on when to use which goes like this:

❑   Use SET when you are performing a simple assignment of a variable – where your value is already known in the form of an explicit value or some other variable

❑   Use SELECT when you are basing the assignment of your variable on a query

I'm not going to pick any bones about the fact that you'll see me violate this last convention in many places in this book. Using SET for variable assignment first appeared in version 7.0, and I must admit that I haven't completely adapted yet. Nonetheless, this seems to be something that's really being pushed by Microsoft and the SQL Server community, so I strongly recommend that you start out on the right foot and adhere to the convention.

Reviewing System Functions

There are over 30 parameterless system functions available. Some of the ones you should be most concerned with are in the table that follows:

Variable	Purpose	Comments
@@CURSOR_ROWS	returns how many rows are currently in the last cursor set opened on the current connection.	SQL 7 can populate cursors asynchronously. Be aware that the value in this variable may change if the cursor is still in the process of being populated.
@@DATEFIRST	Returns what is currently set as the first day of the week (say, Sunday vs. Monday).	Is a system wide setting – if someone changes the setting, you may not get the result you expect.
@@DBTS	Returns the last used timestamp for the current database.	The value changes based on any change in the database, not just the table you're working on. The value is more of a true "global" than is @@IDENTITY – *any* timestamp change in the database is reflected, not just those for the current connection.

Table continued on following page

Variable	Purpose	Comments
@@ERROR	Returns the error number of the last T-SQL statement executed on the current connection. Returns 0 if no error.	Is reset with each new statement. If you need the value preserved, move it to a local variable immediately after the execution of the statement for which you want to preserve the error code.
@@FETCH_STATUS	Used in conjunction with a FETCH statement.	Returns 0 for valid fetch, –1 for beyond end of cursor set, –2 for a missing (deleted) row. Typical gotcha is to assume that any non-zero value means you are at the end of the cursor – a –2 may just mean one missing record.
@@IDENTITY	Returns the last identity value inserted as a result of the last INSERT or SELECT INTO statement.	Is set to NULL if no identity value was generated. This is true even if the lack of an identity value was due to a failure of the statement to run. If multiple inserts are performed by just one statement, then only the last identity value is returned.
@@LANGID and @@LANGUAGE	Returns the language or the ID of the language currently in use.	Handy for localization situations.
@@LOCK_TIMEOUT	Returns the current amount of time in milliseconds before the system will time-out waiting on a blocked resource.	Connection default is system default, but unless you manually set it, the value returned is –1. Use SET LOCK_TIMEOUT if you want to change it for the current connection.
@@NESTLEVEL	Returns the current nesting level for nested stored procedures.	Returns 1 for non-nested stored procedures, and a higher number for each additional nesting level. You cannot nest beyond 32 levels.
@@OPTIONS	Returns information about options that have been set using the SET command.	Since you only get one value back, but can have many options set, SQL Server uses binary flags to indicate what values are set. In order to test whether the option you are interested is set, you must use the option value together with a bitwise operator.
@@REMSERVER	Used only in stored procedures. Returns the value of the server that called the stored procedure.	Handy when you want the sproc to behave differently depending on the remote server (often a geographic location) from which it was called.

Variable	Purpose	Comments
@@ROWCOUNT	One of the most used system functions. Returns the number of rows affected by the last statement.	Commonly used in non run-time error checking. For example, if you try to DELETE a row using a WHERE clause, and no rows are affected, then that would imply that something unexpected happened. You can then raise an error manually.
@@SERVERNAME	Returns the name of the local server that the script is running from.	Can be changed by using sp_addserver and then restarting SQL Server, but rarely required.
@@TRANCOUNT	Returns the number of active transactions – essentially the transaction nesting level – for the current connection.	A ROLLBACK TRAN statement decrements @@TRANCOUNT to 0 unless you are using savepoints. BEGIN TRAN increments @@TRANCOUNT by 1, COMMIT TRAN decrements @@TRANCOUNT by 1.
@@VERSION	Returns the current version of SQL Server as well as the date, processor and O/S architecture.	Unfortunately, this doesn't return in the information into any kind of structured field arrangement, so you have to parse it if you want to use it to test for specific information.

Don't worry if you don't recognize some of the terms in a few of these. They will become clear in due time, and you will have this table to look back on for reference at a later date. The thing to remember is that there are sources you can go to in order to find out a whole host of information about the current state of your system and your activities.

Using @@IDENTITY

@@IDENTITY is one of the most important of all the system functions. Remember when we saw identity values all the way back in Chapter 6? An identity column is one where we don't supply a value, and SQL Server inserts a numbered value automatically.

In our example case, we obtain the value of @@IDENTITY right after performing an insert into the Orders table. The issue is that we don't supply the key value for that table – it's automatically created as we do the insert. Now we want to insert a record into the Order Details table, but we need to know the value of the primary key in the associated record in the Orders table (remember, there is a foreign key constraint on the Order Details table that references the Orders table). Since SQL Server generated that value instead of us supplying it, we need to have a way to retrieve that value for use in our dependent inserts later on in the script. @@IDENTITY gives us that automatically generated value since it was the last statement run.

In the case of our example, we could have easily gotten away with not moving @@IDENTITY to a local variable – we could have just referenced it explicitly in our next INSERT query. I make a habit of always moving it to a local variable though, to avoid errors on the occasions when I do need to keep a copy. An example of this kind of situation would be if we had yet another INSERT that was dependent on the identity value from the INSERT into the Orders table. If I hadn't moved it into a local variable, then it would be lost when I did the next INSERT, because it would have been overwritten with the value from the Order Details table, which, since Order Details has no identity column, means that @@IDENTITY would have been set to NULL. Moving the value of @@IDENTITY to a local variable also let me keep the value around for the statement where I printed out the value for later reference.

Let's create a couple of tables to try this out:

```
CREATE TABLE TestIdent
(
    IDCol    int    IDENTITY
    PRIMARY KEY
)

CREATE TABLE TestChild1
(
    IDcol    int
    PRIMARY KEY
    FOREIGN KEY
            REFERENCES TestIdent(IDCol)
)

CREATE TABLE TestChild2
(
    IDcol    int
    PRIMARY KEY
    FOREIGN KEY
            REFERENCES TestIdent(IDCol)
)
```

What we have here is a parent table – it has an identity column for a primary key (as it happens, that's the only column it has). We also have two child tables. They each are the subject of an identifying relationship – that is, they each take at least part (in this case all) of their primary key by placing a foreign key on another table (the parent). So what we have is a situation where the two child tables need to get their key from the parent. Therefore, we need to insert a record into the parent first, and then retrieve the identity value generated so we can make use of it in the other tables.

Now that we have some tables to work with, we're ready to try a little test script:

```
/******************************************
 * This script illustrates how the identity
 * value gets lost as soon as another INSERT
 * happens
 ****************************************** */

DECLARE @Ident    int   -- This will be a holding variable
                        -- We'll use it to show how we can
                        -- move values from system functions
                        -- into a safe place.

INSERT INTO TestIdent
        DEFAULT VALUES

SET @Ident = @@IDENTITY
PRINT "The value we got originally from @@IDENTITY was " +
        CONVERT(varchar(2),@Ident)
PRINT "The value currently in @@IDENTITY is " + CONVERT(varchar(2),@@IDENTITY)
```

```
/* On this first INSERT using @@IDENTITY, we're going to get lucky.
** We'll get a proper value because there is nothing between our
** original INSERT and this one. You'll see that on the INSERT that
** will follow after this one, we won't be so lucky anymore. */
INSERT INTO TestChild1
VALUES
      (@@IDENTITY)

PRINT "The value we got originally from @@IDENTITY was " +
      CONVERT(varchar(2),@Ident)
IF (SELECT @@IDENTITY) IS NULL
    PRINT "The value currently in @@IDENTITY is NULL"
ELSE
    PRINT "The value currently in @@IDENTITY is " + CONVERT(varchar(2),@@IDENTITY)

-- The next line is just a spacer for our print out
PRINT ""

/* The next line is going to blow up because the one column in
** the table is the primary key, and primary keys can't be set
** to NULL. @@IDENTITY will be NULL because we just issued an
** INSERT statement a few lines ago, and the table we did the
** INSERT into doesn't have an identity field. Perhaps the biggest
** thing to note here is when @@IDENTITY changed - right after
** the next INSERT statement. */
INSERT INTO TestChild2
VALUES
      (@@IDENTITY)
```

What we're doing in this script, is seeing what happens if we depend on @@IDENTITY directly rather than moving the value off to a safe place. When we execute the script above, everything's going to work just fine until the final INSERT. That final statement is trying to make use of @@IDENTITY directly, but the preceding INSERT statement has already changed the value in @@IDENTITY. Since that statement is on a table with no identity column, the value in @@IDENTITY is set to NULL. Since we can't have a NULL value in our primary key, the last INSERT fails:

```
(1 row(s) affected)

The value we got originally from @ @IDENTITY was 5
The value currently in @ @IDENTITY is 5

(1 row(s) affected)

The value we got originally from @ @IDENTITY was 5
The value currently in @ @IDENTITY is NULL

Server: Msg 515, Level 16, State 2, Line 43
Cannot insert the value NULL into column 'IDcol', table 'Northwind.dbo.TestChild2'; column does not
allow nulls. INSERT fails.
The statement has been terminated.
```

If we make just one little change (to save the original @@IDENTITY value):

```
/*****************************************
* This script illustrates how the identity
* value gets lost as soon as another INSERT
* happens
***************************************** */

DECLARE @Ident    int   -- This will be a holding variable
                        -- We'll use it to show how we can
                    -- move values from system functions
                    -- into a safe place.

INSERT INTO TestIdent
        DEFAULT VALUES

SET @Ident = @@IDENTITY
PRINT "The value we got originally from @@IDENTITY was " +
        CONVERT(varchar(2),@Ident)
PRINT "The value currently in @@IDENTITY is " + CONVERT(varchar(2),@@IDENTITY)

/* On this first INSERT using @@IDENTITY, we're going to get lucky.
** We'll get a proper value because there is nothing between our
** original INSERT and this one. You'll see that on the INSERT that
** will follow after this one, we won't be so lucky anymore. */
INSERT INTO TestChild1
VALUES
        (@@IDENTITY)

PRINT "The value we got originally from @@IDENTITY was " +
        CONVERT(varchar(2),@Ident)
IF (SELECT @@IDENTITY) IS NULL
    PRINT "The value currently in @@IDENTITY is NULL"
ELSE
    PRINT "The value currently in @@IDENTITY is " + CONVERT(varchar(2),@@IDENTITY)

-- The next line is just a spacer for our print out
PRINT ""

/* This time all will go fine because we are using the value that
** we have placed in safekeeping instead of @@IDENTITY directly.*/
INSERT INTO TestChild2
VALUES
        (@Ident)
```

this time everything runs just fine:

(1 row(s) affected)

The value we got originally from @ @IDENTITY was 1
The value currently in @ @IDENTITY is 1

(1 row(s) affected)

The value we got originally from @@IDENTITY was 1
The value currently in @@IDENTITY is NULL

(1 row(s) affected)

> In this example, it was fairly easy to tell that there was a problem because of the attempt at inserting a NULL into the primary key. Now, imagine a far less pretty scenario – one where the second table did have an identity column – you could easily wind up inserting bogus data into your table and not even knowing about it – at least not until you already had a very serious data integrity problem on your hands!

Using @@ROWCOUNT

In the many queries that we ran up to this point, it's always been pretty easy to tell how many rows a statement affected – Query Analyzer tells us. For example, if we run:

```
USE Northwind

SELECT * FROM Categories
```

Then we see all the rows in Categories, but we also see a count on the number of rows affected by our query (in this case, it's all the rows in the table):

(8 row(s) affected)

But what if we need to *programmatically* know how many rows were affected? Much like @@IDENTITY, @@ROWCOUNT is an invaluable tool in the fight to know what's going on as your script runs – but this time the value is how many rows were affected rather than our identity value.

Let's examine this just a bit further with an example:

```
USE Northwind
GO

DECLARE @RowCount int -- Notice the single @ sign

SELECT * FROM Categories

SELECT @RowCount = @@ROWCOUNT

PRINT 'The value of @@ROWCOUNT was ' + CAST(@RowCount AS varchar(5))
```

This again shows us all the rows, but notice the new line that we got back:

The value of @@ROWCOUNT was 8

We'll take a look at ways this might be useful when we look at stored procedures later in the book. For now, just realize that this provides us with a way to learn something about what a statement did, and it's not limited to use SELECT statements – UPDATE, INSERT, and DELETE also set this value.

> **If you look through the example, you might notice that, much as I did with @@IDENTITY, I chose to move the value off to a holding variable. @@ROWCOUNT will be reset with a new value the very next statement, so, if you're going to be doing multiple activities with the @@ROWCOUNT value, you should move it into a safe keeping area.**

Batches

A **batch** is a grouping of T-SQL statements into one logical unit. All of the statements within a batch are combined into one execution plan, so all statements are parsed together and must pass a validation of the syntax or none of the statements will execute. Note, however, that this does not prevent run-time errors from happening. In the event of a run-time error, any statement that has been executed prior to the run-time error will still be in effect. To summarize, if a statement fails at parse-time, then nothing runs – if a statement fails at run-time, then all statements until the statement that generated the error have already run.

All the scripts we have run up to this point are made up of one batch each. Even the script we've been analyzing so far this in chapter is just one batch. To separate a script into multiple batches, we make use of the GO statement. The GO statement:

❑ Must be on its own line (nothing other than a comment can be on the same line); there is an exception to this discussed below, but think of a GO as needing to be on a line to itself

❑ Causes all statements since the beginning of the script or the last GO statement (whichever is closer) to be compiled into one execution plan and sent to the server independently of any other batches

❑ Is not a T-SQL command, but, rather, a command recognized by the various SQL Server command utilities (OSQL, ISQL, and the Query Analyzer)

A Line to Itself

The GO command should stand alone on its own line. Technically, you can start a new batch on the same line after the GO command, but you'll find this puts a serious damper on readability. T-SQL statements cannot precede the GO statement, or the GO statement will often be misinterpreted and cause either a parsing error or some other unexpected result. For example, if I use a GO statement after a WHERE clause:

```
SELECT * FROM Customers WHERE CustomerID = 'ALFKI' GO
```

The parser becomes somewhat confused:

Server: Msg 170, Level 15, State 1, Line 1
Line 1: Incorrect syntax near 'GO'.

Each Batch is Sent to the Server Separately

Because each batch is processed independently, an error in one batch does not preclude another batch from running. To illustrate, take a look at some code:

```
USE Northwind

DECLARE @MyVarchar varchar(50)   --This DECLARE only lasts for this batch!

SELECT @MyVarchar = "Honey, I'm home..."

PRINT 'Done with first Batch...'

GO

PRINT @MyVarchar  --This generates an error since @MyVarchar
                  --isn't declared in this batch
PRINT 'Done with second Batch'

GO

PRINT 'Done with third batch'    -- Notice that this still gets executed
                                 -- even after the error

GO
```

If there were any dependencies between these batches, then either everything would fail – or, at the very least, everything after the point of error would fail – but it doesn't. Look at the results if you run the above script:

```
Done with first Batch...
Server: Msg 137, Level 15, State 2, Line 2
Must declare the variable '@MyVarchar'.
Done with third batch
```

Again, each batch is completely autonomous in terms of run-time issues. Keep in mind though that you can build in dependencies in the sense that one batch may try to perform work that depends on the first batch being complete – we'll see some of this in the next section when we talk about what can and can't span batches.

GO is Not a T-SQL Command

Thinking that GO is a T-SQL command is a common mistake. GO is a command that is only recognized by the editing tools (Query Analyzer, Enterprise Manager, OSQL). If you use a third party tool, then it may or may not support the GO command.

When the editing tool (Isql, Osql, or the Query Analyzer) encounters a GO statement, it sees it as a flag to terminate that batch, package it up, and send it as a single unit to the server – *without* including the GO. That's right, the server itself has absolutely no idea what GO is supposed to mean.

If you try to execute a GO command in a pass-through query using ODBC, OLE DB, ADO, DB-LIB, or any other access method, you'll get an error message back from the server. The GO is merely an indicator to the tool that it is time to end the current batch, and time, if appropriate, to start a new one.

Errors in Batches

Errors in batches fall into two categories:

- ❑   Syntax errors
- ❑   Run-time errors

If the query parser finds a **syntax error**, processing of that batch is cancelled immediately. Since syntax checking happens before the batch is compiled or executed, a failure during the syntax check means none of the batch will be executed – regardless of the position of the syntax error within the batch.

Run-time errors work quite a bit differently. Any statement that has already executed before the run-time error was encountered is already done, so anything that statement did will remain intact unless it is part of an uncommitted transaction (transactions are covered in Chapter 14, but the relevance here is that they imply an all or nothing situation). What happens beyond the point of the run-time error depends on the nature of the error. Generally speaking, run-time errors will terminate execution of the batch from the point where the error occurred to the end of the batch. Some run-time errors, such as a referential-integrity violation will only prevent the offending statement from executing – all other statements in the batch will still be executed. This later scenario is why error checking is so important – we will cover error checking in full in our chapter on stored procedures (Chapter 12).

When to Use Batches

Batches have several purposes, but they all have one thing in common – they are used when something has to happen either before or separately from everything else in your script.

Statements that Require their Own Batch

There are several commands that absolutely must be part of their own batch. These include:

- ❑   CREATE DEFAULT
- ❑   CREATE PROCEDURE
- ❑   CREATE RULE
- ❑   CREATE TRIGGER
- ❑   CREATE VIEW

If you want to combine any of these statements with other statements in a single script, then you will need to break them up into their own batch by using a GO statement.

> Note that, if you **DROP** an object, you may want to place the **DROP** in its own batch or at least with a batch of other **DROP** statements. Why? Well, if you're going to later create an object with the same name, the **CREATE** will fail during the parsing of your batch unless the **DROP** has already happened. That means you need to run the **DROP** in a separate and prior batch so it will be complete when the batch with the **CREATE** statement executes.

Using Batches to Establish Precedence

Perhaps the most likely scenario for using batches is when precedence is required – that is, you need one task to be completely done before the next task starts. Most of the time, SQL Server deals with this kind of situation just fine – the first statement in the script is the first executed, and the second statement in the script can rely on the server being in the proper state when the second statement runs. There are times however, when SQL Server can't resolve this kind of issue.

Let's take the example of creating a database together with some tables:

```
CREATE DATABASE Test

CREATE TABLE TestTable
(
    col1    int,
    col2    int
)
```

Execute this and, at first, it appears that everything has gone well:

The **CREATE DATABASE** process is allocating 0.75 MB on disk 'TEST'.
The **CREATE DATABASE** process is allocating 0.49 MB on disk 'TEST_log'.

However, things are not as they seem – check out the INFORMATION_SCHEMA in the Test database, and you'll notice something is missing:

```
SELECT TABLE_CATALOG FROM INFORMATION_SCHEMA.TABLES WHERE TABLE_NAME =
    'TestTable'
```

TABLE_CATALOG
\---
master

(1 row(s) affected)

Hey! Why was the table created in the wrong database? The answer lies in what database was current when we ran the CREATE TABLE statement. In my case, it happened to be the master database, so that's where my table was created.

> Note that you may have been somewhere other than the master database when you ran this, so you may get a different result. That's kind of the point though – you could be in pretty much any database. That's why making use of the USE statement is so important.

When you think about it, this seems like an easy thing to fix – just make use of the USE statement, but before we test our new theory, we have to get rid of the old (OK, not that old) database

```
USE MASTER
DROP DATABASE Test
```

We can then run our newly modified script:

```
CREATE DATABASE Test

USE Test

CREATE TABLE TestTable
(
    col1    int,
    col2    int
)
```

Unfortunately, this has its own problems:

Server: Msg 911, Level 16, State 1, Line 3
Could not locate entry in sysdatabases for database 'TEST'. No entry found with that name. Make sure that the name is entered correctly.

The parser tries to validate your code and finds that you are referencing a database with your USE command that doesn't exist. Ahh, now we see the need for our batches. We need the CREATE DATABASE statement to be completed before we try to use the new database:

```
CREATE DATABASE Test
GO


USE Test

CREATE TABLE TestTable
(
    col1    int,
    col2    int
)
```

Now things work a lot better. Our immediate results look the same:

The CREATE DATABASE process is allocating 0.75 MB on disk 'Test'.
The CREATE DATABASE process is allocating 0.49 MB on disk 'Test_log'.

But when we run our INFORMATION_SCHEMA query, things are confirmed:

```
TABLE_CATALOG
--------------------------------------------------------------------------------
Test

(1 row(s) affected)
```

Let's move on to another example that shows an even more explicit need for precedence.

When you use an ALTER TABLE statement that significantly changes the type of a column or adds columns, you cannot make use of those changes until the batch that makes the changes has completed.

If we add a column to our `TestTable` table in our `Test` database and then try to reference that column without ending the first batch:

```
USE Test

ALTER TABLE TestTable
   ADD col3 int

INSERT INTO TestTable
(col1, col2, col3)
VALUES
(1,1,1)
```

We get an error message – SQL Server cannot resolve the new column name, and therefore complains:

Server: Msg 207, Level 16, State 1, Line 1
Invalid column name 'col3'.

Add one simple `GO` statement after the `ADD col3 int` though and everything is working fine:

(1 row(s) affected)

OSQL

OSQL – usually spoken as "OH-Sequel" – is a utility that allow you to run scripts from a command prompt in an NT command box or Win 9x DOS prompt. This can be very nice for executing conversion or maintenance scripts, as well as a quick and dirty way to capture a text file (beginning with SQL Server 2000, you can also capture a text file directly from within QA).

OSQL replaces the older ISQL with a new 32-bit engine. ISQL is still included with SQL Server for backward compatibility only.

The syntax for running OSQL from the command line includes a large number of different switches, and looks like this:

```
osql -U<login id> [-e] [-E] [-p] [-n] [-d<database name>]
[-Q "query text"] [-q "query text"] [-c<cmd terminator>]
[-h<headers>] [-w<column width>] [-s<column separator>]
[-t<time out>] [-m<error level>] [-I] [-L] [-?] [-r {0 | 1}]
[-H<workstation name>] [-P<password>] [-R] [-S<server name>]
[-i<input file>] [-o<output file>] [-u] [-a<packet size>]
[-b] [-O] [-l<time out>]
```

The single biggest thing to keep in mind with these flags is that many of them (but, oddly enough, not all of them) are case sensitive. For example, both "-Q" and "-q" will execute queries, but the first will exit OSQL when the query is complete, and the second won't. The other big thing in running OSQL is to run the arguments for each flag right against the flag (don't put a space in between). The exception to this later rule is when the parameter argument is quoted, it which case you do want a space between the flag and the first quote, for example:

```
oqsl -URobV -PMyPassword -Q "My Query"
```

So, let's try a quick query direct from the command line. Again, remember that this is meant to be run from the NT command prompt or a DOS box in Win9x (don't try it in QA):

```
osql -Usa -P -Q "SELECT * FROM Northwind..Shippers"
```

> *The –P is the flag that indicates the password. If your server is configured with something other than a blank password (and it should be!), then you'll need to provide that password immediately following the –P with no space in between.*

If you run this from a command prompt, you should get something like:

```
C:\>Osql -Usa -P -Q "SELECT * FROM Northwind..Shippers"
ShipperID      CompanyName                     Phone
---------------- ------------------------------- --------------------
1              Speedy Express                  (503) 555-9831
2              United Package                  (503) 555-3199
3              Federal Shipping(503) 555-9931
```

(3 rows affected)

C:\>

Now, let's create a quick text file to see how it works when including a file. At the command prompt (or DOS box in Win9x), type the following:

```
C:\>copy con testsql.sql
```

This should take you down to a blank line (with no prompt of any kind), where you can enter in this:

```
SELECT * FROM Northwind..Shippers
```

Then press *F6* and *Return* (this ends the creation of our text file). You should get back a message like:

1 file(s) copied.

Now let's retry our earlier query using a script file this time. The command line at the prompt only has a slight change to it:

```
C:\>Osql -Usa -P -i testsql.sql
```

This should get us exactly the same results as we had when we ran the query using –Q. The major difference is, of course, that we took the command from a file. The file could have had hundreds – if not thousands – of different commands in it.

There are a wide variety of different parameters, but the most important are the login, the password, and the one that says what you want to do (straight query or input file).

Dynamic SQL: Generating Your Code on the Fly with the EXEC Command

OK, so all this saving stuff away in scripts is all fine and dandy, but what if you don't know what code you need to execute until run time?

SQL Server allows us, with a few gotchas, to build our SQL statement on the fly using string manipulation. The need to do this usually stems from not being able to know the details about something until run time. The syntax looks like this:

```
EXEC ({<string variable>|'<literal command string>'})
```

Or:

```
EXECUTE ({<string variable>|'<literal command string>'})
```

As with executing a stored proc, whether you use the EXEC or EXECUTE makes no difference.

Let's build an example in the Northwind database by creating a dummy table to grab our dynamic information out of:

```
USE Northwind
GO

--Create The Table. We'll pull info from here for our dynamic SQL
CREATE TABLE DynamicSQLExample
(
    TableID    int    IDENTITY    NOT NULL
        CONSTRAINT PKDynamicSQLExample
                PRIMARY KEY,
    TableName varchar(128)      NOT NULL
)
GO

/* Populate the table. In this case, We're grabbing every user
** table object in this database                               */
INSERT INTO DynamicSQLExample
SELECT TABLE_NAME
    FROM Information_Schema.Tables
    WHERE TABLE_TYPE = 'BASE TABLE'
```

This should get us a response something like:

(17 row(s) affected)

> *To quote the old advertising disclaimer: "actual results may vary". It's going to depend on which examples you've already followed along with in the book, which ones you haven't, and for which ones you took the initiative and did a DROP on once you were done with them. In any case, don't sweat it too much.*

OK, so what we now have is a list of all the tables in our current database. Now let's say that we wanted to select some data from one of the tables, but we wanted to identify the table only at run time by using its ID. For example, I'll pull out all the data for the table with an ID of 1:

```
/* First, declare a variable to hold the table name. Remember,
** object names can be 128 characters long
*/
DECLARE @TableName       varchar(128)

-- Now, grab the table name that goes with our ID
SELECT @TableName = TableName
   FROM DynamicSQLExample
   WHERE TableID = 1

-- Finally, pass that value into the EXEC statement
EXEC ('SELECT * FROM ' + @TableName)
```

If your table names went into the DynamicSQLExample table the way mine did, then a TableID of 1 should equate to the Categories table. If so, you should wind up with something like this (the rightmost columns have been snipped for brevity):

CategoryID	CategoryName	Description	
1	Beverages	Soft drinks, coffees, teas, beers, and ales	...
2	Condiments	Sweet and savory sauces, relishes, spreads, and seasonings	...
3	Confections	Desserts, candies, and sweet breads	...
4	Dairy Products	Cheeses	...
5	Grains/Cereals	Breads, crackers, pasta, and cereal	...
6	Meat/Poultry	Prepared meats	...
7	Produce	Dried fruit and bean curd	...
8	Seafood	Seaweed and fish	...

The Gotchas of EXEC

Like most things that are of interest, using EXEC is not without its little trials and tribulations. Among the gotchas of EXEC are:

❑ It runs under a separate scope than the code that calls it – that is, the calling code can't reference variables inside the EXEC statement, and the EXEC can't reference variables in the calling code after they are resolved into the string for the EXEC statement.

❑ It runs under the same security context as the current user – not that of the calling object.

❑ It runs under the same connection and transaction context as the calling object (we'll discuss this further in Chapter 14).

❑ Concatenation that requires a function call must be performed on the EXEC string prior to actually calling the EXEC statement – you can't do the concatenation of function in the same statement as the EXEC call.

❑ EXEC can not be used inside a User Defined Function.

Each of these can be a little difficult to grasp, so let's look at each individually.

The Scope of EXEC

Determining variable scope with the EXEC statement is something less than intuitive. The actual statement line that calls the EXEC statement has the same scope as the rest of the batch or procedure that the EXEC statement is running in, but the code that is performed as a result of the EXEC statement is considered to be in its own batch. As is so often the case, this is best shown with an example:

```
USE Northwind

/* First, we'll declare to variables. One for stuff we're putting into
** the EXEC, and one that we think will get something back out (it won't)
*/
DECLARE @InVar    varchar(50)
DECLARE @OutVar   varchar(50)

-- Set up our string to feed into the EXEC command
SET @InVar = 'SELECT @OutVar = FirstName FROM Employees WHERE EmployeeID = 1'

-- Now run it
EXEC (@Invar)

-- Now, just to show there's no difference, run the select without using a in
variable
EXEC ('SELECT @OutVar = FirstName FROM Employees WHERE EmployeeID = 1')

-- @OutVar will still be NULL because we haven't been able to put anything in it
SELECT @OutVar
```

Now, look at the output from this:

```
Server: Msg 137, Level 15, State 1, Line 1
Must declare the variable '@OutVar'.
Server: Msg 137, Level 15, State 1, Line 1
Must declare the variable '@OutVar'.


---------------------------------------------------
NULL

(1 row(s) affected)
```

SQL Server wastes no time in telling us that we are scoundrels and clearly don't know what we're doing. Why do we get a "Must Declare" error message when we have already declared @OutVar? Because we've declared it in the outer scope – not within the EXEC itself.

Let's look at what happens if we run things a little differently:

```
USE Northwind

-- This time, we only need one variable. It does need to be longer though.
DECLARE @InVar    varchar(200)

/* Set up our string to feed into the EXEC command. This time we're going
** to feed it several statements at a time. They will all execute as one
** batch.
*/
SET @InVar = 'DECLARE @OutVar varchar(50)
            SELECT @OutVar = FirstName FROM Employees WHERE EmployeeID = 1
            SELECT ''The Value Is '' + @OutVar'

-- Now run it
EXEC (@Invar)
```

This time we get back results closer to what we expect:

```
----------------------------------------------------------------
The Value Is Nancy
```

> *Notice the way that I'm using two quote marks right next to each other to indicate that I really want a quote mark rather than to terminate my string.*

So, what we've seen here is that we have two different scopes operating, and nary the two shall meet. There is, unfortunately, no way to pass information between the inside and outside scopes without using an external mechanism such as a temporary table. If you decide to use a temp table to communicate between scopes, just remember that any temporary table created within the scope of your EXEC statement will only live for the life of that EXEC statement.

> This behavior of a temp table only lasting the life of your **EXEC** procedure will show up again when we are dealing with triggers and sprocs.

A Small Exception to the Rule

There is one thing that happens inside the scope of the EXEC that can be seen after the EXEC is done – system functions – so, things like @@ROWCOUNT can still be used. Again, let's look at a quick example:

```
USE Northwind

EXEC('SELECT * FROM Customers')
SELECT 'The Rowcount is ' + CAST(@@ROWCOUNT as varchar)
```

Yields us (after the result set):

The Rowcount is 91

Security Contexts and EXEC

This is a tough one to cover at this point because we haven't covered the issues yet with stored procedures and security. Still, the discussion of the EXEC command belonged here rather than in the sprocs chapter, so here we are (this is the only part of this discussion that gets wrapped up in sprocs, so bear with me).

When you give someone the right to run a stored procedure, you imply that they also gain the right to perform the actions called for within the sproc. For example, let's say we had a stored procedure that lists all the employees hired within the last year. Someone who has rights to execute the sproc can do so (and get results back) even if they do not have rights to the Employees table directly. This is really handy for reasons we will explore later in our sprocs chapter.

Developers usually assume that this same implied right is valid for an EXEC statement also – it isn't. Any reference made inside an EXEC statement will be run under the security context of the current user. So, let's say I have the right to run a procedure called spNewEmployees, but I do not have rights to the Employees table. If spNewEmployees gets the values by running a simple SELECT statement, then everything is fine. If, however, spNewEmployees uses an EXEC statement to execute that SELECT statement, the EXEC statement will fail because I don't have the rights to perform a SELECT on the Employees table.

Since we don't have that much information on sprocs yet, I'm going to bypass further discussion of this for now, but we will come back to it when we discuss sprocs later on.

Use of Functions in Concatenation and EXEC

This one is actually more of a nuisance than anything else, since there is a reasonably easy workaround. Simply put, you can't run a function against your EXEC string in the argument for an EXEC. For example:

```
USE Northwind

-- This won't work
DECLARE @NumberOfLetters int
SET @NumberOfLetters = 15
EXEC('SELECT LEFT(CompanyName,' + CAST(@NumberOfLetters AS varchar) + ') AS
ShortName
FROM Customers')
GO

-- But this does
DECLARE @NumberOfLetters AS int
SET @NumberOfLetters = 15
DECLARE @str AS varchar(255)
SET @str = 'SELECT LEFT(CompanyName,' + CAST(@NumberOfLetters AS varchar) + ') AS
ShortName FROM Customers'
EXEC(@str)
```

The first instance gets us an error message because the CAST function needs to be fully resolved prior to the EXEC line:

Server: Msg 170, Level 15, State 1, Line 6
Line 6: Incorrect syntax near 'CAST'.

But the second line works just fine because it is already a complete string:

ShortName

Alfreds Futterk
Ana Trujillo Em
...
...
Wolski Zajazd

EXEC and UDF's

This is a tough one to touch on since we haven't gotten to User Defined Functions as yet, but suffice to say that you are not allowed to use EXEC within a UDF – period.

Summary

Understanding scripts and batches is the cornerstone to an understanding of programming with SQL Server. The concepts of scripts and batches lay the foundation for a variety of functions from scripting complete database builds to programming stored procedures and triggers.

Local variables have scope for only one batch. Even if you have declared the variable within the same overall script, you will still get an error message if you don't re-declare it (and start over with assigning values) before referencing it in a new batch.

There are over 30 system functions. We provided a listing of some of the most useful system functions, but there are many more. Try checking out the Books Online or Appendix A at the back of this book for some of the more obscure ones. System functions do not need to be declared, and are always available. Some are scoped to the entire server, while others return values specific to the current connection.

You can use batches to create precedence between different parts of your scripts. The first batch starts at the beginning of the script, and ends at the end of the script or the first GO statement – whichever comes first. The next batch (if there is another) starts on the line after the first one ends and continues to the end of the script or the next GO statement – again, whichever comes first. The process continues to the end of the script. The first batch from the top of the script is executed first; the second is executed second, and so on. All commands within each batch must pass validation in the query parser, or none of that batch will be executed; however, any other batches will be parsed separately and will still be executed (if they pass the parser).

Finally, we also saw how we can create and execute SQL dynamically. This can afford us the opportunity to deal with scenarios that aren't always 100% predictable or situations where something we need to construct our statement is actually itself a piece of data.

In the next couple of chapters, we will take the notions of scripting and batches to the next level, and apply them to stored procedures and triggers –the closest things that SQL Server has to actual programs.

12

Stored Procedures

Ah, the good stuff. If you're a programmer coming from a procedural language, then this is probably the part you've been waiting for. It's time to get down to the "code" of SQL Server, but before we get going too far down that road, I need to prepare you for what lies ahead – there's probably a lot less than you're expecting, and, at the very same time, a whole lot more.

You see, a **stored procedure**, sometimes referred to as a **sproc** (which I usually say as one word, but I've sometimes heard this pronounced as "ess-proc"), is really just something of a script – or more correctly speaking, a **batch** – that is stored in the database rather than in a separate file. Now this comparison is not an exact one by any means – sprocs have things such as input parameters, output parameters, and return values that a script doesn't really have, but the comparison is not that far off either.

For now, SQL Server's only "programming" language continues to be T-SQL, and that leaves us miles short of the kind of procedural horsepower that you expect when you think of a true programming language. However, T-SQL blows C, C++, Visual Basic, Java, Delphi, or whatever away when it comes to what T-SQL is supposed to do – work on data definition, manipulation, and access. But T-SQL's horsepower stops right about there – at data access and management. From there, it has an adequate amount of power to get most simple things done, but it's not always the place to do it.

> *At the time of writing, rumors persist regarding the possibility that SQL Server will support other languages in the next release (code named Yukon). I for one will be waiting anxiously, but I also won't hold my breath – the first time I heard about this it was going to either be VBScript or VBA that was be supported in 7.0. We're now a full release beyond that point and it still isn't here. Still – I'm hoping…*

For this chapter, however, we're not going to worry all that much about T-SQL's shortcomings – instead, we'll focus on how to get the most out of T-SQL. We'll take a look at parameters, return values, control of flow, looping structures, both basic and advanced error trapping, and more. In short, this is a big chapter that deals with many subjects. All of the major subject areas are broken up into their own sections, so you can take them one step at a time, but let's start right out with the basics of getting a sproc created.

Creating the Sproc: Basic Syntax

Creating a sproc works pretty much the same as creating any other object in a database, except that it uses the AS keyword that you first saw when we took a look at views. The basic syntax looks like this:

```
CREATE PROCEDURE|PROC <sproc name>
   [<parameter name> <data type> [VARYING] [= <default value>] [OUTPUT] [,
    <parameter name> <data type> [VARYING] [= <default value>] [OUTPUT] [,
    ...
    ...
       ]]
[WITH
   RECOMPILE|ENCRYPTION|RECOMPILE, ENCRYPTION]
[FOR REPLICATION]
AS
   <code>

GO
```

As you can see, we still have our basic CREATE <Object Type> <Object Name> syntax that is the backbone of every CREATE statement. The only oddity here is the choice between PROCEDURE and PROC. Either option works just fine, but as always, I recommend that you be consistent regarding which one you choose (personally, I like the saved keystrokes of PROC). The name of your sproc must follow the rules for naming as outlined in Chapter 2.

After the name comes a list of parameters. Parameterization is optional, and we'll defer that discussion until a little later in the chapter.

Last, but not least, comes your actual code following the AS keyword.

An Example of a Basic Sproc

Perhaps the best examples of basic sproc syntax is to get down to the most basic of sprocs – a sproc that returns all the columns in all the rows on a table – in short, everything to do with a table's data.

I would hope that, by now, you have the query that would return all the contents of a table down cold (HINT: SELECT * FROM...) – if not, then I would suggest a return to the chapter on basic query syntax. In order to create a sproc that performs this basic query, we just add the query in the code area of the sproc syntax:

```
USE Northwind

GO
CREATE PROC spShippers
AS
    SELECT * FROM Shippers
```

Not too rough – eh? If you're wondering why I put the GO keyword in before the CREATE syntax (if we were just running a simple SELECT statement, we wouldn't need it), it's because most non-table CREATE statements cannot share a batch with any other code. Indeed, even with a CREATE TABLE statement leaving out the GO can become rather dicey. In this case, having the USE command together with our CREATE PROC statement would have been a no-no, and would have generated an error.

Now that we have our sproc created, let's execute it to see what we get:

```
EXEC spShippers
```

We get exactly what we would have got if we had run the SELECT statement that's embedded in the sproc:

```
ShipperID         CompanyName                       Phone
----------------  --------------------------------  --------------------
1                 Speedy Express                    (503) 555-9831
2                 United Package                    (503) 555-3199
3                 Federal Shipping                  (503) 555-9931
```

(3 row(s) affected)

You've just written your first sproc. It was easy of course, and frankly, for most situations, sproc writing isn't nearly as difficult as most database people would like to have you think (job preservation), but there are lots of possibilities, and we've only seen the beginning.

Changing Stored Procedures with ALTER

I'm going to admit something here – I cut and pasted almost all the text you're about to read in this and the next section (*Dropping Sprocs*), from the chapter on views. What I'm pointing out by telling you this is that they work almost identically from the standpoint of what an ALTER statement does.

The main thing to remember when you edit sprocs with T-SQL is that you are completely replacing the existing sproc. The only differences between using the ALTER PROC statement and the CREATE PROC statement are:

❑   ALTER PROC expects to find an existing proc, where CREATE doesn't.

❑   ALTER PROC retains any permissions that have been established for the proc. It keeps the same object ID within system objects and allows the dependencies to be kept. For example, if procedure A calls procedure B and you drop and re-create procedure B, you no longer see the dependency between the two. If you use ALTER it is all still there.

❑   ALTER PROC retains any dependency information on other objects that may call the sproc being altered.

The latter of these two is the biggy.

> If you perform a **DROP** and then use a **CREATE**, you have almost the same effect as using an **ALTER PROC** statement with one rather big difference – if you **DROP** and **CREATE** then you will need to entirely re-establish your permissions on who can and can't use the sproc.

Dropping Sprocs

It doesn't get much easier than this:

```
DROP PROC|PROCEDURE <sproc name>
```

And it's gone.

Parameterization

A stored procedure gives you some procedural capability, and also gives you a performance boost (more on that later), but it wouldn't be much help in most circumstances if it couldn't accept some data to tell it what to do. For example, it doesn't do much good to have an spDeleteShipper stored procedure if we can't tell it what shipper we want to delete, so we use an **input parameter**. Likewise, we often want to get information back out of the sproc – not just one or more recordsets of table data, but also information that is more direct. An example here might be where we update several records in a table and we'd like to know just how many we updated. Often, this isn't easily handed back in recordset form, so we make use of an **output parameter**.

From outside the sproc, parameters can be passed in either by position or by reference. From the inside, it doesn't matter which way they come in – they are declared the same either way.

Declaring Parameters

Declaring a parameter requires two to four of these pieces of information:

❑ The name
❑ The data type
❑ The default value
❑ The direction

The syntax is:

```
@parameter_name [AS] datatype [= default|NULL] [VARYING] [OUTPUT|OUT]
```

The name has a pretty simple set of rules to it. First, it must start with the @ sign. Other than that, the rules for naming are pretty much the same as the rules for naming described in Chapter 2, except that they cannot have embedded spaces.

The data type, much like the name, must be declared just as you would for a variable – with a valid SQL Server data type.

> *The one special thing in declaring the data type is to remember that, when declaring a parameter of type CURSOR, you must also use the VARYING and OUTPUT options. However, the use of this type of parameter is pretty unusual. We will take a good look at output parameters in this chapter, but we will defer our look at outputting cursors until our chapter on cursors later in the book.*

> *Note also that OUTPUT can be abbreviated to OUT.*

The default is the first place we start to see any real divergence from variables. Where variables are always initialized to a NULL value, parameters are not. Indeed, if you don't supply a default value, then the parameter is assumed to be required, and a beginning value must be supplied when the sproc is called. To supply a default, you simply add an = sign after the data type and then provide the default value. Once you've done this, the users of your sproc can decide to supply no value for that parameter, or they can provide their own value.

Let's create another sproc, only this time we'll make use of a few input parameters to create a new record in the Shippers table:

```
USE Northwind
GO

CREATE PROC spInsertShipper
    @CompanyName    nvarchar(40),
    @Phone          nvarchar(24)
AS
    INSERT INTO Shippers
    VALUES
        (@CompanyName, @Phone)
```

Our last sproc told us what data is currently in the Shippers table, but let's use our new sproc to insert something new:

```
EXEC spInsertShipper 'Speedy Shippers, Inc.', '(503) 555-5566'
```

If this is executed from the Query Analyzer, we see the results of our stored procedure run just as if we had run the INSERT statement ourselves:

(1 row(s) affected)

Now let's run our first sproc again and see what we get:

```
EXEC spShippers
```

ShipperID	CompanyName	Phone
1	Speedy Express	(503) 555-9831
2	United Package	(503) 555-3199
3	Federal Shipping	(503) 555-9931
4	Speedy Shippers, Inc.	(503) 555-5566

(4 row(s) affected)

Sure enough, our record has been inserted, and a new identity has been filled in for it.

Since we didn't supply any default values for either of the parameters, both parameters are considered to be required. That means that, in order to have success running this sproc, we *must* supply both parameters. You can easily check this out by executing the sproc again with only one or no parameters supplied:

```
EXEC spInsertShipper 'Speedy Shippers, Inc.'
```

SQL Server wastes no time in informing you of the error of your ways:

Server: Msg 201, Level 16, State 1, Procedure spInsertShipper, Line 0
Procedure 'spInsertShipper' expects parameter '@Phone', which was not supplied.

Supplying Default Values

To make a parameter optional, you have to supply a default value. To do this, you just add an = together with the value you want to use for a default after the data type but before the comma.

Let's try building our INSERT sproc again, only this time we won't require the phone number:

```
USE Northwind
GO

CREATE PROC spInsertShipperOptionalPhone
    @CompanyName    nvarchar(40),
    @Phone          nvarchar(24) = NULL
AS
    INSERT INTO Shippers
    VALUES
        (@CompanyName, @Phone)
```

Now we're ready to re-issue our command, only using the new sproc this time:

```
EXEC spInsertShipperOptionalPhone 'Speedy Shippers, Inc'
```

This time everything works just fine, and our new row is inserted:

(1 row(s) affected)

```
EXEC spShippers
```

ShipperID	CompanyName	Phone
1	Speedy Express	(503) 555-9831
2	United Package	(503) 555-3199
3	Federal Shipping	(503) 555-9931
4	Speedy Shippers, Inc.	(503) 555-5566
5	Speedy Shippers, Inc.	NULL

(5 row(s) affected)

In this particular case, we set the default to NULL, but the value could have been anything that was compatible with the data type of the parameter for which we are establishing the default. Also, notice that we didn't have to establish a default for both values – we can make one have a default, and one not – we decide which parameters are required (have no default), and which are not (have a default).

Creating Output Parameters

Sometimes, you want to pass non-recordset information out to whatever called your sproc. One example of this would create a modified version of our last two sprocs.

Let's say, for example, that we are performing an insert into a table (like we did in the last example), but we are planning to do additional work using the inserted record.

Or more specifically, maybe we're inserting a new record into our Orders table in Northwind, but we also need to insert detail records in the Order Details table. In order to keep the relationship intact, we have to know the identity of the Orders record before we can do our inserts into the Order Details table. The sproc will look almost exactly like our spInsertShipper did, except that it will have parameters that match up with the different columns in the table and, most importantly of all, it will have an output parameter for the identity value that is generated by our insert:

```
USE Northwind
GO

CREATE PROC spInsertOrder
    @CustomerID         nvarchar(5),
    @EmployeeID         int,
    @OrderDate          datetime       = NULL,
    @RequiredDate       datetime       = NULL,
    @ShippedDate        datetime       = NULL,
    @ShipVia            int,
    @Freight            money,
    @ShipName           nvarchar(40)   = NULL,
    @ShipAddress        nvarchar(60)   = NULL,
    @ShipCity           nvarchar(15)   = NULL,
    @ShipRegion         nvarchar(15)   = NULL,
    @ShipPostalCode     nvarchar(10)   = NULL,
    @ShipCountry        nvarchar(15)   = NULL,
    @OrderID            int       OUTPUT

AS
    /* Create the new record */
    INSERT INTO Orders
    VALUES
        (
            @CustomerID,
            @EmployeeID,
            @OrderDate,
            @RequiredDate,
            @ShippedDate,
            @ShipVia,
            @Freight,
            @ShipName,
            @ShipAddress,
            @ShipCity,
            @ShipRegion,
            @ShipPostalCode,
            @ShipCountry
        )

    /* Move the identity value from the newly inserted record into
       our output variable */
    SELECT @OrderID = @@IDENTITY
```

Now, let's try this baby out, only this time, let's set our parameter values by reference rather than by position. In order to see how our output parameter is working, we'll also need to write a little bit of test code in the script that executes the sproc:

```
USE Northwind
GO

DECLARE    @MyIdent    int

EXEC spInsertOrder
     @CustomerID = 'ALFKI',
     @EmployeeID = 5,
     @OrderDate = '5/1/1999',
     @ShipVia = 3,
     @Freight = 5.00,
     @OrderID = @MyIdent OUTPUT

SELECT @MyIdent AS IdentityValue

SELECT OrderID, CustomerID, EmployeeID, OrderDate, ShipName
FROM Orders
WHERE OrderID = @MyIdent
```

Notice that we didn't supply all of the parameters. Some of them were optional, and we decided to leave some of those off – which would take the default value. If we had been calling the sproc and passing values in using positional parameters, then we would have had to address each position in the parameter list at least until the last parameter for which we wanted to supply a value.

Let's see what this gives us – keep in mind that your identity value may vary from mine depending on what modifications you've already made in the Orders table:

(1 row(s) affected)

IdentityValue

11078

(1 row(s) affected)

OrderID	CustomerID	EmployeeID	OrderDate	ShipName
11078	ALFKI	5	1999-05-01 00:00:00.000	NULL

(1 row(s) affected)

The first row affected line is really feedback from the sproc itself – it inserted one row. The second resultset provides us with the identity value that was inserted – for me, this value was 11078 – this is positive proof that our identity value was indeed passed out of the sproc by the output parameter. Finally, we selected several columns from that row in the Orders table to verify that the row was indeed inserted using the data we expected.

There are several things that you should take note of between the sproc itself, and the usage of it by the calling script:

❑ The OUTPUT keyword was required for the output parameter in the sproc declaration.

❑ You must use the OUTPUT keyword when you call the sproc, much as you did when you declared the sproc. This gives SQL Server advance warning about the special handling that parameter will require. Be aware, however, that forgetting to include the OUTPUT keyword won't create a run-time error (you won't get any messages about it), but the value for the output parameter won't be moved into your variable (you'll just wind up with what was already there – most likely a NULL value). This means that you'll have what I consider to be the most dreadful of all computer terms – unpredictable results.

❑ The variable you assign the output result to does *not* have to have the same name as the internal parameter in the sproc. For example, in our previous sproc, the internal parameter was called @OrderID, but the variable the value was passed to was called @MyIdent.

❑ The EXEC (or EXECUTE) keyword was required since the call to the sproc wasn't the first thing in the batch (you can leave off the EXEC if the sproc call is the first thing in a batch) – personally, I recommend that you train yourself to use it regardless.

Control-of-Flow Statements

Control-of-flow statements are a veritable must for any programming language these days. I can't imagine having to write my code where I couldn't change what commands to run depending on a condition. T-SQL offers most of the classic choices for control of flow situations, including:

❑ IF...ELSE

❑ GOTO

❑ WHILE

❑ WAITFOR

We also have the CASE statement (aka SELECT CASE, DO CASE, and SWITCH/BREAK in other languages), but it doesn't have quite the level of control of flow capabilities that you've come to expect from other languages.

The IF...ELSE Statement

IF...ELSE statements work much as they do in any language, though I equate them closest to C in the way they are implemented. The basic syntax is:

```
IF <Boolean Expression>
   <SQL statement> | BEGIN <code series> END
[ELSE
   <SQL statement> | BEGIN <code series> END]
```

The expression can be pretty much any expression that evaluates to a Boolean.

> **This brings us back to one of the most common traps that I see SQL programmers fall into – improper user of NULLs. I can't tell you how often I have debugged stored procedures only to find a statement like:**
>
> ```
> IF @myvar = NULL
> ```
>
> **This will, of course, never be true on most systems (see below), and will wind up bypassing all their NULL values. Instead, it needs to read:**
>
> ```
> IF @myvar IS NULL
> ```
>
> **Don't forget that NULL doesn't equate to anything – not even NULL. Use IS instead of =**
>
> **The exception to this is dependent on whether you have set the ANSI_NULLS option ON or OFF. The default is that this is ON, in which case you'll see the behavior described above. You can change this behavior by setting ANSI_NULLS to OFF. I strongly recommend against this since it violates the ANSI standard (it's also just plain wrong).**

Note that only the very next statement after the IF will be considered to be conditional (as per the IF). You can include multiple statements as part of your control-of-flow block using BEGIN...END, but we'll discuss that one a little later in the chapter.

Let's create a new edition of our last query, and deal with the situation where someone supplies an OrderDate that is older than we want to accept.

Our sales manager is upset because someone has been putting in orders long after she has already completed her sales analysis for the time-period in which that order is. She has established a new policy that says that an order must be entered into the system within seven days after the order is taken, or the order date is considered to be invalid and is to be set to NULL.

How do we change the value of the order date? That's where our IF...ELSE statement comes in.

We need to perform a simple test, in which we'll need to make use of the DATEDIFF function. The syntax for DATEDIFF is:

```
DATEDIFF(<datepart>, <startdate>, <enddate>)
```

DATEDIFF compares our two dates – in this case the supplied order date and the current date. It can actually compare any part of the datetime data supplied from the year down to the millisecond. In our case, a simple dd for day will suffice, and we'll put it together with an IF statement:

```
IF DATEDIFF(dd, @OrderDate, GETDATE()) > 7
```

In the event that our returned value is over 7 – that is, over 7 days old – then we want to change the value that we insert:

```
SELECT @OrderDate = NULL
```

Now that we've got ourselves set with our IF statement, let's write that new version of the spInsertOrder sproc:

```
USE Northwind
GO

CREATE PROC spInsertDateValidatedOrder
    @CustomerID         nvarchar(5),
    @EmployeeID         int,
    @OrderDate          datetime    = NULL,
    @RequiredDate       datetime    = NULL,
    @ShippedDate        datetime    = NULL,
    @ShipVia            int,
    @Freight            money,
    @ShipName           nvarchar(40) = NULL,
    @ShipAddress        nvarchar(60) = NULL,
    @ShipCity           nvarchar(15) = NULL,
    @ShipRegion         nvarchar(15) = NULL,
    @ShipPostalCode     nvarchar(10) = NULL,
    @ShipCountry        nvarchar(15) = NULL,
    @OrderID            int         OUTPUT

AS

/* Test to see if supplied date is over seven days old, if so
   replace with NULL value                                   */
IF DATEDIFF(dd, @OrderDate, GETDATE()) > 7
    SELECT @OrderDate = NULL

/* Create the new record */
INSERT INTO Orders
VALUES
(
    @CustomerID,
    @EmployeeID,
    @OrderDate,
    @RequiredDate,
    @ShippedDate,
    @ShipVia,
    @Freight,
    @ShipName,
    @ShipAddress,
    @ShipCity,
    @ShipRegion,
    @ShipPostalCode,
    @ShipCountry
)

/* Move the identity value from the newly inserted record into
   our output variable */
SELECT @OrderID = @@IDENTITY
```

Now let's run the same test script as we used for the original `spInsertOrder` sproc with only minor modifications to deal with our new situation:

```
USE Northwind
GO

DECLARE    @MyIdent    int

EXEC spInsertDateValidatedOrder
    @CustomerID = 'ALFKI',
    @EmployeeID = 5,
    @OrderDate = '5/1/1999',
    @ShipVia = 3,
    @Freight = 5.00,
    @OrderID = @MyIdent OUTPUT

SELECT @MyIdent AS IdentityValue

SELECT OrderID, CustomerID, EmployeeID, OrderDate, ShipName
FROM Orders
WHERE OrderID = @MyIdent
```

This time, even though most of the sproc is the same, we change what we put into the database, and therefore, what we see in our selected results:

(1 row(s) affected)

IdentityValue

11079

(1 row(s) affected)

OrderID	CustomerID	EmployeeID	OrderDate	ShipName
11079	ALFKI	5	NULL	NULL

(1 row(s) affected)

Even though we supplied the same date as last time (5/1/1999), that isn't the value that was inserted – our `IF` statement picked off the illegal value and changed it before the insert.

The ELSE Clause

Now this thing about being able to change the data on the fly is just great, but it doesn't really deal with all the scenarios we might want to deal with. Quite often – indeed, most of the time – when we deal with an `IF` condition, we have specific statements we want to execute not just for the true condition, but also a separate set of statements that we want to run if the condition is false – or the `ELSE` condition.

> *You will run into situations where a Boolean cannot be evaluated – that is, the result is unknown (for example, if you are comparing to a NULL). Any expression that returns a result that would be considered as an unknown result will be treated as FALSE.*

The ELSE statement works pretty much as it does in any other language. The exact syntax may vary slightly, but the nuts and bolts are still the same – the statements in the ELSE clause are executed if the statements in the IF clause are not.

To expand our example just a bit, let's look at the oldest records that are currently in the Orders table of Northwind:

```
USE Northwind
GO

SELECT TOP 5 OrderID, OrderDate
FROM Orders
WHERE OrderDate IS NOT NULL
ORDER BY OrderDate
```

There's something interesting about the results:

OrderID	OrderDate
10248	1996-07-04 00:00:00.000
10249	1996-07-05 00:00:00.000
10250	1996-07-08 00:00:00.000
10251	1996-07-08 00:00:00.000
10252	1996-07-09 00:00:00.000

(5 row(s) affected)

None of the dates has a time component – OK, technically they're all at midnight, but I suspect you get the picture. It's likely that this was done on purpose, as it makes date (without time) comparisons much easier.

What we want to do is convert our sproc to make sure that we store all dates as just dates – no times. The current sproc won't work because it will insert the entire date, including time – but to verify that, let's test it out:

```
USE Northwind
GO

DECLARE    @MyIdent    int
DECLARE    @MyDate     smalldatetime

SELECT @MyDate = GETDATE()

EXEC spInsertDateValidatedOrder
    @CustomerID = 'ALFKI',
    @EmployeeID = 5,
    @OrderDate  = @MyDate,
    @ShipVia    = 3,
    @Freight = 5.00,
    @OrderID = @MyIdent OUTPUT

SELECT @MyIdent AS IdentityValue

SELECT OrderID, CustomerID, EmployeeID, OrderDate, ShipName
FROM Orders
WHERE OrderID = @MyIdent
```

When we insert our date, the time comes along with it:

```
(1 row(s) affected)

IdentityValue
-------------
11080

(1 row(s) affected)
```

OrderID	CustomerID	EmployeeID	OrderDate	ShipName
11080	ALFKI	5	2000-07-22 16:48:00.000	NULL

```
(1 row(s) affected)
```

So, what we have is an either/or situation. Either we now want the date changed to NULL, or we want the time truncated from the date. Unfortunately, SQL Server doesn't give us a function that does it automatically (another severe let down in my not so humble opinion). Fortunately, however, we again have a workaround.

Truncating the Time from a Datetime Field

In order to truncate a date, we can either take the date apart piece by piece and reassemble it without the time, or, as I prefer, we can use the CONVERT function on it, to convert it to a timeless day and then convert it back.

CONVERT() is just one of many functions that are available to us in SQL Server. Originally, it was the one and only method to convert data between data types. These days, CONVERT should be getting much less use in scripts because much of its functionality is duplicated by CAST(), which is ANSI-compliant (whereas CONVERT isn't). Still, CONVERT has some special date formatting capabilities that can't be duplicated by CAST.

CONVERT works with this syntax:

```
CONVERT(<target data type>, <expression to be converted>, <style>)
```

The first two parameters are pretty self-describing, but the last one isn't – it only applies when dealing with dates and its purpose is to tell SQL Server in which format you want the date to be. Examples of common date formats include 1, for standard US mm/dd/yy format and 12 for the standard ISO format (yymmdd). Adding 100 to any of the formats adds the full century to the date scheme (for example, standard US format with a four digit year – mm/dd/yyyy – has a style of 101).

For example, it would look something like this for the GETDATE function:

```
SELECT CONVERT(datetime,(CONVERT(varchar,GETDATE(),112)))
```

This takes things to an ANSI date format and then back again:

```
--------------------------------
2000-06-06 00:00:00.000

(1 row(s) affected)
```

Implementing the ELSE Statement In Our Sproc

Now that we've figured out how to do the pieces, it's time to move that into our actual sproc. This time, however, we're going to make use of the ALTER command rather than creating a separate procedure. Remember that, even when using an ALTER statement, we must entirely re-define the procedure:

```
USE Northwind
GO

ALTER PROC spInsertDateValidatedOrder
    @CustomerID         nvarchar(5),
    @EmployeeID         int,
    @OrderDate          datetime      = NULL,
    @RequiredDate       datetime      = NULL,
    @ShippedDate        datetime      = NULL,
    @ShipVia            int,
    @Freight            money,
    @ShipName           nvarchar(40) = NULL,
    @ShipAddress        nvarchar(60) = NULL,
    @ShipCity           nvarchar(15) = NULL,
    @ShipRegion         nvarchar(15) = NULL,
    @ShipPostalCode nvarchar(10) = NULL,
    @ShipCountry        nvarchar(15) = NULL,
    @OrderID            int       OUTPUT

AS

/* I don't like altering input parameters - I find that it helps in debugging
** if I can refer to their original values at any time. Therefore, I'm going
** to declare a separate variable to assign the end value we will be
** inserting into the table. */
DECLARE    @InsertedOrderDate    smalldatetime

/* Test to see if supplied date is over seven days old, if so
** replace with NULL value
** otherwise, truncate the time to be midnight */
IF DATEDIFF(dd, @OrderDate, GETDATE()) > 7
    SELECT @InsertedOrderDate = NULL
ELSE
    SELECT @InsertedOrderDate =
        CONVERT(datetime,(CONVERT(varchar,@OrderDate,112)))

    /* Create the new record */
INSERT INTO Orders
VALUES
(
    @CustomerID,
    @EmployeeID,
    @InsertedOrderDate,
    @RequiredDate,
    @ShippedDate,
    @ShipVia,
    @Freight,
    @ShipName,
    @ShipAddress,
    @ShipCity,
    @ShipRegion,
    @ShipPostalCode,
    @ShipCountry
)

/* Move the identity value from the newly inserted record into
    our output variable */
SELECT @OrderID = @@IDENTITY
```

Now, if we re-run the original batch, we have the affect we were after:

```
(1 row(s) affected)

IdentityValue
-------------
11081

(1 row(s) affected)

OrderID          CustomerID            EmployeeID            OrderDate                        ShipName
----------------  --------------------  --------------------  -------------------------------  --------------
11081            ALFKI                 5                     2000-07-22 00:00:00.000 NULL

(1 row(s) affected)
```

We now have a sproc that handles the insert differently depending on the specific values that are given to the sproc.

> If you look closely, you'll note that I changed more than just the **IF...ELSE** statement for this version of the sproc – I also changed things so that a holding variable was declared for the order date.
>
> The purpose behind this has to do with a general philosophy I have about changing input parameter values. With the exception of where you are changing parameter values for the express purpose of passing out a changed value, I don't think you should change parameter values. Why? Well, part of it is a clarity issue – I don't want people to have to look in multiple places for where my variables are declared if possible. The other reason is perhaps a more convincing one – debugging. I like to retain my input values for as long as possible so that, when I need to debug, I can easily check my input value against the various places in the code I make use of the input value. That is, I want to simplify being able to tell if things are working correctly.

Grouping Code into Blocks

Sometimes you need to treat a group of statements as though they were all one statement (if you execute one, then you execute them all – otherwise, you don't execute any of them). For instance, the IF statement will, by default, only consider the very next statement after the IF to be part of the conditional code. What if you want the condition to require several statements to run? Life would be pretty miserable if you had to create a separate IF statement for each line of code you wanted to run if the condition holds.

Thankfully, SQL Server gives us a way to group code into blocks that are considered to all belong together. The block is started when you issue a BEGIN statement, and continues until you issue an END statement. It works like this:

```
IF <Expression>
BEGIN    --First block of code starts here - executes only if
         --expression is TRUE
    Statement that executes if expression is TRUE
    Additional statements
    …
    …
    Still going with statements from TRUE expression
    IF <Expression>    --Only executes if this block is active
        BEGIN
            Statement that executes if both outside and inside
                expressions are TRUE
            Additional statements
            …
            …
            Still statements from both TRUE expressions
        END
    Out of the condition from inner condition, but still
        part of first block
END      --First block of code ends here
ELSE
BEGIN
    Statement that executes if expression is FALSE
    Additional statements
    …
    …
    Still going with statements from FALSE expression
END
```

Notice our ability to nest blocks of code. In each case, the inner blocks are considered to be part of the outer block of code. I have never heard of there being a limit to how many levels deep you can nest your BEGIN…END blocks, but I would suggest that you minimize them. There are definitely practical limits to how deep you can keep them readable – even if you are particularly careful about the formatting of your code.

Just to put this notion into play, let's make yet another modification to our last order insert sproc. This time, we're going to provide a little bit of useful information to our user as we go through code that alters what the caller of the sproc has provided. This can act as something of a lead-in for the upcoming section on error handling.

Any time we decide to change the data we're inserting to be something other than what the user supplied, then we also need to inform the user of exactly what we're doing. We'll use a PRINT statement to output the specifics of what we've done. We'll add these PRINT statements as part of the code in our IF…ELSE statement so the information can be topical. Note that a PRINT statement doesn't generate any kind of error – it just provides textual information regardless of error status.

We'll discuss this further in the error handling section.

```
USE Northwind
GO

ALTER PROC spInsertDateValidatedOrder
    @CustomerID        nvarchar(5),
    @EmployeeID        int,
    @OrderDate         datetime    = NULL,
    @RequiredDate      datetime    = NULL,
    @ShippedDate       datetime    = NULL,
    @ShipVia           int,
    @Freight           money,
    @ShipName          nvarchar(40) = NULL,
    @ShipAddress       nvarchar(60) = NULL,
    @ShipCity          nvarchar(15) = NULL,
    @ShipRegion        nvarchar(15) = NULL,
    @ShipPostalCode    nvarchar(10) = NULL,
    @ShipCountry       nvarchar(15) = NULL,
    @OrderID           int       OUTPUT

AS

/* I don't like altering input paramters - I find that it helps in debugging
** if I can refer to their original value at any time. Therefore, I'm going
** to declare a separate variable to assign the end value we will be
** inserting into the table. */
DECLARE    @InsertedOrderDate    smalldatetime

/* Test to see if supplied date is over seven days old, if so
** replace with NULL value
** otherwise, truncate the time to be midnight*/
IF DATEDIFF(dd, @OrderDate, GETDATE()) > 7
BEGIN
    SELECT @InsertedOrderDate = NULL
    PRINT 'Invalid Order Date'
    PRINT 'Supplied Order Date was greater than 7 days old.'
    PRINT 'The value has been reset to NULL'
END
ELSE
BEGIN
    SELECT @InsertedOrderDate =
        CONVERT(datetime,(CONVERT(varchar,@OrderDate,112)))
        PRINT 'The Time of Day in Order Date was truncated'
END

/* Create the new record */
INSERT INTO Orders
VALUES
(
    @CustomerID,
    @EmployeeID,
    @InsertedOrderDate,
    @RequiredDate,
    @ShippedDate,
```

```
        @ShipVia,
        @Freight,
        @ShipName,
        @ShipAddress,
        @ShipCity,
        @ShipRegion,
        @ShipPostalCode,
        @ShipCountry
    )

    /* Move the identity value from the newly inserted record into
       our output variable */
    SELECT @OrderID = @@IDENTITY
```

Now when we execute our test batch, we get slightly different results. First, the test batch using the current date:

```
USE Northwind
GO


DECLARE     @MyIdent    int
DECLARE     @MyDate     smalldatetime

SELECT @MyDate = GETDATE()

EXEC spInsertDateValidatedOrder
    @CustomerID = 'ALFKI',
    @EmployeeID = 5,
    @OrderDate  = @MyDate,
    @ShipVia    = 3,
    @Freight    = 5.00,
    @OrderID    = @MyIdent OUTPUT

SELECT OrderID, CustomerID, EmployeeID, OrderDate, ShipName
FROM Orders
WHERE OrderID = @MyIdent
```

Note that we've deleted the line SELECT @MyIdent AS IdentityValue *from the test batch for brevity's sake.*

And we can see that not only was our value truncated in terms of the actual data, but we also have the message that explicitly tells us:

The Time of Day in Order Date was truncated

(1 row(s) affected)

OrderID	CustomerID	EmployeeID	OrderDate	ShipName
11080	ALFKI	5	1999-08-30 00:00:00.000	NULL

(1 row(s) affected)

Next, we run the older version of the test batch that manually feeds an older date:

```
USE Northwind
GO

DECLARE   @MyIdent    int

EXEC spInsertDateValidatedOrder
    @CustomerID = 'ALFKI',
    @EmployeeID = 5,
    @OrderDate  = '1/1/1999',
    @ShipVia    = 3,
    @Freight    = 5.00,
    @OrderID    = @MyIdent OUTPUT

SELECT OrderID, CustomerID, EmployeeID, OrderDate, ShipName
FROM Orders
WHERE OrderID = @MyIdent
```

Again we see an explicit indication of what happened to our data:

Invalid Order Date
Supplied Order Date was greater than 7 days old.
The value has been reset to NULL

(1 row(s) affected)

OrderID	CustomerID	EmployeeID	OrderDate	ShipName
11085	ALFKI	5	NULL	NULL

(1 row(s) affected)

The CASE Statement

The CASE statement is, in some ways, the equivalent of one of several different statements depending on the language from which you're coming. Statements in procedural programming languages that work in a similar way to CASE include:

- Switch – C, C++, Delphi
- Select Case – Visual Basic
- Do Case – Xbase
- Evaluate – COBOL

I'm sure there are others – these are just from the languages that I've worked with in some form or another over the years. The big drawback in using a CASE statement in T-SQL is that it is, in many ways, more of a substitution operator than a control-of-flow statement.

There is more than one way to write a CASE statement – with an input expression or a Boolean expression. The first option is to use an input expression that will be compared with the value used in each WHEN clause. The SQL Server documentation refers to this as a **simple CASE**:

```
CASE <input expression>
WHEN <when expression> THEN <result expression>
[...n]
[ELSE <result expression>]
END
```

Option number two is to provide an expression with each WHEN clause that will evaluate to TRUE/FALSE. The docs refer to this as a **searched CASE**:

```
CASE
WHEN <Boolean expression> THEN <result expression>
[...n]
[ELSE <result expression>]
END
```

Perhaps what's nicest about CASE is that you can use it "inline" with (that is, as an integral part of) a SELECT statement. This can actually be quite powerful.

Let's move away from our previous example (the searched CASE) for the time being (don't worry, we'll be back to it), and look at a simple CASE statement from a couple of different perspectives.

A Simple CASE

A simple CASE takes an expression that equates to a Boolean result. Let's get right to an example:

```
USE Northwind
GO

SELECT TOP 10 OrderID, OrderID % 10 AS 'Last Digit', Position =
CASE OrderID % 10
    WHEN 1 THEN 'First'
    WHEN 2 THEN 'Second'
    WHEN 3 THEN 'Third'
    WHEN 4 THEN 'Fourth'
    ELSE 'Something Else'
END
FROM Orders
```

For those of you who aren't familiar with it, the % operator is for a **modulus**. A modulus works in a similar manner to the divide by (/), but it only gives you the remainder. Therefore, 16 % 4 = 0 (4 goes into 16 evenly); but 16 % 5 = 1 (16 divided by 5 has a remainder of 1). In the example, since we're dividing by ten, using the modulus is giving us the last digit of the number we're evaluating.

Let's see what we got with this:

OrderID	Last Digit	Position
10249	9	Something Else
10251	1	First
10258	8	Something Else
10260	0	Something Else
10265	5	Something Else
10267	7	Something Else
10269	9	Something Else
10270	0	Something Else
10274	4	Fourth
10275	5	Something Else

(10 row(s) affected)

Notice that whenever there is a matching value in the list, the THEN clause is invoked. Since we have an ELSE clause, any value that doesn't match one of the previous values will be assigned whatever we've put in our ELSE. If we had left the ELSE out, then any such value would be given a NULL.

Let's go with one more example that expands on what we can use as an expression. This time, we'll use another column from our query:

```
USE Northwind
GO

SELECT TOP 10 OrderID % 10 AS "Last Digit",
    ProductID,
    "How Close?" = CASE OrderID % 10
        WHEN ProductID THEN 'Exact Match!'
        WHEN ProductID - 1 THEN 'Within 1'
        WHEN ProductID + 1 THEN 'Within 1'
        ELSE 'More Than One Apart'
    END
FROM [Order Details]
WHERE ProductID < 10
ORDER BY OrderID DESC
```

Notice that we've used equations at every step of the way on this one, yet it still works...

Last Digit	ProductID	How Close?
7	8	Within 1
7	7	Exact Match!
7	6	Within 1
7	4	More Than One Apart
7	3	More Than One Apart
7	2	More Than One Apart
6	6	Exact Match!
5	2	More Than One Apart
2	2	Exact Match!
1	7	More Than One Apart

(10 row(s) affected)

As long as the expression evaluates to a specific value that is of compatible type to the input expression, then it can be analyzed, and the proper THEN clause applied.

A Searched CASE

This one works pretty much the same as a simple CASE, with only two slight twists:

❑ There is no input expression (remember that's the part between the CASE and the first WHEN)

❑ The WHEN expression must evaluate to a Boolean value (whereas in the simple CASE examples we've just looked at we used values such as 1, 3, and ProductID + 1)

Perhaps what I find the coolest about this kind of CASE is that we can completely change around what is forming the basis of our expression – mixing and matching column expressions depending on our different possible situations.

As usual, I find the best way to get across how this works is via an example:

```
USE Northwind
GO

SELECT TOP 10 OrderID % 10 AS "Last Digit",
    ProductID,
    "How Close?" = CASE
        WHEN (OrderID % 10) < 3 THEN 'Ends With Less Than Three'
        WHEN ProductID = 6 THEN 'ProductID is 6'
        WHEN ABS(OrderID % 10 - ProductID) <= 1 THEN 'Within 1'
        ELSE 'More Than One Apart'
    END
FROM [Order Details]
WHERE ProductID < 10
ORDER BY OrderID DESC
```

This is substantially different from our simple CASE examples, but it still works:

Last Digit	ProductID	How Close?
7	8	Within 1
7	7	Within 1
7	6	ProductID is 6
7	4	More Than One Apart
7	3	More Than One Apart
7	2	More Than One Apart
6	6	ProductID is 6
5	2	More Than One Apart
2	2	Ends With Less Than Three
1	7	Ends With Less Than Three

(10 row(s) affected)

There are a couple of things to pay particular attention to in how SQL Server evaluated things:

❑ Even when two conditions evaluate to TRUE, only the first condition is used. For example, the second to last row meets both the first (the last digit is smaller than 3) and third (the last digit is within 1 of the ProductID) conditions. For many languages including Visual Basic, this kind of statement always works this way. If you're from the C world though, you'll need to remember this when you are coding; no "break" statement is required – it always terminates after one condition is met.

❑ You can mix and match what fields you're using in your condition expressions. In this case, we used OrderID, ProductID, and both together.

❑ You can perform pretty much any expression as long as, in the end, it evaluates to a Boolean result.

Let's try this out with a slightly more complex example. In this example, we're not going to do the mix and match thing – instead, we'll stick with just the one column we're looking at (we could change columns being tested – but, most of the time, we won't need to). Instead, we're going to deal with a more real-life scenario that I helped solve for a rather large e-commerce site.

The scenario is this: marketing people really like nice clean prices. They hate it when you apply a 10% markup over cost, and start putting out prices like $10.13, or $23.19. Instead, they like slick prices that end in numbers like 49, 75, 95, or 99. In our scenario, we're supposed to create a possible new price list for analysis, and they want it to meet certain criteria.

If the new price ends with less than 50 cents (such as our $10.13 example above), then marketing would like the price to be bumped up to the same dollar amount but ending in 49 cents ($10.49 for our example). Prices ending with 50¢ to 75¢ should be changed to end in 75¢, and prices ending with more than 75¢ should be changed to end with 95¢. Let's look at some examples of what they want:

If the new price would be	Then it should become
$10.13	$10.49
$17.57	$17.75
$27.75	$27.75
$79.99	$79.95

Technically speaking, we could do this with nested IF...ELSE statements, but:

❑ It would be much harder to read – especially if the rules were more complex

❑ We would have to implement the code using a cursor (*bad!*) and examine each row one at a time

In short – *yuck!*

A CASE statement is going to make this process relatively easy. What's more, we're going to be able to place our condition inline to our query and use it as part of a set operation – this almost always means that we're going to get much better performance than we would with a cursor.

Our marketing department has decided they would like to see what things would look like if we increased prices by 10%, so we'll plug a 10% markup into a CASE statement, and, together with a little extra analysis, we'll get the numbers we're looking for:

```
USE Northwind
GO

/* I'm setting up some holding variables here. This way, if we get asked
** to run the query again with a slightly different value, we'll only have
** to change it in one place.
*/
DECLARE @Markup     money
DECLARE @Multiplier money

SELECT @Markup = .10                 -- Change the markup here
SELECT @Multiplier = @Markup + 1     -- We want the end price, not the amount
                                     -- of the increase, so add 1


/* Now execute things for our results. Note that we're limiting things
** to the top 10 items for brevity - in reality, we either wouldn't do this
** at all, or we would have a more complex WHERE clause to limit the
** increase to a particular set of products
*/
SELECT TOP 10 ProductID, ProductName, UnitPrice,
    UnitPrice * @Multiplier AS "Marked Up Price", "New Price" =
    CASE WHEN FLOOR(UnitPrice * @Multiplier + .24)
            > FLOOR(UnitPrice * @Multiplier)
                THEN FLOOR(UnitPrice * @Multiplier) + .95
        WHEN FLOOR(UnitPrice * @Multiplier + .5) >
            FLOOR(UnitPrice * @Multiplier)
                THEN FLOOR(UnitPrice * @Multiplier) + .75
        ELSE FLOOR(UnitPrice * @Multiplier) + .49
    END
FROM Products
ORDER BY ProductID DESC        -- Just because the bottom's a better example
                              -- in this particular case
```

The FLOOR function you see here is a pretty simple one – it takes the value supplied and rounds down to the nearest integer.

Now, I don't know about you, but I get very suspicious when I hear the word "analysis" come out of someone's lips – particularly if that person is in a marketing or sales role. Don't get me wrong – those people are doing their jobs just like I am. The thing is, once they ask a question one way, they usually want to ask the same question another way. That being the case, I went ahead and set this up as a script – now all we need to do when they decide they want to try it with 15% is make a change to the initialization value of @Markup. Let's see what we got this time with that 10% markup though:

ProductID	ProductName	UnitPrice	Marked Up Price	New Price
77	Original Frankfurter grüne Soße	13.0000	14.3000	14.4900
76	Lakkalikööri	18.0000	19.8000	19.9500
75	Rhönbräu Klosterbier	7.7500	8.5250	8.7500
74	Longlife Tofu	10.0000	11.0000	11.4900
73	Röd Kaviar	15.0000	16.5000	16.7500
72	Mozzarella di Giovanni	34.8000	38.2800	38.4900
71	Flotemysost	21.5000	23.6500	23.7500
70	Outback Lager	15.0000	16.5000	16.7500
69	Gudbrandsdalsost	36.0000	39.6000	39.7500
68	Scottish Longbreads	12.5000	13.7500	13.7500

(10 row(s) affected)

Look these over for a bit, and you'll see that the results match what we were expecting. What's more, we didn't have to build a cursor to do it.

Now, for one final example with this CASE statement, and to put something like this more into the context of sprocs, let's convert this to something the marketing department can call themselves.

In order to convert something like this to a sproc, we need to know what information is going to be changing each time we run it. In this case, the only thing that will change will be the markup percentage. That means that only the markup percent needs to be accepted as a parameter – any other variables can remain internal to the sproc.

To change this particular script then, we only need to change one variable to a parameter, add our CREATE statements, and we should be ready to go. However, we are going to make just one more change to clarify the input for the average user:

```
USE Northwind
GO

CREATE PROC spMarkupTest
    @MarkupAsPercent    money
AS

    DECLARE @Multiplier money

-- We want the end price, not the amount
SELECT @Multiplier = @MarkupAsPercent / 100 + 1 /*of the increase, so add 1

** Now execute things for our results. Note that we're limiting things
** to the top 10 items for brevity - in reality, we either wouldn't do this
** at all, or we would have a more complex WHERE clause to limit the
** increase to a particular set of products
*/
SELECT TOP 10 ProductId, ProductName, UnitPrice,
    UnitPrice * @Multiplier AS "Marked Up Price", "New Price" =
    CASE WHEN FLOOR(UnitPrice * @Multiplier + .24)
            > FLOOR(UnitPrice * @Multiplier)
                    THEN FLOOR(UnitPrice * @Multiplier) + .95
        WHEN FLOOR(UnitPrice  * @Multiplier + .5) >
            FLOOR(UnitPrice * @Multiplier)
                    THEN FLOOR(UnitPrice * @Multiplier) + .75
        ELSE FLOOR(UnitPrice * @Multiplier) + .49
    END
FROM Products
ORDER BY ProductID DESC    -- Just because the bottom's a better example
                           -- in this particular case
```

Now, to run our sproc, we only need to make use of the EXEC command and supply a parameter:

```
EXEC spMarkupTest 10
```

Our results should be exactly as they were when the code was in script form. By putting it into sproc form though, we:

❑ Simplified the use for inexperienced users

❑ Sped up processing time

The simplified use for the end user seems pretty obvious. They probably would be pretty intimidated if they had to look at all that code in the script – even if they only had to change just one line. Instead, they can enter in just three words – including the parameter value.

The performance boost is actually just about nothing in an interactive scenario like this case, but, rest assured, the process will run slightly faster (just milliseconds in many cases – longer in others) as a sproc – we'll look into this much further before the chapter's done.

Looping with the WHILE Statement

The WHILE statement is one of those Catch-22 kinds of statements. It's a control-of-flow statement, so I need to address it here. At the same time, the WHILE statement is rarely used in SQL except when dealing with cursors, so it makes a lot of sense to address it there.

We're going to do a little of both. We'll get the basics down here and go through an example of where we might want to make use of a WHILE in a non-cursor construct.

The WHILE statement works much as it does in other languages to which you have probably been exposed. Essentially, a condition is tested each time you come to the top of the loop. If the condition is still TRUE, then the loop executes again – if not, you exit.

The syntax looks like this:

```
WHILE <Boolean expression>
      <sql statement> |
[BEGIN
      <statement block>
      [BREAK]
      <sql statement> | <statement block>
      [CONTINUE]
END]
```

While you can just execute one statement (much as you do with an IF statement), you'll almost never see a WHILE that isn't followed by a BEGIN...END with a full statement block.

The BREAK statement is a way of exiting the loop without waiting for the bottom of the loop to come and the expression to be re-evaluated.

I'm sure I won't be the last to tell you this, but using a BREAK is generally thought of as something of bad form in the classical sense. I tend to sit on the fence on this one. I avoid using them if reasonably possible. Most of the time, I can indeed avoid them just by moving a statement or two around while still coming up with the same results. The advantage of this is usually more readable code. It is simply easier to handle a looping structure (or any structure for that matter) if you have a single point of entry and a single exit. Using a BREAK violates this notion.

All that being said, sometimes you can actually make things worse by reformatting the code to avoid a BREAK. In addition, I've seen people write much slower code for the sake of not using a BREAK statement – bad idea.

The CONTINUE statement is something of the complete opposite of a BREAK statement. In short, it tells the WHILE loop to go back to the beginning. Regardless of where you are in the loop, you immediately go back to the top and re-evaluate the expression (exiting if the expression is no longer TRUE).

We'll go ahead and do something of a short example here just to get our feet wet. As I mentioned before, WHILE loops tend to be rare in non-cursor situations, so forgive me if this example seems lame.

What we're going to do is create something of a monitoring process using our WHILE loop and a WAITFOR command (we'll look at the specifics of WAITFOR in our next section). We're going to be automatically updating our statistics once per day:

```
WHILE 1 = 1
BEGIN
    WAITFOR TIME '01:00'
    EXEC sp_updatestats
    RAISERROR('Statistics Updated for Database', 1, 1) WITH LOG
END
```

This would update the statistics for every table in our database every night at 1AM and write a log entry of that fact to both the SQL Server log and the Windows NT application log. If you want check to see if this works, leave this running all night and then check your logs in the morning.

Note that an infinite loop like this isn't the way that you would normally want to schedule a task. If you want something to run everyday, set up a job in EM (see Chapter 30 for more details). In addition to not keeping a connection open all the time (which the above example would do), you also get the capability to make follow up actions dependent on the success or failure of your script. Also, you can e-mail or net-send messages regarding the completion status.

The WAITFOR Statement

There are often things that you either don't want to or simply can't have happen right this moment, but you also don't want to have to hang around waiting for the right time to execute something.

No problem – use the WAITFOR statement and have SQL Server wait for you. The syntax is incredibly simple:

```
WAITFOR
    DELAY <'time'> | TIME <'time'>
```

The WAITFOR statement does exactly what it says it does – that is, it waits for whatever you specify as the argument to occur. You can specify either an explicit time of day for something to happen, or you can specify an amount of time to wait before doing something.

The DELAY Parameter

The DELAY parameter choice specifies an amount of time to wait. You cannot specify a number of days – just time in hours, minutes, and seconds. The maximum allowed delay is 24 hours. So, for example:

```
WAITFOR DELAY '01:00'
```

Would run any code prior to the WAITFOR, then reach the WAITFOR statement, and stop for one hour, after which execution of the code would continue with whatever the next statement was.

The TIME Parameter

The TIME parameter choice specifies to wait until a specific time of day. Again, we cannot specify any kind of date – just the time of day using a 24-hour clock. Once more, this gives us a one-day time limit for the maximum amount of delay. For example:

```
WAITFOR TIME '01:00'
```

Would run any code prior to the WAITFOR, then reach the WAITFOR statement, and stop until 1AM, after which execution of the code would continue with whatever the next statement was after the WAITFOR.

Confirming Success or Failure with Return Values

You'll see return values used in a couple of different ways. The first is to actually return data, such as an identity value or the number of rows that the sproc affected – consider this an evil practice from the dark ages. Instead, move on to the way that return values should be used and what they are really there for – determining the execution status of your sproc.

> If it sounds like I have an opinion on how return values should be used, it's because I most definitely do. I was actually originally taught to use return values as a "trick" to get around having to use output parameters – in effect, as a shortcut. Happily, I overcame this training. The problem is that, like most shortcuts, you're cutting something out, and, in this case, what you're cutting out is rather important.
>
> Using return values as a means of returning data back to your calling routine clouds the meaning of the return code when you need to send back honest-to-goodness error codes. In short – don't go there!

Return values are all about indicating success or failure of the sproc, and even the extent or nature of that success or failure. For the C programmers among you, this should be a fairly easy strategy to relate to – it is a common practice to use a function's return value as a success code, with any non-zero value indicating some sort of problem. If you stick with the default return codes in SQL Server, you'll find that the same rules hold true.

How to Use RETURN

Actually, your program will receive a return value whether you supply one or not. By default, SQL Server automatically returns a value of zero when your procedure is complete.

To pass a return value back from our sproc to the calling code, we simple use the RETURN statement:

```
RETURN [<integer value to return>]
```

> Note that the return value must be an integer.

Perhaps the biggest thing to understand about the RETURN statement is that it unconditionally exits from your sproc. That is, no matter where you are in your sproc, not one single more line of code will execute after you have issued a RETURN statement.

By unconditionally, I don't mean that a RETURN statement is executed regardless of where it is in code – on the contrary, you can have many RETURN statements in your sproc, and they will only be executed when the normal conditional structure of your code issues the command. Once that happens however, there is no turning back.

Let's illustrate this idea of how a RETURN statement affects things by writing a very simple test sproc:

```
USE Northwind
GO

CREATE PROC spTestReturns
AS
    DECLARE @MyMessage          varchar(50)
    DECLARE @MyOtherMessage     varchar(50)

    SELECT @MyMessage = 'Hi, it''s that line before the RETURN'
    PRINT @MyMessage
    RETURN
    SELECT @MyOtherMessage = 'Sorry, but we won''t get this far'
    PRINT @MyOtherMessage
RETURN
```

OK, now we have a sproc, but we need a small script to test out a couple of things for us. What we want to see is:

❑   What gets printed out

❑   What value the RETURN statement returns

In order to capture the value of a RETURN statement, we need to assign it to a variable during our EXEC statement. For example, the following code would assign whatever the return value is to @ReturnVal:

```
EXEC @ReturnVal = spMySproc
```

Now let's put this into a more useful script to test out our sproc:

```
DECLARE @Return int

EXEC @Return = spTestReturns
SELECT @Return
```

Short but sweet – when we run it, we see that the RETURN statement did indeed terminate the code before anything else could run:

Hi, it's that line before the RETURN

0

(1 row(s) affected)

We also got back the return value for our sproc, which was zero. Notice that the value was zero even though we didn't specify a specific return value – that's because the default is always zero.

> **Think about this for a minute – if the return value is zero by default, then that means that the default return is also, in effect, "No Errors". This has some serious dangers to it. The key point here is to make sure that you always explicitly define your return values – that way, you are reasonably certain to be returning the value you intended rather than something by accident.**

Now, just for grins, let's alter that sproc to verify that we can send whatever integer value we want back as the return value:

```
USE Northwind
GO

ALTER PROC spTestReturns
AS
    DECLARE @MyMessage          varchar(50)
    DECLARE @MyOtherMessage     varchar(50)

    SELECT @MyMessage = 'Hi, it''s that line before the RETURN'
    PRINT @MyMessage
    RETURN 100
    SELECT @MyOtherMessage = 'Sorry, but we won''t get this far'
    PRINT @MyOtherMessage
RETURN
```

Now re-run your test script, and you'll get the same result save for that change in return value:

Hi, it's that line before the RETURN

```
-----------
100
```

(1 row(s) affected)

Dealing with Errors

Sure. We don't need this section. I mean, our code never has errors, and we never run into problems, right? OK, well, now that we've had our moment of fantasy for today, let's get down to reality. Things go wrong – it's just the way that life works in the wonderful world of software engineering. Fortunately, we can do something about it. Unfortunately, you're probably not going to be happy with the tools you have. Fortunately again, there are ways to make the most out of what you have, and ways to hide many of the inadequacies of error handling in the SQL world.

Three common error types can happen in SQL Server:

❑ Errors that create run-time errors and stop your code from proceeding further.

❑ Errors that SQL Server knows about, but that don't create run-time errors such that your code stops running. These can also be referred to as "inline" errors.

❑ Errors that are more logical in nature and to which SQL Server is essentially oblivious.

The first thing to understand about handling errors in SQL Server is that there is no "error handler" mechanism available. You don't have an option that essentially says, "If any error happens, go run this code over in this other spot." This is probably going to be something of a real shock for you if you've come from a more modern procedural or event-driven programming language. Errors that have enough severity to generate a run-time error are problematic from the SQL Server side of the equation. On the bright side, all the current data access object models pass through the message on such errors, so you know about them in your client application and can do something about them there. This leaves us with the other two kinds of errors.

Handling Inline Errors

Inline errors are those pesky little things where SQL Server keeps running as such, but hasn't, for some reason, succeeded in doing what you wanted it to do. For example, let's try to insert a record into the Order Details table that doesn't have a corresponding record in the Orders table:

```
USE Northwind
GO

INSERT INTO [Order Details]
    (OrderID, ProductID, UnitPrice, Quantity, Discount)
VALUES
    (999999,11,10.00,10, 0)
```

SQL Server won't perform this insert for us because there is a FOREIGN KEY constraint on Order Details that references the PRIMARY KEY in the Orders table. Since there is no record in the Orders table with an OrderID of 999999, the record we are trying to insert into Order Details violates that constraint and is rejected:

Server: Msg 547, Level 16, State 1, Line 1
INSERT statement conflicted with COLUMN FOREIGN KEY constraint 'FK_Order_Details_Orders'.
The conflict occurred in database 'Northwind', table 'Orders', column 'OrderID'.
The statement has been terminated.

Pay attention to that error 547 up there – that's something of which we can make use.

Making Use of @@ERROR

We've already talked some about this bad boy when we were looking at scripting, but it's time to get a lot friendlier with this particular system function.

To review, @@ERROR contains the error number of the last T-SQL statement executed. If the value is zero, then no error occurred.

> The caveat with **@@ERROR** is that it is reset with each new statement – this means that if you want to defer analyzing the value, or you want to use it more than once, you need to move the value into some other holding bin – a local variable that you have declared for this purpose.

Let's play with this just a bit using our INSERT example from before:

```
USE Northwind
GO
```

```
DECLARE    @Error    int

-- Bogus INSERT - there is no OrderID of 999999 in Northind
INSERT INTO [Order Details]
    (OrderID, ProductID, UnitPrice, Quantity, Discount)
VALUES
    (999999,11,10.00,10, 0)
```

```
-- Move our error code into safe keeping. Note that, after this statement,
-- @@Error will be reset to whatever error number applies to this statement
SELECT @Error = @@ERROR

-- Print out a blank separator line
PRINT ''

-- The value of our holding variable is just what we would expect
PRINT 'The Value of @Error is ' + CONVERT(varchar, @Error)

-- The value of @@ERROR has been reset - it's back to zero
PRINT 'The Value of @@ERROR is ' + CONVERT(varchar, @@ERROR)
```

Now execute our script, and we can examine how @@ERROR is affected:

```
Server: Msg 547, Level 16, State 1, Line 0
INSERT statement conflicted with COLUMN FOREIGN KEY constraint 'FK_Order_Details_Orders'.
The conflict occurred in database 'Northwind', table 'Orders', column 'OrderID'.
The statement has been terminated.

The Value of @Error is 547
The Value of @@ERROR is 0
```

This illustrates pretty quickly the issue of saving the value from @@ERROR. The first error statement is only informational in nature. SQL Server has thrown that error, but hasn't stopped our code from executing. Indeed, the only part of that message that our sproc has access to is the error number. That error number resides in @@ERROR for just that next T-SQL statement – after that it's gone.

> Notice that **@Error** and **@@ERROR** are two separate and distinct variables, and can be referred to separately. This isn't just because of the case difference (depending on how you have your server configured, case sensitivity can affect your variable names), but rather because of the difference in scope. The @ or @@ is part of the name, so just the number of @ symbols on the front makes each one separate and distinct from the other.

Using @@ERROR in a Sproc

Let's go back to our `spInsertDateValidatedOrder` stored procedure that we started back when we were dealing with `IF...ELSE` statements. All the examples we worked with in that sproc ran just fine. Of course they did – they were well-controlled examples. However, that's not the way things work in the real world. Indeed, you never have any idea what a user is going to throw at your code. The world is littered with the carcasses of programmers who thought they had thought of everything, only to find that their users had broken something (you might say they thought of something else) within the first few minutes of operation.

We can break that sproc in no time at all by just changing one little thing in our test script:

```
USE Northwind
GO

DECLARE    @MyIdent    int
DECLARE    @MyDate     smalldatetime

SELECT @MyDate = GETDATE()

EXEC spInsertDateValidatedOrder
    @CustomerID = 'ZXZXZ',
    @EmployeeID = 5,
    @OrderDate  = @MyDate,
    @ShipVia    = 3,
    @Freight    = 5.00,
    @OrderID    = @MyIdent OUTPUT

SELECT OrderID, CustomerID, EmployeeID, OrderDate, ShipName
FROM Orders
WHERE OrderID = @MyIdent
```

This seemingly simple change creates all kinds of havoc with our sproc:

```
The Time of Day in Order Date was truncated
Server: Msg 547, Level 16, State 1, Procedure spInsertDateValidatedOrder, Line 44
INSERT statement conflicted with COLUMN FOREIGN KEY constraint 'FK_Orders_Customers'. The
conflict occurred in database 'Northwind', table 'Customers', column 'CustomerID'.
The statement has been terminated.
OrderID         CustomerID            EmployeeID            OrderDate            ShipName
--------------- --------------------  --------------------  -------------------- --------------

(0 row(s) affected)
```

Our row wasn't inserted. It shouldn't have been – after all, isn't that why we put in constraints – to ensure that bad records don't get inserted into our database?

The nasty thing here is that we get a big ugly message that's almost impossible for the average person to understand. What we need to do is test the value of `@@ERROR` and respond accordingly.

We can do this easily using an `IF...ELSE` statement together with either `@@ERROR` (if we can test the value immediately and only need to test it once), or a local variable, into which we have previously moved the value of `@@ERROR`.

Personally, I like my code to be consistent, so I always move it into a local variable and then do all my testing with that – even when I only need to test it once. I have to admit to being in the minority on that one though. Doing this when you don't need to takes up slightly more memory (the extra variable) and requires an extra assignment statement (to move @@ERROR to your local variable). Both of these pieces of overhead are extremely small and I gladly trade them for the idea of people who read my code knowing that they are going to see the same thing done the same way every time.

In addition, it doesn't make much sense to still select out the inserted row, so we'll want to skip that part since it's irrelevant.

So let's add a couple of changes to deal with this referential integrity issue and skip the code that doesn't apply in this error situation.

```
USE Northwind
GO

ALTER PROC spInsertDateValidatedOrder
    @CustomerID         nvarchar(5),
    @EmployeeID         int,
    @OrderDate          datetime    = NULL,
    @RequiredDate       datetime    = NULL,
    @ShippedDate        datetime    = NULL,
    @ShipVia            int,
    @Freight            money,
    @ShipName           nvarchar(40) = NULL,
    @ShipAddress        nvarchar(60) = NULL,
    @ShipCity           nvarchar(15) = NULL,
    @ShipRegion         nvarchar(15) = NULL,
    @ShipPostalCode     nvarchar(10) = NULL,
    @ShipCountry        nvarchar(15) = NULL,
    @OrderID            int          OUTPUT

AS

-- Declare our variables
DECLARE    @Error                   int
DECLARE    @InsertedOrderDate       smalldatetime

/* Test to see if supplied date is over seven days old, if so
** replace with NULL value
** otherwise, truncate the time to be midnight*/
IF DATEDIFF(dd, @OrderDate, GETDATE()) > 7
BEGIN
    SELECT @InsertedOrderDate = NULL
    PRINT 'Invalid Order Date'
    PRINT 'Supplied OrderDate was greater than 7 days old.'
    PRINT 'The value has been reset to NULL'
END
ELSE
BEGIN
    SELECT @InsertedOrderDate =
        CONVERT(datetime,(CONVERT(varchar,@OrderDate,112)))
        PRINT 'The Time of Day in Order Date was truncated'
END
```

```
/* Create the new record */
INSERT INTO Orders
VALUES
(
    @CustomerID,
    @EmployeeID,
    @InsertedOrderDate,
    @RequiredDate,
    @ShippedDate,
    @ShipVia,
    @Freight,
    @ShipName,
    @ShipAddress,
    @ShipCity,
    @ShipRegion,
    @ShipPostalCode,
    @ShipCountry
)

-- Move it to our local variable and check for an error condition
SELECT @Error = @@ERROR

IF @Error != 0
BEGIN
    -- Uh, oh - something went wrong.

    IF @Error = 547
    -- The problem is a constraint violation. Print out some informational
    -- help to steer the user to the most likely problem.
    BEGIN
        PRINT 'Supplied data violates data integrity rules'
        PRINT 'Check that the supplied customer number exists'
        PRINT 'in the system and try again'
    END
    ELSE
    -- Oops, it's something we haven't anticipated, tell them that we
    -- don't know, print out the error.
    BEGIN
        PRINT 'An unknown error occurred. Contact your System Administrator'
        PRINT 'The error was number ' + CONVERT(varchar, @Error)
    END
    -- Regardless of the error, we're going to send it back to the calling
    -- piece of code so it can be handled at that level if necessary.
    RETURN @Error
END

/* Move the identity value from the newly inserted record into
     our output variable */
SELECT @OrderID = @@IDENTITY

RETURN
```

Now we need to run our test script again, but it's now just a little inadequate to test our sproc – we need to accept the return value so we know what happened. In addition, we have no need to run the query to return the row just inserted if the row couldn't be inserted – so we'll skip that in the event of error.

```
USE Northwind
GO

DECLARE    @MyIdent    int
DECLARE    @MyDate     smalldatetime
DECLARE    @Return     int

SELECT @MyDate = GETDATE()

EXEC @Return = spInsertDateValidatedOrder
    @CustomerID = 'ZXZXZ',
    @EmployeeID = 5,
    @OrderDate  = @MyDate,
    @ShipVia    = 3,
    @Freight    = 5.00,
    @OrderID    = @MyIdent OUTPUT

IF @Return = 0
    SELECT OrderID, CustomerID, EmployeeID, OrderDate, ShipName
    FROM Orders
    WHERE OrderID = @MyIdent
ELSE
    PRINT 'Value Returned was ' + CONVERT(varchar, @Return)
```

Realistically, not much changed – just five lines. Nonetheless, the behavior is quite a bit different when we have an error. Run this script, and we wind up with a different result than before we had our error checking:

The Time of Day in Order Date was truncated
Server: Msg 547, Level 16, State 1, Procedure spInsertDateValidatedOrder, Line 42
INSERT statement conflicted with COLUMN FOREIGN KEY constraint 'FK_Orders_Customers'. The conflict occurred in database 'Northwind', table 'Customers', column 'CustomerID'.
The statement has been terminated.
Supplied data violates data integrity rules
Check that the supplied customer number exists
in the system and try again
Value Returned was 547

We didn't have an error handler in the way most languages operate these days, but we were able to handle it nonetheless.

Handling Errors Before They Happen

Sometimes you have errors that SQL Server doesn't really have an effective way to even know about, let alone tell you about. Other times we want to prevent the errors before they happen. These we need to check for and handle ourselves.

Sticking with the main example sproc we've used for this chapter, let's address some business rules that are logical in nature, but not necessarily implemented in the database. For example, we've been allowing nulls in the database, but maybe we don't want to do that so liberally anymore. We've decided that we should no longer allow a null OrderDate. We still have records in there that we don't have values for, so we don't want to change over the column to disallowing nulls at the table level. What to do?

The first thing we need to take care of is editing our sproc to no longer allow NULL values. This seems easy enough – just remove the NULL default from the parameter, right? That has two problems to it:

❑ SQL Server will generate an error if the parameter is not supplied, but will still allow a user to explicitly supply a NULL

❑ Even when the user fails to provide the parameter, the error information is vague

We get around these problems by actually continuing with our NULL default just as it is, but this time we're testing for it. If the parameter contains a NULL, we then know that one was either not supplied or the value supplied was NULL (which we don't allow anymore) – then we act accordingly. So the question becomes, "How do I test to see if it's a NULL value?" Simple, just the way we did in our WHERE clauses in queries:

```
IF @OrderDate IS NULL
    <abort the INSERT and print a message>
```

Let's make the modifications to our now very familiar sproc:

```
USE Northwind
GO

ALTER PROC spInsertDateValidatedOrder
    @CustomerID         nvarchar(5),
    @EmployeeID         int,
    @OrderDate          datetime = NULL,
    @RequiredDate       datetime = NULL,
    @ShippedDate        datetime = NULL,
    @ShipVia            int,
    @Freight            money,
    @ShipName           nvarchar(40) = NULL,
    @ShipAddress        nvarchar(60) = NULL,
    @ShipCity           nvarchar(15) = NULL,
    @ShipRegion         nvarchar(15) = NULL,
    @ShipPostalCode     nvarchar(10) = NULL,
    @ShipCountry        nvarchar(15) = NULL,
    @OrderID            int       OUTPUT

AS

-- Declare our variables
DECLARE     @Error                  int
DECLARE     @InsertedOrderDate      smalldatetime

/* Here we're going to declare our constants. SQL Server doesn't really
** have constants in the classic sense, but I just use a standard
** variable in their place. These help your code be more readable
** - particularly when you match them up with a constant list in your
** client. */

DECLARE     @INVALIDDATE    int

/* Now that the constants are declared, we need to initialize them.
** Notice that SQL Server ignores the white space in between the
** variable and the "=" sign. Why I put in the spacing would be more
** obvious if we had several such constants - the constant values
** would line up nicely for readability */
```

```
*/
SELECT @INVALIDDATE = -1000

/* Test to see if supplied date is over seven days old, if so
** it is no longer valid. Also test for NULL values.
** If either case is true, then terminate sproc with error
** message printed out. */
IF DATEDIFF(dd, @OrderDate, GETDATE()) > 7 OR @OrderDate IS NULL
BEGIN
    PRINT 'Invalid Order Date'
    PRINT 'Supplied Order Date was greater than 7 days old '
    PRINT 'or was NULL. Correct the date and resubmit.'
    RETURN @INVALIDDATE
END

-- We made it this far, so it must be OK to go on with things.
SELECT @InsertedOrderDate =
    CONVERT(datetime,(CONVERT(varchar,@OrderDate,112)))
    PRINT 'The Time of Day in Order Date was truncated'
```

```
/* Create the new record */
INSERT INTO Orders
VALUES
(
    @CustomerID,
    @EmployeeID,
    @InsertedOrderDate,
    @RequiredDate,
    @ShippedDate,
    @ShipVia,
    @Freight,
    @ShipName,
    @ShipAddress,
    @ShipCity,
    @ShipRegion,
    @ShipPostalCode,
    @ShipCountry
)

-- Move it to our local variable, and check for an error condition
SELECT @Error = @@ERROR

IF @Error != 0
BEGIN
    -- Uh, oh - something went wrong.

    IF @Error = 547
    -- The problem is a constraint violation. Print out some informational
    -- help to steer the user to the most likely problem.
    BEGIN
        PRINT 'Supplied data violates data integrity rules'
        PRINT 'Check that the supplied customer number exists'
        PRINT 'in the system and try again'
    END
    ELSE
```

```
    -- Oops, it's something we haven't anticipated, tell them here that we
    -- don't know, print out the error.
    BEGIN
        PRINT 'An unknown error occurred. Contact your System Administrator'
        PRINT 'The error was number ' + CONVERT(varchar, @Error)
    END
    -- Regardless of the error, we're going to send it back to the calling
    -- piece of code so it can be handled at that level if necessary.
    RETURN @Error
END


/* Move the identity value from the newly inserted record into
        our output variable */
SELECT @OrderID = @@IDENTITY

RETURN
```

We're going to want to test this a couple of different ways, first, we need to put back in a valid customer number, then we need to run it. Assuming it succeeds, then we can move on to supplying an unacceptable date:

```
USE Northwind
GO

DECLARE    @MyIdent    int
DECLARE    @MyDate     smalldatetime
DECLARE    @Return     int

SELECT @MyDate = '1/1/1999'

EXEC @Return = spInsertDateValidatedOrder
    @CustomerID = 'ALFKI',
    @EmployeeID = 5,
    @OrderDate = @MyDate,
    @ShipVia = 3,
    @Freight = 5.00,
    @OrderID = @MyIdent OUTPUT

IF @Return = 0
    SELECT OrderID, CustomerID, EmployeeID, OrderDate, ShipName
    FROM Orders
    WHERE OrderID = @MyIdent
ELSE
    PRINT 'Value Returned was ' + CONVERT(varchar, @Return)
```

This time, when we run it, we get an error message:

Invalid Order Date
Supplied Order Date was greater than 7 days old
or was NULL. Correct the date and resubmit.
Value Returned was -1000

Note that this wasn't a SQL Server error – as far as SQL Server's concerned, everything about life is just fine. What's nice though, is that, were we using a client program (say one you wrote in VB, C++, or some other language), we would be able to track the -1000 against a known constant and send a very specific message to the end user.

Manually Raising Errors

Sometimes we have errors that SQL Server doesn't really know about, but we wish it did. For example, perhaps in our previous example we don't want to return -1000. Instead, we'd like to be able to create a run-time error at the client end that the client would then use to invoke an error handler and act accordingly. To do this, we make use of the RAISERROR command in T-SQL. The syntax is pretty straightforward:

```
RAISERROR (<message ID | message string>, <severity>, <state>
[, <argument>
[,<...n>]] )
[WITH option[,...n]]
```

Message ID/Message String

The message ID or message string you provide determines what message is sent out to the client.

Using a message ID creates a manually raised error with the ID that you specified and the message that is associated with that ID as found in the sysmessages table in the master database.

> *If you want to see what your SQL Server has as predefined messages, you can always perform a SELECT*
> *FROM master..sysMessages. This will include any messages you've manually added to your*
> *system using the sp_addmessage stored procedure or through the Enterprise Manager.*

You can also just supply a message string in the form of ad hoc text without creating a more permanent message in sysmessages. For example:

```
RAISERROR ('Hi there, I''m an error', 1, 1)
```

Raises a rather simple error message:

Msg 50000, Level 1, State 50000
Hi there, I'm an error

Notice that the assigned message number, even though we didn't supply one, is 50000. This is the default error value for any ad hoc error. It can be overridden using the WITH SETERROR option.

Severity

For those of you already familiar with NT, severity should be an old friend. Severity is an indication of just how bad things really are based on this error. For SQL Server, however, what severity codes mean can get a little bizarre. They can range from essentially being informational (severities 1-18), to being considered as system level (19-25), and even catastrophic (20-25). If you raise an error of severity 19 or higher (system level), then the WITH LOG option must also be specified. 20 and higher will automatically terminate the users' connections (they *hate* that!).

So, let's get back to what I meant by bizarre. SQL Server actually varies its behavior into more ranges than NT does – or even than the Books Online will tell you about. They fall into six major groupings:

1-9	Purely informational only, but will return the specific error code in the message information. No matter what you set the state (discussed next) to in your RAISERROR, it will wind up coming out with the same value as the error number (don't ask me why – it just does).
10	Also informational, but will not raise an error in the client and will not provide any specific error information other than the error text.
11-16	These terminate execution of the procedure and raise an error at the client. From this point forward, the state is shown to be whatever value you set it to.
17	Usually, only SQL Server should use this severity. Basically, it indicates that SQL Server has run out of resources (for example tempdb was full) and can't complete the request.
18-19	Both of these are severe errors, and imply that the underlying cause requires system administrator attention. With 19, the WITH LOG option is required, and the event will show up in the NT or Win2K Event Log if you are using that OS family.
20-25	Your world has just caved in – so has the users connection. Essentially, this is a fatal error. The connection is terminated. As with 19, you must use the WITH LOG option, and a message will, if applicable, show up in the Event Log.

State

State is an ad hoc value. It is something that recognizes that exactly the same error may occur at multiple places within your code. The notion is that this gives you an opportunity to send something of a place marker for where exactly the error occurred.

State values can be between 1 and 127. If you are troubleshooting an error with Microsoft tech support, they apparently have some arcane knowledge that hasn't been shared with us of what some of these mean. I'm told that, if you make a tech support call to MS, they are likely to ask and make use of this state information.

Error Arguments

Some pre-defined errors will accept arguments. These allow the error to be somewhat more dynamic in nature by changing to the specific nature of the error. You can also format your error messages to accept arguments.

When you want to make use of dynamic information in what is otherwise a static error message, you need to format the fixed portion of your message such that it leaves room for the parameterized section of the message. This is done using placeholders. If you're coming from the C or C++ world, then you'll recognize the parameter placeholders immediately – they are very similar to the printf command arguments. If you're not from the C world, these may seem a little odd to you. All of the placeholders start with the % sign, and are then coded for what kind of information you'll be passing to them:

Placeholder Type Indicator	Type of value
D	Signed integer – note that Books Online also indicates that i is an OK choice, but I've had problems getting it to work as expected
O	Unsigned octal
P	Pointer
S	String
U	Unsigned integer
X or x	Unsigned hexadecimal

In addition, there is the option to prefix any of these placeholder indicators with some additional flag and width information:

Flag	What it does
– (dash or minus sign)	Left justify – only makes a difference when you supply a fixed width.
+ (plus sign)	Indicate the positive or negative nature if the parameter is a signed numeric type.
0	Tells SQL Server to pad the left side of a numeric value with zeroes until it reaches the width specified in the width option.
# (pound sign)	Only applies to octal and hex values. Tells SQL Server to use the appropriate prefix (0 or 0x) depending on whether it is octal or hex.
' '	Pad the left of a numeric value with spaces if positive.

Last, but not least, you can also set the width, precision, and long/short status of a parameter:

- ❑ Width: set by simply supplying an integer value for how much space we want to hold for the parameterized value. You can also specify a *, in which case SQL Server will automatically determine the width depending on the value you've set for precision.

- ❑ Precision: determines the maximum number of digits output for numeric data.

- ❑ Long/Short: set by using an h (short) or I (long) when the type of the parameter is an integer, octal, or hex value.

To use this in an example:

```
RAISERROR ("This is a sample parameterized %s, along with a zero
padding and a sign%+010d",1,1, "string", 12121)
```

If you execute this, you get back something that looks a little different from what's in the quotes:

Msg 50000, Level 1, State 50000
This is a sample parameterized string, along with a zero
padding and a sign+000012121

The extra values supplied were inserted, in order, into our placeholders, with the final value being reformatted as specified.

WITH <option>

There are currently three options that you can mix and match when you raise an error:

- ❑ LOG
- ❑ SETERROR
- ❑ NOWAIT

WITH LOG

This tells SQL Server to log the error to the SQL Server error log and the NT application log (the latter applies to installations on NT only). This option is required with severity levels that are 19 or higher.

WITH SETERROR

By default, a RAISERROR command does not set @@ERROR with the value of the error you generated – instead, @@ERROR reflects the success or failure of your actual RAISERROR command. SETERROR overrides this and sets the value of @@ERROR to be equal to your error ID.

WITH NOWAIT

Immediately notifies the client of the error.

Adding Your Own Custom Error Messages

We can make use of a special system stored procedure to add messages to the system. The sproc is called sp_addmessage, and the syntax looks like this:

```
sp_addmessage [@msgnum =] <msg id>,
[@severity =] <severity>,
[@msgtext =] <'msg'>
[, [@lang =] <'language'>]
[, [@with_log =] [TRUE|FALSE]]
[, [@replace =] 'replace']
```

All the parameters mean pretty much the same thing that they did with RAISERROR, except for the addition of the language and replace parameters and a slight difference with the WITH LOG option.

@lang

This specifies the language to which this message applies. What's cool here is that you can specify a separate version of your message for any language supported in syslanguages.

@with_log

This works just the same as it does in RAISERROR in that, if set to TRUE the message will be automatically logged to both the SQL Server error log and the NT application log when raised (the latter only when running under NT). The only trick here is that you indicate that you want this message to be logged by setting this parameter to TRUE rather than using the WITH LOG option.

> Be careful of this one in the Books Online. Depending on how you read it, it would be easy to interpret it as saying that you should set @with_log to a string constant of 'WITH_LOG', when you should set it to TRUE. Perhaps even more confusing is that the REPLACE option looks much the same, and it must be set to the string constant rather than TRUE.

@replace

If you are editing an existing message rather than creating a new one, then you must set the @replace parameter to 'REPLACE'. If you leave this off, you'll get an error if the message already exists.

> Creating a set list of additional messages for use by your applications can greatly enhance reuse, but more importantly, it can significantly improve readability of your application. Imagine if every one of your database applications made use of a constant list of custom error codes. You could then easily establish a constants file (a resource or include library for example) that had a listing of the appropriate errors – you could even create an include library that had a generic handling of some or all of the errors. In short, if you're going to be building multiple SQL Server apps in the same environment, consider using a set list of errors that is common to all your applications.

Using sp_addmessage

As has already been indicated, sp_addmessage creates messages in much the same way as we create ad hoc messages using RAISERROR.

As an example, let's add our own custom message that tells the user about the issues with their order date:

```
sp_addmessage
    @msgnum = 60000,
    @severity = 10,
    @msgtext = '%s is not a valid Order date.
Order date must be within 7 days of current date.'
```

Execute the sproc and it confirms the addition of the new message:

(1 row(s) affected)

> No matter what database you're working with when you run **sp_addmessage**, the actual message is added to the **sysmessages** table in the **master** database. The significance of this is that, if you migrate your database to a new server, the messages will need to be added again to that new server (the old ones will still be in the **master** database of the old server). As such, I strongly recommend keeping all your custom messages stored in a script somewhere so they can easily be added into a new system.
>
> It's also worth noting that you can add and delete custom messages using Enterprise Manager (right-click on a server, then go to **All Tasks | Manage SQL Server messages**). While this is quick and easy, it makes it more problematic to create and test the scripts I recommend in the paragraph above. In short, I don't recommend its use.

Removing an Existing Custom Message

To get rid of the custom message, use:

```
sp_dropmessage <msg num>
```

Putting Our Error Trap to Use

Now it's time to put all the different pieces we've been talking about to use at once.

First, if you tried out the sp_dropmessage on our new error 60000 – quit that! Add the message back so we can make use of it in this example.

What we want to do is take our sproc to the next level up. We're going to modify our sproc again so that it takes advantage of the new error features we know about. When we're done, we'll be able to generate a trappable run-time error in our client so we can take appropriate action at that end.

All we need to do is change our PRINT statement to have a RAISERROR:

```
USE Northwind
GO

ALTER PROC spInsertDateValidatedOrder
    @CustomerID          nvarchar(5),
    @EmployeeID          int,
    @OrderDate           datetime      = NULL,
    @RequiredDate        datetime      = NULL,
    @ShippedDate         datetime      = NULL,
    @ShipVia             int,
    @Freight             money,
    @ShipName            nvarchar(40) = NULL,
    @ShipAddress         nvarchar(60) = NULL,
    @ShipCity            nvarchar(15) = NULL,
    @ShipRegion          nvarchar(15) = NULL,
    @ShipPostalCode      nvarchar(10) = NULL,
    @ShipCountry         nvarchar(15) = NULL,
    @OrderID             int        OUTPUT

AS

-- Declare our variables
DECLARE     @Error              int
DECLARE     @BadDate            varchar(12)
DECLARE     @InsertedOrderDate  smalldatetime

/* Test to see if supplied date is over seven days old, if so
** it is no longer valid. Also test for null values.
** If either case is true, then terminate sproc with error
** message printed out. */
IF DATEDIFF(dd, @OrderDate, GETDATE()) > 7 OR @OrderDate IS NULL
BEGIN
    --RAISERROR doesn't have a date data type, so convert it first
    SELECT @BadDate = CONVERT(varchar, @OrderDate)
    RAISERROR (60000,1,1, @BadDate) WITH SETERROR
    RETURN @@ERROR
END

-- We made it this far, so it must be OK to go on with things.
SELECT @InsertedOrderDate =
    CONVERT(datetime,(CONVERT(varchar,@OrderDate,112)))
    PRINT 'The Time of Day in Order Date was truncated'
```

```
/* Create the new record */
INSERT INTO Orders
VALUES
(
    @CustomerID,
    @EmployeeID,
    @InsertedOrderDate,
    @RequiredDate,
    @ShippedDate,
    @ShipVia,
    @Freight,
    @ShipName,
    @ShipAddress,
    @ShipCity,
    @ShipRegion,
    @ShipPostalCode,
    @ShipCountry
)

-- Move it to our local variable, and check for an error condition
SELECT @Error = @@ERROR

IF @Error != 0
BEGIN
    -- Uh, Oh - something went wrong.

    IF @Error = 547
    -- The problem is a constraint violation. Print out some informational
    -- help to steer the user to the most likely problem.
    BEGIN
        PRINT 'Supplied data violates data integrity rules'
        PRINT 'Check that the supplied customer number exists'
        PRINT 'in the system and try again'
    END
    ELSE
    -- Oops, it's something we haven't anticipated, tell them that we
    -- don't know, print out the error.
    BEGIN
        PRINT 'An unknown error occurred. Contact your System Administrator'
        PRINT 'The error was number ' + CONVERT(varchar, @Error)
    END
    -- Regardless of the error, we're going to send it back to the calling
    -- piece of code so it can be handled at that level if necessary.
    RETURN @Error
END


/* Move the identity value from the newly inserted record into
        our output variable */
SELECT @OrderID = @@IDENTITY

RETURN
```

What a Sproc Offers

Now that we've spent some time looking at how to build a sproc, we probably ought to ask the question as to why to use them. Some of the reasons are pretty basic; others may not come to mind right away if you're new to the RDBMS world. The primary benefits of sprocs include:

❑   Making processes that require procedural action callable

❑   Security

❑   Performance

Creating Callable Processes

As I've already indicated, a sproc is something of a script that is stored in the database. The nice thing is that, since it is a database object, we can call to it – you don't have to manually load it from a file before executing it.

Sprocs can call to other sprocs (called **nesting**). For SQL Server 2000, you can nest up to 32 levels deep. This gives you the capability of reusing separate sprocs much as you would make use of a subroutine in a classic procedural language. The syntax for calling one sproc from another sproc is exactly the same as it is calling the sproc from a script. As an example, let's create a mini sproc to perform the same function as the test script that we've been using for most of this chapter:

```
USE Northwind
GO

CREATE PROC spTestInsert
    @MyDate    smalldatetime
AS
DECLARE    @MyIdent    int
DECLARE    @Return    int

EXEC @Return = spInsertDateValidatedOrder
    @CustomerID = 'ALFKI',
    @EmployeeID = 5,
    @OrderDate  = @MyDate,
    @ShipVia    = 3,
    @Freight    = 5.00,
    @OrderID    = @MyIdent OUTPUT

IF @Return = 0
    SELECT OrderID, CustomerID, EmployeeID, OrderDate, ShipName
    FROM Orders
    WHERE OrderID = @MyIdent
ELSE
    PRINT 'Error Returned was ' + CONVERT(varchar, @Return)
```

Now just call the sproc supplying a good date, then a bad date (to test the error handling). First the good date:

```
DECLARE @Today smalldatetime

SELECT @Today = GETDATE()

EXEC spTestInsert
    @MyDate = @Today
```

Using today's date gets what we expect:

The Time of Day in Order Date was truncated

(1 row(s) affected)

OrderID	CustomerID	EmployeeID	OrderDate	ShipName
11097	ALFKI	5	2000-09-18 00:00:00.000	NULL

(1 row(s) affected)

Then a bad date:

```
EXEC spTestInsert '1/1/1999'
```

Again, this yields us what we expect – in this case an error message:

Msg 60000, Level 1, State 60000
Jan 1 1999 is not a valid Order date.
Order date must be within 7 days of current date.
Error Returned was 60000

Note that local variables are just that – local to each sproc. You can have five different copies of @MyDate, one each in five different sprocs and they are all independent of each other.

Using Sprocs for Security

Many people don't realize the full use of sprocs as a tool for security. Much like views, we can create a sproc that returns a recordset without having to give the user authority to the underlying table. Granting someone the right to execute a sproc implies that they can perform any action within the sproc, provided that the action is taken within the context of the sproc. That is, if we grant someone authority to execute a sproc that returns all the records in the Customers table, but not access to the actual Customers table, then the user will still be able to get data out of the Customers table provided they do it by using the sproc (trying to access the table directly won't work).

What can be really handy here is that we can give someone access to modify data through the sproc, but then only give them read access to the underlying table. They will be able to modify data in the table provided that they do it through your sproc (which will likely be enforcing some business rules). They can then hook directly up to your SQL Server using Excel, Access, or whatever to build their own custom reports with no risk of "accidentally" modifying the data.

> **Setting users up to directly link to a production database via Access or Excel has to be one of the most incredibly powerful and yet stupid things you can do to your system. While you are empowering your users, you are also digging your own grave in terms of the resources they will use and long running queries they will execute (naturally, they will be oblivious to the havoc this causes your system).**
>
> **If you really must give users direct access, then consider using replication or backup and restores to create a completely separate copy of the database for them to use. This will help insure you against record locks, queries that bog down the system, and a whole host of other problems.**

Sprocs and Performance

Generally speaking, sprocs can do a lot to help the performance of your system. Keep in mind though that, like most things in life, there are no guarantees – indeed, some processes can be created in sprocs that will substantially slow the process if the sproc hasn't been designed intelligently.

Where does that performance come from? Well, when we create a sproc, the process works something like this:

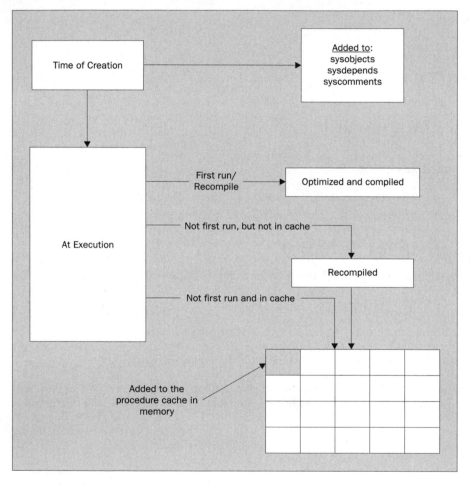

We start by running our CREATE PROC procedure. This parses the query to make sure that the code should actually run. The one difference versus running the script directly is that the CREATE PROC command can make use of what's called **deferred name resolution**. Deferred name resolution ignores the fact that you may have some objects that don't exist yet. This gives you the chance to create these objects later.

After the sproc has been created, it sits in wait for the first time that it is executed. At that time, the sproc is optimized, and a query plan is compiled and cached on the system. Subsequent times that we run our sproc will, unless we specify otherwise using the WITH RECOMPILE option, use that cached query plan rather than creating a new one. This means that whenever the sproc is used it can skip much of the optimization and compilation process. Exactly how much time this saves varies depending on the complexity of the batch, the size of the tables involved in the batch, and the number of indexes on each table. Usually, the amount of time saved is seemingly small – say, perhaps one second for most scenarios – yet that difference can really add up in terms of percentage (1 second is still 100% faster than 2 seconds). The difference can become even more extreme when we have the need to make several calls or when we are in a looping situation.

When a Good Sproc Goes Bad

Perhaps one of the most important things to recognize on the downside of sprocs is that, unless you manually interfere (using the WITH RECOMPILE option) they are optimized based on either the first time that they run, or when the statistics have been updated on the table(s) involved in any queries.

That "optimize once, use many times" strategy is what saves the sproc time, but it's a double-edged sword. If our query is dynamic in nature (the query is built up as it goes using the EXEC command), then the sproc may be optimized for the way things ran the first time, only to find that things never run that way again – in short, it may be using the wrong plan!

It's not just dynamic queries in sprocs that can cause this scenario either. Imagine a web page that lets us mix and match several criteria for a search. For example, let's say that we wanted to add a sproc to the Northwind database that would support a web page that allows users to search for an order based on:

❑   Customer number

❑   Order ID

❑   Product ID

❑   Order date

The user is allowed to supply any mix of the information, with each new piece of information supplied making the search a little more restricted and theoretically faster.

The approach we would probably take to this would be to have more than one query, and select the right query to run depending on what was supplied by the user. The first time that we execute our sproc, it is going to run through a few IF...ELSE statements and pick the right query to run. Unfortunately, it's just the right query for that particular time we ran the sproc (and an unknown percentage of the other times). Any time after that first time the sproc selects a different query to run, it will still be using the query plan based on the first time the sproc ran. In short, the query performance is really going to suffer.

Using the WITH RECOMPILE Option

We can choose to use the security and compartmentalization of code benefits of a sproc but still ignore the pre-compiled code side of things. This lets us get around this issue of not using the right query plan because we're certain that a new plan was created just for this run. To do this, we make use of the WITH RECOMPILE option, which can be included in two different ways.

First, we can include the WITH RECOMPILE at run time. We simply include it with our execution script:

```
EXEC spTestInsert '1/1/1999'
   WITH RECOMPILE
```

This tells SQL Server to throw away the existing execution plan, and create a new one – but just this once. That is, just for this time that weve executed the sproc using the WITH RECOMPILE option.

We can also choose to make things more permanent by including the WITH RECOMPILE option right within the sproc. If we do things this way, we add the WITH RECOMPILE option immediately before our AS statement in our CREATE PROC or ALTER PROC statements.

If we create our sproc with this option, then the sproc will be recompiled each time that it runs, regardless of other options chosen at run time.

Extended Stored Procedures (XPs)

There are times where basic T-SQL and the other features of SQL Server just won't give you what you need. These are usually situations where you need to communicate with something outside of your SQL Server installation, but there may also be situations where you want to provide a level of procedural functionality you just can't get from T-SQL. For these times, there are **extended stored procedures**.

Where standard sprocs have a naming convention that usually includes an sp somewhere in the title of the sproc, extended stored procedures *usually* make use of an xp to show that they are different. However, perhaps the biggest thing to know about extended stored procedures is that they can only exist in the master database – this has several impacts:

❑ If the master database is not current when you run the XP, then you will need to fully qualify the XP (for example, master..xp_sendmail)

❑ If you move your application's database, you will need to re-run any scripts to build the XPs on the new server (the existing XPs will have been left behind in the old server's master database)

❑ Rights to execute the XP are granted in the master database rather than your application database

XPs are actually created outside your SQL Server using some form of low-level programming language. Currently, the only languages actively supported are C and C++. The SQL Server API does not currently support Visual Basic in any way. XPs run in-process to (in the same memory space as) your SQL Server and can be very fast.

XPs are rarely used these days, as there is almost always an alternative that is both easier to code and fits better with today's modern architectures. Most things that might have been created as an XP in the past are now created as a client-side COM object instead.

XPs are a broad topic, and require a serious understanding of C++. Since they are very complex and only apply to a very small subset of the users of SQL Server, we will consider XPs to be out of the scope of this book other than to point out a couple of useful examples.

xp_cmdshell

You can use xp_cmdshell to run O/S command-line commands from within SQL Server. Since this one requires no special setup, let's go ahead and run a quick example. The syntax looks like this:

```
xp_cmdshell <'command_string'> [, no_output]
```

The command_string is exactly what you would have typed into the command line if you were at the DOS prompt in Win 9x or in a command box in NT. The no_output parameter suppresses any results that would have been returned (this lets you execute a command without any feedback that might, in some cases, confuse the user).

Therefore, if we wanted to run a quick directory listing of the main SQL directory, we could do that by issuing a simple command through xp_cmdshell:

```
EXEC master..xp_cmdshell 'Dir "C:\Program Files\Microsoft SQL Server\MSSQL"'
```

The Results pane of the Query Analyzer would quickly show us the same thing as if we had been at a command prompt:

```
output
-------------------------------------------------------------------------------
 Volume in drive C is WIN 98
 Volume Serial Number is 0922-18E6
NULL
 Directory of C:\Program Files\Microsoft SQL Server\MSSQL
NULL
04/27/2000   05:46p   <DIR>          .
04/27/2000   05:46p   <DIR>          ..
04/27/2000   05:49p   <DIR>            Binn
04/27/2000   05:49p   <DIR>            Data
04/27/2000   05:49p   <DIR>            Install
08/06/2000   01:51a            151,609 sqlsun.dll
08/20/2000   12:09p                841 sqlsunin.ini
08/05/2000   06:52p             47,815 readme.txt
04/27/2000   05:52p   <DIR>            LOG
04/27/2000   05:54p   <DIR>            JOBS
04/27/2000   05:54p   <DIR>            BACKUP
04/27/2000   05:54p   <DIR>            REPLDATA
04/27/2000   05:54p<DIR>               FTDATA
08/20/2000   12:18p            820,914 Uninst.isu
       4 File(s)         1,021,179 bytes
      10 Dir(s)     55,181,312 bytes free
NULL

(22 row(s) affected)
```

We could also run any other command that is legal from the command prompt – including any executables we may feel the need to execute.

> **BEWARE OF THIS XP.** I usually lock this XP down because of the potential security risk associated with it. Quite often, we will give the account(s) that SQL Server's services run under a lot of authority in our network. Now, keep in mind that `xp_cmdshell` runs in the security context of SQLAgentCmdExec – a special account used for running SQL Server tasks. That may mean that a user who would have no rights of their own could have major access available through `xp_cmdshell` if you're not careful. How bad can this get? Well, let me make an admission just to prove a point.
>
> A few years ago, I used to work very closely with a SQL Server DBA for a product that I was supporting and augmenting. That DBA had gone to reasonable lengths to make sure that his server was well protected from users accidentally (or deliberately) deleting files from the server. You can imagine the DBA's frustration when he kept finding files moved, deleted, or totally new files added to the server. Who could have been doing all that? How could they do that (no one had rights but the aforementioned DBA)? Well, someone (I'm not admitting – uh, saying – who) was actually issuing the commands through `xp_cmdshell` as part of a joke on our DBA. I finally had to tell him to close that loophole.
>
> In this example, things were pretty innocuous, but it could have easily been very important files that were deleted or altered in some way. Think about this before you leave `xp_cmdshell` open.

xp_msver

This is a largely unknown and yet very handy one to keep in the back of your mind. As the name implies, it returns version information. Beyond that, however, it returns a host of other information. Let's take a look at what it provides:

I can just hear a few people quickly saying, "Hey, why use an extended sproc for this? Won't @@VERSION provide that same info?" The answer is both yes and no. A large amount (but not all) of the info that's available in xp_msver is also available by just performing a SELECT on the @@VERSION global. Unfortunately, that global returns a string – not a result set. The upshot of that is that you can't query it effectively – it's a real pain to have to query for what version or build of the product you're running. You can get that out of xp_msver though.

```
EXEC master..xp_msver
```

And the results:

Index	Name	Internal_Value	Character_Value
1	ProductName	NULL	Microsoft SQL Server
2	ProductVersion	524288	8.00.194
3	Language	1033	English (United States)
4	Platform	NULL	NT INTEL X86

Index	Name	Internal_Value	Character_Value
5	Comments	NULL	NT INTEL X86
6	CompanyName	NULL	Microsoft Corporation
7	FileDescription	NULL	SQL Server Windows NT
8	FileVersion	NULL	2000.080.0194.00
9	InternalName	NULL	SQLSERVR
10	LegalCopyright	NULL	© 1988-2000 Microsoft Corp. All rights reserved.
11	LegalTrademarks	NULL	Microsoft® is a registered trademark of Microsoft Corporation. Windows(TM) is a trademark of Microsoft Corporation
12	OriginalFilename	NULL	SQLSERVR.EXE
13	PrivateBuild	NULL	NULL
14	SpecialBuild	65536	NULL
15	WindowsVersion	143851525	5.0 (2195)
16	ProcessorCount	1	1
17	ProcessorActiveMask	1	00000001
18	ProcessorType	586	PROCESSOR_INTEL_PENTIUM
19	PhysicalMemory	128	128 (133746688)
20	Product ID	NULL	47315-111-1111111-12375

By querying for a specific name and value, we can programmatically check the nature of our server (for verification that the system we're installing on meets the system requirements for example). Let's look at a quick example:

```
CREATE TABLE #VersionTable
(
    [Index] int
        PRIMARY KEY,
    Name varchar(30),
    Internal_Value int,
    Character_Value varchar(250)
)
GO

INSERT INTO #VersionTable
EXEC master..xp_msver

DECLARE @Version int

SELECT @Version = (SELECT Internal_Value
                        FROM #VersionTable
                        WHERE Name = 'ProductVersion')
```

```
IF (@Version) >= 524288
    PRINT 'Running SS2K Beta 2 or Later'
ELSE
    IF @Version >= 458752
        PRINT 'Running 7.0 RTM or Later'
    ELSE
        PRINT 'Running Pre 7.0 RTM Version'

DROP TABLE #VersionTable
```

If I run this on a SQL Server 2000 box, I get the following:

(20 row(s) affected)

Running SS2K Beta 2 or Later

For a SQL Server 7.0 box, I get:

(20 row(s) affected)

Runninng 7.0 RTM or Later

> *This should invite the question, "How did he know what value to hunt for in what version?" The answer is pretty simple – I tried it out. Basically, you should experiment to serve your needs.*

System Stored Procedures

As was discussed earlier in the book, SQL Server comes with a raft of "built-in" stored procedures to take care of this need or that. One of the nice things about these is that they are generally non-database specific. That is, you can call them by name regardless of what database is current.

Well, that notion of being non-database specific may sound appealing to you in some situations, so you may ask the question, "Can I create my own 'system' sprocs?" I'm glad you asked!

There are only a couple of things that differentiate a system sproc from a normal user sproc when you are creating them:

❑   They all start with sp_
❑   They all reside in the master database

Way back in Chapter 9 I set forth a script to perform a DBCC SHOWCONTIG on an index. At the time, I indicated that I would come back to that and show you how to create that script as a system stored procedure that you could easily call to monitor indexes in your system. Let's take a quick look at the code to do that:

```
USE master
GO

CREATE PROC sp_showcontig @TableName sysname, @IndexName sysname
AS
```

```
-- Declare my holding variables
DECLARE @ID int,
    @IdxID int

-- Set what I'm looking for
SET @ID = OBJECT_ID(@TableName)
-- Get the index id values
SELECT @IdxID = IndID
FROM sysindexes
WHERE id = @ID
    AND name = @IndexName

-- Get the info I'm really after
DBCC SHOWCONTIG (@id, @IdxID)
GO
```

Notice that I changed a couple of variables into parameters. Other than that change, I didn't really need to do anything special to make a sproc out of my script. Then I just created it in the master database and made sure to name it with an sp_ and voilà.

As I mentioned back in Chapter 9, the purpose this particular sproc serves – showing us the SHOWCONTIG output by table name – has now been incorporated right into SQL Server 2000. That said, this is still a handy one to keep around in case you are dealing with older versions of the product.

Let's test it to make sure that it really does run from anywhere:

```
USE Northwind

EXEC sp_showcontig [Order Details], PK_Order_Details
```

This should get us the expected results:

```
DBCC SHOWCONTIG scanning 'Order Details' table...
Table: 'Order Details' (325576198); index ID: 1, database ID: 6
TABLE level scan performed.
- Pages Scanned................................: 13
- Extents Scanned..............................: 2
- Extent Switches..............................: 1
- Avg. Pages per Extent........................: 6.5
- Scan Density [Best Count:Actual Count].......: 100.00% [2:2]
- Logical Scan Fragmentation ..................: 0.00%
- Extent Scan Fragmentation ...................: 50.00%
- Avg. Bytes Free per Page.....................: 2957.2
- Avg. Page Density (full).....................: 63.46%
DBCC execution completed. If DBCC printed error messages, contact your system administrator.
```

Some things to remember about system sprocs though:

❑ Since they reside in your master database rather than your application database, you need to think of them as part of a separate backup plan.

❑ Use them sparingly – you never know when Microsoft is going to decide to change something about how system sprocs work or even name one the same thing that you named yours! As such, you should only use them when you're really looking for one instance of a sproc to serve across multiple databases.

A Brief Look at Recursion

Recursion is one of those things that aren't used very often in programming. Still, it's also one of those things for which, when you need it, there never seems to be anything else that will quite do the trick. As a "just in case", a brief review of what recursion is seems in order.

The brief version is that **recursion** is the situation where a piece of code calls itself. A piece of code that calls itself is said to be **recursing**. The dangers here should be fairly self-evident – if it calls itself once, then what's to keep it from calling itself over and over again? The answer to that is *you*. That is, *you* need to make sure that if your code is going to be called recursively, you provide a **recursion check** to make sure you bail out when it's appropriate.

I'd love to say that the example I'm going to use is all neat and original – but it isn't. Indeed, for an example, I'm going to use the classic recursion example that's used with about every textbook recursion discussion I've ever seen – please accept my apologies now – it's just that it's an example that can be understood by just about anyone, so here we go.

So what is that classic example? Factorials. For those who have had a while since math class (or their last recursion discussion), a factorial is the value you get when you take a number and multiply it successively by that number less one, then the next value less one, and so on until you get to 1. For example, the factorial of 5 is 120 – that's 5*4*3*2*1.

So, let's look at an implementation of such a recursive sproc:

```
CREATE PROC spFactorial
@ValueIn int,
@ValueOut int OUTPUT
AS
DECLARE @InWorking int
DECLARE @OutWorking int
IF @ValueIn != 1
BEGIN
    SELECT @InWorking = @ValueIn - 1

    EXEC spFactorial @InWorking, @OutWorking OUTPUT

    SELECT @ValueOut = @ValueIn * @OutWorking
END
ELSE
BEGIN
    SELECT @ValueOut = 1
END
RETURN
GO
```

When you run this CREATE script, you will wind up with an informational message that indicates that:

Cannot add rows to sysdepends for the current stored procedure because it depends on the missing object 'spFactorial'. The stored procedure will still be created.

> Whenever SQL Server creates objects, it stores away dependency information so it knows which objects are dependent on what other objects. In this case, our sproc is dependent upon itself – but how can SQL Server set the dependency information on a sproc that doesn't exist yet? It's something of a "What came first, the chicken or the egg" kind of thing. For the most part, this is informational and not really something to worry about.

So, what we're doing is accepting a value in (that's the value we want a factorial of), and providing a value back out (the factorial value we've computed). The surprising part is that our sproc does not, in one step, do everything it needs to calculate the factorial. Instead, it just takes one number's worth of the factorial, and then turns around and calls itself. The second call will deal with just one number's worth, and then again call itself. This can go on and on up to a limit of 32 levels of recursion. Once SQL Server gets 32 levels deep, it will raise an error and end processing.

Let's try out our recursive sproc with a little script:

```
DECLARE @WorkingOut int
DECLARE @WorkingIn int
SELECT @WorkingIn = 5
EXEC spFactorial @WorkingIn, @WorkingOut OUTPUT

PRINT CAST(@WorkingIn AS varchar) + ' factorial is ' + CAST(@WorkingOut AS
varchar)
```

This gets us the expected result of 120:

5 factorial is 120

You can try different values for `@WorkingIn`, and things should work just fine with two rather significant hitches:

❑　Arithmetic overflow when our factorial grows too large for the int (or even bigint) data type

❑　The 32 level recursion limit

You can test the arithmetic overflow easily by putting any large number in – anything bigger than about 13 will work for this example.

Testing the 32 level recursion limit takes a little bit more modification to our sproc. This time, we'll determine the **triangular** of the number. This is very similar to finding the factorial, except that we use addition rather than multiplication. Therefore, 5 triangular is just 15 (5+4+3+2+1). Let's create a new sproc to test this one out – it will look almost just like the factorial sproc with only a few small changes:

```
CREATE PROC spTriangular
@ValueIn int,
@ValueOut int OUTPUT
AS
DECLARE @InWorking int
DECLARE @OutWorking int
IF @ValueIn != 1
BEGIN
        SELECT @InWorking = @ValueIn - 1
```

```
        EXEC spTriangular @InWorking, @OutWorking OUTPUT

        SELECT @ValueOut = @ValueIn + @OutWorking
END
ELSE
BEGIN
        SELECT @ValueOut = 1
END
RETURN
GO
```

As you can see, there weren't that many changes to be made. Similarly, we only need to change our sproc call and the PRINT text for our test script:

```
DECLARE @WorkingOut int
DECLARE @WorkingIn int
SELECT @WorkingIn = 5
EXEC spTriangular @WorkingIn, @WorkingOut OUTPUT

PRINT CAST(@WorkingIn AS varchar) + ' Triangular is ' + CAST(@WorkingOut AS
varchar)
```

Running this with a @ValueIn of 5 gets our expected 15:

5 Triangular is 15

However, if you try to run it with a @ValueIn of more than 32, you get an error:.

Server: Msg 217, Level 16, State 1, Procedure spTriangular, Line 11
Maximum stored procedure, function or trigger nesting level exceeded (limit 32).

I'd love to say there's some great workaround to this, but, unless you can somehow segment your recursive calls (run it 32 levels deep, then come all the way back out of the call stack, then run down it again), you're pretty much out of luck. Just keep in mind that most recursive functions can be rewritten to be a more standard looping construct – which doesn't have any hard limit. Be sure you can't use a loop before you force yourself into recursion.

Debugging

New in SQL Server 2000 is the addition of real-live debugging tools. Prior to this release, our primary form of debugging was something that many ASP programmers would relate to a Response.Write – that is, we would just stick PRINT or SELECT statements in here and there to print out the current value of variables as different code was being executed in the sproc. Often you would wind up moving these around repeatedly until you finally homed in on the particular piece of code that was causing the problems.

Thankfully, those days are pretty much gone. The new tools are perhaps not as robust as those found for debugging VB or C++ code, but they are a positively mammoth step forward, and include such debugging favorites as a call stack (as it implies, you can step from one sproc into another), a locals window, and even step debugging.

Setting up SQL Server for Debugging

Depending on the nature of your installation, you may have to do absolutely nothing in order to get debugging working. If, however, you took the default path and installed your SQL Server to run using the LocalSystem account, then debugging will either not work at all or will have problems. The upshot of this is that, if you want to use debugging, then you really need to configure the SQL Server service to run using an actual user account – preferably one with admin access to the box the SQL Server is running on.

If you try to run the T-SQL Debugger while SQL Server is set up to use the LocalSystem account, then you should wind up with a dialog box coming up that looks like this:

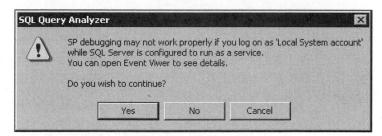

If this happens, you'll need to make the change to having your SQL Server use an actual user account (either that or go without debugging!). Technically, the Debugger will still function while using the LocalSystem account, but you'll find enough of the functions non-functional to make it worthless (for example, you can't set a breakpoint or use the step debugger – which gives you no way to stop and look at things).

> *Having SQL Server run using an account with admin access is definitely something that most security experts would gag, cough, and choke at. It's a major security loophole. Why? Well, there are things, such as running xp_cmdshell, which would wind up running with admin access also. Imagine any user who could get to xp_cmdshell also being able to delete any file on your box, move things around, or possibly worse. This is a "Development System Only" kind of thing. Also, make sure that you're using a local admin account rather than a domain admin.*

To deal with the issue of having SQL Server use an actual login account, use Enterprise Manger. To set the startup account using the Enterprise Manager, just right-click on your server and select **Properties**, then navigate to the **Security** tab:

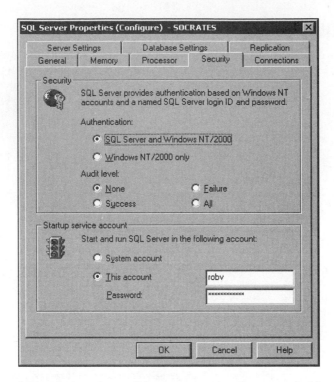

In the lower section of this tab, type in a valid user account and password. After this is done, the Debugger should function normally.

Starting the Debugger

Much of using the Debugger works as it does in VB or C++ – probably like most modern debuggers for that matter.

Before we get too far into this, I'm going to warn you that, while the Debugger is great in many respects, it leaves something to be desired in terms of how easy it is to find it. Pay attention to the steps we'll have to walk through in order to find it and you'll see what I mean.

OK, to get the Debugger going, the first thing that you need to do is make sure that you have the Object Browser open in the Query Analyzer. In case you closed down the Object Browser (most likely to get back a little screen real estate), you can reopen it with the Object Browser icon on the toolbar or by going to the Tools | Object Browser menu option, or by simply pressing *F8*.

Next comes the relatively tricky part – we need to navigate in the Object Browser to the sproc (or UDF) that we want to debug and right-click. In our case, we want to navigate to the spTriangular stored procedure that we created in the last section, and right-click on it:

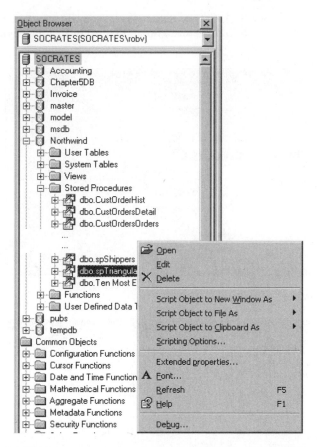

As you might guess, the Debug option is the one we're looking for. When it's selected, it brings up a dialog box that we can use to get our sproc going:

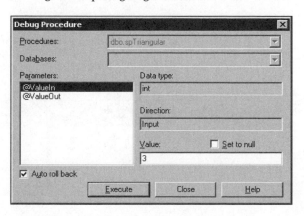

We need to set each non-optional parameter's value before the sproc can run. For the @ValueIn, we'll just set it to 3 – that will allow us to recurse just a bit and let us look into a few extra features. For the @ValueOut, let's use the **Set to null** option:

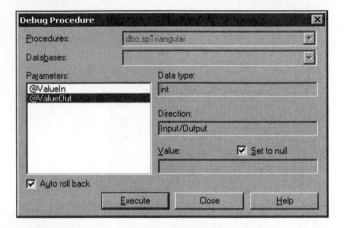

Then just click on **Execute**:

Parts of the Debugger

Several things are worth noticing when the Debugger window first comes up:

- ❑ The yellow arrow on the left indicates the **current row** – this is the next line of code that will be executed if we do a "go" or we start stepping through the code.

- ❑ There are icons at the top to indicate our different options, including:

  - ❑ Go: this will run to the end of the sproc. After you click this, the only thing that will stop execution is a run-time error or hitting a breakpoint.

  - ❑ Toggle Breakpoints and Remove All Breakpoints: these are points that you set to tell SQL Server to "stop here!" when the code is running in debug mode. This is handy in big sprocs or functions where you don't want to have to deal with every line – you just want it to run up to a point and stop every time it gets there.

  - ❑ Step Into: this executes the next line of code and stops prior to running the next line of code regardless of what procedure or function that code is in. If the line of code being executed is calling a sproc or function, then Step Into has the effect of calling that sproc or function, adding it to the call stack, changing the locals window to represent the newly nested sproc rather than the parent, and then stopping at the first line of code in the nested sproc.

  - ❑ Step Over: this executes every line of code required to take us to the next statement that is at the same level in the call stack. If you are not calling another sproc or a UDF, then this command will act just like a Step Into. If, however, you are calling another sproc or a UDF, then a Step Over will take you to the statement immediately following where that sproc or UDF returned its value.

  - ❑ Step Out: this executes every line of code up to the next line of code at the next highest point in the call stack. That is, we will keep running until we reach the same level as whatever code called the level we are currently at.

  - ❑ Run To Cursor: this works pretty much like the combination of a breakpoint and a Go. When this choice is made, the code will start running and keep going until it gets to the current cursor location. The only exceptions are if there is a breakpoint prior to the cursor location (then it stops at the breakpoint instead) or if the end of the sproc comes before the cursor line is executed (such as when you place the cursor on a line that has already occurred or is in part of a control-of-flow statement that does not get executed).

  - ❑ Restart: this does exactly what it says it does. It sets the parameters back to their original values, clears any variables and the call stack, and starts over.

  - ❑ Stop Debugging: again, this does what it says – it stops execution immediately. The debugging window does remain open, however.

  - ❑ Auto Rollback: this automatically wraps the executed code in a transaction and, when processing terminates, automatically rolls back the transaction. The importance of this will become more clear when we get to our chapter on transactions. This is the default option.

There are also four of what we'll call "status" windows, let's go through these one by one...

The Locals Window

As I indicated back at the beginning of the book, I'm pretty much assuming that you have experience with some procedural language out there. As such, the Locals window probably isn't all that new of a concept to you. The simple rendition is that it shows you the current value of all the variables that are currently in scope. The list of variables in the Locals window may change (as may their values) as you step into nested sprocs and back out again. Remember – these are only those variables that are in scope as of the next statement to run.

Three pieces of information are provided for each variable or parameter:

- ❏ The name
- ❏ The current value
- ❏ The data type

However, perhaps the best part to the Locals window is that you can edit the values in each variable. That means it's a lot easier to change things on the fly to test certain behaviors in your sproc.

The Globals Window

The Globals window provides basically the same information as the Locals window does, only this time, for global variables. The downside is that you can't edit global variables the way you can with local variables.

The Callstack Window

The Callstack window provides a listing of all the sprocs and functions that are currently active in the process that you are running. The handy thing here is that you can see how far in you are when you are running in a nested situation, and you can change between the nesting levels to verify what current variable values are at each level.

The Output Window

Much as this one sounds, the Output window is the spot where SQL Server prints any output. This includes resultsets as well as the return value when your sproc has completed running.

Using the Debugger once It's Started

Now that we have the preliminaries out of the way and the Debugger window up, we're ready to start walking through our code.

The first executable line of our sproc is the IF statement, so that's the line that is current when the Debugger starts up. You should notice that none of our variables has had any values set in it yet except for the @ValueIn that we passed in as a parameter to the sproc – it has the value of 3 that we passed in when we filled out the Debug Procedure dialog earlier.

Step forward one line by pressing *F11* or using the Step Into icon or menu choice.

Since the value of @ValueIn is indeed not equal to 1, we step into the BEGIN...END block specified by our IF statement. Specifically, we move to our SELECT statement that initializes the @InWorking parameter. As we'll see later, if the value of @ValueIn had indeed been one, we would have immediately dropped down to our ELSE statement.

Again, step forward one line by pressing *F11* or using the Step Into icon or menu choice:

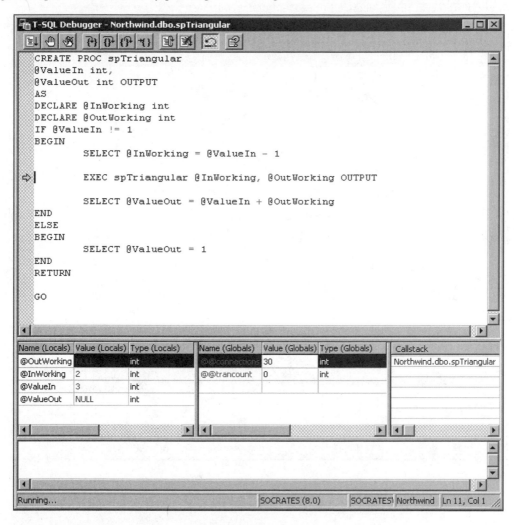

Pay particular attention to the value of @InWorking in the Locals window. Notice that it changed to the correct value (@ValueIn is currently 3, so 3-1 is 2) as set by our SELECT statement. Also notice that our Callstack window only has the current instance of our sproc in it – since we haven't stepped down into our nested versions of the sproc yet, we only see one instance.

Now go ahead and step into our next statement. Since this is the execution of a sproc, we're going to see a number of different things change in our Debugger window:

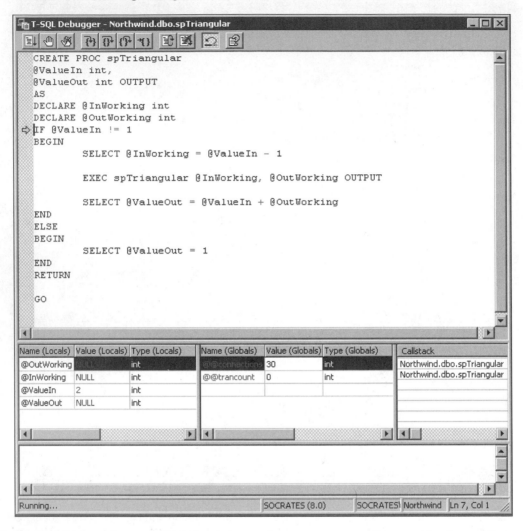

Notice that it *appears* that our arrow that indicates the current statement jumped back up to the IF statement. Why? Well, this is a new instance of our sproc. We can tell this based on our Callstack window – notice that it now has two instances of our sproc listed. The blue one at the top is the current instance. Notice also that the @ValueIn parameter has the value of 2 – that is the value we passed in from the outer instance of the sproc.

If you want to see the value of variables in the scope of the outer instance of the sproc, just click on that instance's line in the Callstack window (the one with the black font) and you'll see several things change again:

There are two things to notice here. First, the values of our variables have changed back to those in the scope of the outer (and currently selected) instance of the sproc. Second, the icon for our current execution line is different. This new green arrow is meant to show that this is the current line in this instance of the sproc, but it is not the current line in the overall callstack.

Go back to the current instance by clicking on the top item in the Callstack window. Then step in three more times. This should bring you to the top line (the IF statement) in our third instance of the sproc. Notice that our callstack has become three deep, and that the values of our variables and parameters in the Locals window have changed again. Last, but not least, notice that this time our @ValueIn parameter has a value of 1.

Step into the code one more time, and you'll see a slight change in behavior. This time, since the value in @ValueIn is indeed equal to 1, we move into the BEGIN...END block defined with our ELSE statement:

Since we've reached the bottom, we're ready to start going back up the callstack. Two more steps will find you back out to the second level in our stack:

Notice that our callstack is back to only two levels. Also, notice that our output parameter (@OutWorking) has been appropriately set.

This time, let's do something different and do a **Step Out** (*Shift+F11*). If you're not careful, it will look like absolutely nothing has changed:

In this case, to use the old cliché, looks are deceiving. Again, notice the change in the **Callstack** window and in the values in the **Locals** window – we stepped *out* of what was then the current instance of the sproc and moved up a level in the callstack. If you now keep stepping into the code (*F11*), then our sproc has finished running and we'll see the final version of our status windows and their respective finishing values:

A *big* word of caution here! If you want to be able to see the truly final values (such as an output parameter being set), make *sure* that you use the **Step Into** option to execute the last line of code.

If you use an option that executes several lines at once, such as a **Go** or **Step Out**, what you'll see in the final values list will be the values as of the last time you had a pause in execution. This is a known issue with the dev team, so it could possibly be fixed in a service pack, but the RTM product has no fix in place for this.

A workaround is to place a break point on the last point at which you expect to perform a RETURN in the outermost instance of your sproc. That way, you can run in whatever debug mode you want, but use the **Step Into** option to execute that final line.

The grayed out Locals window is our hint that we have completed the full execution of the sproc we're running. If you need something more explicit, just check out the bottom left of the window (in the status bar), notice that it indicates that we have Completed our run.

So, you should now be able to see how the Debugger can be very handy indeed.

Summary

Wow! That's a lot to have to take in for one chapter. Still, this is among the most important chapters in the book in terms of being able to function as a developer in SQL Server.

Sprocs are the backbone of code in SQL Server. We can create reusable code, and get improved performance and flexibility at the same time. We can use a variety of programming constructs that you might be familiar with from other languages, but sprocs aren't meant for everything.

Pros to sprocs include:

- ❑ Usually better performance

- ❑ Possible use as a security insulation layer (control how a database is accessed and updated)

- ❑ Reusable code

- ❑ Compartmentalization of code (can encapsulate business logic)

- ❑ Flexible execution depending on dynamics established at run time

Cons to sprocs include:

- ❑ Not portable across platforms (Oracle, for example has a completely different kind of implementation of sprocs)

- ❑ May get locked into the wrong execution plan in some circumstances (actually hurting performance)

Sprocs are not the solution to everything, but they are still the cornerstones of SQL Server programming. In the next chapter, we'll take a look at the sprocs brand new, and very closely related cousin – the UDF.

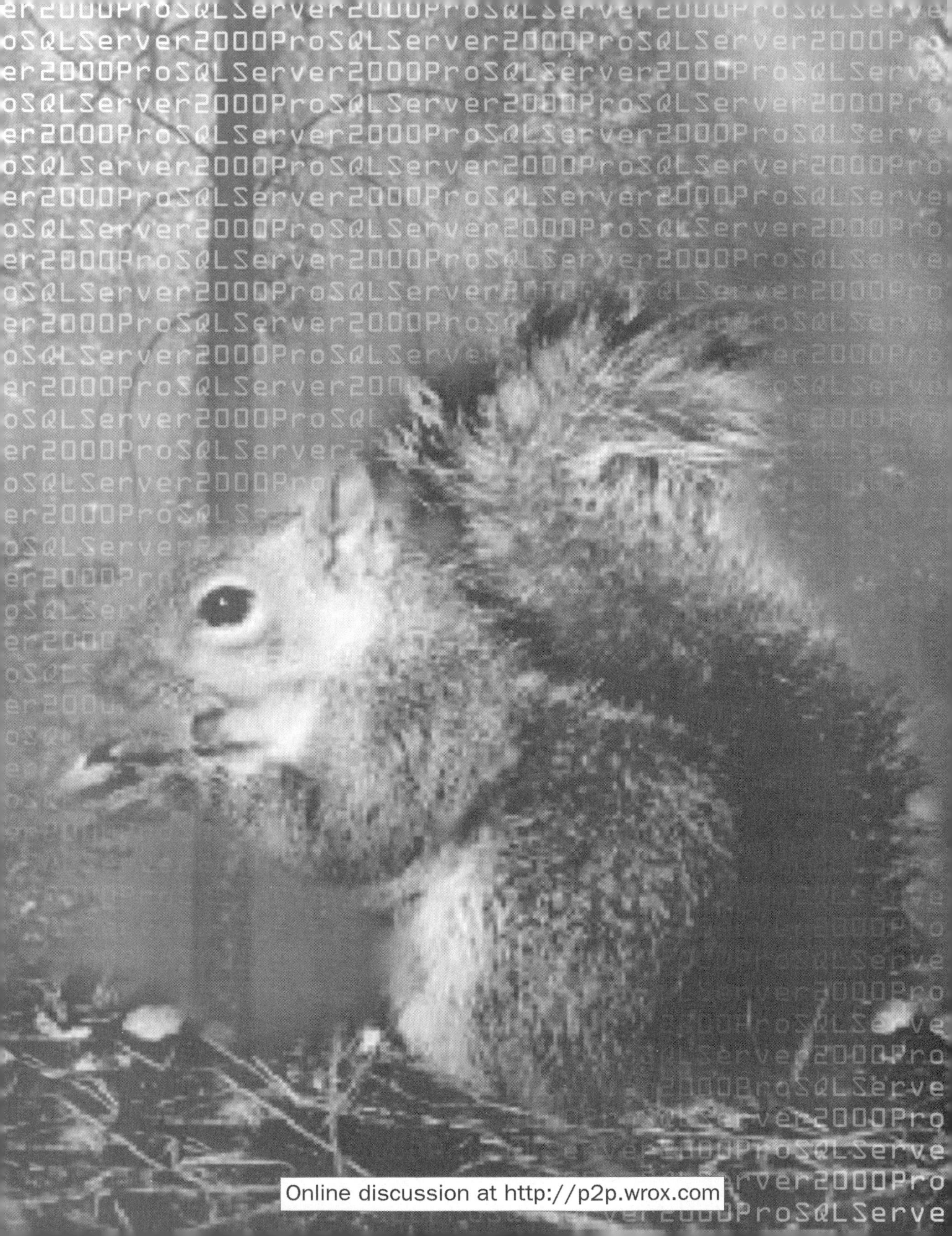
Online discussion at http://p2p.wrox.com

13

User Defined Functions

Those who know me have seen me jump up and down and do about everything short of downright squeal with joy to finally have this topic to talk (or in this case write) about. I know, I know – a pretty silly behavior for a grown man, but I've been waiting for these a long time (if you haven't guessed, they are new with this release). Add in the fact that Microsoft made them even better than I expected, and you have one very happy database dude.

Another nice thing about **User Defined Functions** – or **UDF**s – beside the fact that they are actually finally here, is that, provided you've done the book in order, you already know most of what you need to know to write them. They are actually very, very similar to stored procedures – they just have certain behaviors and capabilities about them that set them apart and make them *the* answer in many situations.

In this chapter, we're not only going to introduce what UDFs are, but we're also going to take a look at the different types of UDFs, how they vary from stored procedures, and, of course, what kind of situations we might want to use them in.

What a UDF Is

A user-defined function is, much like a sproc, an ordered set of T-SQL statements that are pre-optimized and compiled and can be called to work as a single unit. The primary difference between them is how results are returned. Due to things that need to happen in order to support these different kinds of returned values, UDFs have a few more limitations to them than sprocs do.

> *OK, so I've said what a UDF is, so I suspect I ought to take a moment and say what it is not. A UDF is definitely NOT a replacement for a sproc – they are just a new option that offers us a new kind of code flexibility that we never had before.*

With a sproc, you can pass parameters in, and also get values in parameters passed back out. You can return a value, but that value is really intended to indicate success or failure rather than return data. You can also return result sets, but you can't really use those result sets in a query without first inserting them into some kind of table (usually a temporary table) to work with them further.

With a UDF, however, you can pass parameters *in*, but not out. Instead, the concept of output parameters has been replaced with a much more robust return value. As with system functions, you can return a scalar value. What's nice is that this value is not limited to just the integer data type as it would be for a sproc. Instead, you can return most SQL Server data types (more on this in the next section).

As they like to say in late night television commercials: "But Wait! There's more!" The "more" is that you are actually not just limited to returning scalar values – you can also return tables. This is wildly powerful, and we'll look into this fully later in the chapter.

So, to summarize, we have two types of UDFs:

❑   Those that return a scalar value

❑   Those that return a table

Let's take a look at the general syntax for creating a UDF:

```
CREATE FUNCTION [owner_name.]function_name
    ( [ <@parameter name> <scalar data type> [ = <default value>]
    [ ,...n ] ] )
RETURNS {<scalar type>|TABLE}
    [ WITH {ENCRYPTION|SCHEMABINDING|}]
AS
BEGIN
    [<function statements>]
    {RETURN <type as defined in RETURNS clause>|RETURN (<SELECT statement>)}
END
```

This is kind of a tough one to explain because parts of the optional syntax are dependent on the choices you make elsewhere in your CREATE statement. The big issue here is whether you are returning a scalar data type or a table, so let's look at each type individually.

UDFs Returning a Scalar Value

This type of UDF was originally the only type I was expecting Microsoft to give us (but, in this case, I like surprises), and is probably the most like what you might expect a function to be. Much like SQL Server's own built-in functions, they will return a scalar value to the calling script or procedure; the functions that are built into SQL Server (such as `GETDATE()` or `USER()`) return scalar values.

As I indicated earlier, one of the truly great things about a UDF is that you are not limited to an integer for a return value – instead, it can be of any valid SQL Server data type, except for BLOBs, cursors, and timestamps. Even if you wanted to return an integer, a UDF should look very attractive to you for two different reasons:

1. Unlike sprocs, the whole purpose of the return value is to serve as a meaningful piece of data – for sprocs, a return value is meant as an indication of success or failure, and, in the event of failure, to provide some specific information about the nature of that failure.

2. You can perform functions in-line to your queries (for instances, include it as part of your `SELECT` statement) – you can't do that with a sproc.

So, that said, let's create a simple UDF to get our feet wet on the whole idea of how we might utilize them differently from a sproc. I'm not kidding when I say this is a simple one from a code point of view, but I think you'll see how it illustrates my sprocs versus UDFs point.

One of the most common function-like requirements I see is a desire to see if an entry in a datetime field occurred on a specific day. The usual problem here is that your datetime field has specific time-of-day information that prevents it from easily being compared with just the date. Indeed, we've already seen this problem in some of our comparisons in previous chapters.

Let's go back to our Accounting database that we created in an earlier chapter. Imagine for a moment that we want to know all the orders that came in today. Let's start by adding a few orders in with today's date. We'll just pick customer and employee IDs we know already exist in their respective tables (if you don't have any records there, you'll need to insert a couple of dummy rows to reference). I'm also going to create a small loop to add in several rows:

```
USE Accounting

DECLARE @Counter   int

SET @Counter = 1
WHILE @Counter <= 10
BEGIN
    INSERT INTO Orders
        VALUES (1, DATEADD(mi,@Counter,GETDATE()), 1)
    SET @Counter = @Counter + 1
END
```

So, this gets us 10 rows inserted, with each row being inserted with today's date, but one minute apart from each other.

OK, if you're running this just before midnight, some of the rows may dribble over into the next day, so be careful – but it will work fine for everyone except the night owls.

So, now we're ready to run a simple query to see what orders we have today. We might try something like:

```
SELECT *
FROM Orders
WHERE OrderDate = GETDATE()
```

Unfortunately, this query will not get us anything back at all. This is because GETDATE() gets the current time down to the millisecond – not just the day. This means that any query based on GETDATE() is very unlikely to return us any data – even if it happened on the same day (it would have had to have happened within in the same minute for a smalldatetime, and within a millisecond for a full datetime field).

The typical solution is to convert the date to a string and back in order to truncate the time information, then perform the comparison.

It might look something like:

```
SELECT *
FROM Orders
WHERE CONVERT(varchar(12), OrderDate, 101) = CONVERT(varchar(12), GETDATE(), 101)
```

This time, we will get back every row with today's date in the OrderDate column – regardless of what time of day the order was taken. Unfortunately, this isn't exactly the most readable code. Imagine you had a large series of dates you needed to perform such comparisons against – it can get very ugly indeed.

So now let's look at doing the same thing with a simple user-defined function. First, we'll need to create the actual function. This is done with the new CREATE FUNCTION command, and it's formatted much like a sproc. For example, we might code this function like this:

```
CREATE FUNCTION dbo.DayOnly(@Date datetime)
RETURNS varchar(12)
AS
BEGIN
    RETURN CONVERT(varchar(12), @Date, 101)
END
```

where the date returned from GETDATE() is passed in as the parameter and the task of converting the date is included in the function body and the truncated date is returned.

To see this function in action, let's reformat our query slightly:

```
SELECT *
FROM Orders
WHERE dbo.DayOnly(OrderDate) = dbo.DayOnly(GETDATE())
```

We get back the same set as with the stand-alone query. Even for a simple query like this one, the new code is quite a bit more readable. The call works pretty much as it would from most languages that support functions. There is, however, one hitch – the schema (owner) is required. SQL Server will, for some reason, not resolve functions the way it does with other objects.

As you might expect, there is a lot more to UDFs than just readability though. You can embed queries in them and use them as an encapsulation method for subqueries. Almost anything you can do procedurally that returns a discrete value could also be encapsulated in a UDF and used inline with your queries.

Let's take a look at encapsulating the stock subquery example that is used in books online. The subquery version looks like this:

```
USE pubs
SELECT Title,
    Price,
    (SELECT AVG(Price) FROM Titles) AS Average, Price - (SELECT AVG(Price) FROM
Titles)
        AS Difference
FROM Titles
WHERE Type='popular_comp'
```

This gets us back a pretty simple set of data:

Title	Price	Average	Difference
But Is It User Friendly?	22.9500	14.7662	8.1838
Secrets of Silicon Valley	20.0000	14.7662	5.2338
Net Etiquette	NULL	14.7662	NULL

(3 row(s) affected)

Warning: Null value is eliminated by an aggregate or other SET operation.

Let's try it again, only this time we'll encapsulate both the average and the difference into two functions. The first encapsulates the task of calculating the average and the second does the subtraction.

```
CREATE FUNCTION dbo.AveragePrice()
RETURNS money
WITH SCHEMABINDING
AS
BEGIN
    RETURN (SELECT AVG(Price) FROM dbo.Titles)
END
GO

CREATE FUNCTION dbo.PriceDifference(@Price money)
RETURNS money
AS
BEGIN
    RETURN @Price - dbo.AveragePrice()
END
```

Notice that it's completely legal to embed one UDF in another one.

Note that the WITH SCHEMABINDING *option works for functions just the way that it did for views – if a function is built using schema-binding, then any object that function depends on cannot be altered or dropped without first removing the schema-bound function. In this case, schema-binding wasn't really necessary, but I wanted to point out its usage and also prepare this example for something we're going to do with it a little later in the chapter.*

Now let's run our query using the new functions instead of the old subquery model:

```
USE pubs
SELECT Title,
    Price,
    dbo.AveragePrice() AS Average,
    dbo.PriceDifference(Price) AS Difference
FROM Titles
WHERE Type='popular_comp'
```

This yields us the same results we had with our subquery, but without the warning!

Note that, beyond the readability issue, we also get added benefit of reuse out of this. For a little example like this, it probably doesn't seem like a big deal, but as your functions become more complex, it can be quite a time saver.

UDFs that Return a Table

SQL Server's new user-defined functions are not limited to just returning scalar values. They can return something far more interesting – tables. Now, while the possible impacts of this are sinking in on you, I'll go ahead and add that the table that is returned is, for the most part, usable much as any other table is. You can perform a JOIN against it and even apply WHERE conditions against the results. It's *very* cool stuff indeed.

To make the change to using a table as a return value is not hard at all – a table is just like any other SQL Server data type as far as a UDF is concerned. To illustrate this, we'll build a relatively simple one to start:

```
USE pubs
GO

CREATE FUNCTION dbo.fnAuthorList()
RETURNS TABLE
AS
RETURN (SELECT au_id,
            au_lname + ', ' + au_fname AS au_name,
            address AS address1,
            city + ', ' + state + ' ' + zip AS address2
        FROM authors)
GO
```

This function returns a table of SELECTed records and does a little formatting: joining the last and first names, separating them with a comma, and concatenating the three components to fill the address2 column.

At this point, we're ready to use our function just as we would use a table – the only exception is that, as was discussed with scalar functions, we *must* use the two-part naming convention:

```
SELECT *
FROM dbo.fnAuthorList()
```

The results are a bit lengthy, so I've clipped out the middle of them, but you should get the picture:

au_id	au_name	address1	address2
172-32-1176	White, Johnson	10932 Bigge Rd.	Menlo Park, CA 94025
213-46-8915	Green, Marjorie	309 63rd St. #411	Oakland, CA 94618
238-95-7766	Carson, Cheryl	539 Darwin Ln.	Berkeley, CA 94705
...			
...			
893-72-1158	McBadden, Heather	301 Putnam	Vacaville, CA 95688
899-46-2035	Ringer, Anne	67 Seventh Av.	Salt Lake City, UT 84152
998-72-3567	Ringer, Albert	67 Seventh Av.	Salt Lake City, UT 84152

Now, let's add a bit more fun into things. What we did with this table up to this point could have been done just as easily – easier in fact – with a view. But what if we wanted to parameterize a view? What if we only wanted this to show authors who had sold at least certain quantity of books? We could do this with a view by joining with another table or two, but, then again, things get a bit messy and we would wind up having to include a column in our view we don't necessarily want (the sales quantity) and then use a WHERE clause. It might look something like this:

```
--CREATE our view
CREATE VIEW vSalesCount
AS
    SELECT au.au_id,
        au.au_lname + ', ' + au.au_fname AS au_name,
        au.address,
        au.city + ', ' + au.state + ' ' + zip AS address2,
        SUM(s.qty) As SalesCount
    FROM authors au
    JOIN titleauthor ta
        ON au.au_id = ta.au_id
    JOIN sales s
        ON ta.title_id = s.title_id
    GROUP BY au.au_id,
        au.au_lname + ', ' + au.au_fname,
        au.address,
        au.city + ', ' + au.state + ' ' + zip
GO
```

This would yield us what was asked for, with a few twists. First, we can't parameterize things right in the view itself, so we're going to have to include a WHERE clause in our query. Second, we'll need to provide a specific SELECT list to filter out the vSalesCount column (remember, we want to show the authors who sold over a specific value, but not necessarily their actual sales):

```
SELECT au_name, address, Address2 FROM vSalesCount
WHERE SalesCount > 25
```

This should get you results that look something like this:

au_name	address	Address2
Green, Marjorie	309 63rd St. #411	Oakland, CA 94618
Carson, Cheryl	589 Darwin Ln.	Berkeley, CA 94705
O'Leary, Michael	22 Cleveland Av. #14	San Jose, CA 95128
Dull, Ann	3410 Blonde St.	Palo Alto, CA 94301
DeFrance, Michel	3 Balding Pl.	Gary, IN 46403
MacFeather, Stearns	44 Upland Hts.	Oakland, CA 94612
Panteley, Sylvia	1956 Arlington Pl.	Rockville, MD 20853
Hunter, Sheryl	3410 Blonde St.	Palo Alto, CA 94301
Ringer, Anne	67 Seventh Av.	Salt Lake City, UT 84152
Ringer, Albert	67 Seventh Av.	Salt Lake City, UT 84152

To simplify things a bit, we'll encapsulate everything in a function instead:

```
USE pubs
GO

CREATE FUNCTION dbo.fnSalesCount(@SalesQty bigint)
RETURNS TABLE
AS
RETURN (SELECT au.au_id,
           au.au_lname + ', ' + au.au_fname AS au_name,
           au.address,
           au.city + ', ' + au.state + ' ' + zip AS Address2
       FROM authors au
       JOIN titleauthor ta
           ON au.au_id = ta.au_id
       JOIN sales s
           ON ta.title_id = s.title_id
       GROUP BY au.au_id,
           au.au_lname + ', ' + au.au_fname,
           au.address,
           au.city + ', ' + au.state + ' ' + zip
       HAVING SUM(qty) > @SalesQty
       )
GO
```

Now we're set up pretty well – to execute it, we just call the function and provide the parameter:

```
SELECT *
FROM dbo.fnSalesCount(25)
```

And we get back the same result set – no WHERE clause, no filtering the SELECT list, and, as our friends down under would say, "no worries", we can use this over and over again without having to use the old "cut and paste" trick. Note, also, that while you could have achieved similar results with a sproc and an EXEC command, you couldn't directly join the results of the sproc to another table.

To illustrate this, let's take our example just one step further. Let's say that you have a manager who wants a report listing the author and the publisher(s) for every author who's sold over 25 books. With a stored procedure, you couldn't join to the results, so you would pretty much be out of luck (I can think of one several step processes to do this, but it isn't pretty at all). With our function, this is no problem:

```
SELECT DISTINCT p.pub_name, a.au_name
FROM dbo.fnSalesCount(25) AS a
JOIN titleauthor AS ta
   ON a.au_id = ta.au_id
JOIN titles AS t
   ON ta.title_id = t.title_id
JOIN publishers AS p
   ON t.pub_id = p.pub_id
```

We get back our author listing along with all the different publishers that they have:

pub_name	au_name
Algodata Infosystems	Carson, Cheryl
Binnet & Hardley	DeFrance, Michel
Algodata Infosystems	Dull, Ann
Algodata Infosystems	Green, Marjorie
New Moon Books	Green, Marjorie
Algodata Infosystems	Hunter, Sheryl
Algodata Infosystems	MacFeather, Stearns
Binnet & Hardley	MacFeather, Stearns
Algodata Infosystems	O'Leary, Michael
Binnet & Hardley	O'Leary, Michael
Binnet & Hardley	Panteley, Sylvia
New Moon Books	Ringer, Albert
Binnet & Hardley	Ringer, Anne
New Moon Books	Ringer, Anne

As you can see, we joined to the function just as if it were a table or view. The only real difference is that we were allowed to parameterize it.

Well, all this would probably be exciting enough, but sometimes we need more than just a single SELECT statement. Sometimes, we want more than just a parameterized view. Indeed, much as we saw with some of our scalar functions, we may need to execute multiple statements in order to achieve the results that we want. User-defined functions support this notion just fine. Indeed, they can return tables that are created using multiple statements, as we've seen in a single statement function – the only big difference is that you must both name and define the meta-data (much as you would a temporary table) for what you'll be returning.

For this example, we'll deal with a very common problem in the relational database world – hierarchies. Imagine for a moment that you are working in the Human Resources department for Northwind. You have an Employees table, and it has a unary relationship that relates each employee to their boss through the ReportsTo column – that is, the way you know who someone's boss is by relating the ReportsTo column back to another EmployeeID. A very common need in a scenario like this is to be able to create a reporting "tree" – that is, a list of all of the people who exist below a given manager in an organization chart.

At first blush, this would seem pretty easy. If we wanted to know all the people who report to Andrew Fuller, we might write a query that would join the Employees table back to itself – something like:

```
Use Northwind

SELECT Emp.EmployeeID, Emp.LastName, Emp.FirstName, Emp.ReportsTo
FROM Employees AS Emp
JOIN Employees AS Mgr
    ON Mgr.EmployeeID = Emp.ReportsTo
WHERE Mgr.LastName = 'Fuller'
    AND Mgr.FirstName = 'Andrew'
```

Again, at first glance, this might appear to give us what we want:

EmployeeID	LastName	FirstName	ReportsTo
1	Davolio	Nancy	2
3	Leverling	Janet	2
4	Peacock	Margaret	2
5	Buchanan	Steven	2
8	Callahan	Laura	2

(5 row(s) affected)

But, in reality, we have a bit of a problem here. At issue is that we want all of the people in Andrew Fuller's reporting chain – not just those who report to Andrew Fuller, but those who report to people who report to Andrew Fuller, and so on. You see that if you look at all the records in Northwind, you'll find a number of employees who report to Steven Buchanan, but they don't appear in the results of this query.

OK, so some of the quicker or more experienced among you may now be saying something like, "Hey, no problem! I'll just join back to the Employees table one more time!" You could probably make this work for such a small data set, or any situation where the number of levels of your hierarchy is fixed – but what if the number of hierarchy levels isn't fixed? What if people are reporting to Steven Buchanan, and still others report to people under Steven Buchanan – it could go on virtually forever. Now what? Glad you asked...

What we really need is a function that will return all the levels of the hierarchy below whatever `EmployeeID` (and, therefore, `ManagerID`) we provide. To do this, we have a classic example of **recursion**. A block of code is said to recurse anytime it calls itself. We saw an example of this in our last chapter with our `spFactorial` and `spTriangular` stored procedures. Let's think about this scenario for a moment:

1. We need to figure out all the people who report to the manager that we want

2. For each person in #1 above, we need to know who reports to them

3. Repeat # 2 until there are no more subordinates

This is recursion all the way. What this means is that we're going to need several statements to make our function work. Some statements to figure out the current level, and at least one more to call the same function again to get the next lowest level.

> *Keep in mind that UDFs are going to have the same recursion limits that sprocs had – that is, you can only go to 32 levels of recursion, so, if you have a chance of running into this limit, you'll want to get creative in your code to avoid errors.*

Let's put it together. Notice the couple of changes in the declaration of our function. This time, we need to associate a name with the return value (in this case, `@Reports`) – this is required anytime you're using multiple statements to generate your result. Also, we have to define the table that we will be returning – this allows SQL Server to validate whatever we try to insert into that table before it is returned to the calling routine.

```
CREATE FUNCTION dbo.fnGetReports
     (@EmployeeID AS int)
     RETURNS @Reports TABLE
     (
     EmployeeID     int          NOT NULL,
     ReportsToID    int          NULL
     )
AS
BEGIN

/* Since we'll need to call this function recursively - that is once for each
reporting
** employee (to make sure that they don't have reports of their own), we need a
holding
** variable to keep track of which employee we're currently working on. */
DECLARE @Employee AS int

/* This inserts the current employee into our working table. The significance here
is
** that we need the first record as something of a primer due to the recursive
nature
** of the function - this is how we get it. */
INSERT INTO @Reports
    SELECT EmployeeID, ReportsTo
    FROM Employees
    WHERE EmployeeID = @EmployeeID
```

```
/* Now we also need a primer for the recursive calls we're getting ready to start
making
** to this function. This would probably be better done with a cursor, but we
haven't
** gotten to that chapter yet, so.... */
SELECT @Employee = MIN(EmployeeID)
FROM Employees
WHERE ReportsTo = @EmployeeID

/* This next part would probably be better done with a cursor but we haven't
gotten to
** that chapter yet, so we'll fake it. Notice the recursive call to our function!
*/
WHILE @Employee IS NOT NULL
    BEGIN
        INSERT INTO @Reports
            SELECT *
            FROM fnGetReports(@Employee)

            SELECT @Employee = MIN(EmployeeID)
            FROM Employees
            WHERE EmployeeID > @Employee
                AND ReportsTo = @EmployeeID
    END

RETURN

END
GO
```

I've written this one to provide just minimal information about the employee and their manager – I can join back to the Employees table if need be to fetch additional information. I also took a little bit of liberty with the requirements on this one, and added in the selected manager to the results. This was done primarily to support the recursion scenario and also to provide something of a base result for our result set. Speaking of which, let's look at our results – Andrew Fuller is EmployeeID #2, so we'll feed that into our function:

```
SELECT * FROM fnGetReports(2)
```

This gets us not only the original 5 people who reported to Andrew Fuller, but also those who report to Steven Buchanan (who reports to Mr. Fuller) and Mr. Fuller himself (remember, I added him in as something of a starting point).

EmployeeID	ReportsToID
2	NULL
1	2
3	2
4	2
5	2
6	5
7	5
9	5
8	2

(9 row(s) affected)

As it happens, this is all of the employees in Northwind (unless you've added some yourself), but, if you play around with the data in the ReportsTo column some, you'll see we are indeed getting back the expected results. To test just a little further though, you can feed in Steven Buchanan's ID (which is 5):

```
SELECT * FROM fnGetReports(5)
```

EmployeeID	ReportsToID
5	2
6	5
7	5
9	5

(4 row(s) affected)

We get the limited results we expected. Now, let's go the final step here and join this back to actual data. We'll use it much as we did our original query looking for the reports of Andrew Fuller:

```
DECLARE @EmployeeID int

SELECT @EmployeeID = EmployeeID
    FROM Employees
    WHERE LastName = 'Fuller'
    AND FirstName = 'Andrew'

SELECT Emp.EmployeeID, Emp.LastName, Emp.FirstName, Mgr.LastName AS ReportsTo
FROM Employees AS Emp
JOIN dbo.fnGetReports(@EmployeeID) AS gr
    ON gr.EmployeeID = Emp.EmployeeID
JOIN Employees AS Mgr
    ON Mgr.EmployeeID = gr.ReportsToID
```

This gets us back all 8 employees who are under Mr. Fuller:

EmployeeID	LastName	FirstName	ReportsTo
1	Davolio	Nancy	Fuller
3	Leverling	Janet	Fuller
4	Peacock	Margaret	Fuller
5	Buchanan	Steven	Fuller
6	Suyama	Michael	Buchanan
7	King	Robert	Buchanan
9	Dodsworth	Anne	Buchanan
8	Callahan	Laura	Fuller

(8 row(s) affected)

This should have you asking why Mr. Fuller didn't show up in the query – after all, we've already proven that he shows up in the results of the function. The reason that he doesn't show up is that the value in the ReportsTo column for his record is NULL, and so there's nothing to join back to the Employees table based on. The filtering happened because of the query, not because of the function.

So, as you can see, we can actually have very complex code build our table results for us, but it's still a table that results, and, as such, it can be used just like any other table.

Understanding Determinism

Any coverage of UDFs would be incomplete without discussing determinism. Determinism was not really all that important prior to SQL Server 2000, but, with the addition of indexing to views and computed columns, it has now become a big deal. If SQL Server is going to build an index over something, it has to be able to deterministically define (define with certainty) what the item being indexed is.

User-defined functions can be either deterministic or non-deterministic. The determinism is not defined by any kind of parameter, but rather by want the function is doing. If, given a specific set of valid inputs, the function will return exactly the same value every time, then the function is said to be deterministic. An example of a built-in function that is deterministic is SUM(). The sum of 3, 5, and 10 is always going to be 18 – *every* time the function is called with those values as inputs. The value of GETDATE(), however, is non-deterministic – it changes pretty much every time you call it.

To be considered deterministic, a function has to meet four criteria:

❑ The function must be schema-bound. This means that any objects that the function depends on will have a dependency recorded and no changes to those objects will be allowed without first dropping the dependent function.

❑ All other functions referred to in your function, regardless of whether they are user- or system-defined, must also be deterministic.

❑ You cannot reference tables that are defined outside the function itself (use of table variables and temporary tables is fine, as long as the table variable or temporary table was defined inside the scope of the function).

❑ You cannot use an extended stored procedure inside the function.

The importance of determinism shows up if you want to build an index on a view or computed column – both of which are new with SQL Server 2000. Indexes on views or computed columns are only allowed if the result of the view or computed column can be reliably determined. This means that, if the view or computed column refers to a non-deterministic function, no index will be allowed on that view or column. This situation isn't necessarily the end of the world, but you will want to think about whether a function is deterministic or not before creating indexes against views or columns that use that function.

> So, this should beget the question: "How do I figure out whether my function is deterministic or not?" Well, beyond checking the rules we've already described, you can also have SQL Server tell you whether your function is deterministic or not – it's stored in the **IsDeterministic** property of the object.

To check this out, you can make use of the OBJECTPROPERTY function. For example, we could check out the determinism of our DayOnly function that we used earlier in the chapter:

```
USE Accounting

SELECT OBJECTPROPERTY(OBJECT_ID('DayOnly'), 'IsDeterministic')
```

It may come as a surprise to you (or maybe not), that the response is that this function is *not* deterministic:

```
-----------
0

(1 row(s) affected)
```

Look back through the list of requirements for a deterministic function and see if you can figure out why this one doesn't meet the grade.

> When I was working on this example, I got one of those not so nice little reminders about how it's the little things that get you. You see, I was certain this function should be deterministic, and, of course, it wasn't. After too many nights writing until the morning hours, I completely missed the obvious – SCHEMABINDING. Thanks go out, in print, to Micle in the sqlserver.programming newsgroup for seeing what was right before my too tired eyes.

Fortunately, we can fix the only problem this one has. All we need to do is add the WITH SCHEMABINDING option to our function, and we'll see better results:

```
ALTER FUNCTION DayOnly(@Date datetime)
RETURNS varchar(12)
WITH SCHEMABINDING
AS
BEGIN
    RETURN CONVERT(varchar(12), @Date, 101)
END
```

Now, we just re-run our OBJECTPROPERTY query:

```
-----------
1

(1 row(s) affected)
```

And voilà – a deterministic function!

We can compare this, however, with our AveragePrice function that we built in the pubs database. It looked something like this:

```
USE Pubs
GO

CREATE FUNCTION dbo.AveragePrice()
RETURNS money
WITH SCHEMABINDING
AS
BEGIN
    RETURN (SELECT AVG(Price) FROM dbo.Titles)
END
```

In this function we used schema-binding right from the beginning, so let's look at our OBJECTPROPERTY:

```
SELECT OBJECTPROPERTY(OBJECT_ID('AveragePrice'), 'IsDeterministic')
```

Despite being schema-bound, this one still comes back as being non-deterministic. That's because this function references a table that isn't local to the function (a temporary table or table variable created inside the function).

Under the heading of "one more thing", it's also worth noting that the PriceDifference function we created at the same time as AveragePrice is also non-deterministic. For one thing, we didn't make it schema-bound, but, more importantly, it references AveragePrice – if you reference a non-deterministic function, then the function you're creating is non-deterministic by association.

Creating "System" Functions

System stored procedures and functions are rather handy for obvious reasons, but one particular benefit they have is that you can use them in any database without having to fully qualify them. Even though they exist in the master database, they can be called from any database and function just as if they existed within that database.

"OK," you say, "what's that got to do with me?" Well, many SQL programmers have enjoyed being able to create their own system stored procedures, so it follows that some of you will also want to create your own "system" functions – that is, functions callable from any database and that do not need to be qualified with the source database or even the owner name (remember, regular UDFs must be owner qualified in order to resolve at all).

To create a system defined UDF, you must do the following:

- ❑ CREATE it in the master database
- ❑ Use the prefix fn_
- ❑ Change the owner to system_function_schema using sp_changeobjectowner

Once you do this, your function should be callable from any database on your SQL Server. To illustrate this, let's review our first function. Originally, it looked like this:

```
CREATE FUNCTION DayOnly(@Date datetime)
RETURNS varchar(12)
WITH SCHEMABINDING
AS
BEGIN
    RETURN CONVERT(varchar(12), @Date, 101)
END
```

This time, let's run things again but change the CREATE database to master, include the fn_, and change the ownership to system_function_schema:

```
USE master
GO

CREATE FUNCTION fn_DayOnly(@Date datetime)
RETURNS varchar(12)
WITH SCHEMABINDING
AS
BEGIN
    RETURN CONVERT(varchar(12), @Date, 101)
END
GO

EXEC sp_changeobjectowner 'fn_DayOnly', 'system_function_schema'

USE Northwind
GO

SELECT fn_DayOnly(GETDATE())
```

This should yield you the current date – even though you were in a different database from that in which you created the function and didn't owner qualify it. Very handy!

> You should also get a warning that is generated by the sp_changeobjectowner system stored procedure. This warning is normal, and is just reminding you that, when you change the owner of an object, you change a piece of the four part name (server.database.owner.object) – because changing the name, you always run the risk of some piece of code being out there that fully qualifies a reference to the object – such a reference would no longer find the object because part of the name has changed.

Deleting the "System" Functions after You Create Them

The catch to creating your own system functions comes when you want to get rid of them later. You'll find that, if you try and drop your function after changing the owner name, you'll get a "doesn't exist" error from SQL Server and your function won't be deleted – that's because SQL Server doesn't like the notion of you deleting system functions.

To drop a system function that you have created, you must turn on the "allow updates" option for your server by using sp_configure.

> **Two quick words of warning here:**
>
> **First, turning on this option is extremely dangerous – you could easily "accidentally" delete rows from system tables that might disable your server or drop functions/procedures that you really need – if this happens, the only way to safely reinstall it will likely be to reload your SQL Server from the CD – be sure to turn the option back off after you've done what you needed to do.**
>
> **Second, don't add system procedures and functions for everything – like any system table or function update, it deserves careful thought and planning before messing with such an important area of your system.**

So, to drop our newly created system function, we would simply execute:

```
USE master
GO

EXEC sp_configure 'allow updates', 1
GO

RECONFIGURE WITH OVERRIDE
GO

DROP FUNCTION system_function_schema.fn_DayOnly
GO

EXEC sp_configure 'allow updates', 0
GO

RECONFIGURE WITH OVERRIDE
```

And it's gone.

Summary

What we added in this chapter was, in many ways, not new at all. Indeed, much of what goes into user-defined functions is the same set of statements, variables, and general coding practices that we have already seen in scripting and stored procedures. However, UDFs still provide us a wonderful new area of functionality that was not previously available in SQL Server. We can now encapsulate a wider range of code, and even use this encapsulated functionality inline with our queries. What's more, we can now also provide parameterized views and dynamically created tables.

User-defined functions are, in many ways, the most exciting of all the new functionality added to SQL Server. In pondering their uses, I have already come to realize that I'm only scratching the surface of their potential. Over the life of this next release, I suspect that developers will implement UDFs in ways I have yet to dream of – hopefully, you'll be one of those developers!

Online discussion at http://p2p.wrox.com

14

Transactions and Locks

This is one of those chapters that, when you go back to work, makes you sound like you've had your Wheaties today. Nothing in what we're going to cover in this chapter is wildly difficult, yet transactions and locks tend to be two of the most misunderstood areas in the database world.

In this chapter, we're going to:

❑ Demystify transactions

❑ Examine how the SQL Server log and "checkpoints" work

❑ Unlock your understanding of locks

We'll learn why these topics are so closely tied to each other, and how to minimize problems with each.

Transactions

Transactions are all about **atomicity**. Atomicity is the concept that something should act as a unit. From our database standpoint, it's about the smallest grouping of one or more statements that should be considered to be "all or nothing".

Often, when dealing with data, we want to make sure that if one thing happens, another thing happens, or that neither of them do. Indeed, this can be carried out to the degree where 20 things (or more) all have to happen together or nothing happens. Let's look at a classic example:

Imagine that you are a banker. Sally comes in and wants to transfer $1000 from checking to savings. You are, of course, happy to oblige, so you process her request.

Behind the scenes, we have something like this happening:

```
UPDATE checking
    SET Balance = Balance - 1000
    WHERE Account = 'Sally'
UPDATE savings
    SET Balance = Balance + 1000
    WHERE Account = 'Sally'
```

This is a hyper-simplification of what's going on, but it captures the main thrust of things: you need to issue two different statements – one for each account.

Now, what if the first statement executes and the second one doesn't? Sally would be out of a thousand dollars! That might, for a short time, seem OK from your perspective (heck, you just made a 1000 bucks!), but not for long. By that afternoon you'd have a steady stream of customers leaving your bank – it's hard to stay in the bank business with no depositors.

What you need is a way to be certain that, if the first statement executes, the second statement executes. There really isn't a way that we can be certain of that – all sorts of things can go wrong from hardware failures to simple things like violations of data integrity rules. Fortunately though, there is a way to do something that serves the same overall purpose – we can essentially forget that the first statement ever happened. We can enforce at least the notion that if one thing didn't happen then nothing did – at least within the scope of our **transaction**.

In order to capture this notion of a transaction though, we need to be able to define very definite boundaries. A transaction has to have very definitive begin and end points. Actually, every SELECT, INSERT, UPDATE, and DELETE statement you issue in SQL Server is part of an implicit transaction. Even if you only issue one statement, that one statement is considered to be a transaction – everything about the statement will be executed, or none of it will. Indeed, by default, that is the length of a transaction – one statement.

But what if we need to have more than one statement be all or nothing – such as our bank example above? In such an occasion, we need a way of marking the beginning and end of a transaction, as well as the success or failure of that transaction. To that end, there are several T-SQL statements that we can use to "mark" these points in a transaction. We can:

- ❏ BEGIN a transaction – set the starting point

- ❏ COMMIT a transaction – make the transaction a permanent, irreversible part of the database

- ❏ ROLLBACK a transaction – essentially saying that we want to forget that it ever happened

- ❏ SAVE a transaction – establishing a specific marker to allow us to do only a partial rollback

Let's look over all of these individually before we put them together into our first transaction.

BEGIN TRAN

The beginning of the transaction is probably one of the easiest concepts to understand in the transaction process. Its sole purpose in life is to denote the point that is the beginning of a unit. If, for some reason, we are unable to or do not want to commit the transaction, this is the point to which all database activity will be rolled back. That is, everything beyond this point that is not eventually committed, will effectively be forgotten as far as the database is concerned.

The syntax is:

```
BEGIN TRAN[SACTION] [<transaction name>|<@transaction variable>]
```

COMMIT TRAN

The committing of a transaction is the end of a completed transaction. At the point that you issue the COMMIT TRAN the transaction is considered to be what is called **durable**. That is, the effect of the transaction is now permanent, and will last even if you have a system failure (as long as you have a backup or the database files haven't been physically destroyed). The only way to "undo" whatever the transaction accomplished is to issue a new transaction that, functionally speaking, is a reverse of your first transaction.

The syntax for a COMMIT looks pretty similar to a BEGIN:

```
COMMIT TRAN[SACTION] [<transaction name>|<@transaction variable>]
```

ROLLBACK TRAN

Whenever I think of a ROLLBACK, I think of the movie The Princess Bride. If you've ever seen the film (if you haven't, I highly recommend it), you'll know that the character Vizzini (considered a genius in the film) always said, "If anything goes wrong – go back to the beginning."

That was some mighty good advice. A ROLLBACK does just what Vizzini suggested – it goes back to the beginning. In this case, it's your transaction that goes back to the beginning. Anything that happened since the associated BEGIN statement is effectively forgotten about. The only exception to going back to the beginning is through the use of what are called **save points** – which we'll describe next.

The syntax again looks pretty much the same, with the exception of allowance for a save point.

```
ROLLBACK TRAN[SACTION] [<transaction name>|<save point name>|
     <@transaction variable>|<@savepoint variable>]
```

SAVE TRAN

To save a transaction is essentially to create something of a bookmark. You establish a name for your bookmark (you can have more than one). After this "bookmark" is established, you can reference it in a rollback. What's nice about this is that you can roll back to the exact spot in the code that you want to – just by naming a save point to which you want to roll back. This is truly great if you have a long process that gets an error at the end. You could, for example, use a WAITFOR and wait briefly before trying again (for example, if the problem was a deadlock – that is two transactions fighting over the same record – the odds are a second try will get your transaction through).

The syntax is simple enough:

```
SAVE TRAN[SACTION] [<save point name>| <@savepoint variable>]
```

The thing to remember about save points is that they are cleared on ROLLBACK – that is, even if you save five save points, once you perform one ROLLBACK they are all gone. You can start setting new save points again, and rolling back to those, but whatever save points you had when the ROLLBACK was issued are gone.

> Save points were something of a major confusion area for me when I first came across them. Books Online indicates that, after rolling back to a save point, you must run the transaction to a logical conclusion (this is technically correct). Where the confusion came from was the way that Books Online was written that seemed to indicate that you had to go to a ROLLBACK or COMMIT without using any more save points. This is not the case – you just can't use the save points that were declared prior to the ROLLBACK – save points after this are fine.

Let's test this out with a bit of code to see what happens when we mix the different types of TRAN commands. Type the following code in and then we'll run through an explanation of it:

```
USE Northwind

-- Start the transaction
BEGIN TRAN TranStart

-- Insert our first piece of data using default values. Consider this record
-- No1.
-- This record stays after all the rollbacks are done.
INSERT INTO Orders
    DEFAULT VALUES

-- Create a "Bookmark" to come back to later if need be
SAVE TRAN FirstPoint

-- Insert some more default data (this one will disappear after the
-- rollback).
-- Consider this record No2.
INSERT INTO Orders
    DEFAULT VALUES

-- Roll back to the first save point . Anything up to that point will still
-- be part of the
-- transaction. Anything beyond is now toast.
ROLLBACK TRAN FirstPoint

-- Insert some more default data. Consider this record No3. This record
-- stays
-- after all the rollbacks are done.
INSERT INTO Orders
    DEFAULT VALUES

-- Create another point to roll back to.
SAVE TRAN SecondPoint

-- Yet more data. This one will also disappear, only after the second
-- rollback this time.
-- Consider this record No4.
INSERT INTO Orders
    DEFAULT VALUES

-- Go back to second save point
ROLLBACK TRAN SecondPoint
```

```
-- Insert a little more data to show that things are still happening.
-- Consider this record No5. This record stays after all the rollbacks are
-- done.
INSERT INTO Orders
    DEFAULT VALUES

-- Commit the transaction
COMMIT TRAN TranStart

-- See what records were finally committed.
SELECT TOP 3 OrderID
FROM Orders
ORDER BY OrderID DESC
```

First, we begin the transaction. This starts our grouping of "all-or-nothing" statements. We then INSERT a row. At this juncture, we have just one row inserted:

```
Use Northwind

-- Start the transaction
BEGIN TRAN TranStart

-- Insert our first piece of data using default values. Consider this record --
No1.
-- This record stays after all the rollbacks are done.
INSERT INTO Orders
    DEFAULT VALUES
```

Next, we establish a save point called FirstPoint and insert another row. We have two rows inserted at this point, but remember that they are not committed yet, so the database doesn't consider them to really be part of the data:

```
-- Create a "Bookmark" to come back to later if need be
SAVE TRAN FirstPoint

-- Insert some more default data (this one will disappear after the
-- rollback)
-- Consider this record No2.
INSERT INTO Orders
    DEFAULT VALUES
```

We then ROLLBACK – explicitly saying that it is *not* the beginning that we want to rollback to, but just to FirstPoint. With the ROLLBACK, everything between our ROLLBACK and the FirstPoint save point is undone. Since we have one INSERT statement between the ROLLBACK and the SAVE, that statement is rolled back. At this juncture, we are back down to just one row inserted. Any attempt to reference a save point would now fail since all save points have been reset with our ROLLBACK:

```
-- Roll back to the first save point. Anything up to that point will still
-- be part of the
-- transaction. Anything beyond is now toast.
ROLLBACK TRAN FirstPoint
```

We add another row, putting us back up to a total of two rows inserted at this point. We also create a brand new save point. This is perfectly valid, and we can now refer to this save point since it is established after the ROLLBACK:

```
-- Insert some more default data. Consider this record No3.
-- This record stays after all the rollbacks are done.
INSERT INTO Orders
    DEFAULT VALUES

-- Create another point to roll back to.
SAVE TRAN SecondPoint
```

Time for yet another row to be inserted, bringing our total number of still-valid inserts up to three:

```
-- Yet more data. This one will also disappear, only after the second
-- rollback this time.
-- Consider this record No4.
INSERT INTO Orders
    DEFAULT VALUES
```

Now we perform another ROLLBACK – this time referencing our new save point (which happens to be the only one valid at this point since FirstPoint was reset after the first ROLLBACK). This one undoes everything between it and the save point it refers to – in this case just one INSERT statement. That puts us back at two INSERT statements that are still valid:

```
-- Go back to second save point
ROLLBACK TRAN SecondPoint
```

We then issue yet another INSERT statement, bringing our total number of INSERT statements that are still part of the transaction back up to three:

```
-- Insert a little more data to show that things
-- are still happening.
-- Consider this record No5. This record stays
-- after all the rollbacks are done.
INSERT INTO Orders
    DEFAULT VALUES
```

Last (for our transaction anyway), but certainly not least, we issue the COMMIT TRAN statement that locks our transaction in and makes it a permanent part of the database:

```
-- Commit the transaction
COMMIT TRAN TranStart

-- See what records were finally committed.
SELECT TOP 3 OrderID
FROM Orders
ORDER BY OrderID DESC
```

> Note that if either of these ROLLBACK statements had not included the name of a save
> point, or had included a name that had been set with the BEGIN statement, then the entire
> transaction would be rolled back, and the transaction would be considered to be closed.

The end of our script is just a little statement that shows us our three rows. When you look at this, you'll
be able to see what's happened in terms of rows being added and then removed from the transaction:

```
OrderID
----------
11148
11146
11144

(3 row(s) affected)
```

Sure enough, three rows have been inserted, though you might get different order IDs from mine.

> I've pointed out this issue before, but, if you've skipped chapters at all, some of you'll
> probably be confused as to why the values of the OrderID skip some numbers. After all,
> doesn't the identity field automatically insert numbers sequentially for us – keeping
> track of which one was last?
>
> Indeed, it does just that, but you have to remember that we did have a couple of other rows
> – they were just "undone". The change in identity value cannot be reversed since other
> inserts may (and, in this case have) already drawn the next value out before the ROLLBACK
> occurred. The inserted records were reversed – essentially removed from any history – but
> not without a trace. Identity and timestamp values are still incremented.

How the SQL Server Log Works

You definitely must have the concept of transactions down before you get into trying to figure out the
way that SQL Server tracks what's what in your database. You see, what you *think* of as your database is
only rarely a complete version of all the data. Except for rare moments when it happens that everything
has been written to disk, the data in your database is made up of not only the data in the physical
database file(s), but also any transactions that have been committed to the log since the last checkpoint.

In the normal operation of your database, most activities that you perform are "logged" to the
transaction log rather than written directly to the database. A **checkpoint** is a periodic operation that
forces all dirty pages for the database currently in use to be written to disk. Dirty pages are log or data
pages that have been modified after they were read into the cache, but the modifications have not yet
been written to disk. Without a checkpoint the log would fill up and/or use all the available disk space.
The process works something like this:

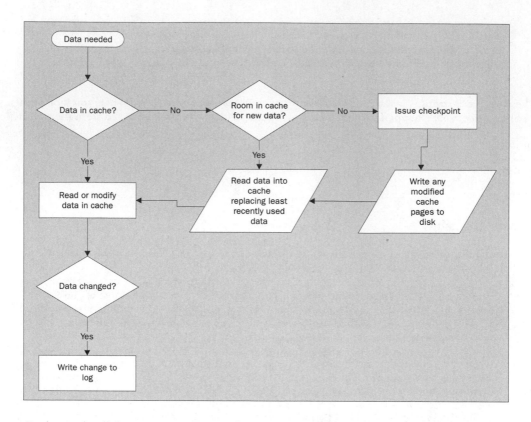

Don't mistake all this as meaning that you have to do something special to get your data out of the cache. SQL Server handles all of this for you. This information is only provided here to facilitate your understanding of how the log works, and, from there, the steps required to handle a transaction. Whether something is in cache or not can make a big difference to performance, so understanding when things are logged and when things go in and out of the cache can be a big deal when you are seeking maximum performance.

Note that the need to read data into a cache that is already full is not the only reason that a checkpoint would be issued. Checkpoints can be issued under the following circumstances:

❑   By a manual statement – using the CHECKPOINT command

❑   At normal shutdown of the server (unless the WITH NOWAIT option is used)

❑   When you change any database option (for example, single user only, dbo only, etc.)

❑   When, for SQL Server 2000, the Simple Recovery option is used and the log becomes 70% full, or, for version 7.0 and older, the database option Truncate Log On Checkpoint is set, and the log becomes 70% full

❑   When the amount of data in the log since the last checkpoint (often called the **active** portion of the log) exceeds the size that the server could recover in the amount of time specified in the **recovery interval** option

Let's look at each of these more carefully:

Using the CHECKPOINT Command

One way (but probably the least often used) for the database to have a checkpoint issued is for it to be done manually. You can do this anytime by just typing in the word:

```
CHECKPOINT
```

It's just that simple.

SQL Server does a very good job of managing itself in the area of checkpoints, so the times when issuing a manual checkpoint makes sense would be fairly rare.

> *One place that I will do this is during the development cycle when I have the Simple Recovery option turned on for my database (you would not want that option active on a production database). It's not at all uncommon during the development stage of your database to perform actions that are long running and fill up the log rather quickly. While I could always just issue the appropriate command to truncate the log myself, CHECKPOINT is a little shorter and faster and, when the Simple Recovery option is active, has the same effect.*

At Normal Server Shutdown

Ever wondered why SQL Server sometimes takes a very long time to shut down? Besides the de-allocation of memory and other destructor routines that have to run to unload the system, SQL Server must also first issue a checkpoint before the shutdown process can begin. This means that you'll have to wait for any data that's been committed in the log to be written out to the physical database before your shutdown can continue. Checkpoints also occur when the server is stopped:

❑ Using Service Manager

❑ Using Enterprise Manager

❑ Running the net stop mssqlserver NT command at the command prompt

❑ Using the **Services** option from the Windows 2000 **Administrative Tools** menu (or the **Services** icon of the Windows NT control panel), selecting the **MSSQLSERVER** service, and clicking the **Stop** button

There is a way you can get around the delay if you so choose. To use it, you must shut down using the SHUTDOWN command in T-SQL. To eliminate the delay associated with the checkpoint (and the checkpoint itself for that matter), you just add the WITH NOWAIT key phrase to your shutdown statement:

```
SHUTDOWN [WITH NOWAIT]
```

Note that I recommend highly *against* using this unless you have some programmatic need to shut down your server. It will cause the subsequent restart to take a longer time than usual to recover the databases on the server.

At a Change of Database Options

A checkpoint is issued any time you issue a change to your database options regardless of how the option gets changed (using sp_dboption or ALTER DATABASE). The checkpoint is issued prior to making the actual change in the database.

When You are Using Simple Recovery (SQL Server 2000) or the Truncate Log on Checkpoint Option is Active (7.0 And Earlier)

If you are using the Simple Recovery option (as of SQL Server 2000) or have turned on the Truncate On Checkpoint database option (7.0 and prior), then SQL Server will automatically issue a checkpoint any time the log becomes more than 70% full. Using these options is fairly common during a development phase, but I recommend against their use on production servers.

When Recovery Time Would Exceed the Recovery Interval Option Setting

As we saw briefly earlier (and will see more closely next), SQL Server performs a process called recovery every time the SQL Server is started up. SQL Server will automatically issue a checkpoint anytime the estimated time to run the recovery process would exceed the amount of time set in a database option called recovery interval. By default, the recovery interval is set to zero – which means that SQL Server will decide for you (in practice, this means about 1 minute).

Failure and Recovery

A recovery happens every time that SQL Server starts up. SQL Server takes the database file, and then applies (by writing them out to the physical database file) any committed changes that are in the log since the last transaction. Any changes in the log that do not have a corresponding commit are rolled back – that is, they are essentially forgotten about.

Let's take a look at how this works depending on how transactions have occurred in your database. Imagine five transactions that span the log as pictured:

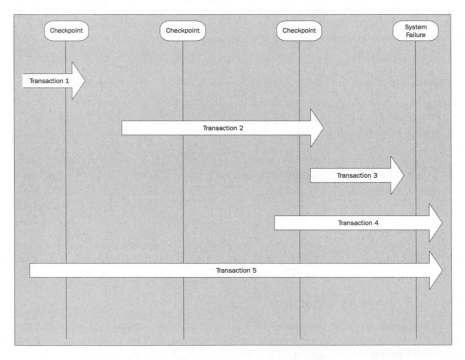

Let's look at what would happen to these transactions one by one.

Transaction 1

Absolutely nothing would happen. The transaction has already been through a checkpoint, and has been fully committed to the database. There is no need to do anything at recovery, because any data that is read into the data cache would already reflect the committed transaction.

Transaction 2

Even though the transaction existed at the time that a checkpoint was issued, the transaction had not been committed (the transaction was still going). Without that commitment, the transaction does not actually participate in the checkpoint. This transaction would, therefore, be "rolled forward". This is just a fancy way of saying that we would need to read all the related pages back into cache, and then use the information in the log to re-run all the statements that we ran in this transaction. When that's finished, the transaction should look exactly as it did before the system failed.

Transaction 3

It may not look the part, but this transaction is exactly the same as Transaction 2 from the standpoint of what needs to be done. Again, because Transaction 3 wasn't finished at the time of the last checkpoint, it did not participate in that checkpoint just like Transaction 2 didn't. The only difference is that Transaction 3 didn't even exist at that time, but, from a recovery standpoint, that makes no difference – it's where the commit is issued that makes all the difference.

Transaction 4

This transaction wasn't completed at the time of system failure, and must, therefore, be rolled back. In effect, it never happened from a row data perspective. The user would have to re-enter any data, and any process would need to start from the beginning.

Transaction 5

This one is no different than Transaction 4. It appears to be different because the transaction has been running longer, but that makes no difference. The transaction was not committed at the time of system failure, and must therefore be rolled back.

Implicit Transactions

Primarily for compatibility with other major RDBMS systems such as Oracle or DB2, SQL Server supports the notion of what is called an **implicit transaction**. Implicit transactions do not require a BEGIN TRAN statement – instead, they are automatically started with your first statement. They then continue until you issue a COMMIT TRAN or ROLLBACK TRAN statement. The next transaction then begins with your next statement.

Theoretically, the purpose behind this is to make sure that every statement is part of a transaction. SQL Server also wants every statement to be part of a transaction, but takes a different approach by default – if there is no BEGIN TRAN, then SQL Server assumes you have a transaction of just one statement, and automatically begins and ends that transaction for you. With some other systems though, you'll find the implicit transaction approach. Those systems will assume that any one statement is only the beginning of the transaction, and therefore require that you explicitly end every transaction with a COMMIT or ROLLBACK.

By default, the `IMPLICIT_TRANSACTIONS` option is turned off (and the connection is in autocommit transaction mode). You can turn it on by issuing the command:

```
SET IMPLICIT_TRANSACTIONS ON
```

After that, any of the following statements will initiate a transaction:

- ❏ CREATE
- ❏ ALTER TABLE
- ❏ GRANT
- ❏ REVOKE
- ❏ SELECT
- ❏ UPDATE
- ❏ DELETE
- ❏ INSERT
- ❏ TRUNCATE TABLE
- ❏ DROP
- ❏ OPEN
- ❏ FETCH

The transaction will continue until you COMMIT or ROLLBACK. Note that the implicit transactions option will only affect the current connection – any other users will still have the option turned off unless they have also executed the SET statement.

> Implicit transactions are something of a dangerous territory, and I highly recommend that you leave this option off unless you have a very specific reason to turn it on (such as compatibility with code written in another system).
>
> Here's a common scenario: a user calls up and says, "I've been inserting data for the last half hour, and none of my changes are showing." You run a DBCC OPENTRAN (see the Admin Chapter), and discover that there's a transaction that's been there for a while. You can take a guess at what's happened. The user has a transaction open, and his or her changes won't appear until that transaction is committed. They may have done it using an explicit BEGIN TRANS statement, but they may also have executed some code that turned implicit transactions on, and then didn't turn it off. A mess follows. A bad case scenario would be that the database will gradually become more and more locked with these open transactions and would eventually become unusable.

Locks and Concurrency

Concurrency is a major issue for any database system. It addresses the notion of two or more users each trying to interact with the same object at the same time. The nature of that interaction may be different for each user (updating, deleting, reading, inserting), and the ideal way to handle the competition for control of the object changes depending on just what all the users in question are doing and just how important their actions are. The more users – more specifically, the more transactions – that you can run with reasonable success at the same time the higher your concurrency is said to be.

In the OLAP environment, concurrency is usually the first thing we deal with in data and it is the focus of most of the database notions put forward in this book (OLAP is usually something of an afterthought – it shouldn't necessarily be that way, but it is). Dealing with the issue of concurrency can be critical to the performance of your system. At the foundation of dealing with concurrency in databases is a process called **locking**.

Locks are a mechanism for preventing a process from performing an action on an object that conflicts with something already being done on that object. That is, you can't do some things to an object if someone else got there first. What you can and cannot do depends on what the other user is doing. It is also a means of describing what is being done, so the system knows if the second process action is compatible with the first process or not. For example, 1, 2, 10, 100, 1000, or whatever number of user connections the system can handle are usually all able to share the same piece of data at the same time as long as they all only want the record on a read-only basis. Think of it as being like a crystal shop – lots of people can be in looking at things – even the same thing – as long as they don't go to move it, buy it, or otherwise change it. If more than one person does that at the same time, you're liable to wind up with broken crystal. That's why the shopkeeper usually keeps a close eye on things, and they will usually decide who gets to handle it first.

The SQL Server **lock manager** is that shopkeeper. When you come into the SQL Server "store", the lock manager asks what is your intent – what it is you're going to be doing. If you say "just looking," and no one else already there is doing anything but "just looking," then the lock manager will let you in. If you want to "buy" (update or delete) something, then the lock manager will check to see if anyone's already there. If so, then you must wait, and everyone who comes in behind you will also wait. When you are let in to "buy", no one else will be let in until you are done.

By doing things this way, SQL Server is able to help us avoid a mix of different problems that can be created by concurrency issues. We will examine the possible concurrency problems and how to set a **transaction isolation level** that will prevent each, but for now, let's move on to what can and cannot be locked, and what kinds of locks are available.

What Problems Can Be Prevented by Locks

Locks can address four major problems:

- ❑ Dirty reads
- ❑ Unrepeatable reads
- ❑ Phantoms
- ❑ Lost updates

Each of these presents a separate set of problems, and can be handled by mix of solutions that usually includes proper setting of the transaction isolation level. Just to help make things useful as you look back at this chapter later, I'm going to include information on which transaction isolation level is appropriate for each of these problems. We'll take a complete look at isolation levels shortly, but for now, let's first make sure that we understand what each of these problems is all about.

Dirty Reads

Dirty reads occur when a transaction reads a record that is part of another transaction that isn't complete yet. If the first transaction completes normally, then it's unlikely there's a problem. But what if the transaction was rolled back? You would have information from a transaction that never happened from the database's perspective!

Let's look at it in an example series of steps:

Transaction 1 Command	Transaction 2 Command	Logical Database Value	Uncommitted Database Value	What Transaction 2 Shows
BEGIN TRAN		3		
UPDATE col = 5	BEGIN TRAN	3	5	
SELECT anything	SELECT @var = col	3	5	5
ROLLBACK	UPDATE anything SET whatever = @var	3		5
Oops – problem!!!				

Transaction 2 has now made use of a value that isn't valid! If you try to go back and audit to find where this number came from, you'll wind up with no trace and an extremely large headache.

Fortunately, this scenario can't happen if you're using the SQL Server default for the transaction isolation level (called READ COMMITTED which will be explained later in the section "*Setting the Isolation Level*").

Unrepeatable Reads

It's really easy to get this one mixed up with a dirty read. Don't worry about that – it's only terminology. Just get the concept.

An **unrepeatable read** is caused when you read the record twice in a transaction, and a separate transaction alters the data in the interim. For this one, let's go back to our bank example. Remember that we don't want the value of the account to go below 0 dollars:

Transaction 1	Transaction 2	@Var	What Transaction 1 *Thinks* Is In The Table	Value in Table
BEGIN TRAN		NULL		125
SELECT @Var = value FROM table	BEGIN TRAN	125	125	125

Transaction 1	Transaction 2	@Var	What Transaction 1 *Thinks* Is In The Table	Value in Table
	UPDATE value, SET value = value – 50			75
IF @Var >=100	END TRAN	125	125	75
UPDATE value, SET value = value – 100		125	125 (waiting for lock to clear)	75
(Finish, wait for lock to clear, then continue)		125	75	Either: -25 (If there isn't a CHECK constraint enforcing > 0) Or: Error 547 (If there is a CHECK)

Again, we have a problem. Transaction 1 has pre-scanned (which can be a good practice in some instances – remember that section, *Handling Errors Before They Happen* in Chapter 12?) to make sure that the value is valid, and that the transaction can go through (there's enough money in the account). The problem is that, before the UPDATE was made, Transaction 1 was beaten to the punch by Transaction 2. If there isn't any CHECK constraint on the table to prevent the negative value, then it would indeed be set to -25 – even though it logically appeared that we prevented this through the use of our IF statement.

We can only prevent this problem two ways:

- ❏ Create a CHECK constraint and monitor for the 547 Error
- ❏ Set our ISOLATION LEVEL to be REPEATABLE READ or SERIALIZABLE

The CHECK constraint seems fairly obvious. The thing to realize here is that you are taking something of a reactive rather than a proactive approach with this method. Nonetheless, in most situations we have a potential for unrepeatable reads, so this would be my preferred choice in most circumstances.

We'll be taking a full look at isolation levels shortly, but for now, suffice to say that there's a good chance that setting it to REPEATABLE READ or SERIALIZABLE is going to cause you as many headaches (or more) as it solves. Still – it's an option.

Phantoms

No – we're not talking the "of the opera" kind here – what we're talking about are records that appear mysteriously, as if unaffected by an UPDATE or DELETE statement that you've issued. This can happen quite legitimately in the normal course of operating your system, and doesn't require any kind of elaborate scenario to illustrate. Here's a classic example of how this happens:

Let's say you are running a fast food restaurant. If you're typical of that kind of establishment, you probably have a fair number of employees working at the "minimum wage" as defined by the government. The government has just decided to raise the minimum wage from $5.00 to $5.50 per hour, and you want to run an update on the Employees table to move anyone making less than $5.50 per hour up to the new minimum wage. No problem you say, and you issue the rather simple statement:

```
UPDATE Employees
SET HourlyRate = 5.50
WHERE HourlyRate < 5.50

ALTER TABLE Employees
    ADD ckWage CHECK (HourlyRate >= 5.50)
GO
```

That was a breeze, right? *Wrong!* Just for illustration, we're going to say that you get an error message back:

Server: Msg 547, Level 16, State 1, Line 1
ALTER TABLE statement conflicted with COLUMN CHECK constraint 'ckWage'. The conflict occurred in database 'FastFood', table 'Employees', column 'HourlyRate'.

So you run a quick SELECT statement checking for values below $5.50, and sure enough you find one. The question is likely to come rather quickly, "How did that get there! I just did the UPDATE which should have fixed that!" You did run the statement, and it ran just fine – you just got a **phantom**.

The instances of phantom reads are rare, and require just the right circumstances to happen. In short, someone performed an INSERT statement at the very same time your UPDATE was running. Since it was an entirely new row, it didn't have a lock on it, and it proceeded just fine.

The only cure for this is setting your transaction isolation level to SERIALIZABLE, in which case any updates to the table must not fall within your WHERE clause, or they will be locked out.

Lost Updates

Lost updates happen when one update is successfully written to the database, but is accidentally overwritten by another transaction. I can just hear you right about now, "Yikes! How could that happen?"

Lost updates can happen when two transactions read an entire record, then one writes updated information back to the record, then the other writes updated information back to the record. Let's look at an example:

Let's say that you are a credit analyst for your company. You get a call that customer X has reached their credit limit, and would like an extension, so you pull up their customer information to take a look. You see that they have a credit limit of $5,000, and that they appear to always pay on time.

While you're looking, Sally, another person in your credit department, pulls up customer X's record to enter a change in the address. The record she pulls up also shows the credit limit of $5,000.

At this point, you decide to go ahead and raise customer X's credit limit to $7,500, and press enter. The database now shows $7,500 as the credit limit for customer X.

Sally now completes her update to the address, but she's using the same edit screen that you are – that is, she updates the entire record. Remember what her screen showed as the credit limit? $5,000. Oops, the database now shows customer X with a credit limit of $5,000 again. Your update has been lost!

The solution to this depends on your code somehow recognizing that another connection has updated your record between when you read the data and when you went to update it. How this recognition happens varies depending on what access method you're using.

Detecting Updates Using ADO

Detecting that someone else has updated things under ADO is about as easy as it gets – do nothing. Well, not quite, you just need to set an error handler. You see, ADO will raise an error when you issue an `Update` or `UpdateBatch` method and one or more records in your recordset have already been updated. Indeed, it can even detect whether the particular columns you're updating have been changed – if the column that you're updating wasn't the one changed, it can then just do the update without any errors or any problems.

There are complete books on ADO, so I'm not going to go deep down that alley here, but keep in mind that it has some nice features in this regard.

Detecting Updates Using Non-ADO Access Methods

Some of the other data access models have their own methods for helping to detect changes in the data before your edit is applied, but the most common method makes use of the `rowversion` (formerly `timestamp`) data type.

Remember that a time stamp is a number based on the activity of your server, and is guaranteed to be unique within any given database (it's actually very unlikely that you'd find duplicates on the same server, but Microsoft only promise it at the database level). What's even more unique about the `rowversion` data type is that the column of this type (you can only have one per table) in a table is automatically updated whenever any change is made to a row. Checking for changes is therefore not a problem – you just read the time stamp in with the rest of the data, and, before updating the row, make sure that the time stamp hasn't changed. If the time stamp has changed, then someone else has beaten you to the row, and you'll want to abort the update – usually giving the user the chance to either see the exact change or to start over after refreshing to the new data.

Lockable Resources

There are six different **lockable resources** for SQL Server, and they form a hierarchy. The higher level the lock, the less **granularity** it has (that is, you're choosing a higher and higher number of objects to be locked in something of a cascading action just because the object that contains them has been locked). These include, in ascending order of granularity:

Database

The entire database is locked. This happens usually during database schema changes.

Table

The entire table is locked. This includes all the data-related objects associated with that table including the actual data rows (every one of them) and all the keys in all the indexes associated with the table in question.

Extent

The entire extent is locked. Remember than an extent is made up of eight pages, so an extent lock means that the lock has control of the extent, the eight data or index pages in that extent, and all the rows of data in those eight pages.

Page

All the data or index keys on that page are locked.

Key

There is a lock on a particular key or series of keys in an index. Other keys in the same index page may be unaffected.

Row or Row Identifier (RID)

The addition of this little gem may be the most celebrated feature enhancement in SQL Server version 7.0. Although the lock is technically placed on the row identifier (an internal SQL Server construct), it essentially locks the entire row.

Lock Escalation and Lock Effects on Performance

For years developers using SQL Server had been asking – no, pleading – for row-level locking. You see, prior to version 7.0 the granularity only went down to page-level locking. This meant that if you were placing a lock to do with one row, you were actually affecting the availability of all the other rows on that same page. This led to a lot of contention issues where users were prevented from accessing records that weren't being used because the page on which the records were located contained another record that was being accessed by another user.

Microsoft had a classic marketing answer to this, and, like most Microsoft marketing ploys, it had some supposed basis in reality. The answer to the row-level locking question went something like this:

"Locking a page takes up fewer resources than locking a row. If you lock the page, then you don't need to check every row in a page to see whether it's locked or not – if the page is locked the row is locked. What's more, if you only lock the page, then you don't waste the memory, CPU, and other resources associated with keeping track of every row on the page that's locked – you just keep track of the one page."

That argument didn't hold a lot of water with those of us trying to fight off contention issues related to two separate rows in a table. Still, it has a lot of relevance in terms of thinking about performance and understanding the concept of escalation.

Escalation is all about recognizing that maintaining a finer level of granularity (say a row-lock instead of a page lock) makes a lot of sense when the number of items being locked is small. However, as we get more and more items locked, then the overhead associated with maintaining those locks actually hinders performance. It can cause the lock to be in place longer (thus creating contention issues – the longer the lock is in place, the more likely that someone will want that particular record). When you think about this for a bit, you'll realize there's probably a balancing act to be done somewhere, and that's exactly what the lock manager uses escalation to do.

When the number of locks being maintained reaches a certain threshold, then the lock is escalated to the next highest level, and the lower level locks do not have to be so tightly managed (freeing resources, and helping speed over contention).

Note that the escalation is based on the number of locks rather than the number of users. The importance here is that you can single-handedly lock a table by performing a mass update – a row-lock can graduate to a page lock which then escalates to a table lock. That means that you could potentially be locking every other user out of the table. If your query makes use of multiple tables, it's actually quite possible to wind up locking everyone out of all of those tables.

While you certainly would prefer not to lock all the other users out of your object, there are times when you still need to perform updates that are going to have that effect. There is very little you can do about escalation other than to keep your queries as targeted as possible. Recognize that escalations will happen, so make sure you've thought about what the possible ramifications of your query are.

Lock Modes

Beyond considering just what resource level you're locking, you also should consider what lock mode your query is going to acquire. Just as there are a variety of resources to lock, there is also a variety of **lock modes**.

Some modes are exclusive of each other (which means they don't work together). Some modes do nothing more than essentially modify other modes. Whether modes can work together is based on whether they are **compatible** (we'll take a closer look at compatibility between locks later in this chapter).

Just as we did with lockable resources, let's take a look at lock modes one by one:

Shared Locks

This is the most basic type of lock there is. A **shared lock** is used when you only need to read the data – that is you won't be changing anything. A shared lock wants to be your friend, as it is compatible with other shared locks. That doesn't mean that it still won't cause you grief – while a shared lock doesn't mind any other kind of lock, there are other locks that don't like shared locks.

Shared locks tell other locks that you're out there. It's the old, "Look at me! Ain't I special?" thing. They don't serve much of a purpose, yet they can't really be ignored. However, one thing that shared locks do is prevent users from performing dirty reads.

Exclusive Locks

Exclusive locks are just what they sound like. Exclusive locks are not compatible with any other lock. They cannot be achieved if any other lock exists, nor will they allow a new lock of any form to be created on the resource while the exclusive lock is still active. This prevents two people from updating, deleting, or whatever at the same time.

Update Locks

Update locks are something of a hybrid between shared locks and exclusive locks. An update lock is a special kind of placeholder. Think about it – in order to do an UPDATE, you need to validate your WHERE clause (assuming there is one) to figure out just what rows you're going to be updating. That means that you only need a shared lock, until you actually go to make the physical update. At the time of the physical update, you'll need an exclusive lock.

Update locks indicate that you have a shared lock that's going to become an exclusive lock after you've done your initial scan of the data to figure out what exactly needs to be updated. This acknowledges the fact that there are two distinct stages to an update:

❑ First, the stage where you are figuring out what meets the WHERE clause criteria (what's going to be updated). This is the part of an update query that has an update lock.

❑ Second, the stage where, if you actually decide to perform the update, the lock is upgraded to an exclusive lock. Otherwise, the lock is converted to a shared lock.

What's nice about this is that it forms a barrier against one variety of **deadlock**. A deadlock is not a type of lock in itself, but rather a situation where a paradox has been formed. A deadlock would arise if one lock can't do what it needs to do in order to clear because another lock is holding that resource – the problem is that the opposite resource is itself stuck waiting for the lock to clear on the first transaction.

Without update locks, these deadlocks would crop up all the time. Two update queries would be running in shared mode. Query A completes its query and is ready for the physical update. It wants to escalate to an exclusive lock, but it can't because Query B is finishing its query. Query B then finishes the query, except that it needs to do the physical update. In order to do that, Query B must escalate to an exclusive lock, but it can't because Query A is still waiting. This creates an impasse.

Instead, an update lock prevents any other update locks from being established. The instant that the second transaction attempts to achieve an update lock, they will be put into a wait status for whatever the lock timeout is – the lock will not be granted. If the first lock clears before the lock timeout is reached, then the lock will be granted to the new requester, and that process can continue. If not, an error will be generated.

Update locks are compatible only with shared locks and intent shared locks.

Intent Locks

An **intent lock** is a true placeholder, and is meant to deal with the issue of object hierarchies. Imagine a situation where you have a lock established on a row, but someone wants to establish a lock on a page, or extent, or modify a table. You wouldn't want another transaction to go around yours by going higher up the hierarchy, would you?

Without intent locks, the higher level objects wouldn't even know that you had the lock at the lower level. Intent locks improve performance, as SQL Server needs to examine intent locks only at the table level, and not check every row or page lock on the table, to determine if a transaction can safely lock the entire table. Intent locks come in three different varieties:

❑ **Intent shared lock** – a shared lock has or is going to be established at some lower point in the hierarchy. For example, a page is about to have a page level shared lock established on it. This type of lock only applies to tables and pages.

❑ **Intent exclusive lock** – this is the same as intent shared, but with an exclusive lock about to be placed on the lower level item.

❑ **Shared with intent exclusive lock** – a shared lock has or is about to be established lower down the object hierarchy, but the intent is to modify data, so it will become an intent exclusive at some point.

Schema Locks

These come in two flavors:

- **Schema modification lock (Sch-M)** – a schema change is being made to the object. No queries or other CREATE, ALTER, or DROP statements can be run against this object for the duration of the Sch-M lock.

- **Schema stability lock (Sch-S)** – this is very similar to a shared lock, this lock's sole purpose is to prevent a Sch-M since there are already locks for other queries (or CREATE, ALTER, DROP statements) active on the object. This is compatible with all other lock types.

Bulk Update Locks

A **bulk update lock** (**BU**) is really just a variant of a table lock with one little (but significant) difference. Bulk update locks will allow parallel loading of data – that is, the table is locked from any other "normal" (T-SQL Statements) activity, but multiple BULK INSERT or bcp operations can be performed at the same time.

Lock Compatibility

The table below shows the compatibility of the resource lock modes (listed in increasing lock strength). Existing locks are shown by the columns; requested locks by the rows:

	IS	S	U	IX	SIX	X
Intent Shared (IS)	YES	YES	YES	YES	YES	NO
Shared (S)	YES	YES	YES	NO	NO	NO
Update (U)	YES	YES	NO	NO	NO	NO
Intent Exclusive (IX)	YES	NO	NO	YES	NO	NO
Shared with Intent Exclusive (SIX)	YES	NO	NO	NO	NO	NO
Exclusive (X)	NO	NO	NO	NO	NO	NO

Also:

- The Sch-S is compatible with all lock modes except the Sch-M.
- The Sch-M is incompatible with all lock modes.
- The BU is compatible only with schema stability and other bulk update locks.

Specifying a Specific Lock Type – Optimizer Hints

Sometimes you want to have more control over how the locking goes either in your query, or perhaps in your entire transaction. You can do this by making use of what are called **optimizer hints**.

Optimizer hints are ways of explicitly telling SQL Server to escalate a lock to a specific level. They are included right after the name of the table (in your SQL Statement) that they are to effect, and are designated as follows:

Optimizer Hint	Description
SERIALIZABLE / HOLDLOCK	Once a lock is established by a statement in a transaction, that lock is not released until the transaction is ended (via ROLLBACK or COMMIT). Inserts are also prevented if the inserted record would match the criteria in the WHERE clause in the query that established the lock (no phantoms). This is the highest isolation level, and guarantees absolute consistency of data.
READUNCOMMITTED / NOLOCK	Obtains no lock (not even a shared lock), and does not honor other locks. While a very fast option, it can generate dirty reads as well as a host of other problems.
READCOMMITTED	The default hint. Honors all locks, but releases any locks held as soon as the object in question is no longer needed. Performs the same as the READ COMMITTED isolation level.
REPEATABLEREAD	Once a lock is established by a statement in a transaction, that lock is not released until the transaction is ended (via ROLLBACK or COMMIT). New data can be inserted.
READPAST	Rather than waiting for a lock to clear, skips all locked rows. The skip is limited to row locks (still waits for page, extent, and table locks) and can only be used with a SELECT statement.
ROWLOCK	Introduced in SQL 7.0, this tells SQL Server to use row-level locking instead of page locks for inserts. It forces the initial level of the lock to be at the row-level even if the optimizer would have otherwise selected a less granular locking strategy. It does not prevent the lock from being escalated to those less granular levels if the number of locks reaches the system's lock threshold.
PAGLOCK	Uses a page-level lock regardless of the choice that would otherwise have been made by the optimizer. The usefulness of this can go both ways: sometimes you know that a page lock is more appropriate than a row lock for resource conservation; other times you want to minimize contention where the optimizer might have chosen a table lock.
TABLOCK	Forces a full-table lock rather than whatever the lock manager would have used. Can really speed up known table scan situations, but creates big contention problems if other users want to modify data in the table.

Optimizer Hint	Description
TABLOCKX	Similar to TABLOCK, but creates an exclusive lock – locks all other users out of the table for the duration of the statement or transaction depending on how the TRANSACTION ISOLATION LEVEL is set.
UPDLOCK	Uses an update lock instead of a shared lock. This is a highly underutilized tool in the war against deadlocks, as it still allows other users to obtain shared locks, but ensures that no data modification (other update locks) are established until you end the statement or transaction (presumably after going ahead and updating the rows).
XLOCK	With its roots in TABLOCKX, this one is new with SQL Server 2000. The advantage here is that, for the first time, we can specify an exclusive lock regardless of what lock granularity we have chosen (or not chosen) to specify.

Most of these have times where they can be very useful, but, before you get too attached to using these, make sure that you also check out the concept of isolation levels later in the chapter.

The syntax for using these optimizer hints is fairly easy – just add it after the table name, or after the alias if you're using one:

```
...
FROM <table name> [AS <alias>][[WITH](<hint>)]
```

So to put this into a couple of examples, any of these would be legal, and all would force a table lock (rather than the more likely key or row lock) on the Orders table:

```
SELECT * FROM Orders AS ord WITH (TABLOCKX)
```

```
SELECT * FROM Orders AS ord (TABLOCKX)
```

```
SELECT * FROM Orders WITH (TABLOCKX)
```

```
SELECT * FROM Orders (TABLOCKX)
```

Now look at it from a multiple table perspective. The queries below would do the same thing as those above in terms of locking – they would force an exclusive table lock on the Orders table. The thing to note, however, is that they do *not* place any kind of special lock on the Order Details table – the SQL Server lock manager is still in complete control of that table.

```
SELECT *
FROM Orders AS ord WITH (TABLOCKX)
JOIN [Order Details] AS od
   ON ord.OrderID = od.OrderID
```

```
SELECT *
FROM Orders AS ord (TABLOCKX)
JOIN [Order Details] AS od
   ON ord.OrderID = od.OrderID
```

```
SELECT *
FROM Orders WITH (TABLOCKX)
JOIN [Order Details] AS od
   ON Orders.OrderID = od.OrderID
```

```
SELECT *
FROM Orders (TABLOCKX)
JOIN [Order Details] AS od
   ON Orders.OrderID = od.OrderID
```

We also could have done something completely different here and placed a totally separate hint on the Order Details table – it's up to you.

Using sp_lock – and an Extra Surprise

Sometimes you want to know which locks are active in the system. If you go ask your buddy who's already a DBA, then he'll probably tell you, "No problem! Use sp_lock." I have one word for that DBA – *yuck*! Let's look at sp_lock and I think you'll see what I mean.

We'll open two separate query windows in the Query Analyzer, and use one of the queries that we just used to illustrate optimizer hints. (OK, so I'm cheating here with two demos in one, but hey, it works and it's probably how you'd check things in real life.)

In the first Query Analyzer window, we'll set up our query:

```
SELECT *
FROM Orders AS ord (TABLOCKX)
JOIN [Order Details] AS od
   ON ord.OrderID = od.OrderID
```

Now, in the second window, set up the sp_lock system stored proc:

```
EXEC sp_lock
```

Make sure that both windows are visible. Execute the first window (the query), and then, while the first command is still executing (you may need to be very quick if you have a fast system), switch to the second window and execute sp_lock. Your sp_lock return should look something like this:

spid	dbid	ObjId	IndId	Type	Resource	Mode	Status
52	6	0	0	DB		S	GRANT
52	6	325576198	1	PAG	1:213	IS	GRANT
52	6	21575115	0	TAB		X	GRANT
52	6	325576198	0	TAB		IS	GRANT
52	6	325576198	1	KEY	(8700210 aa3b6)	S	GRANT
54	1	85575343	0	TAB		IS	GRANT
54	6	0	0	DB		S	GRANT

It doesn't take a rocket scientist to figure out that this isn't (immediately speaking) much help. It does, however, take a rocket scientist – well, not really, but it seems like it – to figure out what it all means.

Part of it is relatively easy. The Type tells us whether it's a table, database, row, page, extent, etc. The Mode tells us whether it's a shared, update, exclusive, etc. lock, with an "I" at the front indicating that it's an intent lock. Finally (as far as the easy stuff goes), it tells us the status – almost always that's going to be that the lock has actually been granted, though it may still be pending.

Now things become more difficult – what exactly has these locks on it? The information is there, but you have to know how to get it. You need to decipher the dbid (the database ID) by querying the sysdatabases table in the master database (or using the DB_NAME() function), and the ObjId (the object ID) and IndId (the index ID) by querying the sysobjects and sysindexes tables respectively in the appropriate database. The ObjId can be determined using OBJECT_NAME().

Using spDBLocks

I find all that deciphering rather annoying, so I'm giving you a little present on the Wrox web site. The present is called spDBLocks. Just pull up the script and run it. I've made it into a system stored procedure (so you can call it everywhere after only creating it once).

The specific syntax is (assuming you build it in the master database):

```
EXEC spDBLocks [<database name> [, '<object name>']]
```

If you don't provide a database name, then it will assume you want the current database. If you supply an object name, then you'll get just the locks related to that object.

If you run the previous example using this new sproc, you'll get a result that is a little more useful:

spid	dbid	ObjId	Object Name	IndId	Type	Resource	Mode	Status
55	6	21575115	Orders	0	TAB		X	GRANT
55	6	325576198	Order Details	1	PAG	1:362	IS	GRANT
55	6	325576198	Order Details	0	TAB		IS	GRANT
55	6	325576198	Order Details	1	KEY	(bd00e2e 36aa0)	S	GRANT

If you look at the messages, you'll see that it knew what database we were interested in (on a production server, a mix of databases and larger user counts can make using sp_lock a real nightmare).

If you like, you can modify the sproc to eliminate information that you may not be interested in (such as the dbid, or, if you're not looking to track the lock to a particular process, the spid). Feel free to use it as you wish as long as you don't redistribute it.

The reason I built this sproc is pretty simple – I wanted to be able to trim the list down to just the database I was interested in, and, if necessary, just the object I was interested in. When I'm looking for a block, I'd like to see the object name rather than the object ID – maybe Microsoft will "borrow" this code and give us something more useful next time...

If you go ahead and analyze the results, you'll also see a nice example of why locking with less granularity can actually be a good thing if contention isn't your concern – it takes fewer resources. Even in this rather brief example where we aren't using a HOLDLOCK (which means that as soon as the resource is not needed any more, the lock is released), we still have three locks related to the Order Details table, but only one for the Orders table. In a transaction situation, this could be even more dramatic.

Because we started out with a table lock on the Orders table, there were no intent locks required. Even if we touched 20,000 rows, the single table lock would be enough to protect our cause. The Order Details table, however, has to establish either a row identifier lock (if there's no cluster key) or a key lock (if a cluster key is available), plus the intent locks for the page and table. In short, we can see that, by obtaining the table lock straight off the bat, we were able to save resources – that usually translates into a somewhat faster query – exactly how much depends on the query (usually not much, but every little bit helps).

Determining Locks Using EM

Perhaps the nicest way of all to take a look at your locks is by using the Enterprise Manager. EM will show you locks in two different sorts – by **process ID** or by **object**.

To make use of EM's lock display, just navigate to the Management I Current Activity node of your server:

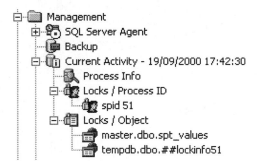

Just expand the node that you're interested in (either the Process ID or the Object), and you'll see various locks.

> **Perhaps the coolest feature in this shows itself when you double-click on a specific lock in the right-hand pane of EM. A dialog box that will come up and tell you the last statement that was run by that process ID. This can be very handy when you are troubleshooting deadlock situations.**

Setting the Isolation Level

We've seen the several different kinds of problems that can be prevented by different locking strategies. We've also seen what kinds of locks are available and how they impact on the availability of resources. Now it's time to take a closer look at how these process management pieces work together to ensure overall data integrity – to make certain that you can get the results you expect.

The first thing to understand about the relationship between transactions and locks is that they are inextricably linked with each other. By default, any lock that is data modification related will, once created, be held for the duration of the transaction. If you have a long transaction, this means that your locks may be preventing other processes from accessing the objects you have a lock on for a rather long time. It probably goes without saying that this can be rather problematic.

However, that's only the default. In fact, there are actually four different **isolation levels** that you can set:

- ❑ READ COMMITTED (the default)
- ❑ READ UNCOMMITTED
- ❑ REPEATABLE READ
- ❑ SERIALIZABLE

The syntax for switching between them is pretty straightforward:

```
SET TRANSACTION ISOLATION LEVEL <READ COMMITTED|READ UNCOMMITTED
    |REPEATABLE READ|SERIALIZABLE>
```

The change in isolation level will affect only the current connection – so you don't need to worry about adversely affecting other users (or them affecting you).

Let's start by looking at the default situation (READ COMMITTED) a little more closely.

READ COMMITTED

With READ COMMITTED, any shared locks you create will be automatically released as soon as the statement that created them is complete. That is, if you start a transaction, run several statements, run a SELECT statement, and then run several more statements, the locks associated with the SELECT statement are freed as soon as the SELECT statement is complete – SQL Server doesn't wait for the end of the transaction.

Action queries (UPDATE, DELETE, and INSERT) are a little different. If your transaction performs a query that modifies data, then those locks will be held for the duration of the transaction (in case you need to roll-back).

By keeping this level of default, with READ COMMITTED, you can be sure that you have enough data integrity to prevent dirty reads. However, unrepeatable reads and phantoms can still occur.

READ UNCOMMITTED

READ UNCOMMITTED is the most dangerous of all isolation level choices, but also has the highest performance in terms of speed.

Setting the isolation level to READ UNCOMMITTED tells SQL Server not to set any locks, and not to honor any locks. With this isolation level, it is possible to experience any of the various concurrency issues we discussed earlier in the chapter (most notably a dirty read).

Why would one ever want to risk a dirty read? When I watch the newsgroups on Usenet, I see the question come up on a regular basis. It's surprising to a fair number of people, but there are actually good reasons to have this isolation level, and they are almost always to do with reporting.

In an OLAP environment, locks are both your protector and your enemy. They prevent data integrity problems, but they also often prevent, or block, you from getting at the data you want. It is extremely commonplace to see a situation where the management wants to run reports regularly, but the data entry people are often prevented from or delayed in entering data because of locks held by the manager's reports.

By using READ UNCOMMITTED, you can often get around this problem – at least for reports where the numbers don't have to be exact. For example, let's say that a sales manager wants to know just how much has been done in sales so far today. Indeed, we'll say he's a micro-manager, and asks this same question (in the form of re-running the report) several times a day.

If the report happened to be a long running one, then there's a high chance that his running it would damage the productivity of other users due to locking considerations. What's nice about this report though, is that it is a truly nebulous report – the exact values are probably meaningless. The manager is really just looking for ballpark numbers.

By having an isolation level of READ UNCOMMITTED, we do not set any locks, so we don't block any other transactions. Our numbers will be somewhat suspect (because of the risk of dirty reads), but we don't need exact numbers anyway, and we know that the numbers are still going to be close even on the off chance that a dirty read is rolled back.

You can get the same effect as READ UNCOMMITTED by adding the NOLOCK optimizer hint in your query. The advantage to setting the isolation level is that you don't have to use a hint for every table in your query, or use it in multiple queries. The advantage to using the NOLOCK optimizer hint is that you don't need to remember to set the isolation level back to the default for the connection (With READ UNCOMMITTED you do).

REPEATABLE READ

The REPEATABLE READ escalates your isolation level somewhat, and provides an extra level of concurrency protection by preventing not only dirty reads (the default already does that), but also preventing unrepeatable reads.

That prevention of unrepeatable reads is a big upside, but holding even shared locks until the end of the transaction can block users' access to objects, and therefore hurt productivity. Personally, I prefer to use other data integrity options (such as a CHECK constraint together with error handling) rather than this choice, but it remains an available option.

The equivalent optimizer hint for the REPEATABLE READ isolation level is REPEATABLEREAD (these are the same, only no space).

SERIALIZABLE

SERIALIZABLE is something of the fortress of isolation levels. It prevents all forms of concurrency issues except for a lost update. Even phantoms are prevented.

When you set your isolation to SERIALIZABLE, you're saying that any UPDATE, DELETE, or INSERT to the table or tables used by your transaction must not meet the WHERE clause of any statement in that transaction. Essentially, if the user was going to do something that your transaction would be interested in then it must wait until your transaction has been completed.

The SERIALIZABLE isolation level can also be simulated by using the SERIALIZABLE or HOLDLOCK optimizer hint in your query. Again, like the READ UNCOMMITTED and NOLOCK debate, the option of not having to set it every time versus not having to remember to change the isolation level back is the big issue.

> *Going with an isolation level of SERIALIZABLE would, on the surface, appear to be the way you want to do everything. Indeed, it does provide your database with the highest level of what is called **consistency** – that is, the update process works the same for multiple users as it would if all your users did one transaction at a time (processed things serially).*

> *As with most things in life, however, there is a trade-off. Consistency and concurrency can, from a practical sense, be thought of as polar opposites. Making things SERIALIZABLE can prevent other users from getting to the objects they need – that equates to lower concurrency. The reverse is also true – increasing concurrency (by going to a REPEATABLE READ for example) reduces the consistency of your database.*

> *My personal recommendation on this is to stick with the default (READ COMMITTED) unless you have a specific reason not to.*

About Isolation Levels and MTS/COM+

I'm going to formalize something that otherwise might have just been shown elsewhere as a caution – that is, I'm going to give an appropriate heading to the topic of Microsoft Transaction Server and its successor COM+. Discussion of these two transaction managers is beyond the scope of this book, however since they alter SQL Server's default behavior in a way I never see discussed anywhere, I'm going to take the time to mention that here.

When you are working with MTS/COM+, it's important to realize that both of these transaction managers alter the default isolation level that is being used on your SQL Server. Instead of the relatively contention free READ COMMITTED, MTS and COM+ both set the isolation level to SERIALIZABLE. It's the safest from a pure data integrity point of view, but it can wreak havoc on your system due to concurrency issues.

Unfortunately, there is no way to change this from within ADO. The only API exposure robust enough to override this is found in the form of OLE DB, which means two things:

❑ You're probably writing it in C++ (VB can't address the OLE DB API directly)

❑ Even if you're an experienced C++ developer, you're probably in pain (OLE DB is *not* fun!)

The only way to get around this from a VB perspective is to use optimizer hints in your queries – just keep in mind that doing so is going to cut into your portability to other platforms (the hints are not ANSI compliant).

Dealing with Deadlocks (aka "A 1205")

OK. So now you've seen locks, and you've also seen transactions. Now that you've got both, we can move on to the rather pesky problem of dealing with **deadlocks**.

As we've already mentioned, a deadlock is not a type of lock in itself, but rather a situation where a paradox has been formed by other locks. Like it or not, you'll bump into these on a regular basis (particularly when you're just starting out), and you'll be greeted with an error number **1205**. So prolific is this particular problem that you'll hear many a database developer refer to them simply by the number.

Deadlocks are caused when one lock can't do what it needs to do in order to clear because a second lock is holding that resource, and vice versa. When this happens, somebody has to win the battle, so SQL Server chooses a deadlock **victim**. The deadlock victim's transaction is then rolled back and is notified that this happened through the 1205 error. The other transaction can continue normally (indeed, it will be entirely unaware that there was a problem, other than seeing an increased execution time).

How SQL Server Figures out there's a Deadlock

Every five seconds SQL Server checks all the current transactions for what locks they are waiting on but haven't yet been granted. As it does this, it essentially makes a note that the request exists. It will then re-check the status of all open lock requests again, and, if one of the previous requests has still not been granted, it will recursively check all open transactions for a circular chain of lock requests. If it finds such a chain, then one or more deadlock victims will be chosen.

How Deadlock Victims Are Chosen

By default, a deadlock victim is chosen based on the "cost" of the transactions involved. The transaction that costs the least to rollback will be chosen (in other words SQL Server has to do the least number of things to undo it). However, you can override this by setting the DEADLOCK_PRIORITY to LOW for your connection. The syntax is pretty simple:

```
SET DEADLOCK_PRIORITY <LOW|NORMAL>
```

If you set your DEADLOCK_PRIORITY to LOW, then any transactions on the current connection will be treated as a preferred choice to become the deadlock victim. If there is a deadlock, and there is only one connection that has a low priority, then that will be the one chosen. If there are two at the same priority, then the standard, least-cost method will be used between those connections. NORMAL specifies the default deadlock-handling mechanism.

> The **DEADLOCK_PRIORITY** can be problematic if not used properly. Since the **SET** option applied to the entire connection, any other transactions run for this connection will also adhere to that priority setting. As such, I would classify it as nothing short of critical that you make sure to change the option back prior to exiting your sproc. Make certain that, if you have multiple exit points, that you reset this option prior to each one.

Avoiding Deadlocks

Deadlocks can't be avoided 100% of the time in complex systems, but you can almost always totally eliminate them from a practical standpoint – that is, make them so rare that they have little relevance to your system.

To cut-down or eliminate deadlocks, follow these simple (OK, usually simple) rules:

- ❑ Use your objects in the same order
- ❑ Keep your transactions as short as possible and in one batch
- ❑ Use the lowest transaction isolation level necessary
- ❑ Do not allow open-ended interruptions (user interactions, batch separations) within the same transaction
- ❑ In controlled environments, use bound connections (described briefly below)

Nearly every time I run across deadlocking problems, at least one (usually more) of these rules has been violated. Let's look at each one individually.

Use Objects in the Same Order

This is the most common problem area within the few rules that I consider to be basic. What's great about using this rule is that it almost never costs you anything to speak of – it's more a way of thinking. You decide early in your design process how you want to access your database objects – including order – and it becomes a habit in every query, procedure, or trigger that you write for that project.

Think about it for a minute – if our problem is that our two connections each have what the other wants, then it implies that we're dealing with the problem too late in the game. Let's look at a simple example.

Consider that we have two tables: Suppliers and Products. Now say that we have two processes that make use of both of these tables. The Process 1 accepts inventory entries, updates Products with the new amount of product on hand, and then updates Suppliers with the total amount of product that we've purchased. Process 2 records sales; it updates the total amount of product sold in the Suppliers table, and then decreases the inventory quantity in Products.

If we run these two processes at the same time, we're begging for trouble. Process 1 will grab an exclusive lock on the Products. Process 2 grabs an exclusive lock on the Suppliers table. Process 1 then attempts to grab a lock on the Suppliers table, but it will be forced to wait for Process 2 to clear its existing lock. In the mean time, Process 2 tries to create a lock on the Products table, but it will have to wait for Process 1 to clear its existing lock. We now have a paradox – both processes are waiting on each other. SQL Server will have to pick a deadlock victim.

Now let's rearrange that scenario, with Process 2 changed to first decrease the inventory quantity in Products, and then update the total amount of product sold in the Suppliers table. This is a functional equivalent to the first way we organized the processes, and it will cost us nothing to perform it this new way. The impact though, will be stunning – no more deadlocks (at least not between these two processes)! Let's walk through what will now happen.

When we run these two processes at the same time, Process 1 will grab an exclusive lock on the `Products` table (so far, it's the same). Process 2 then also tries to grab a lock on the `Products` table, but will be forced to wait for Process 1 to finish (notice that we haven't done anything with `Suppliers` yet). Process 1 finishes with the `Products` table, but doesn't release the lock because the transaction isn't complete yet. Process 2 is still waiting for the lock on `Products` to clear. Process 1 now moves on to grab a lock on the `Suppliers` table. Process 2 continues to wait for the lock to clear on `Products`. Process 1 finishes and commits or rolls back the transaction as required, but frees all locks in either case. Process 2 now is able to obtain its lock on the `Products` table, and moves through the rest of its transaction without further incident.

Just swapping the order in which these two queries are run has eliminated a potential deadlock problem. Keep things in the same order wherever possible and you too will experience far less in the way of deadlocks.

Keeping Transactions as Short as Possible

This is another of the basics. Again, it should become just an instinct – something you don't really think about, something you just do.

This is one that never has to cost you anything really. Put what you need to put in the transaction, and keep everything else out – it's just that simple. Why this works isn't rocket science – the longer the transaction is open, and the more it touches (within the transaction), then the higher the likelihood that you're going to run into some other process that wants one or more of the objects that you're using (reducing concurrency). If you keep your transaction short, you minimize the number of objects that can potentially cause a deadlock, plus you cut down on the time that you have your lock on them. It's as simple as that.

Keeping transactions in one batch minimizes network roundtrips during a transaction, reducing possible delays in completing the transaction and releasing locks.

Use the Lowest Transaction Isolation Level Possible.

This one is considerably less basic, and requires some serious thought. As such, it isn't surprising just how often it isn't thought of at all. Consider it Rob's axiom – that which requires thought is likely not to be thought of. Be different – think about it.

We have several different transaction isolation levels available. The default is READ COMMITTED. Using a lower isolation level holds shared locks for a shorter duration than a higher isolation level, thereby reducing locking contention.

No Open-Ended Transactions

This is probably the most common sense out of all the recommendations here – but it's one that's often violated due to past practices.

One of the ways we used to prevent lost updates (mainframe days here folks!), was just to grab the lock and hold it until we were done with it. I can't tell you how problematic this was (can you say *yuck*!).

Imagine this scenario (it's a real-life example): someone in your service department likes to use update (exclusive locks) screens instead of display (shared locks) screens to look at data. He goes on to look at a work order. Now his buddy calls and asks if he's ready for lunch. "Sure!" comes the reply, and the service clerk heads off to a rather long (1½-2hr) lunch. Everyone who is interested in this record is now locked out of it for the duration of this clerk's lunch.

Wait – it gets worse. In the days of the mainframe, you used to see the concept of queuing far more often (it actually can be quite efficient). Now someone submits a print job (which is queued) for this work order. It sits in the queue waiting for the record lock to clear. Since it's a queue environment, every print job your company has for work orders now piles up behind that first print job (which is going to wait for that person's lunch before clearing).

This is a rather extreme example – but I'm hoping that it clearly illustrates the point. Don't ever create locks that will still be open when you begin some form of open-ended process. Usually we're talking user interaction (like our lunch lover), but it could be any process that has an open-ended wait to it.

Bound Connections

Hmm. I had to debate even including this one, because it's something of a can of worms. Once you open it, you're never going to get them all back in. I'll just say that bound connections are used extremely rarely, and are not for the faint-hearted.

It's not that they don't have their uses; it's just that things can become rather convoluted rather quickly, so you need to manage things well. It's my personal opinion that there is usually a better solution.

That brings on the question of what is a bound connection. Bound connections are connections that have been associated together, and are allowed to essentially share the same set of locks. What that means is that the two transactions can operate in tandem without any fear of deadlocking each other or being blocked by one another. The flip side is that it means that you essentially are on your own in terms of dealing with most concurrency issues – locks aren't keeping you safe anymore.

Given my distaste for these for 99.9% of situations, we're going to forget that they exist now even though we know they are an option. If you're going to insist on using them, just remember that you're going to be dealing with an extremely complex relationship between connections, and you need to manage the activities in those connections rather closely if you are going to maintain data integrity within the system.

Summary

Transactions and locks are both cornerstone items to how SQL Server works, and, therefore, to maximizing your development of solutions in SQL Server.

By using transactions, you can make sure that everything you need to have happen as a unit happens, or none of it does. SQL Server's use of locks ensures that we avoid the pitfalls of concurrency to the maximum extent possible (you'll never avoid them entirely, but it's amazing how close you can come with a little – OK a lot – of planning). By using the two together, you are able to pass what the database industry calls the **ACID** test. If a transaction is ACID, then it has:

❑   **Atomicity**: the transaction is all or nothing.

❑   **Consistency**: all constraints and other data integrity rules have been adhered to, and all related objects (data pages, index pages) have been updated completely.

❑   **Isolation**: each transaction is completely isolated from any other transaction. The actions of one transaction cannot be interfered with by the actions of a separate transaction.

❑   **Durability**: after a transaction is completed, its effects are permanently in place in the system. The data is "safe", in the sense that things like a power outage or other non-disk system failure will not lead to data that is only half written.

In short, by using transactions and locks, you can minimize deadlocks, ensure data-integrity, and improve the overall efficiency of your system.

In our next chapter, we'll be looking at triggers. Indeed, we'll see that, for many of the likely uses of triggers, the concepts of transactions and rollbacks will be at the very center of the trigger.

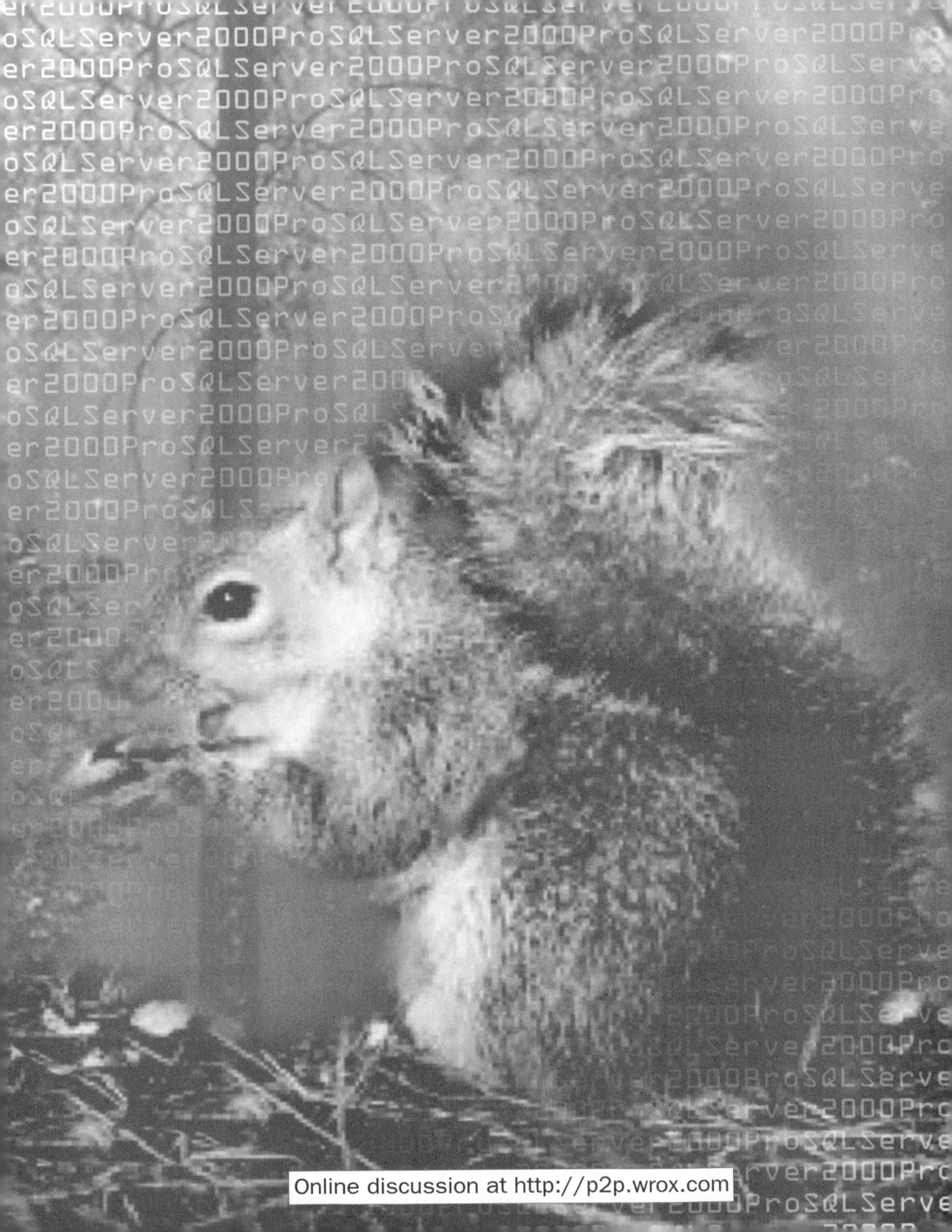
Online discussion at http://p2p.wrox.com

15

Triggers

Ah, triggers. Triggers are cool, triggers are neat, and triggers are our friends. At the very same time, triggers are evil, triggers are ugly, and triggers are our enemy. In short, I am often asked, "Should I use triggers?" The answer is, like most things in SQL, "It depends." There's little that's black and white in the wonderful world of SQL Server – triggers are definitely a very plain shade of gray.

In this chapter, we'll try to look at triggers in all of their colors – from black all the way to white and a whole lot in between. The main issues we'll be dealing with include:

- ❑ What is a trigger?
- ❑ Using triggers instead of DRI (Declarative Referential Integrity)
- ❑ Using triggers for more flexible referential integrity
- ❑ Using triggers to create flexible data integrity rules
- ❑ Using INSTEAD OF triggers to create more flexible updateable views
- ❑ Other common uses for triggers
- ❑ Controlling the firing order of triggers
- ❑ Performance considerations

By the time we're done, you should have an idea of just how complex the decision about when and when not to use triggers is. You'll also have an inkling of just how powerful and flexible they can be.

Most of all, if I've done my job well, you won't be a trigger extremist (which *so* many SQL Server people I meet are) with the distorted notion that triggers are evil and should never be used. Neither will you side with the other end of the spectrum, who think that triggers are the solution to all the world's problems. The right answer in this respect is that triggers can do a lot for you, but they can also cause a lot of problems. The trick is to use them when they are the right things to use, and not to use them when they aren't.

Some common uses of triggers include:

❑ Referential Integrity: though I recommend using Declarative Referential Integrity (DRI) whenever possible, there are many things that DRI won't do (for example, referential integrity across databases or even servers, many complex types of relationships, etc.).

❑ Creating Audit Trails: writing out records that keep track of not just the most current data, but also the actual change history for each record.

❑ Functionality similar to a CHECK constraint, but which works across tables, databases, or even servers.

❑ Substituting your own statements in the place of a user's action statement (usually used to enable inserts in complex views).

And these are just a few. So, with no further ado, let's look at exactly what a trigger is.

What is a Trigger?

A trigger is a special kind of stored procedure that responds to specific events.

Triggers are pieces of code that you attach to a particular table. Unlike sprocs, where you needed to explicitly invoke the code, the code in triggers is automatically run whenever the event(s) you attached the trigger to occur in the table. Indeed, you *can't* explicitly invoke triggers – the only way to do this is by performing the required action in the table that they are assigned to.

> **Beyond not being able to explicitly invoke a trigger, you'll find two other things that exist for sprocs but are missing from triggers: parameters and return codes.**
>
> **While triggers take no parameters, they do have a mechanism for figuring out what records they are supposed to act on (we'll investigate this further later in the chapter). And, while you can use the RETURN keyword, you cannot return a specific return code (since you didn't explicitly call the trigger, what would you return a return code to?).**

What events can you attach triggers to? – the three "action" query types you use in SQL. So, there are three types of triggers, plus hybrids that come from mixing and matching the events and timing that fire them:

1. INSERT triggers

2. DELETE triggers

3. UPDATE triggers

4. A mix and match of any of the above

> It's worth noting that there are times when a trigger will not fire – even though it seems that the action you are performing falls into one of the above categories. At issue is whether the operation you are doing is in a logged activity or not. For example, a **DELETE** statement is a normal, logged activity that would fire any delete trigger, but a **TRUNCATE TABLE**, which has the effect of deleting rows, just deallocates the space used by the table – there is no individual deletion of rows logged, and no trigger is fired.
>
> Data inserted into tables from the Bulk Copy Program (bcp) also used to work this way (no triggers fired). With SQL Server 2000, bcp activity is now logged by default, which in turn causes your triggers to fire.

The syntax for creating triggers looks an awful lot like all of our other CREATE syntax, except that it has to be attached to a table – a trigger can't stand on its own. The complexity of the various CREATE TRIGGER syntaxes has, however, increased quite a bit in this release to support INSTEAD OF triggers and creating triggers against views (neither of which existed prior to SQL Server 2000).

Let's take a look:

```
CREATE TRIGGER <trigger name>
    ON <table or view name>
    [WITH ENCRYPTION]
    {{{FOR|AFTER} <[DELETE] [,] [INSERT] [,] [UPDATE]>} |INSTEAD OF}
    [WITH APPEND]
    [NOT FOR REPLICATION]
AS
    <sql statements
    ...
    ...
    ...>
```

As you can see, the all too familiar CREATE <object type> <object name> is still there – we've just added the ON clause to indicate the table to which this trigger is going to be attached, as well as when and under what conditions it fires.

ON

This part just names what object you are creating the trigger against. Keep in mind that, if the type of the trigger is an AFTER trigger (if it uses FOR or AFTER to declare the trigger), then the target of the ON clause must be a table – AFTER triggers are not supported for views.

WITH ENCRYPTION

This works just as it does for views and sprocs. If you add this option, you can be certain that no one will be able to view your code (not even you!). This is particularly useful if you are going to be building software for commercial distribution, or if you are concerned about security and don't want your users to be able to see what data you're modifying or accessing. Obviously, you should keep a copy of the code required to create the trigger somewhere else, in case you want to re-create it sometime later.

As with views and sprocs, the thing to remember when using the WITH ENCRYPTION option is that you must re-apply it every time you ALTER your trigger. If you make use of an ALTER TRIGGER statement and do not include the WITH ENCRYPTION option, then the trigger will no longer be encrypted.

The FOR|AFTER vs. the INSTEAD OF Clause

Beginning with SQL Server 2000, you have the ability to run what is called an INSTEAD OF trigger. Alternatively (and, in most cases, preferably), you can use the historical FOR trigger. A FOR trigger can also now be declared using the AFTER keyword in the place of the FOR.

Confusing? Probably. Let's try it a different way with a diagram that shows where each choice fires:

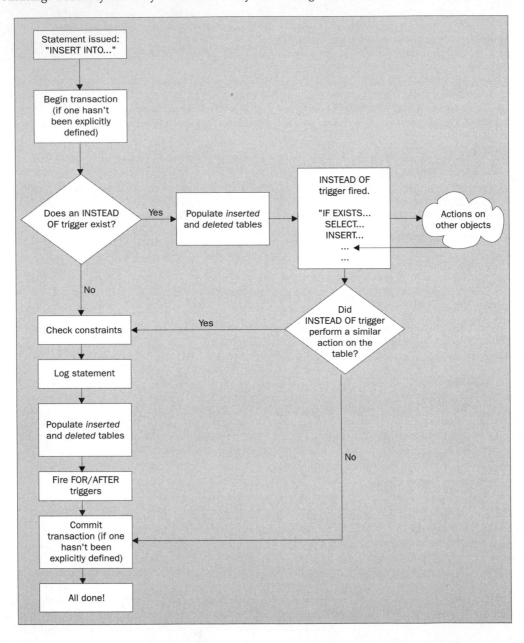

The thing to note here is that, regardless of which choice you make, SQL Server will put together two working tables – one holding a copy of the records that were inserted (and, incidentally, called INSERTED) and one holding a copy of any records that were deleted (called DELETED). We'll look into the details of the uses of these working tables a little later. For now realize that, with INSTEAD OF triggers, the creation of these working tables will happen *before* any constraints are checked – this is wildly different from the behavior found in 7.0 and previous versions. The key to this behavior is that you can actually run your own code in the place of whatever the user requested. This means we can clean up ambiguous insert problems in views (remember the problem back in Chapter 10 with inserting when there was a JOIN in the view?). It also means that we can take action to clean up constraint violations before the constraint is even checked.

Triggers using the FOR and AFTER declaration behave identically to each other. The big difference between them and INSTEAD OF triggers is that they build their working tables *after* any constraints have been checked.

INSTEAD OF triggers can be used to perform *before trigger* functionality.

FOR|AFTER

The FOR (or, alternatively, you can use AFTER) clause indicates under what type of action(s) you want this trigger to fire. You can have the trigger fire whenever there is an INSERT, UPDATE, or DELETE, or any mix of the three. So, for example, your FOR clause could look something like:

```
FOR INSERT, DELETE
```

...or:

```
FOR UPDATE, INSERT
```

...or:

```
FOR DELETE
```

As was stated in the section about the ON clause, triggers declared using the FOR or AFTER clause can only be attached to tables – no views are allowed (see INSTEAD OF triggers for those).

INSERT Trigger

The code for any trigger that you mark as being FOR INSERT will be executed anytime that someone inserts a new row into your table. For each row that is inserted, SQL Server will create a copy of that new row and insert it in a special table that exists only within the scope of your trigger. That table is called INSERTED, and we'll see much more of it over the course of this chapter. The big thing to understand is that the INSERTED table only lives as long as your trigger does. Think of it as not existing before your trigger starts or after your trigger completes.

DELETE Trigger

This works much the same as an INSERT trigger does, save that the INSERTED table is not created. Instead, a copy of each record that was deleted is inserted into another table called DELETED that, like the INSERTED table, is limited in scope to just the life of your trigger.

UPDATE Trigger

More of the same, save for a twist. The code in a trigger declared as being FOR UPDATE will be fired whenever an existing record in your table is changed. The twist is that there's no such table as UPDATED. Instead, SQL Server treats each row as if the existing record had been deleted, and a totally new record was inserted. As you can probably guess from that, a trigger declared as FOR UPDATE contains not one but two special tables called INSERTED and DELETED. The two tables have exactly the same number of rows, of course.

WITH APPEND

WITH APPEND is something of an oddball and, in all honesty, you're pretty unlikely to use it; nonetheless, we'll cover it here for that "just-in-case" scenario. WITH APPEND only applies when you are running in 6.5 compatibility mode (which can be set using sp_dbcmptlevel).

SQL Server 6.5 and prior did not allow multiple triggers of the same type on any single table. For example, if you had already declared a trigger called trgCheck to enforce data integrity on updates and inserts, then you couldn't create a separate trigger for cascading updates. Once one update (or insert, or delete) trigger was created, that was it – you couldn't create another trigger for the same type of action.

This was a real pain. It meant that you had to combine logically different activities into one trigger. Trying to get what amounted to two entirely different procedures to play nicely together could, at times, be quite a challenge. In addition, it made reading the code something of an arduous task.

Along came SQL Server 7.0 and the rules changed substantially. No longer do we have to worry about how many triggers we have for one type of action query – you can have several if you like. When running our database in 6.5 compatibility mode though, we run into a problem – our database is still working on the notion that there can only be one trigger of a given type on a given table.

WITH APPEND gets around this problem by explicitly telling SQL Server that we want to add this new trigger even though we already have a trigger of that type on the table – both will be fired when the appropriate trigger action (INSERT, UPDATE, DELETE) occurs. It's a way of having a bit of both worlds.

NOT FOR REPLICATION

Adding this option slightly alters the rules for when the trigger is fired. With this option in place, the trigger will not be fired whenever a replication-related task modifies your table. Usually a trigger is fired (to do the housekeeping/cascading/etc.) when the original table is modified and there is no point in doing it again.

AS

Exactly as it was with sprocs, this is the meat of the matter. The AS keyword tells SQL Server that your code is about to start. From this point forward, we're into the scripted portion of your trigger.

Using Triggers for Referential Integrity

Up to this point, the only way presented to perform referential integrity checks has been through the use of declarative referential integrity– or DRI – but that's not the only option. Indeed, DRI wasn't even an option until SQL Server 6.5. Before that everything was done with triggers.

Triggers are still often an excellent choice for your referential integrity needs. While they are a bit slower (more on that later), they are considerably more flexible in the way they enforce data integrity. As such, there are actually some types of relationships (and treatments thereof) that can only be enforced by means of a trigger.

Examples of relationship uses where triggers shine include:

❏   One-to-one relationships

❏   Exclusive subcategory

❏   Any situation where your enforcement needs to cross database or server boundaries

As game show announcers often say, there are "these and many, many more!" It just depends on your particular requirements. That's what's great about triggers – they are the ultimate in flexibility.

Using Triggers for Simple Referential Integrity

Besides all those tricky things we just listed, triggers can be used for the same plain and simple referential integrity that DRI can. Generally speaking, this isn't the way you want to do things, but there are times when it's the thing to do, or you might just want to understand how they work in case you bump into these kinds of triggers in legacy code.

Let's not waste any more time with the theory and get right to the code. Before we create the actual trigger though, we'll need to create a test area. What we'll do is make use of a copy of the `Northwind` database that doesn't have any DRI in it. Indeed, when we start, it won't have any referential integrity at all.

Make sure you've downloaded the file `NorthwindTriggers.dts` from www.wrox.com or my personal web site www.ProfessionalSQL.com before you start working with this example.

> *Be careful as you go through the examples in this chapter! Unless otherwise stated, all examples should be run in the* `NorthwindTriggers` *database that is created by the* `NorthwindTriggers.dts` *script. If you run these examples in the regular* `Northwind` *database, you're liable to see some rather strange results as you bump into the foreign key constraints that exist there.*

To create `NorthwindTriggers` – our test database for triggers – you'll want to go to the **Data Transformation Services** node in EM, and right-click:

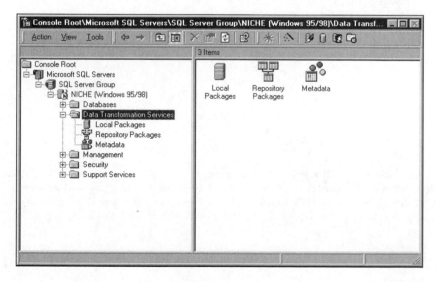

Select the **Open Package** menu choice. Open the file `NorthwindTriggers.dts` and then execute it (by clicking on the green arrow).

> **If you've set your sa password to something other than blank (which I actually recommend that you do – even for a test machine), this DTS package will fail. Just double-click on each of the two icons called Connection, enter your correct sa password, and then execute the package again.**

Now that we've got something to work with, let's go for one of the relationships that was enforced with DRI in the original `Northwind` database. What we're going to do is add back the relationship between `Customers` and `Orders`. This relationship made sure that we couldn't add orders into our table if they didn't refer to a `CustomerID` that already exists in the `Customers` table.

First though, let's make sure that the old integrity isn't there:

```
INSERT Orders
    DEFAULT VALUES
```

When we run this we get exactly what we expect, but also exactly what we don't want – an inserted record that doesn't meet our `CustomerID` constraint (which doesn't exist at the moment as far as the database is concerned).

(1 row(s) affected)

Now we'll create a simple trigger to take care of this:

```
CREATE TRIGGER OrderHasCustomer
    ON Orders
    FOR INSERT, UPDATE
AS
    IF EXISTS
        (
        SELECT 'True'
        FROM Inserted i
        LEFT JOIN Customers c
            ON i.CustomerID = c.CustomerID
        WHERE c.CustomerID IS NULL
        )
    BEGIN
        RAISERROR('Order Must Have Valid CustomerID',16,1)
        ROLLBACK TRAN
    END
```

This will actually catch two different situations. First, if the user or any sproc tries to insert a record without a matching `CustomerID`, the insert will fail. Second, if they try to update an existing order to a `CustomerID` that doesn't exist, then that will also fail. We are enforcing the very same one-to-zero, -one, or -many relationship that DRI did in the original `Northwind` database.

Let's try to insert that data now that the trigger is in place:

```
INSERT Orders
    DEFAULT VALUES
```

This time we get an error message:

```
Server: Msg 50000, Level 16, State 1, Line -1074284106
Order Must Have Valid CustomerID
```

Ah, isn't life grand?

But wait – this error is quite uninformative. It doesn't tell the user much about what actually constitutes a valid `CustomerID`.

This is actually one of the nice things about using triggers instead of DRI – you're in control of how the error message reads. If you're in a client-server environment, this isn't always a big thing (you'll often use some form of resource file to change the actual text of the error that the user sees anyway) but, in some instances, you would really like to be able to just pass through the text of the error to the end user. With triggers, we can easily do this with custom messages – just as we did with our sprocs.

Let's go ahead and enter in a custom message for use with our trigger above:

```
sp_addmessage 60000, 16, 'Error. Value for field %s in table %s must have matching
value in field %s of table %s'
```

Notice that our new custom message accepts four parameters corresponding to the column and table names for the relevant fields in each of our two tables. Also note that, if we were dealing with a composite key (two or more fields in the key), we would need to create a separate message for those or modify this message to be a bit more flexible.

Let's alter our trigger to make use of this new error. Note that the syntax for the `ALTER TRIGGER` command is exactly the same as the `CREATE TRIGGER`, save that there isn't any need for the `WITH APPEND` option.

```
ALTER TRIGGER OrderHasCustomer
    ON Orders
    FOR INSERT, UPDATE
AS
    IF EXISTS
        (
        SELECT 'True'
        FROM Inserted i
        LEFT JOIN Customers c
            ON i.CustomerID = c.CustomerID
        WHERE c.CustomerID IS NULL
        )
    BEGIN
        RAISERROR(60000,16,1,'CustomerID','Orders','CustomerID','Customers')
        ROLLBACK TRAN
    END
```

Now we'll run our little test again:

```
INSERT Orders
    DEFAULT VALUES
```

And, sure enough, we get our new error message:

Server: Msg 60000, Level 16, State 1, Line -1074284106
Error. Value for field CustomerID in table Orders must have matching value in field CustomerID of table Customers

Now let's move on to dealing with the other direction. DRI doesn't just deal with records being inserted into the destination table – it also deals with the concept of orphans by dealing with deletions from the referenced table (in our case, Customers). This is one of the minor pitfalls of triggers – in order to ensure that we do not create orphan records in a one-to-one table relationship, we have to prevent an insertion and/or deletion procedure that results in a one-to-zero relationship. For triggers, this often means placing a trigger at both ends of the relationship.

Let's get right to it again by adding in a trigger to prevent deletions from the Customers table:

```
CREATE TRIGGER CustomerHasOrders
    ON Customers
    FOR DELETE
AS
    IF EXISTS
        (
        SELECT 'True'
        FROM Deleted d
        JOIN Orders o
            ON d.CustomerID = o.CustomerID
        )

    BEGIN
        RAISERROR('Customer has Order History. Delete failed!',16,1)
        ROLLBACK TRAN
    END
```

We will test it out by trying to delete a customer that has orders:

```
DELETE Customers
    WHERE CustomerID = 'WHITC'
```

We get the expect error – and the record is not deleted:

Server: Msg 50000, Level 16, State 1, Line -1074284106
Customer has Order History. Delete failed!

It's just that simple. The only additional trick would be if our relationships were one-to-zero or many-to-many rather than one-to-many. In that case we would need to modify our triggers to only run the test query if CustomerID in the inserted table was NOT NULL.

Note that, just like with our previous trigger, we could have (and should have) created a custom error message to use with the DELETE statement – I'll leave that for you to experiment with on your own.

Using Triggers for More Flexible Referential Integrity

Plain old DRI enforces only two kinds of relationships: one-to-one or -many, or one-to-zero, -one, or -many. That's it. Another instance of a common requirement that can't be met with DRI is an **exclusive subcategory relationship**. In this relationship, the parent table holds information that is similar between several possible child tables but, for each row in the parent, there is a match in only one of the child tables (we look at subcategories in Chapter 24) – you definitely can't deal with this using DRI.

For these types of relationships, triggers are our only answer. While you'll hear me push DRI for performance reasons, DRI doesn't deal with the oddball stuff such as our subcategory example. Triggers become our salvation, and they actually do quite well at it.

One-to-One Relationships

Exact one-to-one relationships are far from the most common kind of relationship you'll find – but they aren't at all unheard of either. Perhaps the most common usage of one-to-one relationships is to establish a point of commonality between two separate systems.

For example, let's say that you have a system that is tracking all purchases that you make with your vendors. To further complicate this though, add the notion that you are a conglomerate – running several smaller companies that all have their own systems suited to their specific business. You want your top-level system to make sure that you know all the things that you're buying so you can make sure to use that information when bargaining with your vendors.

To do this, you would probably want to make sure that each system was using the same vendor numbers as well as the same part numbers for items that are the same. You want to make sure that your subsidiaries don't add records that you don't know about, and you want to make sure that they have all the options that are available to the parent company.

The implementation of this is a set of tables (one to each system for each of the vendors and part numbers) that all have a one-to-one relationship with the copy of the table on the master system. Every system gets a certain level of local performance and control over their tables, and they get to run the table within the context of their particular system. Still, you are certain that each system is working from some level of common ground.

For an example, we're going to pretend that our `NorthwindTriggers` database has a second system to which it's relating. First, we'll create a second `Orders` table to relate to:

```
CREATE TABLE Orders2 (
    OrderID            int             NOT NULL,
    CustomerID         nchar (5)       NULL,
    EmployeeID         int             NULL,
    OrderDate          datetime        NULL,
    RequiredDate       datetime        NULL,
    ShippedDate        datetime        NULL,
    ShipVia            int             NULL,
    Freight            money           NULL
        CONSTRAINT DF_Orders2_Freight DEFAULT (0),
    ShipName           nvarchar (40)   NULL,
    ShipAddress        nvarchar (60)   NULL,
    ShipCity           nvarchar (15)   NULL,
    ShipRegion         nvarchar (15)   NULL,
```

```
    ShipPostalCode    nvarchar (10) NULL,
    ShipCountry       nvarchar (15) NULL,
      CONSTRAINT PK_Orders2 PRIMARY KEY  CLUSTERED
      (OrderID)
)
GO
```

Note that we've removed the IDENTITY option from the OrderID column, since the Orders table will drive this table in the master system.

Next, we'll populate it with some data from the existing Orders table:

```
INSERT INTO Orders2
SELECT * FROM Orders
```

It's just that quick to make something to play with.

Now, in a one-to-one relationship, there are a couple of ways things can work. We can either have one table be a true master (as we will here), where all the inserting happens in one table, and then is propagated out to the other tables, or we can allow both tables to accept inserts and propagate to the other tables.

As I just indicated, we're going to take the model of having the Orders table be the master table, and the Orders2 table be a dependent table. We want Orders2 to reject any inserts that aren't already in the Orders table. Likewise, we need the Orders table to insert any new records it receives into the Orders2 table as well. To do this, we'll actually need to create two triggers – one for each table:

```
CREATE TRIGGER OrdersFeedsOrder2
    ON Orders
    FOR INSERT, UPDATE, DELETE
AS
    DECLARE @Count int
    SELECT @Count = COUNT(*) FROM DELETED

-- Check if any rows were deleted. If so, delete from the dependent table
    IF @Count  > 0
    BEGIN
        DELETE FROM Orders2
            FROM DELETED i
            JOIN Orders2 o2
                ON i.OrderID = o2.OrderID
    END

-- If anything went wrong, roll the transaction back
    IF @@ERROR != 0
        ROLLBACK TRAN

    SELECT @Count = COUNT(*) FROM Inserted

-- Now check for inserts. If there are any, copy to the dependent table
    IF @Count > 0
    BEGIN
```

```
        INSERT INTO Orders2
            SELECT i.*
            FROM Inserted i
            LEFT JOIN Orders2 o2
                ON i.OrderID = o2.OrderID
            WHERE o2.OrderID IS NULL
    END

-- Again, if problems, roll it back
    IF @@ERROR != 0
        ROLLBACK TRAN
```

Here's the second:

```
CREATE TRIGGER Order2DependsOnOrders
    ON Orders2
    FOR INSERT, UPDATE, DELETE
AS
    DECLARE @Count int

-- Do not allow a delete unless it's already been deleted from the parent table
    SELECT @Count = COUNT(*) FROM DELETED
    IF @Count > 0
    BEGIN
        IF NOT EXISTS
            (
             SELECT 'True'
             FROM Deleted d
             LEFT JOIN Orders o
                ON d.OrderID = o.OrderID
             WHERE o.OrderID IS NULL
            )
        BEGIN
            RAISERROR('Record Exists In Orders Table. Delete Cancelled.',16,1)
            ROLLBACK TRAN
        END
    END

-- Do not allow insert unless there's a match in the parent table
    IF @@ERROR != 0
        ROLLBACK TRAN
    SELECT @Count = COUNT(*) FROM INSERTED
    SELECT 'Count is ' + CONVERT(varchar,@Count) + ' Before Delete'
    IF @Count > 0
    BEGIN
        IF EXISTS
            (
             SELECT 'True'
             FROM Inserted i
             LEFT JOIN Orders o
                ON i.OrderID = o.OrderID
             WHERE o.OrderID IS NULL
            )
        BEGIN
            RAISERROR('Inserted Record Must exist in the Orders Table',16,1)
            ROLLBACK TRAN
        END
    END
    IF @@ERROR != 0
        ROLLBACK TRAN
```

Now we're ready to do some testing again. Let's start with an insert into the Orders table, and make sure that it propagates to the Orders2 table:

```
INSERT Orders
    (CustomerID, OrderDate)
VALUES
    ('ALFKI', '1/1/2000')
```

Then select back the values from both tables:

```
SELECT OrderID, CustomerID FROM Orders WHERE OrderDate = '1/1/2000'
SELECT OrderID, CustomerID FROM Orders2 WHERE OrderDate = '1/1/2000'
```

...and we see that, even though we only inserted the value into the Orders table, we also had data inserted into the other table:

```
OrderID          CustomerID
---------------- ---------------
11098            ALFKI
```

(1 row(s) affected)

```
OrderID          CustomerID
---------------- ---------------
11098            ALFKI
```

(1 row(s) affected)

Now let's test out a couple of deletes – first from the Orders2 table:

```
DELETE Orders2
WHERE  OrderDate = '1/1/2000'
```

This yields us an error:

Server: Msg 50000, Level 16, State 1, Line -1074284106
Record Exists In Orders Table. Delete Cancelled.

(0 row(s) affected)

The deletion was rejected since we've set things up such that it has to go through the master table.

Now we'll delete it from the master table by just changing our last DELETE query:

```
DELETE Orders
WHERE  OrderDate = '1/1/2000'
```

...and then re-run our search for our two records:

```
SELECT OrderID, CustomerID FROM Orders WHERE OrderDate = '1/1/2000'
SELECT OrderID, CustomerID FROM Orders2 WHERE OrderDate = '1/1/2000'
```

OrderID   CustomerID
--------------- ----------------

(0 row(s) affected)

OrderID   CustomerID
--------------- ----------------

(0 row(s) affected)

Note that this is just one of many possible one-to-one examples.

Exclusive Subcategories

Back when we were working on design issues, we discussed the notion of exclusive subcategories. Remember that these are when you have a base type that provides the basic information about a certain class of item, and then subcategories that are built on and extend that base type with information that is specific to that subcategory only. This kind of relationship can only be enforced through the use of triggers.

We're going to build a simple example since Northwind doesn't really have anything to offer us in this regard. We'll just say that we have a concept of an *activity*. This Activity has a few common pieces of information, and looks like this:

```
CREATE TABLE Activity
(
    ActivityID        int    IDENTITY (1, 1)    NOT NULL,
    ActivityType      int                       NOT NULL,
    ActivityDate      datetime                  NOT NULL,
    ActivityComplete  bit NOT                   NULL,
    CONSTRAINT PK_Activity
        PRIMARY KEY  NONCLUSTERED (ActivityID)
)
```

Football and softball are both activities that are exclusive subcategories of activities – that is, you can have one or the other, but not both. We'll create them like this:

```
CREATE TABLE ActivityFootball
(
    ActivityID      int       NOT NULL,
    InstantReplay   bit       NOT NULL,
    FlagTackle      bit       NOT NULL,
    TwoPointPlay    bit       NOT NULL
    CONSTRAINT PK_ActivityFootball
        PRIMARY KEY  NONCLUSTERED (ActivityID)
)
GO

CREATE TABLE ActivitySoftball
(
    ActivityID      int       NOT NULL,
    NoOfRefs        tinyint   NOT NULL,
    DiamondSize     tinyint   NOT NULL,
    StealingAllowed bit       NOT NULL
    CONSTRAINT PK_ActivitySoftball
        PRIMARY KEY  NONCLUSTERED (ActivityID)
)
GO
```

Now we're ready to deal with enforcing our exclusive subcategory relationship. First, we'll add a trigger to the `ActivityFootball` table. It will look a lot like our standard referential integrity trigger, except that it will take its check one step further and make sure there aren't any softball records:

```sql
CREATE TRIGGER FootballIsExclusiveActivity
    ON ActivityFootball
    FOR INSERT, UPDATE
AS
--Check for ActivityID (Must Be In Activity Table)
    IF EXISTS
        (
        SELECT 'True'
        FROM Inserted i
        LEFT JOIN Activity a
            ON i.ActivityID = a.ActivityID
        WHERE a.ActivityID IS NULL
        )
    BEGIN
        RAISERROR('Football item Must Have Corresponding Activity',16,1)
        ROLLBACK TRAN
    END
--Check for Softball Record (Must NOT be one)
    IF EXISTS
        (
        SELECT 'True'
        FROM Inserted i
        LEFT JOIN ActivitySoftball asb
            ON i.ActivityID = asb.ActivityID
        WHERE asb.ActivityID IS NOT NULL
        )
    BEGIN
        RAISERROR('Matching Softball Record Exists.',16,1)
        ROLLBACK TRAN
    END
```

Now we need a nearly identical trigger for softball:

```sql
CREATE TRIGGER SoftballIsExclusiveActivity
    ON ActivitySoftball
    FOR INSERT, UPDATE
AS
--Check for ActivityID (Must Be In Activity Table)
    IF EXISTS
        (
        SELECT 'True'
        FROM Inserted i
        LEFT JOIN Activity a
            ON i.ActivityID = a.ActivityID
        WHERE a.ActivityID IS NULL
        )
    BEGIN
        RAISERROR('Softball item Must Have Corresponding Activity',16,1)
        ROLLBACK TRAN
    END
```

```
--Check for Football Record (Must NOT be one)
    IF EXISTS
        (
        SELECT 'True'
        FROM Inserted i
        LEFT JOIN ActivityFootball afb
            ON i.ActivityID = afb.ActivityID
        WHERE afb.ActivityID IS NOT NULL
        )
    BEGIN
        RAISERROR('Matching Football Record Exists.',16,1)
        ROLLBACK TRAN
    END
```

Now we're ready to go. Let's insert a couple of records:

```
DECLARE @Identity int

INSERT Activity
VALUES
    (1,'1/1/1980',1)

SELECT @Identity = @@IDENTITY

INSERT ActivityFootball
VALUES
    (@Identity, 0,0,0)

SELECT 'New ActivityID is ' + CONVERT(varchar,@Identity)
```

This gets us started. Both records should go in just fine, and we get back some information about what the `ActivityID` assigned was. Now we'll run an `INSERT` on the `SoftballActivity` table to get our expected failure (since a record already exists in `FootballActivity`):

```
INSERT ActivitySoftball
VALUES
    (1,3,90,1)
```

Note that the value inserted into the first column may change – fill it in with whatever the previous command said was the identity value used. When you do that, you should get an error message saying that your insert into `ActivitySoftball` has failed:

Server: Msg 50000, Level 16, State 1, Line -1074284106
Matching Football Record Exists.

This is something we could never do with DRI.

Using Triggers for Data Integrity Rules

Much as a trigger can enforce relationships like a Foreign Key constraint can, a trigger can also perform the same functionality as a CHECK constraint or even a DEFAULT. Again, as with triggers vs. DRI, the triggers vs. CHECK constraints question is answered by "it depends". If a CHECK can do the job, then it's probably (but not always) the preferable choice. There are times, however, when a CHECK constraint just won't do the job, or when something inherent in the CHECK process makes it less desirable than a trigger. Examples of where you would want to use a trigger over a CHECK include:

❑ Your business rule needs to reference data in a separate table

❑ Your business rule needs to check the **delta** (difference between before and after) of an update

❑ You require a customized error message

A summary table of when to use what type of data integrity mechanism is provided at the end of Chapter 7.

This really just scratches the surface of things. Since triggers are highly flexible, deciding when to use them really just comes down to whenever you need something special done.

Dealing with Requirements Sourced from Other Tables

CHECK constraints are great – fast and efficient – but they don't do everything you'd like them to. Perhaps the biggest shortcoming shows up when you need to verify data across tables.

To illustrate this, let's take a look at the Products and Order Details tables in the NorthwindTriggers database that we created earlier in the chapter. If we still had our DRI in place, the relationship looks like this:

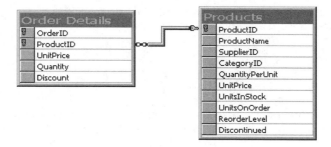

So, under DRI (which we've removed for this chapter), you could be certain that no Order Detail item could be entered into the Order Details table unless there was a matching ProductID in the Products table.

Since we have removed our declarative referential integrity, we'll go ahead and quickly add back in the referential integrity side of things before dealing with our constraint:

```
CREATE TRIGGER OrderDetailIsProduct
    ON [Order Details]
    FOR INSERT, UPDATE
AS
    IF EXISTS
        (
        SELECT 'True'
        FROM Inserted i
        LEFT JOIN Products p
            ON i.ProductID = p.ProductID
        WHERE p.ProductID IS NULL
        )
    BEGIN
        RAISERROR('Order Item Must Be a Valid Product',16,1)
        ROLLBACK TRAN
    END
```

OK. Now that we have got that little item out of the way, let's deal with our business requirements that can't be met with a CHECK constraint.

Our Inventory department has been complaining that our Customer Support people keep placing orders for products that are marked discontinued. They would like to have such orders rejected before they get into the system.

We can't deal with this using a CHECK constraint because the place where we know about the discontinued status (the Products table) is in a separate table from where we are placing the restriction (the Order Details table). Don't sweat it though – you can tell the Inventory department, "No problem!" You just need to use a trigger:

```
CREATE TRIGGER OrderDetailNotDiscontinued
    ON [Order Details]
    FOR INSERT, UPDATE
AS
    IF EXISTS
        (
        SELECT 'True'
        FROM Inserted i
        JOIN Products p
            ON i.ProductID = p.ProductID
        WHERE p.Discontinued = 1
        )
    BEGIN
        RAISERROR('Order Item is discontinued. Transaction Failed.',16,1)
        ROLLBACK TRAN
    END
```

Notice that this trigger is entirely separate from the previous trigger that we wrote on this table. Under SQL Server 6.5 and previous versions, we could not have written this separate trigger as there was already one trigger for either inserts or updates (in this case, it was both). We would have had to combine all the logic into one trigger. In this case, that probably wouldn't have been that big a deal but, for complex triggers, it can really make the trigger convoluted and difficult to debug. Thankfully, under 7.0 and 2000, we can just go ahead and add the additional trigger.

Let's go ahead and test out our handiwork. First, we need a record or two that will fail when it hits our trigger:

```
SELECT ProductID, ProductName FROM Products WHERE Discontinued = 1
```

ProductID	ProductName
5	Chef Anton's Gumbo Mix
9	Mishi Kobe Niku
17	Alice Mutton
24	Guaraná Fantástica
28	Rössle Sauerkraut
29	Thüringer Rostbratwurst
42	Singaporean Hokkien Fried Mee
53	Perth Pasties

(8 row(s) affected)

So let's go ahead and add an `Order Details` item that violates this constraint:

```
INSERT [Order Details]
    (OrderID, ProductID, UnitPrice, Quantity, Discount)
VALUES
    (10000, 5, 21.35, 5, 0)
```

This gets the rejection that we expect:

Server: Msg 50000, Level 16, State 1, Line -1074284106
Order Item is discontinued. Transaction Failed.

Remember that we could, if desired, also create a custom error message to raise, instead of the ad hoc message that we used with the `RAISERROR` command.

Using Triggers to Check the Delta of an Update

Sometimes, you're not interested as much in what the value was or is as you are in how much it changed. While there isn't any one column or table that gives you that information, you can calculate it by making use of both the `Inserted` and `Deleted` tables in your trigger.

To check this out, let's take a look at the `Products` table again. `Products` has a column called `UnitsInStock`. Recently, there has been a rush on several products, and Northwind has been selling out of several things. Since Northwind needs more than just a few customers to stay in business in the long run, it has decided to institute a rationing system on their products. The Inventory department has requested that we prevent orders from being placed that try to sell more than half of the units in stock for any particular product.

To implement this, we make use of both the Inserted and Deleted tables:

```
CREATE TRIGGER ProductIsRationed
    ON Products
    FOR UPDATE
AS
    IF EXISTS
        (
        SELECT 'True'
        FROM Inserted i
        JOIN Deleted d
            ON i.ProductID = d.ProductID
        WHERE (d.UnitsInStock - i.UnitsInStock) > d.UnitsInStock / 2
            AND d.UnitsInStock - i.UnitsInStock > 0
        )
    BEGIN
        RAISERROR('Cannot reduce stock by more than 50%% at once.',16,1)
        ROLLBACK TRAN
    END
```

Before we test this out, let's analyze what we're doing here.

First, we're making use of an IF EXISTS just as we have throughout this chapter. We only want to do the rollback if something exists that meets the evil, mean, and nasty criteria that we'll be testing for.

Then we join the INSERTED and DELETED tables together – this is what gives us the chance to compare the two.

Our WHERE clause is the point where things might become a bit confusing. The first line of it is pretty straightforward. It implements the nominal statement of our business requirement; updates to the UnitsInStock column that are more than half the units we previously had on hand will meet the criterion, and ready the transaction to be rejected.

The next line, though, is not quite so straightforward. As with all things in programming, we need to think beyond the nominal statement of the problem, and think about other ramifications. The requirement really only applies to reductions in orders – we certainly don't want to restrict how many units be put *in* stock – so we make sure that we only worry about updates where the number in stock after the update is less than before the update.

If both of these conditions have been met (over 50%, and a reduction rather than addition to the inventory), then we raise the error. Notice the use of two % signs, rather than one, in the RAISERROR. Remember that a % works as a placeholder for a parameter, so one % by itself won't show up when your error message comes out. By putting two in a row, %%, we let SQL Server know that we really did want to print out a percent sign.

OK – let's check out how it works. We'll just pick a record and try to do an update that reduces the stock by more than 50%:

```
UPDATE Products
    SET UnitsInStock = 2
    WHERE ProductID = 8
```

I just picked out "Northwoods Cranberry Sauce" as our victim, but you could have chosen any ProductID as long as you set the value to less than 50% of its previous value. If you do, you'll get the expected error:

Server: Msg 50000, Level 16, State 1, Line -1074284106
Cannot reduce stock by more than 50% at once.

Note that we could have also implemented this in the Order Details table by referencing the actual order quantity against the current UnitInStock amount, but we would have run into several problems:

❑   Is the process that's creating the Order Details record updating Products before or after the Order Details record? That makes a difference in how we make use of the UnitsInStock value in the Products table to calculate the effect of the transaction.

❑   Updates that change the inventory external to the Order Details table updates would not be affected – they could still reduce the inventory by more than half (this may actually be a good thing in many circumstances, but it's something that has to be thought about).

Using Triggers for Custom Error Messages

We've already touched on this in some of our other examples, but remember that triggers can be handy for when you want control over the error message or number that gets passed out to your user or client application.

With a CHECK constraint for example, you're just going to get the standard 547 error along with its rather nondescript explanation. As often as not, this is less than helpful in terms of the user really figuring out what went wrong – indeed, your client application often doesn't have enough information to make an intelligent and helpful response on behalf of the user.

In short, sometimes you create triggers when there is already something that would give you the data integrity that you want, but won't give you enough information to handle it.

Other Common Uses for Triggers

In addition to the straight data integrity uses, triggers have a number of other uses. Indeed, the possibilities are fairly limitless, but here are a few common examples:

❑   Updating summary information

❑   Feeding de-normalized tables for reporting

❑   Setting condition flags

Updating Summary Information

Sometimes we like to keep aggregate information around to help with reporting, or to speed performance when checking conditions.

Take, for instance, the example of a customer's credit limit vs. their current balance. The limit is a fairly static thing, and is easily stored with the rest of the customer information. The current balance is another matter. We can always figure out the current balance by running a query to total all of the unpaid balances for any orders the customer has, but think about that for a moment. Let's say that you work for Sears & Roebuck, and you do literally millions of transactions every year. Now think about how your table is going to have many millions of records for your query to sort through, and that you're going to be competing with many other transactions in order to run your query. Things would perform an awful lot better if we could just go to a single place to get that total – but how to maintain it?

We certainly could just make sure that we always use a stored procedure for adding and paying order records, and then have the sproc update the customer's current balance. But that would mean that we would have to be sure that every sproc that has a potential effect on the customer's balance would have the update code. If just one sproc leaves it out, then we have a major problem, and figuring out which sproc is the offending one is a hassle at best, and problematic at worst. By using a trigger, however, the updating of the customer balance becomes pretty easy.

We'll go ahead and implement an extremely simplified version of this. It probably isn't quite the way we'd build our tables in a real life accounts receivable situation, but it will have all the basics.

First, we need to add a current balance column to our Customers table:

```
ALTER TABLE Customers
    ADD CurrentBalance money NOT NULL
    CONSTRAINT CurrentBalanceDefault
    DEFAULT 0 WITH VALUES
```

Make sure you get all four lines in, or you'll wind up with NULL values in the CurrentBalance column. That wouldn't be that big a deal, except that when we go to do math on the column later, a NULL plus anything equals a NULL – so we wouldn't get far.

Now we'll add a trigger to our Order Details table to adjust the balance:

```
CREATE TRIGGER OrderDetailAffectsCustomerBalance
    ON [Order Details]
    FOR INSERT, UPDATE, DELETE
AS
    UPDATE c
        SET c.CurrentBalance = c.CurrentBalance + i.UnitPrice * i.Quantity *
                               (1 - Discount)
    FROM Customers c
JOIN Orders o
    ON c.CustomerID = o.CustomerID
JOIN Inserted i
    ON o.OrderID = i.OrderID
```

```
        UPDATE c
           SET c.CurrentBalance = c.CurrentBalance - d.UnitPrice * d.Quantity *
                                   (1 - d.Discount)
        FROM Customers c
        JOIN Orders o
           ON c.CustomerID = o.CustomerID
        JOIN Deleted d
           ON o.OrderID = d.OrderID
```

Before we get going here, we should probably also initialize our values for CurrentBalance in the Customers table. Note that this isn't quite the way things would be in reality since we're going to assume that none of our customers has ever made a payment (we wouldn't stay in business long if that were the case!):

```
    SELECT c.CustomerID, CAST(SUM(od.UnitPrice * od.Quantity * (1 - Discount))
        AS Money) AS CurrentBalance
    INTO #Totals
       FROM Customers c
       JOIN Orders o
          ON c.CustomerID = o.CustomerID
       JOIN [Order Details] od
          ON o.OrderID = od.OrderID
    GROUP BY c.CustomerID

    UPDATE c
    SET c.CurrentBalance = t.CurrentBalance
    FROM Customers c
    JOIN #Totals t
       ON c.CustomerID = t.CustomerID
```

OK, so you should now have some data in the CurrentBalance column of the Customers table. So we're ready to do something more real. We'll start by figuring out the existing balance of a customer:

```
    SELECT CustomerID, CurrentBalance
    FROM Customers
    WHERE CustomerID = 'BLAUS'
```

It turns out that Blauer See Delikatessen has a balance of $3,329.80:

CustomerID	CurrentBalance
BLAUS	3239.8000

(1 row(s) affected)

Now let's modify an existing order. Blauer See Delikatessen already has an order 10614 with three line items on it for a total of $464:

```
    SELECT o.CustomerID, ProductID, od.Quantity * od.UnitPrice AS ExtendedPrice
    FROM Orders o
    JOIN [Order Details] od
       ON o.OrderID = od.OrderID
    WHERE o.OrderID = 10614
    COMPUTE  SUM( od.Quantity * od.UnitPrice)
```

CustomerID	ProductID	ExtendedPrice
BLAUS	11	294.0000
BLAUS	21	80.0000
BLAUS	39	90.0000
		sum
		===========
		464.0000

(4 row(s) affected)

Now we'll make an addition to this order:

```
INSERT [Order Details]
    (OrderID, ProductID, UnitPrice, Quantity, Discount)
VALUES
    (10614, 1, 18.00, 5, 0)
```

If everything worked correctly, then we should have a current balance that is $90 ($18 x 5) higher than it was before – or $3,329.80. Let's find out:

```
SELECT CurrentBalance
FROM Customers
WHERE CustomerID = 'BLAUS'
```

Hooray! We get what we're looking for:

CurrentBalance

3329.8000

(1 row(s) affected)

Now we'll make sure that the deletion part of the query is working OK:

```
DELETE [Order Details]
WHERE OrderID = 10614 AND ProductID = 1
```

Rerun the SELECT statement again, and we see this puts us right back where we started (as we should be):

CurrentBalance

3239.8000

(1 row(s) affected)

Now we will know that we always have up-to-date information on the customer's current balance.

We can do something like this for pretty much any aggregation that we want to keep track of. Keep in mind, however, that every trigger that you add increases the amount of work that has to be done to complete your transactions. That means that you are placing an additional burden on your system and increasing the chances that you will run into deadlock problems.

Feeding Data into De-Normalized Tables for Reporting

I'm going to start right off by saying this isn't the way you should do things in most circumstances. Usually, this kind of data transfer should be handled as part of a batch process run at night or during non-peak hours for your system. Replication may also be an excellent answer, depending upon the nature of what you are moving. We will be discussing replication in detail in Chapter 23.

That being said, sometimes you need the data in your reporting tables to be right up-to-the-minute. The only real way to take care of this is either to modify all your sprocs and other access points into your system to update the reporting tables at the same time as they update the OLTP tables (yuck!), or to use triggers to propagate any updates to records.

I'm going to skip the specific example on this one because it works pretty much the same as our last example for aggregation – just copy the data to the new table rather than aggregating it.

What's nice about using this method to propagate data is that you are always certain to be up-to-the-minute on what's happening in the OLTP tables. That being said, it defeats a large part of the purpose of keeping separate reporting tables. While keeping the data in a de-normalized format can greatly improve query performance, one of its main goals, in most installations, is to clear reporting needs out of the main OLTP database and minimize concurrency issues. If all your OLTP updates still have to update information in your reporting tables, then all you've done is to move which database the actual deadlock or other concurrency issue is happening in. From the OLTP standpoint, you've added work without gaining any benefits.

The thing you have to weigh here is whether you're going to gain enough performance in your reporting to make it worth the damage you're going to do to performance on your OLTP system.

Setting Condition Flags

This situation is typically used much as aggregation is – to maintain a flag as changes are made rather than having to look for a certain condition across a complete table. Lookup flags are one of the little things that, while they usually break the rules of normalization (you're not supposed to store data that can be derived elsewhere), can really boost system performance substantially.

For our example on this topic, let's assume that we maintain a variety of information on the products that we sell. Material Safety Data Sheets (MSDS), nutritional information, information on suppliers – there can be an unlimited number of different documents that all provide some sort of information on our products. Now imagine that we have something more than the mere 77 products that are in the Northwind database. The number of possible informational records could get extremely large.

We want to be able to show flags on our Customer Support screens that tell the order takers whether there is any additional information available for this product. If we were living by the rules of a normalized database, we would have to look in the ProductInformation table to see if it had any records that matched up with our ProductID.

Rather than do that lookup, we can just place a bit field in our Products table that is a yes/no indicator on whether other information is available. We would then put a trigger on the ProductInformation table that updates the bit flag in the Products table. If a record is inserted into ProductInformation, then we set the bit flag to TRUE for the corresponding product. When a ProductInformation record is deleted, we look to see whether it was the last one and, if so, set the bit flag in the Products table back to FALSE.

Again, this looks an awful lot like our aggregation update, so we'll go for an ultra quick example. First, we need to set up a bit by creating the bit flag field and `ProductInformation` table:

```
CREATE TABLE ProductInformation
(
    InformationID    int              NOT NULL    IDENTITY
        PRIMARY KEY,
    ProductID        int              NOT NULL
        REFERENCES Products(ProductID),
    Information       varchar(7500)    NOT NULL
)

ALTER TABLE Products
    ADD InformationFlag bit    NOT NULL
    CONSTRAINT InformationFlagDefault
        DEFAULT 0 WITH VALUES
```

Then we're ready to add our trigger:

```
CREATE TRIGGER InformationBelongsToProduct
    ON ProductInformation
    FOR INSERT, DELETE
AS
    DECLARE @Count    int

    SELECT @Count = COUNT(*) FROM Inserted

    IF @Count > 0
        BEGIN
            UPDATE Products
                SET InformationFlag = 1
                FROM Inserted i
                JOIN Products p
                    ON i.ProductID = p.ProductID
        END

    IF @@ERROR != 0
        ROLLBACK TRAN

    SELECT @Count = COUNT(*) FROM Deleted
    IF @Count > 0
    BEGIN
        UPDATE Products
            SET InformationFlag = 0
            FROM Inserted i
            RIGHT JOIN Products p
                ON i.ProductID = p.ProductID
            WHERE i.ProductID IS NULL
    END

    IF @@ERROR != 0
        ROLLBACK TRAN
```

...and we're ready to test:

```
INSERT ProductInformation
    (ProductID, Information)
VALUES
    (1, 'Yatta, Yatta, Yatta')

SELECT InformationFlag
FROM Products
WHERE ProductID = 1
```

This yields us the proper update:

InformationFlag

1

(1 row(s) affected)

...and the delete:

```
DELETE ProductInformation
WHERE InformationID = 1

SELECT InformationFlag
FROM Products
WHERE ProductID = 1
```

...again gets up the proper update:

InformationFlag

0

(1 row(s) affected)

Now we can find out whether there's ProductInformation right in the very same query with which we grab the base information on the product. We won't incur the overhead of the query to the ProductInformation table unless there really is something out there for us to retrieve.

Other Trigger Issues

You have most of it now but if you're thinking you are finished with triggers, then think again. As I indicated early in the chapter, triggers create an awful lot to think about. The sections below attempt to point out some of the biggest issues you need to consider, plus provide some information on additional trigger features and possibilities.

Triggers Can Be Nested

A nested trigger is one that did not fire directly as a result of a statement that you issued, but rather because of a statement that was issued by another trigger.

This can actually set off quite a chain of events – with one trigger causing another trigger to fire which, in turn, causes yet another trigger to fire, and so on. Just how deep the triggers can fire depends on:

1. Whether nested triggers are turned on for your system (this is a system wide, not database level option; it is set using EM or sp_configure, and defaults to on).

2. There is a limit of nesting to 32 levels deep.

3. A trigger can, by default, only be fired once per trigger transaction. Once fired, it will ignore any other calls as a result of activity that is part of the same trigger action. Once you move on to an entirely new statement (even within the same overall transaction), the process can start all over again.

In most circumstances, you actually want your triggers to nest (thus the default), but you need to think about what's going to happen if you get into a circle of triggers firing triggers. If it comes back around to the same table twice, then the trigger will not fire the second time, and something you think is important may not happen, for example, the referential integrity may be destroyed. It's also worth noting that, if you do a ROLLBACK anywhere in the nesting chain, then entire chain is rolled back. In other words, the entire nested trigger chain behaves as a transaction.

Triggers Can Be Recursive

Recursive triggers are rare. Indeed, by default, recursive triggers are turned off. This is, however, a way of dealing with the situation just described where you are nesting triggers and you want the update to happen the second time around. Recursion, unlike nesting, is a database level option, and can be set using the sp_dboption system sproc.

What is a recursive trigger? A trigger is said to be recursive when something the trigger does eventually causes that same trigger to be fired. It may be directly (by an action query done to the table on which the trigger is set), or indirectly (through the nesting process).

The danger in recursive triggers is that you'll get into some form of unintended loop. As such, you'll need to make sure that you get some form of recursion check in place to stop the process if necessary.

Triggers Don't Prevent Architecture Changes

This is a classic good news/bad news story.

Using triggers is positively great in terms of making it easy to make architecture changes. Indeed, I often use triggers for referential integrity early in the development cycle (when I'm more likely to be making lots of changes to the design of the database), and then change to DRI late in the cycle when I'm close to production.

When you want to drop a table and re-create it using DRI, you must first drop all of the constraints before dropping the table. This can create quite a maze in terms of dropping multiple constraints, making your changes, and then adding back the constraints again. It can be quite a wild ride trying to make sure that everything drops that is supposed to so that your changed scripts will run. Then it's just as wild a ride to make sure that you've got everything back on that needs to be. Triggers take care of all this because they don't care that anything has changed until they actually run.

There's the rub though – when they run. You see, it means that you may change architecture and break several triggers without even realizing that you've done it. It won't be until the first time that those triggers try to address the object(s) in question that you find the error of your ways. By that time, you may find difficulty in piecing together exactly what you did and why.

Both sides have their hassles – just keep the hassles in mind no matter which method you're employing.

Triggers Can Be Turned Off Without Being Removed

Sometimes, just like with CHECK constraints, you want to turn off the integrity feature so you can do something that will violate the constraint, but still has a valid reason for happening (importation of data is probably the most common of these).

Another common reason for doing this is when you are performing some sort of bulk insert (importation again), but you are already 100% certain the data is valid. In this case, you may want to turn off the triggers to eliminate their overhead and speed up the insert process.

You can turn a trigger off and on by using an ALTER TABLE statement. The syntax looks like this:

```
ALTER TABLE <table name>
    <ENABLE|DISABLE> TRIGGER <ALL|<trigger name>>
```

As you might expect, my biggest words of caution in this area are, "Don't forget to re-enable your triggers!"

One last thing. If you're turning them off to do some form of mass importation of data, I highly recommend that you kick out all your users and go either to single-user mode, dbo-only mode, or both. This will make sure that no one sneaks in behind you while you had the triggers turned off.

Trigger Firing Order

In every single SQL Server 7.0 class that I taught, a student would always ask whether you could control firing order. The answer was, of course, "No." Under 7.0, you were allowed the multiple triggers, but you had no control over the firing order of those triggers. With SQL Server 2000, you now have a limited amount of control. For any given table (not views, since firing order can only be specified for AFTER triggers and views only accept INSTEAD OF triggers), you can, if you choose, elect to have one (and only one) trigger fired first. Likewise, you may elect to have one (and only one) trigger fired last. All other triggers are considered to have no preference on firing order – that is, you have no guarantee in what order a trigger with a firing order of "none" will fire in other than that they will fire after the FIRST trigger (if there is one) is complete and before the LAST trigger (again, if there is one) begins:

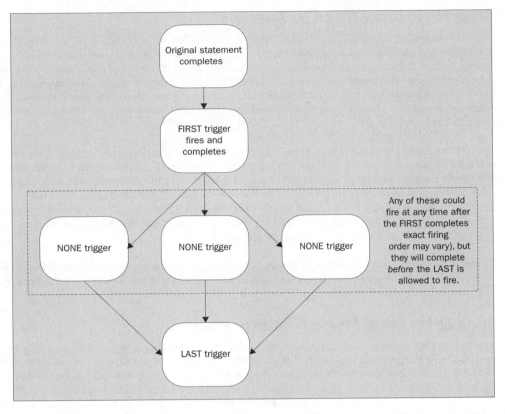

The creation of a trigger that is to be first or last works just the same as any other trigger. You state the firing order preference after the trigger has already be created using a special system stored procedure, sp_settriggerorder.

The syntax of sp_settriggerorder looks like this:

```
sp_settriggerorder[@triggername =] '<trigger name>',
    [@order =] '{FIRST|LAST|NONE}',
    [@stmttype =] '{INSERT|UPDATE|DELETE}'
```

There can only be one trigger that is considered to be "first" for any particular action (INSERT, UPDATE, or DELETE). Likewise, there can only be one "last" trigger for any particular action. Any number of triggers can be considered to be "none" – that is, the number of triggers that don't have a particular firing order is unlimited.

So, the question should be, "Why do I care what order they fire in?" Well, often you won't care at all. At other times, it can be important logic-wise or just a good performance idea. Let's consider what I mean in a bit more detail.

Controlling Firing Order for Logic Reasons

Why would you *need* to have one trigger fire before another? The most common reason would be that the first trigger lays some sort of foundation for, or otherwise validates, what will come afterwards. Under SQL Server 6.5 and earlier, we didn't have to think about this kind of thing much – we were only allowed one trigger of any particular type (UPDATE, DELETE, or INSERT) for a given table. This meant that having one thing happen before another wasn't really a problem. Since you combined all logic into one trigger, you just put the first thing that needed to happen first in the code and the last part last (no real rocket science there at all).

Version 7.0 came along and made things both better and worse than they were before. You were no longer forced to jam all of your logic into one trigger. This was really cool because it meant that you could physically separate parts of your trigger code that were logically different, which, in turn, both made the code much easier to manage and also allowed one part of the code to be disabled (remember that NO CHECK thing we did a few sections ago?) while other parts of the code continued to function. The downside was that, if you went ahead and separated out your code that way, you lost the logical stepping order that the code had when it was in one trigger.

By gaining at least a rudimentary level of control over firing order, we now have something of the best of both worlds – we can logically separate our sprocs, but still maintain necessary order of precedence on what piece of code runs first or last.

Controlling Firing Order for Performance Reasons

On the performance front, a FIRST trigger is the only one that really has any big thing going for it. If you have multiple triggers, but only one of them is likely to generate a rollback (for example, it may be enforcing a complex data integrity rule that a constraint can't handle), you would want to consider making such a trigger a FIRST trigger. This makes certain that your most likely cause of a rollback is already complete before you invest any more activity in your transaction. The more you do before the rollback is detected, the more that will have to be rolled back. Get the highest possibility of that rollback happening determined before performing additional activity.

INSTEAD OF Triggers

This variety of trigger is entirely new with SQL Server 2000. While it can work against tables, the primary purpose of an INSTEAD OF trigger is usually to allow updates to views in places where it was previously not possible.

Essentially, an INSTEAD OF trigger is a block of code we can use as an interceptor for anything that anyone tries to do to our table or view. We can either elect to just go ahead and do whatever the user requests or, if we choose, we can go so far as doing something that is entirely different.

INSTEAD OF triggers come in three different flavors – INSERT, UPDATE, and DELETE. For each of the different flavors, you can only have one trigger per table or view.

Let's explore each.

INSTEAD OF INSERT Triggers

The INSTEAD OF INSERT trigger allows us to examine the data that is about to go into our table or view, and decide what we want to do with it prior to the insert physically occurring. The typical use of this will usually be on a view – where getting to manipulate the data before the actual physical insert is attempted can mean the difference between the insert succeeding or failing.

Let's look at an example by creating an updateable view – specifically, one that will accept INSERTs where, before INSTEAD OF INSERT triggers, we wouldn't have been able to do it.

In this case, we'll use a view we created way back in Chapter 10. We'll need to create a copy of it for our NorthwindTriggers database:

```
USE NorthwindTriggers
GO
CREATE VIEW CustomerOrders_vw
WITH SCHEMABINDING
AS
SELECT    cu.CompanyName,
          o.OrderID,
          o.OrderDate,
          od.ProductID,
          p.ProductName,
          od.Quantity,
          od.UnitPrice
FROM      dbo.Customers AS cu
INNER JOIN    dbo.Orders AS o
          ON cu.CustomerID = o.CustomerID
INNER JOIN    dbo.[Order Details] AS od
          ON o.OrderID = od.OrderID
INNER JOIN    dbo.Products AS p
          ON od.ProductID = p.ProductID
```

The view is not updateable in its current state – how would SQL Server know which data went to which table? Sure, one could make a case for a straight update statement working, but we don't have the Primary Key for every table here. Even worse – what if we wanted to do an insert (which, as it happens, we do)?

The answer is something that SQL Server can't give you by itself – you need to provide more instructions on what you want to do in such complex situations. That's where INSTEAD OF triggers really shine.

Let's take a look at an example order:

```
SELECT *
FROM CustomerOrders_vw
WHERE OrderID = 11000
```

This gets us back three rows:

Company Name	Order ID	OrderDate	ProductID	ProductName	Quantity	Unit Price
Rattlesnake Canyon Grocery	11000	1998-04-06 00:00:00.000	4	Chef Anton's Cajun Seasoning	25	22
Rattlesnake Canyon Grocery	11000	1998 1998-04-06 00:00:00.000	24	Guaraná Fantástica	30	4.5
Rattlesnake Canyon Grocery	11000	1998 1998-04-06 00:00:00.000	77	Original Frankfurter grüne Soße	30	13

Now, just to prove it doesn't work, let's try to INSERT a new Order Details record:

```
INSERT INTO CustomerOrders_vw
    (
    OrderID,
    OrderDate,
    ProductID,
    Quantity,
    UnitPrice
    )
VALUES
    (
    11000,
    '1998-04-06',
    5,
    10,
    21.35
    )
```

As expected, it doesn't work:

Server: Msg 4405, Level 16, State 2, Line 1
View or function 'CustomerOrders_vw' is not updatable because the modification affects multiple base tables.

It's time for us to take care of this with an INSTEAD OF trigger. What we need to do here is decide ahead of time what scenarios we want to handle (in this case, just the insert of new OrderDetail records) and what we want to do about it.

We're going to treat any INSERT as an attempt to add a new order item. We're going to assume for this example that the customer already exists (if we wanted to get complex, we could break things up further) and that we have an OrderID available. Our trigger might look something like:

```
CREATE TRIGGER trCustomerOrderInsert ON CustomerOrders_vw
INSTEAD OF INSERT
AS
BEGIN
    -- Check to see whether the INSERT actually tried to feed us any rows.
    -- (A WHERE clause might have filtered everything out)
```

```
        IF (SELECT COUNT(*) FROM Inserted) > 0
        BEGIN
            INSERT INTO [Order Details]
                SELECT      i.OrderID,
                            i.ProductID,
                            i.UnitPrice,
                            i.Quantity,
                            0
                FROM Inserted AS i
                JOIN Orders AS o
                    ON i.OrderID = o.OrderID
            -- If we have records in Inserted, but no records could join to
            -- the orders table, then there must not be a matching order
            IF @@ROWCOUNT = 0
                RAISERROR('No matching Orders. Cannot perform insert',10,1)
        END
    END
```

So, let's try that insert again:

```
INSERT INTO CustomerOrders_vw
    (
    OrderID,
    OrderDate,
    ProductID,
    Quantity,
    UnitPrice
    )
VALUES
    (
    11000,
    '1998-04-06',
    5,
    10,
    21.35
    )
```

Oops – more errors, but notice that they've changed in nature:

Server: Msg 233, Level 16, State 2, Line 1
The column 'CompanyName' in table 'CustomerOrders_vw' cannot be null.
Server: Msg 233, Level 16, State 1, Line 1
The column 'ProductName' in table 'CustomerOrders_vw' cannot be null.

This time, the complaint isn't about the ambiguity of the view, but rather the acceptability of the
individual rows being inserted. The view determines whether rows can contain NULLs or not based on
their underlying columns. If the base table the column is sourced from does not accept NULLs, then
neither will the view. Anything that contains a computation or function that could return a NULL is
assumed to accept NULLs. We have two choices for how to deal with this:

❏   Require that all of our INSERT statements include the CompanyName and ProductName
    columns – even though we won't be using them in the actual INSERT that happens inside the view

❏   Alter our view so that rows with NULL in CompanyName or ProductName are filtered out

525

The first of these is pretty easy – we basically do nothing other than add the additional information to our INSERT statement. The odd thing is that we could really use any value (for example, "I love the works of Shakespeare") in our INSERT statement, and it would make no difference – our final INSERT doesn't include those columns, so the data would be meaningless.

The second is slightly trickier. It requires that we go back and update our view. What we're going to do here is make use of the NULLIF() function. This function returns a NULL if the two provided values match.

```
ALTER VIEW CustomerOrders_vw
WITH SCHEMABINDING
AS
SELECT    NULLIF(cu.CompanyName, NULL) AS CompanyName,
          o.OrderID,
          o.OrderDate,
          od.ProductID,
          NULLIF(p.ProductName, NULL) AS ProductName,
          od.Quantity,
          od.UnitPrice
FROM      dbo.Customers AS cu
INNER JOIN    dbo.Orders AS o
      ON cu.CustomerID = o.CustomerID
INNER JOIN    dbo.[Order Details] AS od
      ON o.OrderID = od.OrderID
INNER JOIN    dbo.Products AS p
      ON od.ProductID = p.ProductID
```

Now we're ready to try our insert yet again:

```
INSERT INTO CustomerOrders_vw
    (
    OrderID,
    OrderDate,
    ProductID,
    Quantity,
    UnitPrice
    )
VALUES
    (
    11000,
    '1998-04-06',
    5,
    10,
    21.35
    )
```

There is a chance that you'll have a problem with this last INSERT. If you get a message indicating that your have the wrong setting for ARITHABORT, just run a SET ARITHABORT ON and retry the INSERT.

OK, so this time things should be fine, but let's check it out by re-running our SELECT statement:

```
SELECT *
FROM CustomerOrders_vw
WHERE OrderID = 11000
```

Our original data now contains our new row:

Company Name	Order ID	OrderDate	Product ID	ProductName	Quantity	Unit Price
Rattlesnake Canyon Grocery	11000	1998-04-06 00:00:00.000	4	Chef Anton's Cajun Seasoning	25	22
Rattlesnake Canyon Grocery	11000	1998-04-06 00:00:00.000	5	Chef Anton's Gumbo Mix	10	21.35
Rattlesnake Canyon Grocery	11000	1998-04-06 00:00:00.000	24	Guaraná Fantástica	30	4.5
Rattlesnake Canyon Grocery	11000	1998-04-06 00:00:00.000	77	Original Frankfurter grüne Soße	30	13

What we've done is alter both of our previously offending columns so that SQL Server sees them as accepting NULL values. The reality is that they never would accept a NULL (we're comparing a value that doesn't accept NULLs to NULL, so how could they ever be equal?), but what SQL Server doesn't know won't hurt it.

Keep in mind that, by using this latter approach (rather than requiring those columns to be filled in), we've made things easier for the user, but harder for SQL Server. The server now has to perform two worthless operations (the two NULLIF comparisons) that only have the usability value – keep this in mind if you're in a performance-focused situation.

INSTEAD OF UPDATE Triggers

We've now seen how INSERT statements against views can lead to ambiguous situations and also how to fix then with an INSTEAD OF INSERT trigger – but what about updates?

Even on the update side of things our statements can become ambiguous – if we were to update the ProductName in CustomerOrders_vw, does that mean we want to change the actual name on the product or does it mean that we want to change what product this line item is selling? The answer, of course, is that it depends on the situation. For one system, changing the ProductName might be the correct answer – for another system, changing the product sold might be the thing.

In previous versions of SQL Server, we wouldn't have had any choice in how to address this other than force the user to go directly to the appropriate table. With INSTEAD OF UPDATE triggers, we can now interpret what the user wants for SQL Server so it can carry on with the task at hand.

Let's carry on with our CustomerOrders_vw scenario in Northwind for a moment. We need to allow some of the fields to be updated. For example, it would be perfectly reasonable to allow a change in price or quantity.

```
CREATE TRIGGER trCustomerOrderUpdate ON CustomerOrders_vw
INSTEAD OF UPDATE
AS
BEGIN

    -- Check to see whether the UPDATE actually tried to feed us any rows
    -- (A WHERE clause might have filtered everything out)
    IF (SELECT COUNT(*) FROM Inserted) > 0
    BEGIN
        UPDATE [Order Details]
            SET     UnitPrice = i.UnitPrice,
                    Quantity = i.Quantity
            FROM [Order Details] AS od
            JOIN Inserted AS i
                ON i.OrderID = od.OrderID
               AND i.ProductID = od.ProductID
    END
END
```

Now we're ready for a little testing.

```
SELECT ProductID, UnitPrice, Quantity
FROM CustomerOrders_vw
WHERE OrderID = 11000
```

This gets us back our expected four rows:

ProductID	UnitPrice	Quantity
4	22	25
5	21.35	10
24	4.5	30
77	13	30

Now we'll run a quick update to check our work:

```
UPDATE CustomerOrders_vw
SET UnitPrice = 22, Quantity = 8
WHERE OrderID = 11000
  AND ProductID = 5
```

Re-run the SELECT, and sure enough, our changes go through:

ProductID	UnitPrice	Quantity
4	22	25
5	22	8
24	4.5	30
77	13	30

A Couple of Gotchas and Provisos

Before you get too carried away with INSTEAD OF UPDATE triggers, I need to warn you that not all is necessarily well in Gotham City, Batman. You see there are some situations where INSTEAD OF UPDATE triggers won't work, and there are things you can do (or fail to do) that are not great practice. So, when doing INSTEAD OF UPDATE triggers, remember:

❏ They are not allowed on tables that have referential integrity actions defined on them (if you have CASCADE actions set in foreign keys).

❏ If you're going to allow updates at all, then provide some sort of handler for all columns (we actually just violated this rule on our last example). If you fail to address each column, then it will be possible for users to run UPDATE statements that name those columns, but actually do nothing. While this doesn't appear to do any harm, it can mean that the user thinks they have done something they haven't – and that can lead to trouble. Basically, add code to address the columns you want to make updateable, and then use the IF UPDATE and COLUMNS_UPDATED functions described a little later in the chapter to test for the other columns and return errors accordingly.

Not all that much to think about, but big things nonetheless.

> *Just for clarification, note that the issue with referential integrity action is only applicable when you are defining INSTEAD OF triggers on base tables. Since most INSTEAD OF triggers are defined against views, you shouldn't run into this problem very often. INSTEAD OF triggers defined on views are not constrained by any referential integrity actions that exist on underlying tables.*

INSTEAD OF DELETE Triggers

OK, the last of our INSTEAD OF triggers and, most likely, the one that you'll run into the least often. As with the other two INSTEAD OF trigger types, these are used almost exclusively to allow views to delete data in one or more underlying tables.

So, continuing with our CustomerOrders_vw example, we'll add some delete functionality. This time, however, we're going to raise the complexity bar a bit. We want to delete all the rows for a given order but, if deleting those rows means that the order has no detail items left, then we also want to delete the order header.

We know from our last section (assuming you've been playing along), that we have four rows in order 11000 but, before we start trying to delete things, let's build our trigger:

```
CREATE TRIGGER trCustomerOrderDelete ON CustomerOrders_vw
INSTEAD OF DELETE
AS
BEGIN

    -- Check to see whether the DELETE actually tried to feed us any rows
    -- (A WHERE clause might have filtered everything out)
    IF (SELECT COUNT(*) FROM Deleted) > 0
    BEGIN
        DELETE [Order Details]
            FROM [Order Details] AS od
            JOIN Deleted AS d
                ON d.OrderID = od.OrderID
                AND d.ProductID = od.ProductID
```

```
            DELETE Orders
                FROM Orders AS o
                JOIN Deleted AS d
                    ON o.OrderID = d.OrderID
                LEFT JOIN [Order Details] AS od
                    ON od.OrderID = d.OrderID
                    AND od.ProductID = d.OrderID
                WHERE od.OrderID IS NULL
        END

    END
```

And now we're ready to test. We'll start off by deleting just a single row from our CustomerOrders_vw view:

```
DELETE CustomerOrders_vw
WHERE OrderID = 11000
    AND ProductID = 5
```

We're ready to run our select again:

```
SELECT ProductID, UnitPrice, Quantity
FROM CustomerOrders_vw
WHERE OrderID = 11000
```

Sure enough, our row that we first inserted in our INSTEAD OF INSERT section is now gone:

ProductID	UnitPrice	Quantity
4	22	25
24	4.5	30
77	13	30

So our deleting of individual detail lines is working just fine. Now let's get a bit more cavalier and delete the entire order:

```
DELETE CustomerOrders_vw
WHERE OrderID = 11000
```

To really check that this worked OK, we need to go all the way to our Orders table:

```
SELECT * FROM Orders WHERE OrderID = 11000
```

Sure enough – the order has been removed.

One More Proviso

While we don't have to think about individual columns with INSTEAD OF DELETE triggers (you delete by row, not by column), we do need to be aware of any referential integrity actions that exist on any table (not view) that we are defining an INSTEAD OF DELETE trigger for. Just like INSTEAD OF UPDATE triggers, INSTEAD OF DELETE triggers are not allowed on tables that have referential integrity actions.

Performance Considerations

I've seen what appear almost like holy wars happen over the pros and cons, evil and good, and light and dark of triggers. The worst of it tends to come from purists – people who love the theory, and that's all they want to deal with, or people that have figured out how flexible triggers are and want to use them for seemingly everything.

My two bits worth on this is, as I stated early in the chapter, use them when they are the right things to use. If that sounds sort of non-committal and ambiguous – good! Programming is rarely black and white, and databases are almost never that way. I will, however, point out some facts for you to think about.

Triggers are Reactive rather than Proactive

What I mean here is that triggers happen after the fact. By the time that your trigger fires, the entire query has run and your transaction has been logged (but not committed and only to the point of the statement that fired your trigger). This means that, if the trigger needs to roll things back, it has to undo what is potentially a ton of work that's already been done. *Slow!* Keep this knowledge in balance though. How big an impact this adds up to depends strongly on how big your query is.

"So what?" you say. Well, compare this to the notion of constraints, which are proactive – that is, they happen before your statement is really executed. That means that they prevent things that will fail happening before the majority of the work has been done. This will usually mean that they will run at least slightly faster – much faster on more complete queries. Note that this extra speed really only shows itself to any significant extent when a rollback occurs.

What's the end analysis here? Well, if you're dealing with very few rollbacks, and/or the complexity and run-time of the statements affected are low, then there probably isn't much of a difference between triggers and constraints. There's some, but probably not much.

Triggers don't have Concurrency Issues with the Process that Fires them

You may have noticed throughout this chapter that we often make use of the ROLLBACK statement, even though we don't issue a BEGIN TRAN. That's because a trigger is always implicitly part of the same transaction as the statement that caused the trigger to fire.

If the firing statement was not part of an explicit transaction (one where there was a BEGIN TRAN), then it would still be part of its own one-statement transaction. In either case, a ROLLBACK TRAN issued inside the trigger will still rollback the entire transaction.

Another upshot of this part-of-the-same-transaction business is that triggers inherit the locks already open on the transaction they are part of. This means that we don't have to do anything special to make sure that we don't bump into the locks created by the other statements in the transaction. We have free access within the scope of the transaction, and we see the database based on the modifications already placed by previous statements within the transaction.

Using IF UPDATE() and COLUMNS_UPDATED

In an UPDATE trigger, we can often limit the amount of code that actually executes within the trigger by checking to see whether the column(s) we are interested in are the ones that have been changed. To do this, we make use of the UPDATE() or COLUMNS_UPDATED() functions. Let's look at each.

The UPDATE() Function

The UPDATE() function only has relevance within the scope of a trigger. Its sole purpose in life is to provide a Boolean response (true/false) to whether a particular column has been updated or not. You can use this function to decide whether a particular block of code needs to run or not – for example, if that code is only relevant when a particular column is updated.

Let's run a quick example of this by modifying one of our earlier triggers (in NorthwindTriggers):

```
ALTER TRIGGER ProductIsRationed
    ON Products
    FOR UPDATE
AS
    IF UPDATE(UnitsInStock)
    BEGIN
    IF EXISTS
        (
        SELECT 'True'
        FROM Inserted i
        JOIN Deleted d
            ON i.ProductID = d.ProductID
        WHERE (d.UnitsInStock - i.UnitsInStock) > d.UnitsInStock / 2
            AND d.UnitsInStock - i.UnitsInStock > 0
        )
    BEGIN
        RAISERROR('Cannot reduce stock by more than 50%% at once.',16,1)
        ROLLBACK TRAN
    END
    END
```

With this change, we will now limit the rest of the code to only run when the UnitsInStock column (the one we care about) has been changed. The user can change the value of any other column, and we don't care. This means that we'll be executing fewer lines of code and, therefore, this trigger will perform more quickly than our previous version.

The COLUMNS_UPDATED() Function

This one works somewhat differently from UPDATE(), but has the same general purpose. What COLUMNS_UPDATED() gives us is the ability to check multiple columns at one time. In order to do this, the function uses a bit mask that relates individual bits in one or more bytes of varbinary data to individual columns in the table. It ends up looking something like this:

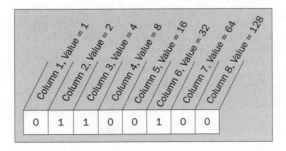

In this case, our single byte of data is telling us that the second, third, and sixth columns were updated – the rest were not.

In the event that there are more than eight columns, SQL Server just adds another byte on the right hand side and keeps counting:

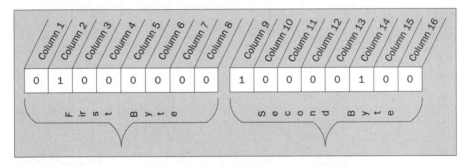

This time the second, ninth, and fourteenth columns were updated.

I can hear you out there, "Gee, that's nice – but how do I make any use of this?" Well, to answer that, we have to get into the world of Boolean algebra.

Making use of this information means that you need to add up the binary value of all the bytes, considering the leftmost digit to be the least significant. So, if you want your comparison to take into account 2, 5, and 7, then you need to add the binary value of each bit: $2 + 16 + 64$. Then you need to compare the sum of the binary values of your columns to the bitmask by using bitwise operators:

|	represents bitwise OR
&	represents bitwise AND
^	represents bitwise Exclusive OR

As I read back over what I've just written, I realize that it is correct, but about as clear as mud, so let's look a little closer at what I mean with a couple of examples.

Imagine that we updated a table that contained five columns. If we updated the first, third, and fifth columns, the bitmask used by COLUMNS_UPDATED would contain 10101000, from $1 + 4 + 16 = 21$. We could use:

❑ COLUMNS_UPDATED() > 0 to find out if any column was updated

❑ COLUMNS_UPDATED() ^ 21 = 0 to find out if *all* of the columns specified (in this case 1, 3, and 5) were updated and nothing else was

❑ COLUMNS_UPDATED() & 21 = 21 to find out if all of the columns specified were updated, but the state of other columns doesn't matter

❑ COLUMNS_UPDATED | 21 != 21 to find out if any column *other* than those we're interested in was updated

So let's go back a section or two and put this into practice against our INSTEAD OF UPDATE trigger that we built on our CustomerOrders_vw view in Northwind. In the *Gotchas and Provisos* section, I mentioned that it's a bad idea to just ignore columns – the user might think an update had happened when it had really just been ignored. We could use our COLUMNS_UPDATED() function to check all of the other columns for updates, and report an error back to the user if they attempted to update an unsupported column.

It might look something like this:

```
ALTER TRIGGER trCustomerOrderUpdate ON CustomerOrders_vw
INSTEAD OF UPDATE
AS
BEGIN

    -- Check to see whether the UPDATE actually tried to feed us any rows.
    -- (A WHERE clause might have filtered everything out)
    IF (SELECT COUNT(*) FROM Inserted) > 0
    BEGIN
        -- Make sure we're not going to need to undo things before we start
        -- our update. We're only supporting updates to columns 6 & 7, so
        -- our comparison value is 32 + 64, or 96.
        IF (COLUMNS_UPDATED() | 96) != 96
        BEGIN
            RAISERROR('Updates only supported for UnitPrice and Quantity', 16,1)
        END
        ELSE        BEGIN
            UPDATE [Order Details]
                SET     UnitPrice = i.UnitPrice,
                        Quantity = i.Quantity
                FROM [Order Details] AS od
                JOIN Inserted AS i
                    ON i.OrderID = od.OrderID
                    AND i.ProductID = od.ProductID
        END
    END
END
```

Now let's test this further. First, we'll select a couple of values from our view:

```
SELECT ProductID, Quantity, UnitPrice
FROM CustomerOrders_vw
WHERE OrderID = 11001
```

Unless you've been messing with the data, this should yield you four rows:

ProductID	Quantity	UnitPrice
7	60	30
22	25	21
46	25	12
55	6	24

So let's try two updates – the first should work (it will be to just the columns we support), and the other will not:

```
-- This one should work
UPDATE CustomerOrders_vw
SET UnitPrice = 35
WHERE ProductID = 7

-- This one should not
UPDATE CustomerOrders_vw
SET ProductID = 8
WHERE ProductID = 7

-- Now, see what changed and what didn't
SELECT ProductID, Quantity, UnitPrice
FROM CustomerOrders_vw
WHERE OrderID = 11001
```

We see that the second update generated an error and, in looking at our data, only the UnitPrice column was updated:

ProductID	Quantity	UnitPrice
7	60	35
22	25	21
46	25	12
55	6	24

Boolean math is not exactly the easiest of concepts to grasp for most people, so check things carefully and TEST, TEST, TEST!

Keep it Short and Sweet

I feel like I'm stating the obvious here, but it's for a good reason.

I can't tell you how often I see bloated, stupid code in sprocs and triggers. I don't know whether it's that people get in a hurry, or if they just think that the medium they are using is fast anyway, so it won't matter.

Remember that a trigger is part of the same transaction as the statement in which it is called. This means the statement is not complete until your trigger is complete. Think about it – if you write long running code in your trigger, this means that every piece of code that you create that causes that trigger to fire will, in turn, be long running. This can really cause heartache in terms of trying to figure out why your code is taking so long to run. You write what appears to be a very efficient sproc, but it performs terribly. You may spend weeks and yet never figure out that your sproc is fine – it just fires a trigger that isn't.

Don't Forget Triggers when Choosing Indexes

Another common mistake. You look through all your sprocs and views figuring out what the best mix of indexes is – and totally forget that you have significant code running in your triggers.

This is the same notion as the *Short and Sweet* section – long running queries make for long running statements which, in turn, lead to long running everything. Don't forget your triggers when you optimize!

JOINs in Triggers Count towards the Pre-7.0 Table Limit

It doesn't apply in SQL Server 7.0 and beyond, but you used to have a limit of 16 tables involved in a query at one time. If you're working with version 6.5 or prior, make sure to include tables you access in your trigger in your table count.

Try Not to Rollback within Triggers

This one's hard since rollbacks are so often a major part of what you want to accomplish with your triggers.

Just remember that AFTER triggers (which are far and away the most common type of trigger) happen after most of the work is already done – that means a rollback is expensive. This is where DRI picks up almost all of its performance advantage. If you are using many ROLLBACK TRAN statements in your triggers, then make sure that you pre-process looking for errors before you execute the statement that fires the trigger. That is, since SQL Server can't be proactive in this situation, be proactive for it. Test for errors beforehand rather than waiting for the rollback.

Dropping Triggers

Dropping triggers is as easy as it has been for almost everything else this far:

```
DROP TRIGGER <trigger name>
```

And it's gone.

Debugging Triggers

If you try to navigate to the debugger for triggers the way that you navigate to the debugger for sprocs (see Chapter 12 for that), then you're in for a rude awakening – you won't find it. Since trigger debugging is such a pain, and I'm not very good at taking "no" for an answer, I decided to make the debugger work for me – it isn't pretty, but it works.

Basically, what we're going to do is create a wrapper procedure to fire off the trigger we want to debug. Essentially, it's a sproc whose sole purpose in life is to give us a way to fire off a statement that will let us step into our trigger with the debugger.

For example purposes, I'm going to take a piece of the last bit of test code that we used in this chapter and just place it into a sproc so I can watch the debugger run through it line by line:

```
CREATE PROC spTestTriggerDebugging
AS
BEGIN
    -- This one should work
    UPDATE CustomerOrders_vw
    SET UnitPrice = 35
    WHERE ProductID = 7

    -- This one should not
    UPDATE CustomerOrders_vw
    SET ProductID = 8
    WHERE ProductID = 7
END
```

Now I just navigate to this sproc in the **Object Browser** of Query Analyzer, right-click on it, and start the debugger:

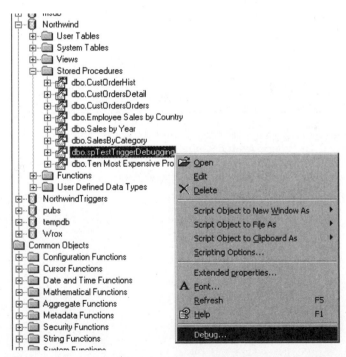

Click **Execute** at the dialog (we don't need to enter any parameters). At first, you'll just be in the debugger at the beginning of the sproc, but "step into" the lines that cause your trigger to fire, and you'll get a nice surprise!

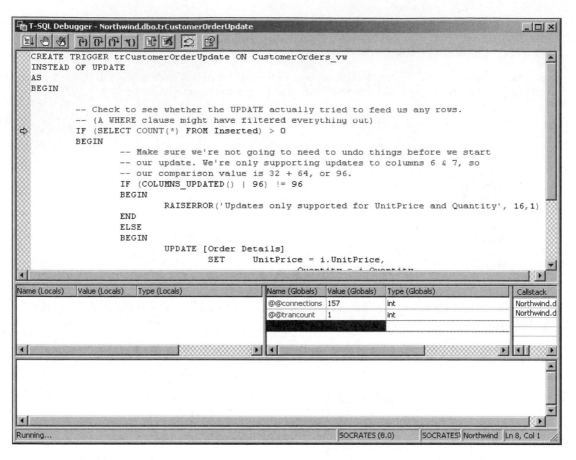

From here, there's no real rocket science in using the debugger – it works pretty much as it did when we looked at it with sprocs. The trigger even becomes an active part of your call stack.

Keep this in mind when you run into those sticky trigger debugging situations. It's a pain that it has to be done this way, but it's better than nothing.

Summary

Triggers are an extremely powerful tool that can add tremendous flexibility to both your data integrity and the overall operation of your system. That being said, they are not something to take lightly. Triggers can greatly enhance the performance of your system if you use them for proper summarization of data, but they can also be the bane of your existence. They can be very difficult to debug (even now that we have the debugger), and a poorly written trigger affects not only the trigger itself, but any statement that causes that trigger to fire.

Before you get too frustrated with triggers – or before you get too bored with the couple of trigger templates that fill about 90% of your trigger needs – keep in mind that there are a large number of tools out there that will auto-generate triggers for you that meet certain requirements. We will be looking at this a bit further in Appendix C of this book.

16

Advanced Queries

It was a tough decision. Advanced query design before cursors, or cursors before advanced query design? You see, it's something of a chicken and egg thing (which came first?). Not that you need to know anything about cursors to make sure of the topics covered in this chapter, but rather because we'll be discussing some benefits of using different query methods that avoid cursors – and it really helps to understand the benefits if you know what you're trying to avoid.

That said, I went for the advanced queries first notion. In the end, I figured I wanted to try to get you thinking about non-cursor based queries as much as possible before we start talking cursors. Since I figure that a large percentage of the readers of this book will already have experience in some programming language, I know that you're going to have a natural tendency to think of things in a procedural fashion, rather than a "set" fashion. Since cursors are a procedural approach, the odds are you're going to think of more complex problems in terms of cursors first rather than using a single query.

Suffice to say that I want to challenge you in this chapter. Even if you don't have that much procedural programming experience, the fact is that your brain has a natural tendency to break complex problems down into smaller parts (sub-procedures – logical steps) as opposed to as a whole (the "set", or SQL way). My challenge to you is to first try to see the question as a whole. Be certain that you can get it into a single query. Even if you can't think of a way, quite often you can break it up into several smaller queries and then combine them one at a time back into a larger query that does it all in one task. Try to see it as a whole, and, if you can't, then go ahead and break it down, after which re-assemble it to be whole again to the largest extent possible.

In this chapter, we're going to be looking at ways to ask what amounts to multiple questions in just one query. Essentially, we're going to look at ways of taking what seem like multiple queries and placing them into something that will execute as a single unit. In addition, we'll also be taking a look at query performance, and what you can do to get the most out of queries.

Among the topics we'll be covering in this chapter are:

- ❑ Nested subqueries
- ❑ Correlated subqueries
- ❑ Derived tables
- ❑ Making use of the EXISTS operator
- ❑ Optimizing query performance

We'll see how using subqueries can make the seemingly impossible completely possible, and how an odd tweak here and there can make a big difference in your query performance.

What is a Subquery?

A **subquery** is a normal T-SQL query that is nested inside another query – using parentheses – created when you have a SELECT statement that serves as the basis for either part of the data or the condition in another query.

Subqueries are generally used to fill one of a number of needs:

- ❑ To break a query up into a series of logical steps
- ❑ To provide a listing to be the target of a WHERE clause together with [IN | EXISTS | ANY | ALL]
- ❑ To provide a lookup driven by each individual record in a parent query

Some subqueries are very easy to think of and build, but some are extremely complex – it usually depends on the complexity of the relationship between the inner (the sub) and outer (the top/parent) query.

It's also worth noting that most subqueries (but definitely not all) can also be written using a join. In places where, among other options, it is possible to use a join, the join is usually the preferable choice.

I once got into a rather lengthy debate (perhaps 20 or 30 e-mails flying back and forth with examples, reasons, etc. over a few days) with a co-worker over the joins vs. subqueries issue.

> **Traditional logic says to always use the join, and that was what I was pushing (due to experience rather than traditional logic – you've already seen several places in this book where I've pointed out how traditional thinking can be misleading). My co-worker was pushing the notion that a subquery would actually cause less overhead. I decided to try it out.**
>
> **What I found was essentially (as you might expect), that we were both right in certain circumstances. We will explore these circumstances towards the end of the chapter.**

Now that we know what a subquery is in theory, let's look at some specific types and examples of subqueries.

Building a Nested Subquery

A **nested subquery** is one that goes in only *one* direction – returning either a single value for use in the outer query, or perhaps a full list of values to be used with the IN operator. If you want to use an explicit "=" operator, then you're going to be using a query that returns a single value – that means one column from one row. If you are expecting a list back, then you'll need to use the IN operator with your outer query.

In the loosest sense, your query syntax is going to look something like one of these two syntax templates:

```
SELECT  <SELECT list>
FROM    <SomeTable>
WHERE   <SomeColumn> = (
        SELECT <single column>
        FROM <SomeTable>
        WHERE <condition that results in only one row returned>)
```

Or:

```
SELECT  <SELECT list>
FROM    <SomeTable>
WHERE   <SomeColumn> IN (
          SELECT <single column>
          FROM <SomeTable>
          [WHERE <condition>])
```

Obviously, the exact syntax will vary – not just for substituting the SELECT list and exact table names, but also because you may have a multi-table join in either the inner or outer query – or both.

Nested Queries Using Single Value SELECT Statements

Let's get down to the nitty-gritty with an explicit example. Let's say, for example, that we wanted to know the ProductIDs of every item sold on the first day that any product was purchased from the system.

If you already know the first day that an order was placed in the system, then it's no problem; the query would look something like this:

```
USE Northwind

SELECT DISTINCT o.OrderDate, od.ProductID
FROM Orders o
JOIN [Order Details] od
  ON o.OrderID = od.OrderID
WHERE OrderDate = '7/4/1996'   --This is first OrderDate in the system
```

This yields us the correct results:

```
OrderDate                              ProductID
------------------------------------   -------------
1996-07-04 00:00:00.000                11
1996-07-04 00:00:00.000                42
1996-07-04 00:00:00.000                72

(3 row(s) affected)
```

But let's say, just for instance, that we are regularly purging data from the system, and we still want to ask this same question as part of an automated report.

Since it's going to be automated, we can't run a query to find out what the first date in the system is and manually plug that into our query.

No problem, you say. Just add in a variable and make it part of a batch:

```
DECLARE @FirstDate smalldatetime

SELECT @FirstDate = MIN(OrderDate) FROM Orders

SELECT DISTINCT o.OrderDate, od.ProductID
FROM Orders o
JOIN [Order Details] od
    ON o.OrderID = od.OrderID
WHERE o.OrderDate = @FirstDate
```

While this works (you should get back exactly the same results), we can actually clean things up a bit by putting it all into one statement:

```
SELECT DISTINCT o.OrderDate, od.ProductID
FROM Orders o
JOIN [Order Details] od
    ON o.OrderID = od.OrderID
WHERE o.OrderDate = (SELECT MIN(OrderDate) FROM Orders)
```

It really is that quick and easy. The inner query (SELECT MIN...) retrieves a single value for use in the outer query. Since we're using an equals sign and surrounding the inner query in parentheses, the inner query absolutely must return only one column from one single row, or you will get a run-time error.

Nested Queries Using Subqueries that Return Multiple Values

Perhaps the most common of all subqueries that are implemented in the world are those that retrieve some form of domain list and use it as a basis for a query.

For this one, let's switch over to using the pubs database as we did in Chapter 5 (*Joining Tables*). What we want is a list of all the stores that have discount records. The stores are, not surprisingly, in a table called stores. The discounts are in a table called, appropriately enough, discounts.

We might write something like this:

```
USE pubs

SELECT stor_id AS "Store ID", stor_name AS "Store Name"
FROM stores
WHERE stor_id IN (SELECT stor_id FROM discounts)
```

As it happens, this only gets us back one row – but what's interesting is that it is exactly the same row we saw doing an inner join in a query in Chapter 5. That query was:

```
SELECT discounttype, discount, s.stor_name
FROM discounts d
JOIN stores s
  ON d.stor_id = s.stor_id
```

With either approach, we get the same row (although with slightly different columns):

Store ID	Store Name
8042	Bookbeat

(1 row(s) affected)

Queries of the type shown here almost always fall into the category of one that can be done using an INNER JOIN rather than a nested SELECT. For example, we could get the same results as the previous subquery by running this simple join:

```
SELECT s.stor_id AS "Store ID", stor_name AS "Store Name"
FROM stores s
JOIN discounts d
  ON s.stor_id = d.stor_id
```

For performance reasons you should use the join method as your default solution if you don't have a specific reason for using the nested SELECT – we'll discuss this more before the chapter's done.

Using a Nested SELECT to Find Orphaned Records

In the following example, the use of a nested SELECT is nearly identical to our previous example, except that we add the NOT operator. The difference this makes when you are converting to join syntax is that you are equating to an outer join rather than an inner join.

Before we do the nested SELECT syntax, let's review one of our examples of an outer join from Chapter 5. In this query, we were trying to identify all the stores in the pubs database that didn't have matching discount records:

```
USE pubs

SELECT s.stor_name AS "Store Name"
FROM discounts d
RIGHT OUTER JOIN stores s
            ON d.stor_ID = s.stor_ID
WHERE d.stor_ID IS NULL
```

This gave us five rows:

```
Store Name
--------------------------------------------------
Eric the Read Books
Barnum's
News & Brews
Doc-U-Mat: Quality Laundry and Books
Fricative Bookshop

(5 row(s) affected)
```

Typically speaking, things should be done this way. I can't say, however, that it's the way that things are usually done. The join usually takes a bit more thought, so we usually wind up with the nested SELECT instead.

See if you can write this nested SELECT on your own – but I'll warn you, this one has something of a gotcha in it. Once you're done, come back and take a look below.

It should wind up looking like this:

```
SELECT stor_id AS "Store ID", stor_name AS "Store Name"
FROM stores
WHERE stor_id NOT IN
    (SELECT stor_id FROM discounts WHERE stor_id IS NOT NULL)
```

This yields us exactly the same five records, with the addition of the store_id field for each record. I'm guessing though, that you probably didn't use the NOT NULL comparison in the inner query the first time you tried it.

Whether you need to include the NOT NULL qualification or not depends on whether your table accepts NULLs and what exactly you want for results. In our case, if we leave the comparison off, we will, in error, wind up thinking that there aren't any stores that don't have discounts (when there really are). The reason has to do with how NULLs compare. If we left NOT NULL off, our list would wind up with NULLs in it. If your list has a NULL value in it, then the comparison will always yield a false result (remember – comparing anything to a NULL yields a NULL). This means that the WHERE clause will evaluate to NULL for every row. You need to be extremely careful when dealing with the possibility of NULL values in your IN list.

The ANY, SOME, and ALL Operators

Up to this point, we've only been looking for an item that was IN a list – that is, where at least one value in the list was an exact match to what we were looking for. Ah, but life isn't that simple. What if we want to do something other than an exact match – something that isn't quite equivalent to an equals (=) sign? What if we want a more complete list of operators? No problem!

"Wait, hold on!" you say. "What if I want to see if *every* value in a list matches something – what then?" Again – no problem!

ANY and SOME

ANY and SOME are functional equivalents; if you choose to use either one of these (you'll see later why I don't recommend them), then I would suggest using SOME, as it is the ANSI-compliant one of the two. In all honesty, for the rest of this section, I'm only going to use SOME, but feel free to substitute ANY in its place – you should get the same results.

The ANY and SOME operators allow you to use a broader range of other operators against the lists created by your subqueries. They can also be used with any of the other operators that you would typically use for comparisons (such as >=, <=, <>, !>, etc.).

Taking > as an example; >SOME means greater than any one value – in other words, greater than the minimum. So >SOME (1,2,3) means greater than 1. If you use SOME or ANY with an equals sign (=), then they are functionally equivalent to the IN operator.

Let's try this out with a simple rehash of the NOT IN query we just looked at. We'll use this one to show how close SOME is to the IN operator, but then we'll play with it to see the additional flexibility SOME gives us. The syntax only requires two changes (NOT IN becomes != SOME):

```
SELECT stor_id AS "Store ID", stor_name AS "Store Name"
FROM stores
WHERE stor_id != SOME
     (SELECT stor_id FROM discounts WHERE stor_id IS NOT NULL)
```

Run this and you should get the same five rows back yet again:

Store ID	Store Name
6380	Eric the Read Books
7066	Barnum's
7067	News & Brews
7131	Doc-U-Mat: Quality Laundry and Books
7896	Fricative Bookshop

(5 row(s) affected)

That works fine, but let's mess around with it some, and see how we can change things. This time, we'll change our comparison:

```
SELECT stor_id AS "Store ID", stor_name AS "Store Name"
FROM stores
WHERE stor_id < SOME
     (SELECT stor_id FROM discounts WHERE stor_id IS NOT NULL)
```

Yet again this gives us these five rows:

Store ID	Store Name
6380	Eric the Read Books
7066	Barnum's
7067	News & Brews
7131	Doc-U-Mat: Quality Laundry and Books
7896	Fricative Bookshop

(5 row(s) affected)

The results of this query would be any stores that have a `stor_id` that is less than the largest `stor_id` with no discount.

Actually, I'm not a big fan of this keyword. The reason is that I find it functionally useless, and it can also be a little confusing. The things you can do with `SOME` (or `ANY`) fall into two categories. The first of these doesn't include anything you can do with `SOME` that you can't do with some other syntax (the other syntax has always been more succinct in my experience). The second is the case of `<> SOME`. Where the `NOT IN (A, B, C)` clause gets you a logical expansion of `<>A AND <> B AND <> C`, `<> SOME` gets you `<>A OR <> B OR <> C`. This last option is a positively useless construct. Think about it for a minute – any comparison you run against `<> SOME` is going to yield you a non-filtered list. By definition, anything that is `= A` is `<> B`.

In short, if you find a reason to use this, great – I'd love to hear about it – but, to date, I haven't seen anything done with `SOME` that can't be done more clearly and with better performance using a different construct (which one depends on the nature of the `SOME` you're trying to match).

ALL

The `ALL` operator is similar to the `SOME` and `ANY` operators in that it allows you to work with a broader range of comparison operators. However, applying our previous `>` example to the `ALL` statement, we see the difference between them. `> ALL` means greater than every value that has been specified, for example, `"> ALL (1, 2, 3)"` means "greater than 3".

Correlated Subqueries

Two words for you on this section: *pay attention*! This is another one of those little areas that, if you truly get it, you are really set apart from the crowd. By "get it" I don't just mean that you understand how it works, but also that you understand how important and useful the following information can be.

Correlated subqueries are one of those things that make the impossible possible. What's more, they often turn several lines of code into one, and often create a corresponding increase in performance. The problem with them is that they require a substantially different way of thinking from that which you're probably used to. Correlated subqueries are probably the single easiest concept in SQL to learn, understand, and then promptly forget because it simply goes against the grain of how you think. If you're one of the few who choose to remember it as an option, then you will be one of the few who figure out that particularly difficult problem. You'll also be someone with a far more complete toolset when it comes to squeezing every ounce of performance from your queries.

How Correlated Subqueries Work

What makes correlated subqueries different from the nested subqueries we've been looking at is that the information travels in *two* directions rather than one. In a nested subquery, the inner query is only processed once, and that information is passed out for the outer query, which will also execute just once – essentially providing the same value or list that you would have provided if you had typed it in yourself.

With correlated subqueries, however, the inner query runs on information provided by the outer query, and vice versa. That may seem a bit confusing (that chicken or the egg thing again), but it works in a three-step process:

❑   The outer query obtains a record and passes it into the inner query

❑   The inner query executes based on the value(s) passed in

❑   The inner query then passes the values from its results back out to the outer query, which uses them to finish its processing

Correlated Subqueries in the WHERE Clause

I realize that this is probably a bit confusing, so let's look at it in an example.

We'll go back to the Northwind database and look again at the query where we wanted to know the orders that happened on the first date that any order was placed in the system. However, this time we want to add a new twist: We want to know the OrderID(s) and OrderDate of the first order in the system for each customer, that is, we want to know the first day that a customer placed an order and the IDs of those orders. Let's look at it piece by piece.

First, we want the OrderDate, OrderID, and CustomerID for each of our results. All of that information can be found in the Orders table, so we know that our query is going to be based, at least in part, on that table.

Next, we need to know what the first date in the system was for each customer. That's where the tricky part comes in. When we did this with a nested subquery, we only looked for the first date in the entire file – now we need a value for each individual customer.

This wouldn't be that big a deal if we were to do it in two separate queries – we could just create a temporary table, and then join back to it – like this:

```
USE Northwind

SELECT CustomerID, MIN(OrderDate) AS OrderDate
INTO #MinOrderDates
FROM Orders
GROUP BY CustomerID
ORDER BY CustomerID

SELECT o.CustomerID, o.OrderID, o.OrderDate
FROM Orders o
JOIN #MinOrderDates t
   ON o.CustomerID = t.CustomerID
   AND o.OrderDate = t.OrderDate
ORDER BY o.CustomerID

DROP TABLE #MinOrderDates
```

We get back 89 rows:

(89 row(s) affected)

CustomerID	OrderID	OrderDate
ALFKI	10643	1997-08-25 00:00:00.000
ANATR	10308	1996-09-18 00:00:00.000
ANTON	10365	1996-11-27 00:00:00.000
AROUT	10355	1996-11-15 00:00:00.000
BERGS	10278	1996-08-12 00:00:00.000
...		
...		
...		
WHITC	10269	1996-07-31 00:00:00.000
WILMK	10615	1997-07-30 00:00:00.000
WOLZA	10374	1996-12-05 00:00:00.000

(89 row(s) affected)

As previously stated, don't worry if your results are slightly different from those shown here – it just means you've been playing around with the Northwind data a little more or a little less than I have.

The fact that we are building two completely separate result sets here is emphasized by the fact that you see two different row(s) affected statements in the results pane (one at the top and one at the bottom). That, more often that not, has a negative impact on performance. We'll explore this further after we've discussed our options a little more.

Sometimes using this two query approach is simply the only way to get things done without using a cursor – this is not one of those times.

OK, so if we want this to run in a single query, we need to find a way to look up each individual customer. We can do this by making use of an inner query that performs a lookup based on the current CustomerID in the outer query. We will then need to return a value back out to the outer query so it can match things up based on the earliest order date.

It looks like this:

```
SELECT o1.CustomerID, o1.OrderID, o1.OrderDate
FROM Orders o1
WHERE o1.OrderDate = (SELECT Min(o2.OrderDate)
                      FROM Orders o2
                      WHERE o2.CustomerID = o1.CustomerID)
ORDER BY CustomerID
```

With this, we get back the same 89 rows:

CustomerID	OrderID	OrderDate
ALFKI	10643	1997-08-25 00:00:00.000
ANATR	10308	1996-09-18 00:00:00.000
ANTON	10365	1996-11-27 00:00:00.000
AROUT	10355	1996-11-15 00:00:00.000
BERGS	10278	1996-08-12 00:00:00.000
...		
...		
...		
WHITC	10269	1996-07-31 00:00:00.000
WILMK	10615	1997-07-30 00:00:00.000
WOLZA	10374	1996-12-05 00:00:00.000

(89 row(s) affected)

There are a couple of key things to notice in this query:

❑ We only see the **89 row(s) affected** statement once; that's because only one query plan had to be executed, thereby affecting the rows on only one occasion. Just by observation, we can guess that this version probably runs faster than the two query version, and in reality, it does. Again, we'll look into this in a bit more depth later.

❑ The outer query (in this example) looks pretty much just like a nested subquery. The inner query, however, has an explicit reference to the outer query (notice the use of the "o1" alias).

❑ Aliases are used in both queries – even though it looks like the outer query shouldn't need one – that's because they are required whenever you explicitly refer to a column from the other query (the inner query refers to a column on the outer query and vice versa).

The latter point of needing aliases is a big area of confusion. The fact is that sometimes you need them, and sometimes you don't. While I don't tend to use them at all in the types of nested subqueries that we looked at in the early part of this chapter, I alias everything when dealing with correlated subqueries.

> **The hard and fast "rule" is that you must alias any table (and its related columns) that's going to be referred to by the other query. The problem with this is that this can quickly become very confusing. The way to be on the safe side is to alias everything – that way you're positive of which table in which query you're getting your information from.**

In this particular query, the outer query only references the inner query in the WHERE clause – it could also have requested data from the inner query to include in the SELECT list.

Normally, it's up to us whether we want to make use of an alias or not, but with correlated subqueries, they are required. This particular query is a really great one for showing why because the inner and outer queries are based on the same table. Since both queries are getting information from each other, without aliasing, how would they know which instance of the table data you were interested in?

Correlated Subqueries in the SELECT List

Subqueries can also be used to provide a different kind of answer in your selection results. This kind of situation is often found where the information you're after is fundamentally different from the rest of the data in your query (for example, you want an aggregation on one field, but you don't want all the baggage from that to affect the other fields returned).

To test this out, let's just run a modified version of the query that we used in the last section. What we're after here is just the name of the customer and the date on which he or she first ordered something.

This query requires a more significant change than would be expected. We're now asking for the customer's name, which means that we have to bring the Customers table into play. In addition, we no longer need to build any kind of condition into the query – we're asking for all customers (no restrictions), and all we want to know is when their first order date was.

The query actually ends up being a little simpler than the last one, and it looks like this:

```
SELECT cu.CompanyName,
    (SELECT Min(OrderDate)
        FROM Orders o
        WHERE o.CustomerID = cu.CustomerID)
        AS "Order Date"
FROM Customers cu
```

This gets us data that looks something like this:

CompanyName	Order Date
Alfreds Futterkiste	1997-08-25 00:00:00.000
Ana Trujillo Emparedados y helados	1996-09-18 00:00:00.000
Antonio Moreno Taquería	1996-11-27 00:00:00.000
Around the Horn	1996-11-15 00:00:00.000
Berglunds snabbköp	1996-08-12 00:00:00.000
Blauer See Delikatessen	1997-04-09 00:00:00.000
…	
…	
…	
White Clover Markets	1996-07-31 00:00:00.000
Wilman Kala	1997-07-30 00:00:00.000
Wolski Zajazd	1996-12-05 00:00:00.000

(91 row(s) affected)

Note that, if you look down through all the data, there are a couple of rows that have a NULL in the OrderDate column. Why do you suppose that is? It is because there is no record in the Orders table that matches the then current record in the Customers table (the outer query).

This brings us to a small digression to take a look at a particularly useful function for this situation – ISNULL().

Dealing with NULL Data – The ISNULL Function

There are actually a few functions that are specifically meant to deal with NULL data, but the one of particular use to us at this point is ISNULL(). ISNULL() accepts a variable or expression and tests it for a NULL value. If the value is indeed NULL, then the function returns some other pre-specified value. If the original value is not NULL, then the original value is returned. This syntax is pretty straightforward:

```
ISNULL(<expression to test>, <replacement value if null>)
```

So, for example:

ISNULL Expression	Value Returned
ISNULL(NULL, 5)	5
ISNULL(5, 15)	5
ISNULL(@MyVar, 0) where @MyVar IS NULL	0
ISNULL(@MyVar, 0) where @MyVar =3	3
ISNULL(@MyVar, 0) where @MyVar ='Fred Farmer'	Fred Farmer

Now let's see this at work in our query:

```
SELECT cu.CompanyName,
    ISNULL(CAST ((SELECT MIN(o.OrderDate)
            FROM Orders o
            WHERE o.CustomerID = cu.CustomerID)AS varchar), 'NEVER ORDERED')
            AS "Order Date"
FROM Customers cu
```

Now, in our two lines that had NULL values as the OrderDate, we go from:

...
FISSA Fabrica Inter. Salchichas S.A.   NULL
...
Paris spécialités   NULL
...

To something substantially more useful:

...
FISSA Fabrica Inter. Salchichas S.A.   NEVER ORDERED
...
Paris spécialités   NEVER ORDERED
...

Notice that I also had to put the CAST() function into play to get this to work. The reason has to do with casting and implicit type conversion. Since the first row starts off returning a valid date, the OrderDate column is assumed (for the whole result set) to be of type DateTime. However, when we get to our first NULL, there is an error generated since the ISNULL function substitutes 'NEVER ORDERED' and that can't be converted to the DateTime data type. Keep CAST() in mind – it can help you out of little troubles like this one. This is covered further later in the chapter.

So, at this point, we've seen correlated subqueries that provide information for both the WHERE clause, and for the SELECT list. You can mix and match these two in the same query if you wish.

Derived Tables

Sometimes you get into situations where you need to work with the results of a query in a way that doesn't really lend itself to the kinds of subqueries that we've discussed up to this point. An example would be where, for each row in a given table, you may have multiple results in the subquery, but you're looking for a more complex action than the IN operator provides. Essentially, what I'm talking about here are situations where you would want to use a JOIN operator on your subquery.

It's at times like these that we turn to a somewhat lesser known construct in SQL – a **derived table**. A derived table is made up of the columns and rows of a result set from a query (with columns, rows, data types, etc. just like normal tables, so why not use them as such?).

Imagine for a moment that you want to get a list of customers that ordered a particular product – say, Chocolade. No problem! Your query might look something like this:

```
USE Northwind
SELECT c.CompanyName
FROM Customers AS c
JOIN Orders AS o
   ON c.CustomerID = o.CustomerID
JOIN [Order Details] AS od
   ON o.OrderID = od.OrderID
JOIN Products AS p
   ON od.ProductID = p.ProductID
WHERE p.ProductName = 'Chocolade'
```

OK, so that was easy. Now, let's add a twist to the end – let's now say that I want to know all the customers that ordered not only Chocolade, but also Vegie-spread. Note that I said that they had to have ordered both these products. Now you have a problem. Your first inclination might be to write something like this in place of WHERE p.ProductName = 'Chocolade':

```
WHERE p.ProductName = 'Chocolade' AND p.ProductName = 'Vegie-spread'
```

However, that's not going to work at all – each row is for a single product, so how can it have both Chocolade and Vegie-spread as the name at the same time? It can't – so you will not get back what you want (indeed, while this query will run, you'll never get any rows back at all).

What we really need here is to join the results of a query to find buyers of Chocolade with the results of a query to find buyers of Vegie-spread. How do we join results though? Well, as you might expect given the title of this section, you use derived tables.

To create our derived table, we need two things:

❑   To enclose our query that generates the result set in parentheses

❑   To alias the results of the query

So, the syntax looks something like this:

```
SELECT <select list>
FROM (<query that returns a regular result set>) AS <alias name>
JOIN <some other base or derived table>
```

So let's take this now and apply it to our requirements. Again, what we want is the names of all the companies that have ordered both Chocolade and Vegie-spread. Our query should look something like this:

```
SELECT DISTINCT c.CompanyName
FROM Customers AS c
JOIN
    (SELECT CustomerID
          FROM Orders o
          JOIN [Order Details] od
            ON o.OrderID = od.OrderID
          JOIN Products p
            ON od.ProductID = p.ProductID
          WHERE p.ProductName = 'Chocolade') AS spen
            ON c.CustomerID = spen.CustomerID
JOIN
    (SELECT CustomerID
          FROM Orders o
          JOIN [Order Details] od
            ON o.OrderID = od.OrderID
          JOIN Products p
            ON od.ProductID = p.ProductID
          WHERE ProductName = 'Vegie-spread') AS spap
            ON c.CustomerID = spap.CustomerID
```

As it happens, we only get one customer:

CompanyName

Ernst Handel

(1 row(s) affected)

If you want to check things out on this, just run the queries for the two derived tables separately and compare the results.

For this particular query, we needed to use the DISTINCT keyword. If we hadn't, then we would have potentially received multiple rows for each customer – for example, Ernst Handel ordered Vegie-spread on two occasions, so we would have gotten one record for each. We only wanted to know which customers had ordered both, not how many times they had ordered.

As you can see, we were able to take a seemingly impossible query and make it possible – and it even performs reasonably well.

Bear in mind that derived tables are not the solution to every problem. For example, if the result set is going to be fairly large and you're going to have lots of joined records, then you may want to look at using a temporary table and building an index on it (derived tables have no indexes). Every situation is different, but now you have one more tool in your arsenal.

The EXISTS Operator

I call EXISTS an operator, but all you'll hear the Books Online call it is a keyword. That's probably because it defies description in some senses. It's an operator much like the IN keyword is, but it works a little differently.

When you use EXISTS, you don't really return data – instead, you return a simple TRUE/FALSE regarding the existence of data that meets the criteria established in the query which the EXISTS statement is operating against.

Let's go right to an example, so you can see how the EXISTS operator is applied. What we're going to query here is a list of customers that have placed at least one order (we don't care how many):

```
USE Northwind
SELECT CustomerID, CompanyName
FROM Customers cu
WHERE EXISTS
    (SELECT OrderID
            FROM Orders o
            WHERE o.CustomerID = cu.CustomerID)
```

This gets us what amounts to the same 89 records that we've been dealing with throughout this chapter:

```
CustomerID                 CompanyName
-------------------------  ----------------------------------------------
ALFKI                      Alfreds Futterkiste
ANATR                      Ana Trujillo Emparedados y helados
ANTON                      Antonio Moreno Taquería
AROUT                      Around the Horn
BERGS                      Berglunds snabbköp
BLAUS                      Blauer See Delikatessen
...
...
...
WHITC                      White Clover Markets
WILMK                      Wilman Kala
WOLZA                      Wolski Zajazd
```

(89 row(s) affected)

We could have easily done the same thing using a join:

```
USE Northwind
SELECT DISTINCT cu.CustomerID, cu.CompanyName
FROM Customers cu
JOIN Orders o
    ON cu.CustomerID = o.CustomerID
```

This second syntax, for example, would have yielded us exactly the same results (subject to possible sort differences). So why, then, would we need this new syntax? The reason is performance – plain and simple.

When you use the EXISTS keyword, SQL Server doesn't have to perform a full row by row join. Instead, it can look through the records until it finds the first match, and stop right there. As soon as there is a single match, the value of EXISTS is TRUE, so there is no need to go further.

Let's take a brief look at things the other way around – what if we want the customers who have not ordered anything? Under the join method that we looked at back in Chapter 5, we would have had to make some significant changes in the way we went about getting this data. First, we would have to use an outer join. Then we would perform a comparison to see whether any of the Order records were NULL.

It looked like this:

```
USE Northwind

SELECT c.CustomerID, CompanyName
FROM Customers c
LEFT OUTER JOIN Orders o
          ON c.CustomerID = o.CustomerID
WHERE o.CustomerID IS NULL
```

And it returned two rows:

CustomerID	CompanyName
PARIS	Paris spécialités
FISSA	FISSA Fabrica Inter. Salchichas S.A.

(2 row(s) affected)

To do the same change over when we're using EXISTS we only add one word – NOT:

```
SELECT CustomerID, CompanyName
FROM Customers cu
WHERE NOT EXISTS
    (SELECT OrderID
           FROM Orders o
           WHERE o.CustomerID = cu.CustomerID)
```

And we get back those exact same two rows:

CustomerID	CompanyName
FISSA	FISSA Fabrica Inter. Salchichas S.A.
PARIS	Paris spécialités

(2 row(s) affected)

The difference in performance here is even more marked than with the inner join. SQL Server just applies a little reverse logic on the EXISTS statement. In the case of the NOT EXISTS we're now using, SQL will still stop looking as soon as it finds one matching record – the only difference being that it returns FALSE for the lookup rather than TRUE. As far as performance is concerned, everything else about the query is the same.

Using EXISTS in Other Ways

If you use the Enterprise Manager to create any scripts, one of the options it gives you is whether to include DROP statements. Assuming you select that option, you'll notice something peculiar that it adds to the creation script for each table. It will look something like this:

```
IF EXISTS (SELECT * FROM sysobjects WHERE id = object_id(N'[dbo].[Shippers]')
AND OBJECTPROPERTY(id, N'IsUserTable') = 1)
DROP TABLE [dbo].[Shippers]
GO

CREATE TABLE [dbo].[Shippers] (
    [ShipperID] [int] IDENTITY (1, 1) NOT NULL ,
    [CompanyName] [nvarchar] (40) NOT NULL ,
    [Phone] [nvarchar] (24) NULL
)
GO
```

Actually, it's kind of funny that they still do it this way as opposed to using the INFORMATION SCHEMA as they tell you to, but it's still handy for illustrating a very common use for EXISTS – that is, with an IF...ELSE statement, as we'll see later.

Since EXISTS returns nothing but TRUE or FALSE, it works as an excellent conditional expression. The previous example will only run the DROP TABLE code if the table exists; otherwise, it skips over that part and moves right into the CREATE statement. This avoids one of two errors showing up when you run the script. First, it would not be able to run the CREATE statement because the object already exists. If the CREATE statement were to be run, this would probably create other problems if you were running this in a script where other tables were depending on this being done first. Second, it would not be able to DROP the table because it didn't exist (this pretty much just creates a message that might be confusing to a customer who installs your product). You're covered for both instances.

As for an example of this, let's write our own CREATE script for something that's often skipped in the automation effort – the database itself. Because Enterprise Manager will generate the table scripts for you (assuming that you've already created the table with the New Table... command, or scripts, etc.), that part tends to get done – it's easy, so people are willing to do it. However, the creation of the database is often left as part of some cryptic directions that say something like "create a database called 'xxxx'". The fun part is when the people who are actually installing it (who often don't know what they're doing) start including the quotes, or create a database that is too small, or perhaps make a host of other possible errors which can be very easily done in these circumstances. This is the point where I hope you have a good technical support department.

Instead, we'll just build a script to create the database object that could go with Northwind. For safety's sake, we'll call it NorthwindCreate. We'll also keep the statement to a minimum since we're interested in the EXISTS operator rather than the CREATE command:

```
USE master

GO

IF NOT EXISTS (SELECT 'True' FROM INFORMATION_SCHEMA.SCHEMATA WHERE
    CATALOG_NAME = 'NorthwindCreate')
BEGIN
```

```
    CREATE DATABASE NorthwindCreate
    ON
    ( NAME = NorthwindCreate,
      FILENAME = 'c:\Program Files\Microsoft SQL
Server\mssql\data\NorthwindCreate.mdf' )
END
ELSE
BEGIN
    PRINT 'Database already exists. Skipping CREATE DATABASE Statement'
END
GO
```

The first time you run this, there won't be any database called NorthwindCreate (unless by sheer coincidence you created something called that before we got to this point), so you'll get a response back that looks like this:

The CREATE DATABASE process is allocating 0.63 MB on disk 'NorthwindCreate'.
The CREATE DATABASE process is allocating 0.49 MB on disk 'NorthwindCreate_log'.

If the sizes seem small, that's because we didn't specify a size, so the files were created based on the size of the model database. In a real-life situation, you'd specify whatever size was appropriate.

Now run the script a second time, and you'll see a change:

Database already exists. Skipping CREATE DATABASE Statement

So, without much fanfare or fuss, we've added a rather small script, that will make things much simpler for the installer of your product. That may be an end user who bought your off-the-shelf product, or it may be you – in which case it's even better that it's fully scripted.

EXISTS is a very handy keyword indeed. It can make some queries run much faster, and it can also simplify some queries and scripts.

> **A word of caution here – this is another one of those places where it's easy to get trapped in "traditional thinking". While EXISTS blows other options away in a large percentage of queries where EXISTS is a valid construct, it's not always the case. For example, the query we used as a derived table example can also be written with a couple of EXISTS operators (one for each product). Though the derived table happens to run more than twice as fast, in this case, that is definitely the exception not the rule – EXISTS will normally outdo a derived table where performance is concerned; just remember that rules are sometimes made to be broken.**

Mixing Data Types: CAST and CONVERT

You'll see both CAST and CONVERT used frequently. Indeed, we've touch briefly on both of these in several places throughout the book. This seems like a good time to look a little closer at what these two functions can do for you.

Both CAST and CONVERT perform data type conversions for you. In most respects, they both do the same thing, with the exception that CONVERT also does some date formatting conversions that CAST doesn't offer.

So, the question probably quickly rises to your mind – hey, if CONVERT does everything that CAST does, and CONVERT also does date conversions, why would I ever use CAST? I have a simple answer for that – ANSI compliance. CAST is ANSI compliant, and CONVERT isn't – it's that simple.

Let's take a look for the syntax for each.

CAST (*expression* AS *data_type*)

CONVERT(*data_type*, *expression*[, *style*])

With a little flip-flop on which goes first, and the addition of the formatting option on CONVERT (with the *style* argument), they have basically the same syntax.

CAST and CONVERT can deal with a wide variety of data type conversions that you'll need to do when SQL Server won't do it implicitly for you. For example, converting a number to a string is a very common need. To illustrate:

```
USE Northwind
SELECT 'The Customer has an Order numbered ' + OrderID
FROM Orders
WHERE CustomerID = 'ALFKI'
```

Will yield an error message:

Server: Msg 245, Level 16, State 1, Line 1
Syntax error converting the varchar value 'The Customer has an Order numbered ' to a column of data type int.

But change the code to convert the number first:

```
USE Northwind
SELECT 'The Customer has an Order numbered ' + CAST(OrderID AS varchar)
FROM Orders
WHERE CustomerID = 'ALFKI'
```

And you get a much different result:

```
-----------------------------------------------------------
The Customer has an Order numbered 10643
The Customer has an Order numbered 10692
The Customer has an Order numbered 10702
The Customer has an Order numbered 10835
The Customer has an Order numbered 10952
The Customer has an Order numbered 11011

(6 row(s) affected)
```

The conversions can also get a little less intuitive. Suppose for example, that you wanted to convert a `timestamp` column into a regular number. A `timestamp` is just a binary number, so the conversion isn't really a big deal:

```
CREATE TABLE ConvertTest
(
    ColID    int    IDENTITY,
    ColTS    timestamp
)

INSERT INTO ConvertTest
    DEFAULT VALUES

SELECT ColTS AS "Unconverted", CAST(ColTS AS int) AS "Converted"
FROM ConvertTest
```

Yields us something like (your exact numbers will vary):

(1 row(s) affected)

Unconverted	Converted
0x00000000000000C9	201

(1 row(s) affected)

We can also convert dates:

```
SELECT OrderDate, CAST(OrderDate AS varchar) AS "Converted"
FROM Orders
WHERE OrderID = 11050
```

This yields us something similar to the following (your exact format may change depending on system date configuration):

OrderDate	Converted
1998-04-27 00:00:00.000	Apr 27 1998 12:00AM

(1 row(s) affected)

Notice that CAST can still do date conversion, you just don't have any control over the formatting as you do with CONVERT. For example:

```
USE Northwind
SELECT OrderDate, CONVERT(varchar(12), OrderDate, 111) AS "Converted"
FROM Orders
WHERE OrderID = 11050
```

Yields us:

OrderDate	Converted
1998-04-27 00:00.00	2000/10/11

(1 row(s) affected)

Which is quite a bit different from what CAST did. Indeed, we could have converted to any one of thirty-four two-digit or four-digit year formats. For example:

```
USE Northwind
SELECT OrderDate, CONVERT(varchar(12), OrderDate, 5) AS "Converted"
FROM Orders
WHERE OrderID = 11050
```

Gives us:

OrderDate	Converted
1998-04-27 00:00:00.000	27-04-98

(1 row(s) affected)

All you need is to supply a code at the end of the CONVERT function (111 in the previous example gave us the JAPAN standard, with a four-digit year; and 5 the Italian standard, with a two-digit year) that specifies which format you want. Anything in the 100s is a four-digit year, anything less than 100, with a few exceptions, is a two-digit year. The available formats can be found in Books Online under the topic of CONVERT or CASE.

> *Bear in mind that some changes have needed to be made to things in order to deal with the infamous Y2K issue. One of the changes is that you can now set a **split point** that SQL Server will use to determine whether a 2 digit year should be have a 20 added on the front or a 19. The default breaking point is 49/50 – a two-digit year of 49 or less will be converted by prefixing it with 20, anything higher will be prefixed by 19. These can be changed using sp_configure, or by setting them in the Server Settings tab of the Properties dialog for your server in Enterprise Manager.*

Performance Considerations

We've already touched on some of the macro-level "what's the best thing to do?" stuff as we've gone through the chapter, but, like most things in life, it's not as easy as all that. What I want to do here is provide something of a quick reference regarding performance issues for your queries. I'll try and steer you towards the right kind of query for the right kind of situation.

> **Yes, it's time again, folks, for one of my now famous soapbox diatribes. At issue this time, is the concept of blanket use of blanket rules.**
>
> **What we're going to be talking about in this section is about the way that things** *usually* **work. The word usually is extremely operative here. There are very few rules in SQL that will be true 100% of the time. In a world full of exceptions, SQL has to be at the pinnacle of the exception world – exceptions are a dime a dozen when you try to describe the performance world in SQL Server.**
>
> **In short, you need to gauge just how important the performance of a given query is. If performance is critical, then don't take these rules too seriously – instead, use them as a starting point, and then TEST, TEST, TEST!!!**

JOINs vs. Subqueries vs. ?

This is that area where, as I mentioned earlier in the chapter, I had a heated debate with a co-worker. And, as you might expect when two people have such conviction, with such contrasting points of view, both of us were correct up to a point (and it follows, wrong up to a point).

The long-standing and traditional viewpoint about subqueries has always been that you are much better off using joins instead (if you can). This is absolutely correct – well, sometimes. In reality, it depends on a large number of factors. The following table discusses some of the issues that performance will depend on, and which favor joins, subqueries, or whatever:

Situation	Favors...
The value returned from a subquery is going to be the same for every row in the outer query.	Pre-query. Declaring a variable, and then selecting the needed value into that variable will allow the would-be subquery to be executed just once rather than once for every record in the outer table.
Both tables are relatively small (say 10,000 records or less).	Subqueries. I don't know the exact reasons, but I've run several tests on this, and subqueries have had the edge pretty much every time. I suspect that the issue is the lower overhead of a lookup vs. a join.
The match, after considering all criteria, is only going to return one value.	Subqueries. Again, there is much less overhead in going and finding just one record and substituting it, than having to join the entire table.
The match, after considering all criteria, is only going to return relatively few values and there is no index on the lookup column.	Subqueries. A single lookup or even a few lookups will usually take less overhead than a hash join.
The lookup table is relatively small, but the base table is large.	Nested subqueries if applicable; joins if vs. a correlated subquery. With subqueries the lookup will only happen once, and is relatively low overhead. With correlated subqueries, however, you will be cycling the lookup many times – in this case, the join would be a better choice in most cases.
Correlated subquery vs. join	Join. Internally, a correlated subquery is going to create a nested loop situation. This can create quite a bit of overhead. Subqueries are substantially faster than cursors in most instances, but slower than other options that might be available.
Using derived tables	Derived tables typically carry a fair amount of overhead, so proceed with caution. The thing to remember is that they are run (or derived) once, and then they are in memory, so, most of the overhead is in the initial creation and, in larger result sets, the lack of indexes. They can be fast or slow – it just depends. Think before coding on these.
Using EXISTS	EXISTS. It does not have to deal with multiple lookups for the same match – once it finds one match for that particular row, it is free to move on to the next lookup – this can seriously cut down on overhead.

These are just the highlights. The possibilities of different mixes and additional situations are endless.

> I can't stress enough how important it is, that when you are in doubt – or even when you're not in doubt but performance is everything – to make reasonable tests of competing solutions to the problem. Most of the time, the blanket rules will be fine, but not always. By performing reasonable tests, you can be certain you've made the right choice.

Summary

The query options you learned back in Chapters 4 and 5 cover perhaps 80% or more of the query situations that you run into, but it's that other 20% that can kill you. Sometimes the issue is whether you can even find a query that will give you the answers you need. Or you might have a particular query or sproc that has unacceptable performance. Whatever the case, you'll run across plenty of situations where simple queries and joins just won't work as you require them to. You need something more, and, hopefully, the options covered in this chapter have given you a little extra arsenal to deal with those tough situations.

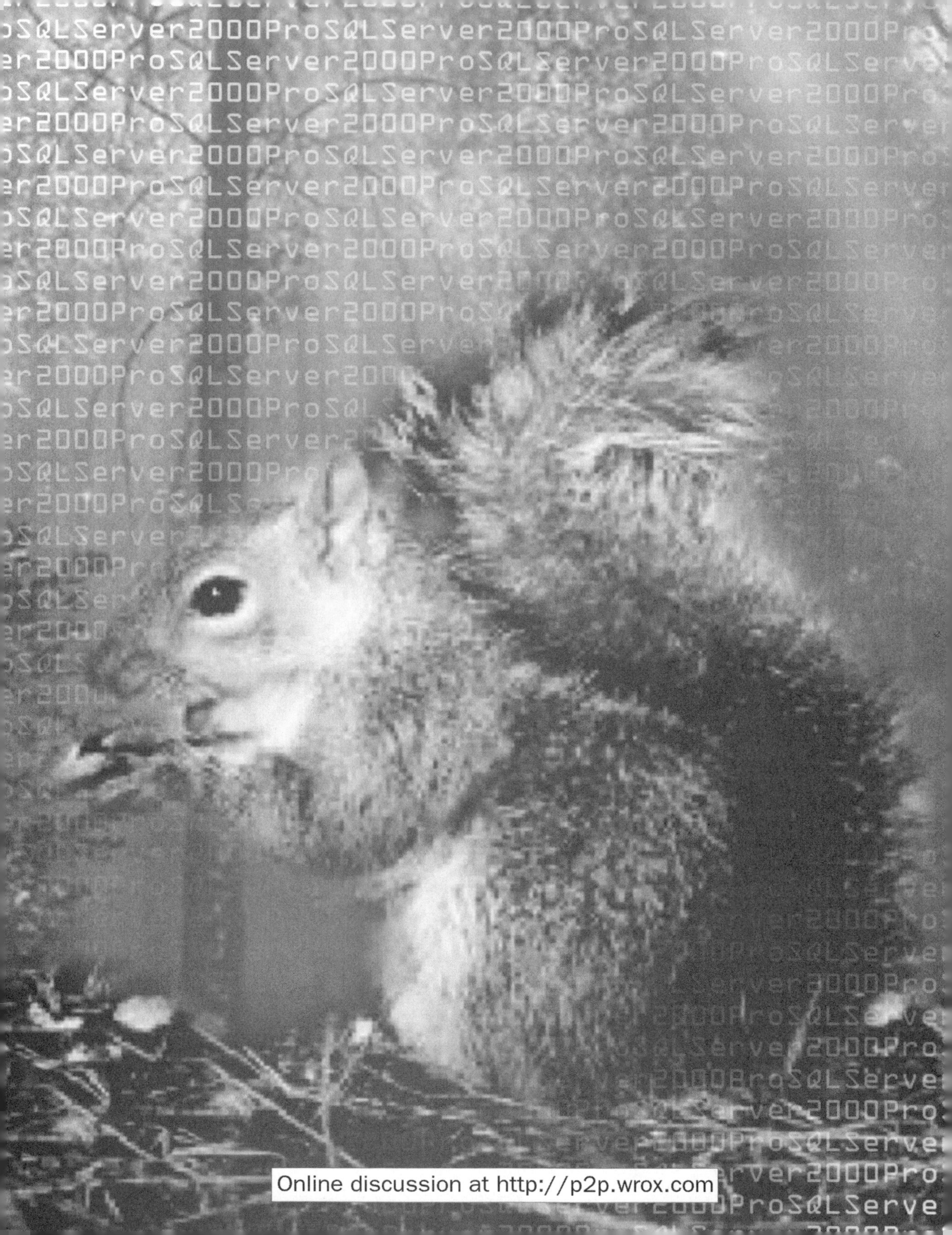
Online discussion at http://p2p.wrox.com

17

Distributed Queries and Transactions

Wouldn't it be nice if everything, everywhere could run on just one machine? Of course, everyone would need to have bandwidth to the machine such that it seemed local. And security – oops, that would be a problem. And this is, of course, just the start of things. Nope – we don't want every application for everyone running on the same server at all.

Indeed, sometimes dealing with multiple servers is a must. Reasons for operating on separate servers include geographical requirements, loading (too much for one machine), redundancy (not "having all your eggs in one basket", as the old saying goes), and more. Often we can let those servers live in their own little autonomous world, but quite often we keep things separate because it seems like too much of a hassle to bring them together.

You can think of a distributed transaction as being any transaction (such as we've already discussed using one SQL Server), where you need to have that same reliability across multiple servers.

In addition to continued support for distributed transactions, version 7.0 added features that make querying information across servers – re-phrase that – data sources, extremely easy for many providers (in all honesty, others can be a real bear to get working). You can now perform heterogeneous (mixed data source) joins on SQL Server. That means that you can query information from SQL Server A and SQL Server B, plus join that information with any OLEDB data source – including Excel, Access, dBase, Active Directory – anything that has an OLEDB provider.

SQL Server 2000 now provides the ability to set up these remote servers is such a way that you can spread data across multiple tables and multiple servers, yet make them all look as if they are one. Microsoft has long held the best cost per transaction numbers from the Transaction Performance Council (TPC). As SQL Server 2000 came through beta, Microsoft also began making a lot of noise and posting excellent numbers in the total performance ratings. Microsoft achieved these numbers by making use of the "virtual table" concept known as **distributed partitioned views** – which, in plain English, means a bunch of tables with a view built over them which makes them act like they are all one table. Very cool stuff when you think about it – yes, the rules have changed.

In this chapter, we'll take a look at these distributed features.

Distributed Transactions

To make use of all the basic SQL Server transaction features (BEGIN, SAVE, ROLLBACK, COMMIT), the transaction must only deal with objects local to the server the transaction is running on.

SQL Server does, however, offer another choice for transactions that is especially made for situations where you need to have absolute assurance that data is committed at both ends of an unreliable connection. (Phone lines can easily go down even in the same city – so imagine if your line is from Virginia to Malaysia. You would definitely want a safety net.) It is called **Microsoft Distributed Transaction Coordinator** (**MS DTC**) and comes not only with SQL Server, but also with Microsoft Transaction Server (MTS). MS DTC can be described as a "vote collector" and coordinator of transactions between different servers and different RDBMSs.

MS DTC makes use of what is called a **two-phase commit protocol** (**2PC**). Much as its name implies, a 2PC has two distinct phases to guarantee that a transaction that is indicated as committed really did get committed at both ends:

❑ Prepare

❑ Commit

The Prepare Phase

In the prepare phase of the transaction, the server (more technically, the transaction manager for that server – for SQL Server, it will be DTC) that is the source of the request for a transaction sends a command to the other servers involved in the transaction. These other servers do not need to be SQL Servers as such, but can actually be any other servers that provide transaction managers which support a protocol used by MTS (X/Open and OLE Transactions are currently supported) – which is pretty much all of the mainstream data sources.

At the point that the prepare command is received by the remote servers, those servers do whatever is necessary to create the transaction at their end – including ensuring the durability and atomicity of the transaction. When this is completed, a confirmation or failure message is sent to the originating server as appropriate. As each remote server completes the prepare phase, it returns success or failure of the prepare to the originating server.

The Commit Phase

Assuming that all remote servers involved in the transaction reply with a success message, then the transaction can proceed. The originating server will then send out a message that signals to go ahead and commit the transaction. The remote servers then commit the transaction, and again report back the success or failure of the transaction. Assuming that all remote servers return a success message to the commit command, then the originating server will report the transaction as complete.

If at any point in this process one of the servers fails to send the required reply, then the entire transaction is terminated, and, if it has gotten far enough to require it, rolled back.

> *If any of the remote servers fail to respond to DTC in the prepare phase, as a result of a failed connection between the two servers, for instance, then the other remote servers which have signalled their readiness to commit, are said to be in doubt. This situation can be resolved by forcing the in-doubt transactions to abort.*

Unfortunately, starting out a distributed transaction is a little bit different from starting regular transactions. On the bright side though, the commands to invoke the distributed transaction engine look almost like those for the regular SQL Server transaction engine. The comparison looks like this:

SQL Server Native Command	Distributed Command
BEGIN TRAN	BEGIN DISTRIBUTED TRAN
SAVE TRAN	(Not Supported)
ROLLBACK TRAN	ROLLBACK TRAN
COMMIT TRAN	COMMIT TRAN

Notice that things are almost the same. The BEGIN just requires an extra word. The commands are otherwise syntactically the same except for the lack of support for saved transactions.

There are, however, some other differences to be aware of:

❑ Distributed transactions cannot be nested.

❑ Local transactions can automatically be escalated if you issue a distributed query – use sp_configure with the remote proc trans option to set your preference.

❑ MS DTC must be running locally to your SQL Server in order to use distributed transactions with it.

❑ The remote server must support transactions in order for the transaction process to succeed. DTC will attempt to manage this for you, and even provides a level of transitioning not inherent in the base product in some instances. There are, however, instances where transactions will not be an option with a given data source.

❑ Distributed transactions create much more in the way of overhead, and, therefore, should be used only as a relative last resort versus other options that may be available. (Use them because they are the thing to use – not "just because".)

Other than that, distributed transactions work pretty much as regular transactions do.

Distributed Queries

Along with SQL Server 7.0 came a whole host of new features, and what they've done in the way of querying distributed data is quite a gift. If you're coming from the Access world, then a lot of this will look somewhat familiar – not the same, but definitely familiar.

There are a few new features in this realm. These include the ability to:

❑ "Link" to another server and reference its objects directly by merely qualifying the object with a server name.

❑ Open a query on the fly – without using a linked server – and join the result set of that query with other objects in yet another query.

❑ Open a query on a linked server making use of a pass-through query to avoid certain compatibility issues.

Let's take a look at each of these in turn.

Creating Linked Servers

This is probably the least interesting part of this whole chapter, but it's a necessary evil on your way to putting some great horsepower in your query options.

To create a **linked** server is essentially to inform the SQL Server to which you're connected how to make contact with another individual server. What this amounts to is telling your server how to become a client to yet another server. I guess you could say that you're creating something of a controlled schizophrenia.

To create a linked server and make it usable involves two steps:

❑ Telling SQL Server the name and contact information for the new linked server

❑ Providing login mapping information to the new server

Using sp_addlinkedserver

To add a linked server, you execute a special stored procedure called sp_addlinkedserver. This special sproc stores away the information on where to find and how to connect with another data source. It accepts up to seven parameters, although only one is actually required. The syntax looks like this:

```
sp_addlinkedserver [@server =] '<server>'
    [, [@srvproduct =] '<product name>']
    [, [@provider =] '<provider name>']
    [, [@datasrc =] '<data source path>']
    [, [@location =] '<location>']
    [, [@provstr =] '<connection string>']
    [, [@catalog =] '<database or equivalent for datasource>']
```

Let's take a look at each of the parameters:

Parameter	Required?	Description
@server	Yes	Internal name for the linked server you are creating. This will be the name you use when referring to this linked server in queries. For example: `NorthwindRemote.Northwind.dbo.Orders`
@srvproduct	No	A user-friendly name for `@provider` below. For example, SQL Server OLEDB Provider or Oracle OLEDB Provider.
@provider	No	OLEDB provider name (`PROGID`). For example, `SQLOLEDB` is the OLEDB name for the SQL Server provider and `MSDAORA` is the name for the Oracle OLEDB provider.
@datasrc	No	Name of the data source as interpreted by the OLEDB provider. For Access, this will be the full path to the `.mdb` file. For Oracle and SQL Server, this would be the name of the server. For the ODBC provider, this would be the name of the ODBC data source.
@location	No	The location of the data source as interpreted by the OLEDB provider (exactly meaning varies).
@provstr	No	Any connection string information required by your OLEDB provider.
@catalog	No	The catalog as interpreted by the OLEDB provider. For many providers this is used to change the default database (the one that is set to current when you fist log on) for the connection.

I've seen a variety of documentation on this, and about half of it was wrong on the parameter names. This isn't that big of deal if you're passing your parameters positionally, but, if you're passing them by name, then it could cause you lots of grief. The parameter names listed here are taken directly from the `sp_addlinkedserver` system sproc itself – I suspect they'll keep these names forever at this point.

Note that, even though there's only one required parameter (the name that you will refer to the server by internally), this sproc is pretty much useless without some of the other parameters – most notably `@provider` and `@datasrc`. If you're using the OLEDB provider for ODBC, then the `@provstr` parameter is also very important.

Deleting a Linked Server

Deleting a linked server entry is pretty straightforward – just execute the `sp_dropserver` sproc and supply the name of the linked server you want to drop.

Using sp_addlinkedsrvlogin

In addition to providing the link to the actual server, you must also provide a mapping of what user information to use on the remote server. SQL Server provides us a reasonably easy means of doing this through the use of a system sproc called sp_addlinkedsrvlogin. It accepts five parameters:

Parameter	Required?	Description
@rmtsrvname	Yes	Name of the remote server as you defined it in sp_addlinkedserver
@useself	No	If True, automatically maps all the current user information straight through to the remote server. In this case, the remaining parameters become irrelevant.
@locallogin	No	The name of the user for which you are creating the map. Whatever login ID you specify here will be, when contacting the server named in the first parameter above, aliased to the login ID and password supplied in the next two parameters.
@rmtuser	No	Name of the alias that you want to use when the user supplied in @locallogin performs a linked query to the server supplied in @rmtsrvname.
@rmtpassword	No	Password that goes with @rmtuser

The default for everything is for @useself to be True – that is, if you don't set up any kind of linked server login information, then SQL Server will still try to contact the remote server using the current user's login ID and password such as it is on the local system.

> This is an area where using NT integrated security really shines. Think about it for a moment – imagine managing the user names and passwords for 1000 users. Not a big deal – right? Now imagine that all 1000 users need to be able to link to 10 servers – that's 10,000 logins to maintain, right? Wrong! Actually, you're going to be maintaining 19,000 login entries. The 10,000 logins local to each server, plus 9 linked server login entries for each user – or another 9,000.
>
> Of course, you can just make sure that they have the same login ID on every server, and that the password is the same on every server; then just keep the @useself option set to True. However, I think you'll find keeping all those passwords in synch will be quite a chore.
>
> Thankfully, SQL Server's integration with NT security is *much* better than it has been in the past. If you just use NT security, then you only have to worry about the one user ID and one password in NT – you get to avoid all the work associated with setting up additional logins for every SQL Server you have.

Deleting Linked Server Login Information

Deleting an entry made by `sp_addlinkedsrvlogin` is easy – just use the `sp_droplinkedsrvlogin` sproc and supply the name of the linked server along with the local login ID.

Seeing What You Already Have

In order to verify that your linked server exists (or check out what's already there), use the `sp_linkedservers` system sproc. The syntax looks like this:

```
EXEC sp_linkedservers
```

No parameters, so it's an easy one.

Using a Linked Server

Let's go ahead and work a quick example by actually linking to another SQL Server. Since I'm guessing you are going to have to work on this at home (if you're like me, you learn lots of new stuff at work, but never get the chance to do it as formally as working through the examples in a book), you probably don't have the resources to have multiple machines at home to test with, so it's worth noting that this example will work by looping back to your original. In other words, if you use your own server name in the `@datasrc` field shown in the following code fragment, you'll get a loop back to yourself that should work just fine for limited testing purposes.

Let's start our example by getting the linked server definition in place. Remember that this is what tells SQL Server where to go to find the local name we're going to create:

```
EXEC sp_addlinkedserver @Server = 'MyLocalServer',
    @srvproduct = 'SQLServer OLEDB Provider',
    @provider = 'SQLOLEDB',
    @datasrc  = 'SOCRATES'
```

To verify that your new server was added, just use `sp_linkedservers`:

```
EXEC sp_linkedservers
```

And you'll quickly see the servers you have available for linked queries.

If you're looped back to your own server (for example, if I was running this on SOCRATES), then you could actually stop right here – you know that your own login is going to work fine on your own machine. Indeed, this example is usable right away as long as the remote server (SOCRATES in this case) has a matching login and password to the current user on the local machine (remember that the current login information is passed to the linked server automatically if you haven't set something specific up using `sp_addlinkedsrvlogin`).

Let's test it out:

```
SELECT CustomerID, CompanyName
FROM MyLocalServer.Northwind.dbo.Customers
WHERE CustomerID < 'C'
```

Notice, since I wanted to go to the linked server rather than the local server, I needed to explicitly provide the server's name. If I don't fully qualify the name, then the query parser will assume I want the local server. OK, that being said, we can see that we do indeed get data back!

```
CustomerID       CompanyName
---------------  --------------------------------------------
ALFKI            Alfreds Futterkiste
ANATR            Ana Trujillo Emparedados y helados
ANTON            Antonio Moreno Taquería
AROUT            Around the Horn
BERGS            Berglunds snabbköp
BLAUS            Blauer See Delikatessen
BLONP            Blondesddsl père et fils
BOLID            Bólido Comidas preparadas
BONAP            Bon app'
BOTTM            Bottom-Dollar Markets
BSBEV            B's Beverages
```

(11 row(s) affected)

But it doesn't stop there. We could also join information together from two different servers – even if both servers were linked:

```
SELECT mnw.CustomerID, mnw.CompanyName, nw.OrderID
FROM MyLocalServer.Northwind.dbo.Customers mnw
JOIN Northwind..Orders nw
    ON mnw.CustomerID = nw.CustomerID
WHERE mnw.CustomerID LIKE 'AN%'
```

This gets us:

```
CustomerID       CompanyName                               OrderID
---------------  ----------------------------------------  ---------
ANATR            Ana Trujillo Emparedados y helados        10308
ANATR            Ana Trujillo Emparedados y helados        10625
ANATR            Ana Trujillo Emparedados y helados        10759
ANATR            Ana Trujillo Emparedados y helados        10926
ANTON            Antonio Moreno Taquería                   10365
ANTON            Antonio Moreno Taquería                   10507
ANTON            Antonio Moreno Taquería                   10535
ANTON            Antonio Moreno Taquería                   10573
ANTON            Antonio Moreno Taquería                   10677
ANTON            Antonio Moreno Taquería                   10682
ANTON            Antonio Moreno Taquería                   10856
```

(11 row(s) affected)

Now this example was really dealing with the simplest of worlds – so perhaps we better get a reality check.

In this scenario, I'm assuming that you are actually linking back to yourself – this doesn't have even the slightest hint of real life to it, other than seeing that you can link to a server. The cold hard facts are that you are always going to be linking to some other server – which is going to have its own login information.

To check out how to deal with this, we need to add another user to our remote server. Even if your remote server is the same as your local server (the home test if you will), you still, for testing purposes at least, want to create a separate user to which you can map. Then we'll test out that user with some special permissions to see how things work.

First, we have to create the user and give it a little different permission set than is the default for Northwind users:

```
EXEC sp_addlogin 'rmtuser','rmtpass'

USE Northwind

EXEC sp_adduser 'rmtuser'

EXEC sp_addrolemember 'db_denydatawriter','rmtuser'
```

> **These are all sprocs that help us set up and manage users in the system. For the time being, I'm not going to elaborate on exactly how they work (they are covered in our chapter on security). If you really feel the need to know exactly how they work, feel free to skip ahead to Chapter 28. Otherwise, just take my word for it that you need to run the previous code fragment to get our test user added.**

You should now have a new user called rmtuser added to the Northwind database. It will have the same rights that everyone belonging to the public (default) group has, save that this user also belongs to db_denydatawriter – which means that they can't do any kind of updates to the Northwind database.

Before we implement the rest of this though – let's verify that, before we make the changes, that we have the authority to make an update:

```
SELECT OrderID, ProductID, Quantity, UnitPrice
FROM MyLocalServer.Northwind.dbo.[Order Details]
WHERE OrderID = 10250

UPDATE MyLocalServer.Northwind.dbo.[Order Details]
SET Quantity = Quantity + 5
WHERE OrderID = 10250
AND ProductID = 41

SELECT OrderID, ProductID, Quantity, UnitPrice
FROM MyLocalServer.Northwind.dbo.[Order Details]
WHERE OrderID = 10250
```

It's quite possible that, when running this, you'll get an error indicating that a SET option is not properly set. In particular, it's likely to be the ARITHABORT option. If you run into this, I guarantee confusion – sorry, but there's no way for me to make this all that easy on you, as SQL Server will tell you virtually nothing about the source of the problem. You may find that, regardless of what you set ARITHABORT to, you get no change in effect. If this happens, then you'll need to focus on the 'arithabort' db option, which can be set using sp_dboption. If you find that sp_dboption still doesn't do the trick, then look for objects (such as indexed views) that are SCHEMABOUND and require the ARITHABORT option to be on when they are created. You'll need to drop those objects before your database option change can be set (even though SQL Server won't give you any error or warning about problems before you drop the objects in question). It's a big bad ugly confusing mess in SQL Server 2000 (it wasn't a problem in version 7.0), but we're stuck with it for now.

This should show you a before and after shot for that order:

OrderID	ProductID	Quantity	UnitPrice
10250	41	10	7.7000
10250	51	35	42.4000
10250	65	15	16.8000

(3 row(s) affected)

(1 row(s) affected)

OrderID	ProductID	Quantity	UnitPrice
10250	41	15	7.7000
10250	51	35	42.4000
10250	65	15	16.8000

(3 row(s) affected)

That pretty well proves that we currently have the right to update the records – even though we haven't explicitly provided the remote server with any users. We can now be pretty sure that it has just passed through our existing user and login information – that the same information (login ID and password) exists on the remote server (it does in this case, since the remote and the local are the same system) – and that the login ID in question has update rights.

Now let's bring sp_addlinkedsrvlogin into the picture by mapping our current user to the different role:

```
EXEC sp_addlinkedsrvlogin MyLocalServer, FALSE, 'sa', 'rmtuser', 'rmtpass'
```

If you're using a login other than sa to login to your SQL Server (for example, you may be using NT security), then you'll need to substitute the appropriate login in the place of sa above.

Now we re-run our query:

```
SELECT OrderID, ProductID, Quantity, UnitPrice
FROM MyLocalServer.Northwind.dbo.[Order Details]
WHERE OrderID = 10250

UPDATE MyLocalServer.Northwind.dbo.[Order Details]
SET Quantity = Quantity + 5
WHERE OrderID = 10250
AND ProductID = 41

SELECT OrderID, ProductID, Quantity, UnitPrice
FROM MyLocalServer.Northwind.dbo.[Order Details]
WHERE OrderID = 10250
```

Only we get a different result this time:

OrderID	ProductID	Quantity	UnitPrice
10250	41	15	7.7000
10250	51	35	42.4000
10250	65	15	16.8000

(3 row(s) affected)

Server: Msg 229, Level 14, State 5, Line 5
UPDATE permission denied on object 'Order Details', database 'Northwind',
owner 'dbo'.

So, things have indeed changed – but what? Even though we're logged in locally as sa, that is not the login ID that is being used on the linked server. Instead, the linked server is now using the security context of rmtuser – the login that we used sp_addlinkedsrvlogin to map our sa user to.

> *It's worth noting that there isn't any way to update an existing linked server login. The only option is to drop the current instance and create an entirely new one.*

Executing Sprocs on a Linked Server

You can also execute stored procedures that reside on your remote server. There really isn't any significant trick to it – you just need to fully qualify the sproc when you run your EXEC statement.

Before we can make use of this though, we need to enable remote procedure calls (RPC). This is done by enabling one or both of two server options. The rpc option enables RPC calls from the remote to the local server, and the rpc out option enables RPC from the local server to the remote server. We'll go ahead and turn them both on:

```
EXEC sp_serveroption 'MyLocalServer', 'rpc', TRUE
EXEC sp_serveroption 'MyLocalServer', 'rpc out', TRUE
```

We are then ready to run our sproc:

```
EXEC MyLocalServer.Northwind.dbo.CustOrderHist 'BLAUS'
```

This sproc lists the product by product order history for our customer:

```
ProductName            Total
-------------------------------------------
Camembert Pierrot        21
Carnarvon Tigers         10
Chartreuse verte          5
Lakkalikööri             14
Manjimup Dried Apples     8
Queso Cabrales           14
Ravioli Angelo            4
Rössle Sauerkraut         3
Sir Rodney's Scones      23
Sirop d'érable            4
Tourtière                20
Zaanse koeken            14

(12 row(s) affected)
```

It's easy as can be.

Gathering Meta-data Information from the Remote Server

Now all of this is well and good so far – but how do you deal with the situation where you don't really know (or more likely, can't remember the specifics of) what the linked server has to offer?

You see, most of the system sprocs that we use in order to retrieve meta-data don't work against a remote data source. Fortunately, SQL Server offers a series of separate sprocs that are meant to deal with just this situation. Here's a list of the main sprocs for retrieving information about linked servers.

Sproc Name	Syntax	Description
sp_linkedservers	sp_linkedservers	Lists all the servers that currently have linked server entries on the local system.
sp_catalogs	sp_catalogs [@server_name =] <linked server>	Lists all the databases (catalogs is the ANSI term, and also fits well in that it doesn't necessarily mean quite the same thing as a database) that exist on the linked server.
sp_tables_ex	sp_tables_ex [@table_server =] <linked server> [, @table_name =] <table> [, @table_schema =] <owner> [, @table_catalog =] <database> [, @table_type =] <table type>	Lists all the tables in the requested server and catalog.

Sproc Name	Syntax	Description
sp_columns_ex	sp_columns_ex [@table_server =] <linked server> [, @table_name =] <table> [, @table_schema =] <owner> [, @table_catalog =] <database> [, @column_name =] '<column>'] [, @ODBCVer = '<ODBCVer>']	Lists all the columns and data types for the server. If you leave off parameters, then all values for that parameter will be included. Do *not* leave out the catalog name. It will run without it – but it may never end (very long running) and won't respond to a stop request.
sp_table_privileges_ex	sp_table_privileges_ex [@table_server =] '<linked server>' [, [@table_name =] '<table name>'] [, [@table_schema =] '<owner>' [, [@table_catalog =] '<database>']	Provides a listing of what security permissions have been established on a specific table on a linked server.
sp_columnprivileges_ex	sp_column_privileges_ex [@table_server =] '<linked server>' [, [@table_name =] '<table name>'] [, [@table_schema =] '<owner>'] [, [@table_catalog =] '<database>'] [, [@column_name =] '<column name>']	Provides column level permissions for a table on a linked server.
sp_primarykeys	sp_primarykeys [@table_server =] '<linked server>' [, [@table_name =] '<table name>'] [, [@table_schema =] '<owner>'] [, [@table_catalog =] '<database>']	Provides the name of the column(s) that serve as the primary key for the requested table.

Table continued on following page

Sproc Name	Syntax	Description
sp_foreignkeys	sp_foreignkeys [@table_server =] '<linked server>' [, [@pktab_name =] '<primary key table>'] [, [@pktab_schema =] '<primary key owner>'] [,[@pktab_catalog =] <primary key database>'] [, [@fktab_name =] '<foreign key table>'] [, [@fktab_schema =] '<foreign key owner>'] [, [@fktab_catalog =] '<foreign key database>']	This one is somewhat similar to sp_primarykeys except that it is focused on foreign keys rather than primary keys. As such, you may see it return entirely separate key values (since you can have more than one), whereas all of the output from sp_primarykeys would relate to just one key.
sp_indexes	sp_indexes [@table_server =] '<linked server>' [, [@table_name =] '<table name>'] [, [@table_schema =] '<owner>'] [, [@table_catalog =] <database>'] [, [@table_catalog =] '<database>'] [, [@index_name =] '<index name>'] [, [@is_unique =] '<is unique>']	Lists one or more of the indexes on the requested table (if one is specified – otherwise on all tables). Listing can also be limited by whether a unique constraint (unique or primary key) is imposed or not.

You can mix and match these to obtain a wide variety of information about the schema on your linked servers.

In reality, you would pretty much only want to use these for non-SQL Server data sources and when you need to get some sort of result set back programmatically. Beyond these needs, I'm sure you'll find it much easier – not to mention more informative – to register the linked server in EM and examine things from there.

Creating and Using Pass-Through Queries

Sometimes you'll have the need to send a command directly through to the linked server without any pre-processing by the local server. The reasons for this vary, but the most common would be that you need to issue a command that is completely valid to the remote server, but does not pass the SQL Server query parser (legal on the remote server, but not on the local server). What's nice is that, if your command produces a result set, that result set can be joined to and otherwise treated as though it were a table.

To perform these pass-throughs, we make use of a command called OPENQUERY. The syntax looks a little odd in use, but it works like this:

```
OPENQUERY(<linked server name>, <'query string'>)
```

It's quite strange to see this in a SELECT statement since it gets used just like a table, but doesn't really look like one. Here's a very simple example using our MyLocalServer linked server:

```
SELECT *
FROM OPENQUERY(MyLocalServer, 'SELECT CustomerID, CompanyName
                               FROM Northwind.dbo.Customers
                               WHERE CustomerID < ''b''')
```

This yields us four quick rows:

```
CustomerID   CompanyName
------------ ----------------------------------------------
ALFKI    Alfreds Futterkiste
ANATR    Ana Trujillo Emparedados y helados
ANTON    Antonio Moreno Taquería
AROUT    Around the Horn
```

(4 row(s) affected)

We can also join results with objects from the local server – or even with another pass-through query:

```
SELECT ptq.CustomerID, ptq.CompanyName, o.OrderID, o.OrderDate
FROM OPENQUERY(MyLocalServer, 'SELECT CustomerID, CompanyName
           FROM Northwind.dbo.Customers
           WHERE CustomerID < ''b''') ptq
JOIN Orders o
   ON ptq.CustomerID = o.CustomerID
WHERE YEAR(o.OrderDate) = 1998
```

CustomerID	CompanyName	OrderID	OrderDate
ALFKI	Alfreds Futterkiste	10835	1998-01-15 00:00:00.000
ALFKI	Alfreds Futterkiste	10952	1998-03-16 00:00:00.000
ALFKI	Alfreds Futterkiste	11011	1998-04-09 00:00:00.000
ANATR	Ana Trujillo Emparedados y helados	10926	1998-03-04 00:00:00.000
ANTON	Antonio Moreno Taquería	10856	1998-01-28 00:00:00.000
AROUT	Around the Horn	11016	1998-04-10 00:00:00.000
AROUT	Around the Horn	10864	1998-02-02 00:00:00.000
AROUT	Around the Horn	10920	1998-03-03 00:00:00.000
AROUT	Around the Horn	10953	1998-03-16 00:00:00.000

(9 row(s) affected)

This is really cool stuff – particularly when you are dealing with more unorthodox data sources, such as Active Directory or Index Server.

Notice, by the way, that we had multiple WHERE clauses in operation. The first was with the pass-through query. This WHERE executes with the pass-through query, and affects the pass-through related recordset before it is available for the join. The second belongs to the outer query, and is the last filter to run in this particular query.

> *You can also include pass-through queries as the target in action statements (INSERT, UPDATE, DELETE). The trick here is whether your OLEDB provider will allow it or not. SQL Server will; others, such as Access, will as long as the query is formatted right (some are considered updateable, some aren't).*

Play with this – there are odd instances where these and a close relative (which we'll discuss next) can be lifesavers.

Using Ad Hoc Queries Against Remote Data Sources

Pass-through queries and linked servers are all well and good. They refer to something that is essentially a constant connection (it isn't, but whether it's connected or not is relatively invisible to the query, so, from the query's standpoint, it appears to be a constant connection). Sometimes, however, that just doesn't fit the bill. Occasionally, you need something that's going to go together better in an "on the fly situation" – the situation where your query is more ad hoc, and you want to create the connection manually at the time it's needed. OPENQUERY has a close relative that was made for just this kind of situation.

The most flexible, albeit tedious, query option is achieved through the use of a command called OPENROWSET. The syntax looks like a cross between sp_addlinkedserver, sp_addlinkedsrvlogin, and OPENQUERY – and it is indeed a little bit of all of these. It looks like this:

```
OPENROWSET
(
    <'provider name'>,
    <'data source'>;<'login ID'>,<'password'>,<'provider string'>,
    <'query'>
)
```

Just like a pass-through query, this should return a tabular result set that can be used in a join or otherwise much like a table. What's different is that there isn't any information stored about the server that you're connecting to – you're basically making things up as you go along.

Here's the final pass-through query that we did, redone to be an ad hoc query:

```
SELECT ptq.CustomerID, ptq.CompanyName, o.OrderID, o.OrderDate
FROM OPENROWSET('SQLOLEDB', 'SOCRATES'; 'rmtuser'; 'rmtpass',
                'SELECT CustomerID, CompanyName
                FROM Northwind.dbo.Customers
                WHERE CustomerID < ''b''') ptq
JOIN Orders o
    ON ptq.CustomerID = o.CustomerID
WHERE YEAR(o.OrderDate) = 1998
```

Execute it, and you probably won't be surprised to see the same nine rows.

Pretty much all the same rules apply. You can perform action queries on the OPENROWSET results as long as your OLEDB provider supports it, and, as we've show with this example, you can also perform joins against the results.

Other Distributed Query Points to Ponder

There are some other things to think about when running distributed queries. The biggies among these are:

❑   Some activities can't be done on a remote server

❑   Collation compatibility

❑   Shared names with "remote" servers

Let's quickly look at each one of these.

Some Activities Can't Be Done Via Links

Some commands can't be executed via a linked server arrangement. These include:

❑   DDL Statements (CREATE, DROP, ALTER), or anything that implies any one of these (SELECT INTO, for example). You can, in most instances, get away with this using OPENROWSET (which just does a pass through on whatever code you supply it, so, as long as it's valid at the other end, it should work), but I advise you against doing this since the error handling is so poor.

❑   In some cases, ORDER BY statements. ORDER BYs are fine as long as your query doesn't include a BLOB field. Note that it doesn't matter whether the BLOB is part of the ORDER BY (you can't even do that in a local server – at least without pulling some tricks). If the BLOB is part of the query at all, then the query cannot have an ORDER BY.

❑   Any of the BLOB-related statements (READTEXT, WRITETEXT, UPDATETEXT).

These are situations that you shouldn't run into that often, so I wouldn't worry about them too much. Still, you need to be aware that they exist.

Collation Compatibility

By default, the collation compatibility option is turned off. What this gem does for you is tell SQL Server that the local and remote servers both play by the same rules when it comes to sort order and accent sensitivity. This may not seem like that big of a deal – but it can be.

Normally (without collation compatibility set), the local SQL Server requests all the data to be retuned to the local server (the WHERE clause isn't applied until the data arrives at the local server). This is because the local server has to make sure that the query is playing by the local rules (since that's where the query came from). If, however, the local server knows that the remote server plays by the right set of rules (has the same collation order), then it can defer the comparison testing to the remote server.

The benefits of this should be readily apparent. First, since the comparisons are happening at the remote server, only the data that meets the comparison criteria needs to be passed back to the local server – that means an awful lot less data transfer over the network. Second is the whole notion of distributed work. If the remote server can do a portion of the analysis work, then you're taking some load off your local server – it can work on other things while it's waiting. Since SQL Server can run queries asynchronously, the distribution factor alone may help speed up your query.

To turn on collation compatibility, use the sp_serveroption system sproc. The syntax looks like this:

```
EXEC sp_serveroption '<server name>', 'collation compatible', 'true'
```

Making a "Remote" Server also Act as a Linked Server

"What?" you say, "I thought a linked server *was* a remote server." It is – sort of. It is a remote server in that it is a separate box from the local server. In SQL Server however, we also have the notion of a remote server – this is a type of server used with replication (we'll look at replication in Chapter 23). Remote servers are registered with the system in much the same way as linked servers are. Just because you have a server configured as being a remote server, that does not also make it configured to be a linked server (only linked servers have all the various remote querying that wc've looked at in this chapter). It's a bit early for the whole remote server game, but suffice to say for now that you can configure a remote server to also work as a linked server.

If you have a server that you've been using in replication, which you now also want to show as a linked server, just execute sp_serveroption and set the data access option to True.

Adding a Linked Server Using EM

Adding a linked server in EM is, as you might expect, a little easier (but you can't script it, so keep sp_addlinkedserver in mind).

Linked servers can be found inside the Security node for your server. Just right-click on the Linked Server sub-node and choose New Linked Server... You should get a dialog box that looks something like this:

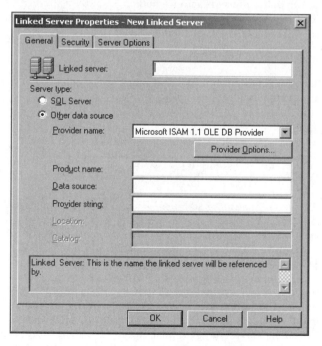

The information matches up well to sp_addlinkedserver. If you want to link to a SQL Server, just check that option box and most of the other parameter boxes will be grayed out (SQL Server already knows how to fill them out). If you want to link to something other than a SQL Server, then choose Other data source and select the appropriate OLEDB provider.

Adding a Linked Server Login Using EM

This is just another tab on the linked server dialog box you've already seen:

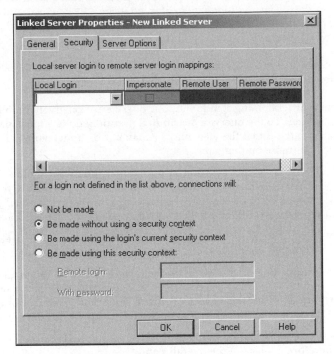

Again, you can do all the same things that you can do using the sp_addlinkedsrvlogin, but, again, you can't script Enterprise Manager, so, if you need to have an install script, EM is out of the question.

Federated Servers (Distributed Partitioned Views)

By now, you've probably heard (or read) the term distributed partitioned view many more times than you'd care to think of. But, you really haven't seen much in terms of the "How do I do it?" and "What's it useful for?" questions and their answers – well, if you want to know the basics of distributed partitioned views, then you've come to the right place. So, what is a distributed partitioned view? And what, exactly, does it have to do with this "Federated Server" term that's also flying about? Let's explore these questions and more....

In it's simplest terms, a distributed partitioned view is not terribly different than any other view – it is something of a virtual table built based on a query against "real" data that resides in a physical table somewhere. The big difference with distributed partitioned views is hinted at in the extra parts of the name. That is, they are:

❑ Distributed: They usually access data that is spread across multiple servers. This is facilitated by the servers being linked (much as we covered in our last section).

❑ Partitioned: The data that the view is providing access to is broken up into predictable physical chunks of responsibility – that is, one table is responsible for one piece – or partition – of the overall data represented by the view, and one or more other tables are responsible for the remaining data. This partitioning is enforced using CHECK constraints, so there is no doubt as to which table is responsible for which block of data. The distributed partitioned view is able to tell which is which by looking at the meta-data for the underlying tables.

Let's look at the mechanics of this a bit further by looking at a diagram that breaks apart the various pieces when a distributed partitioned view is utilized. We have:

❑ Query: From a programming standpoint, our queries are relatively oblivious to how the data is physically stored. To the query, a distributed partitioned view looks pretty much like any table. The only catch is that the view may or may not be updateable depending on how the view was created (more on that later).

❑ Partitioned View: This is the piece that pulls together the physical tables and makes them appear to the query as if they were just one table. The actual syntax of the view is pretty simple – it's just a series of queries to each table, appropriately qualified (with a four part name if on a separate server), and then a UNION ALL to hook all the data together.

❑ Federated Servers: Essentially, these are just a series of servers have been linked together, and are sharing the load for data that is distributed across the set of servers.

❑ Databases: By convention, these will actually have the same name on all of the participating servers – the notion is that it's easier to write queries across the servers in question (you don't have to worry about which database is on which server), and reduces bugs in general – frankly, after playing with these for a while, I have to agree with the convention here.

❑ Tables: Each table participating in the distributed partitioned view is carrying a piece of the load, and, therefore, a piece of the overall data.

❑ Constraints: A CHECK constraint *must* be defined on each table that defines a specific range of data that each particular table will accept. For each partitioned view, no more than one table can accept that range of data (if there is a range that no table accepts, then data in that range is rejected by the view).

All of these work together to form up the distributed partitioned view.

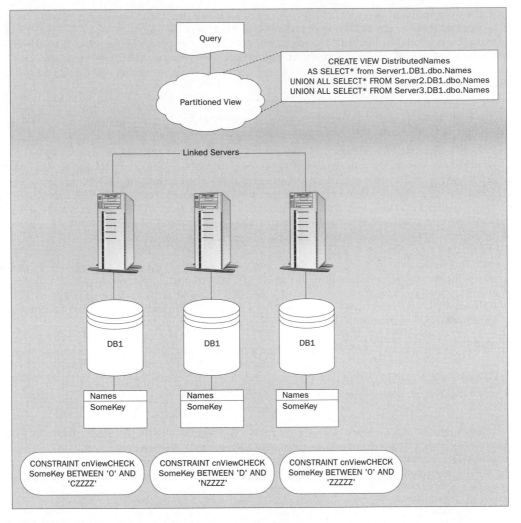

OK, let's look into this further still, by using an example.

You will need to have at least two servers in order to effectively run this example. I have tried to get it to work in a single server example (such as the looped-back linked server we used last section), but, to date, I have not found any way to perform such an example (indeed, it turns out that the rules for partitioned servers explicitly say you can't do it – but I keep hoping to find a way).

In addition, you will need to be running either the Developer Edition or the Enterprise Edition of SQL Server on both systems – updateable distributed partitioned views are not supported in the Standard and Desktop versions of SQL Server.

So, imagine for a moment that our little `Northwind` company has a world-wide advertising campaign coming out, and that we are expecting the number of customers on our database to increase to millions. We're concerned about the load that's going to be placed on our servers as we scale up to these large table sizes, and of course, about the query time to retrieve information about our customers. We're going to start by adding an additional server to the mix – we've decided that we're going to distribute the data across two servers instead of one.

Keep in mind that, although we're only going up to two servers for this particular example, it could have been 3, 5, 25 – whatever. Two is just our starting point for this example.

The first thing we need to do is decide how we're going to partition the data. We know we're only going to spread it out across two servers (we've already said that). For our purposes, we're going to assume that the customers are fairly evenly distributed, and try to split them roughly 50-50. Since there really aren't many customers that have a `CustomerID` starting with a number, I'm just going to choose the M's as my partition point – that is, anyone whose name starts with an M or after (alphabetically speaking) will go in one table, and everyone else will go in the other table.

So, we need to set up both servers to see each other as linked servers. In addition, we need to create the database we'll be using as well as adding the tables and constraints we'll need. In addition, we're going to set a server option – lazy schema validation – that will help our performance out a bit, by telling the query optimizer not to request any information from a server/table unless it's already been determined that data will come from that server/table.

Here's some code to set up a first server. Again, remember to change your server names as necessary.

```
-- CREATE the database on the local server
CREATE DATABASE NorthwindDistributed
GO


/* CREATE the table we're going to use on the local server
** Notice the CHECK constraint restricts this table's range
** down to a particular set of values
*/

USE NorthwindDistributed
CREATE TABLE dbo.Customers
(CustomerID char(5),
 CompanyName nvarchar(40),
 CONSTRAINT PKCustomerID
   PRIMARY KEY (CustomerID),
 CONSTRAINT CKIDRange
   CHECK (CustomerID BETWEEN '0' AND 'LZZZZ') )

-- Set up linked server
EXEC sp_addlinkedserver @Server = 'FederatedServer',
    @srvproduct = 'SQLServer OLEDB Provider',
    @provider = 'SQLOLEDB',
    @datasrc  = 'ARISTOTLE'

-- Add a remote user if it doesn't already exist
IF NOT EXISTS (SELECT 'True' FROM master.dbo.syslogins WHERE Name = 'rmtuser')
    EXEC sp_addlogin 'rmtuser','rmtpass'
```

```
USE NorthwindDistributed

EXEC sp_adduser 'rmtuser'

EXEC sp_addrolemember 'db_owner','rmtuser'

EXEC sp_addlinkedsrvlogin @rmtsrvname = FederatedServer,
    @useself = FALSE,
    @rmtuser = 'rmtuser',
    @rmtpassword = 'rmtpass'

EXEC sp_serveroption @SERVER = FederatedServer,
        @OPTNAME = 'lazy schema validation',
        @OPTVALUE = 'TRUE'
```

Now we need to set up the second server by using nearly identical code:

```
-- CREATE the database on the local server
CREATE DATABASE NorthwindDistributed
GO

/* CREATE the table we're going to use on the local server.
** Notice the CHECK constraint restricts this table's range
** down to a particular set of values that is different
** from what we see in the table we created on the other
** server.
*/

USE NorthwindDistributed
CREATE TABLE dbo.Customers
(CustomerID char(5),
 CompanyName nvarchar(40),
 CONSTRAINT PKCustomerID
   PRIMARY KEY (CustomerID),
 CONSTRAINT CKIDRange
   CHECK (CustomerID BETWEEN 'M' AND 'ZZZZZ') )


-- Set up linked server
EXEC sp_addlinkedserver @Server = 'FederatedServer',
    @srvproduct = 'SQLServer OLEDB Provider',
    @provider = 'SQLOLEDB',
    @datasrc = '216.254.48.186'


-- Add a remote user if it doesn't already exist
IF NOT EXISTS (SELECT 'True' FROM master.dbo.syslogins WHERE Name = 'rmtuser')
    EXEC sp_addlogin 'rmtuser','rmtpass'

USE NorthwindDistributed

EXEC sp_adduser 'rmtuser'

EXEC sp_addrolemember 'db_owner','rmtuser'
```

```
EXEC sp_addlinkedsrvlogin @rmtsrvname = FederatedServer,
    @useself = FALSE,
    @rmtuser = 'rmtuser',
    @rmtpassword = 'rmtpass'

EXEC sp_serveroption @SERVER = FederatedServer,
        @OPTNAME = 'lazy schema validation',
        @OPTVALUE = 'TRUE'
```

Everything up to this point is essentially just preliminary in nature – we need to make sure we have all of this done *before* we create the actual distributed partitioned view. With the formalities out of the way, however, we can now create the actual view:

```
USE NorthwindDistributed
GO

CREATE VIEW AllCustomers
AS
SELECT *
FROM Customers

UNION ALL

SELECT *
FROM FederatedServer.NorthwindDistributed.dbo.Customers
```

> It's worth noting that you could create a view with the same name on both servers – thus making the view all that much more transparent across servers. In our case, we could actually run exactly the same code on both servers, but, if you're running across more than two servers, then there's a good chance that the view on each server is going to be slightly different (due to the different names of the servers that need to be referenced).

Now – let's test things out a bit with a few queries. We'll begin by inserting some data into our distributed partitioned view:

```
INSERT INTO AllCustomers
    SELECT CustomerID, CompanyName
    FROM Northwind.dbo.Customers
```

This should insert the `CustomerID` and `CompanyName` from all the rows in your current `Northwind` `Customers` table (it should be somewhere around 91 rows depending on how much playing around you've been doing). We could, of course, have created our tables and the view will contain all of the matching columns, but I left them out for the sake of brevity and hard disk space.

> It's quite possible that, in running your first statement that requires a transaction (INSERT, UPDATE, DELETE), that you'll get an error message about not being able to nest a transaction. If this happens, run a SET XACT_ABORT ON. This tells SQL Server to automatically abort any transaction that has a run-time error occur within the transaction, and it is required for distributed partitioned views to work correctly.

Now let's run three queries to see what we end up with:

```
-- Start by showing all the customers that got inserted
SELECT * FROM AllCustomers

-- Now look at just the rows physically stored on the local server
SELECT * FROM NorthwindDistributed.dbo.Customers

-- And, of course, just the rows stored physically on the remote server
SELECT * FROM FederatedServer.NorthwindDistributed.dbo.Customers
```

The first query gets you back all of the rows you inserted:

CustomerID	CompanyName
ALFKI	Alfreds Futterkiste
ANATR	Ana Trujillo Emparedados y helados
ANTON	Antonio Moreno Taquería
...	
...	
...	
WHITC	White Clover Markets
WILMK	Wilman Kala
WOLZA	Wolski Zajazd

(91 row(s) affected)

Then things get more interesting as we move on to looking at the underlying tables. Right away we see what our distributed partitioned view has done for us – they completely handle all of the tasks necessary to break one logical table up into multiple physical tables.

It begins with what is roughly the first half of our customers – everything through the "L's":

CustomerID	CompanyName
ALFKI	Alfreds Futterkiste
ANATR	Ana Trujillo Emparedados y helados
ANTON	Antonio Moreno Taquería
...	
...	
...	
LILAS	LILA-Supermercado
LINOD	LINO-Delicateses
LONEP	Lonesome Pine Restaurant

(48 row(s) affected)

Then the next query picks up the rest:

CustomerID	CompanyName
MAGAA	Magazzini Alimentari Riuniti
MAISD	Maison Dewey
MEREP	Mère Paillarde
...	
...	
...	
WHITC	White Clover Markets
WILMK	Wilman Kala
WOLZA	Wolski Zajazd

(43 row(s) affected)

Again, I can't stress enough that, in "real life", the data could be spread out across several servers – indeed, Microsoft's early SQL Server 2000 postings to the Transaction Performance Council (TPC) were based on federations of 8 and 12 servers. How much benefit you get from the partitioning of the data is going to depend largely on the nature of the queries run against it and how well you've designed your partitions.

A Few More Things About Distributed Partitioned Views

OK, so now we've got our basic distributed partitioned view down, and, hopefully, you're ready to get barraged with the details. There are a ton of little gotchas in distributed partitioned views – some we've already discussed, and some we haven't – so let's try to summarize them for you.

General Gotchas and Recommendations

❑ Don't forget to SET XACT_ABORT ON if the statements you'll run against the view will be part of a transaction.

❑ Turn on LAZY SCHEMA VALIDATION using sp_serveroption. The view will work without it, but the performance difference is substantial. With LAZY SCHEMA VALIDATION, SQL Server doesn't request any meta-data from the underlying tables/servers until it is absolutely needed – this can save a lot of time and network bandwidth if something less than all of the actual servers are to be enlisted in the transaction.

❑ Create, using the same name, a functional equivalent of your distributed partitioned views on each server in the federation. This helps make the view that much more transparent no matter what server the end user is actually connected to.

❑ All tables referenced in the view must have been created using the same ANSI_PADDING setting. That is, if ANSI_PADDING was turned on for one table in the view that was created, then it must have been turned on for each of the views in the table.

❑ You can't reference a specific instance of a table more than once in the view.

❑ You can't reference any particular column more than once in the view.

❑ You can't have a timestamp column in the view if you plan to perform INSERT or UPDATE statements against the view.

❑ The view must have at least one partitioning column – more info on the rules and recommendations for partitions in a moment.

❏ Construct all of the underlying tables to be identical to each other with the exception of the CHECK constraint. While they can, technically speaking, look different, you will quickly learn to hate life if you try and use such a mix of structures, as ordinal position and explicit compatibility between data types are both very important factors in distributed partitioned views.

Gotchas Surrounding INSERTs

❏ You can't perform an INSERT if one or more of the underlying tables have an IDENTITY column.

❏ An INSERT will also not be allowed if the specific value you are inserting does not fall into the valid range for at least one of the underlying tables as defined by their CHECK constraints.

❏ You must specify an *explicit* value for every column in the view – even if that value allows a NULL value (but you can explicitly provide NULL as the value). The DEFAULT keyword cannot be used.

Gotchas Surrounding UPDATEs

These tend to have a lot in common with the rules we've already seen for the INSERT statement, but there are few that are new:

❏ You *can* perform an UPDATE on a view where the underlying tables contain an IDENTITY column – but you *cannot* update the IDENTITY column itself.

❏ An UPDATE will not be allowed if the underlying tables have a column with a timestamp datatype.

Rules for Partitioning Columns

I'm going to defer discussion of how to choose your partitions until we get to our *Advanced Design* chapter, but there are some rules surrounding the column you use to partition your data that fall into the *must* category – that is, you need to observe these rules if you want *any* partitioning scheme to work.

❏ The partitioning column must be made up of all or part of the PRIMARY KEY of the underlying tables.

❏ You can only use operators that establish a range or a specific Boolean set of data (<, >, =, >=, <=, BETWEEN, AND, and OR – notice the lack of ! = and =).

❏ The column used for partitioning must be in the same ordinal position for each of the tables.

Keep in mind that many of these rules are possible to circumvent through the use of an INSTEAD OF trigger as we discussed in Chapter 15, but the overhead is considerable, and you'll also find the solution to be much less scalable as you are forced to change a substantial portion of code in order to alter partitions (instead of just changing the CHECK constraint and moving the data to the appropriate server/table).

Summary

In this chapter, we've looked closely at the notion of distributed environments as they relate to SQL Server in a transaction and query context.

Distributed transactions are transactions that in any way cross the boundary to operate outside of the local system. For SQL Server, they are managed by MS DTC (which, in addition to being included with SQL Server, is also installed with MTS). Distributed transactions make use of a two-phase commit (2PC) to ensure atomicity and durability even across unreliable connections. Transactions that start out as local can be "escalated" to be distributed automatically.

SQL Server 7.0 added a whole new means of making use of distributed transactions. Developers were given the option to make use of linked servers for a semi-permanent connection, and OPENROWSET when they need a more ad hoc query.

SQL Server 2000 now adds distributed partitioned views – the ability to spread data across multiple tables, databases, and servers but have all the separate physical tables work together to form one highly scalable, logical table.

We will be seeing more and more about working with data outside SQL Server in the chapters to come, but first, we need to take a look at a somewhat different concept – cursors.

Online discussion at http://p2p.wrox.com

18

SQL Cursors

It was a tough decision. Advanced query design before cursors, or cursors before advanced query design? Well, I guess that we've already seen how I answered that question.

Throughout this book thus far, we've been dealing with data in sets. This tends to go against the way that the more procedure-driven languages go about things. Indeed, when the data gets to the client end, they almost always have to take our set, and then deal with it row by row. What they are dealing with is a **cursor**.

In this chapter, we will be looking at:

- ❑ What a cursor is
- ❑ The lifespan of a cursor
- ❑ Cursor types (sensitivity and scrollability)
- ❑ Uses for cursors

We'll discover that there's a lot to think about when creating cursors.

> **Perhaps the biggest question to ask yourself when creating cursors is, "Is there a way I can get out of doing this?" If you ask yourself that every time you're about to create a cursor, then you will be on the road to a better performing system. That being said, we shall see that there are times when nothing else will do.**

What Is a Cursor?

Cursors are a way of taking a set of data, and being able to interact with a single record at a time in that set. It doesn't happen nearly as often as one tends to think, but there are indeed times where you just can't obtain the results you want to by modifying or even selecting the data in an entire set. The set is generated by something all of the rows have in common (as defined by a SELECT statement), but then you need to deal with those rows on a one by one basis.

The result set that you place in a cursor has several distinct features that set it apart from a normal SELECT statement:

- ❑ You declare the cursor separately from actually executing it
- ❑ The cursor and, therefore its result set, is named at declaration – you then refer to it by name
- ❑ The result set in a cursor, once opened, stays open until you close it
- ❑ Cursors have a special set of commands used to navigate the recordset

While SQL Server has its own engine to deal with cursors, there are actually a few different object libraries that can also create cursors in SQL Server:

- ❑ OLE DB (used by ADO)
- ❑ ODBC (used by RDO, DAO, and in some cases, OLE DB/ADO)
- ❑ DB-Lib (used by VB-SQL)

Client applications will typically use these libraries to access individual records. Each provides its own syntax for navigating the recordset and otherwise managing the cursor. Each, however, shares in the same set of basic concepts, so, once you have got one object model down for cursors, you're most of the way there for all of them.

> *Every data access API out there (ADO, RDO, ODBC, OLE DB, etc.) returns data to a client application or component in a cursor – it's simply the only way that non-SQL programming languages can currently deal with things. This is the source of a big difference between this kind of cursor and SQL Server cursors. With SQL Server cursors, you usually have a choice to perform things as a set operation, which is what SQL Server was designed to do. With the API-based cursors, all you have is cursors, so you don't have the same cursor vs. no cursor debate that you have in your server-side activities.*
>
> *The client-side part of your data handling is going to be done using cursors – that's a given, so don't worry about it. Instead, worry about making the server side of your data access as efficient as possible – that means not using cursors on the server side if you can possibly help it.*

The Lifespan of a Cursor

Cursors have lots of little pieces to them, but I think that it's best if we get right into looking at the most basic form of cursor, and then build up from there.

Before we get into the actual syntax though, we need to understand that using a cursor requires more than one statement – indeed, it takes several. The main parts include:

❑   The declaration

❑   Opening

❑   Utilizing/navigating

❑   Closing

❑   Deallocating

That being said, the basic syntax for declaring a cursor looks like this:

```
DECLARE <cursor name> CURSOR
FOR <select statement>
```

Keep in mind that this is the super simple rendition – create a cursor using defaults wherever possible. We'll look at more advanced cursors a little later in the chapter.

The cursor name is just like any other variable name, and must obey the rules for SQL Server naming accordingly. The SELECT statement can be any valid SELECT statement that returns a result set. Note that some result sets will not, however, be updateable. (For example, if you use a GROUP BY then what part of the group is updated? The same holds true for calculated fields for much the same reason.)

We'll go ahead and start building a reasonably simple example. For now, we're not really going to use it for much, but we'll see later that it will be the beginning of a rather handy tool for administering your indexes:

```
DECLARE @TableName varchar(255)
DECLARE TableCursor CURSOR FOR
    SELECT TABLE_NAME FROM INFORMATION_SCHEMA.TABLES
        WHERE TABLE_TYPE = 'BASE TABLE'
```

Note that this is just the beginning of what we will be building. One of the first things you should notice about cursors is that they require a lot more code than the usual SELECT statement.

We've just declared a cursor called TableCursor that is based on a SELECT statement that will select all of the tables in our database. We also declare a holding variable that will contain the values of our current row while we are working with the cursor.

Just declaring the cursor isn't enough though – we need to actually open it:

```
OPEN TableCursor
```

This actually executes the query that was the subject of the FOR clause, but we still don't have anything in place we can work with it. For that, we need to do a couple of things:

❑ Grab – or FETCH – our first record

❑ Loop through, as necessary, the remaining records

We issue our first FETCH – this is the command that says we want to retrieve a particular record. We must also say into what variable we want to place the value:

```
FETCH NEXT FROM TableCursor INTO @TableName
```

Now that we have a first record, we're ready to move on to performing actions against the cursor set:

```
WHILE @@FETCH_STATUS = 0
BEGIN
    PRINT @TableName
    FETCH NEXT FROM TableCursor INTO @TableName
END
```

You may remember @@FETCH_STATUS from our brief discussion of globals earlier in the book. Every time we fetch a row, @@FETCH_STATUS is updated to tell us how our fetch went. The possible values are:

❑ 0: fetch succeeded – everything's fine.

❑ –1: fetch failed –you're beyond the last (or before the first) record in the cursor. We'll see more of this later in the chapter.

❑ –2: fetch failed – this time it's because the record is missing (you're not at the end, but a record has been deleted since you opened the cursor). We'll look at this in more detail later in the chapter.

Once we exit this loop, we are, for our purposes, done with the cursor, so we'll close it:

```
CLOSE TableCursor
```

However, closing the cursor does not free up the memory associated with that cursor. It does free up the locks associated with it. In order to be sure that you've totally freed up the resources used by the cursor, you must deallocate it:

```
DEALLOCATE TableCursor
```

So let's bring it all together just for clarity:

```
DECLARE @TableName varchar(255)
DECLARE TableCursor CURSOR FOR
    SELECT TABLE_NAME FROM INFORMATION_SCHEMA.TABLES
        WHERE TABLE_TYPE = 'BASE TABLE'
OPEN TableCursor
FETCH NEXT FROM TableCursor INTO @TableName
WHILE @@FETCH_STATUS = 0
BEGIN
    PRINT @TableName
    FETCH NEXT FROM TableCursor INTO @TableName
END
CLOSE TableCursor
DEALLOCATE TableCursor
```

As we've created it at the moment, it's really nothing more than if we had just run the SELECT statement by itself (technically, this isn't true since we can't "PRINT" a SELECT statement, but you could do what amounts to the same thing). What's different is that, if we so chose, we could have done nearly anything to the individual rows. Let's go ahead and illustrate this by completing our little utility.

In SQL Server there is, unfortunately, no single statement that will rebuild all the indexes in your system, yet there are several reasons that you might want to do this (if you don't recall any, take a look back at Chapter 9 on indexes, or look forward to the performance tuning round up, Chapter 29).

The only real tool that we have for rebuilding our indexes is to either drop and recreate them, or use DBCC DBREINDEX. The syntax for the latter looks like this:

```
DBCC DBREINDEX ('<table name>' [, index_name [, fillfactor ] ] )
```

The problem with trying to use this statement to rebuild all the indexes on all of your tables is that it is designed to work on one table at a time. You can leave off the index name if you want to build all the indexes for a table, but you can't leave off the table name to build all the indexes for all the tables.

Our cursor can get us around this by just dynamically building the DBCC command:

```
DECLARE @TableName varchar(255)
DECLARE TableCursor CURSOR FOR
    SELECT TABLE_NAME FROM INFORMATION_SCHEMA.TABLES
        WHERE TABLE_TYPE = 'BASE TABLE'
DECLARE @Command varchar(255)

OPEN TableCursor
FETCH NEXT FROM TableCursor INTO @TableName
WHILE @@FETCH_STATUS = 0
BEGIN
    PRINT 'Reindexing ' + @TableName
    DBCC DBREINDEX(@TableName)
    FETCH NEXT FROM TableCursor INTO @TableName
END
CLOSE TableCursor
DEALLOCATE TableCursor
```

We've now done what would be impossible using only set-based commands. The DBCC command is expecting a single argument – providing a recordset won't work. We get around the problem by combining the notion of a set operation (the SELECT that forms the basis for the cursor), with single data point operations (the data in the cursor).

In order to mix these set based and individual data point operations, we had to walk through a series of steps. First, we declared the cursor and any necessary holding variables (in this case just one, but we'll see more in use at one time as we continue through the chapter). We then "opened" the cursor – it was not until this point that the data was actually retrieved from the database. Next, we used the cursor by navigating through it. In this case, we only navigated forward, but, as we shall see, we could have created a cursor that can scroll forwards and backwards. Moving on, we closed the cursor (any locks were released at this point in time), but memory continues to be allocated for the cursor. Finally, we deallocated the cursor. At this point, all resources in use by the cursor are freed for use by other objects in the system.

So, just that quick, we have our first cursor. Still, this is really only the beginning. There is much more to cursors than meets the eye in this particular example. Next, we'll go on and take a closer look at some of the powerful features that give cursors additional flexibility.

Types of Cursors and Extended Declaration Syntax

Cursors come in a variety of different flavors (we'll visit them all before we're done). The default cursor is forward-only (you can only move forwards through the records, not backwards) and read-only, but cursors can also be scrollable and updateable. They can also have a varying level of sensitivity to changes that are made to the underlying data by other processes.

> *The forward-only, read-only cursor is the default type of cursor in not only the native SQL Server cursor engine, it is also the default in pretty much all the cursor models I've ever bumped into. It is extremely low in overhead, by comparison to the other cursor choices, and is usually referred to as being a "fire hose" cursor because of the sheer speed with which you can enumerate the data. Fire hose cursors simply blow away the other cursor-based options in most cases, but don't mistake this as a performance choice over set operations – even a fire hose cursor is slow by comparison to most equivalent set operations.*

Let's start out by taking a look at a more extended syntax for cursors, and then we'll look at all of the options individually:

```
DECLARE <cursor name> CURSOR
[LOCAL|GLOBAL]
[FORWARD_ONLY|SCROLL]
[STATIC|KEYSET|DYNAMIC|FAST_FORWARD]
[READ_ONLY|SCROLL_LOCKS|OPTIMISTIC]
[TYPE_WARNING]
FOR <SELECT statement>
[FOR UPDATE [OF <column name >[,...n]]]
```

At first glance, it really looks like a handful, and indeed, there are a good many things to think about when declaring cursors (as I've said, probably the most important is along the lines of, "Do I really need to be doing this?"). The bright side is that several of these options imply one another, so once you've made one choice the others often start to fall into place quickly.

Let's go ahead and apply the specific syntax in a step-by-step manner that attaches each part to the important concepts that go with it.

Scope

The LOCAL vs. GLOBAL option determines the scope of the cursor, that is, what connections and processes can "see" the cursor. Most items that have scope will default to the more conservative approach, that is, the minimum scope (which would be LOCAL in this case). SQL Server cursors are something of an exception to this – the default is actually GLOBAL. Before we get too far into the ramifications of the LOCAL vs. GLOBAL scope question, we had better digress for a moment as to what I mean by local and global in this context.

We are already dealing with something of an exception in that the default scope is set to what we're calling global rather than the more conservative option of local. The exception doesn't stop there though. In SQL Server, the notion of something being global vs. local usually indicates that it can be seen by all connections rather than just the current connection. For the purposes of our cursor declaration, however, it refers to whether all processes (batches, triggers, sprocs) in the current connection can see it vs. just the current process.

The figure below illustrates this:

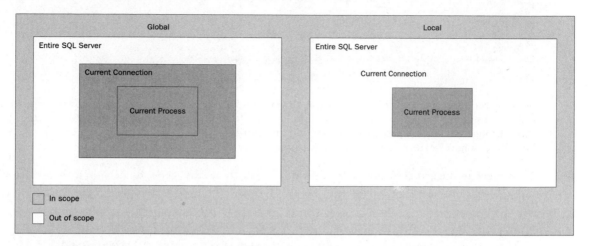

Now let's think about what this means, and test it out a bit.

The ramifications to the global default fall, as you might expect, on both the pro and the con side of things. Being global, it means that you can create a cursor within one sproc and refer to it from within a separate sproc – you don't necessarily have to pass references to it. The down side of this though is that, if you try to create another cursor with the same name, you're going to get an error.

Let's test this out with a brief sample. What we're going to do here is create a sproc that will create a cursor for us:

```
USE Northwind
GO

CREATE PROCEDURE spCursorScope
AS

DECLARE @Counter      int,
        @OrderID      int,
        @CustomerID   varchar(5)


DECLARE CursorTest  CURSOR
GLOBAL
FOR
    SELECT OrderID, CustomerID
    FROM Orders

SELECT @Counter = 1
OPEN CursorTest
FETCH NEXT FROM CursorTest INTO @OrderID, @CustomerID
PRINT 'Row ' + CONVERT(varchar,@Counter) + ' has an OrderID of ' +
    CONVERT(varchar,@OrderID) + ' and a CustomerID of ' + @CustomerID
```

```
WHILE (@Counter<=5) AND (@@FETCH_STATUS=0)
BEGIN
    SELECT @Counter = @Counter + 1
    FETCH NEXT FROM CursorTest INTO @OrderID, @CustomerID
    PRINT 'Row ' + CONVERT(varchar,@Counter) + ' has an OrderID of ' +
    CONVERT(varchar,@OrderID) + ' and a CustomerID of ' + @CustomerID
END
```

Notice several things in this sproc. First, we've declared holding variables to do a few things for us. The first, @Counter, will just keep tabs on things so we only have to move through a few records rather than moving through the entire recordset. The second and third, @OrderID and @CustomerID respectively, will hold the values retrieved from the query as we go row by row through the result set.

Next, we declare the actual cursor. Note that we've explicitly set the scope. By default, if we had left off the GLOBAL keyword, then we would have still received a cursor that was global in scope.

> You do not have to live by this default. You can use **sp_dboption** to set the "default to local cursor" option to **True** (set it back to **False** if you want to go back to global).
>
> This happens to be yet another great example of why it makes sense to always explicitly state the options that you want – don't rely on defaults. Imagine if you were just relying on the default of **GLOBAL**, and then someone changed that option in the system! I can just hear plenty of you out there saying, "Oh, no one would ever change that." WRONG! This is exactly the kind of "small change" that people make to fix some problem somewhere. Depending on the obscurity of your cursor usage, it may be weeks before you run into the problem – by which time you've totally forgotten that the change was made.

We then go ahead and open the cursor and step through several records. Notice, however, that we do not close or deallocate the cursor – we just leave it open and available as we exit the sproc.

> *I can't help but think of the old show "Lost in Space" here, with the robot constantly yelling "DANGER Will Robinson! DANGER!" Leaving cursors open like this willy-nilly will lead you to a life of sorrow, frustration, and severe depression.*
>
> *I'm doing it here to fully illustrate the concept of scope, but you need to be extremely careful about this kind of usage. The danger lies in the notion that you would call this sproc without realizing that it doesn't clean up after itself. If you don't clean up (close and deallocate) the cursor outside the sproc, then you will create something of a resource leak in the form of this abandoned, but still active cursor. You will also expose yourself to the possibility of errors should you call the same sproc again (it will try to declare and open the cursor again, but it already exists).*
>
> *When we look into declaring our cursor for output, we will see a much more explicit and better choice for situations where we want to allow outside interaction with our cursors.*

Now that we've enumerated several records and proven that our sproc is operating, we will then exit the sproc (remember, we haven't closed or deallocated the cursor). We'll then refer to the cursor from outside the sproc:

```
EXEC spCursorScope

DECLARE @Counter      int,
        @OrderID      int,
        @CustomerID   varchar(5)

SET @Counter=6

WHILE (@Counter<=10) AND (@@FETCH_STATUS=0)
BEGIN
    PRINT 'Row ' + CONVERT(varchar,@Counter) + ' has an OrderID of ' +
    CONVERT(varchar,@OrderID) + ' and a CustomerID of ' + @CustomerID
    SELECT @Counter = @Counter + 1
    FETCH NEXT FROM CursorTest INTO @OrderID, @CustomerID
END

CLOSE CursorTest
DEALLOCATE CursorTest
```

OK, so let's walk through what's happening here.

First, we execute the sproc. As we've already seen, this sproc builds the cursor and then enumerates several rows. It exits leaving the cursor open.

Next, we declare the very same variables that were declared in the sproc. Why do we have to declare them again, but not the cursor? Because it is only the cursor that is global by default. That is, our variables went away as soon as the sproc went out of scope – we can't refer to them anymore, or we'll get a variable undefined error. We must redeclare them.

The next code structure looks almost identical to one in our sproc – we're again looping through to enumerate several records.

Finally, once we've proven our point that the cursor is still alive outside the realm of the sproc, we're ready to close and deallocate the cursor. It is not until we close the cursor that we free up the memory or `tembdb` space from the result set used in the cursor, and it is not until we deallocate that the memory taken up by the cursor variable and its query definition is freed.

Now, go ahead and create the sproc in the system (if you haven't already) and execute the script. You should wind up with a result that looks like this:

```
Row 1 has an OrderID of 10248 and a CustomerID of VINET
Row 2 has an OrderID of 10249 and a CustomerID of TOMSP
Row 3 has an OrderID of 10250 and a CustomerID of HANAR
Row 4 has an OrderID of 10251 and a CustomerID of VICTE
Row 5 has an OrderID of 10252 and a CustomerID of SUPRD
Row 6 has an OrderID of 10253 and a CustomerID of HANAR

Row 7 has an OrderID of 10254 and a CustomerID of CHOPS
Row 8 has an OrderID of 10255 and a CustomerID of RICSU
Row 9 has an OrderID of 10256 and a CustomerID of WELLI
Row 10 has an OrderID of 10257 and a CustomerID of HILAA
```

So, you can see that the cursor stayed open, and our loop outside the sproc was able to pick up right where the code inside the sproc had left off.

Now let's see what happens if we alter our sproc to have local scope:

```
ALTER PROCEDURE spCursorScope
AS

DECLARE @Counter      int,
        @OrderID      int,
        @CustomerID   varchar(5)


DECLARE CursorTest cursor
LOCAL
FOR
    SELECT OrderID, CustomerID
    FROM Orders

SELECT @Counter = 1
OPEN CursorTest
FETCH NEXT FROM CursorTest INTO @OrderID, @CustomerID
PRINT 'Row ' + CONVERT(varchar,@Counter) + ' has an OrderID of ' +
      CONVERT(varchar,@OrderID) + ' and a CustomerID of ' + @CustomerID

WHILE (@Counter<=5) AND (@@FETCH_STATUS=0)
BEGIN
    SELECT @Counter = @Counter + 1
    FETCH NEXT FROM CursorTest INTO @OrderID, @CustomerID
    PRINT 'Row ' + CONVERT(varchar,@Counter) + ' has an OrderID of ' +
    CONVERT(varchar,@OrderID) + ' and a CustomerID of ' + @CustomerID
END
```

It seems like only a minor change, but the effects are significant when we execute our script again:

```
Row 1 has an OrderID of 10248 and a CustomerID of VINET
Row 2 has an OrderID of 10249 and a CustomerID of TOMSP
Row 3 has an OrderID of 10250 and a CustomerID of HANAR
Row 4 has an OrderID of 10251 and a CustomerID of VICTE
Row 5 has an OrderID of 10252 and a CustomerID of SUPRD
Row 6 has an OrderID of 10253 and a CustomerID of HANAR

Server: Msg 16916, Level 16, State 1, Line 13
A cursor with the name 'CursorTest' does not exist.
Server: Msg 16916, Level 16, State 1, Line 16
A cursor with the name 'CursorTest' does not exist.
Server: Msg 16916, Level 16, State 1, Line 17
A cursor with the name 'CursorTest' does not exist.
```

Things ran just as they did before until we got out of the sproc. This time the cursor was no longer in scope as we came out of the sproc, so we were unable to refer to it, and our script ran into several errors. Later on in the chapter, we'll take a look at how to have a cursor with local scope, but still be able to access it from outside the procedure in which it was created.

The big thing that you should have gotten out of this section is that you need to think about the scope of your cursors. They do not behave quite the way that other items for which you use the DECLARE statement do.

Scrollability

Like most of the concepts that we'll be talking about throughout this chapter, **scrollability** applies to pretty much any cursor model you might face. The notion is actually fairly simple: can I navigate in relatively any direction, or am I limited to only moving forward? The default is no – you can only move forward.

Forward-Only

A forward-only cursor is exactly what it sounds. Since it is the default method, it probably doesn't surprise you to hear that it is the only type of cursor that we've been using up to this point. When you are using a forward-only cursor, the only navigation option that is valid is FETCH NEXT. You need to be sure that you're done with each record before you move on to the next because, once it's gone, there's no getting back to the previous record unless you close and reopen the cursor.

Scrollable

Again, this is just as it sounds. You can "scroll" the cursor backwards and forwards as necessary. If you're using one of the APIs (ODBC, OLE DB, DB-Lib), you can often navigate right to a specific record – depending on what object model you're dealing with. Indeed, with ADO you can even easily re-sort the data and add additional filters.

The cornerstone of scrolling is the FETCH keyword. You can use FETCH to move forward and backward through the cursor, as well as move to specific positions. The main arguments to FETCH are:

❑ NEXT – Move to the next record

❑ PRIOR – Move to the previous record

❑ FIRST – Move to the first record

❑ LAST – Move to the last record

We'll take a more in-depth look at FETCH later in the chapter, but, for now, be aware that FETCH exists and is what controls your navigation through the cursor set.

Let's do a brief example to get across the concept of a scrollable cursor. We'll actually just use a slight variation of the sproc we created a little earlier in the chapter:

```
CREATE PROCEDURE spCursorScroll
AS

DECLARE @Counter     int,
        @OrderID     int,
        @CustomerID  varchar(5)


DECLARE CursorTest cursor
LOCAL
SCROLL
FOR
    SELECT OrderID, CustomerID
    FROM Orders
```

```
SELECT @Counter = 1
OPEN CursorTest
FETCH NEXT FROM CursorTest INTO @OrderID, @CustomerID
PRINT 'Row ' + CONVERT(varchar,@Counter) + ' has an OrderID of ' +
      CONVERT(varchar,@OrderID) + ' and a CustomerID of ' + @CustomerID

WHILE (@Counter<=5) AND (@@FETCH_STATUS=0)
BEGIN
    SELECT @Counter = @Counter + 1
    FETCH NEXT FROM CursorTest INTO @OrderID, @CustomerID
    PRINT 'Row ' + CONVERT(varchar,@Counter) + ' has an OrderID of ' +
    CONVERT(varchar,@OrderID) + ' and a CustomerID of ' + @CustomerID
END

WHILE (@Counter>1) AND (@@FETCH_STATUS=0)
BEGIN
    SELECT @Counter = @Counter - 1
    FETCH PRIOR FROM CursorTest INTO @OrderID, @CustomerID
    PRINT 'Row ' + CONVERT(varchar,@Counter) + ' has an OrderID of ' +
    CONVERT(varchar,@OrderID) + ' and a CustomerID of ' + @CustomerID
END

CLOSE CursorTest
DEALLOCATE CursorTest
```

The big differences are:

❏ The cursor is declared with the SCROLL option

❏ We added a new navigation keyword – PRIOR – in the place of NEXT

❏ We went ahead and closed and deallocated the cursor in the sproc rather than using an outside procedure (been there, done that).

The interesting part comes in the results. This one doesn't require the fancy test script – simply execute it:

```
EXEC spCursorScroll
```

And you'll see how the order values scroll forward and back:

Row 1 has an OrderID of 10249 and a CustomerID of TOMSP
Row 2 has an OrderID of 10251 and a CustomerID of VICTE
Row 3 has an OrderID of 10258 and a CustomerID of ERNSH
Row 4 has an OrderID of 10260 and a CustomerID of OTTIK
Row 5 has an OrderID of 10265 and a CustomerID of BLONP
Row 6 has an OrderID of 10267 and a CustomerID of FRANK
Row 5 has an OrderID of 10265 and a CustomerID of BLONP
Row 4 has an OrderID of 10260 and a CustomerID of OTTIK
Row 3 has an OrderID of 10258 and a CustomerID of ERNSH
Row 2 has an OrderID of 10251 and a CustomerID of VICTE
Row 1 has an OrderID of 10249 and a CustomerID of TOMSP

As you can see, we were able to successfully navigate not only forwards, as we did before, but also backwards.

A forward-only cursor is far and away the more efficient choice of the two options. Think about the overhead for a moment – if it is read-only, then SQL Server really only needs to keep track of the next record – à la linked list. In a situation where you may reposition the cursor in other ways, extra information must be stored in order to reasonably seek out the requested row. How exactly this is implemented depends on the specific cursor options you choose.

Some types of cursors imply scrollability; others do not. Some types of cursors are sensitive to changes in the data, and some are not. We'll look at some of these issues in the next section.

Cursor Types

The various APIs generally break cursors into four types:

- ❑   Static
- ❑   Keyset-driven
- ❑   Dynamic
- ❑   Fast-forward-only

How exactly these four types are implemented (and what they're called) will sometimes vary slightly between the various APIs and object models, but the general nature of them is usually pretty much the same.

What makes the various cursor types different is their ability to be scrollable and their **sensitivity** to changes in the database over the life of the cursor. We've already seen what scrollability is all about, but the term "sensitivity" probably sounds like something you'd be more likely to read in *Men are from Mars, Women are from Venus* than in a programming book. Actually though, the concept of sensitivity is a rather critical one to think about when choosing your cursor type.

Whether a cursor is sensitive or not defines whether it notices changes in the database or not after the cursor is opened. It also defines just what it does about it once the change is detected. Let's look at this in its most extreme versions – static vs. dynamic cursors. The static cursor, once created, is absolutely oblivious to any change to the database. The dynamic cursor, however, is effectively aware of every change (inserted records, deletions, updates, you name it) to the database as long as the cursor remains open. We'll explore the sensitivity issue as we look at each of the cursor types.

Static Cursors

A static cursor is one that represents a "snapshot" in time. Indeed, at least one of the data access object models refers to it as a snapshot recordset rather than a static one.

When a static cursor is created, the entire recordset is created in what amounts to a temporary table in `tempdb`. After the time that it's created, a static cursor changes for no one and nothing. That is, it is set in stone. Some of the different object models will let you update information in a static cursor, some won't, but the bottom line is always the same: you cannot write updates to the database via a static cursor.

Before we get too far into this brand of cursor, I'm going to go ahead and tell you that the situations where it makes sense to use a static cursor on the server-side are extremely rare. I'm not saying they don't exist – they do – but they are very rare indeed.

Before you get into the notion of using a static cursor on the server side, ask yourself:

❑ Can I do this with a temporary table?

❑ Can I do this entirely on the client side?

Remember that SQL Server keeps a static cursor in a private table in tembdb. If that's how SQL Server is going to be storing it anyway, why not just use a temporary table yourself? There are times when that won't give you what you need (record rather than set operations). However, if you are just after the concept of a snapshot in time, rather than record-based operations, build your own temporary table using SELECT INTO and save yourself (and SQL Server) a lot of overhead.

If you're working in a client-server arrangement, static cursors are often better dealt with on the client side. By moving the entire operation to the client, you can cut the number of network round-trips to the server substantially. Since you know that your cursor isn't going to be affected by changes to the database (after all, isn't that why you chose a static cursor in the first place), there's no reason to make contact with the server again regarding the cursor after it is created.

OK, so let's move on to an example of a static cursor. What we're going to do in this example is play around with the notion of creating a static cursor, then make changes, and see what happens. We'll play with variations of this throughout the remainder of this part of the chapter as we look at each cursor type.

We'll start with building a table to test with, and then we'll build our cursor and manipulate it to see what's in it. Don't forget that, since we're using a SELECT INTO here, you'll need to have the SELECT INTO/BULK COPY option turned on (sp_dboptions) for the Northwind database:

```
USE Northwind
/* Build the table that we'll be playing with this time */
SELECT OrderID, CustomerID
INTO CursorTable
FROM Orders
WHERE OrderID BETWEEN 10701 AND 10705


-- Declare our cursor
DECLARE CursorTest CURSOR
GLOBAL                      -- So we can manipulate it outside the batch
SCROLL                      -- So we can scroll back and see the changes
STATIC                      -- This is what we're testing this time
FOR
SELECT OrderID, CustomerID
FROM CursorTable


-- Declare our two holding variables
DECLARE @OrderID      int
DECLARE @CustomerID   varchar(5)


-- Get the cursor open and the first record fetched
OPEN CursorTest
FETCH NEXT FROM CursorTest INTO @OrderID, @CustomerID


-- Now loop through them all
WHILE @@FETCH_STATUS=0
BEGIN
     PRINT CONVERT(varchar(5),@OrderID) + '   ' +  @CustomerID
     FETCH NEXT FROM CursorTest INTO @OrderID, @CustomerID
END
```

```
-- Make a change. We'll see in a bit that this won't affect the cursor.
UPDATE CursorTable
     SET CustomerID = 'XXXXX'
     WHERE OrderID = 10703

-- Now look at the table to show that the update is really there.
SELECT OrderID, CustomerID
FROM CursorTable

-- Now go back to the top. We can do this since we have a scrollable cursor
FETCH FIRST FROM CursorTest INTO @OrderID, @CustomerID

-- And loop through again.
WHILE @@FETCH_STATUS=0
BEGIN
    PRINT CONVERT(varchar(5),@OrderID) + '   ' +  @CustomerID
    FETCH NEXT FROM CursorTest INTO @OrderID, @CustomerID
END

-- Now it's time to clean up after ourselves
CLOSE CursorTest

DEALLOCATE CursorTest

DROP TABLE CursorTable
```

Let's take a look at what this gets us:

(5 row(s) affected)

```
10701     HUNGO
10702     ALFKI
10703     FOLKO
10704     QUEEN
10705     HILAA
```

(1 row(s) affected)

(5 row(s) affected)

```
OrderID         CustomerID
--------------- ---------------
10701           HUNGO
10702           ALFKI
10703           XXXXX
10704           QUEEN
10705           HILAA

10701           HUNGO
10702           ALFKI
10703           FOLKO
10704           QUEEN
10705           HILAA
```

611

There are several things to notice about what happened during the run on this script.

First, even though we had a result set open against the table, we were still able to perform the update. In this case, it's because we have a static cursor – once it was created, it was disconnected from the actual records and no longer maintains any locks.

Second, although we can clearly see that our update did indeed take place in the actual table, it did not affect the data in our cursor. Again, this is because, once created, our cursor took on something of a life of its own – it is no longer associated with the original data in any way.

Under the heading of "one more thing", you might also have noticed that we made use of a new argument to the FETCH keyword – this time we went back to the top of our result set by using FETCH FIRST.

Keyset-Driven Cursors

When we talk about keysets with cursors, we're not talking your local locksmith. Instead, we're talking about maintaining a set of data that uniquely identifies the entire row in the database.

Keyset-driven cursors have the following high points:

- ❏ They require a unique index to exist on the table in question
- ❏ Only the keyset is stored in tempdb – not the entire dataset
- ❏ They are sensitive to changes to the rows that are already part of the keyset including the possibility that they have been deleted
- ❏ They are, however, not sensitive to new rows that are added after the cursor is created
- ❏ Keyset cursors can be used as the basis for a cursor that is going to perform updates to the data

Given that it has a name of "keyset" and that I've already said that the keyset uniquely identifies each row, it probably doesn't shock you in any way that you must have a unique index of some kind (usually a primary key, but it could also be any index that is explicitly defined as unique) to create the keyset.

The keys are all stored in a private table in tempdb. SQL Server uses this key as a method to find its way back to the data as you ask for a specific row in the cursor. The point to take note of here is that the actual data is being fetched, based on the key, at the time that you issue the FETCH. The great part about this is that the data for that particular row is up-to-date as of when the specific row is fetched. The downside (or upside depending on what you're using the cursor for) is that it uses the keyset that is already created to do the lookup. Hence, once the keyset is created, that is all the rows that will be included in your cursor. Any rows that were added after the cursor was created – even if they meet the conditions of the WHERE clause in the SELECT statement – will not be seen by the cursor. The rows that are already part of the cursor can, depending on the cursor options you chose, be updated by a cursor operation.

Let's modify our earlier script to illustrate the sensitivity issue when we are making use of keyset-driven cursors:

```
USE Northwind
/* Build the table that we'll be playing with this time */
SELECT OrderID, CustomerID
INTO CursorTable
FROM Orders
WHERE OrderID BETWEEN 10701 AND 10705
```

```
-- Now create a unique index on it in the form of a primary key
ALTER TABLE CursorTable
     ADD CONSTRAINT PKCursor
     PRIMARY KEY (OrderID)

/* The IDENTITY property was automatically brought over when
** we did our SELECT INTO, but we want to use our own OrderID
** value, so we're going to turn IDENTITY_INSERT on so that we
** can override the identity value.
*/
SET IDENTITY_INSERT CursorTable ON


-- Declare our cursor
DECLARE CursorTest CURSOR
GLOBAL                     -- So we can manipulate it outside the batch
SCROLL                     -- We can scroll back to see if the changes are there
KEYSET                     -- This is what we're testing this time
FOR
SELECT OrderID, CustomerID
FROM CursorTable


-- Declare our two holding variables
DECLARE @OrderID       int
DECLARE @CustomerID    varchar(5)


-- Get the cursor open and the first record fetched
OPEN CursorTest
FETCH NEXT FROM CursorTest INTO @OrderID, @CustomerID


-- Now loop through them all
WHILE @@FETCH_STATUS=0
BEGIN
     PRINT CONVERT(varchar(5),@OrderID) + '    ' +  @CustomerID
     FETCH NEXT FROM CursorTest INTO @OrderID, @CustomerID
END


-- Make a change. We'll see that it does affect the cursor this time.
UPDATE CursorTable
     SET CustomerID = 'XXXXX'
     WHERE OrderID = 10703


-- Now we'll delete a record so we can see how to deal with that
DELETE CursorTable
     WHERE OrderID = 10704


-- Now insert a record. We'll see that the cursor is oblivious to it.
INSERT INTO CursorTable
     (OrderID, CustomerID)
VALUES
     (99999, 'IIIII')


-- Now look at the table to show that the update is really there.
SELECT OrderID, CustomerID
FROM CursorTable
```

```
-- Now go back to the top. We can do this since we have a scrollable cursor
FETCH FIRST FROM CursorTest INTO @OrderID, @CustomerID
```

```
/* And loop through again.
** This time, notice that we changed what we're testing for.
** Since we have the possibility of rows being missing (deleted)
** before we get to the end of the actual cursor, we need to do
** a little bit more refined testing of the status of the cursor.
*/
WHILE @@FETCH_STATUS != -1
BEGIN
    IF @@FETCH_STATUS = -2
    BEGIN
        PRINT '  MISSING! It probably was deleted.'
    END
    ELSE
    BEGIN
        PRINT CONVERT(varchar(5),@OrderID) + '    ' +  @CustomerID
    END
    FETCH NEXT FROM CursorTest INTO @OrderID, @CustomerID
END
```

```
-- Now it's time to clean up after ourselves
CLOSE CursorTest

DEALLOCATE CursorTest

DROP TABLE CursorTable
```

The changes aren't really all that remarkable. We've gone ahead and added the required unique index. I happened to choose to do it as a primary key since that's what matches up best with the table we got this information out of, but it also could have been a unique index without the primary key. We also added something to insert a row of data so we can clearly see that the keyset doesn't see the row in question.

Perhaps the most important thing that we've changed is the condition for the WHILE loop on the final run through of the cursor. Technically speaking, we should have made this change to both loops, but there is zero risk of a deleted record the first time around in this example, and I wanted the difference to be visible right within the same script.

The change was made to deal with something new we've added – the possibility that we might get to a record only to find that it's now missing. More than likely, someone has deleted it.

Let's take a look then at the results we get after running this:

(5 row(s) affected)

```
10701        HUNGO
10702        ALFKI
10703        FOLKO
10704        QUEEN
10705        HILAA
```

(1 row(s) affected)

(1 row(s) affected)

(1 row(s) affected)

```
OrderID        CustomerID
---------------  ---------------
10701        HUNGO
10702        ALFKI
10703        XXXXX
10705        HILAA
99999        IIIII
```

(5 row(s) affected)

```
10701        HUNGO
10702        ALFKI
10703        XXXXX
  MISSING! It probably was deleted.
10705        HILAA
```

OK, let's walk through the highlights here.

Everything starts out pretty much as it did before. We see the same five rows in the first result set as we did last time. We then see an extra couple of "affected" messages – these are for the INSERT, UPDATE, and DELETE statements that we added. Next comes the second result set. It's at this point that things get a bit more interesting.

In this next result set, we see the actual results of our UPDATE, INSERT, and DELETE statements. Just as we think we're done, OrderID 10704 has been deleted, and a new order with an OrderID of 99999 has been inserted. That's what's in the table, but things don't appear quite as cozy in the cursor.

The next (and final) result set tells the tale on some differences in the way that things are presented in the cursor vs. actually rerunning the query. As it happens, we have exactly five rows – just like we started out with and just like our SELECT statement showed are in the actual table. But that's entirely coincidental.

In reality, there are a couple of key differences between what the cursor is showing and what the table is showing. The first presents itself rather boldly – our result set actually knows that a record is missing. You see, the cursor continues to show the key position in the keyset, but, when it went to do the lookup on the data, the data wasn't there anymore. Our @@FETCH_STATUS was set to −2, and we were able to test for it and report it. The SELECT statement showed us what data was actually there without any remembrance of the record ever having been there. The INSERT, on the other hand, is an entirely unknown quantity to the cursor. The record wasn't there when the cursor was created, so the cursor has no knowledge of its existence – it doesn't show up in our result set.

Keyset cursors can be very handy for dealing with situations where you need some sensitivity to changes in the data, but don't need to know about every insert right up to the minute. They can, depending on the nature of the result set you're after and the keyset, also provide some substantial savings in the amount of data that has to be duplicated and stored into tempdb – this can have some favorable performance impacts for your overall server.

> **WARNING!!!** If you define a cursor as being of type **KEYSET** but do so on a table with no unique index, then SQL Server will implicitly convert your cursor to be **STATIC**. The fact that the behavior gets changed would probably be enough to ruffle your feathers a bit, but it doesn't stop there – it doesn't tell you about it. That's right; by default, you get absolutely no warning about this conversion. Fortunately, you can watch out for this sort of thing by using the **TYPE_WARNING** option in your cursor. We'll look at this option briefly towards the end of the chapter.

Dynamic Cursors

Don't you just wish that you could be on a quiz show and have them answer a question like, "What's so special about a dynamic cursor?" Hmmm, then again, I suppose their pool of possible contestants would be small, but those that decided to go for it would probably have the answer right away, "They are **dynamic** – right?" Exactly.

Well, almost exactly. Dynamic cursors fall just short of what I would call dynamic in the sense that they won't proactively tell you about changes to the underlying data. What gets them close enough to be called dynamic is that they are sensitive towards all changes to the underlying data. Of course, like most things in life, all this extra power comes with a high price tag.

If you want inserted records to be added to the cursor – no problem. If you want updated rows to appear properly updated in the cursor – no problem. If you want deleted records to be removed from the cursor set – no problem (although you can't really tell that something's been deleted since you won't see the missing record that you saw with a keyset cursor type). If, however, you want to have concurrency – uh oh, big problem (you're holding things open longer, so collisions with other users are more likely). If you want this to be low overhead – uh oh, big problem again (you are effectively requerying with every FETCH). Yes, dynamic cursors can be the bane of your performance existence, but, hey, that's life isn't it?

The long and the short of it is that you usually should avoid dynamic cursors.

Why all the hype and hoopla? Well, in order to understand some of the impacts that a dynamic cursor can have, you just need to realize a bit about how they work. You see, with a dynamic cursor, your cursor is essentially rebuilt every single time you issue a FETCH. That's right, the SELECT statement that forms the basis of your query, complete with its associated WHERE clause is effectively re-run. Think about that when dealing with large data sets. It brings just one word to mind – ugly. Very ugly indeed.

One of the things I've been taught since the dawn of my RDBMS time is that dynamic cursors are a performance pig – I've found this not to always be the case. This seems to be particularly true when the underlying tables are not very large in size. If you think about it for a bit, you might be able to come up with why a dynamic cursor can actually be slightly faster in terms of raw speed.

My guess as to what's driving this is the use of tempdb *for keyset cursors. While a lot more work has to be done with each* FETCH *in order to deal with a dynamic cursor, the data for the re-query will often be completely in cache (depending on the sizing and loading of your system). This means the dynamic cursor gets to work largely from RAM. The keyset cursor, on the other hand, is stored in* tempdb, *which is on disk (in other words, much, much slower) for most systems.*

As your table size gets larger, there is more diverse traffic hitting your server, the memory allocated to SQL Server gets smaller, and the more that keyset-driven cursors are going to have something of an advantage over dynamic cursors. In addition, raw speed isn't everything – you really need to think about concurrency issues too (we will look at the options for concurrency in detail later in the chapter), which can be more problematic in dynamic cursors. Still, don't count out dynamic cursors for speed alone if you're dealing with a server-side cursor with small data sets.

Let's go ahead and rerun our last script with only one modification – the change from KEYSET to DYNAMIC:

```
USE Northwind
/* Build the table that we'll be playing with this time */
SELECT OrderID, CustomerID
INTO CursorTable
FROM Orders
WHERE OrderID BETWEEN 10701 AND 10705

-- Now create a unique index on it in the form of a primary key
ALTER TABLE CursorTable
      ADD CONSTRAINT PKCursor
      PRIMARY KEY (OrderID)

/* The IDENTITY property was automatically brought over when
** we did our SELECT INTO, but we want to use our own OrderID
** value, so we're going to turn IDENTITY_INSERT on so that we
** can override the identity value.
*/
SET IDENTITY_INSERT CursorTable ON

-- Declare our cursor
DECLARE CursorTest CURSOR
GLOBAL                 -- So we can manipulate it outside the batch
SCROLL                 -- So we can scroll back and see if the changes are there
DYNAMIC                -- This is what we're testing this time
FOR
SELECT OrderID, CustomerID
FROM CursorTable

-- Declare our two holding variables
DECLARE @OrderID       int
DECLARE @CustomerID    varchar(5)
```

```
-- Get the cursor open and the first record fetched
OPEN CursorTest
FETCH NEXT FROM CursorTest INTO @OrderID, @CustomerID


-- Now loop through them all
WHILE @@FETCH_STATUS=0
BEGIN
     PRINT CONVERT(varchar(5),@OrderID) + '   ' + @CustomerID
     FETCH NEXT FROM CursorTest INTO @OrderID, @CustomerID
END


-- Make a change. We'll see that it does affect the cursor this time.
UPDATE CursorTable
       SET CustomerID = 'XXXXX'
       WHERE OrderID = 10703


-- Now we'll delete a record so we can see how to deal with that
DELETE CursorTable
       WHERE OrderID = 10704


-- Now insert a record. We'll see that the cursor is oblivious to it.
INSERT INTO CursorTable
       (OrderID, CustomerID)
VALUES
       (99999, 'IIIII')


-- Now look at the table to show that the update is really there.
SELECT OrderID, CustomerID
FROM CursorTable


-- Now go back to the top. We can do this since we have a scrollable cursor
FETCH FIRST FROM CursorTest INTO @OrderID, @CustomerID


/* And loop through again.
** This time, notice that we changed what we're testing for.
** Since we have the possibility of rows being missing (deleted)
** before we get to the end of the actual cursor, we need to do
** a little bit more refined testing of the status of the cursor.
*/
WHILE @@FETCH_STATUS != -1
BEGIN
     IF @@FETCH_STATUS = -2
     BEGIN
          PRINT '  MISSING! It probably was deleted.'
     END
     ELSE
     BEGIN
          PRINT CONVERT(varchar(5),@OrderID) + '   ' + @CustomerID
     END
     FETCH NEXT FROM CursorTest INTO @OrderID, @CustomerID
END



-- Now it's time to clean up after ourselves
CLOSE CursorTest

DEALLOCATE CursorTest

DROP TABLE CursorTable
```

And the results:

(5 row(s) affected)

```
10701        HUNGO
10702        ALFKI
10703        FOLKO
10704        QUEEN
10705        HILAA
```

(1 row(s) affected)

(1 row(s) affected)

(1 row(s) affected)

```
OrderID          CustomerID
---------------  ---------------
10701            HUNGO
10702            ALFKI
10703            XXXXX
10705            HILAA
99999            IIIII
```

(5 row(s) affected)

```
10701        HUNGO
10702        ALFKI
10703        XXXXX
10705        HILAA
99999        IIIII
```

The first two recordsets look exactly as they did last time. The change comes when we get to the third (and final) result set:

❑   There is no indication of a failed fetch, even though we deleted a record (no notification)

❑   The updated record shows the update (just as it did with a keyset)

❑   The inserted record now shows up in the cursor set

Dynamic cursors are the most sensitive of all cursors. They are affected by everything you do to the underlying data. The downside is that they can provide some extra concurrency problems, and they can pound the system when dealing with larger data sets.

Technically speaking, and unlike a keyset cursor, a dynamic cursor can operate on a non-unique index. Avoid this at all costs (in my opinion, it should prevent you from doing this and throw an error). Under certain circumstances, it is quite possible to create an infinite loop because the dynamic cursor cannot keep track of where it is in the cursor set. The only sure-fire way of avoiding this is to either stay away from dynamic cursors or only work on tables with a truly unique index available.

Fast-Forward Cursors

Fast (from a cursor standpoint – queries make this or any other cursor look like a snail) is the operative word on this one. This one is the epitome of the term "fire hose cursor" that is often used around forward-only cursors. I've always taken the analogy to imply the way that the data sort of spews forth – once out, you can't put it back in. In short, you're simply awash with data. With FAST_FORWARD cursors, you open the cursor, and do nothing else but deal with the data, move forward, and deallocate it (note that I didn't say close it).

Now, it's safe to say that calling this a cursor "type" is something of a misnomer. This kind of cursor has several different circumstances where it is automatically converted to other cursor types, but I think of them as being most like a keyset-driven cursor in the sense that membership is fixed – once the members of the cursor are established, no new records are added. Deleted rows show up as a missing record (@@FETCH_STATUS of –2). Keep in mind though that, if the cursor is converted to something else (via automatic conversion), it will take on the behavior of that new cursor type.

> The nasty side here is that SQL Server doesn't tell you that the conversion has happened unless you have the **TYPE_WARNING** option added to your cursor definition.

As I said before, there are a number of circumstances where a FAST_FORWARD cursor is implicitly converted to another cursor type. Below is a table that outlines these conversions:

Condition	Converted to
The underlying query requires that a temporary table be built	Static
The underlying query is distributed in nature	Keyset
The cursor is declared as FOR UPDATE	Dynamic
A condition exists that would convert to keyset-driven, but at least one underlying table does not have a unique index	Static

I've heard that there are other circumstances where a cursor will be converted, but I haven't seen any documentation of this, and I haven't run into it myself.

> If you find that you are getting that most dreadful of all computer-related terms (unpredictable results), you can make use of **sp_describe_cursor** (a system stored procedure) to list out all the currently active options for your cursor.

It's worth noting that all FAST_FORWARD cursors are read-only in nature. You can explicitly set the cursor to have the FOR UPDATE option, but, as suggested in the implicit conversion table above, the cursor will be implicitly converted to dynamic.

OK, so what exactly does a FAST_FORWARD cursor have that any of the other cursors wouldn't have if they were declared as being FORWARD_ONLY? Well, a FAST_FORWARD cursor will implement at least one of two tricks to help things along:

❑   The first is to pre-fetch data. That is, at the same time that you open the cursor, it automatically fetches the first row – this means that you save a round trip to the server if you are operating in a client-server environment using ODBC. Unfortunately, this is only available under ODBC.

❑   The second is the one that is a sure thing – auto-closing of the cursor. Since you are running a cursor that is forward-only, SQL Server can assume that you want the cursor closed once you reach the end of the recordset. Again, this saves a round trip and squeezes out a tiny bit of additional performance.

Oddly enough, cursors declared as being FAST_FORWARD are not allowed to also be declared as FORWARD_ONLY (or SCROLL for that matter) – you need to leave the scrolling vs. forward-only option out when specifying a cursor of type FAST_FORWARD.

Choosing a cursor type is one of the most critical decisions when structuring a cursor. Choices that have little apparent difference in the actual output of the cursor task can have major differences in performance. Other effects can be seen in sensitivity to changes, concurrency issues, and updateability.

Concurrency Options

We got our first taste of concurrency issues back in our chapter on transactions and locks. As you will recall, we deal with concurrency issues whenever there are issues surrounding two or more processes trying to get to the same data at essentially the same time. When dealing with cursors, however, the issue becomes just slightly stickier.

The problem is multi-fold:

❑   The operation tends to last longer (more time to have a concurrency problem)

❑   Each row is read at the time of the fetch, but someone may try to edit it before you get a chance to do your update

❑   You may scroll forwards and backwards through the result set for what could be an essentially unlimited amount of time (I hope you never do that, but it's possible to do)

As with all concurrency issues, this tends to be more of a problem in a transaction environment than when running in a single statement situation. The longer the transaction, the more likely you are to have concurrency problems.

SQL Server gives us three different options for dealing with this issue:

❑   READ_ONLY

❑   SCROLL_LOCKS (equates to "pessimistic" in most terminologies)

❑   OPTIMISTIC

Each of these has their own thing they bring to the party, so let's look at them one by one.

READ_ONLY

In a read-only situation, you don't have to worry about whether your cursor is going to try and obtain any kind of update or exclusive lock. You also don't have to worry about whether anyone has edited the data while you've been busy making changes of your own. Both of these make life considerably easier.

READ_ONLY is just what it sounds like. When you choose this option, you cannot update any of the data, but you also skip most (but not all) of the notion of concurrency entirely.

SCROLL_LOCKS

Scroll locks equate to what is more typically referred to as pessimistic locking in the various APIs and object models. In its simplest form, it means that, as long as you are editing this record, no one else is allowed to edit it. The specifics of implementation of duration of this vary depending on:

❏   Whether you're in a transaction or not

❏   What transaction isolation level you've set

Note that this can be different from what we saw with update locks back in our locking and transaction chapter.

With update locks, we prevented other users from updating the data. This lock was held for the duration of the transaction. If it was a single statement transaction, then the lock was not released until every row affected by the update was complete.

Scroll locks work identically to update locks with only one significant exception – the duration the lock is held. With scroll locks, there is much more of a variance depending on whether the cursor is participating in a multi-statement transaction or not. Assuming for the moment that you do not have a transaction wrapped around the cursor, the lock is held only on the current record in the cursor. That is, from the time the record is first fetched until the next record (or end of the result set) is fetched. Once you move on to the next record, the lock is removed from the prior record.

Let's take a look at this through a significantly pared down version of the script we've been using through much of this chapter:

```
USE Northwind
/* Build the table that we'll be playing with this time */

SELECT OrderID, CustomerID
INTO CursorTable
FROM Orders
WHERE OrderID BETWEEN 10701 AND 10705

-- Now create a unique index on it in the form of a primary key
ALTER TABLE CursorTable
      ADD CONSTRAINT PKCursor
      PRIMARY KEY (OrderID)
```

```
/* The IDENTITY property was automatically brought over when
** we did our SELECT INTO, but I want to use my own OrderID
** value, so I'm going to turn IDENTITY_INSERT on so that I
** can override the identity value.
*/
SET IDENTITY_INSERT CursorTable ON

-- Declare our cursor
DECLARE CursorTest CURSOR
GLOBAL                  -- So we can manipulate it outside the batch
SCROLL                  -- So we can scroll back and see if the changes are there
DYNAMIC                 -- This is what we're testing this time
SCROLL_LOCKS
FOR
SELECT OrderID, CustomerID
FROM CursorTable

-- Declare our two holding variables
DECLARE @OrderID        int
DECLARE @CustomerID     varchar(5)

-- Get the cursor open and the first record fetched
OPEN CursorTest
FETCH NEXT FROM CursorTest INTO @OrderID, @CustomerID
```

You'll not see much of our usual gray (to indicate that changes were made on that line) because only one line was added. The remainder of the changes were deletions of lines, so there's nothing for me to make gray for you. Just make sure that you've made the appropriate changes if you're going to try and run this one.

What we've done is toss out most of the things that were happening, and we've refocused ourselves back on the cursor. Perhaps the biggest thing to notice though is a couple of key things that we have deliberately omitted even though they are things that would normally cause problems if we try to operate without them:

❑   We do not have a CLOSE on our cursor, nor do we deallocate it at this point

❑   We don't even scroll any farther than getting the first row fetched

The reason we've left the cursor open is to create a situation where the state of the cursor being open lasts long enough to play around with the locks somewhat. In addition, we only fetch the first row because we want to make sure that there is an active row (the way we had things before, we would have been to the end of the set before we started running with other, possibly conflicting, statements).

What you want to do is execute the above and then open a completely separate connection window with Northwind active. Then run a simple test in the new connection window:

```
SELECT * FROM CursorTable
```

If you haven't been grasping what I've been saying in this section, you might be a tad surprised by the results:

```
OrderID          CustomerID
---------------  ----------------
10701            HUNGO
10702            ALFKI
10703            FOLKO
10704            QUEEN
10705            HILAA
```

(5 row(s) affected)

Based on what we know about locks (from our chapter on the subject), you would probably expect the SELECT statement above to be blocked by the locks on the current record. Not so with scroll locks. The lock is only on the record that is currently in the cursor, and, perhaps more importantly, the lock only prevents updates to the record. Any SELECT statements (such as ours) can see the contents of the cursor without any problems.

Now that we've seen how things work, go back to the original window and run the code to clean things up. This is back to the same code we've worked with for much of this chapter:

```
-- Now it's time to clean up after ourselves
CLOSE CursorTest

DEALLOCATE CursorTest

DROP TABLE CursorTable
```

Don't forget to run the clean up code above!!! If you forget, then you'll have an open transaction sitting in your system until you terminate the connection. SQL Server should clean up any open transactions (by rolling them back) when the connection is broken, but I've seen situations where you run the database consistency checker (DBCC) and find that you have some really old transactions – SQL Server missed cleaning up after itself.

OPTIMISTIC

Optimistic locking creates a situation where no scroll locks of any kind are set on the cursor. The assumption is that, if you do an update, you want people to still be able to get at your data. You're being optimistic because you are essentially guessing (hoping may be a better word) that no one will edit your data between when you fetched it into the cursor and when you applied your update.

The optimism is not necessarily misplaced. If you have a lot of records and not that many users, then the chances of two people trying to edit the same record at the same time are very small (depending on the nature of your business processes). Still, if you get this optimistic, then you need to also be prepared for the possibility that you will be wrong – that is, that someone has altered the data in between when you performed the fetch and when you went to actually update the database.

If you happen to run into this problem, SQL Server will issue an error with a value in @@ERROR of 16394. When this happens, you need to completely re-fetch the data from the cursor (so you know what changes were being made) and either rollback the transaction or try the update again.

Detecting Conversion of Cursor Types: TYPE_WARNING

This one is really pretty simple. If you add this option to your cursor, then you will be notified if an implicit conversion is made on your cursor. Without this statement, the conversion just happens with no notification. If the conversion wasn't an anticipated behavior, then there's a good chance that you're going to see the most dreaded of all computer terms (unpredictable results).

This is one of those that is perhaps best understood with an example, so let's go back and run a variation again of the cursor that we've been using throughout most of the chapter.

In this instance, we're going to take out the piece of code that creates a key for the table. Remember that without a unique index on a table, a keyset will be implicitly converted to a static cursor:

```
USE Northwind
/* Build the table that we'll be playing with this time */
SELECT OrderID, CustomerID
INTO CursorTable
FROM Orders
WHERE OrderID BETWEEN 10701 AND 10705


-- Declare our cursor
DECLARE CursorTest CURSOR
GLOBAL                  -- So we can manipulate it outside the batch
SCROLL                  -- So we can scroll back and see the changes
KEYSET
TYPE_WARNING
FOR
SELECT OrderID, CustomerID
FROM CursorTable


-- Declare our two holding variables
DECLARE @OrderID      int
DECLARE @CustomerID   varchar(5)


-- Get the cursor open and the first record fetched
OPEN CursorTest
FETCH NEXT FROM CursorTest INTO @OrderID, @CustomerID


-- Now loop through them all
WHILE @@FETCH_STATUS=0
BEGIN
    PRINT CONVERT(varchar(5),@OrderID) + '   ' + @CustomerID
    FETCH NEXT FROM CursorTest INTO @OrderID, @CustomerID
END


-- Now it's time to clean up after ourselves
CLOSE CursorTest

DEALLOCATE CursorTest

DROP TABLE CursorTable
```

There's nothing particularly special about this one. I'm considering it to be something of a complete rewrite only because we've deleted so much from the original and it's been so long since we've seen it. The creation of the table and cursor is pretty much the same as when we did our keyset-driven cursor much earlier in the chapter. The major changes are the removal of blocks of code that we don't need for this illustration along with the addition of the TYPE_WARNING option in the cursor declaration.

Now we come up with some interesting results:

(5 row(s) affected)

Cursor created was not of the requested type.
```
10701     HUNGO
10702     ALFKI
10703     FOLKO
10704     QUEEN
10705     HILAA
```

Everything ran OK – we just saw a statement that was meant solely as a warning. The results may not be what you expected given that the cursor was converted.

> *The down side here is that you get a message sent out, but no error. Programmatically speaking, there is essentially no way to tell that you received this message – which makes this option fairly useless in a production environment. Still, it can often be quite handy when you're trying to debug a cursor to determine why it isn't behaving in the expected fashion.*

FOR <SELECT>

This section of the cursor declaration is at the very heart of the matter. This is a section that is required under even the most basic of cursor syntax, and that's because it's the one and only clause that determines what data should be placed in the cursor.

Almost any SELECT statement is valid – even those including an ORDER BY clause. As long as your SELECT statement provides a single result set, you should be fine. Examples of options that would create problems would be any of the summary options such as a CUBE or ROLLUP.

FOR UPDATE

By default, any cursor that is updateable at all is completely updateable – that is, if one column can be edited then any of them can.

The FOR UPDATE <column list> option allows you to specify that only certain columns are to be editable within this cursor. If you include this option, then only the columns in your column list will be allowed to be updateable. Any columns not explicitly mentioned will be considered to be read-only.

Navigating the Cursor: the FETCH Statement

I figure that whoever first created the SQL cursor syntax must have really liked dogs. They probably decided to think of the data they were after as being the bone, with SQL Server the faithful bloodhound. From this I'm guessing, the FETCH keyword was born.

It's an apt term if you think about it. In a nutshell, it tells SQL Server to "go get it boy!" With that, our faithful mutt (in the form of SQL Server) is off to find the particular bone (row) we were after. We've gotten a bit of a taste of the FETCH statement in some of the previous cursors in this chapter, but it's time to look at this very important statement more closely.

FETCH actually has many more options than what we've seen so far. Up to this point, we've seen three different options for FETCH (NEXT, PREVIOUS, and FIRST). These really aren't a bad start. Indeed, we really only need to add one more for the most basic set of cursor navigation commands, and a few after that for the complete set.

Let's look at each of the cursor navigation commands and see what they do for us:

FETCH Option	Description
NEXT	This moves you forwards exactly one row in the result set, and is the backbone option. 90% or more of your cursors won't need any more than this. Keep this in mind when deciding to declare as FORWARD_ONLY or not. When you try to do a FETCH NEXT and it results in moving beyond the last record, you will have a @@FETCH_STATUS of –1.
PRIOR	As you have probably surmised, this one is the functional opposite of NEXT. This moves backwards exactly one row. If you performed a FETCH PRIOR when you were at the first row in the result set, then you will get a @@FETCH_STATUS of –1 just as if you had moved beyond the end of the file.
FIRST	Like most cursor options, this one says what it is pretty clearly. If you perform a FETCH FIRST then you will be at the first record in the recordset. The only time this option should generate a @@FETCH_STATUS of –1 is if the result set is empty.
LAST	The functional opposite of FIRST, FETCH LAST moves you to the last record in the result set. Again, the only way you'll get a –1 for @@FETCH_STATUS on this one is if you have an empty result set.
ABSOLUTE	With this one, you supply an integer value that indicates how many rows you want from the beginning of the cursor. If the value supplied is negative, then it is that many rows from the end of the cursor. Note that this option is not supported with dynamic cursors (since the membership in the cursor is redone with every fetch, you can "really know where you're at"). This equates roughly to navigating to a specific "absolute position" in a few of the client access object models.
RELATIVE	No – this isn't your mother-in-law kind of thing. Instead, this is about navigating by moving a specified number of rows forward or backward relative to the current row.

We've already gotten a fair look at a few of these in our previous cursors. The other navigational choices work pretty much the same.

Altering Data within your Cursor

Up until now, we've kind of glossed over the notion of changing data directly in the cursor. Now it's time to take a look at updating and deleting records within a cursor.

Since we're dealing with a specific row rather than set data, we need some special syntax to tell SQL Server that we want to update. Happily, this syntax is actually quite easy given that you already know how to perform an UPDATE or DELETE.

Essentially, we're going to update or delete data in the table that is underlying our cursor. To do this, it's as simple as running the same UPDATE and DELETE statements that we're now used to, but qualifying them with a WHERE clause that matches our cursor row. We just add one line of syntax to our DELETE or UPDATE statement:

```
WHERE CURRENT OF <cursor name>
```

Nothing remarkable about it at all. Just for grins though, we'll go ahead and implement a cursor using this syntax:

```
USE Northwind
/* Build the table that we'll be playing with this time */
SELECT OrderID, CustomerID
INTO CursorTable
FROM Orders
WHERE OrderID BETWEEN 10701 AND 10705

-- Now create a unique index on it in the form of a primary key
ALTER TABLE CursorTable
      ADD CONSTRAINT PKCursor
      PRIMARY KEY (OrderID)

/* The IDENTITY property was automatically brought over when
** we did our SELECT INTO, but we want to use our own OrderID
** value, so we're going to turn IDENTITY_INSERT on so that we
** can override the identity value.
*/
SET IDENTITY_INSERT CursorTable ON

-- Declare our cursor
DECLARE CursorTest CURSOR
SCROLL            -- So we can scroll back and see if the changes are there
KEYSET
FOR
SELECT OrderID, CustomerID
FROM CursorTable

-- Declare our two holding variables
DECLARE @OrderID      int
DECLARE @CustomerID   varchar(5)

-- Get the cursor open and the first record fetched
OPEN CursorTest
FETCH NEXT FROM CursorTest INTO @OrderID, @CustomerID
```

```
-- Now loop through them all
WHILE @@FETCH_STATUS=0
BEGIN
    IF (@OrderID % 2 = 0)    -- Even number, so we'll update it
    BEGIN
        -- Make a change. This time though, we'll do it using cursor syntax
        UPDATE CursorTable
            SET CustomerID = 'EVEN'
            WHERE CURRENT OF CursorTest
    END

    ELSE                          -- Must be odd, so we'll delete it.
    BEGIN
        -- Now we'll delete a record so we can see how to deal with that
        DELETE CursorTable
            WHERE CURRENT OF CursorTest
    END
    FETCH NEXT FROM CursorTest INTO @OrderID, @CustomerID
END

-- Now go back to the top. We can do this since we have a scrollable cursor
FETCH FIRST FROM CursorTest INTO @OrderID, @CustomerID

-- And loop through again.
WHILE @@FETCH_STATUS != -1
BEGIN
    IF @@FETCH_STATUS = -2
    BEGIN
        PRINT '  MISSING! It probably was deleted.'
    END
    ELSE
    BEGIN
        PRINT CONVERT(varchar(5),@OrderID) + '   ' +  @CustomerID
    END
    FETCH NEXT FROM CursorTest INTO @OrderID, @CustomerID
END

-- Now it's time to clean up after ourselves
CLOSE CursorTest

DEALLOCATE CursorTest

DROP TABLE CursorTable
```

Again, I'm treating this one as an entirely new cursor. We've done enough deletions, additions, and updates that I suspect you'll find it easier to just key things in a second time rather than having to look through row by row to see what you might have missed.

We are also again using the modulus operator (%) that we saw earlier in the book. Remember that it gives us nothing but the remainder. Therefore, if the remainder of any number divided by two is zero, we know the number was an even number.

The rest of the nuts and bolts of this don't require any rocket science, yet we can quickly tell that we got some results:

(5 row(s) affected)

(1 row(s) affected)

(1 row(s) affected)

(1 row(s) affected)

(1 row(s) affected)

(1 row(s) affected)

```
  MISSING! It probably was deleted.
10702  EVEN
  MISSING! It probably was deleted.
10704  EVEN
  MISSING! It probably was deleted.
```

You can see the multiple "1 row affected" that is the returned message for any row that was affected by the UPDATE and DELETE statements. When we get down to the last result set enumeration, you can quickly tell that we deleted all the odd numbers (which is what we told our code to do), and that we updated the even numbered rows with a new CustomerID.

No tricks – just a WHERE clause that makes use of the WHERE CURRENT argument.

Summary

Cursors give us those memories of the old days – when we could address things row by row. Ahhh, it sounds so romantic with that "old days" kind of thought. WRONG! I'd stick to set operations any day if I thought I could get away with it.

The fact is that set operations can't do everything. Cursors are going to be the answer anytime a solution must be done on a row-by-row basis. Notice that I used the word "must" in there, and that's the way you should think of it. Cursors are great of taking care of some problems that can't be solved by any other means.

That being said, remember to avoid cursor use wherever possible. Cursors are a resource pig, and will almost always produce 100 times or worse negative performance impact. It is extremely tempting – especially if you come from the mainframe world or from a dBase background – to just keep thinking in that row-by-row method. Don't fall into that trap! Cursors are meant to be used only when no other options are available.

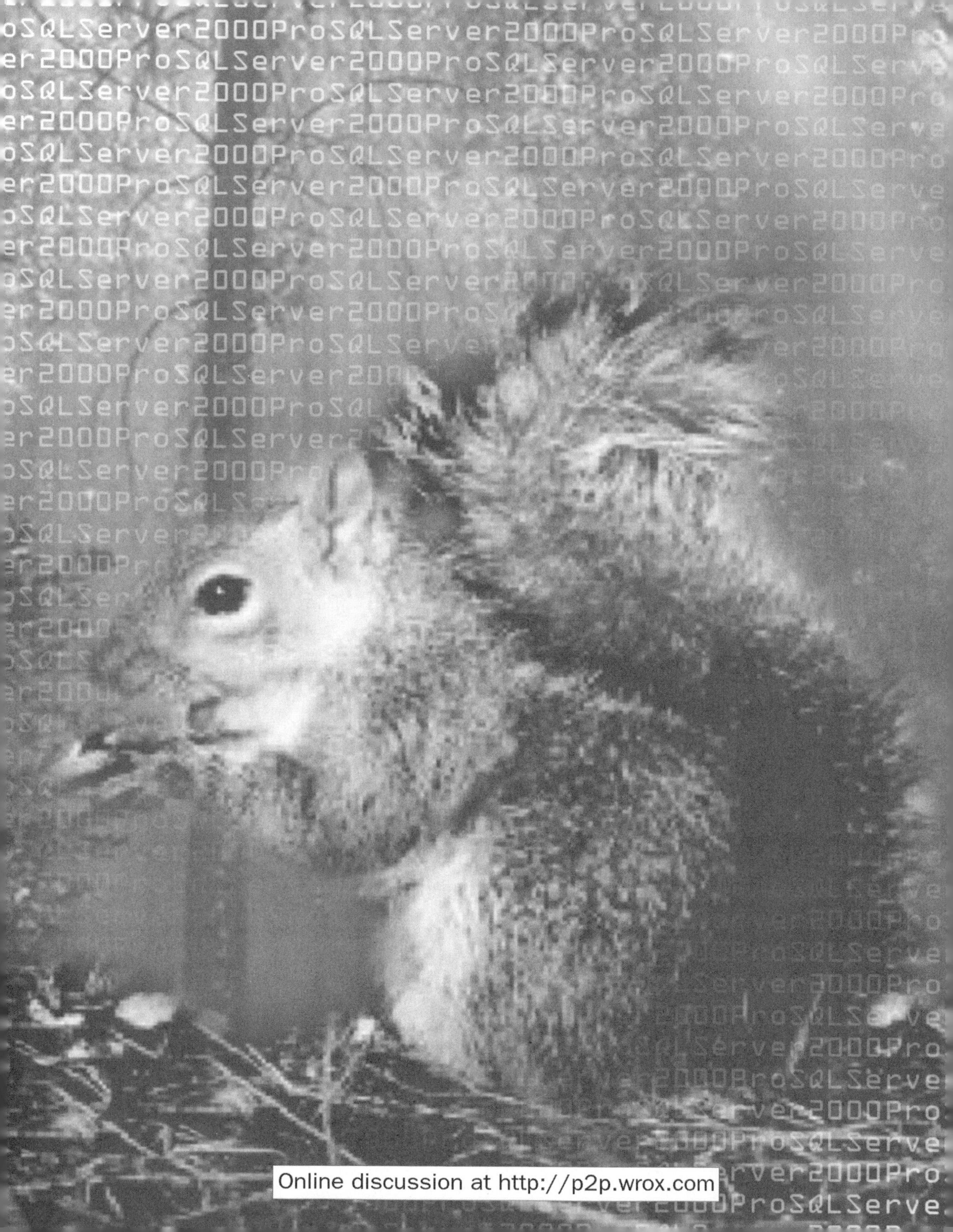
Online discussion at http://p2p.wrox.com

19

A Brief XML Primer

So, here we are – most of our structural stuff is done at this point, and we're ready to start moving on to the peripheral stuff. That is, we're ready to start looking at what I would consider to be the "extras" of SQL Server. It's not that some of the items still to be covered aren't things that you would normally expect out of an RDBMS system – it's just that we don't really *need* these in order to have a functional SQL Server.

This chapter will present some background for the first of these "extras", and it is entirely new with this release of SQL Server – XML integration. The catch here is that XML is really entirely its own animal – it's a completely different kind of thing from the relational system we've been working with up to this point. Why, then, has it been added? Well, XML, quite simply, is taking the world by storm and it is probably the most important thing to happen to data since the advent of data warehousing.

XML has actually been around for a few years now but, while the talk was big, its actual usage was not what it could have been. At issue was the fact that there was very little in the way of standards to deal with XML. Now that these well-defined standards exist, the third party support (XML parsers, integration into mainstream products, standardized XML implementations within major industries, etc.) is exploding.

While databases are really good for storing persistent data, XML is good for transient data. In addition, XML is a positively spectacular way of making data *useful*. As such, the ways of utilizing XML will likely continue to grow, and grow, and grow.

So, with all that said, in this chapter we'll look at:

- ❑ What exactly is XML?
- ❑ What other technologies are closely tied to XML?

If you're already reasonably comfortable with XML, then you may want to skip this chapter and move into the nitty-gritty of SQL Server's new XML integration features in the next chapter. For the rest of you – let's get started.

XML Basics

There are tons and tons of books out there on XML – for example, *Beginning XML*, Wrox Press, ISBN 1-861003-41-2, or *Professional XML*, Wrox Press, ISBN 1-861003-11-0. Given how full up this book already is, my first inclination was to shy away from much information about XML itself, and assume that you already knew something about it. Fortunately, I've come to realize that I know an awful lot of database people who think that XML "is just some web technology" and, therefore, have spent zero time on it – they couldn't be more wrong.

XML is first and foremost an *information* technology. It is *not* a web-specific technology at all. Instead, it just tends to be thought of that way (usually by people who don't understand XML) for several reasons – such as:

- ❑ XML is a **markup** language, and looks a heck of a lot like HTML to the untrained eye.

- ❑ XML is often easily **transformed** into HTML. As such, it has become a popular way to keep the information part of a page, with a final transformation into HTML only on request – a separate transformation can take place based on criteria (such as what browser is asking for the information).

- ❑ One of the first widely used products to support XML was Microsoft's Internet Explorer.

- ❑ The Internet is quite often used as a way to exchange information, and that's something that XML is ideally suited for.

Like HTML, XML is a text-based markup language. Indeed, they are both derived from the same original language, called SGML. SGML has been around for much longer than the Internet (at least as we think of it today), and is most often used in the printing industry or in government related documentation. Note that the "S" in SGML doesn't stand for simple – SGML is anything but intuitive and is actually a downright pain to learn. XML, on the other hand, tends to be reasonably easy to decipher.

So, this might have you asking the question, "Great – where can I get a listing of XML tags?" Well, you can't – at least, not in the sense that you're thinking of when you ask the question. XML has very few tags that are actually part of the language. Instead, it provides ways for defining your own tags and for utilizing tags as defined by others (such as industry groups). XML is largely about flexibility – which includes the ability for you to set your own rules for your XML through the use of either a **Document Type Definition (DTD)** or, as an alternative, an **XML schema**.

> *As of this writing, the W3C (see http://www.w3c.org) has not finalized the standard for XML schemas. It is, however, in what they call "Last Call" draft status, so the basic structure is unlikely to change much. In a nutshell, an XML schema is really just an XML document whose sole purpose in life is to set the rules for other XML documents.*

An XML document has very few rules placed on it just because it happens to be XML. The biggie is that it must be what is called **well formed**. We'll look into what "well formed" means shortly. Now, just because an XML document meets the criteria of being well formed, it doesn't mean that it would be classified as being **valid**. Valid XML must not only be well formed, but must also live up to any restrictions placed on the XML document by DTDs or XML schemas that the document references. We will briefly examine DTDs and XML schemas later on in the chapter.

XML can also be transformed. The short rendition of what this means is that it is relatively easy for you to turn XML into a completely different XML representation or even a non-XML format. One of the most common uses for this is to transform XML into HTML for rendering on the Web. The need for this transformation presents us with our first mini-opportunity to compare and contrast HTML vs. XML. In the simplest terms, XML is about information, and HTML is about presentation.

The information stored in XML is denoted through the use of what are called **elements** and **attributes**. Elements are usually created through the use of both an opening and a closing tag (there's an exception, but we'll see that later) and are identified with a case sensitive name (no spaces allowed). Attributes are items that further describe elements, and are embedded in the element's start tag. Attribute values must be in matched single or double quotes.

Parts of an XML Document

Well, a few of the names have already flown by, but it makes sense, before we get too deep into things, to stop and create something of a glossary of terms that we're going to be utilizing for the rest of this chapter.

What we're really going to be doing here is providing a listing of all the major parts of an XML document that you will run into. Many of the parts of the document are optional, though a few are not. In some cases, having one thing means that you have to have another. In other cases, the parts of the document are relatively independent of each other.

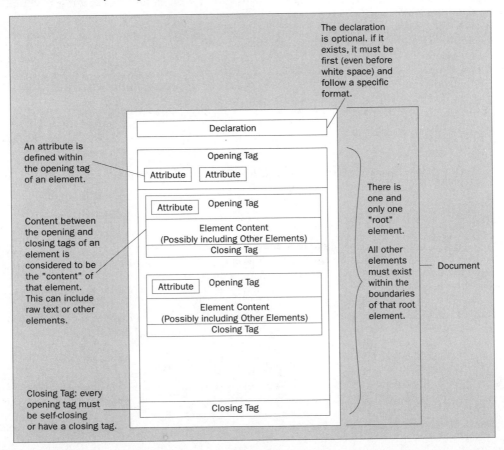

We will take things in something of a hierarchical approach and, where it makes sense, in the order you'll come across them in a given XML document.

The Document

The **document** encompasses everything from the very first character to the last. When we refer to an XML document, we are referring to both the structure and the content of that particular XML document.

Declaration

The **declaration** is optional. If it exists, it must be the very first thing in the document. *Nothing* can be before the declaration, not even white space (spaces, carriage returns, tabs, whatever) – nothing.

The declaration is made with a special tag that begins with a question mark (which indicates that this tag is a preprocessor directive) and the xml moniker:

```
<?xml version="1.0"?>
```

The declaration has one required attribute (something that further describes the element) – the **version**. In the above example, we've declared that this is an XML document and also that it is to comply with version 1.0 of the XML specification.

The declaration can optionally have one additional attribute – this one is called **encoding**, and it describes the nature of the character set this XML document utilizes. XML can handle a few different character sets, most notably UTF-16 and UTF-8. UTF-16 is essentially the Unicode specification, which is a 16 bit encoding specification that allows for most characters in use in the world today. The default encoding method is UTF-8, which is backward compatible to the older ASCII specification. A full declaration would look like this (note that I'm using single quotes this time, just because I can!):

```
<?xml version='1.0' encoding='UTF-8'?>
```

> *Elements that start with the letters* xml *are strictly forbidden by the specification – they are reserved for future expansion of the language.*

Elements

Elements serve as pieces of glue to hold together descriptive information about something – it honestly could be anything. Elements define a clear start and end point for your descriptive information. Usually, elements exist in matched pairs of tags, known as an opening tag and a closing tag. Optionally, however, the opening tag can be **self-closing** – essentially defining what is known as an **empty element**.

The structure for an XML element looks pretty much as HTML tags do. An opening tag will begin with an opening angle bracket (<), contain a name and possibly some attributes, and then a closing angle bracket (>):

```
<ATagForANormalElement>
```

The exception to the rule is if the element is self-closing, in which case the closing angle bracket of the opening tag is preceded with a "/":

```
<ASelfClosingElement/>
```

Closing tags will look exactly like the opening tag (case sensitive), but start with a slash (/) before the name of the element it's closing:

```
<ATagForANormalElement >      <== Opening Tag
    Some data or whatever can go in here.
</ATagForANormalElement >   <== Closing Tag
```

This element contains some data. The **document object model** (**DOM**) for Microsoft's MSXML defines specific ways of navigating to all of the information (including the contents of the element).

Elements can also contain attributes (which we'll look at shortly) as part of the opening (but not the closing) tag for the element. Finally, elements can contain other elements, but if they do, the inner element must be closed before closing the outer element:

```
<OuterElement>
   <InnerElement>
   </InnerElement>
</OuterElement>
```

We will come back to elements shortly when we look at what it means to be "well formed".

Nodes

When you map out the hierarchies that naturally form in an XML document, they follow the familiar tree model that you see in just about any hierarchical relationship. Each intersection point in the tree is referred to as a **node**.

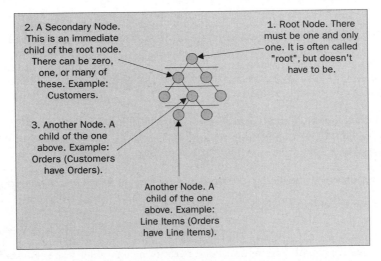

The contents of an XML document can be navigated based on node levels and the values in the attributes and elements of particular nodes.

The "Root" Node

Perhaps one of the most common points of confusion in XML documents is over what is called the **root node**. Every XML document must have exactly one (no more, no less) root node. The root node is an element that contains any other elements in the document (if there are any). You can think of the root node as being the unification point that ties all the nodes below it together and gives them structure within the scope of any particular XML document. So, what's all the confusion about? Well, the confused fall into two camps: those who don't know that they need to have a singular root node (which *you* now know); and those who don't understand how root nodes are named (which you will in a moment).

Because the general statement is usually, "You must have a root node", people usually interpret that to mean that they must have a node that is called root. Indeed, you'll find that a very large percentage of XML documents do indeed name their root node Root (or root or ROOT). The reality, however, is that root nodes follow the exact same naming scheme as any other element with only one exception – the name must be unique throughout the document. That is, no other element in the entire document can have the same name as the root.

Attributes

Attributes exist only within the context of an element. They are implemented as a way of further describing an element, and are placed within the boundaries of the opening tag for the element:

```
<SomeElement MyFirstAttribute="Hi There" MySecondAttribute="25">
```

Regardless of the data type of the information in the value for the attribute, the value must be enclosed in either single or double quotes.

> *By default, XML documents have no concept of data type. We will investigate ways of describing the rules of individual document applications later in this chapter. At that time, we'll see that there are some ways of ensuring data type – it's just that you, not XML, set the rules for it.*

No Defects – Being "Well Formed"

The part of the rules that defines how XML must "look" – that is, what elements are OK, how they are defined, what parts they have – is about whether an XML document is "well formed" or not.

Actually, all SGML based languages have something of the concept of being well formed. Heck, even HTML has this concept – it's just that it has been largely lost in the facts that HTML is naturally more forgiving and that the browsers ignore many errors.

If you're used to HTML at all, then you've seen some pretty sloppy stuff as far as a tag-based language goes. XML has much more strict rules about what is and isn't OK. The short rendition looks like this:

❑ Every XML document *must* have a unique "root" node.

❑ Every tag must have a matching (case sensitive) closing tag unless the opening tag is self-closing.

❑ Tags cannot straddle other tags.

❑ You can't use restricted characters for anything other than what they indicate to the XML parser. If you need to represent any of these special characters, then you need to use an escape sequence (which will be translated back to the character you requested).

The following is an example of a document that is "well formed":

```
<?xml version="1.0" encoding="UTF-8"?>

<ThisCouldBeCalledAnything>
   <AnElement>
     <AnotherElement AnAttribute="Some Value">
       <AselfClosingElement AnAttributeThatNeedsASpecialCharacter=
       "Fred&quot;s flicks"/>
     </AnotherElement>
   </AnElement>
</ThisCouldBeCalledAnything>
```

Notice that we didn't need to have a closing tag at all for the declaration. That's because the declaration is a preprocessor directive – not an element. Essentially, it is telling the XML parser some things it needs to know before the parser can get down to the real business of dealing with our XML.

So, this has been an extremely abbreviated version of what's required for your XML document to be considered well formed, but it pretty much covers the basics for the limited scope of our XML coverage in this book.

Understanding these concepts is going to be absolutely vital to your survival (well, comprehension at least) in the next chapter. The XML example that is covered next should reinforce things for you, but if, after looking at it, you find you're still confused, then read the above again or check out Beginning XML. *Your sanity depends on knowing this stuff before you move on to the styling and schema issues at the end of this chapter – let alone the next chapter.*

An XML Example

If there's one continuing theme throughout this book, it's got to be that I don't like explaining things without tossing in an example or two. As I've said earlier, this isn't an XML book, so I'm not going to get carried away with my examples here, but let's at least take a look at what we're talking about.

Throughout the remainder of this chapter and the next, you're going to find that life is an awful lot easier if you have some sort of XML editing tool. Since XML is text based, you can easily open and edit XML documents in Notepad – the problem is that you're not going to get any error checking. How are you going to know that your document is well formed? Sure, you can just look it over if it's just a few lines, but get to a complete document or an XSL document and life will quickly become very difficult.

I normally try to make a point out of not promoting any particular product in my writing. Because you need something – because this product has a 30 day free trial (I suspect you'll buy it before time runs out) and because it's clearly the best thing on the market at the moment – for purposes of this book, I'm going to go ahead and say I'll be utilizing a tool called XML Spy. As one of my coworkers is fond of saying (referring to the team at XML Spy), "Those guys ROCK!" You can find them at http://www.xmlspy.com.

For this example, we're going to look at an XML representation of some of our `Northwind` data. In this case, I'm going to take a look at some order information. We're going to start with just a few things and grow from there.

First, we know that we need a root node for any XML document that we're going to have. The root node can be called anything we want, as long as it is unique within our document. A common way of dealing with this is to call the root `root`. More frequently, the root is called something representative of what the particular XML document is all about, `Northwind`.

For our purposes, we'll start off with something really simple, and just use root:

```
<root>
</root>
```

Just that quick, we've created our first well-formed XML document. Notice that it didn't include the `<?xml>` tag that we saw in the earlier illustration. We could have put that in, but it's actually an optional item. The only restriction related to it is that, if you include it, it must be first. Just for clearness, we'll go ahead and add it:

```
<?xml version="1.0" encoding="UTF-8"?>
<root>
</root>
```

Actually, by the rules of XML, any tag starting with ?xml is considered to be a reserved tag – that is, you shouldn't name your tags that, as they are reserved for the current or future use of the W3C as XML goes into future versions.

So, moving on, we have our first well-formed XML document. Unfortunately, this document is about as plain as it can get – it doesn't really tell us anything. Well, for our example, we're working on describing order information, so we might want to start putting in some information that is descriptive of an order. Let's start with a (self-closing) Order tag:

```
<?xml version="1.0" encoding="UTF-8"?>
<root>
   <Order/>
</root>
```

OK – so this is getting monotonous – isn't it? We now know that we have one order in our XML document, but we still don't know anything about it. Let's expand on it by adding a few attributes:

```
<?xml version="1.0" encoding="UTF-8"?>
<root>
   <Order CustomerID="ALFKI" OrderID="10643" OrderDate="1997-08-25T00:00:00" />
</root>
```

Well, it doesn't really take a brain surgeon at this point to be able to discern the basics about our order at this point:

❑ The customer's ID number is ALFKI

❑ The order ID number was 10643

❑ The order was placed on August 25th, 1997

Basically, as we have things, it equates to a row in the Orders table in Northwind in SQL Server. If the customer had several orders, it might look something like:

```
<?xml version="1.0" encoding="UTF-8"?>
<root>
   <Order CustomerID="ALFKI" OrderID="10643" OrderDate="1997-08-25T00:00:00" />
   <Order CustomerID="ALFKI" OrderID="10692" OrderDate="1997-10-03T00:00:00" />
   <Order CustomerID="ALFKI" OrderID="10702" OrderDate="1997-10-13T00:00:00" />
   <Order CustomerID="ALFKI" OrderID="10835" OrderDate="1998-01-15T00:00:00" />
</root>
```

While this is a perfectly legal – and even well-formed – example of XML, it doesn't really represent the hierarchy of the data as we might wish. We might, for example, wish to build our XML a little differently, and represent the notion that customers are usually considered to be higher in the hierarchical chain (they are the "parents" of orders, if you will). We could represent this by changing the way we express customers. Instead of an attribute, we could make a customer an element in its own right – including having its own attributes – and nest a particular customer's orders inside its customer element:

```
<?xml version="1.0" encoding="UTF-8"?>
<root>
    <Customer CustomerID="ALFKI" CompanyName="Alfreds Futterkiste">
        <Order OrderID="10643" OrderDate="1997-08-25T00:00:00" />
        <Order OrderID="10692" OrderDate="1997-10-03T00:00:00" />
        <Order OrderID="10702" OrderDate="1997-10-13T00:00:00" />
        <Order OrderID="10835" OrderDate="1998-01-15T00:00:00" />
    </Customer>
</root>
```

If we have more than one customer, that's not a problem – we just add another customer node:

```
<?xml version="1.0" encoding="UTF-8"?>
<root>
    <Customer CustomerID="ALFKI" CompanyName="Alfreds Futterkiste">
        <Order OrderID="10643" OrderDate="1997-08-25T00:00:00" />
        <Order OrderID="10692" OrderDate="1997-10-03T00:00:00" />
        <Order OrderID="10702" OrderDate="1997-10-13T00:00:00" />
        <Order OrderID="10835" OrderDate="1998-01-15T00:00:00" />
    </Customer>
    <Customer CustomerID="ANTON" CompanyName="Antonio Moreno Taquería">
        <Order OrderID="10365" OrderDate="1996-11-27T00:00:00" />
        <Order OrderID="10507" OrderDate="1997-04-15T00:00:00" />
        <Order OrderID="10535" OrderDate="1997-05-13T00:00:00" />
        <Order OrderID="10573" OrderDate="1997-06-19T00:00:00" />
    </Customer>
</root>
```

Indeed, this can go to unlimited levels of hierarchy (subject, of course, to whatever your parser can handle). We could, for example, add a level for individual line items in the order.

Determining Elements vs. Attributes

The first thing to understand here is that there is no hard and fast rule for determining what should be an element or an attribute. An attribute describes something of the properties of the element that it is an attribute of. Child elements – or child "nodes" – of an element do much the same thing. So how, then, do we decide which should be which? Why are attributes even necessary? Well, like most things in life, it's something of a balancing act.

Attributes make a lot of sense in situations where the value has a one-to-one relationship with, and is inherently part of, the element. In Northwind, for example, we have only one company name per customer ID – this is ideal for an attribute. As we are transforming our relational data to XML, the columns of a table will often make good attributes for an element which is directly related to an individual row in a table.

Elements tend to make more sense if there is a one-to-many relationship between the element and what's describing it. In our example earlier in the chapter, there are many orders for each customer. Technically speaking, we could have had each order be an attribute of a customer element, but then we would have needed to repeat much of the customer element information over and over again. Similarly, if our Northwind database allowed for the notion of customers having aliases (multiple names), then we may have wanted to have a "name" element under the customer, and have its attribute describe individual instances of names.

Namespaces

With all this freedom to create your own tags, to mix and match data from other sources, and to do your own thing, there are bound to be a few collisions here and there about what things are going to use which names where. For example, an element with a name of letter might have entirely different structure, rules, and meaning in an application built for libraries (for which a letter is probably a document written from one person to another person) from that which it would in another application describing fonts (which might relate the association between a character set and a series of glyphs).

To take this example a little further, the nature of XML is such that industry organizations around the world are slowly agreeing on naming and structure conventions to describe various types of information in their industry. Library organizations may have agreed on element formats describing books, plays, movies, letters, essays, etc. At the same time, the operating systems and/or graphics industries may have agreed on element formats describing pictures, fonts, and document layouts.

Now, imagine that we, the poor hapless developers that we are, have been asked to write an application that needs to render library content. Obviously, library content makes frequent use of things like fonts – so, when you refer to something called letter in our XML, are we referring to something to do with the font or is it a letter from one person to another (say, from Thomas Jefferson to George Washington)? We have a conflict, and we need a way to resolve it.

That's where **namespaces** come in. Namespaces describe a domain of elements and attributes, and what their structure is. The structure that supports letters in libraries would be described in a libraries namespace. Likewise, the graphics industry would likely have their own namespace(s) that would describe letters as they relate to that industry. The information for a namespace is stored in a reference document and can be found using a Uniform Resource Identifier (URI) – a special name, not dissimilar to a URL – that will eventually resolve to our reference document.

When we build our XML documents that refer to both library and graphics constructs, we simply reference the namespaces for those industries. In addition, we qualify elements and attributes whose nature we want described by the namespace. By qualifying our names using namespaces, we make sure that, even if a document has elements that are structurally different but have the same name, we can refer to the parts of our document with complete confidence that we are not referring to the wrong kind of element or attribute.

To reference a namespace, we simply add the reference as a special attribute (called xmlns) to our root. The reference will provide both a local name (how we want to refer to the namespace) and the URI that will resolve to our reference document.

Below is an example of an XML document (technically, this is what we call a "schema") that we will be utilizing in our next chapter. Notice several things about it as relates to namespaces:

❏ The document references three namespaces – one for XDR (this happens to be an XDR document), a Microsoft datatype namespace (this one builds a list about the number and nature of different data types), and, last but not least, a special sql namespace used for working with SQL Server XML integration.

❏ Some attributes (including one in the root) are qualified with namespace information (see the sql:relation attribute for example.

```
<?xml version="1.0" encoding="UTF-8"?>
<Schema xmlns="urn:schemas-microsoft-com:xml-data"
            xmlns:dt="urn:schemas-microsoft-com:datatypes"
            xmlns:sql="urn:schemas-microsoft-com:xml-sql"
            sql:xsl='../Customers.xsl'>
    <ElementType name="Root" content="empty"  />
    <ElementType name="Customers" sql:relation="Customers">
        <AttributeType name="CustomerID"/>
        <AttributeType name="CompanyName"/>
        <AttributeType name="Address"/>
        <AttributeType name="City"/>
        <AttributeType name="Region"/>
        <AttributeType name="PostalCode"/>
        <attribute type="CustomerID" sql:field="CustomerID"/>
        <attribute type="CompanyName" sql:field="CompanyName"/>
        <attribute type="Address" sql:field="Address"/>
        <attribute type="City" sql:field="City"/>
        <attribute type="Region" sql:field="Region"/>
        <attribute type="PostalCode" sql:field="PostalCode"/>
    </ElementType>
</Schema>
```

The `sql` namespace references a couple of special attributes. We do not have to worry about whether the Microsoft `datatypes` namespace also has a field or relation data type because we are fully qualifying our attribute names. Even if the `datatypes` namespace does have an attribute called field, our XML parser will still know to treat this element by the rules of the `sql` namespace.

Element Content

Another notion of XML and elements that deserves mentioning is the concept of element content.

Elements can contain data beyond the attribute level and nested elements. While nested elements are certainly one form of element content (one element contains the other), XML also allows for row text information to be contained in an element. For example, we could have an XML document that looked something like:

```
<?xml version="1.0" encoding="UTF-8"?>
<root>
  <Customer CustomerID="ALFKI" CompanyName="Alfreds Futterkiste">
   <Note Date="1997-08-25T00:00:00">
   The customer called in today and placed another order. Says they really like
our work and would like it if we would consider establishing a location closer to
their base of operations.
   </Note>
   <Note Date="1997-08-26T00:00:00">
   Followed up with the customer on new location. Customer agrees to guarantee us
$5,000 per month in business to help support a new office.
   </Note>
  </Customer>
</root>
```

The contents of the `Note` elements, such as "`The customer called...`" are neither an element nor an attribute, yet they are valid XML data.

Be aware that such data exists in XML, but SQL Server will not output data in this format natively. The row/column approach of RDBMS systems lends itself far more strongly to elements and attributes. To output data such as our notes above, you would need to transform the data into the new format. We will look at transformations as the last item in this chapter.

Valid vs. Well Formed – DTDs and Schemas

Just because an XML document is well formed does not mean that it is **valid** XML. Now, while that is sinking in, I'll tell you that *no* XML is considered valid unless it has been validated against some form of specification document. Currently, there are only two recognized types of specification documents (OK, as I write this, it's technically only one, but be patient with me) – a Document Type Definition, or DTD, and an XML schema.

> *As mentioned earlier: at the time of writing, the W3C specification on XML schemas is still only considered to be in "Last Call" and is not a formal recommendation as yet. This should change soon. In the mean time, Microsoft has implemented its own brand of XML schemas in anticipation of the standard. There will definitely be some differences between the Microsoft implementation and the most likely final recommendation from the W3C, so keep this in mind if you are going to learn about XML schemas (and I suspect you will be).*

The basic premise behind both varieties of validation documents is much the same. DTDs and XML schemas seek to define what the rules are for a particular *class* of XML document. The two approaches are implemented somewhat differently and each offers distinct advantages over the other:

❑ DTDs: This is the old tried and true. DTDs are utilized in SGML (XML is an SGML application – you can think of SGML as being a superset of XML, but incredibly painful to learn), and have the advantage of being a very well known and accepted way of doing things. There are tons of DTDs already out there that are just waiting for you to use them.

The downside to DTDs (you knew there had to be one – right?) is the word "old" in my "old tried and true" statement above. Not that being old is a bad thing but, in this case, DTDs are definitely not up to speed with what else has happened in document technology. DTDs do not really allow for such seemingly rudimentary things as restricting data types.

❑ XML schemas: The new kid in town. XML schemas have the distinct advantage of being strongly typed. What's cool about them is that you can effectively establish your own **complex data types** – types that are made up based on combinations of one or more other data types (including other complex data types) or require specialized pattern matching. For example, a Social Security Number is just a number, but it has special formatting that you could easily enforce via an XML schema. XML schemas also have the advantage, as their name suggests, of being an XML document themselves. This means that a lot of the skills in writing your XML documents also apply to writing schemas (though there's still plenty to learn) and that schemas can, themselves, be self describing – right down to validating themselves against yet another schema.

The downside to schemas is largely the fact that there is still no formal recommendation from the W3C, so, while there are a fair number of tools that work against the spec as it is now, a lot of those tools may be broken (due to changes) when the final version is recommended. This can include your XML parser! XML schemas are intrinsically better than DTDs, but DTDs still have their well-tested nature on their side.

DTDs

Document Type Definitions are actually fairly simple in structure. For example, let's review an earlier example of some XML:

```
<?xml version="1.0" encoding="UTF-8"?>
<root>
  <Customer CustomerID="ALFKI" CompanyName="Alfreds Futterkiste">
    <Note Date="1997-08-25T00:00:00">
    The customer called in today and placed another order. Says they really like
our work and would like it if we would consider establishing a location closer to
their base of operations.
    </Note>
    <Note Date="1997-08-26T00:00:00">
    Followed up with the customer on new location. Customer agrees to guarantee us
$5,000 per month in business to help support a new office.
    </Note>
  </Customer>
</root>
```

Here's a DTD that might have gone with this example:

```
<!ELEMENT Customer (Note*)>
<!ATTLIST Customer
    CustomerID (ALFKI | XXXXI) #REQUIRED
    CompanyName CDATA #REQUIRED
    Address CDATA #IMPLIED
>
<!ELEMENT Note (#PCDATA)>
<!ATTLIST Note
    Date (1997-08-25T00:00:00 | 1997-08-26T00:00:00) #REQUIRED
>
<!ELEMENT root (Customer+)>
```

If you peruse this for a bit, there are several things worth noticing:

❑   There is an element type called `root` – it requires one or more sub-elements of the name `Customer`.

❑   `Customer` also has sub-elements, but the difference is that the `Note` sub-element is not required.

❑   The `CustomerID` attribute in the `Customer` element has a limited list of acceptable values – that is, the value in that attribute needs to be either `ALFKI` or `XXXXI`. One value is required. If we changed this to `CDATA` (which, by the way, stands for Character Data), then we could place any value in `CustomerID`.

❑   Because of the `(#PCDATA)` type, the element called `Note` is free-form text (no validation). However, `Note` does have a required attribute in the form of `Date`.

Perhaps the biggest thing to note is the lack of strong type enforcement – we can limit to specific lists of values, but we can't do general restrictions based on data type.

XML Schemas

This is a tough part for me to write because the specification isn't final, and most likely won't be until after this book has gone to press.

That said, I highly recommend that you keep an eye on the W3C web site and Microsoft offerings for when XML schemas are formalized. XML schemas have the advantage of much better data type enforcement. In addition, they are themselves XML documents, which means that you can do things like transform them into some other restrictive format. For example, it's quite possible that you will see some transformation templates written to transform XML schemas written under the working draft to be compliant with the new spec – time will tell.

Just for comparison purposes, we'll take a look at an XML schema that loosely matches the DTD we just looked at. Keep in mind that this has been produced before the spec is finalized.

```
<?xml version="1.0" encoding="UTF-8"?>
<!DOCTYPE xsd:schema PUBLIC "-//W3C//DTD XMLSCHEMA 19991216//EN" "" [
    <!ENTITY % p 'xsd:'>
    <!ENTITY % s ':xsd'>
]>
<xsd:schema xmlns:xsd="http://www.w3.org/1999/XMLSchema">
    <xsd:complexType name="CustomerType" content="elementOnly">
        <xsd:sequence>
            <xsd:element name="Note" type="NoteType" minOccurs="0"
             maxOccurs="unbounded"/>
        </xsd:sequence>
        <xsd:attribute name="CustomerID" use="required">
            <xsd:simpleType base="xsd:NMTOKEN">
                <xsd:enumeration value="ALFKI"/>
                <xsd:enumeration value="XXXXI"/>
            </xsd:simpleType>
        </xsd:attribute>
        <xsd:attribute name="CompanyName" type="xsd:string" use="required"/>
        <xsd:attribute name="Address" type="xsd:string"/>
    </xsd:complexType>
    <xsd:complexType name="NoteType" base="xsd:string">
        <xsd:attribute name="Date" use="required">
            <xsd:simpleType base="xsd:NMTOKEN">
                <xsd:enumeration value="1997-08-25T00:00:00"/>
                <xsd:enumeration value="1997-08-26T00:00:00"/>
            </xsd:simpleType>
        </xsd:attribute>
    </xsd:complexType>
    <xsd:element name="root">
        <xsd:complexType content="elementOnly">
            <xsd:sequence>
                <xsd:element name="Customer" type="CustomerType" minOccurs="1"
                 maxOccurs="unbounded"/>
            </xsd:sequence>
            <xsd:attribute name="xmlns:xsi" type="xsd:uriReference"
             use="default" value="http://www.w3.org/1999/XMLSchema-instance"/>
            <xsd:attribute name="xsi:noNamespaceSchemaLocation"
             type="xsd:string"/>
            <xsd:attribute name="xsi:schemaLocation" type="xsd:string"/>
        </xsd:complexType>
    </xsd:element>
</xsd:schema>
```

The length of this document and the number of tags may be a little intimidating, but it's my guess that, once you sit down and adjust to the new way of doing things, you'll find this actually easier to read. It's more verbose for sure, but most of the things that actually place requirements on our XML document are in easy-to-read attributes.

From reading this document, we can see that:

- ❑ We can set more precise controls on the number of sub-elements any particular element has.
- ❑ We can build types on top of types – for example, the `CustomerType` here makes use of the `NoteType` that is defined in the same document. We can set up enumerated lists to choose from.

All this without even breaking into a sweat.

A Quick Word on DTDs/Schemas and Performance

All that work of checking and double-checking a document can really add some serious overhead to your system (I've heard as much as 30%, but I can't say that I've tested it). With this in mind, you may want to think about how to get the best of both worlds – data that you feel comfortable about (that usually means validating) and performance your users can live with.

Generally speaking, a good way to approach things is to only apply DTDs and schemas during the test phase as long as the data you're dealing with is coming from a controlled source. For example, if you have a program that is generating the XML, then, if you test and don't ever find validation errors, your code is probably going to consistently give you good XML. Think about just "trusting" things and removing the validation (by removing the reference to the DTD).

While this is great for data that you have a lot of control over – for example on the SQL Server based queries that we'll be looking at in the next chapter – avoid removing validation if the XML you're dealing with comes from some other source. For example, you may be accepting an XML document that you plan to parse in the DOM and then update some things on your system – who knows when the information that is being sent to you is going to change? Keeping the validation on in these scenarios can save you a fortune in updates that corrupt your system.

Transformations – XSLT

This takes us to the last but by far and away the most complex of the things we're dealing with in this chapter.

The **Extensible Stylesheet Language Transformation** side of things is something of a little extra toss into the XML world that increases the power of XML multifold. You see, using **XSLT**, we can transform our XML document into other forms.

To get us going with a quick start here, let's take a look at an XML document that I've produced from the `Northwind` database:

```
<?xml version="1.0" encoding="iso-8859-1"?>
<root>
    <Customer CustomerID="ALFKI" CompanyName="Alfreds Futterkiste">
        <Products ProductID="28" ProductName="Rössle Sauerkraut"/>
        <Products ProductID="39" ProductName="Chartreuse verte"/>
```

```
            <Products ProductID="46" ProductName="Spegesild"/>
    </Customer>
    <Customer CustomerID="BLONP" CompanyName="Blondesddsl père et fils">
        <Products ProductID="28" ProductName="Rössle Sauerkraut"/>
        <Products ProductID="29" ProductName="Thüringer Rostbratwurst"/>
        <Products ProductID="31" ProductName="Gorgonzola Telino"/>
        <Products ProductID="38" ProductName="Côte de Blaye"/>
        <Products ProductID="39" ProductName="Chartreuse verte"/>
        <Products ProductID="41" ProductName="Jack&apos;s New England Clam
          Chowder"/>
        <Products ProductID="46" ProductName="Spegesild"/>
        <Products ProductID="49" ProductName="Maxilaku"/>
    </Customer>
</root>
```

What we have here is something XML does very well – keep hierarchies. In this case, we have a situation where customers have ordered different products. What our XML document is laid out to tell us is what products our customers have purchased. It seems like a reasonable question – doesn't it?

Now, time for me to twist things on you a bit – what if I change the question to be more along the lines of, "Which customers have ordered each product?" Now our perspective has changed mightily. At this point, a much better hierarchy would be one that had the products on the outside and the customers on the inside. Under that scenario, it would be our customers (rather than our products) that were repeated multiple times (once for each product), but it would get more to the root of our question.

With XML coupled with XSL transformations, this is no big deal. You see, I don't want to change the data that I'm looking at – I just need to *transform* my XML document so that I can look at it differently.

> *Don't confuse my saying the way I "look" at the data to mean how I visually look at it – what I'm talking about is more of how the data is perceived. Part of that is just how ready the data is to be used in a particular fashion. With our customers at the top of the hierarchy, our data doesn't seem very ready to answer questions that are product focused. What I need is to change the data so it is product focused – just like my questions.*

The code that will transform our piece of XML is the following XSL stylesheet. As it's also an XML-based solution, needless to say, it has a lot of tags in it:

```
<?xml version="1.0"?>
<xsl:stylesheet version="1.0" xmlns:xsl="http://www.w3.org/1999/XSL/Transform">
<xsl:output method="xml" indent="yes"/>

<xsl:template match="/">
<root>
<xsl:for-each
select="//Customer/Products[not(@ProductID=preceding::Products/@ProductID)]">
    <Products><xsl:apply-templates select="@*"/>
    <xsl:variable name="prod-code" select="@ProductID"/>
    <xsl:for-each select="//Customer[Products/@ProductID = $prod-code]">
        <Customer><xsl:apply-templates select="@*"/></Customer>
    </xsl:for-each>
    </Products>
</xsl:for-each>
```

```
    </root>
  </xsl:template>


  <xsl:template match="@*">
    <xsl:attribute name="{name()}"><xsl:value-of select="."/></xsl:attribute>
  </xsl:template>

</xsl:stylesheet>
```

Combining our original XML file with this XSL stylesheet gives the following output. It's the exact same data, but with it transformed into another look:

```
<?xml version="1.0" encoding="utf-8"?>
<root>
<Products ProductID="28" ProductName="Rössle Sauerkraut">
<Customer CustomerID="ALFKI" CompanyName="Alfreds Futterkiste"/>
<Customer CustomerID="BLONP" CompanyName="Blondesddsl père et fils"/>
</Products>
<Products ProductID="39" ProductName="Chartreuse verte">
<Customer CustomerID="ALFKI" CompanyName="Alfreds Futterkiste"/>
<Customer CustomerID="BLONP" CompanyName="Blondesddsl père et fils"/>
</Products>
<Products ProductID="46" ProductName="Spegesild">
<Customer CustomerID="ALFKI" CompanyName="Alfreds Futterkiste"/>
<Customer CustomerID="BLONP" CompanyName="Blondesddsl père et fils"/>
</Products>
<Products ProductID="29" ProductName="Thüringer Rostbratwurst">
<Customer CustomerID="BLONP" CompanyName="Blondesddsl père et fils"/>
</Products>
<Products ProductID="31" ProductName="Gorgonzola Telino">
<Customer CustomerID="BLONP" CompanyName="Blondesddsl père et fils"/>
</Products>
<Products ProductID="38" ProductName="Côte de Blaye">
<Customer CustomerID="BLONP" CompanyName="Blondesddsl père et fils"/>
</Products>
<Products ProductID="41" ProductName="Jack's New England Clam Chowder">
<Customer CustomerID="BLONP" CompanyName="Blondesddsl père et fils"/>
</Products>
<Products ProductID="49" ProductName="Maxilaku">
<Customer CustomerID="BLONP" CompanyName="Blondesddsl père et fils"/>
</Products>
</root>
```

Again, this is the same data – just from a different perspective.

This output was obtained using a parser called **xt**, an open source XSLT processor developed by James Clark, the editor of the XSLT spec. It can be downloaded from http://www.jclark.com/xml/xt.html. (Note that the encoding in the original XML file is set to iso-8859-1 as opposed to the usual UTF-8, to cope with the foreign characters.)

> **Don't get bogged down in the details of this code. Remember, this isn't an XSLT book –
> you can check out *XSLT Programmer's Reference* (Wrox, ISBN 1-861003-12-9) for that.
> Instead, what you should be focusing on is what can be done using XSLT. We will be
> applying some real-life examples of this directly to our SQL output in the next chapter.**

OK, so let's move on to an example that you can actually test out yourself. You can either enter this
code directly or just download it from www.wrox.com and watch it fly.

What we want to do is focus in on a few XSLT basics that we can use to cover a fair number of
circumstances. This will at least let you get a feel for what XSLT is all about, and you can then decide
for yourself whether it's something you need to be learning more of.

First of all, let's start with a little XML. This particular document is pretty simple, but it will meet our
needs for this example:

```xml
<?xml version="1.0" encoding="UTF-8"?>
<Root>
    <Products ProductName="Aniseed Syrup" UnitPrice="10" UnitsInStock="13"/>
    <Products ProductName="Boston Crab Meat" UnitPrice="18.4"
     UnitsInStock="123"/>
    <Products ProductName="Camembert Pierrot" UnitPrice="34"
     UnitsInStock="19"/>
    <Products ProductName="Carnarvon Tigers" UnitPrice="62.5"
     UnitsInStock="42"/>
</Root>
```

What we're going to do in this example is twofold. If you haven't downloaded the code from Wrox, save
this off to a file called `CatalogTransform.xml` – that's step 1. Now navigate directly to the file using
Internet Explorer. IE should bring up the file and show it to you in a form that isn't much different from
what you see above. IE is showing you the raw XML, with the exception of a little color-coding that IE
does to all XML files that it reads in directly:

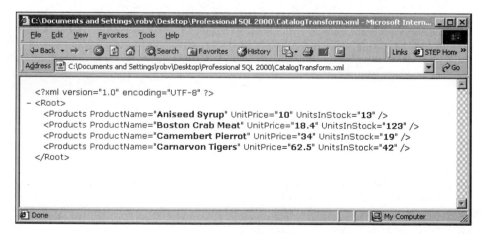

Next, we need to create our XSLT document. We'll start by looking at the code, and then go through what it does for us:

```xml
<?xml version='1.0' encoding='UTF-8'?>
<xsl:stylesheet xmlns:xsl="http://www.w3.org/1999/XSL/Transform" version="1.0">

    <xsl:template match = '*'>
        <xsl:apply-templates />
    </xsl:template>
    <xsl:template match = "Products">
       <TR>
         <TD><xsl:value-of select = '@ProductName' /></TD>
         <TD align="right" width="75">
           <B>
           <xsl:value-of select = "format-number(@UnitPrice, '#.00')" />
           </B>
         </TD>
          <td align="right" width="75">
            <xsl:value-of select='@UnitsInStock' />
          </td>
       </TR>
    </xsl:template>
    <xsl:template match = '/'>
      <HTML>
        <HEAD>
          <TITLE>Northwind Traders Online Catalog</TITLE>
          <STYLE>th { background-color: #CCCCCC }</STYLE>
        </HEAD>
        <BODY>
            <TABLE border='0' width="*">
                    <TR><TH colspan='3'>Products</TH></TR>
                    <TR>
                      <TH>Product Name</TH>
                       <th>Price</th><th>Quantity On Hand</th>
                    </TR>
                    <xsl:apply-templates select = 'Root' />
            </TABLE>
        </BODY>
      </HTML>
    </xsl:template>
</xsl:stylesheet>
```

OK, the first two lines of the stylesheet are references that identify it as an XML document (which it is) and provide a reference back to the rules of XSLT (which are kept at the W3C web site).

Next up is the beginning of our effort to match things up to templates that can be applied to parts of the document. This first attempt at a match includes a wild card:

```xml
<xsl:template match = '*'>
    <xsl:apply-templates />
</xsl:template>
```

What we're saying here is that we want to run this template against everything. It, in turn, kicks off the other templates in our stylesheet:

```
<xsl:template match = "Products">
  <TR>
    <TD><xsl:value-of select = '@ProductName' /></TD>
    <TD align="right" width="75">
      <B>
      <xsl:value-of select = "format-number(@UnitPrice, '#.00')"/>
      </B>
    </TD>
    <td align="right" width="75">
      <xsl:value-of select='@UnitsInStock' />
    </td>
  </TR>
</xsl:template>
```

Now things are getting more interesting. For this block of code (beginning of the xsl:template element to its ending tag), we're saying that we only want to run this template for elements of the type Products. For each product we have, we need to retrieve the value in the attribute called ProductName. Likewise, we will also retrieve the values for the attributes called UnitPrice and UnitsInStock.

What's happening here is a substitution process. We have a template that will be applied to every product. The value looked up for each of the value-of tags will be substituted in the place of that tag. A slight formatting change is made before one of the substitutions (UnitPrice is made consistently two decimal places) and, beyond that, the regular HTML tags I've inserted are just passed through to the client.

Next comes a match value that doesn't seem to agree with anything:

```
<xsl:template match = '/'>
  <HTML>
    <HEAD>
      <TITLE>Northwind Traders Online Catalog</TITLE>
      <STYLE>th { background-color: #CCCCCC }</STYLE>
    </HEAD>
    <BODY>
          <TABLE border='0' width="*">
            <TR><TH colspan='3'>Products</TH></TR>
            <TR>
             <TH>Product Name</TH>
             <th>Price</th><th>Quantity On Hand</th>
            </TR>
            <xsl:apply-templates select = 'Root' />
          </TABLE>
    </BODY>
  </HTML>
</xsl:template>
```

The slash symbol (/) is a substitute for the root node. If we say that we want our template to apply on a match of "/", then that match will be applied to the root node (and, since root nodes are unique, that means the template in question will only be applied once). This gives us a way of matching the all important root node without necessarily having to know what it was called.

In this case, we are applying our header HTML and then making reference to our other matches.

Reviewing some Key XSL Elements

Just to review, let's look back at a couple of key tags that we'll use repeatedly in the next chapter:

`<xsl:template match=?????>`	Provides the layout to be outputted whenever a match is found. If there are multiple matches, then the values will be sent out multiple times.
`<xsl:value-of select="@?????">`	Looks up a named attribute value for the current node and substitutes it for the current tag.
`<xsl:apply-templates select="?????">`	Applies the templates that match all nodes below the select argument.
`format-number(value, format)`	Formats a numeric value as specified by the format expression.

Summary

Well, there you have an extreme whirlwind tour of XML, DTDs, schemas, and XSL transformations. It is impossible in one chapter to address a topic as broad as XML and its related technologies – however, hopefully this chapter has at least provided an insight into what XML is all about and what is involved in making use of it at the most basic level.

All of these issues should be beaten into your brain a little bit more as we go through the next chapter, where we will get some real experience dealing with XML data and utilizing a special breed of XML documents to create queries and return web pages directly from the SQL Server.

XML is one of the most important technologies to hit the industry in the last 10 years or more. It provides a flexible, very transportable way of describing data. This ease of description will help to facilitate not only the web site development that you hear so much about, but also the kind of behind-the-scenes information exchange that businesses have wanted for a very long time indeed.

In our next chapter, we will be focusing on what SQL Server can do for us specifically in the area of XML integration. We will explore all the different options that are available, their security ramifications, and how we can utilize them to create real solutions.

Online discussion at http://p2p.wrox.com

20

Integration of XML into SQL Server

Well, we've done some of the preliminaries. Our last chapter was a very, very brief look at XML, and the technologies that most closely surround it that relate to our little SQL Server world. With that now accomplished, we're ready to turn the coolness factor up to maximum and maybe even add in an extra power amp to hit all new levels of cool.

New with SQL Server 2000 is a substantial level of direct integration between the old SQL Server that we know and love and the new world of XML. The concept is multi-faceted, but still pretty simple:

❑   XML is all about information

❑   XML is here to stay

❑   SQL Server is all about information

❑   XML does some things better than SQL Server

❑   Ah, but SQL Server still does a lot of things better than XML

❑   SQL Server is here to stay

❑   The two will need to interact in some fashion – let's take as much out of the middle of that interaction as possible!

People interact with XML in a lot of different ways. Obviously, the most public of these methods is via some sort of web activity. Indeed, to a large extent, we will make use of web examples in this chapter. But that's really only one way of many.

Perhaps the biggest opportunity for XML lies in business-to-business communication. If two businesses can agree on how they are going to format their XML, then they can trade information. Even if they can't agree, as long as they can output/input XML (and there's *always* some way to do that) and the same basic content is in their XML output, then one side or the other (or both) can always style the XML into whatever format they need.

So, how do these businesses communicate? Well, in just about any fashion imaginable:

❑   e-Mail

❑   FTP

❑   HTTP

❑   Leased line

❑   Yes, even floppy disk or CD-ROM with your favorite air express service (a.k.a. "sneaker-net")

There are probably a thousand more variations on this basic theme.

SQL Server addresses this issue by offering to serve up and accept XML in multiple ways. The one getting all the press is HTTP access directly in the URL, but SQL Server has more to offer than just HTTP access. The ADO 2.6 library has added streaming functionality, which allows us to escape much of the overhead associated with ADO recordsets and, instead, stream the actual XML directly to a client.

It really doesn't stop there though – Microsoft has elected to take the XML integration portion of SQL Server and change it to a "Web Release" format. Microsoft's notion here is that changes in XML-related technologies are simply moving too fast for the multi-year release cycles used by most products. What this means is that the functionality in the XML-integration side of SQL Server is going to be changing and expanding regularly.

> *Let me leverage this last bit of information to apologize in advance for any material that becomes out of date over the life of this book. Microsoft was changing the way some things worked even as I was writing the final chapters of this book (and the RTM had been out for a while at the time). What I'm presenting here is a relatively complete and accurate portrayal of the functionality as it was available when I wrote this, but be sure to check out SQL Server sites such as* http://msdn.microsoft.com/sqlserver *to see what updates have been added. I also hope to keep my web site reasonably up to date with information on newer functionality that Microsoft adds, but I simply can't promise that at this time.*

In this chapter, we'll be taking a look not only at the access methods that are available to us, but also the different options in terms of how to format our data requests and updates. Among the things we'll cover are:

❑   Syntactical issues, including:

   ❑   The FOR XML clause

   ❑   OPENXML

❑   Interaction methods, including:

   ❑   HTTP access

   ❑   Streaming access

❑   Ways of wrapping our request, including:

    ❑   Direct queries

    ❑   XML Templates

    ❑   XML Schemas

❑   And last, but not least, we'll also look at styling approaches:

    ❑   XSL directly associated through the template

    ❑   XSL applied through a DOM object

I feel the need to apologize for the client code that's going to appear in a couple of places from here until the end of the book. It was very much my goal, since the first version of this book was conceptualized, that I would remain language agnostic. I don't want the VB, C++, Java, and other. bigots of the world to decide that this isn't a book for them because it utilizes that "other" language in a few places. In the 7.0 version of this book, the only large-scale use of a client-side language was in the English Query chapter – which would make no sense without client-side code.

That said, it's impossible to be everything to everyone, and features in this release (such as XML integration) and a general desire to expand the depth of the book (more advanced DTS coverage and WMI) have forced me to include more client-side code this time. Regardless of the client language you see used here, realize that it's the concepts – which are basically the same in all languages – that I want to get across. Since I can't do it in every language, I'm going to take the ugly least common denominator approach and just use VB. While the C++ and Java enthusiasts among you may guffaw at that choice, the primary strength of VB is that it is fairly readable and cuts out most of the "set-up" stuff that is not important to the concepts that I need to get across here. In addition, some of these examples very much call for an ASP example, and that's going to force a VB approach anyway. Frankly, I'd love to do it in all the languages, but that simply is not practical – please accept my apologies for subjecting you to "that VB stuff". If any reader wants to take the time to convert the examples provided in this book to C++, Delphi, Java, or whatever, I will be more than happy (grateful too) to add them to my web site (with appropriate credits) for other users to learn from.

The FOR XML Clause

This clause is at the root of most of the different integration models currently available. With the exception of XML Mapping Schemas and the use of XPath, FOR XML will serve as the actual way of telling SQL Server that it's XML that you want back, not the more typical result set. It is essentially just an option added onto the end of the existing T-SQL SELECT statement.

Let's look back at the SELECT statement syntax from Chapter 4:

```
SELECT <column list>
[FROM <source table(s)>]
[WHERE <restrictive condition>]
[GROUP BY <column name or expression using a column in the SELECT list>
[HAVING <restrictive condition based on the GROUP BY results>]
[ORDER BY <column list>]
[FOR XML {RAW|AUTO|EXPLICIT}[, XMLDATA][, ELEMENTS][, BINARY base64]]
[OPTION (<query hint>, [, ...n])]
```

Most of this should seem pretty trivial by now – after all, we've been using this syntax throughout a lot of hard chapters by this time – but it's time to focus in on that FOR XML line…

FOR XML provides three different initial options for how you want your XML formatted in the results:

❏ RAW: This sends each row of data in your result set back as a single data element, with the element name of "row" and with each column listed as an attribute of the "row" element. Even if you join multiple tables, RAW outputs the results with the same number of elements as you would have rows in a standard SQL query.

❏ AUTO: This option labels each element with either the name or alias of the table that the data is sourced from. If there is data output from more than one table in the query, the data from each table is split into separate, nested elements. If AUTO is used, then an additional option, ELEMENTS, is also supported if you would like column data presented as elements rather than as attributes.

❏ EXPLICIT: This one is certainly the most complex to format your query with, but the end result is that you have a high degree of control over what the XML looks like in the end. With this option, you define a hierarchy to the data that's being returned, and then format your query such that each piece of data belongs to a specific hierarchy level (and gets assigned a tag accordingly) as desired.

> *Note that none of these options provide the required root element. If you want the XML document to be considered to be "well formed", then you will need to wrap the results with a proper opening and closing tag for your root element. While this is in some ways a hassle, it is also a benefit – it means that you can build more complex XML by stringing multiple XML queries together and wrapping the different results into one XML file.*

In addition to the three major formatting options, there are three other optional parameters that further modify the output that SQL Server provides in an XML Query:

❏ XMLDATA: This tells SQL Server that you would like to apply an XML schema onto the front of the results. The schema will define the structure (including data types) and rules of the XML data that follows. Keep in mind that this schema, while similar, is not an exact match to the W3C spec as it is proposed at the time of this writing.

❏ ELEMENTS: This option is only available when you are using the AUTO formatting option. It tells SQL Server that you want the columns in your data returned as nested elements rather than as attributes.

❏ BINARY BASE64: This tells SQL Server to encode any binary columns (binary, varbinary, image) in base64 format. This option is implied (SQL Server will use it even if you don't state it) if you are also using the AUTO option. It is not implied, but is currently the only effective option for EXPLICIT and RAW queries – eventually, the plan is to have these two options automatically provide a URL link to the binary data (unless you choose to do the base64 encoding), but this has not yet been implemented.

Let's explore all these options in a little more detail.

RAW

This is something of the "no fuss, no muss" option. The idea here is to just get it done – no fanfare, no special formatting at all – just the absolute minimum to translate a row of relational data into an element of XML data. The element is named "row" (creative, huh?), and each column in the select list is added as an attribute using whatever name the column would have appeared with, if you had been running a more traditional SELECT statement.

> *One downside to the way in which attributes are named is that you need to make certain that every column has a name. Normally, SQL Server will just show no column heading if you perform an aggregation or other calculated column and don't provide an alias – when doing XML queries, everything MUST have a name, so don't forget to alias calculated columns.*

So, let's start things off with something relatively simple. Imagine that our manager has asked us to provide a query that lists a few customers' orders – say CustomerIDs ALFKI and ANTON. After cruising through just the first five or so chapters of the book, you would probably say "No Problem!" and supply something like:

```
USE Northwind

SELECT Customers.CustomerID,
  Customers.CompanyName,
  Orders.OrderID,
  Orders.OrderDate
FROM Customers
JOIN Orders
  ON Customers.CustomerID = Orders.CustomerID
WHERE Customers.CustomerID = 'ALFKI' OR Customers.CustomerID = 'ANTON'
```

So, you go hand your boss the results:

ANTON Antonio Moreno Taquería	10365	1996-11-27 00:00:00.000	
ANTON Antonio Moreno Taquería	10507	1997-04-15 00:00:00.000	
...			
...			
ALFKI Alfreds Futterkiste	11081	2000-07-22 00:00:00.000	
ALFKI Alfreds Futterkiste	11087	2000-08-05 17:37:52.520	

Easy, right? Well, now the boss comes back and says, "Great – now I'll just have Billy Bob write something to turn this into XML – too bad that will probably take a day or two." This is your cue to step in and say, "Oh, why didn't you say so?" and simply add three key words:

```
USE Northwind

SELECT Customers.CustomerID,
  Customers.CompanyName,
  Orders.OrderID,
  Orders.OrderDate
FROM Customers
JOIN Orders
  ON Customers.CustomerID = Orders.CustomerID
WHERE Customers.CustomerID = 'ALFKI' OR Customers.CustomerID = 'ANTON'
FOR XML RAW
```

You have just made the boss very happy. The output is a one-to-one match versus what we would have seen in the result set had we ran just a standard SQL query:

```
<row CustomerID="ANTON" CompanyName="Antonio Moreno Taquería" OrderID="10365" OrderDate="1996-11-27T00:00:00" />
<row CustomerID="ANTON" CompanyName="Antonio Moreno Taquería" OrderID="10507" OrderDate="1997-04-15T00:00:00" />
<row CustomerID="ANTON" CompanyName="Antonio Moreno Taquería" OrderID="10535" OrderDate="1997-05-13T00:00:00" />
<row CustomerID="ANTON" CompanyName="Antonio Moreno Taquería" OrderID="10573" OrderDate="1997-06-19T00:00:00" />
<row CustomerID="ALFKI" CompanyName="Alfreds Futterkiste" OrderID="10643" OrderDate="1997-08-25T00:00:00" />
<row CustomerID="ANTON" CompanyName="Antonio Moreno Taquería" OrderID="10677" OrderDate="1997-09-22T00:00:00" />
<row CustomerID="ANTON" CompanyName="Antonio Moreno Taquería" OrderID="10682" OrderDate="1997-09-25T00:00:00" />
<row CustomerID="ALFKI" CompanyName="Alfreds Futterkiste" OrderID="10692" OrderDate="1997-10-03T00:00:00" />
<row CustomerID="ALFKI" CompanyName="Alfreds Futterkiste" OrderID="10702" OrderDate="1997-10-13T00:00:00" />
<row CustomerID="ALFKI" CompanyName="Alfreds Futterkiste" OrderID="10835" OrderDate="1998-01-15T00:00:00" />
<row CustomerID="ANTON" CompanyName="Antonio Moreno Taquería" OrderID="10856" OrderDate="1998-01-28T00:00:00" />
<row CustomerID="ALFKI" CompanyName="Alfreds Futterkiste" OrderID="10952" OrderDate="1998-03-16T00:00:00" />
<row CustomerID="ALFKI" CompanyName="Alfreds Futterkiste" OrderID="11011" OrderDate="1998-04-09T00:00:00" />
```

Be aware that, if you cut and paste this from Query Analyzer into an XML parser of some kind, you may wind up with an error. Query Analyzer has a nasty habit of inserting a carriage return once the output for any particular line goes beyond a certain length. If this happens to you, you'll need to take the carriage return out manually in order for the parser to consider the XML to be well formed. Also, Query Analyzer will truncate any column where the length exceeds the number set in the Results tab (maximum is 8,192). Both of these problems exist in the Results window (grid or text) and if you output directly to a file. This is a problem with the tool – not SQL Server itself. If you use another method to retrieve results (HTTP access, stream object in ADO), you shouldn't encounter either of these problems.

We have one element in XML for each row of data our query produced. All column information, regardless of what table was the source of the data, is represented as an attribute of the "row" element. The downside of this is that we haven't represented the true hierarchical nature of our data – orders are only placed by customers. The upside, however, is that the XML DOM – if that's the model you're using – is going to be much less deep and, hence, will have a slightly smaller footprint in memory and perform better, depending on what you're doing.

AUTO

AUTO takes a somewhat different approach to our data from RAW. AUTO tries to format things a little better for us – naming elements based on the table (or the table alias if you use one). In addition, AUTO recognizes the notion that our data probably has some underlying hierarchical notion to it that is supposed to be represented in the XML.

Let's go back to our customer orders example from the last section. This time, we'll make use of the AUTO option, so we can see the difference versus the rather plain output we got with RAW:

```
USE Northwind

SELECT Customers.CustomerID,
Customers.CompanyName,
   Orders.OrderID,
   Orders.OrderDate
FROM Customers
JOIN Orders
   ON Customers.CustomerID = Orders.CustomerID
WHERE Customers.CustomerID = 'ALFKI' OR Customers.CustomerID = 'ANTON'
FOR XML AUTO
```

The first apparent difference is that the element name has changed to be that of the name or alias of the table that is the source of the data, but, another even more significant difference appears when we look at the XML more thoroughly (I have again cleaned up the output a bit for clarity):

```
<Customers CustomerID="ANTON" CompanyName="Antonio Moreno Taquería">
  <Orders OrderID="10365" OrderDate="1996-11-27T00:00:00" />
  <Orders OrderID="10507" OrderDate="1997-04-15T00:00:00" />
  <Orders OrderID="10535" OrderDate="1997-05-13T00:00:00" />
  <Orders OrderID="10573" OrderDate="1997-06-19T00:00:00" />
</Customers>
<Customers CustomerID="ALFKI" CompanyName="Alfreds Futterkiste">
  <Orders OrderID="10643" OrderDate="1997-08-25T00:00:00" />
</Customers>
<Customers CustomerID="ANTON" CompanyName="Antonio Moreno Taquería">
  <Orders OrderID="10677" OrderDate="1997-09-22T00:00:00" />
  <Orders OrderID="10682" OrderDate="1997-09-25T00:00:00" />
</Customers>
<Customers CustomerID="ALFKI" CompanyName="Alfreds Futterkiste">
  <Orders OrderID="10692" OrderDate="1997-10-03T00:00:00" />
  <Orders OrderID="10702" OrderDate="1997-10-13T00:00:00" />
  <Orders OrderID="10835" OrderDate="1998-01-15T00:00:00" />
</Customers>
<Customers CustomerID="ANTON" CompanyName="Antonio Moreno Taquería">
  <Orders OrderID="10856" OrderDate="1998-01-28T00:00:00" />
</Customers>
<Customers CustomerID="ALFKI" CompanyName="Alfreds Futterkiste">
  <Orders OrderID="10952" OrderDate="1998-03-16T00:00:00" />
  <Orders OrderID="11011" OrderDate="1998-04-09T00:00:00" />
</Customers>
```

Data that is sourced from our second table (as determined by the SELECT list) is nested inside the data sourced from the first table. In this case, our Orders elements are nested inside our Customers elements. If a column from the Orders table were listed first in our select list, then Customers would be nested inside Orders.

Pay attention to this business of the ordering of your SELECT *list! In our last chapter, I showed examples of XML with* Customers *being the parent of* Products. *I also showed you how we could style that same data into a different hierarchy –* Products *being the parent of* Customers. *Think about the primary question your XML query is meant to solve. Arrange your* SELECT *list such that the style that it produces is fitting for the goal of your XML. Sure, you could always style it into the different form – but why do that if SQL Server could have just produced it for you that way in the first place?*

The downside to using AUTO is that the resulting XML data model ends up being slightly more complex. Also, AUTO is currently not compatible with a GROUP BY clause. The upside is that the data is more explicitly broken up into a hierarchical model. This makes life easier for situations where the elements are more significant breaking points – such as where you have a doubly sorted report (e.g. **Orders** sorted within **Customers**).

EXPLICIT

The word "explicit" is an interesting choice for this option – it loosely describes the kind of language you're likely to use while trying to create your query. The EXPLICIT option takes much more effort to prepare, but it also rewards that effort with very fine granularity of control over what's an element and what's an attribute, as well as what elements are nested in what other elements.

EXPLICIT enables you to define each level of the hierarchy and how each level is going to look. In order to define the hierarchy, you create what is internally called the **universal table**. The universal table is, in many respects, just like any other result set you might produce in SQL Server. It is usually produced by making use of UNION statements to piece it together one level at a time, but you could, for example, build much of the data in a UDF and then make a SELECT against that to produce the final XML. The big difference between the universal table and a more traditional result set is that you must provide sufficient meta-data right within your result set so that SQL Server can then transform that result set into an XML document in the schema you desire.

What do I mean by sufficient meta-data? Well, to give you an idea of just how complex this can be, let's look at a real universal table – one used by a code example we'll examine a little later in the section:

Tag	Parent	Customer!1!CustomerID	Customer!1!CompanyName	Order!2!OrderID	Order!2!OrderDate
1	NULL	ALFKI	Alfreds Futterkiste	NULL	NULL
2	1	ALFKI	Alfreds Futterkiste	10643	1997-08-25 00:00:00.000
2	1	ALFKI	Alfreds Futterkiste	10692	1997-10-03 00:00:00.000
2	1	ALFKI	Alfreds Futterkiste	10702	1997-10-13 00:00:00.000
2	1	ALFKI	Alfreds Futterkiste	10835	1998-01-15 00:00:00.000
2	1	ALFKI	Alfreds Futterkiste	10952	1998-03-16 00:00:00.000
2	1	ALFKI	Alfreds Futterkiste	11011	1998-04-09 00:00:00.000
2	1	ALFKI	Alfreds Futterkiste	11078	1999-05-01 00:00:00.000
2	1	ALFKI	Alfreds Futterkiste	11079	NULL
2	1	ALFKI	Alfreds Futterkiste	11080	2000-07-22 16:48:00.000

Tag	Parent	Customer!1!CustomerID	Customer!1!CompanyName	Order!2!OrderID	Order!2!OrderDate
2	1	ALFKI	Alfreds Futterkiste	11081	2000-07-22 00:00:00.000
2	1	ALFKI	Alfreds Futterkiste	11087	2000-08-05 17:37:52.520
1	NULL	ANTON	Antonio Moreno Taquería	NULL	NULL
2	1	ANTON	Antonio Moreno Taquería	10365	1996-11-27 00:00:00.000
2	1	ANTON	Antonio Moreno Taquería	10507	1997-04-15 00:00:00.000
2	1	ANTON	Antonio Moreno Taquería	10535	1997-05-13 00:00:00.000
2	1	ANTON	Antonio Moreno Taquería	10573	1997-06-19 00:00:00.000
2	1	ANTON	Antonio Moreno Taquería	10677	1997-09-22 00:00:00.000
2	1	ANTON	Antonio Moreno Taquería	10682	1997-09-25 00:00:00.000
2	1	ANTON	Antonio Moreno Taquería	10856	1998-01-28 00:00:00.000

This is what the universal table we would need to build would look like in order to make our EXPLICIT return exactly the same results as we received with our AUTO query in the last example.

> *Your first inclination might be to say, "Hey, if this is just producing the same thing as AUTO, why use it?" Well, this particular example happens to be producible using AUTO – I'm using this one on purpose to illustrate some functional differences compared with something you've already seen. We will, however, see later in this section that EXPLICIT will allow us to do the "extras" in formatting that aren't possible with AUTO or RAW – so please bear with me on this one...*

You should note several things about this result set:

❑ It has two special meta-data columns – **Tag** and **Parent** – added to it that do not, otherwise, relate to the data (they didn't come from table columns)

❑ The actual column names are adhering to a special format (which happens to supply additional meta-data)

❑ The data has been ordered based on the hierarchy

Each of these items is critical to our end result, so, before we start working a complete example, let's look at what we need to know to build it.

Tag and Parent

We saw in our last chapter that elements can contain other elements, but that they cannot overlap. This means that XML is naturally hierarchical in nature (elements are contained within other elements, which essentially creates a parent-child relationship). Tag and Parent are columns that define the relationship of each row to the element hierarchy. Each row is assigned to a certain tag level (which will later have an element name assigned to it) – that level, as you might expect, goes in the Tag column. Parent then supplies reference information that indicates what the next highest level in the hierarchy is – by doing this, SQL Server knows at what level this row needs to be nested or assigned to as an attribute (what it's going to be – element or attribute – will be figured out based on the column name – but we'll get to that in our next section). If Parent is NULL, then SQL Server knows that this row must be a top-level element or an attribute of that element.

So, if we had data that looked like this:

Tag	Parent
1	NULL
2	1

...then the first row would be related to a top-level element (an attribute of the outer element or the element itself), and the second would be related to an element that was nested inside the top-level element (its Parent value of 1 matches with the Tag value of the first.

Column Naming

Frankly, this was the most confusing part of all when I first started looking at EXPLICIT. While Tag and Parent have nice neat demarcation points (they are each their own column), the name takes several pieces of meta-data and crams them together as one thing – the only way to tell where one stops and the next begins is that we separate them by an exclamation mark (!).

The naming format looks like this:

```
<element name>!<tag>![<attribute name>]
    [!{element|hide|ID|IDREF|IDREFS|xml|xmltext|cdata}]
```

The element name is, of course, just that – what you want to be the name of the element in the XML. For any given tag level, once you define a column with one name, any other column with that same tag must have the same name as the previous column(s) with that tag number. So: if we have a column already defined as [MyElement!2!MyCol], then another column could be named [MyElement!2!MyOtherCol] but [SomeOtherName!2!MyOtherCol] could not be.

The tag relates the column to rows with a matching tag number. When SQL Server looks at the universal table, it reads the tag number, and then analyzes the columns with the same tag number. So, when SQL Server sees the row:

Tag	Parent	Customer!1!CustomerID	Customer!1!CompanyName	Order!2!OrderID	Order!2!OrderDate
1	NULL	ALFKI	Alfreds Futterkiste	NULL	NULL

...it can look at the tag number, see that it is 1, and know that it should process Customer!1!CustomerID and Customer!1!CompanyName, but that it doesn't have to process Order!2!OrderID, for example.

That takes us to the attribute name, which begins the next phase of getting more complex (hey, we still have one more to go after this!). If you do not specify a directive (which comes next), then the attribute is required and is the name of the XML attribute that this column will supply a value for. The attribute will be in the XML as part of the element specified in the column name.

If you do specify a directive, then the attribute falls into one of three different camps:

❑   It's prohibited – that is, you must leave the attribute blank (you do still use an exclamation mark (!) to mark its place though). This is the case if you use a CDATA directive.

❑   It's optional – that is, you can supply the attribute, but don't have to. What happens in this case varies depending on the directive that you've chosen.

❑   It's still required – this is true for the elements and xml directives. In this case, the name of the attribute will become the name of a totally new element that will be created as a result of the elements or xml directive.

So, now that we have enough of the naming down to meet the minimum requirements for a query, let's go ahead and look at an example of what kind of a query produces what kind of results.

We will start with a query to produce the same basic data that we used in our RAW and AUTO examples. You will notice that EXPLICIT has a much bigger impact on the code than we saw when we went with RAW and AUTO. With both RAW and AUTO, we added the FOR XML clause at the end, and we were largely done. With EXPLICIT, we will quickly see that we need to entirely rethink the way our query comes together.

It looks like this (yuck):

```
USE Northwind

SELECT 1                          as Tag,
       NULL                       as Parent,
       Customers.CustomerID       as [Customer!1!CustomerID],
       Customers.CompanyName       as [Customer!1!CompanyName],
       NULL                       as [Order!2!OrderID],
       NULL                       as [Order!2!OrderDate]
FROM Customers
WHERE Customers.CustomerID = 'ALFKI' OR Customers.CustomerID = 'ANTON'

UNION ALL

SELECT 2,
       1,
       Customers.CustomerID,
       Customers.CompanyName,
       Orders.OrderID,
       Orders.OrderDate
FROM Customers
JOIN Orders
ON Customers.CustomerID = Orders.CustomerID
WHERE Customers.CustomerID = 'ALFKI' OR Customers.CustomerID = 'ANTON'
ORDER BY [Customer!1!CustomerID], [Order!2!OrderID]
FOR XML EXPLICIT
```

> Notice that we only use the **FOR XML** clause once – after the last query in the **UNION**.

I reiterate – yuck! But, ugly as it is, with just a few changes, I could change my XML into forms that AUTO wouldn't give me.

As a fairly simple illustration, let's make a couple of small alterations to our requirements for this query. What if we decided that we wanted the CompanyName information to be an attribute of the Order element rather than (or, if we wished, in addition to) the Customer element? With AUTO, we would need some trickery in order to get this (for every row, we would need to look up the Company again using a correlated subquery – AUTO won't let you use the same value in two places). If you had these multiple lookups, your code could get very complex – indeed, you might not be able to get what you're after at all. With EXPLICIT, this is all relatively easy (at least, by EXPLICIT's definition of easy).

To do this with EXPLICIT, we just need to reference the CompanyName in our SELECT list again, but associate the new instance of it with Orders instead of Customers:

```
USE Northwind

SELECT 1                        as Tag,
      NULL                      as Parent,
      Customers.CustomerID      as [Customer!1!CustomerID],
      Customers.CompanyName     as [Customer!1!CompanyName],
      NULL                      as [Order!2!OrderID],
      NULL                      as [Order!2!OrderDate],
      NULL                      as [Order!2!CompanyName]
FROM Customers
WHERE Customers.CustomerID = 'ALFKI' OR Customers.CustomerID = 'ANTON'

UNION ALL

SELECT 2,
      1,
      Customers.CustomerID,
      Customers.CompanyName,
      Orders.OrderID,
      Orders.OrderDate,
      Customers.CompanyName
FROM Customers
JOIN Orders
ON Customers.CustomerID = Orders.CustomerID
WHERE Customers.CustomerID = 'ALFKI' OR Customers.CustomerID = 'ANTON'
ORDER BY [Customer!1!CustomerID], [Order!2!OrderID]
FOR XML EXPLICIT
```

Execute this, and we get pretty much the same results as before, only this time we receive the additional attribute we were looking for in our Order element:

```
<Customer CustomerID="ALFKI" CompanyName="Alfreds Futterkiste">
  <Order OrderID="10643" OrderDate="1997-08-25T00:00:00" CompanyName="Alfreds Futterkiste"
/>
  <Order OrderID="10692" OrderDate="1997-10-03T00:00:00" CompanyName="Alfreds Futterkiste"
/>
  <Order OrderID="10702" OrderDate="1997-10-13T00:00:00" CompanyName="Alfreds Futterkiste"
/>
  <Order OrderID="10835" OrderDate="1998-01-15T00:00:00" CompanyName="Alfreds Futterkiste"
/>
  <Order OrderID="10952" OrderDate="1998-03-16T00:00:00" CompanyName="Alfreds Futterkiste"
/>
  <Order OrderID="11011" OrderDate="1998-04-09T00:00:00" CompanyName="Alfreds Futterkiste"
```

```
/>
  <Order OrderID="11078" OrderDate="1999-05-01T00:00:00" CompanyName="Alfreds Futterkiste"
/>
  <Order OrderID="11079" CompanyName="Alfreds Futterkiste" />
  <Order OrderID="11080" OrderDate="2000-07-22T16:48:00" CompanyName="Alfreds Futterkiste"
/>
  <Order OrderID="11081" OrderDate="2000-07-22T00:00:00" CompanyName="Alfreds Futterkiste"
/>
  <Order OrderID="11087" OrderDate="2000-08-05T17:37:52.520" CompanyName="Alfreds
Futterkiste" />
  </Customer>
<Customer CustomerID="ANTON" CompanyName="Antonio Moreno Taquería">
  <Order OrderID="10365" OrderDate="1996-11-27T00:00:00" CompanyName="Antonio Moreno
Taquería" />
  <Order OrderID="10507" OrderDate="1997-04-15T00:00:00" CompanyName="Antonio Moreno
Taquería" />
  <Order OrderID="10535" OrderDate="1997-05-13T00:00:00" CompanyName="Antonio Moreno
Taquería" />
  <Order OrderID="10573" OrderDate="1997-06-19T00:00:00" CompanyName="Antonio Moreno
Taquería" />
  <Order OrderID="10677" OrderDate="1997-09-22T00:00:00" CompanyName="Antonio Moreno
Taquería" />
  <Order OrderID="10682" OrderDate="1997-09-25T00:00:00" CompanyName="Antonio Moreno
Taquería" />
  <Order OrderID="10856" OrderDate="1998-01-28T00:00:00" CompanyName="Antonio Moreno
Taquería" />
  </Customer>
```

> **Notice the fact that our OrderDate attribute is completely missing – you'll see that on any row where the value was NULL. XML represents NULL values by the non-existence of those values.**

This example is really just for starters. We can utilize **directives** to achieve far more flexibility – shaping and controlling both our data and our schema output (if we use the XMLDATA option).

Directives are a real pain to understand. Once you do understand them though, they aren't all that bad to deal with, although they can still be confusing at times (some of them work pretty counter-intuitively and behave differently in different situations). My personal opinion (and the members of the dev team I know are going to shoot me for saying this) is that someone at Microsoft had a really bad day and decided to make something that would inflict as much pain as he/she was feeling, but would be so cool that people wouldn't be able to help themselves but use it.

All together, there are eight possible directives you can use. Some can be used in the same level of the hierarchy – others are mutually exclusive within a given hierarchy level.

The purpose behind directives is to allow you to tweak your results. Without directives, the EXPLICIT option would have little or no value (AUTO will take care of most "real" things that you can do with EXPLICIT if you don't use directives, even though, as I indicated earlier, you sometimes have to get a little tricky). So, with this in mind, let's look at what directives are available.

Element

This is probably the easiest of all the directives to understand – all it does is indicate that you want the column in question to be added as an element rather than an attribute. The element will be added as a child to the current tag. For example, let's say that our manager from the previous examples has indicated that he needs the `OrderDate` to be represented as its own element. This can be accomplished as easily as adding the element directive to the end of our `OrderDate` field:

```
SELECT 1                        as Tag,
       NULL                     as Parent,
       Customers.CustomerID     as [Customer!1!CustomerID],
       Customers.CompanyName    as [Customer!1!CompanyName],
       NULL                     as [Order!2!OrderID],
       NULL                     as [Order!2!OrderDate!element]
FROM Customers
WHERE Customers.CustomerID = 'ALFKI' OR Customers.CustomerID = 'ANTON'

UNION ALL

SELECT 2,
       1,
       Customers.CustomerID,
       Customers.CompanyName,
       Orders.OrderID,
       Orders.OrderDate
FROM Customers
JOIN Orders
ON Customers.CustomerID = Orders.CustomerID
WHERE Customers.CustomerID = 'ALFKI' OR Customers.CustomerID = 'ANTON'
ORDER BY [Customer!1!CustomerID], [Order!2!OrderID]
FOR XML EXPLICIT
```

Suddenly, we have an extra element instead of an attribute:

```
<Customer CustomerID="ALFKI" CompanyName="Alfreds Futterkiste">
  <Order OrderID="10643">
   <OrderDate>1997-08-25T00:00:00</OrderDate>
  </Order>
  <Order OrderID="10692">
   <OrderDate>1997-10-03T00:00:00</OrderDate>
  </Order>
  <Order OrderID="10702">
   <OrderDate>1997-10-13T00:00:00</OrderDate>
  </Order>
  <Order OrderID="10835">
   <OrderDate>1998-01-15T00:00:00</OrderDate>
  </Order>
  <Order OrderID="10952">
   <OrderDate>1998-03-16T00:00:00</OrderDate>
  </Order>
  <Order OrderID="11011">
   <OrderDate>1998-04-09T00:00:00</OrderDate>
  </Order>
</Customer>
<Customer CustomerID="ANTON" CompanyName="Antonio Moreno Taquería">
```

```
<Order OrderID="10365">
  <OrderDate>1996-11-27T00:00:00</OrderDate>
</Order>
<Order OrderID="10507">
    <OrderDate>1997-04-15T00:00:00</OrderDate>
</Order>
<Order OrderID="10535">
  <OrderDate>1997-05-13T00:00:00</OrderDate>
</Order>
<Order OrderID="10573">
    <OrderDate>1997-06-19T00:00:00</OrderDate>
</Order>
<Order OrderID="10677">
    <OrderDate>1997-09-22T00:00:00</OrderDate>
</Order>
<Order OrderID="10682">
  <OrderDate>1997-09-25T00:00:00</OrderDate>
</Order>
<Order OrderID="10856">
  <OrderDate>1998-01-28T00:00:00</OrderDate>
</Order>
</Customer>
```

Xml

This directive is essentially just like the `element` directive. It causes the column in question to be generated as an element rather than as an attribute. The differences between the `xml` and `element` directives will only be seen if you have special characters that require encoding – for example, the "=" sign is reserved in XML. If you need to represent an =, then you need to **encode** it (for =, it would be encoded as &eq). With the `element` directive, the content of the element is automatically encoded. With `xml`, the content is passed straight into the resulting XML without encoding. If you use the `xml` directive, no other item at this level (the number) can have a directive other than `hide`.

Hide

`Hide` is another simple one that does exactly what it says it does – it hides the results of that column.

Why in the world would you want to do that? Well, sometimes we include columns for reasons other than output. For example, in a normal query, we can perform an ORDER BY based on columns that do not appear in the SELECT list. For UNION queries, however, we can't do that – we have to specify a column in the SELECT list because it's the one thing that unites all the queries that we are performing the UNION on.

Let's use a little example of tracking some `Product` sales. We'll say that we want a list of all of our products as well as the `OrderID`s of the orders they shipped on, and the date that they shipped. We only want the `ProductID`, but we want the `ProductID` to be sorted such that any given product is near similar products – that means we need to sort based on the `CategoryID`, but we do not want the `CategoryID` to be included in the end results.

We can start out by building the query without the directive – that way we can see that our sort is working:

```
SELECT 1              as Tag,
    NULL              as Parent,
    ProductID         as [Product!1!ProductID],
    CategoryID        as [Product!1!CategoryID],
```

```
        NULL              as [Order!2!OrderID],
        NULL              as [Order!2!OrderDate]
FROM Products

UNION ALL

SELECT 2,
      1,
      p.ProductID,
      p.CategoryID,
      od.OrderID,
      o.OrderDate
FROM Products AS p
JOIN  [Order Details] AS od
   ON p.ProductID = od.ProductID
JOIN Orders AS o
   ON od.OrderID = o.OrderID
WHERE o.OrderDate BETWEEN '1998-01-01' AND '1998-01-07'
ORDER BY [Product!1!CategoryID],[Product!1!ProductID], [Order!2!OrderID]
FOR XML EXPLICIT
```

Be sure to check out the way we dealt with the OrderDate *on this one. Even though I needed to fetch that information out of the* Orders *table, it was easy (since we're using* EXPLICIT *anyway) to combine that information with the* OrderID *from the* Order Details *table. As it happens, I could have also just grabbed the* OrderID *from the* Orders *table too, but sometimes you need to mix data from multiple tables in one element, and this query is yet another demonstration of how we can do just that.*

We can see from the results that we are indeed getting the sort we expected:

```
<Product ProductID="1" CategoryID="1" />
<Product ProductID="2" CategoryID="1">
<Order OrderID="10813" OrderDate="1998-01-05T00:00:00" />
</Product>
<Product ProductID="24" CategoryID="1" />
<Product ProductID="34" CategoryID="1" />
<Product ProductID="35" CategoryID="1" />
<Product ProductID="38" CategoryID="1">
<Order OrderID="10816" OrderDate="1998-01-06T00:00:00" />
<Order OrderID="10817" OrderDate="1998-01-06T00:00:00" />
</Product>
<Product ProductID="39" CategoryID="1" />
<Product ProductID="43" CategoryID="1">
<Order OrderID="10814" OrderDate="1998-01-05T00:00:00" />
<Order OrderID="10819" OrderDate="1998-01-07T00:00:00" />
</Product>
<Product ProductID="67" CategoryID="1" />
<Product ProductID="70" CategoryID="1">
<Order OrderID="10810" OrderDate="1998-01-01T00:00:00" />
</Product>
<Product ProductID="75" CategoryID="1">
<Order OrderID="10819" OrderDate="1998-01-07T00:00:00" />
</Product>
```

```
<Product ProductID="76" CategoryID="1">
<Order OrderID="10808" OrderDate="1998-01-01T00:00:00" />
</Product>
<Product ProductID="3" CategoryID="2" />
<Product ProductID="4" CategoryID="2" />
...
```

Note that I've trimmed my results a bit for brevity.

Now we'll add our `hide` directive to get rid of the category information:

```
SELECT 1              as Tag,
       NULL           as Parent,
       ProductID      as [Product!1!ProductID],
       CategoryI      as [Product!1!CategoryID!hide],
       NULL           as [Order!2!OrderID],
       NULL           as [Order!2!OrderDate]
FROM Products

UNION ALL

SELECT 2,
       1,
       p.ProductID,
       p.CategoryID,
       od.OrderID,
       o.OrderDate
FROM Products AS p
JOIN  [Order Details] AS od
   ON p.ProductID = od.ProductID
JOIN Orders AS o
   ON od.OrderID = o.OrderID
WHERE o.OrderDate BETWEEN '1998-01-01' AND '1998-01-07'
ORDER BY [Product!1!CategoryID!hide],[Product!1!ProductID],
   [Order!2!OrderID]
FOR XML EXPLICIT
```

And we get the same results, only this time our `Category` information is indeed hidden:

```
<Product ProductID="1" />
<Product ProductID="2">
<Order OrderID="10813" OrderDate="1998-01-05T00:00:00" />
</Product>
<Product ProductID="24" />
<Product ProductID="34" />
<Product ProductID="35" />
<Product ProductID="38">
<Order OrderID="10816" OrderDate="1998-01-06T00:00:00" />
<Order OrderID="10817" OrderDate="1998-01-06T00:00:00" />
</Product>
<Product ProductID="39" />
<Product ProductID="43">
<Order OrderID="10814" OrderDate="1998-01-05T00:00:00" />
```

```
<Order OrderID="10819" OrderDate="1998-01-07T00:00:00" />
</Product>
<Product ProductID="67" />
<Product ProductID="70">
<Order OrderID="10810" OrderDate="1998-01-01T00:00:00" />
</Product>
<Product ProductID="75">
<Order OrderID="10819" OrderDate="1998-01-07T00:00:00" />
</Product>
<Product ProductID="76">
<Order OrderID="10808" OrderDate="1998-01-01T00:00:00" />
</Product>
<Product ProductID="3" />
<Product ProductID="4" />
...
```

Id, Idref, and Idrefs

None of these three have any affect whatsoever unless you also make use of the XMLDATA option (it goes after the EXPLICIT in the FOR clause) or validate against some other schema that has the appropriate declarations. This makes perfect sense when you think about what they do – they add things to the schema to enforce behavior, but, without a schema, what do you modify?

You see, XML has the concept of an id. An id in XML works much the same as a primary key does in relational data – it designates a unique identifier for that element name in your XML document. For any element name, there can be no more than one attribute specified in the id. What attribute is to serve as the id is defined in the schema for the XML. Once you have one element with a given value for your id attribute, no other element with the same element name is allowed to have the same attribute.

> **Note, however, that unlike primary keys in SQL, you cannot have multiple attributes make up your id in XML.**

Since XML has a concept that is similar to a primary key, it probably comes as no surprise that XML also has a concept that is similar to a foreign key – that's where idref and idrefs come in. Both are used to create a reference from an attribute in one element to an id attribute in another element.

What do these directives do for us? Well, if we didn't have these, there would only be one way to create a relationship between two elements – nest them. By giving a certain element an id and then making reference to it from an attribute declared as being an idref or idrefs attribute, we gain the ability to link the two elements, regardless of their position in the document.

This should bring on the question, "OK – so why are there two of them?" The answer is implied in their names: idref provides for a single value that must match an existing element's id value. idrefs provides a multi-valued, white space separated list – again, the values must *each* match an existing element's id value. The result is that you use idref if you are trying to establish a one-to-many relationship (there will only be one of each id value, but potentially many elements with that value in an attribute of idref). Use idrefs when you are trying to establish a many-to-many relationship (each element with an idrefs can refer to many ids, and those values can be referred to by many ids).

To illustrate this one, we'll go with a slight modification of our last query. We'll start with the `idref` directive:

```
SELECT 1                as Tag,
        NULL            as Parent,
        ProductID       as [Product!1!ProductID!ID],
        Cate            as [Product!1!CategoryID!hide],
        NULL            as [Order!2!OrderID],
        NULL            as [Order!2!ProductID!idref],
        NULL            as [Order!2!OrderDate]
FROM Products

UNION ALL

SELECT 2,
      1,
      p.ProductID,
      p.CategoryID,
      od.OrderID,
      od.ProductID,
      o.OrderDate
FROM Products AS p
JOIN  [Order Details] AS od
    ON p.ProductID = od.ProductID
JOIN Orders AS o
    ON od.OrderID = o.OrderID
WHERE o.OrderDate BETWEEN '1998-01-01' AND '1998-01-07'
ORDER BY [Product!1!CategoryID!hide],[Product!1!ProductID!ID],
    [Order!2!OrderID]
FOR XML EXPLICIT, XMLDATA
```

When we look at the results, there are really just two pieces that we are interested in – the **Schema** and our **Product** element:

```
<Schema name="Schema2" xmlns="urn:schemas-microsoft-com:xml-data" xmlns:dt="urn:schemas-
microsoft-com:datatypes">
<ElementType name="Product" content="mixed" model="open">
<AttributeType name="ProductID" dt:type="id" />
<attribute type="ProductID" />
</ElementType>
<ElementType name="Order" content="mixed" model="open">
<AttributeType name="OrderID" dt:type="i4" />
<AttributeType name="ProductID" dt:type="idref" />
<AttributeType name="OrderDate" dt:type="dateTime" />
<attribute type="OrderID" />
<attribute type="ProductID" />
<attribute type="OrderDate" />
</ElementType>
</Schema>
```

In the schema, you can see some fairly specific type information. Our **Product** is declared as a type of element, and you can also see that **ProductID** has been declared as being the `id` for this element type. Likewise, we have an **Order** element with the **ProductID** declared as an `idref`.

The next piece that we're interested in is a **Product** element:

```
<Product xmlns="x-schema:#Schema2" ProductID="2">
<Order OrderID="10813" ProductID="2" OrderDate="1998-01-05T00:00:00"/>
</Product>
```

In this case, notice that SQL Server has referenced our in-line schema in the **Product** element. This declares that the **Product** element and everything within it must comply with our schema – thereby ensuring that our `id` and `idrefs` will be enforced.

When we try to use the `idrefs` directive, we have to be a little more cunning. SQL Server requires that the query that we use to build our `idrefs` list be separate from the query that builds the elements with the `ids`. In addition, we must add another query to our `UNION` to supply the `idrefs` (the list of possible `ids` has to be known before we can build the `idrefs` list – but the actual `ids` will come after the `id` list). The query to generate the `idrefs` must immediately precede the query that generates the `ids`. This makes the query look pretty convoluted:

```
SELECT 1                     as Tag,
       NULL                  as Parent,
       ProductID             as [Product!1!ProductID],
       Category              as [Product!1!CategoryID!hide],
       NULL                  as [Product!1!OrderList!idrefs],
       NULL                  as [Order!2!OrderID!id],
       NULL                  as [Order!2!OrderDate]
FROM Products

UNION ALL

SELECT 1,
       NULL,
       p.ProductID,
       p.CategoryID,
       'id' + CAST(od.OrderID AS varchar),
       NULL,
       NULL
FROM Products AS p
JOIN  [Order Details] AS od
   ON p.ProductID = od.ProductID
JOIN Orders AS o
   ON od.OrderID = o.OrderID
WHERE o.OrderDate BETWEEN '1998-01-01' AND '1998-01-07'

UNION ALL

SELECT 2,
       1,
       p.ProductID,
       p.CategoryID,
       NULL,
       'id' + CAST(od.OrderID AS varchar),
       o.OrderDate
FROM Products AS p
JOIN  [Order Details] AS od
   ON p.ProductID = od.ProductID
JOIN Orders AS o
   ON od.OrderID = o.OrderID
WHERE o.OrderDate BETWEEN '1998-01-01' AND '1998-01-07'
ORDER BY [Product!1!CategoryID!hide],[Order!2!OrderID!id],
    [Product!1!OrderList!idrefs]
FOR XML EXPLICIT, XMLDATA
```

The schema winds up looking an awful lot like the one we got for `idref`:

```
<Schema name="Schema9" xmlns="urn:schemas-microsoft-com:xml-data" xmlns:dt="urn:schemas-microsoft-com:datatypes">
<ElementType name="Product" content="mixed" model="open">
<AttributeType name="ProductID" dt:type="i4" />
<AttributeType name="OrderList" dt:type="idrefs" />
<attribute type="ProductID" />
<attribute type="OrderList" />
</ElementType>
<ElementType name="Order" content="mixed" model="open">
<AttributeType name="OrderID" dt:type="id" />
<AttributeType name="OrderDate" dt:type="dateTime" />
<attribute type="OrderID" />
<attribute type="OrderDate" />
</ElementType>
</Schema>
```

But the elements couldn't be much more different:

```
<Product xmlns="x-schema:#Schema9" ProductID="76" OrderList="id10808 id10810 id10813 id10814 id10816 id10817 id10819 id10819">
   <Order OrderID="id10808" OrderDate="1998-01-01T00:00:00"/>
   <Order OrderID="id10810" OrderDate="1998-01-01T00:00:00"/>
   <Order OrderID="id10813" OrderDate="1998-01-05T00:00:00"/>
   <Order OrderID="id10814" OrderDate="1998-01-05T00:00:00"/>
   <Order OrderID="id10816" OrderDate="1998-01-06T00:00:00"/>
   <Order OrderID="id10817" OrderDate="1998-01-06T00:00:00"/>
   <Order OrderID="id10819" OrderDate="1998-01-07T00:00:00"/>
   <Order OrderID="id10819" OrderDate="1998-01-07T00:00:00"/>
</Product>
```

Using `id`, `idref`, and `idrefs` is very complex. Still, they allow us to make our output strongly typed. For most situations, this level of control and the hassles that go with it simply aren't necessary, but, when they are, these three can be lifesavers.

Xmltext

`Xmltext` expects the content of the column to be XML, and attempts to insert it as an integral part of the XML document you are creating.

While, on the surface, that may sound simple enough (OK, so they're inserting some text in the middle – big deal!), the rules of where, when, and how it inserts the data are a little strange:

❑ As long as the XML you're trying to insert is well-formed, then the root element will be stripped out – but the attributes of that element will be retained and applied depending on the following few rules.

❑ If you did not specify an attribute name when using the `xmltext` directive, then the retained attributes from the stripped element will be added to the element that contains the `xmltext` directive. The names of the retained attributes will be used in the combined element. If any attribute names from the retained attribute data conflict with other attribute information in the combine element, then the conflicting attribute is left out from the retained data.

❑ Any elements nested inside the stripped element will become nested elements of the combined element.

❑ If an attribute name is provided with the xmltext directive, then the retained data is placed in an element of the supplied name. The new element becomes a child of the element that made the directive.

❑ If any of the resulting XML is not well-formed, there is no defined behavior. Basically, the behavior will depend on how the end result looks, but I would figure that you're going to get an error (I haven't seen an instance where you can refer to data that is not well-formed and escape without an error).

CDATA

The term CDATA is a holdover from DTDs and SGML. Basically, it stands for character data. XML acknowledges a CDATA section as something of a no man's land – it completely and in all ways ignores whatever is included inside a properly marked CDATA section. Since there is no validation on the data in a CDATA section, no encoding of the data is necessary. You would use CDATA anytime you need your data to be completely untouched (you can't have encoding altering the data) or, frankly, when you want to move the data but have no idea what the data is (so you can't know if it's going to cause you problems or not).

For this one, we'll just take a simple example – the Northwind Employees table. This table has a field that has a text data type. The contents are basically unknown. A query to generate the notes on employees into XML might look something like this:

```
SELECT 1                    as Tag,
       NULL                 as Parent,
       Employees.EmployeeID as [Employee!1!EmployeeID],
       Employees.Notes      as [Employee!1!!CDATA]
FROM Employees
ORDER BY [Employee!1!EmployeeID]
FOR XML EXPLICIT
```

The output is pretty straightforward:

```
<Employee EmployeeID="1">
<![CDATA[
   Education includes a BA in psychology from Colorado State University in 1970.  She
      also completed "The Art of the Cold Call."  Nancy is a member of Toastmasters
      International.
]]>
</Employee>
<Employee EmployeeID="2">
<![CDATA[
   Andrew received his BTS commercial in 1974 and a Ph.D. in international marketing
      from the University of Dallas in 1981.  He is fluent in French and Italian and reads
      German.  He joined the company as a sales representative, was promoted to
      sales manager in January 1992 and to vice president of sales in March 1993.
      Andrew is a member of the Sales Management Roundtable, the Seattle Chamber
      of Commerce, and the Pacific Rim Importers Association.
]]>
</Employee>
<Employee EmployeeID="3">
```

```
<![CDATA[
    Janet has a BS degree in chemistry from Boston College (1984).  She has also
        completed a certificate program in food retailing management.  Janet was hired
        as a sales associate in 1991 and promoted to sales representative in February
        1992.
]]>
</Employee>
```

If you look at EmployeeID="1", you'll see right away that there is indeed no encoding going on (otherwise the " symbols would be encoded to &quot).

Basically – this was a pretty easy one.

OPENXML

We've spent pages and pages dealing with how to turn our relational data into XML. It seems reasonably intuitive then that SQL Server must also allow you to open a string of XML and represent it in the tabular format that is expected in SQL. Such functionality has indeed been added to this release as a match to the FOR XML clause that we've already seen.

OPENXML is a rowset function that opens your string, much as other rowset functions (such as OPENQUERY and OPENROWSET) work. This means that you can join to an XML document, or even use it as the source of input data by using an INSERT...SELECT or a SELECT INTO. The major difference is that it requires you to use a couple of system stored procedures to prepare your document and clear the memory after you're done using it.

To set up your document, you use sp_xml_preparedocument. This moves the string into memory and pre-parses it for optimal query performance. The XML document will stay in memory until you explicitly say to remove it or you terminate the connection that sp_xml_preparedocument was called on. The syntax is pretty simple:

```
sp_xml_preparedocument @hdoc = <integer variable> OUTPUT,
[, @xmltext = <character data>]
[, @xpath_namespaces = <url to a namespace>]
```

> Note that, if you are going to provide a namespace URL, you need to wrap it in the
> "<" and ">" symbols at both ends (for example '<root xmlns:sql ="run:
> schemas-microsoft-com:xml-sql>').

The parameters of this sproc are fairly self-describing:

❑   @hdoc: If you've ever programmed to the Windows API (and to tons of other things, but this is a common one), then you've seen the "h" before – it's Hungarian notation for a handle. A handle is effectively a pointer to a block of memory where something (could be about anything) resides. In our case, this is the handle to the XML document that we've asked SQL Server to parse and hold onto for us. This is an output variable – the variable you reference here will, after the sproc returns, contain the handle to your XML – be sure to store it away, as you will need it when you make use of OPENXML.

❑   @xmltext: Is what it says it is – the actual XML that you want to parse and work with.

❑   @xpath_namespaces: Any namespace reference(s) your XML needs to operate correctly.

After calling this sproc and saving away the handle to your document, you're ready to make use of OPENXML. The syntax for it is slightly more complex:

```
OPENXML(<handle>,<XPath to base node>[, <mapping flags>])
[WITH (<Schema Declaration>|<Table Name>)]
```

We have already discussed the handle – this is going to be an integer value that you received as an output parameter for your sp_xml_preparedocument call.

When you make your call to OPENXML, you must supply a path to a node that will serve as a starting point for all your queries. The schema declaration can refer to all parts of the XML document by navigating relative to the base node you set here.

Next up are the mapping flags. These assist us in deciding whether you want to favor elements or attributes in your OPENXML results. The options are:

Byte Value	Description
0	Same as 1 except that you can't combine it with 2 or 8 (2 + 0 is still 2). This is the default.
1	Unless combined with 2 below, only attributes will be used. If there is no attribute with the name specified, then a NULL is returned. This can also be added to either 2 or 8 (or both) to combine behavior, but this option takes precedence over option 2. If XPath finds both an attribute and an element with the same name, the attribute wins.
2	Unless combined with 1 above, only elements will be used. If there is no element with the name specified, then a NULL is returned. This can also be added to either 1 or 8 (or both) to combine behavior. If combined with 1, then the attribute will be mapped if it exists. If no attribute exists, then the element will be used. If no element exists, then a NULL is returned.
8	Can be combined with 1 or 2 above. Consumed data should not be copied to the overflow property @mp:xmltext (you would have to use the MetaProperty schema item to retrieve this). If you're not going to use the MetaProperties – and most of the time you won't be – I recommend this option. It cuts a small (OK, *very* small) amount of overhead out of the operation.

Finally comes the schema or table. If you're defining a schema and are not familiar with XPath, this part can be a bit tricky. Fortunately, this particular XPath use isn't very complex and should become second nature fairly quickly (it works a lot like directories do in Windows).

The schema can vary somewhat in the way you declare it. The definition is declared as:

```
WITH (
<Column Name> <data type> [{<Column XPath>|<MetaProperty>}]
[,<Column Name> <data type> [{<Column XPath>|<MetaProperty>}]
   ...
```

❑ The Column Name is just that – the name of the attribute or element you are retrieving. This will also serve as the name you refer to when you build your SELECT list, perform JOINs, etc.

❑ The data type is any valid SQL Server data type. Since XML can have data types that are not equivalents of those in SQL Server, an automatic coercion will take place if necessary, but this is usually predictable.

❑ The Column XPath is the XPath pattern (relative to the node you established as the starting point for your OPENXML function) that gets you to the node you want for your column – whether an element or attribute gets used is dependent on the flags parameter as described above. If this is left off, then SQL Server assumes you want the current node as defined as the starting point for your OPENXML statement.

❑ MetaProperties are a set of special variables that you can refer to in your OPENXML queries. They describe various aspects of whatever part of the XML DOM you're interested in. To use them, just enclose them in single quotes and put them in the place of the column XPath. Available MetaProperties include:

   ❑ @mp:id: Don't confuse this with the XML id that we looked at with EXPLICIT. While this property serves a similar function, it is a unique identifier (within the scope of the document) of the DOM node. The difference is that this value is system-generated – as such, you can be sure it is there. It is guaranteed to refer to the same XML node as long as the document remains in memory. If the id is zero, it is the root node (its @mp:parentid property, as referred to below, will be NULL).

   ❑ @mp:parentid: This is the same as above, only for the parent.

   ❑ @mp:localname: Provides the non-fully qualified name of the node. It is used with prefix and namespace URI (Uniform Resource Identifier – you'll usually see it starting with URN) to name element or attribute nodes.

   ❑ @mp:parentlocalname: This is the same as above, only for the parent.

   ❑ @mp:namespaceuri: Provides the namespace URI of the current element. If the value of this attribute is NULL, no namespace is present.

   ❑ @mp:parentnamespacerui: This is the same as above, only for the parent.

   ❑ @mp:prefix: Stores the namespace prefix of the current element name.

   ❑ @mp:prev: Stores the mp:id of the previous sibling relative to a node. Using this, you can tell something about the ordering of the elements at the current level of the hierarchy. For example, if the value of @mp:prev is NULL, then you are at the first node for this level of the tree.

   ❑ @mp:xmltext: This MetaProperty is used for processing purposes, and contains the actual XML for the current element.

Of course, you can always save yourself a ton of work by bypassing all these parameters. You get to do this if you have a table that relates directly (names and data types) to the XPath starting point that you've specified in your XML. If you do have such a table, you can just name it and SQL Server will make the translation for you!

OK, that's a lot to handle, but we're not quite finished yet. You see, when you're all done with your XML, you need to call sp_xml_removedocument to clean up the memory where your XML document was stored. Thankfully, the syntax is incredibly easy:

```
sp_xml_removedocument [hdoc = ]<handle of XML doc>
```

I can't stress enough how important it is to get in the habit of always cleaning up after yourself. I know that, in saying that, I probably sound like your mother. Well, like your mother, SQL Server will clean up after you some, but, like your mother, you can't count on SQL Server to clean up after you every time. SQL Server will clean things up when you terminate the connection, but what if you are using connection pooling? Some connections may never go away if your system is under load. It's an easy sproc to implement, so do it – every time!

OK, I'm sure you've been bored waiting for me to get to how you really make use of this – so now it's time for the all-important example.

Imagine that you are merging with another company and need to import some of their data into your system. For this example, we'll say that we're working on importing a few Shippers that they have and our company (Northwind) doesn't. A sample of what our script might look like to import these from an XML document is:

```
USE Northwind

DECLARE @idoc      int
DECLARE @xmldoc    nvarchar(4000)

-- define the XML document
SET @xmldoc = '
<ROOT>
<Shipper ShipperID="100" CompanyName="Billy Bob&apos;s Pretty Good
  Shipping"/>
<Shipper ShipperID="101" CompanyName="Fred&apos;s Freight"/>
</ROOT>
'

--Load and parse the XML document in memory
EXEC sp_xml_preparedocument @idoc OUTPUT, @xmldoc

--List out what our shippers table looks like before the insert
SELECT * FROM Shippers

-- ShipperID is an IDENTITY column, so we need to allow direct updates
SET IDENTITY_INSERT Shippers ON

--See our XML data in a tabular format
SELECT * FROM OPENXML (@idoc, '/ROOT/Shipper', 0) WITH (
    ShipperID       int,
    CompanyName     nvarchar(40))

--Perform and insert based on that data
INSERT INTO Shippers
(ShipperID, CompanyName)
SELECT * FROM OPENXML (@idoc, '/ROOT/Shipper', 0) WITH (
    ShipperID       int,
    CompanyName     nvarchar(40))

--Set things back to normal
SET IDENTITY_INSERT Shippers OFF

--Now look at the Shippers table after our insert
SELECT * FROM Shippers

--Now clear the XML document from memory
EXEC sp_xml_removedocument @idoc
```

The final result set from this looks just like what we wanted:

ShipperID	CompanyName	Phone
1	Speedy Express	(503) 555-9831
2	United Package	(503) 555-3199
3	Federal Shipping	(503) 555-9931
4	Speedy Shippers, Inc.	(503) 555-5566
5	Speedy Shippers, Inc	NULL
100	Billy Bob's Pretty Good Shipping	NULL
101	Fred's Freight	NULL
102	Readyship	(503)555-1234
103	MyShipper	(503)555-3443

Well, that's all well and good for such an easy example, but let's get a few more of OPENXML's options going.

This time, we'll make use of a subset of an XML block we generated with our FOR XML EXPLICIT clause earlier in the chapter. This time, we want to retrieve the ProductID, CategoryID, OrderID, and OrderDate. To make things a little more interesting, try retrieving the @mp:previous property too.

Before you get into the code here, it seems like a good time to remind you – remember your root element! SQL Server doesn't put it in for you on FOR XML queries in order to allow you to put multiple queries in one document. You need to manually add it before you try to send it to sp_xml_preparedocument.

```
DECLARE @idoc int
DECLARE @doc varchar(4000)
-- XML that came from our FOR XML EXPLICIT
SET @doc ='
<root>
<Product ProductID="1" CategoryID="1" />
<Product ProductID="2" CategoryID="1">
    <Order OrderID="10813" OrderDate="1998-01-05T00:00:00" />
</Product>
<Product ProductID="24" CategoryID="1" />
<Product ProductID="34" CategoryID="1" />
<Product ProductID="35" CategoryID="1" />
<Product ProductID="38" CategoryID="1">
    <Order OrderID="10816" OrderDate="1998-01-06T00:00:00" />
    <Order OrderID="10817" OrderDate="1998-01-06T00:00:00" />
</Product>
<Product ProductID="39" CategoryID="1" />
<Product ProductID="43" CategoryID="1">
    <Order OrderID="10814" OrderDate="1998-01-05T00:00:00" />
    <Order OrderID="10819" OrderDate="1998-01-07T00:00:00" />
</Product>
<Product ProductID="67" CategoryID="1" />
<Product ProductID="70" CategoryID="1">
    <Order OrderID="10810" OrderDate="1998-01-01T00:00:00" />
</Product>
</root>
'
-- Create an internal representation of the XML document.
EXEC sp_xml_preparedocument @idoc OUTPUT, @doc
```

```
-- Execute a SELECT statement using OPENXML rowset provider.
SELECT *
FROM OPENXML (@idoc, '/root/Product/Order', 1)
      WITH (ProductID int '../@ProductID',
            Category int '../@CategoryID',
            OrderID int '@OrderID',
            OrderDate varchar(19) '@OrderDate',
            Previous varchar(10) '@mp:prev')
EXEC sp_xml_removedocument @idoc
```

Really pay attention to the relative pathing in our XPath references when we build the meta-data. Compare it to the hierarchy in the XML. If you think about it, it works an awful lot like a DOS/Windows directory structure.

So let's take a look at what our hard work has wrought:

ProductID	Category	OrderID	OrderDate	Previous
2	1	10813	1998-01-05T00:00:00	NULL
38	1	10816	1998-01-06T00:00:00	NULL
38	1	10817	1998-01-06T00:00:00	23
43	1	10814	1998-01-05T00:00:00	NULL
43	1	10819	1998-01-07T00:00:00	35
70	1	10810	1998-01-01T00:00:00	NULL

As you can see, we were able to grab XML data from different points in the hierarchy. We can use XPath to navigate us to any point in the XML tree that we need to retrieve our data from.

So, now that we have a way to get XML query results, and a way to get XML turned into relational data, it's time to start looking at even more cool stuff – ways to interact with SQL Server's XML features.

HTTP Access

So far, we've been accessing all of our XML through Query Analyzer. As it happens, QA is a terrible tool for XML work. It adds white space (in the form of a carriage return) right in the middle of our elements and has no XML validation capabilities, so doing XML in QA isn't real fun. That's OK though, because QA wasn't really designed for that task; but there are a few tools that are, and we'll be looking at them in this section and the next.

Access to XML-formatted results is also available semi-directly through HTTP access. This access requires that you also run IIS (though not necessarily on the same server). SQL Server provides an excellent management tool to facilitate the set up of HTTP-based access, and we will be looking into that shortly.

The architecture of the URL/HTTP-based access is fairly complex:

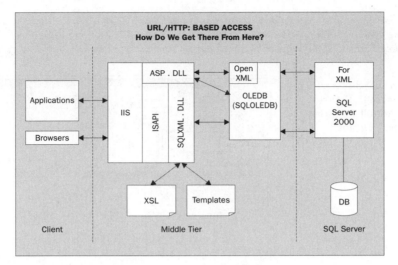

As you can see, a special ISAPI DLL is required for HTTP access. There are plans to fully integrate this functionality into SQL Server at some later date but, for now, the ISAPI solution is effective and allowed this functionality to ship much sooner than might have otherwise been possible. Frankly, it's amazing they could get such diverse access methods all plumbed in without more dramatic measures.

Well, seeing the picture is nice, but before we can explore HTTP access very far, we need to get some access set up on our system.

Setting Up HTTP Access

SQL Server provides a tool to take care of a large degree of the set up of HTTP access. The actual access happens through the use of a virtual directory on the web server. This virtual directory is how IIS figures out that you want access to the special ISAPI DLL that's required for HTTP access to SQL Server.

To set up such a virtual directory, we need to go select Configure SQL XML Support in IIS, reached through the SQL Server Start | Programs menu.

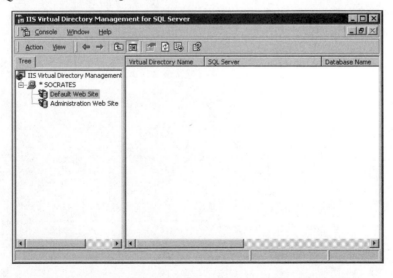

All of the examples in this HTTP access section are going to assume that you are accessing IIS through the default web site. SQL Server will, however, do just fine on a non-default web (indeed, the first time I set up HTTP support, it was through a separate web on a non-standard port).

To create the virtual directory we will use to access SQL Server, right-click on Default Web Site and choose New | Virtual Directory:

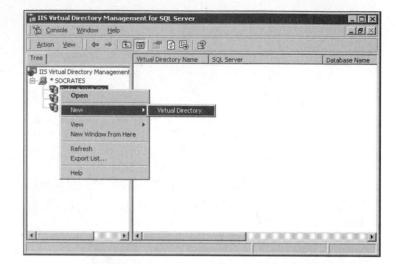

This brings us up the dialog we'll use to build our access to SQL Server. On the General tab, name the virtual directory Northwind (creative – aren't I?) and choose a location to store any files related to the virtual directory. This particular directory choice is something of a farce – we won't be storing anything there – but it can be any directory.

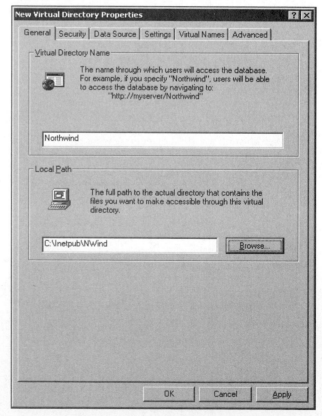

Go ahead and move on to the **Security** tab. It is at this point that we have our first need to do something special. The account you utilize for this security setting will dictate a tremendous amount about what access users have to your server. If you're in an internal environment (no Internet to deal with), then you can probably choose Windows security – definitely the more secure choice.

If, however, you need Internet users to have anonymous access (you're not setting up individual login accounts), then you have some problems ahead of you. At issue is how to balance their level of access with the need for security, but still be able to make effective use of the HTTP access that we know is so cool. We will be looking into how to address some of these issues as we examine the individual access methods available to us in detail.

For now, enter in a user account that has at least read access to the Northwind database. This can be the sa account, or some account that you've set up especially for this purpose (which is what I recommend, but we also haven't gotten to the security chapter yet). Since we're going to be doing all kinds of different demos in this chapter, you'll want this user to have reasonably full access to the Northwind database. I'm going to set mine up with a user called NWindXML and a password of NWindXML. You can provide any user account you wish, as long as it has access to all the objects in the Northwind database. To create a user just like my NWindXML login, you can use the following code (this will also be available from the Wrox web site in a script called CreateNWindXML.sql):

```
USE Northwind
GO

IF NOT EXISTS (SELECT * FROM master.dbo.syslogins WHERE loginname =
  N'NWindXML')
BEGIN
    DECLARE @logindb nvarchar(132), @loginlang nvarchar(132)
      SELECT @logindb = N'Northwind', @loginlang = N'us_english'
    IF @logindb IS NULL OR NOT EXISTS (SELECT * FROM master.dbo.sysdatabases WHERE
name = @logindb)
        SELECT @logindb = N'master'
    EXEC sp_addlogin N'NWindXML', N'NWindXML', @logindb, @loginlang
END

GO

IF NOT EXISTS(SELECT 'True' FROM Northwind..sysusers WHERE name = N'NWindXML')
EXEC sp_grantdbaccess @loginame   = N'NWindXML'
GO


IF NOT EXISTS(SELECT 'True' FROM Northwind..sysusers AS su
                    JOIN Northwind..sysmembers AS sm
                        ON su.uid = sm.memberuid
                    JOIN Northwind..sysusers AS su2
                        ON su2.uid = sm.groupuid
                        WHERE su.name = N'NWindXML' AND su2.name = 'db_owner')
EXEC sp_addrolemember @rolename = db_owner,
        @membername = N'NWindXML'
GO
```

I've granted this particular user access to the built-in db_owner security role – this means that this user will be able to do about anything within the scope of this database.

For production systems, you would not want a generic user like this to have the kind of carte blanche access that the db_owner *group has – I'm only doing that here to facilitate the wide variety of examples we have in this chapter (there are a bunch of them!).*

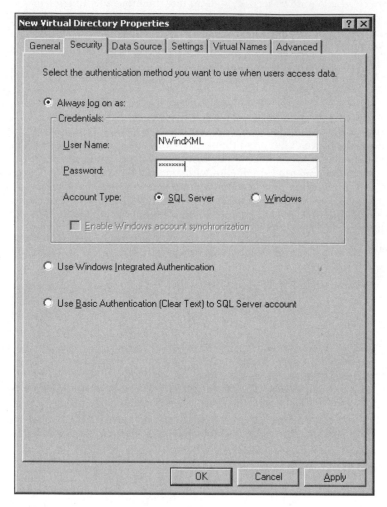

As you move off to the next tab, **Data Source**, you will be prompted (if you used SQL Security as I did) to confirm the user's password. Re-enter it, click **OK**, and you will then be at the next tab.

Choose the name of the database server you want to connect to (I use one local to my web server, but you don't have to) and also the default database you want that user logged into (in this case, **Northwind**):

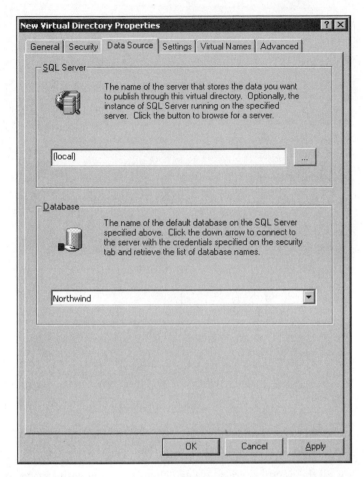

Next up is the **Settings** tab. This is where we will determine what kinds of access we want to allow to our server. We will use the various options here, together with user rights and the security method chosen (Windows vs. SQL Server), to try to secure our server to the highest degree possible.

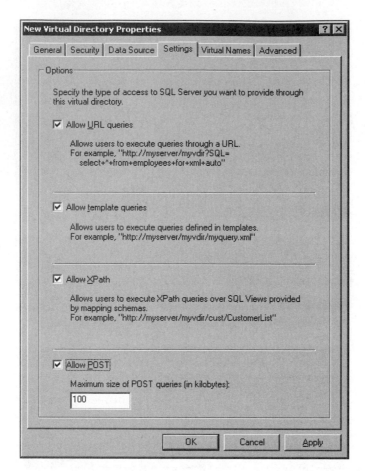

I'm choosing to allow all the options here so we can check them out with examples, but let's take a moment and examine each of them:

❑ **Allow URL queries**: If this is on, queries can be entered right on the URL in the user's browser. Think a little deeper though – if you can code an HTTP request, then you can programmatically issue queries with this method too, and get the results back as XML. I could see something like this used over the Internet as a business-to-business thing if you had the right routing restrictions, but it's definitely a risky choice.

❑ **Allow template queries**: You establish a template as an XML document and the user gets the templated query results (which can be styled too) back – they don't even see what the actual query looked like. These can be straight templates that have a raw, fixed query, or you can also parameterize them.

❑ **Allow XPath**: Under this model, you construct mapping schemas that provide a mapping of your relational data into a form that can be queried using XPath. It's a dynamic query language, but users can also only get at what you have provided mappings for, unless you allow direct access to the database objects (I wouldn't do this unless you truly don't care about the security of your data!).

❑ **Allow Post**: Allows you to do any of the above, only through a POST. This one is a huge disappointment to me. It would have been great if you were still restricted by the other three options – that is, if it was set to no URL queries, then you couldn't run queries through POST either (but still could for templates if they were enabled) – but that's not the way it works. When POST is on, an HTML form can submit just about anything – including the text of a template – and get the query results back. I suggest *really* watching out on this one. I suspect they will get this one right in a future release, but it's way too wide open at this point for my tastes.

Now we're ready to move on to the heart of things – setting up the virtual names. This part can be kind of confusing – after all, isn't setting up a virtual directory for our HTTP access what we're already doing? Well, yes – this is just a further breakdown of that. This lets you determine where you're going to store your templates and mapping schemas, as well as whether you're going to allow XPath queries to go directly against your database objects or not. Only schemas and templates map to physical locations (the database objects map directly to the database), but this separate physical location allows you to place separate security at the directory level regarding who has access to what (you could always manage at the file level, but that's tedious at best).

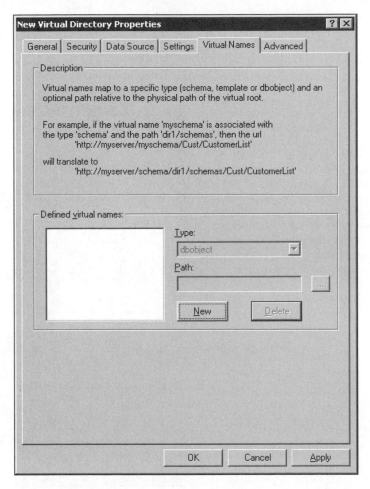

Click on New here, and you get yet another
dialog:

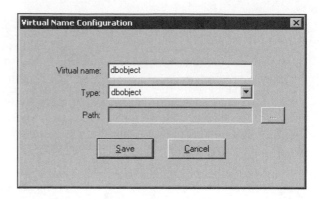

The virtual name used here will become part of the URL path you'll use when accessing the particular
virtual functionality you're enabling. In this case, I'm setting up direct access to database objects, and
calling it dbobject.

> *Again, we're setting this up because we need to know how it works, but I can't reiterate enough that
> you are leaving the barn doors of your system wide open – so don't be surprised if the cows come out!
> Keep this functionality locked down unless you either don't care about the security of the data, or the
> server is sitting at the bottom of Fort Knox with no network connections – get it?*

Go ahead and also set up virtual names to
match up for templates and schemas (call them
templates and schemas respectively). For each
of these, you'll need to specify a directory that
you want to physically store your templates
and schemas in. Unfortunately, the tool doesn't
let you create these on the fly, so you'll need to
have created the physical directories before
you get to the Virtual Name Configuration
dialog box. Remember, the physical location
doesn't really matter much – the users will map
to it through the virtual name you assign.

Go ahead and click on Apply, and then move
over to our last tab:

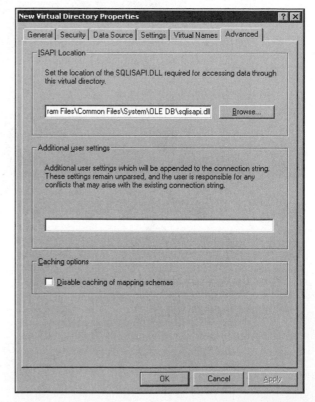

We won't change anything on this tab – indeed, it's very rare that you will want to change things here. This tab is all about setting up specifics of the ISAPI DLL that is used for HTTP access. My advice is simply – "Don't Touch!"

We've done what we need to do. Now we're ready to move on and start putting it to work!

URL-Based Queries

As we've already seen, URL-based queries are an optional part of HTTP access. That is, you can allow queries to be entered right into the URL request from the browser. This clearly has security concerns that should be carefully considered prior to allowing such queries. That said – let's see how they work.

A sample query to provide the same results we saw with RAW previously in the chapter would look as follows:

http://localhost/Northwind?SQL=SELECT+Customers.CustomerID,+Customers.CompanyName,+Orders.OrderID,+Orders.OrderDate+FROM+Customers+JOIN+Orders+ON+Customers.CustomerID+=+Orders.CustomerID+WHERE+Customers.CustomerID+=+'ALFKI'+OR+Customers.CustomerID+=+'ANTON'+FOR+XML+RAW&root=ROOT

If you have IE5 or better, you can enter this in the URL and SQL Server will immediately generate what should be, by now, some pretty familiar XML:

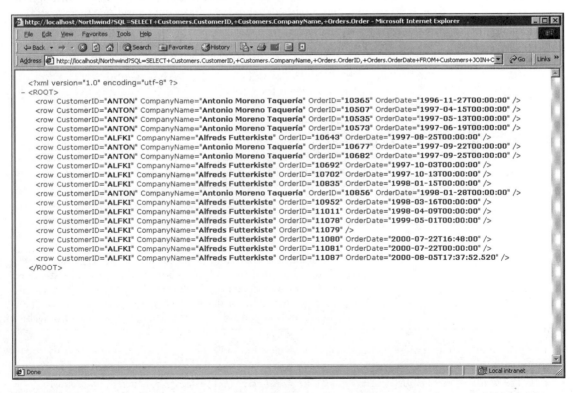

IE5 will automatically render XML into its natural hierarchy complete with color-coding for attributes and values.

Several things about this query are worth noting:

❑ The &root=ROOT at the end explicitly defined a root element called ROOT. It doesn't need to be called ROOT – it could have been called BillClinton if that's what we wanted it to be – it just needs to be unique. SQL Server takes care of wrapping our new root element at both ends of the XML before passing it to the client.

❑ The + signs take the place of spaces. The %20 that is somewhat more common in URL encoding is also valid.

❑ The SQL= parameter marks the beginning of our query.

❑ It produces exactly the same output as our original RAW query from earlier in the chapter, with the exception of this query providing the root element according to our instructions.

We could also simulate our AUTO and EXPLICIT queries from the last section by substituting the appropriate SQL.

We can apply a number of other parameters to affect our output. These include:

Parameter	Description
?template	This would take the place of ?SQL. This allows you to send through the raw text that serves as a template for our query and XML generation. Templates are more commonly stored in files, but the content of a Template file can just as easily be put directly on the URL (it just isn't as secure). We will look at templates in the next section.
&xsl	The path to a style sheet to be applied to the resulting XML. You can use XSL to transform the output into HTML, to another XML format, and even to change the encoding scheme (also see the outputencoding parameter).
&root	As we saw in our example, this provides a name for a root element. If provided, SQL Server will create a root element and name it the value of this parameter. If &root is not specified, then the client needs to be aware that the XML will not be well formed and will require additional manipulation.
&outputencoding	Changes the character encoding for the output document. The default is UTF-8, but any W3C recognized encoding scheme should work.
&contenttype	Supplies the value of the content-type HTTP header information. This can make a huge difference to how your client perceives your data. For example, IE5 will assume that a document with an extension of .xml is an XML file and render it accordingly. You can use this option to indicate to the client that you want the data treated in some other fashion.

You can mix and match these parameters as necessary, but only the template parameter is truly required.

You'll always want to use &root in any URL based query that you perform directly in a browser – otherwise the browser won't see it as well formed XML (no root). If, however, you're writing an application that makes the HTTP request, you may very well want to get back the data without the root element – adding it later (presumably after you added additional XML to the document).

Using Templates

Using templates allows us to encapsulate much of the query logic both for ease of maintenance and for security purposes. Creating a template is as simple as defining an XML document that lists the basic structure of your XML document and also provides the one or more queries you want to make up the results.

The basic layout of a template should take the form of:

```
[<literal values>]
 [<sql:header>
   [ <sql:parameter <<parameter name>><default value>
       </<parameter name>></sql:parameter>]
   [ <sql:parameter
       <<parameter name>><default value></<parameter name>>
     </sql:parameter>]
   [ <sql:parameter
       <<parameter name>><default value></<parameter name>>
     </sql:parameter>]
   ...
 </sql:header>]
 <sql:query>
  <query text>
 </sql:query>
[<literal values>]
 [
  <sql:query>
   <query text>
  </sql:query>
 ]
[<literal values>]
...
```

To stick with the example that has formed the basis of many of our queries thus far, here is a template that would achieve the same results:

```
<Root xmlns:sql="urn:schemas-microsoft-com:xml-sql">
  <sql:query>
    SELECT Customers.CustomerID,
      Customers.CompanyName,
      Orders.OrderID,
      Orders.OrderDate
    FROM Customers
    JOIN Orders
      ON Customers.CustomerID = Orders.CustomerID
    WHERE Customers.CustomerID = 'ALFKI' OR Customers.CustomerID = 'ANTON'
    ORDER BY Customers.CustomerID
    FOR XML AUTO
  </sql:query>
</Root>
```

The xmlns attribute in the Root element is indicating that the content in this element (in this case, the Root element) makes use of the xml-sql namespace managed by Microsoft. Its purpose is just to make sure that when we use the word query later in the document, we do not create a conflict with some other namespace that might also use the word query to mean something. Keep in mind that we can have multiple namespaces represented in a single XML document. Each namespace must have a definition indicating where to find the reference document that sets the rules for that namespace.

If we were to add the template code above into a template called `CustomerOrders.xml` and store it in the directory you used for physical storage of your "templates" virtual name then we could call it by the URL reference: http://localhost/Northwind/templates/CustomerOrders.xml.

The results contain the same data as the URL query we did a page or two ago (it's the same query).

Parameterizing Templates

The possibilities do not end there though – we can parameterize our templates if we need to. For example, we could alter our query to accept a parameter to look for a specific customer:

```
<Root xmlns:sql="urn:schemas-microsoft-com:xml-sql">
  <sql:header>
    <sql:param name="CustomerID">ALFKI</sql:param>
  </sql:header>
  <sql:query>
    SELECT Customers.CustomerID,
      Customers.CompanyName,
      Orders.OrderID,
      Orders.OrderDate
    FROM Customers
    JOIN Orders
      ON Customers.CustomerID = Orders.CustomerID
    WHERE Customers.CustomerID = @CustomerID
    ORDER BY Customers.CustomerID
    FOR XML AUTO
  </sql:query>
</Root>
```

Adding the parameter to our URL works much as it does for parameters passed in to an HTTP GET through the URL. Save this as `CustomerOrdersParam.xml` in the same folder as `CustomerOrders.xml`, and navigate to:

http://localhost/Northwind/templates/CustomerOrdersParam.xml?CustomerID=ANTON

Now we receive only one CustomerID at a time, but we can change it to any customer we want:

```
<Root xmlns:sql="urn:schemas-microsoft-com:xml-sql">
<Customers CustomerID="ANTON" CompanyName="Antonio Moreno Taquería">
<Orders OrderID="10365" OrderDate="1996-11-27T00:00:00" />
<Orders OrderID="10507" OrderDate="1997-04-15T00:00:00" />
<Orders OrderID="10535" OrderDate="1997-05-13T00:00:00" />
<Orders OrderID="10573" OrderDate="1997-06-19T00:00:00" />
<Orders OrderID="10677" OrderDate="1997-09-22T00:00:00" />
<Orders OrderID="10682" OrderDate="1997-09-25T00:00:00" />
<Orders OrderID="10856" OrderDate="1998-01-28T00:00:00" />
</Customers>
</Root>
```

> It's probably worth the reminder at this point that, since XML is case sensitive, your parameter names will also be case sensitive. Whether the actual parameters are case sensitive or not will depend on your SQL Server settings (that part will work just like it would in a query in the Query Analyzer).

Since we supplied a default (in this case, ALFKI), we can even leave the parameter out and still receive the information on our default customer.

Stored Procedures and UDF's Within Templates

All this talk of parameters might have you thinking about sprocs and UDFs. Using such blocks of code within our templates could not be much easier. You just use the procedure or function call much as you would to get results back in Query Analyzer.

For example, let's just encapsulate our query from our parameter template example into a sproc. The sproc should be pretty straightforward:

```
USE Northwind
GO

CREATE PROC spCustomerOrdersXML @CustomerID nchar(5)
AS
    SELECT Customers.CustomerID,
           Customers.CompanyName,
           Orders.OrderID,
           Orders.OrderDate
    FROM Customers
    JOIN Orders
      ON Customers.CustomerID = Orders.CustomerID
    WHERE Customers.CustomerID = @CustomerID
    ORDER BY Customers.CustomerID
    FOR XML AUTO

GO
GRANT EXECUTE ON spCustomerOrdersXML TO NWindXML
```

I would recommend that you add recognition of XML output to the naming conventions for your stored procs. Because their use is different, I suspect that many applications are going to find that they have two versions of some sprocs – the "regular" version and one that outputs XML. You will want to adopt a strategy for easily telling them apart.

So, now that we have a sproc to work with, we can just substitute it for the query in our parameterized template example, to give:

```
<Root xmlns:sql="urn:schemas-microsoft-com:xml-sql">
  <sql:header>
    <sql:param name="CustomerID">ALFKI</sql:param>
  </sql:header>
  <sql:query>
      EXEC spCustomerOrdersXML @CustomerID
  </sql:query>
</Root>
```

This time, we'll save the file as `CustomerOrdersParamSP.xml`. Once you have it constructed, just navigate to it much as we did with `CustomerOrdersParam.xml` and supply **ANTON** as the **CustomerID** parameter:

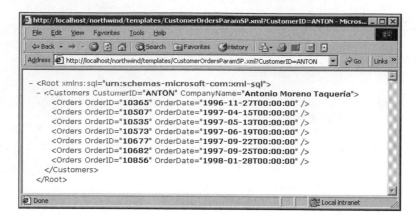

Presto – we now have a sproc to return our XML. Beyond the performance and encapsulation benefits that a stored procedure offers, you could also have your sproc run multiple XML queries and they would all be returned into the one document. You could use this as an alternative to placing multiple queries right in your XML template – which we will look at next.

Building XML from Multiple Queries

Easy, easy, easy. The only real trick to it all is to remember that your document can only have one root node – so all your results need to be inside that one root. Other than that, just keep adding multiple queries (within separate query tags) to your template.

So, if we wanted a single XML file that not only had a listing of all the orders that a customer had made, but also a list of what products they had purchased and how many they had purchased in total (all orders), we could just add one more query to our template.

We'll start with the template from our last section, and just add a query to get a product list and quantity count for our customer:

```
<Root xmlns:sql="urn:schemas-microsoft-com:xml-sql">
  <sql:header>
    <sql:param name="CustomerID">ALFKI</sql:param>
  </sql:header>
  <sql:query>
    EXEC spCustomerOrdersXML @CustomerID
  </sql:query>
  <sql:query>
    SELECT    1                        AS Tag,
              NULL                     AS Parent,
              Product.ProductID        AS [Product!1!ProductID],
              Product.ProductName      AS [Product!1!ProductName],
              COUNT(od.Quantity)       AS [Product!1!TotalPurchases]
    FROM   Products AS Product
    JOIN [Order Details] AS od
      ON Product.ProductID = od.ProductID
    JOIN Orders AS o
      ON o.OrderID = od.OrderID
    WHERE o.CustomerID = @CustomerID
    GROUP BY Product.ProductID, Product.ProductName
    FOR XML EXPLICIT
  </sql:query>
</Root>
```

If you're wondering why I chose an EXPLICIT *option, remember that* GROUP BY *clauses are not supported when using* AUTO.

Save this as CustomerPurchases.xml and supply ANTON as the CustomerID parameter again. This time, we get back our more complex XML document:

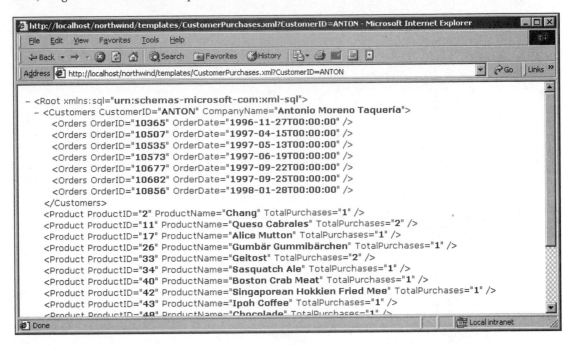

POST

You can also "post" templates. There are two pieces of functionality that are enabled when you allow posts in the virtual directory setup:

- ❑ Treatment of HTTP POST form variables the same as HTTP GET (the same as URL-based template use)
- ❑ The ability to post templates from your HTTP forms

While the first point is *highly* desirable, the second one is a major security problem in situations where you aren't able to perform some form of NT security. It is extremely unfortunate that you can't do one without the other.

The main thing to keep in mind if you activate POST queries is that anyone who can send an HTTP stream to your server will effectively have all the rights of the user that the virtual directory is aliased to. The only limitations are the restrictions that you placed on the virtual directory user and a length limit on the size of the accepted post.

If you elect to enable this option, it is highly recommended that you set the accepted POST length to the smallest size your application can function with. This will at least limit the amount of damage that can be created by individual rogue queries.

So, as always, let's get to testing this baby out. In order to do that, we have to venture into the wonderful world of HTML. We need to create a form that we can use to submit a query for us. The HTML to do this is pretty simple:

```
<head>
<TITLE>Sample Form submit for template query</TITLE>
</head>
<body>
For a given CustomerID, the Company Name and Orders are retrieved.
<form action="Northwind/templates/CustomerOrdersParam.xml" method="POST">
<B>CustomerID</B>
<input type=text name=CustomerID value="ALFKI">
<input type="submit">
</form>
</body>
```

You can type this in through notepad or your favorite HTML editor, and save it in the root directory of your web server (normally C:\Inetpub\wwwroot) as something like TestTemplates.htm. Then navigate to it through the web server as shown in the following screenshot (*not* through the regular file system):

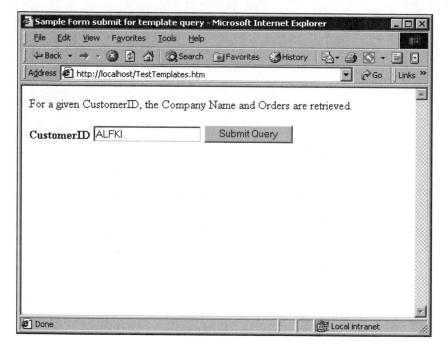

Choose your favorite **CustomerID** and then submit the query:

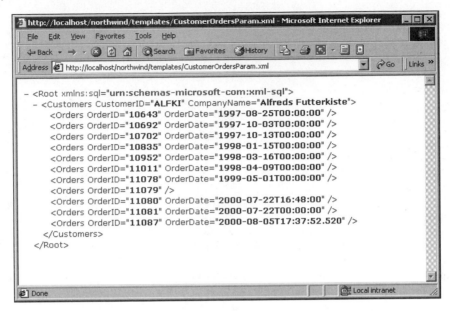

What's nice about this is that you don't see the parameter on the URL. If we were really worried about security, we could wrap the whole thing in a Secure Sockets transaction and it would be relatively protected from the user (still fairly hackable, but now it would take a significant amount of work instead of a simple URL change). There is an unfortunate side effect of this however; enabling POST seems to enable just about everything to be done through a post regardless of other settings.

To illustrate this problem, let's build another HTML form. This will largely be the same form, only this time we're going to submit the XML template directly from the form rather than referencing a file. We'll explore the effect of turning off the XML template option, and how POST will still process the template as long as the template was sent via POST rather than through a file.

Let's get that new HTML form built utilizing the contents of CustomerOrdersParam.xml:

```
<head>
<TITLE>Sample Form submit for template query</TITLE>
</head>
<body>
For a given CustomerID, the Company Name and Orders are retrieved.
<form action="northwind/" method="POST">
<input type=hidden name=contenttype value=text/xml>
<input type=hidden name=template value='<Root xmlns:sql="urn:schemas-
  microsoft-com:xml-sql">
  <sql:header>
    <sql:param name="CustomerID">ALFKI</sql:param>
  </sql:header>
  <sql:query>
    SELECT Customers.CustomerID,
           Customers.CompanyName,
           Orders.OrderID,
           Orders.OrderDate
```

```
      FROM Customers
      JOIN Orders
        ON Customers.CustomerID = Orders.CustomerID
      WHERE Customers.CustomerID = @CustomerID
      ORDER BY Customers.CustomerID
      FOR XML AUTO
    </sql:query>
  </Root>
  '>
<B>CustomerID</B>
<input type=text name=CustomerID value="ALFKI">

<input type="submit">
</form>
</body>
```

This is a fully parameterized query, just as it was when we ran it in the templates section. Realize, however, that we could have put just about anything in this form. What's more, if we accept templates in this manner, there is absolutely nothing to stop the user from drawing up their own HTML (like we just did here), but putting a different command in it – say, DELETE * FROM [Order Details].

OK, just to prove it works, go ahead and save this away to `TestTemplates2.htm` in the root directory of your web server – then navigate to that web page, and submit it.

We end up with the exact same results as we did when we used the saved template file, with only one notable exception:

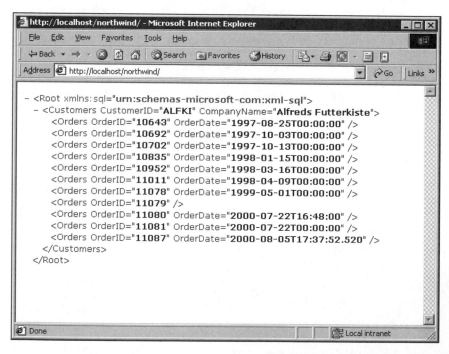

We haven't navigated to any particular new page – to a user, it looks like we didn't go anywhere.

So far, this is all cool but, as I pointed out earlier, this has now become a function of the POST security rather than template security – that is, we could turn off template access but, since we are submitting the template through POST, SQL Server would still accept it.

Let's explore this just to make sure. Go into the Configure SQL XML Support in IIS management utility again and switch to the Settings tab for our virtual directory:

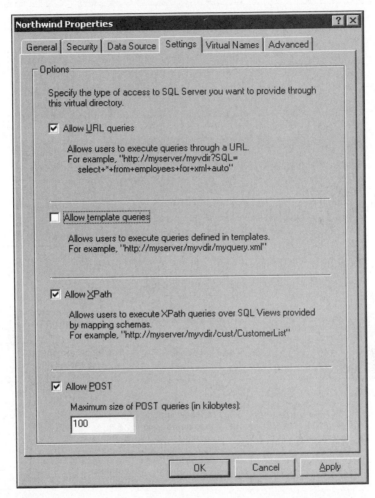

Turn template access off and apply it. Now navigate back to the template (not the POST yet) we used in the last section:

http://localhost/Northwind/templates/CustomerOrdersParam.xml?CustomerID=ANTON

Since we've turned templates off, IIS doesn't serve up the page – we get a page error:

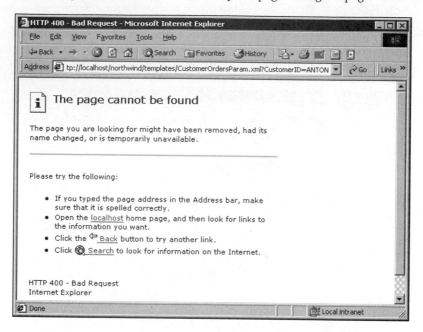

Now, we could easily think that *all* forms of templates have been disabled – but that's not the case. Let's go ahead and navigate back to our TestTemplates2.htm page, and we'll see that we can still submit a template, as long as it comes directly through the post rather than referencing a file:

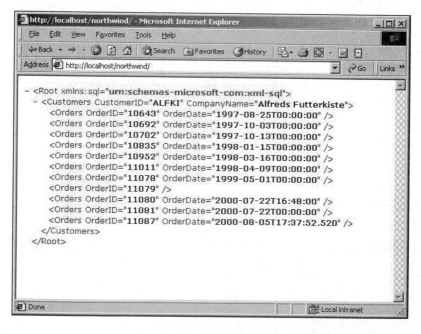

Even though we've said we do not want to allow templates, one has still been allowed through. This means that the person submitting the form, provided they know how to build an HTML form, can submit any query they want and, as long as the login you used to set up HTTP access (NWindXML is what I used at the beginning of this chapter) has adequate permissions, the person submitting the form can get whatever they want.

I'm really, really hoping that this gets fixed (yes, I consider it something that's "broken"). I very much like the notion of being able to submit my template request and parameters via POST – it hides that information from the user. You can then also keep some parameter information (such as things that filter to the current user and prevent them from seeing other users' information). If you're particularly concerned about locking it down, then you could use secure sockets to prevent sniffing of the information sent to the server. But, unfortunately, the hole created by the acceptance of ad hoc templates is simply too large – as such, I highly recommend against the use of the POST feature. Turn it OFF!

So, now that we've seen that, please turn template access back on to support examples that come later in the chapter.

XPath

> **I need to start this section off with a positively *huge* disclaimer. As I mentioned at the beginning of the chapter, parts of the XML integration continue to be in a constant state of flux due to the new Web Release format for XML integration. XPath functionality is, next to Updategrams, perhaps the most unfinished part of the product, with only a fraction of the XPath dialect supported as of writing this. This section attempts to cover most of the functionality that existed at the time that SQL Server 2000 went to manufacturing but, even as this book went to press, a new web release was due that would put some of the information out of date. Be sure to check out the Microsoft web sites to get the latest information.**

SQL Server 2000 also now supports the widely recognized XPath query language. XPath can be particularly useful for dealing with complex XML queries. XPath does not exist as a W3C recommendation in its own right (it made it as far as being a "proposed" recommendation in late 1999). Instead, for W3C purposes, the elements of XPath have been broken out for use in both XSLT (which is now a formal recommendation) and XPointer (a Candidate Recommendation as of this writing). XPath can allow many (but not all) of the same flexibility options that FOR XML EXPLICIT offers, but in what some people find to be a somewhat easier query format.

Use of XPath in SQL Server falls into two categories:

❑ Queries directly against underlying database objects.

❑ Queries against annotated schemas – these allow an XPath query to be made against a schema that "maps" to fields in your database. The fields do not need to be in the same table.

Each of these types of query requires a little extra setup to be completed beyond simply checking the XPath box in the SQL XML setup utility. Let's look at each individually.

XPath Against Database Objects

We have actually already performed the little bit of extra set up necessary to allow XPath against your database objects. The requirements are:

❑   You must have enabled the **Allow XPath** option on the **Settings** tab when you set up your SQL virtual root (you can edit it by going to the properties of your virtual root).

❑   You must have set up a virtual name, which, when referenced, will let SQL Server and IIS know that you intend to go directly against the database objects.

Once you have your virtual name set up and XPath enabled, you should be ready to issue your first query – for example, by typing:

http://localhost/northwind/dbobject/Customers[@CustomerID='ALFKI']/@CompanyName

I get back a simple text result (not XML):

Alfreds Futterkiste

Currently, the XPath implementation does not support some fairly common XPath operators – including such things as the union (|) operator. This means that you are pretty much limited to a single attribute at a time when performing queries directly against the database object.

As of this writing, the direct access has little practical use with one highly notable exception – links to binary data.

In the past, we would have had to do what is called "chunking" in ADO, or some other client library, to retrieve our binary data and serve it up on the Web or to some other destination. Now, you can just include a straight link to it, and the picture or other binary data that is embedded in the database comes right up.

Let's check this out quickly by making a very simple HTML page that refers to Nancy DaValio (Northwind EmployeeID 1):

```
<html>
<head>
 <TITLE>Sample xpath</TITLE>
</head>
<body>
 Hi! This is Nancy:
<img src="northwind/dbobject/Employees[@EmployeeID='1']/@Photo" />
</body>
</html>
```

Save this as Nancy.html in the root directory of your web server again (probably C:\Inetpub\wwwroot) and navigate to http://localhost/Nancy.html.

It's actually a very handy way to link to binary data, but you would want to be very careful about your security on something like this – unless the user is restricted to just this column in this one database object, then they could put in their own XPath and probably see things you would rather they didn't see... Still, it has some possibilities.

In the long run, as Microsoft adds additional XPath support, the URL-based XPath should become fairly attractive to developers who are relatively new to SQL but have significant XPath experience.

Using Annotated Schemas

The main concept of using XPath with SQL Server Annotated Schemas is essentially similar to that of a view (rather than the direct object approach that we've already seen). A mapping or **annotated schema** is needed to relate the relational structure of a table or query to that of an **XML Data Reduced** – or **XDR** – schema. XDR is also used by BizTalk Server (which is something very definitely worth looking at if you need to deal with outside data sources). XDR is easily a full topic in itself and, as such, we won't spend much time beyond the basics and how to specify your mapping.

> *Much like XPath, Microsoft is going with something of a past proposal on this one. The concepts related to XDR have been migrated into the XML schemas recommendation that is being worked on by the W3C. XDR is, as such, a Microsoft-only implementation of XML schemas. Microsoft indicates that it plans to utilize the more industry-standard XML schemas but, since that doesn't have a recommendation yet, Microsoft has apparently decided to go with what's available and deal with the changes later.*

Annotated schemas are just like any other XDR document, with two major exceptions:

❏ They make use of Microsoft's data types and xml-sql namespaces.

❏ They use annotations to tell SQL Server how to "map" XPath nodes to SQL Server tables and columns. Mappings are optional – that is, you can choose to map only some columns of your table or view, or you can choose to map them all.

There are a couple of attributes and one element that these namespaces give us that are key to building even the simplest of schemas:

❏ From the datatype namespace:

    ❏ dt:type: This associates our data with a particular data type.

❏ From the xml-sql namespace:

    ❏ sql:relation: This associates an element with a particular table or view.

    ❏ sql:field: This associates an attribute within the element to a specific field. The named field must exist within the table or view indicated by the relation attribute on the element.

    ❏ sql:relationship: This is an element that will contain the attributes that define our relationship. It is nested within the element definition for the element that is to be the child of the relationship.

    ❏ sql:key-relation: This attribute of sql:relationship will be the name of a table that is to be the referenced (parent) table in a foreign key relationship.

    ❏ sql:key: The referenced column in the foreign key relationship. This is an attribute of sql:relationship and the column must exist within the table specified in the key-relation attribute.

    ❏ sql:foreign-relation: This attribute of sql:relationship is the referencing (child) table in the relationship.

    ❏ sql:foreign-key: This attribute of sql:relationship indicates which column has the foreign key restriction placed on it.

Note that all of the foreign key related attributes are placed in the element declaration of the referencing element.

705

So, let's start off with an extremely simple mapping – the `Employees` table that we have already used to retrieve some binary data. In this case, I'm going to map most of the rows, but I'll leave off the `Photo` field for the sake of brevity in the results:

```xml
<?xml version="1.0" ?>
<Schema     xmlns="urn:schemas-microsoft-com:xml-data"
            xmlns:dt="urn:schemas-microsoft-com:datatypes"
            xmlns:sql="urn:schemas-microsoft-com:xml-sql" >
  <ElementType name="Employee" content="mixed" sql:relation="Employees">
    <AttributeType name="EmployeeID" dt:type="int" />
    <AttributeType name="LastName" dt:type="string" />
    <AttributeType name="FirstName" dt:type="string" />
    <AttributeType name="Title" dt:type="string" />
    <AttributeType name="TitleOfCourtesy" dt:type="string" />
    <AttributeType name="BirthDate" dt:type="date" />
    <AttributeType name="HireDate" dt:type="date" />
    <AttributeType name="Address" dt:type="string" />
    <AttributeType name="City" dt:type="string" />
    <AttributeType name="Region" dt:type="string" />
    <AttributeType name="PostalCode" dt:type="string" />
    <AttributeType name="Country" dt:type="string" />
    <AttributeType name="HomePhone" dt:type="string" />
    <AttributeType name="Extension" dt:type="string" />
    <AttributeType name="Notes" dt:type="string" />
    <AttributeType name="ReportsTo" dt:type="int" />
    <AttributeType name="PhotoPath" dt:type="string" />

    <attribute type="EmployeeID" sql:field="EmployeeID"/>
    <attribute type="LastName" sql:field="LastName"/>
    <attribute type="FirstName" sql:field="FirstName"/>
    <attribute type="Title" sql:field="Title"/>
    <attribute type="TitleOfCourtesy" sql:field="TitleOfCourtesy"/>
    <attribute type="BirthDate" sql:field="BirthDate"/>
    <attribute type="HireDate" sql:field="HireDate"/>
    <attribute type="Address" sql:field="Address"/>
    <attribute type="City" sql:field="City"/>
    <attribute type="Region" sql:field="Region"/>
    <attribute type="PostalCode" sql:field="PostalCode"/>
    <attribute type="Country" sql:field="Country"/>
    <attribute type="HomePhone" sql:field="HomePhone"/>
    <attribute type="Extension" sql:field="Extension"/>
    <attribute type="Notes" sql:field="Notes"/>
    <attribute type="ReportsTo" sql:field="ReportsTo"/>
    <attribute type="PhotoPath" sql:field="PhotoPath"/>
  </ElementType>
</Schema>
```

Save this as `employees.xdr` in whatever physical directory you pointed your "schema" virtual root to back when we set up HTTP: access (for me, it was `C:\Inetpub\NWind\schemas`).

Now let's look at how we would navigate such a schema. It looks much like our straight database object query did, but now we are allowed to leave off some information that can be implied from our schema. For example, the direct object query requires us to name one (and only one) attribute. When querying against a schema, we can leave the attribute off, and SQL Server will assume that we want all of the mapped attributes:

http://localhost/northwind/schemas/employees.xdr/Employee[@EmployeeID='1']

This queries for just Employee elements with an EmployeeID of 1:

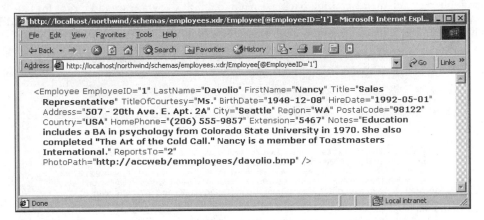

Now try something a little different – Employees with an EmployeeID that is less than 5. This gets us a little nastygram:

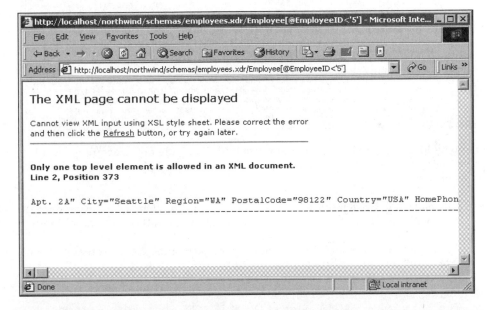

> If you are seeing a different error page than this (for example, a **500 error**), then you will need to go into the **Advanced** tab of the **Tools | Internet Options** menu choice in Internet Explorer. Uncheck the option that says, **show friendly HTTP error messages** and apply the change. This will greatly shorten your debugging time when working with anything that gets rendered in the browser.

Why? Well, if you go to View | Source and look over the XML, you should quickly see that we have multiple `Employee` elements, but no root element to encapsulate them. When we only had one `Employee` element (`EmployeeID 1`), that element served both as the root and to provide our data. With multiple outer elements coming back, we need to tell SQL Server to add a root for us – we do that pretty much as we did back in the URL-based queries we looked at a few sections ago – by adding a parameter of ?root=ROOT on the end of our query:

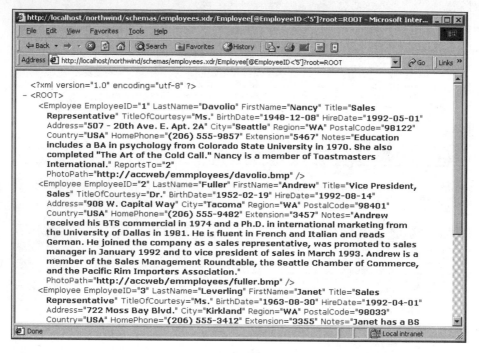

We can also build more complex views of our data by defining the full structure of what is to be returned in the schema. In order to do this, we need to define multiple elements and the relationships between them.

Let's go a little more step-by-step this time. For example, using a schema we can produce the same basic result as we did with `FOR XML` when we looked at `RAW`, `AUTO`, and `EXPLICIT` earlier in the chapter.

To start, we need to create `ElementType` definitions for each of the elements that we want to include in our query. We could, for instance, start out with:

```
<?xml version="1.0" encoding="UTF-8"?>
<Schema    xmlns="urn:schemas-microsoft-com:xml-data"
           xmlns:dt="urn:schemas-microsoft-com:datatypes"
           xmlns:sql="urn:schemas-microsoft-com:xml-sql">

  <ElementType name="Customer" >
  </ElementType>
  <ElementType name="Order" >
  </ElementType>
</Schema>
```

Next, we want to establish what tables our elements relate to:

```xml
<?xml version="1.0" encoding="UTF-8"?>
<Schema    xmlns="urn:schemas-microsoft-com:xml-data"
           xmlns:dt="urn:schemas-microsoft-com:datatypes"
           xmlns:sql="urn:schemas-microsoft-com:xml-sql">

  <ElementType name="Customer" sql:relation="Customers" >
  </ElementType>
  <ElementType name="Order" sql:relation="Orders" >
  </ElementType>
</Schema>
```

Now we're ready to add our fields:

```xml
<?xml version="1.0" encoding="UTF-8"?>
<Schema    xmlns="urn:schemas-microsoft-com:xml-data"
           xmlns:dt="urn:schemas-microsoft-com:datatypes"
           xmlns:sql="urn:schemas-microsoft-com:xml-sql">

  <ElementType name="Customer" sql:relation="Customers" >
      <AttributeType name="CustomerID" />
      <AttributeType name="CompanyName" />
      <attribute type="CustomerID" sql:field="CustomerID" />
      <attribute type="CompanyName" sql:field="CompanyName" />
  </ElementType>
  <ElementType name="Order" sql:relation="Orders" >
      <AttributeType name="CustomerID" />
      <AttributeType name="OrderID" />
      <AttributeType name="OrderDate" />
      <attribute type="CustomerID" sql:field="CustomerID" />
      <attribute type="OrderID" sql:field="OrderID" />
      <attribute type="OrderDate" sql:field="OrderDate" />
  </ElementType>
</Schema>
```

Next up (almost done!), we need to add in our nesting structure. Our `Customer` element type is to have an `Orders` element nested within it. Naturally, that nested element will be of type `"Order"` – which is also defined in our schema:

```xml
<?xml version="1.0" encoding="UTF-8"?>
<Schema    xmlns="urn:schemas-microsoft-com:xml-data"
           xmlns:dt="urn:schemas-microsoft-com:datatypes"
           xmlns:sql="urn:schemas-microsoft-com:xml-sql">

  <ElementType name="Customer" sql:relation="Customers" >
      <AttributeType name="CustomerID" />
      <AttributeType name="CompanyName" />
      <attribute type="CustomerID" sql:field="CustomerID" />
      <attribute type="CompanyName" sql:field="CompanyName" />
          <element type="Order" >
          </element>
  </ElementType>
  <ElementType name="Order" sql:relation="Orders" >
<AttributeType name="CustomerID" />
      <AttributeType name="OrderID" />
      <AttributeType name="OrderDate" />
<attribute type="CustomerID" sql:field="CustomerID" />
      <attribute type="OrderID" sql:field="OrderID" />
      <attribute type="OrderDate" sql:field="OrderDate" />
  </ElementType>
</Schema>
```

Since we've declared our nested element as being of a type that we've already declared (the ElementType called Order), we do not need to specify any of the attributes – those are inherited from the ElementType definition. What we do still need to do, however, is define the relationship between our Customer ElementType and the nested element – Order. To do this, we add in our relationship definition:

```xml
<?xml version="1.0" encoding="UTF-8"?>
<Schema    xmlns="urn:schemas-microsoft-com:xml-data"
           xmlns:dt="urn:schemas-microsoft-com:datatypes"
           xmlns:sql="urn:schemas-microsoft-com:xml-sql">

  <ElementType name="Customer" sql:relation="Customers" >
      <AttributeType name="CustomerID" />
      <AttributeType name="CompanyName" />
      <attribute type="CustomerID" sql:field="CustomerID" />
      <attribute type="CompanyName" sql:field="CompanyName" />
       <element type="Order" >
         <sql:relationship key-relation="Customers" key="CustomerID"
            foreign-key="CustomerID" foreign-relation="Orders" />
       </element>
  </ElementType>
  <ElementType name="Order" sql:relation="Orders" >
      <AttributeType name="CustomerID" />
      <AttributeType name="OrderID" />
      <AttributeType name="OrderDate" />
      <attribute type="CustomerID" sql:field="CustomerID" />
      <attribute type="OrderID" sql:field="OrderID" />
      <attribute type="OrderDate" sql:field="OrderDate" />
  </ElementType>
</Schema>
```

OK – we're done! Save this file in our schemas directory as CustomerOrders.xdr, and you're ready to run a query against it:

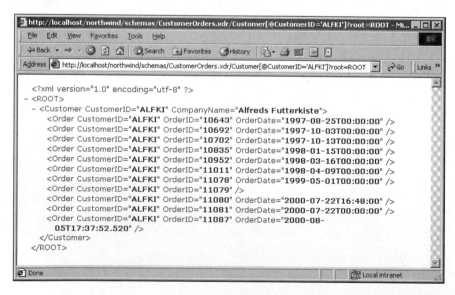

Too cool!

Styling Your Results

One of the nice things about XML is that it can so easily be "styled" into some other form. That form can be HTML (a very common application of styling), a different XML format, or even something completely different.

In this section, we're going to take a whirlwind look at how to apply styling to our HTTP based queries.

It's probably time for me to reiterate that this isn't an XML, XPath, or XLST book. While I will be showing some of the XSLT scripting used in this section, the focus is entirely on how we reference our XSL documents. For more information on XSL, I recommend the XSLT Programmer's Reference by Michael Kay, which – I'm sure this will totally surprise you – is available from Wrox Press (ISBN 1-861003-12-9).

Styling URL Based Queries

This one is pretty easy – you just need to add the XSL parameter, in the form of:

```
&xsl=<{path to xsl file}>
```

To use an example of this, you can build the following style sheet and name it customers.xsl:

```
<?xml version='1.0' encoding='UTF-8'?>
<xsl:stylesheet xmlns:xsl="http://www.w3.org/1999/XSL/Transform"
  version="1.0">

    <xsl:template match = '*'>
        <xsl:apply-templates />
    </xsl:template>
    <xsl:template match = 'Customers'>
      <TR>
        <TD valign="top"><a>
          <xsl:attribute name="href">../../Login.asp?CustomerID=
            <xsl:value-of select='@CustomerID'/>
          </xsl:attribute>
          <xsl:value-of select="@CustomerID"/></a></TD>
          <TD align="left" width="300"><B>
      <xsl:value-of select = '@CompanyName'/><br/>
      <xsl:value-of select='@Address'/><br/>
      <xsl:value-of select="@City"/>,
      <xsl:value-of select="@Region"/>
      <xsl:value-of select="@PostalCode"/>
      </B>
  </TD>
      </TR>
    </xsl:template>
    <xsl:template match = '/'>
      <HTML>
        <HEAD>
<TITLE>Northwind Traders Customers</TITLE>
        </HEAD>
        <BODY>
<TABLE cellpadding="0" cellspacing="0" border="0">
```

```
    <TR>
      <TD>
      <IMG alt="Northwind Traders" src="../../images/NorthwindLogo.jpg"
        border="0"/>
      </TD>
      <TD><FONT face="Arial" size="6" > Northwind Traders Online</FONT>
      </TD>
    </TR>
    <TR>
      <TD bgcolor="Aqua" colspan="2">
        <HR width="*"/>
      </TD>
    </TR>
    <TR>
    <TD valign="top" bgcolor="Aqua">
    </TD>
    <td>
    <TABLE border='1'  width="*">
            <TR><TH colspan='2'>Customers</TH></TR>
            <TR><TH>Customer ID</TH><th>Company</th></TR>
            <xsl:apply-templates select = 'Root' />
        </TABLE>
    </td>
  </TR>
</TABLE>
    </BODY>
    </HTML>
   </xsl:template>
</xsl:stylesheet>
```

This needs to be saved in whatever you designated as being the storage location for your Northwind virtual directory.

You can also download this file from the Wrox web site or ProfessionalSQL.com. That will save you an awful lot of typing, and also guard against typos – remember, XSL and XML are case sensitive, so even the little things can get you! Also, if you want to see the graphic that this refers to, you'll need to download that from Wrox or my web site too, and install the graphic in a directory called images, which should be right under your web site's root directory.

With this created and saved appropriately, we're ready to run our query. This query is going to supply data for a web page listing our Northwind customers:

http://localhost/Northwind?sql=SELECT+CustomerID,+CompanyName,+Address,+City,+Region,+PostalCode+FROM+Customers+ORDER+BY+CustomerID+FOR+XML+AUTO&xsl=customers.xsl&root=Root

If all has been saved and stored in the right place, you should wind up with something that looks like this:

We have a web page and, as yet, not a single line of ASP code!

Styling Templates

OK, so if the last one was easy (just saving the XSLT document in the right place and adding the xsl parameter on the query), you might consider this one even easier. All we need to do is add an attribute to our root element in our template. This attribute will reference our XSLT document. The attribute should have the form of:

```
sql:xsl="<path to style sheet>"
```

For an example this time, let's turn our URL query into a Customers template that we'll call customers.xml. We will make use of the same XSLT document, and we'll need to change the path accordingly:

```
<Root xmlns:sql="urn:schemas-microsoft-com:xml-sql" sql:xsl="../customers.xsl">
  <sql:query>
    SELECT CustomerID,
        CompanyName,
        Address,
        City,
        Region,
        PostalCode
    FROM Customers
    ORDER BY CustomerID
    FOR XML AUTO
  </sql:query>
</Root>
```

Now, we should be able to call our customers.xml file and get back a web page just like the one we saw with the URL-based query. But we'll run into a small problem:

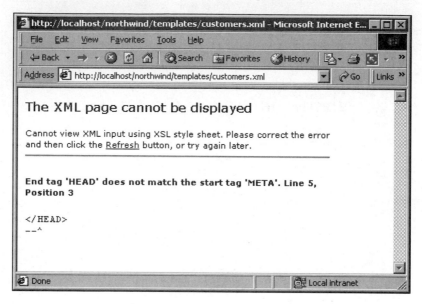

At this stage you may get something that resembles HTML tags; this is another manifestation of the same error message. The probable cause of this is different server configurations.

The problem here is with something called the **content-type**. The content-type is something that is embedded in the HTTP header information, and it is what tells your browser what kind of data it is dealing with. For much of what we have done so far in this chapter, SQL Server has made sure that the right content-type information was associated with our documents, so we haven't had to worry about it. Now, however, we are applying transformations, so SQL Server has no way of knowing for sure what content-type you want – you have to explicitly say so somewhere. There are two ways of specifying the content-type:

- ❏ The contenttype parameter in your URL

- ❏ A special element called xsl:mediatype near the top (right after the namespace declaration) of your XSLT document

The contenttype parameter makes the most sense when you want to be able to output in multiple content-types. An example of where you might want to do this is if you are transforming to XHTML (normally, you would want to have a content-type of text/HTML for this so the browser thinks it's HTML), but you have instances where you really want to treat the XHTML as XHTML (maybe you're going to perform a secondary transformation on it). To make use of contenttype, just add it to the end of your URL using a ? prefix if it will be the first or only parameter, and & if it is a subsequent parameter:

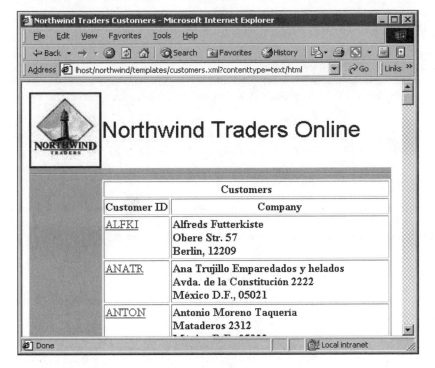

At this stage, we could employ the `media-type` attribute of the `xsl:output` element to modify our `customers.xsl` file. This defines the media type of the output file and would therefore enable us to run the previous query and obtain the same results, but without needing to incorporate the `contenttype` parameter in the query.

Not that hard at all.

We can also override an XSLT transformation in our templates by providing a new XSLT document reference on the URL – if an XSLT document is referenced both in the template and in the URL, the URL version wins.

A Brief Word About Updategrams

Well, this one is downright painful to me. You see, **updategrams** are on the way as I write this, but they are not here yet, so few things I write about them are likely to be the same once the official release happens. Updategrams are a method of sending XML back to the server and having SQL Server figure out what it's supposed to update. This is something of an alternative to and far more powerful approach than `OPENXML`.

Updategrams essentially supply SQL Server with a before and after image of the data that we want updated. SQL Server is then able to look over the supplied information, figure out what changes need to be made, and then make those changes.

Updategrams are on web release, and will be offered and then updated regularly at Microsoft's web site. I will be making information on updategrams available on my web site at some point shortly after they are officially released.

Streaming XML

Using newer versions of ADO (2.6 and beyond), the results of a query that needs to end up in XML can now be streamed to a client without having to build all the meta-data that goes with a full result set. Once at a client or a web server, the XML can then be transformed into just about anything you would like – for example, an XHTML web page or a data file for pickup/transmission to a customer or vendor.

> *As with when we were dealing with XSLT, I'm going to assume that you already know something about ADO. Check out Dave Sussman's* ADO 2.6 Programmer's Reference *(Wrox, ISBN: 1-861004-63-X), and Thearon Willis'* Beginning SQL Server 2000 for Visual Basic Developers *(Wrox, ISBN: 1-861004-67-2) for getting to know the basic connectivity between Visual Basic and SQL Server using ADO.*

What we are going to do in this section is race through building a component in Visual Basic that can execute a query for you and then provide a block of XML back for use in whatever your needs are. We will also take a look at how we could do much the same thing from ASP.

A Quick Look at the Stream Object

This object, in most ways, takes the place of the `Recordset` object when you are dealing with XML using SQL Server XML integration. It doesn't really stop there though – you see, you also use the `Stream` object to submit your queries.

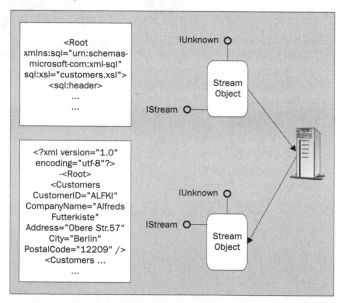

The `Stream` object is quite a bit different from a `Recordset`. You see, a `Recordset` has a ton of things going on under the covers that allow you to specifically address each field, know its data type, know whether it's been updated – the list goes on and on. With `Stream`s however, what you see is pretty much what you get. With the exception of you indicating a dialect (to tell the recipient things like whether you're using T-SQL or XPath), there is little descriptive information associated with a `Stream` object. You provide a serial string (or "stream") of text. SQL Server parses that text based on the dialect you have chosen, and then sends you back another serial line of text – that is, another stream. In our case, the return stream is either going to be XML or something else that we've applied a style to achieve.

Implementing a Stream Object into a Component

What we're going to do here is teach almost solely by example. It is my hope that you'll be able to glean a lot out of this quickly because it would take a whole additional book to explain it in detail – still, you will see that, like most things, the basics (what you need 90% of the time) are not that difficult.

Start by opening Visual Basic and creating a new ActiveX DLL project – we will be saving this later as Northwind:

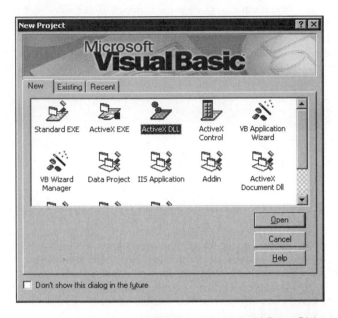

Once your project is open, set a reference to the Microsoft ActiveX Data Objects Library by navigating to the Projects | References menu choice:

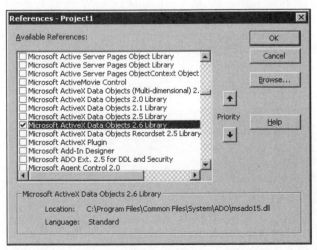

Next, change the name of your project in the Project Properties to Northwind. Change the Class1 module's name to Orders.cls.

Now we're ready to do a little coding. We will start by setting up some header information, by declaring a couple of constants:

```
Option Explicit

Const XML_HEADER = "<Root xmlns:sql='urn:schemas-microsoft-com:xml-sql'>"
Const XML_FOOTER = "</Root>"
```

What we are going to do here is implement a simple function that will accept a Customer ID and provide a list of the customer's orders and the date the orders were placed (getting a sense of déjà vu here?). We'll set up our function header to accept a `CustomerID` parameter as a string (`CustomerID` is an `nchar(5)` in the database). We also need to declare several variables – including a couple of `Stream` objects. We will see how these are utilized as we continue through the code:

```
Public Function GetCustomerOrdersXML(CustomerID As String) As String
Dim cn As ADODB.Connection
Dim Cmd As ADODB.Command
Dim sQuery As String
Dim sXML As String
Dim sResult As String
Dim adoStreamQuery As ADODB.Stream
Dim ResultStream As ADODB.Stream

End Function
```

Next up, we're ready to establish a connection. Notice that I'm passing in a different user login and password from those we used in our virtual root. There is nothing to say that we couldn't use the same thing over again, but I want to make it clear that you could have a different user here that you would probably grant more significant access to than you might in a situation like the virtual root. Anonymous users can usually only instantiate objects like this one via an ASP page, which means that you should have some degree of control over when it is instantiated.

> *In real life, I would want to wait to establish the connection until my query was 100% ready to go – remember, don't start using resources until you need them! I've created my connection early here to get it out of the way. We're not here for connections, but Streams, so I don't want to stick something like connections in the middle of the more interesting stuff later in the code.*

```
Public Function GetCustomerOrdersXML(CustomerID As String) As String
Dim cn As ADODB.Connection
Dim Cmd As ADODB.Command
Dim sQuery As String
Dim sXML As String
Dim sResult As String
Dim adoStreamQuery As ADODB.Stream
Dim ResultStream As ADODB.Stream

'Fire up the Connection
Set cn = CreateObject("ADODB.Connection")

cn.ConnectionString = "Provider=SQLOLEDB;Data Source=(local);Initial
Catalog=Northwind;User ID=NorthwindSecure;Password=NorthwindSecure;"
```

```
        cn.CursorLocation = adUseClient
        cn.Open

        'Create a Command Object
        Set Cmd = CreateObject("ADODB.Command")
        Set Cmd.ActiveConnection = cn

End Function
```

OK – now we're ready for things to get a tad more interesting. What we are going to do here is build what amounts to a query template. Indeed, if you take a look back at our `CustomerOrders.xml` file, you'll see that I've pretty much just cut and pasted that template right into our Visual Basic code. To SQL Server, this isn't really going to be much different from when it came through the web site – after all, the `SQLISAPI.DLL` library is simply performing many of these same tasks for us.

```
    . . .
    . . .
    'Create a Command Object
    Set Cmd = CreateObject("ADODB.Command")
    Set Cmd.ActiveConnection = cn

    'Build the XML Query
    sXML = XML_HEADER
    sXML = sXML & "<sql:query>"
    sXML = sXML & "SELECT Customer.CustomerID, Customer.CompanyName, "
    sXML = sXML & "Orders.OrderID, Orders.OrderDate,
    (SELECT SUM(Quantity * UnitPrice) FROM [Order Details]
       WHERE OrderID = Orders.OrderID) AS OrderTotal "
    sXML = sXML & "FROM Customers AS Customer
       JOIN Orders ON Customer.CustomerID = Orders.CustomerID "
    sXML = sXML & "WHERE Customer.CustomerID = '" & CustomerID & "' FOR XML
       AUTO"
    sXML = sXML & "</sql:query>"
    sXML = sXML & XML_FOOTER

End Function
```

The reason I'm using constants for a header and footer here is that it makes it easy for me to include them if I write multiple functions for this class. That way, if one of the URNs changes or any other slight alterations are desired, I only have to make them in one place.

So, now things get even meatier. We are now going to instantiate the first of two `Stream` objects. The `Stream` object has a method called `WriteText` – this accepts either string or binary data and places the data into the `Stream`. We're going to use the `adWriteChar` enum value, which tells the `Stream` object that we're dealing with character data rather than binary. As we place data into the `Stream`, a pointer is kept so we know where we want to insert the next chunk of data into the stream. Once we're done adding our `Stream` data, we want to set the `Position` value back to zero – this will make sure that our data `Stream` is sent to the server from the very beginning.

Finally, with our output `Stream` all prepared, we associate our `Stream` with a `Command` object by utilizing the new `CommandStream` property of the ADO `Command` object. This accepts a `Stream` object as a parameter – in this case, the `Stream` object that contains our XML template:

```
. . .
. . .
sXML = sXML & "</sql:query>"
sXML = sXML & XML_FOOTER

'Set up a Stream for the query
Set adoStreamQuery = CreateObject("ADODB.Stream")
adoStreamQuery.Open
adoStreamQuery.WriteText sXML, adWriteChar
adoStreamQuery.Position = 0

'Assign the Stream to the Command
Set Cmd.CommandStream = adoStreamQuery

End Function
```

Now we're ready to wrap things up. We need to instantiate one more `Stream`. This time we won't be sending anything – instead, we will be receiving back a stream of XML! We still need to open the `Stream` as we did last time, but this time we're setting the `Stream` up to read (rather than write) data. We then associate this `Stream` with the `Command` object, but this time it's not a `CommandStream` – indeed, it's quite the opposite. Our `ResultStream` is going to be the recipient of our XML data when we execute the `Command`. Once we have both `Streams` (`Command` and `Result`) set up and properly associated with the `Command`, we can execute it. Be sure to recognize that ADO now has more options in the nature of the `Execute` method. In our case, we need to make use of the `adExecuteStream` enum value to tell the `Command` object to use the `Streams` rather than the methods and properties used for more standard ADO `Recordsets`.

Finally, we read the results of the now populated `Stream`, and pass those into our return value:

```
Public Function GetCustomerOrdersXML(CustomerID As String) As String
Dim cn As ADODB.Connection
Dim Cmd As ADODB.Command
Dim sQuery As String
Dim sXML As String
Dim sResult As String
Dim adoStreamQuery As ADODB.Stream
Dim ResultStream As ADODB.Stream

'Fire up the Connection
Set cn = CreateObject("ADODB.Connection")

cn.ConnectionString = "Provider=SQLOLEDB;Data Source=(local);Initial
Catalog=Northwind;User ID=NorthwindSecure;Password=NorthwindSecure;"

cn.CursorLocation = adUseClient
cn.Open

'Create a Command Object
Set Cmd = CreateObject("ADODB.Command")
Set Cmd.ActiveConnection = cn

'Build the XML Query
sXML = XML_HEADER
sXML = sXML & "<sql:query>"
```

```
sXML = sXML & "SELECT Customer.CustomerID, Customer.CompanyName, "
sXML = sXML & "Orders.OrderID, Orders.OrderDate,
(SELECT SUM(Quantity * UnitPrice) FROM [Order Details]
  WHERE OrderID = Orders.OrderID) AS OrderTotal "
sXML = sXML & "FROM Customers AS Customer
 JOIN Orders ON Customer.CustomerID = Orders.CustomerID "
sXML = sXML & "WHERE Customer.CustomerID = '" & CustomerID & "' FOR XML
  AUTO"
sXML = sXML & "</sql:query>"
sXML = sXML & XML_FOOTER

'Set up a Stream for the query
Set adoStreamQuery = CreateObject("ADODB.Stream")
adoStreamQuery.Open
adoStreamQuery.WriteText sXML, adWriteChar
adoStreamQuery.Position = 0

'Assign the Stream to the Command
Set Cmd.CommandStream = adoStreamQuery

'Create a Stream to receive the results
Set ResultStream = CreateObject("ADODB.Stream")
ResultStream.Open
Cmd.Properties("Output Stream") = ResultStream

'Execute the query
Cmd.Execute , , adExecuteStream
sResult = ResultStream.ReadText
GetCustomerOrdersXML = sResult
End Function
```

At this point, the object is ready for use. You can test it by using any client language that will accept a string from VB (ASP, VB, C++). Just call the function passing in a Customer ID, and you should get back a list of that customer's orders.

For example, here is the code from a little tester I wrote in VB:

```
Option Explicit

Private Sub cmdGo_Click()
Dim ResultStream As String
Dim objData As Northwind.Orders

Set objData = CreateObject("NorthWind.Orders")
ResultStream = objData.GetCustomerOrdersXML(txtCustomerID)
txtResponse = ResultStream
End Sub
```

This just ran inside a little form that looks like this:

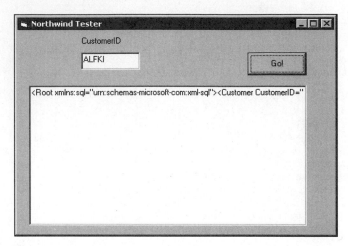

The output looked like this:

```
<Root xmlns:sql="urn:schemas-microsoft-com:xml-sql">
<Customer CustomerID="ALFKI" CompanyName="Alfreds Futterkiste">
  <Orders OrderID="10643" OrderDate="1997-08-25T00:00:00" OrderTotal="1086" />
  <Orders OrderID="10692" OrderDate="1997-10-03T00:00:00" OrderTotal="878" />
  <Orders OrderID="10702" OrderDate="1997-10-13T00:00:00" OrderTotal="330" />
  <Orders OrderID="10835" OrderDate="1998-01-15T00:00:00" OrderTotal="851" />
  <Orders OrderID="10952" OrderDate="1998-03-16T00:00:00" OrderTotal="491.2" />
  <Orders OrderID="11011" OrderDate="1998-04-09T00:00:00" OrderTotal="960" />
</Customer>
</Root>
```

So, without much fuss or fanfare, we are able to submit our templates not only from HTTP, but also from more traditional sources. HTTP access does not need to be turned on in order for this last approach to work and, as such, it is inherently more secure.

Summary

Wow, huh? A lot of stuff there to comprehend, and a lot to think about in terms of the classic, "Yeah, but what does it mean to me?" question.

XML is simply the biggest thing going on in the development world right now. While it's conceivable that .NET will give XML a challenge for impact on the industry in the next couple of years, one can still be certain that XML is going to be sitting at the core of an awful lot of things that are going on – particularly relating to data and web technologies.

SQL Server has added a wide array of fairly powerful integration points with XML. Microsoft has gone to a web release format for XML functionality and this will ensure that there are new things to learn and changes in functionality coming at the SQL Server world at a very high rate.

Online discussion at http://p2p.wrox.com

21

The Bulk Copy Program (bcp)

If your system is going to be operating in something of a bubble, then you can probably skip this chapter and move on. Unfortunately, the real world doesn't work that way, so you probably ought to hang around for a while.

Sometimes, reality just gets in the way. There will be times when you need to move around large blocks of data. You need to bring in data that's in the wrong format or that's sitting in another application's data files. The good thing is, SQL Server has two tools to help you move large blocks of data fast – the **bulk copy program** (**bcp**) and **Data Transformation Services** (**DTS**). In this chapter, we'll be looking at the first of these. In addition, we'll take a look at bcp's close cousin – the BULK INSERT command. We will examine DTS in the next chapter.

The bcp is something of an old friend. You know the one – the friend whom you hardly ever see anymore, but when you do, you reminisce on all the crazy things you used to do together. It was, for a very long time, *the* way large blocks of data were moved about – and it did so (still does as far as that goes) amazingly fast. What it lacks, however, is sex appeal – well, frankly, since version 7.0, it has lacked appeal in a whole lot of areas.

So, why then am I even spending a chapter on it? Well, because bcp still definitely has its uses.

Among it's advantages are:

- ❏ It's very compact
- ❏ It can move a lot of data very quickly
- ❏ It's legacy – that is, there may be code already running that is making effective use of it, so why change it?
- ❏ It uses a cryptic, yet very traditional scripting style (which will probably appeal to some of you)
- ❏ It is very consistent (none of those nagging interface changes that come with COM-based methods such as DTS)

The bcp is used for transferring text and SQL Server native format data to and from SQL Server tables. It has changed very little in the last several versions, though there are some changes both in terms of functionality and behavior under SQL Server 2000. You can think of the bcp as being like a data pump, with little functionality other than moving data from one place to the other as efficiently as possible.

The bcp Utility

bcp runs from an operating system command prompt to import or export native data (specific to SQL Server), ASCII text, or Unicode text. This means that you can execute bcp from an operating system batch file, or user-defined stored procedure, as well as from other places. bcp can also be run as part of a scheduled job, or executed from a COM-based object through the use of a shell command.

Like most command line utilities, options can be specified using a hyphen (–) or forward slash (/); however, unlike most DOS or Windows family utilities, option switches are case sensitive; –c and –C do different things so be careful.

bcp Syntax

```
bcp {[[<database name>.][<owner>].]{<table name>|<view name>}|"<query>"}
    {in | out | queryout | format} <data file>
    [-m <maximum no. of errors>] [-f <format file>] [-e <error file>]
    [-F <first row>] [-L <last row>] [-b <batch size>]
    [-n] [-c] [-w] [-N] [-V (60 | 65 | 70)] [-6]
    [-q] [-C <code page>] [-t <field term>] [-r <row term>]
    [-i <input file>] [-o <output file>] [-a <packet size>]
    [-S <server name>[\<instance name>]] [-U <login id>] [-P <password>]
    [-T] [-v] [-R] [-k] [-E] [-h "<hint> [,...n]"]
```

Gee – that's a lot to take in, so let's go through them one by one (thankfully, most of them are optional, so you will usually only include just a fraction of them).

Parameter	Description
Database name	Exactly what it sounds like. Basically, this is a standard part of the four-part naming scheme. If not specified, the user's default database is assumed.
Owner	More of the four-part naming scheme stuff. Again, exactly what it sounds like.
Table name or View name or a SQL query	Required. Can only be one – table, view, or query. This is the input destination or output source table or view. A SQL Server query can only be used as a bcp output destination, and only when queryout is specified. If the query returns multiple result sets, only the first result set is used by bcp.

Parameter	Description
in data file *or* out data file *or* queryout data file *or* format data file	Required. Again, there can only be one of these specified. If using any of these, you must also supply a source or destination file. Establishes the direction of the bcp action. in indicates that you are importing data from a source file into a table or view. out indicates that you are exporting data from table or view into the destination file. Use queryout only for output to the destination file using a query as its source. Use format to create a format file based on the format option you've selected. You must also specify -f, as well as format options (-n, -c, -w, -6, -C, or -N) or you will have to answer prompts from interactive bcp. The source or destination path and filename is specified as <data file>, and cannot include more than 255 characters.
-m <maximum errors>	You can specify a maximum number of errors that you will allow before SQL Server cancels the bulk copy operation, defaulting to 10 errors. Each row that cannot be copied by bcp is counted as one error.
-f <format file>	A format file contains responses saved from a previous bcp operation on the same table or view. This parameter should include the full path and filename to the format file. This option is used primarily with the in and format options to specify the path and filename when making use of or creating a format file.
-e <error file>	You can specify the full path and filename for an error file to store any rows that bcp is not able to transfer. Otherwise, no error file is created. Any error messages will be displayed at the client station.
-F first row	Use this option if you want to specify the first row to be copied by the bulk copy operation. If not specified, bcp defaults to a value of 1 and begins copying with the first row in the source data file. This option can be handy if you want to handle your loading in chunks, and can be used to pick back up where you left off in a previous loading run.
-L last row	This option is the complement of -F. It provides for determining what is the last row you want loaded as part of this bcp execution. If not specified, bcp defaults to a value of 0, the last row in the source file. When used in conjunction with -F, this option can allow you to load your data one chunk at a time – loading small blocks of data and then picking up next time where the previous load left off.
-b batch size	You can specify the number of rows copied as a batch. A batch is copied as a single transaction. Like all transactions, the rows of the batch are committed in an "all-or-nothing" fashion – either every row is committed or the transaction is rolled back and it is as if the batch never happened. The -h (hint) switch has a similar option (ROWS_PER_BATCH), which should be considered to be mutually exclusive with -b (use either one of them, but not both).

Table continued on following page

Parameter	Description
-n	Native data types (SQL Server data types) are used for the copy operation. Using this option avoids the need to answer the questions regarding the data types to be used in the transfer (it just picks up the native type and goes with it).
-c	This specifies that the operation uses character data (text) for all fields, and, as such, does not require a separate data type question for each field. A tab character is assumed as field delimiter unless you use the -t option, and a new line character as row separator unless you specify different terminator using -r.
-w	The -w option is similar to -c, but specifies Unicode data type instead of ASCII for all fields. Again, unless you override with -t and -r, the tab character and row separator are assumed to be the field delimiter and new line character respectively. This option cannot be used with SQL Server version 6.5 or earlier.
-N	This is basically the same as -w – using Unicode for character data, but uses native data types (database data types) for non-character data. This option offers higher performance when going from SQL Server to SQL Server. As with -w, this option cannot be used with SQL Server version 6.5 or earlier.
-V (60|65|70)	Causes bcp to utilize data type formats that were only available in previous versions of SQL Server. 60 uses 6.0 data types, 65 uses 6.5 data types, and 70 uses 7.0 data types. This replaces the -6 option.
-6	Use this option to force bcp to use SQL Server 6.0 or 6.5 data types. This option is used in conjunction with the -c or -n format options for backward compatibility reasons only – use -V whenever possible.
-q	Use -q to specify that a table or view name includes non-ANSI characters. This effectively executes a SET QUOTED_IDENTIFIERS ON statement for the connection used by bcp. The fully qualified name, database, owner, and table or view must be enclosed in double quotation marks, in the format "database name.owner.table".
-C <code page>	This option is used to specify the code page for the data-file data. It is only necessary to use this option with char, varchar, or text data having ASCII character values of less than 32 or greater than 127. A code page value of ACP specifies ANSI/Microsoft Windows (ISO 1252). OEM specifies the default client code page. If RAW is specified, there will be no code page conversion. You also have the option of providing a specific code page value. Avoid this option where possible – instead, use a specific collation in the format file or when asked by bcp.
-t <field terminator>	This option allows you to override the default field terminator. The default terminator is the tab character. You can specify the terminator as tab (\t), new line (\n), carriage return (\r), backslash (\\), null terminator (\0), any printable character, or a string of up to ten printable characters. For example, you would use '-t,' for a comma-delimited text file.

Parameter	Description
-r <row terminator>	This option works just like -t except that it allows you to override the default row terminator (as opposed to the field terminator). The default terminator is \n, the newline character. The rules are otherwise the same as -t.
-i <input file>	You have the option of specifying a response file, as input file, containing the responses to be used when running bcp in interactive mode (this can save answering a ton of questions!).
-o <output file>	You can redirect bcp output from the command prompt to an output file. This gives you a way to capture command output and results when executing bcp from an unattended batch or stored procedure.
-a <packet size>	You have the option of overriding the default packet size for data transfers across the network. Larger packet sizes tend to be more efficient when you have good line quality (few CRC errors). The specified value must be between 4,096 and 65,535, inclusive and overrides whatever default has been set up for the server. At installation, the default packet size is 4,096 bytes. This can be overridden using the SQL Server Enterprise Manager or the sp_configure system stored procedure.
-S <server name>	If running bcp from a server, the default is the local SQL Server. This option lets you specify a different server and is required in a network environment when running bcp from a remote system.
-U <login name>	Unless connecting to SQL Server through a trusted connection, you must provide a valid username for login.
-P password	When you supply a username, you must also supply a password. Otherwise, you will be prompted for a password. Include -P as your last option with no password to specify a null password.
-T	You have the option of connecting to the server using network user credentials through a trusted connection. If a trusted connection is specified, there is no need to provide a login name or password for the connection.
-v	When this option is used, bcp returns the version number and copyright information.
-R	Use this option to specify that the regional format for clients' local settings is used when copying currency, date, and time data. The default is that regional settings are ignored.
-k	Use this option to override the use of column default values during bulk copy, ignoring any default constraints. Empty columns will retain a null value rather than the column default.
-E	This option is used during import when the import source file contains identity column values, and is essentially equivalent to SET IDENTITY_INSERT ON. If not specified, SQL Server will ignore the values supplied in the source file and automatically generate identity column values. You can use the format file to skip the identity column when importing data from a source that does not include identity values and have SQL Server generate the values.

Table continued on following page

Parameter	Description
-h "hint[, …]"	The hint option lets you specify one or more hints to be used by the bulk copy operation. Option -h is not supported for SQL Server version 6.5 or earlier.
ORDER column [ASC|DESC]	You can use this hint to improve performance when the sort order of the source data file matches the clustered index in the destination table. If the destination table does not have a clustered index or if the data is sorted in a different order the ORDER hint is ignored.
ROWS_PER_BATCH=nn	This can be used in place of the -b option to specify the number of rows to be transferred as a batch. Do not use this hint with the -b option.
KILOBYTES_ PER_BATCH=nn	You can optionally specify batch size as the approximate number of kilobytes of data to be transferred in a batch.
TABLOCK	This will cause a table-level lock to be acquired for the duration of the operation. Default locking behavior is set by the table lock on bulk load table option.
CHECK_CONSTRAINTS	By default, check constraints are ignored during an import operation. This hint forces check constraints to be checked during import.
FIRE_TRIGGERS	New with SQL Server 2000 and similar to CHECK_CONSTRAINTS, this option causes any triggers on the destination table to fire for the transaction. By default, triggers are not fired on bulk operations. This option is not supported in prior versions of SQL Server.

bcp runs in interactive mode, prompting for format information, unless -f, -c, -n, -w, -6, or -N is specified when the command is executed. When running in interactive mode, bcp will also prompt to create a format file after receiving the format information.

bcp Import

OK, so up to this point we've been stuck in the preliminaries. Well, it's time to get down to the business of what bcp is all about.

Probably the most common use of bcp is to import bulk data into existing SQL Server tables and views. To import data, you must have access permissions to the server, either through a login ID or a trusted connection, and you must have INSERT and SELECT permissions on the destination table or view.

The source file can contain native code, ASCII characters, Unicode, or mixed native and Unicode data. Remember to use the appropriate option to describe the source data. Also, for the data file to be usable, you must be able to describe the field and row terminators (using -t and -r) or the fields and rows must be terminated with the default tab and new line characters respectively.

Be sure you know your destination before you start. bcp has a few quirks that can affect data import. Values supplied for timestamp or computed columns are ignored. If you have values for those columns in the source file, they'll be ignored. If the source file doesn't have values for these columns, you'll need a format file (which we'll see later in this chapter), so you can skip over them.

This is one of those really bizarre behaviors that you run across from time to time in just about any piece of software that you ever use. In this case, if your destination table contains them, you're required to have columns to represent timestamp or computed data even though SQL Server will just ignore that data – silly, isn't it? Again, the way around this is to use a format file that explicitly says to skip the columns in question.

For bcp operations, rules are ignored. Any triggers and constraints are ignored unless the `FIRE_TRIGGERS` and/or `CHECK_CONSTRAINTS` hints are specified. Unique constraints, indexes, and primary/foreign key constraints are enforced. Default constraints are enforced unless the `-k` option is specified.

Data Import Example

The easiest way to see how bcp import works is to look at an example. Let's start with a simple example, a tab-delimited file containing shipper information for the `Northwind` database. Here's how the data looks:

```
47      Readyship      (503)555-1234
48      MyShipper      (503)555-3443
```

To import this into the `Shippers` table using a trusted connection at the local server, you run:

```
bcp northwind.dbo.shippers in c:ProfessionalSQL\newship.txt -c -T
```

Two things are important here: first, up to this point, everything we've ran has been done either in Query Analyzer or the Enterprise Manger. For bcp however, you type your command into a DOS or command box. Second, you'll need to change the command line above to match wherever you've downloaded the sample files/data for this book.

Because the first column in the `Shippers` table is an identity column and the `-E` option wasn't specified, SQL Server will ignore the identity values in the file and generate new values. The `-c` option identifies the source data as character data and `-T` specifies to use a trusted connection.

Note that, if you have not been using NT authentication and haven't set your network login up with appropriate rights in SQL Server, then you may need to modify the above example to utilize the `-S`, and `-P` options.

When we execute it, SQL Server quickly tells us some basic information about how our bulk copy operation went:

Starting copy...

2 rows copied.
Network packet size (bytes): 4096
Clock Time (ms.): total   951

We can go back into our old friend the Query Analyzer and verify that the data went into the shippers table as expected:

```
USE Northwind

SELECT * FROM Shippers
```

Which gets us back several rows – most importantly, the two we expect from our bcp operation:

```
ShipperID    CompanyName                              Phone
-----------  ---------------------------------------  ------------------
1            Speedy Express                           (503) 555-9831
2            United Package                           (503) 555-3199
3            Federal Shipping                         (503) 555-9931
4            Speedy Shippers, Inc.                    (503) 555-5566
5            Speedy Shippers, Inc                     NULL
100          Billy Bob's Pretty Good Shipping         NULL
101          Fred's Freight                           NULL
102          Readyship                                (503)555-1234
103          MyShipper                                (503)555-3443
```

As always, note that, other than the two rows we just imported, your data may look a bit different depending on which parts of this book you've done the examples for, which you haven't, and how much playing around of your own you've done. For this example, you just want to see that Readyship and MyShipper made it into the table with the appropriate phone number – the identity values will have been reassigned to whatever was next for your particular server.

Now let's look at a more involved example. This time, the file is a comma-delimited file (in the same format as a .csv file) with new customer information. This time, the file looks like:

```
XWALL,Wally's World,Wally Smith,Owner,,,,,,(503)555-8448,,
XGENE,Generic Sales and Services,Al Smith,,,,,,,(503)555-9339,,
XMORE,More for You,Paul Johnston,President,,,,,,(573)555-3227,,
```

> **What's with all the commas in the source file?** Those are place holders for columns in the **Customers** table. The source file doesn't provide values for all of the columns, so commas are used to skip over those columns. This isn't the only way to handle a source file that doesn't provide values for all of the columns. You can use a format file to map the source data to the destination. We'll be covering format files a little later in the chapter.

Imagine for a moment that are going to run bcp to import the data to a remote system. The command this time is:

```
bcp northwind.dbo.customers in c:\ProfessionalSQL\newcust.txt -c -t, -r\n
-Ssocrates -Usa -Pbubbagump
```

The line wrapping shown here was added to make the command string easier to read. Do not press ENTER to wrap if you try this example yourself. Type the command as a single string and allow it to wrap itself inside the command prompt.

Once again, the data is being identified as character data. The −t, option identifies the file as comma delimited (terminated) data and −r\n identifies the new line character as the row delimiter. Server connection information was also provided for a little variety this time, using sa as the login and supplying the appropriate password.

Again, bcp confirms the transfer along with basic statistics:

Starting copy...

3 rows copied.
Network packet size (bytes): 4096
Clock Time (ms.): total   420

And again we'll also verify that the data got there as expected:

```
USE Northwind

SELECT CustomerID, CompanyName, ContactName
FROM Customers
WHERE CustomerID LIKE 'X%'
```

And, sure enough, all our data is there...

```
CustomerID CompanyName                          ContactName
---------- ------------------------------------ ------------------
XGENE      Generic Sales and Services           Al Smith
XMORE      More for You                         Paul Johnston
XWALL      Wally's World                        Wally Smith
```

Logged vs. Non-logged

bcp can run in either fast mode (not logged) or slow mode (logged operation). Each has its advantages. Fast mode gives you the best performance, but slow mode provides maximum recoverability. Since slow mode is logged, you can run a quick transaction log backup immediately after the import and be able to recover the database should there be a failure.

Fast mode is usually your best option when you need to transfer large amounts of data. Not only does the transfer run faster, but since the operation isn't logged you don't have to worry about running out of space in the transaction log. What's the catch? There are several conditions that must be met for bcp to run as non-logged:

- ❏   The target table cannot be replicated
- ❏   If the target table is indexed, it must not have any rows before the bcp operation takes place
- ❏   If the target table already has rows, it must not have any indexes
- ❏   The TABLOCK hint must be specified
- ❏   The target table must have no triggers
- ❏   For versions prior to SQL Server 2000, the select into/bulkcopy option must be set to TRUE

Obviously, if you want to do a fast mode copy into an indexed table with data, you will need to:

- ❑ Drop the indexes
- ❑ Drop any triggers
- ❑ Run bcp
- ❑ Re-index the target table
- ❑ Re-create any triggers

You need to immediately back up the destination database after a non-logged bcp operation.

If the target table doesn't meet the requirements for fast bcp, then the operation will be logged. This means that you can run the risk of filling the transaction log when transferring large amounts of data. You can run BACKUP LOG using the WITH TRUNCATE_ONLY option to clear the transaction log. The TRUNCATE_ONLY option truncates the inactive portion of the log without backing up any data.

> *I can't stress enough how deadly bcp operations can be to the size of your log. If you can't achieve a minimally logged operation, then consider adjusting your batch size down and selecting the* **Simple** *recovery option for the duration of the operation. Another solution is to use the −F and −L options to pull things one block at a time.*

Format Files

The use of format files was mentioned earlier. Format files can be thought of as import templates and make it easier to support recurring import operations when:

- ❑ Source file and target table structures or collations do not match
- ❑ You want to skip columns in the target table

To get a better idea of how format files work, let's look at some specific examples. First, you'll see how the file is structured when the source and destination match. Next, you can compare this to situations where the number of source file fields doesn't match the number of table columns or where source fields are ordered differently from the table columns.

You can create a default format file to use as your source when you run bcp in interactive mode. After prompting for column value information, you're given the option of saving the file. The default filename is bcp.fmt, but you can give the format file any valid filename.

To create a default format like this for the Northwind database Customers table, you could run:

```
bcp northwind.dbo.customers out c:\ProfessionalSQL\cust.txt -t, -r\n -T
```

This is a handy way of creating a quick format file that you can then edit as needed. You can do this with any table, so you can use bcp to get a jump-start on your format file needs.

Enter prefix length and data length information and, in this case, a comma as the field terminator and \n as the row terminator. SQL Server will prompt you to save the format file after you've entered all of the format information; save it as say, cust.fmt. You can then edit the format file to meet your particular needs with any text editor, such as Windows Notepad.

Let's take a look at the format file we just produced:

```
8.0
11
1    SQLNCHAR    2    10    ","    1     CustomerID      SQL_Latin1_General_CP1_CI_AS
2    SQLNCHAR    2    80    ","    2     CompanyName     SQL_Latin1_General_CP1_CI_AS
3    SQLNCHAR    2    60    ","    3     ContactName     SQL_Latin1_General_CP1_CI_AS
4    SQLNCHAR    2    60    ","    4     ContactTitle    SQL_Latin1_General_CP1_CI_AS
5    SQLNCHAR    2    120   ","    5     Address         SQL_Latin1_General_CP1_CI_AS
6    SQLNCHAR    2    30    ","    6     City            SQL_Latin1_General_CP1_CI_AS
7    SQLNCHAR    2    30    ","    7     Region          SQL_Latin1_General_CP1_CI_AS
8    SQLNCHAR    2    20    ","    8     PostalCode      SQL_Latin1_General_CP1_CI_AS
9    SQLNCHAR    2    30    ","    9     Country         SQL_Latin1_General_CP1_CI_AS
10   SQLNCHAR    2    48    ","    10    Phone           SQL_Latin1_General_CP1_CI_AS
11   SQLNCHAR    2    48    ","    11    Fax             SQL_Latin1_General_CP1_CI_AS
```

The first two lines in the file identify the bcp version number and the number of fields in the host file. The remaining lines describe the host data file and how the fields match up with target columns and collations.

The first column is the host file field number. Numbering starts with 1 through the total number of fields. Next is the host file data type. The example file is an Unicode text file, so the data type of all fields is SQLNCHAR – given that there are no special characters in this data, we could have just as easily gone with an ASCII format.

The next two columns describe the prefix and data length for the data fields. The prefix is the number of prefix characters in the field. The prefix describes the length of the data in the actual bcp file, and allows the data file to be compacted to a smaller size. The data field is the maximum length of the data stored in the field. Next is the field terminator (delimiter). In this case, a comma is used as the field terminator and new line as the row terminator. The next two columns describe the target table columns by providing the server column order and server column name. Since there is a direct match between the server columns and host fields in this example, the column and field numbers are the same. Last, but not least, comes the collation for each column (remember that, with SQL Server 2000, we now can have a different collation for every column in a table).

Next let's deal with the situation where the data file has fewer fields than the destination table. We need to modify the format file to identify which columns do not exist in the data file and, accordingly, which columns in our table should be ignored. This is done by setting the prefix and data length to 0 for each missing field and the table column number to 0 for each column we are going to skip.

For example, if the host data only has CustomerID, CompanyName, ContactName, ContactTitle, Phone, and Fax, you would modify the file as:

```
8.0
11
1    SQLNCHAR    2    10    ","    1     CustomerID      SQL_Latin1_General_CP1_CI_AS
2    SQLNCHAR    2    80    ","    2     CompanyName     SQL_Latin1_General_CP1_CI_AS
3    SQLNCHAR    2    60    ","    3     ContactName     SQL_Latin1_General_CP1_CI_AS
4    SQLNCHAR    2    60    ","    4     ContactTitle    SQL_Latin1_General_CP1_CI_AS
5    SQLNCHAR    0    0     ","    0     Address         SQL_Latin1_General_CP1_CI_AS
6    SQLNCHAR    0    0     ","    0     City            SQL_Latin1_General_CP1_CI_AS
7    SQLNCHAR    0    0     ","    0     Region          SQL_Latin1_General_CP1_CI_AS
8    SQLNCHAR    0    0     ","    0     PostalCode      SQL_Latin1_General_CP1_CI_AS
9    SQLNCHAR    0    0     ","    0     Country         SQL_Latin1_General_CP1_CI_AS
10   SQLNCHAR    2    48    ","    10    Phone           SQL_Latin1_General_CP1_CI_AS
11   SQLNCHAR    2    48    ","    11    Fax             SQL_Latin1_General_CP1_CI_AS
```

As you can see, the `Address`, `City`, `Region`, `PostalCode`, and `Country` fields and columns have been zeroed out.

The scenario for a data file that has more columns than the table does is actually amazingly similar to the short data file scenario we just looked at. The only trick here is that you must add column information for the additional fields, but the prefix length, data length, and column number fields are all set to 0:

```
8.0
11
1    SQLNCHAR    2    10     ","    1     CustomerID      SQL_Latin1_General_CP1_CI_AS
2    SQLNCHAR    2    80     ","    2     CompanyName     SQL_Latin1_General_CP1_CI_AS
3    SQLNCHAR    2    60     ","    3     ContactName     SQL_Latin1_General_CP1_CI_AS
4    SQLNCHAR    2    60     ","    4     ContactTitle    SQL_Latin1_General_CP1_CI_AS
5    SQLNCHAR    2    120    ","    5     Address         SQL_Latin1_General_CP1_CI_AS
6    SQLNCHAR    2    30     ","    6     City            SQL_Latin1_General_CP1_CI_AS
7    SQLNCHAR    2    30     ","    7     Region          SQL_Latin1_General_CP1_CI_AS
8    SQLNCHAR    2    20     ","    8     PostalCode      SQL_Latin1_General_CP1_CI_AS
9    SQLNCHAR    2    30     ","    9     Country         SQL_Latin1_General_CP1_CI_AS
10   SQLNCHAR    2    48     ","    10    Phone           SQL_Latin1_General_CP1_CI_AS
11   SQLNCHAR    2    48     ","    11    Fax             SQL_Latin1_General_CP1_CI_AS
12   SQLNCHAR    0    0      ","    0     eMail           SQL_Latin1_General_CP1_CI_AS
13   SQLNCHAR    0    0      ","    0     MobilePhone     SQL_Latin1_General_CP1_CI_AS
```

This time, the host file includes fields for an e-mail address and a mobile phone. The target table doesn't have any columns to receive this information. The fields are added to the original format file, as well as two dummy columns with a column number of 0. This will force `bcp` to ignore the fields.

Mismatched Field Order

Another possibility is that the host and target have the same fields, but the field orders don't match. This is corrected by changing the server column order to match the host file order:

```
8.0
11
1    SQLNCHAR    2    10     ","          CustomerID      SQL_Latin1_General_CP1_CI_AS
2    SQLNCHAR    2    80     ","    2     CompanyName     SQL_Latin1_General_CP1_CI_AS
3    SQLNCHAR    2    60     ","    4     ContactTitle    SQL_Latin1_General_CP1_CI_AS
4    SQLNCHAR    2    60     ","    3     ContactName     SQL_Latin1_General_CP1_CI_AS
5    SQLNCHAR    2    120    ","    5     Address         SQL_Latin1_General_CP1_CI_AS
6    SQLNCHAR    2    30     ","    6     City            SQL_Latin1_General_CP1_CI_AS
7    SQLNCHAR    2    30     ","    7     Region          SQL_Latin1_General_CP1_CI_AS
8    SQLNCHAR    2    20     ","    8     PostalCode      SQL_Latin1_General_CP1_CI_AS
9    SQLNCHAR    2    30     ","    9     Country         SQL_Latin1_General_CP1_CI_AS
10   SQLNCHAR    2    48     ","    10    Phone           SQL_Latin1_General_CP1_CI_AS
11   SQLNCHAR    2    48     ","    11    Fax             SQL_Latin1_General_CP1_CI_AS
```

In this case, the contact title is listed before the contact name in the host file. The server column order has been changed to reflect this. Notice, the order in which the server columns are listed has not changed, but the server column numbers have been swapped.

Using Format Files

As an example, let's use a format file for an import. This command will copy records into the Customers table based on a format file named shortcust.fmt:

```
bcp northwind.dbo.customers in c:\ProfessionalSQL\shortcust.txt -
fc:\ProfessionalSQL\shortcust.fmt -Ssocrates -Usa -Pbubbagump
```

The sample files used in this example, SHRTCUST.TXT and SHRTCUST.FMT, are available for download from the Wrox web site.

Maximizing Import Performance

One obvious way of maximizing bcp performance is to make sure that the target table meets all the requirements for running bcp as a non-logged operation. This may mean you need to:

❑ Drop any existing indexes on the target table. While this is only actually required if you want a minimally logged operation, the fact is that leaving indexes off during bulk operation is greatly beneficial performance-wise regardless of the logging status. Be sure, however, to rebuild you indexes after the bulk operation is complete.

❑ Attempt to have your source data files created in the same order that your clustered index (if there is one) is in. During your index rebuild, this will allow you to make use of the SORTED_DATA_REORG option, which greatly speeds index creation (and thus the overall time of your bcp operation). Even if you have to leave a clustered index in place, performing the bcp with sorted data will allow the use of the ORDER column option (within the -HINT option).

❑ Make sure your maintenance properties are set to Simple or non-logged. If they are set to Full Recovery, then bcp will not be allowed a minimally logged operation.

If you're looking for additional improvement when importing data into a table, you can run **parallel data loads** from multiple clients. To do this, you must:

❑ Use the TABLOCK hint

❑ Remove all indexes (you can rebuild them after the operation is complete)

❑ Set the server recovery option to Bulk-Logged

How would this work? Rather than importing one very large file, break it up into smaller files. Then you launch bcp from multiple client systems, each client importing one of the smaller files. Obviously, you will only be interested in doing this if the expected performance increase saves more time on the import than you'll spend preparing the source files and copying them to the clients.

> *Just because you are running two or three (or more) simultaneous bulk loading operations, don't expect the two or three times (or more) performance increase – it will be something less than that. There is overhead that still has to be shared between all the separate loads you have running, so you will not see a linear performance increase.*

Parallel loads are not supported for SQL Server 6.5 or earlier.

> **With either of these operations, it will be necessary to re-create any indexes on the target table after completing the operation. Re-create the target table clustered index (if any) before any non-clustered indexes.**

You can get additional performance improvement by letting SQL Server ignore check constraints and triggers, which is the default option. Keep in mind that this can result in loading data that violates the table's check constraints and any data integrity rules that are enforced by your triggers.

bcp Export

If you're going to be accepting data in via bulk operations, then it follows that you probably want to be able to pump data out too.

bcp allows you to export data from a table, view, or query. You must specify a destination filename – if the file already exists, it will be overwritten. Unlike import operations, you are not allowed to skip columns during export. Timestamp and computed columns are exported in the same manner (just as if they were "real" data) as any other SQL Server columns. To run an export, you must have appropriate SELECT authority to the source table or tables.

Let's look at a couple of quick examples using the Shippers table in the Northwind database.

To export to a data file using the default format, you could run:

```
bcp northwind.dbo.shippers out d:\data\shipout.txt -c -T
```

This would create a file that looks like:

```
1      Speedy Express         (503) 555-9831
2      United Package         (503) 555-3199
3      Federal Shipping       (503) 555-9931
4      Speedy Shippers, Inc.  (503) 555-5566
5      Speedy Shippers, Inc
100    Billy Bob's Pretty Good Shipping
101    Fred's Freight
102    Readyship              (503)555-1234
103    MyShipper              (503)555-3443
```

This creates an ASCII text file with tab as a field terminator and new line as the row terminator (the defaults). To modify this to create a comma-delimited file, you just make use of the -t option, for example you could run:

```
bcp northwind.dbo.shippers out C:\ProfessionalSQL\shipout.txt -c -t, -T
```

This would give you something like:

```
1,Speedy Express,(503) 555-9831
2,United Package,(503) 555-3199
3,Federal Shipping,(503) 555-9931
4,Speedy Shippers, Inc.,(503) 555-5566
5,Speedy Shippers, Inc,
100,Billy Bob's Pretty Good Shipping,
101,Fred's Freight,
102,Readyship,(503)555-1234
103,MyShipper,(503)555-3443
```

> **Keep in mind that the destination file will be overwritten if it already exists – this will happen without any kind of prompt or warning.**

In this case, we didn't have to use a format file, nor were we prompted for any field lengths or similar information – the use of the -c option indicated that we just wanted everything – regardless of type – exported as basic ASCII text in a default format.

BULK INSERT

Entirely new with SQL Server 2000 is the BULK INSERT command. In order to make use of this new command, you must be a member of either the sysadmin or bulkadminserver role.

What BULK INSERT does is essentially operate like a limited version of bcp that is available directly within T-SQL. The syntax looks like this:

```
BULK INSERT [['<database name>'.]['<owner>'].]'<table name>'
FROM '<data file>'
    [WITH
      (
        [BATCHSIZE [ = <batch size>]]
        [, CHECK_CONSTRAINTS]
        [, CODEPAGE [={'ACP'|'OEM'|'RAW'|'<code page>'}]]
        [, DATAFILETYPE [={'char'|'native'|'widechar'|'widenative'}]]
        [, FIELDTERMINATOR [= '<field terminator>' ]]
        [, FIRSTROW [= <first row>]]
        [, FIRE_TRIGGERS]
        [, FORMATFILE = '<format file path>' ]
        [, KEEPIDENTITY]
        [, KEEPNULLS]
        [, KILOBYTES_PER_BATCH [= <no. of kilobytes>]]
        [, LASTROW [ = <last row no.>]]
        [, MAXERRORS [ = <max errors>]]
        [, ORDER ({column [ASC|DESC]} [ ,...n ] )]
        [, ROWS_PER_BATCH [= <rows per batch>]]
        [, ROWTERMINATOR [ = '<row terminator>']]
        [, TABLOCK]
      )
    ]
```

Now, if you are getting a sense of déjà vu, then you're on top of things for sure – these switches pretty much all have equivalents in the basic bcp import syntax that we started the chapter with.

The special permission requirements of BULK INSERT are something of a hassle (not everyone belongs to sysadmin or bulkinsert), but BULK INSERT does carry with it a couple of distinct advantages:

❑ It can be enlisted as part of a user defined transaction using BEGIN TRAN and its associated statements.

❑ It runs in-process to SQL Server, so it should pick up some performance benefits there (I'm sorry to say I haven't done enough testing on this one to know for sure yet).

❑ It's slightly (very slightly) less cryptic than the command line syntax used by bcp.

BULK INSERT is not for everyone, but it is a nice new option.

Summary

In this chapter, we looked at the first of our two major data import/export utilities. bcp is used primarily for importing and exporting data stored as text files to and from our SQL Server.

As a legacy utility, bcp will be familiar to most people who have worked with SQL Server for any length of time. The addition of trigger support and other new twists with SQL Server 2000 demonstrates that Microsoft has not given up on this old friend, and bcp is clearly here to stay.

That said, bcp is quite often not your best option. In our next chapter, we will take a look at bcp's major competitor – DTS. DTS has the glamour and glitz that bcp is missing, but it also has its own quirks that can occasionally make the simplicity of bcp seem downright appealing.

Online discussion at http://p2p.wrox.com

22

Introduction to Data Transformation Services

Perhaps the strongest feedback I got regarding the last version of this book was, "More DTS!" I have listened. I have heard.

And so we begin – this time with the first of, not one, but *two* chapters on DTS. We'll make a start in this chapter on how to get around in the DTS Package Editor, and how to do basic transformations. Then, later in the book, we'll come back and add some additional functionality, programmability, and options to see how much of a pro you can become.

In the previous chapter, we took a close look at the bulk copy program, or bcp. The bcp gave us the opportunity to move large blocks of data around rather efficiently. DTS is designed for much the same purpose and more. DTS offers a graphical user interface approach (which will be the focus of this chapter), and also allows for direct programming to an object model through COM support (which we will examine in Chapter 31). DTS also offers additional functionality in the form of what are called **transformations**. A transformation is when you take data in one form, and then change it to another form.

Our fun with DTS doesn't stop there, however, as DTS has a robust branching model, and even allows for parallel actions – that is, you can have multiple operations occurring at once within your package. In addition, DTS isn't limited to operations on SQL Server data – it can support just about any OLE DB or ODBC data source.

In short, DTS is all about the steps – whether there are one or many – that are needed to move data from place to place.

The DTS Package Editor

Let's start things off by starting up and examining the DTS Package Editor. You start it by navigating to the Data Transformation Services node of the server that you want to work on the package with:

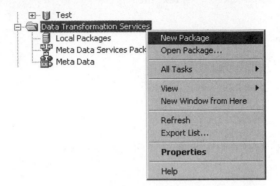

Right-click and look at our options. As you might expect, we could edit an existing package by using the Open Package option. For now, select New Package – this brings up the DTS Package Editor:

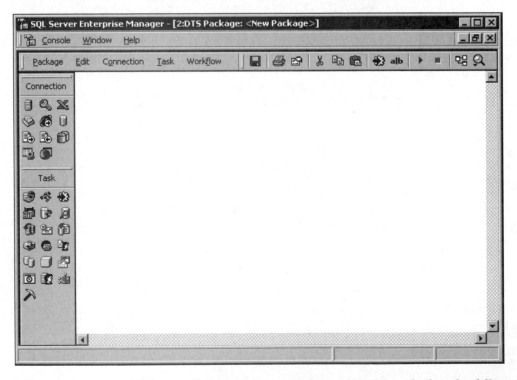

It would be pretty easy to get lost in all these options, so let's start by taking a look at the different sections on the screen.

Connection

A **connection** is just what it sounds like – a pipeline to a given SQL Server or other data source. There are eleven connection choices that come along with SQL Server and which cover a wide range of data sources from SQL Servers to Oracle, from text files to any ODBC data source – the possibilities are fairly endless.

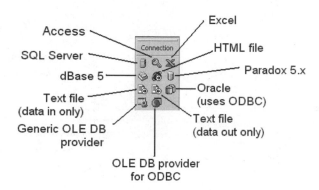

Most of the properties inside each of these are fairly self-describing. Much of the time you'll find yourself connecting to SQL Server (quite often the very SQL Server that you're creating the package on).

> *While, for the vast majority of the time, you will be making at least one connection to the local SQL Server, there is actually no restriction that forces you to do this. I'm aware of companies that run on DB2 only, for example, but have purchased and installed a copy of SQL Server just so they can have DTS around to move data between their DB2 servers! I've seen Oracle data moved to Access, and text file information sent to FoxPro.*

While many of the connection properties are the same among the different connection methods, some are not, and there definitely tends to be a difference between RDBMS-stored data and the file-based data:

❑ RDBMS data: These kinds of connections are going to focus on the server and connection information. They may or may not ask for a specific database to become the default database (SQL Server does). The primary examples here would be SQL Server and Oracle – though you can get OLE DB and ODBC drivers for DB2, Informix, Sybase, Ingress, and more.

❑ File-based data: As you might expect, the connection managers for file-based data systems are going to be focused on the file location for the data you want. Sometimes the manager will want you to specify a specific file (as is the case for text files and Access), others will just want a directory (where they will access many different files as though each was a table). Examples here range from the older xBase formats (dBase, FoxPro, and Clipper mostly) to Access and text files.

> *The key thing to remember about connections is to ask yourself how many different things are going to be going on with that connection at once. For example, if you are moving data to and from the same server (say from one database to another), then, if you use just one connection, you'll have a bottleneck at the connection since the data going each way (to and from) will have to contend with data going the other direction for connection time. If you use separate connections for each direction, you'll find that you get higher throughput – even if the data is all going to the same server.*

Task

A **task** is a unit of work that you want DTS to perform. There are a wide variety of tasks that are already set up in the DTS Package Editor when you first install SQL Server, and you can also create your own custom tasks. Several of the tasks that come along with DTS are used quite regularly, and we will examine them in some detail later in the chapter. For now, however, let's take a brief look at what all of the tasks do.

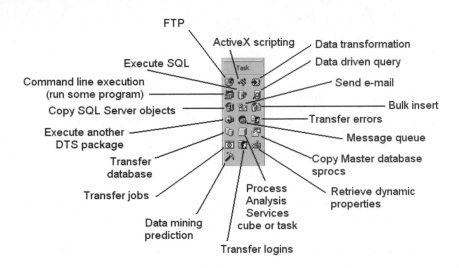

FTP

The **FTP task** allows you to download and upload files to and from FTP sites. This is pretty cool since it will log you into the site, navigate to the appropriate file, and retrieve (or upload) it. This means that you can trade information with a remote site both efficiently and securely.

ActiveX Script

The **ActiveX Script task** allows you to use VBScript or JScript (or you can even install other scripting languages, such as PerlScript) to create custom tasks inside your package that may be beyond the functionality of the other tasks available. This could be complex data conversions or formatting – whatever your heart (reasonably) desires.

Transform Data

The **Transform Data task** is a retrieval and storage function, but with a twist. Most of the time we just copy data from one place to another, but the Data Transformation task allows us to alter the data as we are converting it. For example, if we were retrieving data that contained NULL values, but the destination did not accept NULLS, then we could make use of the ISNULL() Visual Basic function to programmatically decide what it is that we want to change the value to before inserting it in the destination (we could even elect to tell DTS to skip that particular record).

Execute Process (Command Line)

The **Execute Process task** allows us to run programs that we would normally have to run from a command prompt or by manually selecting them in Windows. This option allows us to supply parameters to be included in the command line when DTS executes the program for us.

Execute SQL

The **Execute SQL task** is what it sounds like. It allows us to run one or more T-SQL statements in a relatively free-form manner.

Data Driven Query

The **Data Driven Query task** allows us to query data, based on one or more dynamic query conditions. If we wanted to build something that would behave differently depending on the nature of the data in each row, then this would be our task.

Copy SQL Server Objects

The **Copy SQL Server Objects task** is a fairly free-form way of copying objects. Pretty much any object that can be in a SQL Server database can be copied using this task. The task defaults to copying all objects in a database, but we can select individual objects if we so choose.

Send Mail

Again, the **Send Mail task** is what it sounds like. This task allows us to send an e-mail message to one or more recipients. The only catch here is that you must have a MAPI client and appropriate mail server and login information set up on your system for the user that SQL Server is using to run DTS.

Bulk Insert

The **Bulk Insert task** basically performs the BULK INSERT command as we saw in our last chapter. Keep in mind that this is not bcp – it's just something that looks and acts an awful lot like bcp.

Execute Package

The **Execute Package task** is a rather cool addition in SQL Server 2000 that allows for package reuse and modularization. Using this task, we can create master packages that in turn make use of other packages we have created.

Message Queue

The **Message Queue task** allows us to insert a message into a queue as set up in Microsoft Message Queue. In order to use this task, you must have the Microsoft Message Queue client installed.

Transfer Error Messages

The **Transfer Error Messages task** allows us to transfer system messages between servers.

Transfer Databases

The **Transfer Databases task,** what part of this name is there to not understand? This allows us to transfer one or more databases from one server to another. We can alter the file locations (they don't have to have exactly the same physical file path on both servers) if we wish. The only catch is that you must have different source and destination servers – this makes sense if you think about the fact that we need to have a unique database name on each server.

Analysis Services Processing

The **Analysis Services Processing task** allows us to perform our update tasks. All three processing models are supported (full process, refresh data, and incremental update).

Transfer Master Stored Procedures

The **Transfer Master Stored Procedures task** allows us to copy system stored procedures from the `master` database on one server to the `master` database on another server. The source servers can be either version 7.0 or 2000, but the destination must be 2000.

Transfer Jobs and Logins

The **Transfer Jobs task** and **Transfer Logins task** do what their names imply – they transfer one or more jobs or users from one server to another. Much like several of the tasks we've looked at thus far, these are largely meant to help in upgrade and deployment situations.

Dynamic Properties

The **Dynamic Properties task** allows us to retrieve information from outside the package (in a table for example), and store the result as custom properties in our package – we can then use this information to conditionally drive other parts of our package or a data driven query. Other sources we can retrieve information from include `.ini` files and system functions such as `@@SERVERNAME`. The only rule here is that each one of these tasks can only retrieve a single discrete value – so any query you write should return only one column and one row.

Data Mining Prediction

Another one of those "does what it sounds like" things – the **Data Mining Prediction task** allows us to retrieve a result from a data mining predictive task. We will look at data mining much more closely in Chapter 25 (it has been added to Analysis Services). The catch on this one is that the data mine must be local to the server where you will be running the DTS package.

Workflow

Workflow is the last of the three major topics we need to get familiar with in the DTS Package Editor (the other two are connections and tasks – which we've already seen). Workflow is really just about controlling what happens under what conditions and in what order. You can establish an order of precedence for your various tasks, and also set up branching rules based on the success or failure of any particular task. Some tasks may be executed only if one or more other tasks succeeded. Other tasks may serve only to clean up if something fails.

The workflow side of things doesn't have its own pretty toolbar like connections and tasks do, but it does have its own menu:

Each of these options establishes a link between two different tasks. One task will be run prior to the other task. The second task will run only after the first task is complete and only based on the rules you establish as part of the workflow (completion, success, or failure). Let's look at how each of these affects our DTS package at run time.

On Completion

With the On Completion option the second (or **dependent**) task will run after the first task is complete. Whether the first task succeeds or fails is irrelevant – as soon as the first task is done, the second task executes.

On Success

If On Success is selected the dependent task will run after the first task, but only if the first task completed successfully. Generally, we would use this kind of option in conjunction with an On Failure workflow – this makes sure we don't waste time trying to perform dependent tasks if the parent task that the other tasks depend on has failed.

On Failure

With On Failure the dependent task will run after the first task, but only if the first task did not complete successfully. This is usually used in conjunction with some form of error handling or notification process. This might range from making another attempt to perform a task to simply e-mailing an administrator.

Using the Import/Export Wizard

To help us get our first package built, and to see how powerful even a simple package can be, we're going to make use of the import side of the **DTS Import/Export Wizard**. This will also get you familiar with an easy to use but rather handy tool that you'll probably make use of over and over again in your SQL Server endeavors.

The Import/Export Wizard can be found in Enterprise Manager, and can be started up in a number of ways. For example, you can try right-clicking at almost any level of the Databases node in SQL Server and navigate to All Tasks | Import Data. You can also get there through Tools.

Navigate past the first screen and you should come to a dialog that helps you create your first connection. We will see a little later that this dialog is being used to create a SQL Server connection (just like we discussed in the *Connection* section earlier in this chapter) in a DTS package:

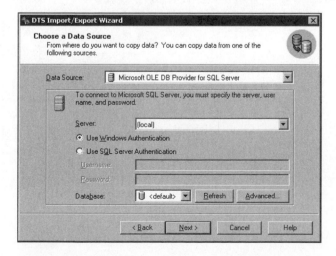

This dialog is self-describing in most respects – after all, you've connected up to SQL Server many times before you got to this point in the book. However, we should take the time to look at the values in the drop-down box labeled Data Source:

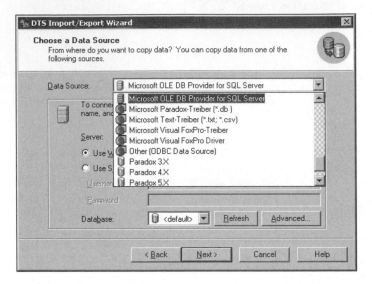

We have a wide range of data sources available to us. These correspond to the list of connections we saw earlier in the chapter, with the difference being that we have separate entries here for separate versions of some of the potential data sources.

Let's stay with SQL Server, and choose Northwind as our source database (from whatever server you choose to source the data from):

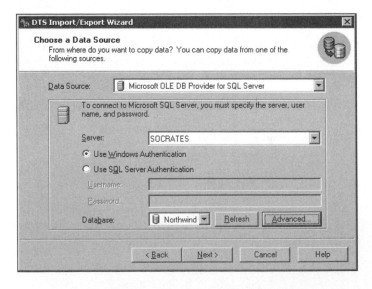

Now click Next and move on to identifying the destination for this data:

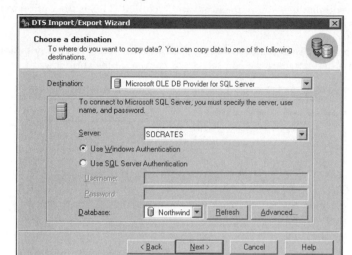

When it first comes up, the only change in the dialog is the heading (which is now referencing a destination instead of a source)! For this example, we'll leave the destination as Northwind, but it could have been just about any OLE DB or ODBC compliant data source.

Move on to the next dialog and we are presented with a few choices:

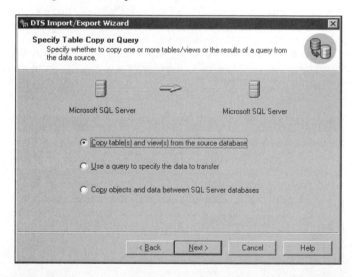

- ❑ **Copy table(s) and view(s):** This is, by default, a straight table-to-table copy. We are allowed to select multiple tables to be copied, and the initial setup will call for each to be an exact copy of the original (column for column).

- ❑ **Use a query:** This is what it sounds like – we specify a query to be the source instead of a table. This one is really cool for doing basic transformations – often you can put the data in the form the destination expects just by making a SELECT statement that retrieves the data in the right way.

❑ Copy objects and data: This allows us to move more than just tables and views; sprocs, UDFs, rules, defaults – you name it, it can be copied. This is the option to use if you want to move anything (even triggers and indexes) other than a table or view.

For this first transform, we're going to keep it simple and just select the Copy table(s) option. Click on Next and we reach a dialog where we can select our source tables and views:

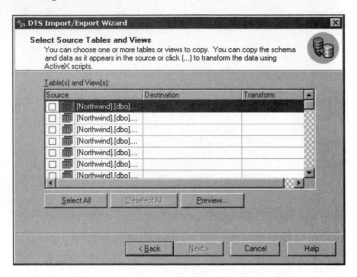

For our example, we're going to be "importing" three different tables: Customers, Orders, and Order Details. The start of that process is as simple as just selecting the checkbox to the left of each of those tables (note that you'll need to play with the column widths in this dialog to be able to see the table names). As you check the tables you want, the dialog will populate the Destination names with a default equivalent to the original table name. Obviously, since we've selected the same source and target database, we probably don't want to use the same name. For our example, we'll take that pesky space out of the name of the Order Details table, and we'll also rename the tables with a DTS after the original name:

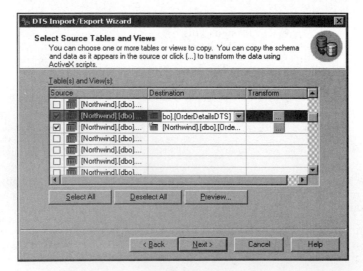

Now we're ready to move on to the Transform column. For just the Orders table, click on the button labeled with an ellipsis (...) in the Transform column and take a look at the dialog that comes up:

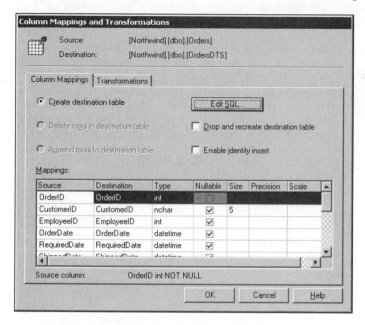

Let's examine the options in this dialog:

- ❑ **Create destination table**: This allows us to create the target table on the fly. It will not be created until the package is actually executed. What if we select this option and the table already exists at run time? Well, the behavior will depend on what we've chosen for the **Drop and recreate destination table** option – if that option is turned on, then the transformation will complete normally after first dropping the existing version of the destination table. If the option is turned off, then SQL Server will raise an error if the destination object already exists.

- ❑ **Delete rows in destination table**: While this is grayed out in the dialog above, it would be enabled if the object already existed. This option just allows us to make use of the existing instance of the destination table, but to truncate any existing data in that table.

- ❑ **Append rows to destination table**: The functional opposite of the previous two choices, this option leaves the existing table and data intact and just adds any new rows to what's already there.

- ❑ **Drop and recreate destination table**: This one is only valid if we're also using the **Create destination table** option. This just makes sure that, in the event the table already exists, it is dropped, and a new version created from this transformation. All existing data is lost, as is the structure of the original table (SQL Server doesn't care if the column names didn't match).

- ❑ **Enable identity insert**: This just helps deal with the situation where you are transferring a table that has an identity column. If you want to keep your original identity column values intact, then you'll want to use this option – it will operate as a functional equivalent to SET IDENTITY_INSERT ON, and will automatically set IDENTITY_INSERT back to normal after the import/export is complete.

On the "row movement" side of things, we only have the choice of **Create destination table**. We do, however, want to turn the **Enable identity insert** option on for this table so that the original identity values will be retained (remember that `Orders` has an identity column – we'd hate to accidentally lose our order numbers!).

Since we're here, let's go ahead and take a brief look at the **Transformations** tab:

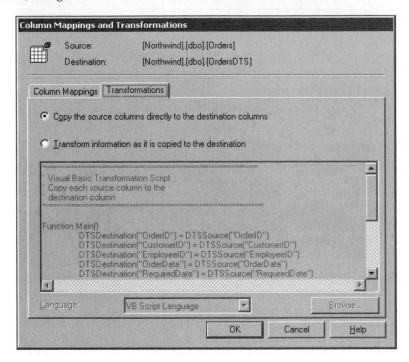

We won't be using this tab for this particular example (patience!), but this is the place that we could go to provide some ActiveX scripting to further control the movement of data. Later in the chapter, we'll examine how we can use this tab to provide reasonably complex alterations to our data.

We want to stick with the **Copy the source columns directly to the destination columns** option, but you can get a glimpse here of what our ActiveX scripting code might look like if we had needed to do something more elaborate.

Click **OK**, and you should be back at the **Select Source Tables and Views** dialog.

If you want, you could check out the Preview option on the Select Source Tables and Views dialog – it gives you something of a preview of what your data might look like. The emphasis is on "might" here – this preview is not very thorough. Still, I find that taking a quick look at it sometimes helps me catch blunders I've made before they get committed to the database. In our example here, however, there's not really much to see (straight copies aren't that exciting to preview!).

Clicking Next takes us to the Save, schedule, and replicate package dialog:

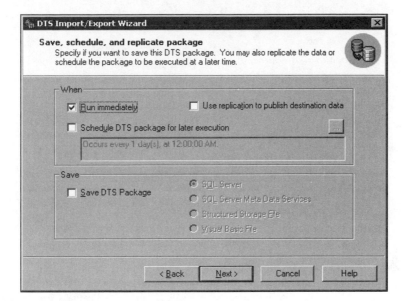

We've reached the last of our main dialogs. This is, in many respects, the first clear signal that our wizard does more than just import or export data itself. Instead, it creates a DTS package so we can, if we choose, save and repeat the process.

The options here are:

❑ Run immediately: Well – there isn't much to say about this one. Check it, and the package will run as soon as you go through one more dialog and then click Next.

❑ Use replication to publish destination data: This one just indicates that you are going to use the target as a source for replication. If this option is selected, then the publication wizard will automatically come up as soon as we click Next. This one is kind of interesting because it points out a common use for DTS – to move a clean copy of data off to a safe location prior to replication.

❑ Schedule DTS package for later execution: This pulls up the job scheduler so we can set up our package to run automatically based on some schedule. The job scheduler is examined in detail in Chapter 30.

❑ Save DTS Package: A key option for sure. This just says that what we've done in our wizard isn't necessarily a one-time thing, and we would like to save the package for editing/reuse at some other time. If we select this option, then we are presented with additional options about where we want to store our package (we will examine these later in the chapter).

For now, select both the Run immediately and the Save DTS Package options (accept the default, SQL Server, option for where the DTS package is saved) and click Next.

This brings us to the last dialog we can edit at all – the naming and security of our DTS package:

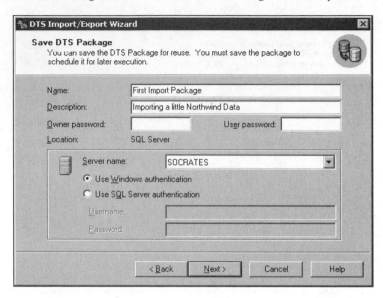

Most of this isn't that amazing. We have login information because we've said that we want to store this package in our SQL Server – if we had chosen to save it as a file, we would have had a more traditional **Save As** dialog. The only interesting information is the **Owner** and **User** password information. These allow us to protect our package from editing and use. We will explore these options just a tad more when we look at our storage options later in the chapter.

OK, so now we're ready to click **Next** again and provide final confirmation before having our package execute:

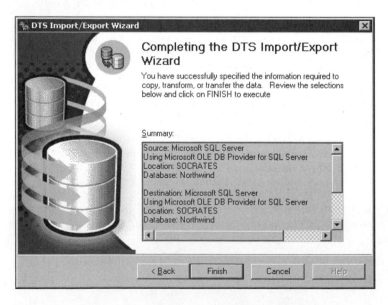

Click **Finish** and the package executes (because we chose the **Run** immediately option a dialog or two ago). While it's executing, SQL Server shows you the progress of what's taking place. Notice that some of the tasks seem to be happening in parallel (at the same time):

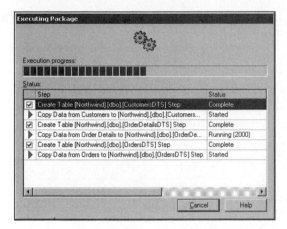

SQL Server runs tasks in parallel where possible to speed up performance. The impact of this can be particularly large on systems with multiple CPUs and fast disk I/O subsystems. When we're all done with the "import", we get a confirmation dialog:

Three tables were what we wanted moved, and that's what we got.

> *Be aware that you won't necessarily always get this confirmation dialog. It shows up when using the Import/Export Wizard, but it doesn't show up if you just re-run the package later.*

After you click the **OK** button, you get a far more interesting dialog:

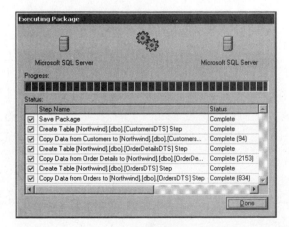

This dialog tells us that the various steps completed and shows how many rows were moved. If any individual step failed, we would see a red X rather than a green checkmark. In addition, the Status would indicate an error. To learn more about the error, just double-click the step where the error occurred.

So, it's that quick to get our first DTS job done. Now all that's left to do for this section is to look at the DTS package that was actually produced to do this work.

To see our package, click Done and then navigate to the Data Transformation Services tab under your server in EM. Click on the Local Packages option:

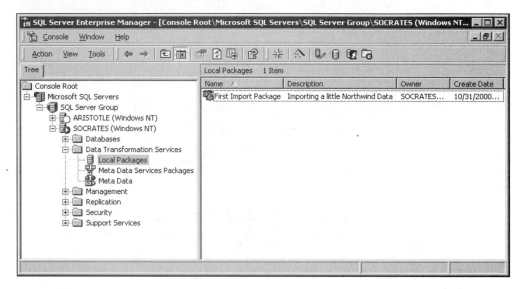

Now double-click on our package in the right pane, and the DTS Package Editor will be displayed. We looked at this at the beginning of the chapter:

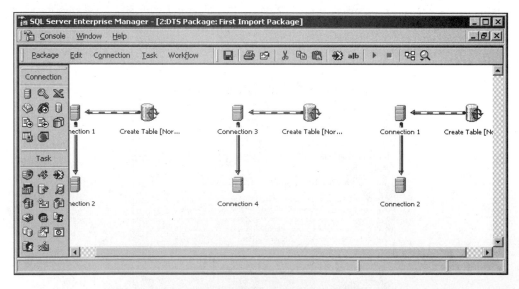

What we have here are a few different logical sets of operations. Essentially, each table creation and transformation has been shown in its own little task group.

Let's focus in on the two connections and the SQL task that are related to the OrderDetailsDTS table. For me, this happens to be the set of tasks in the middle of the diagram, but yours could easily be any of the three. Double-click on the SQL task (or right-click and select Properties) to tell which is which.

There are a total of five distinct items shown:

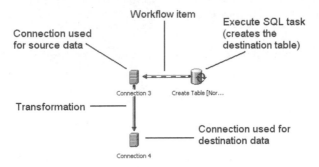

Execute SQL

The Execute SQL task (labeled Create Table under the icon) can execute almost any T-SQL statement. In our case, we can double-click it and see what the command is all about:

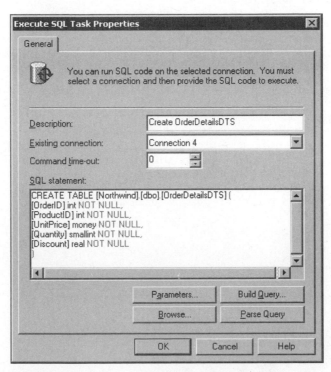

I've started by renaming the task to something more likely to be visible in the DTS Package Editor. You can also see that this task is making use of the connection called Connection 4 and is executing a basic CREATE TABLE statement, much like the one we saw back in Chapter 6.

> **Pay close attention to the fact that there aren't any constraints showing here – not even a primary key! The basic Copy table(s) and view(s) option in the Import/Export Wizard does not have any options that allow us to copy all the supporting objects (triggers, indexes, constraints, etc.). If we need to copy such supporting objects, then we need to use the Copy objects option in the first dialog after the connection information is established.**

This CREATE TABLE statement must come before any data can be inserted – which brings us to the next item in our diagram.

Workflow

Our workflow item is blue with white stripes. This indicates that it is an On Completion workflow item (check out the arrows in the Workflow menu if you need a handy reminder of which color is what). This means that our Execute SQL task must be finished before our transformation will take place. In this case, there is no requirement as to whether that Execute SQL task was successful or had errors, but our On Completion workflow constraint makes certain that our OrderDetailsDTS table is created before the transformation attempts to insert data.

The Connection Objects

We have one connection that is used for the source data (Connection 3), and one for the destination data (Connection 4). All these objects do is establish the connection information – what server, database, and login information is to be used. We could, for example, use one connection to drive many tasks. Indeed, Connection 4 is used both for the transform (it's the connection to the destination) and for the Execute SQL task.

The Transform

The transform is the workhorse as far as actually moving our data is concerned. If we double-click on the black line that represents our transform (the arrow points in the direction of the flow of our data), we come to a dialog that has defined our source data:

I've again shortened the description somewhat compared with what the Import/Export Wizard put in there, but the really important thing to notice here is that the Import/Export Wizard chose to use a **SQL query** rather than just directly sourcing from the table. For our example here, we were moving all columns, so, if we had been building this from scratch, we could have chosen the **Table/View** based connection rather than a query – either way works just fine and the performance differences are negligible. Don't worry about the other tabs for the moment – we will come back to those in a more complex example later in the chapter.

Click **OK** to close up the transform, save the package, and we're pretty much done with our tour of what the Import/Export Wizard did for us. In the next section, we'll look at what it takes to create our own package from scratch and do a genuine transformation (this import example was more of a copy than anything else).

Creating a Simple Transformation Package

Creating packages isn't really all that difficult. Indeed, we've already seen one of a number of SQL Server wizards that are available to walk you through a difficult process.

What we're going to do in this section is combine the issues of creating a package from scratch with a look at some basic transformations. We'll be making a copy of a portion of the Northwind database, (the Customers, Orders, and Order Details tables, as well as several tables they depend on), but this time we'll be bringing across a number of supporting objects in addition to our tables. This is going to also have elements of a data warehouse, so we'll be adding in a table or two that has been deliberately denormalized.

Start by creating an empty database called NorthwindCopy that we can use to move our copied data into:

```
CREATE DATABASE NorthwindCopy
```

Then fire up the DTS Package Editor using the New Package option that we saw at the beginning of the chapter. Add two connections to the package – to add a connection, just drag and drop from the toolbar on the left. The first connection should be named Northwind Source and its default database set to Northwind:

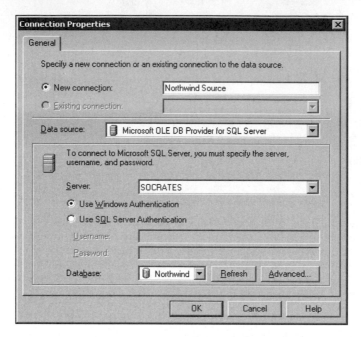

For the second connection, set the name to NorthwindCopy Target and set the default database to NorthwindCopy.

Since not everyone can afford to have multiple systems lying around just waiting for them to work through a book, I'm going to assume that you need to run this on one server. That's fine. Just keep in mind that we could easily run this same logic against multiple servers by naming them appropriately in the connection dialog.

At this point, our package looks both sparse and boring:

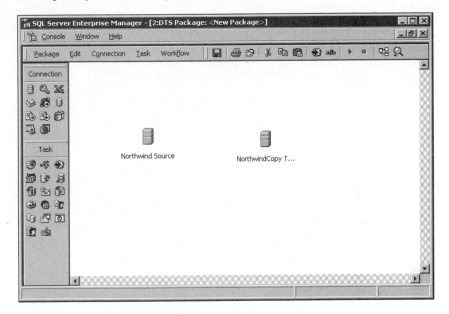

We're going to be doing a transformation on our Customers table. To do this, we need to add a Transform Data task to our package. Start by performing a drag and drop of the Transform Data task from the toolbar into the work area of the package. As you do this, your mouse icon will change to one that indicates for you to **Select source connection**. Do just that by clicking on our **Northwind Source** connection. When you do this, the mouse icon will again change – this time to one that indicates for you to **Select destination connection**. Again, do just that – this time by clicking on our **NorthwindCopy Target** connection. When you're done, you'll wind up with a black arrow pointing from **Northwind Source** to **NorthwindCopy Target**:

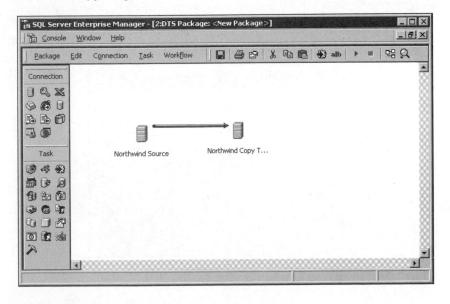

We've added a transform, but the transform doesn't know what to do. We must double-click on the transform and set several properties within it:

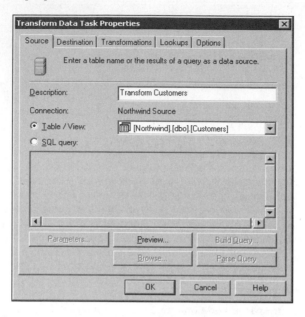

Provide a somewhat clearer name for our transform, **Transform Customers**, and define that the source will be a table (we could also have made it a query). We're now ready to move on to the **Destination** tab – as we do this, however, we get a dialog.

SQL Server provides a CREATE TABLE statement that will generate a copy of the columns and data types used in the source table. The default CREATE statement will be based on matching up with the column names and data types of the source table (constraints are not, however, included). In our case, however, we are going to split the contacts' names into first and last names using a transformation, so we want to eliminate the **ContactName** column from our table and replace it with **ContactFirstName** and **ContactLastName**. We'll set both of these to **nvarchar(20)**. In addition, we want to make sure that our new table has a primary key (remember, keys are not included in the default statement), so we'll add that in too:

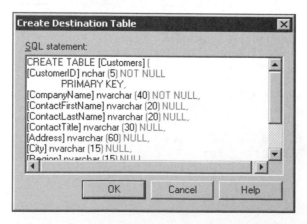

When you've changed the ContactName field to allow for both a first and last name, and added the PRIMARY KEY constraint, click OK to return to the Destination tab.

Be aware that, as soon as you click OK in the Create Destination Table dialog, the table is created immediately – it doesn't wait for your package to run. The upshot of this is that your package doesn't create the table, but instead expects the table to be there when the package runs. Keep this in mind if you migrate the package from one server to another. In addition to changing connection information, you'll also need to make sure the target table already exists the first time you run the package.

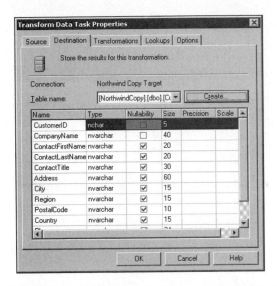

Notice that our destination table now includes all the column information from our new table – including the new ContactFirstName and ContactLastName columns.

Go ahead and move on to the Transformations tab:

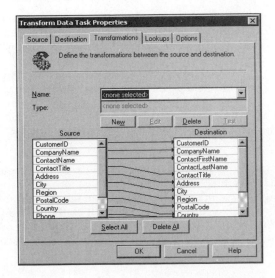

Here we see a number of different things going on. You can see that most of the rows in the **Source** and **Destination** tables have already been mapped to one another. SQL Server has made a guess on which column goes where based on column name and positioning. Each of the black arrows in the dialog represents a separate transformation, and will be handled independently. If you click on the **Name** drop-down box, you'll see that there is a separate transformation name that goes with each line on the dialog:

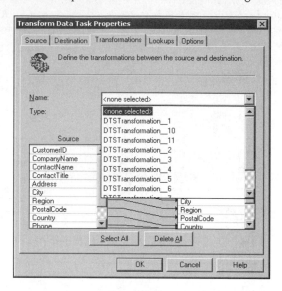

While things appear to be virtually set up for us, there are actually a number of things to dislike about the way that SQL Server has chosen to do things:

❑ Each transform is effectively its own process. This is highly inefficient compared to the notion of one process that moves all of the columns at once.

❑ The transformation names are indecipherable – if you want to alter a transformation, how do you know which is which?

❑ The ContactName has been mapped to the ContactFirstName column in the destination table, which, while partially correct, isn't going to give us quite the results we want (we want the first and last name separate – not the entire name in the first name column!).

> **This deserves to be stressed from a performance point of view. The default is for each transformation (one per column by default) to be handled as what amounts to a separate process and to receive its own transformation name. Things will perform much better if we can combine as much as possible to run as one unit.**

What we want to do here is effectively start over. To do this, we click **Delete All** and all of our transformation arrows (and the actual transformations for that matter) disappear. Now we're ready to begin anew. Go ahead and click **Select All**. Next, hold down the *Ctrl* key and then click on ContactName in the **Source** column, and both the **ContactFirstName** and **ContactLastName** items in the **Destination** column. At this point, you have all columns selected except for those related to the ContactName. Now release *Ctrl* and click **New**, and SQL Server will show us the **Create New Transformation** dialog:

In our case, we're going to want to make use of Copy Column at this point (we'll use another type of transform shortly). Before we do that, however, let's take a quick run through these transform types – they really only fall into three categories:

❑ ActiveX Script: This is a fairly free-form way of manipulating the data between source and destination. You can, using some special condition flags, even do row-by-row operations – including some rows and throwing others out, for example.

❑ Copy Column: This just takes data from a column in the source and copies it to the destination without any change whatsoever.

❑ Everything else: The rest are all essentially ActiveX scripts, but have already had common functions added in to save you work. Most of these are limited to only one source and one destination column per transform (remember, you can have multiple transforms inside this one transformation task).

Again, what we're focused on is the Copy Column option, so select it and click OK:

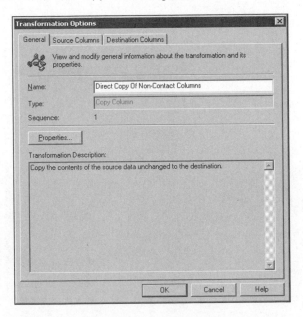

Actually, all we're going to change in this dialog is just the name to Direct Copy Of Non-Contact Columns (I've never been fond of names like DTS_Transformation_1 – it doesn't really tell you much, does it?), but, since we're here, let's look around at things a bit.

Let's start by checking out the Properties dialog:

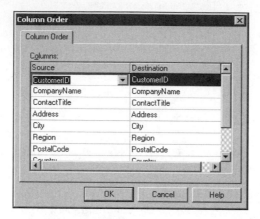

There's nothing too exciting in this dialog because we're doing a straight Copy Column. If we were doing an ActiveX operation, there would be a bit more of interest. Still, we can use this dialog, if we choose, to provide column mappings between the source and destination tables. However, we're going to move on and see the more typical place to fill in this information – in the Source Columns and Destination Columns tabs of the Transformation Options dialog.

Press Cancel and click on the Source Columns tab:

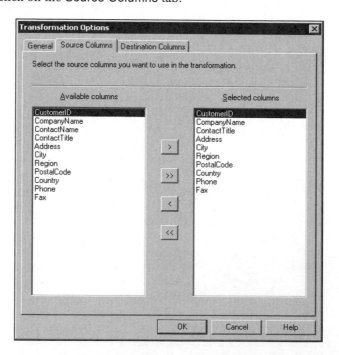

If you look closely at this dialog, you'll notice that the only columns that were moved into the Selected columns side of the dialog were those that we had selected prior to clicking New in the main transform dialog.

The Destination Columns tab looks almost exactly the same:

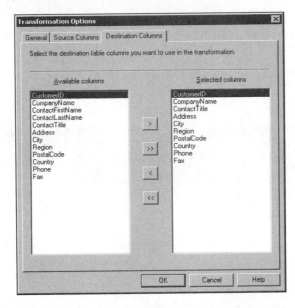

After seeing the Source Columns tab, there's not really much to say about this one (the rules work the same).

After we click OK, however, there is something more interesting to look at:

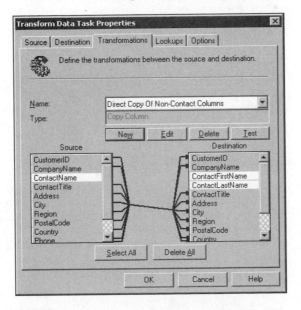

We have our arrows back, but they've changed rather radically!

This time, SQL Server is showing us all the rows involved in the transform, but we can also see that they are all moved as one gigantic transfer. This is actually more efficient and should be faster than doing things on a column-by-column basis.

Now what we need is to address our final two destination columns. Since we're populating these columns by splitting a Source column, we will need a little more power to be available to us – this is where our ActiveX transforms come in handy.

To set up our ActiveX transform, select the ContactName in the Source list of things, and the ContactFirstName and ContactLastName from the Destination list. Then click on New and select ActiveX Script:

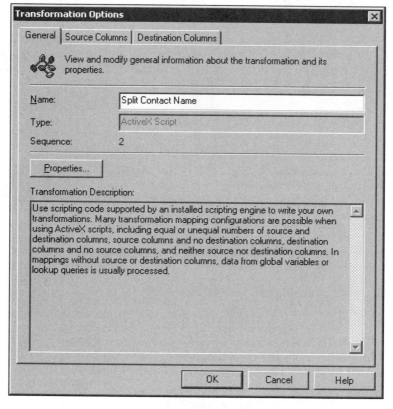

To start with, there's very little of interest. All I've done here is change the name to Split Contact Name to make it somewhat more descriptive than the default is. The Source and Destination Columns tabs work exactly as they did in our first transform – the real difference shows up when we click on Properties:

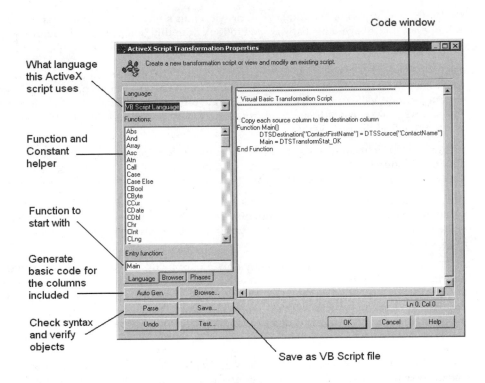

Code window

What language this ActiveX script uses

Function and Constant helper

Function to start with

Generate basic code for the columns included

Check syntax and verify objects

Save as VB Script file

Wow! This is totally different from what the **Properties** dialog looked like in our last transform. What we have here is a mini version of a Visual Basic development environment. Technically speaking, you can use just about any scripting language, though VBScript and JScript are the only built-in languages at this time.

> *DTS is a fairly far-reaching topic so, even though there's a ton of new information on DTS in this version of the book, please forgive me for skirting over details in some places. My goal here is to give you the absolute basics – what you need to know to do 80-90% of the DTS operations you're likely to require. Between this chapter and Chapter 31, I think you'll get there. If you need to dive in still deeper (for that other 10-20%), consider picking up a copy of* Professional SQL Server 2000 DTS (Data Transformation Services) *also from Wrox Press, ISBN 1-861004-41-9.*

Let's move right into the code to split up our contact name. SQL Server came up with auto-generated code that looks like this:

```
'*****************************************************************
'   Visual Basic Transformation Script
'*****************************************************************


'   Copy each source column to the destination column
Function Main()
    DTSDestination("ContactLastName") = DTSSource("ContactName")
    Main = DTSTransformStat_OK
End Function
```

For our needs, this is pretty worthless, other than providing us a nice template for what we need to do. There are, however, a few key items that we need to look at in this "template" code before we go on to writing our own version of it:

❑ `Function Main()`: This is the default function name that will be put on any auto-generated code. It's also the default start-up function for an ActiveX script in DTS. Like any other place you might code VBScript, we can create separate functions and subroutines if we so choose. We can even make one of them the startup function by naming it in the Entry function text box to the left of the code window.

❑ `DTSSource()` collection: This contains values for each of our source fields. The format for obtaining a source value is `DTSSource("<column name>")`. This is going to be used in almost any DTS transformation that you create using ActiveX scripting.

❑ `DTSDestination()` collection: Much like the `DTSSource()` collection, only this is where we supply values for each of our destination fields. The format for assigning a destination value is `DTSDestination("<column name>")`. This is also going to be used in almost any DTS transformation that you create using ActiveX scripting.

❑ `DTSTransformStat_OK`: This is actually only one of many possible status codes that you can pass back to SQL Server. By placing this at the end of our function, we are saying to SQL Server that each row it passes into our function is OK to store away. If, for example, we were doing error checking or wanted to skip rows that didn't meet a condition, we might want to make use of some `IF` statements and perhaps `DTSTransformStat_Error` or `DTSTransformStat_SkipRow`.

Now that we've looked at the basic pieces that show up in pretty much any ActiveX transform, let's make the changes that we need to in order to split up our `ContactName` column.

The algorithm that I'm going to use is based on the notion that there will be a space between the first and last names, and that the first name will always be first and the last name last.

> *Note that this algorithm is certainly not foolproof. If, for example, one of our contact names included a middle initial or middle name, then those would get lumped in with the last name in error. Still, for our data this works fairly well, and it's fine for illustrating that we can use VBScript to add a tremendous amount of flexibility to our transforms.*

What I'll do is first look for the space and identify its position in the overall name. I'll then use that position to grab the portions of the name to the left (the first name) and right (the last name) of the space:

```
'***********************************************************************
'  Visual Basic Transformation Script
'***********************************************************************

'  Copy each source column to the destination column
Function Main()
   Dim iPosition

   iPosition = InStr(DTSSource("ContactName") , " " )
   DTSDestination("ContactLastName") = Mid(DTSSource("ContactName"), iPosition + 1)
   DTSDestination("ContactFirstName") = Left(DTSSource("ContactName"), iPosition)
   Main = DTSTransformStat_OK
End Function
```

In this case, we're not expecting anything to happen that might cause an error. Nor do we have any need to skip rows. If we did, we could add additional logic to test for those conditions and change the return value from `DTSTransformStat_OK` to some other value as necessary.

We can do two things before we close this to make sure that the code is going to run OK. First, we can simply click on the Parse button – this will parse our code and make sure that we do not have any syntax errors. Finally, we can click on the Test button and SQL Server will literally run our code and give us the opportunity, by clicking on View Results, to see whether the output looks as we expect or not:

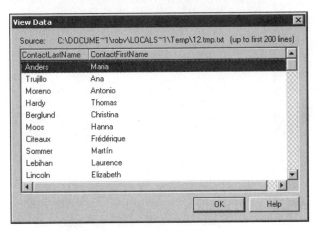

From our test data, it looks like everything is pretty much in order, and we should be ready to move on with our package with confidence that this transform is ready to go.

Notice the changes in our main Transform Data Task Properties dialog now:

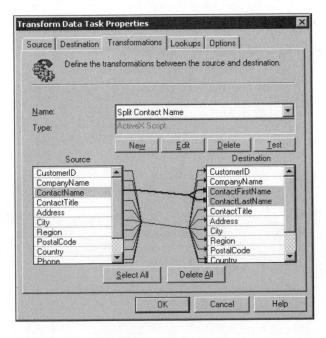

We've taken what were a dozen or so transformations and turned them into just two. At the same time, we've actually increased the power of our transform dramatically.

Let's take a quick look at the last two tabs in our transform task. First, there's the Lookups tab:

We won't be using this tab now, but the gist of what it does is that it allows you to look up values using a completely separate connection (this means a different server and database, potentially). This can be handy when you need to drive part of your transform from data that exists outside the realm of the standard source and target.

Next comes the very important Options tab:

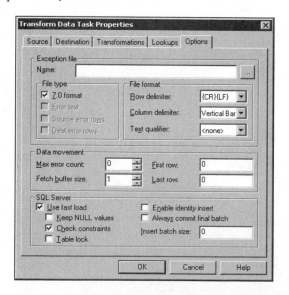

This one has some pretty important stuff:

- ❑ **Exception file**: This allows you to specify the location where a text file will be written, which contains any exceptions that occurred during the running of this transformation. If the file doesn't exist it will be created. Any existing data in the file will be truncated to make room for data from the new run.

- ❑ **File type**: Using 7.0 format can be handy if you already have exception files out there and you want to view them (by hand or programmatically) in the same layout as existed under version 7.0. The other three options are only available if you turn off the 7.0 format option. They determine the degree of information that will be stored in the event of an error.

- ❑ **File format**: The row and column delimiter options here basically equate to what we saw last chapter when we were dealing with bcp. The text qualifier can be useful in allowing you to get minimal data typing when dealing with text files. All character fields will be qualified with quotes when this option is selected.

- ❑ **Max error count**: The maximum error count is a setting that allows SQL Server to decide how many rows must have problems before SQL Server aborts the transformation. If the package completes with errors, but fewer than the threshold set here, then the task will be considered as having completed successfully (think of this when planning workflow).

- ❑ **Fetch buffer size**: This just decides how many rows are grabbed up front. The **First row** and **Last row** options allow you to specify a particular starting point (for situations where you are loading data in chunks or, more commonly, when you need to skip a header row – this doesn't happen much in SQL Server but happens in text files all the time).

- ❑ **SQL Server**: Among the options here are:

  - ❑ **Use fast load**: Using fast bulk copy operations to speed the transfer.

  - ❑ **Keep NULL values**: Set this and any NULLs in the old table will become NULLs in the new table. Turn this off, and any row that tries to insert will use the target table's default (if there is one) instead.

  - ❑ **Check constraints**: By default, SQL Server will bypass constraints if you are using fast load. This means that you can have bogus data getting into your system. On the bright side, the bogus data will be loaded *very* fast! Actually, this is an OK option if you can be certain of where you are getting the data from and are sure that it meets the criteria.

  - ❑ **Table lock**: Grabs a table-level lock right from the beginning. If you turn both this and **Use fast load** off, then row-level locking will be used (not usually a good idea on large data movements).

  - ❑ **Enable identity insert**: This has the effect of executing a SET IDENTITY_INSERT ON. It automatically sets this IDENTITY_INSERT option back to normal when the DTS task is complete.

  - ❑ **Always commit final batch**: This commits all rows that were successful before an error rather than rolling them back.

  - ❑ **Insert batch size**: This decides how many rows are loaded "together". 0 is the default, and means that all rows are loaded. Any other positive number indicates the number of rows you want to accept before the system commits the transaction in the event of failure (rather than the standard rollback).

Now we're ready to click **OK** and close our transformation.

Let's move on rather quickly and look at copying the other objects that we're interest in. To do this, we'll add in a Copy SQL Server Objects task. Again, to add that task, just click and drag it into the main DTS Package Editor window. This will bring up something of an "all-in-one" dialog – one tab for the source, one for the destination, and one for the details of our copy:

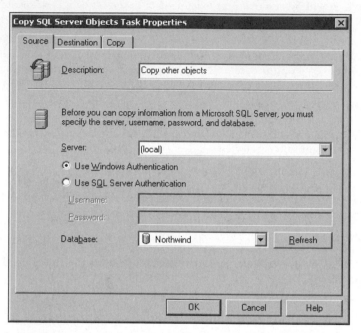

Again, I've played with the name a little. Make sure you set up the Northwind database as the source and NorthwindCopy as the destination, then move on to the Copy tab:

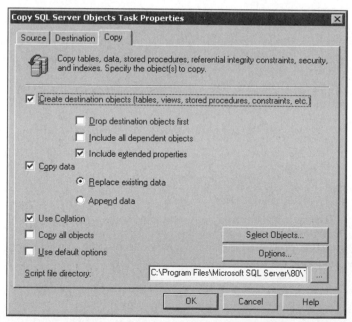

Most of these options are self-describing, so we'll just focus on a couple:

❑ **Include all dependent objects**: This means that anything your object depends on will be copied, in addition to the objects you specify. Furthermore, there can be a dependency chain on this (for example, `view1` depends on `view2`, which depends on `table1`). Be sure you know what you're going to get before choosing this option.

❑ **Include extended properties**: This includes the notes associated with a table or column. Extended properties are new with SQL Server 2000.

Uncheck the **Copy all objects** and **Use default options** checkboxes – doing this will enable the **Select Objects** and **Options** buttons. In addition, uncheck the **Include all dependent objects** and **Drop destination objects first** options, and check **Include extended properties**. Now click on the **Select Objects** button:

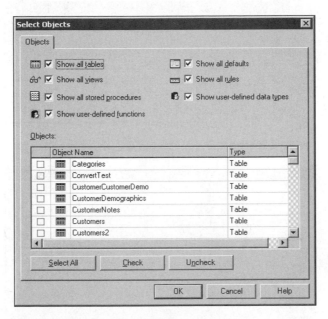

This gives us a rather complete list of all the objects in our `Northwind` database. Uncheck all the options except for **Show all tables**, and then select the following tables: **Categories, Employees, Orders, Order Details, Products, Shippers**, and **Suppliers**.

All of these tables could have been copied simply by selecting the Order Details table and leaving the last screen's Include all dependent objects option turned on – the dependency chain would end up with the above list in it. So why did I not do it that way? Well, because we did something special with Customers, and Customers would be in the dependency chain too. The result is that making use of the dependency chain to copy all the tables would, in this case, create a conflict when both tasks try to copy in records for the Customers table. That being the case, we have to state all the tables manually.

777

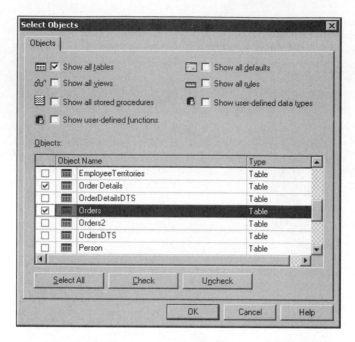

Select **OK** and then move on to **Options**:

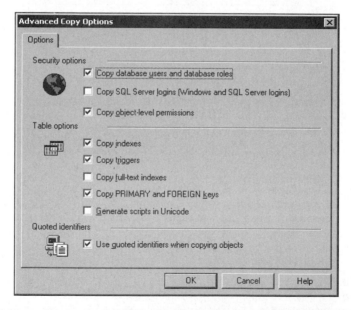

This is the side of things that lets us decide whether to include things like constraints, triggers, and indexes (remember how the Import/Export Wizard wouldn't do that for us?).

We'll go ahead and take the defaults on this one, and then click **OK** – we're done with this task.

Setting up Workflow

The only problem with our latest task is that it has some dependencies on our Customers table. For example, we're not going to be able to insert records from the Orders table if the Customers table doesn't already have rows in it. So what we're going to do here is establish a workflow requirement that flows from our NorthwindCopy Target connection to our Copy other objects task.

To do this, we first click on the NorthwindCopy Target connection. Then hold down the *Shift* key and click on the Copy other objects task (the order that they get selected is important here!). With both items now selected, click on Workflow and select On Success:

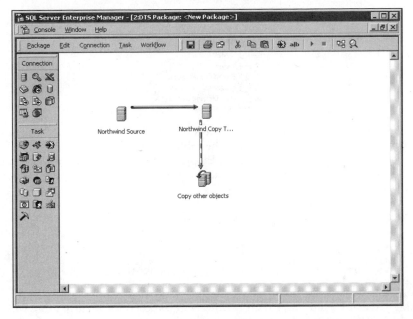

Now we're ready to execute our package. To do this, just click on the green arrow up at the top of the package designer. Assuming that we've done everything correctly, you should see things chug away for a bit (how long depends on your server configuration), and eventually come up with a confirmation:

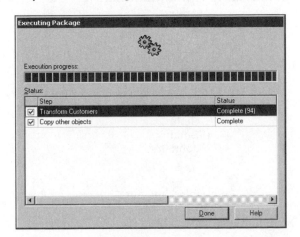

Now fire up Query Analyzer, and let's check out a thing or two about what we just did with DTS.

First, let's examine what tables got moved into our `NorthwindCopy` database. We can do that by making use of the Object Browser in Query Analyzer (if you've closed down the Object Browser, it can be easily added back by pressing *F8*):

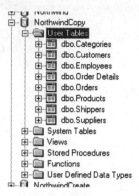

We have our **Customers**, **Orders**, and **Order Details** tables. SQL Server also automatically followed the dependency chain in order to figure out what other objects needed to be created (for example, **Orders** has a foreign key that references **Employees**, so **Employees** was created to satisfy that dependency). If you expand the tables and look at their indexes and constraints, you'll see that all of our requested information was copied into the new database.

Next, let's look at the actual data in the `Customers` table:

```
USE NorthwindCopy

SELECT CustomerID, ContactFirstName, ContactLastName
FROM Customers
```

We can quickly see that we now have slightly different `Customers` table from that which we had in the original `Northwind` database:

```
CustomerID    ContactFirstName                  ContactLastName
-----------   -------------------------------   ----------------------
ALFKI         Maria                             Anders
ANATR         Ana                               Trujillo
ANTON         Antonio                           Moreno
AROUT         Thomas                            Hardy
BERGS         Christina                         Berglund
...
...
...
XXALL         Wally                             Smith
XXENE         Al                                Smith
XXORE         Paul                              Johnston

(94 row(s) affected)
```

Our data has moved between all of our tables, and our `Customers` table has had the data customized during the move. A fairly powerful concept!

Saving a Package

Saving a package is fairly easy – you just click on the little disk icon in the toolbar or choose **Package |
Save** from the menu.

What's a little more confusing is the manner in which you can save your packages. SQL Server offers
four storage methods for DTS packages:

- ❑ **Meta Data Services**: This is a cool option, but you must have Meta Data Services installed to
  make use of it. What's cool about it is that it allows you to track the versioning of a package as
  well as things like what columns it updates and where it gets its data. The versioning issue is
  particularly slick since not only can you keep different versions of a DTS package, but you can
  also keep track of what version of the package loaded what blocks of data.

- ❑ **SQL Server**: This is the default. Basically, the package is stored in a table in the msdb
  database. This option is rather handy since there is no question of where the package is
  (packages stored as files can sometimes get "lost" in the sea of other files in the O/S).

- ❑ **Structured Storage file**: This is file-based storage. What's nice about this is that you can ship
  copies of the package around, store it in version control software (such as Source Safe), and
  easily load it up again for additional editing.

- ❑ **Visual Basic file**: This is another cool option in that, rather than storing the actual package, it
  instead scripts out the package in Visual Basic. Think about this option if you need a starting
  point for your packages after you read Chapter 31.

So, for the package we created in the last section, we could simply click on the save icon (the little
floppy disk), and fill out the dialog that comes up:

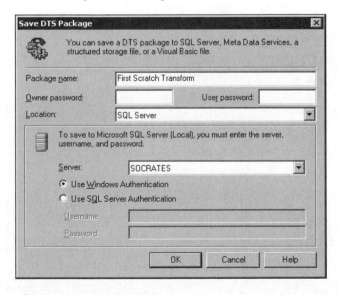

Click **OK** and it's saved.

Using DTS in the place of bcp

DTS can be used in the place of most any bulk copy operation. The advantage of doing this is that you have a GUI tool to work with and, perhaps more importantly, you are working with a consistent interface – there will be things you might want to do where DTS is your only option.

To illustrate DTS in the place of bcp, let's quickly run through one of the exports that we did in our last chapter. You may recall us exporting to a .csv file using bcp:

```
BCP northwind.dbo.shippers out C:\ProfessionalSQL\shipout.txt -c -t, -T
```

This created the following output:

```
1,Speedy Express,(503) 555-9831
2,United Package,(503) 555-3199
3,Federal Shipping,(503) 555-9931
4,Speedy Shippers, Inc.,(503) 555-5566
5,Speedy Shippers, Inc,
100,Billy Bob's Pretty Good Shipping,
101,Fred's Freight,
102,Readyship,(503)555-1234
103,MyShipper,(503)555-3443
```

To do this with DTS, I just need to start up the package designer, and add three things:

❑ A SQL Server connection

❑ A text (output) connection

❑ A transformation

Let's add them one at a time.

First, the SQL Server connection – this is basically the same as our previous connection objects:

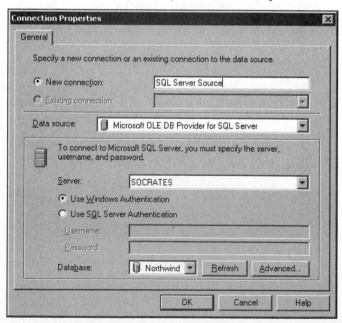

Now just add in a Text File (Destination) connection:

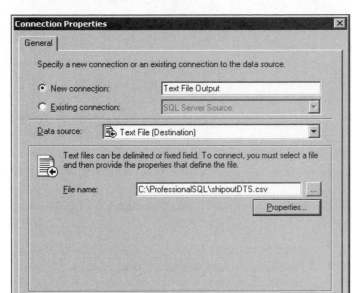

We'll call this one **shipoutDTS.csv**. Now, we need to check out the values for the Properties:

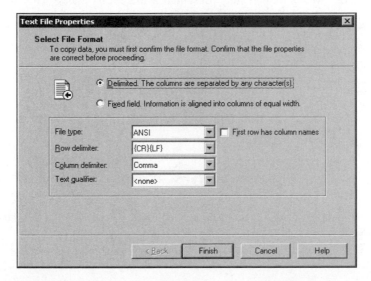

Our only change here is to turn the **Text qualifier** off (so we can match the previous output).

At this point, we're done with our connections and we just need to set up our transformation task. As with the last example, just use drag-and-drop to pick up the Transform Data task, click first on the SQL Server connection (since it is the source) and then on the text connection (since it is the destination). Now, double-click on the transformation arrow, and up comes the now familiar dialog:

Just like with the bcp, we're going to pull things directly from the Shippers table without any special treatment, so we're ready to move on to the Destination tab.

When we go to this tab, we are immediately presented with another dialog. This one is basically meant to define the columns in the destination, and the default will be based on the source table:

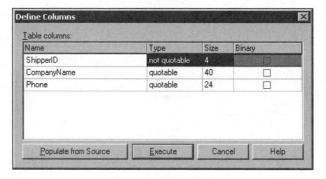

As I indicated earlier, we're not doing anything special on this export, so the defaults are fine. Just click Execute and it will finish populating the Destination tab:

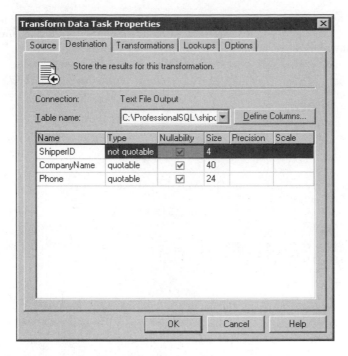

Now go ahead and move on to the Transformations tab:

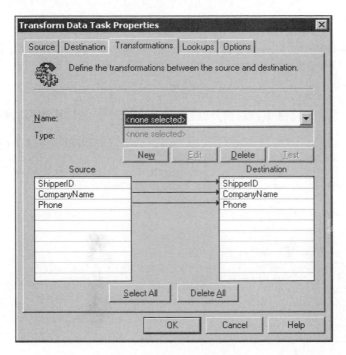

Once again, SQL Server has set things up as separate transforms. You can either leave this as is or, for better performance, you can delete these transforms and remap them into one (similarly to how we did in the package that we set up earlier).

> *Here's my two units of your chosen unit of currency on this one. For something like the tiny table that we're moving here, clearing out the transformations and setting them up as one is probably not worth the effort (even though it will only take a minute or two, tops). There are only three rows in the default Northwind database (we've added several more in the course of the book), so I don't think performance is really an issue. If we were, however, moving tens or hundreds of thousands of rows – it would be worth it. In the end, it's up to you.*

Click **OK** and we're ready for our export. Just run the package, and you should find your new text file wherever you chose to create it:

```
1,Speedy Express,(503) 555-9831
2,United Package,(503) 555-3199
3,Federal Shipping,(503) 555-9931
4,Speedy Shippers, Inc.,(503) 555-5566
5,Speedy Shippers, Inc,
100,Billy Bob's Pretty Good Shipping,
101,Fred's Freight,
102,Readyship,(503)555-1234
103,MyShipper,(503)555-3443
```

> *This kind of "create the file on the fly and populate it" is not limited to just text files – you can even create an Excel spreadsheet and load data into it – all from your DTS package!*

Go ahead and save this as DTSExport.dts, a structured storage file, in your file system somewhere (make it easy to get to – we'll be using it in the next section).

Running from the Command Line – dtsrun.exe

Before we end this chapter, I need to get you using one last tool. This one will let you execute DTS packages from a command prompt – which means that you can execute a DTS package from just about anywhere. You could shell out from some other program you wrote, use the Windows scheduler, use the SQL Server job manager, or set up batch files. It has major flexibility.

The utility in question is called dtsrun.exe, and the syntax for using it looks like this:

```
dtsrun [/?]|[
    [   /[~]S <server name>[\<instance name>]
        { {/[~]U <user name> [/[~]P <password>]} | /E }]
    {/[~]N <package name>|/[~]G <package GUID string>|
     /[~]V <package version GUID string>}
    [/[~]M <package password>]
    [/[~]F <filename>]
    [/[~]R <repository database name>]
    [/A <global variable name>:<typeid>=<value>]
    [/L <log file name>]
    [/W <NT event log completion status>]
    [/Z] [/!X] [/!D] [/!Y] [/!C]
]
```

Well, this is a big mess, so let's look at what all this means:

Option	Explanation
?	Help – prints out the list you see above.
~	Indicates that the parameter that follows is in Hex rather than decimal.
S (optionally followed by instance name)	Specifies the server name and, optionally, the instance name.
U	Specifies the user name to log in as.
P	Password.
E	Indicates that you want to use a trusted connection (don't need /U or /P).
N	The package name.
G	Package GUID string – this is a GUID that uniquely identifies this package. Don't confuse this with the version ID.
V	Another GUID, but this time it's for the specific version of the DTS package.
M	DTS package password. This is a password placed on the package itself, not the user.
F	The filename of the DTS package if it is stored using structured storage rather than SQL Server or Meta Data Services.
R	The repository name if the package is in Meta Data Services.
A	Specifies a package global variable – the global variable will take on the value supplied.
L	Log file name – a text file that you want logged results sent to.
W	If followed by the word True, then the execution will be logged to the Windows Event Log.
Z	Tells SQL Server that the command line is encrypted using SQL Server 2000 encryption (much stronger than previous versions).
!X	Blocks execution of the script – allows for test running of the script without physical execution of said script. Used when figuring out the encryption schema if you're going to use one.
!D	Deletes a package from a SQL Server.
!Y	When you use this with a dtsrun command, !Y provides back the encrypted command line to be used in future calls to DTS.
!C	Takes the entire command that invoked dtsrun and copies it to the clipboard.

OK! For a quick example, we're going to re-run the code from the last section. Before we do, however, either delete or move the shipoutDTS.csv file that we created in the last section.

Now try running things again:

```
C:\ProfessionalSQL>dtsrun /F DTSExport.dts
```

Since the default is a trusted connection, I didn't need to use any login information – if you've been using the sa password or something similar, then you'll probably need to use the /S and /U switch.

This run should provide some feedback:

```
DTSRun: Loading...
DTSRun: Executing...
DTSRun OnStart: DTSStep_DTSDataPumpTask_1
DTSRun OnProgress: DTSStep_DTSDataPumpTask_1; 9 Rows have been transformed or c
opied.; PercentComplete = 0; ProgressCount = 9
DTSRun OnFinish: DTSStep_DTSDataPumpTask_1
DTSRun: Package execution complete.
```

If you check out the directory where your shipoutDTS.csv file should be, it will now be there again!

Summary

Data Transformation Services was definitely one of the coolest features that debuted in version 7.0. With SQL Server 2000, some additional flexibility and parameterization support has been added. In addition, there is now a two-stage data pump (which we will learn more about in Chapter 31), and some overall improvements to the object model.

DTS is, in many respects, a replacement for bcp. That said, bcp is still lighter weight and very, very fast. In addition, there is still a very substantial amount of legacy code out there for bcp. The bottom line? Get familiar with and make use of DTS, but don't forget bcp.

What we've seen in this chapter is just the real basics of DTS. DTS is a very, very large topic that could easily be a book of its own (oops, wait a minute – it *is* in a book of its own!). Hopefully, though, the information provided here should get you off to a good start and help you determine if DTS is right for your particular needs. In Chapter 31, we will be exploring more facets of the engine behind DTS and how to code directly against the object model.

Online discussion at http://p2p.wrox.com

23

Replication

The problem seems relatively straightforward. You've got multiple SQL Servers and you want to keep data between the servers current and accurate. DTS or the bulk copy program might work, but they would require too much interaction and overhead. You've considered doing everything through distributed transactions, but there are timing, bandwidth, and reliability issues going out to the remote links. Trying to manage the process through careful use of backups and restores is out of the question. Latency of backup transmissions, along with the general inability to merge backup data, forces DBAs to look to replication as the source for managing distributed databases within the enterprise.

Does this sound familiar to you? The problem is distributed data. The solution, quite often, is **replication**. In most cases, Microsoft SQL Server will provide the functionality and flexibility to support your distributed data environment.

Supporting Distributed Data

You may be wondering how you ended up supporting distributed data in the first place. It could be that you started with autonomous servers and later discovered a need to duplicate data between servers. It could come about as an organization grows and you want to keep data geographically close to the users. It might even have been planned that way from the outset, but it's probably more likely that distributed data requirements "just happened".

If you're just at the planning stage, you actually have an advantage. You can design your databases from the beginning with replication in mind. If you're working with existing servers, you're going to find yourself working around design decisions that were made in the past. You'll probably have to make some changes to the way data is organized on some of the servers.

What changes? That will depend on how you implement replication. As I said at the beginning of the chapter, the problem *seems* relatively straightforward. "Seems" is the key word here.

Considerations when Planning for Replication

If you've come this far, then you've probably decided that you need to at least consider replication. Even if you don't need it now, you may have a need for it in the future.

That decided, let's start looking at some of the details. First, what are some of the factors that you have to consider when planning for replication? Key considerations include:

❑ Autonomy

❑ Latency

❑ Data consistency

❑ Schema consistency

Let's take a quick look at each of these.

Autonomy

You have to consider the level of **autonomy** or **server independence** that you want to support at each site. Determine what data needs to be replicated and at what frequency. For example, you could be supporting a sales application where each site keeps separate customer records. You would want to have these replicated to a central database, but you may only need to make daily updates.

Latency

Latency refers to the time delay between updates; in other words, the time taken for a change at the publishing server to be made available at the subscribing server. The higher the autonomy between sites, the greater the latency between updates. You need to determine the acceptable delay. This will typically depend on the particular data and different latency values that may be acceptable for different types of data.

Data Consistency

Obviously, **data consistency** is going to be critical. Data consistency can be accomplished through data convergence or transactional consistency:

❏ **Data convergence** means that all sites eventually end up with the same values. However, the values aren't necessarily the same as they would be if all of the changes had taken place on one server.

❏ **Transactional consistency** is a little different. The results at any server are the same as if all transactions were executed on a single server.

Replication can ensure data consistency, but you will have to keep potential latency in mind. How data consistency is managed and maintained is somewhat dependent on the replication method you select.

Schema Consistency

Many developers in non-replicated environments take an ability to easily change the database schema for granted. If they need to add a new column, drop a column, add a new table or constraint – no problem. Life is not quite so "no problem" in a replicated world.

The good news is that SQL Server 2000 now supports schema changes during replication. Fields that are added or dropped on the publisher may be propagated to all subscribers during future replication operations. The bad news is that your change procedures need to be much more strict. You must, for example, make use of the special `sp_repladdcolumn` and `sp_repldropcolumn` system sprocs rather than the more familiar `ALTER TABLE` command. See the *Replication and Schema Changes* section towards the end of this chapter.

The bottom line is that, if you need to make frequent schema changes, you'll want to fully plan what your change strategy is going to be before implementing replication at all.

Other Considerations

Finally, you have to consider the geographic locations of your servers, the type of connection between the servers, and the connection bandwidth. You're not going to want to constantly saturate your connection with replication traffic, so you may need to adjust your initial autonomy and latency decisions to match real-world capabilities.

One of the advantages to replication that is new in SQL Server 2000 is the ability to compress the replication files as well as to use alternative media for data transfer. Removable media is now a valid location for replication databases. We can now use media such as recordable CDs to transfer data to disconnected networks.

The Publishing Metaphor

Before we can look more closely at how replication works, you need to understand some of the basic terms and concepts. Replication is built around a **publishing metaphor** for distributing data.

The source database is maintained at the **Publisher**, which also owns the source data. The Publisher identifies the data items to be published (made available for replication) and the **Distributor** collects them from the publisher's transaction log.

The Distributor can be on the same server as the Publisher or can be set up on a different server, as in the following figure. Note that one Distributor can support multiple Publishers:

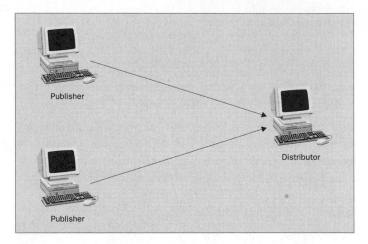

Changes to published data are stored on the Distributor where they are held until forwarded to **Subscribers**. Not only can a Distributor support multiple Publishers, it can also support multiple Subscribers:

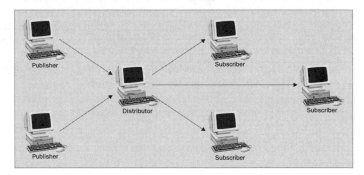

A key component of the Distributor is the **distribution database**. The distribution database stores any transactions awaiting distribution and tracks the replication status.

A copy of the published data is maintained on the Subscriber. Changes to the data are sent to the Subscriber on a periodic basis. In some situations, you may want to configure replication so that changes can occur on both the Publisher and Subscriber.

Subscriptions

Under SQL Server 2000, the subscriptions that the Subscriber receives are called **publications**. A publication will contain one or more **articles**. An article is most commonly a table or part of the data from a table, but it can be a stored procedure or a group of stored procedures. By subscribing to a publication, the Subscriber is subscribing to all of the articles in the publication – the Subscriber cannot subscribe to individual articles alone.

Subscriptions can be set up as **push** subscriptions or **pull** subscriptions.

With push subscriptions:

- ❏ The Publisher determines when updates go out to the Subscriber
- ❏ You usually want to keep latency to a minimum or you want to keep full control at the Publisher

With pull subscriptions:

- ❏ The Subscriber requests updates
- ❏ You allow for a higher level of autonomy since the Subscriber decides when updates occur

A publication can simultaneously support both push and pull subscriptions. However, any one Subscriber can either have a push or pull subscription to a publication, but cannot have both to the same publication.

Types of Subscribers

SQL Server supports three types of Subscribers:

- ❏ The default is a **local** Subscriber. The Publisher is the only server that knows the Subscriber. Local Subscribers are often used as a security mechanism or when you want to maximize autonomy between servers.
- ❏ There are also **global** Subscribers, where all servers know the Subscribers. Global Subscribers are commonly used in a multi-server environment where you want to be able to combine data from different Publishers at the Subscriber.
- ❏ Finally, there are **anonymous** Subscribers. The Publisher is only aware of an anonymous Subscriber while it is connected. This is useful when setting up Internet-based applications.

Filtering Data

We aren't just limited to publishing an entire table as an article. We also have the option of horizontally or vertically filtering tables.

Horizontal filtering (you may come across the term **horizontal partitioning** for this as well) identifies rows within the table for publication. For example, you could divide inventory information by warehouse as a way of maintaining separate warehouse totals.

Vertical filtering (also known as **vertical partitioning**) identifies the columns to be replicated. For example, you might want to publish quantity on hand information from an inventory table, but not quantity on order.

Types of Replication

SQL Server supports various types of replication, letting us pick the type that best meets our needs; which to choose is something of a balancing act between:

❑   The need for connectivity vs. independence: Is there a constant connection available between the servers? If so, what kind of bandwidth is available? How many transactions will be replicating?

❑   The need to minimize conflict: What is the risk that the same data will be edited in multiple locations either at the same time or in-between replicated updates? What is the tolerance for data on one or more of the replicated servers?

Some replication scenarios don't allow for connectivity except on a sporadic basis – others may never have connectivity at all except through what is often referred to as "sneaker net", which is where you run, mail, fly, etc. a disk (CD-ROM, ZIP disk, and so on) from one site to another. Other replication scenarios have an absolute demand for consistent data at all sites with zero data loss.

From highest to lowest server independence they are:

❑   **Snapshot** replication

❑   **Merge** replication

❑   **Transactional** replication

We're going to look at potential benefits and drawbacks of each replication type, and at situations where it would be an appropriate solution, and outline any data concerns that might arise.

It's important that you know that you can mix and match the replication types as necessary to meet your implementation requirements. There are going to be some publications where you want to allow greater autonomy between sites. There will be other publications where minimizing latency is critical.

Snapshot Replication

With **snapshot replication**, a "picture" is taken at the source of all of the data to be replicated. This is used to replace the data at the destination server.

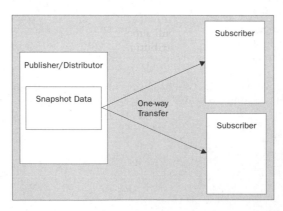

Snapshot replication can be the easiest type of replication to set up and manage. Complete tables or table segments (for partitioned tables) are written to the Subscribers during replication. Since updates occur on a periodic basis only, most of the time, there is minimal server or network overhead required to support replication.

In its simplest form, snapshot replication is used to update read-only tables on Subscriber systems. It allows for a high level of autonomy at the Subscriber, but at the cost of relatively high latency.

You are able to keep tight control on when periodic updates occur when using snapshot replication. This means that you can schedule updates to occur when network and server activity is at a lull.

There is a potential concern about the time and resources to complete replication during the periodic updates. As source tables grow, the amount of data that has to be transferred during each update increases. Over time it may become necessary to either change the replication type or partition the table to reduce the amount of data replicated to keep traffic to manageable levels.

A variation of snapshot replication is **snapshot replication with immediate-updating subscribers**. With this, changes can be made to the data at the Subscriber. Those changes are sent to the publishing server on a periodic basis unless immediate updating has been implemented, and then distributed transactions are executed in real time.

How Snapshot Replication Works

Snapshot replication is implemented through **replication agents**. Each plays a vital role in the replication process.

Snapshot Agent

The **Snapshot Agent** supports snapshot replication and initial synchronization of data tables for replication (for more about synchronization, see Appendix C). All types of replication require that the source and destination tables must be synchronized, either by the replication agents or through manual synchronization, before replication can begin. In either case, the Snapshot Agent has the same responsibility. It takes the "picture" of the published data and stores the files on the Distributor.

Distribution Agent

The **Distribution Agent** is responsible for moving transactions and snapshots from the Publisher to the Subscriber(s). The Distribution Agent is used for moving data for initial synchronization and snapshot replication (and, as we'll see later, for transactional replication). For push subscriptions, the Distribution Agent typically runs on the Distributor. For pull subscriptions, the Distribution Agent typically runs on the Subscriber. The actual location of the Distribution Agent is an option that can be configured within Enterprise Manager.

The Process of Snapshot Replication

Snapshot replication uses periodic updates. During the updates, schema and data files are created and sent to the Subscribers. Let's step through the basic procedure:

1. The Snapshot Agent places a shared lock on all articles in the publication to be replicated, ensuring data consistency.

2. A copy of each article's table schema is written to the distribution working folder on the Distributor.

3. A snapshot copy of table data is written to the snapshot folder.

4. The Snapshot Agent releases the shared locks from the publication articles.

5. The Distribution Agent creates the destination tables and database objects, such as indexes, on the Subscriber. It then copies in the snapshot data, overwriting the existing tables, if any.

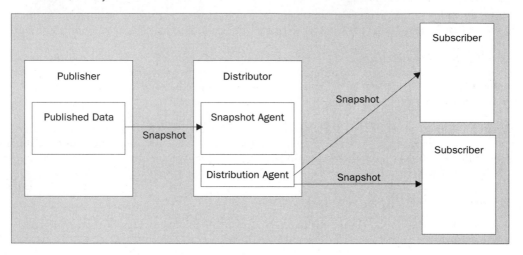

Snapshot data is stored as a native bcp file if all of the Subscribers are Microsoft SQL Servers. If you are supporting heterogeneous (non-SQL Server) data sources, character mode files will be created instead.

When to Use Snapshot Replication

Use snapshot replication to update look-up data or read-only copies of data on remote servers. You can use snapshot replication when you want (or need) to connect to the Publisher intermittently.

Think of how servers might be managed for a chain of garden supply stores. You have stores in several cities. Some larger cities have multiple stores. What are some good candidates for snapshot replication?

Customer records are an obvious choice. A customer, such as a landscape gardener, may turn up at different locations. In most cases, it won't matter if there's a delay updating customer information. This would also give you a way to make sure that only users who have access to the publishing server can change customer records.

Inventory records could be a little more of a problem. The items you keep in inventory are somewhat constant with most changes taking place by season. Even then, you would probably keep the items in file, but with a zero quantity on hand. The problem is, you may want to replicate more up-to-date inventory records between stores. This would let you search for items you might not have on hand without having to call each of the stores. Timely updates would probably mean transactional replication.

Special Planning Requirements

An important issue when setting up snapshot replication is timing. You need to make sure that users are not going to need write access to any published tables when the Snapshot Agent is generating its snapshot. You also want to be sure that the traffic generated by replication does not interfere with other network operations.

Storage space can also become an issue as published tables grow. You have to verify that you have enough physical disk space available on the destination folder (disk, CD-ROM, ZIP, etc.) to support the snapshot folder.

Merge Replication

Another way of managing data changes taking place at multiple servers is with **merge replication**. The changes from all of the sites are merged when they are received by the Publisher. Updates take place either periodically or on demand:

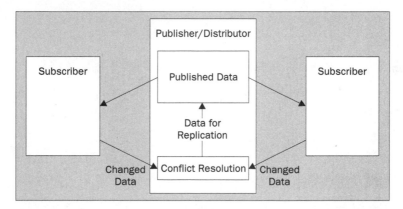

Merge replication has a high level of autonomy, but also has the highest latency and runs a risk of lower transactional consistency. Unlike transactional and snapshot replication, which guarantee consistency, merge replication does not. This is one of the more critical design considerations that you need to make when implementing merge replication – how important is consistency.

In a way, roles tend to get somewhat blurred in merge replication. The Publisher is the initial source for the merge data, but changes can be made at the Publisher or at the Subscribers. Changes can be tracked by row or by column. Transactional consistency is not guaranteed because conflicts can occur when different systems make updates to the same row. Data consistency is maintained through conflict resolution based on criteria you establish. You can determine whether conflicts are recognized by row or by column.

The Snapshot Agent prepares the initial snapshot for synchronization. An agent called the Merge Agent then performs the synchronization and applies any changes made since the initial snapshot.

How Merge Replication Works

As with the other forms of replication, an agent implements the merge replication.

Merge Agent

The **Merge Agent** is used with merge replication. It copies the changes from all Subscribers and applies them to the Publisher. The Merge Agent copies all changes at the Publisher (including those made by the Merge Agent) to the Subscribers. The Merge Agent typically runs on the Distributor for push subscriptions and on the Subscriber for pull subscriptions, but as with the snapshot and transactional replication, it can be configured to run remotely:

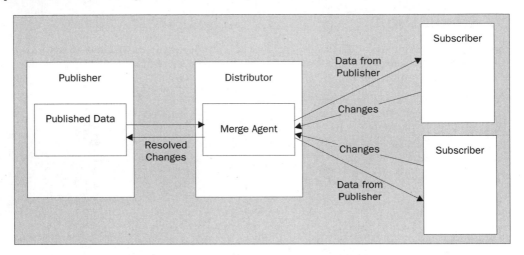

The Process of Merge Replication

Assuming that the initial synchronization has already taken place, here's what happens during merge replication:

❑   Triggers installed by SQL Server track changes to published data

❑   Changes from the Publisher are applied to Subscribers

❑   Changes from Subscribers are applied to the Publisher and any conflicts resolved

> **Note that merge triggers do not interfere with the placement or use of user-defined triggers.**

The Merge Agent applies the changes, whether they occurred at the Publisher or Subscribers. Conflicts are resolved automatically through the Merge Agent. The Merge Agent tracks every row update for conflicts at the row or column level, depending on how you have configured conflict resolution. You must define the priority scheme to be used when conflicts occur between new (arriving) and current data values.

When to Use Merge Replication

One way of using merge replication is to support partitioned tables. Going back to the garden supply business, you could set up filtering (partitioning) so that each store can view inventory information for any store, but would only be able to directly update its own inventory. Changes would be propagated through merge replication. Data can be filtered horizontally or vertically. You can exclude rows to be replicated from a table and you can exclude any table columns. Merge replication watches for changes to any column in a replicated row.

Special Planning Requirements

When implementing merge replication, there are checks that you need to make to ensure that your data is ready for replication. While setting up merge replication, some changes will be made automatically by SQL Server to your data files.

You Need to...

❑ Use care when selecting the tables to be published. Any tables required for data validation must be included in the publication.

❑ Include any tables that are referenced by a foreign key as part of the publication.

❑ Avoid the use of WRITETEXT or UPDATETEXT to update text or image data. Only changes made using the UPDATE statement will be recognized and propagated.

The Server Will...

SQL Server will identify a column as a globally unique identifier for each row in a published table. If the table already has a uniqueidentifier column, SQL Server will automatically use that column. Otherwise, it will add a rowguid column to the table and create an index based on the column.

There will be triggers created on the published tables at both the Publisher and the Subscribers. These are used to track data changes based on row or column changes. These are used to allow the Merge Agent to identify changes.

There will also be several tables added for tracking purposes. These tables are used by the server to manage:

❑ Conflict detection and resolution

❑ Data tracking

❑ Synchronization

❑ Reporting

For example, conflicts are detected through a column in the MSmerge_contents table, one of the tables created when you set up merge replication.

Transactional Replication

The difference between transactional and snapshot replication is that incremental changes, rather than full tables, are replicated to the Subscribers during **transactional replication**. Any logged changes to published articles, such as INSERT, UPDATE, and DELETE statements, are tracked and replicated to Subscribers. In transactional replication, only changed table data is distributed, maintaining the transaction sequence. In other words, all transactions are applied to the Subscriber in the same order that they were applied to the Publisher.

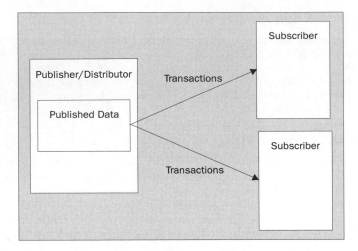

In its simplest form, changes can only be made at the Publisher. Changes can be replicated to Subscribers at set intervals or as near-real-time updates. While you may have less control over when replication occurs, you are typically moving less data with each replication. Updates are occurring much more often and latency is kept to a minimum. Reliable and consistent near-real time Subscriber updates (immediate transactional consistency) require a network connection between the Publisher and Subscriber.

Before transactional replication can take place, the published articles must be initially synchronized between the Publisher and the Subscriber. This is typically managed through automatic synchronization using snapshot replication. In situations where automatic synchronization is neither practical nor efficient, manual synchronization can be used to prepare the Subscriber. This is a relatively simple process:

- ❑   Run BACKUP DATABASE to back up the Publisher's database
- ❑   Deliver the tape backup to the Subscribers' systems
- ❑   Run RESTORE DATABASE to create the database and database objects, and to load the data
- ❑   The Publisher and Subscriber are synchronized as of the point when the backup was run

Transactional replication can also be used to replicate stored procedures. In its simplest implementation, changes can only be made at the publishing server. This means that you don't have any worries about conflicts.

You can also implement transactional replication as **transactional replication with immediate-updating subscribers**. This means that changes can be made at the Publisher or at the Subscriber. Transactions occurring at the Subscriber are treated as distributed transactions. MS DTC (Microsoft Distributed Transaction Coordinator) is used to ensure that both the local data and the data on the Publisher are updated at the same time to avoid update conflicts. Queued updating can be used as a fallback in the event that there is a network connectivity issue such as a disconnection or if the network is physically offline. See the *Queued Updating* section later in this chapter.

Note that you would have to implement distributed transactions to get a lower latency than that provided with transactional replication with immediate-updating subscribers. You still have the distribution delay in getting changes posted at the Publisher, either locally or from a Subscriber, out to all of the Subscribers. Distributed transactions would provide near immediate updates to all servers when data is changed at any server. Depending on the connection speed between servers, this could result in performance problems, including locking conflicts.

How Transactional Replication Works

Transactional replication is also impl mented through replication agents.

Log Reader Agent

The **Log Reader Agent** is used in transactional replication. After a database is set up for transactional replication, its transaction log is monitored for changes to published tables. The Log Reader Agent then has responsibility for copying the transactions marked for replication from the Publisher to the Distributor.

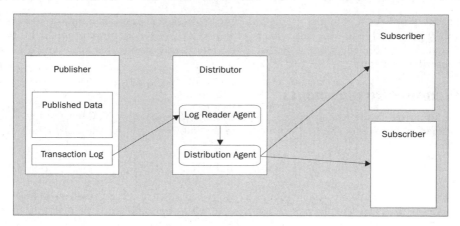

Distribution Agent

The **Distribution Agent** is also used in transactional replication and is responsible for moving transactions from the Distributor to the Subscriber(s).

The Process of Transactional Replication

Assuming that initial synchronization has already taken place, transactional replication follows these basic steps:

1. Modifications are posted to the Publisher's transaction log.

2. The Log Reader Agent reads the transaction log and identifies changes marked for replication.

3. Changes taken from the transaction log are written to the distribution database on the Distributor.

4. The Distribution Agent applies the changes to the appropriate database tables.

5. You can set up the Log Reader Agent to read the transaction log continuously or on a schedule that you specify. As before, the Distribution Agent typically runs at the Publisher for push subscriptions and at the Subscriber for pull subscriptions, but this can be changed through Enterprise Manager to run the Distribution Agent remotely.

When to Use Transactional Replication

You should use transactional replication when you want to reduce latency and provide Subscribers with relatively up-to-date information. Near-real-time updates usually require a LAN connection, but scheduled replication can often be managed through scheduled updates. If you choose to use scheduled updates, latency increases, but you gain control over when replication occurs.

Let's go back to our garden supply store and the inventory problem discussed earlier. You want each of the stores to have up-to-date, or at the very least, relatively up-to-date inventory information. You would probably use scheduled replication to pass data to the Subscribers.

Now let's see if we can make things a little more difficult. Not only do you have a chain of stores, you also have traveling sales people who visit and take orders from your largest customers. They need to have at least relatively up-to-date inventory information, but can spend their days sitting around and waiting for updates from the Publisher. For systems of this type, you may want to use pull subscriptions, letting the sales people decide when they connect to the server and download recent transactions.

You've probably noticed a potential problem in both of these scenarios. The remote servers can receive data, but they are not able to make any changes to the data. We'll cover that problem a little later. Transactional replication, when implemented in this manner, is used to support read-only copies of the data at Subscriber systems.

Special Planning Requirements

Space is an important issue when planning for transactional replication. You have to make sure that you allow adequate space for the transaction log on the Publisher and for the distribution database on the Distributor.

Check each of the tables that you are planning to publish. For a table to be published under transactional replication, it must have a primary key. There are also potential concerns if you are supporting text or image data types in any of the tables. INSERT, UPDATE, and DELETE are supported as for any data type, but you must be sure to use the WITH LOG option if using WRITETEXT or UPDATETEXT to update a published table.

You may encounter problems with the max text repl size parameter, which sets the maximum size of text or image data that can be replicated. Make sure that this parameter is set to a high enough value to support your replication requirements.

Immediate-Update Subscribers

We have the option of setting up Subscribers to snapshot or transactional publications as immediate-update subscribers. Immediate-update subscribers have the ability to update subscribed data, as long as the updates can be immediately reflected at the Publisher. This is accomplished using the two-phase commit protocol managed by the MS DTC.

There is, effectively, no latency in updating the Publisher. Updates to other Subscribers are made normally, as if the change was initiated at the Publisher, so latency when going to other Subscribers will depend on the rate at which they are updated.

You should consider immediate-updating subscribers when you need to post changes to replicated data at one or more Subscribers and propagate near-immediate updates. You might be using multiple servers to support an online transaction processing (OLTP) application as a way of improving performance and providing near-real-time redundancy. When a transaction is posted to any server, it will be sent to the Publisher, and through the Publisher, to the remaining servers.

There is a possibility of conflicts arising when using immediate-updating subscribers. A uniqueidentifier column will be added to any published tables that do not already have one.

Here's how the timestamp column is used. Let's say we have two Subscribers, SubOne and SubTwo. SubOne sends an immediate-update transaction to the Publisher. Before that transaction is sent to SubTwo, the Publisher will check the timestamp value on any affected row to verify that it has not changed since it was replicated to SubTwo. In other words, it won't change a row that has been modified locally.

A high-speed, *reliable* connection is required between the Publisher and any immediate-updating subscribers, such as a LAN connection, unless queued updates are used. A reliable connection is not required if queued updates are implemented, since the replication will take place once there is a connection between the networks. You may still want to have a high-speed connection for your replication as SQL Server 2000 still doesn't have an option to increase your network bandwidth.

Mixing Replication Types

We can also mix and match replication types as needed. Not only can we have different replication types on the same server, we can even have different replication types for the same table.

Here's a possible situation where you might want to publish a table in different ways. A heavy equipment warehouse wants to have up-to-date inventory information and reference copies of invoices available at each of its locations. Each location has its own local SQL Server. Invoices are posted to a central location using an Internet-based application. These are replicated to all local servers through transactional replication so that inventory records are updated.

You want to have invoice and inventory information replication-updated on a separate server weekly. This information is used for business analysis and running weekly reports. This server is updated weekly through a separate snapshot publication referencing the same tables.

Replication Model Scenarios

Microsoft has defined a number of replication topology models (which represent the logical and physical connectivity) to describe how replication can be implemented. These are provided as reliable topology suggestions, not as hard and fast rules for implementation. It is not only possible to mix and modify these models; it's actually quite common.

Your decisions about the type of replication you need to use and your replication model topology can be made somewhat independent of each other. That said; there is a chance that restrictions imposed by your physical topology, such as transmission bandwidth, will influence your decisions.

Standard Models

Let's start with a look at the standard models. Once you've got the basic idea, we can move on to some variations.

Central Publisher/Distributor

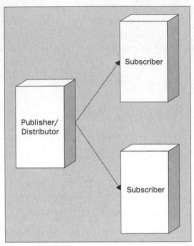

The **Central Publisher/Distributor** scenario is the default SQL Server model. We have one system acting as Publisher and as its own Distributor. This Publisher/Distributor supports any number of Subscribers. The Publisher/Distributor owns all replicated data and is the sole data source for replication. The most basic model assumes that all data is being published to the Subscribers as read-only data. Read-only access can be enforced at the Subscriber by giving users SELECT permission only on the replicated tables.

Since this is the easiest model to set up and manage, you should consider its use in any situation where it fits. If you have a single Publisher, one or more Subscribers, and read-only access to data at the Subscriber, this is your best choice.

Central Publisher/Remote Distributor

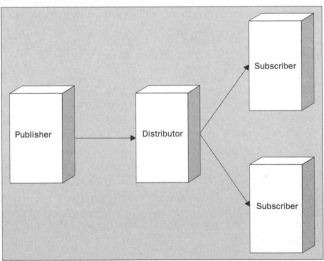

Depending upon the volume of replicated data and the amount of activity at the Publisher, it may be necessary to implement the Publisher and Distributor as separate systems using the **Central Publisher/Remote Distributor** model. Operationally, this is effectively the same as the Publisher/Distributor model. The Publisher is still the owner of, and only source for, replicated data. Once again, the basic model assumes that the data will be treated as read-only at the Subscriber.

Obviously, you will use this model when a single Publisher/Distributor cannot handle both production activity and replication to Subscribers.

Central Subscriber

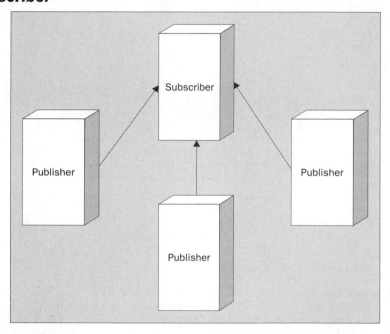

In the **Central Subscriber** model, you only have one Subscriber receiving data, but you have multiple Publishers. The Publishers can be configured as Publisher/Distributor systems. This model provides a way to keep just local data at the local server, but still have a way of consolidating the data at one central location. Horizontal filtering may be necessary to keep Publishers from overwriting each other's data at the Subscriber.

This is the model to use when you have data consolidation requirements.

Mixed Models

Now let's look at a few variations to the basic models. These are just suggestions and are not meant to imply a complete list of possibilities.

Publishing Subscriber

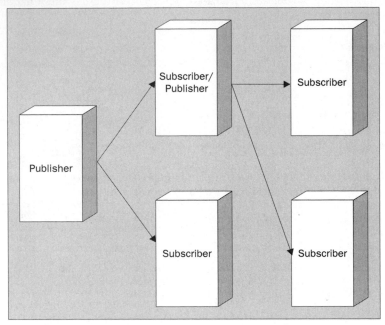

Publishing Subscribers (that is Subscribers that are also configured as Publishers) can be added to any of the basic models. This model has two Publishers publishing the same data. The original Publisher replicates data to its Subscribers, one of which is a Publishing Subscriber. The Publishing Subscriber can then pass the same data along to its Subscribers.

This model is useful when you have pockets of servers or when you have an especially slow or expensive link between servers. Another possibility is that you don't have a direct link between the initial Publisher and all of the potential Subscribers. The Publisher only needs to pass data to one system on the far side of the link, and the Publisher Subscriber can then pass the data along to the other subscribers.

Publisher/Subscriber

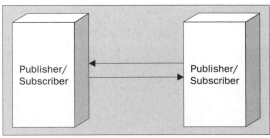

The **Publisher/Subscriber** model is another case where we have SQL Servers acting as both Publishers and Subscribers. Each server has its own set of data for which it is responsible. This model can be used when you have data changes taking place at both locations and you want to keep both servers updated. This is different from Publishing Subscribers in that each server is generating its own data, not just passing along updates received from another server.

Multiple Subscribers/Multiple Publishers

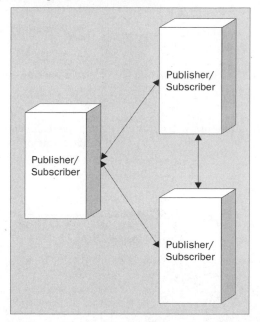

This is where things can start getting complicated. In the **Multiple Subscribers/Multiple Publishers** model we have multiple Publishers and multiple Subscribers. Each system may or may not act as a Publisher/Subscriber or Publishing Subscriber. This model requires very careful planning to provide optimum communications and to ensure data consistency.

One More Issue...

Before leaving topology models there is another issue that needs to be raised.

Publish to Self

SQL Server allows a server to subscribe to its own published articles. Before you dismiss this as just an interesting quirk, there are a number of situations where this could be a part of a business solution. One obvious example is that you want to segregate the data used for online transaction processing from the data used for decision-making. You can use replication to make separate read-only copies of your data (updated on any schedule you consider appropriate) to be used as a reference.

Implementation Examples

Are you ready to try some examples of how we might put these replication types and topology models into practice to build a business solution? Note that the sample solutions provided here are not necessarily the only possible solutions to the problem.

Contractor Supply

Contractor Supply has three warehouses in addition to its home office in San Francisco. The warehouses are located in Los Angeles, Denver, and Boston. Currently, each warehouse manages its own sales and inventory. If there is a request for an out-of-stock item, the warehouse will dial into each of the other warehouses through RAS servers to check inventory levels and request an overnight shipment.

Proposed Changes

It's been decided that each warehouse will continue to manage its inventory, customer, and sales information. All business activity needs to be reported to the home office on a weekly basis for analysis and reporting. Each warehouse's business will be kept in a separate database at the home office.

Proposed Solution

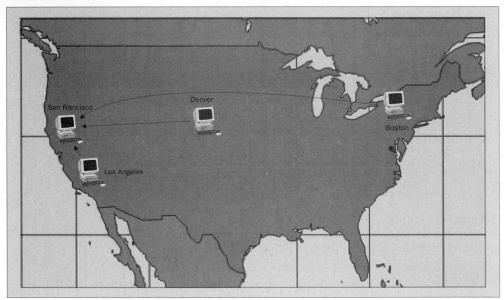

Action points:

- ❑ Set up each of the warehouses as Publisher/Distributors.

- ❑ Create a snapshot publication on each warehouse server containing all of the business activity tables.

- ❑ Define push subscriptions from each of the warehouses to separate databases on a server at the home office with updates going out on a weekly basis.

Cleanzit

Cleanzit is a cleaning service with its main office in New York and satellite offices along the United States eastern seaboard. Currently, the satellite offices send hard copies of customer invoices to the home office daily by overnight mail. Updated customer information is e-mailed as an Excel spreadsheet weekly.

Proposed Changes

Cleanzit is installing SQL Server Personal Edition at each of the satellite offices. Customer invoices will be posted locally as they are created. The invoices do not update local copies of customer balances. All updates take place at the home office. Updated customer records need to go out to the satellite offices nightly.

Proposed Solution

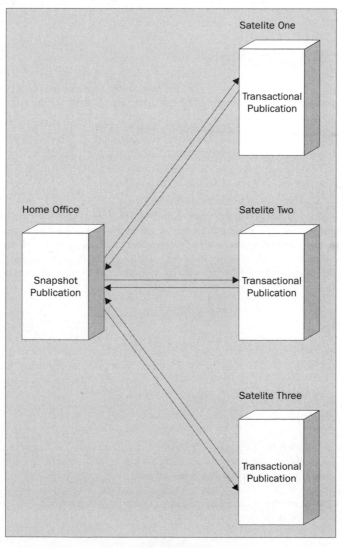

This solution is a little more involved, the action points are:

❑   Set up transactional replication on each of the satellite servers.

❑   The home office will be the Subscriber for all of the satellites.

❑   Configure push subscriptions to send updates to the home office hourly.

> **Depending on the traffic levels generated by the transactional updates, you may want to stagger the updates so that they arrive at different times.**

❑   Set up the customer table at the home office as a snapshot publication.

❑   Create push subscriptions to each of the satellite offices to run nightly.

Planning for Replication

Now we're ready to step through the procedures for setting up replication. The first step *must* be planning. The time you spend in planning will more than pay off in the long run. Planning considerations include:

❑   Replication data

❑   Replication type

❑   Replication model

Along with these are other factors that will influence your decision, such as current network topologies, current server configurations, server growth potential, activity levels, and so forth. Each replication method has its advantages and disadvantages and there is not a one-size-fits-all approach to replicating data. For instance, if you have a slow network or unreliable connection then you may not want to implement transactional replication. Instead, you may opt to use merge replication that runs during a scheduled connection time.

Data Concerns

First, you have to consider what you are going to publish and to whom. You need to identify your articles (that's tables to be published remember) and how you plan to organize them into publications. In addition, there are some other data issues of which you need to be aware. Some of these have already been mentioned, but it's worth our time to review them here.

timestamp

Include a timestamp column for transaction publications. That gives you a way of detecting conflicts on updates. By having a timestamp column already in place, you've already met part of the requirements for adding immediate-updating Subscribers.

Prior to SQL Server 2000, merge replication could not handle timestamp columns. One of the new features of SQL Server 2000 is the ability to handle timestamps in all replication scenarios.

uniqueidentifier

A unique index and globally unique identifier are required for merge replication. Remember, if a published table doesn't have a `uniqueidentifier` column, a globally unique identifier column will be added.

User-Defined Data Types

User-defined data types are not supported unless they exist on the Subscriber destination database. Alternatively, you can have user-defined data types converted to base data types during synchronization.

NOT FOR REPLICATION

The `NOT FOR REPLICATION` clause lets us disable table features on Subscribers. We can disable:

❑ The `IDENTITY` property

❑ `CHECK` constraints

❑ Triggers

These features are disabled when replication processes data on the Subscriber. The features remain enabled when user applications change data.

Replication Type

It may be more accurate to say that you need to consider replication types. It's not uncommon to be supporting more than one type of replication.

Replication Wizards

We're almost ready to start setting up replication. SQL Server Enterprise Manager provides several wizards to help simplify the process:

❑ Configure Publishing and Distribution Wizard

❑ Create Publication Wizard

❑ Disable Publishing and Distribution Wizard

❑ Pull Subscription Wizard

❑ Push Subscription Wizard

To launch any of the replication wizards, select your server in the Enterprise Manager and run Tools | Wizards. Expand the Replication list and select the wizard that you want to run.

Enabling Publishing and Distribution

The first step is setting up our Distributor. We can do this through the **Configure Publishing and Distribution Wizard**. We can also use the Configure Publishing and Distribution Wizard to modify Distributor and Publisher properties. Launch the wizard from the Select Wizard dialog or run Tools | Replication | Configure Publishing and Subscribers:

Starting the Wizard

The opening screen lists our options. The Configure Publishing and Distribution Wizard can be used to:

- ❑ Specify a server as a Distributor
- ❑ Configure Distributor properties
- ❑ Configure Publishing properties

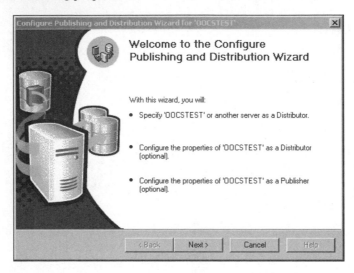

First, we have to identify the system that we are configuring as a Distributor. We can specify the default server or another registered server. We can also select to register servers from this dialog if we've chosen to use a different server:

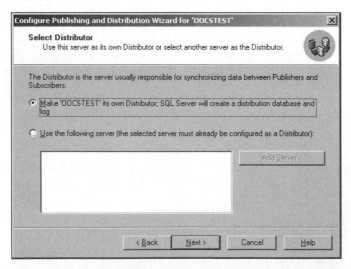

Click Next to reach the Configure SQL Server Agent screen. We are prompted to choose whether the SQL Server Agent service is configured to start automatically on our server or not. Click on Yes and Next, and then Next again to skip through the Specify Snapshot Folder window, accepting its defaults.

Default Configuration

The wizard then prompts us to customize the configuration. At this point, we are basically choosing whether to accept the default configuration, which is to:

❏ Configure the server as a Distributor

❏ Configure all registered servers as Subscribers

❏ Configure the start-up of Microsoft SQL Server Agent

❏ Configure the location of the snapshot folder

❏ Name the distribution database `distribution` and create it on `C:\Program Files\Microsoft SQL Server\MSSQL\data`

❏ Enable the specified server to use itself as Distributor when configured later as a Publisher

This figure shows configuration information based on SQL Server installed to the standard destination directory on drive `C:`. The default location will be the SQL Server 2000 directory on the installation drive, wherever that might actually be:

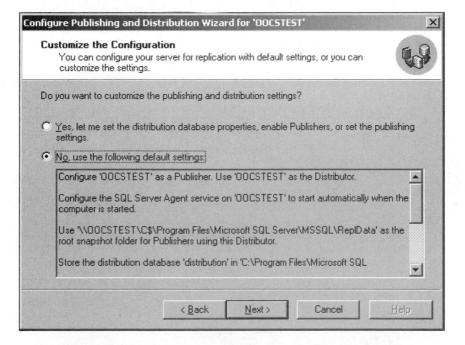

If we continue on at this point, the wizard will prompt us to complete the configuration:

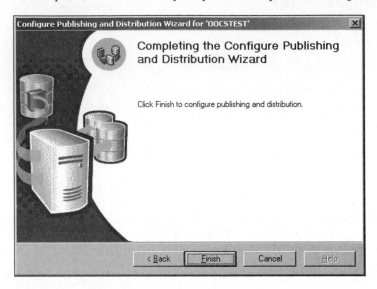

The wizard then steps through the configuration steps as it configures the server as a Distributor and prompts you when finished.

SQL Server will also add the Replication Monitor to your Enterprise Manager after it finishes configuring the server:

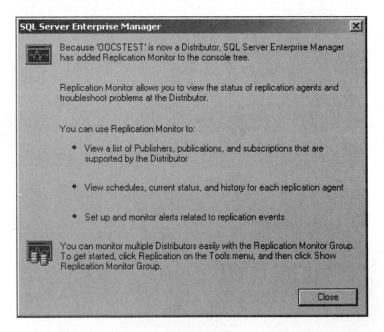

Custom Configuration

If you choose to set the configuration information yourself, you are taken through a separate series of prompts:

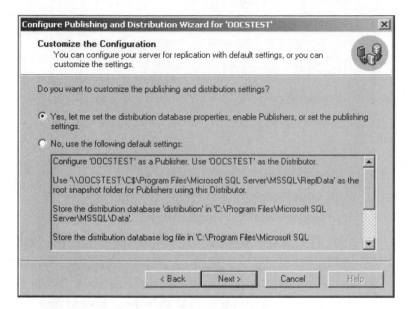

First, you are prompted to provide the distribution database name, the folder in which it will be stored, and the folder in which the distribution log will be stored:

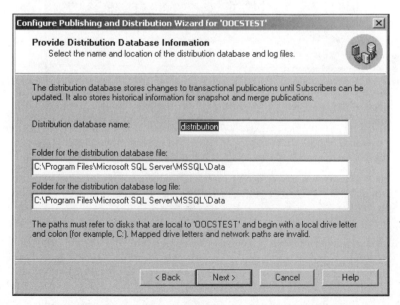

Next, you are prompted to enable Publishers. Click on the properties button (the ...) to display the server properties:

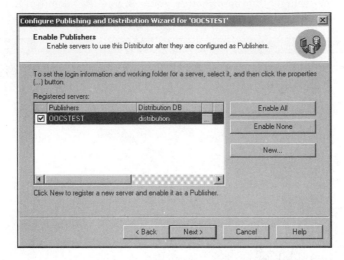

The Properties dialog lets you identify the distribution database to be used as well as the location of the snapshot folder. Make sure that the location specified for the snapshot folder has sufficient space to meet your storage requirements.

You can also specify how replication agents log into the Publisher, either by impersonating the SQL Server agent account through a trusted connection or by using a SQL Server Authentication connection:

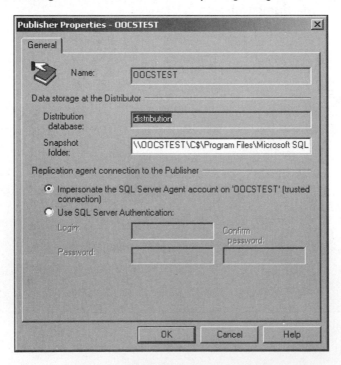

Return to the wizard by clicking OK and then Next. Now you need to enable databases for replication. You can enable a database for transactional replication, merge replication, or both. Enabling a database for transactional replication also enables the database for snapshot replication.

> **SQL Server 2000 Personal Edition and below does not support publishing via transactional replication. You can only have snapshot and merge running from a SQL Server Personal Edition Publisher. SQL Server Personal Subscribers can subscribe to transactional replication publications.**

The figure shows the Northwind database, enabled for both transactional and merge replication:

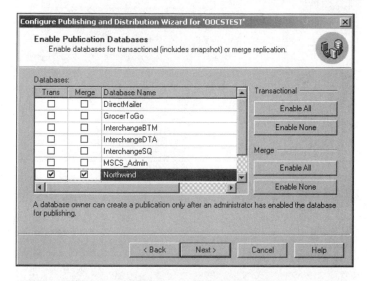

On the next screen, you can identify authorized Subscribers to the database. You can choose from a list of registered servers. Click on New if you want to register additional servers:

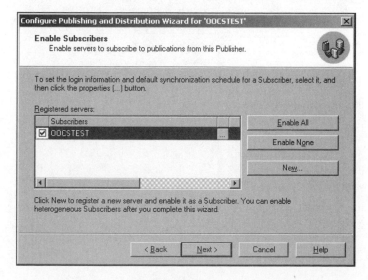

Clicking on Next at the Enable Subscribers window takes you to the final screen. Now you're ready to finish configuration based on your configuration settings. The dialog describes your configuration. SQL Server keeps you informed as it completes the configuration process. You will be prompted if the SQL Server Agent service is not configured to start automatically:

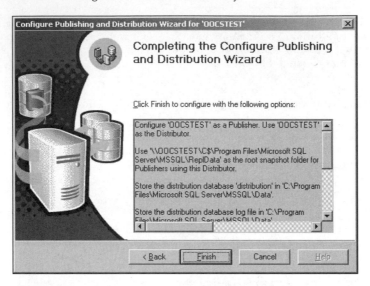

After Configuration

Once you have identified a database as publishing, the Enterprise Manager will show the database as shared – by placing a hand on the database icon. You can also see the Replication Monitor in the Enterprise Manager:

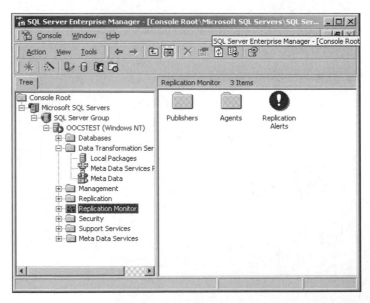

SQL Server 2000 adds a new Replication folder in Enterprise Manager. This new folder is designed to organize all replication packages within a server.

Disabling Distribution

A Distributor can be uninstalled using the **Disable Publishing and Distribution Wizard**. Uninstalling a Distributor will automatically delete its distribution databases and disable any Publishers using the Distributor. Subscribers and publications on disabled Publishers are deleted. Any data that has been replicated to Subscribers is not deleted from the Subscribers. To launch this wizard, select your database in Enterprise Manager and run Tools | Replication | Disable Publishing, or select Disable Publishing and Distribution Wizard from the Select Wizard dialog.

You can review and modify Publisher and Distributor properties at any time by running Tools | Replication | Configure Publishing, Subscribers, and Distribution. You can view and modify the following property pages:

- ❑ Distributor: Distribution databases and replication agent profiles
- ❑ Publishers: All Publishers including snapshot folder and login method for Distribution Agents
- ❑ Publication Databases: Enable or disable databases for publication
- ❑ Subscribers: Register or remove Subscribers

In the examples throughout the rest of this chapter, we will walk through the process of configuring publications and articles, as well as setting up Subscribers. We'll cover transactional and snapshot replication first, and then merge replication.

Transact-SQL Procedures

The following table is a list of Transact-SQL system stored procedures that we can use to set up Publishers and Distributors, as well as identifying Subscribers:

Stored Procedure	Description
Sp_adddistributor	Run sp_adddistributor at the server to configure the server as a Distributor.
Sp_adddistributiondb	Run at the Distributor to create the distribution database(s).
Sp_adddistpublisher	Run at each server that you will be configuring as a Publisher to identify its Distributor.
Sp_addsubscriber	Run at the Publisher to register a Subscriber.

These stored procedures have extensive input parameters and options; please refer to SQL Server Books Online for detailed information about these procedures.

Transactional/Snapshot Publications

Note that you will see the same prompts when setting up either a snapshot or transactional publication.

You can create publications by launching the **Create Publication Wizard** from the Select Wizard dialog or by running Tools | Replication | Create and Manage Publications.

The Create and Manage Publications Wizard

First, we need to select the database for which we want to define publications in this instance let's select Northwind, then click on Create Publication to continue:

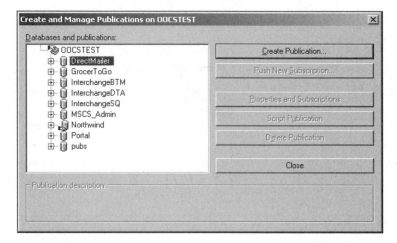

The opening dialog explains that you can create a publication, filter data, and set publication properties through the wizard. Select Show advanced options in this wizard, and hit Next:

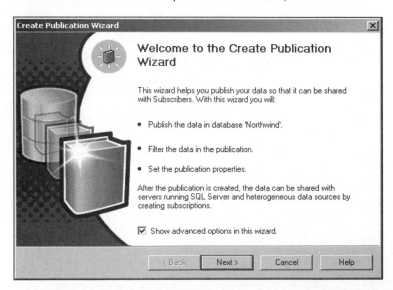

Select the database that will be used for the replication, Northwind, and click on Next:

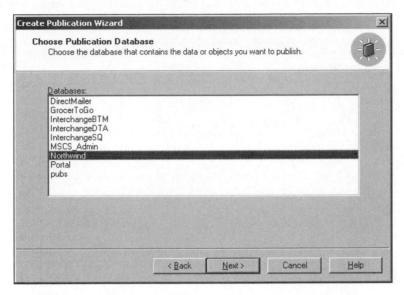

If you have already created a publication for this database, you will be prompted as to whether or not to use the existing publication as a template for the new publication. For this example, select No.

After clicking on Next, we reach the Select Publication Type screen. We're going to choose Transactional for this example:

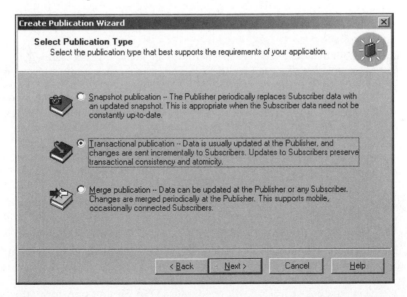

Remember that SQL Server Personal Edition and below cannot be configured to publish for transactional replication.

After clicking Next, we have to decide whether or not we are going to support immediate-updating subscriptions. Alternatively, SQL Server 2000 has added the ability to implement queued updating for both snapshot and transactional replication:

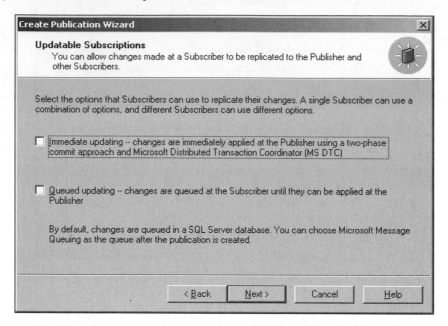

Queued Updating

We'll take a short break now from our Create Publication Wizard example to examine queued updating in a bit more detail.

With **queued updating**, all database changes are held in a queue and processed when connectivity to the SQL Server database is possible. This is ideal for systems (with snapshot and transactional replication) that do not have persistent connections but still need the ability to replicate data across servers. All changes to data are stored in a queue where they remain until a network connection from the subscriber to the publisher is restored. Once the connection is restored, all changes are applied asynchronously to the publisher server.

Queued updating is designed for systems that have few updates on the subscribers since conflict resolution is important to consider. You can change the conflict resolution policy for the subscription by going to the Properties of a queued update publication in Enterprise Manager. The Updatable tab contains a Conflict Resolution Policy entry that will allow you to set or change the logic to be used.

Back to the Wizard

Returning to our Create Publication Wizard example, we'll decide not to support immediate updates or queued updating, and click on Next.

Now we need to select whether or not we will need to use DTS for any transformation services during the replication process example. Select Yes and click on Next:

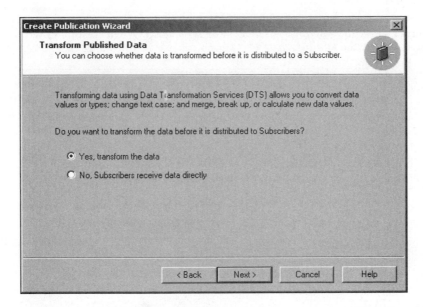

The next screen asks us to tell SQL Server what type of database servers will be subscribing: SQL Server 2000, SQL Server 7.0, or others. This specification makes it relatively easy to set up replication support in a heterogeneous networking environment. All of our subscribers are running SQL Server:

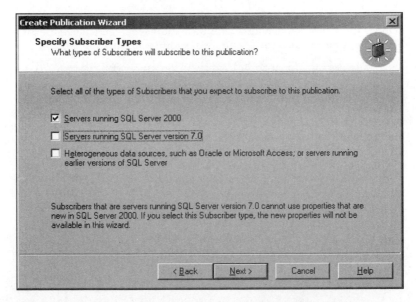

Click Next and we're ready to select the tables to be published. For this example, we're going to publish the Employees table. We can choose whether to include tables, stored procedures, views, or all three in our publication. We're limiting the publication to Tables here.

By default, the dialog lists all user-defined tables in the database. If you deselect the Show unpublished objects option, only tables marked for publication will be displayed in the list.

As a special note on stored procedures, you may be creating stored procedures at some time that will be used for filtering tables and will only be executed by replication. When creating stored procedures of this type, be sure to specify the FOR REPLICATION option as part of your CREATE PROCEDURE statement.

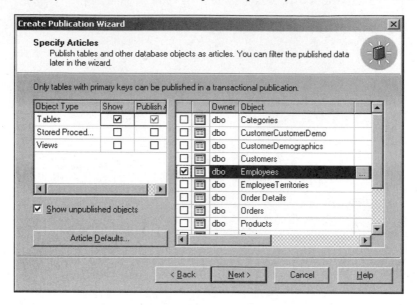

Click on the properties button (marked with ...) to view the Table Article Properties dialog. The General tab includes the article name and table information. You can change the article name and destination table name. You can also specify an owner for the destination table:

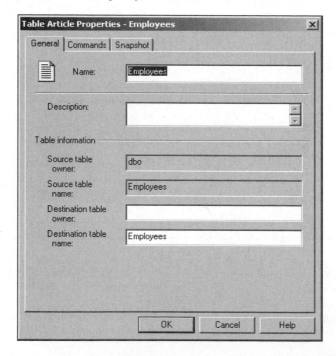

The **Commands** tab shows the stored procedures that will be used instead of INSERT, DELETE, and UPDATE commands at the Subscriber. We also have the option of selecting the stored procedure and the calling method that you would like to use. Our options are CALL, MCALL, and XCALL. CALL will pass all values for inserted and deleted columns, MCALL passes only the affected records, and XCALL passes the values for all columns along with the original values for the columns. The stored procedures will be created at the Subscriber during synchronization:

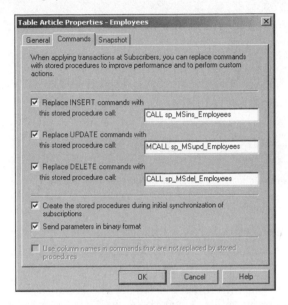

The **Snapshot** tab lets us modify snapshot options. We can specify what to do if the destination table already exists, identify whether to copy clustered and non-clustered indexes, set whether user-defined data types should be converted to base data types, and whether declared referential integrity on primary keys is included:

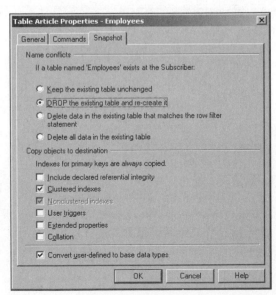

If a table contains an identity column then you will receive a warning informing you that the identity column will be converted to an integer.

Return to the wizard by clicking OK, then hit Next. Accept the defaults on the Article Issues screen and click Next again:

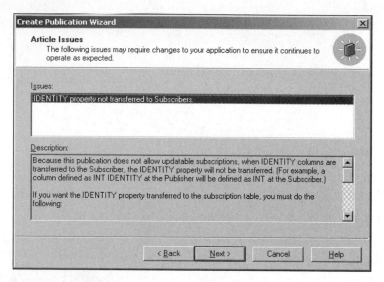

Now we reach the Select Publication Name and Description screen. The publication name defaults to the database name. We're changing the name to NorthTran here to allow us to easily recognize the publication. You can name your publication as you wish. If you are going to be supporting several publications, pick names that will help remind you what is being published. It will probably be helpful to include the source database name – and, possibly, the name of one of the source tables – as part of the publication name:

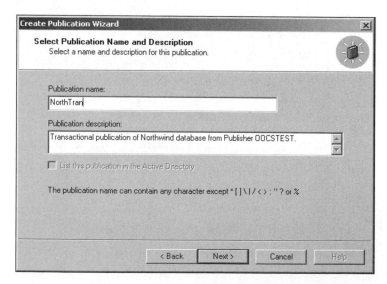

Click on **Next** and we reach the point where we can accept default properties for the article or set custom properties. Default properties include:

❏ Do not filter the publication

❏ Do not allow anonymous Subscribers to create pull subscriptions

❏ Run the snapshot once at a specified time

We're going to define custom options for our publication:

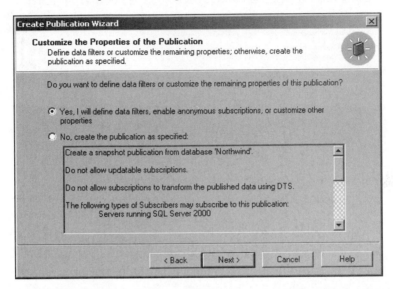

Next we determine how to filter the publication. Leaving both options unselected will include all rows and columns with the selected tables.

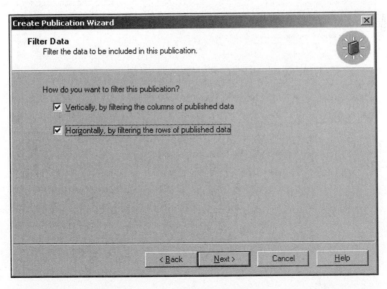

We will check both filtering options, however, and click **Next**.

If you've worked with earlier versions of SQL Server, don't forget that what is being referred to now as "filtering" was previously referred to as "partitioning". When you see "filter", think "partition" and you should be fine. Note that the Create and Manage Publications Wizard uses the term column filtering to refer to vertical filtering and row filtering to refer to horizontal filtering.

To filter undesired columns (vertical filtering) so they are not included in the article, remove the check beside them. We're filtering out the columns containing employee information, such as last name, first name, title, and so on. In this example, we are including all of the data for this particular table, but we could remove the check box from BirthDate to prevent this field from replicating:

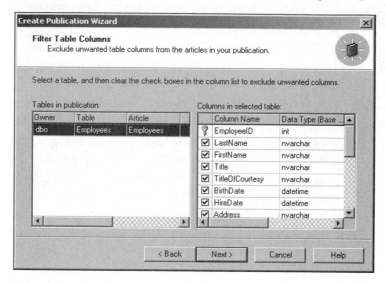

Row (horizontal) filtering is selected on the next screen:

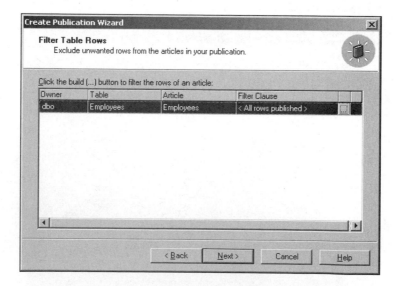

Click on the ... button next to the **Filter Clause** to define filters. Row filtering is defined by entering a filtering clause as a WHERE clause in a SELECT statement. The next screenshot gives an example of a row filter we could use, but we're not going to use any row filtering in this example so click **Cancel**:

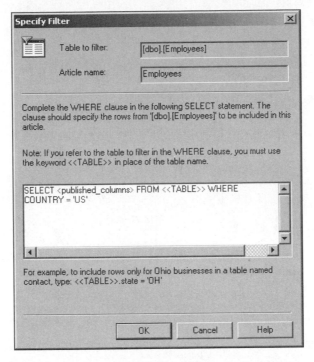

Hit Next and we reach the **Allow Anonymous Subscriptions** dialog. We're not going to allow anonymous Subscribers in this example:

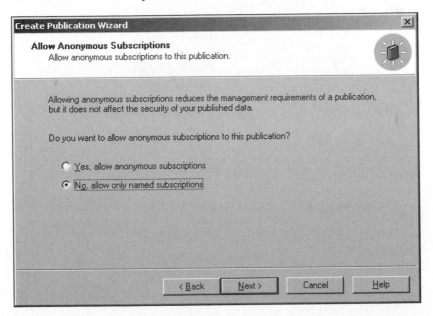

Next, we need to set the Snapshot Agent schedule. By default, the first snapshot will be created at the first scheduled run of the Snapshot Agent:

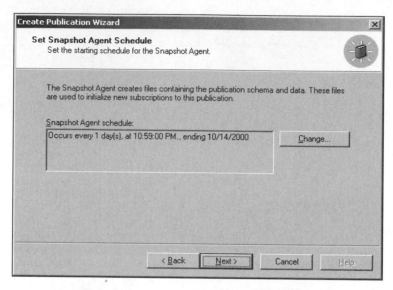

Click on Change to alter the default schedule. We can have replication occur daily, weekly, or monthly, and can set the time of day for replication. We can even define the start and end date. Additionally, this dialog can be used to configure a recurring snapshot, even if we are supporting transactional replication. This will force periodic resynchronization between the Publisher and Subscriber:

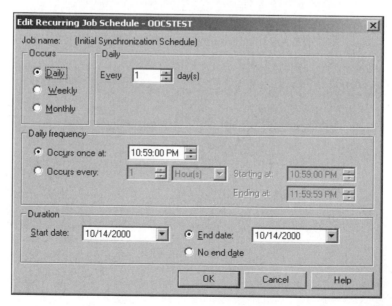

Accept the defaults by clicking Cancel and then Next. Now we're ready to create the publication. The Wizard summarizes the options we've selected for our review. Hit Finish:

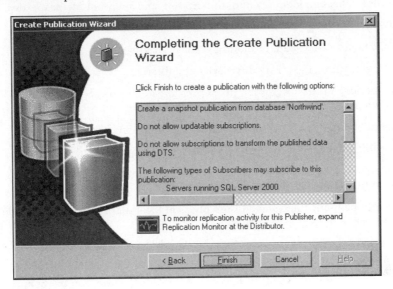

After Configuration

We can now see the publication listed under the Northwind database. From here, you can push a subscription out to Subscribers, modify properties and subscriptions, or delete the publication:

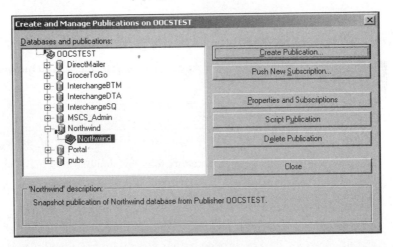

Select the Northwind publication from under the Northwind database and click on the Properties and Subscriptions button. Alternatively, if you close this dialog, you can run Tools | Replication | Create and Manage Publications to reach the Publication Properties.

The publication property pages include:

- ❏ **General**: Publication identification, description, and snapshot file properties.
- ❏ **Articles**: Modify properties for published articles, add articles to the publication, and delete articles.
- ❏ **Filter Columns**: View, add, or modify vertical filtering.
- ❏ **Filter Rows**: View, add, or modify horizontal filtering.
- ❏ **Subscriptions**: View subscription properties, create new push subscriptions, delete subscriptions, and force resynchronization between the Publisher and Subscribers.
- ❏ **Subscription Options**: View and set subscription options, including Internet support.
- ❏ **Updateable**: Provides information on immediate and queued update settings.
- ❏ **Snapshot**: View and modify the replication format (native or bulk copy program) and any scripts to be run before or after the replication.
- ❏ **Snapshot Location**: View and edit the physical location of the replication file and any FTP settings.
- ❏ **Publication Access List**: View and modify logins used by pull and immediate-update subscriptions.
- ❏ **Status**: View Snapshot Agent and service status information, run the Snapshot Agent, and start services.
- ❏ **Scripts**: View and modify script options and format.

You will have to remove any subscriptions from the publication to be able to modify some publication options.

Transact-SQL Procedures

The following system stored procedures are used to define snapshot and transactional publications and articles:

Stored Procedure	Description
sp_replicationdboption	Run this procedure to enable publication of the current database.
sp_addpublication	Use this procedure to define a publication in the current database.
sp_addpublication_ snapshot	This is used to create a Snapshot Agent for a publication.
sp_addarticle	Run for each article you wish to add to the publication.
Sp_articlefilter	This procedure lets you set up horizontal filtering for an article.
sp_articlecolumn	Use this procedure to set up vertical filtering for an article.
sp_articleview	This is used to create the synchronization object for a filtered article.

As before, refer to SQL Server Books Online for detailed information about these procedures.

Merge Publications

Now we're going to step through creating a merge publication.

You can create publications by launching the Create Publication Wizard from the Select Wizard dialog or by running Tools | Replication | Create and Manage Publications.

The Create and Manage Publications Wizard

When we use the Create and Manage Publications Wizard to create a merge publication we start out the same, by selecting the database from which we want to publish. The opening screen of the wizard is also the same, so we won't show it here, but be sure to select Show advanced options in this wizard at this point. If you do not select this option then you will not see all of the following screens.

Again, if you have already created a publication for this database, you will be prompted as to whether or not to use the existing publication as a template for the new publication. For this example, select No.

This time, we're selecting to create a Merge publication:

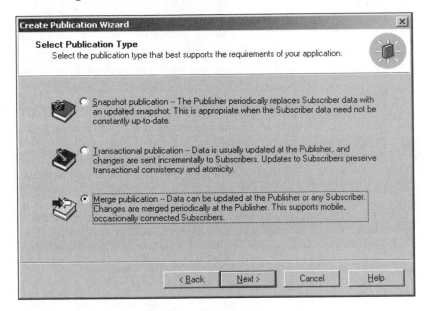

As before, we have to identify whether or not all of the Subscribers are running Microsoft SQL Server. Notice the addition of SQL Server CE (hmmm, the possibilities):

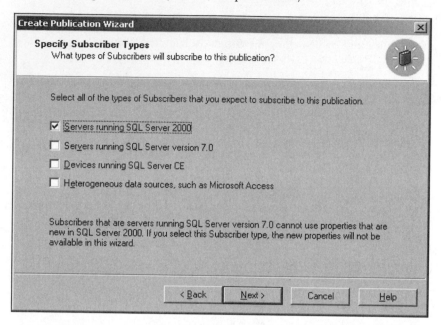

Next, we have to identify the tables that we wish to publish. When defining a merge publication we can only select to publish tables, views, and stored procedures. Don't forget, a table can be identified as an article in more than one publication:

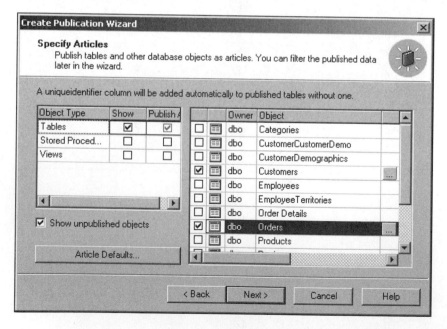

Hitting the properties button (...) shows us that the article properties are a little different for merge publications. The General tab lets us determine whether changes to the same row, or changes to the same column in a row, are considered as conflicts:

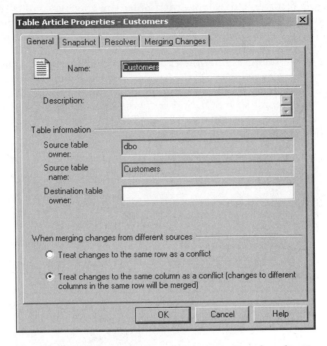

The Snapshot properties are the same as for snapshot/transactional replication:

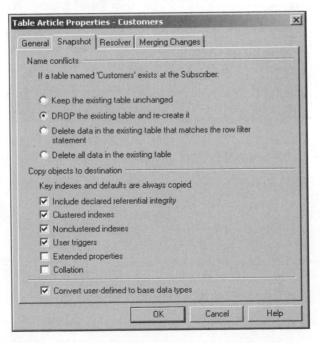

The **Resolver** properties let us choose to use either the default resolver or a custom resolver.

Custom resolvers are COM components that have been designed using the `ICustomResolver` interface. With a custom resolver, a developer can implement specific conflict resolution that may not be a default option within SQL Server 2000. If you chose to install the developer samples for SQL Server then you will find a compressed file under `Program Files\Microsoft SQL Server\80\Tools\DevTools\Samples\sqlrepl`. If you run the file `unzip_sqlrepl.exe`, it will extract all of the replication samples. After the extraction you will have an additional series of folders with one of the folders being named `resolver\subspres`. Here you will find a Visual C++ sample resolver (sorry VB programmers, there is no VB sample for you to browse). You can also use one of the many built-in resolvers that come with SQL Server. These resolvers will use specific defaults when implementing conflict resolution. For instance, the DATETIME resolver uses "first in wins" or "last in wins" logic for resolving conflicts:

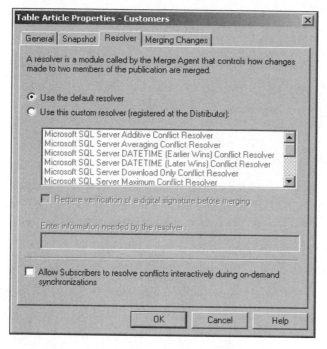

Finally, the **Merging Changes** tab allows us to add a security check for the replication package, along with the ability to make all changes to the data in a row as a single UPDATE statement:

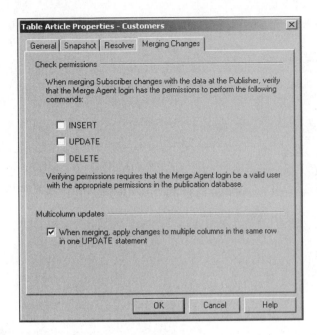

Return to the wizard and hit **Next**. If any of the published tables do not include a `uniqueidentifier` column, you will be notified that the column will be created for you. Now the Article Issues screen appears:

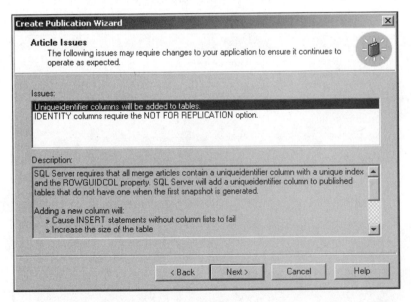

Accept the defaults and move on. As in the last example, the article needs to be given a name and description. This time, we're calling the article NorthMerge:

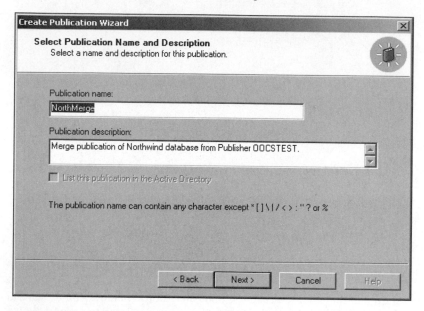

Next, you can choose to create the publication using the default properties or define customized properties. Check Yes and click on Next. You'll see very nearly the same screens as for snapshot and transactional publications:

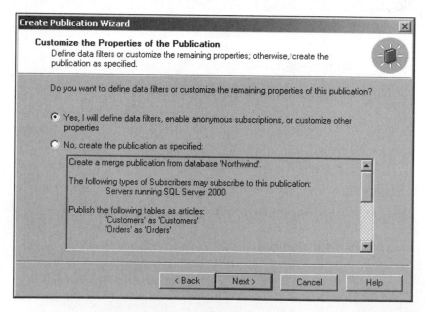

The default is that you do not want to use filtering, but we will check both options:

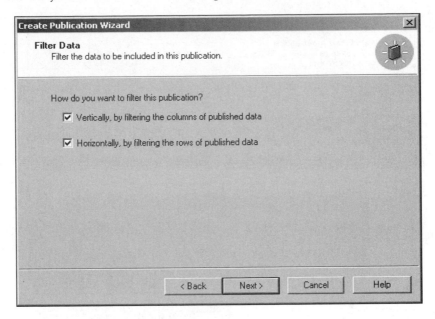

Hit Next to skip the Filter Table Columns screen. Now we have to choose whether to enable dynamic filters or not. A static filter sends the same data to all subscribers. If we want to send different parts of the data to different subscribers, we need to use dynamic filters. For this example, we're going to use static filters:

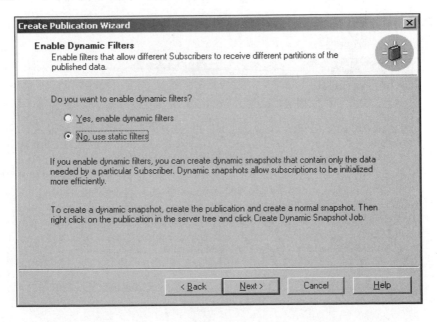

We're going to create a static filter limiting the rows to just those customers in the USA:

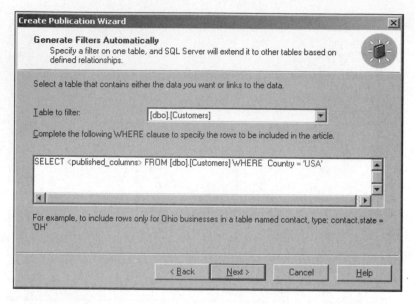

SQL Server will create the filters for us before continuing to the next wizard prompt.

We can also set up joins between filtered tables. We have added a filter criterion to the **Customers** table; now we want to filter the orders table for that specific list of customers. If we do not do this, then we will replicate all of the order data, which is much more than we are looking for.

Select the **Customers** table from the **Filtered Table** cell and then select the **Orders** table from the **Table to Filter** cell:

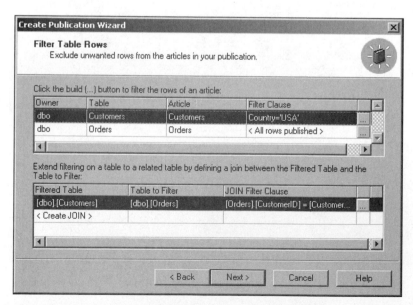

Select the ... button in the JOIN Filter Clause cell to bring up the Specify JOIN window:

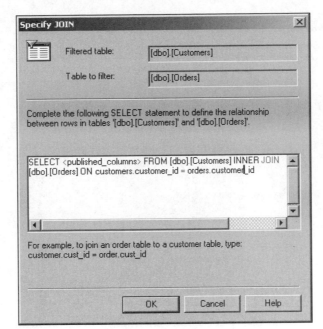

We'll not do anything here so return to the wizard and select Next. Now we need to decide whether or not we would like SQL Server to minimize the network traffic used by the replication package. Selecting Yes will increase the size of the database on the publisher, but will reduce the amount of data sent to a subscriber. We will choose No here:

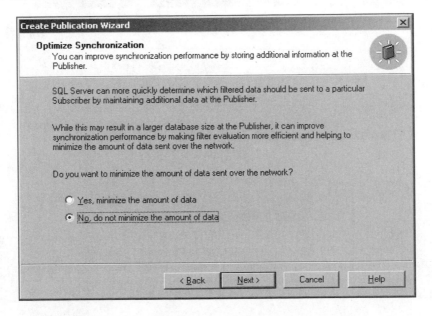

As before, we can choose whether or not we want to support anonymous subscribers:

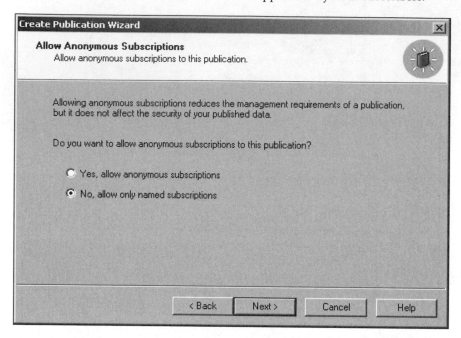

We can also make changes to the default snapshot schedule. By default, the snapshot will only run once per week:

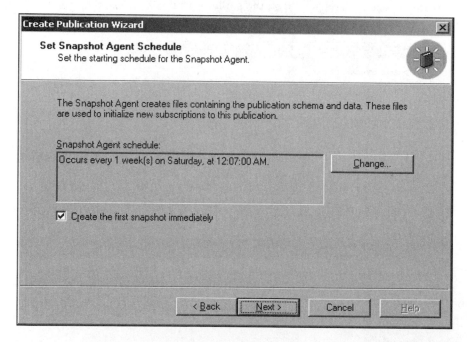

Now we're ready to create the publication. Hit Finish and SQL Server will show us as it completes each step of the process:

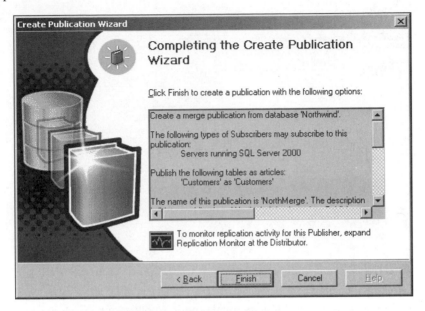

We will be informed of any errors or anything that might result in data corruption:

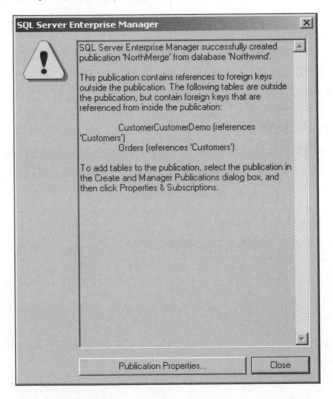

After Configuration

As you can see, NorthMerge is now listed as a publication:

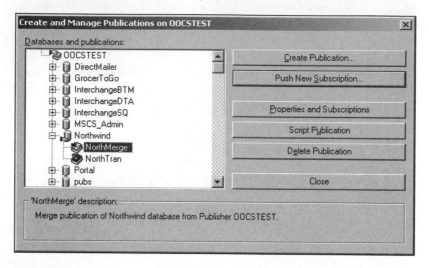

After creating a publication, we can display its property pages to view or modify publication and article properties. Run Tools | Replication | Create and Manage Publications. Select the publication you wish to view from under its database and click on Properties & Subscriptions. The property pages include:

❑   General: Publication identification and description.

❑   Articles: Modify properties for published articles, add articles to the publication, and delete articles.

❑   Filter Columns: View, add, or modify vertical filtering.

❑   Filter Rows: View, add, or modify horizontal filtering.

❑   Subscriptions: View subscription properties, create new push subscriptions, delete subscriptions, and force resynchronization between the Publisher and Subscribers.

❑   Subscription Options: View and set subscription options, including Internet support.

❑   Snapshot: Set the pre and post replication scripts and set the data format (native SQL Server or character mode).

❑   Snapshot Location: View and set the location of the snapshot file. If publishing to an FTP server the settings will be edited here.

❑   Publication Access List: View and modify logins used by pull and immediate-update subscriptions.

❑   Sync Partners: View and modify alternative synchronization partners.

❑   Status: View Snapshot Agent and service status information, run the Snapshot Agent, and start services.

You will have to remove any subscriptions from the publication to be able to modify some publication options.

Transact-SQL Procedures

The following system stored procedures are used to define merge publications and articles:

Stored Procedure	Description
sp_replicationdboption	Run this procedure to enable publication of the current database.
Sp_addmergepublication	Use this procedure to define a publication in the current database.
Sp_addpublication_snapshot	This is used to create a Snapshot Agent.
Sp_addmergearticle	Run for each article you wish to add to the publication.
Sp_addmergefilter	This procedure lets you set up horizontal filtering for an article. Merge articles do not support vertical filtering.

Refer to SQL Server Books Online for detailed information about these procedures.

Push Subscriptions

We can configure push subscriptions by selecting the **Push Subscription Wizard** from the Select Wizard dialog or by running Tools | Replication | Push Subscriptions to Others.

Push Subscription Wizard

Select the publication for which you want to push a subscription; let's use NorthTran:

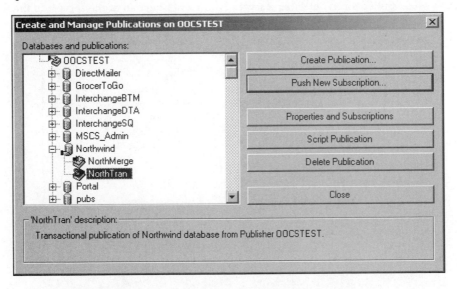

The Push Subscription Wizard lets us:

❑   Select Subscribers

❑   Select the destination database

❑   Set the initialization and synchronization schedule

❑   Set subscription properties

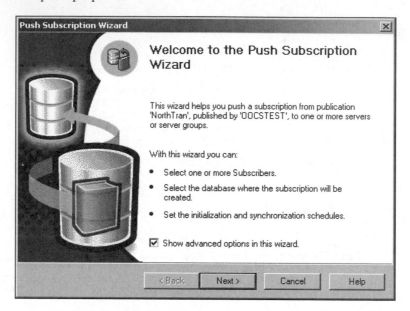

Don't forget to select **Show advanced options on this wizard**. Then click on Next. We are now prompted to select Subscribers. Selecting a server group will select all of the servers in that group:

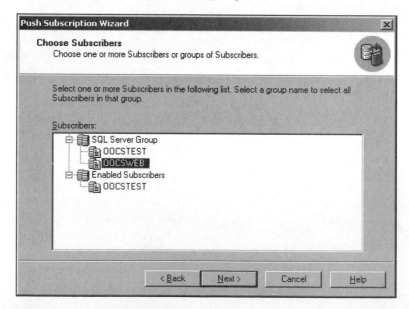

Next, we need to select the destination database. Click on Browse or Create to view a list of available databases:

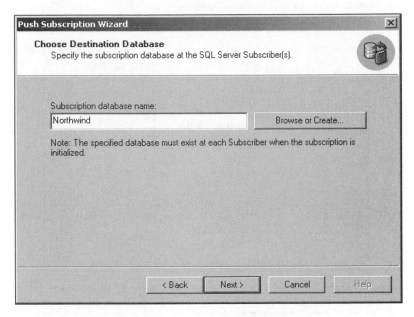

We can either pick from an existing database or create a new database on the Subscriber. We will create a new database to test our subscription by selecting Create New:

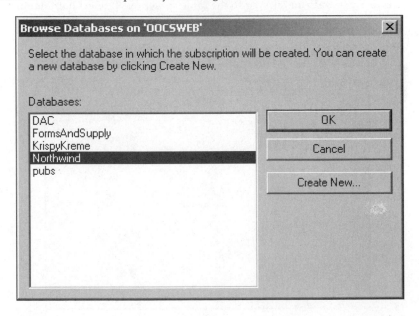

Call the new database PushTest and click OK:

This is a transactional publication, so we're prompted to set the Distribution Agent schedule in the wizard's next screen. Since we're publishing to the same server, we'll select continuous updates for our test. The default schedule is to update every 5 minutes, but you can set the schedule to meet your particular needs and available network bandwidth:

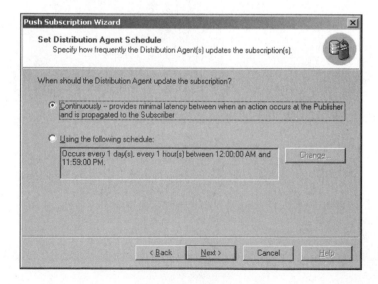

Next we need to set the initialization schedule. The default is to initialize the Subscriber. We've also selected to start the process immediately. If you are using manual synchronization, you should specify that the Subscriber already has the schema and data:

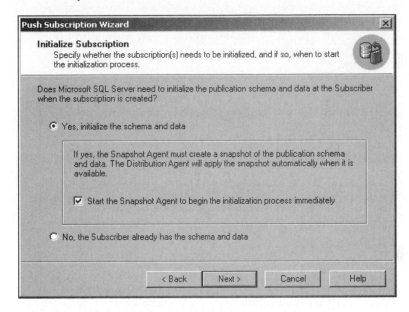

Next, services that need to be running for the subscription will be listed. The check indicates that the service will be started automatically if it is not already running:

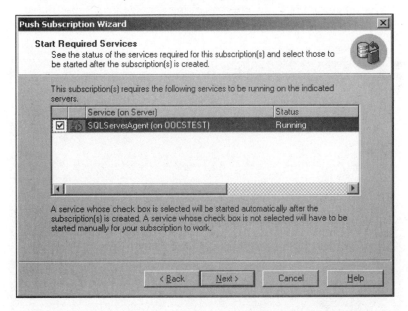

The Wizard is now ready to complete the subscription. You will receive a verifying dialog when the subscription is created:

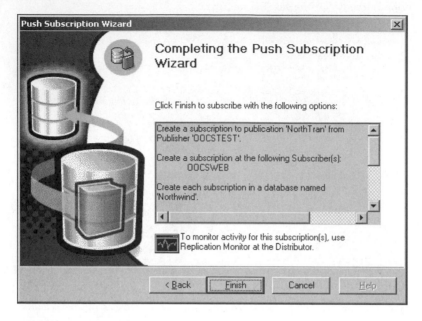

About Merge Subscriptions

You will see an additional prompt if you are configuring a merge push subscription. You will be prompted to set the priority for resolving conflicts using either the Publisher setting or a different value that you specify:

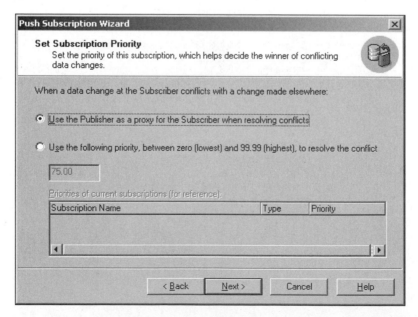

Transact-SQL Procedures

The following system stored procedures are used to define push subscriptions:

Stored Procedure	Description
sp_addsubscription	Run at the Publisher to create a snapshot or transactional push subscription.
sp_addmergesubscription	Run at the Publisher to create a merge push subscription.

Refer to SQL Server Books Online for detailed information about these procedures.

Pull Subscriptions

Pull subscriptions, as the name implies, are initiated from the Subscriber. Select the **Pull Subscription Wizard** from the Select Wizard dialog or run Tools | Replication | Pull Subscription.

A Subscriber can only have one subscription to an article. If the Subscriber is already subscribed through a push subscription, the subscription must be deleted before a pull subscription can be created. To drop a push subscription, run Tools | Replication | Create and Manage Publications, select the database containing the publication, click on Properties and Subscriptions, then on the Subscriptions tab. This will display the push subscriptions list. Click on the subscription you want to delete, then on Delete.

Pull Subscription Wizard

The first step is to select a database, let's use Northwind again, and click on Pull New Subscription:

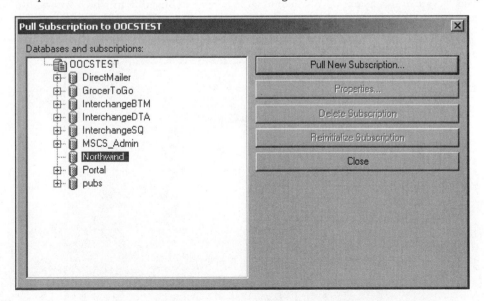

The Pull Subscription Wizard lets us:

❏ Select the Publisher and publication

❏ Select the destination database

❏ Set the initialization and synchronization schedule

❏ Set subscription properties

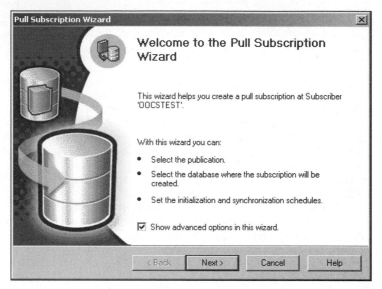

Click on Next to skip past the Look for Publications screen – we will look at publications from registered servers in this example. We then have to select a publication to which we want to subscribe. This tree shown will only list Publishers that recognize the destination server as a Subscriber and servers that allow anonymous Subscribers:

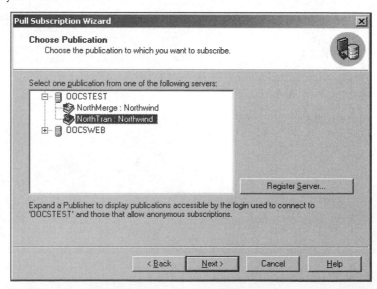

If the Publisher is set up for SQL Server Authorization, you will be prompted for login information. Otherwise, you will be taken directly to a list of available databases. Select the destination database from this list. If you wish, you can click on New Database to create a new database on the Subscriber:

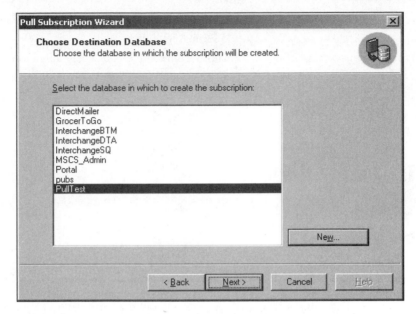

The remaining dialogs are the same as for a push subscription, as shown earlier. You will be prompted to:

❏ Initialize the subscription

❏ Set the Distribution Agent schedule

❏ Configure required services to start

❏ Create the subscription

If you are creating a merge subscription, you will also be prompted to set subscription priority.

Transact-SQL Procedures

The following system stored procedures are used to add pull subscriptions:

Stored Procedure	Description
sp_addsubscription	Run at the Publisher to create a subscription.
sp_addpullsubscription	Run at the Subscriber to create the pull subscription.
sp_addpullsubscription_agent	This procedure will create a scheduled job for the Subscriber's Distribution Agent. Run this procedure at the Subscriber.

Table continued on following page

Stored Procedure	Description
sp_addmergesubscription	Run at the Publisher to create a subscription.
sp_addmergepullsubscription	This procedure is run at the Subscriber to create a merge subscription.
sp_addmergepullsubscription_agent	This procedure will create a scheduled job for the Subscriber's Distribution Agent. Run this procedure at the Subscriber.

Refer to SQL Server Books Online for detailed information about these procedures.

Managing Replication

Before we can leave the subject of replication, there are a few additional issues that deserve special mention.

Replication Scripts

SQL Server gives us a way of generating **replication scripts**, which are Transact-SQL scripts based on the replication configuration. Replication scripts let us document our configuration and give us an easy way to recover and reinstall replication. If you need to set up multiple servers with identical configurations, you can set up one server, generate a script, and use the script to configure the remaining servers.

To generate a replication script run Tools | Replication | Generate SQL Scripts. You have the option of previewing the script before it is created. This dialog will not only allow you to create the script for creating a replication package, but you have the option of generating the code to drop the package as well.

Supporting Heterogeneous Replication

SQL Server supports replication with other databases, including Microsoft Access databases, Oracle databases, as well as other databases as long as they comply with SQL Server ODBC Subscriber requirements. The ODBC driver for Subscribers must:

- ❏ Allow updates
- ❏ Support transactions
- ❏ Support Transact-SQL data definition language statements (such as CREATE, ALTER, and DROP)
- ❏ Conform to ODBC level 1
- ❏ Be 32-bit and thread-safe

> **Only SQL Server subscribers can request pull subscriptions. All other subscribers are supported by push subscriptions.**

This isn't to say there aren't potential problems with heterogeneous Subscribers. For example, where there are differences in data types supported, data is mapped to the nearest match on the Subscriber. Depending on naming conventions, you can even run into problems just trying to configure Subscribers. The Subscriber ODBC data source name (DSN) must be a valid SQL Server identifier.

Publishing to the Internet

SQL Server supports replication across the Internet, but publishing to the Internet requires careful planning. You need to understand the requirements and restrictions before you start.

First, there are some basic requirements for all subscriptions. An obvious one is TCP/IP. TCP/IP is required for Internet communications. You have to make sure that the Publisher and Distributor, if installed on separate systems, have a direct network connection and are on the same side of your firewall.

Pull subscriptions are supported through FTP. This means that the Distributor and Microsoft Internet Information Server can be installed on separate systems with the FTP home directory set to the distribution working folder. The Subscriber Distribution and Merge Agents will need the FTP's IP address.

You need to make some changes in the Properties dialog for a publication to allow it to support Internet subscriptions. Run Tools | Replication | Create and Manage Publications, select the publication from its database, and click on Properties and Subscriptions.

❑   In the Subscription Options tab, allow anonymous Subscribers to pull subscriptions by checking Allow pull subscriptions and Allow anonymous subscriptions

❑   In the Snapshot Location tab, allow snapshots to be downloaded using FTP

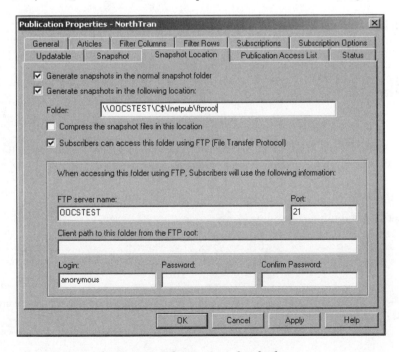

Don't forget to re-create any subscriptions after you are finished.

After you've set up a publication to support pull subscriptions over the Internet, you will see additional prompts when running the Pull Subscription Wizard. You will be asked whether or not the Subscriber will be using FTP to copy the snapshot files:

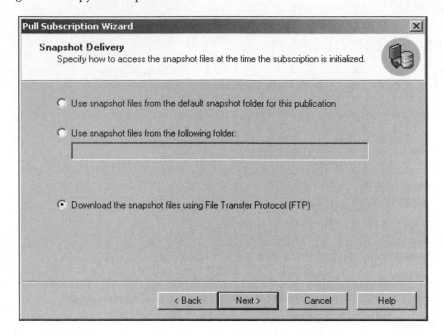

Replication and Schema Changes

One of the new features of SQL Server 2000 is the ability to replicate schema changes to the subscribers of a publication. This allows us to include schema changes with distributions and avoids the need to drop tables and re-subscribe to the publication. This area was one of the more difficult areas to manage with previous versions of SQL Server.

In order to provide this functionality, a DBA must take special steps to implement schema changes for replicated tables. The new stored procedures named sp_repladdcolumn and sp_repldropcolumn are used to add and drop columns respectively. These stored procedures are added at the publisher on the publication database and both procedures are used for all types of replication. Let's take a look at them.

sp_repladdcolumn

The prototype of this function is as follows:

```
sp_repladdcolumn source_object, column, typetext, [publication_to_add],
                 [schema_change_script], [force_invalidate_snapshot],
                 [force_reinit_subscription]
```

There are several parameters to this command, some optional and others accepting a single value. The following table gives the details.

Parameter	Values	Purpose
source_object		Name of the table that is being changed.
Column		Name of the column to be added.
Typetext		Field definition including any Null flags and defaults.
publication_to_add		Name of the publication that the change should be added to. The default for this parameter is all.
schema_change_script		Name of the SQL script to be executed. Null by default.
force_invalidate_snapshot	Bit, 0 or 1 (default=1)	Invalidates a snapshot (1) and forces a new snapshot to be generated. Setting this to 0 does not invalidate the snapshot.
force_reinit_subscription	Bit, 0 or 1 (default=0)	A value of 0 (default) will not re-initialize the subscription while a value of 1 will cause the subscription to be re-initialized.

This procedure returns 0 for success and 1 for failure.

For example, if you wanted to add a column called MiddleName to the employee table that is a varchar(30) nullable field, then you would use sp_repladdcolumn, paying particular attention to the typetext field:

```
sp_repladdcolumn 'employee', 'MiddleName', 'varchar(30) null'
```

This implements the change through all of the replication publications.

One issue with this approach is that DTS packages are not handled automatically. You will need to re-create the DTS packages manually in order to accept the new schema changes. If you do not update the package then the distribution agent may fail to apply future data changes.

sp_repldropcolumn

On the other hand, if you want to drop a column within a table then you will need to execute the sp_repldropcolumn stored procedure. This procedure, like sp_repladdcolumn, must be run on the Publisher on the publication database. The prototype is almost identical to the sp_repladdcolumn procedure:

```
sp_repldropcolumn source_object, column, [schema_change_script],
                  [force_invalidate_snapshot],
                  [force_reinit_subscription]
```

Parameter	Values	Purpose
source_object		Name of the table that is being changed.
column		Name of the column being dropped.
schema_change_script		Name of the SQL script to be executed. Null by default.
force_invalidate_snapshot	Bit, 0 or 1 (default=1)	Invalidates a snapshot (1) and forces a new snapshot to be generated. Setting this to 0 does not invalidate the snapshot.
Force_reinit_subscription	Bit, 0 or 1 (default=0)	A value of 0 (default) will not re-initialize the subscription while a value of 1 will cause the subscription to be re-initialized.

The sp_repldropcolumn also has a return value of 0 for success and 1 for failure.

If we wanted to drop the MiddleName column from our employee table, we would issue the sp_repldropcolumn procedure:

```
sp_repldropcolumn 'employee', 'MiddleName'
```

This would drop the employee.MiddleName column from all of the publications for this database. Dropping a column has the same issues with DTS packages that adding columns has. You will need to rebuild your DTS packages manually to prevent the Distribution Agent from failing.

There are some issues with dropping columns that you should be aware of. Not all columns can be dropped from replicated tables using the sp_repldropcolumn stored procedure:

❑　Columns that are the primary key or part of a primary key or a unique constraint

❑　Columns that are UNIQUEIDENTIFIER columns or ROWGUID columns

❑　Columns that are part of a filter criterion for a replication publication

Columns that contain constraints will prompt you for verification of the drop operation. Once the operation is confirmed, the constraints and then the column will be dropped.

Remember that using the visual data tools or ALTER TABLE statements will not replicate the changes. You can use the replication publication properties dialog in SQL Server's Enterprise Manager.

Replication Monitor

The **Replication Monitor** is added to Enterprise Monitor when a server is configured as a Distributor. It is only available on the Distributor. You can use the Replication Monitor to view Publishers, publications, Subscribers, agents, and agent and job history. You can also set agent priorities, and set up and monitor replication event alerts:

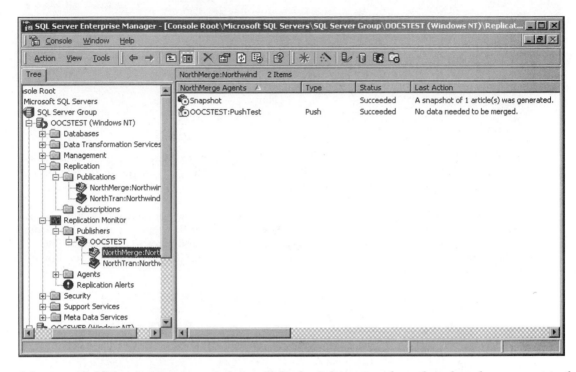

Selecting a Publisher, publication, or agent will display information about the selected component in the Enterprise Manager window. You can also display this information in a separate window by running Action | New window from Here or right-clicking on the Publisher, publication, or agents and running New window from Here:

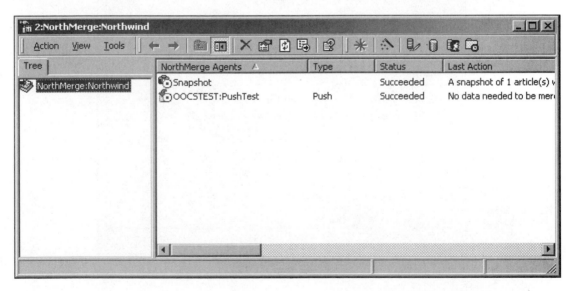

Selecting an agent displays history information for that agent. You can also view agent history by querying the agent histories in the distribution database. These are:

❑ MSsnapshot_history

❑ MSlogreader_history

❑ MSdistribution_history

❑ MSmerge_history

Each table includes entries for the local distributor. Table columns track agent-specific information, including date and time stamps for each row. By querying the table, you can view activity over a period of time, as well as check for specific conditions.

You can modify the Replication Monitor refresh rate and performance monitor information. Select a Publisher, publication, or agent and run Action | Refresh Rate and Settings or right-click and run Refresh Rate and Settings. The General tab sets the refresh rate and inactivity threshold. The Performance Monitor tab sets the path to the file containing settings that Performance Monitor will use to monitor replication performance:

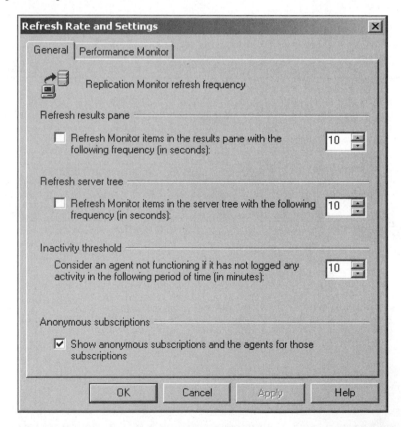

Keeping it Going

Of course, there's more to keeping replication running smoothly than checking Replication Monitor on occasion. Replication may be an automatic process, but unfortunately, some of its required upkeep isn't.

Disk Space

SQL Server Agents clean up after themselves on a regular basis to help keep storage space requirements to a minimum. You need to check the clean-up jobs on occasion to make sure that they are running.

In addition, you need to keep an eye on the distribution database and transaction log to keep them from growing too large. You can help keep the distribution database to a manageable size by adjusting the retention period.

You can limit the size and growth characteristics of the distribution database as in any other database. However, you need to exercise caution to make sure it is large enough to store all of your replication jobs.

Error Logs

Sooner or later, you can expect that problems will arise with replication. When they do, it helps to know where to look for information. You've already been introduced to Replication Monitor, but you have other sources available.

One source is the SQL Server Agent Error Log. Right-click on the **SQL Server Agent** node under the **Management** node in Enterprise Manager and run **Display Error Log**. Entries are identified as errors, warnings, and informational messages:

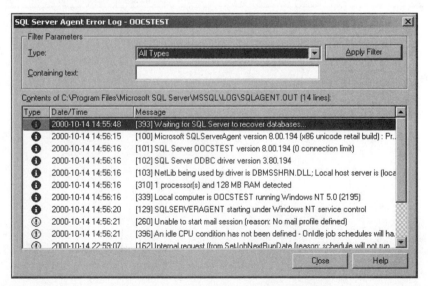

You can get detailed information about server activity through the agent logs in Enterprise Manager. Click on an agent to view the activity log. You can run Actions | New window from Here or right-click on a log and run New window from Here to open the log in a separate window.

A source that is sometimes overlooked is the Windows NT Event Viewer. In Windows NT you can find SQL Server information and error messages by selecting Log | Application from Event Viewer's menu. If you are using Windows 2000, you just need to select the Application Log node from the Tree window:

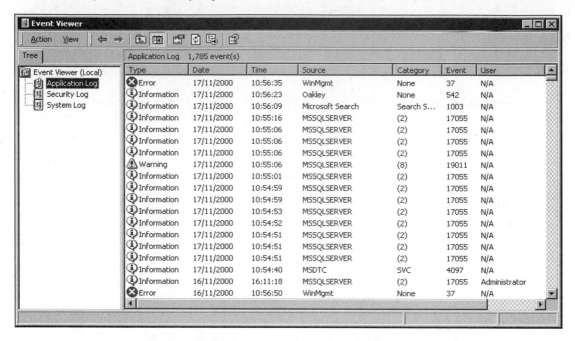

Summary

This chapter gave you a relatively detailed look at SQL Server replication. You were introduced to some general terms and concepts, including the terms relating to components in the replication publishing metaphor. You saw how different types of replication work and were given guidelines on when and how to use replication types and models. This included data requirements and restrictions for snapshot, transactional, and merge publications.

The chapter also stepped you through the process for setting up replication. You saw how to use the replication wizards to configure Distributors, Publishers, Subscribers, publications, and articles. You were also given a brief introduction to heterogeneous environments and the procedures for publishing to the Internet.

Online discussion at http://p2p.wrox.com

24

Advanced Design

OK, so now you're an expert – right? I mean, we've looked at all sorts of stuff up to this point: normalization, sprocs, triggers, UDFs, views, transactions, XML, linked servers, and more. Hard to believe we still have nine chapters to go, eh? That's the way the database thing is though – it's a big thing to swallow. What's worse, you really need to understand a significant percentage of it before you can be truly productive.

In this chapter, we'll be adding to the database design issues that we've talked about thus far. Most (but not quite all) of what we'll deal with after this chapter sits on the periphery of our database design, so it seems like a good time to try to pull some of what we've learned together to the point of seeing how to deal with certain situations. This chapter is going to be about identifying solutions to several common database problems, and seeing how we can mix and match the functionality within SQL Server to end up with good answers to some tough problems.

Some of the topics we'll look over in this chapter include:

- ❑ More on diagramming
- ❑ Logical vs. physical design
- ❑ Dealing with large-file-based information
- ❑ Subcategories
- ❑ Database reusability

More on Diagramming and Relationships

As I said way back in Chapter 8, SQL Server doesn't really give us all that much in terms of diagramming tools (before SQL Server 7.0, it didn't give us anything at all), and what there is doesn't adhere to either of the most common diagramming paradigms – IE and IDEF1X. You'll find both of these in widespread use, but I'm going to limit things here to a once over of the basics of **IE** (also called **Information Engineering**). For the record, **IDEF1X** is a perfectly good diagramming paradigm, and was first put forth by the US Air Force. IE (Information Engineering – *not* Internet Explorer) is, however, the method I use personally, and I do so for just one reason – it is far more intuitive for the inexperienced reviewer of your diagrams.

So why, if SQL Server doesn't provide anything to do this, am I providing information on IE? Well, even if you're using the daVinci tools to do your diagramming, I'm going to strongly encourage you to create a logical model for all your databases. Since the daVinci tools don't have a mechanism for logical modeling, I'm going to give you some of the rules of the road in case you decide to:

❑ Draw them out by hand

❑ Use a simple diagramming program such as Visio

❑ Upgrade to a real Entity Relationship Diagram (ERD) tool

If nothing else, it will really help you out when you're working on the white board with a co-worker.

> I can't say enough about the importance of having the right tools. While the daVinci tools are a tremendous step forward from what we had before, it is largely because we didn't have anything before. We'll be talking in this chapter about the importance of physical modeling – well, daVinci has absolutely nothing in the way of logical modeling – just physical.
>
> ERD tools are anything but cheap – running from somewhere over $1,000 to just under $3,500 (that's per seat!). They are also something of a language unto themselves. Don't plan on just sitting down and going to work with any of the major ER tools – you had better figure on some spin-up time to get it to do what you expect.
>
> Don't let the high price of these tools keep you from building a logical model. While Visio (the low cost editions anyway) is not the answer to the world's database design problems, it does do OK in a pinch for light logical modeling. That said; if you're serious about database design, and are going to be doing a lot of it, you really need to find the budget for a real ERD tool.

Expense aside, there is no comparison between the productivity possible in the third party tools out there and the built-in tools. Depending on the ER tool you select, they give you the capability to do things like:

❑ Create logical models, then switch back and forth between the logical and physical model

❑ Work on the diagram off-line – then propagate all your changes to the physical database at one time (when you're ready, as opposed to when you need to log off)

❑ Reverse engineer your database from any one of a number of mainstream RDBMS systems (even some ISAM databases), then forward engineer them to a completely different RDBMS

❑ Create your physical model on numerous different systems

This really just scratches the surface. We'll review some of these tools a bit further in Appendix C – but I wanted to hop on the soapbox here to make sure that you don't forget to look at what you're missing!

A Couple of Relationship Types

Before we get going too far in more diagramming concepts, we want to explore two types of relationships: **identifying** and **non-identifying**.

Identifying Relationships

For some of you, I'm sure the term "identifying relationship" brings back memories of some boyfriend or girlfriend you've had in the past that got just a little over possessive – this is not that kind of relationship. Instead, we're dealing with the relationships that are defined by foreign keys.

An identifying relationship is one where the column or columns (remember, there can be more than one) being referenced (in the parent table) are used as all or part of the referencing (child) table's primary key. Since a primary key serves as the identity for the rows in a table, and all or part of the primary key for the child table is dependent on the parent table – the child table can be said to, at least in part, be "identified" by the parent table.

Non-Identifying Relationships

Non-identifying relationships are those that are created when you establish a foreign key that does not serve as part of the referencing (child) table's primary key. This is extremely common in situations where you are referencing a domain table – where essentially the sole purpose of the referenced table is to limit the referencing field to a set list of possible choices.

The Entity Box

One of the many big differences you'll see in both IE and IDEF1X vs. SQL Server's own brand of diagramming comes in the **entity box**. The entity box, depending on whether you're dealing with logical or physical models, equates roughly to a table. By looking over the entity box, you should be able to easily identify the entity's name, primary key, and any attributes (effectively columns) that entity has. In addition, the diagram may expose other information such as the attribute's data type or whether it has a foreign key defined for it. As an example, here is the entity box for our Orders table from back in Chapter 8 (remember all that first design and normalization stuff?):

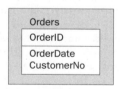

The name of our entity is kept on the top outside the box. Then, in the top area of the overall box, but in a separate box of its own, we have the primary key OrderID (we'll look at an example with more than one column in the primary key shortly), and last, but not least, come the attributes OrderDate and CustomerNo of the entity.

Let's look at a slightly different entity:

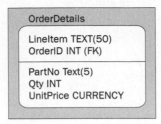

Several new things appear:

- ❑ The data types (I've turned on the appropriate option)
- ❑ Foreign keys (if any – again I've turned on the option to make this show)
- ❑ We have multiple columns in the primary key (everything above the line is part of the primary key)
- ❑ This time, the entity is rounded on the corners (this tells us that this table is identified (remember identifying relationships?) by at least one other table)

Depending on the ER tool, the data types can be defined right within the ER diagram. Also, as we draw the lines that form our relationships (we'll look at those shortly), we are able to define foreign keys that can also be shown. For most available ER tools, you can even tell the tool to automatically define the referenced field(s) in the foreign key relationship as being part (or possibly all) of the primary key in the referencing table.

The Relationship Line

There are two kinds of relationship line, and they match 100% with our relationship types:

A solid line indicates an identifying relationship: ————————————

A broken or dashed line indicates a non-identifying relationship: — — — — — — — — — — — —

An identifying relationship is one where the column that is referencing another table serves as all or part of the primary key of the referencing table. In a non-identifying relationship, the foreign key column has nothing to do with the primary key in the referencing table.

Terminators

Ahh, this is where things become slightly more interesting. The **terminators** we're talking about here are, of course, not the kind you'd see Arnold Schwarzenegger play in a movie – they are the end caps that we put on our relationship lines.

The terminators on our lines will communicate as much or more about the nature of our database as the entities themselves will. They are the things that will tell us the most information about the true nature of the relationship, including the **cardinality** of the relationship.

Cardinality is, in its most basic form, the number of records on both sides of the relationship. When we say it is a one-to-many relationship, then we are indicating cardinality. Cardinality can, however, be much more specific than the zero, one, or many naming convention that we use more generically. Cardinality can address specifics, and is often augmented in a diagram with two numbers and a colon, such as:

❑ 1:M

❑ 1:6 (which, while meeting a one-to-many criteria, is more specific and says there is a maximum of six records on the *many* side of the relationship)

Let's walk through a couple of the parts of a terminator and examine what they mean:

> **Just as a reminder, the terminators that follow are the ones from the IE diagramming methodology. There is another diagramming standard that is in widespread use (though I see it much less than IE) called IDEF1X. While its entity boxes are much like IE's, its terminators on the relationship lines are entirely different.**

The top half of the terminator is indicating the first half of our relationship. In this case, we have a zero. For the bottom half, we are indicating the second half of our relationship – in this case, a many. In this example, then, we have a zero, one, or many side of a relationship:

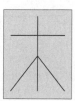

This time, we're not allowing nulls at this end of the relationship – this is a one or many end to a relationship:

This time around, we're back to allowing a zero at this end of the relationship, but we are now allowing a maximum of one. This is a zero or one side of a relationship:

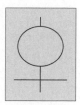

And this one is pretty restrictive – it's simply a "one" side of a relationship:

Since it's probably pretty confusing to look at these just by themselves, let's look at a couple of example tables and relationships.

First, we'll stick with our original couple of tables from when we were working with normalization back in Chapter 8.

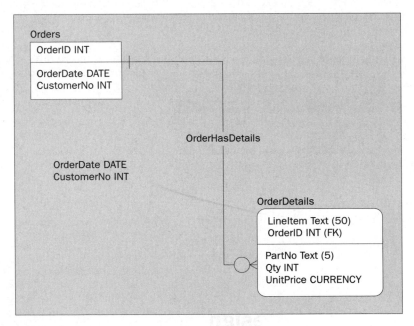

This is a diagram that shows not only our **Orders** and **OrderDetails** tables, but also depicts a one (the **Orders** side) to zero, one, or many (the **OrderDetails** side) relationship between the two tables. The relationship is an identifying relationship (depicted by the solid, rather than dashed, line), and the relationship is called **OrderHasDetails**.

Now, let's toss in the Products table:

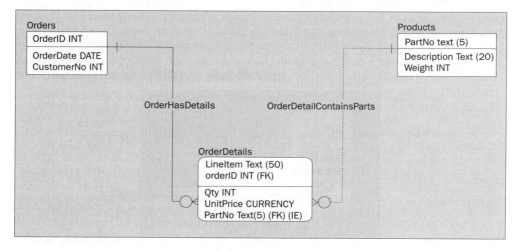

This new relationship is very similar to the relationship that we have already looked at. It is again a one (**Products** this time) to zero, one, or many (**OrderDetails** again) relationship, but this is it is non-identifying (as represented by the broken line). The IE indicates that, for this table, **PartNo** is an **inversion entry**, or an index that is not associated with anything other than a foreign key. The inversion entry has been added since it usually makes sense to have an index on a field that is a foreign key (since it is a frequent target of lookups).

By looking at all three together, we can see that there is a many-to-many relationship between **Orders** and **Products** by virtue of their relationship through the **OrderDetails** table.

As I've indicated before, we are still really only scratching the surface of the different information that your ER diagrams can convey. Still, by now you should have a good idea of the fact that the more accepted methodologies out there have an awful lot more information to convey than what is offered by the tools in SQL Server. In addition, just the nature of how tables are displayed makes information such as keys more visible and easier to read.

Logical vs. Physical Design

As you move forward in your database endeavors, you're likely to hear about the concepts of logical vs. physical models. In this section, we'll be exploring the differences between the two.

The physical model is one that's probably pretty easy to grasp. It is essentially what you have been working with up to this point in the book. You can think of anything that you can perform a CREATE statement on as being part of the physical model. Indeed – if you run any statements in SQL Server on it at all then it must be part of the physical model.

That being said, a logical model is a means to a number of different things – the physical model in particular. This means that, as you work on the logical model, you are working your way towards being able to generate DDL (Data Definition Language – or things like CREATE, ALTER, and DROP statements).

Purpose of a Logical Model

The first thing to understand about logical models is that they have somewhat different goals from physical models. A logical model does several things for you:

❑ Allows you to begin to build abstracts of complex, data-related business issues as well as provide a high-level beginning effort at identifying your entities

❑ Allows you to use these abstracts to effectively communicate about business rules and content as relates to data

❑ Represents the purest form of the data (before you start introducing the realities of what will really work)

❑ Serves as a major piece of documentation in the data requirements portion of your project

Because logical models aren't strictly rooted in the exact syntax to create the database, they give you a flexibility that you can't obtain from a physical model. You can attach dialogs and rules to the logical model regardless of whether your particular RDBMS will support those rules or not. In short, it lets you squeeze in all the facts before you start paring down your design to a more specific implementation.

What's nice about this is that logical models allow you to capture all of your data rules in one place regardless of where that rule will be actually implemented. You will frequently run into situations where you cannot sensibly implement your rules in the databases. The rules in question may be data related, but due to some constraint or requirement, you need to implement them using more procedural code in your client or in some form of middle tier. With logical models – you go ahead and include the data related rules anyway.

As an example of something that might be in the logical model, but not in your physical model, imagine for a moment that you are running an online stock brokerage. Obviously, you need to keep track of your users account balances and trades – those will be in both the logical and physical models. But what about the "extras" that you give the customer? Things like news feeds and links to financial advice columns. These are things that you may very well outsource – that is; you contract with a financial news service to provide news feeds. The news service worries about the physical storage of the news stories – and that means you don't have to. You would have no news feed representation in your physical model, but your logical model should still show this data so you can conceptualize where that data fits into your system as a whole.

Regardless of its source, you include all data-related information in a first logical design to create one or more abstracts of the data in your system. These abstracts can then be used as a representation to your customer about what you really are intending to store and what rules you believe you have captured. Using such a representation early (and often) can save your projects valuable time and money by opening extra doors of communication. Even a customer who is not very data savvy can often look at the highest level diagrams and say things like, "Where are the purchase requisitions?" Usually, you have some handy dandy explanation of why you called them something else and you can point to them on the diagram – other times, however, you find yourself uttering those most fearsome of words – "Oops!" I don't know about you, but I'd rather utter those words in the first weeks of a project rather than the first weeks of deployment. Logical modeling, when properly shared with the customer, can help avoid those deployment time "oops" statements.

I can't do enough to stress the importance of sharing your logical design (there had better be one!) with your customer both early and often. With a little education of the customer in how to read your logical model (this should also include good documentation on cause and purpose of the entities and relationships of the model), you can save a fortune in both time and money.

I haven't met a developer with any real experience who hadn't, at least once (and probably far more often than that), learned the hard way about the cost of late changes to your system. Changing code is very expensive, but that typically doesn't even begin to touch on what happens when you need to change your database late in a project. If you haven't done a good job of abstracting your database (3-tier or n-tier design), then every change you make to your database is going to cascade through tons of code. In other words, one little change in your database can potentially cost several – possibly hundreds or even thousands (depending on the size of the system) of changes in the code that accesses the database.

In short, communication is everything, and logical modeling should be a huge part of your tool set for communicating with your customer.

Parts of a Logical Model

A logical model contains three major parts:

- ❑ Structure
- ❑ Constraints
- ❑ Rules

The combination of these three should completely describe the requirements of the data in your system, but they may not translate entirely to the physical model. Some of the issues identified in the logical model may need to be implemented in some procedural form (such as in a middle-tier component). Other times, the entire logical model can be implemented through the various features of your RDBMS.

This is a really important point, and I want to stress it again – just because it's in your logical model doesn't mean that it will be in your physical database. A logical model should take into account all of your data requirements – even those that are not possible to implement in your RDBMS (for example, data that you might be retrieving from a third party source – perhaps in an XML document or some other storage medium). Having everything in your logical model allows you to plan the physical design in such a way that you can be sure that you have addressed all data issues – not just those that will physically reside in the database.

Structure

Structure is that part of the logical design that deals with the concept of actually storing the data. When we deal with the structure of the database, we're talking about entities – most of which will translate to tables that will store our data – and the particular columns we are going to need to maintain the atomicity of our data.

Constraints

Constraints, from a logical model standpoint, are a bit broader than the way that we've used the word "constraint" up until now. Prior to now, when we used the word constraint, we were talking about a specific set of features to limit data to certain values.

From a logical standpoint, a constraint is anything that defines the "what" question for our data – that is, what data is valid. A logical model includes constraints, which is to say that it includes things like:

❑ Data types (notice that this is really a separate thought from the notion that a column needs to exist or what the name of that column should be).

❑ Constraints in the form we're used to up until now – that is, CHECK constraints, foreign keys, even primary keys, and UNIQUE constraints (alternate keys). Each of these provides a logical definition of what data can exist in our database. This area would also include things like domain tables (which we would reference using foreign keys) – which restrict the values in a column to a particular "domain" list.

Rules

If constraints were the "what" in our data, then rules are the "when and how much" in our data.

When you define logical rules, you're defining things like, "Do we require a value on this one?" (which equates to a "do we allow nulls?") and, "How many of these do we allow?" (which defines the cardinality of our data – "do we accept one or many?").

It's worth noting yet again that any of these parts may not be implemented in the physical part of our database – we may decide that the restrictions that we want to place on things will be handled entirely at the client – regardless of where the requirement is implemented, it should still be part of our comprehensive logical data model. It is only when we achieve this complete modeling of our data that we can really know that we have addressed all the issues (regardless of where we addressed them).

Dealing with File-Based Information

BLOBs! You haven't really seen enough to them to hate them yet – and I do mean *yet*. BLOBs (**Binary Large Objects**) are slow – very slow and big. Hey, did I mention they were slow?

BLOBs are nice in the sense that they let you break the 8K barrier on row size (BLOBs can be up to about 2GB in size). The problem is that they are painfully slow (I know, I'm repeating myself, but I suspect I'm also making a point here). In the race between the BLOB and the tortoise (the sequel to the tortoise and the hare), the BLOB won only after the tortoise stopped for a nap.

OK, so we've beaten the slow thing into the ground, and you still need to store large blocks of text or binary information. Normally, you'd do that using a BLOB – but we do have the option of not doing it that way. Instead, we can go around the problem by storing things as files instead.

> **OK, so by now some of you have to be asking the question of, "Isn't a database going to be a faster way of accessing data than the file system?" My answer is quite simply, "No!" There is an exception to this that I'll get to before the chapter is done, but, by and large, using files is going to be much faster.**

I'm going to warn you right up front that, in order to pull this off, you need to be planning for this in your client – this isn't a "database server only" kind of thing to do. Indeed, we'll be removing most of the work from the database server and putting it into your middle tier and file system.

Let's start by looking at what we need to do on the server's file system side. The only thing that we need is to make sure that we have at least one directory to store the information in. Depending on the nature of our application, we may also need to have logic in a middle-tier object that will allow it to create additional directories as needed.

All of the Windows operating systems have limits on the number of files they can store in one directory. As such, you need to think about how many files you're going to be storing. If it will be many (say, over 500), then you'll want to create a mechanism in the object that stores your BLOB so that it can create new directories either on an as-needed basis, or based on some other logical criteria.

Your business component will be in charge of copying the BLOB information to the file you're going to store it in. If it is already in some defined file format, you're on easy street – just run your language's equivalent to a copy command (with a twist we'll go over shortly) and you're in business. If it is streamed data, then you'll need to put the logic in your component to store the information in a logical format (such as COM structured storage) for later retrieval.

> **One big issue with this implementation is that of security. Since you're storing the information in a file that's outside SQL Server's realm that means that it is also outside SQL Server's protection security-wise. Instead, you have to rely on your network security.**
>
> **There are several "wow, that's scary!" things that should come to mind for you here. First, if someone's going to read data out of the directory that you're storing all this in, doesn't that mean they can see other files that are stored in there? Yes, it does (you could get around this by changing the NT security for each file, but it would be very tedious indeed – in the case of a web application, you would need to do something like implementing an ISAPI DLL). Second, since you'd have to give people rights to copy the file into the directory, wouldn't there be a risk of someone altering the file directly rather than using the database (potentially causing your database to be out of synch with the file)? Absolutely!**
>
> **The answer to these, and the many other questions that you could probably come up with, lies in your data access layer (I'm assuming an n-tier approach here). Using MTS, you can have the access component run under a different security context from the end user. This means that you can create a situation where the user can access their data – but only when they are using the data access component to do it (they don't have any rights to the directory themselves – indeed, they probably don't even know where the files are stored).**
>
> **Doing things this way in not nearly as difficult as it may first sound, and Wrox has a number of good books on MTS to help you figure it out.**

So then, where does SQL Server come into play in all this? It keeps track of where you stored the information in question. Theoretically, the reason why you were trying to store this information in the database in the first place is because it relates to some other information in the row you were going to store it as part of. But instead of saving the actual data in the row in the form of a BLOB, you will now store a path to the file that you saved. The process for storage will look something like this:

1. Determine the name you're going to store it as.

2. Copy the file to the location that you're going to store it at.

3. Save the full name and path in a varchar(255) (which also happens to be the maximum size for a name in a Windows NT directory) along with the rest of the data for that row.

4. To retrieve the data, run your query much as you would have if you were going to retrieve the data direction from the table, only this time, retrieve the path to where the actual BLOB data is stored.

5. Retrieve the data from the file system.

In general, this approach will run approximately 2-3 times faster than if we were using BLOBs. There are, however, some exceptions to the rule of wanting to use this approach:

❑ The BLOBs you are saving are consistently small (less than 64K) in size

❑ The data is text or some format that MS Search has a filter for, and you want to be able to perform full-text searches against it

If the size of your BLOBs is consistently less than 64K, then the data is all able to fit on one data page. This significantly reduces the overhead in dealing with your BLOB. While the file system approach is still probably going to be faster, the benefits will be sharply reduced so that it doesn't make as much sense. If you're in this scenario, and speed is everything, then all I can suggest is to experiment.

If you want to perform full-text searches, you're probably going to be better off going ahead and storing the large blocks of text as a TEXT data type (which is a BLOB) in SQL Server. If the text is stored in a binary format that has a MS Search filter available (or you could write your own if you're desperate enough), then you can store the file in an image data type and MS Search will automatically use the filter to build the full-text index. Don't get me wrong, it's still very possible to do full-text searches against the text in the file, but you're going to have to do substantially more coding to keep your relationships intact if you want non-BLOB data from the same functional row. In addition, you're most likely going to wind up having to program your middle tier to make use of index server (which is what supports SQL Server's full-text search).

> *If push comes to shove, and you need to make a full-text search against file-system-based information, you could take a look at accessing the index server via a query directly. Remember from our chapter on remote queries that we can potentially access any OLEDB data source – well, the Index Server service has an OLEDB provider and can be used at the target as a linked server or in an OPENQUERY. The bad news, however, is that performing an index server query against an index server that is not on the same physical box as your SQL Server really doesn't work. The only workaround is to have index server on the system local to SQL Server, but have it catalog files stored on another system. The problem with this is the network chatter during the cataloging process and the fact that it doesn't let you offload the cataloging work (which hurts scalability).*

Subcategories

A **subcategory** is a logical construct that provides us another type of relationship (sometimes called a "supertype" or "subtype" relationship) to work with. On the physical side of the model, a subcategory is implemented using a mix the types of relationships that we've already talked about (we'll see the specifics of that before we're done).

A subcategory deals with the situation where you have a number of what may at first seem like different entities, but which share some, although not all, things in common.

I think the best way to get across the concept of a subcategory is to show you one. To do this, we'll take the example of a document in a company.

A document has a number of attributes that are common to any kind of document. For example:

- ❏ Title
- ❏ Author
- ❏ Date Created
- ❏ Date Last Modified
- ❏ Storage Location

I'm sure there are more. Note that I'm not saying that every document has the same title, rather that every document has a title. Every document has an author (possibly more than one actually, but, for this example, we'll assume a limit of one). Every document was created on some date. You get the picture – we're dealing with the attributes of the concept of a document, not any particular instance of a document.

However, there are lots of different kinds of documents. From things like legal forms (say your mortgage documents) to office memos, to report cards – there are lots of document types. Still, each of these can still be considered to be a document – or a subcategory of a document. Let's consider a few examples:

For our first example, we'll look at a lease. A lease has all the characteristics that we expect to find our in documents category, but it also has information that is particular to a lease. A lease has things like:

- ❏ Leasor
- ❏ Leasee
- ❏ Term (how long the lease is for)
- ❏ Rate (how much per month or week)
- ❏ Security deposit
- ❏ Start date
- ❏ Expiration date
- ❏ Option (which usually offers an extension at a set price for a set additional term)

The fact that a lease has all of these attributes does not preclude the fact that it is still a document. We can come up with a few more examples, and I'll stay with my legal document trend – let's start with a divorce document. It has attributes such as:

- ❑ Plaintiff (the person suing for a divorce)
- ❑ Defendant (the plaintiff's spouse)
- ❑ Separation date
- ❑ Date the plaintiff files for the divorce
- ❑ Date the divorce was considered "final"
- ❑ Alimony (if any)
- ❑ Child support (if any)

We could also have a bill of sale – our bill of sale might include attributes such as:

- ❑ Date of sale
- ❑ Amount of the sale
- ❑ Seller
- ❑ Purchaser
- ❑ Warranty period (if any)

Again, the fact that divorces and bills of sale both have their own attributes does not change the fact that they are documents.

In each case – leases, divorces, and bills of sale – we have what is really a subcategory of the category of *documents*. A document really has little or no meaning without also belonging to a subcategory. Likewise, any instance of a subcategory has little meaning without the parent information that is found only in the supercategory – documents.

Types of Subcategories

Subcategories fall into two separate classifications of their own – exclusive and non-exclusive.

When we refer to a subcategory as simply a subcategory (without saying "exclusive"), then we are usually referring to a non-exclusive subcategory arrangement. In this situation, we have a record in a table that represents the supercategory (a document in our previous example), and a matching record in at least one of the subcategories.

This kind of subcategory is represented with a symbol that appears rather odd compared to those we've seen thus far:

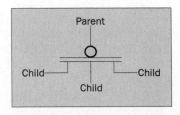

Even though there are three subcategories depicted both here and in the document example, don't misconstrue this as being any kind of official limit to the number of subcategories – there isn't one. You could have a single subcategory or ten of them – it doesn't really make any difference.

Far more common is the situation where we have an **exclusive subcategory**. An exclusive subcategory works exactly as a category did with only one exception – for every record in the supercategory, there is only one matching record in any of the subcategories. Each subcategory is deemed to be mutually exclusive, so a record to match the supercategory exists as exactly one row in exactly one of the subcategory tables.

The diagramming for an exclusive subcategory looks odder yet:

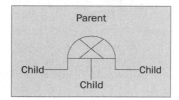

Implementing Subcategories

The thing that's really cool about subcategories is that they allow you to store all of a similar construct in one place. Before learning this concept, we would have taken one of two approaches to implement our document model:

1. Add all of the attributes into one column and just leave the columns null for the information that doesn't fit the specific type of document we're interested in for a given record.

2. Have separate tables for each type of document. The columns that are essentially the same between document types would be repeated for each table (each table stores its own copy of the document information as it applies to the records in that particular table).

Using the notion of a subcategory, we can now store all documents, regardless of type, such that they all begin in one place. Any query that you have that is looking for information about all the documents in your system can now run against just one table instead of having to do something like using the UNION operator on three (maybe more, maybe less) different tables. It probably goes without saying, then, that implementing this kind of situation using a subcategory can provide a serious performance enhancement over the other options.

There is a catch though (you knew there would be, right?) – you need to provide some mechanism to point to the rest of the information for that document. Your query of all documents may provide the base information on the specific document that you're looking for, but when you want the rest of the information for that document (the things that are unique to that document type), then how does your application know which of the subcategory tables to search for the matching record in? To do this, just add a field to your supercategory that indicates what the subcategory is for that record. In our example, we would probably implement another column in our documents table called DocumentType. From that type, we would know which of our other tables to look through for the matching record with more information. Furthermore, we might implement this using a domain table – a table to limit the values in our DocumentType column to just those types that we have subcategories for – and a foreign key to that table.

Keep in mind that, while what we're talking about here is the physical storage and retrieval of the data, there is no reason why you couldn't abstract this using either a sproc or a series of views (or both). For example, you could have a stored procedure call that would pull together the information from the Documents table and then join to the appropriate subcategory.

Oh – for those of you who are thinking, "Wait, didn't that other text that I read about n-tier architecture say to never use sprocs?" Well, that's a garbage recommendation in my not so humble opinion (which I indicated to some degree back in Chapter 12). It's foolish not to use the performance tools available – just remember to access them only through your data access layer – don't allow middle tier or client components to even know your sprocs exist. Follow this advice, and you'll get better performance, improved overall encapsulation, shorter development times, and, even with all that, still live within the real theory of a separate data access layer that is so fundamental to n-tier design.

In addition to establishing a pointer to the type of document, we also need to determine whether we're dealing with a plain subcategory or an exclusive subcategory. In our document example, we have what should be designed as an exclusive subcategory. We may have lots of documents, but we do not have documents that are both a lease and a divorce (a non-exclusive subcategory would allow any mix of our subcategories). Even if we had a lease with a purchase option, the bill of sale would be a separate document created at the time the purchase option was exercised.

So now we're ready to implement our logical model:

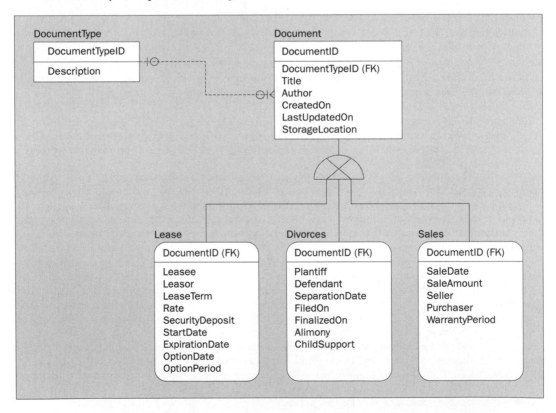

OK, so we have an entity called **Document**. These documents are of a specific type, and that type is limited to a domain – **DocumentType** sets the boundaries of that domain. In addition, each of the types is represented by its own entity – or subcategory. The symbol in the middle of it all (the half circle with an "X" through it), tells us that the three subcategories are exclusive in nature (you have one, and only one for each instance of a document).

This is an excellent place to step back and reflect on what our logical model can do for us. As we discussed earlier in the chapter, our logical model, among other things, provides us with a way to communicate the business rules and requirements of our data. In this case, with a little explanation, someone (a customer perhaps?) can look at this and recognize the concept that we are saying that Leases, Divorces, and Sales are all variations on a theme – that they are really the same thing. This gives the viewer the chance to say, "Wait – no, those aren't really the same thing." Or perhaps something like, "Oh, I see – you know, we also have wills and power-of-attorney documents – they are pretty much the same, aren't they?" These are little pieces of information that can save you a bundle of time and money later.

The Physical Implementation of Subcategories

On the physical side of things, there's nothing quite as neat and clean as it looks in the logical model. Indeed, all we do for the physical side is implement a series of one to zero or one relationships. We do, however, draw them out as being part of a single, multi-table relationship:

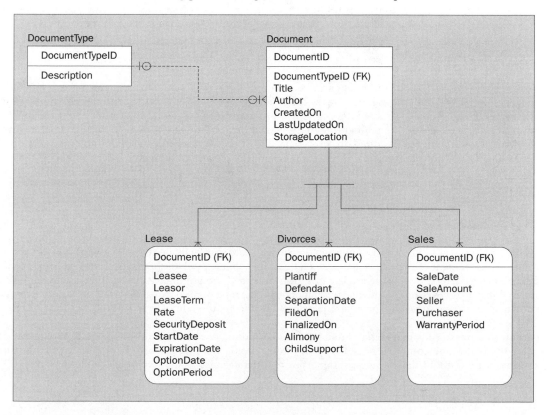

The only real trick in the game occurs if you have an exclusive subcategory (which is actually the case much more often than not). In this case, you also need to put some logic into the subcategory tables (in the form of triggers) to ensure that, if any row is to be inserted, there is not already another matching row in one of the other subcategories. For example, you would need to place an insert trigger in `Leases` that queried the `Divorces` and `Sales` tables for records with the same `DocumentID`. If one was found, then the trigger should reject inserted record with an appropriate error message and a `ROLLBACK`.

How Subcategories Add to Extensibility

Subcategories are one of those concepts that can make a huge difference in the success of your database design. If used when appropriate, you can cut significant time off your queries and significantly simplify pulling together aggregate information for related but different pieces of information. Yet these aren't the only benefits to subcategories.

Subcategories can provide a pathway to making your database more extensible. If you need to add another subcategory, the only queries you need to deal with are those that are specific to your new subcategory. Any of your queries that worked only with the parent table will still work fine – what's more, they'll pick up the information on your new subcategory without any changes!

In short, you're picking up two major scalability benefits:

❑ The information for your supercategory (documents in the example) can be scanned from just one table rather than using a `UNION` operator. This means less joins and faster relative query performance – especially as your tables grow larger or you have more and more subcategories.

❑ The addition of new subcategories often does not take as much development time as it would have if you where developing the framework for that category from scratch.

Now, just like most things, you do need to keep in mind one down side – subcategories can create a bottleneck at the parent table. Every query that you run against all the tables and data involved in the overall set of categories is probably going to need to access the parent table – think about the locking implications there. If you are not careful about your index and query strategies, this can lead to some very bad blocking and/or deadlocking problems. That said, with intelligent planning and query writing, this is usually not a problem. Also, if the sheer size of the parent table becomes a problem, SQL Server 2000 now gives us the option of using distributed partitioned views to scale out the table.

Database Reuse

This is almost never thought of, but you can create databases that facilitate reuse. Why do I say that it's almost never thought of? Well, just trust me on this – developers think of things like reusable components. Things such as objects to validate credit cards, distribute mail, stream binary information in and out – these are all things that you would immediately think about placing in a repository and using over and over again. For whatever reason, however, databases just don't seem to get thought of in that way.

Perhaps one reason for this is that databases, by definition, store data. Data is normally thought of as being unique to one company or industry and, most of all, as being private. I'm guessing that we then automatically think of the storage container for that data as also being personal – who knows?

Contrary to popular belief, however, databases can be built to be reusable. Surprisingly, to do this you apply a lot of the same concepts that make code components reusable – most of all compartmentalization and the use of common interfaces.

Just as many of the concepts of how to implement reusability of code components also apply to database reuse, so too does the concept of efficiency in the cost and time departments. Databases that are already designed save the design time and the associated costs. This can shorten product schedules and help in the ever-present battle with the budget.

> *Just remember to make sure there's really a good fit before you try to reuse an existing database structure. Like most things in programming that I've seen reuse of, it's very possible to have your reuse become a situation where you are trying to use the wrong tool for the job, and things can actually become even more expensive then they would have been if you had written things from scratch to begin with.*

Candidates for Reusable Databases

The databases that have the best chance of being reusable are those that can be broken up into separate subject areas (much like components are usually broken up into functional groupings). Each subject area is kept as generic as is feasible. An example would be something like an accounting database. You could have separate subject areas that match up with the functional areas in accounting:

❑   Purchasing

❑   Accounts Receivable (which in turn may be broken up into Invoicing and Cash Receipts)

❑   Inventory

❑   Accounts Payable

❑   General Ledger

❑   Cash Management

The list could go on. One can also take the approach down to a more granular level and create many, many databases down to the level of things like persons, commercial entities (ever noticed how similar customers are to vendors), orders – there are lots of things that have base constructs that are used repeatedly. You can roll these up into their own "mini-database", then plug them into a larger logical model (tied together using sprocs, views, or other components of your data access layer).

How to Break Things Up

This is where the logical vs. physical modeling really starts to show its stuff. When we're dealing with databases that we're trying to make reusable, we often have one logical database (that contains all the different subject areas) that contains many physical databases. Sometimes we'll choose to implement our logical design by referencing each of the physical implementations directly. Other times we may choose an approach that does a better job of hiding the way that we've implemented the database – we can create what amounts to a "virtual" database in that it holds nothing but views that reference the data from the appropriate physical database.

Let me digress long enough to point out that this process is essentially just like encapsulation in object-oriented programming. By using the views, we are hiding the actual implementation of our database from the users of the view. This means that we can remove one subject area in our database and replace it with an entirely different design – the only trick in doing this is to map the new design to our views – from that point on, the client application and users are oblivious to the change in implementation.

Breaking things up into separate physical databases and/or virtualizing the database places certain restrictions on us, and many of these restrictions contribute to the idea of being able to separate one subject area from the whole, and reuse it in another environment.

Some of the things to do are:

❑ Minimize or eliminate direct references to other functional areas. If you've implemented the view approach, connect each physically separate piece of the database to the logical whole only through the views.

❑ Don't use foreign key constraints – where necessary, use triggers instead. Foreign key constraints can't span databases, but triggers can.

The High Price of Reusability

All this reuse comes at a price. Many of the adjustments that you make to your design in order to facilitate reuse have negative performance impacts. Some of these are:

❑ Foreign key constraints are faster than triggers overall, but triggers are the only way to enforce referential integrity that crosses database boundaries.

❑ Using views means two levels of optimization run on all your queries (one to get at the underlying query and mesh that into your original query, another to sort out the best way to provide the end result) – that's more overhead and it slows things down.

❑ If not using the virtual database approach (one database that has views that map to all the other databases), maintaining user rights across many databases can be problematic.

In short, don't look for things to run as fast unless you're dealing with splitting the data across more servers than you can with the single database model.

Reusing your database can make lots of sense in terms of reduced development time and cost, but you need to balance those benefits against the fact that you may suffer to some degree in the performance category.

Partitioning for Scalability

Beginning with SQL Server 2000, we have picked up the marvelous ability to create one logical table from multiple physical tables – **partitioned views**. That is, the data from one logical table is partitioned such that is stored in a separate well-defined set of physical tables. However, the notion of partitioning your data has been around a lot longer than partitioned views have been. Indeed, keeping your main accounting system on one server and your order entry and inventory systems on another is a form of partitioning – you are making sure that the load of handling the two activities is spread across multiple servers.

The simple notion of having linked servers, first seen in version 7.0, really got partitioning going in the SQL Server world. While we didn't have the nice ability to partition individual tables, it was not uncommon to see a particularly highly loaded system broken up where one group of tables was located on one server and another group was on a completely different server.

The question of just *how* to partition your data should be a very big one indeed. The tendency is going to be to take the hyper-simplistic approach as we did back when we first introduced distributed partitioned views back in Chapter 17 – that is, to just divide things up equally based on the possible values in your partitioning column. This approach may work fine, but it is also a little short-sighted for two big reasons:

❑   Data rarely falls into nice, evenly distributed piles. Often, predicting the distribution requires a lot of research and sampling up front.

❑   It fails to take into account the way the data will actually be used once stored.

The way that you partition your data does a lot more than determine the volume of data that each partition will receive – much more importantly, it makes a positively huge difference to how well your overall system is going to perform. Keep in mind:

❑   Tables rarely live in a bubble. Most of the time you are going to be joining data from any given table with other data in the system – is how the "other" data is partitioned compatible (from a performance perspective)?

❑   Network bandwidth tends to be a huge bottleneck in overall system performance – how are you taking that into account when designing your partitions?

So, with all this in mind, here are a couple of rules for you:

❑   Keep data that will be used together, stored together. That is, if certain tables are going to be used together frequently in queries, then try to partition those tables such that data that is likely to be returned as part of a query will most likely reside on the same server. Obviously, you won't be able to make that happen 100% of the time, but, with careful thought and a recognition of how your data gets used, you should find that you can arrange things so that most queries will happen local to just one server. For example, for a given order, all the related order detail rows will be on the same server.

❑   When you design your application, you should ideally make it partition aware – that is, you should code the routines that execute the queries such that they know which server most likely has their data. The data may be broken out across multiple machines – wouldn't it be nice if the database server your application made the request to was the right one from the start, and there was no need for the request to be forwarded to another server?

If you've got as far as deciding that you need to go with a partitioned system, then you must really have one heck of a load you're planning on dealing with. How you partition your data is going to have a huge impact on how well your system is going to deal with that load. Remember to take the time to fully plan out your partitioning scheme. After you think you've decided what you're going to do – Test! Test! Test!

Summary

In this chapter, we've added some more things to think about in your database designs. We've seen how a logical model can help us truly understand our database rules and requirements before we are committed to a physical database design. We also looked into an alternative way of storing large file based information. Using this alternative method will often yield you increased throughput and performance. We've taken a solid look at subcategories and the very important role they can and should play in your database design strategy. We also took a look over some of the concepts of reusability of databases. Last, but certainly not least, we examined some of the things that you need to think about when partitioning data. Frankly, the number of different things to think about in design is virtually unlimited, but, hopefully, you now have some additional tools in your attempts to make the right choices about your database design.

In our next chapter, we'll toss in more design information yet. We'll be checking into the concepts that surround OLAP rather than the OLTP that has so dominated the book thus far. We'll see that the needs of OLAP are wildly different from those of an OLTP environment. By the time we're done, you'll see why you need to think of OLTP and OLAP as two completely separate problems, and you'll refuse to yield to the user to solve them both with one solution (it just doesn't work).

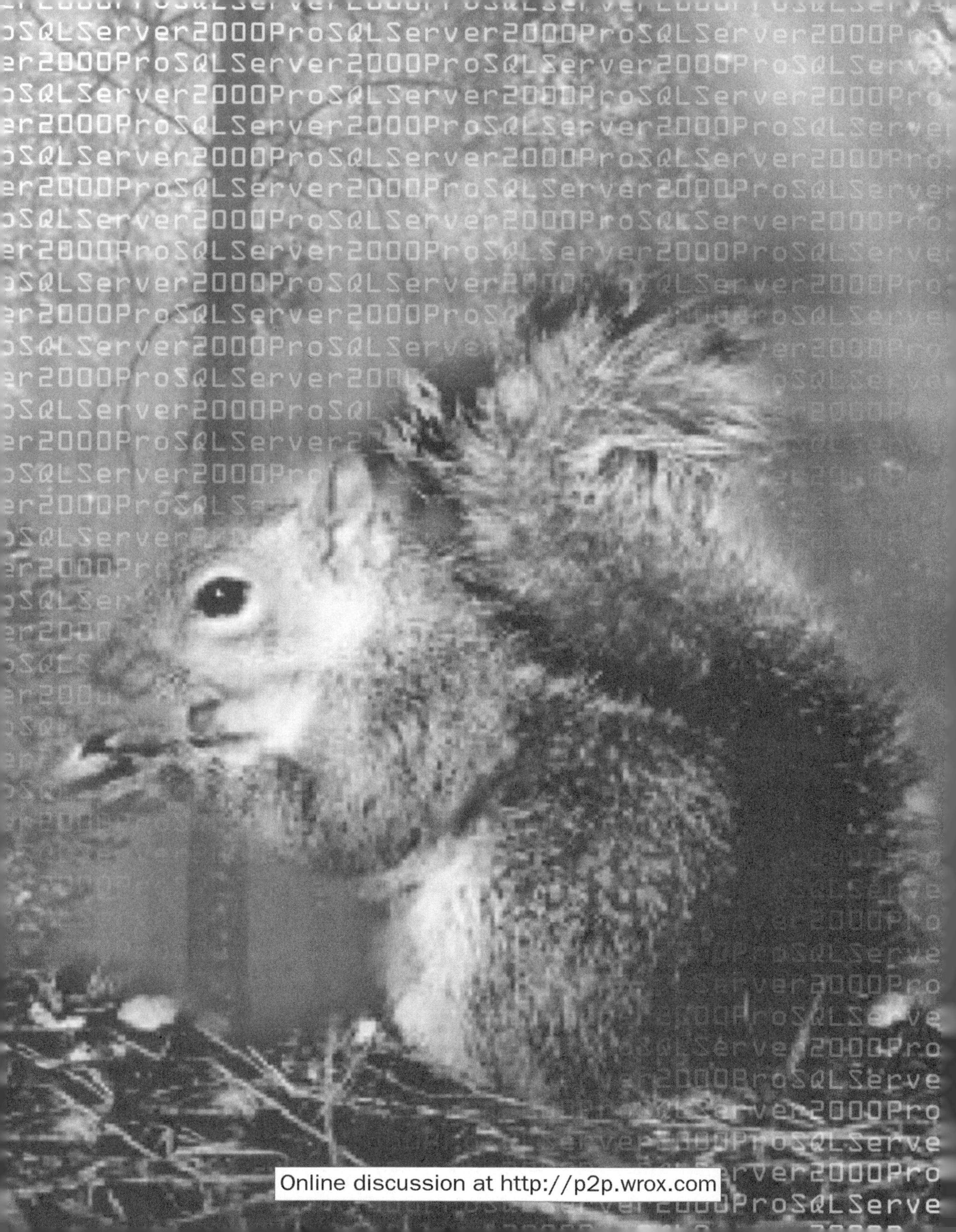
Online discussion at http://p2p.wrox.com

25

Analysis Services

Here we are, twenty-five chapters in. You've learned all the great and fantastic stuff – now forget most of it.

Up to this point, we've been thinking in terms of transactions – we've been working primarily in the world of **Online Transaction Processing**, or **OLTP**. Now, however, it's time to get dimensional – to start thinking in terms of analysis and **Online Analytical Processing**, or **OLAP**.

SQL Server 7.0's OLAP Services has now become part of SQL Server 2000's Analysis Services package, which is installed separately from the CD ROM after installing SQL Server itself. Analysis Services also contains new data mining support, which extends the help OLAP offers in making decisions for your business.

In this chapter we will:

❑ Discuss the differences between the needs of transaction processing vs. analysis processing

❑ Discuss how these differences necessarily lead to substantially different solutions

❑ Dispel the myth that your OLTP solution can also work as a great OLAP solution

❑ Define the concept of a data cube, and indicate how data cubes can help provide a solution to the special requirements of an OLAP environment

❑ Be introduced to the new data mining support in SQL Server 2000, including the new wizards and user interface you can use to conduct your analysis

❑ Look at some other aspects of Analysis Services that come as part of SQL Server 2000

The Requirements of End Users

As corporations build business applications and store their daily data in back-end databases associated with their applications, the databases grow in size. This growth eventually has negative impacts on the applications themselves – slowing them down, hampering concurrency, reducing scalability, and even causing them to crash at times.

End users may use data sources differently from one another. Three main categories of users can be distinguished:

❑ Those who want to access the data sources on a daily basis, retrieving certain records, adding new records, updating, or deleting existing records

❑ Those who want to make sense of the enormous amounts of data piling in the database, generating reports that will help them come up with the right decisions for the corporation and give it the competitive edge that will make it succeed in the marketplace

❑ The third category represents a group of users who want to take the knowledge they gained from their OLAP or transactional systems a step further by predicting business performance and analyzing trends for the future

The separate OLTP and OLAP systems help satisfy the different requirements of the first two categories of users. Data mining, an evolving technology, helps satisfy the requirements of the third category. The following sections present the characteristics of these systems and technologies, and how and when each of them can be used.

Online Transaction Processing (OLTP)

As I mentioned previously, OLTP systems are designed to allow for high concurrency, making it possible for many users to access the same data source and conduct the processing they need. As the name implies, these systems allow transactions (in other words, controlled changes to the data in the tables, due to inserts, updates, and deletes during the conduction of business processes) to be processed against the database. The following figure depicts a basic OLTP system:

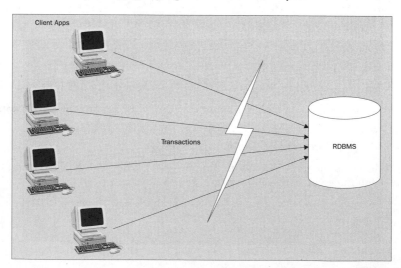

The figure shows that numerous client applications are accessing the database to get small pieces of information, add new data, update, or delete existing data. The broken line between the client applications and the server symbolizes that these connections can physically take place in many different ways. For instance, client applications could be accessing the database through a transaction monitor or application server, or they could be connected directly through the network.

Examples of OLTP systems include data-entry programs such as banking, ticket reservation, online sales applications, etc. No matter what the application is, OLTP systems are usually built with the following objectives in mind:

- ❑ Process data generated by transactions
- ❑ Maintain a high degree of accuracy by eliminating data redundancy
- ❑ Ensure data and information integrity
- ❑ Produce timely documents and reports, such as receipts and invoices
- ❑ Increase work efficiency
- ❑ Improve and enhance offered services to build and maintain customer loyalty

These objectives are usually accomplished by keeping the database in third normal form (or better), eliminating redundancy in the system, and maximizing relationships among the business entities as represented by the tables.

Online Analytical Processing (OLAP)

OLAP systems fall under the broader scope of **Decision Support Systems (DSS)** and **Executive Information Systems (EIS)**. The goal of OLAP systems is to analyze huge amounts of data, generating summaries and aggregations in many different ways, to help decision makers find patterns and trends that will allow them to improve the performance of their corporations, gain a competitive edge, and optimize business processes.

With OLAP systems, you need to forget about nicely keeping your relational database in the third normal form. You'll need to break this form and de-normalize the database (or flatten it) to some extent, allowing some redundancy with improved query performance in mind. This is because data stored in OLAP systems is rarely changed. The data is kept there for query purposes; to generate reports that would help decision makers plan the future of their enterprises. With this established, the database no longer conforms to the highly normalized relational database definition and conditions; it becomes what is called a **dimensional database** that follows a specific structure or schema. OLAP databases are used to build **data cubes**, which are multi-dimensional representations of the data that facilitate online business analysis and query performance. The dimensions of a cube represent distinct categories for analyzing business data. Such categories include time, geography, or product line, among others.

> **SQL Server 2000's Analysis Manager, part of Analysis Services, allows you to build up to 64 dimensions for each data cube.**

Data Mining

Traditional querying techniques, including OLAP, help you find information from your data that is not otherwise obvious to you. For instance, you can use queries or OLAP to find the number of customers who bought a certain product in a certain period of time per state or city. The information you are seeking is already in your database. It is just buried in a way that makes it difficult to see by just looking at the data. The query helps you extract the information by re-organizing your data.

Data mining, on the other hand, will take the information that you get from your data a step further, allowing you to discover hidden relationships among your data, find out new trends, speculate on causes for certain events, or even forecast the performance or direction of certain aspects of your data. For example, data mining can help you find why a certain product is selling more than another product in a certain region. Alternatively, it can help you forecast the sales of a certain product over the next few quarters.

SQL Server 2000 strongly supports data mining through the support of two widely used algorithms – decision trees and data clustering – that allow specific grouping and classification of data as a means to discover trends and predict future behavior. Analysis Service's Analysis Manager provides a new user interface with wizards that make data mining easy to do based on both relational data and OLAP data. The support to data mining is also extensible through new functions added in **MultiDimensional Expression language** (**MDX**), the SQL extension that handles OLAP data. Finally, the new OLE DB provider for data mining is the engine that provides data mining support and extensibility in SQL Server 2000.

OLTP or OLAP?

Now that you have seen the general ideas behind the two systems of OLAP and OLTP, let's consider the banking business, for example. During the bank's working hours, bank tellers help customers to perform their much needed transactions, like depositing funds into their accounts, transferring funds between accounts, and withdrawing funds from these accounts. The customers may also conduct their own transactions using an ATM (Automatic Teller Machine), or a phone-based and/or computer-based banking service. In other words, such transactions are not limited to a particular part of the day but can take place around the clock. All of these operations lead to changes in the data stored in the database. These changes could be inserts of new records, updating, or deleting existing records.

OLTP is built to allow these transactions to be made by a large number of users accessing the database concurrently. Databases serving OLTP systems are usually highly normalized relational databases (third normal form or higher), and their table indexes need to be selected carefully for the right fields. OLTP databases should be built to promote performance, allow high frequency of transactions, and represent tables in a relational fashion with parent-child relationships. Transactions held in such systems include inserts, updates, deletes, and selects.

Let's now look at a different scenario with the banking example. Suppose that the bank managers are conducting future planning. They definitely need to look at current and historical performance data of the bank. If they were to query the database that is used for the OLTP system, they will face big difficulties and cause major problems to other users who are conducting their transactions.

These issues arise because the queries used to build management reports will usually be summary, or aggregation queries. For example, they might want to know the total number of transactions conducted by all customers in a certain region. Such queries will have to sift through large amounts of data that is fragmented and scattered over many joined tables. For example, an accounting general ledger transaction could be stored in a dozen different tables. The queries will have to pull fields from these joined tables to build the views needed by the management, grouping and performing aggregations as they do so. All of this will impose a large overhead on the database management system (DBMS), slowing down the OLTP applications and the report generation process for the managers as well.

To face these challenges, it is necessary to isolate the managers who use existing bank data to build their future outlook and planning, and have them use a different system based on OLAP principals. This means creating two different systems: an OLTP system for transaction processing by bank staff and customers, and an OLAP system to help with the decision-making.

Now we have two different systems, should these systems use the same database with separate tables for each system, or should they use two completely different databases? The answer to this question depends on how much effect one of the systems will have on the performance of the other, and also depends on the management and administration plans of these systems. It is very likely that the two systems will be used at the same time. This causes performance problems even if the tables are separate. This is because the two systems still share many resources on the database server, and these resources may be depleted quickly with the two systems in use. These two systems are usually optimized differently. If we optimize for OLAP, we may adversely affect the performance of the OLTP system, and vice versa. In addition, the two systems may have to be administered differently, with different user accounts, backup and maintenance strategies, etc. Therefore, even though it is theoretically possible to tap into the same database, it is a good idea to keep separate databases on separate database servers for the two systems. With this, each system will have its own resources, and optimizing it will not affect the other system.

Querying an OLTP System

Although the relational model allows great flexibility in defining ways to look at and process the data in the database, we often find that the way data is processed in a business solution is different, especially when processed by decision makers. Decision makers are not interested in the details of every single transaction recorded in the database; they are interested in looking at the big picture instead. Let's consider a `sales` database for a bookseller, for instance. The database is likely to include a `sales` table, such as the one presented here:

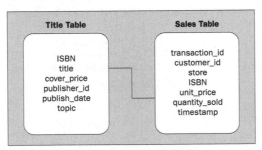

As the OLTP system is used over time, the table grows in size and becomes full of sales data, sometimes for the same customers, buying the same goods at different prices. Thus, the table becomes a good candidate for analysis.

The business analyst may be interested in finding out the effect the price had on the sales of programming-related books. In this case, she would be looking for the results in a table similar to the table below or even in graph format.

Price	Quantity Sold	Revenue
$20	7,000	140,000
$30	3,500	105,000
$40	2,500	100,000
$50	2,000	100,000

To get such results, the business analyst may ask a SQL developer to write a complex query for her that would extract the data from the OLTP system and put it in the format she wants. Such a query may look like:

```
SELECT      unit_price AS Price,
            SUM(quantity_sold) AS 'Quantity Sold',
            unit_price * SUM(quantity_sold) AS Revenue
FROM        sales, title
WHERE       title.ISBN = sales.ISBN
        AND title.topic = 'programming book'
GROUP BY    unit_price;
```

Needless to say, it's very time and resource consuming for the business analyst to have to follow this path whenever she wants to get some summaries and aggregations of data. Yet, this is a simplified version of what could happen in the real world. In production OLTP systems, such a query may be much larger, involving many table joins that affect the speed at which the results will return and affect the performance of other users of the database.

Dimensional Databases

The solution to the problems inherent in requesting complex queries from OLTP systems is to build a separate database that represents the business facts more accurately. The structure of this database will not be relational – instead, it will be **dimensional**.

The Fact Table

The central table of a dimensional database is called the **fact table**. Its rows are known as **facts** and they are **measures** of activities.

For example, we may build a `sales` fact table to record daily sales transactions of products offered by a given store. The `sales` table includes the facts of the business activities. `quantity` and `total_price` are the measures of facts in the `sales` table, just as they usually are in a typical relational database.

The Dimension Tables

Dimensions help put the facts in context and represent such things as time, product, customer, and location. The dimensions describe the data in the fact table. Continuing with our sales example, it would make sense to have time, store, customer, and product line dimensions.

The fact table, `sales`, captures transactions on a daily level for each store, for all customers, and for all books. This table, therefore, will grow to be very large. To improve the efficiency with which data is retrieved from the database, aggregates are pre-computed at different levels and stored in the database or in an optimized format, as we will see later in the chapter.

The tables linked to the fact table are called **dimension tables** and each represents a dimension. They are used to generate the aggregations from the fact table. For instance, we could find the total monthly sales of all books to all customers by all stores if we were to query the `sales` table grouping by month of the year. Alternatively, we could find the total sales by state at all times, for all customers, and for all books if we queried the `sales` table grouping on state. We can also have aggregations on a combination of the dimensions in the `sales` fact table. For example, we could find the total sales for a particular book category by state on a monthly basis for a certain type of customer by grouping on state and month and adding the appropriate criteria in the WHERE clause for the customer and book category.

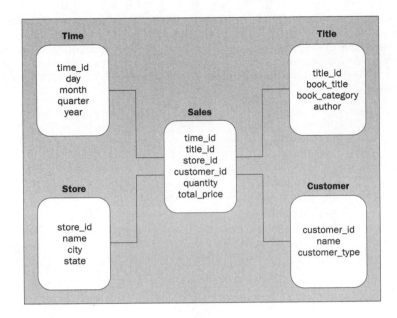

The Star and Snowflake Schemas

The database schema above, where there is a single fact table with a number of dimension tables linked directly to it, is an example of the **star schema**.

Another schema the dimensional database can follow is the **snowflake schema**. In a snowflake schema, multiple tables define one or more of the dimensions. What this means is that the snowflake schema is an extension of the star schema, where extra dimension tables are linked, not to the fact table directly, but to dimension tables.

Data Cubes

So far, we have seen that data is moved from the transactional system into the star or snowflake schemas, which represent the OLAP database.

The OLAP database is used as the basis for constructing what are known as OLAP cubes. To understand what OLAP cubes are, think of the data in the OLAP database as the transformed raw data for your analysis. In other words, if you look at the example in the previous section, you notice that the fact table includes the transaction information and pointers (foreign keys) to the dimensions along which we want to conduct our analysis.

The reports we generate based on the schema above are usually something like total sales for customers in a particular region over a particular period of time for a specific line of products. To obtain such a result, you have to aggregate the values in the fact table based on the dimensions you are using to construct the needed report. SQL Server's Analysis Services allows you to pre-calculate such results and store them in what is called an OLAP cube. Hence, the OLAP cube is a structure that stores the data aggregations from the OLAP database by combining all possible dimension values with the sales facts in the fact table. With this, retrieving the final reports becomes much more efficient, since no complex queries are evaluated at run time.

To visualize what a cube looks like, look at the figure below. The dimensions of the cube represent the dimensions of the fact table. Each cell in the cube represents a fact corresponding to a level of detail for the different dimensions of the cube. Although the graphical representation of the cube can only show three dimensions, a data cube can have up to 64 dimensions when using Analysis Services. The following figure shows a representation of a data cube for the sales table, with the store, title, and time dimensions shown:

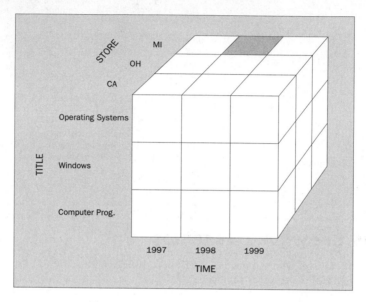

If you want to use this cube to find out the total sales for stores in Michigan during 1998 for the Operating Systems book category, you need to look at the shaded cell in the figure, which is the resulting cell from the intersection of those three dimensions. That cell should contain the quantity of books sold and the total price, which are the facts identified in the fact table.

Analysis Services allows you to build your cube from any source of data that has an OLE DB provider. This source can be a relational database in any database management system that has an ODBC driver (such as Oracle or Sybase SQL Server) or a native OLE DB provider (such as SQL Server, Oracle, or MS Access). The data source for the cube can also be a dimensional database, text files, or LDAP data source.

OLAP Storage Types

Based on the cube data storage method, three OLAP options are allowed by the decision support systems that ship with SQL Server 2000. These options are:

- ❑ Multi-dimensional OLAP (MOLAP)
- ❑ Relational OLAP (ROLAP)
- ❑ A hybrid of the previous two options (HOLAP)

Each of these options provides certain benefits, depending on the size of your database and how the data will be used.

MOLAP

MOLAP is a high-performance, multi-dimensional data storage format. The OLAP data supporting the cubes, along with the cubes themselves, are stored with this option on the OLAP server in multi-dimensional structures (OLAP structures). MOLAP gives the best query performance because it is specifically optimized for multi-dimensional data queries. Performance gains stem from the fact that the fact tables are compressed with this option and bitmap indexing is used for them.

Since MOLAP requires that all of the data be copied, converting its format appropriately to fit the multi-dimensional data store, MOLAP is appropriate for small to medium-sized data sets. Copying all of the data for such data sets would not require significant loading time nor would it utilize large amounts of disk space.

ROLAP

Relational OLAP storage keeps the OLAP data that feeds the cubes, along with the cube data (aggregations), in relational tables located in the relational database. In this case, a separate set of relational tables is used to store and reference aggregation data (cube data) in this OLAP system. These tables are not downloaded to the DSS server. The tables that hold the aggregations of the data are called **materialized views**. These tables store data aggregations as defined by the dimensions when the cube is created.

With this option, aggregation tables have fields for each dimension and measure. Each dimension column is indexed. A composite index is also created for all of the dimension fields. Due to its nature, ROLAP is ideal for large databases or legacy data that is infrequently queried.

HOLAP

A combination of MOLAP and ROLAP is also supported by the DSS server. This combination is referred to as HOLAP. With HOLAP, the OLAP data feeding the cubes is kept in its relational database tables similarly to ROLAP. Aggregations of the data (cube data) are performed and stored in a multi-dimensional format. An advantage of this system is that HOLAP provides connectivity to large data sets in relational tables while taking advantage of the faster performance of the multi-dimensional aggregation storage. A disadvantage of this option is that the amount of processing between the ROLAP and MOLAP systems may affect its efficiency.

Data Warehouse Concepts

Now we have seen what OLAP and dimensional databases are, let's define what a data warehouse is and how it can be built in SQL Server 2000.

A **data warehouse** is a data store that holds the data collected during the company's conduction of business over a long period of time. The data warehouse uses the OLTP systems that collect the data from everyday activities and transactions as its source. The data warehouse concept also includes the processes that scrub (see *Data Scrubbing* later in the chapter) and transform the data, making it ready for the data warehouse. It also includes the repository of summary tables and statistics, as well as the dimensional database. Finally, it also includes the tools needed by the business analysts to present and use the data. These tools include OLAP tools (such as Analysis Manager), as well as data mining and reporting tools. The figure overleaf depicts the conceptual structure and components of a data warehouse solution:

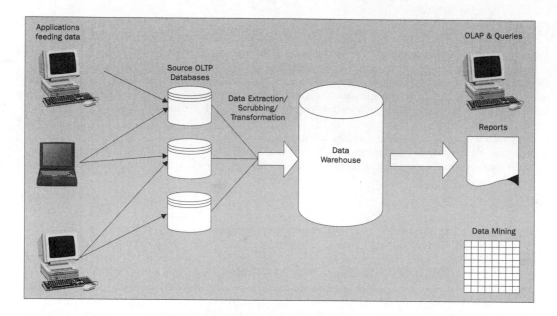

Data Warehouse Characteristics

A data warehouse is usually built to support decision-making and OLAP because it is designed with the following unique characteristics:

- **Consolidated and consistent data**: In a data warehouse, data is collected from different sources and consolidated and made consistent in many ways, including the use of naming conventions, measurements, physical attributes, and semantics. This is important because business analysts, accessing the data warehouse and using its data for their decision-making processes, have to use consistent standards. For example, date formats may all follow one standard, showing day, month, quarter, and year. Data should be stored in the data warehouse in a single, acceptable format. This allows the referencing, consolidating, and cross-referencing of data from numerous heterogeneous sources, such as legacy data on mainframes, data in spreadsheets, or even data from the Internet, giving the analysts a better understanding of the business.

- **Subject-oriented data**: The data warehouse organizes key business information from OLTP sources so that it is available for business analysis. In the process, it weeds out irrelevant data that might exist in the source data store. The organization takes place based on the subject of the data, separating customer information from product information, which may have been intermingled in the source data store.

- **Historical data**: Unlike OLTP systems, the data warehouse represents historical data. In other words, when you query the data warehouse, you use data that had been collected using the OLTP system in the past. The historical data could cover a long period of time compared to the OLTP system, which contains current data that accurately describes the present situation.

- **Read-only data**: After data has been moved to the data warehouse, you may not be able to change it unless the data was incorrect in the first place. The data in the data warehouse cannot be updated because it represents historical data, which cannot be changed. Deletes, inserts, and updates (other than those involved in the data loading process) are not applicable in a data warehouse. The only operations that occur in a data warehouse once it has been set up are loading of additional data and querying.

Data Marts

You may find out, after building your data warehouse, that many people in your organization only access certain portions of the data in the data warehouse. For instance, the sales managers may only access data relevant to their departments. Alternatively, they may only access data for the last year. In this case, it would be inefficient to have these people query the whole data warehouse to get their reports. Instead, it would be wise to partition the data warehouse in smaller units, called **data marts**, which are based on their business needs.

In addition, some people in your organization may want to be able to access the data in the data warehouse in remote areas far from the company buildings. For instance, a sales manager may want to access data about products and sales particular to his or her market area while on a sales venture. People such as this would benefit from a data mart, as they would be able to carry a section of the data warehouse on their laptop computers, allowing them to access the data they need at any time.

Of course, with data marts, the data should be kept in synch with the data warehouse at all times. This can be done in a variety of ways, such as using DTS, ActiveX scripting, or programs. The following diagram shows the structure of the data warehouse concept with data marts included:

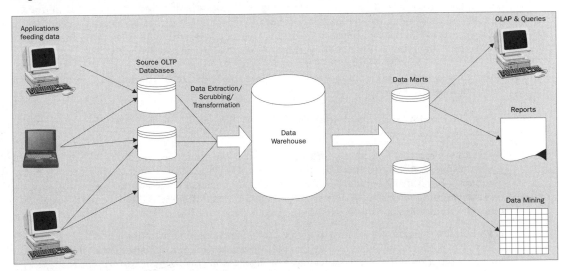

Data Transformation Services

Many organizations need to centralize data to improve decision-making. However, this data can be stored in a large variety of formats in a number of different sources. The row data that exists in these sources has to be reconciled and transformed in many cases before it can be stored in the data warehouse. Data Transformation Services (DTS), which we saw back in Chapter 22, conducts this function providing a means to move data from the source OLTP database to the destination data warehouse while validating, cleaning up, consolidating, and transforming the data when needed.

Data Validation

It is extremely important to conduct data validation before the data is extracted from the source OLTP databases and transferred to the destination data warehouse. If the data is not valid, the integrity of the business analysis conducted with it will be in question. For example, if one of the fields is a currency field, and the OLTP data sources exist in multiple countries around the globe, one has to make sure that the data in this currency field is always transferred in the currency of the destination data warehouse. If you transfer 500 French francs as 500 US dollars, you will be misrepresenting the data in the data warehouse, and any report that includes this value will not be valid.

Another thing you need to pay close attention to when validating the data is information related to geographical regions; you need to make sure that referenced cities have the right countries as the country field. Yet another example of validating data is making sure that the products (books in our example) are represented in a similar manner in all data sources.

Data Scrubbing

Data reconciliation has to take place between multiple sources feeding the same data warehouse. The reconciliation process is referred to as **data scrubbing**. For example, if a book is classified in one OLTP database under the *database* category, and in another OLTP database under a category called *database systems*, aggregations in the data warehouse involving this category will yield inaccurate results unless the two data sources have been reconciled during the data transformation process.

Data scrubbing can be achieved in different ways. These methods are beyond the scope of this book, but are mentioned briefly here:

❑ Using DTS import and export wizards to modify data as it is copied from the source to the destination data store.

❑ By writing a Microsoft ActiveX script or program. This may use the DTS API to connect to the data source and scrub the data. Such a technique is not the easiest for performing data scrubbing, but it provides a great deal of flexibility because it uses the power of the scripting or programming language to access the data, which can often provide a tremendous amount of control and manipulation across heterogeneous data sources.

❑ DTS Lookup provides the ability to perform queries using one or more named, parameterized query strings. This allows the building of custom transformation schemes to retrieve data from locations other than the immediate source or destination row being transformed.

Data Migration

Ideally, when migrating data from OLTP data sources to a data warehouse, data is copied to an intermediate database before it is finally copied to the data warehouse. This intermediate process is necessary to allow data scrubbing and validation to occur.

Special care should be taken when performing the data migration. The migration process should be performed during periods of low activity at the operational OLTP system to minimize the impact on the users of that system. If the migration is done from multiple data sources that are replicas or participate in replication processes, the migration should happen when all these sources are synchronized to make sure that consistent data is copied from these sources.

A commonly deployed strategy is to execute data migration procedures after the nightly database backups occur. This ensures that, if a migration procedure crashes the system, the backup was just performed.

Data Transformation

When you move the data from the source OLTP databases to the destination data warehouse, you may find yourself performing many transformations of existing data to make it more operational and practical when used in the destination warehouse. Below are examples of data transformations you may want to consider when moving data from the OLTP databases to the data warehouse:

❑　You may break a column into multiple columns, such as dividing a date or timestamp field into its components of day, month, quarter, and year.

❑　You may also find yourself having to calculate new fields based on the values in source fields, such as creating a `total_price` field in the destination data warehouse, which is a result of multiplying the `unit_price` by the `quantity_sold` fields in the source database.

❑　You may need to merge separate fields into one field, such as merging the `first_name` and `last_name` fields in the source database in one `name` column in the destination data warehouse.

❑　You may also want to map data from one representation to another, such as translation of code to literal values and converting values from decimal numerical values (1, 2, 3, etc.) to Roman numerals (I, II, III, etc.).

DTS Components

DTS includes the import/export wizard and COM programming interfaces that allow the creation of custom import/export and transformation applications. A detailed discussion of these topics is presented in Chapters 22 and 31.

Meta-data and the Repository

Meta-data is, by definition, data about data. In other words, the information about the way storage is structured in the data warehouse, OLAP, and DTS services is all kept as meta-data, which is stored in the Microsoft Repository. The repository is built to maintain such technical information about the data sources involved with the services mentioned above.

Repository information is stored by default in the SQL Server `msdb` database. The repository is the preferred means of storing DTS packages in a data warehousing scenario because it is the only method of providing data lineage for packages.

Access to the repository is possible through the interfaces exposed by the Analysis Manager's graphical user interface (GUI) and programming interfaces (APIs) that ship with SQL Server 2000 as part of the Meta Data Services. These APIs are known as the **Repository API**. Meta-data can also be accessed through the **Decision Support Objects** (**DSO**), and through programs that use interfaces to the repository. Unless you are an experienced programmer, Microsoft recommends only using the Repository API, DSO, or Analysis Manager's GUI to access the meta-data. It can be risky and could be damaging to access the repository database directly, because incorrect changes to the repository data may affect the whole SQL Server installation. In addition, the repository is subject to change in new releases, which may render any programs you build to access the repository directly unusable.

Note that multiple repositories can exist in a single SQL Server installation. However, DTS supports only a single repository database per server in the Enterprise Manager tree.

Data Mining Models

As I mentioned earlier in the chapter, SQL Server 2000 brings new support for data mining. This is evident in extensions made to the graphical tool that comes with Analysis Services, the Analysis Manager (the OLAP Manager in the previous release of SQL Server), in extensions to some of the programming object models and tools, such as decision support objects (DSO) and multidimensional expressions language (MDX), and extensions to the PivotTable service.

A **data mining model** is a virtual structure that stores the data used by the data mining extensions in SQL Server. The data in this model is stored in a similar fashion to a database, except that instead of storing the raw data, rules and patterns about the data are stored in the model. Such rules and patterns are interpretations of the multidimensional data in the form of statistical information, and are used to predict future directions and changes to certain aspects of such data. Datasets in the data mining models are referred to as **case sets**.

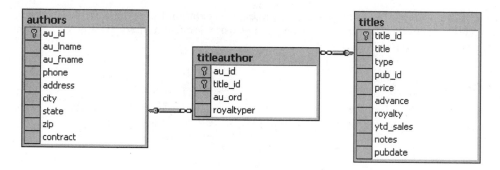

To understand this better, look at the example shown in the previous diagram, which is derived from the sample `pubs` database that ships with SQL Server. It is clear that an author can have multiple books and a single book can be written by multiple authors. Let's take the case where an author can have multiple books published. Each author record in the `authors` table and its corresponding title record in the `titles` table is treated as a **case** in the data mining model. Hence, the case is represented in one table in the model. In this table, you will see columns relating to the author and one column that represents the information relating to the books that the author has published. Each row in the model table represents a case, and a collection of rows relating to the same author is called a case set:

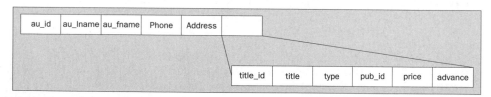

In the figure above, you will notice that the three tables are flattened into one table and the records are looked at from a different perspective. You can, for instance, change the way you look at the cases by taking each book title and the associated authors who worked on it instead. That would give you a different insight into the data in question, especially if you added fields that represent other attributes of the author and the book that you can use in your analysis, such as author age, marital status, etc.

Data Mining Algorithms

The data mining algorithms are logical representations that determine how to analyze the cases in a data mining model. SQL Server 2000 comes with support for two widely used data mining algorithms, decision trees and data clustering.

Decision Trees

Decision trees have been used for a long time to find out a series of characteristics or rules and the effects of these rules on a target variable. For example, if you want to find out the characteristics of the person who is most likely to respond to a direct mail, you may translate these characteristics into a set of rules.

Let's say, for example, that you are designing a direct mail campaign to introduce a new bookstore to an area and induce more book sales. Knowing who is most likely to respond to the direct mail will help build a more focused campaign and cut down the costs associated with it. To start the campaign, you would first analyze combinations of demographic variables distinguishing potential responders. The figure below shows the decision tree you would follow to determine who would be most likely to respond to your direct mail:

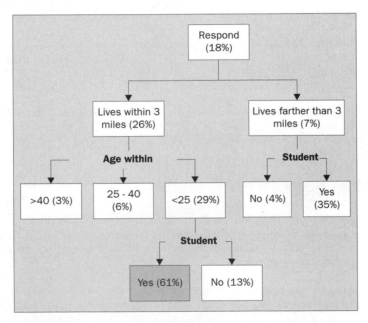

In the figure above, you will notice that the decision tree helps us segment the potential recipients of the mail promotion into groups and helps us find out which of these groups or segments is most likely to respond to our campaign. In the case above, 18% of the people who received our promotion responded. However, 26% of those who live within 3 miles of the new bookstore responded, as opposed to only 7% of those living further than 3 miles away. Continuing with the segmentation process, we find out that the people who would most likely respond to our campaign are students below 25 years of age who live within 3 miles of the new bookstore.

Clustering

Clustering is a technique that aims at data reduction. With clustering, data is grouped based on similar characteristics. The result of this technique is data segments with each segment having members similar in certain characteristics. This technique is useful for finding customer segments based on characteristics such as demographic and financial information or purchase behavior.

For example, suppose a bookstore wants to find segments of customers based on their education. A cluster analysis gave three groups of customers as shown in the diagram below. The three groups are: people with post-graduate degrees, people with college degrees, and people with high school degrees. After identifying the three groups, characteristics of each group are added, such as marital status, any children, frequently go to public libraries, last book purchased, etc. These characteristics are then combined with the groupings to find out their distribution among the group:

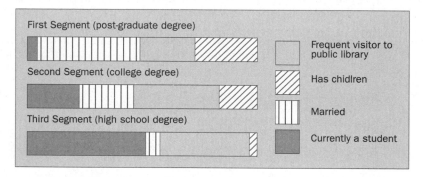

The figure above clearly shows that the first segment has more married people and people with children (who they may bring to the bookstore) than the other two segments. The third segment includes the highest percentage of students compared with the other two segments.

Analysis Manager

The **Analysis Manager** is installed separately from the SQL Server CD ROM after installing SQL Server. This tool is a graphical user interface that allows the user to build an OLAP solution based on existing data sources. This section will demonstrate how this tool can be used while presenting an OLAP solution example at the same time.

To run Analysis Manager, you need to select the Microsoft SQL Server group from the Start | Programs menu, then select Analysis Services | Analysis Manager. You'll see the following screen:

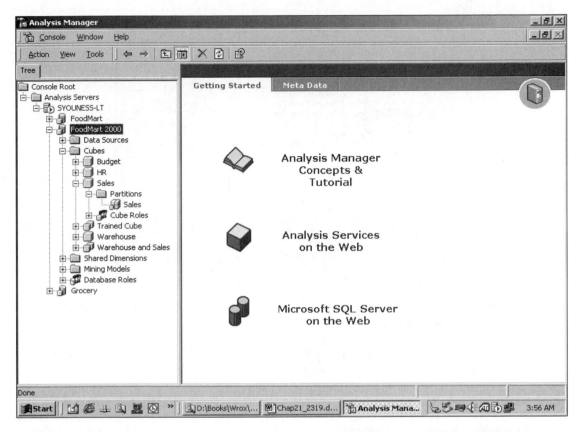

The Analysis Manager is a snap-in of the Microsoft Management Console. Like the SQL Server Enterprise Manager, it consists of two panes. The left pane contains a tree structure that depicts the available OLAP servers, databases, cubes, etc. The right pane contains details of the selected items in the left pane, whenever such details are available. The Analysis Manager allows you to manage databases, data sources, cubes, dimensions, measures, etc.

Creating an OLAP Solution

In this section, we will look at an example OLAP database that ships with SQL Server 2000 Analysis Services. This database is already full of data that can be used to show how the different OLAP and data warehouse tools work together. The database is called FoodMart 2000 and contains information about the sales and inventory of a national food chain. The database is an Access database that is installed when you install the OLAP server, and its default location is C:\Program Files\Microsoft Analysis Services\Samples\FoodMart.mdb.

An ODBC Data Source Name (DSN) is also created for this database at the time you install the Analysis Services. The name of the DSN is also FoodMart 2000. To verify that this DSN exists, select the ODBC32 applet from the Control Panel if you are running Windows 9x, Windows Me, or Windows NT, or select Data Sources (ODBC) from the Control Panel | Administrative Tools menu if you are running Windows 2000. Then click on the System DSN tab, and you'll see a screen similar to this:

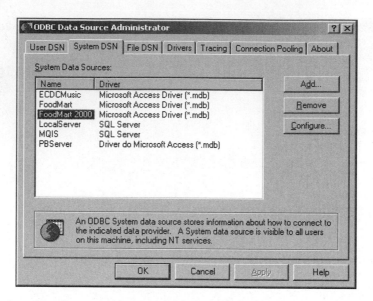

The goal here is to present the sales data for the stores, broken down by region, product, date, and customer for the year 1998.

> *If you want to look at the database in Microsoft Access, you need to close the Analysis Manager first because, when it is open, it accesses the* `FoodMart` *database in an exclusive mode.*

Let's now examine the database tables that we will need for our example. We will have a fact table for the year 1998 linked to the dimension tables: `product`, `store`, `time_by_day`, and `customer`. The `product` table is also linked to a `product_class` table.

The fact table (`sales_fact_1998`) is the main table with which we need to concern ourselves. This table contains the fields that link it to the dimension tables mentioned above, as well as the measures we need to find eventually. These measures are the `store_sales`, `store_cost`, and `unit_sale`. The screenshot opposite shows the database schema that we will need to use:

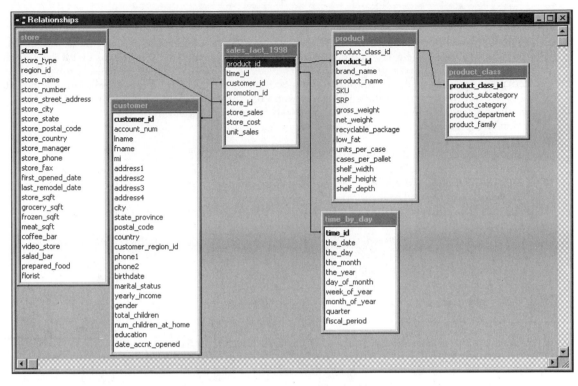

The links that the fact table has to the dimension tables allow us to produce the aggregations we want, rolling up the data to any level of these dimensions, as we shall see later in the chapter.

Before we move to the next section, notice that in the `customer` dimension table, there is no field that holds the customer name. Instead, there is a field for first name (fname), a field for middle initial (mi), and a field for last name (lname). It would be better to combine the fname and lname fields in one field called `cust_name`. This makes it easier to define the levels of the dimension later on country, state, city, and name. To do this, we will run the following two queries in the `FoodMart` database in Access (using **SQL View** mode):

```
/* To add the new field, run the following query */
ALTER TABLE customer ADD cust_name text(80);
```

```
/* To update the name column, run the next query */
UPDATE customer SET customer.cust_name = [fname] & ' ' & [lname];
```

Once you have run the queries, you will see that a new field called `cust_name` has been created and populated by concatenating the fname and lname fields.

How Did We Get to this Schema?

You may be wondering how the schema shown above was reached. It is most likely that the original production database was a relational database in the third normal form. This means that it is likely that the store table did not exist in this structure. The store.store_manager field was probably called store_manager_id originally, and linked to a table that held the employee information, maybe called employee. Information about the employees would be stored in such a table, including their titles. When the store table linked to the employee table, it only needed to have the employee_id field as a foreign key pointing to the primary key in the employee table.

Also in the same table are the fields: grocery_sqft, frozen_sqft, and meat_sqft. These fields were probably in a middle table between the store table and another table, perhaps called departments. The relationship between the store table and the departments table is a many-to-many relationship. A middle table would be used to transform the many-to-many relationship into two one-to-many relationships. The structure of the middle table and its relationships might have looked like this:

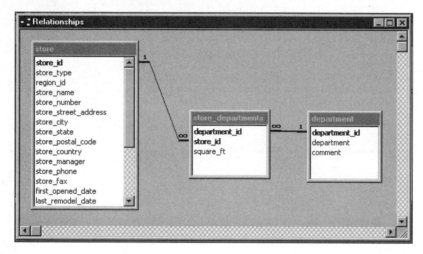

The kind of de-normalization in this particular case is described as de-normalization by flattening the data structures.

In summary, you can analyze the remaining dimension tables and normalize them to reach what could be the original relational database used in the transactional system. The resulting database would represent the production database responsible for feeding the data warehouse.

Creating the OLAP Database in the Analysis Manager

To create the database we will be using, right-click the analysis server name (which happens to be the same name as your machine) in the left pane of the Analysis Manager, and select New Database. Add the following information:

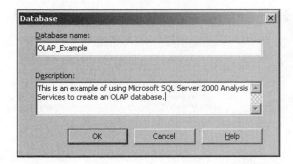

The new database will appear in the tree-view pane of the Analysis Manager. The database will have no cubes yet, no dimensions, no measures, etc. This will become apparent as you expand the tree view for the database by clicking on the + signs that correspond to it and its components:

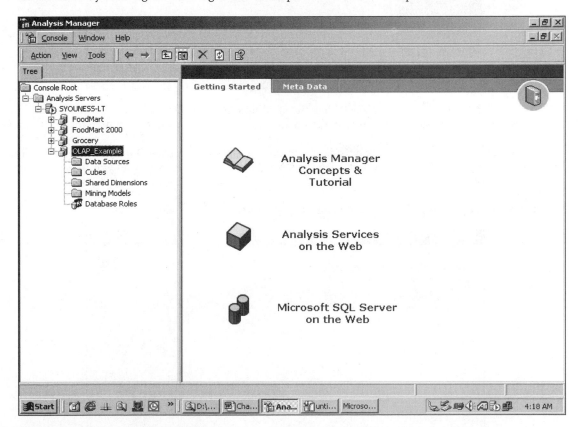

Adding the Data Sales Cube

To add the first data cube in the database we just created, you need to right-click on the Cubes item in the left pane underneath the OLAP_Example database we have just created, and select New Cube from the context-sensitive menu. You will be presented with a submenu that has two commands: Wizard and Editor. Select Wizard, and you will be presented with the first screen of the Cube Wizard:

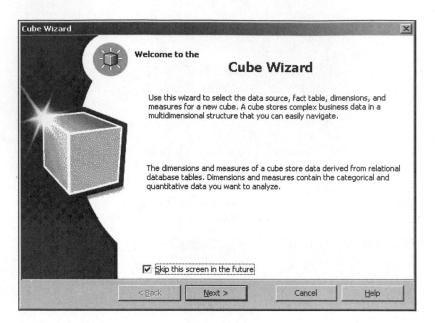

On the first screen of the Cube Wizard, click the Next button. The following screen will allow you to add a new data source to use for building the data cube, or use an existing data source for this purpose.

You can also add new data sources outside this wizard by right-clicking the Data Sources item in the left pane of the Analysis Manager and selecting New Data Source. This will lead you directly to the Data Link Properties screen.

As for our example, click the New Data Source button on the wizard screen:

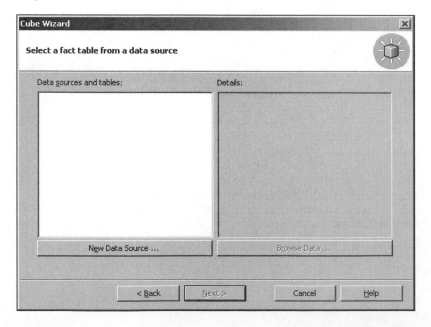

The Data Link Properties dialog will appear, allowing you to set up a data link using an OLE DB provider you have selected from the list. Select the Microsoft JET 4.0 OLE DB Provider, and click the Next button:

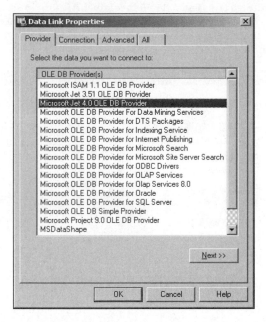

When you do so, you will be presented with the same dialog set to the Connection tab. This tab allows you to specify the properties of the connection or data link, such as the database name, user name, and password. Once you have connected to FoodMart.mdb, test the connection by clicking on the Test Connection button. This will ensure that the database server is up and running, that the database name is valid, and that the user name and password are also valid:

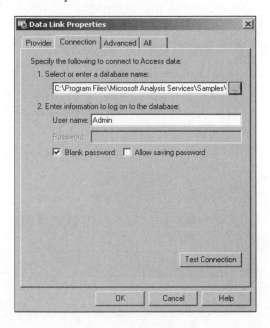

Click **OK** after testing the connection, and then select the newly added data source on the Cube Wizard screen, then click the + sign next to it to expand it. This will show you all the tables available from the selected database. Select the `sales_fact_1998` fact table. As you do so, you will notice that the right side of the wizard screen shows the fields existing in the selected fact table. You will also see a button called **Browse Data**. Clicking this button will actually bring a spreadsheet showing the data in your fact table. You can navigate through the records at this point.

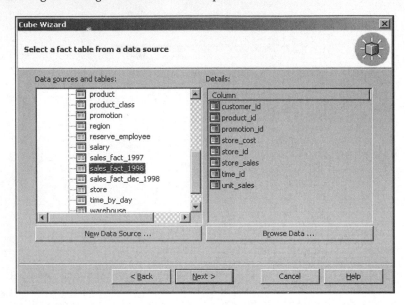

However, let's proceed with the Cube Wizard for now. Click the **Next** button. The next screen will allow you to define your measures. On the left-hand side of the screen there is a list of available columns in the fact table. Select the store_cost, store_sales, and unit_sales fields individually, double-clicking each one to transfer it to the right-hand side list, the **Cube measures** list:

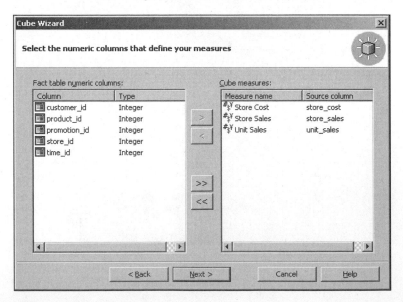

Click the Next button. The next screen will allow you to establish the cube dimensions. When you create dimensions for a cube, you have the option of making each dimension a shared dimension. Since the database has just been created, there are no dimensions defined in it yet, and the list of shared dimensions is empty. Therefore, let's create new dimensions to use for our cube. Click on the New Dimension button to launch the Dimension Wizard:

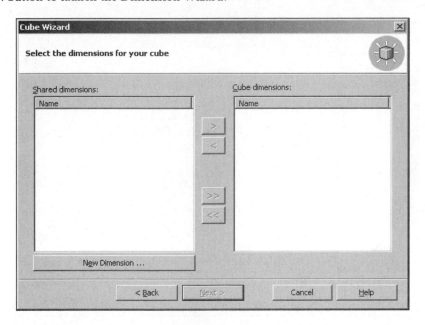

Hit Next to skip the Welcome Screen (which isn't shown here). The next screen allows you to specify one of five options: Star Schema, Snowflake Schema, Parent-Child, Virtual Dimension, Mining Model. Let's select the first Star Schema option, and click the Next button:

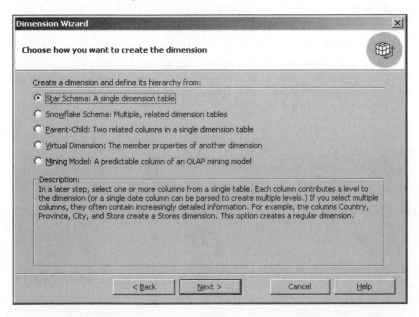

The next screen in the Dimension Wizard allows you to select the dimension table. A list on the left-hand side shows all the available tables from which you can pick. Once a table is selected, a list on the right-hand side shows the fields in the selected table. Similar to the fact table, a Browse Data button allows you to browse the data in the selected dimension table in a spreadsheet format when you click it. For our example, select the customer table, and click the Next button:

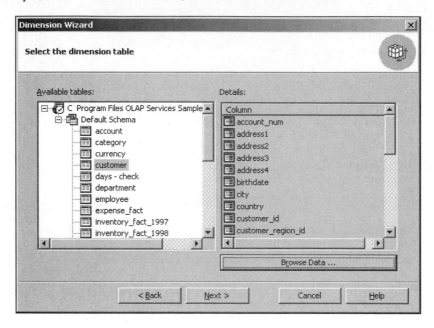

The next screen asks you whether the dimension you selected is a time or a standard dimension. Select Standard dimension and click the Next button:

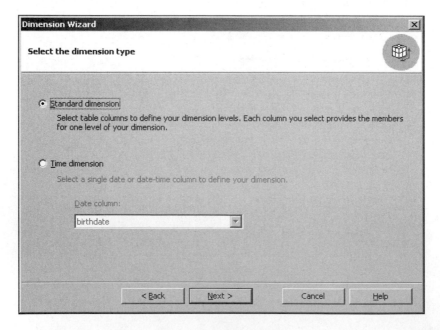

The next screen allows you to select the fields you want to use for your dimension levels. The fields in the customer table are presented on the left-hand list. Select the country, state_province, city, and cust_name fields, double-clicking on them individually to transfer them to the Dimension levels list on the right-hand side. Note that the cust_name field is the one that we added prior to creating our OLAP database and running the Cube Wizard. It makes more sense to select this field for our dimension level than selecting any of the two fields used to create it, namely fname and lname:

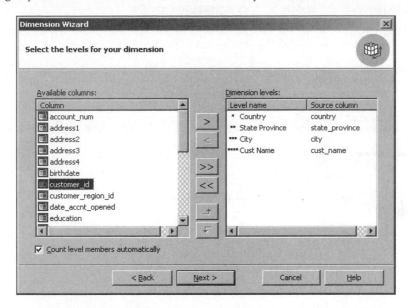

Click Next and the following screen shows you the member keys for your dimensions. You may change these fields as you see fit. You only need to change the column if you suspect that the current default value does not make the record unique. Leave the selections as they are and click the Next button:

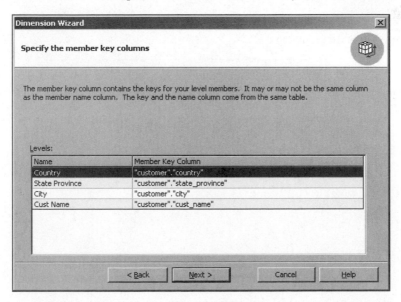

The next screen will present you with three advanced options that you can specify through the wizard if you choose to. The options are:

❑ **Changing dimension:** This option allows you to specify that the dimension is a dynamically changing dimension. In other words, the dimension data can be changed and the dimension processed without the need to process the whole cube. Cube processing is the process that leads to populating the cube with its aggregation data.

❑ **Ordering and uniqueness of members:** This option specifies the order and sorting properties of the dimensions, as well as the uniqueness of the level keys and names.

❑ **Storage mode and member groups:** This option allows you to specify in which mode the dimension data is stored – in multidimensional structures (MOLAP) or in relational tables (ROLAP).

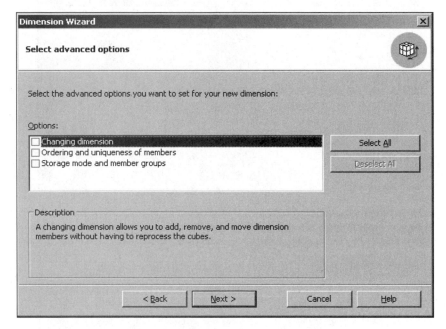

Selecting the third checkbox in the screenshot above leads us to the next screen. The checkbox in the screenshot opposite, **Create member groups for the lowest level**, is a new feature in Analysis Services that allows automatic creation of a grouping level if the lowest level of the dimension contains more than 64,000 members. We'll leave this unchecked, and then click **Next**:

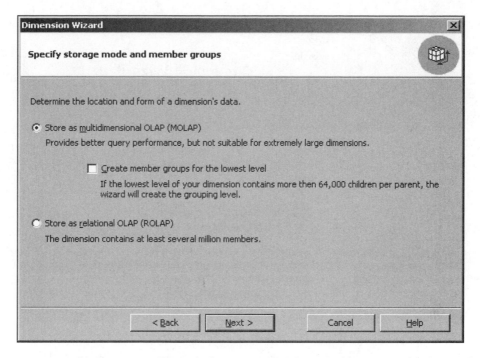

The next screen in the Dimension Wizard, shown overleaf, lets us select a name for the newly created dimension. Let's call it Customer. Notice how a small window within the screen allows you to preview the data in the customer table in terms of the levels you selected. If you click the + signs to expand the view, you can clearly see the hierarchy that follows the selected levels for the dimension, starting with the country at the top level, followed by the state/province, then city, and then name at the lowest level. This view shows you that three countries exist in the customer dimension table and that California is one of the US states for which there is data in the table. The cities within California that have related customers are shown. When you select one of these cities, you can see a list of the customers whose addresses are in that city.

Please note the checkbox that asks you whether you want to Share this dimension with other cubes in the database. Usually you should make sure it is checked, because it is always a good idea to share these dimensions, rather than re-inventing the wheel every time you need to create a similar dimension (for our example, we will keep this checkbox unchecked because there is already a shared dimension named customer). One new feature is that, using this screen of the wizard, you can now specify hierarchies in the dimension. This is done by checking the Create a hierarchy of a dimension checkbox. This feature comes in handy for dimensions that have multiple hierarchies, such as the time dimension.

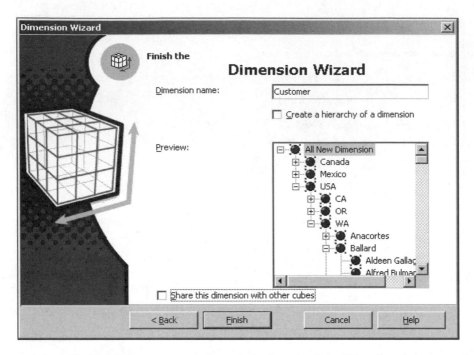

When you click on the Finish button, you are brought back to the Cube Wizard, at the screen where you started the Dimension Wizard, with the new dimension already selected in the right-hand list of dimensions:

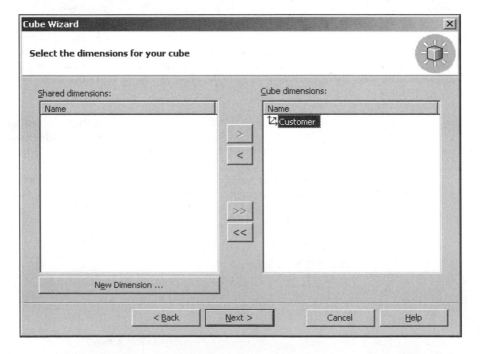

Follow the same steps we have just done to create the store dimension. Make sure you select the following levels for the store dimension: store_country, store_state, store_city, and store_name.

Creating the time dimension is a little different in the Dimension Wizard. From the Select the dimension table screen, select the time_by_day table from the Available tables list to be the table for the time dimension, and click the Next button:

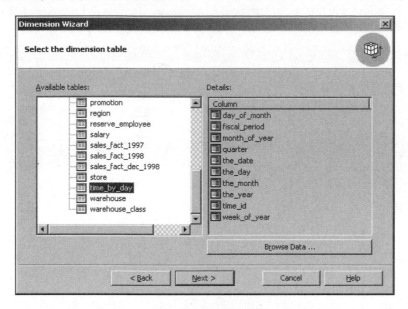

The screen asking you whether this is a time dimension or a standard dimension will pop up. Select the Time dimension radio button, and make sure the date-formatted column, the_date, is selected in the Date column drop-down list. Then click the Next button:

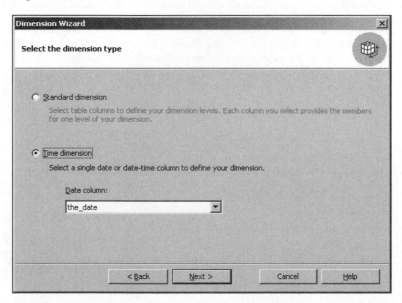

The next screen allows you to define the time dimension levels. From the Select time levels drop-down list, select Year, Quarter, Month, Day. A list below the drop-down list will then show you the dimension structure.

Two drop-down lists called Year starts on allow you to specify the month and day of the start of the fiscal year, in case they are different from the calendar year. This is a great feature. Just imagine how much work this feature will save you compared to having to program this yourself. Let's select the defaults and click the Next button:

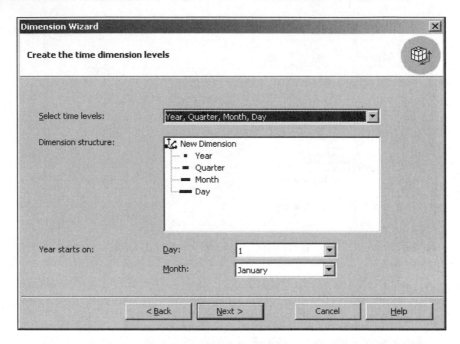

Click Next again at the Select advanced options screen. Finally, name the dimension as the time dimension, and continue until you get back to the Cube Wizard screen that launched the Dimension Wizard. Once there, you should see three dimensions selected in the Cube dimensions list.

Launch the Dimension Wizard one last time to create the product dimension. On the first screen of the Dimension Wizard, select Snowflake Schema: Multiple, related dimension tables, because the levels we will be selecting exist in two tables, product and product_class:

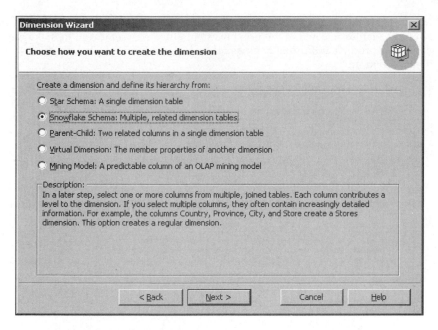

This is a good example of the snowflake schema because we have the `product_class` dimension indirectly linked to the fact table. Clicking the Next button after you make the selection mentioned above will lead you to the following screen:

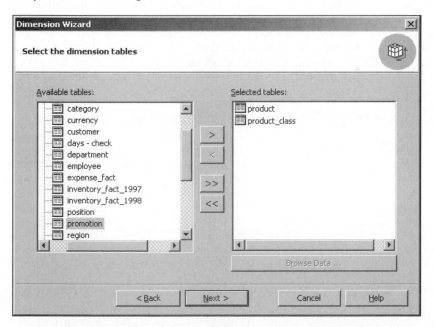

After selecting the product and product_class tables from the Available tables list, click on the Next button.

At this point, you will be presented with the following screen. This allows you to specify and/or modify the join between the tables selected in the previous step. Since we don't need to make any changes to the join between the product and product_class tables (they're joined on the product_class_id field), let's click the Next button:

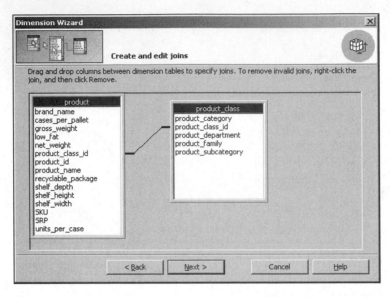

The next screen will allow you to specify the levels of the product dimension. These levels are: Product Family, Product Department, Product Category, Product Subcategory, Brand Name, and Product Name. The number of blue dots shown to the left of the selected levels in the Dimension levels list indicates the ordinal number for the corresponding level. For our example, the first level is the Product Family whereas the fifth level is the Brand Name. Click the Next button until you get to the screen where you can name the dimension as product, and proceed with creating the dimension until you reach the Cube Wizard again:

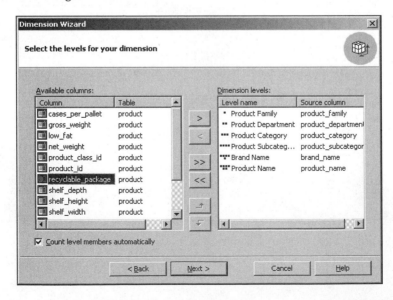

Continue with the Cube Wizard until you get to the screen where you can name your cube. Let's name it Sales_1998. Notice the small window on this screen that shows you the structure of the newly created cube. You can expand and collapse the view to make sure you did everything correctly:

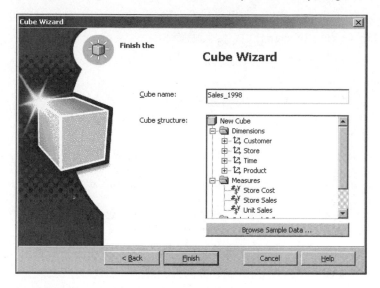

When you click the Finish button on the Cube Wizard screen, you get the Cube Editor screen:

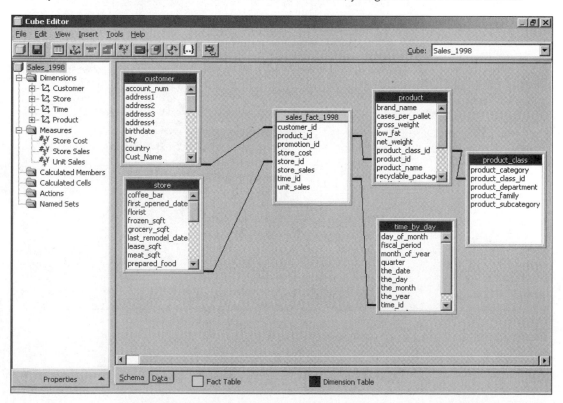

As the name implies, this editor can be used for many useful tasks, such as:

- ❑ Modifying the cube structure
- ❑ Designing the cube storage (we will see how this is done in the next section)
- ❑ Validating the cube schema
- ❑ Optimizing the cube schema
- ❑ Managing the cube roles
- ❑ Processing the cube so that we can browse its data

Designing Cube Storage

After the cube has been created, we need to design its storage. Will the cube data be kept in a new dimensional database, stored in the original OLTP database, or in both databases? These three options correspond to whether we want to use MOLAP or ROLAP storage, or a hybrid of the two, HOLAP.

For the purpose of our example, we will be using MOLAP storage to optimize query performance. To design the storage, select Tools | Design Storage from the Cube Editor menu.

This will start the Storage Design Wizard. Skip the first screen and select the MOLAP option in the next screen, as shown below:

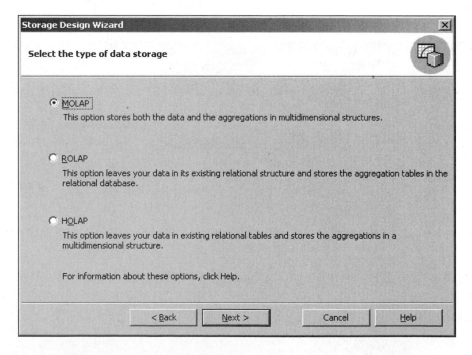

The following screen will allow you to set the aggregation options. These options include:

❑ **Estimated storage reaches X MB**: With this option, you can limit the amount of disk space used to store the aggregation results. This option is useful if you have limited disk space, but it may affect query performance if not all possible aggregations are saved on disk. With this option, SQL Server's OLAP server will choose which aggregates will be stored.

❑ **Performance gain reaches X %**: This means that you are allowing as much disk space as needed to store aggregations, until performance gains due to the aggregation storage reaches x% of the original performance with no storage.

❑ **Until I click Stop**: This option allows you to manually set the points that disk storage and performance gains can reach. You do so by watching the **Performance vs. Size** graph and clicking when you see a point that you think would be optimal for you.

Set the estimated storage to 100 MB, click the Start button, and watch the **Performance vs. Size** graph change. At the bottom of the graph, the number of aggregations, the storage needed for them, and the performance gains are indicated. At the end of the run, you will notice that, in our case, the maximum number of aggregations is 332. The needed disk space is 44.2 MB. At this point, we will get 100% performance gains. Based on this, let's select the default option and click the **Next** button:

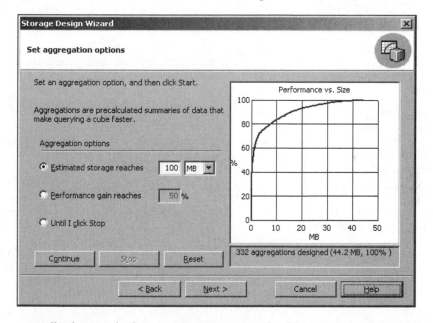

The next screen will ask you whether you want to process the data, or just save the storage design (and process the aggregations later). Processing the data actually creates and stores the aggregations for you. Let's select **Process now**, and click **Finish** to process the data.

While processing the data, the Wizard will show you a screen that includes information on the progress of the operation:

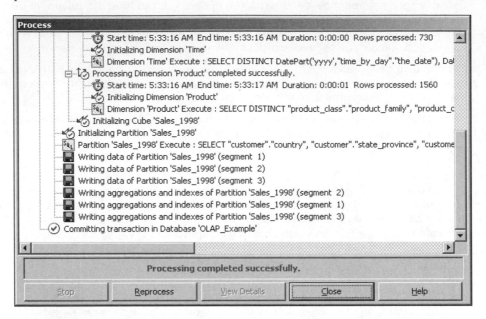

Cube Security

Since the data presented by the cube could be sensitive historical data about the performance of your company, you may want to set up a security scheme to control who can access the cube and use it, and who cannot do so. Cube security is tightly integrated with Windows NT/2000 security. In Analysis Services 2000, you can specify security down to the cell level, which is a great improvement over the previous version, which allowed you to specify security on the cube level.

To set up security for the cube you have just created, you need to create a **role**. The role will have certain access privileges to the cube. The role will then be assigned to groups of Windows NT users, setting permissions for them accordingly.

Let's create a new role. To do so, right-click on the Cube Roles node in the Analysis Manager, by expanding the Cubes node and the Sales_1998 node. Select Manage Roles. This will launch a Cube Role Manager window:

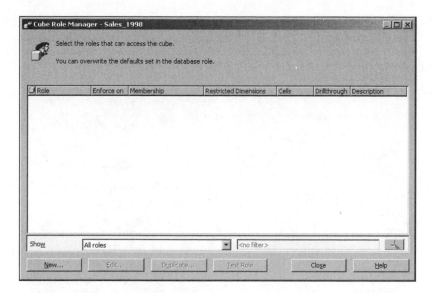

Click on the New button. In the next screen, you can click the Add button on the Membership tab to add Windows NT/2000 users and/or groups. Let's add the Everyone group as shown below:

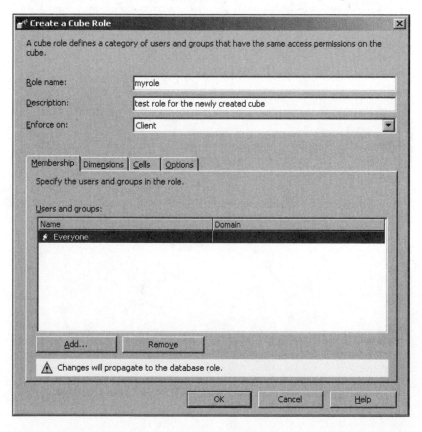

Now we can grant privileges to the new role at virtually any level or piece of data in the cube. For instance, select the Dimensions tab and select the Customer dimension. In the Rule drop-down, you can elect to have unrestricted access, fully restricted access, or custom. Select Custom and click the ellipsis (...) button in the Custom Settings column:

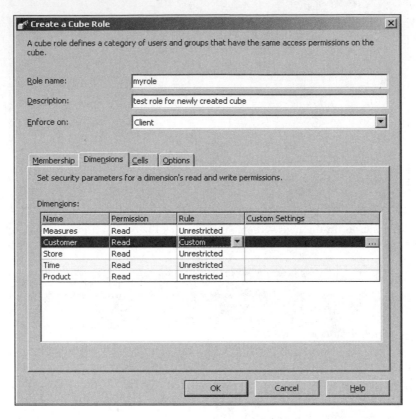

This will present you with a Custom Dimension Security dialog box. In the Members pane, you can expand the hierarchy to show the countries level. Make sure you select only the USA. This will ensure that this role will have access to only USA data in the customer dimension. This is a really powerful feature that allows you to restrict the users' access to permitted data:

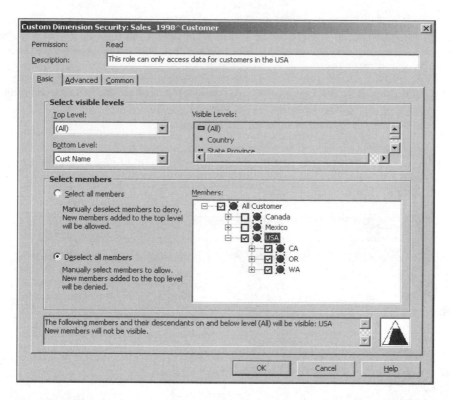

Browsing the Cube Data

Now the Sales_1998 cube has been created, its storage set up, and security taken care of, let's browse the data in it so we can see how the aggregations have been done.

Right-click the Sales_1998 cube from the Analysis Manager's tree view menu, and click Browse Data. The following dialog will be shown:

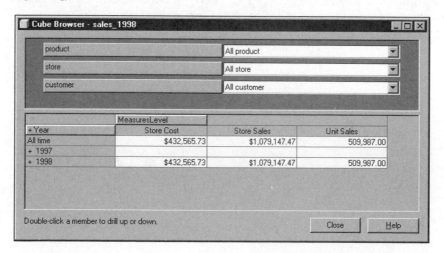

This dialog shows you a spreadsheet with the values of the measure in which we are interested. The left column of the spreadsheet represents one of the dimensions (time in this case) and, in the top pane, you can see the remaining dimensions created for the sales_1998 cube. These dimensions are product, store, and customer.

You can drag and drop these dimensions the way you like onto the spreadsheet to show them on the left, and to show how the aggregations are taking place.

Since the fact table in our example stores data for 1998 only, we can see that the measures for 1997 are blank.

To see the measure values by quarter of 1998, for food products sold to customers in stores in Los Angeles, California, you need to make the selections shown in the drop-down lists and in the time dimension column as shown:

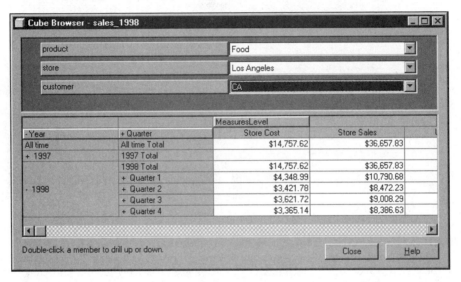

You can also browse data by quarter, by product family, and store country by dragging the **product and store** dimensions to the spreadsheet and expanding them appropriately, as shown:

Cube Browser - sales_1998

customer | CA

-Year	+Quarter	+Product Family	+Store Country	MeasuresLevel Store Cost	Store Sales	Unit Sales
+1998	1998 Total	All product	+USA	$61,936.33	$154,513.49	73,017.00
			All store	$5,523.57	$13,755.12	6,871.00
		+Drink	+Canada			
			+Mexico			
			+USA	$5,523.57	$13,755.12	6,871.00
			All store	$44,676.82	$111,467.82	52,515.00
		+Food	+Canada			
			+Mexico			
			+USA	$44,676.82	$111,467.82	52,515.00
			All store	$11,735.95	$29,290.55	13,631.00
		+Non-Consumable	+Canada			
			+Mexico			
			+USA	$11,735.95	$29,290.55	13,631.00
-1998	+Quarter 1	All product	All store	$17,007.27	$42,396.97	19,969.00
			+Canada			
			+Mexico			
			+USA	$17,007.27	$42,396.97	19,969.00
		+Drink	All store	$1,506.30	$3,767.55	1,855.00
			+Canada			
			+Mexico			
			+USA	$1,506.30	$3,767.55	1,855.00
		+Food	All store	$12,282.25	$30,594.05	14,383.00
			+Canada			
			+Mexico			
			+USA	$12,282.25	$30,594.05	14,383.00
		+Non-Consumable	All store	$3,218.73	$8,035.37	3,731.00
			+Canada			
			+Mexico			
			+USA	$3,218.73	$8,035.37	3,731.00
	+Quarter 2	All product	All store	$14,879.27	$37,028.41	17,546.00
			+Canada			
			+Mexico			
			+USA	$14,879.27	$37,028.41	17,546.00
		+Drink	All store	$1,400.16	$3,464.49	1,695.00
			+Canada			
			+Mexico			

Double-click a member to drill up or down.

Close | Help

Building a Data Mining Model

This section will show you how to build a data mining model using the Analysis Manager. In this example, we will use the Microsoft Decision Tree algorithm to build the data model. The model will be based on the customer dimension and the data in that dimension will be used to "train" the model. Model training is the process through which existing data in the tables feeding the model is used to create the cases needed by the model. For example, the data in the customer dimension – including income, marital status, etc. – is used to create cases that will be used as the data for the mining model.

To build our first data mining model, we will use the Sales cube that ships as part of the Analysis Services sample OLAP application, FoodMart 2000. This cube is rich in many components and elements that we can utilize in our analysis. It has many more dimensions than the cube we built in this chapter, and it has more elements – such as member properties – that we can use to evaluate our goal.

Right-click the Mining Models item in the tree pane of the Analysis Manager for the FoodMart 2000 database. Select New Mining Model from the context-sensitive menu. This will launch the Mining Model wizard:

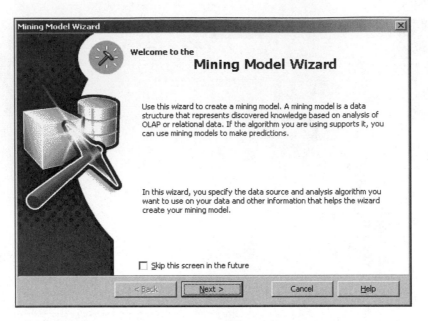

Click the Next button. This will show you a screen with a choice between using OLAP data or relational data for the data mining model. Analysis Services allows you to build your model based on either of these data models. The wizard screens will be different based on your selection in this page. However, we will not go into such depth in this chapter and, for our purposes, select OLAP data and click Next:

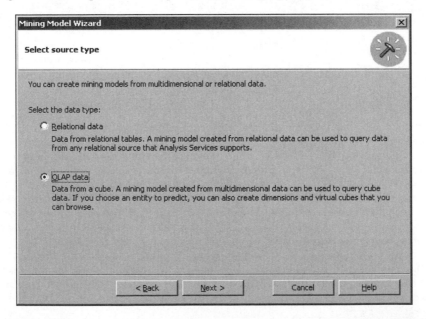

The next screen will allow us to select the cube that contains the OLAP data. Select the Sales cube in the Cube list. You will see that the dimensions of the Sales cube are listed on the right-hand side in the Dimensions list. Click Next to go to the next screen:

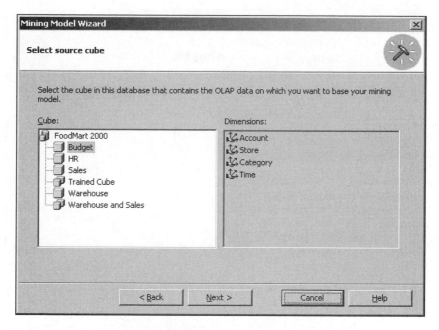

The next screen will allow us to select the data mining algorithm. The two choices are Microsoft Decision Trees and Microsoft Clustering. We have already explained what these two algorithms are earlier in the chapter. Select Microsoft Decision Trees and click Next:

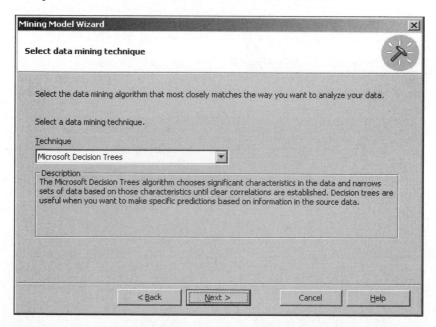

The next screen will allow you to select the dimension and level of the dimension at which you want to conduct your analysis. Select the Customers dimension and the Name level:

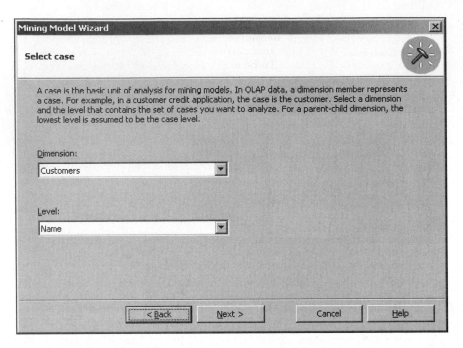

The next screen in the wizard allows you to specify the predictable entity. This entity can be one of three values: a measure, a member property, or a member in another dimension. A **member property** is a custom property that you can set for a particular level in your dimension. For instance, for the Name level in the customer dimension, you can set member properties that describe the customer's gender, martial status, or education level. Select the Store Sales measure and click Next:

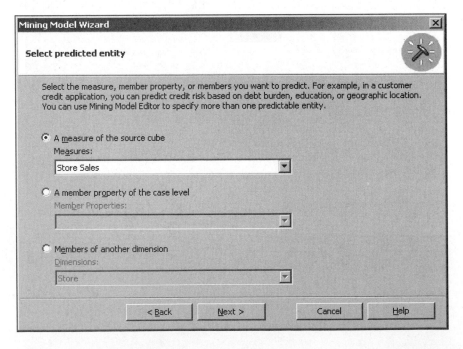

The next screen is very important. It allows us to select the training data for our model. Make sure you select the Name level of the customer dimension, and the member properties that you want to use in your model. Also, select other dimensions that correspond to some of the member properties on the Name level of the Customers dimension. To be exact, make sure you select the Education Level, Gender, and Marital Status dimensions:

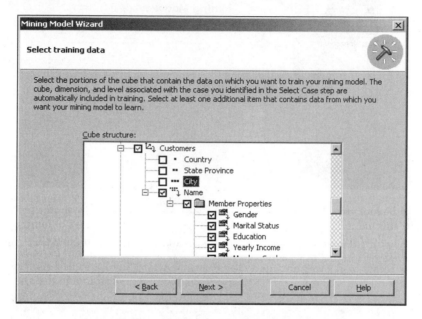

The next screen gives us the option to create a new dimension based on the model. Deselect this option and click Next:

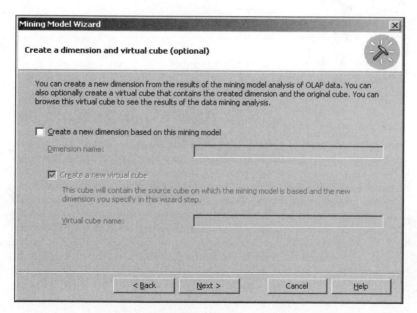

The next screen allows us to give a name to our model and process it, which means calculate its cases and predictions:

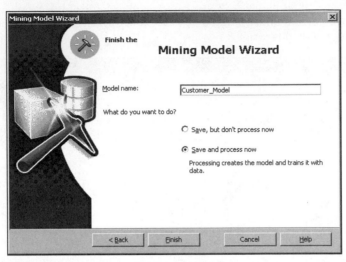

Once finished, the wizard will open the OLAP Mining Model Editor, which allows us to make changes to the model, add tables, remove tables, etc. It will also allow us to view the decision tree and make decisions on whether we need to modify it or not:

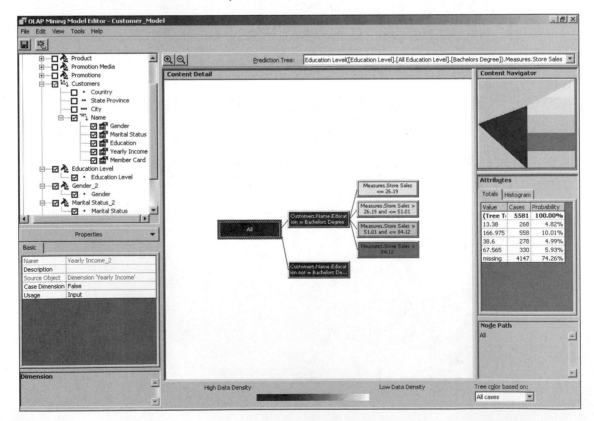

Now you have the data mining model, you might be asking yourself, "How can I use it, or even read it?" In the screenshot, you see that a tree-like structure is presented along with a coloring scheme. The tree structure shows you the distribution of your customers in terms of education level. It also shows you the sales distribution of those who had bachelors degrees. You can notice that a large number of them had sales in excess of $40. Therefore, this model can help you see which group of people would be most responsive to a promotion campaign.

In addition, notice on the top right side of the screen a drop-down list labeled as **Prediction Tree**. This list allows you to change the tree in the **Content Detail** section of the Model Editor to show the tree in terms of other criteria. For instance, you can select to see the tree in terms of the High School member of the Education Level dimension, or you can select to see the tree in terms of gender or marital status. Also, now you have your model in the OLAP Mining Model Editor screen, you can tweak it and change it. For instance, you could add new dimensions to your analysis and re-process the model.

Summary

This was an introductory chapter about Analysis Services in SQL Server 2000. Analysis Services and data warehousing in SQL Server really deserve much more than one chapter. There are many more topics I wish I could cover. These include data mining using MDX – the SQL language equivalent for data cubes – and using programming languages to build custom cube browsers. However, I hope that this chapter will only be a start for you and will entice you to learn more about this technology and the powerful tools that come with it.

We covered the basics of data warehousing and OLAP at the beginning of the chapter. Then I introduced you to the Microsoft SQL Server Analysis Manager and the great wizards and tools that come with it. The example we followed was detailed and probably looked like a tutorial at some points, but I hope that it will put you on the right track in your endeavor to explore this technology further.

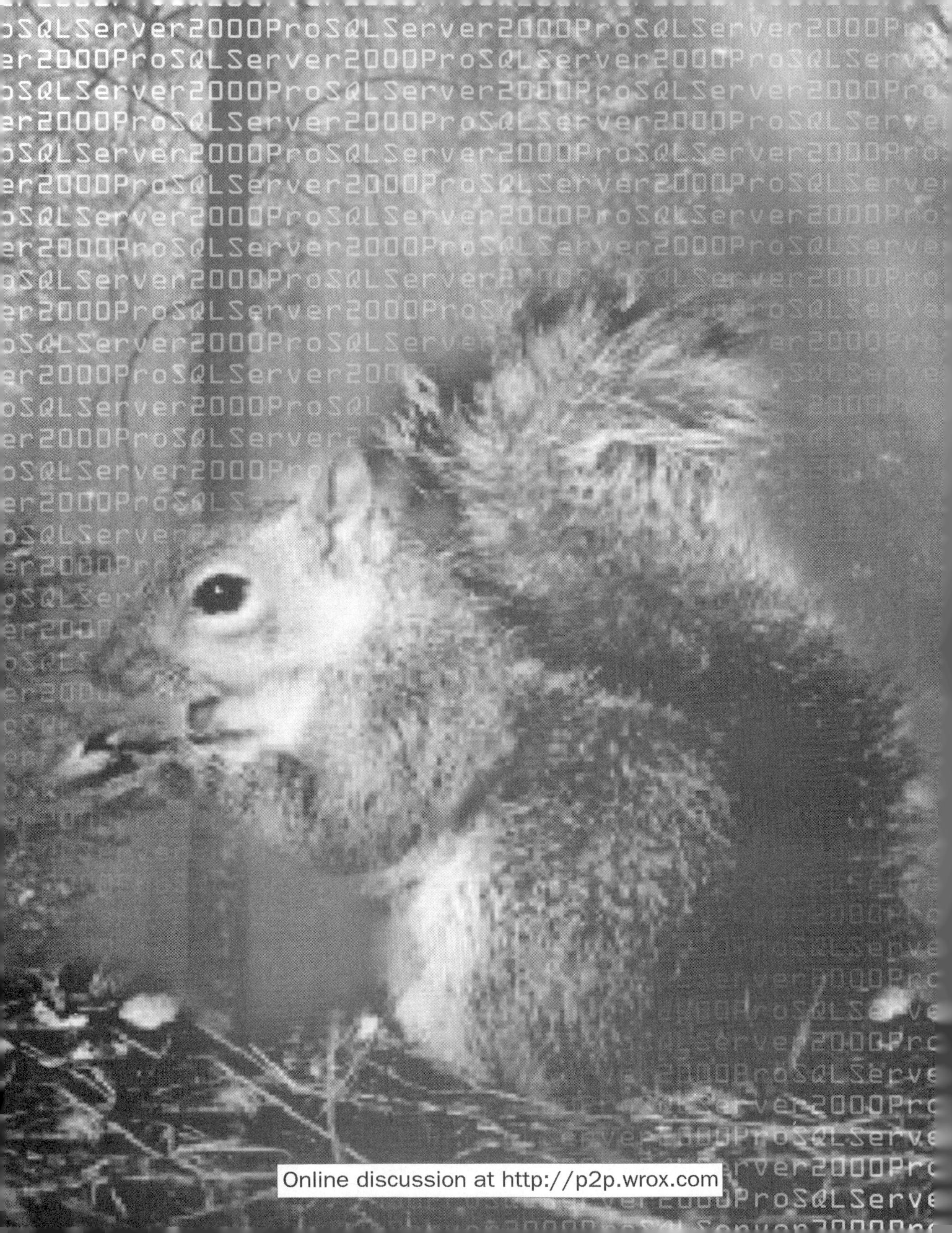
Online discussion at http://p2p.wrox.com

26

Full-Text Search

In the last revision of this book, we combined this topic with English Query – an odd pairing, admittedly, but we were looking to group a couple of "extra" features that SQL Server had added to allow extra power through non-standard queries. Well, both of these features have grown in functionality and use, and it now seems that they each deserve a place of their own in this version of the book.

Using plain old T-SQL (without Full-Text functionality), our options for querying text information are somewhat limited. Indeed, we only have a couple of options:

❑   Use a `LIKE` clause. This is generally woefully inefficient, and is not able to utilize any kind of index structure unless the search pattern starts with an explicit value. If the search starts with a wildcard (say "%" or "_"), then SQL Server wouldn't know which spot in the index to begin with, so any indexes become worthless.

❑   Use some other form of pattern matching, such as `PATINDEX` or `CHARINDEX`. This is generally even more inefficient, but this can allow us to do things that `LIKE` will not.

With Full-Text Search, however, we gain the ability to index the contents of the text – essentially keeping a word list that lets us know what words we can find and in what rows. In addition, we are not limited to just pattern matching algorithms. We can search for the inflectional forms of words – for example, we might use the word university, but have SQL Server also find the word universities, or, even better, SQL Server can still find a work like drunk when the word we asked for was drink. It's up to us to decide how precise we want to be, but even if the word we are searching for is located deep in the middle of a large text block, SQL Server can quickly find the rows that contain the word in question.

New with SQL Server 2000 is the ability to build full-text indexes on data that isn't necessarily in raw text form. Full-Text Search also supports any document type that is supported by Microsoft Index Server – this means that you can store things like Word, Excel, PowerPoint, and other supported files in an image data type, but still perform full-text searches against that data! For SQL Server 2000, five file types are supported:

❑ Word (*.doc)

❑ Excel (*.xls)

❑ PowerPoint (*.ppt)

❑ Text (*.txt)

❑ HTML (*.htm or *.html)

In addition to the built-in supported filters, many third party software vendors (Adobe for example, the maker of Acrobat) make filters for Index Server (which, again, is related to Full-Text Search, and uses the same filters) available for purchase or download. Indeed, the format for building index server filters to support new document types is a published API, so you could even write your own extensions to support other document types if necessary.

> *Personally, I think this latter point is extremely cool. As we saw back in Chapters 19 & 20, we're now living in an XML world. We can use OPENXML to query XML on the fly, but there isn't currently any way to index the contents. Since Index Server file extensions are now supported, we could, for example, build an extension that knows the format of your XML document, store the document in a image data type using the extension, and, whammo, we can now use FTS to be able to quickly search a large store of XML documents for those that contain certain data. It's not an ideal query model by any means – searching for the existence of a text string in an XML document rather than querying individual columns as we can in a relational data store – still, it has some slick possibilities to it.*

In this chapter, we'll take a look at all of these FTS features. Full-Text is something of a different animal from the kinds of things that we've seen in SQL Server thus far, living partly in SQL Server itself, and partly as an autonomous unit that leverages non-SQL Server technologies. We'll examine some of the issues that are unique to full-text indexing and search, and explore the special syntax that is used in Full-Text queries.

Among the sections we'll look at are:

❑ Full-Text Search (FTS) architecture

❑ Setting up Full-Text indexes and catalogs

❑ Full-Text query syntax

❑ Full-Text quirks

By the time we're done, you should be prepared for the hassles that FTS creates for you, but you should also be ready to utilize what can be some wonderful functionality in return.

> *Be aware that, in version 7.0, the FTS engine and functionality was not installed in the default installation – you needed to select a custom installation and specifically choose to install FTS. With SQL Server 2000, FTS is installed by default.*

Full-Text Search Architecture

The architecture surrounding FTS is something that confuses a lot of people. When you realized how the different pieces play together to make FTS happen, the confusion isn't that surprising.

The first thing to recognize is that the core of FTS isn't really part of SQL Server at all. Actually, it is a shared technology item that originally comes from Microsoft Index Server and Site Server. The technology is implemented through a service known as MSSearch. MSSearch is excellent at examining raw text data and aggregating word lists. An association is then maintained between the individual words and phrases and the places that MSSearch encountered them; for Index Server, this will be file locations, for Site Search this is a mix of file locations and web page URLs, and for FTS in SQL Server the word list is associated with rows of data.

FTS is about marrying the file-based storage architecture of MSSearch with the RDBMS architecture in SQL Server. In order to perform full-text queries against any SQL Server table, you must build a full-text index for that table. The construction and maintenance of this full-text index – or the population of the index – is done through a process in which SQL Server passes text streams to the MSSearch engine, the words in the stream being catalogued, and an association being made between each catalog entry and the row the word was sourced from.

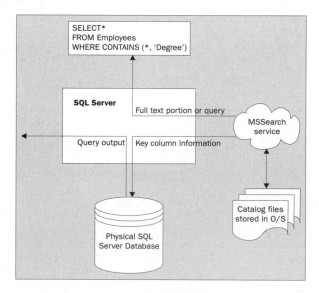

By default, tables have no full-text functionality at all. The fact that there is a table and that it has text and/or character data types is no guarantee that there is a full-text index on the table – if you want it, you need to create it. Even after you create the full-text index, the index will have nothing in it – in order to make the index fully functional, you need to **populate** the index.

The population process looks over the columns specified by the index and builds the word list that is going to be used. Much like standard indexes in SQL Server, only the columns you specify to include in the index will become part of the index. Unlike normal indexes in SQL Server, however, you are only allowed one full-text index per table – so every column you want to participate in full-text queries needs to be part of the index.

The differences don't stop there though – actually there are several. The major differences include:

- ❑ Storage Location: SQL Server indexes are stored as part of the main database file(s). Full text indexes, however, are stored in what is called a Full-Text Catalog. This makes it very easy to store the full-text catalog on a separate physical device from the rest of the database (which can help performance), but it also means that database backups do not include the full-text indexes for that database (backups do include normal SQL Server indexes).

- ❑ Method of Creation: SQL Server indexes are created using the CREATE INDEX command in T-SQL, SQL-DMO, or WMI (you can also use EM, but it just uses SQL-DMO). Full-text indexes are created through the use of special system stored procedures (again, you can use EM, but it uses the special system sprocs).

- ❑ Method of Update: SQL Server indexes are automatically updated in the normal course of changes to the underlying SQL Server data. Full text indexes are only populated on demand (with SQL Server 2000, you can now make them *seem* to be immediately updated, but it's still more similar to an on-demand process).

So that's the quick lesson in Full-Text Architecture 101. As we move through the rest of the chapter, the impact of the differences should become apparent compared with the more "normal" way things are implemented in SQL Server.

Setting up Full-Text Indexes and Catalogs

As we saw in the last section, each table in SQL Server can have zero or one full-text indexes. These full-text indexes are stored in a file – called a **full-text catalog** – that is external to the SQL Server database and system files. A catalog can store multiple full-text indexes. The indexes must be from the same database – you may, however, want to store indexes from one database in multiple catalogs so you can manage the population of those indexes on separate schedules.

Enabling Full-Text for Your Database

By default, your database will not have FTS enabled at all. SQL Server will not allow full-text catalogs or indexes to be created until you enable FTS for the database in question.

To do this, we make use of a special system stored procedure called sp_fulltext_database. The syntax is amazingly simple:

```
EXEC sp_fulltext_database [@action =] '{enable|disable}'
```

The enable option turns on full-text indexing for the current database. If there are any full-text catalogs already existing for the current database, they are deleted, as are any associations your tables have with those catalogs.

> *Really be careful of this latter point. There is no prompting and no warning – anything to do with full-text in the current database is immediately and irrevocably destroyed to make way for a fresh start. This means you need to be careful in two ways: 1) be sure this is something you really want to do; 2) make SURE, for positive, that the correct database is current when you execute this sproc.*

The disable option turns off full-text operations for the current database and removes any current catalogs and indexes.

As a quick example, let's enable full-text operations for the `Northwind` database:

```
USE Northwind

EXEC sp_fulltext_database @action = 'Enable'
```

And it's done.

> *Be warned that SQL Server doesn't really tell you much to confirm that full-text operations have been successfully enabled. All you'll see are a few messages about rows being affected – there isn't even a print statement that says "done enabling full-text search" or something like that. You should, however, get some form of an error message if there is a problem.*

Creating a Full-Text Catalog

The first logical step in enabling your database for full-text operations is to create at least one catalog in which to store full-text indexes. Since full-text indexes must reside in a full-text catalog, it follows that you need to already have the full-text catalog created when you try to create the index.

To create the full-text catalog, we use a special system stored procedure called `sp_fulltext_catalog`. Technically speaking, this sproc does about everything needed to manage the catalog – unlike many T-SQL statements, we do not use a totally different command to manage or update the object. Instead, we use just this one stored procedure with a mixture of parameters to fit our particular situation.

The general syntax is:

```
EXEC sp_fulltext_catalog [@ftcat =] '<name of catalog>' ,
    [@action =] '{create|drop|start_incremental|start_full|stop|rebuild}'
    [,[@path =] '<root directory>' ]
```

The three arguments to the stored procedure are as follows:

Argument	Description
@ftcat	Does what it says. If you are using the CREATE option for the @action parameter, this is what will be used as the name for your full-text catalog.
@action	This is basically a "What do you want to do?" parameter. Since sp_fulltext_catalog can do about everything we need, we use this parameter to indicate what action we want done this time. It has six possible options: create OK – who can figure this one out? Tick, tick, tick – bzzzzt! That's right! It means that we want to create a full-text catalog. When this option is used, the name specified with the @ftcat parameter must not already exist in the database or the create will fail.

Table continued on following page

Argument	Description
@action	drop Another toughie for sure. Choose this option and your full-text catalog is gone. Note that you must delete all indexes that were in the catalog before you try to drop it or the drop operation will fail. start_incremental This one starts the catalog population process (think of it as the indexing process) for an incremental build – we'll explore incremental versus full builds shortly. start_full This one starts the catalog population process for a full build. The existing populated indexes (if there are any) will be truncated and rebuilt from scratch. Again, we will explore full builds shortly. stop Stops any population process that is already in progress. rebuild Effectively deletes and recreates the specified catalog. The catalog is left in an empty (unpopulated) state – if you want to populate the catalog after a rebuild, then you must explicitly call sp_fulltext_catalog again and specify the START_FULL option.
@path	This optional argument specifies the path to the root directory that will contain the catalog. If the path is not specified, it is the ..\MSSQL\FTDATA directory under wherever your installation of SQL Server went.

OK, so now we're armed and ready to fire away with a full-text catalog. For our examples in this chapter, it probably won't come as any surprise to learn that I'm going to point you at the Northwind database.

We'll start off with a catalog to hold the full-text indexes we'll be working with:

```
USE Northwind

EXEC sp_fulltext_catalog @ftcat = 'NorthwindFullText', @action = 'CREATE'
```

Again there is little to no feedback from SQL Server about the completion of this action.

Now that we have our catalog created, we're going to go away from it for the time being. We'll come back to the other options of our sp_fulltext_catalog sproc after we've laid some more groundwork.

Enabling Full-Text Search for Individual Tables

Well, we've enabled full-text for our database and created our catalog – everything should be ready to go now, right? Wrong! All we've accomplished through this tedious work thus far is to prepare ourselves to enable whatever tables we want to perform full-text operations against. So, it's time to get down to the business of figuring out what tables we want to be able to run full-text queries against and creating full-text indexes on those tables.

As you might expect, we're going to use another system sproc to create our actual indexes for us. Following the same general naming theme as our previous two sprocs, this one is called sp_fulltext_table, and the syntax looks like this:

```
EXEC sp_fulltext_table [@tabname =] '[<owner>.]<table>', [@action =]
   '{create|drop|activate|deactivate|start_change_tracking|
   stop_change_tracking|start_background_updateindex|
   stop_background_updateindex|update_index|start_full|start_incremental|stop}'
   [,[@ftcat = ] '<fulltext catalog>',[@keyname =] '<index name>']
```

Let's take a brief look at each of the parameters:

@tabname	The name of the table. Optionally, the two-part name in the form of owner.object. The table is assumed to exist in the current database. If no such object exists in the database, an error message is returned.
@action	The "What do you want done?" question again. This parameter has a long list of possible choices – we will explore each next.
@ftcat	The name of the full-text catalog that this index is to be created in. This should only be provided if the option for @action was 'create'; otherwise, leave this option off.
@keyname	Name of a single column unique key for this table. Usually the Primary Key but, if you have a composite key, you may use a column with a UNIQUE constraint (you may need to add an identity column or similar mechanism just for this purpose).

The @action parameter has several options to it, so let's look at those:

create	Enables FTS for the table specified in @tabname.
drop	Deactivates full-text for this table and deletes the full-text index from the catalog.
activate	If the table has had full-text deactivated, this option reactivates it. If change tracking is turned on, then running this option will also start population the next time a scheduled population run begins.
deactivate	Disables the table from participating in FTS activity, but leaves any population data in place for use if the table is reactivated.

Table continued on following page

start_change_tracking	If the table contains a timestamp column (required for incremental updates), this starts an incremental population of the full-text index. If no timestamp column exists, then this starts a full population of the full-text index. Repopulates (incremental or full as appropriate) automatically (may be immediate or next scheduled population run, depending on other settings) if any changes happen to the table for non-BLOB columns.
stop_change_tracking	Ceases change tracking. Does not affect populations already in progress, but eliminates the automatic population based on changes.
start_background_updateindex	Begins immediate population of index with any changes found as a result of change tracking. Any subsequent updates are added to the index immediately.
stop_background_updateindex	Stops the immediate population process.
update_index	Causes any tracked changes not already applied to the full-text index to be applied immediately.
start_full	Immediately begins a full population for the target index.
start_incremental	Immediately begins an incremental population for the target index.
stop	Stops any population in progress.

So, now that we have these lovelies under our belt, let's add a full-text index to our Employees table. We'll add this index to our NorthwindFullText catalog and utilize the Primary Key that exists on EmployeeID column as our unique key. The only problem we have is that we know our column name, but not our index name (which is what we really need). To get that information, we'll quickly look at the indexes on the Employees table:

```
USE Northwind

EXEC sp_helpindex Employees
```

This gets us back three indexes:

index_name	index_description	index_keys
LastName	Nonclustered located on PRIMARY	LastName
PK_Employees	Clustered, unique, primary key located on PRIMARY	EmployeeID
PostalCode	Nonclustered located on PRIMARY	PostalCode

So, the index called PK_Employees is the one that will give us our unique column to reference our full-text index to. Now we're ready to create that index:

```
USE Northwind

EXEC sp_fulltext_table @tabname = 'Employees',
    @action = 'create',
    @ftcat = 'NorthwindFullText',
    @keyname = 'PK_Employees'
```

Again, there is little confirmation from SQL Server that things worked other than the lack of error messages.

At this point it would be really easy to think that we were done – that we could run full-text queries and life would be grand. Sorry – no dice. We're still missing something – columns in the index. Unlike in T-SQL, where we defined the columns that were part of the index as part of the index creation, with full-text indexes the creation process is really just about making the association between the catalog that's going to be used and the unique index that's going to identify each row in our table. It is only after the table has been created that we can add indexes to it and make the index truly usable.

So, how do we add columns? Well, we again stick with the naming scheme that we've been using all along, and use a system stored procedure called sp_fulltext_column. The syntax is as follows:

```
sp_fulltext_column [@tabname =] '[<owner>.]<table>',
    [@colname =] '<column name>' ,
    [@action =] '{add|drop}'
    [,[ @language =] '<language>']
    [,[ @type_colname =] '<type column name>']
```

@tabname	The name of the table that the full-text index exists on.
@colname	The name of the column you wish to add to or drop from the index.
@action	Whether to add a column or drop one.
@language	The Locale ID for the native language used in the column being indexed. The default is language neutral.
@type_colname	This should be the name of the column that will hold the document type (.doc, .pdf, .xls, etc.) of the data stored in the column named in @colname. This only applies to image data where you are planning to use the index server filter for the appropriate document type.

OK, we're nearing the home stretch on this. Let's add a column to the full-text index that we created on our Employees table:

```
USE Northwind

EXEC sp_fulltext_column @tabname = 'Employees',
    @colname = 'Notes',
    @action = 'add'
```

We get the now familiar nothing (or very little) back to confirm the success of our column being added.

At this point the full-text index is almost ready – all that is left to do is to populate it and we'll be in business. Before we do that though, I want to perform a small exercise in futility. Why? Well, I want you to see how something works (or, one could argue, doesn't work) so you have a chance to recognize it if it happens to you (which, if you do much with FTS, it probably will sooner or later).

Even though we really haven't studied the query syntax as yet, I'd like you to humor me for a moment and run the following query:

```
SELECT EmployeeID, LastName, FirstName
FROM Employees
WHERE CONTAINS(*, 'University')
```

You should get back zero rows.

That said, trust me when I tell you that:

❑ This query should return all rows that contain the word University in the Notes column of the Employees table in the Northwind database.

❑ Despite the fact that our query says otherwise, our Notes column in Northwind does indeed have rows with the word University in them.

Given the above, why did we get zero rows back? Well, you can probably figure it out from what we were preparing to do when we started this whole exercise – we haven't populated our index yet. Full text is enabled and active on our table, and so the full-text commands work just fine; however, we haven't populated the index yet, so there's nothing to return rows back to us. Be very careful of this one – it's really easy to think that you have no matching rows when, in reality, we do have matching rows, but they haven't been populated into the full-text index as yet.

Index Population

Unlike "normal" SQL Server indexes, which are naturally kept up to date by the very nature of SQL Server and the way it stores data, full-text indexes exist partially outside the realm of SQL Server and, as such, require a certain degree of intervention before they will be up to date with the actual data they are supposed to represent.

Population comes in three – well, more like 2½ – flavors. Let's look at each:

❑ Full: What it sounds like. With this kind of population, SQL Server basically forgets anything that it knew about the data previously, and starts over. Every row is rescanned and the index is rebuilt from scratch.

❑ Incremental: Under this option, SQL Server utilizes a column of type timestamp in order to keep track of which columns have changed since the last population. In this scenario, SQL Server only needs to record the changes for those rows that have changed in some manner. This option requires that the table in question have a timestamp column. Any updates that do not cause a change in the timestamp (non-logged operations – usually BLOB activity) will not be detected unless something else in the same row changed.

❑ Change Tracking: This tracks the actual changes since the last population. This option is really just something of a modifier to the previous two options (thus the ½), and can help you keep your full-text indexes up to date at near real time. However, keep in mind that full-text population is very CPU and memory intensive, and can bog down your server – weigh the notion of immediate updates against the notion that you may be able to hold your updates to off peak hours for your server.

Unless you're using Change Tracking, population of your full-text indexes will only occur when you specifically start the process, or according to a population schedule that you establish. With change tracking, you are provided with two options: Scheduled Propagation and Background Update. The former applies the tracked changes at scheduled intervals. The latter is essentially always running in the background and applies changes as soon as possible after the change was made.

Obviously, whenever you first create a full-text index or change the list of columns participating in the index, you need to completely repopulate the index (an incremental change of a previously empty index would mean that every row would have to be scanned in – right?). We can perform this repopulation at either the catalog or the table level. Typically, you'll perform repopulation at the table level for newly added or changed indexes, and repopulate at the catalog level when you are performing routine maintenance.

So, with this in mind, we should now be ready to populate the full-text index we have created on our `Employees` table. Since this is both a new index and a new catalog, it really doesn't matter at what level we perform our repopulation. For this scenario, I'm going to treat it as if we were adding just one index to a catalog that already existed with other indexes in it – as such, I'm going to perform my repopulation at the table level.

Repopulating at the table level makes use of the same sproc we already have seen – `sp_fulltext_table`. We'll run it against our `Employees` table, using a full population:

```
EXEC sp_fulltext_table @tabname = 'Employees',
    @action = 'start_full'
```

Notice that we did not include the full-text catalog and key name options. Those are only for use when creating the full-text index. Afterwards, they should not be used.

> *Given the small size of our data set, this population run will happen fairly quickly for you – probably in well under a minute. Don't let this deceive you. Full text population is extremely CPU and memory intensive and can put quite a load on your server and still take a long time to process. A project I have worked on intermittently took as long as 26 hours for a full population using SQL Server 7. SQL Server 2000 is much more efficient, but it still can be a very long running process – keep this in mind before you start that population job!*

OK, so now that we have that population done, we're ready to re-run that sample query I gave you in the last section:

```
SELECT EmployeeID, LastName, FirstName
FROM Employees
WHERE CONTAINS(*, 'University')
```

This time you should get back something on the order of six rows:

EmployeeID	LastName	FirstName
7	King	Robert
6	Suyama	Michael
5	Buchanan	Steven
2	Fuller	Andrew
1	Davolio	Nancy
8	Callahan	Laura

(6 row(s) affected)

We have a full-text index, and it works! Time to move on to what that query we just ran is supposed to do and what other options we have available.

Full-Text Query Syntax

As has been indicated a couple of times throughout the chapter, FTS has its own brand of query syntax. It adds special commands to extend T-SQL and to clearly indicate that we want the full-text engine to support our query rather than the regular SQL Server engine.

Fortunately, the basics of full-text queries are just that – basic. There are only four base statements to work with in the full-text engine: CONTAINS, CONTAINSTABLE, FREETEXT, and FREETEXTTABLE. They actually fall into two overlapping categories of two statements each:

	Exact or Inflectional Term	**Meaning**
Conditional	CONTAINS	FREETEXT
Ranked Table	CONTAINSTABLE	FREETEXTTABLE

The conditional predicates both work an awful lot like an EXISTS operator. Essentially they provide, for each row, a simple yes or no as to whether the row qualifies against the search condition provided. You use both of these in the WHERE clause of your queries. On the other hand, the two ranked table queries do not provide conditions at all – instead, they return a tabular result set (which you can join to) that includes the key value of all the rows that found matches (that's what you join to), as well as a ranking to indicate the strength of the match.

Let's look more closely at each of our four keywords.

CONTAINS

This term looks for a match based on a particular word or phrase. By default, it's looking for an exact match (that is, swim must be swim – not swam), but it can also use modifiers to look for what are called inflectional matches (words that have the same root, such as swim and swam). CONTAINS recognizes certain keywords.

For now, we're going to stick with the simple form of CONTAINS. We will look at the advanced features after we have the basics of our four statements down (since they share certain modifiers, we'll look at those all at once).

The basic syntax, then, looks like this:

```
CONTAINS({<column>|*} , '<search condition>')
```

You can name a specific column to check or use *, in which case the condition will be compared for matches against any of the indexed columns. In its simplest form, the search condition should only contain a word or phrase.

> *There are two things worth pointing out here. First, remember that you will only get back results against columns that were included in the full-text index. In the index we created on the Employees table, that means the search only includes the Notes column – columns like LastName are not included in the search because they are not included in the index. Second, the search condition can be far more complex than the simple condition that we've shown here – but we'll get to that after you have the basic operations down.*

For an example, let's go back to the query we used to prove that our population exercise had worked.

```
SELECT EmployeeID, LastName, FirstName
FROM Employees
WHERE CONTAINS(*, 'University')
```

What we've said we want here is the `EmployeeID`, `LastName`, and `FirstName` columns for all the rows where any of the columns in the index (the * indicates all columns are to be included in the search) include the word `University`.

Let's modify the query a little:

```
SELECT EmployeeID, LastName, FirstName, Notes
FROM Employees
WHERE CONTAINS(*, 'University')
```

...to return our `Notes` column:

EmployeeID	LastName	FirstName	Notes
7	King	Robert	Robert King served i...
6	Suyama	Michael	Michael is a graduat...
5	Buchanan	Steven	Steven Buchanan gr...
2	Fuller	Andrew	Andrew received his...
1	Davolio	Nancy	Education includes a...
8	Callahan	Laura	Laura received a BA...

(6 row(s) affected)

If you check out the `Notes` column for the results, you'll see that every row has an exact match.

Let's quickly look at another example. This time, we're going to run pretty much the same query, but we're going to look for the word `Course`.

```
SELECT EmployeeID, LastName, FirstName, Notes
FROM Employees
WHERE CONTAINS(*, 'Course')
```

This time we get back just two rows:

EmployeeID	LastName	FirstName	Notes
7	King	Robert	Robert King served in the...
8	Callahan	Laura	Laura received a BA in ps...

(2 row(s) affected)

Again, we got back all the rows where any of the full-text indexed columns (in this case, just `Notes`) had an exact match with the word `Course`. Were you to look through the other rows in the table, however, you would find that there were other variations of the word `Course` ("Courses", for instance), but they were not returned.

Again, the default behavior of `CONTAINS` is an exact match behavior.

FREETEXT

FREETEXT is an incredibly close cousin to CONTAINS. Indeed, their syntax is nearly identical:

```
FREETEXT({<column>|*} , '<search condition>')
```

So, the only real difference is in the results you get back. You see, FREETEXT is a lot more forgiving in just how exact a match it looks for. It is more interested in the meaning of the word than it is in the exact letter-for-letter spelling.

To illustrate my point rather quickly here, let's look at our Course query from the last section, but modify it to use FREETEXT instead of CONTAINS:

```
SELECT EmployeeID, LastName, FirstName, Notes
FROM Employees
WHERE FREETEXT(*, 'Course')
```

When we execute this, we get back slightly different results than we did with CONTAINS:

EmployeeID	LastName	FirstName	Notes
7	King	Robert	Robert King served in the...
6	Suyama	Michael	Michael is a graduate of ...
5	Buchanan	Steven	Steven Buchanan graduated...
8	Callahan	Laura	Laura received a BA in ps...

(4 row(s) affected)

The difference in this case comes in interpretation of the plurals. Our FREETEXT query has picked up the couple of rows that contain the word "Courses" – not just those with the word Course. Though Northwind doesn't offer us the best in examples of this, FREETEXT can handle things like swim versus swam and other word variations.

CONTAINSTABLE

CONTAINSTABLE, in terms of figuring out which rows would be matched, works identically to CONTAINS. The difference is how the results are dealt with.

The syntax is similar, but has the twist of identifying which table the CONTAINSTABLE is going to operate against, plus an optional limitation to just a top set of matches:

```
CONTAINSTABLE (<table>, {column|*}, '<contains search condition>' [, <top
'n'>])
```

Where CONTAINS returns a simple Boolean response suitable for use in a WHERE clause, CONTAINSTABLE returns a table – complete with rankings of how well the search phrase matched the row being returned.

Let's see what I mean here by running our query, but this time with a CONTAINSTABLE:

```
SELECT *
FROM CONTAINSTABLE(Employees, *, 'Course')
```

This gets us back two rows – just as with CONTAINS – but the information provided by the returned values is somewhat different:

```
KEY         RANK
----------- -----------
8           16
7           16
```

(2 row(s) affected)

We are provided with two columns:

❏ KEY: Remember when we said that our full-text index had to be able to relate to a single column key in the indexed table? Well, the KEY returned by CONTAINSTABLE relates exactly to that key column. That is, the value outputted in the column called KEY matches with a single unique row, as identified by the key, in the index table.

❏ RANK: A value from 0 to 1000 that indicates just how well the search result matched the row being returned – the higher the value the better the match.

To make use of CONTAINSTABLE , we simply join our original table back to the CONTAINSTABLE result. For example:

```
SELECT Rank, EmployeeID, LastName, FirstName, Notes
FROM CONTAINSTABLE(Employees, *, 'Course') AS ct
JOIN Employees AS e
    ON ct.[KEY] = e.EmployeeID
```

Notice the use of square brackets around the KEY column name. The reason why is that KEY is also a keyword. Remember from our rules of naming that, if we use a keyword for a column or table name (which you shouldn't do), you need to enclose them in square brackets.

This gets us back our original two rows, but this time we have the extra information from the underlying table:

```
Rank        EmployeeID  LastName             FirstName  Notes
----------- ----------- -------------------- ---------- -------------------------
16          8           Callahan             Laura      Laura received a BA in ps...
16          7           King                 Robert     Robert King served in the...
```

(2 row(s) affected)

In this case, the values in the Rank are the same but, given more diverse values, we could have done things like:

❏ Filter based on some arbitrary Rank value. For example, we could want to return only the best matches based on score.

❏ Order by the Rank (sort the rankings – most likely highest to lowest).

FREETEXTTABLE

Much as FREETEXT was the close cousin to CONTAINS, so FREETEXTTABLE is the close cousin to CONTAINSTABLE. FREETEXTTABLE simply combines the more inexact word matching of FREETEXT with the tabular presentation found in CONTAINSTABLE.

We can then combine some of our previous examples to see how FREETEXTTABLE changes things:

```
SELECT Rank, EmployeeID, LastName, FirstName, Notes
FROM FREETEXTTABLE(Employees, *, 'Course') AS ft
JOIN Employees AS e
    ON ft.[KEY] = e.EmployeeID
```

This gets us the same four rows we had with our original FREETEXT query, but with the kind of rankings we had with our CONTAINSTABLE:

Rank	EmployeeID	LastName	FirstName	Notes
0	6	Suyama	Michael	Michael is a graduate of
0	5	Buchanan	Steven	Steven Buchanan graduated
133	8	Callahan	Laura	Laura received a BA in ps
133	7	King	Robert	Robert King served in the

(4 row(s) affected)

Notice that, although our ranking is low (zero is about as low as it gets), our rows for Buchanan and Suyama are still returned. They meet the rules for matching with FREETEXT or FREETEXTTABLE, but they are not as strong a match as Callahan and King.

Dealing with Phrases

All of our various full-text keywords can deal with the concept of phrases. How the phrases are parsed and handled, however, is somewhat different.

Let's start off with the most basic of examples. We'll go with the simple three-word phrase, the University of California.

```
SELECT EmployeeID, LastName, FirstName, Notes
FROM Employees
WHERE CONTAINS(*, '"University of California"')
```

Notice that the phrase was included in double quotes – we need to do this anytime we want a set of words to be considered as a single unit. This does, however, get us back one row:

EmployeeID	LastName	FirstName	Notes
6	Suyama	Michael	Michael is a graduate of ...

(1 row(s) affected)

Our CONTAINS will check for rows that exactly match the phrase, as long as we enclose that phrase in double quotes (within the single quotes we always need on our search phrase). There's a bit of a catch though, and we'll see an example of that if we alter our query just a bit:

```
SELECT EmployeeID, LastName, FirstName, Notes
FROM Employees
WHERE CONTAINS(*, '"University and California"')
```

Even though we've changed the phrase to something that doesn't exactly exist in our table, we still get back the same row as before:

EmployeeID	LastName	FirstName	Notes
6	Suyama	Michael	Michael is a graduate of …

(1 row(s) affected)

The issue lies in how full-text deals with certain keywords. These include:

❑ AND

❑ NOT

❑ OR

Each works as it does in other programming languages and, if used in the middle of a phrase, will still be treated as a keyword and will operate on the other words in the phrase. In our example above, Michael Suyama's record happens to be the only one that has both the word University and the word California.

It's not quite the same for all free text commands however. FREETEXT ignores keywords and treats them as just the words they are. For example, let's try both of the above queries again, only this time with FREETEXT instead of CONTAINS:

```
SELECT EmployeeID, LastName, FirstName, Notes
FROM Employees
WHERE FREETEXT(*, '"University of California"')
```

EmployeeID	LastName	FirstName	Notes
7	King	Robert	Robert King served in the…
6	Suyama	Michael	Michael is a graduate of …
5	Buchanan	Steven	Steven Buchanan graduated…
2	Fuller	Andrew	Andrew received his BTS c…
1	Davolio	Nancy	Education includes a BA i…
8	Callahan	Laura	Laura received a BA in ps…

(6 row(s) affected)

This time around we received a lot more data – much of which didn't have the phrase University of California. So, what happened?

Well, remember that FREETEXT is substantially less precise than CONTAINS. For FREETEXT, the phrase was broken down into looking for "University", or "of", or "California". The word "of" was then dropped because it is what is referred to as a noise word (we will look at the details of these in a moment, but suffice to say for the moment that they are words that SQL Server ignores). The six rows we see here contain both or at least one of University and California.

Let's try it the other way with FREETEXT:

```
SELECT EmployeeID, LastName, FirstName, Notes
FROM Employees
WHERE FREETEXT(*, '"University and California"')
```

We actually get back exactly the same results we got with the previous FREETEXT query:

EmployeeID	LastName	FirstName	Notes
7	King	Robert	Robert King served in the...
6	Suyama	Michael	Michael is a graduate of ...
5	Buchanan	Steven	Steven Buchanan graduated...
2	Fuller	Andrew	Andrew received his BTS c...
1	Davolio	Nancy	Education includes a BA i...
8	Callahan	Laura	Laura received a BA in ps...

(6 row(s) affected)

What happened this time? *Exactly* the same thing as last time. Remember that FREETEXT treats the keywords that CONTAINS uses (AND, OR, NOT) as regular old words. The reason we received the same results this time is that "and" is a noise word just like "of". The end result is that FREETEXT is looking for the same words as last time – "University" or "California".

Now let's take this one step further and look at the effects this has on our CONTAINSTABLE and FREETEXTTABLE keywords. First CONTAINSTABLE:

```
SELECT Rank, EmployeeID, LastName, FirstName, LEFT(CAST(Notes AS nchar), 25) AS
Notes
FROM CONTAINSTABLE(Employees, *, '"University Of California"') AS ft
JOIN Employees AS e
    ON ft.[KEY] = e.EmployeeID
```

This gets us back just the one row:

Rank	EmployeeID	LastName	FirstName	Notes
21	6	Suyama	Michael	Michael is a graduate of

(1 row(s) affected)

Notice that the rank is just 21. Even though we have an exact match, we do not get a 1000 rank. I have not been able to get the Product Manager for Full-Text to give me the answer as to why this is, other than the notion that the score is relative to a large number of factors. We have a match here, but there are many other words in the note field for this record, so the match isn't exact with the row. Like I said, I don't know all the factors – my point here is to worry about how the ranking is relative to other rows – not the exact number.

Now FREETEXTTABLE:

```
SELECT Rank, EmployeeID, LastName, FirstName, Notes
FROM FREETEXTTABLE(Employees, *, '"University and California"') AS ft
JOIN Employees AS e
    ON ft.[KEY] = e.EmployeeID
```

Rank	EmployeeID	LastName	FirstName	Notes
0	2	Fuller	Andrew	Andrew received his BTS c
0	1	Davolio	Nancy	Education includes a BA i
209	6	Suyama	Michael	Michael is a graduate of
0	5	Buchanan	Steven	Steven Buchanan graduated
0	8	Callahan	Laura	Laura received a BA in ps
0	7	King	Robert	Robert King served in the

(6 row(s) affected)

As an interesting exercise, play around with the case of the words in the search. Even the word "And", which is supposed to be a noise word and automatically filtered out, seems to sometimes (and sometimes not) affect the Rank if you change the case of some of the letters. Again, remember to use the Rank as a relative score compared to other entries in the resultset – do not attach significance to the individual numbers that might be returned.

Proximity

Full-text search also allows us to make use of proximity terms. Currently, the list of supported proximity terms is a whopping one term long – NEAR. NEAR works a lot like it sounds – it says that the terms on either side of the NEAR keyword must be close to each other. Microsoft hasn't told us how close the words have to be to be considered NEAR, but figure around 8-10 words for most situations.

Technically, there is one more "word" on the proximity keyword list, but it isn't a "word" at all – rather a symbol. You can, if you choose, use a tilde (~) instead of the NEAR keyword. It works just the same. Personally, I recommend against this for readability reasons – not too many readers of your code are going to recognize what ~ means, but most of them will at least make a guess at NEAR.

For examples on how NEAR works, we're going to stick with CONTAINSTABLE. NEAR works much the same in the other full-text query operators, so we're going to just focus on what happens to the rankings in a NEAR query as well as what does and doesn't get included in the query.

For this example, we'll look at the words completed and sales:

```
SELECT Rank, EmployeeID, LastName, FirstName, Notes
FROM CONTAINSTABLE(Employees, *, 'completed near sales') AS ft
JOIN Employees AS e
    ON ft.[KEY] = e.EmployeeID
```

Notice that we have different rankings on the two rows returned.

Rank	EmployeeID	LastName	FirstName	Notes
1	3	Leverling	Janet	Janet has a BS degree in
3	5	Buchanan	Steven	Steven Buchanan graduated

(2 row(s) affected)

If you look carefully at the Notes column, you'll see that both rows do indeed have both words, but that the words are slightly closer together in the Buchanan record – thus causing a higher ranking.

> *Don't be surprised to see situations where a record that has your search criteria closer together gets ranked lower than one where the search criteria are not as close. Remember that, even when you use the NEAR keyword, nearness is only one of several criteria that SQL Server uses to rank the rows. Other considerations such as percentage of words that match, case values, and more, can play with the numbers.*

Now, just to be sure this whole NEAR business works, let's compare the results of two queries – an AND and a NEAR:

```
SELECT Rank, EmployeeID, LastName, FirstName, Notes
FROM CONTAINSTABLE(Employees, *, 'received AND Association') AS ft
JOIN Employees AS e
    ON ft.[KEY] = e.EmployeeID
```

This first query gets us back a row:

Rank	EmployeeID	LastName	FirstName	Notes
16	2	Fuller	Andrew	Andrew received his BTS c

(1 row(s) affected)

So, now we know both words exist within that row, but are they close enough to be considered NEAR?

```
SELECT Rank, EmployeeID, LastName, FirstName, Notes
FROM CONTAINSTABLE(Employees, *, 'received NEAR Association') AS ft
JOIN Employees AS e
    ON ft.[KEY] = e.EmployeeID
```

Apparently not:

Rank	EmployeeID	LastName	FirstName	Notes

(0 row(s) affected)

Prefix Terms

In addition to the notion of meaning (as we had with the FREETEXT stuff), the full-text product also allows you to make use of a "Starts with" or **Prefix Term**. Making use of a Prefix Term is as simple as providing the first part of a word or phrase followed by an asterisk (*). The only real catch is that, regardless of whether you are searching for an individual word or a phrase, you must enclose both the word or phrase and the prefix in double quotes (in addition to the usual single quotes).

To demonstrate what I'm talking about here, let's run a fairly simple query using a prefix term:

```
SELECT FirstName, LastName, Notes
FROM Employees e
WHERE CONTAINS(*, 'grad*')
```

This will get back zero rows because Full-Text thinks that you're looking for the exact term "grad*" – including the asterisk. Now, if we use the double quotes:

```
SELECT FirstName, LastName, Notes
FROM Employees e
WHERE CONTAINS(*, '"grad*"')
```

We get back all the rows that have words starting with "grad":

FirstName	LastName	Notes
Michael	Suyama	Michael is a graduate of
Steven	Buchanan	Steven Buchanan graduated

(2 row(s) affected)

Remember those double quotes when using a Prefix Term.

Weighting

These rankings are very cool, but what would we do if one of the words in our search criteria was more important than another?

To deal with situations where you need to give precedence to one or more words, full-text provides us with the ISABOUT() function and WEIGHT keyword. The syntax looks like this:

```
ISABOUT(<weighted term> WEIGHT (<weight value>), <weighted term> WEIGHT
(<weighted term>),…n)
```

Let's say, for example, that you want to rank your employees by their education. You've decided that a Master's Degree is worth twice as much as a Bachelor of Science, which is, in turn, worth twice as much as a Bachelor of Arts. You could get a ranked listing using the following:

```
SELECT Rank, FirstName, LastName, Notes
FROM Employees e
JOIN CONTAINSTABLE(Employees, Notes, 'ISABOUT (BA WEIGHT (.2), BS WEIGHT (.4), MA
WEIGHT (.8) )' ) ct
     ON e.EmployeeID = ct.[KEY]
ORDER BY Rank DESC
```

Now take a look at the results:

```
Rank        FirstName           LastName                      Notes
----------- ----------- -------------------- ------------------------------------
17          Margaret            Peacock              Margaret holds a BA in English...
15          Michael             Suyama               Michael is a graduate of Susse...
10          Janet               Leverling            Janet has a BS degree in chemi...
3           Anne                Dodsworth            Anne has a BA degree in Englis...
2           Laura               Callahan             Laura received a BA in psychol...
2           Nancy               Davolio              Education includes a BA in psy...
```

(6 row(s) affected)

I could have used any decimal value between 0.0 and 1.0 for the WEIGHTs. Essentially, I just chose proportional values within that range. The results showed that Margaret Peacock – who happens to hold both a Master's and a Bachelor's degree – was ranked highest, while the bottom three were ranked lowest since they only had the BA.

Inflectional

This one doesn't really apply to FREETEXT, as FREETEXT is inherently inflectional. What is inflectional you ask? Well, it's basically telling SQL Server that different forms of one word have the same general meaning. The syntax looks like this:

```
FORMSOF(INFLECTIONAL, <term>[, <term>[, ...n]] )
```

So, if we, for example, wanted to return all forms of the word graduate or degree – regardless of whether it was a noun or verb, or whether it was singular or plural – we could write:

```
SELECT FirstName, LastName, Notes
FROM Employees
WHERE CONTAINS (Notes, 'FORMSOF (INFLECTIONAL, graduate, degree)')
```

And we would get back five rows:

```
FirstName   LastName             Notes
----------  -------------------- -----------------------------
Robert      King                 Robert King served in the Peac...
Michael     Suyama               Michael is a graduate of Susse...
Steven      Buchanan             Steven Buchanan graduated from...
Janet       Leverling            Janet has a BS degree in chemi...
Anne        Dodsworth            Anne has a BA degree in Englis...
```

(5 row(s) affected)

If you look through the Notes fields in the results, you'll see that not all of the rows have the word degree or graduate in them – instead, they quite often just have forms of those words (for example, degrees or graduated).

A Brief Word about Rank

Don't get overly focused on the number you see coming back in the Rank column of FREETEXTTABLE and CONTAINSTABLE. I have been asked on many occasions how they come up with that number, and I have, on a few occasions, tried desperately to find a way to get the Product Manager for Full-Text Search to answer that question for me (and, therefore, for you). The answer has always been the same, "The method we use to calculate that number is a trade secret, and I can't say", or something similar.

What you, as a developer who is using that Rank information, need to focus on is that it is relative in nature. A row with a Rank of "x" more than another row is typically going to have met one or more of the following conditions:

- ❏   It has more instances of the word you are searching for

- ❏   If you supplied multiple words, then they where found in the same order you specified, or nearer each other

- ❏   It matched case more accurately

- ❏   It was an exact match as opposed to an inflectional match

Those are just for starters – I'm sure there's a dozen more kinds of things that Microsoft is using to determine that Rank, but they haven't been nice enough to share it with me yet!

Noise Words

There are tons and tons of words in use in different languages (FTS supports more than just US English!). Most languages have certain words that appear over and over again with little intrinsic meaning to them. In the English language, for example, prepositions (to, in, for, etc.), pronouns, (you, she, he, etc.), articles (the, a, an), and conjunctions (and, but, or) are just a few examples of words that appear in many, many sentences but play a relatively minor part in their meaning.

If SQL Server paid attention to those words, and we did searches based on them, then we would drown in the results that SQL Server gave us – quite often, every single row in the table would be returned! The solution comes in the form of what is called a **noise word** list. This is a list of words that SQL Server ignores when considering matches.

The noise word list is, by default, stored in a text file in the path:

```
Program Files\Microsoft SQL Server\MSSQL\FTDATA\SQL Server\Config
```

For US English, the name of the file is noise.eng. Other noise files can be found in the same subdirectory that support several other languages. Which noise word file(s) get used depends on the language setting for your server as determined by its **default full-text language** option. The default language can also be overridden at the column level by using sp_fulltext_column.

You can add and delete words from this list as suits the particular needs of your application. For example, if you are in the business of selling tractor-trailer rigs, then you might want to add words like "hauling" to your noise word list. More than likely, a huge percentage of your customers have that word in their name, so it is relatively unhelpful in searches. To do this, you would just add the word "hauling" to noise.eng (or whatever language noise word file is appropriate for your installation) and, after the next population, hauling would be ignored.

Adding words to and removing words from the noise list is something of a double-edged sword. When you add a word to the list, it means that searches involving that word are no longer going to return the results that users are more than likely going to expect. By the same token, it also, depending on the frequency that the word is used, can dramatically shrink the processing time and size of your catalogs.

Also be aware that, while the Full-Text Search is active, it has a lock on the noise word file at the operating system level – that means you need to shut down FTS to make your noise word changes.

Linguistics

SQL Server's Full-Text Search supports more than just US English. Indeed, it isn't limited to English at all. Besides US and UK English, other supported languages include:

- ❑   Chinese (Simplified and Traditional)
- ❑   Dutch
- ❑   French
- ❑   German
- ❑   Italian
- ❑   Japanese
- ❑   Korean
- ❑   Spanish (Modern)
- ❑   Swedish

By default, the search capabilities are language neutral, which is to say that MSSearch doesn't favor any particular language at all. If you are running a localized version of SQL Server, then the **default full-text language** option is set to one of the languages listed above, as appropriate to the location SQL Server is localized for. If there is no language match between your localized copy of SQL Server and one of the above supported languages, then it will default to being language neutral.

I haven't run any benchmarking on it but, if all your searches are going to be language specific, it makes sense that changing from language neutral to your specific language should speed performance up a bit. Like I said, I can't give you any benchmarks, but doing less work usually means taking less time.

sp_fulltext_service

Why does this one deserve its own heading when none of the other full-text sprocs did? Well, because the others fit together with each other rather nicely, but this one is something of a rogue. `sp_fulltext_service` is all about changing a few different pieces of meta-data in your search service, plus it provides the added bonus of doing some clean-up for you.

The syntax looks like this:

```
sp_fulltext_service [@action=]
'resource_usage|clean_up|connect_timeout|data_timeout'
    [, [@value=]'NULL|<numeric value>']
```

Let's look at the possible values for these:

resource_usage	The name of this one is a little misleading. At first blush, one might think this had something to do with memory or disk usage, but it's actually related to the priority boost concept in Windows 2000/NT. Both of these O/S versions have the concept of priority, which will affect how much of the CPU any particular process gets in comparison to other processes running on the system.
	If you use this option, you must supply a value of 1-5 for the @value parameter. 3 is the default (Normal priority). 1 would mean run full-text at the lowest priority level, and 5 would mean that this system is pretty much dedicated to running full-text searches.
clean_up	This is for dealing with those situations where you change full-text related meta-data while the MSSearch service is not active. For example, you might elect to remove a column from an index or drop one entirely at a time when MSSearch has, for whatever reason, been shut down. Using the clean_up option, the Search Service will look for catalogs or columns that are no longer associated with SQL Server data, and remove them.
	This is the only action that does not require the @value parameter to be filled in.
connect_timeout/ data_timeout	These two are very closely related to each other. Whenever the MSSearch service needs to perform a population, it needs to retrieve data from the SQL Server. The connect_timeout action sets the length of time the MSSearch service will wait to connect to SQL Server before it declares an error. The data_timeout action sets the length of time SQL Server will wait on a particular data request before raising an error.
	If you use this option, you must supply a numeric value of between 1 and 32,767 (which will equate to how many seconds MSSearch will wait for the action you've specified).

Summary

Full-Text runs as a separate service in the SQL Server box, and takes up a separate block of memory. Be sure to keep both services in mind when planning how much memory your system needs, and also when establishing the amount of memory used by the SQL Server service. By default, the MSSQLServer service will be set to a maximum memory usage equal to the amount of RAM in your system, less 1MB. That doesn't leave much for MSSearch. How to balance the actual RAM between the two services will vary widely depending on the size of your full-text and non full-text queries, so it's tough for me to give you guide on that side of things. In addition, if you're running full-text server, you'll want to adjust up your Windows 2000/NT virtual memory size from the fairly standard 1.5 times physical memory to 3 times physical memory.

When you implement full-text, also consider the load the population process is going to place on your server, and balance that against how quickly you need changes reflected in search results. If possible, delay repopulation of full-text indexes until the non-peak hours of your system.

Full-Text Search is a powerful and fast way of referencing the contents of almost any character-based columns. It is substantially more efficient and powerful than a LIKE clause, but comes with additional overhead in terms of both space and processing time.

27

English Query

Originally, SQL was actually SEQUEL – which stood for Structured English QUEry Language. Indeed, SQL does read like basic English – as you read it, you learn in pretty much plain English what exactly the query is going to do. The problem, however, arrives when you try to go the other way – that is, to *write* queries rather than read them. That's where English Query comes in.

English Query translates questions written by users in plain English or natural language into the SQL queries that we've come to know and love as we've moved through this book. It is intended to provide enhanced search support to users while reducing the demands on developers to anticipate users' queries. As a result, users get flexible searches based upon free-form queries entered in the form of questions.

How does this work? Well, we'll investigate this as the chapter goes on, but suffice it to say that, you, as the developer, define **semantics** that describe database tables and the relationships between tables and columns. English Query uses these semantics to translate user queries into standard SQL statements that are then executed by an application program to retrieve results from the database and present them to the user.

English Query, much like Analysis Services, involves a completely separate installation process (though it is on the same CD with SQL Server and Analysis Services) and, while it is often ignored by many SQL developers, it is a very important and powerful tool. It allows us to build applications that provide users with more flexible and powerful data retrieval capabilities than are possible using standard T-SQL queries. English Query – often referred to simply as "EQ" – was introduced in the Enterprise Edition of SQL Server 6.5, but was first put into wide scale distribution with SQL Server 7.0 – where it was available in all editions. It has been thoroughly revised for SQL Server 2000. Several major improvements were added to simplify the development, testing, and deployment of EQ applications:

❑ A SQL Project Wizard automates the creation of basic EQ models from a relational database, using the tables in the database to create table "entities", the fields in those tables to create minor entities, and the relationships to create semantic relationships among these entities.

❑ The EQ authoring system now uses the Microsoft Visual Studio 6.0 Interactive Development Environment (IDE). The IDE will be familiar to developers who have used Visual InterDev.

❑ Model information is now stored in the XML-based Semantic Modeling Format (SMF), reflecting the Microsoft .NET strategy.

❑ A graphical authoring tool displays entities and relationships in the EQ model, and additional relationships can be created by dragging and dropping.

❑ Full-text query is supported.

❑ Analytical services for OLAP databases can be created by a new OLAP Project Wizard, provided that OLAP is installed.

❑ More sample projects are included to assist developers. Sample EQ projects are provided for the Foodmart, Northwind, and Pubs sample databases. Sample programming projects in Visual Basic, Visual C++, and ASP demonstrate how to integrate EQ into these applications using these languages. An Authoring Object Model (AOM) automates model building and updating using existing model files.

This chapter will introduce EQ and provide you with the fundamentals for implementing it with your database. Like most of the major tools that come with SQL Server (DTS, Analysis Services, WMI), EQ really takes more than a single chapter to become an expert at it – it really could be a book in itself. With this in mind, the idea in this chapter is really to give you a good foundation in what EQ is all about, and to give you a feel for whether it's something you want to dig further into or not. In this chapter, we'll cover:

❑ The benefits and limitations of EQ

❑ A tutorial on creating a basic EQ application

❑ Examples of advanced refinements in an application

❑ How to refine the semantics for an EQ application

❑ How to deploy an EQ application and use it in a COM application

What is English Query?

EQ allows application and web site developers to provide users with the ability to retrieve data by asking questions in plain English. It must be used in conjunction with a data access technology such as ActiveX Data Objects (ADO) or Remote Data Objects (RDO). The illustration shows the communication that takes place between a client application, the EQ Engine, and the EQ Application (.eqd file) created by a developer using the EQ Domain Editor:

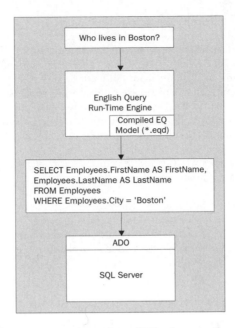

The user asks a question in normal English, such as, "Who lives in Boston?" The client application passes the user's question to the EQ Engine, which then uses the EQ Application's knowledge about the database and its semantics to generate a T-SQL statement. That statement is passed back to the client application. The client application must then issue the query against the database to retrieve a result set.

The term "client application" refers to the application that uses the services of the EQ Engine. As we'll see later in the chapter, this client application can be built in any language that supports ActiveX automation , such as Visual Basic, Visual C++, or Active Server Pages. It can run on the client workstation or it can run as an ActiveX component on an application or database server.

The Benefits and Limitations of English Query

EQ can provide an important enhancement to applications that allows users to retrieve information about a data source. Implementing EQ support provides the following benefits:

- ❑   Users can interact with the application in a more natural way

- ❑   Users can retrieve the information they really want

- ❑   Users can get answers to more complicated questions

- ❑   Developers do not have to write predefined queries for every combination of data users might need, nor build complicated SQL joins from user selections of fields and operators.

The user typically presents a query to the application by typing a question. Another possible scenario to consider when using EQ is one that involves speech recognition, which must be provided by the developer's application to translate spoken words into text that can be presented to an EQ. By using EQ, in conjunction with speech recognition technology, developers can provide users with the ability to ask questions about a data source, almost as naturally as they would ask another person. This provides a distinct advantage for supporting visually impaired users, users who suffer from repetitive motion disorders, and users with other disabilities.

Although EQ opens the door to some exciting possibilities, it is not a panacea. EQ translates the user's question into SQL, a step that involves some overhead. It creates ad hoc queries, which are going to run somewhat slower than one encapsulated in a sproc. This means that it should only be used in situations that can benefit from the type of flexibility it offers users. If the users of your application will typically perform some queries over and over again, you will want to provide them with a more static means of executing the query. For example, if the users are interested in retrieving predefined reports ninety percent of the time, you will want to provide users with a list of those reports and utilize stored procedures to generate those reports. EQ is all about flexibility so use it when flexibility is the goal – but use more defined (and better performing) methods where possible.

Another limitation is that EQ does what its name implies – it translates *English* to a query. At this time, there are no equivalent implementations in other languages.

It is also important to realize that building an effective EQ application is not a trivial task. It requires a careful consideration of how the entities and relationships in your database can be used to answer questions. Testing your application well is essential to ensuring that users won't be frustrated by questions that can't be answered. This chapter will give you some understanding of the work involved in creating an EQ application so that you can make an informed choice about whether or not the effort will create a sufficient return on your investment.

The Architecture of an English Query Application

Before looking at the specifics of how to build an EQ application, let's look at its contents. An EQ application requires two types of information: the database schema and information about how that schema maps to semantic objects.

A **semantic object** can be either an **entity** or a **relationship** between entities. Each semantic object corresponds closely to a standard element of a database. There are three possible types of entities in an EQ project:

❑ Table entities, each referring to a table in the database

❑ Field entities, each referring to a field or column in a table

❑ Analysis Services entities (if Analysis Services is installed)

The short rendition of what entities are takes me back to something that many American readers will remember from "Schoolhouse Rock" (these used to be short educational programmes that aired much like commercials on TV). Entities are nouns – which is to say they are a "Person, Place, or Thing".

Later in this chapter, we will build an application using table and field entities, but many of the concepts learned here will also apply to EQ Applications you build using Analysis Services.

Relationships are expressed as phrases, corresponding to a particular sentence structure. Consider the simplest case – the relationship between a field within a table and the table entity as a whole. A `Customer` table, for instance, might contain a `Customer_City` field. In the relational database, the relationship of `Customer_City` to the `Customer` table is automatically maintained by the RDBMS. We understand that each `Customer` record has a field that contains the `Customer_City` name. But the semantic relationship may need to be more precise. Is the city a location of customers? Or an adjective that describes the customer? The semantic choices are either that customers have cities (adjective) or that customers are in cities (location).

Clearly, for any query purpose, the second relationship is the more relevant. Later, we will see that we may need synonyms for "are in" – such as "live in". We may also find that we need relationships such as "work in" or "travel to", among others.

In RDBMS design, a "relationship" is more commonly interpreted as a relationship between tables, such as `Customers` and `Orders`. Here the primary key in one table (such as the `Customer_ID`) is the foreign key in another table (`Orders`) and is used in joins across the tables. The semantic relationship would be `Customers have Orders`.

To a very large degree, the challenge of developing an EQ project is to define the entities and the relationships. Each entity and relationship has properties that help to determine how the English query is translated into a SQL query. We will begin to build a simple application and use the example to show these properties. It should be clear by now that English queries, like SQL queries, cannot solve problems in the database design. Indeed, the use of EQ in your applications accentuates the importance of sound database design.

The most common EQ problems arise from incomplete normalization of the database. For example, if the database has composite fields, such as `Customer_Name` instead of `Customer_FirstName` and `Customer_LastName`, no query can return customers whose last name is `Jones`. If the `Order` table has multi-valued attributes such as `Item1`, `Item2`, and `Item3`, then no simple query can return a list or a count of orders for `Apples`. The `Order` table must be normalized by setting up a separate `OrderItem` table.

Creating an English Query Project

Now that you understand the fundamental concepts behind EQ, it's time to look at what's involved in creating an EQ project. The steps you need to take to implement an EQ project are:

1. Create a new project, incorporating a connection to a database

2. Define the tables and fields that will become the semantic entities

3. Define the relationships between these entities

4. Test your project

5. Expand and refine the definitions of the entities and relationships

6. Test your project again

7. Repeat steps 5 & 6 above as many times as necessary

8. Compile and distribute your application

If you have Use Case or Unified Modelling Language (UML) documentation for your application, you will be able to use this as a starting point for defining the entities and relationships in your EQ application. However, you will also need significant input from your users. Survey them to determine what questions they are likely to want to ask when analyzing the data and pay particular attention to how they phrase their questions. Your design documentation may refer to Customer objects, but the salespeople may call them Clients and the accounting department may call them Accounts. If you are going to build an application that allows users to ask questions in their own way, you will need to consider small differences like these.

Testing and refining your project is an iterative process. It is a good idea to get users involved in the testing. When working with the product, they may ask questions they didn't think about during the initial design phase. Once you and the group of users whose help you have enlisted are satisfied that your application can answer all of the questions that a user will pose, you can compile and distribute your application.

Let's take a closer look at the steps involved in building an application. We'll do this by building a sample application using the Northwind database.

Create a New Project using SQL Project Wizard

When EQ is installed, a shortcut is created in Start | Programs | Microsoft SQL Server | English Query (provided you have placed English Query in the default location). With SQL Server 2000, three entries are created in this menu, English Query Books Online, English Query Tutorials, and Microsoft English Query.

Launching Microsoft English Query displays a dialog form that is new in SQL Server 2000:

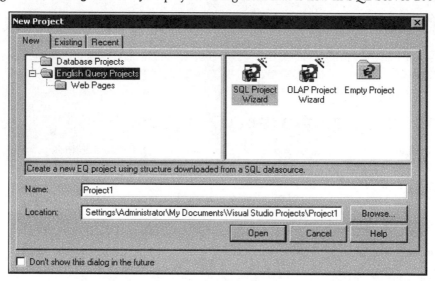

If you do not see the SQL Project Wizard *choice in the right-hand pane, make sure that in the* New Projects *dialog, the* New *tab is selected and that in the left pane,* English Query Projects *is highlighted.*

This form has four major parts requesting the following information:

❑ The dialog has three tabs, which we can use to create a New project, open an Existing project, or select a Recent project. Let's keep the New tab open, and select the English Query Projects.

❑ In the right-hand pane of the New tab, select the SQL Project Wizard.

❑ In the Name text box, we can replace the default name of Project1 with our desired project name. For the purposes of this chapter, we'll name it Northwind.

❑ In the Location text box, we can accept the default or browse to a new location. The default will be a subfolder, usually under My Documents\Visual Studio, with the exact path depending upon your operating system and installation.

Note that we haven't specified which database we will be using yet, although we have named the project and decided on its location.

> *If you choose to create an* Empty Project *at the first step, then you will get an empty project with the default name of* Project1. *You can import tables from a database at the next step, but you will not get any assistance from the wizard and you will have to create each entity and relationship individually. To import tables, first use the* Project Explorer *window and double-click on the module file (*.eqm) *to which the tables are to be added. Next, on the main menu select* Model | Import Tables. *Next you choose a connection, server, and database. In the* New Databases Tables and Views *dialog box, select the tables you want from the* Available *list and add them to the list in the right-hand pane. When you're done, don't forget to click on* OK. *Then begin building entities and relationships.*

Once you've set all the options correctly, click on Open. The SQL Project Wizard now prompts us to select a Data Link Provider. As we're working with a SQL Server database, we need to select the Microsoft OLE DB Provider for SQL Server:

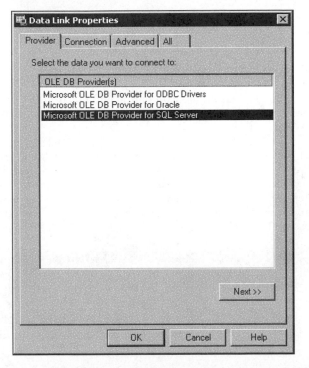

Clicking the Next button, we then move on to the Connection tab. On this tab we select the name of the server to which we want to connect, the login information for this server, and also the database to which we wish to connect. In the example shown, I have selected a test server called SOCRATES, using Windows NT Integrated Security. However, your choices must fit your own network configuration here, so select your desired instance of SQL Server. If you choose to use the Use a specific user name and password option, be sure to enter a user name and password with access to the Northwind database. Then select the Northwind database:

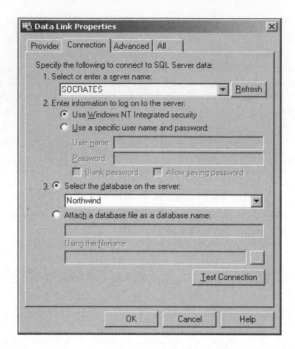

Finally, it is wise to click on the Test Connection button and receive the Test connection succeeded message before proceeding. If your test connection was successful, then you've completed the database connection step. Click OK.

Next, the SQL Project Wizard assists in the selection of the database tables and views that you want to be accessible to the English Query model. It displays a dialog box showing the list of all available tables and views on the left. If you highlight an Available table, you can select it to make it accessible to EQ by clicking the > button. Alternatively, you can select all of the available views and tables by clicking on the >> button. Similarly, you can remove individual or multiple items from the Selected list by using either the < or << buttons. To follow along, select all the files and click on OK.

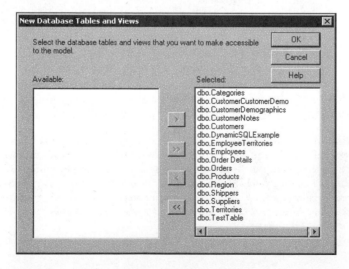

As with many of the other examples we've worked throughout this book, you may see a somewhat different list of tables from that shown here. The list will vary depending on which chapters' examples you've worked through. As long as you have all the original tables that came with Northwind, *then you're OK for this set of examples. If you're in doubt, you can always reinstall* Northwind *from scratch by loading and executing the* instnwnd.sql *file that's in the install sub-directory under your main SQL Server installation directory.*

Next, the SQL Project Wizard offers to automatically create a model from your database. It creates an entity corresponding to each database object, and creates relationships between all of the tables. For each entity, the wizard automatically builds name and trait relationships. It therefore provides automated creation of all of the basic entities and relationships needed in a basic model.

Don't get overly reliant on the automated creation wizard – it's less than foolproof. For example, it will occasionally do things like decide that "Order Details have Orders", but it's really the other way around (Orders have Order Details). Still, it gets a ton of the preliminary work out of the way for you – you just need to keep and eye on things and not blindly accept the defaults (good advice for just about anything – not just EQ). We'll see more of this as we continue through the example.

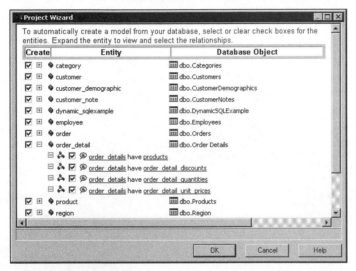

Each entity has a + sign beside it. Clicking the + adjacent to the order_detail entity (which was created for the database table dbo.Order Details) expands the list and shows the default relationships that will be created by the wizard. The check box accompanying each suggested relationship enables us to employ each specific relationship as we require. In addition, the 🕸 icon next to the check mark allows us to edit the nature of the relationship (for example, we could fix entries that had the wrong relationship precedence – such as the "Orders have Order Details" example I used earlier).

At this stage, we can begin to see the EQ capability emerging in relationships such as <u>order details</u> have <u>products</u> and <u>order details</u> have <u>order detail discounts</u>.

You should notice that not all tables suggest relationships that are as clear or as simple as they were for the Order Details table. For example, expand the Customer entity:

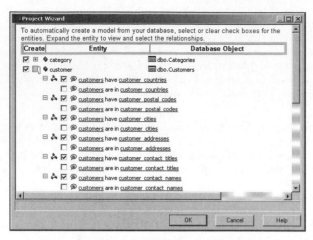

The wizard shows several choices of relationships, such as customers_have_customer_countries and customers_are_in_customer_countries, with the first choice checked. In fact, the second suggested relationship would probably be the better choice because it fits a more typical use of the English language. Feel free to cruise through the list of relationships at this point and make the choices that seem to make more sense to you.

Click on the OK button and the wizard is finally completed. At this point, you will see the EQ authoring tools in the Visual InterDev 6.0 integrated development environment (IDE). In this environment, all components of the project are visible.

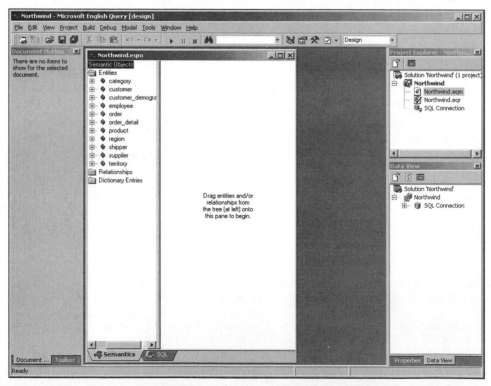

Don't worry if the layout of your IDE environment doesn't exactly match this one. If you've ever opened up Visual InterDev, then changes you made there (windows you closed or changed the position of) will also be reflected in what you see when editing EQ projects.

At this point you've done a fair amount of the construction of your EQ project, so it's probably a good idea to save all of the files in the project by clicking the Save All icon on the tool bar or by going to the File menu and then selecting Save All. The motto, "Save early, save often" applies here – it's rather easy to make changes that cause problems that make you want to revert to an earlier version.

There are a few things worth noticing in the IDE:

❑ In the center is the Model Editor window. This is really the starting point for all development. The caption of the Model Editor window is Northwind.eqm (if you used the same title I did). This corresponds to the Equation Model File, which contains the XML code that defines the entities and relationships that will be used in creating English queries. (Sample contents of this file will be discussed later in this chapter.)

❑ Within the Model Editor, there are two tabs: the Semantics tab and the SQL tab.

❑ The Semantics tab shows the Semantics Objects for the project, consisting of the Entities, the Relationships, and the Dictionary Entries.

❑ The SQL tab shows the list of tables and fields in the database, as well as the default JOINs that EQ has built (using foreign key references). A JOIN from an EQ perspective means that, when EQ needs to access those two tables together, it will use the JOIN information it has stored for the query when the T-SQL is generated.

After this initial construction, most English Query development will be done in the Semantics tab of the Model Editor window. Keep the SQL window in mind, however, when you add new tables or relationships.

Basic English Queries

At this stage, we have the capability to execute very basic English Queries. To do this, start the project either by using the menu command Debug | Start, by clicking the Start arrow icon on the toolbar, or by hitting the *F5* key, exactly as you would in a Visual Basic project. Initially you see the empty Northwind – Model Test window seen in the following screenshot. Click to depress the View Results button so that the results of the query will be displayed.

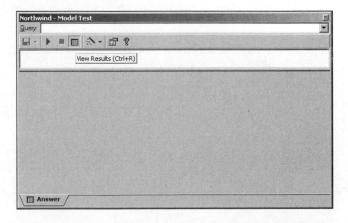

Testing a Basic Query

To conduct a test, click the Start icon or hit the *F5* key to start up the EQ test environment. Then type the simple query List all customers in the Query box at the top of the Model Test form:

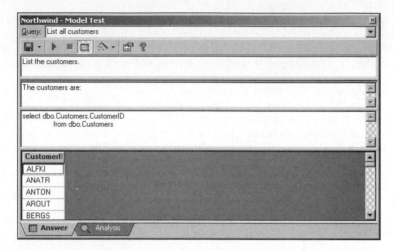

The Model Test form shows the query that you entered, English Query's restatement of your query, a box showing the query as a statement, and the SQL statements generated to execute the query. At the bottom of the Model Test form you see the results of the query, in this case the list of CustomerIDs. Although only a few queries will be successful at this point in time, you should be able to execute "List customers and their phones", "List customers and their cities", and "List customer cities". Note that the query "List customer cities" returns only the unique city names and not the customer identification.

We want to go back and look at the first query we executed, "List all customers". The easiest way to do this is to click on the Query box pull-down menu (above the toolbar right at the top of the Model Test form), and you will then see a list of the executed queries, from which you can select the query we want simply by clicking on it. Now re-execute the "List all customers" query and then click on the Analysis tab at the bottom of the form and you will then see a list of the entities and phrasings used:

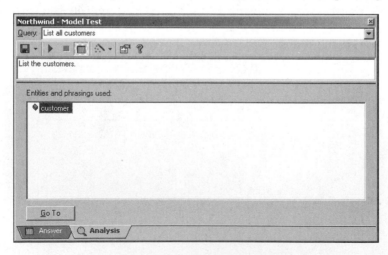

Viewing and Changing Entity Properties

Since we have used only one entity, the Analysis tab shows only the customer semantic entity and seems to be of limited interest. However, if you double-click on the customer entity you will then see the customer entity properties displayed in the Entity: customer dialog.

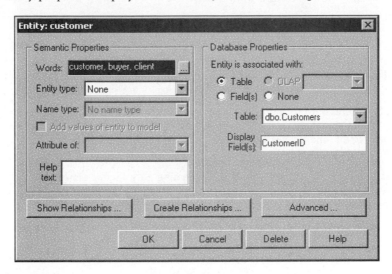

This dialog shows the entity properties that can be modified to increase the power of English queries using it. The frame on the left shows the Semantic Properties, while the frame on the right details the Database Properties. At the bottom, we can modify the relationships between the entities – we shall examine this later on in the chapter.

> *A more direct way to view entity properties is to double-click the entity name in the* Semantics *tab of the of Model Editor window. This is the route to use when you know you need to modify an entity before you can test your queries or when you want to examine the properties of an entity.*

Before we get mired down in the notion of relationships, however, let's look at the parts of the Semantic Properties frame; key properties are:

Words

As you can see, the wizard has provided three synonyms for customer, and they are displayed in the Words list for us: customer, buyer, client. We do not need to add anything to this list, but if we did want to, we could click on the list and type in our new word or phrase (make use of the same comma separator to indicate the beginning and end of the phrase). If we click the ellipsis (…) to the right of the list, we get additional word suggestions:

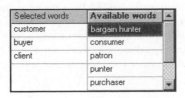

When you put the cursor over any word in the Available words list, the cursor changes to a left arrow. If you perform a single click at this point, EQ adds that word to the Selected words list. Similarly, if you've added a word to the Selected words list and wish to remove it, you can remove it by simply hovering your cursor over the word you wish to remove; a right arrow will then appear – a subsequent mouse click will then remove the word from the list.

Entity Type

The Entity type is currently set to None. Other choices available in the drop-down list are:

- ❑ **Who:** This essentially tells EQ that we're dealing with the concept of a person when dealing with this entity. It allows "Who" kinds of questions – for example, "Who bought fish?"

- ❑ **When:** Someone once told me "It's all about timing, Rob!" – we'll, this entity type is all about questions that somehow relate to time. Among other things, this option allows you to adjust the When, Start, and End options when you are specifying semantic information on the Semantics tab in the Relationship dialog.

- ❑ **Where:** This one lets EQ know that we're dealing with location information. If we wanted, we could ask about the "location" of a customer address or perhaps deal with something like a store location.

- ❑ **Measure:** – This deals with things like quanity (such as "How many pounds of beans were sold?").

For this example, we'll select Who, as it is clearly the best choice for customers in the long run.

Name Type

This one is a bit more of an advanced concept, and is only available if you've selected Field(s) or OLAP from the Database Properites option on the right-hand side of the dialog. Most of the time you won't use this one, but it allows you to deal with certain kinds of names – for example, a "classifier" name defines something that is usually a grouping kind of name such as "the Sales Department".

Add Values of Entity to Model

The "Add Values..." checkbox is only available if you have something other than "No Name Type" in the Name type field above. Essentially, this one tells EQ to adopt the actual row values of the underlying data source into the actual EQ model.

Attribute of

This allows you to identify the fact that your entity serves as an attribute for some other entity – for example, order detail items have characteristics such as weight. This option will generally not be used.

Help Text

Another relatively advanced feature, this one allows you to attach a certain amount of help to the entity. This should probably beg the question "Wait a minute! If I have to write the app that runs this query in the first place, how do I expose this 'help' to the end users?" Glad you asked. EQ makes available to you a special tool called the **Question Builder**. You can expose this tool to the end user to provide extra help and information about the queries that they are writing. In addition to the Help Text, Question Builder also exposes things like word lists that your EQ model recognizes and what entities and relationships they are associated with.

Is Associated With

This one is what it sounds like – it defines what table, OLAP item (level, dimension, measure, property, and fact), or individual Field(s) that this entity is associated with (and, subsequently, what field(s) get displayed or otherwise utilized when you reference this entity). Select "None" to indicate that this entity is independent of specific tables, OLAP cuts, or fields. If you do specify a particular association, then you'll also need to fill out the Table and, perhaps, Field(s) information.

We want to change the display fields to show the ContactName instead of the CustomerID. Click on CustomerID in the Display Field(s) box and you will see a drop-down list showing Selected Fields on the left and Available Fields on the right.

When you put the cursor over the field CustomerID, the cursor turns to a right arrow. Click once to remove the CustomerID. Now put the cursor over ContactName and click once to put ContactName into the Display Field(s) box.

Retesting the Basic Query

Now click OK to close the Entity: customer window, and return to the Answer tab of Model Test form. Then run the query "List all customers and their phones":

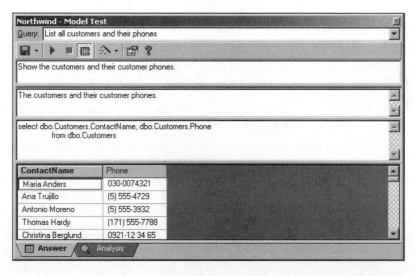

At this stage even minor variations in the wording of queries may produce different query results. The query "List customer phones and cities" gives the expected result listing ContactName, City, and Phone. Try "List customers, phones and cities." You will see that English Query broke that into three different queries with three different Answer tabs, one listing the ContactName, one listing the supplier phones, and one listing customer cities.

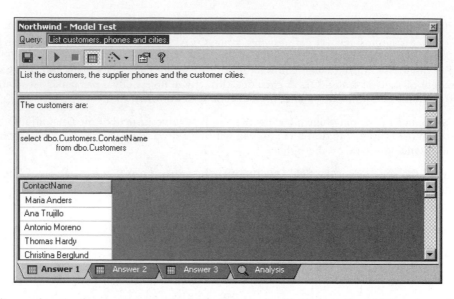

Let's refine and expand our entities and relationships to enable us to make additional queries. Close the Entity: customer and Model Test windows to view the Model Editor. If you have a small monitor you will probably want to close some of the windows to make some screen space for the next development steps. We will not be using the Toolbox or Task List windows so these should be your first choices in windows to close if this applies to you.

Refining and Expanding Entities and Relationships

If you play around with our EQ model for very long, you'll probably quickly figure out that the model is not yet ready for prime time. There are lots of fairly obvious questions you could ask where EQ would respond with something along the lines of, "I don't understand what you mean."

You will generally always want to expand and refine the entity definitions provided by the wizard – rounding out the word associations and adding terminology and synonyms that are specific to your particular application.

For our Northwind example, let's begin this process by considering the **table entity**. In database design, a table contains data about something that is a person, place, thing, action, or state (condition, not location). In other words, an entity is a noun. A semantic table entity corresponds to a table or view in the database. For example, we are building an EQ application that will allow users to retrieve information about customers and the orders they have placed, so we need to expand the definition of the table entity named customer. To do so, double-click on the customer entity in the Model Editor. The Entity: customer dialog will appear, allowing us to view, edit, and expand the Semantic Properties on the left, the Database Properties on the right, or the Relationships at the bottom.

> When you add new words to your entities' selected words list, make sure that you type the word in its singular form. In addition, these words are case-sensitive. Synonyms should be entered as lower case words. If users are likely to use various cases when entering the question, make sure to list all cases of the word here. Otherwise, English Query assumes that any capitalized word in a query is a proper name.

Customers usually relate more closely to the notion of a person rather than anything else, so we're probably going to deal with "Who?" questions (the question "Where bought coffee?" doesn't make sense, but "Who bought coffee?" does). Since the wizard did not make a selection for us, you should therefore select Who as the Entity type.

With our Customers entity, we're dealing with a whole table (as opposed to an OLAP cube or a particular field), so we don't have anything to see for the Name type or Attribute of options. We'll also skip the Help text for the while.

Moving on to the Database Properties frame on the right, the Table property should be already be selected. We changed the Display Field(s) to ContactName a little earlier in the chapter. If, however, we were to leave this option entirely blank, then any query we made that referenced this entity (that is to say, Customers) would display *all* fields from the associated table in the database.

> *Remember that, in the default setting, it was set to* CustomerID *for the* Customers *table – this is because the default is the Primary Key for the table. More often than not, that's not going to be the kind of thing that a user who needs EQ is going to know much about – indeed, it may just be confusing to them. The point here is to really think about what fields are (and are not) appropriate for each entity that you define in EQ.*

We've finished modifying our basic customer entity, so click on the OK button.

Refining and Expanding a Field Entity

In SQL Server 2000, the EQ SQL Project Wizard creates basic entity definitions and relationships automatically by using the primary keys and foreign keys defined in the database. In EQ for SQL Server 7.0, the **autoname** facility allowed us to define the field or fields with which the name of a table entity was identified. Defining an autoname created a relationship with the phrasing "*table entity* names are the Names of *Table Entity*". For example, a default relationship for the employee entity results in a relationship of *employee_names_are_the_names_of_employees*. The SQL Project Wizard provides the equivalent entities and relationships in SQL Server 2000.

Identifying the appropriate entity properties helps the query engine understand when a value for the **field entity** (field entries are the entities based on individual fields in the tables, as opposed to table entities which are based on entire tables) is being specified. This is a two-step process. First, set the properties of the field entity, and then define its relationship to the table entity.

To view the properties of the employee_name field entity, first expand the employee table entity in the Model Editor, then double-click the employee_name field entity. The entity properties created by the wizard will then be displayed:

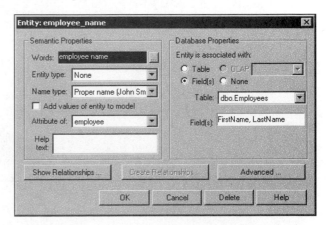

You can see that the properties of the field entity are similar to those of the table entity, but the additional properties Add values of entity to model and Attribute of: have been enabled. Our first step is to set the Entity type to Who. Notice that the wizard has set Name Type to Proper name, based on its analysis of the contents of the table.

As indicated a moment ago, field entities have two more properties than table entities – the Add values of entity to model, and the Attribute of, which specify to which table entity the field belongs. This allows resolution of homonyms – words that are the same but refer to different attributes in different tables (for instance, where a Name field might be the name of a customer, an employee, or a product).

Note that we can associate the employee_name field entity with multiple fields in the database. The wizard has done this for us automatically. An employee may sometimes be referenced by first name, sometimes by last name, and at other times by his or her full name. By creating an employee_name field entity that includes the Firstname and Lastname fields, any query generated will automatically check both fields, allowing users to use the first name, the last name, or both names to locate a match.

> The **Add values of entity to model** option for field entities is *not* checked by default in English Query for SQL Server 2000. Checking this option causes the values in the column associated with this entity to be added to the model for each row of the table. Checking this option is *highly* recommended. If the values of entities are not included in the model, some questions involving these values may be untranslatable or ambiguous. Turning this option off can result in a smaller application, but the English Query Engine may not be able to translate some questions that users pose.

Basic Field Relationships

Next, let's look at the relationship that relates the employee_name field entity to the employee table entity. Click OK to close the Entity: employee_name window and expand the Relationships node in the Model Editor. Since the wizard has already created this relationship, we can double-click on the employee_names_are_the_ names_of_employees relationship in the Model Editor and view the Relationship dialog box. Note in particular the list of entities in the upper pane and the phrasings in the lower pane. We can also add tables or edit the phrasings as needed:

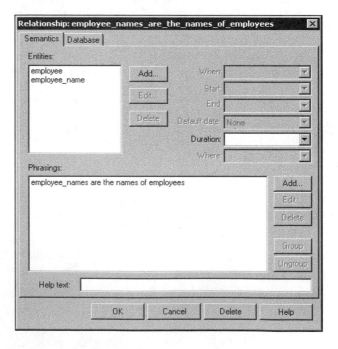

The following table shows the queries that will be generated if an `employee` entity contains a relationship mapped to `FirstName` and `LastName`:

English	SQL
Which employees are named Steven?	`SELECT dbo.Employees.FirstName AS "FirstName", dbo.Employees.LastName AS "LastName" FROM dbo.Employees WHERE dbo.Employees.FirstName ='Steven' OR dbo.Employees.LastName='Steven'`
Who is Steven Buchanan?	`SELECT dbo.Employees.FirstName AS "FirstName", dbo.Employees.LastName AS "LastName" FROM dbo.Employees WHERE dbo.Employees.LastName= 'Buchanan' AND dbo.Employees.FirstName='Steven'`

Although the second query is a little obvious, if more entities and relationships were defined, it would allow users to ask about Steven Buchanan's address, title, or salary.

In the Relationship: employee_names_are_the_names_of_employees window, click on the phrase in the Phrasings list at the bottom of the dialog box. Then click the Edit button – you will see the Name/ID Phrasing dialog showing the field Entity that is the name/ID on the left and the table Entity being named on the right. Click OK or Cancel to close the window, then close the employee_names Relationship window.

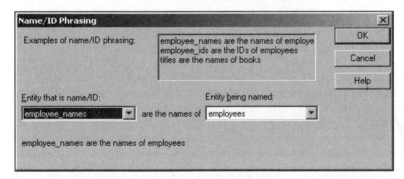

Now try the query Which customers are named Maria?. The response you should get is, Based on the information I've been given about this database, I can't answer: "What are the names of customers?". This seems odd, because previously we were able to list customers, but there is no relationship that defines customer names as proper names (such as customer_contact_names_are_the_names_of_customers). We need to add a new relationship that defines `customer_contact_names` as the names of customers.

To do this, right-click on the Customer entity in the Model Editor window and choose Add Relationship, or choose from the main menu Model I Add Relationship. In the top part of the window next to the Entities list, click the Add button and choose the entity `customer_contact_name`. Both `customer` and `customer_contact_name` should now appear in the Entities list.

In the bottom part of the window next to the Phrasings list (which is now empty), click Add. We are given several choices of phrasings.

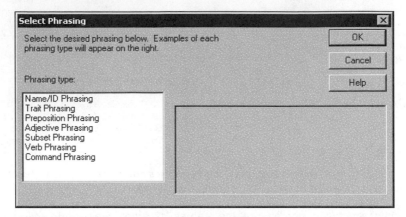

Since we want to associate the customer_contact_name field entity with the customer table entity, choose Name/ID Phrasing. The Name/ID Phrasing window then appears and automatically chooses the desired phrasing: customer_contact_names are the names of customers.

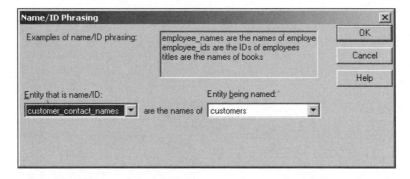

Click OK to save the phrasing, and OK again to save and close the Relationship editor window.

Unfortunately, the query still does not work as expected because the ContactName field includes both first and last names unlike the employee name fields, and EQ will not allow the user to optionally generate a pattern query using the LIKE operator. We can change the default search type for any field to perform pattern or exact match searches.

To change the search type for any field in any table, click on the SQL tab in the Model Editor, expand any table object, double-click the field name, and set the properties for the fields individually.

> *Watch out with this one – we've largely been working with the Semantics tab up to this point – don't forget to change to the SQL tab!*

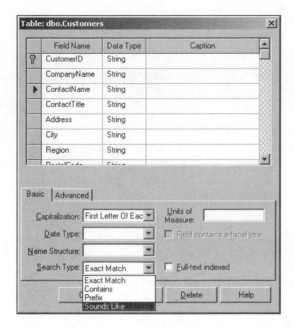

The new default is set for all searches using that field and not only for any single query.

Defining Additional Phrasings

Additional phrasing in relationships can increase the power of EQ when responding to a query. When a field entity is defined, a "have a" relationship will be added to the Relationships folder of the Model Editor. This type of relationship is known as a **trait phrasing**. For example, the wizard created the relationship customers_have_customer_cities.

But, suppose we want to find out which customers are located in certain cities? We need an additional phrasing to implement that relationship.

To define additional phrasings for the entity pair of customer and customer_city, go back to the Model Editor, click on the Semantics tab and double-click on the customers_have_customer_cities relationship. Then, in the Relationships dialog, click on the Add button next to the Phrasings list. The following dialog will appear:

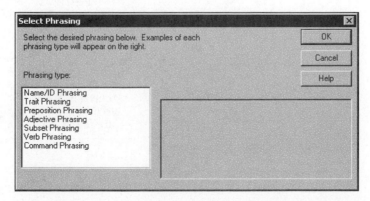

Select the type of phrasing you would like to define. In this case, we want to be able to answer questions like, "Which customers are in London?" Since "in London" is a prepositional phrase, we must double-click on Preposition Phrasing and click on OK. The following dialog appears:

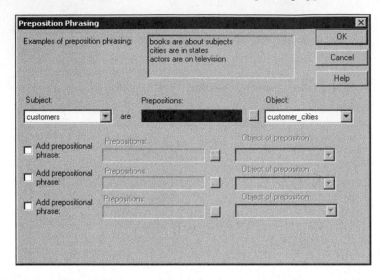

Next, we need to define the prepositional phrases that apply to the pair of entities. Since customers are *in* cities, this would be the only prepositional phrase that would apply, so type in into the Prepositions box and click on OK.

Once you have defined this phrasing, users will be able to get information about customer locations using more natural questions. The following table shows some potential questions and the SQL that is returned by EQ. The comments column describes some of the clauses and functions in the English Query-generated SQL queries:

English	SQL	Comments

Where are the customers located?	`SELECT dbo.Customers.`
	`ContactName,`
	`dbo.Customers.City`
	`FROM dbo.Customers`
		Since we defined `CompanyName` as the Display Field property for the `customer` entity, this query will return a result set containing the company name and the city where the company is located.

Which customers are in London?	`SELECT dbo.Customers.`
	`ContactName FROM`
	`dbo.Customers`
	`WHERE dbo.Customers.`
	`City='London'`	

How many customers are in London?	`SELECT count(*) AS "count"`
	`FROM dbo.Customers`
	`WHERE dbo.Customers.`
	`City='London'`
		This query uses the COUNT aggregate to determine how many customers are in the city of London.

English	SQL	Comments

Which city has the most customers?	`SELECT TOP 1 WITH TIES`
	`    dbo.Customers.City,`
	`    COUNT(*) AS "count"`
	`    FROM dbo.Customers`
	`    WHERE dbo.Customers.`
	`    City IS NOT NULL`
	`    GROUP BY`
	`    dbo.Customers.City`
	`    order by 2 desc`
		The SQL generated to answer this question returns a result set with two columns. The first is the contents of the City column. The second is the number of customers in that city. It then sorts the customers in descending order, by the value in the second column returned (hence the 2).

How many customers are in each city?	`select dbo.Customers.City,`
	`    count(*) as "count"`
	`    from dbo.Customers`
	`    where dbo.Customers.`
	`    City is not null`
	`    group by`
	`    dbo.Customers.City`
		Since this question asks for a sum of customers in each city, the SQL generated uses the COUNT aggregate, in conjunction with the GROUP BY clause, to cause the number of customers to be tallied for each city. The GROUP BY clause ensures that there is only one row per city, regardless of how many times the city appears in the database.

List the customers in London or Paris.	`SELECT dbo.Customers.`
	`    ContactName,`
	`    dbo.Customers.City`
	`    FROM dbo.Customers`
	`    WHERE dbo.Customers.`
	`    City='London'`
	`    OR dbo.Customers.`
	`    City='Paris'`	

As you can see, adding a prepositional phrasing to a relationship provides a great deal more flexibility and allows users to ask much more natural questions. The example also shows how much intelligence is actually built into English Query. Notice that English Query can answer quantitative questions as well as simply searching on defined criteria. This capability is built into the engine, and works automatically when you have defined traits that can be used for categorization.

> One Transact-SQL clause is worth mentioning. Notice that the question, "Which city has the most customers?" generates SQL code that includes the WITH TIES clause. WITH TIES is used to include records that are ranked equally in the result set. For example, in this case, if two cities were tied for the most customers, both would be listed. If the WITH TIES clause was omitted, only the first customer in the list would be included in the result set. It is important to note that English Query uses the WITH TIES clause by default. This means that even if the user requests a particular number of records by asking a question like, "Which ten cities have the most customers?" the application that calls the English Query application and handles the result set cannot count on exactly ten records being returned.

Saving Queries and Regression Testing

Up to this time we have executed several queries and made a few modifications to the model. As the modifications become more extensive and the model more complex, it is always possible that future changes to the model will cause problems. Thus it becomes important to save all successful queries and use them to test the model later.

To save the queries, click the disk icon on the Model Test window toolbar or use *Ctrl Q* on the keyboard. All parts of the query (initial statement, restatement, and SQL) are saved in the regression test file Northwind.eqr. To see the contents of the file, close the Model Test window. The .eqr should be open and the latest question showing. If not, find the Northwind.eqr file name in the **Properties** window and double-click it. All saved queries are in the file, stored in XML format. If this is the first time you have saved a query, you will see only the latest query in the file. Here is a sample of three saved queries:

```xml
<?xml version="1.0"?>
<REGRESSION>
  <QUESTION>List the customers in London or Paris
    <RESTATEMENT>Which customers are in London or are in Paris?</RESTATEMENT>
    <ANSWER>The customers that are in London or are in Paris are:
      <QUERY>
        <![CDATA[select dbo.Customers.ContactName, dbo.Customers.City
      from dbo.Customers
      where dbo.Customers.City='London'
      or dbo.Customers.City='Paris']]>
      </QUERY>
    </ANSWER>
  </QUESTION>
  <QUESTION>Which customers are in London?
    <RESTATEMENT>Which customers are in London?</RESTATEMENT>
    <ANSWER>The customers that are in London are:
      <QUERY>
        <![CDATA[select dbo.Customers.ContactName
      from dbo.Customers
      where dbo.Customers.City='London']]>
      </QUERY>
    </ANSWER>
  </QUESTION>
  <QUESTION>Which city has the most customers?
    <RESTATEMENT>Show the customer city that has the most customers.</RESTATEMENT>
    <ANSWER>The customer city that has the most customers.
      <QUERY>
        <![CDATA[select top 1 with ties dbo.Customers.City, count(*) as "count"
      from dbo.Customers
      where dbo.Customers.City is not null
      group by dbo.Customers.City order by 2 desc]]>
      </QUERY>
    </ANSWER>
  </QUESTION>
</REGRESSION>
```

When you close the .eqr window, EQ prompts you to save the file. Do so. You can maintain as many different regression files as you want in order to test different parts of the application. The regression file(s) can be used for testing at any time. If a regression file is open, the command Run Regression can be seen in the menu. If no regression file is open, you can run a regression test by right-clicking the file name in the Project Explorer and choosing Run Regression.

Once a regression test has been run, you can choose View Output, View Differences, and Promote. The View Differences window compares the queries line by line and highlights any differences between the original .eqr and the .eqr generated by this test. If you want to keep the output of the current test as the reference file, then click Promote to promote the new file as the regression test file.

Defining Relationships between Tables

Since the power in relational databases lies in the ability to generate queries across multiple tables, EQ becomes even more powerful as multiple table entities and the relationships between them are defined. EQ relationships between tables require a join. Implicit joins exist whenever there is a primary key/foreign key relationship in the database, and the SQL Project Wizard imports those joins when the project is created. The database tables and joins can be viewed in the Model Editor by clicking the SQL tab at the bottom of the window, and then expanding the object properties. The screenshot shows the relationships for the Orders table:

In the case of the Northwind database, the Orders table and the Customers table are joined by the CustomerID field. We can also explicitly define joins between tables inside our application if we require relationships that are not already defined by the database schema. The SQL Project Wizard used the Northwind database primary and foreign key definitions to create a relationship between Orders and Customers. Let's see what queries can be executed using the relationships built by the SQL Project Wizard.

English/Restatement	SQL	Comments
Count orders / How many orders are there?	SELECT COUNT(*) AS "count" FROM dbo.Orders	The same syntax works for counting all customers.

Which customers have orders? /
 	
 Who is the customer of orders?
	SELECT distinct
	    dbo.Customers.ContactName
	    FROM dbo.Orders, dbo.Customers
	    WHERE dbo.Orders.CustomerID =
	     dbo.Customers.CustomerID
		Produces the list of customers who have orders.

Table continued on following page

English/Restatement	SQL	Comments

Count orders by customer /
 	
 Show the customers and how many orders have them
	`SELECT dbo.Customers.ContactName,`
	`    COUNT(DISTINCT`
	`    dbo.Orders.OrderID) AS "count"`
	`FROM dbo.Customers`
	`LEFT OUTER JOIN dbo.Orders ON`
	`dbo.Customers.CustomerID=`
	`dbo.Orders.CustomerID`
	`GROUP BY`
	`dbo.Customers.CustomerID,`
	`dbo.Customers.ContactName`
		The restatement is odd, but the result is a correct count of orders for each customer

Which customer placed the most orders?	None. 'Based on the information I've been given about this database, I can't answer: "Which orders did customers place?"'	

To answer the question "Which customer placed the most orders?", we need to enhance the relationship between the `customer` and `order` entities. Let's look at this relationship by right-clicking on the **customer** entity in the Model Editor and selecting **Show Relationships**. In the window that appears you will see that the wizard has created an `orders_have_customers` relationship. This basic relationship allowed us to answer the count questions earlier, but not the **most orders** question. To enhance it:

❑ Double-click on this relationship to open the **Relationship** editor form.

❑ Click on the **Add** button next to the **Phrasings** list.

❑ In this case, we want to define the relationship "Customers place Orders". This type of phrasing is a verb phrasing because *place* is a verb, so double-click on **Verb Phrasing**. You will then see the **Verb Phrasing** dialog.

❑ Now we need to identify the **Sentence type** of the phrasing we are adding. The supported sentence types are listed in the following table, along with an example and the type of question that verb phrasing might answer:

Sentence Type	Example	Answers Question
Subject Verb	Customers shop.	Who shops the most?
Subject Verb Object	Customers place orders.	Who placed the most orders?
Subject Verb Object Object	Employees sell customers products.	Which employees sold Taco Bell the most Corny Tortillas?
Object are Verb	Products are ordered.	How many Corny Tortillas were ordered?
Object are Verb Object	Customers are shipped products.	Who has been shipped Ole Guacamole?

In this case, we want to select **Subject Verb Object**. Next, select **customers** as the **Subject**, type **place** as the **Verb**, and select **orders** as the **Direct object**. The completed phrasing looks like this:

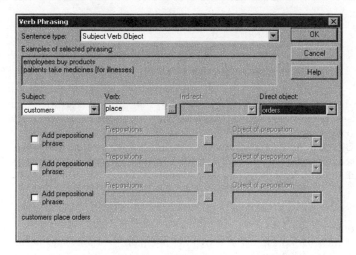

Click **OK** to return to the Model Test window. At this point, our application will be able to translate questions such as those shown in the following table:

English	SQL	Comments
Who placed the most orders?	SELECT TOP 1 WITH TIES dbo.Customers. ContactName, COUNT(*) AS "count" FROM dbo.Orders, dbo.Customers WHERE dbo.Orders.CustomerID= dbo.Customers.Customer ID group by dbo.Orders.CustomerID, dbo.Customers. ContactName ORDER BY 2 DESC	If we want to see more than customer ContactName, we must modify the customer entity and add fields such as CompanyName to the Display Fields property.
Which customers have not placed an order?	SELECT dbo.Customers. ContactName FROM dbo.Customers WHERE dbo.Customers. CustomerID NOT IN (SELECT dbo.Orders. CustomerID FROM dbo.Orders)	In this case, the English Query engine creates a non-correlated subquery. When this query is executed, first a result set containing a list of CustomerIDs of all customers who have placed orders is generated. This query is the inner query. The outer query compares that result set against each CustomerID in the Customers table. Where a match is not found, the customer's CompanyName is included in the final result set.

Table continued on following page

English	SQL	Comments

How many times has Maria Anders placed orders?	`SELECT COUNT(*) AS "count"`
	`FROM dbo.Customers, dbo.Orders`
	`WHERE dbo.Customers.ContactName=`
	`'Maria Anders'`
	`AND dbo.Customers.CustomerID=`
	`dbo.Orders.CustomerID`	

Notice that the phrasing also allows us to add prepositional phrases. Adding the appropriate prepositional phrases to a verb phrasing can allow our application to answer questions that qualify when, where, or how something happened. For example, to allow questions like, "How many orders were placed with Steven?" to be translated we need to add the prepositional phrase, "with Employees". Note that before we can add this prepositional phrase to the phrasing, we need to add the `employee` entity to the relationship. Let's look at how that's done.

Adding a Prepositional Phrase to a Verb Phrasing

To add a prepositional phrase to the `customers_place_orders` relationship, we first need to add the `employee` entity to the relationship. Do this by double-clicking on the relationship to bring up the **Relationships** dialog. Then click on the **Add** button next to the **Entities** list and select **employee** from the list that appears. Now click on **customers place orders** in the **Phrasings** list and then click on **Edit**. This brings up the **Verb Phrasing** dialog that we used to create the relationship. Place a check mark in the first **Add prepositional phrase** box. Type the preposition or prepositions that users will use to describe this relationship and select the object of the preposition from the drop-down list. In this case, we are interested in the prepositional phrase "with employees" so our **Verb Phrasing** dialog should look like this:

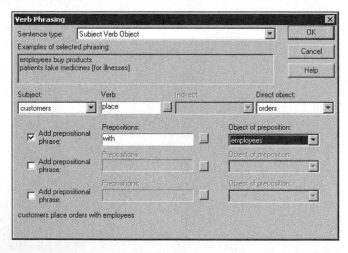

In order to avoid an error when you execute this type of query after making these changes, you must delete the relation "orders_have_customers". This is because, upon defining our relationship "customers place orders with employees", we are implicitly defining a relationship between customers and employees. This implicit way of defining relationships between entities will confuse English Query, as it simply doesn't know which relationship is complete or correct.

Supporting Questions about Time

We can also add support for questions about the time at which a particular relationship occurs. For example, we may want the users to be able to enquire about the number of orders placed in a particular month or year. To do this, we add the appropriate entity to the relationship. Since the `Orders` table includes an `OrderDate` field, we can use the `order_date` field entity. Add this entity to the `customers_place_orders_with_employees` relationship so that the Relationship dialog looks like this:

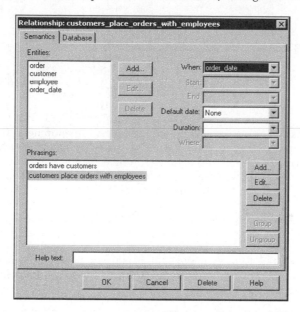

Here we can define whether the relationship *occurs* at the time specified, *starts* at the time specified, or *ends* at the time specified. In this case, the appropriate choice is that the relationship *occurs* at the time specified by the `order_date` field entity. If you want the query to be limited to a particular date if none is specified in the question, you can select a Default date setting. The available choices are None, This Month, This Year, and Today. If the Default date is set to None, the field associated with the date entity will not be qualified in the query. When the query is executed, the results for all dates will be included. If the default date is set to Today, the query will limit the results to those for which the `order_date` was today, when no specific date is included in the user's question.

> **Be careful not to set defaults in your application unless necessary. Make sure that users are aware of any defaults that you have set. Otherwise, a user might think he is asking for a specific set of orders placed over all time, when in fact only the orders placed that day will be returned.**

Relationships Based on Multiple Joins

The EQ Engine is fairly intelligent about the way that defined relationships flow into each other. For example, once the designer has defined that customers are in cities and that customers place orders, it can figure out that customers place orders in cities. This intelligence allows users to ask questions such as, "Where were the most orders placed?" In this case, the transition flows from a relationship defined between tables to a relationship involving database table attributes for which the SQL Project Wizard defined field entities.

Because EQ understands the schema of the database, it is also intelligent enough to handle relationships that involve joins across multiple tables. The best way to understand this is to examine the database relationships:

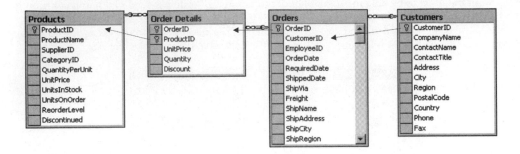

Many of these questions can be answered without any further development. If a field entity is to be used as a searchable identifier, it should, as noted previously, have its Entity type, Name type, and Add values to model set correctly. In previous exercises in this chapter, we set these properties for the Customers ContactName. If you want also to search in CompanyName, you must set its entity type to Who, its Name type to Proper, and Add values of entity to model to yes (that is, check the box).

For example, in order to support questions like, "Which customers ordered Ole Guacamole?" we can use the relationships between the customer and product that use the verb phrasing "customers order products". Although there is no direct foreign key/primary key relationship between the Customers table and the Products table, EQ can analyze the database schema and generate SQL that performs the appropriate join. The following table shows some of the questions that a user can ask based on this relationship and the complex queries they generate:

English	SQL
In what city were the most orders placed?	`SELECT TOP 1 WITH TIES dbo.Customers.City, COUNT(*) AS "count"FROM dbo.Customers, dbo.Orders WHERE dbo.Customers.CustomerID =dbo.Orders.CustomerID group by dbo.Customers.City ORDER BY 2 DESC`
Who ordered Camembert Pierrot?	`SELECT DISTINCT dbo.Customers.ContactName, dbo.Customers.CompanyName FROM dbo.Products, dbo."Order Details", dbo.Orders, dbo.Customers WHERE dbo.Products.ProductName= 'Camembert Pierrot' AND dbo."Order Details".OrderID=dbo.Orders.OrderID`

English	SQL
Which ten products were ordered by the most customers?	SELECT TOP 10 WITH TIES dbo.Products.ProductName, dbo."Order Details".ProductID, dbo.Products.UnitPrice, COUNT(DISTINCT dbo.Orders.CustomerID) AS "count" FROM dbo."Order Details", dbo.Orders, dbo.Products WHERE dbo."Order Details".OrderID=dbo.Orders.OrderID
Which products were ordered by Around the Horn?	SELECT DISTINCT dbo.Products.ProductName, dbo."Order Details".ProductID, dbo.Products.UnitPrice FROM dbo.Customers, dbo."Order Details", dbo.Orders, dbo.Products WHERE dbo.Customers.CompanyName='Around the Horn' AND dbo."Order Details".OrderID=dbo.Orders.OrderID

Complex queries like these involve joins between a number of tables (in this case four). In order to improve performance, you will need to give careful consideration to how your indexes are built.

Phrasings and Relationships among Table and Field Entities

As should be obvious by now, the power of EQ derives from the relationships designed by the developer. While the SQL Project Wizard provides an excellent starting point, the developer will need to add to or refine the relationships. The key to this refinement is to gain a clear understanding of the phrasing that can link across tables or with a table between the table entities and its field entities. These are embodied in the **phrasings** that characterize each relationship.

Trait Phrasings

These are the simplest and most direct, and are built on the structure of the database. They take the form <entities> have <entities>. Within a table, an example is "customers have customer contact names". Across tables, an example is "customers have employees". The SQL Project Wizard defines simple trait phrasing for all table and field entities.

Verb Phrasings

These define relationships based on action words or verbs. Examples are "Customers order products" and "Shippers ship products". The SQL Project Wizard may create some of these, but most must be designed by the developer.

Where possible, verb phrasings should be stated in the active voice (for example, "Customers order products") rather than the passive voice ("Products are ordered by customers"), but, in most cases, if you define a passive voice verb phrasing, EQ will automatically generate the active voice counterpart. This can be confusing when you make modifications, because you may wonder when and how you created the phrasing!

The types of verb phrasings are:

- ❑   Subject verb: "Employees work"

- ❑   Subject verb object: "Employees work for companies"

- ❑   Subject verb object object: "Salespeople sell customers products"

- ❑   Object are verb: "Products are tested"

- ❑   Object are verb object: "Cars are driven on roads"

Prepositional phrases can be added to verb phrasings to refine the relationship. Prepositions are words that combine with a verb phrasing to modify the relationship. Common prepositions are "in", "on", "of", and "with". "People drive cars on roads" is an example.

Adjective Phrasings

These modify a trait or field entity. An example might be, "some people are old", where the adjective is defined on the basis of values in a field.

Subset Phrasings

These are similar to adjective phrasings, but are used to select subsets of records. An example is, "some products are discontinued".

Name/ID Phrasings

These are used to identify the field in a table that will be considered the name field for each record. Examples are, "Category names are the names of categories", and, "Employee names are the names of employees".

Command Phrasings

These expand the list of commands to which EQ will respond. Built in commands such as "List", "Show", and "Count" are usually recognized and translated correctly. However, in a more complex database, you might need a command such as, "Show the paintings by <artist> that are watercolors". If you define command phrasings, you should be careful to avoid reserved words listed in the EQ Books Online.

The following sections give examples of some of the uses of these phrasings.

Defining Subset Phrasings

If you want to allow users to ask questions that categorize entities, you may need to identify the appropriate subset phrasings. Let's look at an example. The Northwind database includes a Categories table that contains various descriptive categories for the types of products in the Products table. In order to allow users to ask questions like, "Which products are beverages?" we need to modify the products_have_categories relationship to create a new categories_categorize_products.

- ❑   Double-click on this relationship in the Model Editor and click on the Add button next to the Phrasings list. Select Subset Phrasing.

- ❑   In this case, we will want to select products as the subject and categories as the entity that contains subset values:

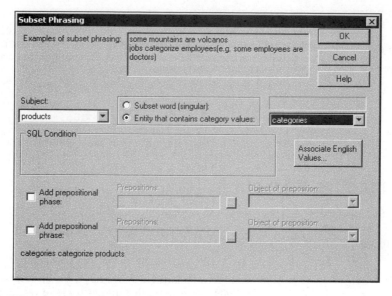

- ❑ Click OK to save the relationship.

- ❑ Now open the Entity dialog window for the category_name field entity in the category table entity.

- ❑ Check the Add values of entity to model box and close the window.

The new subset phrasing we have just created will allow us to translate questions like those shown in the table below:

English	SQL
Who ordered the most seafood?	SELECT TOP 1 WITH TIES dbo.Customers.CompanyName AS "CompanyName", COUNT(DISTINCT dbo."Order Details".ProductID) AS "count" FROM dbo."Order Details", dbo.Orders, dbo.Categories, dbo.Products, dbo.Customers WHERE dbo."Order Details".OrderID=dbo.Orders.OrderID AND dbo.Categories.CategoryName='Seafood'AND dbo.Categories.CategoryID=dbo.Products.CategoryID AND dbo."Order Details".ProductID= dbo.Products.ProductID AND dbo.Orders.CustomerID=dbo.Customers.CustomerID GROUP BY dbo.Orders.CustomerID, dbo.Customers.CompanyName ORDER BY 2 DESC
Which customers ordered dairy products?	SELECT DISTINCT dbo.Customers.CompanyName AS "CompanyName" FROM dbo.Categories, dbo.Products, dbo."Order Details", dbo.Orders, dbo.Customers WHERE dbo.Categories.CategoryName='Dairy Products' AND dbo.Categories.CategoryID= dbo.Products.CategoryID AND dbo."Order Details".OrderID=dbo.Orders.OrderID AND dbo.Products.ProductID=dbo."Order Details".ProductID AND dbo.Orders.CustomerID=dbo.Customers.CustomerID

Table continued on following page

English	SQL
Which cities did not order beverages?	`SELECT DISTINCT dbo.Customers.City AS "City" FROM dbo.Customers WHERE dbo.Customers.CustomerID NOT IN (SELECT dbo.Orders.CustomerID FROM dbo.Categories, dbo.Products, dbo."Order Details", dbo.Orders WHERE dbo.Categories.CategoryName= 'Beverages' AND dbo.Categories.CategoryID= dbo.Products.CategoryID AND dbo."Order Details".OrderID=dbo.Orders.OrderID AND dbo.Products.ProductID=dbo."Order Details".ProductID)`

Defining Adjective Phrasings

In order to enable users to ask qualitative questions about the entities, we need to define some adjective phrasings. An adjective phrasing may be based on the value of a particular entity or it might be a qualitative word such as "best" or "worst".

The `Products` table in the `Northwind` database has a `Discontinued` field that is of the `bit` data type. It is set to `1` if a product has been discontinued and `0` if it has not been discontinued. Let's look at how that field can be used to provide an adjective phrasing that allows users to retrieve information about discontinued products.

Create a brand new relationship and add `product` as the only entity. Now, click on the **Add** button next to the Phrasings list, select Adjective Phrasing, and click on **OK**. Select **products** as the **Subject** and Single adjective as the **Adjective Type**. Enter the word **discontinued** to describe the subject. When your screen looks like this, click on **OK** to close the dialog:

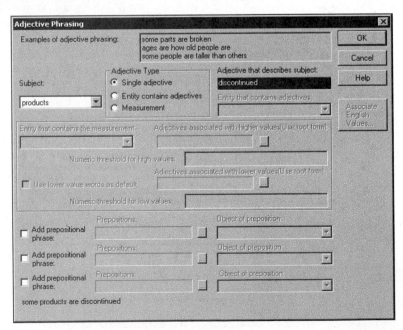

Now we need to let the query engine know under what circumstances the adjective discontinued will describe the product. We will do this on the Database tab of the New Relationship dialog. Select dbo.Products from the drop-down at the top and check the box labeled This relationship is true only when the following SQL condition is true. Then enter the following condition:

```
dbo.Products.discontinued = 1
```

Your Database tab should look like this:

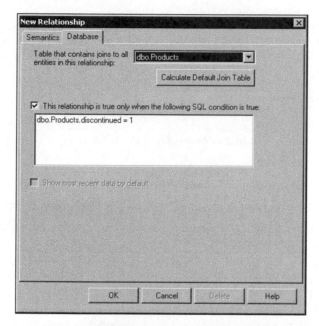

Now the application will be able to interpret questions such as those shown in this table:

English	SQL
Which products have been discontinued?	SELECT dbo.Products.ProductName AS "ProductName" FROM dbo.Products WHERE dbo.Products.Discontinued=1
Who has ordered discontinued products?	SELECT DISTINCT dbo.Customers.CompanyName AS "CompanyName" FROM dbo.Products, dbo."Order Details", dbo.Orders, dbo.Customers WHERE dbo.Products.Discontinued=1 AND dbo."Order Details".OrderID=dbo.Orders.OrderID AND dbo.Products.ProductID=dbo."Order Details".ProductID AND dbo.Orders.CustomerID=dbo.Customers.CustomerID

We can also specify an adjective type that is the value contained in a particular entity. For example, we may have a field for `Color` in a `Houses` database. In that case, we could define an entity for both `Color` and `House`, and establish a relationship between them with an adjective phrase. This would allow users to ask questions like, "Which houses are brown?"

Another way to define an adjective phrasing is by specifying a measurement type. This adjective type is a little more complex than the other two because it allows us to set high and low adjectives, as well as the threshold values for each of them. Let's look at an example.

The `Products` table has a field named `UnitPrice`. Open the `products_have_product_unit_prices` relationship between the `product` and the `product_unit_price` entities and add an adjective phrasing to that relationship, to allow users to ask questions that qualify products as either cheap or expensive. For the sake of this discussion, let's assume that expensive products are those with a unit price over $25.00 and cheap products are those with a unit price under $10.00.

To set up this adjective phrasing:

- ❑ Open the `products_have_product_unit_prices` relationship and click the Add button next to the Phrasings list in the lower part of the form.

- ❑ Choose Adjective phrasing.

- ❑ In the Adjective Phrasing form, choose Measurement as the Adjective Type.

- ❑ Select product_unit_prices as the Entity that contains the measurement.

- ❑ Enter the adjective "expensive" in the Adjectives associated with higher values, and "25" in the Numeric threshold for high values.

- ❑ Enter the adjective "cheap" in the Adjectives associated with lower values, and "10" in the Numeric threshold for lower values.

The Adjective Phrasing window should look like this:

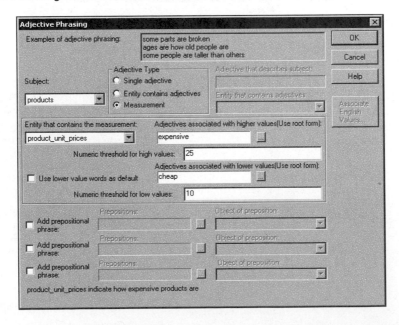

A new relationship `product_unit_prices` to indicate how expensive products are is created in the list of relationships.

The table below shows questions about the cost of products and the SQL that is generated:

English	SQL
Which products are expensive?	SELECT dbo.Products.ProductName AS "ProductName", dbo.Products.UnitPrice AS "UnitPrice" FROM dbo.Products WHERE dbo.Products.UnitPrice>25
Which products are cheap?	SELECT dbo.Products.ProductName AS "ProductName", dbo.Products.UnitPrice AS "UnitPrice" FROM dbo.Products WHERE dbo.Products.UnitPrice<10
Which products are neither expensive nor cheap?	SELECT dbo.Products.ProductName AS "ProductName", dbo.Products.UnitPrice AS "UnitPrice" FROM dbo.Products WHERE dbo.Products.UnitPrice>=10 AND dbo.Products.UnitPrice<=25

Notice that by default the **Use lower value words as default** checkbox is not checked. If it had been, the queries generated would have been significantly different. Let's look at the effect it would have:

English	SQL
Which products are expensive?	SELECT dbo.Products.ProductName AS "ProductName", dbo.Products.UnitPrice AS "UnitPrice" FROM dbo.Products WHERE dbo.Products.UnitPrice>10
Which products are cheap?	SELECT dbo.Products.ProductName AS "ProductName", dbo.Products.UnitPrice AS "UnitPrice" FROM dbo.Products WHERE dbo.Products.UnitPrice<25
Which products are neither expensive nor cheap?	SELECT dbo.Products.ProductName AS "ProductName", dbo.Products.UnitPrice AS "UnitPrice" FROM dbo.Products WHERE dbo.Products.UnitPrice> =25 AND dbo.Products.UnitPrice<=10

The **Use lower value words as default** option in adjective phrasing is not recommended without careful testing. In some queries, this can cause the low threshold to be used with the high adjective and the high threshold to be used with the low adjective. This may not be an appropriate choice because it results in products being described as both expensive and cheap. This option is appropriate in situations where the high adjective and the low adjective are not opposites. For example, consider the words affordable and deluxe. Perhaps deluxe items are considered those that cost $10.00 or more and affordable items are those that cost $25.00 or under. In this case, an item that costs between $10.00 and $25.00 is both affordable and deluxe.

Defining Synonyms

It is essential that you try to account for the synonyms your users will use to describe entities, relationships, and other words they will use in their queries. As you're building your application, you may want to consult a thesaurus for a list of common synonyms. Keep in mind regional differences. Consider, for example, an Employees table that includes a termination date. When a company releases employees in order to cut costs, users in the United States would refer to that person as "laid off". Users in the United Kingdom would refer to that employee as "made redundant". As you think about the different ways users will refer to items, consider the geographic scope of your application and get as much advice from users in those locations as possible.

Synonyms for Entities

We have already seen that entity words are case-sensitive. Different cases can be accounted for by separating the words with commas in the Words list. In a loose sense of the term, we are defining synonyms. We can use the same technique to list additional synonyms for entities. For example, we may want to add the synonym "merchandise" to the list of words that identify the product entity.

Synonyms for Verbs

Synonyms for verbs are defined by adding phrasings. You should think about the different ways users will ask about a set of entities and add phrasings to account for each of them. In the graphic shown here, four alternative phrasings have been provided to allow customers to ask the same question four different ways. If you are working through the example, please add these phrasings to your English Query project:

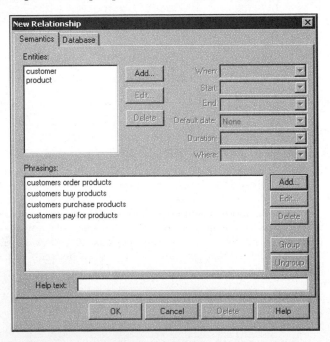

Keep in mind that the synonyms you define are application-specific. Depending on the way the database tracks data, customers ordering products and paying for products may not always mean the same thing.

Dictionary Entries

The English Query built-in dictionary contains words, phrasings, and their synonyms that are commonly used when forming English questions and statements. You can add words and synonyms to your application's dictionary by right-clicking the Dictionary Entries branch of the Semantic Objects tree. While you can do this instead of identifying synonyms and synonymous verb phrasings, keep in mind that the changes you make here are applicable throughout your entire application. They do not depend on the context of an entity or relationship.

Dictionary entries are useful for defining industry-specific jargon words and acronyms, particularly if they use irregular conjugation. English Query is fairly tolerant of incorrect conjugations when generating queries. It will generally try most conjugation rules against a root and if any of them matches the word in the question, it will be used. For example, to generate a past tense of a word, it will add "d" to the root and "ed" to the root, even if it knows that the correct conjugation is irregular. This enables English Query to work well even for users who do not remember irregular conjugations. The table shows how English Query restates the user's questions when "pay" is conjugated correctly and incorrectly. In this case, the primary phrasing is "customers order products" and one of the secondary phrasings is "customers pay for products":

Question	English Query Conjugation	Restatement
Which customers paid for seafood?	Default dictionary conjugation	Which customers paid for seafoods?
Which customers payed for seafood?	Pay + ed	Which customers paid for seafoods?
Which customers payd for seafood?	Pay + d	Which customers paid for seafoods?

Notice that English Query is able to parse the question. Since the irregular conjugation of pay is included in the built-in dictionary, the restatement and the answer text will contain the correctly conjugated form of the word.

However, this answer points out a different problem. The English Query engine is applying standard conjugation rules to the word "seafood". If we want the restatement and the answer text to return the correct plural for seafood, we will need to define a dictionary entry.

To define a dictionary entry, select Model I Add Dictionary Entry from the menu. The New Dictionary Entry form will then be displayed. Since we need to define an irregular plural, we need to select Word as the Dictionary Entry Type. Next, we need to define the root form of the word (seafood) and the part of speech (in this case a Common Noun). Finally, check the Irregular Plural box and enter the correct plural for seafood (seafood). Note that you can only enter irregular inflections for common nouns and verbs.

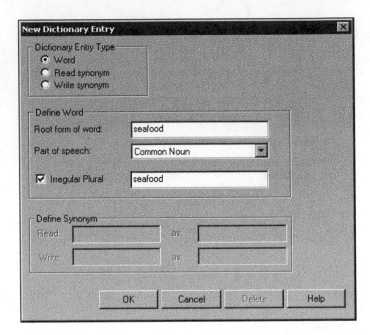

We can also add dictionary entries for read synonyms and write synonyms. A Read synonym tells the English Query Engine that when a particular word is encountered in a question, it should be *read* as its synonym. For example, if we want the word "fish" to be interpreted as "seafood" every time it is encountered in a question, we would enter it as a Read synonym.

A Write synonym tells the English Query Engine that when a particular word would generally be used in the answer text, to substitute the write synonym instead. One use of this is to account for terms that appear plural in the database. Consider the Product categories in the Northwind database. The category name of Condiments is used to identify spices and sauces. When English Query generates the answer text for a question like, "Show me the condiments," it tries to pluralize "condiments" by adding an "es". This results in the answer text, "The condimentses are:" To correct this problem, add a Write synonym to the dictionary. Define the synonym as Write condimentses as condiments. Now the correct answer text will be generated.

Testing Our Application Revisited

Thorough testing of our application is essential to minimize the number of questions that return no results, or worse yet, incorrect results. English Query provides us with two testing tools, an interactive testing tool and a regression tool. While we're developing an English Query application, it is useful to be able to test questions interactively, make a change, and then test again. The interactive test tool is launched by running Debug | Start:

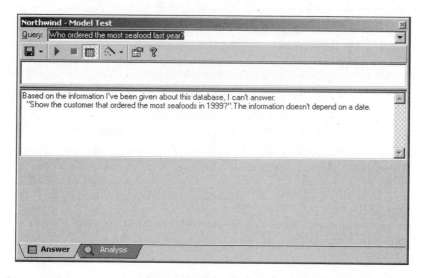

The test application allows you to submit questions by typing them into the box labeled **Query** and clicking on the **Submit Query** button. Questions that are submitted are saved in the drop-down list for later use.

After a question is submitted, the English is translated to SQL and the same types of information are provided as in the regression test output file. In addition, you have the option to execute the SQL. This can be helpful because it sometimes allows you to detect problems without needing to read the SQL. You can also click on the **Analysis** tab to view information about the entities and phrasings that were used to generate the query.

When a question cannot be interpreted, the **Suggestion Wizard** button helps you determine the changes you need to make. When you click on it, you are prompted to identify each entity that English Query cannot interpret:

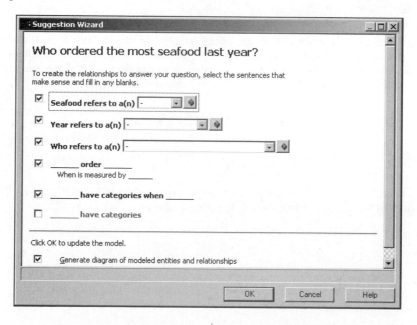

English Query suggests the entities it suspects are the most likely candidates. In this case, since English Query knows that "last year" generally refers to a time or date, it is suggesting the only date/time entity that has been defined. We also have the option of choosing an entity that is not listed or creating a new one. By manipulating the checkboxes and combo boxes in the **Suggestion Wizard**, we provide English Query with as much of the correct information as possible, and click **OK**. The wizard will then deduce relationships between the entities involved, thereby enhancing English Query's ability to answer a wider range of queries.

Once the wizard is finished, submit the query again. This time it is able to execute with no problem:

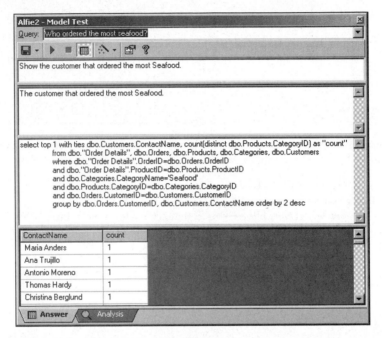

Since the **Execute SQL** option is enabled, the query is executed and the result set is displayed at the bottom of the dialog. While viewing the result set can sometimes help you spot problems more quickly, you should also take a close look at the SQL generated. You can do this on screen, or click on **Add to Question File** to add the question to the .eqr file for regression testing.

> It's a good idea to add all questions you troubleshoot interactively to the question file. Remember, sometimes a change you make to fix one problem may have unexpected repercussions.

The **Analysis** tab allows you to view the entities and phrasings used to build the query. This can provide you with additional information when troubleshooting a query:

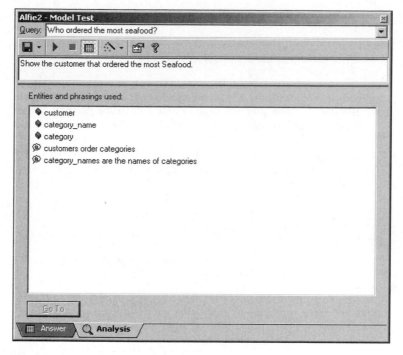

Regression Testing

As discussed earlier in this chapter, after each revision of the application, it is important to retest and assure that all queries still work. This regression testing is carried out using the `Northwind.eqr`. Each time a query is saved, the `.eqr` file is displayed and the latest query is written to it. The file can then be saved and used in regression testing by right-clicking the file name in the Properties window and then choosing Run Regression. You can then choose View Output, View Differences, or Promote. View Differences compares the results of the current regression run with the last saved version. It highlights new queries in blue and changed queries in red. If the results are satisfactory, you can choose Promote to promote the current regression output to replace the previous `.eqr` file.

Deploying an English Query Application

Once you have defined your entities and relationships and tested your application thoroughly, you are ready to deploy your English Query application. Deploying an application consists of the following steps:

- ❑ Building your English Query application
- ❑ Writing the code that uses your English Query application
- ❑ Distributing the English Query application and the English Query engine

We'll look at each of these steps. However, first, let's examine the files in an English Query project.

Project Files

While in development, an English Query project is composed of several files. New in English Query for SQL Server 2000, many of these files are now in XML format.

SLN File

This is the "solution" file that contains pointers to the other files in the project. Developers who typically open projects using Windows Explorer should double-click this file to view its contents.

```
Microsoft Visual Studio Solution File, Format Version 1.00
Project("{3A71645E-EC68-11D1-893C-00C04FC2D0A8}") = "Northwind", "Northwind.eqp",
"{500EF66E-2087-48CF-A494-A6C527AB7EDD}"
EndProject
Global
    GlobalSection(LocalDeployment) = postSolution
        StartupProject = {500EF66E-2087-48CF-A494-A6C527AB7EDD}
    EndGlobalSection
    GlobalSection(BuildOrder) = postSolution
        0 = {500EF66E-2087-48CF-A494-A6C527AB7EDD}
    EndGlobalSection
    GlobalSection(DeploymentRoot) = postSolution
    EndGlobalSection
EndGlobal
```

EQP File

This file is called the **project file**. It contains database connection information and the settings for global variables, such as the names of the regression files. A sample .eqp file is shown below:

```
<?xml version="1.0"?>
<EQPROJECT NAME="Northwind" VERSION="1.2">
  <MODULE ID="MODULE:Northwind">Northwind.eqm</MODULE>
  <PROJECT>
    <DATABASE ID="">
      <DSN>Provider=SQLOLEDB.1;Integrated Security=SSPI;Persist Security
Info=False;Initial Catalog=Northwind;Data Source=WIN2KSVR1</DSN>
      <DBMS TYPE="SQLSERVER" VERSION="08.00.0194"/>
      <OUTERJOINS/>
      <LOADWORDS AMOUNT="500"/>
      <DBMAXROWS>100</DBMAXROWS>
      <DBTIMEOUT>120</DBTIMEOUT>
    </DATABASE>
    <DEFAULTS>
      <SPELLING/>
      <USERCONTEXT/>
    </DEFAULTS>
    <REGRESSION QUESTFILE="Northwind.eqr"/>
  </PROJECT>
</EQPROJECT>
```

EQM File

The .eqm file is the **model file** into which you as the developer have stored all relationship information. It contains the information in the Model Editor pane of the development environment in the same order, including entities, relationships, definitions of tables, fields, joins, phrasings and dictionary entries. Excerpts from the .eqm file are shown below. The first section of the file is the semantics or definitions of the entities.

```xml
<?xml version="1.0"?>
<MODULE ID="MODULE:Northwind" VERSION="1.2">
  <SEMANTICS>
    <ENTITY ID="ENTITY:category">
      <WORD>category</WORD>
      <WORD>class</WORD>
      <WORD>group</WORD>
      <DBOBJECT TABLE="TABLE:dbo.Categories"/>
      <DISPLAY FIELD="FIELD:dbo.Categories.CategoryName"/>
    </ENTITY>
    <ENTITY ID="ENTITY:category_description">
      <WORD>category description</WORD>
      <WORD>description</WORD>
      <DBOBJECT FIELD="FIELD:dbo.Categories.Description"/>
      <ATTRIBUTEOF HREF="ENTITY:category"/>
    </ENTITY>
```

The semantics section is followed by the relationships section, which details the name, the join(s) with tables, the roles and phrasings:

```xml
<RELATIONSHIP ID="RELATIONSHIP:categories_categorize_products">
      <JOINTABLE TABLE="TABLE:dbo.Products"/>
      <ROLE ID="ROLE:categories_categorize_products.category"
HREF="ENTITY:category"/>
      <ROLE ID="ROLE:categories_categorize_products.product"
HREF="ENTITY:product"/>
      <PHRASINGS>
        <SUBSETPHRASING ID=
"PHRASING:categories_categorize_products.categories..20categorize..20products">
          <SUBJECT ROLEREF="ROLE:categories_categorize_products.product"/>
          <OBJECT ROLEREF="ROLE:categories_categorize_products.category"/>
        </SUBSETPHRASING>
      </PHRASINGS>
    </RELATIONSHIP>
...
```

The next section consists of the tables in the database, beginning with the schema and followed by the definitions of each table, each field within the table, and joins representing table relationships:

```xml
<TABLES DATABASE="" SCHEMA="dbo">
    <TABLE ID="TABLE:dbo.Categories">
      <FIELD ID="FIELD:dbo.Categories.CategoryID" DATATYPE="INTEGER">
        <KEY/>
      </FIELD>
      <FIELD ID="FIELD:dbo.Categories.CategoryName" DATATYPE="STRING">
        <CAPITALIZATION TYPE="FIRSTLETTER"/>
```

```
    </FIELD>
    <FIELD ID="FIELD:dbo.Categories.Description" DATATYPE="TEXT">
      <NULLABLE/>
      <CAPITALIZATION TYPE="FIRSTLETTER"/>
    </FIELD>
    <FIELD ID="FIELD:dbo.Categories.Picture" DATATYPE="BINARY">
      <NULLABLE/>
    </FIELD>
  </TABLE>
  <TABLE ID="TABLE:dbo.CustomerCustomerDemo">
```

The field attributes listed are based on the database schema. The capitalization attribute is based on the data in the fields when the field or the table that contains it is added to the project. It can be modified by editing the field properties on the **Database** tab of the IDE.

Join information is determined by examining the primary key and foreign key relationships in the database. Entity information includes values you specifically define, such as the words used to reference the entity and the fields the entity includes. It also may include information discovered from the database, such as a sampling of the data. This sampling helps the English Query engine parse the query.

If any of these entities have special properties, such as designating when an event occurs (time entity) or a SQL condition it depends on, these properties will also be listed. An example of this is:

```
<WHEN ROLEREF="ROLE:customers_order_categories.order_date"/>
```

> The `.eqp` and `.eqm` files are ASCII files and may be viewed directly. However, unless you are very comfortable with what you're doing, editing these files may cause unwanted and unforeseen repercussions. It is generally better to use the IDE to modify your application.

SUD File

Dictionary entries are contained in the `.suo` file, a binary file that cannot be viewed or edited outside the development environment.

EQD File

The `.eqd` file is a **compiled English Query project file**. In SQL Server 2000, this file is a binary file and should not be edited directly. This file is created when building and testing your English Query application. Although it may be used when creating a session with the English Query engine, this is not recommended. Using the `.eqd` file to establish an English Query application is not as efficient as using a fully built binary English Query application. In addition, entity values that should be added to the project are not added until the application is built.

EQR and EQO files

These files contain the latest saved **English Query Regression** file, with all the queries, restatements, and SQL code saved in XML format. The EQO file is the latest **Regression Output** file.

Building an English Query Application

English Query builds each application into the binary .eqd file each time you run a test. You can build the .eqd file at any time using Build in the main menu. If you have selected values for a number of entities and your database has a lot of data, this may take some time. In addition, make sure you have enough disk space. The size of the .eqd file will increase dramatically with the amount of data it needs to include.

Using an English Query Application

A session with an English Query application is established through an in-process ActiveX server, MSEQOLE.DLL. This means that you can use your English Query application in any environment that allows you to use COM automation servers. These environments include:

- Active Server Pages
- Visual Basic
- Visual C++

When choosing the development environment, keep in mind the tools with which your developers have experience, as well as other application and business requirements. If you are using English Query as part of a web solution, you may find that Active Server Pages will meet your needs. However, for performance and scalability, you may be better off building an ActiveX component with either Visual Basic or Visual C++. Let's walk through an example using Visual Basic as the COM controller.

> **Although the example is provided in Visual Basic, using the MSEQOLE.DLL objects from any other COM controller is very similar.**
>
> **The example provided here includes only the most fundamental coding in order to demonstrate the key steps involved in creating an application that can use an English Query application. Code to gracefully handle all possible user input will be much more involved.**

Setting a Reference to the Library

When writing the application in Visual Basic, a reference to the Microsoft English Query 2.0 library or Microsoft English Query Type Library is set by running Project | References. Before you can reference the English Query library, the English Query core components must first be installed on your Visual Basic development machine. If this is the same machine you have been using to build your English Query application, using the IDE, the files will already be installed. Otherwise, you will need to select them by running SQL Server installation.

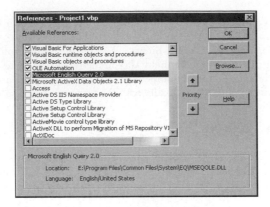

Notice that a reference to the **Microsoft ActiveX Data Objects 2.1 Library** (or higher) is also set. ADO, OLE DB, RDO, or ODBC is required in order to actually run the query returned by Microsoft English Query (MSEQ).

Project Overview

The Visual Basic project has two forms, `frmMain` and `frmClarify`. `frmMain` is shown below:

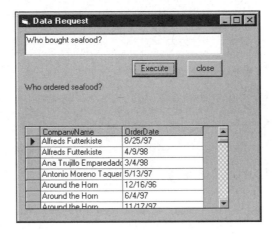

The controls on `frmMain` are described in this table:

Control Class	Control Name
TextBox	txtEnglish
CommandButton	cmdExecute
CommandButton	cmdClose
Label	lblAnswer
DataGrid	DataGrid1

> **You will need to add the Microsoft DataGrid Control 6.0 to your toolbox. To do this, right-click on the toolbox and run Components.**

The sample application will use ADO to execute the queries. We want to prevent users from clicking on the cmdExecute button until the open recordset has been closed. For that reason, code will be added to disable the cmdExecute button after a query has been executed. We'll see that code a little later. To close the recordset and enable the cmdExecute button, the following code has been added to the cmdClose_Click event:

```
Private Sub cmdClose_Click()
    rs.Close
    cmdExecute.Enabled = True
End Sub
```

The other form in the project is frmClarify. It is displayed when clarification about an entity is needed. It is shown below:

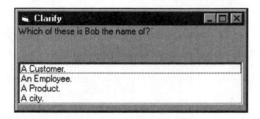

The controls on frmClarify are described here:

Control Class	Control Name
Label	lblClarify
ListBox	lstChoices

Opening a Session

At minimum, we need to declare a Session object and a Response object variable. The Session object is used to initiate the domain and parse the request. The domain information consists of the entities and relationships in the model, as defined in the .eqd file. It is encapsulated in the DomainInfo object. The Response object will hold the results of the ParseRequest method. Their ProgIDs are Mseq.Session and Mseq.Response, respectively. These variables should be declared in the General Declarations section of the frmMain form module. These are declared as shown below:

```
Private eqs As Mseq.Session
Public eqr As Mseq.Response
'Public because it will be referenced from another form

Private rs As ADODB.Recordset
Private conn As ADODB.Connection
```

Before we can use the `Session` object, we will need to create an instance of it. The code below, which should be added to `frmMain`, shows how the `CreateObject` function is used to instantiate the `Session` object. The `Response` object does not need to be instantiated because it is not externally creatable. The only way to set a reference to a `Response` object is through the `ParseRequest` method of the `Session` object:

```
Private Sub Form_Load()
    Set eqs = CreateObject("Mseq.session")
    eqs.InitDomain (App.Path & "\Northwind.eqd")
    Set conn = CreateObject("ADODB.Connection")
    Set rs = CreateObject("ADODB.Recordset")
    conn.CursorLocation = adUseClient
    conn.Open("DRIVER=SQL Server;SERVER=(local);DATABASE=Northwind")
    Set rs.ActiveConnection = conn
    rs.CursorType = adOpenStatic
End Sub
```

> **If are using the English Query application from an ASP, you need to use `Server.CreateObject` to instantiate the `Mseq.Session` object.**
>
> **The `Mseq.Session` object should not be confused with the `Session` object provided by ASP. The `Mseq.Session` object is used to create a session with the English Query Engine.**

The `InitDomain` method of the `Session` object is used to establish a session with a particular application. You need to provide the path and filename of either the `.eqd` file or the `.eqc` file. In this example, the `Path` property of the Visual Basic `App` object was used to indicate that the `Northwind.eqd` file is in the same directory as the executable.

> **The declarations and instantiations for the ADO objects are also shown in order to help you understand the code in the following sections.**

Parsing a Request

After a user enters an English sentence and requests that a query be executed, the first thing we need to do is call the `ParseRequest` method of the `Session` object as shown below:

```
Private Sub cmdExecute_Click()
    Dim doneParsing As Boolean

    Set eqr = eqs.ParseRequest(txtEnglish.Text)
    Do Until doneParsing = True
        doneParsing = HandleResponse
    Loop
End Sub
```

The method accepts the English string to be translated as its only argument. In this case, the string is in the `Text` property of the `txtEnglish` control. The `ParseRequest` method returns a reference to a `Response` object. The `Response` object may be an `ErrorResponse`, a `CommandResponse`, or a `UserClarifyResponse` object.

Handling a Response

The ErrorResponse, CommandResponse, and UserClarifyResponse objects all inherit from the Response object. This means that they all implement the Type property. It also means that a generic Response object can hold references to each of them. However, the ErrorResponse, CommandResponse, and UserClarifyResponse objects implement very different properties and methods. If you want to reference these unique properties and methods through the generic Response object, you will need to code very carefully to avoid run-time errors. Always check the Type property of the Response object before referencing any other property, method, or event.

The Type property lets us know what type of Response object the variable references. Its possible values are stored in the nlResponse enumeration. The three values that concern us here are:

Constant	Value	Response object type
nlResponseCommand	0	CommandResponse
nlResponseError	2	ErrorResponse
nlResponseUserclarify	3	UserClarifyResponse

The code below shows how the ErrorResponse, CommandResponse, and UserClarifyResponse objects can be declared and references to them set to the generic Response object, based on the value of the Type property (add this code to frmMain also):

```
Public Function HandleResponse() As Boolean
    Dim eqCR As Mseq.CommandResponse
    Dim eqUCR As Mseq.UserClarifyResponse
    Dim eqErr As Mseq.ErrorResponse

    Select Case eqr.Type
        Case nlResponseCommand
            Set eqCR = eqr
            HandleResponse = True
        Case nlResponseError
            Set eqErr = eqr
            HandleResponse = True
        Case nlResponseUserclarify
            Set eqUCR = eqr
            HandleResponse = False
    End Select
End Function
```

The HandleResponse function returns True if the CommandResponse is of type nlResponseCommand or nlResponseError. If the CommandResponse object is of type nlResponseUserClarify, the function returns False. You'll see how the return value of this function is used in the application a little later. First, let's take a look at the code that needs to execute for each type of response. As each type of response is discussed, more code will be added to this function.

CommandResponse

A CommandResponse is returned when English Query was able to translate the English into SQL or answer the question directly. An example of the latter is a question that does not depend on the database, such as "What time is it?"

The CommandResponse object exposes a Commands collection, a Restatement property, and a Type property. The Commands collection contains AnswerCommand objects and Command objects. The CmdID property identifies the type of object. The code below shows how the CmdID property is checked to determine if the command returned contains a SQL query or if it is an AnswerCommand. If the command is a query, the following occurs:

- ❑ The Restatement property is displayed in the lblAnswer control
- ❑ The query is executed and the results returned to the rs variable
- ❑ The DataGrid control's DataSource is set to the result set that was returned
- ❑ The cmdExecute control's Enabled property is set to False

> Disabling the **cmdExecute** button prevents users from trying to execute another query before the recordset has been closed (by clicking on the **Close** button). The **cmdClose_Click** event procedure was shown earlier.

If the command is an AnswerCommand, the answer is displayed in the lblAnswer control:

```
Public Function HandleResponse() As Boolean
    Dim eqCR As Mseq.CommandResponse
    Dim eqUCR As Mseq.UserClarifyResponse
    Dim eqErr As Mseq.ErrorResponse

    Select Case eqr.Type
        Case nlResponseCommand
            Set eqCR = eqr
            If eqCR.Commands(0).CmdID = nlCmdQuery Then
                lblAnswer.Caption = eqCR.Restatement
                rs.Open (eqCR.Commands(0).SQL)
                Set DataGrid1.DataSource = rs
                cmdExecute.Enabled = False
            ElseIf eqCR.Commands(0).CmdID = nlCmdAnswer Then
                lblAnswer.Caption = eqCR.Commands(0).Answer
            End If
            HandleResponse = True
        Case nlResponseError
            Set eqErr = eqr
            HandleResponse = True
        Case nlResponseUserclarify
            Set eqUCR = eqr
            HandleResponse = False
    End Select
End Function
```

> It is important to note that the **CommandResponse** object contains a collection of **Command** objects. A sophisticated application will handle every **Command** object in the collection. For simplicity's sake, the code shown here extracts information from only the first instance of the **Command** object.

The handling of the returned data has been simplified by using ADO and the DataGrid control. In a more fully functional application, you would need to iterate through the recordset and check for column names, data types, and values.

ErrorResponse

A reference to an `ErrorResponse` object is returned when English Query is unable to parse the question. This occurs when the question contains entities or verbs the English Query application doesn't know about. The `ErrorResponse` object has a `Description` property that contains a detailed description of the reason English Query could not translate the question. The code below shows how the error description can be displayed in the `lblAnswer` control:

```
Public Function HandleResponse() As Boolean
    Dim eqCR As Mseq.CommandResponse
    Dim eqUCR As Mseq.UserClarifyResponse
    Dim eqErr As Mseq.ErrorResponse

    Select Case eqr.Type
        Case nlResponseCommand
            Set eqCR = eqr
            If eqCR.Commands(0).CmdID = nlCmdQuery Then
                lblAnswer.Caption = eqCR.Restatement
                rs.Open (eqCR.Commands(0).SQL)
                Set DataGrid1.DataSource = rs
                cmdExecute.Enabled = False
            ElseIf eqCR.Commands(0).CmdID = nlCmdAnswer Then
                lblAnswer.Caption = eqCR.Commands(0).Answer
            End If
            HandleResponse = True
        Case nlResponseError
            Set eqErr = eqr
            lblAnswer.Caption = eqErr.Description
            HandleResponse = True
        Case nlResponseUserclarify
            Set eqUCR = eqr
            HandleResponse = False
    End Select
End Function
```

UserClarifyResponse

In some situations, a user may need to be asked to clarify what is meant by certain words or phrases in the question. One situation in which this might occur is if an entity's meaning is ambiguous. Ambiguity is frequently the result of an entity that was defined without including its fields as minor entities. However, it may also result from new data entries or fields that have been added to the database tables after the English Query application was built and distributed. For example, suppose the `Employee` entity and the `Customer` entity both have relationships that define where they are located. If you ask the question, "Where is John Doe?" English Query will examine the domain to determine whether John Doe is an employee or a customer. If it cannot make that determination, a reference to a `UserClarifyResponse` object will be returned.

> It is important to point out that a question may require more than one clarification. For this reason, it is important to continue processing clarifications until the **ParseRequest** method returns a reference to either an **ErrorResponse** or a **CommandResponse** object.

A UserClarifyResponse object contains a collection of UserInput objects. As with the Response object, the UserInput property may contain a reference to one of three object types: the ListInput, StaticInput, and TextInput objects. The StaticInput object contains static informational text that is used in a clarification. The TextInput object is used when the user must enter a value for the clarification. For example, if the user asks, "Who are the new employees?" English Query may ask for a definition of what makes an employee new. The ListInput object is used when the clarification requires a user to choose from a list of entities. Let's look at an example of how code can be added to the HandleResponse function to deal with a ListInput clarification:

```
Public Function HandleResponse() As Boolean
    Dim i As Integer
    Dim Items() As Variant
    Dim eqCR As Mseq.CommandResponse
    Dim eqUCR As Mseq.UserClarifyResponse
    Dim eqErr As Mseq.ErrorResponse

    Dim eqUI As Mseq.UserInput

    Select Case eqr.Type
        Case nlResponseCommand
            Set eqCR = eqr
            If eqCR.Commands(0).CmdID = nlCmdQuery Then
                lblAnswer.Caption = eqCR.Restatement
                rs.Open (eqCR.Commands(0).SQL)
                Set DataGrid1.DataSource = rs
                cmdExecute.Enabled = False
            ElseIf eqCR.Commands(0).CmdID = nlCmdAnswer Then
                lblAnswer.Caption = eqCR.Commands(0).Answer
            End If
            HandleResponse = True

        Case nlResponseError
            Set eqErr = eqr
            lblAnswer.Caption = eqErr.Description
            HandleResponse = True

        Case nlResponseUserclarify
            Set eqUCR = eqr
            Set eqUI = eqUCR.UserInputs(0)
            If eqUI.Type = nlInputList Then
                frmClarify.lblClarify = eqUI.Caption
                For i = 0 To eqUI.ItemCount - 1
                    Items = eqUI.Items
                    frmClarify.lstChoices.AddItem Items(i)
                Next
                frmClarify.Show vbModal
                Set frmClarify = Nothing
            End If
            HandleResponse = False

    End Select
End Function
```

This example tests the value of the `Type` property of the `UserInput` object to ensure that it is an `InputList`. It then displays the `Caption` property in `lblControl` on the `frmClarify` form. The list of choices is stored in an array of variants named `Items`. The `ItemCount` property of the `UserInput` object returns the number of items in the array. The code iterates through the `Items` array, adding each string to the `ListBox` control on `frmClarify`. Finally, `frmClarify` is displayed as a modal dialog:

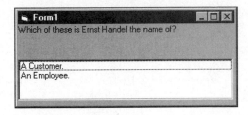

> Notice that a new variable of the type **Mseq.UserInput** is declared and set to reference the first item in the **UserInputs** collection of the **UserClarifyResponse** object. In addition, notice that a reference to the **Items** array is stored in a variant variable named **Items**. This syntax is necessary because the following code generates an error:
>
> **frmClarify.lstChoices.AddItem eqUCR.UserInputs(0).Items(i)**

After the user selects the appropriate entity, we need to add that information to the request. To do so, we set the `Selection` property of the `UserInput` object, then call the `Reply` method of the `Response` object (or `UserClarifyResponse` object). Make sure to set the `Response` object equal to the new reference. The code below shows the syntax for doing this:

```
Private Sub lstChoices_DblClick()
    frmMain.eqr.UserInputs(0).Selection = lstChoices.ListIndex
    Set frmMain.eqr = frmMain.eqr.Reply
    Me.Hide
End Sub
```

In this case, the code is added to the `DblClick` event procedure of the `lstChoices` control on `frmClarify`.

Now the new `Response` object should be processed to determine whether it contains a query, an answer, an error, or another clarification request.

Distribution

Both `MSEQOLE.DLL` and your `.eqd` file must be distributed as part of the application. If you are using the application from within an application built in Visual Basic, you can use the **Package and Deployment Wizard** to ensure that the correct files are included, as shown overleaf:

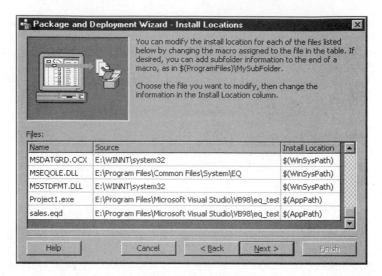

Notice that MSEQOLE.DLL will be installed to the **WinSysPath** location. You can select to install your .eqd file anywhere you want. However, in this case, it should be installed to the same path as the application because the example used the Path property of the App object to locate it in the call to InitDomain.

Regardless of the method you use to build the Setup program, you will need to ensure that MSEQOLE.DLL is properly installed and registered on the server where the application that uses English Query is being run. If you are planning to access English Query from within an ASP, you will need to install MSEQOLE.DLL on the web server.

The location of the .eqd file depends on the implementation inside your code. In an application that is compiled and distributed, you will most likely want to install it to the application directory or a subdirectory beneath it. If you are deploying through ASP, you will locate the .eqd file inside a virtual directory.

Summary

This chapter provided an introduction to English Query for SQL Server 2000. It enables you to build applications that can allow users to retrieve information in a very intuitive way. You have also seen appropriate uses for the technology and examples showing their implementation.

English Query is a powerful way to provide natural language queries against relational data. You saw a very brief introduction to how an English Query application can be built, tested, deployed, and used in a client application. It is safe to say that full development and implement of English Query applications will be labor intensive, but the end result will reward your users with better query responses.

Online discussion at http://p2p.wrox.com

28

Security

There are probably as many ideas on security as there are programmers. It's one of those things where there isn't necessarily a right way to do it, but there are definitely plenty of wrong ones.

The first thing to understand about security is that there is no such thing as a totally secure application. If you can make it secure, rest assured that someone, somewhere, can defeat your efforts and "hack" into the system.

Even with this knowledge, the goal still needs to be to keep unwanted intruders out of your system. The good news about security is that, for most instances, you can fairly easily make it such a hassle that 99.999% of people out there won't want to bother with it. For the other .001%, I can only encourage you to make sure that all your employees have a life so they fall into the 99.999%. The .001% will hopefully find someplace else to go.

In this chapter, we're going to cover:

- ❑ Security basics
- ❑ SQL Server security options
- ❑ Database and server roles
- ❑ Application roles
- ❑ XML integration security issues
- ❑ More advanced security

What we'll discover is that there are a lot of different ways to approach the security problem. Security goes way beyond giving someone a user ID and a password – we'll see many of the things that you need to think about.

Before beginning any of the examples in this chapter, you'll need to load and execute a data package called NorthwindSecure.dts. This builds a special database we'll use throughout this chapter.

OK, so this is another of those chapters where I have to make you create a working database in order for the examples to work – my apologies for that. In the last version of this book, we didn't have to create an extra database to show what I meant, but Microsoft went and changed the default permissions for the Northwind database such that everyone has access to about everything, so most of my previous examples looked pretty useless. The NorthwindSecure database that we'll use throughout this chapter is a more typical database scenario – that is, it has absolutely no permissions added to it beyond what comes naturally with creating tables and objects (which means NONE). We'll learn how to deal with this and explicitly add what permissions we want as the chapter progresses.

To obtain this package you'll need to download it from the Wrox web site at http://www.wrox.com. I suggest that you save it in a new folder called C:/Chapter28/Code/. You can then open the NorthwindSecure.dts package by entering Enterprise Manager and navigating to the Data Transformation Services | Open Package node as shown in the following screenshot:

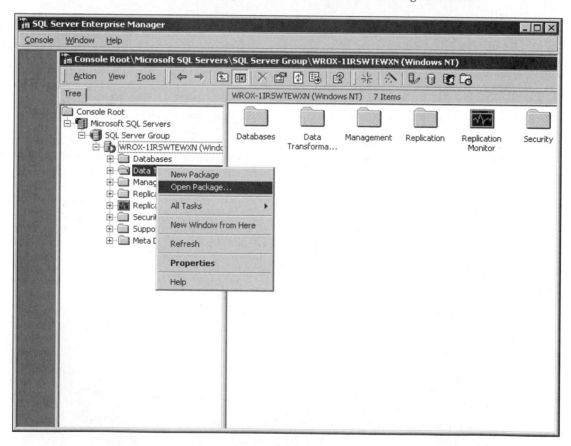

Now navigate to wherever the package is stored; in my case this is the Code subfolder created above:

Clicking on Open will lead you to the following screen:

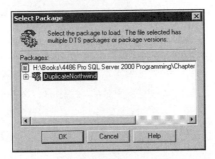

Select the DuplicateNorthwind node and you can go ahead and open the package:

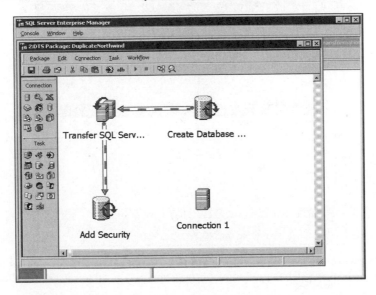

You should now be able to execute the package by clicking on the green arrow in the center of the toolbar. A progress screen will then appear:

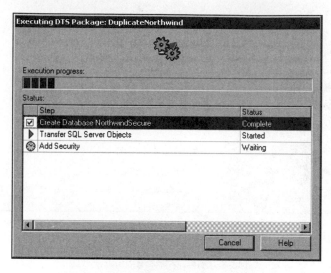

Once the package has been run you should receive a message to say that you have been successful:

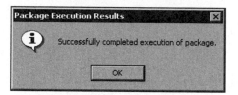

Clicking OK will return you to the execution menu:

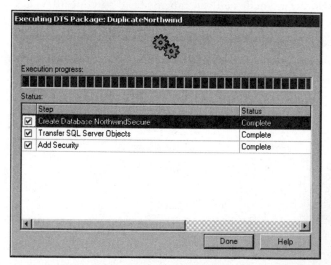

And clicking Done will complete the package execution. The NorthwindSecure database should now be visible in your Enterprise Manager window (though you may need to refresh the Databases node first).

Security Basics

I'm sure that a fair amount of what we're going to look into in this section is going to seem exceedingly stupid – I mean, won't everyone know this stuff? Judging by how often I see violations of even the most simple of these rules, I would say, "No, apparently they don't." All I can ask is that you bear with me, and don't skip ahead. As seemingly obvious as some of this stuff is, you'd be amazed how often it gets forgotten or just plain ignored.

Among the different basics that we'll look at here are:

- ❑ One person, one login ID, one password
- ❑ Password expirations
- ❑ Password length and makeup
- ❑ Number of attempts to log in
- ❑ Storage of user ID and password information

One Person, One Login, One Password

It never ceases to shock me how, everywhere I go, I almost never fail to find that the establishment has at least one "global" user – some login into the network or particular applications that is usually known by nearly everyone in the department or even the whole company. Often, this "global" user has carte blanche (in other words, complete) access. For SQL Server, the common situation is that many installations haven't even bothered to set the sa password to something other than a blank password. Even if they have set it, you'll often find that seemingly everyone knows what the password is. This is a very bad scenario indeed.

> *Prior to SQL Server 2000, the default password for the sa account was null – that is, it didn't have one. Thankfully, SQL Server 2000 has not only changed this default, it will proactively tell you that you are effectively being an idiot if you insist on making it blank – good for the SS2K development team. The thing to watch out for is that, while you're developing, it's really common to still set it to something "easy". You still need to remember to change it before you go into production, or to make it something hard from the beginning if your development server is going to be exposed directly to the Internet or some other non-trustworthy access.*

The first basic then is, if everyone has access to a user ID that is essentially anonymous (if everyone knows it, it could be that anyone has used it) and has access to everything, then you've defeated your security model entirely. The only real benefit that's left is being able to tell who's who as far as who is connected at any point in time (assuming that they are really using their individual login rather than the global login).

Users that have carte blanche access should be limited to just one or two people. Ideally, if you need passwords for such carte blanche access, then you would want separate logins that each have the access, but only one person would know the password for each login.

> *You'll find that users will often share their passwords with someone else in order to let someone temporarily gain some level of access (usually because the owner of the login ID is either out of the office or doesn't have time to bother with doing it themselves at the time) – you should make this nothing short of a hanging offense if possible.*

The problem created by password sharing is multifold. First, some users are getting access to something that you previously decided not to give them (otherwise, why don't they have their own password?) – if you didn't want them to have that access before, why do you want them to have it now? Second, a user that's not supposed to have access probably will now have that access. Since users almost never change their passwords (unless forced to), the person they gave the password to will probably be able to use that login ID indefinitely – and, I assure you, they will! Third, you again lose auditing. You may have something that tracks which user did what based on the login ID. If more than one person has the password for that login ID, how can you be sure which person was logged into that login ID at the time?

This means that if someone is going to be out of the office for some time, perhaps because he is sick or on vacation, and someone else is temporarily going to be doing his job, a new login ID and password should be created specifically for that replacement person (or a modification to the access rights of his existing login ID should be made), and it should be deleted as soon as the original person has returned.

To summarize, stay away from global user accounts whenever possible. If you must have them, keep their use limited to as few people as at all possible – usually this should be kept to just two (one to be a main user, and one person as a backup if the first person isn't available). If you really must have more than one person with significant access, then consider creating multiple accounts (one per user) that have the necessary level of access. By following these simple steps, you'll find you'll do a lot for both the security and auditability of the system.

Password Expiration

Using expiration of passwords tends to be either abused or ignored. That's because it's a good idea that often goes bad.

The principle behind password expiration is to set up your system to have passwords that automatically expire after a certain period of time. After that time, the user must change the password to continue to have access to the account. The concept has been around many years, and if you work in a larger corporation, there's a good chance that the auditors from your accounting firm are already insisting that you implement some form of password expiration.

The problem is that SQL Server does not, natively speaking, support any kind of automatic expiration of passwords. If you want to have automatic password expiration, you have to either use NT-based security (more on that in the next section), or you have to build your own expiration model into your application.

One other caveat here – NT's enforcement of password expiration is somewhat hokey. It will come up and tell the user to change the password, but, by default, the user can choose to enter exactly the same password in and NT will take it. In order for password expiration to be "real", you need to also set up your system or domain to remember the user's old password (you choose how many it will remember), so they can't choose one they've used recently. Again, just because you tell NT to expire the password doesn't mean that it really happened that way – remember to also change the setting for remembering passwords.

What Do You Get for Your Effort?

So, what does password expiration get you? Well, remember that, in the final part of the previous section, I said that once a password is shared, the user would have that access forever? Well, this is the exception. If you expire passwords, then you refresh the level of your security – at least temporarily. The password would have to be shared a second time in order for the user to regain access. While this is far from foolproof (often, the owner of the login ID will be more than happy to share it again), it does deal with the situation where the sharing of the password was really just intended for one-time use. Often, users who share their passwords don't even realize that months later, the other user still has the password, and may be using it on occasion to gain access to something they would not have based on their own security.

Now the Bad News

It is very possible to get too much of a good thing. I mentioned earlier how many audit firms will expect their clients to implement a model where a user's password regularly expires, say, every 30 days – this is a very bad idea indeed.

Every installation that I've seen that does this – without exception – has *worse* security after implementing a 30-day expiration policy. The problem is, as you might expect, multifold in nature.

- ❑ First, technical support calls go way up. When users change passwords that often, they simply can't memorize them all. They can't remember which month's password they are supposed to use, so they are constantly calling for support to reset the password because they forgot what it is.

- ❑ Second, and much more important, the users get tired of both thinking of new passwords and remembering them. Experience has shown me that, for more than 90% of the users I've worked with in installations that use a 30-day expiration, users change their passwords to incredibly predictable (and therefore hackable) words or word/number combinations. Indeed, this often gets to a level where perhaps 50% or more of your users will have the same password – they are all using things like MMMYY where MMM is the month and YY is the year. For example, for January 1996 they might have used JAN96 for their password. Pretty soon, everyone in the place is doing something like that.

I've seen some companies try and deal with this by implementing something of a password sniffer – it checks the password when you go to change it. The sniffing process looks for passwords that incorporate your name or start with a month prefix. These mechanisms are weak at best.

Users are far smarter than we often give them credit for. It took about a week for most users to circumvent the first one of these password sniffers I saw – they simply changed their passwords to have an "X" prefix on them, and otherwise stayed with the same MMMYY format they had been using before. In short, the sniffer wound up doing next to nothing.

The bottom line here is to not get carried away with your expiration policy. Make it short enough to get reasonable turnover and deal with shared or stolen passwords, but don't make it so often that users rebel and start using weak passwords. Personally, I suggest nothing more frequent than 90 days, and nothing longer than 180 days.

Tracking Password Use

If you decide you want to implement this password-tracking functionality on your own, I suggest a couple of things:

❑ Track old passwords to at least ten passwords back – don't let the user use the same password twice over that period. You might also consider checking the first several characters of the new password against old passwords – this can help prevent the user from getting away with only slight changes to the password (changing "hotdog" to "hotdogs" doesn't get you much in the security category).

❑ Track the date the password was changed (as part of the user information), and allow for a system-wide variable that states the number of days that a password can be valid – you can then use the DATEDIFF() function every time the user logs on to your application to make sure the password has been set recently (this assumes that the user has a separate login for each application).

Password Length and Makeup

This is a toughie from the standpoint of both SQL Server and NT based security. Currently, the only real way to implement this is to make your client application the single available route to access the database.

Technically speaking, there is only one way to make your client application the only way into the database. You need to embed the information for a login and password that is dedicated to the application, and then store your user and password information outside the normal security structure of SQL Server. This is something of a real pain. It means that you must manage user access entirely within your application.

The reason that SQL Server or NT security cannot limit access to the database through your application is that they key off the login ID – not the application that passed through that login information. If you are giving users rights to tables and procedures for use with your application, be aware that the users will have those same rights if they log in through the Query Analyzer.

Password Length

If you do indeed make all access driven by your application, then you can implement restrictions on the nature of the password. Realize that, for each possible alphanumeric digit the user includes in the password, they are increasing the number of possible passwords by a factor of 36. That means there are only 36 possible single character passwords, but 1,296 possible two-character passwords. Go up to three characters and you increase the possibilities to 46,656. By the time you add a fourth character, you're well over a million possibilities. The permutations just keep going up as you require more and more characters. The downside though, is that it becomes more and more difficult for your users to remember what their password was and to actually think up passwords. Indeed, I suspect that you'll find that requiring anything more than 5 or 6 characters will generate a full-scale revolt from your end users.

Password Makeup

All right, so I've pointed out that, if you make it a requirement to use at least four alphanumeric characters, you've created a situation where there are over a million possible password combinations. The problem comes when you realize that people aren't really going to use all those combinations – they are going to use words or names that they are familiar with. Considering that the average person only uses about 5,000 words on a regular basis, that doesn't leave you with very many words to try out if you're a hacker.

If you're implementing your own user ID and password scheme, then consider requiring that at least one character be alphabetic in nature (no numbers, just letters), and that at least one character be numeric. This rules out simple numbers that are easy to guess (people really like to use their social security, telephone number or birthday) and all words. The user can still create things that are easy to remember for them – say "77pizzas" – but the password can't be pulled out of a dictionary. Any hacker is forced to truly try each permutation in order to try to break in.

Number of Tries to Login

Regardless of how you're physically storing the user and password information, your login screen should have logic to it that limits the number of tries that someone gets to login. The response if they go over the limit can range in strength, but you want to make sure you throw in some sort of device that makes it difficult to set up a routine to try out all the passwords programmatically.

How many tries to allow isn't really that important as long as it's a reasonably small number – I usually use three times, but I've seen four and five in some places and that's fine too.

What to Do About Login Failure

So, what if they go over? Then what? Well, there are a few different possibilities depending on what extreme you want to go to and how many tech support calls you want:

❑ Stop giving them chances – this is what I most commonly use. I give them their maximum number of tries – each time telling them about their mistake and bringing back up the login dialog. When they hit the limit of failed attempts, I either tell them that was their last chance and close the application, or I just take away the login dialog and make them close the application and restart it on their own. In either case, what I'm trying to do is not stop them from logging in (they can just re-run the application and get another three tries), but rather be enough of a nuisance that they'll want to remember their password correctly next time.

❑ Disable the login ID – you can only do this once if you are using your own security arrangement or if you are using NT/2000. For the former, you can either enable a message to be sent from the client to set something in the database on the third attempt, or you can actually increment a "failed attempts" counter in the user's login information. The outcome of this is to prevent that user from accessing the database with that particular set of login details.

I much prefer the latter of these two choices in this situation. If you're going to go so far as to say that someone's login is disabled on the third failed attempt, then you might as well truly enforce it. If you just send an update from the client to disable login on the final attempt, then it's easy to get around the limit – the user just needs to try one less than the limit, then manually close the application, then start the whole process over again. Each time they close the application it will lose track of the attempts already made. Updating a "failed attempts" column after each such failure ensures that you truly "remember" about all the failed attempts.

Storage of User and Password Information

For the most part, there's no rocket science in how to store user profile and password information. There are, however, a few things to think about:

❑ Since you need to be able to get at the information initially, you will have to do one of the following three things:

    ❑ Compile a password right into the client application or component (and then make sure that the proper login and password is created on any server that you install your application on).

    ❑ Store it in a registry location and have your app retrieve it.

    ❑ Require something of a double password situation – one to get the user as far as the regular password information, and one to get them to the real application. Forcing a user into two logins is generally unacceptable, which pushes you back to one of the other two options in most cases.

❑ If you go with a double password scenario, you'll want the access for the first login to be limited to just a stored procedure execution if possible. By doing this, you can allow the first login to obtain the validation that it needs while not revealing anything to anyone that tries to login through the Query Analyzer. Have your sproc accept a user ID and password, and simply pass back either a Boolean (true/false that they can log in), or pass back a recordset that lists what screens and functions the user can see at the client end. If you use a raw SELECT statement, then you won't be able to restrict what they can see.

One solution I've implemented close to this scenario was to have a view that mapped the current SQL Server login to other login information. In this case, an application role was used that gave the application complete access to everything – the application had to know what the user could and couldn't do. All the user's login had a right to do was execute a stored procedure to request a listing of their rights. The sproc looked something like this:

```
CREATE PROC GetUserRights
AS

DECLARE @User varchar(128)
SELECT @User = USER_NAME()
SELECT * FROM UserPermissions WHERE LoginID = @User
```

❑ If you're going to store password information in the system – encrypt it!!! I can't say enough about the importance of this. Most users will use their passwords for more than one thing – it just makes life a lot easier when you have less to remember. By encrypting the data before you put it in the database, you ensure that no one is going to stumble across a user's password information – even accidentally. They may see it, but what they see is not usable unless they have the key to decrypt it.

Security Options

As far as built-in options go, you now have only two choices in how to set up security under SQL Server. Prior to version 7.0, there were three choices. Just for backward compatibility's sake, let's look at all three types of security that were available for SQL Server 6.x:

❑ NT (or Win 2000) integrated security: the user logs into NT not SQL Server. Authentication is done via NT with trusted connections.

❑ Standard security: the user logs into SQL Server separately from logging into NT. Authentication is done using SQL Server.

❑ Mixed security: an environment in which some users use NT integrated security and others use standard security.

Only the first and last of these are still available. You can still choose a security option that lets you run things as you did with standard security under 6.5 and older versions – it's just that you also have to have NT security as an option. In other words, you can now choose from the following options:

❑ NT (or Win 2000) integrated security

❑ Mix of NT and SQL Server security

You can no longer go only for the old SQL Server-only form of security.

Let's take a look at the two security options available for SQL Server 7 and above.

SQL Server Security

We'll start with SQL Server's built-in login model, as it will have some relevance when we talk about how NT security has worked in the past.

With SQL Server security, you create a **login ID** that is completely separate from your network login information. Some of the pros for using SQL Server security include:

❑ The user doesn't necessarily have to be a domain user in order to gain access to the system

❑ It's easier to gain programmatic control over the user information

❑ In the past, it was much easier to maintain than NT-based or mixed security

Some of the cons are:

❑ Your users have to login twice or more – once into whatever network access they have, and once into the SQL Server for each connection they create from a separate application.

❑ Two logins mean more maintenance for your DBA.

❑ The passwords can easily get out of synch, and that leads to an awful lot of failed logins or forgotten passwords. (Does this sound familiar; "Let's see now, which one was it for this login?")

An example of logging in using SQL Server security would be the use of the sa account that you've probably been using for much of this book. It doesn't matter how you've logged into your network, you log into the SQL Server using a login ID of sa and a separate password (which you've hopefully set to something very secure).

On an ongoing basis, you really don't want to be doing things day-to-day logged in as **sa**. Why? Well, it will probably only take you a minute or two of thought to figure out many of the terrible things you can do by sheer accident when you're using the **sa** account. Using **sa** means you have complete access to everything, that means the DROP TABLE statement you execute when you are in the wrong database will actually do what you told it – drop that table!!! About all you'll be left to say is "oops!" Your boss will probably be saying something completely different.

Even if you do want to always have carte blanche access, just use the **sa** account to make your regular user account a member of the **sysadmins** server role. That gives you the power of **sa**, but gains you the extra security of separate passwords and the audit trail (in Profiler or when looking at system activity) of who is currently logged into the system.

Converting from NT Integrated Security to NT/SQL Server Security

Before we drill down into the specifics of SQL Server security, I want to bring your attention to a bug in SQL Server 2000. If, when you installed, you chose to use only NT integrated security, but decide at a later date that you actually want to have NT and SQL Server security, the sa password will be blanked out and there is no method for entering a new password.

The workaround that Microsoft suggests (at the time of going to press an article was available at http://support.microsoft.com/support/kb/articles/q274/7/73.asp?FR=1) is to make sure that you have a password set up for the sa account *before* you make the switch from NT integrated security to SQL Server security. You can do this by using the sp_password stored procedure:

```
sp_password NULL,'newpassword','sa'
```

Where newpassword should be replaced by the password that you actually want your sa account to have.

Creating a New SQL Server Login

There are currently four ways to create logins on a SQL Server:

- ❑ By using sp_addlogin
- ❑ By using the Enterprise Manager
- ❑ By using SQL Distributed Management Objects (DMO)
- ❑ By using Windows Management Instrumentation (WMI)

SQL DMO is reportedly "going away" after SQL Server 2000 and its replacement is WMI. We'll look at examples of WMI in Chapter 32. For now, let's take a look at the other two options.

sp_addlogin

This sproc does exactly what it says. It only requires one parameter, but most of the time you'll use two or three. There are a couple of additional parameters, but you'll find that you use those far more rarely. The syntax looks like this:

```
EXEC sp_addlogin [@loginame =] <'login'>
    [,[@passwd =] <'password'>]
    [,[@defdb =] <'database'>]
    [,[@deflanguage =] <'language'>]
    [,[@sid =] 'sid']
    [,[@encryptopt =] <'encryption_option'>]
```

Parameter	Description
@loginame	Just what it sounds like – this is the login ID that will be used.
@passwd	Even more what it sounds like – the password that is used to login using the aforementioned login ID.
@defdb	The default database. This defines what is the first "current" database when the user logs in. Normally, this will be the main database your application uses. If left unspecified, the default will be the master database (you usually don't want that, so be sure to provide this parameter).
@deflanguage	The default language for this user. You can use this to override the system default if you are supporting localization.
@sid	A binary number that becomes the **system identifier** (**SID**) for your login ID. If you don't supply a SID, SQL Server generates one for you. Since SIDs must be unique, any SID you supply must not already exist in the system. Using a specific SID can be handy when you are restoring your database to a different server or are otherwise migrating login information.
@encryptopt	The user's login ID and password information is stored in the sysusers table in the master database. The @encryptopt determines whether the password stored in the master database is encrypted or not. By default, (or if you provide a NULL in this parameter), the password is indeed encrypted. The other options are skip_encryption, which does just what it says – the password is not encrypted; and skip_encryption_old, which is only there for backward compatibility, and should not be used.

sp_addlogin gives you the ability to add users as more of a batch function, or to script it right into a client-side administration tool (you could also use SQL DMO for this).

Let's do a quick example with this one:

```
EXEC sp_addlogin UserFromSP, 'password', NorthwindSecure
```

Now create a new connection using the new login of UserFromSP and password of password, and you should be logged in with NorthwindSecure as the first database that shows as current.

Just for ease of use as you go through these exercises, there are two ways you can create a new connection. You can either open up a new instance of Query Analyzer, or you can go to the File | Connect menu option. While the second option can often be easier since you only need to manage windows rather than toggling between QA instances, you must also be careful with it. It's very easy when you use this connect option with multiple logins or servers to forget which one is which and do something that you didn't intend.

sp_password

Once you have that login created, you'll still need to provide a mechanism for changing the password information. The tool to use if you want to do it in T-SQL is `sp_password`. The syntax is pretty straightforward:

```
sp_password [[@old =] <'old password'>,]
   [@new =] <'new password'>
   [,[@loginame =] <'login'>]
```

The new and old password parameters work, of course, just exactly as you would expect. You need to accept those from the user and pass them into the sproc. Note, however, that the login is an optional parameter. If you don't supply it, then it will assume that you want to change the password on the login used for the current connection. Note that `sp_password` cannot be executed as part of a transaction.

> *You might be thinking something like, "Don't most systems require you to enter the new password twice?" Indeed they do. So the follow up question is, "How come `sp_password` doesn't do that?" The answer is a simple one – because SQL Server leaves that up to you. You would include the logic to check for a double entry of the new password in your client application before you ever got as far as using `sp_password`.*

Adding SQL Server Logins Using Enterprise Manager

The most common way that users are added to a SQL Server is with the Enterprise Manager.

To add a login, just open Enterprise Manager and navigate to the server to which you want to add the login. Expand that server's tree, and the **Security** node. Then right-click on **Logins** and select **New Login**:

This brings up the New Login dialog box:

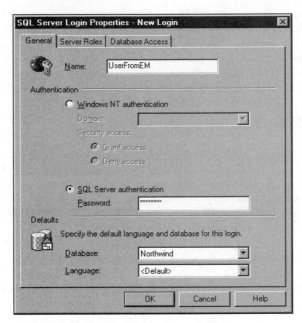

Fill out the fields to match the picture above except use a password of "password". For now, just stick with the defaults on the other two tabs – we'll get to those in the next section.

When you click on OK, you should get another dialog prompting you to re-type the password. This is to be doubly sure that the password you wanted is the one that is really created. Just type the same password in, click on OK, and the login will be created. Now, when you click on the Logins node under the Security node, you should see the UserFromEM login ID listed in the right-hand pane.

In order to improve the apparent performance of the Enterprise Manager, Microsoft changed the way that it updates all the displays of information. Under 6.5 and earlier, the information for each section in EM was constantly refreshed. Under 7.0 and beyond, the information is updated the first time that it's needed, and is then assumed to be stable – that is, EM assumes that nothing has changed.

The benefit of this is that you don't have the overhead of constantly reloading and checking the membership of certain groups of information (logins, databases, tables within the database, etc). The down side, however, is that the lists are often totally unaware of changes on your server.

If you're certain that some changes have been made, but they don't show up in the proper listing, try right-clicking on that node of the tree in the left pane of EM, and then select the Refresh option (you can also select the node you're interested in and then press F5). This will usually clear things up. Note, also, that you'll occasionally bump into errors that say something like "Database MyDB not found in Databases collection". This is a symptom of the same problem. Quit whatever you're doing, right-click on the Databases node and refresh – then try whatever you were doing again.

Changing a Password Using Enterprise Manager

Just as there's a quick and easy way in EM to create a login, there is also a quick and easy way to change a password. Navigate to the Logins node in the left pane – just as you did when you were creating the login, and then just select the node rather than right-clicking on it. Then look in the right-hand pane of the EM window, and double-click the login for which you want to change the password. You'll get exactly the same dialog that you used to create the login. Just type in the new password information and click OK – you'll then get a simple dialog to enter the password again to confirm.

NT Integrated Security

I'm going to do the rather odd thing of starting this section with a comment before we get right down to the nitty-gritty. Prior to 7.0 – NT integrated security was a great idea gone awry (although mixed was even worse). The concept is pretty simple, yet the hassles in both implementation and, in particular, maintenance, rarely made it worth the price of admission. I'm happy to say that was taken care of quite nicely in 7.0. Since then, the model for implementation has been much easier to understand and, in short, works a heck of a lot better. That said, let's get down to it.

NT security gives us the capability to map logins from trusted NT domains into our SQL Server. I can't tell you how cool this notion is, but I can tell you some of the problems that it solves, the things that it simplifies, and why, for versions beyond 7.0, it's just plainly the way to go in many situations.

In this section, we'll look at:

❑   What is NT security?

❑   How do we set it up?

❑   What does (or doesn't) it do for us?

In the end, if you're new to SQL Server, I suspect that you'll think that NT security is pretty cool, and, if you're a user of a version prior to 7.0, then you'll think, "Wow, they finally fixed it!"

What Is NT Security?

NT security is simply a model where you take existing NT domain user accounts or groups and provide SQL Server rights to them directly rather than forcing users to keep separate passwords and make separate logins. Let's again look at examples using both T-SQL and Enterprise Manager.

Granting Access to NT User Accounts

Actually, this is very easy, and works pretty much as it did for SQL Server security. The only real trick is that you need to provide a full domain path to the user profile to which you want to grant access. This is provided through the following syntax:

```
sp_grantlogin [@loginname = ]'<Domain Name>\<NT User Name>'
```

This is one of those things that's perhaps best understood by actually doing it, so let's get right to it.

In order to follow along with this example exactly, you're going to have to have the authority to create users and grant them rights in an NT domain. The domain does not necessarily need to be the main domain that you use at your workplace (for which there's a good chance that you don't have this level of administrative rights), but could be the local domain for your machine if you have administrative rights to it. You should be able to do this example in any domain as long as you have Administrator access to some account that you can substitute in the place of the TestAccount *that we're going to create.*

We'll need to start by creating an NT account with which to test access (we could just use some existing account in a domain somewhere, but I want to be sure of what we're getting, for our purposes in this example). Call the new account TestAccount, and don't give it any special rights of any kind (by default, it will belong to the Everyone built-in NT group).

As soon as we have that account, we're ready to grant some access to it. My TestAccount is in a domain called ARISTOTLE, so I'll need to prefix that domain name when I create the NT login mapping (you will need to replace ARISTOTLE with whatever the name of your NT domain is):

```
EXEC sp_grantlogin 'ARISTOTLE\TestAccount'
```

When you execute sp_grantlogin, you should get a message back indicating that access has been given. However, note that the new user will, by default, not have access to much, if anything, depending on:

❑   Whether any NT group the login belongs to has SQL Server access granted to it

❑   The status of the guest account

We'll look at the specifics of each of these later in the chapter, but if you haven't changed anything security-wise on the server since it was installed, then our NT user TestAccount will have access to the following databases:

❑   Master

❑   Msdb

❑   Northwind

❑   NorthwindBulk

❑   NorthwindCopy

❑   NorthwindCreate

❑   NorthwindDistributed

❑   NorthwindSecure

❑   NorthwindTriggers

❑   Pubs

❑   tempdb

Actually, some of the databases above may not even exist on your system – it's really going to depend on which examples in the book you've run and which you haven't (as well as what you've already deleted!).

For our case, the access is accidental – we haven't granted anything explicitly, so we wind up defaulting to the level of access granted to the guest user. We want to eliminate the access to the NorthwindSecure database so we can do some testing (you'll find out later the reasons why I recommend removing all access from guest). To do this in Enterprise Manager, navigate to the **Users** node under the **NorthwindSecure** database. Right-click on **guest**, and then choose **Delete** (we'll add it back later).

After you've removed the guest access, log into NT using the TestAccount user (or whatever user you're substituting for that account), and start up the Query Analyzer. This time, when you get the login box, choose NT security, and click **OK** to log in. Try changing to the NorthwindSecure database – you shouldn't be allowed access (if you are, then guest must not have been disabled, or some other configuration change has been made).

You now have a valid NT login with SQL Server access – but there isn't a lot you can do with it. This will be the norm on most SQL Servers when you first create a login depending on the factors I mentioned earlier (NT groups, guest account). The login is there, but it has little or no access.

Granting SQL Server access to an NT user account in EM works exactly the same as it did when we were creating SQL Server login accounts. The only difference is that you need to provide the full domain path of the user just as we did with sp_grantlogin.

Why Use NT Security?

Prior to Version 7.0, NT-based security for SQL Server really seemed like nothing more than an afterthought – something of a castaway that nobody really took too seriously. Beginning with 7.0, things became much more usable. Indeed, Microsoft continues to hint that they'd like to see most installations move to using NT security. As we move into the Windows 2000 era, the notion is to have a far more integrated security environment. This makes sense of course – the fewer the logins the tighter and easier it is to maintain security. What's more, it's just plain easier in the long run.

NT security now allows:

❑ Maintenance of a user's access from just one place

❑ Granting of SQL Server rights by simply adding a user to an NT group (this means that you often don't have to even go into SQL Server in order to grant access to a user)

❑ Your users to only need to remember one password and login

The long and the short of it is that NT security now works, for the most part, as it always should have worked.

That being said, let's take a look at how to grant specific rights to specific users.

User Rights

The simplest definition of what a **user right** is would be something like, "what a user can and can't do". In this case, the simple definition is a pretty good one.

User rights fall into three categories:

❑ The right to login

❑ The right to access a specific database

❑ The right to perform specific actions on particular objects within that database

Since we've already looked at creating logins, we'll focus here on the specific rights that a login can have.

Granting Access to a Specific Database

The first thing that you need to do if you want a user to have access to a database is to grant the user the right to access that database. This can be done in EM by adding the user to the **Users** member of the **Databases** node of your server. To add a user using T-SQL, you need to use the sp_grantdbaccess which takes this form:

```
sp_grantdbaccess [@loginame =] <'login'>[, [@name_in_db =]
                <'name in this db'>
```

Note that the access granted will be to the current database – that is, you need to make sure that the database you want the user to have access to is the current database when you issue the command. The login name is the actual login ID that was used to login to SQL Server. The name_in_db parameter allows you to alias this user to another identification. The alias serves for this database only – all other databases will still use the default of the login ID or whatever alias you defined when you granted the user access to that database. The aliasing will affect identification functions such as USER_NAME(). Functions that look at things at the system level, such as SYSTEM_USER will still return the base login ID.

> *Be very careful about aliasing users. It changes the name of that login ID for purposes of the current database. The thing to watch out for is that there can only be one user with a given name in any particular database. This means that if you alias user 'a' to be called 'b' in a given database, then you won't be able to add user 'b' to that database (the database thinks that there is already a user 'b').*

To grant access to the NorthwindSecure database to our ARISTOTLE\TestAccount NT user, we need to use this stored procedure call (using the sa account):

```
USE NorthwindSecure
EXEC sp_grantdbaccess 'ARISTOTLE\TestAccount'
```

If you run this (changing the domain name as appropriate), you should get a confirmation message back that access was granted.

Removing access to a database works pretty much the same – for this, we use the sp_revokedbaccess system sproc:

```
sp_revokedbaccess [@name_in_db =] <'login'>
```

To remove the access we just granted to the NorthwindSecure database, we would execute:

```
USE NorthwindSecure
EXEC sp_revokedbaccess 'ARISTOTLE\TestAccount'
```

You'll get a message back indicating that the user was "dropped" from the database.

> *The login that we just revoked access from is the one we're going to be using as an example throughout the remainder of this chapter. As such, if you're following along with the examples, you'll want to make sure that you grant access back to the user, or none of the rest of the examples will work.*

Granting Object Permissions within the Database

OK, so the user has a login and access to the database you want them to have access to, so now everything's done – right? Ah, if only it were that simple! We are, of course, not done yet.

SQL Server gives us a pretty fine degree of control over what our users can access. Most of the time, you have some information that you want your users to be able to get to, but you also have other information in the database to which you don't want them to have access. For example, you might have a customer service person who has to be able to look at and maintain order information – but you probably don't want them messing around with the salary information. The opposite is also probably true – you need your human resource people to be able to edit employee records, but you probably don't want them giving somebody a major discount on a sale.

SQL Server allows you to assign a separate set of rights to some of the different objects within SQL Server. The objects you can assign rights to include tables, views, and stored procedures. Triggers are implied to have the rights of the person that created them.

User rights on objects fall into six different types:

User Right	Description
SELECT	Allows a user to "see" the data. If a user has this permission, the user has the right to run a SELECT statement against the table or view on which the permission is granted.
INSERT	Allows a user to create new data. Users with this permission can run an INSERT statement. Note that, unlike many systems, having INSERT capability does not necessarily mean that you have SELECT rights.
UPDATE	Allows a user to modify existing data. Users with this permission can run an UPDATE statement. Like the INSERT statement, having UPDATE capability does not necessarily mean that you have SELECT rights.
DELETE	Allows a user to delete data. Users with this permission can run a DELETE statement. Again, having DELETE capability does not necessarily mean that you have SELECT rights.
REFERENCES	Allows a user to insert rows, where the table that is being inserted into has a foreign key constraint, which references another table to which that a user doesn't have SELECT rights.
EXECUTE	Allows a user to EXECUTE a specified stored procedure.

You can mix and match these rights as needed on the particular table, view, or sproc to which you're assigning rights.

You can assign these rights in Enterprise Manager by simply navigating to the Logins option of the Security node of your server. Just right-click on the user and choose Properties. You'll be presented with a different dialog depending on whether you're in the database or security node, but, in either case, you'll have the option of setting permissions. Assigning rights using T-SQL uses three commands that are good to know even if you're only going to assign rights through EM (the terminology is the same).

GRANT

GRANT gives the specified user or role the access specified for the object that is the subject of the GRANT statement.

The syntax for a GRANT statement looks like this:

```
GRANT
    ALL [PRIVILEGES] | <permission>[,...n]
    ON
    <table or view name>[(<column name>[,...n])]
        |<stored or extended stored procedure name>
    TO <login or role name>[,...n]
    [WITH GRANT OPTION]
    [AS <role name>]
```

The ALL keyword indicates that you want to grant all the rights that are applicable for that object type (EXECUTE *never* applies to a table). If you don't use the ALL keyword, then you need to supply one or more specific permissions that you want granted for that object.

PRIVILEGES is a new keyword that has no real function other than to provide ANSI-92 compatibility.

The ON keyword indicates that what comes next is the object for which you want the permissions granted. Note that, if you are granting rights on a table, you can specify permissions down to the column level by specifying a column list to be effected – if you don't supply specific columns, then it's assumed to affect all columns.

> *Microsoft appears to have done something of an about face in their opinion of column level permissions. Being able to say that a user can do a SELECT on a particular table, but only on certain columns seems like a cool idea, but it really convolutes the security process both in its use and in the work it takes Microsoft to implement it. As such, recent literature on the subject, plus what I've been told by insiders, seems to indicate that Microsoft wishes that column level security would go away. They have recommended against its use – if you need to restrict a user to seeing particular columns, consider using a view instead.*

The TO statement does what you would expect – it specifies those to whom you want this access granted. It can be a login ID or a role name.

WITH GRANT OPTION allows the user that you're granting the right to, in turn, also grant access to other users.

> *I recommend against the use of this option since it can quickly become a pain to keep track of who has got access to what. Sure, you can always go into EM and look at the permissions for that object, but then you're in a reactive mode rather than a proactive one – you're looking for what's wrong with the current access levels rather than stopping unwanted access up front.*

Last, but not least, is the AS keyword. This one deals with the issue of a login belonging to multiple roles.

Let's go ahead and move on to an example or two. We'll see later that the TestAccount that we created already has some access based on being a member of the Public role – something that every database user belongs to, and from which you can't remove them. There are, however, a large number of items to which TestAccount doesn't have access (because Public is the only role it belongs to, and Public doesn't have rights either).

Start by logging in with the `TestAccount` user. Then try a `SELECT` statement against the `Region` table:

```
SELECT * FROM Region
```

You'll quickly get a message from SQL Server telling you that you are a scoundrel and you are attempting to go to places that you shouldn't be going:

Server: Msg 229, Level 14, State 5, Line 1
SELECT permission denied on object 'Region', database 'NorthwindSecure', owner 'dbo'.

Login separately as `sa` – you can do this in the same instance of QA if you like by choosing the **File | Connect** menu choice. Then select SQL Server security for the new connection and log in as `sa` with the appropriate password. Now execute a `GRANT` statement:

```
USE NorthwindSecure
GRANT SELECT ON Region TO [ARISTOTLE\TestAccount]
```

Now switch back to the `TestAccount` connection (remember, the information for what user you're connected in as is in the Title Bar of the connection window), and try that `SELECT` statement again. This time, you get better results:

```
RegionID       RegionDescription
-----------------------------------------
1              Eastern
2              Western
3              Northern
4              Southern

(4 row(s) affected)
```

Let's go ahead and try another one. This time, let's run the same tests and commands against the `EmployeeTerritories` table:

```
SELECT * FROM EmployeeTerritories
```

This one fails – again, we don't have rights to it, so let's grant the rights to this table:

```
USE NorthwindSecure
GRANT SELECT ON EmployeeTerritories TO [ARISTOTLE\TestAccount]
```

Now, if you re-run the select statement, things work just fine:

```
EmployeeID     TerritoryID
-------------------------------------------
1              06897
1              19713
...
...
...
9              48304
9              55113
9              55439

(49 row(s) affected)
```

1046

To add an additional twist, however, let's try an INSERT into this table:

```
INSERT INTO EmployeeTerritories
VALUES
    (1, '01581')
```

SQL Server wastes no time in telling us to get lost – we don't have the required permissions, so let's grant them (using the sa connection):

```
USE NorthwindSecure
GRANT INSERT ON EmployeeTerritories TO [ARISTOTLE\TestAccount]
```

Now try that INSERT statement again:

```
INSERT INTO EmployeeTerritories
VALUES
    (1, '01581')
```

Everything works great.

DENY

DENY explicitly prevents the user from the access specified on the targeted object. The key to DENY is that it overrides any GRANT statements. Since a user can belong to multiple roles (discussed shortly), it's possible for a user to be part of a role that's granted access, but also have a DENY in affect. If a DENY and a GRANT both exist in a user's mix of individual and role based rights, then the DENY wins every time. In short, if the user or any role the user belongs to has a DENY for the right in question, then the user will not be able to make use of that access on that object.

The syntax looks an awful lot like the GRANT statement:

```
DENY
    ALL [PRIVILEGES]|<permission>[,...n]
    ON
    <table or view name>[(column[,...n])]
        |<stored or extended stored procedure name>
    TO <login ID or roll name>[,...n]
    [CASCADE]
```

Again, the ALL keyword indicates that you want to deny all the rights that are applicable for that object type (EXECUTE *never* applies to a table). If you don't use the ALL keyword, then you need to supply one or more specific permissions that you want to be denied for that object.

PRIVILEGES is still a new keyword and has no real function other than to provide ANSI-92 compatibility.

The ON keyword indicates that what comes next is the object on which you want the permissions denied.

Everything has worked pretty much the same as with a GRANT statement until now. The CASCADE keyword matches up with the WITH GRANT OPTION that was in the GRANT statement. CASCADE tells SQL Server that you want to also deny access to anyone that this user has granted access to under the rules of the WITH GRANT OPTION.

To run an example on DENY, let's try a simple SELECT statement using the TestAccount login:

```
USE NorthwindSecure
SELECT * FROM Employees
```

This should get you nine records or so. How did you get access when we haven't granted it to TestAccount? TestAccount belongs to Public, and Public has been granted access to Employees.

Let's say that we don't want TestAccount to have access. For whatever reason, TestAccount is the exception, and we don't want that user snooping in that data – we just issue our DENY statement (remember to issue the DENY using the sa login):

```
USE NorthwindSecure
DENY ALL ON Employees TO [ARISTOTLE\TestAccount]
```

When you run the SELECT statement again using TestAccount, you'll get an error – you no longer have access. Note also that, since we used the ALL keyword, the INSERT, DELETE, and UPDATE access that Public has is now also denied from TestAccount.

> Note that **DENY** was new to SQL Server 7.0. The concept of a deny was there in 6.5, but it was implemented differently. Instead of **DENY**, you would issue a **REVOKE** statement twice. The new **DENY** keyword makes things much clearer.

REVOKE

REVOKE eliminates the effects of a previously issued GRANT or DENY statement. Think of this one as like a targeted "Undo" statement.

The syntax is a mix of the GRANT and DENY statements:

```
REVOKE [GRANT OPTION FOR]
    ALL [PRIVILEGES] | <permission>[,...n]
    ON
    <table or view name>[(column name [,...n])]
      |<stored or extended stored procedure name>
    TO | FROM <login ID or roll name>[,...n]
    [CASCADE]
    [AS <role name>]
```

The explanations here are virtually identical to those of the GRANT and DENY statements – I put them here again in case you're pulling the book back off the shelf for a quick lookup on REVOKE.

Once again, the ALL keyword indicates that you want to revoke all the rights that are applicable for that object type. If you don't use the ALL keyword, then you need to supply one or more specific permissions that you want to be revoked for that object.

PRIVILEGES still has no real function other than to provide ANSI-92 compatibility.

The ON keyword indicates that what comes next is the object on which you want the permissions revoked.

The CASCADE keyword matches up with the WITH GRANT OPTION that was in the GRANT statement. CASCADE tells SQL Server that you want also to revoke access from anyone that this user granted access to under the rules of the WITH GRANT OPTION.

The AS keyword again just specifies on which role you want to issue this command based.

Using the sa connection, let's undo the access that we granted to the Region table in NorthwindSecure:

```
REVOKE ALL ON Region FROM [ARISTOTLE\TestAccount]
```

After executing this, our TestAccount can no longer run a SELECT statement against the Region table.

In order to remove a DENY, we also issue a REVOKE statement. This time, we'll regain access to the Employees table:

```
USE NorthwindSecure
REVOKE ALL ON Employees TO [ARISTOTLE\TestAccount]
```

Now that we've seen how all the commands to control access work for individual users, let's take a look at the way we can greatly simplify management of these rights by managing in groupings.

User Rights and Statement-Level Permissions

User permissions don't just stop with the objects in your database – they also extend to certain statements that aren't immediately tied to any particular object. SQL Server gives you control over permissions to run several different statements, including:

❏ CREATE DATABASE

❏ CREATE DEFAULT

❏ CREATE PROCEDURE

❏ CREATE RULE

❏ CREATE TABLE

❏ CREATE VIEW

❏ BACKUP DATABASE

❏ BACKUP LOG

At this point, we've already seen all of these commands at work except for the two backup commands – what those are about is pretty self-explanatory, so I'm not going to spend any time on them here (we'll look at them in Chapter 30) – just keep in mind that they are something you can control at the statement level.

OK, so how do we assign these permissions? Actually, now that you've already seen GRANT, REVOKE, and DENY in action for objects, you're pretty much already schooled on statement-level permissions too. Syntactically speaking, they work just the same as object-level permissions except that they are even simpler (you don't have to fill in as much). The syntax looks like this:

```
GRANT <ALL | statement[,...n]> TO <login ID>[,...n]
```

Easy, hey? To do a quick test, let's start by verifying that our test user doesn't already have authority to CREATE. Make sure you are logged in as your TestAccount, and then run the following command (don't forget to switch your domain name for ARISTOTLE below):

```
USE NorthwindSecure

CREATE TABLE TestCreate
(
    Col1 int Primary Key
)
```

This gets us nowhere fast:

Server: Msg 262, Level 14, State 1, Line 2
CREATE TABLE permission denied, database 'NorthwindSecure', owner 'dbo'.

Now log into SQL Server using the sa account (or another account with dbo authority for NorthwindSecure). Then run our command to grant permissions:

```
GRANT CREATE TABLE TO [ARISTOTLE\TestAccount]
```

You should get confirmation that your command completed successfully. Then just try running the CREATE statement again (remember to log back in using the TestAccount):

```
USE NorthwindSecure

CREATE TABLE TestCreate
(
    Col1 int Primary Key
)
```

This time everything works.

DENY and REVOKE also work the same way as they did for object-level permissions.

Server and Database Roles

Prior to version 7.0, SQL Server had the concept of a "group" – which was a grouping of user rights that you could assign all at once by simply assigning the user to that group. This was quite different from the way NT groups operated, where a user could belong to more than one NT group, so you could mix and match them as needed. In SQL Server 6.5 (and earlier) one user was allowed to belong to only one group per database.

The fallout from the pre-SQL Server 7.0 way of doing things was that SQL Server groups fell into one of three categories:

❑ They were frequently modified by user-level permissions

❑ They were only a slight variation of the main group

❑ They had more access than required (to make the life of the DBA easier)

Basically, they were one great big hassle, albeit a rather necessary one.

Along came version 7.0, and with it some very big changes. Instead of a group, a user now belongs to a **role**. A role is, in the most general sense, the same thing as a group.

> **A role is a collection of access rights that can be assigned to a user en masse simply by assigning the user to that role.**

The similarities begin to fade there though. With roles, a user can belong to several at one time. This can be incredibly handy since you can group access rights into smaller and more logical groups, and then mix and match them into the formula that best fits a user.

Roles fall into two categories:

❑ Server roles

❑ Database roles

> *We'll soon see a third thing that's also called role – though I wish that Microsoft had chosen another name – **application roles**. These are a special way to alias a user into a different set of permissions. An application role isn't something you assign a user to; it's a way of having an application have a different set of rights from the user. For this reason, I don't usually think of application roles as a "role" in the true sense of the word.*

Server roles are limited to those that are already built-in to SQL Server when it ships, and are primarily there for the maintenance of the system as well as granting the capability to do non-database specific things like creating login accounts and creating linked servers.

Much like server roles, there are a number of built-in (or "fixed") database roles, but you can also define your own database roles to meet your particular needs. Database roles are for setting up and grouping specific user rights within a single given database.

Let's look at both of these types of roles individually.

Server Roles

All server roles available are "fixed" roles and are there right from the beginning – all the server roles that you're ever going to have existed from the moment your SQL Server was installed.

Role	Nature
sysadmin	This role can perform any activity on your SQL Server. Anyone with this role is essentially the sa for that server. The creation of this server role provides Microsoft with the capability to one day eliminate the sa login – indeed, the Books Online refers to sa as being legacy in nature. It's worth noting that the NT Administrators group on the SQL Server is automatically mapped into the sysadmin role. This means that anyone who is a member of your server's Administrators group also has sa-level access to your SQL data. You can, if you need to, remove the NT administrators group from the sysadmin role to tighten that security loophole.

Table continued on following page

Role	Nature
serveradmin	This one can set server-wide configuration options or shut down the server. It's rather limited in scope, yet the functions controlled by members of this role can have a very significant impact on the performance of your server.
setupadmin	This one is limited to managing linked servers and startup procedures.
securityadmin	This one is very handy for logins that you create specifically to manage logins, read error logs, and CREATE DATABASE permissions. In many ways, this one is the classic system operator role – it can handle most of the day-to-day stuff, but doesn't have the kind of global access that a true omnipotent superuser would have.
processadmin	Has the capability to manage processes running in SQL Server – this one can kill long running processes if necessary.
dbcreator	Is limited to creating and altering databases.
diskadmin	Manages disk files (what file group things are assigned to, attaching and detaching databases, etc.)
bulkadmin	This one is something of an oddity. It is created explicitly to give rights to execute the BULK INSERT statement, which otherwise is only executable by someone with sysadmin rights. Frankly, I don't understand why this statement isn't granted with the GRANT command like everything else, but it isn't. Keep in mind that, even if a user has been added to the bulkadmin group, that just gives them access to the statement, not the table that they want to run it against. This means that you need, in addition to adding the user to the bulkadmin task, to GRANT them INSERT permissions to any table you want them to be able to perform the BULK INSERT against. In addition, you'll need to make sure they have proper SELECT access to any tables that they will be referencing in their BULK INSERT statement.

You can mix and match these roles to individual users that are responsible for administration roles on your server. In general, I suspect that only the very largest of database shops will use more than the sysadmin and securityadmin roles, but they're still handy to have around.

Earlier in this chapter, I got into a lengthy soapbox diatribe on the evils of global users. It probably comes as no surprise to you to learn that I was positively ecstatic when the new sysadmin role was added back in version 7.0. The existence of this role means that, on an ongoing basis, you should not need to have anyone have the sa login – just let the users that need that level of access become members of the sysadmins role, and they shouldn't ever need to login as sa.

Database Roles

Database roles are limited in scope to just one database – just because a user belongs to the db_datareader role in one database it doesn't mean that they belong to that role in another database. Database roles fall into two subcategories: fixed and user-defined.

Fixed Database Roles

Much as there are several fixed server roles, there are also a number of fixed database roles. Some of them have a special predefined purpose, which cannot be duplicated using normal statements (that is you cannot create a user-defined database role that had the same functionality). However, most exist to deal with the more common situations and make things easier for you.

Role	Nature
db_owner	This role performs as if it were a member of all the other database roles. Using this role, you can create a situation where multiple users can perform the same functions and tasks as if they were the database owner.
db_accessadmin	Performs a portion of the functions similar to the securityadmin server role, except this role is limited to the individual database where it is assigned and the creation of users (not individual rights). It cannot create new SQL Server logins, but members of this role can add NT users and groups as well as existing SQL Server logins into the database.
db_datareader	Can issue a SELECT statement on all user tables in the database.
db_datawriter	Can issue INSERT, UPDATE, and DELETE statements on all user tables in the database.
db_ddladmin	Can add, modify, or drop objects in the database.
db_securityadmin	The other part of the database-level equivalent of the securityadmin server role. This database role cannot create new users in the database, but does manage roles and members of database roles as well as manage statement and object permissions in the database.
db_backupoperator	Backs up the database (gee, bet you wouldn't have guessed that one!).
db_denydatareader	Provides the equivalent of a DENY SELECT on every table and view in the database.
db_denydatawriter	Similar to db_denydatareader, only affects INSERT, UPDATE, and DELETE statements.

Much like the fixed server roles, you're probably not going to see all of these used in anything but the largest of database shops. Some of the roles are not replaceable with your own database roles, and others are just very handy to deal with the quick and dirty situations that seem to frequently come up.

User-Defined Database Roles

The fixed roles that are available are really only meant to be there to help you get started. The real mainstay of your security is going to be the creation and assignment of user-defined database roles. For these roles, you decide what permissions they include.

With user-defined roles, you can GRANT, DENY, and REVOKE in exactly the same way as we did for individual users. The nice thing about using roles is that users tend to fall into categories of access needs – by using roles you can make a change in one place and have it propagate to all the similar users (at least the ones that you have assigned to that role).

Creating a User-Defined Role

To create our own role, we use the `sp_addrole` system sproc. The syntax is pretty simple:

```
sp_addrole [@rolename =] <'role name'>
    [,[@ownername =] <'owner'>]
```

The `role name` is simply what you want to call that role. Examples of common naming schema would include by department (`Accounting`, `Sales`, `Marketing`, etc.) or by specific job (`CustomerService`, `Salesperson`, `President`, etc). Using roles like this can make it really easy to add new users to the system. If your accounting department hires someone new, you can just add them to the `Accounting` role (or, if you're being more specific, it might even be the `AccountsPayable` role) and forget it – no researching, "What should this person have for rights?"

The `owner` is the same thing as it is for all other objects in the system. The default is the database owner, and I strongly suggest leaving it that way (in other words, just ignore this optional parameter).

Let's go ahead and create ourselves a role (using the `sa` login):

```
USE NorthwindSecure
EXEC sp_addrole 'OurTestRole'
```

When you execute this, you should get back a nice and friendly message telling you that the new role has been added.

Now what we need is to add some value to this role in the form of it actually having some rights assigned to it. To do this, we just use our GRANT, DENY, or REVOKE statements just as we did for actual users earlier in the chapter:

```
USE NorthwindSecure
GRANT SELECT ON Territories TO OurTestRole
```

Anyone who belongs to our role now has SELECT access to the `Territories` table (unless they have a DENY somewhere else in their security information).

At this point, you're ready to start adding users.

Adding Users to a Role

Having all these roles around is great, but they are of no use if they don't have anyone assigned to them. Adding a user to a role is as simple as using the `sp_addrolemember` system sproc and providing the database name and login ID:

```
sp_addrolemember [@rolename =] <role name>,
    [@membername =] <Login ID>
```

Everything is pretty self-explanatory on the parameters for this one, so let's move right into an example.

Let's start off by verifying that our `TestAccount` doesn't have access to the `Territories` table:

```
SELECT * FROM Territories
```

Sure enough, we are rejected (no access yet):

Server: Msg 229, Level 14, State 5, Line 1
SELECT permission denied on object 'Territories', database 'NorthwindSecure', owner 'dbo'.

Now we'll go ahead and add our TestAccount NT user to our OurTestRole role (ensuring that you are using the sa account):

```
USE NorthwindSecure
EXEC sp_addrolemember OurTestRole, [ARISTOTLE\TestAccount]
```

Again, we get a friendly confirmation that things have worked properly:

'ARISTOTLE\TestAccount' added to role 'OurTestRole'.

It's time to try to run the SELECT statement again – this time with much more success (you should get about 53 rows back).

Removing a User from a Role

What goes up, must come down, and users that are added to a role will also inevitably be removed from roles.

Removing a user from a role works almost exactly as adding them does, except we use a different system sproc called sp_droprolemember in the form of:

```
sp_droprolemember [@rolename =] <role name>,
    [@membername =] <security account>
```

So let's go right back to our example and remove the TestAccount from the OurTestRole database role:

```
USE NorthwindSecure
EXEC sp_droprolemember OurTestRole, [ARISTOTLE\TestAccount]
```

You should receive another friendly confirmation that things have gone well; now try our SELECT statement again:

```
SELECT * FROM Territories
```

And, sure enough, we are again given the error message that we don't have access.

You can add and drop users from any role this way – it doesn't matter whether the role is user-defined or fixed, or whether it's a system or database role. In any case, they work pretty much the same.

Note also that you can do all of this through Enterprise Manager. To change the rights associated with a role, just click on the Roles member of the Databases node, and assign permissions by using the checkboxes. When you want to add a user to the role, just go to the user properties, select either the Server or Database roles tab, and then put a checkmark in all the roles you want that user to have.

Dropping Roles

Dropping a role is as easy as adding one. Simply change to the database that you want to drop the role from, then the syntax is simply:

```
EXEC sp_droprole <'role name'>
```

And it's gone.

Application Roles

Application roles are something of a different animal from database and server roles. Indeed, the fact that the term "role" is used would make you think that they are closely related – they aren't.

Applications roles are really much more like a security alias for the user. Application roles allow you to define an access list (made up of individual rights or groupings of databases). They are also similar to a user in that they have their own password. They are, however, different from a user login because they cannot "login" as such – a user account must first login, then they can activate the application role.

So what do we need application roles for? For applications – what else? Time and time again, you'll run into the situation where you would like a user to have a separate set of rights depending on under what context they are accessing the database. With an application role, you can do things like grant a user no more than read-only access to the database (SELECT statements only), but still allow them to modify data when they do so within the confines of your application.

> *Note that application roles are a one-way trip – that is, once you've established an application role as being active for a given connection, you can't go back to the user's own security settings for that connection. In order for users to go back to their own security information, they must terminate the connection and login again.*

The process works like this:

1. The user logs in (presumably using a login screen provided by your application)

2. The login is validated, and the user receives his or her access rights

3. The application executes a system sproc called sp_setapprole and provides a role name and password

4. The application role is validated, and the connection is switched to the context of that application role (all the rights the user had are gone – he or she now has the rights of the application role)

5. The user continues with access based on the application role rather than his or her personal login throughout the duration of the connection – the user cannot go back to his or her own access information

You would only want to use application roles as part of a true application situation, and you would build the code to set the application role right into the application. You would also compile the required password into the application or store the information in some local file to be accessed when it is needed.

Creating Application Roles

To create an application role, we use a new system sproc called sp_addapprole. This is another pretty easy one to use; its syntax looks like this:

```
sp_addapprole [@rolename =] <role name>,
    [@password =] <'password'>
```

Much like many of the sprocs in this chapter, the parameters are pretty self-explanatory; so let's move right on to using it by creating ourselves an application role:

```
EXEC sp_addapprole OurAppRole, 'password'
```

Just that quick, our application role is created.

Adding Permissions to the Application Role

Adding permissions to application roles works just like adding permissions to anything else. Just substitute the application role name anywhere that you would use a login ID or regular server or database role.

Again, we'll move to the quick example (using the sa login):

```
GRANT SELECT ON Region TO OurAppRole
```

Our application role now has SELECT rights on the Region table – it doesn't, as yet, have access to anything else.

Using the Application Role

Using the application role is a matter of calling a system sproc (sp_setapprole) and providing both the application role name and the password for that application role. The syntax looks like this:

```
sp_setapprole [@rolename =] <role name>,
    [@password =] {Encrypt N<'password'>}|<'password'>
    [,[@encrypt =] '<encryption style>']
```

The role name is simply the name of whatever application role you want to activate.

The password can either be supplied as is or encrypted using the ODBC encrypt function. If you're going to encrypt the password, then you need to enclose the password in quotes after the Encrypt keyword and precede the password with a capital N – this indicates to SQL Server that you're dealing with a Unicode string, and it will be treated accordingly. Note the use of a curly braces { } rather than parentheses for the encryption parameter. If you don't want encryption, then just supply the password without using the Encrypt keyword.

The encryption style is only needed if you chose the encryption option for the password parameter. If you are encrypting, then supply "ODBC" as the encryption style.

It's worth noting that encryption is only an option with ODBC and OLE DB clients. You cannot use DB-Lib with encryption.

Moving right into the example category, let's start by verifying a couple of things about the status of our `TestAccount` user. At this point in the chapter (assuming you've been following along with all the examples), your `TestAccount` user should not be able to access the `Region` table, but should be able to access the `EmployeeTerritories` table. You can verify this to be the case by running a couple of `SELECT` statements:

```
SELECT * FROM Region
SELECT * FROM EmployeeTerritories
```

The first `SELECT` should give you an error, and the second should return around 50 rows or so.

Now let's activate the application role that we created a short time ago; type this in using `TestAccount` user:

```
sp_setapprole OurAppRole, {Encrypt N'password'}, 'odbc'
```

When you execute this, you should get back a confirmation that your application role is now "active".

Try it out by running our two `SELECT` statements – you'll find that what does and doesn't work has been exactly reversed. That is, `TestAccount` had access to `EmployeeTerritories`, but that was lost when we went to the application role. `TestAccount` did not have access to the `Regions` table, but the application role now provides that access.

There is no way to terminate the application role for the current connection, so you can go ahead and terminate your `TestAccount` connection. Then, create a new connection with NT security for your `TestAccount`. Try running those `SELECT` statements again and you'll find that your original set of rights has been restored.

Getting Rid of Application Roles

When you no longer need the application role on your server, you can use `sp_dropapprole` to eliminate it from the system. The syntax is as follows:

```
sp_dropapprole [@rolename =] <role name>
```

To eliminate our application role from the system, we would just issue the command (from sa):

```
EXEC sp_dropapprole OurAppRole
```

Security with XML

Unless you are in the business of working with HTTP access, then you can skip this section. Indeed, you don't need to worry about HTTP issues to work with SQL Server as it is all taken care of behind the scenes. However, if you do need to work with HTTP, then be warned, HTTP security is very different from any security issues already discussed in this chapter. Since much of the HTTP access stuff is on web release (MS will post updates on the web so you don't need to wait for the next release of SQL Server for additional functionality), I'm hoping to see the security options expanded on.

The best option, if you can use it, is to make use of NT security with HTTP access. This means that whoever is running a query – regardless of whether it's URL-based, template, XPath, or POST – will only be able to see what SQL Server lets them see through any other access method (such as Query Analyzer). Unfortunately, this will often not be the case – you'll often be using some blanket login to deal with anonymous users. In this case, just remember a few key points:

❑ Use XML templates to hide query logic and restrict the particular query being run to what you intended for the situation.

❑ Avoid HTTP POST for now. When combined with XML templates, this had the potential to provide just about everything I wanted in terms of security, but, unfortunately, turning on HTTP POST doesn't just give your templates the ability to accept parameters via POST, but also accepts stand-alone queries via POST.

This is a very bad thing indeed. It took me about 5 minutes after I first turned POST on to create my own HTML page with my own form to submit a query like DELETE * FROM Orders – not good at all.

❑ Also avoid URL-based queries unless you have limited the user your HTTP access uses to permissions that you are comfortable giving to any and everyone.

Be sure to look back at the HTTP set up information in Chapter 20 for more information on how to change what access you are allowing in your HTTP configuration.

More Advanced Security

This section is really nothing more than an "extra things to think about" section. All of these fall outside the realm of the basic rules we defined at the beginning of the chapter, but they address ways around some problems and also how to close some common loopholes in your system.

What to Do about the Guest Account

The guest account provides a way of having default access. When you have the guest account active, then several things happen:

❑ Logins gain guest level access to any database to which they are not explicitly given access.

❑ Outside users can login through the guest account to gain access. This requires that they know the password for guest, but they'll already know the user exists (although, they probably also know that the sa account exists too).

Personally, one of the first things I do with my SQL Server is to eliminate every ounce of access the guest account has. It's a loophole, and it winds up providing access in a way you don't intuitively think of. (You probably think that when you assign rights to someone – that's all the rights they have. With guest active, that isn't necessarily so.) I recommend that you do the same.

There is, however, one use that I'm aware of where the guest account actually serves a fairly slick purpose – when it is used with application roles. In this scenario, you leave the guest account with access to a database, but without any rights beyond simply logging into that database – that is the guest account only makes the logged on database "current". You can then use sp_setapprole to activate an application role, and, boom, you now have a way for otherwise anonymous users to login into your server with appropriate rights. They can, however, only perform any *useful* login if they are using your application.

This is definitely a scenario where you want to be protecting that application role password as if your job depended on it (it probably does). Use the ODBC encryption option – particularly if your connection is via the Internet!

TCP/IP Port Settings

By default when using TCP/IP, SQL Server uses port number 1433. A port can be thought of as something like a radio channel – it doesn't matter what channel you're broadcasting on, it won't do you any good if no one is listening to that channel.

Leaving things with the default value of 1433 can be very convenient – all of your clients will automatically use port 1433 unless you specify otherwise, so this means that you have one less thing to worry about being set right if you just leave well enough alone.

The problem, however, is that just about any potential SQL Server hacker also knows that port 1433 is the one to which 99% of all SQL Servers are listening. If your SQL Server has a direct connection to the Internet, I strongly recommend changing to a non-standard port number – check with your network administrator for what he or she recommends as an available port. Just remember that, when you change what the server is "listening" to, you'll also need to change what all the IP based clients are using. For example, if we were going to change to using port 1402, we would go into the Client Network Utility and set up a specific entry for our server with 1402 as the IP port to use:

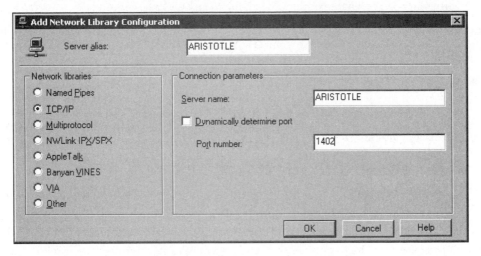

Beginning with SQL Server 2000, we also have the option of telling the client to dynamically determine the port, by checking the Dynamically determine port box.

Don't Use the sa Account

Everyone who's studied SQL Server for more than about ten minutes knows about the system administrator account. Now that SQL Server has the sysadmins fixed server role, I strongly suggest adding true logins to that role, then changing the sa password to something very long and very incomprehensible – something not worth spending the time to hack into. If you only need NT security, then turn SQL Server security off, and that will deal with the sa account issue once and for all.

Keep xp_cmdshell under Wraps

I already mentioned this one back in Chapter 12, but remember to be careful about who you grant access to use xp_cmdshell. It will run any DOS or NT Command Prompt command. The amount of authority that it grants to your users depends on what account SQL Server is running under. If it is a system account (as the majority are), then the users of xp_cmdshell will have very significant access to your server (they could, for example, copy files onto the server from elsewhere on the network, then execute those files). Let's raise the stakes a bit though – there are also a fair number of servers running out there under the context of an NT domain administrator account – anyone using xp_cmdshell now has fairly open access to your entire network!!!

The short rendition here is not to give anyone access to xp_cmdshell that you wouldn't give administrative rights to for your server or possibly even your domain.

Don't Forget Views, Stored Procedures, and UDFs as Security Tools

Remember that views, sprocs, and UDFs all have a lot to offer in terms of hiding data. Views can usually take the place of column-level security. They can do wonders to make a user think they have access to an entire table, when they in reality have access to only a subset of the entire data (remember our example of filtering out sensitive employee information, such as salary?). Sprocs and UDFs can do much the same – you can grant execute rights to a sproc or UDF, but that doesn't mean they get all the data from a table (they only get what the sproc or UDF gives them) – the end user may not even know what underlying table is supplying the data. In addition, views, sprocs, and UDFs have their own implied authority – that is, just because views and sprocs use a table, it doesn't mean that the user has access rights for that table.

Summary

Security is one of those areas that tend to be ignored by developers. Unfortunately, the security of your system is going to be determined by how your client application handles things, so there's only so much a DBA can do after you've shipped your application.

Treat security as if it is the lifeblood for the success or failure of your system at your customer site (which, if you're building internal projects, may be your site) – it probably is a critical factor.

Online discussion at http://p2p.wrox.com

29

Performance Tuning

This is probably the toughest chapter in the book from my perspective as the author, but not for the normal reasons. Usually, the issue is how to relate complex information in a manner that's easy to understand. As we're getting near the end of the book, I hope that I've succeeded there – even if there is still more to come. At this point, you have a solid foundation in everything we're going to discuss in this chapter. That means I'm relatively free to get to the nitty-gritty and not worry quite as much about confusion.

Why then would this be a tough chapter for me to write? Well, because deciding exactly what to put into this chapter is difficult. You see, this isn't a book on performance tuning – that can easily be a book in itself. It is, however, a book about making you successful in your experience of developing with SQL Server. Having a well-performing system is critical to that success. The problem lies in a line from Bob Seger, "What to leave in, what to leave out." What can we focus on here that's going to get you the most bang for your buck?

Perhaps the most important thing to understand about performance tuning is that you are never going to know everything there is to know about it. If you're the average SQL developer, you're going to be lucky if you know 20% of what there is to know. Fortunately, performance tuning is one of those areas where the old 80-20 rule definitely applies (80% of the benefit comes from the right 20% of the work).

With that in mind, we're going to be roaming around quite a bit in this chapter topically speaking. Everything we talk about is going to be performance-related in some fashion, but we'll touch on a wide range of methods for squeezing the most out of the system performance-wise. The topics we'll go into include both new and old subjects. In many cases, we'll revisit a subject we've already covered, but with a particular eye on performance. Some of the fields we'll focus on include:

- ❏ Index choices
- ❏ Client-side vs. server-side processing
- ❏ Strategic de-normalization
- ❏ Routine maintenance
- ❏ Organizing your stored procedures
- ❏ Uses for temporary tables
- ❏ Small gains in repetitive processes vs. big gains in long-running processes
- ❏ Hardware configuration issues
- ❏ Trouble-shooting

Even though we're going to cover all of these, make sure you understand the following – this is only the beginning. The most important concept in performance is to really just stop and think about it. There is, for some strange reason, a tendency when working with SQL to just use the first thing that comes to mind that will work. You need to give the same kind of thought to your queries, sprocs, database designs – whatever – that you would give to any other development work that you're doing. Also, keep in mind that your T-SQL code is only one part of the picture – hardware, client-code, SQL Server configuration, and network issues are examples of things that are "outside the code" and that can have a dramatic impact on your system.

When to Tune

This is probably going to seem a little obvious, but performance needs considering much earlier in the process than when you are writing your code. Indeed, it really should start in the requirements gathering process and then never end.

What's the big deal about performance tuning in the requirements gathering stage? Well, while you obviously can't do anything yet to *physically* tune your system, you can do a lot to *logically* tune your system. For example, is the concern of the customer more towards the side of perceived performance or actual completion of the job? For interactive processes, users will generally be more satisfied and *think* the system is faster if you do something to show them that work is going on (even if it's just a progress bar). In addition, sometimes it's worth having a process that completes a little more slowly as long as the "first response" – that is, when it starts outputting something – is faster. Which of these is preferable is something you should know in the requirements gathering stage. Finally, you should determine what your system's performance requirements are at this time.

> *I often see cases where the developer thinks the system is "fast enough", only to find out that the performance is actually unacceptable to the user. This happens for a lot of reasons, but certainly the most common is that the developer has his or her head buried in the sand.*

> *Find out what's expected! Also, remember to test whether you've met expectations under a realistic load on something resembling the real live hardware – not a load based on one or two developers sitting at their development system.*

Obviously, performance tuning also continues into design. If you design for performance, then you will generally greatly reduce the effort required to tune at completion. What's more, you'll find that you've greatly enhanced the "best" numbers you can achieve.

I'm starting to drone on here, but performance tuning never stops. When you're actually coding, get it working, but then *stop*! Stop and take a look at your code. Once an entire system is together, the actual code will almost never be looked at again, unless:

❑ Something breaks (there's a bug)

❑ You need to upgrade a part of the system

❑ There is a overt performance problem (usually, a *very* bad one)

In the first two of these instances, you probably won't be looking at the performance issues. You'll be concentrating on how to get things fixed or the extra functionality added. The point here is that an extra few minutes of looking at your code and asking yourself, "Could I have done it better?" or, "Hey, have I done anything stupid here?" can shave a little bit here and a little bit there and, occasionally, a whole lot in another place.

> *Simply put: I make stupid mistakes, and so will you. It is, however, amazing how often you can step back from your code for a minute or two, then look at it again with a critical eye and say, "Gee, I can't believe I did that!" Hopefully, those moments will be rare, but, if you take the time to be critical of your own code, you'll find most of those gaffs that could really bog your system down. As for the ones you don't find, hopefully you'll uncover them as you continue down the path we're laying out here.*

The next big testing milestone time is in the Quality Assurance process. At this juncture, you should be establishing general system benchmarks and comparing those against the performance requirements established during the requirements phase.

Last, but not least – never stop. Ask end users where their pain is from a performance perspective. Is there something they say is slow? Don't wait for them to tell you (often, they think "that's just the way it is" and say nothing – except to your boss of course). Go and ask.

Index Choices

Again, this is something that was covered in extreme depth previously, but the topic still deserves more than just a mention here because of its sheer importance to query performance.

People tend to go to extremes with **indexes**. I'm encouraging you not to follow any one rule, but to instead think about the full range of items that your index choices impact upon.

Any table that has a primary key (and they all will have, with very rare exceptions) has at least one index. This doesn't mean, however, that it is a very useful index from a performance perspective. Indexes should be considered for any column that you're going to be frequently using as a target in a WHERE or, to a lesser extent, an ORDER BY clause.

Remember though, that the more indexes you have, the slower your inserts are going to be. When you insert a record, one or more entries (depending on what's going on in the non-leaf levels of the B-Tree) have to be made for that index. That means more indexes and also means more for SQL Server to do on inserts. In an OLTP environment (where you tend to have a lot of inserts, updates, and deletes), this can be a killer. In an OLAP environment, this is probably no big deal since your OLAP data is usually relatively stable (few inserts), and what inserts are made are usually done through a highly repetitive batch process (doesn't have quite the lack of predictability that users have).

> Technically speaking, having additional indexes can also have an impact on updates similar to that for inserts. The problem is much smaller, however. Your indexes only need to be updated if the column that was changed is part of the key for that index. If you do indeed need to update the index though, think about it as a delete and insert – that means that you're exposed to page splits again.
>
> So, what then about deletes? Well, again, when you delete a record you're going to need to delete all the entries from your indexes too, so you do add some additional overhead. Fortunately, you don't have to worry about page splits and having to physically move data around.

The bottom line here is that, if you're doing a lot more querying than modifying, then more indexes are OK. However, if you're making lots of modifications to your data, keep your indexes limited to high use columns.

If you're treating this book as more of a reference than a full "learn how to" book, and haven't taken the time to read the *SQL Server Storage and Index Structures* chapter yet – do it!

Covering Indexes

One little tidbit that I do want to go through into this chapter rather than the index chapter itself is the notion of a **covering index**.

A covering index is any non-clustered index where all the columns referred to in the query exist in the index. By *all* the columns, I really mean *all* – columns in the SELECT list, JOIN clause, and WHERE clause all must be represented in the index.

So what's so special about a covering index? Well, I/O savings is what. You may recall that, in order for SQL Server to navigate a non-clustered index, it must navigate the various levels of the B-Tree. Once at the leaf level of the tree, it must either navigate to the row (using a RID), or navigate the clustered index to find the real data. Well, this isn't actually true quite 100% of the time. You see, if all the information needed to resolve the query exists in the index, why would SQL Server need to go any farther than the index before stopping?

While covering indexes sometimes happen by accident, I would hope that by the time you've made it this far in this book that you're ready to make your own accidents – that is, you're ready to plan for the good things that may have only happened by accident before. In the case of covering indexes, it's just about planning your indexes vs. your queries. If you have an index that includes three columns, but most of your queries only refer to one other column – why not include that one last column in the index? That way, when SQL Server gets to the index row, it's gotten to all the data it needs for many queries.

OK, that said; just like any other index, you need to carefully consider the negative impacts of your index. Covering indexes increase maintenance overhead on your system. Every update to any column in the index means that the index also has to be updated. If you have many queries that can make use of your covering query, then it may be beneficial to add one. On the other hand, if you have tons of inserts and updates that would affect the index, then you may want to shy away from it.

Don't Forget the Index Tuning Wizard

The **Index Tuning Wizard** made its first appearance back in version 7.0. With this tool, you use the SQL Server Profiler to create what's called a **workload file**. A workload file is a trace (created using the SQL Server Profiler) of all the server activity over a given time period. You can place a number of different filters on it (most notably, what database you want to trace), and it "records" what's really happening on the server. What's great about that is that the Index Tuning Wizard can then use that file to help determine what indexes are going to get the biggest bang for the buck.

The Index Tuning Wizard goes through the workload and runs the query optimizer against every query that was run in the workload file. It runs the optimizer not just once but several times, to investigate how the cost estimates would change if there was a change to the indexes on the underlying table(s). If the wizard finds that new indexes might improve the results of the cost estimate, then it balances that information against such things as how many INSERT statements the new index would affect. If there are many INSERTs and the new index offers only minimal performance improvement, then the recommendation to add that index might not be made. If, however, the index provides substantial improvement, then it will add it to a list of recommended indexes. The wizard then gives you the opportunity to implement the suggested indexes at the click of a button. Even better – you don't have to make the change right away – SQL Server gives you the chance to either schedule a job to make the change or to generate a script that you could run at your leisure.

Index Tuning Wizard "Lite"

A version of the Index Turning Wizard is available right within the Query Analyzer by going to Query | Index Tuning Wizard (surprisingly, it's not in the Tools menu) or pressing *Ctrl+I*.

What's nice about this instance of the Index Tuning Wizard is that it is not limited to a workload file. You can run it against the contents of the query window to focus in on indexes that would help that particular query or series of queries.

> *Be very careful with the Index Tuning Wizard. In particular, watch what indexes you let it delete. It makes its recommendations based on the workload you've provided – that workload may not include all of the queries that make up your system. Take a look at the recommendations and ask yourself why those recommendations might help. Particularly with deletions, ask yourself what that index might be used for – does deleting it make sense? Is there some long running report that didn't run when you were capturing the workload file that might make use of that index?*

Client- vs. Server-Side Processing

Where you decide to "do the work" can have a very serious impact – for better or worse – on overall system performance.

When **client/server computing** first came along, the assumption was that you would get more/faster/cheaper by "distributing" the computing. For some tasks, this is true. For others, though, you lose more than you gain.

Here's a quick review of some preferences as to which end to do things at:

Static cursors	Usually much better on the client. Since the data isn't going to change, you want to package it up and send it all to the client in one pass – thus limiting round trips and network impact. The obvious exception is if the cursor is generated for the sole purpose of modifying other records. In such a case, you should try to do the entire process at the server-side – again eliminating round trips.
Forward-only, read-only cursors	Client-side again. The ODBC libraries can take special advantage of the FAST_FORWARD cursor type to gain maximum performance. Just let the server spew the records into the client cursor and then get on with life.
HOLDLOCK situations	Most transactioning works much better on the server than on the client. MTS mitigates some of this (it can make it worse too), but direct client/server transactioning through the different object models is a real pain. RDO is not that bad, but ADO is very problematic – particularly when you are dealing with multiple connections.
Processes that require working tables	This is another of those situations where you want to try to have the finished product created before you attempt to move records to the client. If you keep all of the data server-side until it is really ready to be used, you minimize round trips to the server and speed up performance.
Minimizing client installations	OK, so this isn't "performance" as such, but it can be a significant cost factor. If you want to minimize the number of client installations you have to do, then keep as much of the business logic out of the client as possible. Either perform that logic in sprocs or look at using component-based development with MTS. In an ideal world, you'll have what I like to call "data logic" (logic that exists only for the purpose of figuring out how to get the final data) in sprocs and "business logic" in components.
Significant filtering and/or re-sorting.	Use ADO. It has a great set of tools for receiving the data from the server just once (fewer round trips!), then applying filters and sorts locally using the ADO engine. If you wanted the data filtered or sorted differently by SQL Server, it would run an entirely new query using the new criteria. It doesn't take a rocket scientist to figure out that the overhead on that can get rather expensive.
	Note, however, that with very large result sets, your client computer may not have the wherewithal to deal with the filters and sorts effectively – you may be forced to go back to the server.
	If you want to learn more about ADO, please refer to *ADO 2.6 Programmer's Reference* from Wrox Press (ISBN: 1-861004-63-X).

These really just scratch the surface. The big thing to remember is that round-trips are a killer. What you need to do is move the smallest amount of data back and forth – and only move it once. Usually this means that you'll pre-process the data as much as possible on the server-side, and then move the entire result to the client if possible.

Keep in mind, though, that you need to be sure that your client is going to be able to handle what you give it. Servers are usually much better equipped to handle the resource demands of larger queries. By the same token, you also have to remember that the server is going to be doing this for multiple users – that means the server needs to have adequate resources to store all of the server-side activity for that number of users. If you take a process that was too big for the client to handle and move it server-side for resource reasons, just remember that you may also run out of resources on the server if more than one client goes to use that process at the same time. The best thing is to try to keep result sets and processes the smallest size possible.

Strategic De-Normalization

This section could also be called, "When following the rules can kill you". Normalized data tends to work for both data integrity and performance in an OLTP environment. The problem is that not everything that goes on in an OLTP database is necessarily transaction processing related. Even OLTP systems have to do a little bit of reporting (a summary of transactions entered that day, for example).

Often, adding just one extra column to a table can prevent a large join, or worse, a join involving several tables. I've seen situations where adding one column made the difference between a two-table join and a nine-table join. We're talking the difference between 100,000 records being involved and several million. This one change made the query drop from a run-time of several minutes down to just seconds.

Like most things, however, this isn't something with which you should get carried away. Normalization is the way that most things are implemented for a reason. It adds a lot to maintaining data integrity, and can make a big positive difference performance-wise in many situations. Don't de-normalize just for the sake of it. Know exactly what you're trying to accomplish, and test to make sure that it had the expected impact. If it didn't, then look at going back to the original way of doing things.

Routine Maintenance

I hate it when good systems go bad. It happens on a regular basis though. It usually happens when people buy or build systems, put them into operation, then forget about them.

Maintenance is as much about performance as it is about system integrity. Query plans get out of date, index pages get full (so you have a lot of page splits), fragmentation happens, and the best indexes need changes as usage and the amount of data in various tables alters.

Watch the newsgroups. Talk to a few people who have older systems running. You'll hear the same story over and over again: "My system used to run great, but it just keeps getting slower and slower – we haven't changed anything, so what happened?" Well, systems will naturally become slower as the amount of data they have to search over increases. However, the changes needed to restore speed don't have to be all that remarkable. The cause is usually that the performance enhancements you put in place when you first installed the system don't really apply anymore; as the way your users use the system and the amount of data have changed, so has the mix of things that will give you the best performance.

We'll be looking at maintenance quite a bit in the next chapter. However, we've discussed it here for two reasons. Firstly, to help if you are checking out this chapter because you have a specific performance problem. Secondly, and perhaps more importantly, because there is a tendency to just think about maintenance as being something you do to prevent the system from going down and to ensure backups are available should the worst happen. This simply isn't the case. Maintenance is also critical from a performance perspective.

Organizing Your Sprocs Well

I'm not talking from the outside (naming conventions and such are important, but that's not what I'm getting at here), but rather from a "how they operate" standpoint. Remember to:

Keep Transactions Short

Long transactions can not only cause deadlock situations, but also basic blocking (where someone else's process has to wait for yours because you haven't finished with locks yet). Any time you have a process that is blocked – even if it will eventually be able to continue after the blocking transaction is complete – you are delaying, and therefore hurting the performance of, that blocked procedure. There is nothing that has a more immediate effect on performance than a process simply having to stop and wait.

Use the Least Restrictive Transaction Isolation Level Possible

The tighter you hold those locks, the more likely it is that you're going to end up blocking another process. You need to be sure that you take the amount of locks that you really need to ensure data integrity – but try not to take any more than that.

If you need more information on isolation levels, check out the chapter on Transactions and Locks earlier in the book.

Implement Multiple Solutions if Necessary

An example here is a search query that accepts multiple parameters but doesn't require all of them. It's quite possible to write your sproc so that it just uses one query, regardless of how many parameters were actually supplied – a "one size fits all" approach. This can be a real timesaver from a development perspective, but it is really deadly from a performance point of view. More than likely, it means that you are joining several unnecessary tables for every run of the sproc!

The thing to do here is add a few IF...ELSE statements to check things out. This is more of a "look before you leap" approach. It means that you will have to write multiple queries to deal with each possible mix of supplied parameters but, once you have the first one written, the others can often be cloned and then altered from the first.

This is a real problem area in lots of code out there. Developers are a fickle bunch. We generally only like doing things as long as they are interesting. If you take the situation above, you can probably see that it would get very boring very quickly to be writing what amounts to a very similar query over and over to deal with the nuances of what parameters were supplied.

All I can say about this is – well, not everything can be fun, or everyone would want to be a software developer! Sometimes you just have to grin and bear it for the sake of the finished product.

Avoid Cursors if Possible

If you're a programmer who has come from an ISAM or VSAM environment, doing things by cursor is probably going to be something towards which you'll naturally gravitate. After all, the cursor process works an awful lot more like what you're used to in those environments.

Don't go there!

Almost everything that you first think of as requiring cursors to achieve can actually be done as a set operation. Sometimes it takes some pretty careful thought, but it usually can be done.

By way of illustration, I was asked a year or two ago for a way to take a multi-line cursor-based operation and make it into a single statement if possible. The existing process ran for something like 20 minutes. The run time was definitely problematic, but the customer wasn't really looking to do this for performance reasons (they had accepted that the process was going to take that long). Instead, they were just trying to simplify the code.

They had a large product database and they were trying to set things up to automatically price their available products based on cost. If the markup had been a flat percentage (say 10%) then the UPDATE statement would have been easy – something like:

```
UPDATE Products
SET UnitPrice = UnitCost * 1.1
```

The problem was that it wasn't a straight markup – there was a logic pattern to it. The logic went something like this:

❑ If the pennies on the product after the markup are greater than or equal to .50, then price it at .95

❑ If the pennies are below .50, then mark it at .49

The pseudocode to do this by cursor would look something like:

```
Declare and open the cursor
Fetch the first record
Begin Loop Until the end of the result set
Multiply cost * 1.1
If result has cents of < .50
   Change cents to .49
Else
   Change cents to .95
Loop
```

This is, of course, an extremely simplified version of things. There would actually be about 30 to 40 lines of code to get this done. Instead, we changed it around to work with one single correlated sub-query (which had a CASE statement embedded in it). The run time dropped down to something like 12 seconds.

The point here, of course, is that, by eliminating cursors wherever reasonably possible, we can really give a boost to performance as well as stripping out complexity (as was the original goal here).

Uses for Temporary Tables

The use of **temporary tables** can sometimes help performance – usually by enabling the elimination of cursors.

As we've seen before, cursors can be the very bane of our existence. Using temporary tables, we can sometimes eliminate the cursor by processing the operation as a series of two or more set operations. An initial query creates a working dataset. Then another process comes along and operates on that working data.

We can actually make use of the pricing example we laid out in the last section to illustrate the temporary table concept too. The steps would look something like:

```
SELECT ProductID, FLOOR(UnitCost * 1.1) + .49 AS TempUnitPrice
    INTO #WorkingData
    FROM Products
    WHERE (UnitCost * 1.1) - FLOOR(UnitCost * 1.1) < .50
INSERT INTO #WorkingData
SELECT ProductID, FLOOR(UnitCost * 1.1) + .95 AS TempUnitPrice
    FROM Products
    WHERE (UnitCost * 1.1) - FLOOR(UnitCost * 1.1) >= .50
UPDATE p
    SET p.UnitPrice = t.TempUnitPrice
    FROM Product p
    JOIN #WorkingData t
      ON p.ProductID = t.ProductID
```

With this, we wind up with three steps instead of thirty or forty. This solution wouldn't be quite as good as the correlated sub-query, but it is still quite workable and much faster than the cursor option.

Keep this little interim step using temporary tables in mind when you run into complex problems that you think are going to require cursors. However, try to avoid the temptation of automatically taking this route too – look for the single statement query before choosing this option – but, if all else fails, using temporary tables can really save you a lot of time compared with the cursor option.

Sometimes, it's the Little Things...

A common mistake in all programming for performance efforts is to ignore the small things. Whenever you're trying to squeeze performance, the natural line of thinking is that you want to work on the long running stuff.

It's true that long running processes are the ones in which you stand the biggest chance of getting big one-time performance gains. It's too bad that this often leads people to forget that it's the total time saved that they're interested in – that is, time when the process is really live.

While it's definitely true that a single change in a query can often turn a several minute query into seconds (I've actually seen a few that took literally days trimmed to just seconds by index and query tuning), the biggest gains for your application often lie in getting just a little bit more out of what already seems like a fast query. These are usually tied to often-repeated functions or items that are often executed within a loop.

Think about this for a bit. Say you have a query that currently takes 3 seconds to run, and this query is used every time an order taker looks up a part for possible sale - say 5,000 items looked up a day. Now imagine that you are able to squeeze 1 second off the query time. That's 5,000 seconds, or over an hour and 20 minutes!

Hardware Considerations

Forgive me if I get too bland here – I'll try to keep it interesting, but if you're like the average developer, you'll probably already know enough about this to make it very boring, yet not enough about it to save yourself some grief.

Hardware prices have been falling like a rock over the last few years – unfortunately, so has what your manager or customer is probably budgeting for your hardware purchases. When deciding on a budget for your hardware, remember:

❑ Once you've deployed, the hardware is what's keeping your data safe – just how much is that data worth?

❑ Once you've deployed, you're likely to have many users – if you're creating a public web site, it's possible that you'll have tens of thousands of users active on your system 24 hours per day. What is it going to cost you in terms of productivity loss, lost sales, loss of face, and just general credibility loss if that server is unavailable or – worse – you lose some of your data?

❑ Maintaining your system will quickly cost more than the system itself. Dollars spent early on a mainstream system that is going to have fewer quirks may save you a ton of money in the long run.

There's a lot to think about when deciding who to purchase from and what specific equipment to buy. Forgetting the budget for a moment, some of the questions to ask yourself include:

❑ Will the box be used exclusively as a database server?

❑ Will the activity on the system be processor or I/O intensive? (For databases, it's almost always the latter, but there are exceptions.)

❑ Am I going to be running more than one production database? If so, is the other database of a different type (OLTP vs. OLAP)?

❑ Will the server be on-site at my location, or do I have to travel to do maintenance on it?

❑ What are my risks if the system goes down?

❑ What are my risks if I lose data?

❑ Is performance "everything"?

❑ What kind of long-term driver support can you expect as your O/S and supporting systems are upgraded?

Again, we're just scratching the surface of things – but we've made a good start. Let's look at what these issues mean to us.

Exclusive Use of the Server

I suppose it doesn't take a brain surgeon to figure out that, in most cases, having your SQL Server hardware dedicated to just SQL Server, and having other applications reside on totally separate systems, is the best way to go. Note, however, that this isn't always the case.

If you're running a relatively small and simple application that works with other subsystems (say IIS as a web server for example), then you may actually be better off, performance-wise, to stay with one box. Why? Well, if there are large amounts of data going back and forth between the two subsystems (your database in SQL Server and your web pages or whatever in a separate process), then memory space to memory space communications are going to be much faster than the bottleneck that the network can create – even in a relatively dedicated network backbone environment.

Remember that this is the exception, not the rule, though. The instance where this works best usually meets the following criteria:

- ❑ The systems have a very high level of interaction
- ❑ The systems have little to do beyond their interactions (the activity that's causing all the interaction is the main thing that the systems do)
- ❑ Only one of the two processes is CPU intensive and only one is I/O intensive

If in doubt, go with conventional thinking on this and separate the processing into two or more systems.

I/O vs. CPU Intensive

I can hear a bunch of you out there yelling "Both!" – if that's the case, then I hope you have a very large budget – but we'll talk about that scenario too.

If your system is already installed and running, then you can use a combination of NT's Perfmon (short for Performance Monitor) and SQL Server Profiler to figure out just where your bottlenecks are – in CPU utilization or I/O. CPU utilization can be considered to be high once it starts approaching a consistent 60% level. Some would argue that this number should be as high as 80%, but I'm a believer in the idea that people's time is more expensive than the CPU's, so I tend to set my thresholds a little lower. I/O depends a lot more on the performance characteristics of your drives and controller.

If you haven't installed yet, there's a lot more guesswork involved. While almost anything you do in SQL Server is data based, and will, therefore, certainly require a degree of I/O, how much of a burden your CPU is under varies widely on the types of queries you're running.

Low CPU Load	High CPU Load
Simple, single table queries and updates	Large joins
Joined queries over relatively small tables	Aggregations (SUM, AVG, etc.)
	Sorting of large result sets

With this in mind, let's focus a little closer on each situation.

I/O Intensive

I/O intensive tasks should cause you to focus your budget more on the drive array than on the CPU(s). Notice that I said the drive "array" – I'm not laying that out as an option. In my not-so-humble opinion on this matter, if you don't have some sort of redundancy arrangement on your database storage mechanism then you have certainly lost your mind. Any data worth saving at all is worth protecting – we'll talk about the options there in just a moment.

Before we get into talking about the options on I/O, let's look briefly into what I mean by I/O intensive. In short, I mean that a lot of data retrieval is going on, but the processes being run on the system are almost exclusively queries (not complex business processes) and do not include updates that require wild calculations. Remember – your hard drives are, more than likely, the slowest thing in your system (short of a CD-Rom) in terms of moving data around.

A Brief Look at RAID

RAID; it brings images of barbarian tribes raining terror down on the masses. Actually, most of the RAID levels are there for creating something of a fail-safe mechanism against the attack of the barbarian called "lost data". If you're not a RAID aficionado, then it might surprise you to learn that not all RAID levels provide protection against lost data.

RAID originally stood for **Redundant Array of Inexpensive Disks**. The notion was fairly simple – at the time, using a lot of little disks was cheaper than one great big one. In addition, an array of disks meant that you had multiple drive heads at work and could also build in redundancy (if desired).

Since drive prices have come down so much (I'd be guessing, but I'd bet that drive prices are, dollar per meg, far less than 1% of what they were when the term RAID was coined), I've started to hear new renditions of what RAID stands for. The most common are Random Array of Independent Disks (this one seems like a contradiction in terms to me) and Random Array of Individual Disks (this one's not that bad). The thing to remember, no matter what you think it's an acronym for, is that you have two or more drives working together – usually for the goal of some balance between performance and safety.

There are lots of places you can get information on RAID, but let's take a look at the levels that are most commonly considered:

RAID Level	Description
RAID 0	Also known as Disk Striping Without Parity. Of the three that we are examining here, this is the one you are least likely to know. It requires at least three drives to work just as RAID 5 does. Unlike RAID 5, however, you get no safety net from lost data. (Parity is a special checksum value that allows reconstruction of lost data in some circumstances – as indicated by the time of reconstruction, RAID 0 doesn't have parity.) RAID 0's big claim to fame is giving you maximum performance without loosing any drive space. With RAID zero, the data you store is spread across all the drives in the array (at least three). While this may seem odd, it has the advantage of meaning that you always have three or more disk drives reading or writing your data for you at once. Under mirroring (see RAID 1), the data is all on one drive (with a copy stored on a separate drive). This means you'll just have to wait for that one head to do the work for you.

Table continued on following page

RAID Level	Description
RAID 1	Also known as Mirroring. For each active drive in the system, there is a second drive that "mirrors" (keeps an exact copy of) the information. The two drives are usually identical in size and type, and store all the information to each drive at the same time. (Windows NT has software-based RAID that can mirror any two volumes as long as they are the same size.) Mirroring provides no performance increase when writing data (you still have to write to both drives), but can, depending on your controller arrangement, double your read performance since it will use both drives for the read. What's nice about mirroring is that, as long as only one of the two mirrored drives fails, the other will go on running with no loss of data or performance (well, reads may be slower if you have a controller that does parallel reads). The biggest flaw with mirroring is that you have to buy twice as many drives to get the disk space you need.
RAID 5	The most commonly used. Although, technically speaking, mirroring is a RAID (RAID 1), when people refer to using RAID, they usually mean RAID 5. RAID 5 works exactly as RAID 0 does with one very significant exception – parity information is kept for all the data in the array. Let's say for example that you have a five drive array. For any given write, data is stored across all five of the drives, but a percentage of each drive (the sum of which adds up to the space of one drive) is set aside to store parity information. Contrary to popular belief, no one drive is the parity drive. Instead, some of the parity information is written to each of the drives – it's just that the parity information for a given byte of data is not stored on the same drive as the actual data is. If any one drive is lost, then the parity information from the other drives can be used to re-construct the data that was lost. The great thing about RAID 5 is that you get the multi-drive read performance. The downside is that you lose one drive's worth of space (if you have a three drive array, you'll see the space of two, if it's a seven drive array, you'll see the space of six). It's not as bad as mirroring in the price per megabyte category, but you still see great performance.
RAID 10 (aka RAID 1 + 0 or RAID 0 + 1)	Offers the best of both RAID 0 and RAID 1 in terms of performance and data protection. It is, however, far and away the most expensive of the options discussed here. RAID 10 is implemented in a coupling of both RAID 0 (striping without parity) and RAID 1 (mirroring). The end result: either mirrored sets of striped data or striped sets of mirrored data. The end result in total drive count and general performance is pretty much the same.

The long and the short of it is that RAID 5 is the de facto standard for database installations, and I couldn't agree more. That being said, if you have a loose budget, then I'd actually suggest mixing things up a bit.

RAID 10 is definitely starting to make inroads in larger installations. For the average shop, however, RAID 5 will likely continue to rule the day for at least the next few years – perhaps that will change as we get into the era where drives are measured in Terra, Peta, and even Exa bytes.

What you'd like to have is at least a RAID 5 setup for your main databases, but a completely separate mirrored set for your logs. People who manage to do both usually put both NT and the logs on the mirror set and the physical databases on the RAID 5 array. Since I'm sure inquiring minds want to know why you would want to do this, let's take a brief digression into how log data is read and written.

Unlike database information, which can be read in parallel (this is why RAID 4, 5, or 10 works so well performance-wise), the transaction log is chronology dependent – that is, it needs to be written and read serially to be certain of integrity. I'm not necessarily saying that physically ordering the data in a constant stream is required; rather, I'm saying that everything needs to be logically done in a stream. As such, it actually works quite well if you can get the logs into their own drive where the head of the drive will only seldom have to move from the stream which it is currently reading and writing. The upshot of this is that you really want your logs to be in a different physical device from your data, so the reading and writing of data won't upset the reading and writing of the log.

Logs, however, don't usually take up nearly as much space as the read data does. With mirroring, we can just buy two drives and have our redundancy. With RAID 5, we would have to buy three, but we don't see any real benefit from the parallel read nature of RAID 5. When you look at these facts together, it doesn't make much sense to go with RAID 5 for the logs or OS.

> You can have all the RAID arrays in the world, but they still won't surpass a good backup in terms of the long-term safety of your data. Backups are easy to take off-site, and are not subject to mechanical failure. RAID units, while redundant and very reliable, also become worthless if two (instead of just one) drives fail. Another issue – what if there's a fire? Probably all the drives will burn up – again, without a backup, you're in serious trouble. We'll look into how to back up your databases in our next chapter.

CPU Intensive

On a SQL Server box, you'll almost always want to make sure that you go multi-processor (assuming your OS will utilize them – Win 9x and Me won't), even for a relatively low utilization machine. This goes a long way towards preventing little "pauses" in the system that will drive your users positively nuts, so consider this to be critically important, even if the CPU wasn't your primary focus. Keep in mind that the standard version of SQL Server only supports up to 4 processors – if you need to go higher than that, you'll need to go up to the Enterprise edition which will eventually support up to 32 processors.

Perhaps the biggest issue of all though, is memory. This is definitely one area that you don't want to short change. In addition, remember that if you are in a multiprocessor environment (and you should be), then you are going to have more things going on at once in memory. In these days of cheap memory, no SQL Server worth installing should ever be configured with less than 256MB of RAM – even in a development environment. Production servers should be equipped with no less than 512MB of RAM – quite likely more.

Things to think about when deciding how much RAM to use include:

❑ How many user connections will there be at one time? Each connection takes up about 24K of memory (it used to be even higher). This isn't really a killer since 1,000 users would only take up 24MB, but it's still something to think about.

❑ Will you be doing a lot of aggregations and/or sorts? These can be killers depending on the size of the dataset you're working with in your query.

❑ How large is your largest database? If your database is only 500MB (and, actually, most databases are much smaller than people think), then having 1GB of RAM probably doesn't make much sense.

❑ The Standard edition of SQL Server 2000 only supports addressing of memory up to 4GB. If you need more than this, you'll need to go with the Enterprise edition.

In addition, once you're in operation – or when you get a fully populated test system up and running – you may want to take a look at your cache-hit ratio in Perfmon. We'll talk about how this number is calculated a little bit later in the chapter. For now, it's sufficient to say that this can serve as something of a measurement of how often we are succeeding at getting things out of memory rather that off disk (memory is going to run much, much faster than disk). A low cache-hit ratio is usually a certain indication that more memory is needed. Keep in mind though, that a high ratio does not necessarily mean that you shouldn't add more memory. The read-ahead feature of SQL Server may create what is an artificially high cache hit ratio and may disguise the need for additional memory.

OLTP vs. OLAP

The needs of these two systems are often at odds with each other. In any case, I'm going to keep my recommendation short here:

> **If you are running databases to support both of these requirements, run them on different servers – it's that simple.**

On-Site vs. Off-Site

It used to be that anything that was SQL Server based would be running on-site, next to those who were responsible for its care and upkeep. If the system went down, people were right there to worry about reloads and to troubleshoot.

In the internet era, many installations are co-located to an ISP. The ISP is responsible for making sure that the entire system is backed up – they will even restore according to your directions – but they do not take responsibility for your code. This can be very problematic when you run into a catastrophic bug in your system. While you can always connect remotely to work on it, you're going to run into several configuration and performance issues, including:

❑ Security – remote access being open to you means that you're also making it somewhat more open to others who you may not want to have access. My two bits' worth on this is to make sure that you have very tight routing and port restrictions in place. For those of you not all that network savvy (which includes me), this means that you restrict what IP addresses are allowed to be routed to the remote server.

❑ Performance – you're probably going to be used to the 10MB to 100MB network speeds that you have around the home office. Now you're communicating via VPN over the Internet or, worse, dialup and you're starting to hate life – things are SLOW!

❑ Responsiveness – it's a bit upsetting when you're running some e-commerce site or whatever and you can't get someone at your ISP to answer the phone, or they say that they will get on it right away and hours later you're still down. Make sure you investigate your remote hosting company very closely – don't assume that they'll still think you're important after the sale.

❑ Many co-hosting facilities will not do hardware work for you. If you have a failure that requires more than a reloading, you may have to travel to the site yourself or call yet another party to do the maintenance – that means that your application will be offline for hours or possibly days.

If you're a small shop doing this with an Internet site, then off-site can actually be something of a saving grace. It's expensive, but you'll usually get lots of bandwidth plus someone to make sure that the backups actually get done – just make sure that you really check out your ISP. Many of them don't know anything about SQL Server, so make sure that the expertise is there.

The Risks of Being Down

This may seem like a silly question. When I ask it, I often get this incredulous look. For some installations, the answer is obvious – they can't afford to be down, period. This number is not, however, as high as it might seem. You see, the only true life and death applications are the ones that are in acute medical facilities or are immediately tied to safety operations. Other installations may lose money – they may even cause bankruptcy if they go down – but that's not life and death.

That being said, it's really not as black and white as all that. There is really something of a continuum in how critical downtime is. It ranges from the aforementioned medical applications at the high end, to data-mining operations on old legacy systems at the low end (for some companies, it may be all they have). The thing that pretty much everyone can agree on for every system is that downtime is highly undesirable.

So the question becomes one of just how undesirable is it? How do we quantify that?

If you have a bunch of bean counters working for you (I can get away with saying that since I was one), it shouldn't take you all that long to figure out that there are a lot of measurable costs to downtime. For example, if you have a bunch of employees sitting around saying that they can't do anything until the system comes back up, then the number of affected employees multiplied by their hourly cost (remember, the cost of an employee is more than just their wages) equals the cost of the system being down from a productivity standpoint. But, wait – there's more. If you're running something that has online sales, how many sales did you lose because you couldn't be properly responsive to your customers? Oops – more cost! If you're running a plant with your system, then how many goods couldn't be produced because the system was down, or, even if you could still build them, did you lose quality assurance or other information that might cost you down the line?

I think by now you should be able to both see and sell to your boss the notion that downtime is very expensive – though how expensive depends on your specific situation. Now the thing to do is to determine just how much you're willing to spend to make sure that it doesn't happen.

Lost Data

There's probably no easy way of measuring the cost of this one. In some cases, you can quantify it by the amount of cost you're going to incur reconstructing the data. Sometimes you simply can't reconstruct it, in which case you'll probably never know for sure just how much it cost you.

Again, how much you want to prevent this should affect your budget for redundant systems, as well as things like back-up tape drives and off-site archival services.

Is Performance Everything?

More often than not, the answer is no. It's important, but just how important has something of diminishing returns to it. For example, if buying that extra 100MHz of CPU power is going to save you 2 seconds per transaction, it may be a big deal if you have 50 data entry clerks trying to enter as much as they can each day. Over the course of a day, seemingly small amounts of time saved can add up. If each of those 50 clerks are performing 500 transactions a day, then saving 2 seconds per transaction adds up to over 13 man-hours (that's more than one person working all day!). Saving that time may allow you to delay a little longer in adding staff. The savings in wages will probably easily pay for the extra power.

The company next door may look at the situation a little differently though – they may only have one or two employees; furthermore, the process that they are working in might be one where they spend a lengthy period of time just filling out the form – the actual transaction that stores it isn't that big a deal. In such a case, your extra dollars for the additional speed may not be worth it.

Driver Support

Let's start off by cutting to the chase – I don't at all recommend that you save a few dollars (or even a lot of dollars) when buying your server by purchasing it from some company like "Bob's Pretty Fine Computers". Remember, all those risks! Now, try introducing a strange mix of hardware and driver sets. Now imagine when you have a problem – you're quickly going to find all those companies pointing the finger at each other saying, "It's their fault!" – do you really want to be stuck in the middle?

What you want is the tried and true, the tested, the known. Servers – particularly data servers – are an area to stick with well-known, trusted names. I'm not advocating anyone in particular (no ads in this book!), but I'm talking very mainstream people like Compaq, Dell, IBM, HP, etc. If you need to go to very large systems that are going to exceed the typical four processor limit, then you can look at names like Unisys, Tandem, and Sequent just to name a few (a couple of these are now subsidiaries of names I've already mentioned, but they really operate as a separate unit). Note that, when I say well-known, trusted names, I mean names that are known in the server field. Just because someone sells a billion desktops a year doesn't mean they know anything about servers – it's almost like apples and oranges. They are different.

By staying with well-known equipment, in addition to making sure that you have proper support when something fails, it also means that you're more likely to have that equipment survive upgrades well into the future. Each new version of the OS only explicitly supports just so many pieces of equipment – you want to be sure that yours is one of them.

The Ideal System

Let me preface this by saying that there is no one ideal system. That being said, there is a general configuration (size excluded) that I and a very large number of other so called "experts" seem to almost universally push as where you'd like to be if you had the budget for it. We're talking about drive arrangements here (the CPU and memory tends to be relative chicken feed, budget and setup-wise).

What you'd like to have is a mix of mirroring and RAID 5. You place the OS and the logs on the mirrored drives. You place the data on the RAID 5 array. That way, the OS and logs – which both tend to do a lot of serial operations – have a drive setup all of their own without being interfered with by the reads and writes of the actual data. The data has a multi-head read/write arrangement for maximum performance while maintaining a level of redundancy.

Trouble-Shooting

SQL Server offers a number of options to help with the prevention, detection, and measurement of slow-running queries. The options range from the passive approach of measuring actual performance so you know what's doing what, to the more active approach of employing a query "governor" to automatically kill queries that run over a length of time you set. These tools are very often ignored or used only sparingly, which is something of a tragedy. They can save hours of trouble-shooting by often leading you right to the problematic query, and even the specific portion of your query that is creating the performance issues.

Tools to take a look at include:

- ❑ SHOWPLAN TEXT|ALL and Graphical showplan – looked at in this chapter
- ❑ STATISTICS IO – also in this chapter
- ❑ DBCC – in this chapter
- ❑ The Query Governor – covered in this chapter
- ❑ sp_lock – check out the cool replacement for this in Chapter 14
- ❑ The sysprocesses table – this is where SQL Server keeps track of what's happening!
- ❑ The SQL Server Profiler – in this chapter

Many people are caught up in just using one of these, but the reality is that there is little or no (depending on which two you're comparing) overlap between them. This means that developers and DBAs who try to rely on just one of them are actually missing out on a lot of potentially important information.

Also, keep in mind that many of these are still useful in some form even if you are writing in a client-side language and sending the queries to the server (no sprocs). You can either watch the query come through to your server using the SQL Server Profiler, or you can test the query in QA before moving it back to your client code.

The Various Showplans and STATISTICS

SQL Server gives you a few different SHOWPLAN options. The information that they provide varies a bit depending on what option you choose, but this is one area where there is a fair amount of overlap between your options; however, each one definitely makes its own unique contribution to the overall picture. In addition, there are a number of options available to show query statistics.

SHOWPLAN_TEXT and SHOWPLAN_ALL

When either of these two SHOWPLAN options (they are mutually exclusive) is executed, SQL Server changes what results you get for your query. Indeed, the NOEXEC option (which says to figure out the query plan but to not actually perform the query) is put in place, and you receive no results other than those put out by the SHOWPLAN.

The syntax for turning the SHOWPLAN on and off is pretty straightforward:

```
SET [SHOWPLAN_TEXT|SHOWPLAN_ALL] [ON|OFF]
```

When you use the TEXT option, you get back the query plan along with the estimated costs of running that plan. Since the NOEXEC option automatically goes with SHOWPLAN, you won't see any query results.

When you use the ALL option, you receive everything you received with the TEXT option, plus a slew of additional statistical information including such things as:

- ❑ The actual physical and logical operations planned
- ❑ Estimated row counts
- ❑ Estimated CPU usage
- ❑ Estimated I/O
- ❑ Average row size
- ❑ Whether the query will be run in parallel or not

Let's run a very brief query on the Northwind database, utilizing both of these options (one at a time):

```
SET SHOWPLAN_TEXT ON
GO

SELECT *
FROM Orders
GO

SET SHOWPLAN_TEXT OFF
GO

SET SHOWPLAN_ALL ON
GO

SELECT *
FROM Orders
GO

SET SHOWPLAN_ALL OFF
GO
```

Notice that every statement is followed by a GO, thus making it part of its own batch. The batches that contain the actual query could have had an unlimited number of statements, but the batches setting the SHOWPLAN option have to be in a batch by themselves.

The SHOWPLAN_TEXT portion of the results should look something like this:

```
StmtText
--------------------------------

SELECT *
FROM Orders

(1 row(s) affected)

StmtText
--------------------------------------------------------------------------
  |--Clustered Index Scan(OBJECT:([Northwind].[dbo].[Orders].[PK_Orders]))
```

Results

If we had been running a larger query, say something with several joins, the additional sub-processes would have been listed with indentations to indicate hierarchy.

I'm going to skip showing the ALL results here since they simply will not fit in a book format (it's about 800 characters wide and won't fit in any readable form, even if we flipped things sideways), but they included a host of other information. Which one of these to use is essentially dependent on just how much information you want to be flooded with. If you just want to know the basic plan – such as whether it is using a merge or hash join – you probably just want to use the TEXT option. If you really want to know where the costs are and such, then you want the ALL option.

> The SHOWPLAN options imply the NOEXEC – that means nothing in your query is actually being executed. Before you do anything else, you need to set the option back to off – that even includes switching from one showplan option to the other (e.g. SET SHOWPLAN_ALL ON wouldn't have any effect if you had already run SET SHOWPLAN_TEXT ON and hadn't yet turned it off).
>
> I like to make sure that every script I run that has a SET SHOWPLAN statement in it has both the On and Off within that same script. It goes along way towards keeping me from forgetting that I have it turned on and being confused when things aren't working the way I expect.

Graphical Showplan

The graphical showplan tool combines bits and pieces of SHOWPLAN_ALL and wraps them up into a single graphical format. We looked at this briefly when we were looking at the Query Analyzer back in Chapter 3. Part of the reason for looking at it there is that it is selected through options in the QA rather than through T-SQL syntax – this means that it is only available when using QA.

We have three options to start the graphical showplan tool:

- ❏ Select the Show Execution Plan option from the Query menu
- ❏ Select Show Execution Plan from the Execute mode drop-down list on the tool bar (both this and the option above will execute the query and show the plan)
- ❏ Click on the Display Estimated Execution Plan button on the toolbar and in the Query menu (this option just shows us the plan with the NOEXEC option active)

Personally, I like the option of having the graphical showplan in addition to my normal query run. While it means that I have to put the actual hit of the query on my system, it also means that the numbers I get are no longer just estimates, but based on the actual cost numbers. Indeed, if you run the showplan both ways and wind up with wildly different results, then you may want to take a look at the last time your statistics were updated (using DBCC SHOW_STATISTICS) on the tables on which the query is based. If necessary, you can then update them manually (using UPDATE STATISTICS) and try the process again.

The hierarchy of the different sub-processes is then shown graphically. In order to see the costs and other specifics about any sub-process, just hover your mouse pointer over that part of the graphical showplan and a Tool-tip will come up with the information:

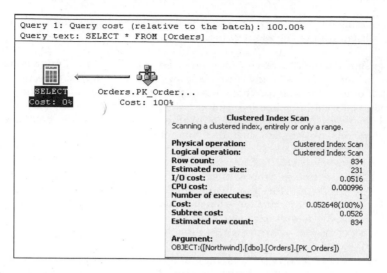

This arrangement can often make it much easier to sort out the different pieces of the plan. The downside is that you can't print it out for reporting in the way that you can with the text versions.

STATISTICS

In addition to using the graphical showplan with actual execution of the query, you have a couple of other options for retrieving the "real" information on the statistics of your query – using SQL Server Profiler and turning on STATISTICS PROFILE.

STATISTICS actually has a couple of options that can be very handy in trouble-shooting query performance including:

SET STATISTICS IO ON|OFF

This one is a very commonly used tool to figure out where and how the query is performing. I find that I'm actually missing the old graphical version of this that used to exist in version 6.5.

STATISTICS IO provides several key pieces of information regarding the actual work necessary to perform your query. Information provided includes:

- ❑ **Physical Reads:** this represents the actual physical pages read from disk. It is never any more than, and is usually less than, the number for logical reads. This one can be very misleading in the sense that it will usually change (be less than the first run) the second time that you run your query. Any page that is already in the buffer cache will not have a physical read done on it, so, the second time you run the query in reasonably short succession, the pages involved will, more than likely, still be in cache. In addition, this number will not be incremented if the page has already been read due to the read-ahead mechanism that is part of SQL Server. This means that your query may be responsible for loading the page physically into cache, but it still may not show up as part of the physical reads.

- ❑ **Logical Reads:** this is the number of times that the page was actually looked at – regardless of from where it came. That is, any page already in the memory cache will still create a logical read if the query makes use of it. Note that I said it is how many times the page was looked at – that means that you may have several logical reads for a single page if the page is needed several times (say for a nested loop that affects a page that has several rows on it).

- **Read-Ahead Reads:** this is the number of pages that SQL Server read into the cache as a result of the read-ahead mechanism anticipating that they would be needed. The page may actually be used – or it may not. In either case, the read still counts as a read ahead. Read-aheads are very similar to physical reads in the sense that they represent data being physically read from disk. The problem is that the number you get is based on the optimistic nature of the read-ahead mechanism, and does not necessarily mean that all that work was actually put to use.

- **Scan Count:** the scan count represents the number of times that a table was accessed. This is somewhat different from logical reads, which was focused on page access. This is another situation where a nested loop is a good example. The outer table that is forming the basis for the condition on the query that is on the inside may only have a scan count of one, while the inner loop table would have a scan count added for every time through the loop – that is, every record in the outer table.

Some of the same information that forms the basis for STATISTICS IO is the information that feeds your cache-hit ratio if you look in Perfmon. The cache-hit ratio is the number of logical reads, less the physical reads, divided by the total actual reads (logical reads).

The thing to look for with STATISTICS IO is for any one table that seems disproportionately high in either physical or logical reads.

A very high physical read count could indicate that the data from the table is being pushed out of the buffer-cache by other processes. If this is a table that you are going to be accessing with some regularity, then you may want to look at purchasing (or, if you're an ISV developing a SQL Server product, recommending) more memory for your system.

If the logical reads are very high, then the real issue may be one of proper indexing. I'll give an example here from a client I had some time back. A query was taking approximately 15 seconds to run on an otherwise unloaded system. Since the system was to be a true OLTP system, this was an unacceptable time for the user to have to wait for information (the query was actually a fairly simple lookup that happened to require a 4 table join). In order to find the problem, I used what amounted to STATISTICS IO – it happened to be the old graphical version that came with 6.5, but the data was much the same. After running the query just once, I could see that the process was requiring less than 20 logical reads from three of the tables, but it was performing over 45,000 logical reads from the fourth table. This is what I liked about the old graphical version, it took about a half a second to see that the bar on one table stretched all the way across the screen when the others were just a few pixels! From there, we knew right where to focus. In about two minutes, I had an index built to support a foreign key (remember, they aren't built by default), and the response time dropped to less than a second. The entire trouble-shooting process on this one took literally minutes. Not every performance trouble-shooting effort is that easy, but using the right tools can often help a lot.

SET STATISTICS TIME ON|OFF

This option is not widely known. It shows the actual CPU time required to execute the query. Personally, I often use a simple SELECT GETDATE() before and after the query I'm testing – as we've done throughout most of the book (it's easier to remember) – but this one can be handy because it separates out the time to parse and plan the query vs. the time to actually execute the query. It's also nice to not have to figure things out for yourself (it will calculate the time in milliseconds; using GETDATE() you have to do that yourself).

Show Client Statistics (Query Analyzer)

New with SQL Server 2000 is the ability to show statistical information about our connection as part of our query run. To make use of this, just select Show Client Statistics from the Query menu. As long as that option is set, every execution you make will produce a Client Statistics tab in the results pane of the Query Analyzer.

Counter	Value	Average
Application Profile Statistics		
Timer resolution (milliseconds)	00	00
Number of INSERT, UPDATE, DELETE statements	00	00
Rows effected by INSERT, UPDATE, DELETE statements	00	00
Number of SELECT statements	00	00
Rows effected by SELECT statements	94	94
Number of user transactions	00	00
Average fetch time	00	00
Cumulative fetch time	00	00
Number of fetches	00	00
Number of open statement handles	00	00
Max number of opened statement handles	00	00
Cumulative number of statement handles	00	00
Network Statistics	00	00
Number of server roundtrips	00	00
Number of TDS packets sent	00	00
Number of TDS packets received	00	00
Number of bytes sent	58	58
Number of bytes received	23597	23597
Time Statistics		
Cumulative client processing time	00	00
Cumulative wait time on server replies	00	00

The Database Consistency Checker (DBCC)

The database consistency checker has a number of different options available to allow you to check the integrity and structural makeup of your database. This is far more the realm of the DBA than the developer, so I am, for the most part, considering the DBCC to be out of scope for this book. The most notable exceptions come in the maintenance of indexes – those are discussed in the next chapter, so I will address DBCC no further at this time.

The Query Governor

The query governor is a tool that's most easily found in Enterprise Manager (you can also set it using `sp_configure`). This sets the maximum amount of time a query can be estimated to take and still have SQL Server execute the query – that is, if the estimated cost of running the query exceeds that allowed in the query governor, then the query will not be allowed to run.

To get to the query governor in EM, right-click on your server, and choose **Properties**. Then choose the **Server Settings** tab:

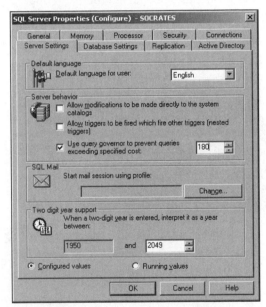

The number you enter into the query governor field loosely (*very* loosely) equates to the number of seconds. So, theoretically, if you set it to 180, that's about 3 minutes. Queries that are estimated to run longer than 3 minutes would not be allowed to run. This can be very handy for keeping just a few rather long queries from taking over your system.

> Did you happen to notice that I slipped the word theoretically into the paragraph above? There's a very important reason for that – the time is just an estimate. What really drives the limit is what the optimizer calculates as the estimated "cost" for that query. The problem is that the time is an estimate based on how cost equates to time. The values used are based on a single test box at Microsoft. You can expect that, as systems get faster, the equation between the query governor setting and the real time factor will get less and less reliable.

The SQL Server Profiler

This is the true lifesaver among the tools provided with SQL Server.

For those of you familiar with SQL Server 6.5, the Profiler used to be called SQL Trace. This version definitely has its differences, but the tools are much the same in the sense that they let you "sniff out" what's really going on with the server.

Profiler can be started remotely if you're in EM (although found in the Tools menu, it still runs as a separate app), or from the Start menu in Windows. There is even something of a "lite" version you can run within Query Analyzer (covered shortly). When you first start it up, you can either load an existing profile template, or create a new one.

> *Be aware that you must be logged in as* sa *or be a member of the* sysadmins *server role in order to perform a trace.*

Let's take a look at some of the key points of the main Profiler (as opposed to the QA version) by walking through a brief example.

Start by choosing New | Trace from the File menu. Log into the server you've been working with, and you should be presented with the following dialog box:

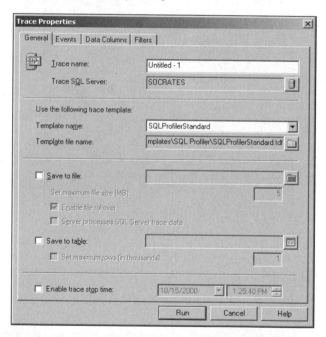

The trace and server names are probably obvious enough, but the template information might not be. A template is a set of pre-established events, data columns, and filters that you want to see in a trace, and the templates provided with SQL Server are named for the kind of situation that you might want to use them in. Any templates that are stored in the default profiler template directory (which is under the tools subdirectory of wherever you installed SQL Server) are included in the Template Name drop-down box. If the template you want isn't in the combo box, then you can choose to navigate to it manually.

Next, you can choose whether to capture the trace to a file on disk or a table in the database. If you save to a file, then that file will be available only to the system that you store it on (or anyone who has access to a network share if that's where you save it). If you save it to a table, then everyone who can connect to the server and has appropriate permissions will be able to examine the trace. You can also opt not to save the results at all and to only show the results while the trace is open in the SQL Server Profiler.

Last but not least on this dialog is the stop time feature – this allows you to leave a trace running (for example for a workload file or some other long-running trace need) and have it shut down automatically at a later time.

Things get somewhat more interesting on the dialog that comes next:

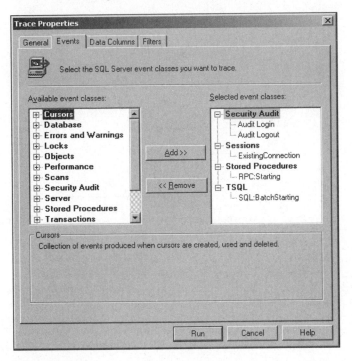

This one is all about what events you are going to track, and, as you can see, there's quite a range. If, for example, you chose the SQLProfilerTSQL trace template, then the initial setup is one that tracks what's needed for the Index Tuning Wizard plus a bit more.

For this example, I'm actually going to leave things just the way they are and move on to the next tab:

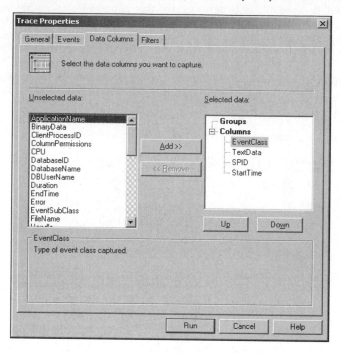

This tab covers what information you want to be kept as part of your trace. The number of options is greatly expanded under SQL Server 2000.

The temptation here is to select everything under the sun so you'll be sure to have all the information. There are a couple of reasons not to do this. First, it means that a lot of additional text has to come back down the pipe to your server. Remember that SQL Server Profiler has to place some audits in the system, and this means that your system is having an additional burden placed on it whenever the Profiler is running – the bigger the trace the bigger the burden. Second, it often means lower productivity for you since you have to wade through a huge morass of data – much of which you probably won't need.

In this particular case, I'm again going to take the defaults, but I want to point out a couple of key fields here before we move on:

- ❑ **Text**: this is the actual text of the statement that the Profiler happens to have added to the trace at that moment in time.

- ❑ **Application Name**: another of those very under-utilized features. The app name is something you can set when you create the connection from the client. With QA, the app name is Query Analyzer, but if you're using ADO or some other data object model and underlying connection method, you can pass the application name as a parameter in your connection string. It can be quite handy for your DBAs when they are trying to trouble-shoot problems in the system.

- ❑ **NT User Name**: this one is what it sounds like – what's great about this is that it can provide a level of accountability.

- ❑ **SQL User Name**: same as NT User Name – only used when operating under SQL Server Security rather than NT Security.

- ❑ CPU: the actual CPU cycles used.
- ❑ Duration: how long the query ran – includes time waiting for locks and such (where the CPU may not have been doing anything, so doesn't reference that load).
- ❑ SPID (SQL Process ID): this one can be nice if your trace reveals something where you want to kill a process – this is the number you would use with your KILL statement.

Moving right along, let's take a look at what I consider to be one of the most important tabs – the **Filters** tab:

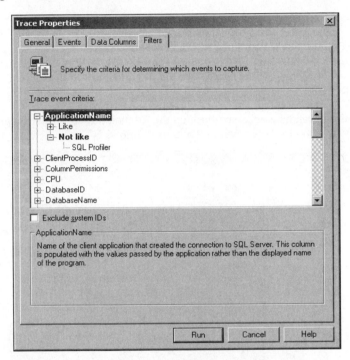

This is the one that makes sure that, on a production or load-test server, you don't get buried in several thousand pages of garbage just by opening a trace up for a few minutes.

With the **Filters** tab, you can select from a number of different options to use to filter out data and limit the size of your result set. By default, Profiler is automatically set up to exclude its own activity in order to try to reduce the Profiler's impact on the end numbers. For our example here, I'm adding in a Duration value where I've set the minimum to 3,000 milliseconds, with no maximum.

Odds are that, if you run this with a query against the Northwind Orders table, you're not going to see it appear in the trace. Why is that? Because that query will probably run very fast and not meet the criteria for being included in our trace – this is an example of how you might set up a trace to capture the query text and user name of someone who has been running very long-running queries on the system. Now try running something a little longer – such as a query that joins the Customers, Orders, and Order Details tables. There's a good chance that you'll now exceed the duration threshold, and your query will show up in the Profiler (if not, then try adjusting down the duration expectation that you set in Profiler).

I can't say enough about how important this tool is in solving performance and other problems. Too many times to count I have been thinking that my sproc was running down one logic path only to find that a totally different branch was being executed. How did I originally find out? I watched it execute in Profiler.

Using Profiler "Lite" (Query Analyzer)

With SQL Server 2000, we now get an extra bonus in the way of a profiling tool. It exists in the Query Analyzer under the Query | Show Server Trace menu option and can be considered to be something like "Profiler Lite". It doesn't have any settable options to it, and it only applies to the current execution window in QA. Still, it's a positively great way to quickly see what code path a stored procedure you're executing is running down, or what a trigger did because of your update statement.

The Performance Monitor (Perfmon)

When you install SQL Server on Windows NT or 2000, SQL Server adds several counters to the NT **performance monitor** (which is sometimes called **Perfmon** because of the executable's file name – perfmon.exe). This can be an excellent tool for finding out where problems are occurring and even determining the nature of some problems.

The performance monitor can be accessed through the Administrative Tools folder from Start | Programs in Windows 2000 in under system tools in Windows NT:

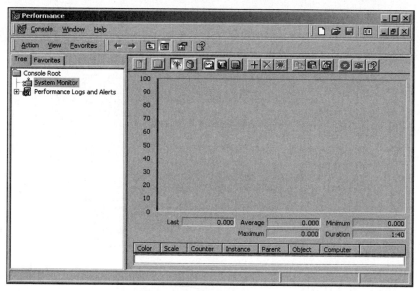

Note that the this image is of the Windows 2000 Performance Monitor – Perfmon in Windows NT is similar, but does look somewhat different.

SQL Server has a number of different Performance Objects and, within each of these, you will find a series of counters related to that object. Historically, some of the important ones have included:

❑ **SQLServer Cache Manager: Buffer Hit Cache Ratio** – this is the number of pages that were available to be read from the buffer cache rather than having to issue a physical read from disk. The thing to watch out for here is that this number can be thrown off depending on how effective the read-ahead mechanism was – anything that the read-ahead mechanism got to and put in cache, before the query actually needed it, is counted as a buffer-cache hit – even though there really was a physical read related to the query. Still, this one is going to give you a decent idea of how efficient your memory usage is. You want to see really high numbers here (in the 90+% range) for maximum performance. Generally speaking, a low buffer hit cache ratio is indicative of needing more memory.

- ❑ **SQLServer General Statistics: User Connections** – pretty much as it sounds, this is the number of user connections currently active in the system.

- ❑ **SQLServer Memory Manager: Total Server Memory** – the total amount of dynamic memory that the SQL Server is currently using. As you might expect, when this number is high relative to the amount of memory available in your system (remember to leave some for the OS!), then you need to seriously consider adding more RAM.

- ❑ **SQLServer SQL Statistics: SQL Compilations/sec** – this is telling you how often SQL Server needs to compile things (sprocs, triggers). Keep in mind that this number will also include recompiles (due to changes in index statistics or because a recompile was explicitly requested). When your server is first getting started, this number may spike for a bit, but it should become stable after your server has been running for a while at a constant set and rate of activities.

- ❑ **SQLServer Buffer Manager: Page Reads/sec** – the number of physical reads from disk for your server. You'd like to see a relatively low number here. Unfortunately, because the requirements and activities of each system are different, I can't give you a benchmark to work from.

- ❑ **SQLServer Buffer Manager: Page Writes/sec** – the number of physical writes performed to disk for your server. Again, you'd like a low number here.

If you want to add or change any of these, just click on the plus (+) sign up on the tool bar. You'll be presented with a dialog that lets you choose between all the different objects and counters available on your system (not just those related to SQL Server):

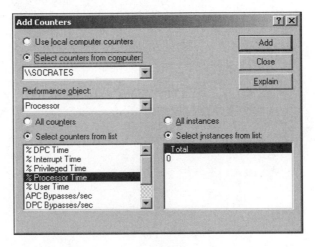

The big thing here is to realize that you can mix and match a wide variety of counters to be able to reach a better understanding of what's going on with your server and make the appropriate adjustments. Much of the time, this kind of task is going to have more to do with the DBA than the developer, but many of these stats can be helpful to you when you are doing load testing for your application.

Summary

Performance could be, and should be, in a book by itself. There's simply too much to cover and get acquainted with to do it all in one or even several chapters. The way I've tried to address this is by pointing out performance issues throughout the book so you could take them on a piece at a time.

The biggest thing is to have a plan – a performance plan. Make performance an issue from the beginnings of your project. Set benchmarks early and continually measure your system against those benchmarks to know where you are improving and what problems you might need to address.

In this chapter, we've reviewed a number of the performance considerations touched on throughout the book, plus added several new tools and ideas to consider.

In our next chapter, we'll be taking a look at administration issues. As you've seen through some of the portions of this chapter, proper administration can also be a key ingredient for performance.

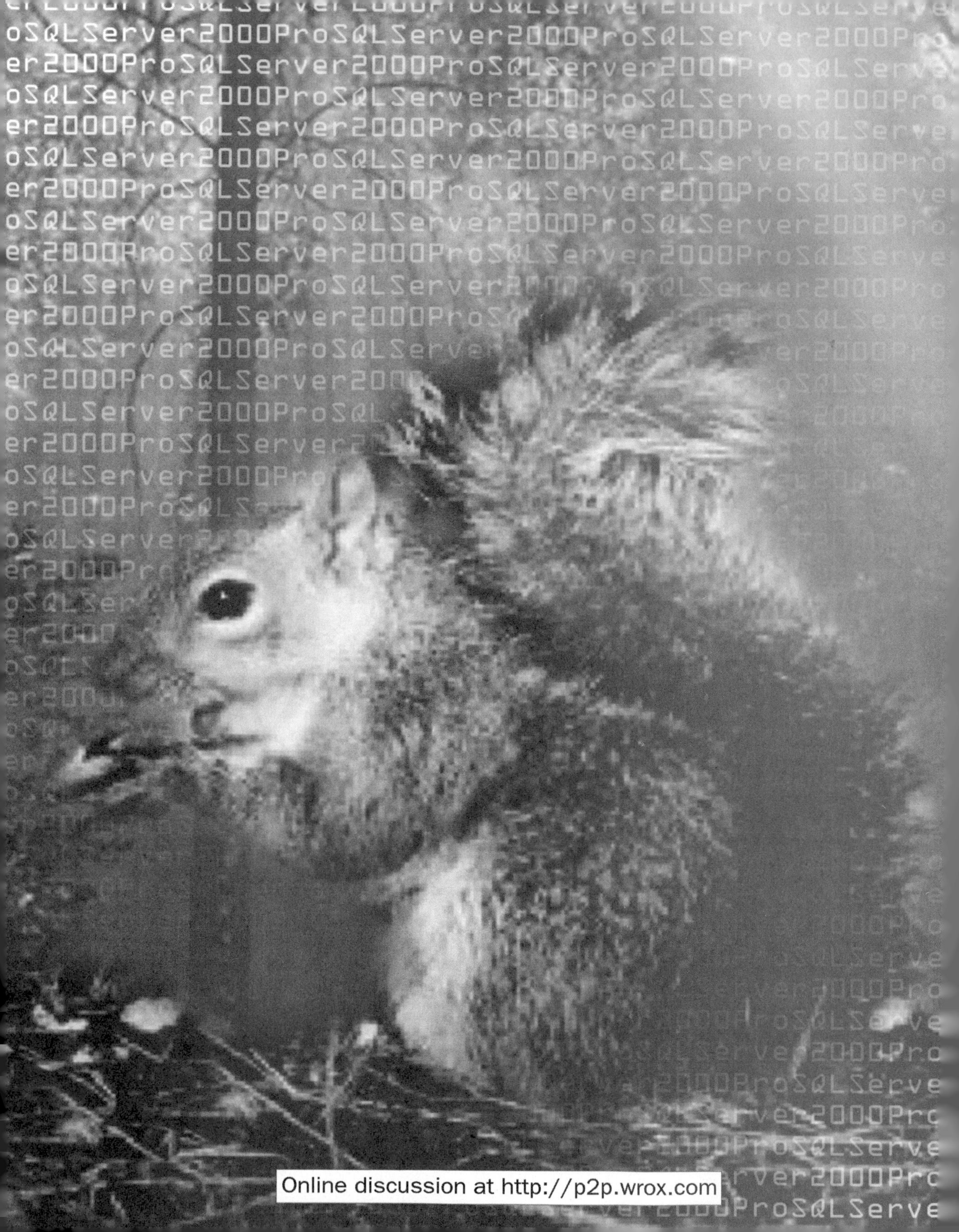
Online discussion at http://p2p.wrox.com

30

Administration Overview

OK, so you're a developer. That means there's a good chance that one of your highest goals in life is not to get sucked into the role of being the permanent Database Administrator (DBA) for your application. If you're building a shrink-wrapped kind of product or building a system to be used by a different company, then you're probably reasonably safe in the long run (but not the short-run). If you're building a system for in-house use, then you'll find yourself constantly involved in some level of problem solving for the system that has little or nothing to do with the code. While this situation is a real pain, I have only three words for you: get over it!

The fact is that, no matter how well you avoid being cast in the DBA role, you're going to need to know a lot of DBA kinds of things in order to build a system that has maximum performance and can be easily administered. Indeed, throughout this book we've already seen how to look into many issues that are more typically thought of as being in the DBA's realm. In each case, we've either focused on the issue in question because it has performance impacts that need to be taken into account in the development of the product, or because not realizing how things work can really make it nearly impossible to administer the system once it's up and running.

In this chapter, we're going to try to do a round up of a number of the administration issues that face any system. While some of these seem more like the day-to-day admin tasks that a DBA will have to handle, you'll want to know about them too, so you can deal with these issues in your operations and setup documentation. If you're in a consulting role, you'll also find that you will invariably end up doing the initial setup and training on any scheduled tasks – that means you had better get it right!

In this chapter, we'll be focusing in on:

- ❑ Scheduling jobs
- ❑ Backup and restore
- ❑ Alerts
- ❑ Full-Text Catalog population
- ❑ Carrying data from one place to another
- ❑ Index rebuilding
- ❑ Archiving of data

These are really just some of the basics – a full coverage of administration issues could create a list of topics hundreds if not thousands of entries long, but that's for another book. In looking at these, we'll cover most of the issues that frequently come up, and allow you to plan for them when you are designing your system, so the DBAs that are eventually put in charge of your system will come to love you rather than hate you.

Scheduling Jobs

Many of the tasks that we'll go over in the remainder of the chapter can be **scheduled**. Scheduling jobs allows you to run tasks that place a load on the system at off-peak hours. It also ensures that you don't forget to take care of things. From index rebuilds to backups, you'll hear of horror stories over and over about shops that "forgot" to do that, or thought they had set up a scheduled job but never checked on it.

SQL Server has always had a job-scheduling tool, but they really beefed things up back in 7.0 with the addition of **SQL Server Agent**. (The previous tool that did this kind of thing was called **SQL Executive**.)

> *If your background is in Windows NT/2000, and you have scheduled other jobs using the Windows NT Scheduler service, you could utilize that scheduling engine to support SQL Server. Doing things all in the Windows Scheduler allows you to have everything in one place, but SQL Server has some more robust branching options.*

There are basically two terms to think about: Jobs and Tasks.

- ❑ **Tasks** – these are single processes that are to be executed, or batches of commands that are to be run. Tasks are not independent – they exist only as members of jobs.

- ❑ **Jobs** – these are groupings of one or more tasks that should be run together. You can, however, set up dependencies and branching depending on the success or failure of individual tasks (for example, task A runs if the previous task succeeds, but task B runs if the previous task fails).

Jobs can be scheduled based on:

- ❑ A daily, weekly, or monthly basis
- ❑ A specific time of the day
- ❑ A specific frequency (say, every 10 minutes, or every hour)
- ❑ When the CPU becomes idle for a period of time
- ❑ When the SQL Server Agent starts
- ❑ In response to an alert

Tasks are run by virtue of being part of a job and based on the branching rules you define for your job. Just because a job runs doesn't mean that all the tasks that are part of that job will run – some may be executed and others not depending on the success or failure of previous tasks in the job and what **branching rules** you have established.

This branching process within a job was added in version 7.0 and is a very cool thing indeed. Previously, developers and DBAs would use a series of tricks to simulate this functionality. The most common approach was to schedule dependent tasks at intervals that were much further apart than would immediately seem necessary. Task A might usually run every 2 minutes, but Task B that was dependent on Task A might not be scheduled to run for an hour – this would be done so that the person who scheduled the job could be absolutely sure that the previous job was complete. The beginning of the second task would often have logic built in to try and detect if the previous job succeeded or failed. It probably doesn't take a rocket scientist to figure out that this kind of approach was problematic at best (and disastrous at worst). First of all, you wind up wasting tremendous amounts of time just from the "buffer" that you place between jobs running. If you had 10 or 15 different dependencies, trying to run all this as a night job could become rather problematic – especially if some of the processes were naturally long-running.

But I digress... The job and task approach addresses the above scenario quite well. SQL Server not only allows one task to automatically fire when another finishes – it also allows for doing something entirely different (such as running some sort of recovery task) if the current task fails.

In addition to branching, you can, depending on what happens, also tell SQL Server to:

❑ Provide notification of the success or failure of a job to an operator; you're allowed to send a separate notification for a network message (which would pop-up on a user's screen as long as they are logged in – NT only), a pager, and an e-mail address to each operator

❑ Write the information to the event log (assuming you're running NT or 2000)

❑ Automatically delete the job (to prevent executing it later and to generally "clean up")

Let's take a quick look at how to create operators and tasks using both EM and T-SQL.

Creating an Operator

If you're going to make use of the notification features of the SQL Agent, then you must have an operator set up to define the specifics for who is notified. This side of things – the creation of operators – isn't typically done through any kind of automated process or as part of the developed code. Operators are usually created manually by the DBA. We'll go ahead and take a rather brief look at this process just to understand how it works in relation to the scheduling of tasks.

Creating an Operator Using EM

To create an operator using EM, you need to navigate to the **SQL Server Agent** sub-node of the **Management** node of the server for which you're creating the operator. Right-click on the **Operators** member and choose **New Operator...**

You should be presented with the following dialog box (mine is partially filled in):

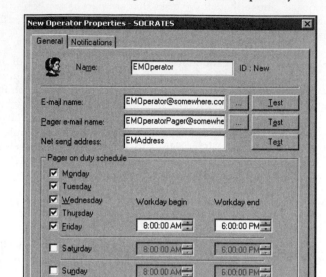

Note that the **Pager on duty schedule** won't be enabled until you supply some form of pager e-mail address. You can then fill out a schedule for what times this operator is to receive e-mail notifications for certain kinds of errors that we'll see on the **Notifications** tab – which looks like this:

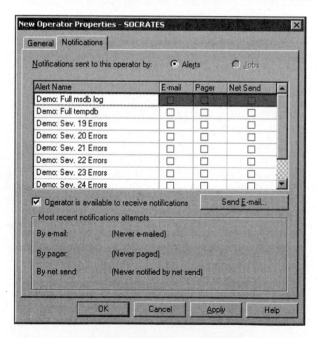

Notice that the operator can be automatically notified of any of the critical system errors that occur (anything above Severity 18). They will only be notified of those messages that you check in this dialog tab. In addition, if we had any scheduled jobs on the system, then the Jobs option could also be enabled so that notifications about these jobs will be sent to this operator.

Creating an Operator Using T-SQL

If you do decide to create operators programmatically, you can make use of the sp_add_operator system sproc. Note that, since this is a SQL Server Agent sproc, you'll find it only in the msdb database.

After seeing all the different things you need to choose in EM, it probably won't surprise you to find out that this sproc has a ton of different parameters. Fortunately, a number of them are optional, so you only need to supply them if you're going to make use of them. The syntax looks like this:

```
sp_add_operator [@name =] '<operator name>'
    [, [@enabled =] <0 for no, 1 for yes>]
    [, [@email_address =] '<email alias or address>']
    [, [@pager_address =] '<pager address>']
    [, [@weekday_pager_start_time =] <weekday pager start time>]
    [, [@weekday_pager_end_time =] <weekday pager end time>]
    [, [@saturday_pager_start_time =] <Saturday pager start time>]
    [, [@saturday_pager_end_time =] <Saturday pager end time>]
    [, [@sunday_pager_start_time =] <Sunday pager start time>]
    [, [@sunday_pager_end_time =] <Sunday pager end time>]
    [, [@pager_days =] <pager days>]
    [, [@netsend_address =] '<netsend address>']
    [, [@category_name =] '<category name>']
```

Most of the parameters in this sproc are self-describing, but there are a few we need to take a closer look at:

❑ @enabled: This is a Boolean value and works just like you would typically use a bit flag – 0 means disable this operator and 1 means enable the operator.

❑ @email_address: This one is a little tricky. In order to use e-mail with your SQL Server, you need to configure SQL Mail to be operational using a specific mail server. This parameter assumes that whatever value you supply is an alias on that mail server. If you are providing the more classic e-mail address type (somebody@SomeDomain.com), then you need to enclose it in square brackets, like so: [somebody@SomeDomain.com]. Note that the entire address – including the brackets – must still be enclosed in quotes.

❑ @pager_days: This is a number that indicates the days that the operator is available for pages. This is probably the toughest of all the parameters. This uses a single-byte bit-flag approach similar to that which we saw with the @@OPTIONS system function that we looked at earlier in the book. You simply add the values together for all the days that you want to set as active days for this operator. The options are:

Value	Day of Week
Sunday	1
Monday	2
Tuesday	4
Wednesday	8
Thursday	16
Friday	32
Saturday	64

OK, so let's go ahead and create our operator using sp_add_operator. We'll keep our use of parameters down:

```
USE msdb
DECLARE @PageDays int

SELECT @PageDays = 2 + 8 + 32 -- Monday, Wednesday, and Friday

EXEC sp_add_operator @name = 'TSQLOperator',
        @enabled = 1,
        @pager_address = 'YourEmail@YourDomain.com',
        @weekday_pager_start_time = 080000,
        @weekday_pager_end_time = 170000,
        @pager_days = @PageDays
```

Now go back into EM and refresh your Operators list. You should see your new operator there – double-click on it to look at the properties:

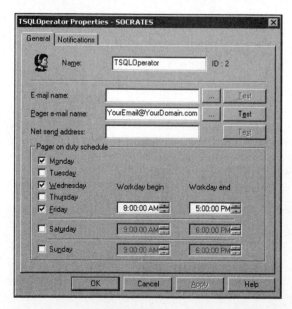

Notice that all our information is exactly as we set it – even the days of the week only include Monday, Wednesday, and Friday, just as we planned in our sproc.

There are three other sprocs that you need to make use of in order to have power over your operator from T-SQL:

❑ `sp_help_operator` – provides information on the current settings for the operator.

❑ `sp_update_operator` – accepts all the same information as `sp_add_operator`; the new information completely replaces the old information.

❑ `sp_delete_operator` – removes the specified operator from the system.

❑ `sp_add_notification` – accepts an alert name, an operator name, and a method of notification (e-mail, pager, netsend). Adds a notification such that, if the alert is triggered, then the specified operator will be notified via the specified method.

Now that we've seen how to create operators, let's take a look at creating actual jobs and tasks.

Creating Jobs and Tasks

As I mentioned earlier, jobs are collections of one or more tasks. A task is a logical unit of work, such as backing up a database or running a T-SQL script. Additionally, even though a job can contain several tasks, this is no guarantee that every task in a job will run, because this can depend on the success or failure of other tasks in the job.

Just like operators, jobs can be created in EM, T-SQL, and DMO (Distributed Management Objects). In this book, we'll cover the quick and dirty creation of tasks and jobs in EM and the automated nature of T-SQL.

Creating Jobs and Tasks Using EM

EM makes it very easy to create scheduled jobs. Just navigate to the **SQL Server Agent** sub-node of the **Management** node of your server in EM. Then right-click on the **Jobs** member and select **New Job...** You should get a four-tab dialog box that will help you build the job one step at a time:

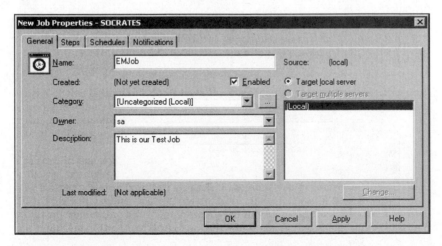

The name can be whatever you like as long as it adheres to the SQL Server rules for naming, as discussed back in Chapter 2.

Most of the rest of the information on this tab is self-explanatory, with a couple of exceptions:

❑ **Category:** This is just one way of grouping jobs together. Many of your jobs that are specific to your application are going to be **Uncategorized,** although you will probably on occasion run into instances where you want to create **Web Assistant, Database Maintenance, Full Text** or **Replication Jobs** – those each go into their own category for easy identification.

❑ The **Target local server** vs. **Target multiple servers** option buttons are only enabled if you've configured remote servers. This is an administrator-only requirement in 99.9% of situations, so we won't cover it here.

We can then move on to tab two. This is the place where we tell SQL Server to start creating our new tasks that will be part of this job. To add a new task, we just click on the New... button and fill in the new dialog box:

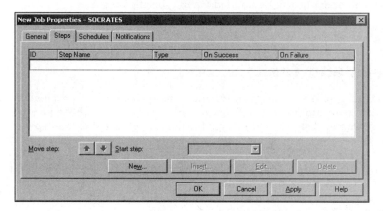

We'll use a T-SQL statement to raise a bogus error just so we can see that things are really happening when we schedule this job. Note, however, that there is an **Open...** button to the left of the command box – you can use this to import SQL Scripts that you have saved in files. It's also worth pointing out that the command box here does provide color-coding (much like QA does), so you get a bit of help with your editing:

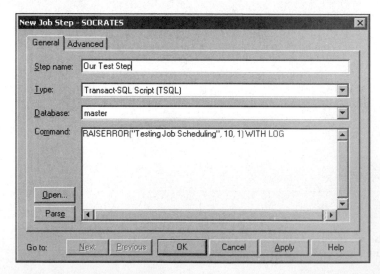

Let's go ahead and move on to the **Advanced** tab for this dialog – it's here that we really start to see some of the cool functionality that our job scheduler offers:

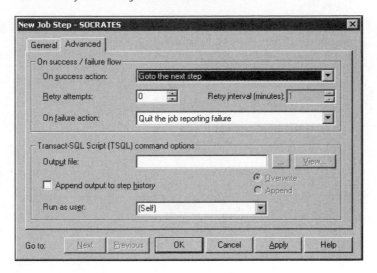

Notice several things in this dialog:

- ❑ You can automatically set the job to retry at a specific interval if the task fails.
- ❑ You can choose what to do if the job succeeds or fails. For each result (success or failure), you can:
    - ❑ Quit reporting success.
    - ❑ Quit reporting failure.
    - ❑ Move on to the next step.
- ❑ You can output results to a file. (This is very nice for auditing.)
- ❑ You can impersonate another user (for rights purposes). Note that you have to have the rights for that user. Since we're logged in as sa, we can run the job as the dbo or using the guest account. The average user would probably only have the guest account available (unless they were the dbo) but, hey, in most cases a general user shouldn't be scheduling their own jobs this way anyway (let your client application provide that functionality).

OK, so there's little chance that our RAISERROR statement is going to fail, so we'll just take the default of **Quit the job reporting failure** on this one (we'll see other possibilities later in the chapter when we come to backups).

That moves us back to the New Job Properties dialog, and we're now ready to move on to the Schedules tab:

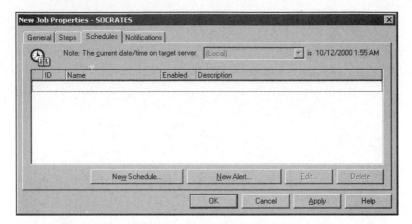

In this dialog, we can manage one or more scheduled times for this job to run. To actually create a new scheduled time for the job to run, we need to click on the New Schedule... button. That brings us up yet another dialog:

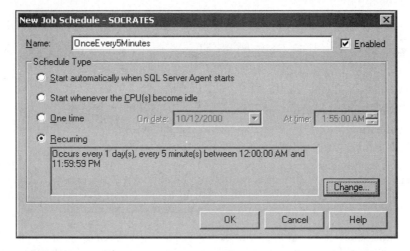

It is from this dialog that we begin the process of creating a new schedule for this job. The first three options can be set entirely from this screen. If you want the job to be recurring, then you need to choose that option and click on the Change button, which takes you to a dialog where you can set how frequently you want the job to run:

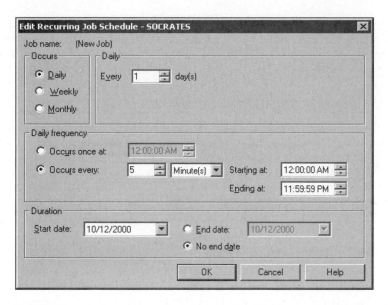

The frequency side of things can be a bit confusing because of the funny way that they've worded things. If you want something to run at multiple times every day, then you need to set the job to Occurs Daily – every 1 day. This seems like it would run only once a day, but then you also have the option of setting whether it runs once or on an interval. In our case, we want to set our job to run every 5 minutes.

Now we're ready to move on to the final tab of our job properties:

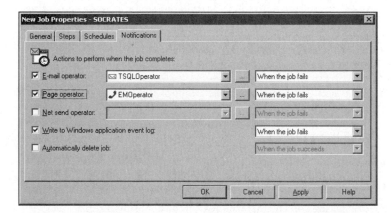

On this last tab, we can select what notifications we want to make depending on what happens. Notice that I was able to choose the couple of operators that we created earlier in the chapter. It is through the definitions of these operators that the SQL Server Agent knows what e-mail address or net send address to make the notification to. Also notice that we have control, on the right-hand side, over when the notification is made.

Since you probably don't have SQL Mail set up (see your DBA about this), and the standard e-mail channels cannot be used as SQL Mail defines how to reach these, I'd recommend turning the notifications other than net send off for now.

At this point, you are ready to apply the changes and exit the dialog. You'll need to wait a few minutes before the task will fire, but you should start to see log entries appear every five minutes in the **Windows NT/2000 event log**. You can look at this by navigating to Start | Programs | Administrative Tools | Event Viewer. You'll need to switch the view to use the Application log rather than the default System log.

Don't forget that, if you're going to be running scheduled tasks like this one, you need to have the SQL Server Agent running in order for them to be executed. You can check the status of the SQL Server Agent by running the Service Manager and selecting the SQL Server Agent service, or by navigating to the SQL Server Agent sub-node of the Management Node for your server in EM.

Also, don't forget to disable this job (right-click on the job in EM and select Disable Job) after you've seen that it's working the way you expect. Otherwise, it will just continue to sit there and create entries in your Application log – eventually, the Application Log will fill up and you can have problems with your system.

Creating Jobs and Tasks Using T-SQL

Before we get started, I want to point out that using T-SQL for this kind of stuff (creating scheduled jobs and tasks) is not usually the way things are done on a day-to-day basis. Most jobs wind up being scheduled by the DBA based on a specific need and a specific schedule that is required. If you're not in a situation where you need to script the installation of tasks, then you may want to just skip this section (it's a lot to learn if you aren't going to use it!). That being said, there can be times where your end users won't have a DBA handy (small shops, for example, often don't have anything even remotely resembling a DBA), so you'll want to script some jobs to help out unsophisticated users.

Automating the creation of certain jobs is a very frequent area of oversight in installation procedures – particularly for shrink-wrap software. If you're working in some form of consulting or private IS shop environment, then there's a good chance that you are going to need to take care of scheduling all the necessary tasks when you do the install. With shrink-wrap software, however, you often aren't at all in control of the installation process – indeed, you may be hundreds or thousands of miles away from the installation and may not even know that it's happening.

How then do you make sure that basic tasks (like backups, for example) get done? You can make it part of your installation process.

Jobs can be added to SQL Server using T-SQL by using three different stored procedures:

- ❑ sp_add_job: This creates the actual job
- ❑ sp_add_job_step: This creates a task within the above job
- ❑ sp_add_jobschedule: This determines when the job will run

Each of these builds a piece of the overall execution of the scheduled task, much as the different tabs in EM did. Let's look at each individually.

> All jobs and tasks are stored in the **msdb** database. As such, you'll need to make sure that **msdb** is the current database (utilizing the **USE** command) when calling any of these sprocs.

sp_add_job

This one creates the top-level of a hierarchy and establishes who owns the job and how notifications should be handled. There are quite a few parameters, but most of them are fairly easy to figure out:

```
sp_add_job [@job_name =] '<job name>'
    [,[@enabled =] <0 for no, 1 for yes>]
    [,[@description =] '<description of the job>']
    [,[@start_step_id =] <ID of the step you want to start at>]
    [,[@category_name =] '<category>']
    [,[@category_id =] <category ID>]
    [,[@owner_login_name =] '<login>']
    [,[@notify_level_eventlog =] <eventlog level>]
    [,[@notify_level_email =] <email level>]
    [,[@notify_level_netsend =] <netsend level>]
    [,[@notify_level_page =] <page level>]
    [,[@notify_email_operator_name =] '<name of operator to email>']
    [,[@notify_netsend_operator_name =] '<name of operator for network
        message>']
    [,[@notify_page_operator_name =] '<name of operator to page>']
    [,[@delete_level =] <delete level>]
    [,[@job_id =] <job id> OUTPUT]
```

Again, most of the parameters here are self-describing, but let's touch on some of the more sticky ones.

❑   @start_step_id: This one is going to default to 1, and that's almost always going to be the way to leave it. We'll be adding steps shortly, but those steps will have identifiers to them, and this just let's the SQL Server Agent know where to begin the job.

❑   @category_name: This one equates directly with the category we saw in the EM. It will often be none (in which case, see @category_ID), but could be Database Maintenance (another common choice), Full Text, Web Assistant, Replication, or a category that you add yourself using sp_add_category.

❑   @category_id: This is just a way of providing a category without being dependent on a particular language. If you don't want to assign any particular category, then I recommend using this option instead of the name and supplying a value of either 0 (Uncategorized, but runs local) or 1 (Uncategorized Multi-Server).

❑   @notify_level_eventlog: For each type of notification, this determines under what condition the notification occurs. In EM, this was the far right combo box in the notification tab. To use this sproc, though, we need to supply some constant values to indicate when we want the notification to happen. The constants are:

Constant Value	When the Notification Occurs
0	Never
1	When the task succeeds
2	When the task fails (this is the default)
3	Every time the task runs

❑   @job_id: This is just a way of finding out what job ID was assigned to your newly created job – you'll need this value when you go to create job steps and the job schedule(s). It is important to remember that:

    ❑   You should receive the value into a variable so you can reuse it.

    ❑   The variable needs to be of type `uniqueidentifier` rather than the types you might be more familiar with at this point.

Note that all the non-level "notify" parameters are expecting an operator name – you should create your operators before running this sproc.

So, let's create a job to test this process out. What we're going to do here is create a job that's nearly identical to our EM-created job. We will use EM as we create the job and the steps so we can watch it come together.

First, we need to create our top-level job. All we're going to do for notifications is to send a message on failure to the NT Event log. If you have got SQL Mail set-up, then feel free to add in notification parameters for your operator.

```
USE msdb

DECLARE @JobID   uniqueidentifier

EXEC sp_add_job
    @job_name = 'TSQLCreatedTestJob',
    @enabled = 1,
    @notify_level_eventlog = 3,
    @job_id = @JobID OUTPUT

SELECT 'JobID is ' + CONVERT(varchar(128),@JobID)
```

Now, execute this and you should wind up with something like this:

```
----------------------------------------------------------------------
JobID is 83369994-6C5B-45FA-A702-3511214A2F8A

(1 row(s) affected)
```

Note that your particular GUID will be different from the one I got here (remember that GUIDs are effectively guaranteed to be unique across time and space). You can either use this value or you can use the job name to refer to the job later (I happen to find this a lot easier, but it can create problems when dealing with multiple servers).

sp_add_jobserver

This is a quick and dirty one. We've now got ourselves a job, but we don't have anything assigned for it to run against. You see, you can create a job on one server, but still run it against a completely different server if you choose.

In order to target a particular server, we'll use a sproc (in `msdb` still) called sp_add_jobserver. The syntax is the easiest by far of any we'll be looking at in this section, and looks like this:

```
sp_add_jobserver [@job_id =] <job id>|[@job_name =] '<job name>',
[@server_name =] '<server>'
```

Note that you supply either the job ID or the job name – not both.

So, to assign a target server for our job, we nee to run a quick command:

```
USE msdb
EXEC sp_add_jobserver
    @job_name = 'TSQLCreatedTestJob',
    @server_name = "(local)"
```

Note that this will just point at the local server regardless of what that server is named. We could have also put the name of another valid SQL Server in to be targeted.

sp_add_jobstep

The second step in the process is to tell the job specifically what it is going to do. At the moment, all we have in our example is just the shell – the job doesn't have any tasks to perform, and that makes it a very useless job indeed. There is a flip side to this though – a step can't even be created without some job to assign it to.

The next step then is to run sp_add_jobstep. This is essentially adding a task to the job. If we had multiple steps we wanted the job to do, then we would run this particular sproc several times.

The syntax looks like this:

```
sp_add_jobstep [@job_id =] <job ID> | [@job_name =] '<job name>']
    [,[@step_id =] <step ID>]
    [,[@step_name =] '<step name>']
    [,[@subsystem =] '<subsystem>']
    [,[@command =] '<command>']
    [,[@additional_parameters =] '<parameters>']
    [,[@cmdexec_success_code =] <code>]
    [,[@on_success_action =] <success action>]
    [,[@on_success_step_id =] <success step ID>]
    [,[@on_fail_action =] <fail action>]
    [,[@on_fail_step_id =] <fail step ID>]
    [,[@server =] '<server>']
    [,[@database_name =] '<database>']
    [,[@database_user_name =] '<user>']
    [,[@retry_attempts =] <retry attempts>]
    [,[@retry_interval =] <retry interval>]
    [,[@os_run_priority =] <run priority>]
    [,[@output_file_name =] '<file name>']
    [,[@flags =] <flags>]
```

Not as many of the parameters are self-describing here, so let's look at the more confusing ones in the list:

- ❏ `@job_id` vs. `@job_name`: This is actually a rather odd sproc in the sense that it expects you to enter one of the first two parameters, but not both. You can either attach this step to a job by its GUID (as we saved from the last sproc run) or by the job name.

- ❏ `@step_id`: All the steps in any job have an ID. SQL Server assigns these IDs automatically as you insert the steps. So why, if it does it automatically, do we have a parameter for it? That's in case we want to insert a step in the middle of a job. If there are already numbers 1-5 in the job, and we insert a new step and provide a step ID of 3, then our new step will be assigned to position number 3. The old step 3 will be moved to position 4, with each succeeding step being incremented by 1 to make room for the previous step.

- ❏ `@step_name`: Is what it says – the name of that particular task. Just be aware that there is no default here – you must provide a step name.

- ❏ `@subsystem`: This ties in very closely to job categories and determines which subsystem within SQL Server (such as the replication engine, the VB Script engine, or the command line – the DOS prompt) is responsible for executing the script. The default is that you're running a set of T-SQL statements. The possible subsystems are:

SubSystem	Description
ACTIVESCRIPTING	The scripting engine (VB Script).
CMDEXEC	Gives you the capability to execute compiled programs or batch files from a command (DOS) prompt.
DISTRIBUTION	The Replication Distribution Agent.
LOGREADER	Replication Log Reader Agent.
MERGE	The Replication Merge Agent.
SNAPSHOT	The Replication Snapshot Agent.
TSQL	A T-SQL batch (this is the default).

- ❏ `@command`: This is the actual command you're issuing to a specific subsystem. In our example, this is going to be the RAISERROR command just like we issued when using EM, but it could be almost any T-SQL command. What's cool here is that there are some system-supplied values you can use in your commands. You place these in the middle of your scripts as needed, and they are replaced at run time (we'll make use of this in our example). The possible system-supplied values are:

Tag	Description
[A-DBN]	Substitutes in the database name.
[A-SVR]	Substitutes the server name in the place of the tag.
[A-ERR]	Error number.
[A-SEV]	Error severity.
[A-MSG]	The message text from the error.

Tag	Description
[DATE]	Supplies the current date (in YYYYMMDD format).
[JOBID]	Supplies the current Job ID.
[MACH]	The current computer name.
[MSSA]	Master SQL Server Agent name.
[SQLDIR]	The directory in which SQL Server is installed (usually C:\Mssql7 for SQL Server 7.0 and C:\Program Files\Microsoft SQL Server\MSSQL for 2000).
[STEPCT]	A count of the number of times this step has executed (excluding retries). You could use this one to keep count of the number of executions and force the termination of a multi-step loop.
[STEPID]	Step ID.
[TIME]	The current time in HHMMSS format.
[STRTTM]	The start time for the job in HHMMSS format.
[STRTDT]	The start date for the job in YYYYMMDD format.

❑ @cmdexec_success_code: This is the value you expect to be returned by whatever command interpreter ran your job if the job ran successfully (only applies to command prompt subsystem). The default is zero.

❑ @on_success_action and @on_fail_action: This is what you actually want doing at the success or failure of your step. Remember that we define what notifications we want to happen at the job level but, at the step level, we can define how we want processing to continue (or end). For this parameter, you need to supply one of the following constant values:

Value	Description
1	Quit with success. This is the default for successful task executions.
2	Quit with failure. This is the default for failed tasks.
3	Go to the next step.
4	Go to a specific step as defined in on_success_step_id or on_fail_step_id.

❑ @on_success_step_id and @on_fail_step_id: What step you want to run next if you've selected option 4 above.

❑ @server: The server that the task is to be run against (you can run tasks on multiple target servers from a single master server).

- ❑ @database_name: The database to be set as current when the task runs.
- ❑ @retry_interval: This is set in minutes.
- ❑ @os_run_priority: Ah, an undocumented feature. The default here is normal, but you can adjust how important NT is going to think that your cmdExec (command line) scheduled task is. The possible values are:

Value	Priority
-15	Run at idle only
-1 through to -14	Increasingly below normal
0	Normal (this is the default)
1 through to 14	Increasingly above normal
15	Time critical

I just can't help but think of the old "Lost In Space" TV show here and think of the robot saying, "DANGER Will Robinson – DANGER!" Don't take messing with these values lightly. If you're not familiar with the issues surrounding NT/2000 thread priorities, I'd suggest staying as far away from this one as possible. Going with the higher values, in particular, can have a very detrimental impact on your system – including creating significant instabilities. If you say that one task is the most important thing, remember that you are taking away some of the importance of other things like operating system functions – not something that it's smart to do. Stay clear of this unless you really know what you're doing.

- ❑ @flags: This one relates to the Output File parameter, and indicates whether to overwrite or append your output information to the existing file. The options are:

Value	Description
0	No option specified (currently, this means your file will be overwritten every time)
2	Append information to the existing file (if one exists)
4	Explicitly overwrite the file

OK, now that we've looked at the parameters, let's add a step to the job we created a short time ago:

```
sp_add_jobstep
    @job_name = 'TSQLCreatedTestJob',
    @step_name = 'This Is The Step',
    @command = 'RAISERROR
        (''RAISERROR (''TSQL Task is Job ID [JOBID] .'',10,1) WITH
            LOG'',10,1)
        WITH LOG',
    @database_name = 'Northwind',
    @retry_attempts = 3 ,
    @retry_interval = 5
```

Technically speaking – our job should be able to be run at this point. The reason I say "technically speaking" is because we haven't scheduled the job, so the only way to run it is to manually tell the job to run. Let's take care of the scheduling issue, and then we'll be done.

sp_add_jobschedule

This is the last piece of the puzzle – we need to tell our job when to run. To do this, we'll make use of `sp_add_jobschedule`, which, like all the other sprocs we've worked on in this section, can only be found in the `msdb` database. Note that we could submit an entry from this sproc multiple times to create multiple schedules for our job. Keep in mind though that getting too many jobs scheduled can lead to a great deal of confusion, so schedule jobs wisely (for example don't schedule one job for each day of the week when you can schedule a single job to run daily).

The syntax has some similarities to what we've already been working with, but adds some new pieces to the puzzle:

```
sp_add_jobschedule
    [@job_id =] <job ID>, | [@job_name =] '<job name>', [@name =]
        '<name>'
[,[@enabled =] <0 for no, 1 for yes>]
[,[@freq_type =] <frequency type>]
[,[@freq_interval =] <frequency interval>]
[,[@freq_subday_type =] <frequency subday type>]
[,[@freq_subday_interval =] <frequency subday interval>]
[,[@freq_relative_interval =] <frequency relative interval>]
[,[@freq_recurrence_factor =] <frequency recurrence factor>]
[,[@active_start_date =] <active start date>]
[,[@active_end_date =] <active end date>]
[,[@active_start_time =] <active start time>]
[,[@active_end_time =] <active end time>]
```

Again, let's look at some of these parameters:

❑   `@freq_type`: This defines the nature of the intervals that are set up in the following parameters. This is another of those parameters that uses bit flags (although you should only use one at a time). Some of the choices are clear, but some aren't until you get to `@freq_interval` (which is next). Your choices are:

Value	Frequency
1	Once
4	Daily
8	Weekly
16	Monthly (fixed day)
32	Monthly (relative to `@freq_interval`)
64	Run at start of SQL Server Agent
128	Run when CPU is idle

❑ @freq_interval: Decides the exact days that the job is executed, but the nature of this value depends entirely on @freq_type (above). This one can get kind of confusing; just keep in mind that it works with both @freq_type and @frequency_relative_interval. The interpretation works like this:

freq_type Value	Matching freq_interval Values
1 (once)	Not used
4 (daily)	Runs every x days, where x is the value in the frequency interval
8 (weekly)	The frequency interval is one or more of the following: 1 (Sunday) 2 (Monday) 4 (Tuesday) 8 (Wednesday) 16 (Thursday) 32 (Friday) 64 (Saturday)
16 (monthly – fixed)	Runs on the exact day of the month specified in the frequency interval
32 (monthly – relative)	Runs on exactly one of the following: 1 (Sunday) 2 (Monday) 3 (Tuesday) 4 (Wednesday) 5 (Thursday) 6 (Friday) 7 (Saturday) 8 (Specific day) 9 (Every weekday) 10 (Every weekend day)
64 (run at Agent startup)	Not used
128 (run at CPU idle)	Not used

❑ @freq_subday_type: Specifies the units for @freq_subday_interval. If you're running daily, then you can set a frequency to run within a given day. The possible value here are:

Value	Description
1	At the specified time
4	Every x **minutes**, where x is the value of the frequency sub-day interval
8	Every x **hours**, where x is the value of the frequency sub-day interval

❑ @freq_subday_interval: This is the number of @freq_subday_type periods to occur between each execution of the job (x in the above table).

❑ @freq_relative_interval: This is only used if the frequency type is monthly – relative (32). If this is the case, then this value determines in which week a specific day of week job is run, or flags things to be run on the last day of the month. The possible values are:

Value	Description
1	First week
2	Second week
4	Third week
8	Fourth week
16	Last week or day

❑ @freq_recurrence_factor: How many weeks or months between execution. The exact treatment depends on the frequency type and is only applicable if the type was weekly or monthly (fixed or relative). This is an integer value and, for example, if your frequency type is 8 (weekly) and the frequency recurrence factor is 3, then the job would run on the specified day of the week every third week.

The default for each of these parameters is 0.

OK, so let's move on to getting that job scheduled to run every five minutes, as we did when using EM.

```
sp_add_jobschedule
    @job_name = 'TSQLCreatedTestJob',
    @name = 'Every 5 Minutes',
    @freq_type = 4,
    @freq_interval = 1,
    @freq_subday_type = 4,
    @freq_subday_interval = 5,
    @active_start_date = 20001012
```

Now, if you go and take a look at the job in EM, you'll find that you have a job that is (other than the name) identical to the job we created directly in EM. Our job has been fully implemented using T-SQL this time.

Maintaining and Deleting Jobs and Tasks

Maintaining jobs in EM is pretty simple – just double-click on the job and edit it just as if you were creating a new job. Deleting jobs and tasks in EM is even simpler – just highlight the job and press the delete button. After one confirmation, your job is gone.

Checking out what you have and editing and deleting are all a bit trickier in T-SQL. The good news, however, is that maintaining jobs, tasks, and schedules works pretty much as creating them did, and deleting any of them is a snap.

Editing and Deleting Jobs with T-SQL

To edit or delete each of the four steps we just covered for T-SQL, you just use (with one exception) the corresponding update sproc – the information provided to the update sproc completely replaces that of the original add sproc (or prior updates) – or delete sproc. The parameters are the same as the add sproc for each:

If the Add was	Then Update with	And Delete with
sp_add_job	sp_update_job	sp_delete_job
sp_add_jobserver	None (drop and add)	sp_delete_jobserver
sp_add_jobstep	sp_update_jobstep	sp_delete_jobstep
sp_add_jobschedule	sp_update_jobschedule	sp_delete_jobschedule

Backup and Restore Operations

I'm not sure that there can be a more fundamental administration role than backing up and restoring, but you would truly be amazed at the percentage of database operations that I've gone into that don't have any kind of reliable backup. Tsk, tsk.

There is one simple rule to follow regarding backing up – do it early and often. The follow up to this to not just backup to a file on the same disk and forget it. You need to make sure that a copy moves to a completely separate place (ideally off-site) to be sure that it's safe. I've personally seen servers catch fire (the stench was terrible, as were all the freaked out staff). You don't want to find out that your backups went up in the same smoke that your original data did.

Backups saw substantially improved operations for version 7.0 and beyond in the sense that they run much faster, put less of a load on the system, and are a little easier to operate with than in previous versions. Restore operations have seen similar improvements. There are three areas to be concerned with when dealing with backups:

- ❏ Backup media and devices
- ❏ Backup operations
- ❏ Restore operations

Let's look at how to back up your data and, of course, how to get it back when you need it.

Backup Media

SQL Server doesn't really care all that much whether your backup is to tape or to a physical hard drive. Still, it does prefer that you pre-define where your backup data is going. This isn't a hard and fast requirement (you can back up directly to a filename if you wish), but it's the way things are supposed to work.

This pre-defined destination for your backup is referred to as a **device**. A device is really nothing more than an alias to help insulate SQL Server from whether you're using a tape drive or a disk file. You can create the backup "device" from T-SQL, EM, DMO, and WMI.

Creating a Device Using EM

To create a backup device using EM, right-click on the Backup member of the Management node for your server. Choose New Backup Device... and you'll be presented with a dialog box:

You can see there is no rocket science here. You simply name the device in the top text box and choose a file name or tape drive from below (mine is grayed out because this system doesn't have a tape drive on it). Be sure to notice the default location and name for your backup – you don't want to delete these by accident. You can also change them at this point, before they are created. After they are created, you need to delete and create a new backup if you need changes.

Click OK and you're done!

Creating a Device Using T-SQL

Creating a device using T-SQL is almost as easy, and brings a touch of nostalgia for when a backup was still called a **dump**. A dump is now a backup – it's that simple. To create the backup device, we use a legacy system sproc called sp_adddumpdevice. The syntax looks like this:

```
sp_adddumpdevice
    [@devtype =] '<type>',
    [@logicalname =] '<logical name>',
    [@physicalname =] '<physical name>'
```

The type is going to be one of the following:

❑ DISK: A local hard drive

❑ PIPE: A named pipe, which can be used for network backups (but they don't work well – the connection or dump fails quite often in my experience)

❑ TAPE: A tape drive

The logical name is the name that you will use in the BACKUP and RESTORE statements that we will look at shortly.

The physical name is either the name of the tape device (must be one on the local server) or the physical path to the disk volume you're backing up to.

As an example, we'll create a backup device called `TSQLBackupDevice`:

```
EXEC sp_addumpdevice 'DISK', 'TSQLBackupDevice',
        'C:\Program Files\Microsoft SQL Server\MSSQL\BACKUP\TSQLBackupDevice.bak'
```

And we're done!

Backing Up

Backing Up Using EM

To back up the database in EM, just right-click on the database, select All Tasks... and then Backup Database. You'll get one of EM's all too common dialog boxes:

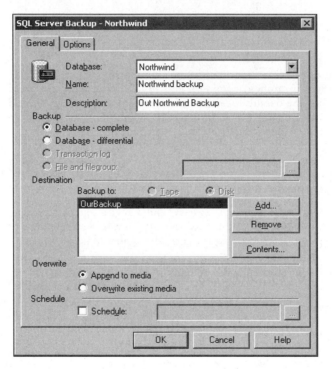

This dialog has everything you need for most situations. We fill it in with the Northwind database, what we want to call our backup, the type of backup, and the destination. The destination will be whatever device(s) we want to back up to. Just click on Add to choose between the existing devices, or to define an on-the-fly file to back up to.

Perhaps one of the coolest features of this dialog is that it will let you create a scheduled backup. You can set that scheduled job to be a once-only or a repetitive task, and it will automatically be added to your job list.

Backing up the logs is just a matter of changing which option button you select.

> There are two other options here for types of backups – differential **and** filegroup.
>
> A differential backup allows you to back up only that which has changed since the last backup – we'll cover this further when we look at backing up using T-SQL.
>
> A filegroup backup allows you to back up just one filegroup, as opposed to the entire database.

Backing Up Using T-SQL

To back up the database or log in T-SQL, we make use of the BACKUP command. The syntax for BACKUP works almost, but not quite, the same depending on whether you're backing up the database or the log:

```
BACKUP DATABASE|LOG <database name>
    -- Next two lines for logs only
    {WITH
    NO_LOG|TRUNCATE_ONLY}
    TO <backup device> [,...n]
    [WITH
    [BLOCKSIZE = <block size>]
    [[,] DESCRIPTION = <description>]
    [[,] DIFFERENTIAL]
    [[,] EXPIREDATE = <expiration date> | RETAINDAYS = <days>]
    [[,] FORMAT|NOFORMAT]
    [[,] INIT|NOINIT]
    [[,] MEDIADESCRIPTION = <description>]
    [[,] MEDIANAME = <media name>]
    [[,] [NAME = <backup set name>]
    [[,] NOSKIP|SKIP]
    [[,] NOUNLOAD|UNLOAD]
    [[,] [RESTART]
    [[,] STATS [= percentage]]]
```

Let's look at some of the parameters:

❑   <backup device>: That's right, you can back up to more than one device. This creates what's called a **media set**. These can really speed up your backups if the media are spread over several disks, as it creates a parallel load situation – you're not bound by the I/O limitations of any of the individual devices. However, beware – you must have the entire media set intact to restore from this kind of backup.

❑   BLOCKSIZE: This is automatically determined in a hard drive backup but, for tape, you need to provide the correct block size – contact your vendor for help on this one.

❑   DIFFERENTIAL: This is to perform a **differential backup**. A differential backup only backs up the data that has changed since your last full backup. Any log or other differential backup is ignored – any row/column changed, added, or deleted since the last full backup in included in the new backup. Differential backups have the advantage of being much faster to create than a full backup and much faster than applying each individual log when restoring.

❑   EXPIREDATE/RETAINDAYS: You can have your backup media expire after a certain time. Doing so lets SQL Server know when it can overwrite the older media.

❑ FORMAT/NOFORMAT: Determines whether the media header (required for tapes) should be re-written or not. Be aware that formatting affects the entire device – this means that formatting for one backup on a device destroys all the other backups on that device as well.

❑ INIT/NOINIT: Overwrites the device data, but leaves the header intact.

❑ MEDIADESCRIPTION and MEDIANAME: Just describe and name the media – maximum of 255 characters for a description and 128 for a name.

❑ SKIP/NOSKIP: Decides whether or not to pay attention to the expiration information from previous backups on the tape. If SKIP is active, then the expiration is ignored so the tape can be overwritten.

❑ UNLOAD/NOUNLOAD: Used for tape only – determines whether to rewind and eject the tape (UNLOAD) or leave it in its current position (NOUNLOAD) after the backup is complete.

❑ RESTART: Picks up where a previously interrupted backup left off.

❑ STATS: Displays a progress bar indicating progress as the backup runs.

Now let's try one out for a true backup:

```
BACKUP DATABASE Northwind
TO TSQLBackupDevice
    WITH
        DESCRIPTION = 'My what a nice backup!',
        STATS
```

We now have a backup of our Northwind database. It's that simple, so let's follow it up with a simple backup of the log:

```
BACKUP LOG Northwind
TO TSQLBackupDevice
    WITH
        DESCRIPTION = 'My what a nice backup of a log!',
        STATS
```

It's worth noting that backups work just fine while there are users in your database. SQL Server is able to reconcile the changes that are being made by knowing the exact point in the log that the backup was begun, and using that as a reference point for the rest of the backup.

Restoring Data

We always hope that we'll never need to restore from backup – reality, of course, works very differently. You can use EM or T-SQL (or DMO) for restoring a database, and the restoration process for each is very much like that of the backup.

Restoring Data Using EM

Restoration of data using EM works almost identically to backing up your data. Right-click on your database and select All Tasks | Restore Database… This will bring up a handy dialog box:

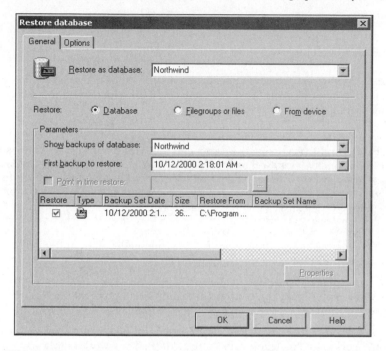

As you can see, EM pretty much holds your hand all the way through this one. If you click on the First backup to restore combo box, you'll probably see additional backups in there from which we could restore.

If you have an existing database that you want to restore over, just click on the Options tab and select Force restore over existing database. It probably goes without saying that this is something you want to be very careful with – once the restore starts, the database that you are restoring over is lost – there isn't any "undo" button for this one!

> **Because I don't want to risk overwriting your Northwind database at this juncture, I recommend just choosing Cancel in this dialog box. We'll have another opportunity when we look at the T-SQL restoration to see the restore in action.**

Restoring Data Using T-SQL

We use the RESTORE command to recover the data that we have in our backups. The syntax looks like this:

```
RESTORE DATABASE|LOG <database name>
    [FROM <backup_device> [,...n]]
    [WITH
    [DBO_ONLY]
    [[,] FILE = <file number>]
    [[,] MEDIANAME = <media name>]
```

```
[[,] MOVE '<logical file name>' TO '<operating system file
    name>'][,...n]
[[,] {NORECOVERY|RECOVERY|STANDBY = <undo file name>}]
[[,] {NOUNLOAD|UNLOAD}]
[[,] REPLACE]
[[,] RESTART]
[[,] STATS [= percentage]]]
```

Let's look at some of these options:

❑   DBO_ONLY: When the restore is done, the database will be set with the dbo_only database option turned on. This gives the dbo a chance to look around and test things out before allowing users back onto the system.

> This is a biggie, and I very strongly recommend that you always use it. You would be amazed at how quickly users will be back on the system once it's backed up for even a moment. When a system is down, you'll find users very impatient to get back to work. They'll constantly be trying to log in, and they won't bother to ask if it's OK or not – they'll assume that, when it's up, it's OK to go into it.

❑   FILE: You can backup multiple times to the same media. This option lets you select a specific version to restore. If this one isn't supplied, SQL Server will assume that you want to restore from the most recent backup.

❑   MOVE: Allows you to restore the database to a different physical file from that which the database was using when it was originally backed up.

❑   NORECOVERY/RECOVERY/STANDBY: RECOVERY and NORECOVERY are mutually exclusive. STANDBY works in conjunction with NORECOVERY. They work as follows:

Option	Description
NORECOVERY	Restores the database, but keeps it marked as off-line. Uncommitted transactions are left intact. This allows you to continue with the recovery process – for example, if you still have additional logs to apply.
RECOVERY	As soon as the restore command is done successfully, the database is marked as active again. Data can again be changed. Any uncommitted transactions are rolled back. This is the default if none of the options are specified.
STANDBY	STANDBY allows you to create an undo file so that the effects of a recovery can be undone. STANDBY allows you to bring the database up for read-only access before you have issued a RECOVERY (which means at least part of your data's been restored, but you aren't considering the restoration process complete yet). This allows users to make use of the system in a read-only mode while you verify the restoration process.

❑   REPLACE: Overrides the safety feature that prevents you from restoring over the top of an existing database.

❑   RESTART: Tells SQL Server to continue a previously interrupted restoration process.

I'm going to go ahead and give you an example run of restoring the `Northwind` database. Do not do this yourself unless you are absolutely certain that your backup was successful and is intact.

> **If, for some reason, you can't get your copy of Northwind to restore, then you can always run the `instnwnd.sql` script that is in the Install directory under your main SQL Server folder. Just keep in mind that it's not going to have any of the other changes you made as you where working through this book. Again, make sure your backup was successful and is intact before running this restore!**

First, I'm going to drop the exiting `Northwind` database:

```
USE master
DROP DATABASE Northwind
```

Once that's done, I'll try and bring it back using my `RESTORE` command:

```
RESTORE DATABASE Northwind
    FROM TSQLBackupDevice
    WITH
        DBO_ONLY,
        NORECOVERY,
        STATS
```

I did my restore with `NORECOVERY` because I want to add another piece to the puzzle. My log will contain any transactions that happened between when my database or log was last backed up and when this log was backed up. I'm going to "apply" this log, and that should bring my database as up to date as I can make it:

```
RESTORE LOG Northwind
    FROM TSQLBackupDevice
    WITH
        DBO_ONLY,
        NORECOVERY,
        STATS
```

Note that if I had several logs to apply from this one device, then I would have to name them as I wanted to apply them. They would also need to be applied in the order in which they were backed up.

Now, I could have turned everything on there, but I wanted to hold off for a bit before making the database active again. Even though I don't have any more logs to apply, I still need to rerun the `RESTORE` statement to make the database active again:

```
RESTORE LOG Northwind WITH RECOVERY
```

I should now be able to test out my database:

```
USE Northwind
SELECT * FROM Region
```

And, sure enough, I get the results I'm looking for:

```
RegionID    RegionDescription
--------------------------------------------
1           Eastern
2           Western
3           Northern
4           Southern
```

(4 row(s) affected)

We're not done yet though. Remember that I chose the DBO_ONLY option for all this. If we run sp_dboption we'll see that no one else is able to get in:

```
EXEC sp_dboption
```

Look for the dbo use only:

```
Settable database options:
-----------------------------------
ANSI null default
ANSI nulls
ANSI warnings
auto create statistics
auto update statistics
autoclose
autoshrink
concat null yields null
cursor close on commit
dbo use only
default to local cursor
merge publish
offline
published
quoted identifier
read only
recursive triggers
select into/bulkcopy
single user
subscribed
torn page detection
trunc. log on chkpt.
```

You must remember to turn that option off or your users won't be able to get into the system:

```
EXEC sp_dboption Northwind, 'dbo use only', 'false'
```

You now have yourself a restored and active database.

Alerts

This tends to be even more of a true DBA task than job scheduling was, but you should know that **alerts** are there and you might even consider adding a few into your installation routines to deal with things like nearly full logs or databases.

Alerts have a definite relationship to jobs in the sense that they define an action that is to take place. The difference is in what causes the defined action to happen. For jobs, the action happened as a result of some schedule being met but, for alerts, the action is taking place as a result of something else happening in the system. The actions that tell an alert to happen are typically errors or performance conditions. When you define the alert, the system monitors for the condition you have specified. Examples of what conditions can be based on include:

- ❑ Error numbers
- ❑ Severity levels
- ❑ Specific databases that the error occurred in
- ❑ Specific event messages
- ❑ Counters – for example, exceeding a certain number of active connections
- ❑ Specific instances – for example, just one server process ID (spid)

You can set any of these up to fire your alert, and then choose how to respond to it by firing a job or notifying an operator.

Creating an Alert in EM

Creating alerts in EM is pretty straightforward. Right-click on the Alerts member in the SQL Server Agent sub-node of the Management node for your server, and choose New Alert... You'll be greeted with a dialog box:

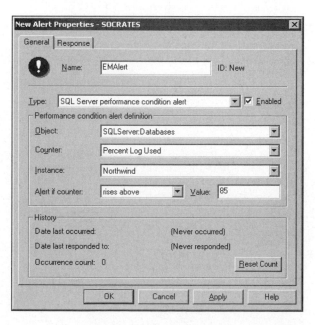

In this case, I have set up an alert that is based on how full the log for the **Northwind** database is. If the log rises above 85% of capacity, then my alert will be fired. We can then click on the **Response** tab to declare what our alert is supposed to do:

I've created a special job to automatically dump the log if it becomes 85% full before I do my normal backups. Although I haven't done it here, I should probably fill in some details in the **Additional notification message to send** pane, so the operator knows what to look at – increasing the size of the log or backing it up more often, maybe.

Creating an Alert in T-SQL

To create an alert in T-SQL, we make use of the sp_addalerts sproc that can be found in the msdb database. The syntax looks like this:

```
sp_add_alert [@name =] '<alert name>'
    [, [@message_id =] <message ID From master..sysmessages>]
    [, [@severity =]<severity>]
    [, [@enabled =] <enabled>]
    [, [@delay_between_responses =] <delay between responses>]
    [, [@notification_message =] '<notification message>']
    [, [@include_event_description_in =] <include event description in>]
    [, [@database_name =] '<database>']
    [, [@event_description_keyword =] '<event description>']
    [, {[@job_id =] <job ID> | [@job_name =] '<job name>'}]
    [, [@raise_snmp_trap =] <raise snmp trap>]
    [, [@performance_condition =] '<performance condition>']
    [, [@category_name =] '<category name>']
```

As usual, let's take a look at the more obscure parameters:

- ❑ @message_id: This would be the system message ID. You can create custom messages just as you do custom errors using sp_addmessage. Creating messages is discussed in detail in the chapter on sprocs.

- ❑ @severity: The severity (1 through 25) that the message has to be at before your alert will fire.

- ❑ @delay_between_responses: Many alerts are set against items that won't change until we do something about them. That means that, if we don't tell the SQL Server Agent to give it a rest, it will keep finding that condition and notifying us over and over again. This interval value tells the Agent that, once we've been notified, it won't tell us again about it for the specified period of time in seconds.

- ❑ @notification_message: The message you want sent with any notifications.

- ❑ @include_event_description_in: This just says whether to include the event description in the notification or not.

- ❑ @event_description_keyword: This is the word or phrase that you're saying the alert message (the one that fires the alert, not the one it sends) has to match up with.

- ❑ @job_id and @job_name: The ID or name (one or the other, but not both) of the job that you want to fire as a result of this alert.

- ❑ @raise_snmp_trap: This one is non-functional for this release – just ignore it.

- ❑ @performance_condition: The is the full evaluator (up to 512 characters in Unicode) to find out whether the performance condition is met or not. These can be a real problem to figure out but, as an example, our performance condition from our EM example would look like this:

```
SQLServer:Databases|Percent Log Used|Northwind|>|85
```

So, to create an example just like the one we did in EM (except for the percentage), the sproc would look like this:

```
USE msdb

EXEC sp_add_alert
    @name = 'Our T-SQL Alert',
    @enabled = 1,
    @delay_between_responses = 300,
    @job_name = 'Dump Northwind Log',
    @performance_condition =
        'SQLServer:Databases|Percent Log Used|Northwind|>|65'
```

> **SQL Server is smart enough to keep you from creating duplicate performance alerts – even if they have different names. Be aware that if you want to have two alerts that do exactly the same thing for some bizarre reason (for instance, you're trying to give a demo), you're out of luck. You'll need to vary them slightly (as I did by changing to 65% instead of 85%).**

Full-Text Catalog Population

This was covered very well back in Chapter 26, but I want to touch on it very briefly here because it can be a major stumbling point in the admin side of things.

Backup and Restore

Don't forget that full-text catalogs are completely separate from your database. They cannot be backed up on their own and they cannot be backed up with your regular database. In short – they can't be backed up at all.

Any time you need to restore your database, you will need to repopulate your full-text catalogs immediately after the recovery is complete. If you fail to do this, your users will be performing full-text queries that return nothing even though there should be matches in the database.

Schedule Your Populations

Now that we've seen how to schedule tasks, make sure you schedule the repopulation of your full-text catalogs. You've probably already taken care of this since the full-text catalog wizards will try to help guide you through setting up such a job, but go check it and make sure. Another key pitfall that often traps unsuspecting developers and DBAs is a full text catalog that has been populated once. It returns some data – but fails to return rows you think it should because it doesn't know anything about the new rows that have been added or changes made to the existing rows in the database.

Copying Data from One Place to Another

There are a few different options available to you when you need to carry a copy of a database from one server to another:

- ❑ Copy Database Wizard
- ❑ Backup and restore
- ❑ `sp_detach_db` and `sp_attach_db`

Which you'll want to use depends on the specifics of your situations and what you're comfortable with.

The Copy Database Wizard

This feature is entirely new with SQL Server 2000. It has the distinct advantage of taking care of almost everything for you with just a couple of mouse clicks and making a combo box choice or two. There are, however, a couple of gotchas in this tool:

- ❑ You can't use it to copy a database on the same server.
- ❑ The two servers must be connected via network.

If you can manage to live within these restrictions, life is good (and fairly easy).

For demonstration purposes, I'm actually going to do a little bit extra and copy a database from a remote server that's only running version 7.0. The copy database wizard has no problem with this, as long as the destination is running SQL Server 2000.

I'll start by choosing Wizards from the Tools menu in EM and by navigating to the Management node in the resulting dialog box:

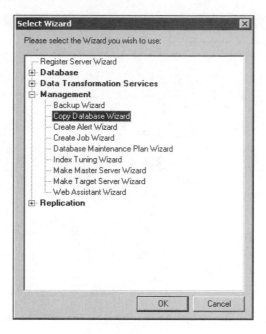

Click OK to start our wizard. If you're following along, go ahead and click Next to navigate to the second dialog:

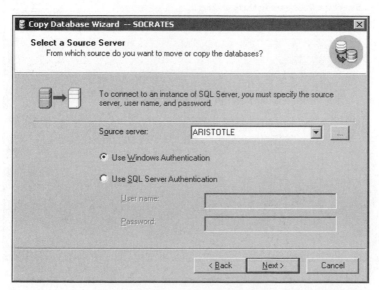

This is where you select the source server. In my case, this is a version 7.0 server called ARISTOTLE (readers of the version 7.0 edition of this book saw a lot of screenshots coming from this box!). I'm going to go ahead and use NT authentication, but you could use whatever you needed to gain the proper level of access – you must be logged in as either sa or a member of the sysadmins server role.

Click Next to move on to the next dialog and set up the destination:

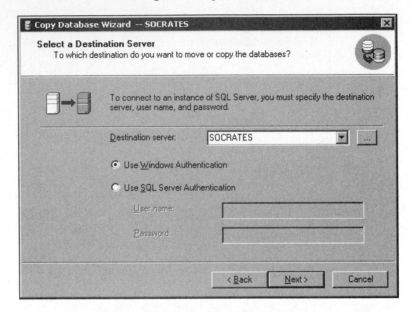

Again, you must authenticate into the destination server. Another click, and things get more interesting:

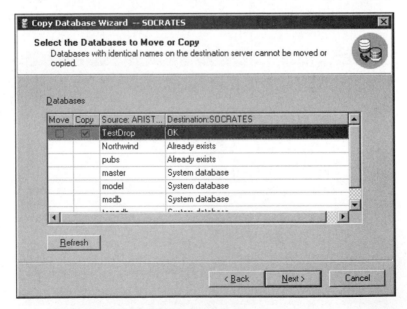

In this case, I'm just moving a test database I had set up quite some time ago. You will need to make sure that the database you move is something that doesn't already have a duplicate name on the destination server. I'm electing to copy the database in question, but I also could elect to move it – in which case SQL Server would drop the database from the source as soon as it was certain that the database had safely arrived at the destination.

Another click of the Next button and we get a chance to modify and/or finish the copy:

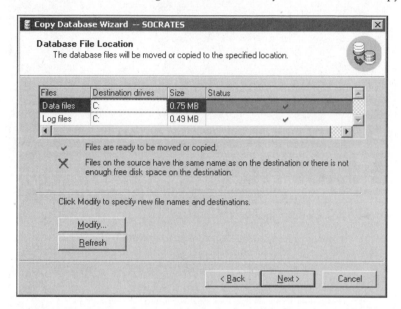

If I click on Modify, I get the opportunity to change file names (but not database names):

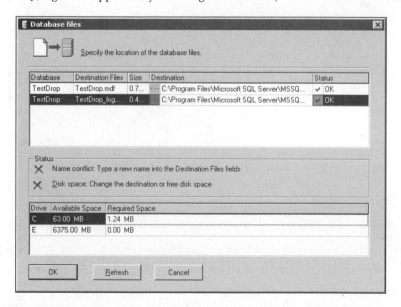

I'm going to leave that as is and move on to the next dialog:

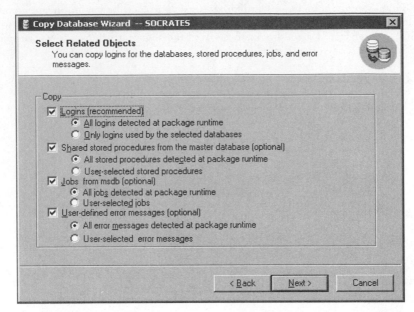

I'm going to take the defaults here and move on to our final dialog:

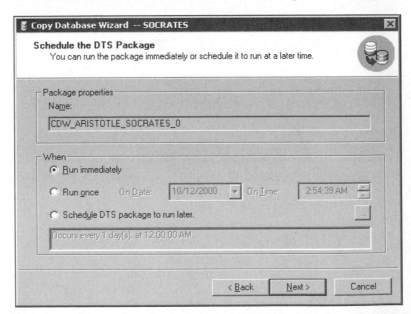

Essentially, SQL Server has just set up a DTS package for us. I'll elect to run it immediately and click through to the finish.

SQL Server then runs through the execution phase much like any other DTS package. If there are any errors, it will bring up a dialog and give you the opportunity to get more specific information.

Backup And Restore

This is pretty much self-explanatory – you backup the database and then restore it to the new location. This has the advantage of working even if the only connection you have is what I call "sneaker net" – that is, no network connection, and data has to move by disk.

There are a few gotchas:

If you restore to a different system, then you are going to need to deal with differences in the security identifiers (SIDs) between the two systems. You can either do this with `sp_change_users_login` (which I find does not always work as intended), or simply drop the users from the database and re-add them.

> *Keep in mind that a backup and restore doesn't move logins for you – just users (which have to be associated with logins). That's why there's the difficulty in dealing with security identifiers – they will vary between servers. Also, and even more importantly, if you take the drop and add approach, you will need to perform the drop using* sp_dropuser *– EM does not correctly show the old users in the database (probably because of the SID mismatch) and, therefore, gives you no way to drop them using that tool.*

Attach/Detach

`sp_detach_db` removes the database from your database entry list – so you don't want to do this on an in-production database. The advantage of this approach, though, is that it is very quick in comparison to backup and restore and it will work in a disconnected environment (just copy the file to CD or whatever). It's great for development databases. The syntax looks like this:

```
sp_detach_db [@dbname =] '<database name>'
    [@skipchecks =] '<true|false>']
```

Making `@skipchecks` true just means that `UPDATE STATISTICS` won't automatically be run as the database is detached.

You can then copy the file and carry it to another location. The syntax for reattaching the database is:

```
sp_attach_db [@dbname =] '<database name>',
    [@filename1 =] '<physical filename>' [,...16]
```

You can re-attach multiple files and they become active immediately as long you have a complete set (which you must have for anything to work at all).

> *The caveat of needing to drop and re-add users also applies to this method.*

Index Rebuilding

This should be part of a set of scripts you should include with your application regardless of what kind of development you're doing. You want to correct any FILLFACTOR problems (too full or too empty) as well as fragmentation issues on a regular basis. How often this is necessary varies by the degree and nature of the activity that goes on in the database. This is one of those things that is often forgotten, and it's frequently the source of performance-related issues. I hear comments from customers such as, "Gee, our database used to run great, but it's turned into a dog recently." You ask questions like, "Did this happen slowly, or all at once?" The response is usually that they only just noticed it, but that it's probably been going on for a while. And the reason? No maintenance!

Just set up this script (it combines many of the skills we've learned in this book, and is actually straight out of Chapter 18) to run on your database on a weekly or monthly basis as seems appropriate:

```
DECLARE @TableName varchar(255)
DECLARE TableCursor CURSOR FOR
    SELECT TABLE_NAME FROM INFORMATION_SCHEMA.TABLES
        WHERE TABLE_TYPE = 'BASE TABLE'
DECLARE @Command varchar(255)

OPEN TableCursor
FETCH NEXT FROM TableCursor INTO @TableName
WHILE @@FETCH_STATUS = 0
BEGIN
    PRINT 'Reindexing ' + @Tablename
    DBCC DBREINDEX(@TableName)
    FETCH NEXT FROM TableCursor INTO @TableName
END
CLOSE TableCursor
DEALLOCATE TableCursor
```

It rebuilds all the indexes in your tables. They should go back to whatever padding level you established when the table was created.

Archiving of Data

Ooh – here's a tricky one. There are as many ways of archiving data as there are database engineers. The OLAP database idea that you saw in Chapter 25 should address what you need to know as far as archiving for long-term reporting goes – but you also need to deal with the issue of when your OLAP data becomes simply too voluminous for your system to perform well.

As I said, there are just too many ways to go about archiving because every database is a little bit different. The key is to think about archiving needs at the time that you create your database. Realize that, as you start to delete records, you're going to be hitting referential integrity constraints and/or orphaning records – design in a logical path to delete or move records at archive time. Here are some things to think about as you write your archive scripts:

❑ If you already have the data in an OLAP database, then you probably don't need to worry about saving it anywhere else – talk to your boss and your attorney on that one.

❑ How often is the data really used? Is it worth keeping? Human beings are natural born pack rats in a larger size. Simply put, we hate giving things up – that includes our data. If you're only worried about legal requirements, think about just saving a copy of never or rarely used data to tape (I'd suggest multiple backups for archive data) and reducing the amount of data you have online – your users will love you for it when they see improved performance.

❑ Don't leave orphans. As you start deleting data, your referential integrity constraints should keep you from leaving many orphans, but you'll end up with some where referential integrity didn't apply. This situation can lead to serious system errors.

❑ Realize that your archive program will probably need a long time to run – plan on running it at a time when your system will not be used.

❑ TEST! TEST! TEST!

Summary

Well, that gives you a few things to think about. It's really easy, as a developer, to think about many administrative tasks and establish what the increasingly inaccurately named *Hitchhiker's Guide To The Galaxy* "trilogy" called an "SEP" field. That's something that makes things like administration seem invisible because it's "somebody else's problem." Don't go there!

> *A project I'm familiar with from several years ago is a wonderful example of taking responsibility for what can happen. A wonderful system was developed for a non-profit group that operates in the Northwestern United States. After about 8 months of operation, an emergency call was placed to the company that developed the software (it was a custom job). After some discussion, it was determined that the database had somehow become corrupted, and it was recommended to the customer that they restore from their backup. Their response? "Backup?" The development company in question missed something very important – they knew they had an inexperienced customer that would have no administration staff – and who was going to tell the customer to do backups and help set it up if the development company didn't? I'm happy to say that the development company in question learned from that experience – and so should you.*

Think about administration issues as you're doing your design and especially in your deployment plan. If you plan ahead to simplify the administration of your system, you'll find that you system is much more successful – that usually translates into rewards for the developer – you!

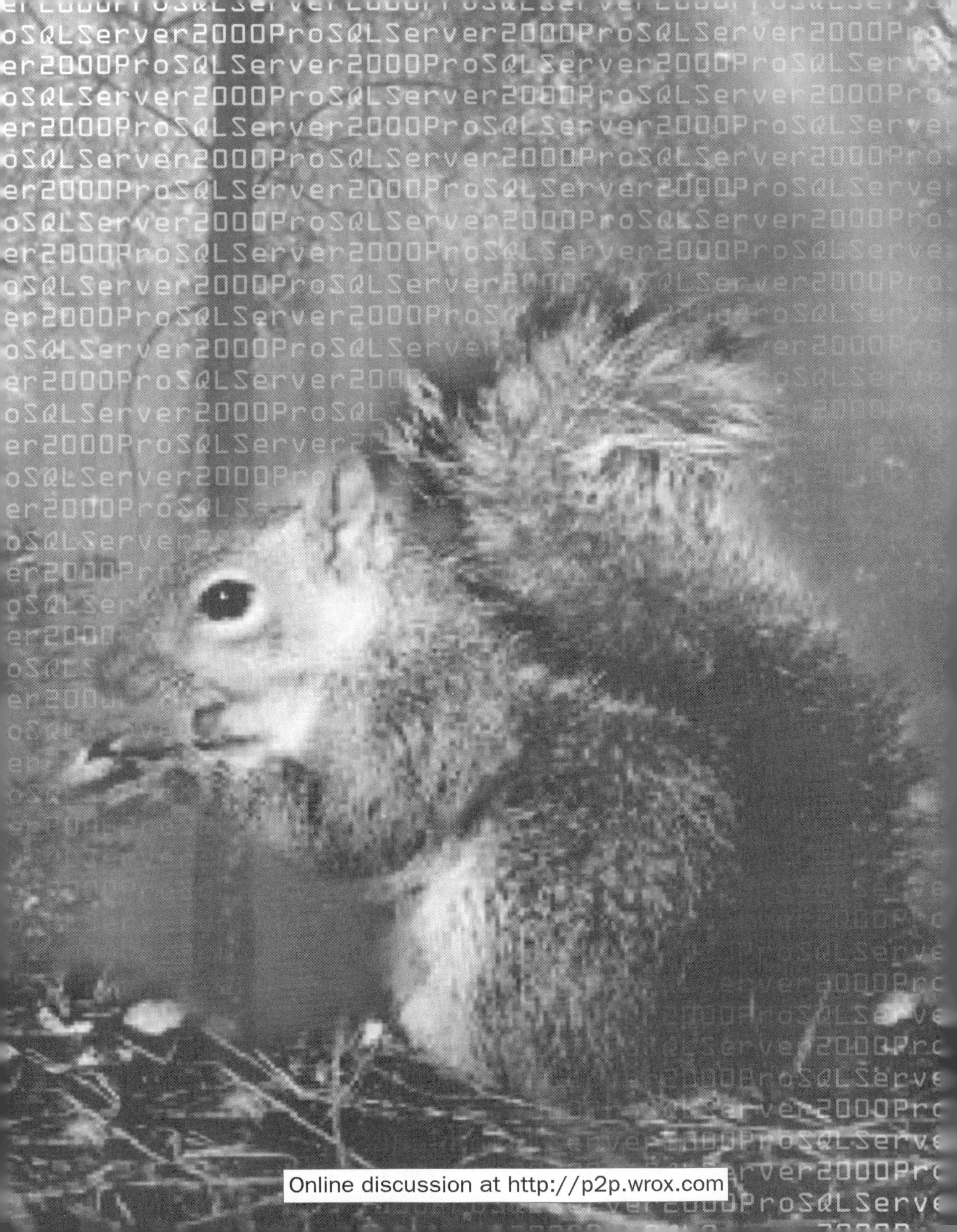

Online discussion at http://p2p.wrox.com

31

Advanced DTS

As a developer, nothing is more frustrating than repetition, whether recreating the same code over and over again or having to fix the same code in multiple locations. Wouldn't it be great to be able to write a DTS package once and then use it multiple times? Wouldn't it be even better to create a process like an auditing process once, and then reuse it from multiple packages? In this chapter we'll discuss doing just that.

In SQL Server 7.0, you would have to program complex scripts around making packages reusable and if you ever made a change to a package's code, you would have to go back and change the code in every location where the code existed. SQL Server 2000 has added tasks to help you with this dilemma and keep you from fat-fingering a code change.

Back in Chapter 22, we saw a little of how DTS works; now we're going to accelerate the pace a little and get into some more advanced topics. SQL Server uses a number of object models in its tools including:

- ❑ Decision Support Objects (DSO): this is the object model that lets us code against the multi-dimensional data store (OLAP Cubes).

- ❑ Distributed Management Objects (SQL-DMO): this is something of a lame duck. This tool is used to manage SQL Server objects (indeed, even Enterprise Manager uses it), but is being replaced by WMI (which we'll look at in our next chapter).

- ❑ SQL Namespace (SQL-NS): this is a set of COM interfaces that go somewhat hand in hand with SQL-DMO. SQL-NS helps programmatically instantiate things like the wizards and dialog boxes that you see in Enterprise Manager.

- ❑ Data Transformation Services (DTS): yep, there's an API here too – one for managing the kinds of things we saw in the Package Editor.

DTS is the easiest of the four object models to use because it's relatively small compared to the others. In this chapter, we'll cover some of the more commonly used objects in DTS. We'll discuss how to execute packages from other applications like Visual Basic and how to pass your packages global variables that can be used to make your packages dynamic. We'll also briefly discuss the multiphase data pump.

Introduction to the DTS Object Model

As we mentioned, the DTS object model is one of the easier object models you'll come across. Many objects, such as the `Package` object, now have another version of the object that has a 2 suffix to allow additional functionality to be added and yet protect backward compatibility with SQL Server 7.0. In SQL Server 7.0, the `Package2` interface did not exist. Instead there was just the `Package` object. The 7.0 object model was preserved in the latest release of SQL Server 2000, but the new objects like `Package2` offer more functionality. The abbreviated basic object model looks like this:

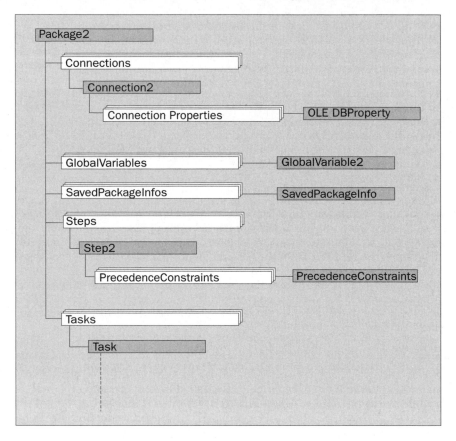

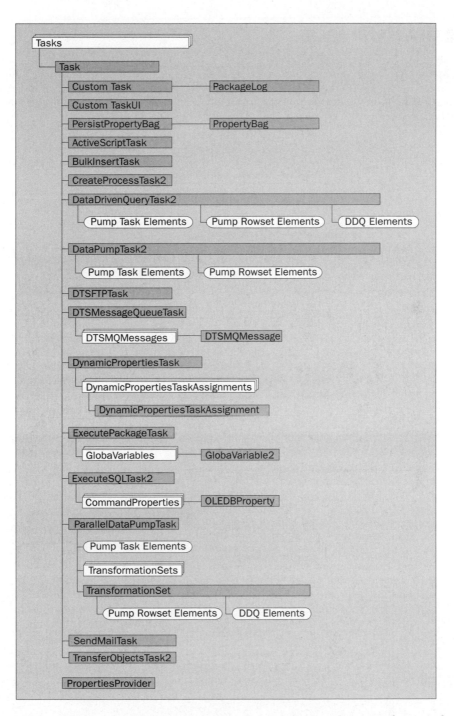

Keep in mind that when you're using the `Package2` extensibility, you lose any chance at backward compatibility with SQL Server 7.0

Setting the Reference

If you're designing your program in Visual Basic or Visual InterDev, you can fully utilize Visual Studio's Intellisense by first setting the references to DTS. This can be done in Visual Basic or Visual InterDev by selecting References under the Project menu. Once in the References screen, select Microsoft DTSPackage Object Library as shown below. If you want to use the object model inside an Active Server Page or inside DTS itself, then there is no need to do this step.

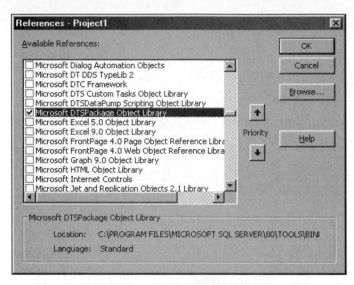

After the reference has been set, you can then browse the entire library of objects by selecting Object Browser under the View menu or pressing the F2 key. You can, at that point, select DTS from the top drop-down box so that only DTS objects are visible:

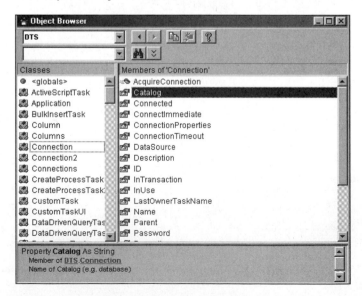

I've selected the **Catalog** property from the **Connection** object. By selecting a member in the right-hand pane, you can view a more logical description of the property in the bottom pane.

So, with our reference set, let's dive into the `Package` object.

If you're new to Visual Basic, then you'll quickly notice that VB likes to give you little "hints" as to what you might type next. This is called Intellisense, and it is based on information from the Type Library of the object you're working with. If you get to working with an object and are not seeing these hints, then double check to make sure that you've set your references as we just looked at doing. The lack of intellisense showing up for your objects in DTS (or any other library for that matter) is a pretty good hint that you didn't properly reference the supporting objects.

The Package Object

The `Package` and `Package2` objects are the foundation of the DTS object model. By defining the `Package` level, you can navigate through the rest of the object model. The next levels you could access would be any connections, global variables, steps or tasks. We will cover these levels shortly.

To demonstrate how to use the `Package2` object, you can create a new package with a single **ActiveX Script Task**. The VBScript below shows the code you can use to present the user with a message box. You can then save the package as `PackageA`.

```
Function Main()
    MsgBox "Hello From PackageA"
Main = DTSTaskExecResult_Success
End Function
```

Once the package is saved, you can execute the package using the following methods:

❑   `LoadFromSQLServer` – Executes packages that are saved locally in the SQL Server.

❑   `LoadFromRepository` – Executes packages that are saved in Meta Data Services.

❑   `LoadFromStorageFile` – Executes packages that are saved as COM-Structured files (`.DTS` files).

With the package saved, you can create a second package with another **ActiveX Script Task** and use the following syntax to execute the package using the `Package2` object:

```
Function Main()
    ' Create a new package.
    Dim objPackage
    Set objPackage = CreateObject("DTS.Package2")

    objPackage.LoadFromSQLServer "ServerName", "username", _
                    "userpassword",,,,,"PackageA"

    objPackage.Execute

    ' Cleanup
    objPackage.Uninitialize
    Set objPackage = nothing

    Main = DTSTaskExecResult_Success
End Function
```

You must first create the object and assign it to the variable using the `CreateObject` function. The variable name `objPackage` is a user-defined name that we choose to represent the instance of the object we created.

```
Dim objPackage
Set objPackage = CreateObject("DTS.Package2")
```

If you're creating a program in Visual Basic and have already set the references in your project, then you would use the code below instead:

```
Dim objPackage As Package2
Set objPackage = New DTS.Package2
```

OK, so technically speaking, the original two lines of code that we used in VBScript would work, but the VB-specific code that I'm saying to change it to will run faster!

Also, if running this in Visual Basic, you will not need to return the `DTSTaskExecResult_Success`, so you can change to a sub instead of a function.

You can then use one of the three methods we mentioned earlier to execute the package. In the example below, our server's name is `ServerName` and our package's name is `PackageA`. You can also specify a certain version to execute. You must load the package before you can perform actions to it like executing it or sending it variables.

```
objPackage.LoadFromSQLServer "ServerName", "username", _
                    "userpassword",,,,,"PackageA"
```

You could also use Windows Authentication to sign into the server and load the package. To do this we set the authentication flag to `256` – this is a constant to use Windows authentication rather than Standard authentication. At this point, you would not need a user name and password in your syntax, as shown below:

```
objPackage.LoadFromSQLServer "ServerName", "", _
                    "","256",,,,"PackageA"
```

You can then execute the package using the `Execute` method. We also clean up our references to the object by uninitializing the object.

```
objPackage.Execute

' Cleanup
objPackage.Uninitialize
Set objPackage = nothing
```

After executing the package, we see the following results:

Although this is a simple example, we will build on it in a later section in this chapter.

Dynamic Packages

A package is like any program – if you go through the trouble of creating a package or a program, you don't want to have to recreate it for another client. In SQL Server 7.0, you would have to create ActiveX Script tasks and write code to manipulate the DTS objects. Because of the complexity of doing this, most DTS developers found themselves creating a package for each client and not reusing any of their code. Those who developed a package to be used by 100 clients would have 100 packages. To solve this problem, Microsoft has added a number of features into DTS to enable you to create a package once and pass variables into the package. DTS has always had global variables (which we will discuss in a moment) but in SQL Server 2000, there is a new task called the Dynamic Properties task that provides a way to easily manipulate your packages through a GUI at design time, and, when the package executes, it will set the properties dynamically.

Global Variables

Global variables can extend the dynamic abilities of DTS. Global variables allow you to set a variable in a single area in your package, and use the variable over and over throughout the package, whether in an ActiveX script or a data transformation. They allow you to communicate with other DTS tasks and pass messages between them. Rowsets can also be stored in a global variable for later use by a different task.

An ideal case for using these variables would be to set up a dynamic database load. For example, say you receive an extract each day from a mainframe. The extract file name changes daily based on the client the extract is for and the date: for example, the filename CLIENT1-010198.txt would mean client 1 run on January 1 1998. By using an ActiveX script, you can read the file name, and change the global variable for the client number and run date based on the name you read. You can later read these two global variables to determine where to insert the data and what security to allow.

Creating a Global Variable using the DTS Designer

The global variables can be set in a variety of ways. The most common method is to right-click on the Design Sheet in the DTS Designer and select Package Properties. They can also be set under Package | Properties by selecting the Global Variables tab. The following dialog appears:

Here you can specify the global variables for your package. You can add variables and remove them. You can reference global variables in VB or VBScript using the `DTSGlobalVariables` collection in the form of:

`DTSGlobalVariables("globalvariablename").value`

For example:

```
MsgBox DTSGlobalVariables("gvMessage").Value
```

Returning to our previous example in VBScript, you can send global variables to the package that you're executing by using the `Item` method. Make sure that you set the global variables after you load the package, but before you execute it. If the global variable does not exist on the package you've loaded, the `Item` method will create the global variable, then set it.

```
Function Main()
    ' Create a new package.
      Set objPackage = CreateObject("DTS.Package2")
       objPackage.LoadFromSQLServer "ServerName", "username", _
            "userpassword",,,,,"PackageA"
    objPackage.GlobalVariables.Item("gvMessage").Value = "New Message"
    objPackage.Execute
    ' Cleanup
    objPackage.Uninitialize()
    Set objPackage = nothing
    Main = DTSTaskExecResult_Success
End Function
```

Again, if you are using NT authentication, make sure you use the code below instead for the `LoadFromSQLServer` method:

```
objPackage.LoadFromSQLServer "ServerName", "", _
        "","256",,,,"PackageA"
```

> **Global variables are case sensitive. If in our above example we try to call gvmessage, but we send gvMessage, then an empty message box will appear.**

The Dynamic Properties Task

Now that you know a little about global variables, you're all set to tackle the Dynamic Properties Task. This task is one of the most important of the tasks that were added to SQL Server 2000. After all, any task that stops you from having to write tons of code has got to be good! In SQL Server 7.0, you would have to write ActiveX scripts to change the properties of a task as shown in the package here:

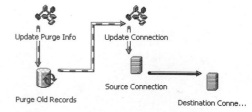

Update Purge Info   Update Connection

Purge Old Records

Source Connection

Destination Conne...

The Dynamic Properties Task allows you to set any property of a DTS package at run time to a number of things, such as a global variable or INI file. This task puts a graphical interface in front of the DTS object model and allows you to take control of your package without having to know how to program. For most DBAs, this is very important.

Dynamic Properties Task Example

In this example, we'll use the Dynamic Properties Task to dynamically change where we bulk insert data. This type of example is quite useful if you want to create one load procedure to be used by every client. You can simply change a few global variables around and then the package will load the data into a different destination.

For our example, we'll first need a flat file to load. The file below represents three columns separated by semicolons. Recreate this file and call it extract.txt, placing it in a directory called C:\Wrox:

```
datacola;datacolb;datacolc
datacola;datacolb;datacolc
datacola;datacolb;datacolc
datacola;datacolb;datacolc
```

Also, create a database (yes, another one) called Wrox:

```
CREATE DATABASE Wrox
```

For this example, you will need to create a new package and create two global variables. Again, you can do this by selecting Package | Properties and then going to the Global Variables tab. Create a global variable called gvCatalog with a value of the database that you'd like to insert into (we choose Wrox). Create another global variable called gvTable that will represent the table you'll be inserting into. You will have to set the latter global variable to the fully qualified table name of extract as shown below. We're inserting into a database called Wrox, but you can insert into anywhere, as our code will show shortly.

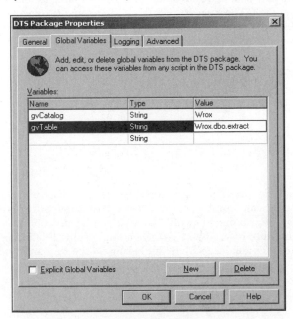

You're now ready to create your first connection as you did in Chapter 22. The connection will be made to the Wrox database that you just created. Below, we have created the connection called Destination to connect to a server that is named SOCRATES:

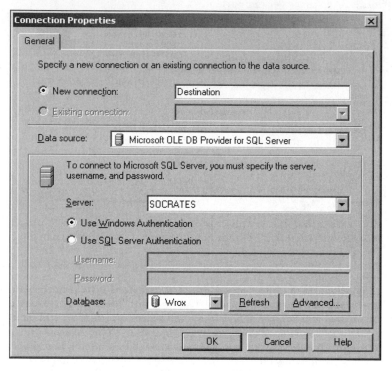

After creating your connection you will need to create a generic table to load the flat file into. This is done through the Execute SQL Task. The Execute SQL Task allows you to execute Transact-SQL statements in your package. We use the code below to detect if the table's already created. If it doesn't exist, then we create it. This is a handy way to dynamically create your schema and makes installations easy.

```
IF NOT EXISTS(SELECT * FROM INFORMATION_SCHEMA.TABLES
                      WHERE TABLE_NAME = 'extract')
BEGIN
CREATE TABLE [extract] (
   [column1] varchar(50) NULL,
   [column2] varchar(50) NULL,
   [column3] varchar(50) NULL )
END
```

As we mentioned this is done through the Execute SQL Task as shown opposite above. Set the connection to the one you created in the previous step called Destination. After you've added this task, go ahead and execute the step so the table will be initially created. You must do this because you won't be able to get through the Bulk Insert Task GUI when there is no table in the Wrox database to insert into. You can execute an individual step by right-clicking on the step and selecting Execute Step.

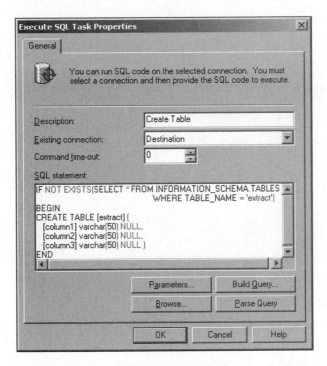

Next, add a **Bulk Insert Task** and enter **Destination**, as used earlier, as the connection. Select your newly created **extract** table as the destination. This table's name will shortly be changed dynamically by the gvTable global variable. If you are running Windows 98, you will have to click the **refresh** button to see a list of tables. The source data file will be the file we created earlier called extract.txt. Lastly, ensure that the column delimiter is a semicolon, not a tab. The row delimiter will be a carriage return, which is the default as shown below:

With the bulk of our package now created, we can jump into the fun part of making it dynamic. You can do this by adding the Dynamic Properties Task from under the Task menu. You are first taken to a summary screen. Since we have not added any dynamic properties, you should see nothing here. We name our task Adjust Properties, as shown below:

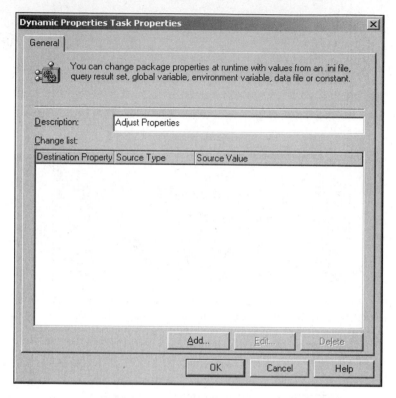

Click on the Add... button to add the first dynamic property. In the left pane, you will be presented with a list of every object being used in your package. You can drill down to each node and explore the various properties in each object. Since we have multiple properties to assign, check the box below labeled Leave this dialog box open after adding a setting. This will ensure that we aren't brought back to the summary screen prematurely. For our first dynamic property we want to assign the database that we will be loading our data into to the global variable gvCatalog. To do this, navigate down the tree on the left to Connections | Destination. On the right pane, you can double-click the Catalog property to make it dynamic. You can also select the property and click the Set... button.

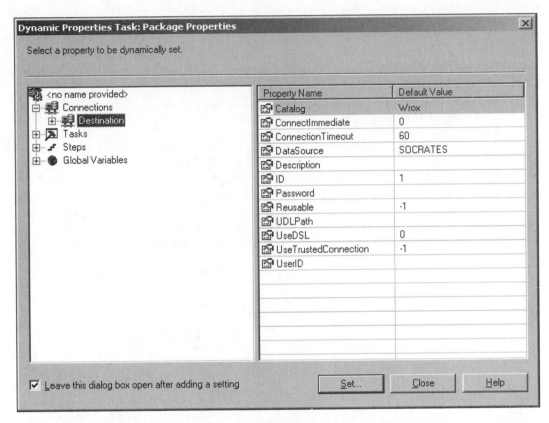

The next screen is the core of this task. By clicking on the Source combo box, you can choose to set your connection to one of the following options:

❑ **Global variable**. The most common way of setting properties dynamically, this method is easy to create and allows you to pass in parameters from outside the package. In a later example, we'll use this method of setting properties to pass in parameters using the Execute Package Task.

❑ **Constant**. Typically used to assign the default value of an item, such as DTSStepExecStat_Completed. This is one way of resetting a value back to the default settings after changing it in another task. The full list of constants and what they mean are shown in the following table:

Constant	Value	Description
DTSStepExecStat_Completed	4	Step execution completed
DTSStepExecStat_Inactive	3	Step execution inactive
DTSStepExecStat_InProgress	2	Step execution in progress
DTSStepExecStat_Waiting	1	Step is waiting to execute

❑ **INI file** – supports a single line property value. This is ideal if you have a program that already uses an INI file to set the program's values (like `ClientID`). This way, you can have one universal INI file that manages your program and your package.

❑ **Data file** – can support multiple lines, but lacks control. Data files are much more an "all-or-nothing" situation.

❑ **Query** that uses the first row returned. For that reason, it's recommended that you design your query in such a way that it only returns one row, like `count`, `sum`, or average queries. This method of setting a property is great when you'd like to retrieve meta-data about a client. For example, if you'd like to find out where the client's extract file is located at before a transformation. We did this before in the Execute SQL Task. By using this method, you may be able to skip that step and simplify your package by skipping global variables altogether.

❑ **Environment variable** from the System or User variables. These can be set in the Control Panel under **System**. Typical environment variables include COMPUTERNAME, TEMP, and PATH. For instance, you can use this method of setting properties to set the server name that you'd like to connect to the COMPUTERNAME environment variable.

For our example, we'll need to set this property to the global variable of **gvCatalog** as shown below:

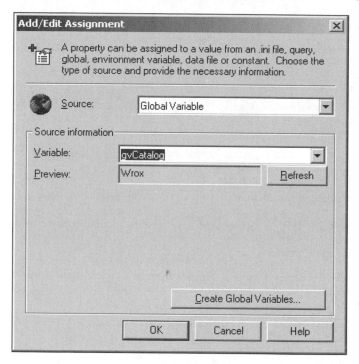

If you have not created the global variables, you can still do this without having to exit the task by clicking the **Create Global Variables…** button. After setting the variable, select **OK** to exit this screen.

Now that you've set the destination database, you'll now need to set which table the data is loaded into. You can do this by drilling down the **Tasks** tree and then selecting the **DTSTask_BulkInsertTask_1** as shown opposite above. You will then need to double-click in the right pane the **DestinationTableName** property to set it:

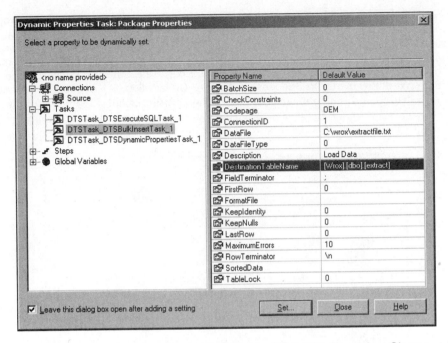

This time set the property to the global variable gvTable. Click OK, then select Close to take you back to the summary screen. The summary screen will display the two properties that you just set. To edit the properties after you've added them, simply double-click on the property you wish to edit:

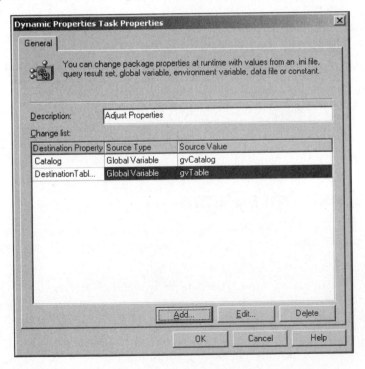

Your package is nearly complete. You now need to ensure that the steps execute in the proper order. For example, you want the Dynamic Properties Task to execute before you begin to insert data. Without these constraints the steps would all execute in parallel. You can set the order in which the steps execute by using precedence constraints. To set a precedence constraint, simply select the source step by clicking on a given task once, then, while holding the *Ctrl* key, select the second step. Then, you can select from the Workflow menu On Success, Failure, or Completion. We're going to use the On Success precedence constraint to make sure that the table is successfully created before we try to insert into it. You also need to create an On Success constraint between the Dynamic Properties Task and the Execute SQL Task. The final package should look like the following:

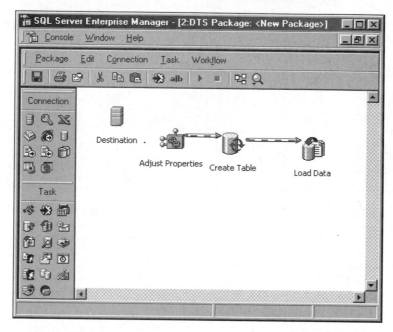

You're now ready to save and execute your package. By executing the package the first time, the data will be loaded into the Wrox database. You can then go and change the global variables of your package to insert into a different database and table, and execute the package again. You have now created your first dynamic package. You can call this from any application that is COM-compliant or through other packages using the ActiveX Scripting Task or the Execute Package Task.

The Multiphase Data Pump

In SQL Server 7.0, we only had one phase when we were transforming data – the Row Transform phase. Now the Row Transform phase has been broken into six functionally different phases to give us more flexibility and control.

Some of the added abilities given through the data pump additions are:

❑ **Transformation Extensibility**. The ability to add logic for your own custom error handling, initialize/free your own COM components, use other script-enabled technologies like ADO (ActiveX Data Objects) programming or perform disparate transformation steps, such as writing header records, rows and footer records.

- ❏ **Transformation Restartability**. The ability to maintain "success points" in your transformations, from which you can then restart from should a complete failure occur.

- ❏ **Data Cleansing** and **Data Awareness**. Provides a mechanism for us to deal with known errors and resubmit data; allows for us to keep accurate counters of the good and bad data, and the types of errors that occur.

Let's first take a look at a diagram of the new phases in SQL Server 2000:

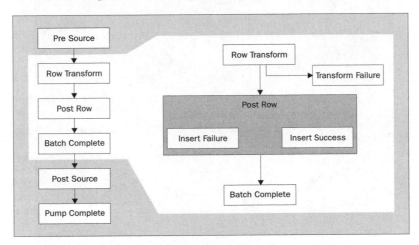

As mentioned and illustrated, there are six phases that comprise the multiphase data pump. The phases are:

- ❏ **Pre Source** – Phase executes only once at the beginning of the transformation. Functions that you script here execute before the first record is fetched from the source. Examples of how you could use this would be to initialize a COM object like ADO or to drop the indexes on the destination table before loading.

- ❏ **Row Transform** – Phase is carried over from SQL Server 7.0. This default phase will copy the records from source to destination.

- ❏ **Post Row Transform** – Phase is executed after each row is transformed. This phase is divided into three sub-phases: Transform Failure, Insert Success, and Insert Failure. Within these three sub-phases, we have the opportunity to address the quality of the data, correct data issues for the transform, maintain counters, and respond to the state of the individual row.

- ❏ **On Batch Complete** – Phase executes after each batch is committed. In DTS there is only one batch by default. Changing the batch size, for example to 50, will mean that the On Batch Complete phase will be called every 50 records. This can be reconfigured though under the Options tab in the Transform Data Task as shown overleaf:

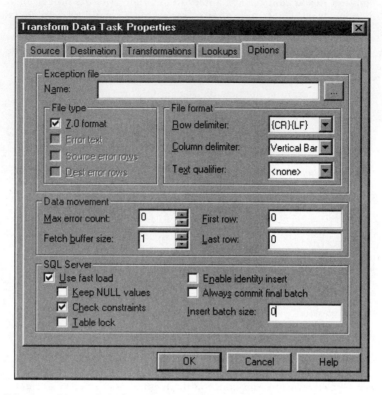

We will look at this more later in the chapter. One example use of this phase would be for auditing the state of a larger, multi-batch table load.

❑ **On Pump Complete** – Phase executes after all rows have been transformed. During this phase, we can perform non data-dependent tasks, like finalizing counter variables, capturing the final status of the pump, freeing memory associated with COM objects or other script-enabled technologies.

❑ **Post Source Data** – Phase executes after all rows are transformed but unlike the On Pump Complete phase, the Post Source Data phase can access data. This can be used to write footer rows to a file if needed or free up resources.

Enabling the Multiphase Data Pump

The multiphase data pump is disabled by default, because it makes your Transform Data task slightly more complex to create for the non-experienced user. You can enable the feature by going to Enterprise Manager and right-clicking on **Data Transformation Services**, and then selecting **Properties**. You will then be given the option to show the feature in DTS Designer:

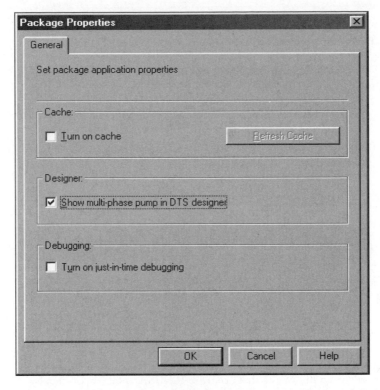

You may also see that you can turn on a few added features here as well. You can also enable DTS to cache packages in this dialog box. DTS is inherently slow when loading packages. One of the reasons for this is that DTS must make a call to the registry each time it opens a package to find out what OLE DB providers are registered to the computer. By enabling SQL Server to cache packages, DTS skips this step and increases your performance substantially.

You can also enable just-in-time debugging on this screen. The Turn on just-in-time debugging option provides you with the control to turn on and off the debugging of ActiveX script. When this option is turned on, DTS will give this information to the Microsoft Scripting Engine, which in turn will call upon one of the debuggers installed with Windows 2000, NT 4.0 Option Pack, or Visual InterDev 6.0, if an error arises. If you have more than one debugger installed, the feature will open whichever debugger you have installed last.

You will need to ensure that the multiphase pump in DTS Designer is turned on for our next example.

Multiphase Data Pump Example

Let's do a quick example using what we've just learned about the multiphase data pump. In this example, we'll log the number of successful batches and rows transformed. This type of example is perfect for those who are outputting this type of information to a GUI front end or logging it into the event log. To start the example, create two connections: one to the Northwind database called Source and one to the Wrox database called Destination. Create a Transform Data Task between the two connections you just created, as shown overleaf:

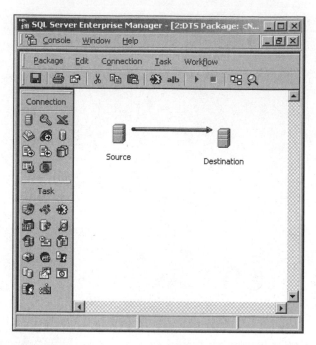

As you may remember from Chapter 22, you can double-click on the arrow joining the two connections to set the Properties of the Transform Data Task. Let's make things a little more interesting by only transforming records from the source that are from the USA. You can do this by selecting the SQL query radio box and then typing the query as shown below:

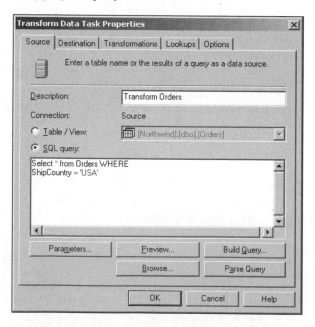

Proceed to the **Destination** tab and click on **Create...** This will provide you with the dialog box to create the **Orders** table in the **Wrox** database. Pay special attention to the table name, which by default is **New Table**. Change the default to **Orders** as shown below:

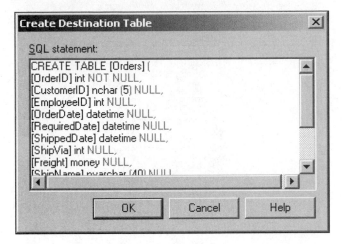

After clicking **OK**, you will be taken back to the original **Destination** tab, but it will now be filled with the proper data:

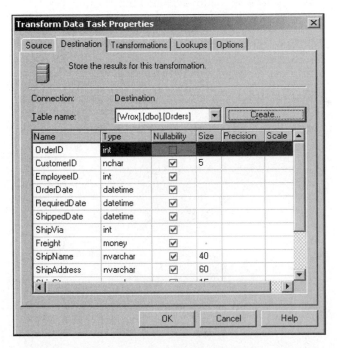

You're ready to proceed to the **Transformations** tab. DTS will automatically map the columns for you, as shown overleaf. This is mapped for the **Row** transform phase:

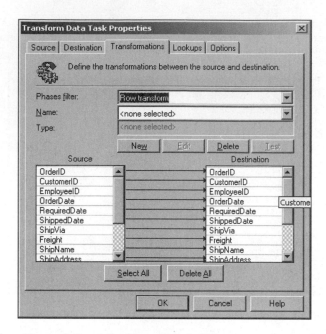

Before we create other phases, let's set the Insert Batch Size to something a little smaller. The batch size specifies the number of records before SQL Server commits these records to the destination. If you have millions of records, it is a good idea to set this to something other than 0. A setting of 0 means that SQL Server won't commit until all the records are written to the destination. A setting of 1 means that SQL Server will commit each record individually and not using a batch method. The batch size can be set on the Options tab – for our example, set the batch size to 50.

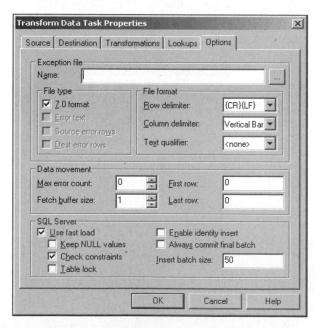

To create other phases, go back to the Transformations tab and select Insert success from the Phases filter drop-down box shown below. Then, click New:

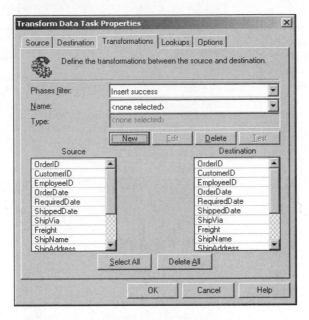

You are first asked what type of transformation you wish to create. We're going to create an ActiveX script to wrap around our current transformation. Select ActiveX Script and then click OK:

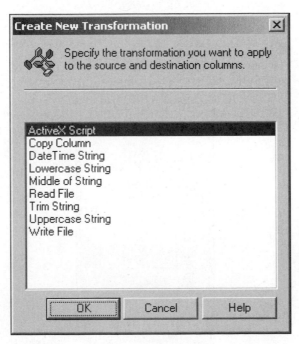

You are now taken to a screen that is not really applicable to our example. If you chose the Copy Column method of transferring data, then this would apply, as we'll show in the next section. For the purpose of our example, accept the defaults and click Properties...:

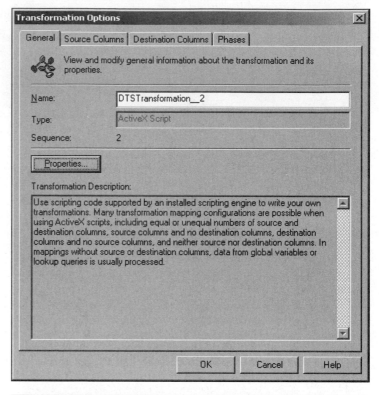

The next screen you'll be taken to is where you'd actually write your script. SQL Server installs VBScript and JScript. You can change what type of scripting language you write in by selecting the language from the language drop-down box. By default, VBScript is selected:

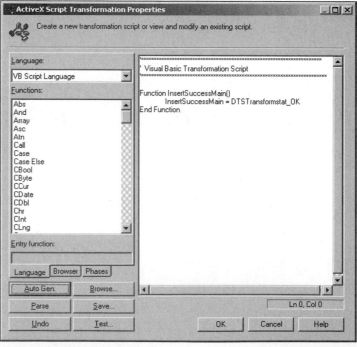

As you can see, the default code that is used for this function looks like the code below. All this code says is that the function has succeeded, by using the `DTSTransformstat_OK` constant. We will add more code in a moment to make the function do something.

```
Function InsertSuccessMain()
    InsertSuccessMain = DTSTransformstat_OK
End Function
```

You can click on the **Browser** tab to view a list of other constants for each DTS object as shown below:

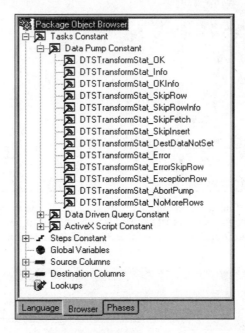

Next, click on the **Phases** tab to view which phases are currently active. As you can see overleaf, only the **On Insert Success** phase is active right now. The **InsertSuccessMain** option below the checkbox signifies which function will be the entry point when the phase is entered:

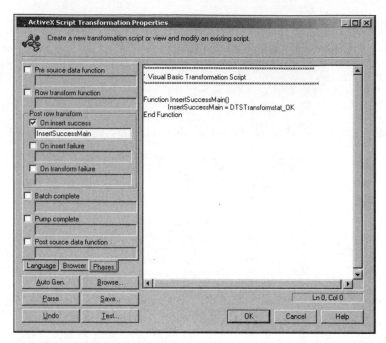

To activate the other phases that we'll use in this example, check the various phases. Check **Pre source data function**, **On insert success**, **On insert failure**, **Batch complete**, and **Pump complete**. You can then click **Auto Gen** to generate the base code for each function and automatically set the entry points as you can see below:

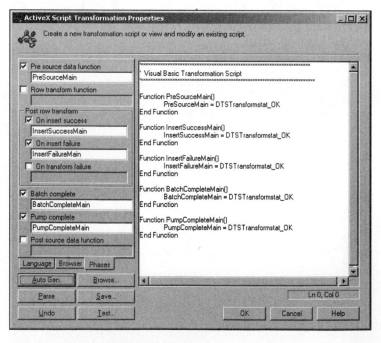

With the basics done, let's begin adding some code.

Pre Source Example

You may recall from our data pump diagram that the Pre Source phase is executed before any transformation occurs. This makes it the perfect place to reset our counters and declare variables. We will use the below code to set all the global variables to 0. When we set the value of any global variable that isn't created yet, it will create it temporarily at run time.

```
Function PreSourceMain()
    ' Sets all the counts to 0
    DTSGlobalVariables("gvRowSuccess").Value = 0
    DTSGlobalVariables("gvRowFailure").Value = 0
    DTSGlobalVariables("gvNumberofBatches").Value = 0
PreSourceMain = DTSTransformstat_OK
End Function
```

We will use these global variables to track how many batches completed and how many records succeeded and failed.

Insert Success Example

We will want to keep an accurate account of how many rows were successfully transformed. The Insert Success phase provides us with an excellent place to increment the counter by 1 each time the phase is raised. The code you can use to do this is below:

```
Function InsertSuccessMain()
    DTSGlobalVariables("gvRowSuccess").Value = _
    DTSGlobalVariables("gvRowSuccess").Value  + 1
    InsertSuccessMain = DTSTransformstat_OK
End Function
```

Insert Failure Example

As we want to know how many records were transformed, we also need to know how many failed. We can do this with almost the same code as we used before. We just change the global variable that's being affected:

```
Function InsertFailureMain()
    DTSGlobalVariables("gvRowFailure").Value = _
    DTSGlobalVariables("gvRowFailure").Value + 1
    InsertFailureMain = DTSTransformstat_OK
End Function
```

Batch Complete Example

You may recall that earlier in this example, we set the Insert batch size to 50. This breaks our 122 records into three separate batches that will process one after another. Why three batches? The last 22 records will create a partial batch. In the real world we would not lower our batch size depending on our data to such a number, but instead use a much higher value, like 100,000. We can use the On Batch Complete phase to report when we complete a batch as shown below:

```
Function BatchCompleteMain()
    DTSGlobalVariables("gvNumberofBatches").Value = _
    DTSGlobalVariables("gvNumberofBatches").Value +1
    BatchCompleteMain = DTSTransformstat_OK
End Function
```

Pump Complete Example

Lastly, we need to report to the client a final status. For our example, we'll use a simple MsgBox function to present a dialog box. In actuality, you may wish to report to the NT Event Log or e-mail yourself this message. The vbCrLf statement signifies to our MsgBox to use a carriage return:

```
Function PumpCompleteMain()
   MsgBox "Transformation Complete!" & vbCrLf & _
   "Batches: " & DTSGlobalVariables("gvNumberofBatches").Value  & vbCrLf & _
   "Successful Rows: " & DTSGlobalVariables("gvRowSuccess").Value & _
   vbCrLf & "Failed Rows: " & DTSGlobalVariables("gvRowFailure").Value
   PumpCompleteMain = DTSTransformstat_OK
End Function
```

The final code should look like that below:

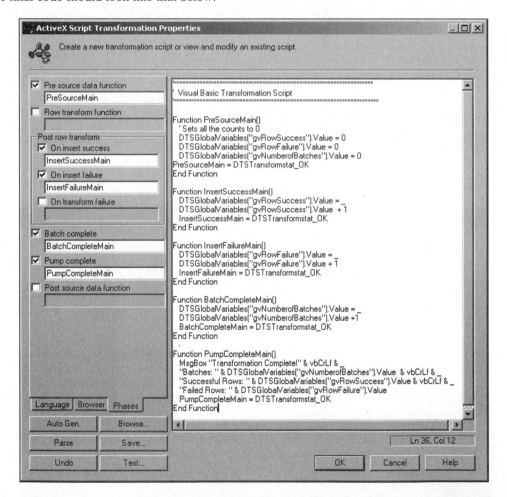

This code should generate a message box like the one below when we execute the package:

This was a simple example on how to use the multiphase data pump. We could become much more elaborate by adding objects to our code to send us a message about the success or failure of our transformation. We could also use this same type of system to clean records that have trouble transforming.

Optimizing Data Loads in DTS

It's important when loading your data to do it quickly. The more you incorporate DTS into your corporate data loading strategy, the more important each second you can save off a data load procedure becomes.

There are a number of tasks that you can use to load the data including the Transform Data Task, the Bulk Insert Task and the Data Driven Query Task. Just to quantify the speed of the various tasks, I loaded a flat file that contains a mailing list with 15,174 records with 30 columns a variety of ways. The same concepts that we discuss in this section would work among any type of data load generally. The first way I loaded the data from the flat file, was by using the Transform Data Task in a simple transformation as shown below:

Source Flat File   Destination

By default, DTS will automatically map the transformation for you between each pair of columns as shown overleaf. Each line represents a COM object that has to be created to transform the data. There is quite a bit of overhead generated to do this and, in our case, because of the number of columns. The number of COM objects is unnecessary as we will see in a moment, since everything maps perfectly. When loading a lot of data, make sure that you temporarily drop indexes on the destination table. When loading a small amount of data, you will not receive a benefit from this. After running this transformation that I just created we noted the time of 5 seconds.

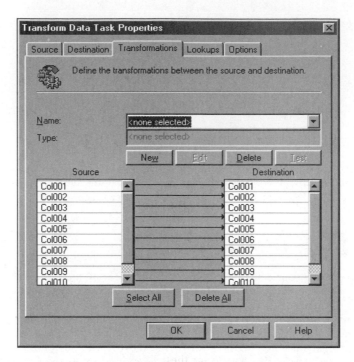

I also ran the same transformation using VBScript and noticed it took 13 seconds. The same transformation written in JScript took 19 seconds. The reason for this is that DTS is no longer using the optimized COM objects that it ships with. Instead it uses interpreted code that I created. Any added logic you place on DTS like this will slow it down further. For example, when I placed some VBScript logic in each field to make it upper case the transformation time of 13 seconds jumped to 24 seconds. If you need to perform custom logic like this, DTS in SQL Server 2000 ships with a number of predefined COM objects that can help perform actions like making a field uppercase.

When running the Import/Export Wizard I noticed that, no matter what type of transformation I selected (VBScript or Copy Columns), the transformation time was almost 50% of the previous transformation time. After saving a package and going to the transformation tab as shown below we can see why. DTS is optimizing itself to use only one COM object to transform all the data. If you're writing a package in the Designer you can do the same thing. Simply delete all the transformation lines and then create a new transformation that uses all the source columns as the source and all the destination columns for the destination. The result should look like this:

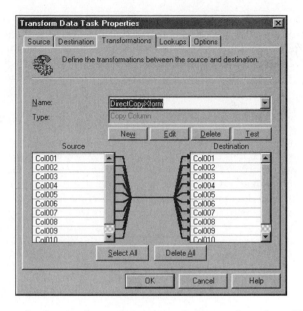

When I did this, the same basic transformation now took 3 seconds and my VBScript transformation took 8. You can also see in the chart below that the Bulk Insert Task was the fastest since no transformations occur in the task. The Bulk Insert Task only took DTS 2 seconds to execute. The chart below covers the results and the time it took for the records to transform for all transformations:

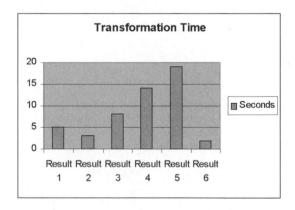

Result 1	Basic
Result 2	Sharing COM Transformation
Result 3	Sharing COM Transformation and VB
Result 4	VBScript for Each Transformations
Result 5	Jscript for Each Transformation
Result 6	Bulk Insert

As you can see, the Bulk Insert Task is much faster for loading data. However the limitations may outweigh any benefits from speed. For example, to use the Bulk Insert Task, the columns' schema on the source must exactly match the columns on the destination other than in length. A great alternative with decent speed is going to be the Transform Data Task when using one COM object. Other options like Fast Load under the Options tab can further increase performance of your data load since it bypasses triggers.

Summary

In this chapter we discussed some of the ways to make DTS much more powerful. We explored the Package object and how to call a DTS package from your applications using the LoadFromSQLServer and Execute methods. We talked about how to make a package dynamic using the Dynamic Properties Task and using the multiphase data pump to break your transformation into multiple phases. The multiphase data pump enabled us to track how many records we successfully transformed in our example. Lastly, we discussed how to optimize DTS transformations to speed up your movement of data. This is only the tip of the iceberg though! If you'd like more information on DTS, you can read *Professional SQL Server 2000 DTS* (Wrox Press, ISBN 1-861004-41-9), which is dedicated to this topic.

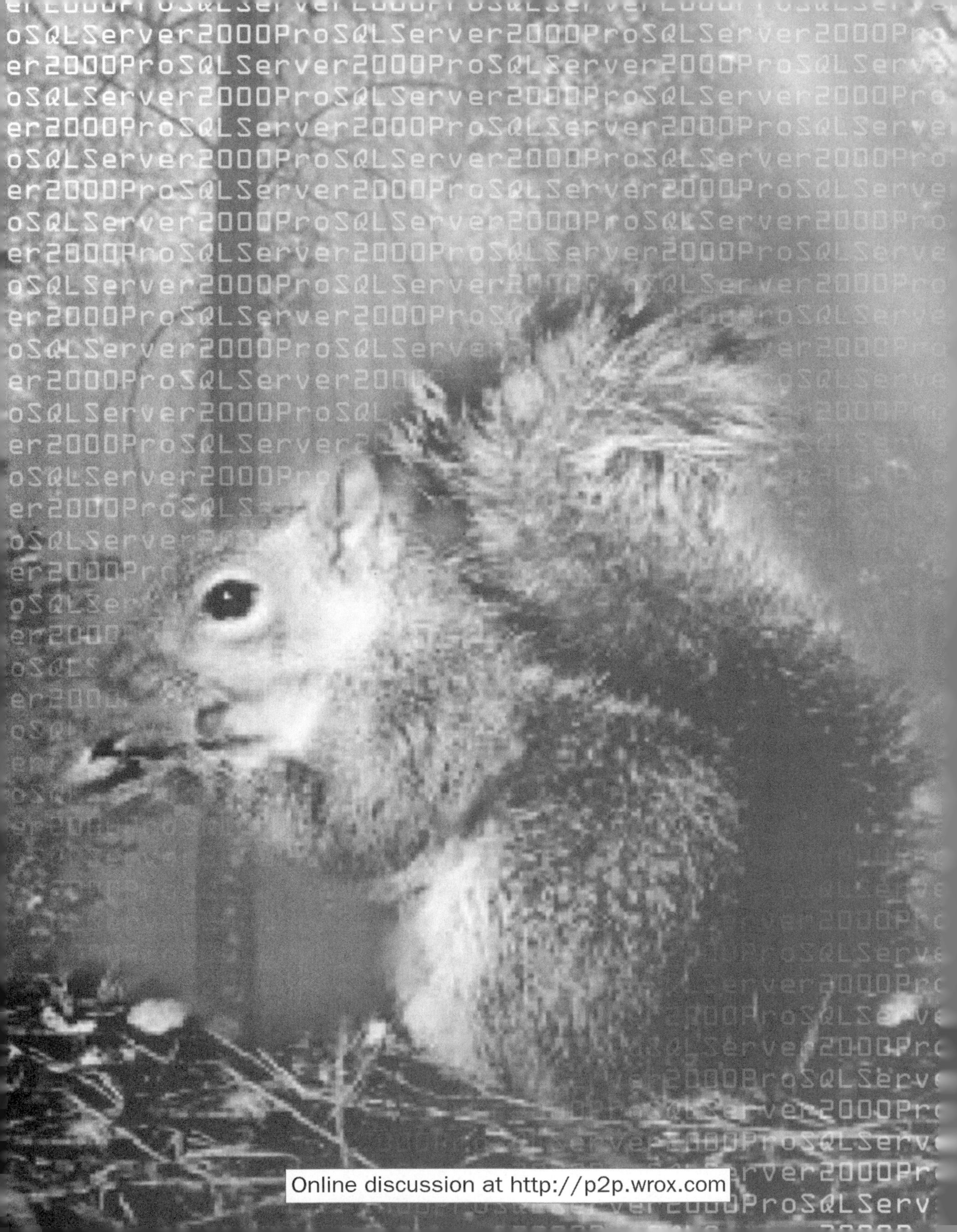
Online discussion at http://p2p.wrox.com

32

Scripting Administrative Functions with WMI

Administration of a SQL Server system is a key part of maintaining optimum performance and availability. SQL Server comes with an administrative user interface, the Enterprise Manager, for configuring service settings, managing databases, users, and so on. While the Enterprise Manager is a powerful tool, like most graphical interfaces, it is not a programmatic interface that can be used from scripts.

As any database administrator will confirm, being able to access management information through scripts, custom applications, or third-party management tools is essential to managing several servers. In addition, most databases are not stand-alone systems these days. Most are part of larger, distributed enterprise and web-based applications. As such, it is important to be able to monitor, configure, and control them as part of the larger system and not as a self-contained entity.

When not using the vendor-supplied tools such as Enterprise Manager, most database administrators use scripts based on the Windows Script Host (WSH) scripting languages to perform routine maintenance and administrative tasks. Scripting is usually easy to become familiar with quickly and provides a fast, flexible way of building custom tools for a variety of needs. With a scriptable interface for SQL Server, even relatively novice database administrators can create a library of useful tools for repetitive tasks and regularly scheduled operations. Additionally, if the scripting interface supports remote access, the management of many or all servers can be centralized and invoked from the database administrator's management console.

The History (and Future) of Scripting Administration for SQL Server

Starting with SQL Server 6.5, the way to manage the system was **SQL-DMO** (**Distributed Management Objects**). SQL-DMO is an object-oriented, COM-based interface for accessing management data about the SQL Server system. For each kind of managed entity in the system – such as databases, tables, users, stored procedures, and so on – it has an object defined which can be used to monitor the state of the entity, configure settings on it, and invoke administrative operations. In fact, the Enterprise Manager tool is built directly on top of the SQL-DMO interface, which will give you some idea of how much functionality is available through it. SQL-DMO is also scriptable and can, of course, be used from other programming languages like C++.

In SQL Server 2000, however, SQL-DMO is no longer the recommended approach to managing your SQL Server system. SQL-DMO is still part of the product and is fully compatible with the version shipped with SQL Server 7.0, but SQL Server 2000 introduces the option of managing the system using **Windows Management Instrumentation** (**WMI**). Moving forward, WMI will become the standard way to manage your databases so any new tools you build today should be based on the WMI interface rather than SQL-DMO. WMI does all that SQL-DMO is capable of and adds significant capabilities not available before, as well as strong integration with the management of the Microsoft Windows operating system itself.

Aside from the unique features that WMI brings to the table, there are a few reasons why SQL-DMO is being phased out in favor of WMI. All of these reasons were driven by customer feedback and the desire to improve the SQL Server administrator's experience when managing the system:

❑ In order to use SQL-DMO with your client application, the SQL-DMO libraries must be installed on the system with the client. This consumes system resources and can be inconvenient for administrators who wish to be able to access their data from any system.

❑ The SQL-DMO object model is very hierarchical. In order to access data about a column in a database table, the client application must first retrieve the SQL Server object, then the database object, the table object, and finally the column object of interest. This approach is obviously quite cumbersome and can make client applications or scripts larger and more complex.

❑ Since SQL-DMO objects are all COM objects, any additions made to SQL-DMO requires a new object to be created to ensure backwards compatibility. The downside of this requirement is that client applications will not be able to benefit from any of the new information being supplied without having to be written to the new object interface.

❑ Many of the features that needed to be delivered in the SQL-DMO object model were already available elsewhere in the system, including through WMI. For example, information about the computer, operating system, Windows NT services, and NT Event Log were all contained in SQL-DMO. As you might expect, WMI was chosen because it resolves all of these issues.

Windows Management Instrumentation

WMI is Microsoft's implementation of the **Web-Based Enterprise Management** (**WBEM**) standard, an industry-driven initiative sponsored by the Distributed Management Task Force (DMTF). Originally called WBEM for Windows, WMI is the Microsoft standard for managing Windows systems, applications, and networks. It ships as a standard part of current Windows operating systems, including Windows 2000 and Windows ME, and is available for previous versions of Windows as well.

The goal of the WBEM initiative is to use standard enterprise technologies to build scaleable, extensible, and object-oriented management systems. WMI is essentially the infrastructure required by client applications to get and set management data and raises events in response to changes in the system in a consistent, structured way. The structure of management data is defined using the **Common Information Model** (**CIM**), another standard overseen by the DMTF.

CIM is made up of classes, which are logical models of managed entities. For example, a class called "File" might model a file on your hard disk. This class would contain properties that describe useful attributes about the file such as its size, when it was created, and its name. The class might also define methods that allow operations to be performed on the file, such as copying it or compressing its contents. For each type of managed object, there is typically a class that models it in this fashion in the CIM model. Generically, these classes are referred to as a **schema**. This schema is not exactly the same as what you might be familiar with as far as a database schema is concerned, but there are certainly many parallels between them. The term schema here refers to the fact that these classes are based on a structured object model, in this case CIM.

The DMTF has defined a large body of basic schema for products to begin from. The figure below depicts how the schema that the DMTF has defined is structured. At the center of the picture is the Core Schema, which contains very simple, generic objects that all others are based upon. Built on these core classes are groups of classes for the various management domains, including applications, users, networks, and databases. CIM makes use of inheritance so that more specific classes can be derived from the general conceptual classes. Each schema area is developed within a technical working group of the DMTF. Typically, the working groups are made up of representatives from all the major operating system, hardware, and management tools vendors, including Microsoft, Sun Microsystems, Cisco, IBM, and Intel. Naturally, in order to build a model that works well for everyone, the classes in each management domain are vendor-neutral and contain no product-specific information. CIM is an extensible model, however, and encourages vendors to start with the standard DMTF schema and extend it to supply any additional information their products can provide.

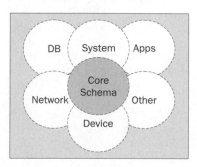

In most operating systems, you will find a large number of APIs for retrieving management data. Typically, these interfaces were built with a relatively narrow scope of requirements and did not attempt to be particularly consistent with those written before them for other parts of the system. For example, in Windows, accessing information about the NT Event Log uses a Win32 function call, but getting data about SQL Server uses a COM-based SQL-DMO function. There are, of course, many other ways data has to be retrieved from the system, including files, the Registry, and the Active Directory. Given this situation, client application writers have to be relatively knowledgeable about the different ways to access data from all these different sources, must write a lot of code to access all the different APIs, and cannot count on a lot of consistency in the way data is returned.

WMI makes use of the CIM model in order to bring consistency to the management data in the Windows system. It does so by modeling all managed objects as CIM-based classes and presenting a single, unified interface through which it is possible to retrieve information. The figure below shows how different client applications all communicate directly with WMI for management data. WMI, in turn, speaks to each of the managed systems (SQL Server, Active Directory, etc.) to get the requested information and return it to the clients. In this way, clients are effectively decoupled from the underlying interfaces each technology has made available. The clients only need to know how to interact with WMI. This is an extremely powerful concept since it allows script and application writers to treat disks, processes, databases, and event logs as objects that look and behave in similar ways:

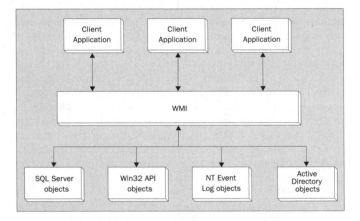

WMI Architecture

In order to make the most of WMI, it is helpful to understand a bit about its architecture. In the previous figure, we saw that WMI acts as an intermediary between clients and the data they seek. Within the WMI box are several components that fulfill this role as well as delivering value-added functions. In the figure opposite, you can see a more detailed version of WMI and how it relates to clients and managed systems:

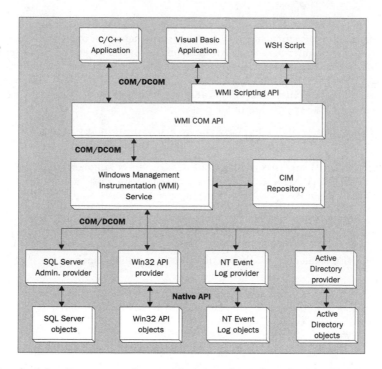

At the lowest level of the diagram are the actual managed systems. As noted before, most of these systems provide different ways for clients to manage them, including Win32 calls, COM interfaces, and so on. Directly above each of these systems is a box representing a **WMI provider**. Essentially, a WMI provider is a set of code that acts as an agent between the main WMI service and the managed system. The provider knows the intimate details of how to retrieve and write data to the managed system and how to receive events from it, if it supports events. When requests come through to the provider for information, it is responsible for gathering the needed data from the underlying system's API, converting it to the appropriate class object, and sending it back to the WMI service.

At the top of the diagram are the various types of clients that can communicate with WMI, including C/C++ applications, Visual Basic programs, and WSH scripts. In general, clients have no need to know about providers. They simply need to know what class they require and how to use the class to get their information. C/C++ clients can call the WMI COM interface, IWbemServices, directly. Visual Basic and script clients call the WMI Scripting layer, SWbemServices, which sits above the native COM interface.

In the center is the WMI service and the CIM repository. Class definitions are typically stored in the CIM repository but management data is not usually stored there. In other words, the definition of the "File" class mentioned earlier would be stored in the repository but the actual information about specific files on the system would not. When a request for a class comes in from a client, the WMI service first looks up the class name in the repository. If it is found, the provider responsible for supplying this class is determined from the class definition. The client request is then redirected to the appropriate provider for processing. When the provider returns the requested data, the WMI service passes it back to the requesting client.

The WMI service introduces several key features between the providers and clients. Since management clients need a consistent experience and way to request management data, WMI must ensure that, no matter what the underlying interfaces support, the client is always given the same set of services. With this in mind, WMI automatically supplies the following standard services:

❑ **Remoting**: All data available in WMI can be accessed remotely even if the native API that supplies it does not support remote access.

❑ **Scripting**: All data available in WMI can be accessed from any of the WSH scripting languages, even if the native API does not have automation support.

❑ **SQL Queries**: WMI supports a subset of the SQL query language called **WMI Query Language** (**WQL**). All data in WMI can be queried using SQL syntax to request the specific information of interest.

❑ **Eventing**: Most interfaces do not support notifications of when objects are created, modified, or deleted, or when other interesting events occur. Using WQL, clients can request specific events to be sent when any data in WMI changes in a way that matches the query. This is supported even if the native API has no internal eventing mechanism.

Note that, while management data can certainly be kept in the repository, most management information changes over time so it makes more sense to retrieve the information on-demand from the source when a client asks for it.

The Basics of WMI Objects

To get the most out of WMI when managing SQL Server, it is helpful to understand the various objects you will encounter, how they are related to one another, and how to use them in practical tasks. Virtually everything in WMI is an object with a well-defined structure. There are four major concepts to be aware of in WMI:

❑ Classes

❑ Instances

❑ Associations

❑ Namespaces

Classes

Classes are essentially the definition of what an object looks like. They don't represent a particular object but, rather, describe what an object of a given kind looks like. In many senses, they are the cookie cutter but not the cookie. Previously, we discussed the `File` class. This class describes the attributes of a file in the file system but does not contain any information about a specific file. In a WMI class definition, called **Managed Object Format** (**MOF**), the basic definition for a simple `File` class might look like the following:

```
Class File {

   [key,read]      String      Name;
   [read]          String      Extension;
   [read]          Uint32      FileSize;
   [read,write]    Boolean     Hidden;

};
```

This class has four properties of various data types, including the full name of the file (with its directory path), the file extension, the size of the file, and finally a Boolean value indicating whether the file is hidden in the file system. Additionally, you will see that each property is marked with an additional set of information in square brackets. These are referred to in CIM as **qualifiers**. Qualifiers can be used on classes, properties, and methods to provide additional useful information about the object. There are many standard qualifiers in CIM and WMI and some used specifically for the WMI SQL Server Administration provider.

The `read` and `write` qualifiers indicate whether or not a property can be read or written by a client application. In this class, all properties can be read but only the `Hidden` property can be changed. Whether or not a property can be written is driven by what is supported by the underlying technology and what the provider has been written to support. The `key` qualifier indicates that the property can be used to uniquely identify specific objects of this class. Here, the name of the file, including the full path to it in the directory structure, uniquely identifies the file; no other file can have this value for its `Name` property. Classes may have no `key` properties or they might have multiple `key` properties, depending on what is needed to uniquely describe a particular object of that class.

If this class supported methods, such as one to copy the file to a new file, it could be changed as follows:

```
Class File {

   [key,read]      String      Name;
   [read]          String      Extension;
   [read]          Uint32      FileSize;
   [read,write]    Boolean     Hidden;

   uint32 Copy([In] string FileName);
};
```

Now the class has a method called `Copy`, which takes a single input parameter (indicated by the `[In]` qualifier) – a string with the name of the file to be created. Note that there is no parameter for the name of the file to be copied from here, just the destination. The reason for this will be discussed in a moment. Methods can have any number of parameters, some being input parameters (as above), others being output parameters (indicated by an `[out]` qualifier). Output parameters are usually used to return useful information back to the caller. The method also sends back an integer return value indicating the success or failure of the method execution.

The CIM model makes heavy use of class inheritance, deriving specific classes from more general ones. The derived classes (referred to as **subclasses**) contain all the properties and methods of the **superclass** (the class they are derived from). The derived classes may also add properties and methods of their own to supply data about their objects. For example, the operating system page files are files in the file system, but have special properties that other files do not have. For example, page files have an initial size and a maximum size that they can take on. Most other files are not constrained in this way. As such, we can create a subclass of the `File` class above that uniquely describes the additional data known about page files:

```
Class PageFile : File  {

[read,write]      Uint32          InitialSize;
[read,write]      Uint32          MaxSize;

};
```

The first thing to notice is that the class is derived from the File class as part of the definition. It automatically gets all the properties and methods defined in File and any of its superclasses, if it had any. The PageFile class only needs to define the new information it will contain beyond what File already supplies.

Classes are the fundamental objects in WMI. Virtually everything you will do in WMI is based on classes or instances of classes.

Instances

Instances are the actual objects that classes describe. Whereas a class is the cookie cutter, the instance is the cookie. For our File class, an instance of this class would be the C:\MYFILE.TXT file on your hard drive. Instances of a class have all the properties defined in the class object and these properties typically contain values for that instance. MOF can be used to specify instances as well as classes. An instance of File for C:\MYFILE.TXT would look something like:

```
Instance of File {

    Name = "C:\\MYFILE.TXT";
    Extension = "TXT";
    FileSize = 278;
    Hidden = False;
};
```

Note that two backslashes are used in the file path since this is required by MOF to identify the backslash character. The important point here is that this is a particular instance of the class, containing data for the specific file. Also, since the Name property is the key, if a client tool asks for the instance of the File class with the Name property containing "C:\\MYFILE.TXT", WMI will return the exact instance shown above, since that is the only one that can match the request.

As for the Copy method defined in the class, when used it will be invoked from the instance object itself. Hence, the source file (the instance) is implicit and therefore only the destination filename needs to be provided in the method. WMI will know from the fact that you are calling the Copy method on the instance, which file you wish to copy from.

Associations

Associations are one of the more powerful concepts in WMI, and the WMI SQL Server Administration provider makes extensive use of them. In general, most objects do not live in isolation but are related to other objects in the system. For example, a database is related to many other objects in the system, not just in SQL Server itself but the operating system as well. Databases contain tables. Databases themselves are contained within an instance of SQL Server. Users are related to a database through the permissions they have to access the database. Databases make use of files in the file system to physically store the data they contain. There are many other similar relationships for objects in SQL Server and throughout a computer system.

The purpose of an association is to describe the relationship between two classes. Associations are classes themselves but they have properties that refer to other class instances. For the relationship between a database and tables, you would have classes called `Database`, `Table`, and `DatabaseTable`. The first two contain instances of the database and table respectively. However, the third class, `DatabaseTable`, would contain instances that show which tables are contained in which databases. A diagram of how these classes would relate to each other would look like this:

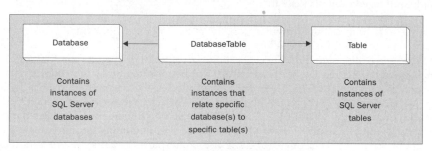

The arrows represent the references to instances of databases and tables. Any given database (for example, `Northwind`), may contain one or more tables (for example, `Customers`). For each table in the `Northwind` database, there will be an instance of `DatabaseTable` with appropriate references to the objects in `Database` and `Table`.

Associations effectively link related pieces of information. More importantly, WMI provides the necessary functionally to discover and traverse these relationships programmatically, enabling many useful management scenarios that were difficult or impossible before because the native API did not expose this data consistently. Finally, associations are not restricted to the boundaries of a given provider. For example, there is an association between the user accounts in SQL Server and the corresponding Windows user accounts. This association spans a class supplied by the WMI SQL Server Administration provider and a provider shipped as part of the Windows operating system. From a client perspective, this transition is transparent.

Associations are also not all the same in the type of relationships that they describe. Objects can be related to each other in different ways, including containment, dependency, and so on. For example, a database is conceptually a grouping of tables, the tables making up the whole of the database. Therefore, the association `DatabaseTable` in the previous example would identify the database instance as the object that groups the table instance. While this information is not necessary in order to use associations in your scripting, it is helpful to understand that the model not only indicates there is a relationship between two objects but also tells you what the relationship is and which role each object plays. We look at this information in more detail when we look at the SQL Server classes.

Namespaces

WMI partitions its data into logical groupings called **namespaces**. They are primarily used to put related information from a management domain in a single place and to avoid having an overwhelming number of classes in one place with no organization. There are several namespaces by default on a Windows 2000 system. The most well known of these is called `root/cimV2`. This namespace is defined as the place where classes reflecting information about the basic computer, and the operating system state and configuration, are kept. Most classes that would be of interest for general system management are stored in `root/cimv2`.

Since SQL Server is an additional product and not part of the basic operating system, its classes are stored in a separate namespace called `root/MicrosoftSQLServer`. From a user perspective, this has little impact other than that your tool or script needs to specify this namespace when initially connecting to WMI.

Installing the WMI SQL Server Administration Provider

The WMI SQL Server Administration provider is not installed as part of the standard SQL Server 2000 installation. Instead, it must be installed using a separate setup program located on the SQL Server 2000 CD in the `\x86\OTHER\wmi` folder. Run the `SETUP.EXE` file in this folder and the provider will be installed and configured on your system.

The provider setup will install the provider quickly and then exit. Unless there is an error, you will not get any further confirmation dialogs. When installed, the provider file (`SQLPROV.DLL`) will be placed in the `BINN` folder under the main SQL Server installation directory. The schema file (`SQLServer.MOF`) will also be located here. Samples for the provider will be installed under `DevTools\Samples\WMI` and the documentation file (`WMISQL.CHM`) will be installed in the `Books` folder, both under the main SQL Server installation directory. Finally, a link to the documentation is created in the Start menu under Microsoft SQL Server | WMI SQL Admin Provider. The documentation discusses the various features of the provider, explains how to use the provider, and contains a complete class references for all classes kept in the `root/MicrosoftSQLServer` namespace. You may read about the classes in the documentation or use the CIM Studio tool supplied in the WMI SDK to interactively browse classes and instances in WMI.

> *If you are installing on a Windows 98 or NT 4.0 system, the WMI core components must already be installed on the system to add and use the provider. The WMI core components and the WMI SDK may be freely downloaded from Microsoft at http://msdn.microsoft.com/downloads/sdks /wmi/default.asp. Both Windows 2000 and Windows ME have WMI included natively, so no additional WMI components need to be installed on these operating systems.*

The provider is also fully supported on SQL Server 7.0 installations as well as mixed SQL Server 7.0 and 2000 systems. There is no additional configuration necessary to use the provider with SQL Server 7.0. Simply install it on the server system where SQL Server is installed and start managing SQL Server!

The SQL Server Provider Schema

All of the classes that make up the SQL Server schema are stored in the `root\MicrosoftSQLServer` namespace. There are well over one hundred classes available for managing the SQL Server service, database, tables, stored procedures, and just about every other facet of the system. Each of these classes has a name that identifies what object it represents. In addition, the name of the class has a prefix that describes what overall schema it belongs to. The SQL Server classes are prefixed with `MSSQL_` to ensure it is clear that they represent objects for SQL Server. So, the class representing a database is called `MSSQL_Database`, tables are accessed via `MSSQL_Table`, and the association between these two classes is called `MSSQL_DatabaseTable`.

As you browse through the class reference for the provider in the SQL Server Administration provider documentation or look around the `root\MicrosoftSQLServer` namespace using CIM Studio, you will find that there are other classes in the namespace that are not prefixed with `MSSQL_`. Specifically you will find classes beginning with `CIM_` and `Win32_`. For example, the `CIM_LogicalElement` class is a standard CIM class defined by the DMTF. It is called an **abstract class** because it has no instances of its own. This class represents generic logical system objects and serves as a base class for many of the MSSQL classes. The `Win32_UserAccount` class, on the other hand, is a **concrete class** (meaning it is not abstract and can have instances) that is related to the `MSSQL_Login` class through an association. `Win32_UserAccount` contains instances of user accounts, as they are known by the Windows operating system. By linking this class with `MSSQL_Login`, which contains SQL Server user login information, it is possible to relate a given SQL Server user account with its Windows counterpart and vice versa.

There are several other CIM and Win32 classes within the SQL Server namespace. They are a mix of abstract and concrete classes. Some are association classes and some are not. You will find that most of these classes are being mirrored from the `root\cimv2` namespace by a special WMI provider called the **view provider**. This is done for convenience so that you can access all the classes relevant to SQL Server management in a single namespace. As you explore the SQL Server schema, you will see how these classes relate to SQL Server objects and provide you will valuable links between the database system and the operating system.

WMI SQL Server Administration Provider Schema Reference

The following tables contain descriptions of the more useful classes that the WMI SQL Server Administration provider supports. There are more classes that serve as base classes for other classes, but these are not included here, as they are not usually used directly. If you want to learn about all the classes, you can browse through detailed explanations in the provider documentation.

This table gives all the SQL Server instance classes in `root\MicrosoftSQLServer`. For each class name a description of what information the class represents is provided. In addition, if a class is abstract (meaning that it has no instances) it is marked with an X in the *Abstract* column:

Class Name	Description	Abstract
MSSQL_BackupHeader	Describes backup header information for a backup set.	X
MSSQL_BackupSetting	Describes settings for a backup operation.	
MSSQL_BulkCopyDevice	Describes settings for a bulk copy operation.	
MSSQL_CandidateKey	Describes a key that can uniquely identify a row in a table. Used as a base class for other key classes.	X
MSSQL_Check	Describes a SQL Server integrity constraint.	
MSSQL_Column	Describes a column in a SQL Server table.	
MSSQL_ConfigValue	Describes configuration settings for SQL Server.	
MSSQL_Database	Describes a SQL Server database.	
MSSQL_DatabaseFile	Describes a file that stores data for a SQL Server database.	
MSSQL_DatabaseRole	Describes a database role (security group).	
MSSQL_DatabaseSetting	Describes configuration settings for a SQL Server database.	
MSSQL_Default	Describes a SQL Server default.	
MSSQL_DRIDefault	Describes a SQL Server DRI default.	
MSSQL_ErrorLog	Describes a SQL Server error log.	

Table continued on following page

Class Name	Description	Abstract
MSSQL_ErrorLogEntry	Describes an entry in a SQL Server error log.	
MSSQL_FileGroup	Describes a SQL Server filegroup.	
MSSQL_ForeignKey	Describes a foreign key.	
MSSQL_FullTextCatalog	Describes a SQL Server full-text catalog.	
MSSQL_FullTextCatalog Service	Describes the SQL Server full-text catalog service.	
MSSQL_Index	Describes a SQL Server table index.	
MSSQL_IndexTable Information	Describes statistical information about a SQL Server table index.	
MSSQL_ IntegratedSecurity Setting	Describes Windows NT user security settings for WMI to use when communicating with SQL Server.	
MSSQL_Key	Describes keys for SQL Server tables. Serves as a base class for other key classes.	X
MSSQL_LanguageSetting	Describes localized date and day of the week settings for SQL Server.	
MSSQL_Login	Describes user authentication records for SQL Server.	
MSSQL_MediaHeader	Describes the header information present on physical media.	X
MSSQL_MethodRtnVal	Used to return detailed error information from method calls.	X
MSSQL_PrimaryKey	Describes a SQL Server primary key for a table.	
MSSQL_Process	Describes an internal process of SQL Server. Not necessarily the same as an operating system process.	
MSSQL_ProviderStatus	Used to return detailed WMI provider error information when an internal error occurs.	X
MSSQL_RegistrySetting	Describes settings for SQL Server stored in the system Registry.	
MSSQL_RestoreSetting	Describes settings for a restore operation.	
MSSQL_Rule	Describes a SQL Server data integrity rule.	
MSSQL_SQLServer	Describes the instances of SQL Server on the system.	

Class Name	Description	Abstract
MSSQL_SQLServer ConnectionSetting	Describes the connection parameters WMI should use when connecting to SQL Server.	
MSSQL_SQLServerRole	Describes a SQL Server role that is not limited to a single database.	
MSSQL_StoredProcedure	Describes a SQL Server stored procedure.	
MSSQL_StoredProcedure Parameter	Describes input/output parameters for a SQL Server stored procedure.	
MSSQL_SystemDatatype	Describes a SQL Server system-defined data type.	
MSSQL_Table	Describes a SQL Server table.	
MSSQL_TransactionLog	Describes a SQL Server database transaction log.	
MSSQL_TransferSetting	Describes settings for a transfer operation.	
MSSQL_Trigger	Describes a SQL Server trigger.	
MSSQL_UniqueKey	Describes a unique key in a SQL Server database.	
MSSQL_User	Describes a SQL Server database user.	
MSSQL_UserDatatype	Describes a SQL Server user-defined data type.	
MSSQL_UserDefined Function	Describes a SQL Server user-defined function.	
MSSQL_View	Describes a SQL Server view.	
CIM_DataFile	Describes a file on a disk drive.	
Win32_Group	Describes Windows NT group accounts.	
Win32_Process	Describes processes running on the system as seen by the Windows operating system.	
Win32_Service	Describes all Windows NT services installed on the system.	
Win32_UserAccount	Describes Windows NT user accounts.	

This table gives SQL Server association classes in root\MicrosoftSQLServer:

Class Name	Description
MSSQL_BaseDatatype	Describes the relationship between a system-defined and a user-defined data type.
MSSQL_ColumnDatatype	Describes the relationship between a column and its data type.
MSSQL_ColumnDefault	Describes the relationship between a column and a default.
MSSQL_ColumnDRIDefault	Describes the relationship between a column and a DRI default.
MSSQL_ColumnRule	Describes the relationship between a column and a rule.
MSSQL_DatabaseCandidate Key	Describes the relationship between a database and a candidate key.
MSSQL_DatabaseDatabase Role	Describes the relationship between a database and a database role.
MSSQL_DatabaseDatabase Setting	Describes the relationship between a database and its settings.
MSSQL_DatabaseDatatype	Describes the relationship between a database and the data types it defines.
MSSQL_DatabaseDefault	Describes the relationship between a database and the defaults it defines.
MSSQL_DatabaseFileData File	Describes the relationship between a database file and the equivalent operating system file.
MSSQL_DatabaseFileGroup	Describes the relationship between a database and the filegroup that contains its data.
MSSQL_DatabaseFullText Catalog	Describes the relationship between a database and a full-text catalog.
MSSQL_DatabaseLogin	Describes the relationship between a database and a login for a user in the database.
MSSQL_ DatabaseOwnerLogin	Describes the relationship between a database and the login for the owner of the database.
MSSQL_DatabaseRole DatabasePermission	Describes the access permissions a database role has for a database.
MSSQL_ DatabaseRoleStored ProcedurePermission	Describes the access permissions a database role has for a stored procedure.
MSSQL_DatabaseRoleTable Permission	Describes the access permissions a database role has for a table.

Class Name	Description
MSSQL_DatabaseRoleUser DefinedFunction Permission	Describes the access permissions a database role has for a user-defined function.
MSSQL_DatabaseRoleView Permission	Describes the access permissions a database role has for a view.
MSSQL_DatabaseRule	Describes the relationship between a database and a rule it defines.
MSSQL_DatabaseStored Procedure	Describes the relationship between a database and a stored procedure it defines.
MSSQL_DatabaseTable	Describes the relationship between a database and a table.
MSSQL_Database TransactionLog	Describes the relationship between a database and a transaction log.
MSSQL_DatabaseUser	Describes the relationship between a database and a user.
MSSQL_DatabaseUser DefinedFunction	Describes the relationship between a database and a user-defined function it defines.
MSSQL_DatabaseView	Describes the relationship between a database and a view it contains.
MSSQL_DBMSObjectOwner	Describes the relationship between a database object and the user that owns it.
MSSQL_ErrorLogDataFile	Describes the relationship between a SQL error log file and the equivalent operating system file.
MSSQL_ ErrorLogErrorEntry	Describes the relationship between a SQL error log file and the error entries the log contains.
MSSQL_FileGroupDatabase File	Describes the relationship between a database filegroup and the database files it contains.
MSSQL_FullTextWin32 Service	Describes the relationship between the SQL Server full-text service and the equivalent Windows NT service.
MSSQL_IndexColumn	Describes the relationship between an index and a column.
MSSQL_IndexFileGroup	Describes the relationship between an index and the filegroup that stores it.
MSSQL_IndexStatistics	Describes the relationship between an index and statistics about the index.
MSSQL_KeyColumn	Describes the relationship between a key and a column.
MSSQL_KeyFileGroup	Describes the relationship between a key and the filegroup that stores it.

Table continued on following page

Class Name	Description
MSSQL_LoginDefault Database	Describes the relationship between a login and its default database.
MSSQL_LoginWin32Group	Describes the relationship between a SQL Server login and the Windows group account it belongs to.
MSSQL_LoginWin32User	Describes the relationship between a SQL Server login and the equivalent Windows user account.
MSSQL_ MemberDatabaseRole	Describes the relationship between two database roles where one is a member of the other.
MSSQL_MemberLogin	Describes the relationship between a database role and a SQL Server login that is a member of the role.
MSSQL_MemberUser	Describes the relationship between a database role and a SQL Server user that is a member of the role.
MSSQL_ReferencedKey	Describes the relationship between a candidate key and a foreign key.
MSSQL_ReferencedTable	Describes the relationship between a foreign key and a table.
MSSQL_SQLServerBackup Device	Describes the relationship between a SQL Server installation and backup devices it is aware of.
MSSQL_SQLServerConfig Value	Describes the relationship between a SQL Server installation and its configuration settings.
MSSQL_SQLServerDatabase	Describes the relationship between a SQL Server installation and databases it contains.
MSSQL_SQLServerErrorLog	Describes the relationship between a SQL Server installation and the error logs it uses.
MSSQL_SQLServer IntegratedSecurity Setting	Describes the relationship between a SQL Server installation and the security settings used when interacting with WMI.
MSSQL_SQLServerLanguage Setting	Describes the relationship between a SQL Server installation and its current language settings.
MSSQL_SQLServerLogin	Describes the relationship between a SQL Server installation and the SQL Server logins it defines.
MSSQL_SQLServerRegistry	Describes the relationship between a SQL Server installation and its Registry settings.
MSSQL_SQLServerServer Role	Describes the relationship between a SQL Server installation and the security roles it contains.
MSSQL_ SQLServerSQLServer ConnectionSetting	Describes the relationship between a SQL Server installation and the connection settings used by the WMI provider.

Class Name	Description
MSSQL_SQLServerUser	Describes the relationship between a SQL Server installation and SQL Server users.
MSSQL_StoredProcedure StoredProcedure Parameter	Describes the relationship between a stored procedure and parameters used by the stored procedure.
MSSQL_TableCheck	Describes the relationship between a table and the checks it uses.
MSSQL_TableColumn	Describes the relationship between a table and the columns it contains.
MSSQL_TableFileGroup	Describes the relationship between a table and the filegroup that stores it.
MSSQL_TableIndex	Describes the relationship between a table and an index.
MSSQL_TableKey	Describes the relationship between a table and a key.
MSSQL_ TableTextFileGroup	Describes the relationship between a table and the filegroup that stores text data in the table.
MSSQL_TableTrigger	Describes the relationship between a table and a trigger.
MSSQL_ TransactionLogDataFile	Describes the relationship between a transaction log and the equivalent operating system file.
MSSQL_UserDatabase Permission	Describes the access permissions a user has for a database.
MSSQL_UserDatatype Default	Describes the relationship between a user-defined data type and a default.
MSSQL_UserDatatypeRule	Describes the relationship between a user-defined data type and a rule.
MSSQL_UserLogin	Describes the relationship between a user and a login record.
MSSQL_UserStored ProcedurePermission	Describes the access permissions a user has for a stored procedure.
MSSQL_UserTable Permission	Describes the access permissions a user has for a table.
MSSQL_UserUserDefined FunctionPermission	Describes the access permissions a user has for a user-defined function.
MSSQL_ UserViewPermission	Describes the access permissions a user has for a view.
Win32_GroupUser	Describes the relationship between a Windows user account and a Windows group account.

Connecting to WMI

The essential first step in starting to write scripts for WMI is connecting to its service on the system you wish to manage. To do so, you simply connect to the server and namespace you are interested in using the SWbemLocator object in the WMI scripting layer. Below is an example of connecting to WMI on the local machine and the root\CIMv2 namespace.

> **Virtually all the following samples can be put in a text file, saved with a .VBS extension, and used from the command line interface or by double-clicking in the graphical user interface. Since many of them can return relatively large sets of data, it is *highly recommended* that you use the command line approach (for example, CSCRIPT MyScriptName.VBS) unless you like clicking "OK" on a lot of dialog boxes. Moreover, in many cases you will need to change the values of parameters to match the names on your system.**

The first step is to get an object for the Wbemscripting.SWbemlocator interface to access the WMI scripting layer. Next, this locator object is used to connect to the WMI service on the specified machine and namespace, here the local (".") machine and root\CIMv2. The result of the ConnectServer call is an SWbemServices object, which gives us general access to the WMI objects in that namespace:

```
' Get the WMI scripting locator object
Set ObjLocator = CreateObject("Wbemscripting.SWbemlocator")

' Connect to the local system, root\CIMv2 namespace
Set ObjServices = ObjLocator.ConnectServer(".", "root\CIMv2")
```

Since WMI is fully remotable, the ConnectServer call can be easily changed to connect to a machine other than the one you are physically logged in to. If you have a machine named MyServer, the second line of the script can be modified as follows to redirect the request to that machine:

```
' Connect to the MyServer system, root\CIMv2 namespace
Set ObjServices = ObjLocator.ConnectServer("MyServer", "root\CIMv2")
```

In order to get to pick a different namespace like root\MicrosoftSQLServer on MyServer, modifying this same line brings about the desired result:

```
' Connect to the MyServer system, root\MicrosoftSQLServer namespace
Set ObjServices = ObjLocator.ConnectServer("MyServer", "root\MicrosoftSQLServer")
```

So far we have seen the longhanded way of connecting to WMI through a script. Using monikers, it is possible to combine these lines into a single statement. To connect to the local system and root\CIMv2, the next script sample can be used:

```
Set ObjServices = GetObject("winmgmts:\\.\root\CIMv2")
```

The end result is exactly the same as the longhand approach. The ObjServices variable will contain an SWbemServices object that can be used to execute WMI requests. The name, winmgmts, takes the place of getting the scripting service object. The rest of the string provided to the GetObject call is simply a URI to the machine and namespace desired. There are some limitations to using this shorthand since the ConnectServer call supports several optional parameters, for specifying things like the username and password to use when connecting, which are not available here. Still, the shorthand can be very convenient and compact for simple scripts.

A Few Notes on Security

In order to ensure that any user is given access to only the data they are allowed to see, WMI uses **COM impersonation**. The impersonation level you specify determines how COM represents you on remote systems. By default, WMI uses the `Impersonate` level of impersonation, meaning it tells the remote system to use your current security credentials when making any calls to get information. Essentially, this makes it possible for the remote system to impersonate you as if you were physically logged in there. There are two levels of impersonation below `Impersonate` and one above, as shown in the table below:

Name	Value	Definition
`Anonymous`	1	Hides the credentials of the caller. This level is not recommended, as most WMI providers will not accept this level of impersonation.
`Identify`	2	Allows objects to query the credentials of the caller. This level is not recommended, as most WMI providers will not accept this level of impersonation.
`Impersonate`	3	Allows objects to use the credentials of the caller. This is the most common minimum supported impersonation level by providers and is recommended for all operations with the WMI SQL Server Administration provider.
`Delegate`	4	Delegation mode is used when the remote machine needs to contact a third machine to get information for the caller. There are no calls for the WMI SQL Server Administration provider that require delegation.

In general, with WMI you should simply use the default of `Impersonate` mode, as virtually all providers require this as a minimum. Anything less than this would not provide enough security to ensure that the caller had access to the data being requested. Delegation mode is used when the caller is on one machine, and information needs to come from another remote system. Passing credentials to this additional machine requires additional security measures, which are not allowed under the `Impersonate` level. However, the WMI SQL Server Administration provider has no data that it retrieves from remote systems. All the data available through it is locally stored. Hence, there is no reason to use `Delegate` mode.

Since `Impersonate` mode is the default for WMI version 1.5, the version shipped as part of Windows 2000 and for other platforms, it is not necessary to specify the impersonation level. However, if you want to do so, you may set the value after connecting to the remote system with the `ConnectServer` call, like so:

```
' Get the WMI scripting locator object
Set ObjLocator = CreateObject("Wbemscripting.SWbemlocator")

' Connect to the MyServer system, root\CIMv2 namespace
Set ObjServices = ObjLocator.ConnectServer("MyServer", "root\CIMv2")

' Set the impersonation level to 'impersonate'
ObjServices.Security_.ImpersonationLevel = 3
```

> The WMI object model is much too complex for us to discuss completely in this chapter. If you want to get a full definition of the properties and methods of all of the objects, please refer to the WMI SDK documentation.

The shorthand approach we saw earlier becomes more useful in this situation since we can integrate the impersonation level setting into it, combining three lines into one, as follows:

```
Set ObjServices = _
    GetObject("winmgmts:{impersonationLevel=impersonate}\\MyServer\root\CIMv2")
```

Once you have connected to WMI, you may then start requesting instances and events. The next sections will walk you through each kind of operation.

Instance Retrieval Operations

WMI supports several different mechanisms for accessing data from SQL Server and any other data it supplies. Which of these mechanisms you use depends upon what you are trying to achieve and how your application or script is designed. The following table describes the three main ways of getting instance data:

Function	SWbemServices Method	Description
Enumerating all instances	InstancesOf	Retrieve all instances of a given class
Getting a specific instance	Get	Retrieve a particular instance by supplying its key values
Querying for instances	ExecQuery	Retrieve all instances that match a supplied WQL query

Enumerating All Instances

An easy place to begin getting WMI data is by **enumerating** a class. Enumeration simply means you want to get back all the instances of a given class. For example, to get all the instances for the disks you see in your Windows Explorer user interface, you can enumerate the Win32_LogicalDisk class in the root\CIMv2 namespace using the InstancesOf method:

```
' Get the WMI scripting locator object
Set ObjLocator = CreateObject("Wbemscripting.SWbemlocator")

' Connect to the local system, root\CIMv2 namespace
Set ObjServices = ObjLocator.ConnectServer(".", "root\CIMv2")

' Ask for all the instances of disks on the system
Set DiskSet = ObjServices.InstancesOf("Win32_LogicalDisk")

' Loop through each disk in the set of instances and print its name
For Each Disk in DiskSet
    Wscript.echo Disk.DeviceID
Next
```

The first few lines are the familiar statements needed to connect to the local WMI service. Once the SWbemServices object is retrieved, the script can invoke the InstancesOf method, passing in the name of the desired class, Win32_LogicalDisk. That's really all there is to it! The rest of the script loops through the instances that come back and prints data from them. For each disk object that is returned, we can reference the properties in it directly using standard dot notation. Here, the DeviceID property (which contains the drive letter of the disk instance) is retrieved from the instance but it is just as simple to ask for the total space, free space, drive volume name, or any of the other properties this class can supply.

As with the basic connect operation, shorthand can be used to combine some of the steps into fewer lines. Here, the script does the same thing but the connection step has been compressed into a single line:

```
' Get the WMI scripting locator object
Set ObjServices = GetObject("winmgmts:\\.\root\CIMv2")

' Ask for all the instances of disks on the system
Set DiskSet = ObjServices.InstancesOf("Win32_LogicalDisk")

' Loop through each disk in the set of instances and print its name
For Each Disk in DiskSet
    Wscript.echo Disk.DeviceID
Next
```

We can go further, however, and really reduce the amount of steps by asking for everything at once. The next example integrates the connection process with the request for the instances:

```
' Ask for all the instances of disks on the system
Set DiskSet = _
    GetObject("winmgmts:\\.\root\CIMv2").InstancesOf("Win32_LogicalDisk")

' Loop through each disk in the set of instances and print its name
For Each Disk in DiskSet
    Wscript.echo Disk.DeviceID
Next
```

There are some semantics about InstancesOf that you should be aware of – when you ask for all instances of a given class that means all instances available on the machine. For a class like Win32_LogicalDisk this is perfectly fine on most systems, since you will not typically find a large number of disks on any given system. The same meaning applies for classes that might have very large numbers of instances, such as MSSQL_Table. When enumerating MSSQL_Table you are asking for all instances of *all* tables in *all* databases. On SQL Server 2000, where multiple copies of SQL Server may be running in parallel at once, enumeration will span all of these copies as well, potentially leading to a very large number of instances. Right after installing SQL Server without adding any new tables, a system can already have 300 or more table instances present. Being able to retrieve all this information in a single request is a very powerful concept but must be used wisely so you do not inadvertently and unnecessarily burden the system. The following script retrieves all the instances of MSSQL_Table to demonstrate this issue:

```
' Get the WMI scripting locator object
Set ObjServices = GetObject("winmgmts:\\.\root\MicrosoftSQLServer")

' Ask for all the instances of tables on the system
Set TableSet = ObjServices.InstancesOf("MSSQL_Table")

' Loop through each table in the set of instances and print its name
' and number of rows
For Each Table in TableSet
    Wscript.echo Table.Name, Table.Rows
Next

' Print how many instances of tables were in the set we got back
Wscript.echo "Total number of tables = ",TableSet.Count
```

Notice that the script connects to root\MicrosoftSQLServer as this is where you will find all the SQL Server management classes. We specified MSSQL_Table in the InstancesOf call and the script loops through the returned instances again. The script prints both the name of the table instance and the number of rows the table currently has from the data in the instance. After printing all the table information, the script uses the Count property on the instance object set, TableSet, to display how many instances were returned. You can use this standard property for any set of instances returned from InstancesOf and similar methods.

If you run this example, you will see how many instances you might get for a class like MSSQL_Table. The result set may grow by an order of magnitude or more if you try a class like MSSQL_Column instead. My intent here is not to discourage the use of InstancesOf but to point out that it should be used with care. Rarely is it really necessary or desirable to enumerate all instances of a class like this, however. Most applications and scripts have a more specific purpose in mind when retrieving data and can identify specifics about what they are looking for, which will significantly reduce the result set. The following two ways of accessing instance data are intended to provide the mechanisms to do just this.

Getting a Specific Instance

As described earlier, the key qualifier is used to distinguish the properties that are used to uniquely identify instances. For the disk drive example used above, the key property of Win32_LogicalDisk is the DeviceID property, which contains the letter designation of the drive (A:, C:, etc.). No drives can have the same letter assigned to them, so each instance will be unique, based upon this property alone. For some classes, more than one key property may be needed to uniquely identify instances. For example, databases on SQL Server 2000 (which can have multiple running copies) are uniquely identified by two key properties, the name of the database and the SQL Server instance the database resides in. If databases were only keyed on the name of the database, there would be no way to ensure there is only one instance that matches. When a request comes in for the Northwind database and there are instances using this name in two different SQL Server copies on the same system, which would be the right one to pick? For this reason, key properties must remove all ambiguity and ensure a given set of key values will identify at most one instance of that class.

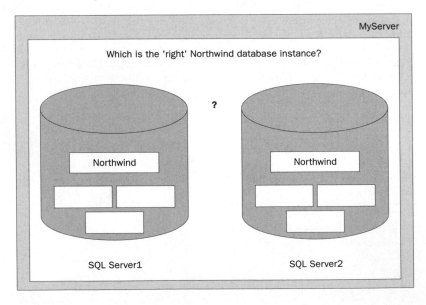

All this means that there is a need to find a way to ask for a specific instance. This allows a script that knows what data it is looking for to avoid enumerating all instances of the class just to get one. To retrieve a single instance, the following script uses the Get method on SWbemServices:

```
' Get the WMI scripting locator object
Set ObjServices = GetObject("winmgmts:\\.\root\CIMv2")

' Ask for the disk instance that has C: for its DeviceID (key)
Set Disk = ObjServices.Get("Win32_LogicalDisk.DeviceID='C:'")

' Print the name of the instance returned
Wscript.echo Disk.Name
```

The input parameter to Get is a WMI object path, essentially the name of the class and the key information for the instance. This object path indicates we want the instance of Win32_LogicalDisk with a key value (the DeviceID property) containing C:.

For classes where there is only a single key property, we can also abbreviate the notation to eliminate the key property name since it is implicit:

```
' Get the WMI scripting locator object
Set ObjServices = GetObject("winmgmts:\\.\root\CIMv2")

' Ask for the disk instance that has C: for its DeviceID (key)
Set Disk = ObjServices.Get("Win32_LogicalDisk='C:'")

' Print the name of the instance returned
Wscript.echo Disk.Name
```

Only one instance at most will be returned so the For...Next loop has been removed. Note that it is possible for no instances to be returned if the key value specified is not valid on the system. If you ask for drive T: and there is no drive with that designation on the system, WMI will return an error message letting you know you have asked for a nonexistent object.

Dealing with classes with multiple key properties is a breeze at this point since we just extend the object path with the additional key values. To get an instance of the Northwind database from the MSSQL_Database class, we need to give the name of the database and the SQL Server to which it belongs. If the name of the desired SQL Server was SQLServer1, the script would look like this:

```
' Get the WMI scripting locator object
Set ObjServices = GetObject("winmgmts:\\.\root\MicrosoftSQLServer")

' Ask for the database instance called Northwind in SQLServer1
Set Database = _
  ObjServices.Get("MSSQL_Database.SQLServerName='SQLServer1',Name='Northwind'")

' Print the name and SQL version compatibility level of the instance returned
Wscript.echo Database.Name, Database.CompatibilityLevel
```

Just like the disk example, the script requests an object path containing the class name and the key property values. Be aware that WMI can be very picky about the syntax of object paths; an extra space character in the path can cause the path to be considered invalid or the object to not be found. It also should be noted that the order that the key properties are listed in the object path is not important and that the values specified for them are case-insensitive. This is true in general for all WMI classes, not just those for SQL Server. The following will return exactly the same number of instances as the last script:

1195

```
' Get the WMI scripting locator object
Set ObjServices = GetObject("winmgmts:\\.\root\MicrosoftSQLServer")

' Ask for the database instance called Northwind in SQLServer1
Set Database = _
    ObjServices.Get("MSSQL_Database.Name='nOrThWiNd',SQLServerName='sqlSERVER1'")

' Print the name and SQL version compatibility level of the instance returned
Wscript.echo Database.Name, Database.CompatibilityLevel
```

Naturally, just like the `InstancesOf` examples, `Get` calls can be reduced to a single line of script although that line does start getting long with the object path added to it:

```
' Ask for the database instance called Northwind in SQLServer1
Set Database = GetObject("winmgmts:\\.\root\MicrosoftSQLServer:MSSQL_Database." _
              & "SQLServerName='SQLServer1',Name='Northwind'")

' Print the name and SQL version compatibility level of the instance returned
Wscript.echo Database.Name, Database.CompatibilityLevel
```

Using `Get` to retrieve particular instances can result in very substantial savings both in processing and network overhead. It is obviously a better idea to ask for the instance you need rather than asking for 100 instances and throwing away all but the one you need. If you know the instance of interest, using `Get` is a good answer but it does not solve every problem. If you only have *some* of the key values or are looking to get instances based on criteria not contained in the keys, `Get` will not suffice. This leads to the next way of accessing instances: queries.

Querying for Instances

WMI includes a subset of SQL called the WMI Query Language (WQL). Using this language, we can submit queries to retrieve data from WMI classes in a very similar fashion to how we would for a SQL Server table. WQL queries take the general form of:

SELECT *<properties>* FROM *<class>* WHERE *<condition>*

For example, to request all stored procedure instances, the query would be something simple like:

```
SELECT * FROM MSSQL_StoredProcedure
```

Throughout this book we've tried to avoid using the asterisk in `SELECT` statements, as it is usually not necessary to get all columns in a table. In WMI, we can identify specific properties we wish to retrieve as well. In most cases, classes have been query-optimized to take advantage of such requests where possible, so asking for a limited set of properties can also result in better performance. To select just the `StartUp` property (which identifies if a stored procedure is run when SQL Server starts), the following WQL query can be used:

```
SELECT StartUp FROM MSSQL_StoredProcedure
```

The instances returned from this query will only contain the `StartUp` property and the key properties populated. The keys will always be populated whether they are specified in the query or not, since the instance would be of little value without this information.

Now that we've demonstrated how to limit the set of properties returned, the next query optimization to look at adding is the WHERE clause, which allows the number of instances returned to be reduced. To limit the previous query to only those stored procedures that have a Type property set to 1 (standard), it can be modified as follows:

```
SELECT StartUp FROM MSSQL_StoredProcedure WHERE Type=1
```

As expected, the result set that you will get from this query will only contain instances that have the Type property set to 1. Just like any other SQL query, you may also add more conditions on the end of this query, use inequality statements, and so on. This power and flexibility makes the query interface extremely valuable and really is the only mechanism you need for instances since it can do all the same things that Get and InstancesOf can do.

For example, the first InstancesOf example enumerated all instances of Win32_LogicalDisk, retrieving all properties. This can easily be replaced with the following query:

```
SELECT * FROM Win32_LogicalDisk
```

Next, we saw that Get can be used to get the C: drive instance by supplying the key value, again asking for all properties to be returned. The same can be done with this query:

```
SELECT * FROM Win32_LogicalDisk WHERE DeviceID='C:'
```

As you can see, queries easily cover the functionality of Get and InstancesOf, but also go well beyond them by allowing us to define exactly the set of data we are interested in receiving. Queries also allow us to minimize the overhead of our request and simplify our client code by eliminating the need to filter out unwanted data. These are not options with Get or InstancesOf.

The other situation where queries can make a big difference is where you only have some of the key values or wish to use the keys to limit the scope of query. An example of this would be if we wanted a list of primary keys in a particular database. As noted before, for SQL Server 2000, databases are unique within the context of a SQL Server instance so both need to be specified. Primary keys also use the table they are contained within as a key, however, so the result set from the following query can include primary keys from more than one table:

```
SELECT * FROM MSSQL_PrimaryKey
WHERE SQLServerName='SQLServer1' AND DatabaseName='Northwind'
```

Even though this query requires the WMI SQL Administration provider to look through a fairly large set of information, it allows the provider to eliminate looking at a lot of unnecessary data. The WHERE clause narrows the scope of the request to a single installation of SQL Server and a particular database in that installation, which can dramatically improve performance and reduce overhead on large database servers.

Making use of queries is much like the other methods for accessing instances. You simply supply the desired query string to the ExecQuery method on the SWbemServices object used in previous examples. In the next example, we use the query to get the set of stored procedures that have a Type property containing 1:

```
' Get the WMI scripting locator object
Set ObjServices = GetObject("winmgmts:\\.\root\MicrosoftSQLServer")

' Ask for all the instances of stored procedures on the system where
' Type=1 (standard). Only retrieve the keys and the Startup property.
Set SPSet = _
  ObjServices.ExecQuery("SELECT Startup FROM MSSQL_StoredProcedure WHERE Type=1")

' Loop through each stored procedure in the set of instances and print its name
For Each SP in SPSet
   Wscript.echo SP.Name
Next
```

So far, we've looked at each of the ways in which we can get instances from WMI, including enumeration, getting specific objects, and queries. While all of them are perfectly good mechanisms for getting data, using queries is clearly the most powerful approach. Queries not only allow us to get the data we want to receive but they give us the opportunity to refine our request to ask for *exactly* what we want and eliminate the need for our code to filter out unwanted data.

> It is strongly recommended that you make the most of queries, using them whenever possible, and only use **InstancesOf** or **Get** calls when necessary.

Association Queries

As described earlier, associations are classes that describe the relationships between instances of other classes. They allow us to discover the connections between related objects, such as disks and disk controllers, views and databases, as well as users and databases. Queries are also used to access association data. Since association classes are much like any other instance class, it is possible to use InstancesOf and Get to access them, but there are some special extensions to WQL that provide convenient access for discovering and traversing these relationships dynamically in our scripts. The WMI SQL Server Administration provider supplies a large number of associations so these functions are particularly useful for managing SQL Server systems.

Associators Of

The first kind of association query uses the WQL statement Associators Of. **Associators** are defined as the classes and instances that are related to the instance specified in the query. For example, for the D: drive on your computer system, the associators would be the instances of Win32_ComputerSystem, Win32_Directory, and Win32_DiskPartition that are related to the D: drive. The following query statement returns three instances, one for each of the related classes:

```
Associators Of {Win32_LogicalDisk.DeviceID='D:'}
```

Behind the scenes, WMI uses the association classes connecting Win32_LogicalDisk with these other classes to discover the data and return it to you. From the client's perspective, the association classes are really just a means to an end and do not have to be known or called out by the script to be used. The instances returned might contain object path data like the following:

```
Win32_Directory.Name="D:\\"
Win32_ComputerSystem.Name="YourSQLComputer"
Win32_DiskPartition.DeviceID="Disk #1, Partition #0"
```

In order to request all the associated instances for the Northwind database, use the following script:

```
' Get the WMI scripting locator object
Set ObjServices = GetObject("winmgmts:\\.\root\MicrosoftSQLServer")

' Ask for all the instances associated to the SQLServer1, Northwind database.
Set AssocSet = ObjServices.ExecQuery("Associators of " _
  & "{MSSQL_Database.SQLServerName='SQLServer1',Name='Northwind'}")

' Loop through each associator in the set of instances and print its name
For Each Assoc in AssocSet
    Wscript.echo Assoc.Path_.Class,Assoc.Path_.RelPath
Next
```

The Associators Of query specifies the object path to the specific database (Northwind in SQLServer1). The results that are returned from this query will be instances from numerous classes including MSSQL_Table, MSSQL_TransactionLog, and MSSQL_User. Since the instances that come back will generally have different sets of properties, the script can only access the common system properties that all instances have. These are accessible via the Path_ property on the instances returned. The script prints the name of the class that the instance belongs to, as well as the object path to it. This same object path can be used in a call to subsequent Associators Of queries in order to discover the instances related to *that* instance. This allows us to move from one object to another, discovering new objects, finding which objects are related to it, and so on.

In a typical initial installation, you will find that there may be well over 100 instances associated to an instance of a MSSQL_Database. Discovering this data can take some time so it can be very useful to refine the query to only get the information in which we are interested. For example, if we wish to know which users have access to this database, we can tune the query using a WHERE clause.

```
' Get the WMI scripting locator object
Set ObjServices = GetObject("winmgmts:\\.\root\MicrosoftSQLServer")

' Ask for all the instances associated to the SQLServer1, Northwind database.
Set UserSet = ObjServices.ExecQuery("Associators of " _
    & "{MSSQL_Database.SQLServerName='SQLServer1',Name='Northwind'}" _
    & "WHERE ResultClass=MSSQL_User")

' Loop through each associator in the set of instances and print its name
For Each User in UserSet
    Wscript.echo User.Name
Next
```

The ResultClass statement in the WHERE clause indicates that the script is only interested in receiving associated instances of the MSSQL_User class. Since we know that only these types of instances will be returned, the script can assume the instances will have a Name property and prints it for each instance received.

To take the next step and find all the instances related to the returned user instances, we just add another nested Associators Of query:

```
' Get the WMI scripting locator object
Set ObjServices = GetObject("winmgmts:\\.\root\MicrosoftSQLServer")
```

```
' Ask for all the user instances associated to the SQLServer1, Northwind
' database.
Set UserSet = _
    ObjServices.ExecQuery("Associators of " _
    & "{MSSQL_Database.SQLServerName='SQLServer1',Name='Northwind'}" _
    & "WHERE ResultClass=MSSQL_User")

' Loop through each user in the set of instances and print its name
For Each User in UserSet
    Wscript.echo "Instances related to: ",User.Name

    ' For each user, do an Associators Of query for instances
    ' by passing the user instance path into the query
    Set UserAssoc = ObjServices.ExecQuery("Associators of {" & _
                                    User.Path_.RelPath & "}")
    For Each Assoc in UserAssoc
        ' As instances come back, print the class name and path
        Wscript.echo Assoc.Path_.Class, Assoc.Path_.Relpath
    Next
Next
```

Now, as each user is returned for the Northwind database, the script looks up instance objects related to that user. This is done by simply taking the RelPath property (which is a valid instance object path) and inserting it into the Associators Of query. Naturally, the second query could be refined to just return MSSQL_View instances rather than any related instances.

Another way of using the WHERE clause for Associators Of queries is to specify the association class we wish to use. For example, the association class between MSSQL_Table and MSSQL_Column (which defines which columns are contained in a table) is called MSSQL_TableColumn:

```
' Get the WMI scripting locator object
Set ObjServices = GetObject("winmgmts:\\.\root\MicrosoftSQLServer")
```

```
' Ask for all the column instances associated to the SQLServer1, Northwind
' [dbo].[Customers] table.
Set ColumnSet = ObjServices.ExecQuery("Associators of " _
        & "{MSSQL_Table.SQLServerName='SQLServer1',DatabaseName='Northwind'," _
        & "Name='[dbo].[Customers]'} WHERE AssocClass=MSSQL_TableColumn")

' Loop through each column in the set of instances and print its name and
' data type
For Each Column in ColumnSet
    Wscript.echo Column.Name,Column.DataType
Next
```

Rather than specifying what other class is of interest, the query uses the AssocClass statement to define the **association class** to use to discover related objects. Like before, since we know that the instances that will be returned have to be MSSQL_Column instances, we know what properties can be accessed ahead of time so can print the name of each column and its data type.

It may be useful to just get a list of the *classes* that have instances that are related to a given instance. In the following example, the query specifies the same instance of MSSQL_Table as before but uses the ClassDefsOnly option in the WHERE clause. This directs WMI to return class objects rather than instances. This is a convenient way of discovering what classes are related to a given instance without retrieving all the related instances themselves:

```
' Get the WMI scripting locator object
Set ObjServices = GetObject("winmgmts:\\.\root\MicrosoftSQLServer")

' Ask for all the instances of table on the system in semi-sync mode
Set TableSet= ObjServices.InstancesOf("MSSQL_Table", _
    wbemFlagForwardOnly+wbemFlagReturnImmediately)

' Loop through each table in the set of instances and print its name
For Each Table in TableSet
    Wscript.echo Table.Name
Next
```

This script enumerates all the instances of MSSQL_Table in semi-synchronous mode. The only real difference here is that we have added flags to the call to request WMI to forward the instances as it gets them. The return immediately flag (wbemFlagReturnImmediately) is the default behavior but must be included as well when explicitly passing in additional flags (such as wbemFlagForwardOnly) to the function.

The same change can be made to the example used earlier for stored procedures:

```
' Define the WMI constants for forwarding only and return immediately
const wbemFlagForwardOnly = &H20
const wbemFlagReturnImmediately = &H10

' Get the WMI scripting locator object
Set ObjServices = GetObject("winmgmts:\\.\root\MicrosoftSQLServer")

' Ask for all the instances of stored procedures on the system that
' Type=1 (standard). Only retrieve the keys and the Startup property.
Set SPSet = ObjServices.ExecQuery("SELECT Startup FROM MSSQL_StoredProcedure" _
    & " WHERE Type=1",,wbemFlagForwardOnly+wbemFlagReturnImmediately)

' Loop through each stored procedure in the set of instances and print its name
For Each SP in SPSet
    Wscript.echo SP.Name
Next
```

> Note that in the **ExecQuery** function there is an additional parameter, between the query string and the flags parameters, which represents the query language being used. The query language is not explicitly supplied and therefore is left as the default (**"WQL"**), which is the only possible choice at this time for WMI.

The performance gain can be substantial for this small change in your scripts and there is rarely a reason why you would not want to use semi-synchronous mode. As noted before, classes with relatively few instances will not necessarily reap large improvements but they will not suffer from using this mode either. In general, it is recommended that you use semi-synchronous mode whenever possible and asynchronous functions if you need to continue processing while your request is being serviced by WMI.

```
' Get the WMI scripting locator object
Set ObjServices = GetObject("winmgmts:\\.\root\MicrosoftSQLServer")

' Ask for all the classes associated to the SQLServer1, Northwind
' [dbo].[Customers] table.
Set AssocSet = ObjServices.ExecQuery("Associators of " _
    & "{MSSQL_Table.SQLServerName='SQLServer1',DatabaseName='Northwind'," _
    & "Name='[dbo].[Customers]'} WHERE ClassDefsOnly")

' Loop through each class in the set returned and print its name
For Each Assoc in AssocSet
    Wscript.echo Assoc.Path_.Class
Next
```

Following in the same vein, Associators Of can be used to find out how classes are related to each other without retrieving any instances, using the SchemaOnly option in the WHERE clause. It should be recognized that WMI simply evaluates the schema when fulfilling this request. This means that WMI does not verify that there are actual instances present for every relationship, just that a relationship *can* exist between the classes as defined by the schema. The following script will print the names of the classes that can be related to the MSSQL_TransactionLog class via associations:

```
' Get the WMI scripting locator object
Set ObjServices = GetObject("winmgmts:\\.\root\MicrosoftSQLServer")

' Ask for all the classes associated to the MSSQL_TransactionLog class
Set AssocSet = ObjServices.ExecQuery("Associators of {MSSQL_TransactionLog}" _
    & " WHERE SchemaOnly")

' Loop through each class in the set returned and print its name
For Each Assoc in AssocSet
    Wscript.echo Assoc.Path_.Class
Next
```

There are several other features supplied by the Associators Of query statement but, as you can see, it enables easy discovery of how one object is related to others within and even outside SQL Server. Using this kind of query, we can leapfrog across management data, dynamically discovering these relationships. Also, as new objects are added to the model, our scripts will automatically be able to access them through this discovery model.

References Of

References Of queries are the functional counterpart to Associators Of queries. Rather than allowing us to find classes that are related to a given instance, References Of identifies instances of association classes where a given instance is referenced. For example, there are three association class instances that refer to the D: drive instance of Win32_LogicalDisk. These association classes are what were used in the Associators Of query to find the related classes:

- ❑ The Win32_SystemDevices association was used to find the Win32_ComputerSystem class
- ❑ The Win32_LogicalDiskRootDirectory association was used to find the Win32_Directory class
- ❑ The Win32_LogicalDiskToPartition association was used to find the Win32_DiskPartition class

In practice, when running a `References Of` query, WMI simply searches for any association instance that has a reference to the requested object path in it.

The following script will find the references for the `D:` drive:

```
' Get the WMI scripting locator object
Set ObjServices = GetObject("winmgmts:\\.\root\CIMv2")

' Ask for all the instances associated to the D: Drive
Set AssocSet = ObjServices.ExecQuery("References of " _
    & "{Win32_LogicalDisk.DeviceId='D:'}")

' Loop through each association in the set of instances and print its name
For Each Assoc in AssocSet
    Wscript.echo Assoc.Path_.Class,Assoc.Path_.RelPath
Next
```

The results returned for this script will be the instances of the association class that have references to the `D:` drive in them.

Tips for Getting the Best Performance from Instance Calls

In the previous section, we've seen that using queries correctly can result in fast, efficient gathering of instances. There are also some ways to improve the speed that WMI *returns* these results to us. So far, in each of the examples above we have not specified any additional flags to WMI and have been using the synchronous versions of the instance calls. WMI actually supports synchronous and asynchronous modes as well as an intermediate mode called semi-synchronous.

Synchronous Calls

Synchronous mode essentially asks WMI to collect up all the instances requested first and then return them all at once to our script. This is not particularly efficient as it can require WMI to allocate a lot of memory to store the instances, adds additional processing to handle the instances, and introduces a delay before the script sees the first instance returned, during which it can only wait. For small numbers of instances, such as the disks on a system, this is not a particular problem but for a class like `Win32_UserAccount`, which can contain all the instances of users in your domain, this can be a very long wait.

Asynchronous Calls

The **asynchronous** mode, as expected, allows our script or application to get back control immediately after sending the request to WMI and continue processing. The script supplies a **sink object**, which points to the subroutine that will be receiving the instances. As WMI gets instances, it sends them to the sink and the script can then process them. Unlike synchronous mode, instances are delivered as they are available and they are not stored by WMI during the process. Using asynchronous mode is done through a different (but familiar sounding) set of methods on the `SWbemServices` object. The asynchronous versions of `InstancesOf`, `Get`, and `ExecQuery` are `InstancesOfAsync`, `GetAsync`, and `ExecQueryAsync`, respectively. Aside from specifying a sink object in the call, using these new calls is pretty much the same. The asynchronous version of the script to retrieve stored procedures with a query follows:

```
' Subroutine to catch the instances and they come in and print them
Sub SINK_OnObjectReady(objObject, objAsyncContext)
    WScript.Echo (objObject.Name)
End Sub

' Create a sink object
Set sink = WScript.CreateObject("WbemScripting.SWbemSink","SINK_")

' Get the WMI scripting locator object
Set ObjServices = GetObject("winmgmts:\\.\root\MicrosoftSQLServer")

' Ask for all the instances of stored procedures on the system
' that Type=1 (standard) using the async version of the function.
' Only retrieve the keys and the Startup property.
ObjServices.ExecQueryAsync sink,"SELECT Startup FROM MSSQL_StoredProcedure" _
                                & " WHERE Type=1"

' Continue on to do more processing as the instances are sent to the subroutine.
' ...
```

At the top of the script is the subroutine that receives the instances as they come in. This routine is called with the instance object as the first parameter. The `Name` property of each instance is printed as it is received, just as before. The main portion of the script creates the sink object, which points to the subroutine by specifying its prefix. The rest of the subroutine name is defined by VBScript to identify what kinds of script events (for example, object ready, operating complete, etc.) should be sent to it. Next, the script connects to WMI and calls the `ExecQueryAsync` method, passing in the sink object and the query string. After this, the script may continue on doing other operations while instances are delivered to the subroutine. Keep in mind that if you do not put additional processing after the `ExecQueryAsync` call, the script will exit and you will get no instances back; the script must continue running in order for the asynchronous processing to take place.

Using asynchronous processing is clearly better than a purely synchronous approach but most scripts are fairly simple and do not have a need to be doing more than one thing at a time (such as repainting a user interface while data is being retrieved). Asynchronous calls can be very powerful tools but also introduce added complexity to the script.

Semi-Synchronous Calls

The **semi-synchronous** mode is really the best of both worlds since it avoids the overhead of synchronous calls but does not add any complexity to the script. This mode basically uses the synchronous calls `InstancesOf` and `ExecQuery`, but instructs WMI to forward instances immediately to the client without storing them, eliminating the wait for all instances to be gathered first. The `Get` function does not have a semi-synchronous mode since, by definition, it is only retrieving a single instance and would not benefit from this approach. Best of all, it is really simple to make your scripts semi-synchronous!

To make a call to `InstancesOf` or `ExecQuery` semi-synchronous, we simply pass in some flag values to the call like so:

```
' Define the WMI constants for forwarding only and return immediately
const wbemFlagForwardOnly = &H20
const wbemFlagReturnImmediately = &H10
```

Modifying Instances

Now that we understand the ways to get instances back from WMI, the next step is to modify them and write them back to WMI. WMI is far from a read-only interface to management data. There are also functions available to change settings and other parameters in the management data. For the WMI SQL Server Administration provider, virtually all properties that make sense to be write-enabled have been made so. There are many properties, however, which just do not make sense to be written, such as the amount of memory a database is currently consuming on disk. These sorts of properties represent the actual state of the managed object rather than something we can modify about it.

In order to modify an instance, we simply retrieve the instance, change the values of one or more write-enabled properties on it, and then write the instance back using the `Put_` function. For example, to modify the settings on the `Northwind` database to disable the auto-shrink feature, the following script can be used:

```
' Get the WMI scripting locator object
Set ObjServices = GetObject("winmgmts:\\.\root\MicrosoftSQLServer")

' Ask for the database instance called Northwind in SQLServer1
Set Database = ObjServices.Get("MSSQL_DatabaseSetting.SettingID='Northwind'," _
                      & "SQLServerName='SQLServer1'")

' Check the AutoShrink property and print a message indicating its
' current state
If Database.AutoShrink = True Then
   Wscript.echo "Auto-Shrink enabled"
Else
   Wscript.echo "Auto-Shrink disabled"
End If

' Set the in-memory instance property value to False (disable auto-shrink)
Database.AutoShrink = False

' Write the change back to WMI and ultimately SQL Server
Database.Put_

' Read the database instance called Northwind in SQLServer1 again to verify
' the change
Set Database = ObjServices.Get("MSSQL_DatabaseSetting.SettingID='Northwind'," _
                      & "SQLServerName='SQLServer1'")

' Check the AutoShrink property again to make sure it was really changed

If Database.AutoShrink = True Then
   Wscript.echo "Auto-Shrink enabled"
Else
   Wscript.echo "Auto-Shrink disabled"
End If
```

This should be getting pretty familiar by now. First, we connect to WMI and retrieve a specific instance of a database – the `Northwind` sample database in the `SQLServer1` instance of SQL Server on the local system. Next, the script checks the `AutoShrink` property and prints a message based on whether it is currently enabled or not. The instance that was retrieved is then modified to disable the `AutoShrink` property. It should be noted that at this point it is only the instance the script has in memory that has been changed; the change has not been written back to WMI yet. To write the change and commit it, the script invokes the `Put_` method on the instance object.

You may be wondering why the call to write the instance is called Put_ *rather than just* Put *(without the underscore). This was done to avoid any possible clashes between property or method names in the class and this call. Underscore characters are strongly discouraged in WMI property and method names so this is a safe way to ensure there is no conflict. As you explore the WMI scripting API, you will find several standard object properties and methods that follow this convention.*

Once completed, the script retrieves the same instance and checks the property to make sure it is set to FALSE (disabled). That's all there is to modifying a property in an instance!

> **Modifying a key property value in WMI means you wish to create a new instance with the new key properties. It does not mean you wish to rename the instance. Renaming is generally not supported in WMI except where the class provides a special mechanism to do so.**

Naturally, we can change more than one property at a time in an instance before writing it back to WMI with Put_. Also, we may work with more than one instance at a time, such as in a loop where we modify all the user databases contained in SQLServer1 to disable the auto-shrink feature:

```
' Get the WMI scripting locator object
Set ObjServices = GetObject("winmgmts:\\.\root\MicrosoftSQLServer")

' Ask for all user database instances in SQLServer1
' NOTE:  We have to filter out the system DBs as they don't allow this
' setting to be changed.

Set DatabaseSet = ObjServices.ExecQuery("SELECT * FROM MSSQL_DatabaseSetting" _
                & " WHERE SQLServerName='SQLServer1'" _
                & " AND SettingID <> 'master'" _
                & " AND SettingID <> 'model'" _
                & " AND SettingID <> 'msdb'" _
                & " AND SettingID <> 'tempdb'")

For Each Database in DatabaseSet
   Database.AutoShrink = False
   Database.Put_
Next
```

All of the properties that are write-enabled in the SQL Server Administration provider are documented. Each will also have the write qualifier assigned to it in the schema. For SQL Server, however, there are many properties that can be written when a new object is created (which we'll tackle in the next section) but become read-only once the object exists. Other properties are write-enabled even after the object has been created. Since the write qualifier does not allow us to distinguish between these two situations, the SQL Server Administration provider has additional qualifiers to clarify what the property supports. Any property that can be modified after the object already exists, will be marked with the WriteAtUpdate qualifier in the class definition. Not only can we use this at design time while writing our script, we may also check these (and any other) qualifiers at run time to determine whether a given property can be written before actually attempting the operation.

Creating Instances

Once you see how to modify an instance, you know just about everything needed to create a new instance in most classes. The standard way to create instances is with the same `Put_` function we learned about in the last section. The difference is that rather than retrieving an instance, we create (or **spawn**) a new instance, fill in our desired values, and then write it to WMI to be instantiated. As mentioned previously, we can also do this by getting an existing instance from WMI, modifying its key values and other property values as needed, and writing it back. From WMI's perspective there is no difference, since it cannot distinguish between getting a new instance this way and us creating a new instance and populating it using script. Generally, however, it is easier and more conceptually familiar to just spawn a new instance.

In the following example, the script creates a new user-defined data type using the `MSSQL_UserDatatype` class:

```
' Get the WMI scripting locator object
Set ObjServices = GetObject("winmgmts:\\.\root\MicrosoftSQLServer")

' Get the user-defined data type *class* object, not an instance
Set UDTClass = ObjServices.Get("MSSQL_UserDatatype")

' Create (spawn) a new instance of the class
Set UDTInst = UDTClass.SpawnInstance_

' Fill in the WriteAtCreate properties and keys

' Keys
UDTInst.SQLServerName = "SQLServer1"
UDTInst.DatabaseName = "Northwind"
UDTInst.Name = "MyUDT"

' WriteAtCreate properties
UDTInst.AllowNulls = False
UDTInst.BaseDataType = "int"

' Length can't be set on a data type based on int
' NumericPrecision and NumericScale don't make sense for an int data type

' Create the new data type
UDTInst.Put_
```

There are a few differences in creating an instance compared to modifying one, but the basics are the same. After connecting to WMI, the script retrieves the class definition. This is an important point, as it is not getting an *instance* of the class, but rather the class definition itself. Next, the `SpawnInstance_` function is called on the class, which returns an empty instance in the `UDTInst` object, based on the class object in `UDTClass`. The next step is to populate the key properties, as these must be filled in to successfully write the instance. Finally, before using `Put_` to commit the new instance, we fill in the needed non-key properties with the desired characteristics of the new data type. Just like the instance modification example, there is a special qualifier on the properties indicating which ones can be used in creating an instance. This qualifier is called `WriteAtCreate`. It does not mean the property *must* be filled in, but that it *may* be used in the creation of the object. As you can see from the script, there are several properties marked as `WriteAtCreate` in the schema for this class, but only two (`AllowNulls` and `BaseDataType`) were actually filled in for this case, as the others (`NumericPrecision` and `NumericScale`) do not apply for an integer data type.

You can view which properties are marked with the `WriteAtCreate` *qualifier using CIM Studio supplied in the WMI SDK.*

Key properties are not marked with this qualifier since it is implicit that they must be written for a creation operation. If this had been a new floating-point data type rather than one being based on an integer, these other properties would have come into play. It does not hurt to provide values for these unneeded values but they will not be written if they do not apply.

For most classes, this is the way you will create new instances. However, there are some times when this mechanism will not apply and a `Create()` method can be used instead. This is typically the case when creation of the object is more complex or requires information for the key values that may not be available to your script. When we discuss how to invoke methods, we will explore this other approach to creating instances.

Deleting Instances

In order to round off the discussion, we need to discuss deleting instances. Fortunately, once you understand creating and modifying instances, deleting is simple. To remove an instance, we simply get the instance object and call `Delete_` on it. For example, to remove the user-defined data type instance created in the previous section the next script can be used:

```
' Get the WMI scripting locator object
Set ObjServices = GetObject("winmgmts:\\.\root\MicrosoftSQLServer")

' Get the user-defined data type instance created before
Set UDTInst = ObjServices.Get("MSSQL_UserDatatype.SQLServerName='SQLServer1'," _
              & "DatabaseName='Northwind',Name='MyUDT'")

' Call Delete_ on the instance received
UDTInst.Delete_
```

Once `Delete_` completes successfully, the instance is removed from SQL Server completely and cannot be restored so consider carefully before deleting instances. Also, unlike create and modify, there is not a specific qualifier on the class or properties to indicate that instances can be deleted. In general, however, it is reasonable to expect that if a class supports creation of instances, it also supports their deletion.

Invoking Methods

Methods are actions we can take on objects, such as compressing a file, rebooting a computer, or clearing an event log. There are actually two types of methods in WMI: dynamic and static.

Dynamic Methods

Operations that apply at the instance level are called **dynamic methods**. Think of a dynamic method as being an action that we wish to perform on a specific instance of a class. Defragmenting a disk, for example, is typically an operation that is performed on a specific disk drive, such as `C:`. You may wish to defragment all your drives, but each one is normally processed individually. Most methods you will come across are dynamic.

UpdateIndexStatistics()

To use a method on an instance, we retrieve an instance and call the method on the instance, providing any necessary parameters. To get started, let's look at a simple method called `UpdateIndexStatistics()` on the `MSSQL_Database` class. This method forces recalculation of index statistics on tables in the database it is invoked upon. It takes no input parameters. In the following example, we select all databases in the `SQLServer1` copy of SQL Server and call `UpdateIndexStatistics()` on each one in turn:

```
' Get the WMI scripting locator object
Set ObjServices = GetObject("winmgmts:\\.\root\MicrosoftSQLServer")

' Ask for all the instances of databases in SQLServer1
Set DBSet = ObjServices.ExecQuery("SELECT * FROM MSSQL_Database" _
            & " WHERE SQLServerName='SQLServer1'")

' Loop through each database in the set of instances and call
' UpdateIndexStatistics() on it
For Each DB in DBSet
    ' Call the method on each database
    Set RtnVal = DB.UpdateIndexStatistics()
    ' Check the return value for errors
    If RtnVal.ReturnValue <> 0 Then
        Wscript.Echo "An error occurred for database: ",DB.Name, _
                     RtnVal.Description
    End If
Next
```

When `UpdateIndexStatistics()` is called on the database, you will notice that we get an object back as the result and store it in the `RtnVal` variable. This object is an instance of the class called `MSSQL_MethodRtnVal`. This class contains three properties:

❑   `ReturnValue`: An integer containing zero if the call was successful, or the error number if a failure occurred

❑   `Description`: A string containing the textual version of the error returned in `ReturnValue`

❑   `Source`: A string containing the SQL Server subsystem that reported the error

In many cases in SQL Server, when an error occurs there is both a numerical and string version of the error information as well as data about where the error occurred. The WMI SQL Server Administration provider passes all this information back in the `MSSQL_MethodRtnVal` object for our script to use as needed.

CheckAllocations()

Next, let's take a look at the same script but use a method with input and output parameters as well. The `CheckAllocations()` method for `MSSQL_Database` has one input parameter used to specify what repair mode should be used if errors are detected. It also has an output parameter, which is used to return error information in an instance of the class we saw in the last example, `MSSQL_MethodRtnVal`. Finally, the method itself returns a string with information about the test and the results of the check:

```
' Get the WMI scripting locator object
Set ObjServices = GetObject("winmgmts:\\.\root\MicrosoftSQLServer")

' Ask for all the instances of databases in SQLServer1
Set DBSet = _
ObjServices.ExecQuery("SELECT * FROM MSSQL_Database WHERE " _
                      & "SQLServerName='SQLServer1'")

' Loop through each database in the set of instances and call
' CheckAllocations() on it
For Each DB in DBSet
   ' Call the method on each database
   strReport = DB.CheckAllocations(0, RtnVal)

   ' Check the return value for errors
   If RtnVal.ReturnValue <> 0 Then
      Wscript.Echo "An error occurred for database: ",DB.Name, _
                   RtnVal.Description
   Else
      Wscript.echo "Check status: ",strReport
   End If
Next
```

For each database that is returned from the query, `CheckAllocations()` is called, passing in 0 for the mode to use (no repairs if errors found) and an object to receive any errors generated during the call. Note, these are errors of the call execution itself, not errors found by the tests `CheckAllocations()` performs.

You might ask why in the first example the error object was the return value of the method and in this one it is an output parameter. The answer is that if a method has output data of its own to return (as `CheckAllocations()` does), that information will be sent back as the return value of the method. In this case, the object reporting errors during execution of the method is returned as an output parameter. If the method does not have its own data to return (as was the case with `UpdateIndexStatistics()`), then the error object is sent back as the return value of the method. As you might expect, it is a good idea to check the `ReturnValue` property of the `MSSQL_MethodRtnVal` instance returned after invoking a method to make sure no failures occurred. If this property is set to 0, the other properties can be safely ignored.

Rename()

I mentioned earlier that changing a key property in an instance and writing it back to WMI is treated as a request to create a new instance. It does not mean we wish to rename the instance. Typically, rename operations are not supported in WMI except through special methods for this purpose. Where possible such methods are supplied, particularly in the WMI SQL Server Administration provider. The following example renames a database called `MyDatabase` to `RenamedDB` using the dynamic method `Rename()` on the `MSSQL_Database` class:

```
' Get the WMI scripting locator object
Set ObjServices = GetObject("winmgmts:\\.\root\MicrosoftSQLServer")

' Need to set the database to single-user mode to rename it
' so first get the database setting instance
Set DBSettingInst = _
ObjServices.Get("MSSQL_DatabaseSetting.SQLServerName='SQLServer1'," _
                & "SettingID='MyDatabase'")
```

```
' Change the mode to single-user and write it back
DBSettingInst.SingleUser = true
DBSettingInst.Put_

' Get the database instance
Set DBInst = _
ObjServices.Get("MSSQL_Database.SQLServerName='SQLServer1'," _
                & "Name='MyDatabase'")

' Call Rename() on the instance received
Set RtnVal = DBInst.Rename("RenamedDB")

' Check the return value for errors
If RtnVal.ReturnValue <> 0 Then
    Wscript.Echo "An error occurred for database: ",DBInst.Name,RtnVal.Description
End If

' Restore the database to multi-user mode, making sure to
' use the new name in the object path
Set DBSettingInst = _
ObjServices.Get("MSSQL_DatabaseSetting.SQLServerName='SQLServer1'," _
                & "SettingID='RenamedDB'")

' Change the mode to single-user and write it back
DBSettingInst.SingleUser = false
DBSettingInst.Put_
```

Static Methods

Methods that apply at the class level are called **static methods**. This means that the operation does not apply to a particular instance or even a set of instances. It applies to the class itself without respect to any instance.

Create()

The most common example of a static method is the Create() method, which can be found in several of the SQL Server classes.

The purpose of Create() is conceptually the same as creating an instance using Put_. The difference is that using Put_ requires that we have all the right information available and that information is modeled in the properties of the class so that we can include it in our new instance. This is not always possible for one reason or another.

When we wish to create a new process (such as launching Notepad), we can use the Win32_Process class in the root\CIMv2 namespace. The key of this class, however, is the process ID, which is assigned by the operating system *after* the process has been created. Therefore, it is not possible for us to have all the information we need ahead of time to write the instance. In this next example, a Create() method has been provided on the class that takes information we can supply (like the path to the binary file to run) as input parameters. The method then returns to us the process ID of the process that has been created once it is done. And, naturally, if we enumerate the instances of Win32_Process after running the Create() method successfully, we will see the new instance. This example looks like:

```
' Get the WMI scripting locator object
Set ObjServices = GetObject("winmgmts:\\.\root\CIMv2")

' Get the process class, not an instance
Set ProcessCls = ObjServices.Get("Win32_Process")

' Create the new process (Run Notepad) and supply a
' return variable for the process ID
RtnVal = ProcessCls.Create("Notepad",,,pid)

' Check if the call was successful and if so print the PID
If RtnVal = 0 Then
   Wscript.echo "Process successfully created: ", pid
End If
```

The same sort of operation is needed when creating a new SQL Server database with the MSSQL_Database class. To create a database we must specify a file to use for the database as well as an initial size. Neither of these parameters is modeled as part of the MSSQL_Database class properties, so it is not possible to create an instance using Put_. The file is not a property in the database class, because it is represented by a class of its own (MSSQL_DatabaseFile). The initial size is not in the class since it is only needed at creation time and serves no purpose afterwards. To create a database using the Create() method, write the following code:

```
' Get the WMI scripting locator object
Set ObjServices = GetObject("winmgmts:\\.\root\MicrosoftSQLServer")

' Get the database file class, not an instance
Set DBFileCls = ObjServices.Get("MSSQL_DatabaseFile")

' Create a new database file instance
Set DBFileInst = DBFileCls.SpawnInstance_

' Instance name and actual file name on disk
DBFileInst.Name = "MyNewDB"
DBFileInst.PhysicalName = "C:\MyNewDB.dat"

'Grow the file in megabytes when needed
DBFileInst.FileGrowthType = 0

'Grow by 1 MB at a time
DBFileInst.FileGrowth = 1

' Max file size is 50MB
DBFileInst.MaximumSize = 50

' Get the database class, not an instance
Set DatabaseCls = ObjServices.Get("MSSQL_Database")

' Create the new database in SQLServer1 with a name of "MyNewDB"
' Give it the file object to create and an initial size of 10MB
Set RtnVal = DatabaseCls.Create("MyNewDB", "SQLServer1", DBFileInst,10)

' Check the return value for errors
If RtnVal.ReturnValue <> 0 Then
   Wscript.Echo "An error occurred: ", RtnVal.Description
End If
```

This particular example is a little more involved since we have to define the file object, based on `MSSQL_DatabaseFile`, that the database will use. Notice that we create an instance of `MSSQL_DatabaseFile` in the script, but it is not written to WMI using `Put_`. The instance is just one of the parameters sent to the `Create()` method of `MSSQL_Database`. When `Create()` executes, it will actually create the file specified in the database file object. Once completed, a new instance of `MSSQL_Database`, as well as `MSSQL_DatabaseFile`, will appear when these classes are queried.

Using Events

A key part of management is being able to receive notifications when interesting things happen in a managed system. For example, it can be very valuable to know when a process has started or stopped on the system or when a new entry has been written to the Windows NT Event Log. Additionally, it can also be important to know when database settings change or when a new login is created to access your SQL Server system. One way of getting this information is to have your script periodically check for these changes by reading all the data and checking for new or changed values. This is clearly undesirable as it introduces significant overhead for your script, can create excessive network traffic if done remotely, and will require a lot of script code to provide flexible detection of changes.

Fortunately, WMI has solved this problem by including a built-in event subsystem so that we can watch for a number of different changes in our management data. This system also uses WQL to allow us to define in detail the events we wish to receive. Just as for instances requested by a query, our scripts will only get events that match our requests. The events we receive (like everything else in WMI) are objects based on classes that can contain properties. WMI supplies two main types of events: instance and non-instance.

> It is important to know that WMI treats events as transient objects in its publication/subscription model. It does not store them or queue them. If an event is fired by an application and no one is registered to receive that event, WMI will immediately and efficiently discard the event. Once discarded, the event cannot be retrieved.

Instance Events

Instance events (also known as **intrinsic events**) allow us to be notified when an instance is created, modified, or deleted. Most events you will use will be of this kind, since most management data is represented by instances in WMI. Instance-related events are reported using the following four system event classes:

Class Name	Description
`__InstanceCreationEvent`	This event reports when a new instance of a class appears or is added.
`__InstanceDeletionEvent`	This event reports when an existing instance of a class disappears or is removed.
`__InstanceModificationEvent`	This event reports when one or more properties change in an instance of a class.
`__InstanceOperationEvent`	This event reports all of the events above. It provides an easy way to get all of the instance events without registering for each type individually.

Instance Creation Events

When a process is created (that is, when we launch a program), this will result in a new instance of the Win32_Process. We can ask WMI to watch for a new instance of this class and send us an __InstanceCreationEvent object when one appears. Registering for such an event is done with a WQL query. The query is passed into the ExecNotificationQuery function on the SWbemServices object.

> It is important to understand that you should use **ExecNotificationQuery** for event queries and **ExecQuery** for instance queries. They are not interchangeable.

```
' Get the WMI scripting locator object
Set ObjServices = GetObject("winmgmts:\\.\root\CIMv2")

' Register for events when a process is created
Set Events = _
   ObjServices.ExecNotificationQuery("SELECT * FROM __InstanceCreationEvent" _
            & " WITHIN 5 WHERE TargetInstance ISA 'Win32_Process'")

' Let the user know the script is waiting for events
Wscript.echo "Waiting for events..."

' As events occur, print the process ID and name
Do
    Set PEvent = Events.nextevent
    WScript.Echo PEvent.TargetInstance.Handle, PEvent.TargetInstance.Name
Loop
```

> Each of these event examples sits in a loop waiting for events forever. To stop the script at the command line, you will need to hit *Ctrl-C*. If you launched the script within the Windows graphical interface, you will need to terminate the associated **WSCRIPT** process to end the script execution. However, I recommend using the command line approach.

After connecting to WMI, this script submits a query asking for an event whenever a new process is created. Let's look at each part of this query in detail.

The first part of the WQL query (shown in bold) requests that instance creation events are sent back, including all properties:

SELECT * FROM __InstanceCreationEvent WITHIN 5 WHERE TargetInstance ISA
'Win32_Process'

Next, the query specifies how often WMI should check for new instances. Since there is no convenient event in the operating system for WMI to use to detect when a new process is started, WMI must poll the Win32_Process class looking for new instances. The WITHIN 5 clause specifies the number of seconds WMI should wait between polling the instances of the class, in this case 5:

SELECT * FROM __InstanceCreationEvent **WITHIN 5** WHERE TargetInstance ISA
'Win32_Process'

While polling does introduce some overhead, keep in mind that all of this typically takes place on the local system where the processes are running and within the WMI process, so the impact on system performance is minimal. This polling introduces no additional traffic between our script and WMI; only when a process is created will traffic occur as the event is sent.

Finally, the query specifies a WHERE clause, identifying what kinds of instances it wishes to get instance creation events from:

```
SELECT * FROM __InstanceCreationEvent WITHIN 5 WHERE TargetInstance ISA
'Win32_Process'
```

Without this clause, the script would be asking for instance creation events for *all* classes, which is not usually desirable due to the sheer number of events that can occur. TargetInstance is a property in the __InstanceModificationEvent class that contains an embedded object. The object will contain the instance that was created and triggered the event to be fired. Using the ISA term (read as "is a") asks that TargetInstance be instances of the Win32_Process class.

Summed up, the query in English might be described as, "Send an instance creation event when the instance created is a Win32_Process instance. Check every five seconds for instances that have been created."

When this script is run, WMI will enumerate all the instances of Win32_Process and save them. Five seconds later, WMI will enumerate all the instances of Win32_Process again and compare that list with the saved list. If a new process is in the later list, an event will be sent. If more than one new process is created during this period, an event will be sent for each one. Within each event, the TargetInstance property will contain a Win32_Process object containing all the data for the new instance. This is convenient as it allows us to get the information about the new process without having to go back to WMI and ask for the instance data ourselves. The script will continue waiting in the loop for new events to come in until we exit the script. At this time, WMI will detect that our script has stopped and, if no other clients are interested in process creation events, it will stop polling the Win32_Process class automatically.

As you would expect, this script can be focused to watch just for specific processes to be started. To make this script watch only for the Windows Calculator being started on a system, it can be easily modified like so:

```
' Get the WMI scripting locator object
Set ObjServices = GetObject("winmgmts:\\.\root\CIMv2")

' Register for events when the Windows calculator is started
Set Events = _
ObjServices.ExecNotificationQuery("SELECT * FROM __InstanceCreationEvent" _
        & " WITHIN 5 WHERE TargetInstance ISA 'Win32_Process' AND " _
        & "TargetInstance.Name='calc.exe'")

' Let the user know the script is waiting for events
Wscript.echo "Waiting for events..."

' As events occur, print the process ID and name
Do
    Set PEvent = Events.nextevent
    WScript.Echo PEvent.TargetInstance.Handle, PEvent.TargetInstance.Name
Loop
```

Since the `TargetInstance` object will contain the new process instance, we can simply check this instance object and its properties for the characteristics desired. In this case, the name of the process instance for the Windows Calculator applet (`calc.exe`) will be contained in the `Name` property of the instance. Now an event will be sent to the script only when a process called `calc.exe` is begun.

Instance Deletion Events

Instance deletion events are very much like creation events. When a program exits, it is the equivalent of a `Win32_Process` instance being deleted. Again, WMI can notify the script when a process ends. Taking the last example, we can update it to watch for when the Windows Calculator ends:

```
' Get the WMI scripting locator object
Set ObjServices = GetObject("winmgmts:\\.\root\CIMv2")

' Register for events when the Windows calculator stops
Set Events = _
ObjServices.ExecNotificationQuery("SELECT * FROM __InstanceDeletionEvent" _
        & " WITHIN 5 WHERE TargetInstance ISA 'Win32_Process' AND " _
        & "TargetInstance.Name='calc.exe'")

' Let the user know the script is waiting for events
Wscript.echo "Waiting for events..."

' As events occur, print the process ID and name
Do
    Set PEvent = Events.nextevent
    WScript.Echo PEvent.TargetInstance.Handle, PEvent.TargetInstance.Name
Loop
```

The only thing that has changed in the script is that `__InstanceCreationEvent` has been replaced in the query string with `__InstanceDeletionEvent`. Everything else is exactly the same. Now, when the Calculator process is stopped, the script will receive an instance deletion event from WMI containing the instance of the process that went away. Note that, in the case of both instance creation and deletion events, how a process is started or stopped does not affect whether or not we will get an event. The process does not have to be started or stopped using WMI. In addition, if a process stops unexpectedly (for example, because of a bug that causes it to abort), we will still get the instance deletion event since WMI is watching the operating system process table and does not depend on the processes themselves to report when they are exiting.

Instance Modification Events

Instance modification events follow much the same process as instance creation and deletion events. Instance modification events allow us to watch for changes in one or more of the property values in the instances of a class. When a change matching the query we have submitted happens, we will get an `__InstanceModificationEvent` object. The only difference is that the `__InstanceModificationEvent` will typically contain two objects, `TargetInstance` and `PreviousInstance`. `TargetInstance` contains the latest state of the instance that has changed. `PreviousInstance` contains the previous values of the instance. By having both instances, our script can not only know that the instance has changed but also determine *how* it has changed.

To watch for any database being set to read-only mode on our SQL Server, we can use the following script:

```
' Get the WMI scripting locator object
Set ObjServices = GetObject("winmgmts:\\.\root\MicrosoftSQLServer")

' Register for events when any database is made read-only
Set Events = _
    ObjServices.ExecNotificationQuery("SELECT * FROM " _
    & "__InstanceModificationEvent WITHIN 60 WHERE TargetInstance ISA " _
    & "'MSSQL_DatabaseSetting' AND TargetInstance.ReadOnly = True")

' Let the user know the script is waiting for events
Wscript.echo "Waiting for events..."

' As events occur, print the database name
Do
    Set PEvent = Events.nextevent
    WScript.Echo PEvent.TargetInstance.SettingID & " set to read-only."
Loop
```

Again, the query has changed very little really. It now requests __InstanceModificationEvent objects for the MSSQL_DatabaseSetting class instances. As part of the query, the circumstances where events are desired are limited to changes to database settings where the new value of the ReadOnly property is True. Therefore, only when a database is set to read-only mode will the event fire. There will be no event if the property is set to False (read/write mode). Also, note that the polling rate has been increased to 60 seconds since it is probably not necessary to check for this kind of change any more often than this. In fact, a much longer interval would be acceptable.

> It is important to consider the polling rate you specify for each query carefully. There really is not a one-size-fits-all polling rate to choose. Management data for the operating system and products such as SQL Server changes at different rates. Some information may need to be monitored each second, some may not change for hours or even days. In addition, if the polling rate is made too long, it is possible to miss changes in the underlying data (that is, if a process starts and stops within the polling window). You must evaluate the polling rate you choose based on how volatile the data is, as well as how quickly you must be notified when monitored data changes.

Using Inequality Tests In Event Queries

Event queries support inequality tests just like instance queries. Your script can perform greater than (>), less than (<), and not equal to (<>) comparisons as well. For instance modification queries, you can also compare the values in the TargetInstance and PreviousInstance objects. For example, to see if a database has grown in size over the time interval, the event query can be along the lines of the following:

```
SELECT * FROM __InstanceModificationEvent WITH 10 WHERE TargetInstance ISA
'MSSQL_Database' AND TargetInstance.Size > PreviousInstance.Size
```

Reporting All Events

If you wish to receive all of the various instance events without restriction, you may just request __InstanceOperationEvent objects. All of the instance events are derived from this class, so by asking for it, you will get all of its subclassed events as well. This can be useful if you wish to watch for new, deleted, and modified instances all at once and act upon them as needed. The events delivered will be the specific events for the changes that happen. For example, if an instance is created in the class you are monitoring, you will receive an __InstanceCreationEvent object, not an __InstanceOperationEvent. This allows your script to act on each kind of event based on what kind of event it is.

Intrinsic Events that don't Require Polling

There are some cases of intrinsic events where polling is not needed. This is based on the fact that the underlying management data supports its own notifications, which WMI can use behind the scenes. The provider in this case becomes a native event provider and takes over the firing of events for WMI, although it is mostly transparent to the client application or script.

An example where polling is not required is when working with the NT Event Log. The NT Event Log service supports a callback mechanism that WMI can take advantage of. Whenever a new event entry is written to a log, WMI is notified without having to poll, which is an obvious performance enhancement.

The following script receives WMI events whenever an event from SQL Server is written to the Application log:

```
' Get the WMI scripting locator object
Set ObjServices = GetObject("winmgmts:\\.\root\CIMv2")

' Register for events for when any SQL Server log event is written to
' the Application log
Set Events = _
ObjServices.ExecNotificationQuery("SELECT * FROM __InstanceCreationEvent " _
            & "WHERE TargetInstance ISA 'Win32_NTLogEvent' AND " _
            & "TargetInstance.LogFile='Application' AND " _
            & "TargetInstance.SourceName='MSSQLServer'")

' Let the user know the script is waiting for events
Wscript.echo "Waiting for events..."

' As events occur, print the log message
Do
    Set NTEvent = Events.nextevent
    WScript.Echo NTEvent.TargetInstance.Message
Loop
```

Since new entries in the NT Event Log mean creation of new instances of the Win32_NTLogEvent class, the query asks for __InstanceCreationEvent objects. No WITHIN clause is specified in the query since, as noted above, WMI does not need to poll for changes in order to provide events in this case. If the WITHIN clause was supplied, WMI would simply ignore it.

As you can see, event queries are extremely easy to use and are well integrated into the object-oriented way that WMI models data. Any instance data in WMI can be used as the basis of events whether or not the underlying managed data supports its own notification mechanism. WMI will simply poll the data for you in as optimal a way possible based on your query. The real power of this system is that it allows you to define exactly what kind of events you wish to receive, what conditions you desire to trigger the event, and how often to monitor for changes.

Non-Instance Events

There are not a lot of events in WMI that do not relate to instance data. Normally, if you wish to get events about a set of management data, you also wish to be able to directly read instances about that data, change it, and so on. There are some cases, however, where some data does not lend itself well to being modeled as instances, or it is useful to create events specific to a particular kind of occurrence in the system such as power management events. In WMI, some events such as power management events (when your system goes into suspend mode, etc.) are available as **non-instance** (also known as **extrinsic**) events, meaning they are pure event classes not based on polling instances. How we interact with these events is nearly identical to how we interact with instance events:

```
' Get the WMI scripting locator object
Set ObjServices = GetObject("winmgmts:\\.\root\CIMv2")

' Register for power management events
Set Events = _
   ObjServices.ExecNotificationQuery("SELECT * FROM Win32_PowerManagementEvent")

' Let the user know the script is waiting for events
Wscript.echo "Waiting for events..."

' As events occur, print the power event type
Do
    Set PEvent = Events.nextevent
    WScript.Echo PEvent.TargetInstance.EventType
Loop
```

The basic logic is the same for this script but you will notice that the event query does not have a WITHIN clause. Since the operating system will notify WMI when a power management event occurs in the system(for example, the system goes into suspend mode or resumes from suspend mode), there is no reason to poll (and there is nothing *to* poll as far as instances are concerned). To see any output from this script, you will need to cause one of these events to occur by causing a suspend/resume operation. As the events happen, WMI will pass them on to anyone registered to listen for them. The WMI SQL Server Administration provider supplies no extrinsic events so you will not have an occasion to use them while managing only SQL Server systems. Still, it is useful to know that they exist in other parts of WMI and may be of use in general system management applications.

Static Settings Classes

Most classes available through the WMI SQL Server Administration provider are **dynamic**, meaning they are read on-demand from SQL Server. However, four classes are **static**, meaning their data is stored in the WMI repository.

Static classes are used to store settings for operations such as backup/restore, bulk copy, and transfers. These classes provide a simple way to submit the numerous parameters to methods for these operations as a single object. In addition, since these settings are stored in the WMI repository, they can be reused and have multiple instances for different purposes. The supplied classes are:

- ❑ MSSQL_BackupSetting

- ❑ MSSQL_BulkCopySetting

- ❑ MSSQL_RestoreSetting

- ❑ MSSQL_TransferSetting

Creating a static instance of one of these classes is identical to doing so for a dynamic class.

To create a set of backup settings for use with the MSSQL_SQLServer.SQLBackup() method, the following demonstrates the basic procedure you would follow:

```
' Get the WMI scripting locator object
Set ObjServices = GetObject("winmgmts:\\.\root\MicrosoftSQLServer")

' Get the backup settings *class* object, not an instance
Set BackUpClass = ObjServices.Get("MSSQL_BackupSetting")

' Create (spawn) a new instance of the class
Set BackUpInst = BackUpClass.SpawnInstance_

' Keys
BackUpInst.SQLServerName = "SQLServer1"
BackUpInst.SettingID = "MyBackupSettings"

' Fill in the rest of the backup setting properties as desired
BackUpInst.BackupSetDescription = "Critical company DB backup"
BackUpInst.BackupSetName = "Daily backup 10-01-2000"
BackUpInst.Database = "Northwind"
BackUpInst.Device = Array("MyBackupDevice")
BackUpInst.FormatMedia = FALSE
BackUpInst.SQLServerName = "SQLServer1"
BackUpInst.TargetType = 0

' Fill in any additional properties of interest...

' Save the settings instance for later use
BackupInst.Put_
```

This creates the backup settings instance, nothing more. No backup operation is invoked by creating this settings data. To make use of this information, we'll use the following script, which creates a backup device (a file to store the backup data) and invokes the backup operation:

```
...
' Get the WMI scripting locator object
Set ObjServices = GetObject("winmgmts:\\.\root\MicrosoftSQLServer")

' Create a backup device (in this case a file)

' Get the backup device *class* object, not an instance
Set BackUpDevClass = ObjServices.Get("MSSQL_BackupDevice")

' Create (spawn) a new instance of the class
Set BackUpDevInst = BackUpDevClass.SpawnInstance_
```

```
' Keys
BackupDevInst.SQLServerName = "SQLServer1"
BackupDevInst.Name = "MyBackupDevice"

' Fill in the rest of the backup device properties as desired
BackupDevInst.PhysicalLocation="C:\\testbak.bak"
BackupDevInst.SkipTapeLabel = FALSE
BackupDevInst.SystemObject = FALSE
BackupDevInst.Type = 2

' Save the settings to create the backup device
'BackupDevInst.Put_

' Get the SQL Server instance for SQLServer1
Set SQLInst = ObjServices.Get("MSSQL_SQLServer='SQLServer1'")

' Get the backup settings instance
Set BackUpInst = _
  ObjServices.Get("MSSQL_BackupSetting.SQLServerName='SQLServer1'," _
              & "SettingID='MyBackupSettings'")

' Invoke the backup method
SQLInst.SQLBackup(BackUpInst)
' Wait for backup to finish and the function to return, check the results,
'...
```

After reviewing the number of properties that can be set in these classes, you will be very thankful to have these convenient classes to simplify and streamline these routine administrative tasks.

Accessing Qualifiers

Qualifiers are additional information added to the schema to convey useful information about classes, properties, method parameters, and so on. Qualifiers are typically name-value pairs. Like properties, qualifiers have data types such as string, Boolean, and integer, as appropriate for the situation. For example, the write qualifier is a Boolean property, having a state of either TRUE or FALSE, depending on whether the property is write-enabled or not. The Values qualifier, on the other hand, is typically an array of strings that allows us to map the value returned from a property into a friendly, human-readable string.

In the case of the MSSQL_Database class, the DatabaseStatus property is marked with the Values and ValueMap qualifiers. The DatabaseStatus property is itself an integer. If we wish to display a friendly string about the status of a database, these numerical values really do not fit the bill. To solve this problem, the Values and ValueMap qualifiers are used to relate the information returned by the property to strings that can be presented to end-users. The ValueMap qualifier contains an array of values the property can take (for DatabaseStatus this would be 0, 32, etc.). The Values qualifier contains an equivalent array of strings that correspond to each entry in the ValueMap qualifier. If the ValueMap qualifier is not present on a property, but the Values qualifier is, the ValueMap is assumed to be a zero-based, sequential numerical index (0, 1, 2, …). The following table shows some of the mappings for DatabaseStatus:

ValueMap Entries	Values Entries
0	Normal
32	Loading
192	Recovering
256	Suspect
...	...

As you can see, if we get the value 192 back from the DatabaseStatus property, we can choose how we wish to present this information to the user. We can just display the numerical value or, by using the Values qualifier, look up and display the corresponding, human-friendly string (in this case Recovering). If your script is just going to use the value of the property to make some decisions, it makes more sense to use the numerical values. If your script is going to present information to users, the string version might be a better choice.

> *When you get a value from a property that has these qualifiers, you can use the WMI scripting features to look up a string that is not only nicer to look at but that has been localized as well. If you retrieve the string version of a property from a Values qualifier on a localized (such as a German language) machine, it will contain the German version of the string, assuming that the user asking for the data also has their locale set to German.*

Accessing these qualifiers and any other qualifiers in the WMI schema is straightforward. Most qualifiers are on the *class* object not the instance, so to get them you must retrieve the class as well. The following example gets the MSSQL_Database class object as well as enumerating all databases on the system. As it loops through each database, it prints the name of the database and the numeric DatabaseStatus value. Following this, it again prints the name and the friendly string version of DatabaseStatus using the GetValuesString function:

```
Const wbemFlagUseAmendedQualifiers = &H20000
Const WbemErrNotFound = &H80041002

' Get the WMI scripting locator object
Set ObjServices = GetObject("winmgmts:\\.\root\MicrosoftSQLServer")

' Ask for the MSSQL_Database class object and ask for localized
' (amended) qualifiers
Set DBClass = ObjServices.Get("MSSQL_Database",wbemFlagUseAmendedQualifiers)

' Ask for the Northwind database instance
Set DBSet = ObjServices.InstancesOf("MSSQL_Database")

For Each DBInst in DBSet
    ' Print value of database status in numeric and then string form
    Wscript.echo DBInst.Name,DBInst.DatabaseStatus
    Wscript.echo DBInst.Name, _
    GetValuesString(DBClass.Properties_("DatabaseStatus"),DBInst.DatabaseStatus)
Next
```

The GetValuesString function (shown below) is a simple function that I put together to look up the equivalent string value for a property and value passed in to it. After verifying that the property object it is given is valid, the routine attempts to find the value it is given in the property's ValueMap. If it finds the value, it saves the position it was found at and uses it later to get the matching Values qualifier entry. If all goes well, the Values string is returned. Otherwise, if the value is not found or some other error occurs, an empty string is returned. Notice that the input value is turned into a string; this remapping from a property value to a string can take place for any data type, including Booleans, integers, or even other strings. This routine will work for virtually any class, so it will be very useful if you would like to present human-readable information from your scripts:

```
' GetValuesString(objProp,value)
'
' For a class and a property value, looks up the VALUES qualifier string
' that maps to the supplied value
'
' IN:
' objProp - a WMI property object
' value   - the value for this property to be mapped to its VALUES
'           qualifier equivalent
'
' RETURNS:
' If value is found in the ValueMap array, returns the equivalent VALUES
' array entry
' If not found, returns an empty string

Function GetValuesString(objProp,value)

' Resume processing if an error occurs
On Error Resume Next

' Init some useful variables
index = 0
QualStringIndex = -1

' Make sure the property value received is not NULL
If Not IsNull(value) then

    ' Convert the property value to a string since VALUEMAP is a string array
    strVal = CStr(value)

    ' Get the VALUEMAP qualifiers for this property
    QualVals = objProp.Qualifiers_.Item("ValueMap")

    ' If the VALUEMAP qualifier isn't there, we can try assuming it is a
    ' zero-based, sequential index and just use the value supplied
    If Err.Number = WbemErrNotFound Then
        QualStringIndex = value

    ' Otherwise, the VALUEMAP qualifier is there, search it for the value we got
    Else
        For Each Val in QualVals

            ' If it's found, save the index
            If strVal = Val Then
                QualStringIndex = index
            End If
            index = index + 1
        Next
    End If
' If we found the value in the VALUEMAP array...
    If QualStringIndex <> -1 Then
```

```
        ' Get the VALUES qualifiers for the property
        Set ValuesQual = objProp.Qualifiers_.Item("Values")

        ' If the VALUES qualifier is missing, there are no strings to
        ' map to here. Send back empty string.
        If Err.Number = WbemErrNotFound Then
            GetValuesString =""
        Else
            ' Use the index we got to retrieve the appropriate VALUES entry
            GetValuesString = ValuesQual.Value(QualStringIndex)
        End If

    ' Didn't find the value in the VALUEMAP array, send back an empty string
    Else
        GetValuesString = ""
    End If
Else
    GetValuesString = ""
End If
End Function
```

Using SQL Server-Specific Qualifiers

There are a number of qualifiers on the classes, properties, and methods of the WMI SQL Server Administration provider. These qualifiers have been added to the schema in order to convey additional information about these objects. This information is not only useful from a documentation perspective but, because they are part of the classes, they can also be accessed from your scripts and used dynamically. There are three main qualifiers you should pay attention to: SQLVersion, WriteAtCreate, and WriteAtUpdate.

SQLVersion

When you find the SQLVersion qualifier on a class, property, method, or method parameter, it will contain an array of the SQL Server versions on which it is supported. Some objects are only available on 7.0 (because they are no longer needed in SQL Server 2000) and some are new to SQL Server 2000. If you find "7.0" in the array, that means the object is supported on SQL Server 7.0. If you find "8.0" in the array, it means the object is supported on SQL Server 2000. In general, you will not find both "7.0" and "8.0" in the array. Instead, to indicate the object is supported on both versions, the SQLVersion qualifier is simply not present on the object. So, if you do not find the qualifier on a given object, you can assume it will be populated on either system.

WriteAtCreate and WriteAtUpdate

There are many cases in SQL Server where a given property can be written when an object is being created (through a Put_ call) but, once it is created, it becomes read-only. Other properties can be modified or updated once an object is created. To distinguish between these cases, objects that have these characteristics are marked with the qualifiers WriteAtCreate, WriteAtUpdate, or both, as appropriate. Both of these qualifiers are Boolean in nature and will therefore either have a value of FALSE (meaning the property cannot be written for the given operation) or TRUE (meaning the property does support being written). By default, if one of these qualifiers is not present, its value is FALSE.

One of these qualifiers being present does not imply anything about the other. In other words, WriteAtUpdate being present and set to TRUE means the property can be modified after it has been created using Put_. WriteAtCreate being present and set to TRUE means the property can be written at the time the object is created. For a property to support both possible ways of being written, it must have both qualifiers set to TRUE.

Summary

In this chapter we have taken a thorough look at the way the WMI SQL Server Administration provider works, what features it supports, and how to access them from the WMI scripting interface.

We have only dealt with the key features that the WMI scripting layer supports, but there are many more properties and methods available that are useful for scripting access to management data. You can find a complete reference to the various WMI scripting API and objects in the WMI SDK documentation (downloadable from http://msdn.microsoft.com/downloads/sdks/wmi/default.asp as part of the overall WMI SDK or as part of the Windows Platform SDK).

Rather than walk through what each class in the provider can do specifically, we have instead reviewed the mechanisms through which you can access instance data, methods, and events for managing SQL Server. As you explorer this provider, and WMI in general, through the documentation and tools such as CIM Studio, you will find that, once you understand how to perform these operations for one class, doing so is virtually identical for any other class. Once you have mastered the various instance and event functions, the key to success is becoming familiar with the schema for the provider and how to best use it for your management tasks.

System Functions

In the paragraphs below, I strive to clarify each of the documented system functions in SQL Server 2000. Some of them are more useful than others, but each has its own little bit to offer.

Do take care if you are used to these functions either in previous versions of SQL Server or in other databases, for example Sybase.

@@CONNECTIONS

Returns the number of connections attempted since the last time your SQL Server was started.

This one is the total of all connection *attempts* made since the last time your SQL Server was started. The key thing to remember here is that we are talking about attempts, not actual connections, and that we are talking about connections as opposed to users.

Every attempt made to create a connection increments this counter regardless of whether that connection was successful or not. The only catch with this is that the connection attempt has to have made it as far as the server. If the connection failed because of NetLib differences or some other network issue, then your SQL Server wouldn't even know that it needed to increase the count – it only counts if the server saw the connection attempt. Whether the attempt succeeded or failed does not matter.

It's also important to understand that we're talking about connections instead of login attempts. Depending on your application, you may create several connections to your server, but you'll probably only ask the user for information once. Indeed, even Query Analyzer does this. When you click for a new window, it automatically creates another connection based on the same login information.

> This, like a number of other global variables, is better served by a system stored procedure, **sp_monitor**. This procedure, in one command, produces the information from the number of connections, CPU busy, through to the total number of writes by SQL Server.

@@CPU_BUSY

Returns the time in milliseconds that the CPU has been actively doing work since SQL Server was last started. This number is based on the resolution of the system timer – which can vary – and can therefore vary in accuracy.

This is another of the "since the server started" kind of functions. This means that you can't always count on the number going up as your application runs. It's possible, based on this number, to figure out a CPU percentage that your SQL Server is taking up. Realistically though, I'd rather tap right into the Performance Monitor for that if I had some dire need for it. The bottom line is that this is one of those really cool things from a "gee, isn't it swell to know that" point of view, but doesn't have all that many practical uses in most applications.

@@CURSOR_ROWS

How many rows are currently in the last cursor set opened on the current connection. Note, that this is for cursors, and not temporary tables.

Keep in mind that this number is reset every time you open a new cursor. If you need to open more than one cursor at a time, and you need to know the number of rows in the first cursor, then you'll need to move this value into a holding variable before opening subsequent cursors.

It's possible to use this to set up a counter to control your WHILE loop when dealing with cursors, but I strongly recommend against this practice – the value contained in @@CURSOR_ROWS can change depending on the cursor type and whether SQL Server is populating the cursor asynchronously or not. Using @@FETCH_STATUS is going to be far more reliable and at least as easy to use.

If the value returned is a negative number larger than –1, then you must be working with an asynchronous cursor, and the negative number is the number of records so far created in the cursor. If however, the value is –1, then the cursor is a dynamic cursor, in that, the number of rows are constantly changing. A returned value of 0 informs you that either no cursor opened has been opened, or the last cursor opened is no longer open. Finally, any positive number indicates the number of rows within the cursor.

> To create an asynchronous cursor, set **sp_configure cursor threshold** to a value greater than 0. Then, when the cursor exceeds this setting, the cursor is returned while the remaining records are placed in to the cursor asynchronously.

@@DATEFIRST

Returns the numeric value that corresponds to the day of the week that the system considers to be the first day of the week.

The default in the US is 7, which equates to Sunday. The values convert as follows:

- ❑ 1 – Monday (the first day for most of the world)
- ❑ 2 – Tuesday
- ❑ 3 – Wednesday
- ❑ 4 – Thursday
- ❑ 5 – Friday
- ❑ 6 – Saturday
- ❑ 7 – Sunday

This can be really handy when dealing with localization issues so you can properly layout any calendar or other day of week dependent information you have.

> Use the **SET DATEFIRST** function to alter this setting.

@@DBTS

Returns the last used timestamp for the current database.

At first look this one seems to act an awful lot like @@IDENTITY in that it gives you the chance to get back the last value set by the system (this time, it's the last timestamp instead of the last identity value). The things to watch out for on this one include:

- ❑ The value changes based on any change in the database, not just the table you're working on
- ❑ *Any* timestamp change in the database is reflected, not just those for the current connection

Because you can't count on this value truly being the last one that you used (someone else may have done something that would change it), I personally find very little practical use for this one.

@@ERROR

Returns the error code for the last T-SQL statement that ran on the current connection. If there is no error, then the value will be zero.

If you're going to be writing stored procedures or triggers, this is a bread and butter kind of system function – you pretty much can't live without it.

> The thing to remember with **@@ERROR** is that its lifespan is just one statement. This means that, if you want to use it to check for an error after a given statement, then you either need to make your test the very next statement, or you need to move it into a holding variable.

A listing of all the system errors can be viewed by using the sysmessages system table in the master database.

To create your own custom errors, use sp_addmessage.

@@FETCH_STATUS

Returns an indicator of the status of the last cursor FETCH operation.

If you're using cursors, you're going to be using @@FETCH_STATUS. This one is how you know the success or failure of your attempt to navigate to a record in your cursor. It will return a constant depending on whether SQL Server succeeded in your last FETCH operation or not, and, if the FETCH failed, why. The constants are:

- ❏ 0 – Success
- ❏ -1 – Failed. Usually because you are beyond either the beginning or end of the cursorset.
- ❏ -2 – Failed. The row you were fetching wasn't found, usually because it was deleted between when the cursorset was created and when you navigated to the current row. Should only occur in scrollable, non-dynamic cursors.

For purposes of readability, I often will set up some constants prior to using @@FETCH_STATUS.

For example:

```
DECLARE @NOTFOUND int
DECLARE @BEGINEND int

SELECT @NOTFOUND = -2
SELECT @BEGINEND = -1
```

I can then use these in my conditional in the WHILE statement of my cursor loop instead of just the row integer. This can make the code quite a bit more readable.

@@IDENTITY

Returns the last identity value created by the current connection.

If you're using identity columns and then referencing them as a foreign key in another table, you'll find yourself using this one all the time. You can create the parent record (usually the one with the identity you need to retrieve), then select @@IDENTITY to know what value you need to relate child records to.

If you perform inserts into multiple tables with identity values, remember that the value in @@IDENTITY will only be for the *last* identity value inserted – anything before that will have been lost, unless you move the value into a holding variable after each insert. Also, if the last column you inserted into didn't have an identity column, then @@IDENTITY will be set to NULL.

@@IDLE

Returns the time in milliseconds (based on the resolution of the system timer) that SQL Server has been idle since it was last started.

You can think of this one as being something of the inverse of @@CPU_BUSY. Essentially, it tells you how much time your SQL Server has spent doing nothing. If anyone finds a programmatic use for this one, send me an e-mail – I'd love to hear about it (I can't think of one).

@@IO_BUSY

Returns the time in milliseconds (based on the resolution of the system timer) that SQL Server has spent doing input and output operations since it was last started. This value is reset every time SQL Server is started.

This one doesn't really have any rocket science to it, and it is another one of those that I find falls into the "no real programmatic use" category.

@@LANGID and @@LANGUAGE

Respectively return the ID and the name of the language currently in use.

These can be handy for figuring out if your product has been installed in a localization situation or not, and if so what language is the default.

For a full listing of the languages currently supported by SQL Server, run a SELECT * on the syslanguages table or use the system stored procedure, sp_helplanguage.

@@LOCK_TIMEOUT

Returns the current amount of time in milliseconds before the system will time-out waiting on a blocked resource.

If a resource (a page, a row, a table, whatever) is blocked, your process will stop and wait for the block to clear. This determines just how long your process will wait before the statement is cancelled.

The default time to wait is 0 (which equates to indefinitely) unless someone has changed it at the system level (using sp_configure). Regardless of how the system default is set, you will get a value of −1 from this global unless you have manually set the value for the current connection using SET LOCK_TIMEOUT.

@@MAX_CONNECTIONS

Returns the maximum number of simultaneous user connections allowed on your SQL Server.

Don't mistake this one to mean the same thing as you would see under the **Maximum Connections** property in the Enterprise Manager. This one is based on licensing, and will show a very high number if you have selected "per seat" licensing.

> *Note that the actual number of user connections allowed also depends on the version of SQL Server you are using and the limits of your application(s) and hardware.*

@@MAX_PRECISION

Returns the level of precision currently set for decimal and numeric data types.

The default is 38 places, but the value can be changed by using the /p option when you start your SQL Server. The /p can be added by starting SQL Server from a command line, or by adding it to the **Startup parameters** for the **MSSQLServer** service in the Windows NT or 2000 **Services** applet (if you're running NT or 2000).

@@NESTLEVEL

Returns the current nesting level for nested stored procedures.

The first stored procedure (sproc) to run has an @@NESTLEVEL of 0. If that sproc calls another, then the second sproc is said to be nested in the first sproc (and @@NESTLEVEL is incremented to a value of 1). Likewise, the second sproc may call a third, and so on up to maximum of 32 levels deep. If you go past the level of 32 levels deep, not only will the transaction be terminated, but you should revisit the design of your application.

@@OPTIONS

Returns information about options that have been applied using the SET command.

Since you only get one value back, but can have many options set, SQL Server uses binary flags to indicate what values are set. In order to test whether the option you are interested in is set, you must use the option value together with a bitwise operator. For example:

```
IF (@@OPTIONS & 2)
```

If this evaluates to True, then you would know that IMPLICIT_TRANSACTIONS had been turned on for the current connection. The values are:

Bit	SET Option	Description
1	DISABLE_ DEF_CNST_CHK	Interim vs. deferred constraint checking.
2	IMPLICIT_ TRANSACTIONS	A transaction is started implicitly when a statement is executed.
4	CURSOR_CLOSE_ ON_COMMIT	Controls behavior of cursors after a COMMIT operation has been performed.
8	ANSI_WARNINGS	Warns of truncation and NULL in aggregates.
16	ANSI_PADDING	Controls padding of fixed-length variables.
32	ANSI_NULLS	Determines handling of nulls when using equality operators.
64	ARITHABORT	Terminates a query when an overflow or divide-by-zero error occurs during query execution.
128	ARITHIGNORE	Returns NULL when an overflow or divide-by-zero error occurs during a query.
256	QUOTED_ IDENTIFIER	Differentiates between single and double quotation marks when evaluating an expression.
512	NOCOUNT	Turns off the row(s) affected message returned at the end of each statement.
1024	ANSI_NULL_ DFLT_ON	Alters the session's behavior to use ANSI compatibility for nullability. Columns created with new tables or added to old tables without explicit null option settings are defined to allow nulls. Mutually exclusive with ANSI_NULL_DFLT_OFF.
2048	ANSI_NULL_ DFLT_OFF	Alters the session's behavior not to use ANSI compatibility for nullability. New columns defined without explicit nullability are defined not to allow nulls. Mutually exclusive with ANSI_NULL_DFLT_ON.
4096	CONCAT_NULL_ YIELDS_NULL	Returns a NULL when concatenating a NULL with a string.
8192	NUMERIC_ ROUNDABORT	Generates an error when a loss of precision occurs in an expression.

@@PACK_RECEIVED and @@PACK_SENT

Respectively return the number of input packets read/written from/to the network by SQL Server since it was last started.

Primarily, these are a network trouble-shooting tools.

@@PACKET_ERRORS

Returns the number of network packet errors that have occurred on connections to your SQL Server since the last time the SQL Server was started.

Primarily a network trouble-shooting tool.

@@PROCID

Returns the stored procedure ID of the currently running procedure.

Primarily a trouble-shooting tool when a process is running and using up a large amount of resources. Is used mainly as a DBA function.

@@REMSERVER

Returns the value of the server (as it appears in the login record) that called the stored procedure.

Used only in stored procedures. This one is handy when you want the sproc to behave differently depending on what remote server (often a geographic location) the sproc was called from.

@@ROWCOUNT

Returns the number of rows affected by the last statement.

One of the most used globals, my most common use for this one is to check for non run-time errors – that is, items that are logically errors to your program, but that SQL Server isn't going to see any problem with. An example would be a situation where you are performing an update based on a condition, but you find that it affects zero rows. Odds are that, if your client submitted a modification for a particular row, then it was expecting that row to match the criteria given – zero rows affected is indicative of something being wrong.

However, if you test this global variable on any statement that does not return rows, then you will also return a value of 0.

@@SERVERNAME

Returns the name of the local server that the script is running from.

If you have multiple instances of SQL Server installed (a good example would be a web hosting service which uses a separate SQL Server installation for each client), then @@SERVERNAME returns the following local server name information if the local server name has not been changed since setup:

Instance	Server Information
Default instance	*<servername>*
Named instance	*<servername\instancename>*
Virtual server – default instance	*<virtualservername>*
Virtual server – named instance	*<virtualservername\instancename>*

@@SERVICENAME

Returns the name of the registry key under which SQL Server is running.

Only returns something under Windows NT/2000, and (under either of these) should always return MSSQLService unless you've been playing games in the registry. Should return nothing if running under Win 9x (Win 9x doesn't have services, so SQL Server can't run as one).

@@SPID

Returns the server process ID (SPID) of the current user process.

This equates to the same process ID that you see if you run sp_who. What's nice is that you can tell the SPID for your current connection, which can be used by the DBA to monitor, and if necessary terminate, that task.

@@TEXTSIZE

Returns the current value of the TEXTSIZE option of the SET statement, which specifies the maximum length, in bytes, returned by a SELECT statement when dealing with text or image data.

The default is 4096 bytes (4KB). You can change this value by using the SET TEXTSIZE statement.

@@TIMETICKS

Returns the number of microseconds per tick. This varies by machines and is another of those that falls under the category of "no real programmatic use".

@@TOTAL_ERRORS

Returns the number of disk read/write errors encountered by the SQL Server since it was last started.

Don't confuse this with run-time errors or as having any relation to @@ERROR. This is about problems with physical I/O. This one is another of those of the "no real programmatic use" variety. The primary use here would be more along the lines of system diagnostic scripts. Generally speaking, I would use Performance Monitor for this instead.

@@TOTAL_READ and @@TOTAL_WRITE

Respectively return the total number of disk reads/writes by SQL Server since it was last started.

The names here are a little misleading, as these do not include any reads from cache – they are only physical I/O.

@@TRANCOUNT

Returns the number of active transactions – essentially the transaction nesting level – for the current connection.

This is a very big one when you are doing transactioning. I'm not normally a big fan of nested transactions, but there are times where they are difficult to avoid. As such, it can be important to know just where you are in the transaction nesting side of things (for example, you may have logic that only starts a transaction if you're not already in one).

If you're not in a transaction, then @@TRANCOUNT is 0. From there, let's look at a brief example:

```
SELECT @@TRANCOUNT As TransactionNestLevel       --This will be zero at this point

BEGIN TRAN
SELECT @@TRANCOUNT As TransactionNestLevel       --This will be one at this point
   BEGIN TRAN
      SELECT @@TRANCOUNT As TransactionNestLevel  --This will be two at this point
   COMMIT TRAN
SELECT @@TRANCOUNT As TransactionNestLevel        --This will be back to one
                                                  --at this point

ROLLBACK TRAN
SELECT @@TRANCOUNT As TransactionNestLevel        --This will be back to zero
                                                  --at this point
```

Note that, in this example, the @@TRANCOUNT at the end would also have reached zero if we had a COMMIT as our last statement.

@@VERSION

Returns the current version of SQL Server as well as the processor type and OS architecture.

For example:

```
SELECT @@VERSION
```

gives:

Microsoft SQL Server 2000 - 8.00.194 (Intel X86)
	Aug 6 2000 01:19:00
	Copyright (c) 1988-2000 Microsoft Corporation
	Developer Edition on Windows NT 5.0 (Build 2195:)

(1 row(s) affected)

Unfortunately, this doesn't return the information into any kind of structured field arrangement, so you have to parse it if you want to use it to test for specific information.

Consider using the xp_msver system sproc instead – it returns information in such a way that you can more easily retrieve specific information from the results.

Online discussion at http://p2p.wrox.com

B

Function Listing

The T-SQL functions available in SQL Server 2000 fall into 10 categories:

- ❑ Aggregate functions
- ❑ Cursor functions
- ❑ Date and time functions
- ❑ Mathematical functions
- ❑ Meta data functions
- ❑ Rowset functions
- ❑ Security functions
- ❑ String functions
- ❑ System functions
- ❑ Text and image functions

Aggregate Functions

Aggregate functions are applied to sets of records rather than a single record. The information in the multiple records is processed in a particular manner and then is displayed in a single record answer. Aggregate functions are often used in conjunction with the GROUP BY clause.

The aggregate functions are:

- ❑ AVG
- ❑ COUNT
- ❑ COUNT_BIG
- ❑ GROUPING
- ❑ MAX
- ❑ MIN
- ❑ STDEV
- ❑ STDEVP
- ❑ SUM
- ❑ VAR
- ❑ VARP

In most aggregate functions, the ALL or DISTINCT keywords can be used. The ALL argument is the default and will apply the function to all the values in the *expression*, even if a value appears numerous times. The DISTINCT argument means that a value will only be included in the function once, even if it occurs several times.

Aggregate functions cannot be nested. The *expression* cannot be a subquery.

AVG

AVG returns the average of the values in *expression*. The syntax is as follows:

```
AVG([ALL | DISTINCT] <expression>)
```

The *expression* must contain numeric values. Null values are ignored.

COUNT

COUNT returns the number of items in *expression*. The data type returned is of type int. The syntax is as follows:

```
COUNT
(
    [ALL | DISTINCT] <expression> | *
)
```

The *expression* cannot be of the uniqueidentifier, text, image, or ntext data types. The * argument returns the number of rows in the table; it does not eliminate duplicate or NULL values.

COUNT_BIG

COUNT_BIG returns the number of items in a group. This is very similar to the COUNT function described above, with the exception that the return value has a data type of bigint. The syntax is as follows:

```
COUNT_BIG
(
    [ALL | DISTINCT ] <expression> | *
)
```

GROUPING

GROUPING adds an extra column to the output of a SELECT statement. The GROUPING function is used in conjunction with CUBE or ROLLUP to distinguish between normal NULL values and those added as a result of CUBE and ROLLUP operations. Its syntax is:

```
GROUPING (<column_name>)
```

GROUPING is only used in the SELECT list. Its argument is a column that is used in the GROUP BY clause and which is to be checked for NULL values.

MAX

The MAX function returns the maximum value from *expression*. The syntax is as follows:

```
MAX([ALL | DISTINCT] <expression>)
```

MAX ignores any NULL values.

MIN

The MIN function returns the smallest value from *expression*. The syntax is as follows:

```
MIN([ALL | DISTINCT] <expression>)
```

MIN ignores NULL values.

STDEV

The STDEV function returns the standard deviation of all values in *expression*. The syntax is as follows:

```
STDEV(<expression>)
```

STDEV ignores NULL values.

STDEVP

The STDEVP function returns the standard deviation for the population of all values in *expression*. The syntax is as follows:

```
STDEVP(<expression>)
```

STDEVP ignores NULL values.

SUM

The SUM function will return the total of all values in *expression*. The syntax is as follows:

```
SUM([ALL | DISTINCT] <expression>)
```

SUM ignores NULL values.

VAR

The VAR function returns the variance of all values in *expression*. The syntax is as follows:

```
VAR(<expression>)
```

VAR ignores NULL values.

VARP

The VARP function returns the variance for the population of all values in *expression*. The syntax is as follows:

```
VARP(<expression>)
```

VARP ignores NULL values.

Cursor Functions

There is only one cursor function (CURSOR_STATUS) and it provides information about cursors.

CURSOR_STATUS

The CURSOR_STATUS function allows the caller of a stored procedure to determine if that procedure has returned a cursor and result set. The syntax is as follows:

```
CURSOR_STATUS
    (
        {'<local>', '<cursor_name>'}
      | {'<global>', '<cursor_name>'}
      | {'<variable>', '<cursor_variable>'}
    )
```

local, *global*, and *variable* all specify constants that indicate the source of the cursor. *Local* equates to a local cursor name, *global* to a global cursor name, and *variable* to a local variable.

If you are using the *cursor_name* form then there are four possible return values:

❏   1 – the cursor is open. If the cursor is dynamic, its result set has zero or more rows. If the cursor is not dynamic, it has one or more rows.

❏   0 – the result set of the cursor is empty.

❏   −1 – the cursor is closed.

❏   −3 – a cursor of *cursor_name* does not exist.

If you are using the *cursor_variable* form, there are five possible return values:

❏   1 – the cursor is open. If the cursor is dynamic, its result set has zero or more rows. If the cursor is not dynamic, it has one or more rows.

❏   0 – the result set is empty.

❏   −1 – the cursor is closed.

❏   −2 – there is no cursor assigned to the *cursor_variable*.

❏   −3 – the variable with name *cursor_variable* does not exist, or if it does exist, has not had a cursor allocated to it yet.

Date and Time Functions

The date and time functions perform operations on values that have datetime and smalldatetime data types or which are character data types in a date form. They are:

❏   DATEADD

❏   DATEDIFF

❏   DATENAME

❏   DATEPART

❏   DAY

❏   GETDATE

❏   GETUTCDATE

❏   MONTH

❏   YEAR

SQL Server recognizes eleven "dateparts" and their abbreviations as shown in the following table:

Datepart	Abbreviations
year	yy, yyyy
quarter	qq, q
month	mm, m
dayofyear	dy, y
day	dd, d
week	wk, ww
weekday	dw
hour	hh
minute	mi, n
second	ss, s
millisecond	ms

DATEADD

The DATEADD function adds an interval to a date and returns a new date. The syntax is as follows:

```
DATEADD(<datepart>, <number>, <date>)
```

The *datepart* argument specifies the time scale of the interval (day, week, month, etc.) and may be any of the dateparts recognized by SQL Server. The *number* argument is the number of dateparts that should be added to the *date*.

DATEDIFF

The DATEDIFF function returns the difference between two specified dates in a specified unit of time (for example: hours, days, weeks). The syntax is as follows:

```
DATEDIFF(<datepart>, <startdate>, <enddate>)
```

The *datepart* argument may be any of the dateparts recognized by SQL Server and specifies the unit of time to be used.

DATENAME

The DATENAME function returns a string representing the name of the specified *datepart* (for example: 1999, Thursday, July) of the specified *date*. The syntax is as follows:

```
DATENAME(<datepart>, <date>)
```

DATEPART

The DATEPART function returns an integer that represents the specified *datepart* of the specified *date*. The syntax is as follows:

```
DATEPART(<datepart>, <date>)
```

The DAY function is equivalent to DATEPART(dd, *<date>*); MONTH is equivalent to DATEPART(mm, *<date>*); YEAR is equivalent to DATEPART(yy, *<date>*).

DAY

The DAY function returns an integer representing the day part of the specified date. The syntax is as follows:

```
DAY(<date>)
```

The DAY function is equivalent to DATEPART(dd, *<date>*).

GETDATE

The GETDATE function returns the current system date and time. The syntax is as follows:

```
GETDATE()
```

GETUTCDATE

The GETUTCDATE function returns the current UTC (Universal Time Coordinate) time. In other words, this returns Greenwich Mean Time. The value is derived by taking the local time from the server, and the local time zone, and calculating GMT from this. Daylight saving is included. GETUTCDATE cannot be called from a user-defined function. The syntax is as follows:

```
GETUTCDATE()
```

MONTH

The MONTH function returns an integer that represents the month part of the specified date. The syntax is as follows:

```
MONTH(<date>)
```

The MONTH function is equivalent to DATEPART(mm, *<date>*).

YEAR

The YEAR function returns an integer that represents the year part of the specified date. The syntax is as follows:

```
YEAR(<date>)
```

The YEAR function is equivalent to DATEPART(yy, *<date>*).

Mathematical Functions

The mathematical functions perform calculations. They are:

- ❏ ABS
- ❏ ACOS
- ❏ ASIN
- ❏ ATAN
- ❏ ATN2
- ❏ CEILING
- ❏ COS
- ❏ COT
- ❏ DEGREES
- ❏ EXP
- ❏ FLOOR
- ❏ LOG
- ❏ LOG10
- ❏ PI
- ❏ POWER
- ❏ RADIANS
- ❏ RAND
- ❏ ROUND
- ❏ SIGN
- ❏ SIN
- ❏ SQRT
- ❏ SQUARE
- ❏ TAN

ABS

The ABS function returns the positive, absolute value of *numeric_expression*. The syntax is as follows:

```
ABS(<numeric_expression>)
```

ACOS

The ACOS function returns the angle in radians for which the cosine is the *expression* (in other words, it returns the arccosine of *expression*). The syntax is as follows:

```
ACOS(<expression>)
```

The value of *expression* must be between -1 and 1 and be of the float data type.

ASIN

The ASIN function returns the angle in radians for which the sine is the *expression* (in other words, it returns the arcsine of *expression*). The syntax is as follows:

```
ASIN(<expression>)
```

The value of *expression* must be between -1 and 1 and be of the float data type.

ATAN

The ATAN function returns the angle in radians for which the tangent is expression (in other words, it returns the arctangent of *expression*). The syntax is as follows:

```
ATAN(<expression>)
```

The *expression* must be of the float data type.

ATN2

The ATN2 function returns the angle in radians for which the tangent is between the two expressions provided (in other words, it returns the arctangent of the two expressions). The syntax is as follows:

```
ATN2(<expression1>, <expression2>)
```

Both *expression1* and *expression2* must be of the float data type.

CEILING

The CEILING function returns the smallest integer that is equal to or greater than the specified expression. The syntax is as follows:

```
CEILING(<expression>)
```

COS

The COS function returns the cosine of the angle specified in *expression*. The syntax is as follows:

```
COS(<expression>)
```

The angle given should be in radians and *expression* must be of the float data type.

COT

The COT function returns the cotangent of the angle specified in *expression*. The syntax is as follows:

COT(<*expression*>)

The angle given should be in radians and *expression* must be of the float data type.

DEGREES

The DEGREES function takes an angle given in radians (*expression*) and returns the angle in degrees. The syntax is as follows:

DEGREES(<*expression*>)

EXP

The EXP function returns the exponential value of the value given in *expression*. The syntax is as follows:

EXP(<*expression*>)

The *expression* must be of the float data type.

FLOOR

The FLOOR function returns the largest integer that is equal to or less than the value specified in *expression*. The syntax is as follows:

FLOOR(<*expression*>)

LOG

The LOG function returns the natural logarithm of the value specified in *expression*. The syntax is as follows:

LOG(<*expression*>)

The *expression* must be of the float data type.

LOG10

The LOG10 function returns the base 10 logarithm of the value specified in *expression*. The syntax is as follows:

LOG10(<*expression*>)

The *expression* must be of the float data type.

PI

The PI function returns the value of the constant. The syntax is as follows:

PI()

POWER

The POWER function raises the value of the specified *expression* to the specified *power*. The syntax is as follows:

POWER(<*expression*>, <*power*>)

RADIANS

The RADIANS function returns an angle in radians corresponding to the angle in degrees specified in *expression*. The syntax is as follows:

RADIANS(<*expression*>)

RAND

The RAND function returns a random value between 0 and 1. The syntax is as follows:

RAND([<*seed*>])

The *seed* value is an integer expression, which specifies the start value.

ROUND

The ROUND function takes a number specified in *expression* and rounds it to the specified length:

ROUND(<*expression*>, <*length*> [, <*function*>])

The *length* parameter specifies the precision to which *expression* should be rounded. The *length* parameter should be of the tinyint, smallint, or int data type. The optional *function* parameter can be used to specify whether the number should be rounded or truncated. If a *function* value is omitted or is equal to 0 (the default), the value in *expression* will be rounded. If any value other than 0 is provided, the value in *expression* will be truncated.

SIGN

The SIGN function returns the sign of the *expression*. The possible return values are +1 for a positive number, 0 for zero and -1 for a negative number. The syntax is as follows:

SIGN(<*expression*>)

SIN

The SIN function returns the sine of an angle. The syntax is as follows:

```
SIN(<angle>)
```

The *angle* should be in radians and must be of the float data type. The return value will also be of the float data type.

SQRT

The SQRT function returns the square root of the value given in *expression*. The syntax is as follows:

```
SQRT(<expression>)
```

The *expression* must be of the float data type.

SQUARE

The SQUARE function returns the square of the value given in *expression*. The syntax is as follows:

```
SQUARE(<expression>)
```

The *expression* must be of the float data type.

TAN

The TAN function returns the tangent of the value specified in *expression*. The syntax is as follows:

```
TAN(<expression>)
```

The *expression* parameter specifies the number of radians and must be of the float or real data type.

Meta Data Functions

The meta data functions provide information about the database and database objects. They are:

- ❑ COL_LENGTH
- ❑ COL_NAME
- ❑ COLUMNPROPERTY
- ❑ DATABASEPROPERTY
- ❑ DB_ID
- ❑ DB_NAME
- ❑ FILE_ID

- ❏ FILE_NAME
- ❏ FILEGROUP_ID
- ❏ FILEGROUP_NAME
- ❏ FILEGROUPPROPERTY
- ❏ FILEPROPERTY
- ❏ FULLTEXTCATALOGPROPERTY
- ❏ FULLTEXTSERVICEPROPERTY
- ❏ INDEX_COL
- ❏ INDEXKEY_PROPERTY
- ❏ INDEXPROPERTY
- ❏ OBJECT_ID
- ❏ OBJECT_NAME
- ❏ OBJECTPROPERTY
- ❏ SQL_VARIANT_PROPERTY
- ❏ TYPEPROPERTY

COL_LENGTH

The COL_LENGTH function returns the defined length of a column. The syntax is as follows:

```
COL_LENGTH('<table>', '<column>')
```

The *column* parameter specifies the name of the column for which the length is to be determined. The *table* parameter specifies the name of the table that contains that column.

COL_NAME

The COL_NAME function takes a table ID number and a column ID number and returns the name of the database column. The syntax is as follows:

```
COL_NAME(<table_id>, <column_id>)
```

The *column_id* parameter specifies the ID number of the column. The *table_id* parameter specifies the ID number of the table that contains that column.

COLUMNPROPERTY

The COLUMNPROPERTY function returns data about a column or procedure parameter. The syntax is as follows:

```
COLUMNPROPERTY(<id>, <column>, <property>)
```

The *id* parameter specifies the ID of the table/procedure. The *column* parameter specifies the name of the column/parameter. The *property* parameter specifies the data that should be returned for the column or procedure parameter. The *property* parameter can be one of the following values:

- ❑ AllowsNull – allows NULL values
- ❑ IsComputed – the column is a computed column
- ❑ IsCursorType – the procedure is of type CURSOR
- ❑ IsFullTextIndexed – the column has been full-text indexed
- ❑ IsIdentity – the column is an IDENTITY column
- ❑ IsIdNotForRepl – the column checks for IDENTITY NOT FOR REPLICATION
- ❑ IsOutParam – the procedure parameter is an output parameter
- ❑ IsRowGuidCol – the column is a ROWGUIDCOL column
- ❑ Precision – the precision for the data type of the column or parameter
- ❑ Scale – the scale for the data type of the column or parameter
- ❑ UseAnsiTrim – the ANSI padding setting was ON when the table was created

The return value from this function will be 1 for True, 0 for False, and NULL if the input was not valid – except for Precision (where the precision for the data type will be returned) and Scale (where the scale will be returned).

DATABASEPROPERTY

The DATABASEPROPERTY function returns the setting for the specified database and property name. The syntax is as follows:

```
DATABASEPROPERTY('<database>', '<property>')
```

The *database* parameter specifies the name of the database for which data on the named property will be returned. The *property* parameter contains the name of a database property and can be one of the following values:

- ❑ IsAnsiNullDefault – the database follows the ANSI-92 standard for NULL values
- ❑ IsAnsiNullsEnabled – all comparisons made with a NULL cannot be evaluated
- ❑ IsAnsiWarningsEnabled – warning messages are issued when standard error conditions occur
- ❑ IsAutoClose – the database frees resources after the last user has exited
- ❑ IsAutoShrink – database files can be shrunk automatically and periodically
- ❑ IsAutoUpdateStatistics – the autoupdate statistics option has been enabled
- ❑ IsBulkCopy – the database allows non-logged operations (such as those performed with the bulk copy program)
- ❑ IsCloseCursorsOnCommitEnabled – any cursors that are open when a transaction is committed will be closed

- ❏ IsDboOnly – the database is only accessible to the dbo
- ❏ IsDetached – the database was detached by a detach operation
- ❏ IsEmergencyMode – the database is in emergency mode
- ❏ IsFulltextEnabled – the database has been full-text enabled
- ❏ IsInLoad – the database is loading
- ❏ IsInRecovery – the database is recovering
- ❏ IsInStandby – the database is read-only and restore log is allowed
- ❏ IsLocalCursorsDefault – cursor declarations default to LOCAL
- ❏ IsNotRecovered – the database failed to recover
- ❏ IsNullConcat – concatenating to a NULL results in a NULL
- ❏ IsOffline – the database is offline
- ❏ IsQuotedIdentifiersEnabled – identifiers can be delimited by double quotation marks
- ❏ IsReadOnly – the database is in a read-only mode
- ❏ IsRecursiveTriggersEnabled – the recursive firing of triggers is enabled
- ❏ IsShutDown – the database encountered a problem during startup
- ❏ IsSingleUser – the database is in single-user mode
- ❏ IsSuspect – the database is suspect
- ❏ IsTruncLog – the database truncates its log on checkpoints
- ❏ Version – the internal version number of the SQL Server code with which the database was created

The return value from this function will be 1 for true, 0 for false, and NULL if the input was not valid – except for Version (where the function will return the version number if the database is open and NULL if the database is closed).

DB_ID

The DB_ID function returns the database ID number. The syntax is as follows:

```
DB_ID(['<database_name>'])
```

The optional *database_name* parameter specifies which database's ID number is required. If the *database_name* is not given, the current database will be used instead.

DB_NAME

The DB_NAME function returns the name of the database that has the specified ID number. The syntax is as follows:

```
DB_NAME([<database_id>])
```

The optional *database_id* parameter specifies which database's name is to be returned. If no *database_id* is given, the name of the current database will be returned.

FILE_ID

The FILE_ID function returns the file ID number for the specified file name in the current database. The syntax is as follows:

FILE_ID('<file_name>')

The file_name parameter specifies the name of the file for which the ID is required.

FILE_NAME

The FILE_NAME function returns the file name for the file with the specified file ID number. The syntax is as follows:

FILE_NAME(<file_id>)

The file_id parameter specifies the ID number of the file for which the name is required.

FILEGROUP_ID

The FILEGROUP_ID function returns the filegroup ID number for the specified filegroup name. The syntax is as follows:

FILEGROUP_ID('<filegroup_name>')

The filegroup_name parameter specifies the filegroup name of the required filegroup ID.

FILEGROUP_NAME

The FILEGROUP_NAME function returns the filegroup name for the specified filegroup ID number. The syntax is as follows:

FILEGROUP_NAME(<filegroup_id>)

The filegroup_id parameter specifies the filegroup ID of the required filegroup name.

FILEGROUPPROPERTY

The FILEGROUPPROPERTY returns the setting of a specified filegroup property, given the filegroup and property name. The syntax is as follows:

FILEGROUPPROPERTY(<filegroup_name>, <property>)

The filegroup_name parameter specifies the name of the filegroup that contains the property being queried. The property parameter specifies the property being queried and can be one of the following values:

- IsReadOnly – the filegroup name is read-only
- IsUserDefinedFG – the filegroup name is a user-defined filegroup
- IsDefault – the filegroup name is the default filegroup

The return value from this function will be 1 for True, 0 for False, and NULL if the input was not valid.

FILEPROPERTY

The FILEPROPERTY function returns the setting of a specified file name property, given the file name and property name. The syntax is as follows:

```
FILEPROPERTY(<file_name>, <property>)
```

The *file_name* parameter specifies the name of the filegroup that contains the property being queried. The *property* parameter specifies the property being queried and can be one of the following values:

- ❑ IsReadOnly – the file is read-only
- ❑ IsPrimaryFile – the file is the primary file
- ❑ IsLogFile – the file is a log file
- ❑ SpaceUsed – the amount of space used by the specified file

The return value from this function will be 1 for True, 0 for False, and NULL if the input was not valid, except for SpaceUsed (which will return the number of pages allocated in the file).

FULLTEXTCATALOGPROPERTY

The FULLTEXTCATALOGPROPERTY function returns data about the full-text catalog properties. The syntax is as follows:

```
FULLTEXTCATALOGPROPERTY(<catalog_name>, <property>)
```

The *catalog_name* parameter specifies the name of the full-text catalog. The *property* parameter specifies the property that is being queried. The properties that can be queried are:

- ❑ PopulateStatus – for which the possible return values are: 0 (idle), 1 (population in progress), 2 (paused), 3 (throttled), 4 (recovering), 5 (shutdown), 6 (incremental population in progress), 7 (updating index)
- ❑ ItemCount – returns the number of full-text indexed items currently in the full-text catalog
- ❑ IndexSize – returns the size of the full-text index in megabytes
- ❑ UniqueKeyCount – returns the number of unique words that make up the full-text index in this catalog
- ❑ LogSize – returns the size (in bytes) of the combined set of error logs associated with a full-text catalog
- ❑ PopulateCompletionAge – returns the difference (in seconds) between the completion of the last full-text index population and 01/01/1990 00:00:00

FULLTEXTSERVICEPROPERTY

The FULLTEXTSERVICEPROPERTY function returns data about the full-text service-level properties. The syntax is as follows:

```
FULLTEXTSERVICEPROPERTY(<property>)
```

The *property* parameter specifies the name of the service-level property that is to be queried. The *property* parameter may be one of the following values:

❑ ResourceUsage – returns a value from 1 (background) to 5 (dedicated)

❑ ConnectTimeOut – returns the number of seconds that the Search Service will wait for all connections to SQL Server for full-text index population before timing out

❑ IsFulltextInstalled – returns 1 if Full-Text Service is installed on the computer and a 0 otherwise

INDEX_COL

The INDEX_COL function returns the indexed column name. The syntax is as follows:

```
INDEX_COL('<table>', <index_id>, <key_id>)
```

The *table* parameter specifies the name of the table, *index_id* specifies the ID of the index, and *key_id* specifies the ID of the key.

INDEXKEY_PROPERTY

This function returns information about the index key.

```
INDEXKEY_PROPERTY(<table_id>, <index_id>, <key_id>, <property>)
```

The *table_id* parameter is the numerical ID of data type int, which defines the table you wish to inspect. Use OBJECT_ID to find the numerical *table_id*. *index_id* specifies the ID of the index, and is also of data type int. *key_id* specifies the index column position of the key, for example, with a key of three columns, setting this value to 2 will determine that you are wishing to inspect the middle column. Finally, the *property* is the character string identifier of one of two properties you wish to find the setting of. The two possible values are ColumnId, which will return the physical column ID, or IsDescending, which returns the order that the column is sorted (1 is for descending and 0 is ascending).

INDEXPROPERTY

The INDEXPROPERTY function returns the setting of a specified index property, given the table ID, index name, and property name. The syntax is as follows:

```
INDEXPROPERTY(<table_ID>, <index>, <property>)
```

The *property* parameter specifies the property of the index that is to be queried. The *property* parameter can be one of these possible values:

- ❑ IndexDepth – the depth of the index
- ❑ IsAutoStatistic – the index was created by the auto create statistics option of sp_dboption
- ❑ IsClustered – the index is clustered
- ❑ IsStatistics – the index was created by the CREATE STATISTICS statement or by the auto create statistics option of sp_dboption
- ❑ IsUnique – the index is unique
- ❑ IndexFillFactor – the index specifies its own fill factor
- ❑ IsPadIndex – the index specifies space to leave open on each interior node
- ❑ IsFulltextKey – the index is the full-text key for a table
- ❑ IsHypothetical – the index is hypothetical and cannot be used directly as a data access path

The return value from this function will be 1 for True, 0 for False, and NULL if the input was not valid, except for IndexDepth (which will return the number of levels the index has) and IndexFillFactor (which will return the fill factor used when the index was created or last rebuilt).

OBJECT_ID

The OBJECT_ID function returns the specified database object's ID number. The syntax is as follows:

OBJECT_ID('<object>')

OBJECT_NAME

The OBJECT_NAME function returns the name of the specified database object. The syntax is as follows:

OBJECT_NAME(<object_id>)

OBJECTPROPERTY

The OBJECTPROPERTY function returns data about objects in the current database. The syntax is as follows:

OBJECTPROPERTY(<id>, <property>)

The *id* parameter specifies the ID of the object required. The *property* parameter specifies the information required on the object. The following *property* values are allowed:

CnstIsClustKey	CnstIsColumn
CnstIsDisabled	CnstIsNonclustKey
CnstIsNotRepl	ExecIsAnsiNullsOn
ExecIsDeleteTrigger	ExecIsInsertTrigger
ExecIsQuotedIdentOn	ExecIsStartup
ExecIsTriggerDisabled	ExecIsUpdateTrigger
IsCheckCnst	IsConstraint
IsDefault	IsDefaultCnst
IsExecuted	IsExtendedProc
IsForeignKey	IsMSShipped
IsPrimaryKey	IsProcedure
IsReplProc	IsRule
IsSystemTable	IsTable
IsTrigger	IsUniqueCnst
IsUserTable	IsView
OwnerId	TableDeleteTrigger
TableDeleteTriggerCount	TableFulltextCatalogId
TableFulltextKeyColumn	TableHasActiveFulltextIndex
TableHasCheckCnst	TableHasClustIndex
TableHasDefaultCnst	TableHasDeleteTrigger
TableHasForeignKey	TableHasForeignRef
TableHasIdentity	TableHasIndex
TableHasInsertTrigger	TableHasNonclustIndex
TableHasPrimaryKey	TableHasRowGuidCol
TableHasTextImage	TableHasTimestamp
TableHasUniqueCnst	TableHasUpdateTrigger
TableInsertTrigger	TableInsertTriggerCount
TableIsFake	TableIsPinned
TableUpdateTrigger	TableUpdateTriggerCount
TriggerDeleteOrder	TriggerInsertOrder
TriggerUpdateOrder	

The return value from this function will be 1 for True, 0 for False, and NULL if the input was not valid, except for:

- ❑ OwnerId (which will return the database user ID of the object owner)

- ❑ TableDeleteTrigger, TableDeleteTriggerCount, TableInsertTrigger, TableInsertTriggerCount, TableUpdateTrigger, TableUpdateTriggerCount (all of which will return the ID of the first trigger with the given type)

- ❑ TableFulltextCatalogId and TableFulltextKeyColumn (both of which will return the full-text catalog ID, or a 0 to indicate that the table has not been full-text indexed, or a NULL to indicate that the input was invalid)

SQL_VARIANT_PROPERTY

SQL_VARIANT_PROPERTY is a powerful function and returns information about a sql_variant. This information could be from BaseType, Precision, Scale, TotalBytes, Collation, MaxLength. The syntax is:

```
SQL_VARIANT_PROPERTY (expression, property)
```

Expression is an expression of type `sql_variant`. *Property* can be any one of the following values:

Value	Description	Base type of sql_variant returned
BaseType	Data types include: char, int, money, nchar, ntext, numeric, nvarchar, real, smalldatetime, smallint, smallmoney, text, timestamp, tinyint, uniqueidentifier, varbinary, varchar	sysname
Precision	The precision of the numeric base data type: datetime = 23 smalldatetime = 16 float = 53 real = 24 decimal (p,s) and numeric (p,s) = p money = 19 smallmoney = 10 int = 10 smallint = 5 tinyint = 3 bit = 1 all other types = 0	int
Scale	The number of digits to the right of the decimal point of the numeric base data type: decimal (p,s) and numeric (p,s) = s money and smallmoney = 4 datetime = 3 all other types = 0	int
TotalBytes	The number of bytes required to hold both the meta data and data of the value. If the value is greater than 900, index creation will fail.	int
Collation	The collation of the particular sql_variant value.	sysname
MaxLength	The maximum data type length, in bytes.	int

TYPEPROPERTY

The TYPEPROPERTY function returns information about a data type. The syntax is as follows:

```
TYPEPROPERTY(<type>, <property>)
```

The *type* parameter specifies the name of the data type. The *property* parameter specifies the property of the data type that is to be queried; it can be one of the following values:

❑ Precision – returns the number of digits/characters

❑ Scale – returns the number of decimal places

❑ AllowsNull – returns 1 for True and 0 for False

❑ UsesAnsiTrim – returns 1 for True and 0 for False

Rowset Functions

The rowset functions return an object that can be used in place of a table reference in a T-SQL statement. The rowset functions are:

❑ CONTAINSTABLE

❑ FREETEXTTABLE

❑ OPENDATASOURCE

❑ OPENQUERY

❑ OPENROWSET

❑ OPENXML

CONTAINSTABLE

The CONTAINSTABLE function is used in full-text queries. Please refer to Chapter 26 for an example of its usage. The syntax is as follows:

```
CONTAINSTABLE (<table>, {<column> | *}, '<contains_search_condition>')
```

FREETEXTTABLE

The FREETEXTTABLE function is used in full-text queries. Please refer to Chapter 26 for an example of its usage. The syntax is as follows:

```
FREETEXTTABLE (<table>, {<column> | *}, '<freetext_string>')
```

OPENDATASOURCE

The OPENDATASOURCE function provides ad hoc connection information. The syntax is as follows:

```
OPENDATASOURCE (<provider_name>, <init_string>)
```

The *provider_name* is the name registered as the ProgID of the OLE DB provider used to access the data source. The *init_string* should be familiar to VB programmers, as this is the initialization string to the OLE DB provider. For example, the *init_string* could look like:

```
"User Id=wonderison;Password=JuniorBlues;DataSource=MyServerName"
```

OPENQUERY

The OPENQUERY function executes the specified pass-through *query* on the specified *linked_server*. The syntax is as follows:

```
OPENQUERY(<linked_server>, '<query>')
```

OPENROWSET

The OPENROWSET function accesses remote data from an OLE DB data source. The syntax is as follows:

```
OPENROWSET('<provider_name>'
    {
     '<datasource>';'<user_id>';'<password>'
     | '<provider_string>'
    },
    {
        [<catalog.>][<schema.>]<object>
        | '<query>'
    })
```

The *provider_name* parameter is a string representing the friendly name of the OLE DB provided as specified in the registry. The *data_source* parameter is a string corresponding to the required OLE DB data source. The *user_id* parameter is a relevant username to be passed to the OLE DB provider. The *password* parameter is the password associated with the *user_id*.

The *provider_string* parameter is a provider-specific connection string and is used in place of the *datasource*, user_id, and *password* combination.

The *catalog* parameter is the name of catalog/database that contains the required object. The *schema* parameter is the name of the schema or object owner of the required object. The *object* parameter is the object name.

The *query* parameter is a string that is executed by the provider and is used instead of a combination of *catalog*, *schema*, and *object*.

OPENXML

By passing in an XML document as a parameter, or retrieving an XML document and defining the document within a variable, OPENXML allows you to inspect the structure and return data, as if the XML document was a table. The syntax is as follows:

```
OPENXML(<idoc_int> [in],<rowpattern> nvarchar[in],[<flags> byte[in]])
[WITH (<SchemaDeclaration> | <TableName>)]
```

The idoc_int parameter is the variable defined using the sp_xml_prepareddocument system sproc. *Rowpattern* is the node definition. The *flags* parameter specifies the mapping between the XML document and the rowset to return within the SELECT statement. *SchemaDeclaration* defines the XML schema for the XML document, if there is a table defined within the database that follows the XML schema, then *TableName* can be used instead.

Before being able to use the XML document, it must be prepared by using the sp_xml_prepareddocument system procedure.

For more information on using OpenXML, please refer to Chapter 20.

Security Functions

The security functions return information about users and roles. They are:

❑ HAS_DBACCESS

❑ IS_MEMBER

❑ IS_SRVROLEMEMBER

❑ SUSER_ID

❑ SUSER_NAME

❑ SUSER_SID

❑ USER

❑ USER_ID

HAS_DBACCESS

The HAS_DBACCESS function is used to determine whether the user that is logged in has access to the database being used. A return value of 1 means the user does have access, and a return value of 0 means that it does not. A NULL return value means the *database_name* supplied was invalid. The syntax is as follows:

```
HAS_DBACCESS ('<database_name>')
```

IS_MEMBER

The IS_MEMBER function returns whether the current user is a member of the specified Windows NT group/SQL Server role. The syntax is as follows:

```
IS_MEMBER ({'<group>' | '<role>'})
```

The *group* parameter specifies the name of the NT group and must be in the form *domain\group*. The *role* parameter specifies the name of the SQL Server role. The role can be a database fixed role or a user-defined role but cannot be a server role.

This function will return a 1 if the current user is a member of the specified group or role, a 0 if the current user is not a member of the specified group or role, and NULL if the specified group or role is invalid.

IS_SRVROLEMEMBER

The IS_SRVROLEMEMBER function returns whether a user is a member of the specified server role. The syntax is as follows:

```
IS_SRVROLEMEMBER ('<role>' [,'<login>'])
```

The optional *login* parameter is the name of the login account to check – the default is the current user. The *role* parameter specifies the server role and must be one of the following possible values:

- sysadmin
- dbcreator
- diskadmin
- processadmin
- serveradmin
- setupadmin
- securityadmin

This function returns a 1 if the specified login account is a member of the specified role, a 0 if the login is not a member of the role, and a NULL if the role or login is invalid.

SUSER_ID

The SUSER_ID function returns the specified user's login ID number. The syntax is as follows:

```
SUSER_ID(['<login>'])
```

The *login* parameter is the specified user's login ID name. If no value for *login* is provided, the default of the current user will be used instead.

> The SUSER_ID system function is included in SQL Server 2000 for backward compatibility, so if possible you should use SUSER_SID instead.

SUSER_NAME

The SUSER_NAME function returns the specified user's login ID name. The syntax is as follows:

```
SUSER_NAME([<server_user_id>])
```

The *server_user_id* parameter is the specified user's login ID number. If no value for *server_user_id* is provided, the default of the current user will be used instead.

> *The SUSER_NAME system function is included in SQL Server 2000 for backward compatibility only, so if possible you should use SUSER_SNAME instead.*

SUSER_SID

The SUSER_SID function returns the security identification number (SID) for the specified user. The syntax is as follows:

```
SUSER_SID(['<login>'])
```

The *login* parameter is the user's login name. If no value for login is provided, the current user will be used instead.

SUSER_SNAME

The SUSER_SNAME function returns the login ID name for the specified security identification number (SID). The syntax is as follows:

```
SUSER_SNAME([<server_user_sid>])
```

The *server_user_sid* parameter is the user's SID. If no value for the *server_user_sid* is provided, the current user's will be used instead.

USER

The USER function allows a system-supplied value for the current user's database username to be inserted into a table if no default has been supplied. The syntax is as follows:

```
USER
```

USER_ID

The USER_ID function returns the specified user's database ID number. The syntax is as follows:

```
USER_ID(['<user>'])
```

The *user* parameter is the username to be used. If no value for *user* is provided, the current user is used.

String Functions

The string functions perform actions on string values and return strings or numeric values. The string functions are:

- ❏ ASCII
- ❏ CHAR
- ❏ CHARINDEX
- ❏ DIFFERENCE
- ❏ LEFT
- ❏ LEN
- ❏ LOWER
- ❏ LTRIM
- ❏ NCHAR
- ❏ PATINDEX
- ❏ QUOTENAME
- ❏ REPLACE
- ❏ REPLICATE
- ❏ REVERSE
- ❏ RIGHT
- ❏ RTRIM
- ❏ SOUNDEX
- ❏ SPACE
- ❏ STR
- ❏ STUFF
- ❏ SUBSTRING
- ❏ UNICODE
- ❏ UPPER

ASCII

The ASCII function returns the ASCII code value of the left-most character in *character_expression*. The syntax is as follows:

```
ASCII(<character_expression>)
```

CHAR

The CHAR function converts an ASCII code (specified in expression) into a string. The syntax is as follows:

CHAR(<*expression*>)

The *expression* can be any integer between 0 and 255.

CHARINDEX

The CHARINDEX function returns the starting position of an *expression* in a *character_string*. The syntax is as follows:

CHARINDEX(<*expression*>, <*character_string*> [, <*start_location*>])

The *expression* parameter is the string, which is to be found. The *character_string* is the string to be searched, usually a column. The *start_location* is the character position to begin the search, if this is anything other than a positive number, the search will begin at the start of *character_string*.

DIFFERENCE

The DIFFERENCE function returns the difference between the SOUNDEX values of two expressions as an integer. The syntax is as follows:

DIFFERENCE(<*expression1*>, <*expression2*>)

This function returns an integer value between 0 and 4. If the two expressions sound identical (for example, blue and blew) a value of 4 will be returned. If there is no similarity a value of 0 is returned.

LEFT

The LEFT function returns the leftmost part of an expression, starting a specified number of characters from the left. The syntax is as follows:

LEFT(<*expression*>, <*integer*>)

The *expression* parameter contains the character data from which the leftmost section will be extracted. The *integer* parameter specifies the number of characters from the left to begin – it must be a positive integer.

LEN

The LEN function returns the number of characters in the specified *expression*. The syntax is as follows:

LEN(<*expression*>)

LOWER

The LOWER function converts any uppercase characters in the *expression* into lowercase characters. The syntax is as follows:

```
LOWER(<expression>)
```

LTRIM

The LTRIM function removes any leading blanks from a *character_expression*. The syntax is as follows:

```
LTRIM(<character_expression>)
```

NCHAR

The NCHAR function returns the Unicode character that has the specified *integer_code*. The syntax is as follows:

```
NCHAR(<integer_code>)
```

The *integer_code* parameter must be a positive whole number from 0 to 65,535.

PATINDEX

The PATINDEX function returns the starting position of the first occurrence of a pattern in a specified expression or zero if the pattern was not found. The syntax is as follows:

```
PATINDEX('<%pattern%>', <expression>)
```

The *pattern* parameter is a string that will be searched for. Wildcard characters can be used, but the % characters must surround the pattern. The *expression* parameter is character data in which the pattern is being searched for – usually a column.

QUOTENAME

The QUOTENAME function returns a Unicode string with delimiters added to make the specified string a valid SQL Server delimited identifier. The syntax is as follows:

```
QUOTENAME('<character_string>'[, '<quote_character>'])
```

The *character_string* parameter is Unicode string. The *quote_character* parameter is a one-character string that will be used as a delimiter. The *quote_character* parameter can be a single quotation mark ('), a left or a right bracket ([]), or a double quotation mark (") – the default is for brackets to be used.

REPLACE

The REPLACE function replaces all instances of second specified string in the first specified string with a third specified string. The syntax is as follows:

```
REPLACE('<string_expression1>', '<string_expression2>',
'<string_expression3>')
```

The *string_expression1* parameter is the expression in which to search. The *string_expression2* parameter is the expression to search for in *string_expression1*. The *string_expression3* parameter is the expression with which to replace all instances of *string_expression2*.

REPLICATE

The REPLICATE function repeats a *character_expression* a specified number of times. The syntax is as follows:

```
REPLICATE(<character_expression>, <integer>)
```

REVERSE

The REVERSE function returns the reverse of the specified *character_expression*. The syntax is as follows:

```
REVERSE(<character_expression>)
```

RIGHT

The RIGHT function returns the rightmost part of the specified *character_expression*, starting a specified number of characters (given by *integer*) from the right. The syntax is as follows:

```
RIGHT(<character_expression>, <integer>)
```

The *integer* parameter must be a positive whole number.

RTRIM

The RTRIM function removes all the trailing blanks from a specified *character_expression*. The syntax is as follows:

```
RTRIM(<character_expression>)
```

SOUNDEX

The SOUNDEX function returns a four-character (SOUNDEX) code, which can be used to evaluate the similarity of two strings. The syntax is as follows:

```
SOUNDEX(<character_expression>)
```

SPACE

The SPACE function returns a string of repeated spaces, the length of which is indicated by *integer*. The syntax is as follows:

SPACE(*<integer>*)

STR

The STR function converts numeric data into character data. The syntax is as follows:

STR(*<numeric_expression>*[, *<length>*[, *<decimal>*]])

The *numeric_expression* parameter is a numeric expression with a decimal point. The *length* parameter is the total length including decimal point, digits, and spaces. The *decimal* parameter is the number of places to the right of the decimal point.

STUFF

The STUFF function deletes a specified length of characters and inserts another set of characters in their place. The syntax is as follows:

STUFF(*<expression>*, *<start>*, *<length>*, *<characters>*)

The *expression* parameter is the string of characters in which some will be deleted and new ones added. The *start* parameter specifies where to begin deletion and insertion of characters. The *length* parameter specifies the number of characters to delete. The *characters* parameter specifies the new set of characters to be inserted into the *expression*.

SUBSTRING

The SUBSTRING function returns part of an expression. The syntax is as follows:

SUBSTRING(*<expression>*, *<start>*, *<length>*)

The *expression* parameter specifies the data from which the substring will be taken, and can be a character string, binary string, text, or an expression that includes a table. The *start* parameter is an integer that specifies where to begin the substring. The *length* parameter specifies how long the substring is.

UNICODE

The UNICODE function returns the UNICODE number that represents the first character in *character_expression*. The syntax is as follows:

UNICODE('*<character_expression>*')

UPPER

The UPPER function converts all the lowercase characters in *character_expression* into uppercase characters. The syntax is as follows:

UPPER(*<character_expression>*)

System Functions

The system functions can be used to return information about values, objects and settings with SQL Server. The functions are as follows:

- ❑ APP_NAME
- ❑ CASE
- ❑ CAST and CONVERT
- ❑ COALESCE
- ❑ COLLATIONPROPERTY
- ❑ CURRENT_TIMESTAMP
- ❑ CURRENT_USER
- ❑ DATALENGTH
- ❑ FORMATMESSAGE
- ❑ GETANSINULL
- ❑ HOST_ID
- ❑ HOST_NAME
- ❑ IDENT_CURRENT
- ❑ IDENT_INCR
- ❑ IDENT_SEED
- ❑ IDENTITY
- ❑ ISDATE
- ❑ ISNULL
- ❑ ISNUMERIC
- ❑ NEWID
- ❑ NULLIF
- ❑ PARSENAME
- ❑ PERMISSIONS
- ❑ ROWCOUNT_BIG
- ❑ SCOPE_IDENTITY
- ❑ SERVERPROPERTY
- ❑ SESSION_USER
- ❑ SESSIONPROPERTY
- ❑ STATS_DATE
- ❑ SYSTEM_USER
- ❑ USER_NAME

APP_NAME

The APP_NAME function returns the application name for the current session if one has been set by the application as an nvarchar type. It has the following syntax:

```
APP_NAME()
```

CASE

The CASE function evaluates a list of conditions and returns one of multiple possible results. It also has two formats:

❑ The simple CASE function compares an expression to a set of simple expressions to determine the result

❑ The searched CASE function evaluates a set of Boolean expressions to determine the result

Both formats support an optional ELSE argument.

Simple CASE function:

```
CASE <input_expression>
   WHEN <when_expression> THEN <result_expression>
   ELSE <else_result_expression>
END
```

Searched CASE function:

```
CASE
    WHEN <Boolean_expression> THEN <result_expression>
    ELSE <else_result_expression>
END
```

CAST and CONVERT

These two functions provide similar functionality in that they both convert one data type into another type.

Using CAST:

```
CAST(<expression> AS <data_type>)
```

Using CONVERT:

```
CONVERT (<data_type>[(<length>)], <expression> [, <style>])
```

Where *style* refers to the style of date format when converting to a character data type.

COALESCE

The COALESCE function is passed an undefined number of arguments and it tests for the first non-null expression among them. The syntax is as follows:

```
COALESCE(<expression> [,...n])
```

If all arguments are NULL then COALESCE returns NULL.

COLLATIONPROPERTY

The COLLATIONPROPERTY function returns the property of a given collation. The syntax is as follows:

```
COLLATIONPROPERTY(<collation_name>, <property>)
```

The *collation_name* parameter is the name of the collation you wish to use, and *property* is the property of the collation you wish to determine. This can be one of three values:

Property Name	Description
CodePage	The non-Unicode code page of the collation.
LCID	The Windows LCID of the collation. Returns NULL for SQL collations.
ComparisonStyle	The Windows comparison style of the collation. Returns NULL for binary or SQL collations.

CURRENT_TIMESTAMP

The CURRENT_TIMESTAMP function simply returns the current date and time as a datetime type. It is equivalent to GETDATE(). The syntax is as follows:

```
CURRENT_TIMESTAMP
```

CURRENT_USER

The CURRENT_USER function simply returns the current user as a sysname type. It is equivalent to USER_NAME(). The syntax is as follows:

```
CURRENT_USER
```

DATALENGTH

The DATALENGTH function returns the number of bytes used to represent *expression* as an integer. It is especially useful with varchar, varbinary, text, image, nvarchar, and ntext data types because these data types can store variable-length data. The syntax is as follows:

```
DATALENGTH(<expression>)
```

FORMATMESSAGE

The FORMATMESSAGE function uses existing messages in sysmessages to construct a message. The syntax is as follows:

FORMATMESSAGE(<msg_number>, <param_value>[,...n])

Where msg_number is the ID of the message in sysmessages.

> FORMATMESSAGE looks up the message in the current language of the user. If there is no localized version of the message, the US English version is used.

GETANSINULL

The GETANSINULL function returns the default nullability for a database as an integer. The syntax is as follows:

GETANSINULL(['<database>'])

The database parameter is the name of the database for which to return nullability information.

When the nullability of the given database allows NULL values and the column or data type nullability is not explicitly defined, GETANSINULL returns 1. This is the ANSI NULL default.

HOST_ID

The HOST_ID function returns the ID of the workstation. The syntax is as follows:

HOST_ID()

HOST_NAME

The HOST_NAME function returns the name of the workstation. The syntax is as follows:

HOST_NAME()

IDENT_CURRENT

The IDENT_CURRENT function returns the last identity value created for a table, within any session or scope of that table. This is exactly like @@IDENTITY, and SCOPE_IDENTITY, however, this has no limit to the scope of its search to return the value.

The syntax is as follows:

IDENT_CURRENT('<table_name>')

The table_name is the table for which you wish to find the current identity.

IDENT_INCR

The IDENT_INCR function returns the increment value specified during the creation of an identity column in a table or view that has an identity column. The syntax is as follows:

```
IDENT_INCR('<table_or_view>')
```

The *table_or_view* parameter is an expression specifying the table or view to check for a valid identity increment value.

IDENT_SEED

The IDENT_SEED function returns the seed value specified during the creation of an identity column in a table or a view that has an identity column. The syntax is as follows:

```
IDENT_SEED('<table_or_view>')
```

The *table_or_view* parameter is an expression specifying the table or view to check for a valid identity increment value.

IDENTITY

The IDENTITY function is used to insert an identity column into a new table. It is used only with a SELECT statement with an INTO table clause. The syntax is as follows:

```
IDENTITY(<data_type>[, <seed>, <increment>]) AS <column_name>
```

Where:

- ❑ *data_type* is the data type of the identity column.
- ❑ *seed* is the value to be assigned to the first row in the table. Each subsequent row is assigned the next identity value, which is equal to the last IDENTITY value plus the *increment* value. If neither *seed* nor *increment* is specified, both default to 1.
- ❑ *increment* is the increment to add to the *seed* value for successive rows in the table.
- ❑ *column_name* is the name of the column that is to be inserted into the new table.

ISDATE

The ISDATE function determines whether an input expression is a valid date. The syntax is as follows:

```
ISDATE(<expression>)
```

ISNULL

The ISNULL function checks an expression for a NULL value and replaces it with a specified replacement value. The syntax is as follows:

```
ISNULL(<check_expression>, <replacement_value>)
```

ISNUMERIC

The `ISNUMERIC` function determines whether an expression is a valid numeric type. The syntax is as follows:

```
ISNUMERIC(<expression>)
```

NEWID

The `NEWID` function creates a unique value of type `uniqueidentifier`. The syntax is as follows:

```
NEWID()
```

NULLIF

The `NULLIF` function compares two expressions and returns a `NULL` value. The syntax is as follows:

```
NULLIF(<expression1>, <expression2>)
```

PARSENAME

The `PARSENAME` function returns the specified part of an object name. The syntax is as follows:

```
PARSENAME('<object_name>', <object_piece>)
```

The *object_name* parameter specifies the object name from the part that is to be retrieved. The *object_piece* parameter specifies the part of the object to return. The *object_piece* parameter takes one of these possible values:

- ❑ 1 – Object name
- ❑ 2 – Owner name
- ❑ 3 – Database name
- ❑ 4 – Server name

PERMISSIONS

The `PERMISSIONS` function returns a value containing a bitmap, which indicates the statement, object, or column permissions for the current user. The syntax is as follows:

```
PERMISSIONS([<objectid> [, '<column>']])
```

The *object_id* parameter specifies the ID of an object. The optional *column* parameter specifies the name of the column for which permission information is being returned.

ROWCOUNT_BIG

The ROWCOUNT_BIG function is very similar to @@ROWCOUNT, in that it returns the number of rows from the last statement. However, the value returned is of a data type of bigint. The syntax is as follows:

```
ROWCOUNT_BIG()
```

SCOPE_IDENTITY

The SCOPE_IDENTITY function returns the last value inserted into an identity column in the same scope (that is, within the same sproc, trigger, function, or batch). This is similar to IDENT_CURRENT, discussed above, although that was not limited to identity insertions made in the same scope.

This function returns a sql_variant data type, and the syntax is as follows:

```
SCOPE_IDENTITY()
```

SERVERPROPERTY

The SERVERPROPERTY function returns information about the server you are running on. The syntax is as follows:

```
SERVERPROPERTY('<propertyname>')
```

The possible values for propertyname are:

Property name	Values returned
Collation	The name of the default collation for the server.
Edition	The edition of the SQL Server instance installed on the server. Returns one of the following nvarchar results: 'Desktop Engine' 'Developer Edition' 'Enterprise Edition' 'Enterprise Evaluation Edition' 'Personal Edition' 'Standard Edition'
Engine Edition	The engine edition of the SQL Server instance installed on the server: 1 – Personal or Desktop Engine 2 – Standard 3 – Enterprise (returned for Enterprise, Enterprise Evaluation, and Developer)
InstanceName	The name of the instance to which the user is connected.

Property name	Values returned
IsClustered	Will determine if the server instance is configured in a failover cluster: 1 – clustered 0 – not clustered NULL – invalid input or error
IsFullText Installed	To determine if the full-text component is installed with the current instance of SQL Server: 1 – full-text is installed 0 – full-text is not installed NULL – invalid input or error
IsIntegrated SecurityOnly	To determine if the server is in integrated security mode: 1 – integrated security 0 – not integrated security NULL – invalid input or error
IsSingleUser	To determine if the server is a single-user installation: 1 – single user 0 – not single user NULL – invalid input or error
IsSync WithBackup	To determine if the database is either a published database or a distribution database, and can be restored without disrupting the current transactional replication: 1 – True 0 – False
LicenseType	What type of license is installed for this instance of SQL Server: PER_SEAT – per-seat mode PER_PROCESSOR – per-processor mode DISABLED – licensing is disabled
MachineName	Returns the Windows NT computer name on which the server instance is running. For a clustered instance (an instance of SQL Server running on a virtual server on Microsoft Cluster Server), it returns the name of the virtual server.
NumLicenses	Number of client licenses registered for this instance of SQL Server, if in per-seat mode. Number of processors licensed for this instance of SQL Server, if in per-processor mode.
ProcessID	Process ID of the SQL Server service. (The ProcessID is useful in identifying which sqlservr.exe belongs to this instance.)

Table continued on following page

Property name	Values returned
ProductVersion	Very much like Visual Basic projects, in that the version details of the instance of SQL Server, are returned, in the form of `'major.minor.build'`.
ProductLevel	Returns the value of the version of the SQL Server instance currently running. Returns: `'RTM'` – shipping version `'SPn'` – service pack version `'Bn'` – beta version
ServerName	Both the Windows NT server and instance information associated with a specified instance of SQL Server.

The SERVERPROPERTY function is very useful for multi-sited corporations where developers need to find out information from a server.

SESSION_USER

The SESSION_USER function allows a system-supplied value for the current session's username to be inserted into a table if no default value has been specified. The syntax is as follows:

```
SESSION_USER
```

SESSIONPROPERTY

The SESSIONPROPERTY function is used to return the SET options for a session. The syntax is as follows:

```
SESSIONPROPERTY (<option>)
```

This function is useful when there are stored procedures that are altering session properties in specific scenarios. This function should rarely be used as you should not alter too many of the SET options during run-time.

STATS_DATE

The STATS_DATE function returns the date that the statistics for the specified index were last updated. The syntax is as follows:

```
STATS_DATE(<table_id>, <index_id>)
```

SYSTEM_USER

The SYSTEM_USER function allows a system-supplied value for the current system username to be inserted into a table if no default value has been specified. The syntax is as follows:

```
SYSTEM_USER
```

USER_NAME

The USER_NAME returns a database username. The syntax is as follows:

```
USER_NAME([<id>])
```

The *id* parameter specifies the ID number of the required username, if no value is given the current user is assumed.

Text and Image Functions

The text and image functions perform operations on text or image data. They are:

- ❑ PATINDEX (this was covered in the *String Functions* section)
- ❑ TEXTPTR
- ❑ TEXTVALID

TEXTPTR

The TEXTPTR function checks the value of the text pointer that corresponds to a text, ntext, or image column and returns a varbinary value. The text pointer should be checked to ensure that it points to the first text page before running READTEXT, WRITETEXT, and UPDATE statements. The syntax is as follows:

```
TEXTPTR(<column>)
```

TEXTVALID

The TEXTVALID function checks whether a specified text pointer is valid. The syntax is as follows:

```
TEXTVALID('<table.column>', <text_ptr>)
```

The *table.column* parameter specifies the name of the table and column to be used. The *text_ptr* parameter specifies the text pointer to be checked.

This function will return 0 if the pointer is invalid and 1 if the pointer is valid.

C

Tools for Our Time

So, here it is – tool time.

I need to start off this appendix by calming expectations a bit. You are not going to hear me make some, "Oh, you *have* to buy this product!" kind of recommendation. Indeed, you're going to find me trying fairly hard to keep from favoring any particular product.

What I'm after in this chapter is more just to show you some of the tools and features that are out there – essentially, I want to show you the possibilities. Realistically speaking, it doesn't matter to me which tool you use as long as you are getting the most from your experience with SQL that you can (a sentimental kind of comment, I know – but a sincere one).

In this appendix, we're going to look at just a couple of the types of different tools that you should be considering adding to your arsenal. The ones I'll touch on here are:

- ❑ ERD (diagramming) tools
- ❑ Coding tools
- ❑ Backup utilities

ERD Tools

ERD stands for **Entity Relationship Diagram**. This is the cornerstone of both understanding and relating your database design to others. If you're serious about database development, then buy a serious ERD tool – end of story.

Now that I've gone and said that, I should probably brace you for what you're going to pay – figure on a $1,000 minimum, and probably double that or more (I'm aware of at least one that goes up to $15K per seat – but it's also a *very* powerful product). What exactly these tools offer you varies by product, but let's take a look at some specific items so you get an idea of what these products can do for you.

Logical and Physical Designs

All of the major products support the concepts of the separation of logical vs. physical design. Logical vs. physical modelling was given a serious overview in Chapter 24 of this book, and I can't stress enough the importance of understanding your logical model before trying to build your physical model.

Your ER tool should facilitate this process. It should allow you to have entities and relationships in the logical model that do not necessarily need to exist in the physical side of things. In Chapter 24, I explained the notion that you may have things that are really part of your data model that can't (or, in some cases, just don't) reside in the traditional database. These can range from query components that are implemented instead of stored procedures, to working tables that only exist in memory somewhere (perhaps using the new **In Memory Database** (**IMDB**) that is part of Windows 2000). Your logical model should be able to pull all of these data constructs together in your logical model, and still be able to easily separate those that won't be in the physical database from those that will.

General Scripting

Pretty much all of the ER tools are capable of converting your physical diagram into scripts to generate your database. Perhaps what's the greatest about this is that most of them also support multiple platforms – this means that you can develop your entity relationships once, but be able to generate the script for multiple back-end servers. You'll find that most support SQL Server, Oracle, and Sybase. Still most, but a fewer number, support DB/2, Access, and Informix. This can be a real time saver when you have to deal with multiple platforms.

Reverse Engineering

OK, so you've been able to create a diagram and generate a database from it – but what if you want to go the other way? The tool you choose should support the notion of **reverse engineering** a database – that is, connect to a database, scan it, and generate a diagram that properly reflects all the tables, views, triggers, constraints, indexes, and relationships.

I say "should" rather than "could", because there may well be times when you do need to reverse engineer a database. It is better to have bought the tool that does this, rather than finding yourself having to buy two ERD tools.

Fortunately, most of the high-end tools I'm talking about in this section will do this for you and actually do a very good job of it. Some will even import sprocs for you.

Synchronization

One of the biggest problem areas in database work is changes made once you have created the physical database. This is even more of a problem once you start getting live data loaded into the database. In short, they are usually a monumental hassle to take care of.

Just the issue of trying to keep track of what you've changed in the model and what has actually been propagated out to the database can be very tedious at best – it is incredibly simple to not get a change out to a database. That's the first place an ERD tool with synchronization can help.

Several of the major ERD vendors have products that will look over your database, compare that to your physical model, and then give you a list of discrepancies. This can be a real lifesaver as you continue to make changes both small (sometimes these are the most dangerous – you tend to forget about them) and large to your database. Another time that this functionality comes into its own is when you are working on a system where remote access is provided for overnight support. Any changes made can then be synchronized back into the ERD. But wait – there's more.

Once you recognize that you have a difference in your design (which should be reflected in the ERD), you have to write the code to make the actual change.

At first, writing the code to make the change to the database may not seem like too big a deal. Indeed, if what you're doing is adding one more column to the end of a table, then it's no big deal at all. Imagine, however, that you want to add a column, but you want it to be in the middle of the column order. Hmmm! That means that you have to:

1. Create the table with the new layout using a different name

2. Copy all the data to the appropriate columns of the new table

3. Delete the old table

4. Rename the new table

That's a few steps – and it's already a hassle. Now let's add a little more reality check to it. Now think about if you have foreign keys that reference the old table. Hmmm, again! Those are going to have to be dropped before the table can be deleted (step number 3 above), plus they (and the statistics) are going to have to be recreated again. Now what have we got?

1. Create the table with the new layout using a different name

2. Copy all the data to the appropriate columns of the new table

3. Drop the foreign keys from any table that is referencing the old table

4. Delete the old table

5. Rename the new table

6. Re-create the foreign keys for all those tables that we just dropped them from

This is starting to get pretty complex, eh?

OK, so that takes us back to the "more" I mentioned before. Some (not all) of the major ERD tools will script this for you. After the comparison phase of the synchronization is complete, they'll give you a dialog to compare – one side for the ERD, and one side for the database. You get to decide which side of the diagram wins for each difference– do you propagate the ERD to the database, or do you accept the difference in the database as needing to be part of the ERD.

In short, this kind of thing can save hours and hours of work.

*Now, after saying all that, I have to give you a word of caution – these tools are **not** foolproof in the way they script the changes. If you're running update scripts against a live database, make sure that you have thoroughly tested the script the ERD tools generates against test databases before you run the change on your live data.*

Macros

Some of the tools give you the capability to build macros in your ERD. These may be used for simplifying repetitive tasks, but they can also do things like automate the generation of stored procedures and triggers by automatically substituting the data names and data types into trigger and sproc templates that you create.

The really great thing about macro-based development is how flexible it is to change – when you change the table, your sprocs and triggers are also automatically changed (depending on how well you've used the macro language).

On the down side of this one is learning time. It takes a while to get to know the macro languages (which are proprietary), and it takes even longer to fully grasp all the places where you can make use of macros once you've learned the language.

Integration with other Tools (Code Generation)

Yes – you can even get versions of ER tools that either have some code generating capabilities of their own, or they integrate with other tools to do so. This can be really useful from a couple of perspectives – prototyping and integration to logical model.

Let's say, for example, that you have a logical model that calls for several non-database data objects – the tool can generate template code for you for those objects. For example, it can create the code to expose properties and provide stubs for method calls. This eliminates a ton of rather tedious work.

Much like the synchronization section above, you need to be a little careful of these tools. Don't just assume that everything in them is going to be correct – proof the code that was generated and make sure that everything that you expect is there. Even with the time spent looking it over, you can still pick up quite a timesaving using these code generators.

Other Things

Some other items to think of or watch out for include:

- ❑ **Automatic loading of domain data**: most databases have several domain tables that need to have data loaded into them that will be constant (a table containing all the states or a list of countries are common examples of this). The problem is that, every time you regenerate your database, you have to reload the domain data. Some of the tools will allow you to build "pre-load" scripts right into the ERD – when you generate the database, these tables are preloaded with the desired data every time.

- ❑ **Cut & Paste**: some of the tools do not support linking and embedding – that is, you can't cut them out of the ERD tool and past them into Word or some other word processor. Needless to say, this can be a huge hassle when you go to document your database.

- ❑ **Diagram methodologies supported**: you'll find that pretty much all the tools support the two most common methodologies –IDEF1X and IE. What's different is the level that they support these methodologies. For example, at least one of the major tools accepts using IE for the physical database, but won't allow it for the logical database (instead, forcing you to use their own proprietary methodology). If you don't mind this – then no big deal – but be sure you know what you're getting.

- ❑ **Subject areas**: some databases get positively huge in the number of separate entities that they have. This can make managing your ERD on a computer screen (which is usually no more than 21" at most – and that's only for the luckier of you out there) virtually impossible. One way that some of the tools get around this is through the concept of subject areas. Subject areas allow you to effectively filter the main drawing. You decide what tables are going to appear in the subject area. This means that you can manage different parts of the database in smaller sections.

- ❑ **Integration with source control**: only the truly high-end tools ($10,000+ a seat) seem to have a decent level of integration with source control utilities (such as Source Safe or PVCS). We can, however, hope this improves in the future.

Coding Tools

In C++, Visual Basic, or any of the other modern programming languages, we have begun to expect very robust development environments. High integration with source control and excellent debugging tools are just the beginning of the things that we now pretty much expect to be there in mainstream development tools. For SQL however, this is an area that is really just beginning to blossom.

Don't expect too much from this area yet, but there are now tools out there that do things like validate code, integrate with Source Safe (hey, source control for your sprocs – what a novel idea!), and even provide debugging capabilities.

> **Microsoft has identified that there was a lack of debugging ability within SQL Server. It addressed this to a great degree with SQL Server 2000's Query Analyzer. The ability to debug stored procedures can now be completed within the Query Analyzer without the need of unnecessary SQL statements.**

It is this last area – debugging – that is winning over the hearts of many SQL Server developers. Debugging triggers, for example, is about as painful as any part of development can be. You can't invoke the code directly (it only fires when you do something to the table the trigger is attached to), and even then, you can't really see what's going on inside the trigger. Some of the newer tools out there will not only let you debug – they will also allow step debugging (walk through one line of code at a time), breakpoints (preset places to stop and look at things), and watch windows (check variable values as of the current line of code). This is a positively huge feature for both sprocs and triggers.

These tools have a much wider range in cost. To some extent, you can find this functionality free, like Query Analyzer, or as part of the Visual Studio package (if you already have it), but even better implementations can be found ranging in price from $299 up to $15,000 (the latter is a complete suite of tools that also includes ER tools among other things).

Backup Utilities

OK, so this is more of a DBA thing than a developer thing, but I would argue that developers still need to think about things like backups. Why? Well, for a lot more than just making sure that you don't lose the data on your development system. Instead, I would argue the biggest motivation here should be to help out your end users – particularly if what you're developing is likely to go into an installation that won't have a true DBA.

SQL Server has its own backup options – just like it has its own ways to diagram a database and enter code. Microsoft has placed some effort in ensuring that backups are easier than in the past, and ensured that, within SQL Server 2000, the backup and restore models are easier to follow. Additionally, backups can be password protected, although this is a double-edged sword; it helps to protect your backup (especially if this is an offsite backup) in case it falls into the wrong hands by mistake, but it does mean you need good documentation defining the backup password, just in case.

Some of the major backup tools provide a much more useful user interface than SQL Server's. In addition, many of these tools will allow you to backup to a tape directly over a network (which SQL Server won't currently do by itself) – this means that you don't have to have a tape drive on every SQL Server that you own. Tape backup is not supported on Windows 98.

Backup utilities are not, as a developer, the first place I would spend my money. However, I still recommend that you take a look at what's available so you're prepared to make recommendations to your customers.

Summary

The tools for SQL Server work pretty much as tools for anything do – you don't necessarily have to have the right tool for the job, but it sure can make a huge difference in both productivity and the level of satisfaction (vs. frustration) you have in your job and in the end product.

Take the time to look at what's available on the market. Even though some of the tools may seem expensive, be sure you think about what they might save you – and how much that saving is worth. I suspect you'll be buying one or more of the tools listed in this chapter.

Online discussion at http://p2p.wrox.com

D

Access Upsizing

If you've started out on Access, and have now decided that it's just not meeting your needs anymore – you're not the first. Don't take that as a bad mark on Access, it's just that Access tends to be used often in places it was never intended for. It starts out honestly enough – we design a simple little database that we're going to use to keep track of some things. After all, there's no sense in going to the expense of a big RDBMS if you already have Access – right?

Then the problems start. Your work colleague figures out that you have some information they want, and so you give them access to your database. Then you decide to add a couple of features, and a few more people want to have access too. It doesn't take long before your database is growing too large, too fast, with too many users connected to it all at once.

A few years ago, Microsoft brought us the **Access Upsizing Wizard,** where you could quite easily and cleanly create a SQL Server database from an Access database. In Access 2000, the wizard is accessed by selecting the Tools | Database Utilities and selecting the Upsizing Wizard from the list.

> However, at the time of publication, there is a problem with the Upsizing Wizard when it comes to creating a SQL Server 2000 database from your Access data.

You are able to specify a SQL Server 2000 server, the name for your new database and a user ID and password combination as follows:

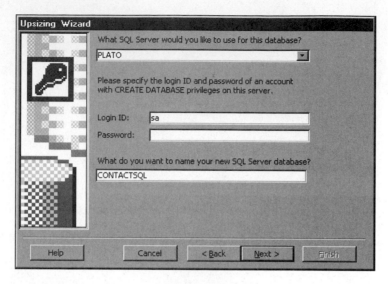

But as soon as you press Next > you get this enigmatic response:

Though this message doesn't give much away, it succeeds in stopping the wizard dead in its tracks.

This error has been reported to Microsoft and information on it can be found at http://support.microsoft.com/support/kb/articles/Q272/3/84.ASP as well as any information on solutions.

To put it simply, the Access Upsizing Wizard cannot be used at the moment to create SQL Server 2000 databases form Access, so you will have to resort to other methods to achieve the same result.

Methods of Upsizing Access Data

The Microsoft support URL shown above suggests several methods of converting your Access data to SQL Server 2000. These are summarized as:

❑ Use the Access Upsizing Wizard to create a SQL Server 7.0 database and then use SQL Server 2000 DTS to migrate the data from SQL 7 to SQL 2000

❑ Use SQL Server 2000 DTS to import the Access database in one step

Unless you really need your data to exist as a SQL Server 7.0 database, you would normally use the second method of data conversion, which is what I'll concentrate on. This process is really quite easy. In Enterprise Manager, right-click on **Databases | All Tasks** and select **Import Data**. The import wizard then guides you through the process. First, you select your source, your Access data, and then a destination database. Note that you do not even need to create a blank database first; in the "Choose a Destination" part of the wizard, select the <new> option from the database list and a window will pop up inviting you supply a name and, if you so wish, you can select the size of the data and log files. Then you select the tables you want importing and a few other options. SQL Server then chugs away for a few moments and creates tables, keys, etc. and inserts data for you. Then refresh the view in Enterprise Manager and see your new database in the list. It's as simple as that.

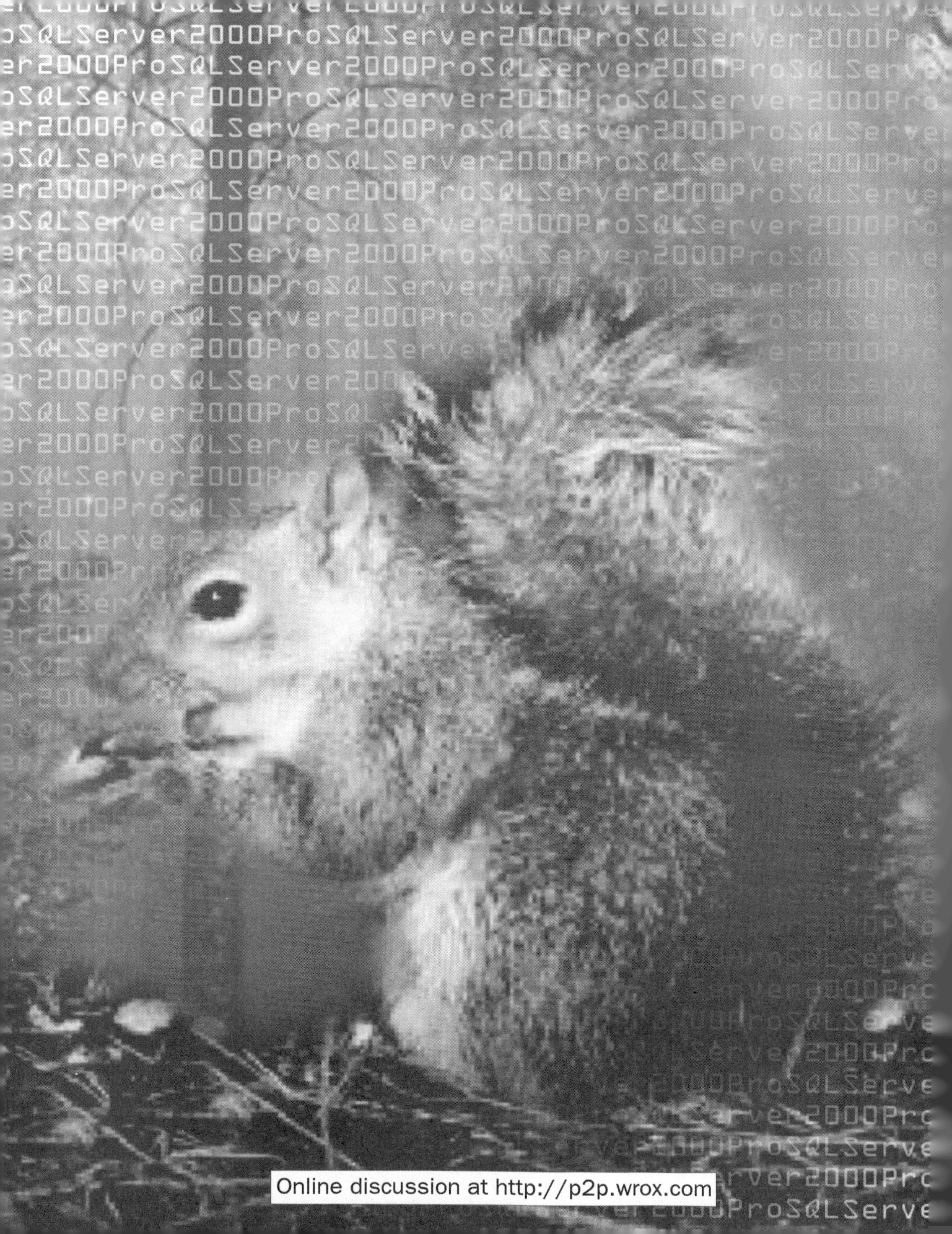
Online discussion at http://p2p.wrox.com

Microsoft Data Transformation Services Package Object Library Reference

The object model is shown diagrammatically overleaf. The gray boxes represent collection objects and the white boxes represent objects.

```
Package2
    Connections
        Connection2
            Connection Properties ──── OLE DBProperty

    GlobalVariables ──── GlobalVariable2
    SavedPackageInfos ──── SavedPackageInfo
    Steps
        Step2
            PrecedenceConstraints ──── PrecedenceConstraints

    Tasks
        Task
```

The hierarchy continues from the Task object as follows:

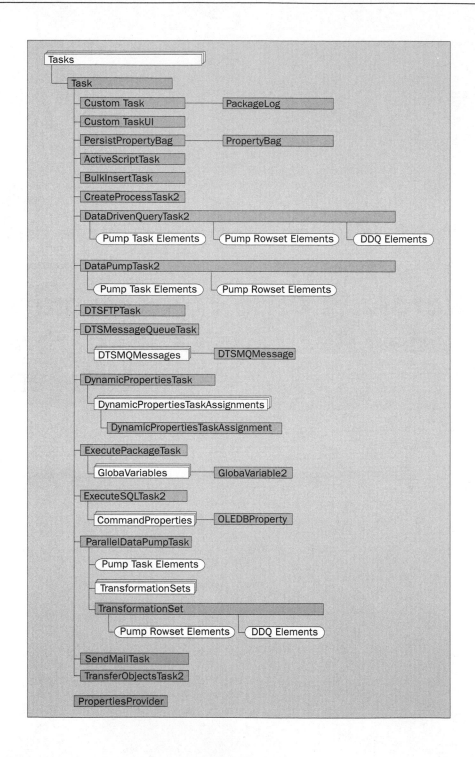

Library File Location

> The source file that contains the Data Transformation Service Object library is located at `<Drive>:\MSSQL7\Binn\Resources\1033\dts.rll`.

Objects

Name	Description
ActiveScriptTask	Defines an ActiveX script task.
BulkInsertTask	Provides an interface for rapid copying of lots of data from a text file.
Column	Contains information about a source or destination column of information.
Connection	Contains information about the connection to the OLE DB service provider.
CreateProcessTask	An object that contains information about running a separate program as a task.
CustomTask	A wrapper object that encapsulates a custom DTS package task.
CustomTaskUI	Allows for the specification of specialized dialog boxes to support DTS tasks.
DataDrivenQueryTask	Contains information regarding the use of individual queries rather than executing an INSERT operation at the destination.
DataPumpTask	Creates and executes an instance of the DTS data pump as a custom task.
ExecuteSQLTask	Allows the execution of a SQL statement on an open connection.
GlobalVariable	Allows the definition of global variables for sharing across scripts or tasks.
IDTSStdObject	The top level hierarchy object for the DTS Package class.
Lookup	Allows the specification of one or more query strings for custom transformation.
OleDBProperty	Used to set OLE DB session properties for the OLE DB service provider.
Package	Main object that defines DTS transformations.
PackageLog	Internal Microsoft use only.

Table continued on following page

Name	Description
Persist PropertyBag	For objects carrying out DTS custom tasks this defines an interface for persistent property storage.
Precedence Constraint	Contains information about the order that steps are executed.
Properties Provider	Defines an object supplying a DTS `Properties` collection.
Property	Defines the attributes of a DTS object.
PropertyBag	Defines an index/name container for DTS custom task implementations.
SavedPackageInfo	Contains information about a saved DTS package.
SendMailTask	Contains information that allows users to send an e-mail as a custom task.
Step	Controls the flow and execution of tasks in a DTS package.
Task	Sets a unit of work within a DTS package.
Transfer ObjectsTask	Allows the transfer of objects between a destination and source SQL Server.
Transformation	Contains information about the source, destination, and transformation of columns of data in a DTS Package.

Collections

Name	Description
Columns	Contains descriptions for columns in a data source.
Connections	Contains information about the OLE DB service providers used in a package.
DTSMQMessages	Defines the messages to be sent by the DTS Message Queue task.
DynamicProperties TaskAssignment	Defines the properties changed by a Dynamic Properties task.
GlobalVariables	A collection of `GlobalVariable` objects.
Lookups	A collection of `Lookup` objects.
OleDBProperties	A collection of `OLEDBProperty` objects.
OLEDBProvider Infos	A collection of information about available OLE DB Providers.
PackageInfos	Provides information about packages stored locally in SQL Server or in Meta Data Services.

Name	Description
PackageLineages	A collection of package lineage records from Meta Data Services.
PackageLogRecords	A collection of package log records from an instance of SQL Server.
Precedence Constraints	A collection of PrecedenceConstraint objects.
Properties	A collection of DTS Property objects.
SavedPackageInfos	A collection of SavedPackageInfo objects.
Scripting LanguageInfos	A collection of information about Microsoft ActiveX scripting languages available on the executing workstation.
StepLineages	A collection of step lineage records from Meta Data Services.
StepLogRecords	A collection of step log records from an instance of SQL Server.
Steps	A collection of Step objects.
TaskInfos	A collection of information about tasks available on the system executing the package.
TaskLogRecords	A collection of task log records from an instance of SQL Server.
Tasks	A collection of Task objects.
Transformation Infos	A collection of information about the DTS transformations available on the system executing the package.
Transformations	A collection of Transformation objects.
Transformation Sets	A collection of transformations used to process components of a hierarchical rowset.

ActiveScriptTask

Methods

Name	Returns	Description
CheckSyntax		Parses the active script for syntax errors.
Execute		Executes an ActiveScriptTask.

Properties

Name	Returns	Description
ActiveXScript	String	Specifies an ActiveX script.
AddGlobal Variables	Boolean	Specifies whether global variables may be used within an ActiveX script.
Description	String	A descriptive string for the ActiveScriptTask.
FunctionName	String	Identifies the function name to call within the ActiveX script.
Name	String	The name of the ActiveScriptTask.
Properties	Properties	Returns the Properties collection for the ActiveScriptTask object.
ScriptLanguage	String	Identifies the scripting language (VBScript, JScript, or PerlScript).

BulkInsertTask

Methods

Name	Returns	Description
Execute		Executes a BulkInsertTask.

Properties

Name	Returns	Description
BatchSize	Long	Sets the number of rows to load in a batch.
CheckConstraints	Boolean	Indicates whether any constraints should be checked while data is loaded.
Codepage	String	Sets code page to use while loading data. Valid values are ACP, OEM (default), RAW or a code page number (like 850).
ConnectionID	Long	Sets the ID of the Connection object.
DataFile	String	Sets the UNC path of the file to be loaded.
DataFileType	DTSBulkInsert _DataFileType	Sets the file type of the data to be inserted.

Name	Returns	Description
Description	String	The descriptive string for the `BulkInsertTask`.
Destination TableName	String	Specifies the name of the table that data will be inserted into.
FieldTerminator	String	Sets the column terminator value for batch inserted files.
FirstRow	Long	Sets the first source row to copy.
FormatFile	String	Specifies a `bcp` format file to use for load operations.
KeepIdentity	Boolean	Shows whether the data in the file should be used as values of an identity column(s).
KeepNulls	Boolean	Sets whether NULL columns should keep NULL values.
LastRow	Long	Identifies the last row to be loaded from a source file.
MaximumErrors	Long	Sets the maximum number of errors that may occur before a load operation is terminated.
Name	String	The name of the `BulkInsertTask`.
Properties	Properties	A list of properties for this object.
RowTerminator	String	Sets the row termination file for the source file.
SortedData	String	Sets the order of the loaded data.
TableLock	Boolean	Sets whether to perform a table lock on the destination table.

Column

Properties

Name	Returns	Description
ColumnID	Variant	Sets/Gets the ID of a source/destination column.
DataType	Long	Sets/Gets the data type of a column object.
Flags	Long	Sets/Gets the `DBCOLUMNFLAGS` value that describes the column.
Name	String	The name of the column object.

Table continued on following page

Name	Returns	Description
Nullable	Boolean	Specifies whether the column is or is not nullable.
NumericScale	Long	Sets/Gets the numeric scale of the column if it is a numeric or decimal value.
Ordinal	Long	Gets the ordinal position of the column within the table.
Parent	IDTSStdObject	The parent object of the Column object.
Precision	Long	Set/Gets the column precision if the column is decimal or numeric data type.
Properties	Properties	A list of properties for the object.
Size	Long	Specifies the maximum size of the column.

Columns

Methods

Name	Returns	Description
Add		Adds a DTS Column object to the collection.
AddColumn		Adds a DTS Column object to the collection by name and ordinal position.
Insert		Inserts a DTS Column object by ordinal position.
Item	Column	Retrieves a DTS Column object from the collection.
New	Column	Creates a new DTS Column object.
Remove		Removes a DTS Column object from the object.

Properties

Name	Returns	Description
Count	Long	Specifies the number of DTS Column objects in the collection.
Parent	IDTSStdObject	The parent object of the Columns object.

Connection

Methods

Name	Returns	Description
Acquire Connection		Allows the acquisition of exclusive use of the OLE DB service provider.
Release Connection		Releases ownership of the OLE DB service provider.

Properties

Name	Returns	Description
Catalog	String	Sets the name of the catalog that the Connection object will be initially established in.
Connected	Boolean	Gets the connection status of the Connection object.
Connect Immediate	Boolean	Identifies whether a package should attempt an immediate connection to the service provider upon starting.
Connection Properties	OleDB Properties	Gets the OleDBProperties object for the established connection.
Connection Timeout	Long	The number of seconds to wait while establishing a connection before generating an error.
DataSource	String	Sets the server name when an application requests an OLE DB provider for SQL Server.
Description	String	A text description of the Connection object.
ID	Long	Unique identifier for the established connection.
InTransaction	Boolean	Identifies whether the connection is involved in a distributed transaction.
InUse	Boolean	Identifies whether the connection is currently in use.
LastOwner TaskName	String	Returns the name of the last Task to utilize the connection.
Name	String	The name of the Connection object.

Table continued on following page

Name	Returns	Description
Parent	IDTSStdObject	Specifies the parent object of the Connection object.
Password	String	The password used while making the connection.
Properties	Properties	A list of properties for this object.
ProviderID	String	The ProgID of the OLE DB provider.
Reusable	Boolean	Identifies whether a connection is reusable by multiple steps within a given task.
UDLPath	String	Path of UDL (data link) file to create connection from, rather than using Connection properties.
UserID	String	The user ID utilized when making a connection.
UseTrusted Connection	Boolean	Specifies whether to use Windows NT Authentication security to establish a connection.

Connections

Methods

Name	Returns	Description
Add		Adds a Connection object to the collection.
BeginAcquire Multiple Connections		Allows the acquisition of multiple connections.
EndAcquire Mutiple Connections		Stops the acquisition of multiple connections.
Insert		Inserts a Connection object into the collection.
Item	Connection	Retrieves a Connection object from the collection.
New	Connection	Creates a new Connection object.
NewDataLink	Connection	Gets a new Connection object to populate prior to adding to this collection, using Microsoft Data Links.
Remove		Removes a Connection object from the collection.

Properties

Name	Returns	Description
Count	Long	Specifies the number of DTS Connection objects in the collection.
Parent	Object	Specifies the parent object of the Connections collection.

CreateProcessTask

Methods

Name	Returns	Description
Execute		Executes a CreateProcessTask.

Properties

Name	Returns	Description
Description	String	A text description of the CreateProcessTask.
FailPackage OnTimeout	Boolean	Identifies whether the DTS package fails within the timeout period.
Name	String	The name of the CreateProcessTask object.
Process CommandLine	String	The UNC file name of the file to execute.
Properties	Properties	A list of properties for this object.
Success ReturnCode	Long	The return code that is returned upon successful completion a task.
Terminate ProcessAfter Timeout	Boolean	Sets whether to terminate a process after a timeout period has expired.
Timeout	Long	The number of seconds in the timeout period.

CustomTask

Methods

Name	Returns	Description
Execute		Executes a `CustomTask`.

Properties

Name	Returns	Description
Description	String	A text description of the `CustomTask`.
Name	String	The name for the `CustomTask`.
Properties	Properties	A list of properties for this object.

CustomTaskUI

Methods

Name	Returns	Description
CreateCustom ToolTip		Creates a tooltip window for a custom tooltip.
Delete		Deletes a `CustomTask` object in the user interface.
Edit		Edits a `CustomTask` object in the user interface.
GetUIInfo		Returns user information about the `CustomTask`.
Help		Used to invoke help about the `CustomTask` object.
Initialize		Initializes the `CustomTaskUI` object.
New		Creates a new custom task.

DataDrivenQueryTask

Methods

Name	Returns	Description
Execute		Executes a `DataDrivenQueryTask`.

Properties

Name	Returns	Description
DeleteQuery	String	Specifies a Transact-SQL statement to delete data from a data source.
DeleteQuery Columns	Columns	Specifies columns to be placed in a parameterized `DeleteQuery`.
Description	String	A text description of the `DataDrivenQueryTask` object.
Destination ColumnDefinitions	Columns	Destination column definitions for a `DTSRowQueue` destination.
Destination CommandProperties	OleDBProperties	The OLE DB command properties for the destination data connection.
Destination ConectionID	Long	Connection object to use for destination.
Destination ObjectName	String	Sets the name of the data destination.
Destination SQLStatement	String	Specifies a SQL statement to execute at the destination.
ExceptionFile ColumnDelimiter	String	The column delimiter for the exception file.
ExceptionFileName	String	The name of the file where exception rows are written.
ExceptionFile RowDelimiter	String	The row delimiter for the data in the exception file.
FetchBufferSize	Long	Sets the number of rows to fetch during a single operation.
FirstRow	Variant	Gets the first source row.
InsertQuery	String	Sets a parameterized SQL statement to insert data at a destination.

Table continued on following page

Name	Returns	Description
InsertQuery Columns	Columns	Sets the column parameters for the InsertQuery parameters.
LastRow	Variant	Gets the last row from the source to copy.
Lookups	Lookups	A collection of lookup values.
MaximumErrorCount	Long	The maximum number of error rows before the data pump terminates operation.
Name	String	The name of the DataDrivenQueryTask object.
ProgressRowCount	Long	Sets the number of rows returned between notifications to the connection point during a DataDrivenQuery execution.
Properties	Properties	A list of properties for this object.
SourceCommand Properties	OleDBProperties	The OLE DB command properties for the data source connection.
Source ConnectionID	Long	The ID for the source OLE DB connection.
SourceObjectName	String	Specifies the source object name if no SQL statement is supplied.
SourceSQL Statement	String	Sets the SQL statement to be executed on the source rowset.
Transformations	Transformations	A collection of Transformation objects.
UpdateQuery	String	Sets a parameterized SQL query to update data.
UpdateQuery Columns	Columns	Specifies the column parameters for the UpdateQuery property.
UserQuery	String	Sets a parameterized user-defined SQL query.
UserQueryColumns	Columns	Specifies the column parameters for the UserQuery property.

DataDrivenQueryTask2

Extended Properties

Name	Returns	Description
Exception FileOptions	Integer	Specifies whether or not to use the SQL Server 7.0 format for exception files as well as specifying whether to keep source and destination error rows.
ExceptionFile TextQualifier	String	Specifies the text qualifier for the exception rows.
InputGlobal VariableNames	String	Specifies a list of package global variable names whose values are to be substituted for the query parameters.
RowsComplete	Integer	Specifies the number of rows that have successfully been transformed.
RowsInError	Integer	Specifies the number of rows that have errors.

DataPumpTask

Methods

Name	Returns	Description
Execute		Executes a `DataPumpTask`.

Properties

Name	Returns	Description
AllowIdentity Inserts	Boolean	Specifies whether the SET IDENTITY_INSERT option is ON or OFF.
Description	String	A text description of the `DataPumpTask` object.
Destination ColumnDefinitions	Columns	Destination column definitions for a `DTSRowQueue` destination.

Table continued on following page

Name	Returns	Description
Destination CommandProperties	OleDBProperties	OLE DB command properties for the destination.
Destination ConnectionID	Long	Connection object to use for destination.
Destination ObjectName	String	Sets the name of the data destination.
Destination SQLStatement	String	Specifies a SQL Statement to execute at the destination.
ExceptionFile ColumnDelimter	String	The column delimiter for the exception file.
ExceptionFileName	String	The name of the file where exception rows are written.
ExceptionFile RowDelimiter	String	The row delimiter for the data in the exception file.
FastLoadOptions	DTSFast LoadOptions	Used for the UseFastLoad property to set SQL OLE DB destination connection options.
FetchBufferSize	Long	Sets the number of rows to fetch during a single operation.
FirstRow	Variant	Gets the first source row from the source.
InsertCommitSize	Long	Number of successful InsertRows between Commits.
LastRow	Variant	Gets the last row from the source to copy.
Lookups	Lookups	A collection of lookup values.
MaximumErrorCount	Long	The maximum number of error rows before the data pump terminates operation.
Name	String	The name of the DataPumpTask object.
ProgressRowCount	Long	The number of rows returned between notifications to the connection point during a data pump execution.
Properties	Properties	A list of properties for this object.
SourceCommand Properties	OleDBProperties	OLE DB command properties for the source.
Source ConnectionID	Long	The ID for the source OLE DB connection.
SourceObjectName	String	Specifies the source object name if no SQL statement is supplied.

Name	Returns	Description
Source SQLStatement	String	Sets the SQL statement to be executed on the source rowset.
Transformations	Transformations	A collection of Transformation objects.
UseFastLoad	Boolean	Specifies whether to use the IRowsetFastLoad interface to insert rows at the data destination.

DataPumpTask2

Extended Properties

Name	Returns	Description
Exception FileOptions	Integer	Specifies whether or not to use the SQL Server 7.0 format for exception files as well as specifying whether to keep source and destination error rows.
Exception FileTextQualifier	String	Specifies the text qualifier for the exception rows.
InputGlobal VariableNames	String	Specifies a list of package global variable names whose values are to be substituted for the query parameters.
RowsComplete	Integer	Specifies the number of rows that have successfully been transformed.
RowsInError	Integer	Specifies the number of rows that have errors.

DynamicPropertiesTask

Methods

Name	Returns	Description
Execute		Executes the Dynamic Properties Task.

Properties

Name	Returns	Description
Assignments		Returns a reference to the Dynamic PropertiesTaskAssignment collection.
Description	String	Optional user-defined text label that helps define the Dynamic Properties Task.
DynamicProperties TaskAssignments	TaskAssignment	Stores the pertinent information about the source and destination properties.
Name	String	Unique user-defined text label for the task.
Properties	Properties	A list of properties for this object.

DynamicPropertiesTaskAssignment

Methods

Name	Returns	Description
Reset		Resets all targets to their defaults.

Properties

Name	Returns	Description
Destination PropertyID	String	Specifies the path through the object model to the property that has been modified.
SourceConstant Value	String	Specifies a value to a constant when the when the SourceType property is DTSDynamic PropertiesSourceType_Constant is set to.
SourceDataFile FileName	String	Specifies the data file that the dynamic property will be set to when the SourceType property is DTSDynamicPropertiesSourceType_ DataFile.

Name	Returns	Description
SourceEnvironment Variable	String	Specifies the name of the environment variable that the dynamic property will be set to if the SourceType property is DTSDynamicPropertiesSourceType_ EnvironmentVariable.
SourceGlobal Variable	String	Specifies the name of the global variable that the dynamic property will be set to if the SourceType property is DTSDynamicPropertiesSourceType_ GlobalVariable.
SourceIniFile FileName	String	Specifies the name of the INI file and path that the dynamic property will be set to if the SourceType property is DTSDynamicPropertiesSourceType_ IniFile.
SourceIniFileKey	String	Specifies the key that will be used in the INI file when the SourceType property is DTSDynamicProperties SourceType_IniFile.
SourceIniFile Section	String	Specifies the section that will be used in the INI file when the SourceType property is DTSDynamic PropertiesSourceType_IniFile.
SourceQuery ConnectionID	String	Specifies the connection ID that the SourceQuerySQL will use.
SourceQuerySQL	String	Specifies the SQL statement that will be used to derive the dynamic property will be set to if the SourceType property is DTSDynamicPropertiesSourceType_ Query.
SourceType	Long	Specifies the method in which the dynamic property will be derived.

DynamicPropertiesTaskAssignments

Methods

Name	Returns	Description
Add		Adds an object to the collection.
Item		Retrieves an object by index.
New		Creates a new object.

Properties

Name	Returns	Description
Count	Long	The number of objects in the collection.
Parent	IDTSStdObject	The parent object of the object.

ExecuteSQLTask

Methods

Name	Returns	Description
Execute		Executes an ExecuteSQLTask.

Properties

Name	Returns	Description
Command Properties	OleDB Properties	Sets the OleDBProperties object for the connection.
Command Timeout	Long	The number of seconds before the command is presumed to have failed.
ConnectionID	Long	The ID for the OLE DB connection.
Description	String	A text description of the ExecuteSQLTask object.
Name	String	The name of the ExecuteSQLTask object.
Properties	Properties	A list of properties for the object.
SQLStatement	String	The SQL statement to execute on the source rowset.

ExecuteSQLTask2

Extended Properties

Name	Returns	Description
InputGlobal VariableNames	String	Specifies a list of package global variable names whose values are to be substituted for the query parameters.
OutputAsRecordSet	Boolean	Specifies whether to output the results of the SQL task into a recordset in a global variable.
OutputGlobal VariableNames	String	Specifies whether to output the results of the SQL task into global variable(s).

GlobalVariable

Properties

Name	Returns	Description
Name	String	The name of the GlobalVariable object.
Parent	IDTSStdObject	The parent object of the GlobalVariable object.
Properties	Properties	A list of properties for the object.
Value	Variant	The value of the GlobalVariable object.

GlobalVariables

Methods

Name	Returns	Description
Add		Adds a GlobalVariable object to the collection.
AddGlobalVariable		Adds a GlobalVariable object to the collection by name.

Table continued on following page

1313

Name	Returns	Description
Insert		Inserts an object at an ordinal position or prior to a named object.
Item	GlobalVariable	Retrieves a GlobalVariable object by index.
New	GlobalVariable	Creates a new GlobalVariable object.
Remove		Removes a GlobalVariable object from the collection.

Properties

Name	Returns	Description
Count	Long	The number of GlobalVariable objects in the collection.
Parent	IDTSStdObject	The parent object of the GlobalVariable object.

IDTSStdObject

There are no methods, events, or properties designed for this object.

Lookup

Properties

Name	Returns	Description
ConnectionId	Long	The ID for the established OLE DB connection.
MaxCacheRows	Long	The maximum number of rows to cache.
Name	String	The name of the Lookup object.
Parent	IDTSStdObject	The parent object of the Lookup object.
Properties	Properties	A list of properties for the object.
Query	String	A parameterized query to execute.

Lookups

Methods

Name	Returns	Description
Add		Adds a Lookup object to the collection.
AddLookup		Adds a Lookup object to the collection by name.
Insert		Inserts a Lookup object into the collection by index.
Item	Lookup	Retrieves a Lookup object by index.
New	Lookup	Creates a new Lookup object.
Remove		Removes a Lookup object from the collection.

Properties

Name	Returns	Description
Count	Long	The number of Lookup objects in the collection.
Parent	IDTSStdObject	The parent object of the Lookup object.

OleDBProperties

Methods

Name	Returns	Description
Item	OleDBProperty	Retrieves an OleDBProperty object by index.

Properties

Name	Returns	Description
Count	Long	The number of OleDBProperty objects in the collection.
Parent	IDTSStdObject	The parent object of the OleDBProperties object.

OleDBProperty

Properties

Name	Returns	Description
Name	String	The name of the OleDBProperty.
Parent	IDTSStdObject	The parent object of the OleDBProperty.
Properties	Properties	A list of properties for the object.
PropertyID	Long	The ID of the OleDBProperty.
PropertySet	String	The GUID of the property.
Value	Variant	The value of the OleDBProperty.

OleDBProperty2

Extended Properties

Name	Returns	Description
IsDefaultValue	Boolean	Set to False if the property has been changed from the default.

Package

Methods

Name	Returns	Description
EndPreparation ForStepsExecuting OnMainThread		Internal Microsoft use only.
Execute		Executes a Package object.
GetDTSVersionInfo		Returns the DTS object version information.
GetLastExecution Lineage	String	Returns information about the lineage of a package stored in the Microsoft Repository.

Name	Returns	Description
GetSaved PackageInfos	SavedPackage Infos	Returns a list of versions in the specified storage location.
LoadFrom Repository		Loads the DTS package from the specified Repository.
LoadFromSQLServer		Loads the DTS package from the specified SQL Server.
LoadFrom StorageFile		Loads the DTS package from the specified storage file.
RemoveFrom Repository		Removes the selected DTS package from the selected Repository.
RemoveFrom SQLServer		Removes the selected DTS package from the selected SQL Server.
SaveAs		Creates a new package ID and assigns a new name to create a new package.
SaveToRepository		Saves a package to a selected Repository.
SaveToSQLServer		Saves a package to a selected SQL Server.
SaveToStorageFile		Saves a package to a selected file.
StartPreparation forStepsExecuting OnMainThread		Internal Microsoft use only.
UnInitialize		Clears all state information and releases all objects.

Properties

Name	Returns	Description
AutoCommit Transaction	Boolean	Sets whether a specified transaction should be committed or terminated upon completion.
Connections	Connections	A collection of Connection objects.
CreationDate	Date	The package creation date.
Creator ComputerName	String	The name of the computer that created the package.
CreatorName	String	The username of the package creator.
Description	String	A descriptive text about the object.

Table continued on following page

Name	Returns	Description
FailOnError	Boolean	Sets whether to stop execution upon package error.
GlobalVariables	Global Variables	A global variable collection.
LineageOptions	DTSLineage Options	Specifies how the execution lineage should be shown.
LogFileName	String	The name of the log file.
MaxConcurrent Steps	Long	The maximum concurrent steps for the package.
Name	String	The name of the Package object.
PackageID	String	The ID value for the package (GUID).
PackagePriority Class	DTSPackage PriorityClass	The Win32 thread priority for the class.
Parent	IDTSStdObject	The parent object (IDTSStdObject) for the Package object.
PrecedenceBasis	DTSStep Precedence Basis	Indicates whether to use step status or result in PrecedenceConstraint.
Properties	Properties	Lists the properties of the object.
Repository MetadataOptions	DTSRepository Metadata Options	Specifies meta data scanning and resolution options when storing the DTS Package to a Repository.
Steps	Steps	A collection of Step objects to be executed for the package.
Tasks	Tasks	A collection of Task objects to be performed during the package execution.
Transaction IsolationLevel	DTSIsolation Level	The isolation level for the transaction for the package.
UseOLEDBService Components	Boolean	Sets whether to use OLE DB components to initialize data sources.
UseTransaction	Boolean	Sets whether the Package object should create a transaction for supporting tasks.
VersionID	String	The GUID of this version of the package.
WriteCompletionSt atusToNTEventLog	Boolean	Whether to write completion status to the Windows NT Event Log.

Events

Name	Returns	Description
OnError		Executes when error condition occurs.
OnFinish		Executes when finish condition occurs.
OnProgress		Executes during progress intervals.
OnQueryCancel		Executes on query cancel status.
OnStart		Executes on start of package.

Package2

Extended Methods

Name	Returns	Description
SaveTo RepositoryAs		Save the package and its objects to a new package in the repository, giving it a new package ID and not a new version ID.
SaveToSQL ServerAs		Saves the package and its objects to the MSDB database locally, giving it a new package ID and not a new version ID.
SaveToStorage FileAs		Saves the package and its objects to a structured storage file and assigns it a new package ID.

Properties

Name	Returns	Description
Explicit GlobalVariables	Boolean	Sets whether the package will use explicit global variables.
FailPackage OnLogFailure	Boolean	Sets or returns a value indicating whether a DTS package will fail if there is a failure during the logging of the package.
LogServerFlags	Boolean	Sets whether Windows NT Authentication is being used to login to the logging server. If this flag is set to False, then standard SQL authentication is used.
LogServerName	String	Sets the server that will hold the logs for the DTS package.

Table continued on following page

Name	Returns	Description
LogServerPassword	String	Sets the password that will be used to authenticate to the server holding the logs.
LogServerUserName	String	Sets the user name that will be used to authenticate to the server holding the logs.
LogToSQLServer	Boolean	Sets whether the logs will be written to a SQL Server's MSDB database. If set to TRUE then the logs will be written to the LogServerName server.
Nested ExecutionLevel	Long	Sets the number of levels deep that a package can call another package through the Execute Package task.
PackageType	Integer	Sets or returns a code that identifies the tool that created the package.

PackageInfo

Properties

Name	Returns	Description
CreationDate	Date	Specifies when the package's version was created.
Description	String	User-defined description for the package.
IsOwner	Boolean	True if the user logging into Package SQL Server is the owner of the package.
Name	String	User-defined name of the package.
Owner	String	Specifies the owner of the package.
PackageDataSize	Long	Specifies the size of the package data for SQL Server packages.
PackageID	String	Specifies a GUID for the package.
PackageType	DTSPackageType	Specifies the tool used to create the package.
Parent	IDTSStdObject	Hierarchical parent object
Properties	Properties	List of properties for the object.
VersionID	String	Specifies a GUID for the version.

PackageInfos

Methods

Name	Returns	Description
Next		Returns the next record in the enumeration.

Properties

Name	Returns	Description
EOF	Boolean	Specifies that the last record has been fetched in the enumeration.

PackageLineage

Properties

Name	Returns	Description
Computer	String	Specifies the server that the package executed on.
ExecutionDate	Date	Specifies the date the package was logged.
LineageFullID	String	Full GUID for the full package lineage.
LineageShortID	Long	Specifies the compressed form of the LineageFullID.
Name	String	Specifies the name of the package.
Operator	String	Specifies the individual who executed the package.
PackageID	String	Specifies the PackageID that was executed.
Parent	IDTSStdObject	Specifies the hierarchical parent object
Properties	Properties	List of properties for the object.
VersionID	String	GUID VersionID of the package that was executed.

PackageLineages

Methods

Name	Returns	Description
Next		Returns the next record in the enumeration.

Properties

Name	Returns	Description
EOF	Boolean	Specifies that the last record has been fetched in the enumeration.

PackageLog

Methods

Name	Returns	Description
WriteStringToLog	String	Writes a string to the log record that is being written for the step.
WriteTaskRecord Method	String	Writes a record to the SQL Server instances' log table for the current task that is being executed. It is formatted for the WriteStringToLog method to write.

PackageLogRecord

Properties

Name	Returns	Description
Computer	String	Specifies the server that the package executed on.
Description	String	User-defined description for the package.
ErrorCode	Long	Error code returned from the Package.Execute method.

Name	Returns	Description
Error Description	String	Full error description returned from the `Package.Execute` method.
ExecutionTime	Double	The total time it took to execute the package in seconds.
FinishTime	Date	Specifies the time at which the package finished execution.
LineageFullID	String	Full GUID for the full package lineage.
LineageShortID	Long	Specifies the compressed form of the `LineageFullID`.
LogDate	Date	Specifies the date the package was logged.
Name	String	Specifies the name of the package.
Operator	String	Specifies the user that is logged in executing the package.
PackageID	String	Specifies the `PackageID` that was executed.
Parent	IDTSStd Object	Specifies the hierarchical parent object
Properties	Properties	List of properties for the object.
StartTime	Date	Specifies the time at which the package started execution.
VersionID	String	GUID `VersionID` of the package that was executed.

PackageLogRecords

Methods

Name	Returns	Description
Next		Returns the next record in the enumeration.

Properties

Name	Returns	Description
EOF	Boolean	Specifies that the last record has been fetched in the enumeration.

PackageRepository

Methods

Name	Returns	Description
EnumPackage Infos		Enumerates the Packages that are stored in the Repository.
EnumPackage Lineages		Enumerates the Package lineages that are stored in the Repository.
EnumStep Lineages		Enumerates the Step lineages that are stored in the Repository.
RemovePackage Lineages		Removes a Package lineage from the Repository.

Properties

Name	Returns	Description
Name	String	Specifies the name of the repository the user is connected to.
Parent	IDTSStdObject	Specifies the hierarchical parent object.
Properties	Properties	List of properties for the object.

PackageSQLServer

Methods

Name	Returns	Description
EnumPackage Infos		Enumerates Packages that are stored in SQL Server.
EnumPackage LogRecords		Enumerates the Package log records that are stored in SQL Server.
EnumStepLog Records		Enumerates the Step log records that are stored in SQL Server.
EnumTaskLog Records		Enumerates the Task log records that are stored in SQL Server.

Name	Returns	Description
RemoveAllLog Records		Removes all log records that are stored in SQL Server.
RemovePackage LogRecords		Removes a Package log record that is stored in SQL Server.
RemoveStepLog Records		Removes a Step log record that is stored in SQL Server.
RemoveTaskLog Records		Removes a Task log record that is stored in SQL Server.

Properties

Name	Returns	Description
Name	String	Specifies the name of the server the user is connected to.
Parent	IDTSStd Object	Specifies the hierarchical parent object.
Properties	Properties	List of properties for the object.

ParallelDataPumpTask

Methods

Name	Returns	Description
Execute		Executes the objects in parallel while other objects in the duration of this call.

Properties

Name	Returns	Description
Description	String	A text description of the ParallelData PumpTask object.
Destination CommandProperties	OleDB Properties	OLE DB command properties for the destination.
Destination ConnectionID	Long	Connection object to use for destination.

Name	Returns	Description
Destination ObjectName	String	Sets the name of the data destination.
Destination SQLStatement	String	Specifies a SQL Statement to execute at the destination.
InputGlobal VariableNames	String	Specifies a delimited string of double-quoted Global Variables that will be passed as input parameters.
Name	String	The name of the `ParallelDataPumpTask` object.
Properties	Properties	A list of properties for this object.
SourceCommand Properties	OleDBProperties	OLE DB command properties for the source.
Source ConnectionID	Long	The ID for the source OLE DB connection.
Source ObjectName	String	Specifies the source object name if no SQL statement is supplied.
SourceSQL Statement	String	Sets the SQL statement to be executed on the source rowset.
Transformations SetOptions	Transformations	Specifies the sequence to copy the rowsets and the options.
Transformation Sets	Transformation Sets	Specifies the `TransformationSets` between each pair of rowsets in the object.

PersistPropertyBag

Methods

Name	Returns	Description
Load		Loads a custom tasks property storage.
Save		Gets a custom task to carry out property storage.

PrecedenceConstraint

Properties

Name	Returns	Description
Parent	IDTSStdObject	The parent object of the PrecedenceConstraint object.
Precedence Basis	DTSStep PrecedenceBasis	Indicates whether to use step status or result in PrecedenceConstraint.
Properties	Properties	The properties of the object.
StepName	String	The name of the Step object that will be evaluated.
Value	Variant	The value of the constraint.

PrecedenceConstraints

Methods

Name	Returns	Description
Add		Adds a PrecedenceConstraint object to the collection.
AddConstraint		Adds a PrecedenceConstraint object to the collection by name.
Insert		Inserts a PrecedenceConstraint object into the collection by index.
Item	Precedence Constraint	Retrieves a PrecedenceConstraint object by index.
New	Precedence Constraint	Creates a new PrecedenceConstraint object.
Remove		Removes a PrecedenceConstraint object from the collection.

Properties

Name	Returns	Description
Count	Long	The number of PrecedenceConstraint objects in the collection.
Parent	IDTSStdObject	The parent object of PrecedenceConstraints collection.

Properties

Methods

Name	Returns	Description
Item	Property	Returns a Property object by index value.

Properties

Name	Returns	Description
Count	Long	The number of Property objects in the collection.
Parent	IDTSStdobject	The parent object of the Properties collection.

PropertiesProvider

Methods

Name	Returns	Description
GetProperties ForObject	Properties	Gets a Properties collection for the specified automation object.

Property

Properties

Name	Returns	Description
Get	Boolean	Retrieves a property value.
Name	String	The name of the property.
Parent	IDTSStdObject	The parent object of the `Property` object.
Properties	Properties	The properties of the object.
Set	Boolean	Returns `True` when a property's value may be changed.
Type	Long	The type property specifies the value type of the `Property` object.
Value	Variant	The value for the `Property` object.

PropertyBag

Methods

Name	Returns	Description
Read		Reads a property value.
Write		Writes a property value.

SavedPackageInfo

Properties

Name	Returns	Description
Description	String	A text description of the `SavedPackageInfo` object.
IsVersion Encrypted	Boolean	Specifies whether this version of the package is encrypted.

Table continued on following page

Name	Returns	Description
Package CreationDate	Date	The package creation date.
PackageID	String	The GUID ID value of the package.
PackageName	String	The name of the package.
VersionID	String	The GUID version ID of the package.
VersionSaveDate	Date	The date and time the package was last saved.

SavedPackageInfos

Methods

Name	Returns	Description
Item	SavedPackageInfo	Retrieves a SavedPackageInfo object by index.

Properties

Name	Returns	Description
Count	Long	The number of SavedPackageInfo objects in the collection.

ScriptingLanguageInfo

Properties

Name	Returns	Description
ClassID	String	Specifies the identifier for the ScriptingLanguage class.
Description	String	Specifies the description of the scripting language.

Name	Returns	Description
Implementation FileName	String	Specifies the implementation file for the scripting language.
Implementation FileVersionString	String	Specifies the implementation file version for the scripting language.
Name	String	The name of the object.
Parent	IDTSStdObject	The parent object of the object.
Properties	Properties	The properties of the object.

ScriptingLanguageInfos

Methods

Name	Returns	Description
Item		Retrieves an object.
Refresh		Executes a refreshes command for the cache and collection.

Properties

Name	Returns	Description
Count	String	Number of items in the collection.
Parent	IDTSStdObject	The parent object of the Step object.
UseCache	String	Specifies whether to cache enumeration information for this collection.

SendMailTask

Methods

Name	Returns	Description
Execute		Executes a `SendMailTask`.
GetDefault ProfileName		Returns the default profile name.
InitializeMAPI		Initializes the MAPI provider.
Logoff		Ends a MAPI session.
Logon	String	Creates a MAPI session.
ResolveName	String	Resolves an e-mail address.
ShowAddressBook	String	Displays the address book user interface.
UnInitializeMAPI		Uninitializes the MAPI provider.

Properties

Name	Returns	Description
CCLine	String	The e-mail addresses for the CC: line.
Description	String	A text description of the `SendMailTask` object.
FileAttachments	String	Set the file attachments.
IsNTService	Boolean	Sets whether the caller is a Microsoft Windows NT Service.
MessageText	String	The message body of the e-mail.
Name	String	The name of the `SendMailTask` object.
Password	String	Specifies the password for making the MAPI connection.
Profile	String	The profile to use to send the e-mail.
Properties	Properties	The properties of the object.
SaveMailInSent ItemsFolder	Boolean	Specifies whether to move the sent e-mail to the Sent Item Folder.
Subject	String	The subject line for the e-mail.
ToLine	String	The TO: line for the e-mail.

Step

Methods

Name	Returns	Description
Execute		Executes the `Step` object.
GetExecution ErrorInfo		Returns the details about the execution if it fails.

Properties

Name	Returns	Description
ActiveXScript	String	The ActiveX script.
AddGlobal Variables	Boolean	Sets whether global variables may be referenced from other ActiveX scripts.
CloseConnection	Boolean	Sets whether to close a connection on step completion.
CommitSuccess	Boolean	Sets whether to commit a step if it completes successfully.
Description	String	A text description of the step.
DisableStep	Boolean	Specifies whether a step should be executed.
ExecuteIn MainThread	Boolean	Whether the step should be executed in the main thread of the package object.
ExecutionResult	DTSStepExec Result	Returns step execution results.
ExecutionStatus	DTSStepExec Status	Returns the status of the step.
ExecutionTime	Double	Specifies the total execution time in seconds.
FinishTime	Date	The date/time when the step was completed.
FunctionName	String	The name of the function from the ActiveX script.
IsPackage DSORowset	Boolean	When the package is a rowset provider, this property sets when the current step executes and returns a rowset.
JoinTransaction IfPresent	Boolean	Whether a step executes within a `Package` object's transaction.

Table continued on following page

1333

Name	Returns	Description
Name	String	The name of the Step object.
Parent	IDTSStdObject	The parent object of the Step object.
Precendence Constraints	Precedence Constraints	The execution constraints for the step.
Properties	Properties	The properties of the object.
RelativePriority	DTSStepRelative Priority	The Win32 thread execution priority.
RollbackFailure	Boolean	Sets whether to roll back a step if there is a failure.
ScriptLanguage	String	The scripting language for the step (VBScript, JScript, or PerlScript).
StartTime	Date	The date/time the step began.
TaskName	String	The name of task to execute in the step.

Step2

Entended Properties

Name	Returns	Description
FailPackage OnError	Boolean	Specifies whether DTS will stop the package's execution on an error in this step.

StepLineage

Properties

Name	Returns	Description
ErrorCode	Long	Specifies the source of the error code from Step.Execute.
ErrorDescription	String	Specifies the source of the error description from Step.Execute.
ErrorHelpContext	Long	Specifies the source of the help context from Step.Execute.

Name	Returns	Description
ErrorHelpFile	String	Specifies the source of the error help file from Step.Execute.
ErrorSource	String	Specifies the source of the error from Step.Execute.
ExecutionTime	Double	Specifies the total time in fractional seconds the step took to execute.
FinishTime	Date	The date/time when the step was completed.
Name	String	The name of the Step object.
Parent	IDTSStd Object	The parent object of the Step object.
Properties	Properties	The properties of the object.
StartTime	Date	Specifies the time at which the step started.
StepExecution Result	DTSStep ExecResult	Specifies the result of the step's execution.
StepExecution Status	DTSStep ExecStatus	Specifies the status of the step.

StepLineages

Methods

Name	Returns	Description
Next		Returns the next record in the enumeration.

Properties

Name	Returns	Description
EOF	Boolean	Indicates that the last record has been fetched in the enumeration.

StepLogRecord

Properties

Name	Returns	Description
ErrorCode	Long	Specifies the source of the error code from Step.Execute.
ErrorDescription	String	Specifies the source of the error description from Step.Execute.
ExecutionTime	Double	Specifies the total time in fractional seconds the step took to execute.
FinishTime	Date	The date/time when the step was completed.
LineageFullID	String	GUID for a Package Lineage.
Name	String	The name of the Step object.
Parent	IDTSStdObject	The parent object of the Step object.
ProgressCount	Variant	Specifies a set of intervals processed by the step. For example, the number of rows that were transformed.
Properties	Properties	The properties of the object.
StartTime	Date	Specifies the time at which the step started.
StepExecutionID	Variant	Specifies the Step execution identifier.
Step ExecutionResult	DTSStep ExecResult	Specifies the result of the step's execution.
Step ExecutionStatus	DTSStep ExecStatus	Specifies the status of the step.

StepLogRecords

Methods

Name	Returns	Description
Next		Returns the next record in the enumeration.

Properties

Name	Returns	Description
EOF	Boolean	Indicates that the last record has been fetched in the enumeration.

Steps

Methods

Name	Returns	Description
Add		Adds a Step object to the collection.
Insert		Adds a Step object to the collection by index.
Item	Step	Retrieves a Step object from the collection.
New	Step	Creates a new Step object.
Remove		Removes a Step object from the collection.

Properties

Name	Returns	Description
Count	Long	The number of Step objects in the collection.
Parent	IDTSStdObject	The parent of the Steps collection.

Task

Methods

Name	Returns	Description
Execute		Executes a Task.

Properties

Name	Returns	Description
CustomTask	CustomTask	Returns the CustomTask object.
CustomTaskID	String	The ProgID or CLSID of the CustomTask object.
Description	String	A descriptive text about the Task object.
Name	String	The name of the Task object.
Parent	IDTSStdObject	The parent object of the Task object.
Properties	Properties	The properties of the object.

Tasks

Methods

Name	Returns	Description
Add		Adds a Task object to the collection.
Insert		Adds a Task object to the collection by index.
Item	Task	Retrieves a Task object from the collection.
New	Task	Creates a new Task object.
Remove		Removes a Task object from the collection.

Properties

Name	Returns	Description
Count	Long	The number of Task objects in the collection.
Parent	IDTSStdobject	The parent of the Tasks collection.

TransferObjectsTask

Methods

Name	Returns	Description
AddObject ForTransfer		Adds an object to the list of objects to be transferred.
CancelExecution		Cancels task execution.
Execute		Executes the `TransferObjectsTask`.
GetObject ForTransfer		Iterates through objects on the list.
ResetObjectsList		Clears the list of objects.

Properties

Name	Returns	Description
CopyAllObjects	Boolean	Sets whether to transfer all objects from the source database.
CopyData	DTSTransfer_ CopyDataOption	Specifies whether data should be copied, and whether existing data should be replaced or appended to.
CopySchema	Boolean	Specifies, based on the `CopyData` property, whether or not data will be copied.
Description	String	A text description of the `TransferObjectTask`.
Destination Database	String	The name of the destination database.
Destination Login	String	The login ID on a destination server.
Destination Password	String	The password for the login ID on a destination server.
Destination Server	String	The destination server name.
Destination UseTrusted Connection	Boolean	Sets whether to use a trusted connection to a destination server.
DropDestination ObjectsFirst	Boolean	Specifies whether to drop objects, if they already exist on the destination.

Table continued on following page

Name	Returns	Description
Include Dependencies	Boolean	Specifies whether dependent objects will be scripted and transferred during an object transfer operation.
IncludeLogins	Boolean	Specifies whether logins will be scripted and transferred during an object transfer operation.
IncludeUsers	Boolean	Specifies whether users will be scripted and transferred during an object transfer operation.
Name	String	The name of the `TransferObjectTask`.
Properties	Properties	The properties of the object.
ScriptFile Directory	String	The directory where the script file and log files are written.
ScriptOption	DTSTransfer_ ScriptOption	Sets the scripting option for the object.
ScriptOptionEx	DTSTransfer_ ScriptOptionEx	Sets the extended scripting option for the object.
SourceDatabase	String	The name of the source database.
SourceLogin	String	The login ID on a source server.
SourcePassword	String	The password for the login ID on a source server.
SourceServer	String	The source server name.
SourceUseTrusted Connection	Boolean	Sets whether to use a trusted connection to a source server.

TransferObjectsTask2

Extended Properties

Name	Returns	Description
DestTranslate Char	Boolean	Determines if translation will be needed for the character data on the destination server. The default setting for this is `True`.
DestUse Transaction	Boolean	Specifies whether to perform operations on the destination server within a transaction. By default, this property is set to `False`.

Name	Returns	Description
SourceTranslate Char	Boolean	Determines if translation will be needed for the character data on the source server. The default setting for this is True.
UseCollation	Boolean	Specifies whether to use column-level collation during the transfer. The default setting for this is True.

Transformation

Properties

Name	Returns	Description
Destination Columns	Columns	The collection of columns for a destination transformation.
ForceBlobs InMemory	Boolean	Specifies whether to always store each source BLOB column in a transformation as a single memory allocation.
ForceSource BlobsBuffered	DTSForceMode	Specifies whether to always buffer each source BLOB column in a transformation.
InMemoryBlob Size	Long	Specifies the size in bytes of per-column allocation for in-memory BLOBs in a transformation.
Name	String	The name of the Transformation object.
Parent	IDTSStdObject	The parent object of the Transformation object.
Properties	Properties	The properties of the object.
SourceColumns	Columns	The collection of columns for a source transformation.
TransformFlags	Long	Sets the transformation flags that indicate characteristics of a transformation.
Transform Server	Object	Contains specification of the dispatch interface of the custom COM server object for a transformation.
Transform ServerID	String	Returns the programmatic identifier (ProgID) or class identifier (CLSID) of the Transformation.

Table continued on following page

Name	Returns	Description
Transform ServerParameter	Variant	Specifies a transform server's initialization parameter.
TransformServer Properties	Properties	Specifies the collection of Automation objects available on the `TransformServer` `IDispatch` interface.

Transformation2

Extended Properties

Name	Returns	Description
TransformPhases	Long	Specifies the phase in which this transform is being called.

TransformationInfo

Properties

Name	Returns	Description
ClassID	String	Specifies the identifier for the `Transformation` class.
Description	String	Specifies the description of the `Transformation` class.
Implementation FileName	String	Specifies the implementation file for the `Transformation` class.
Implementation FileVersionString	String	Specifies the implementation file version for the `Transformation` class.
Name	String	The name of the object.
Parent	IDTSStdObject	The parent object of the object.
Properties	Properties	The properties of the object.

TransformationInfos

Methods

Name	Returns	Description
Item		Retrieves an object.
Refresh		Executes a refresh command for the cache and collection.

Properties

Name	Returns	Description
Count	String	Number of items in the collection.
Parent	IDTSStdObject	The parent object of the Step object.
UseCache	String	Specifies whether to cache enumeration information for this collection.

Transformations

Methods

Name	Returns	Description
Add		Adds a Transformation object to the collection.
Insert		Adds a Transformation object to the collection by index.
Item	Transformation	Retrieves a Transformation object from the collection.
New	Transformation	Creates a new Transformation object.
Remove		Removes a Transformation object from the collection.

Properties

Name	Returns	Description
Count	Long	The number of Transformation objects in the collection.
Parent	IDTSStdObject	The parent of the Transformations collection.

TransformationSet

Properties

Name	Returns	Description
DeleteQuery	String	Specifies the parameterized SQL statement to delete data.
DeleteQuery Columns	Columns	Specifies the column parameters for DeleteQuery.
Description	String	Description of the object.
Destination Column Definitions	Columns	Specifies the destination columns for schema definition.
Exception FileColumn Delimter	String	The column delimiter for the exception file.
Exception FileName	String	The file name where exception rows are written.
Exception FileRow Delimiter	String	The row delimiter for the data in the exception file.
FastLoad Options	DTSFast LoadOptions	Used for the UseFastLoad property to set SQL OLE DB destination connection options.
FetchBuffer Size	Long	Sets the number of rows to fetch during a single operation.
FirstRow	Variant	Gets the first source row from the source.
InsertQuery	String	Specifies the parameterized SQL statement to insert data.
InsertQuery Columns	Columns	Specifies the column parameters for InsertQuery.
LastRow	Variant	Gets the last row from the source to copy.

Name	Returns	Description
Lookups	Lookups	A collection of lookup values.
Maximum ErrorCount	Long	The maximum number of error rows before the data pump terminates operation.
Name	String	The name of the object.
ProgressRow Count	Long	Specifies the frequency at which the progress notification will happen. The default setting for this property is 1000.
Properties	Properties	A list of properties for this object.
Parent	IDTSStdObject	The parent object of the Transformation object.
Properties	Properties	The properties of the object.
Transformations	Transformations	A collection of Transformation objects.
UpdateQuery	String	Specifies the parameterized SQL statement to update data.
UpdateQuery Columns	Columns	Specifies the column parameters for UpdateQuery.
UserQuery	String	Specifies the parameterized SQL statement to user data.
UserQueryColumns	Columns	Specifies the column parameters for UserQuery.

TransformationSets

Methods

Name	Returns	Description
Add		Adds a Transformation object to the collection.
Insert		Adds a Transformation object to the collection by index.
Item	Transformation	Retrieves a Transformation object from the collection.
New	Transformation	Creates a new Transformation object.
Remove		Removes a Transformation object from the collection.

Properties

Name	Returns	Description
Count	Long	The number of `Transformation` objects in the collection.
Parent	IDTSStdObject	The parent of the `Transformations` collection.

Global Constants

For each constant enumeration described in the table below, there is a corresponding enumeration with a prefix of LP that should be used by C++ programmers (for example there is a constant enumeration called LPDTSErrorMode that corresponds to DTSErrorMode).

Name	Description
DTSBulkInsert_DataFileType	Specifies the type of data file used for bulk insert operations.
DTSCustomTaskUIFlags	Indicates the type of user interface supported by a custom task.
DTSErrorMode	Error conditions during step execution of a DTS package.
DTSFastLoadOptions	Specifies fast load options for the `DataPumpTask.UseFastLoad` method.
DTSForceMode	Overrides the default handling of associated properties.
DTSIsolationLevel	The isolation level of a package's transaction.
DTSLineageOptions	Specifies how package execution lineage should be presented and recorded.
DTSPackageError	Error conditions for DTS package creation and execution.
DTSPackagePriorityClass	Win32 process priority class for a DTS package.
DTSRepositoryMetadataOptions	Specifies metadata scanning and resolution options when storing the DTS package to a Repository.
DTSRepositoryStorageFlags	The Repository options when saving or loading the DTS Package.
DTSSQLObjectType	Indicates types of objects available on Microsoft SQL Server.
DTSSQLServerStorageFlags	Specifies Repository options when saving or loading the DTS package.

Name	Description
DTSStepExecResult	The execution result of a DTS Step object.
DTSStepExecStatus	The execution status of a DTS Step object.
DTSStepPrecendenceBasis	The values for a step's precedence value.
DTSStepRelativePriority	The Step object's Win32 thread relative priority.
DTSStepScriptResult	The return code from an ActiveX script step execution.
DTSTaskExecResult	The execution results of a DTS Task.
DTSTransfer_CopyDataOption	Specifies flags indicating whether data should be copied, and whether existing data should be replaced or appended to.
DTSTransfer_ScriptOption	Sets the scripting option for a DTS transfer.
DTSTransfer_ScriptOptionEx	Sets the extended scripting options for a DTS transfer.

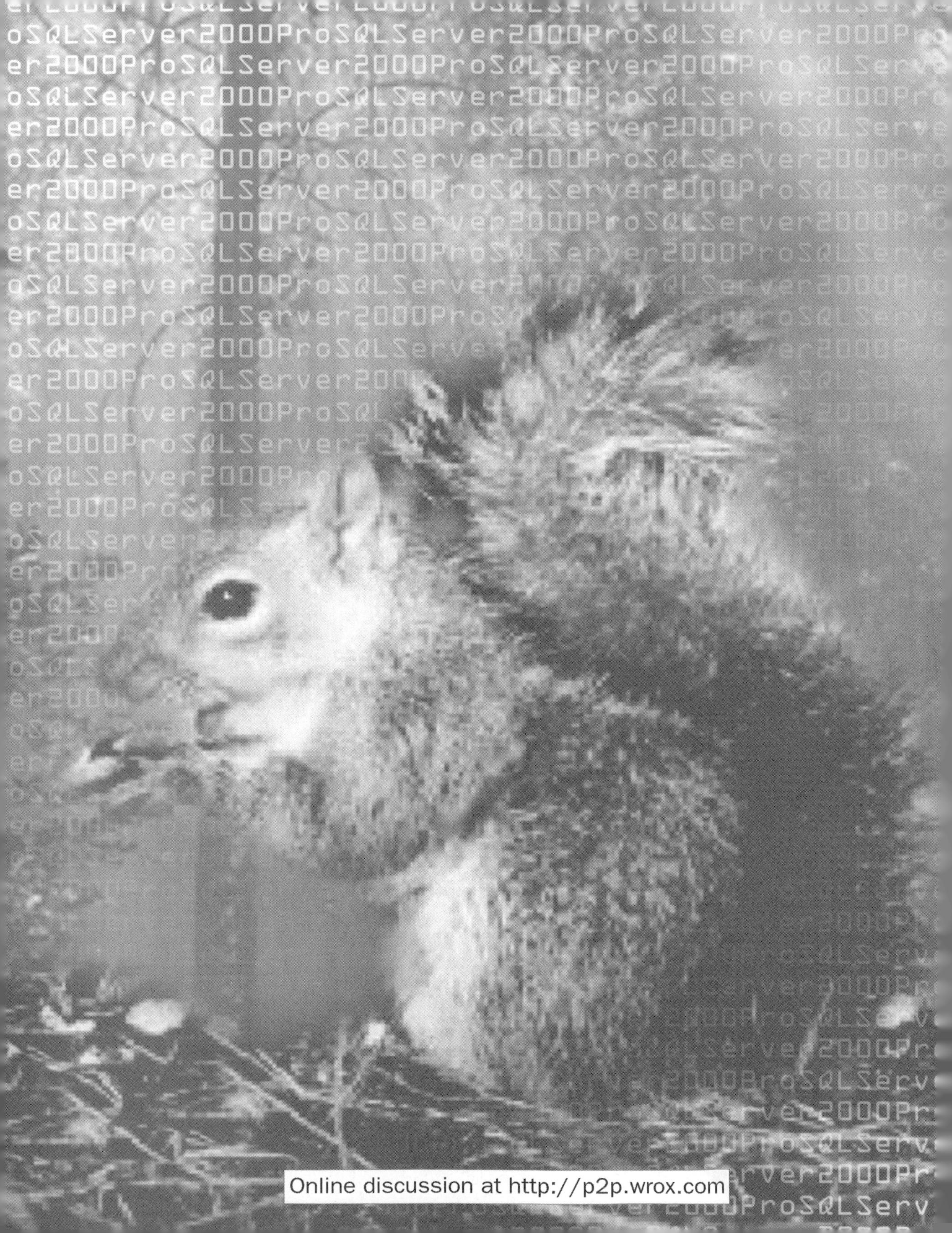

Online discussion at http://p2p.wrox.com

Index

A Guide to the Index

The index is arranged hierarchically, in alphabetical order, with symbols preceding the letter A. Most second-level entries and many third-level entries also occur as first-level entries. This is to ensure that users will find the information they require however they choose to search for it.

P

X

Y

Z

Online discussion at http://p2p.wrox.com

WROX
PROGRAMMER TO PROGRAMMER™

Wrox writes books for you. Any suggestions, or ideas about how you want information given in your ideal book will be studied by our team. Your comments are always valued at Wrox.

Free phone in USA 800-USE-WROX
Fax (312) 893 8001

UK Tel. (0121) 687 4100   Fax (0121) 687 4101

Professional SQL Server 2000 Programming - Registration Card

Name _____

Address _____

_____

_____

City_____ State/Region _____

Country_____ Postcode/Zip _____

E-mail _____

Occupation _____

How did you hear about this book? _____

☐ Book review (name) _____

☐ Advertisement (name) _____

☐ Recommendation _____

☐ Catalog _____

☐ Other _____

Where did you buy this book? _____

☐ Bookstore (name)_____ City _____

☐ Computer Store (name)_____

☐ Mail Order _____

☐ Other _____

What influenced you in the purchase of this book?

☐ Cover Design

☐ Contents

☐ Other (please specify) _____

How did you rate the overall contents of this book?

☐ Excellent   ☐ Good

☐ Average   ☐ Poor

What did you find most useful about this book? _____

What did you find least useful about this book? _____

Please add any additional comments. _____

What other subjects will you buy a computer book on soon? _____

What is the best computer book you have used this year? _____

Note: This information will only be used to keep you updated about new Wrox Press titles and will not be used for any other purpose or passed to any other third party.

4486   *Check here if you DO NOT want to receive support for this book* ☐   **4486**

wrox

PROGRAMMER TO PROGRAMMER™

NB. If you post the bounce back card below in the UK, please send it to:

Wrox Press Ltd., Arden House, 1102 Warwick Road,
Acocks Green, Birmingham B27 6BH. UK.

———— *Computer Book Publishers* ————

BUSINESS REPLY MAIL

FIRST CLASS MAIL   PERMIT#64   CHICAGO, IL

POSTAGE WILL BE PAID BY ADDRESSEE

**WROX PRESS INC.,
29 S. LA SALLE ST.,
SUITE 520
CHICAGO IL 60603-USA**